MANUAL

OF

CHILD PSYCHOLOGY

WILEY PUBLICATIONS IN PSYCHOLOGY

INTRODUCTION TO PSYCHOLOGY. By *Edwin G. Boring, Herbert S. Langfeld,* and *Harry P. Weld.*

STATISTICAL DICTIONARY OF TERMS AND SYMBOLS. By *A. K. Kurtz* and *H. A. Edgerton.*

SOCIAL PSYCHOLOGY. By *Daniel Katz* and *Richard L. Schanck.*

HEARING—ITS PSYCHOLOGY AND PHYSIOLOGY. By *S. Smith Stevens* and *Hallowell Davis.*

MANUAL OF PSYCHIATRY AND MENTAL HYGIENE. Seventh Edition. By *Aaron J. Rosanoff.*

A MANUAL OF PSYCHOLOGICAL EXPERIMENTS. By *Boring, Langfeld,* and *Weld.*

WORKBOOK IN PSYCHOLOGY. By *C. H. Wedell.*

STATISTICAL METHODS IN BIOLOGY, MEDICINE, AND PSYCHOLOGY. Fourth Edition. By *C. B. Davenport* and *Merle P. Ekas.*

MOTIVATION OF BEHAVIOR. By *P. T. Young.*

PSYCHOLOGY—A FACTUAL TEXTBOOK. By *Boring, Langfeld,* and *Weld.*

PSYCHOLOGY IN BUSINESS AND INDUSTRY. By *John G. Jenkins.*

Herbert S. Langfeld
Advisory Editor

MANUAL OF CHILD PSYCHOLOGY. *Leonard Carmichael,* Editor.

EMOTION IN MAN AND ANIMAL. By *P. T. Young.*

UNCONSCIOUSNESS. By *James Grier Miller.*

THE PSYCHOLOGY OF PERSONAL ADJUSTMENT. By *Fred McKinney.*

THE PSYCHOLOGY OF SOCIAL MOVEMENTS. By *Hadley Cantril.*

Manual

OF

Child Psychology

Edited by

LEONARD CARMICHAEL

*President, Tufts College; Director of the Laboratory of
Sensory Psychology and Physiology, Tufts College*

Contributors

John E. Anderson

Leonard Carmichael

Ruth M. Cruikshank

Wayne Dennis

Edgar A. Doll

Arnold Gesell

Florence L. Goodenough

Arthur T. Jersild

Harold E. Jones

Vernon Jones

Kurt Lewin

Dorothea McCarthy

Myrtle B. McGraw

Margaret Mead

Catharine Cox Miles

Norman L. Munn

Karl C. Pratt

Lewis M. Terman

Helen Thompson

New York: JOHN WILEY & SONS, Inc.

London: CHAPMAN & HALL, Limited

PREFACE

It has been said that a most serious need of modern psychology is for advanced scientific manuals to bridge the gap between the excellent and varied elementary textbooks in this field and the scientific periodical literature of psychology. This manual is an advanced-level textbook and is intended to be an addition at just this advanced level to the literature of general as well as child psychology. The book is presented as a series of separate chapters, each written by a recognized authority. Its purpose is to provide an accurate and coherent picture of some of the most important aspects of research in the scientific psychology of human development.

Until comparatively recent years most of those who wrote upon the development of individual mental life elaborated essentially speculative theories. They attempted to describe man's so-called inborn instincts or the allegedly *tabula rasa* character of the mind of the young child. The present book is testimony to the fact that today psychologists and other scientists by the use of appropriate techniques have established a large body of important and reliable facts concerning the details of human mental development. This book is a clear demonstration that the speculative period in child psychology is definitely past.

Many practical as well as theoretical gains have resulted from the empirical study of the growth of the human mind. It will be clear to the reader of these chapters that it has been possible to formulate hypotheses concerning many specific aspects of mental development. These hypotheses have in many instances been tested in the laboratory or in controlled and quantifiable social situations. The conclusions so reached are very different from the vague verbal theories of the prescientific era of child psychology.

One who is interested mainly in securing an understanding of adult mental life can gain many new insights into mental processes in general from a study of these chapters. A knowledge of the way in which adult psychological characteristics develop in each individual is fundamental to a complete understanding of such characteristics. The manual may thus be thought of as a factual introduction to the understanding not only of child psychology but also of the psychology of the normal adult human mind and even of the abnormal human mind.

The editor has not attempted any modification of the separate styles or points of view of the individual chapters as they are presented. The chapters appear essentially as their authors prepared them. It is believed that the extensive bibliographical references included will be of real value to advanced students and to research workers.

The authors of all the chapters wrote for serious advanced undergraduate students and graduate students as well as for specialists in psychology and in such related fields as education, psychiatry, pediatrics, and medicine in general.

Both as editor of the manual and as the author of a special chapter, the writer is indebted to Clark University and to the Clark University Press for their generosity in allowing the reproduction in this book of extensive excerpts and the use of other materials previously published in the *Hand-*

book of Child Psychology, Revised Edition, which was issued in 1933 by that press.

Both the *Handbook of Child Psychology* and the *Handbook of Child Psychology*, Revised Edition, were edited by Dr. Carl Murchison. The present editor wishes to express here his profound appreciation for the pioneer work done by Dr. Murchison in producing these handbooks and other advanced books in psychology. This Manual owes much in spirit and content to the foresight and editorial skill of Dr. Murchison.

This book has been a difficult and expensive one to produce, especially under wartime conditions. The editor cannot resist expressing here his special appreciation to the authors, who have in some cases several times revised chapters and who have also cooperated in making the index. The authors of chapters have been very patient in the face of the many delays in finally setting the publication date of the book. The editor also wishes to express his most sincere gratitude to Miss Ellen Peck of Tufts College, who has handled many of the difficult technical details involved in the editing of the entire volume. Dr. Luberta Harden McCabe of Cambridge has given valuable assistance in the preparation of the manuscript. Dr. Stanley Mikal also deserves special gratitude for his assistance.

The editor and the authors of the chapters in this book express their appreciation to publishers and authors for permission to use excerpts from their works. Great care has been taken in each instance to provide bibliographical references by means of which the reader can identify the author and publisher, to whom credit is thereby given.

LEONARD CARMICHAEL, EDITOR

TUFTS COLLEGE
January, 1946

CONTENTS

Chapter 1

METHODS OF CHILD PSYCHOLOGY [1]

John E. Anderson

A distinction can be made between the content of any science, that is, the facts and generalizations which become welded into a substantial field of knowledge, and the methods of that science—the techniques and procedures by means of which this content is obtained. And back of both content and method lies the framework of thinking within which the science operates. Hence content, method, and theory can never be completely differentiated. In the beginnings of a science, there is little critical analysis of method or much concern with underlying theory. The new techniques produce new content so rapidly that interest centers upon it. But as science matures, interest in method and theoretical substructure increases. And child psychol-

ogy now shows its maturity in an ever-increasing concern with method and theory.

Far from being a uniformly growing body, a science is composed of many parts which grow at different rates and mature at different times. With the discovery of a promising method one area spurts forward rapidly and engrosses many workers, while another remains relatively inactive. In general, progress is from simple description to precise formulation of relations in quantitative terms, and from simple generalizations to explanatory principles that subsume wider and wider ranges of fact. In the beginning simple techniques based on common, everyday observations are used. As clearer conceptions of significant problems arise, new weapons are forged. A method which in one generation is the best available, in another generation becomes obsolete. At the same moment some methods are still in preliminary form; others are very advanced. Little, then, is gained by calling a particular method right or wrong. Rather should we show how better methods give greater insight and more significant generalizations.

In the nineteenth century, so notable for its advance in all fields of science, some observations upon children were made in systematic fashion. The first approach, the baby biography, involved day-by-day recording of the experience and behavior of a single child, usually by an interested scientist, himself a parent or close relative with frequent access to the child. Often

[1] Because of the limited space available for the discussion of the methods of a science so wide in scope as child psychology, the author feels the need of apologizing for the brief and incomplete treatment that, of necessity, must be given many topics. To discuss adequately even one section of method—for example, sampling or indirect measurement—would take as much space as is allotted to the entire chapter. And, since the content chapters which follow will of necessity be somewhat concerned with method in their particular areas, this chapter is limited to a survey which is turned in the direction of extensiveness and representation of the entire field rather than of a minute and detailed analysis in a limited area.

Difficulty is also encountered in citation and bibliography. To cite all the studies which make contributions to method would be the equivalent of listing all the bibliographies in this volume. Hence citations are limited to examples or instances, to summaries that integrate substantial amounts of material, and to major contributions to statistical or research methods.

1

simple experiments and measurements were included. The number of biographies of infants and small children available, both published and unpublished, is great. Among those of historical importance, those of Tiedemann (1787), Darwin (1877), Preyer (1882, 1888, 1889), Shinn (1893, 1899, 1900), the Scupins (1907), and the Sterns (1907, 1909) may be mentioned.

The next stride forward came with a new method, the questionnaire. Starting with Hall's (1891) inquiry into the content of children's minds, a deluge of questionnaires resulted in substantial advances in our knowledge of children, especially at the school ages (Bradbury, 1937). Even more important was the training of a number of scientists, Gesell, Kuhlmann, and Terman, whose lives have been devoted to the study of children.

With Bolton (1892) and Gilbert (1894), extensive tests of school children were undertaken. Unfortunately, however, Gilbert, using simple functions, found only low positive relations with school progress. Had he happened upon complex functions, and obtained significant relations, he might have initiated a development that came twenty years later. Binet and Simon (1905) forged a new method after the turn of the century. Their tests evoked worldwide interest, not only as the outstanding contribution to the measurement of intelligence, but also because of the impetus given to the invention of a wide variety of measurement devices in other areas, such as achievement and personality. Thorndike (1904, 1913a, 1913b, 1914) led in using the techniques with school children and facilitated the development of method in all areas by emphasis upon statistics. For Watson (1919) the crucial observations in a systematic approach to psychology were made upon children rather than adults. By stressing objectivity of method and dismissing introspection, he made infants and children adequate subjects for psychological investigations, a point of view not held by many of his predecessors.

Although clinical notes and descriptions of defective, abnormal, and delinquent children appeared in the medical and psychological literature almost from the beginning, it was not until Freud stressed the relation between neurotic symptoms in adults and childhood experiences that workers were led to the extensive study of past histories to explain present behavior.

In Europe, Gestalt psychology, with its stress upon configuration and organization, reacted strongly against the traditional atomistic view of behavior. In the United States, a biological or organismic point of view, growing out of embryological studies, emphasized the genetic history of each element and pattern of behavior and the principles governing the integration of response.

Some of the older discussions on the appropriateness of children as subjects for psychological investigation, on the need of a special psychological talent for the interpretation of child behavior, and on the limitations with which inferences from the adult mind can be carried over into child behavior now seem to be chiefly of historical interest. Discussions of method in child psychology are found in many sources, among which a few of the more extensive are Koffka (1924), Thomas and Thomas (1928), Goodenough and Anderson (1931), Symonds (1931), Anderson (1931, 1933), Lewin (1935, 1936), Jones and Burks (1936), Bühler (1937), and Murphy, Murphy, and Newcomb (1937). Especially detailed with extensive bibliographies are the Jones and Burks and the Murphy, Murphy, and Newcomb discussions. The Thirty-Seventh (1938) and the Thirty-Eighth (1939) *Yearbooks of the National Society for the Study of Education*, "The Scientific Movement in Education" and "Child Development and Curriculum," respectively, also contain much pertinent material, as does the *Encyclopedia of Educational Research*, Monroe (Ed.), 1941.

With a wealth of material now available on children's behavior, an increased emphasis upon the psychobiological view growing out of animal psychology, and an increased concern with a psychosocial view arising from modern studies of the environment, child psychology is coming into its own. Less and less are the college or graduate students available for research in psychological laboratories looked upon as the representatives of the human species; more and more late adolescent and early adult behavior is viewed as a transition in a developmental cycle that begins with conception and ends with death.

Half a century of child research has given us a very different picture of the nature of the child from that held by earlier investigators (Anderson, 1944). The following brief summary outlines the essentials of the modern point of view from the standpoint of method:

(1) The child is a growing organism who moves by infinitesimal changes from a single cell to the complex organization of structure and function at an adult level. In this progression scientists describe the differentiation of new structures and functions, the changes in the size and form of structures, and the changes in the level and effectiveness of function. They also seek the underlying principles that will bring understanding of these changes and methods of modifying development and function.

(2) The child is a spatially separated unit that functions as an organized whole in the situations he meets. This molar characteristic of behavior needs particular emphasis. In the physical and chemical sciences, units of organization can be broken up into component parts, reassembled, and broken up again. As a result the laws governing organization can be worked out with such preci-

sion and exactness as to give exceptional prediction and control. Since neither the child nor his behavior can so be broken up and reassembled in the literal sense, difficulties arise in the scientific study of the child because both the psychological terms and the measuring devices used to analyze behavior into separate and manipulable symbolic units correspond only to functions which are carried on by the organism as a whole. Thus, when we speak of memory, learning, or emotion, separate acts of behavior are classified on the basis of similarity. They are not discrete phenomena put together because of intrinsic characteristics. Any act may be classified under many different categories, depending upon our scientific purpose. Thus the same behavior may be classified as sensing, as learning, as emotion, as memory, etc. This wholeness of the child forces the use of procedures that seem very devious and indirect to the physical scientist.

(3) The child lives in a context which is itself neither simple nor unitary and which continuously affects his behavior and development. Patterns of stimulation come to him out of this context. In turn, by virtue of his own make-up, he selects from that context. At all times there is a reciprocal relation between the human organism and this biosocial context. Because the child is limited in time, behavior becomes structured, and patterns develop both in the stimulus field and in his own response system. Some stimulus patterns become significant because they modify the developmental stream by affecting practice or social relations with others. Others remain insignificant because they do not affect this web of relations. Why one pattern is significant and another is not is a crucial problem for child psychology.

(4) The child is engaged in an on-going process of development that is not reversible. Because of the interrelations involved, neither the context nor the relations involved can be reproduced a second time in precisely their original form. Behavior at any moment is the resultant of the child's history

and of the stimulation present. The concept of simple and single causes must be replaced by concepts of multiple causation, reciprocal relations, and the progressive cumulation of effect.

The Problems of Child Psychology

The impact of the scientist on the problems of the child may be divided into two major areas or approaches in terms of purpose or function. First, he seeks generalizations or principles of wide scope which will facilitate the understanding, prediction, and control of behavior. In this process he is concerned (a) with the fundamental mechanics of the organism, or the principles intrinsic to the organism itself which determine its function independently of any particular individual or context; (b) with the effects produced by the organism upon the environment, or what organisms of particular constitution and make-up do to the world that is external to them; and (c) with the effects of the environment upon the organism, or how behavior can be modified and changed by modifying and changing the context in which the organism develops.

A second major area common to many sciences is description. The psychologist seeks to describe the developmental process itself in manipulable and understandable symbols. His function is, first, to lay out the general trends common to all individuals. Here there are two approaches: (a) the normative cross-section and (b) the genetic-longitudinal approach. Second, he seeks a description and understanding of individual behavior as such; that is, the uniqueness rather than the commonality of behavior. Here again two attacks may be distinguished: (a) the assessment of the individual at any level and (b) a genetic approach in which an attempt is made to describe the individual in his whole setting.

The Mechanics of the Organism. In any organization of matter that functions as a unit, accomplishing specific results in space and time, science assumes that intrinsic to the organization itself are principles that are lawful, that these principles can be determined more or less independently of the particular mechanism and of its particular context, and that these principles will be found to operate in many different varieties of mechanism and many different contexts. Knowing them, we gain both understanding and control over the particulars; without them, we are left with what seems to be meaningless behavior. Weber's law and the principles of the distribution of effort, of conditioning, of the resumption of interrupted activities, etc., would fall under this head.

This is the traditional content of psychology. In this area the experiment becomes the basic technique of isolating and controlling factors. Understanding and significance increase as (1) studies are made which permit factors to operate within their full range in order to avoid generalizations based on small segments of the relations studied; (2) studies are made on combinations of factors; (3) more attention both in designing experiments and developing principles is paid to interlocking principles and their fit into explanatory systems (not to be confused with systems of psychology in the traditional sense which represent different philosophical approaches to the organism rather than explanatory systems derived empirically from data). In the field of child psychology another question arises—that of the range in terms of age and development through which the principles hold and the degree and nature of their change with age and development.

The Effect of the Organism upon the Environment. The child at any moment may be viewed as a particular pattern of organization of structure and function engaged in meeting an external environment. As he moves forward in time, his relations with the external world will be determined in part by his own make-up. Children differ widely in intelligence, musical capacity, motor coordination, energy level, sensory capacity, and handicapping conditions. If methods can be devised by means of which these characteristics of the individual, both singly and in combination, can be measured, the subsequent accomplishments of individuals separated out early at various levels can be recorded and generalizations made. It is unfortunate that so far such early separations have been made almost wholly in terms of intelligence. There is no reason other than the interest of the particular investigator and the development of appropriate measuring devices why the technique should not be widely extended. The classical example is found in the studies of gifted children, especially those of Terman (1925; Terman and Oden, 1940a, 1940b), who has followed gifted children and control children into adult life. Baller's (1936) study of the adult accomplishments of subnormals tested in childhood also falls in this classification. Problems in differential psychology such as those of sex and race differences might lead to significant generalizations if groups could be separated early and follow-up studies made. As such studies now stand they are complicated by cumulative environmental effects and are difficult to interpret. In this approach, the individual is used as the independent variable and accomplishment or the psychological environment he himself constructs as the dependent variable.

The Effect of the Environment upon the Organism. In the guidance and training of children, society is modifying the contexts in which the child develops. The scientist is concerned with the deliberate and experimental modification of contexts in order to discover underlying principles and practical procedures that can be used for educating and training children. Questions arise, such as the effective method of teaching reading, how to control temper tantrums, what materials to use in geography, and whether motion pictures and visual aids improve learning. Sometimes the modifications of context studied consist of single and readily controlled factors, sometimes of very complex and involved patterns of stimulation. It is clear that experimental design involves setting up parallel groups of children, exposed differentially to the factors to be studied. Because it has been easier to work with simple and single factors, much of the literature consists of relatively isolated experiments. We should not assume, however, that the problems in this area center about only such factors. In fact, the single factor with a particular effect is the limiting case at one end, and a total environment with all its effects is the limiting case at the other end. Our ultimate concern, then, is with all types of environmental combinations in all degrees of complexity. The data in this area usually result in generalizations expressed in actuarial terms and prediction within limits for groups and individuals. In many instances, even though the problems begin at what is essentially a practical level, important generalizations for the mechanics of the organism result.

In the past, child psychology took the results of behavior and worked backward for antecedent or causal factors. Thus delinquent and nondelinquent children, jealous and nonjealous children, etc., are compared. In these studies sampling is in terms of an end result. If, however, progress in our knowledge of children is to come, the environmental context must become the independent variable and behavior the dependent variable in order that we may predict from environment to behavior, not from behavior to environment. But there are difficulties. Sherman and Henry (1933), who selected five contrasting environments in terms of distance from civilization and then measured the children, failed to secure clear-cut results from the standpoint of scientific generalization because any environment that has existed for a long time will have exercised a biologically selective influence upon its population. If environments that differ radically can be set up in advance and children then exposed to them after being matched in advance to control the biologically selective factor, more significant results will be obtained.

Many generalizations on the effect of home discipline and management upon children are derived from working backward from problem and normal children to descriptions of the home and neighborhoods from which they come. If, however, homes of contrasting disciplinary programs equivalent in other respects were observed for some time and the children's behavior measured, more significant results would be obtained. The fundamental scientific question is not "From what home environments do children who show behavior problems or who are well adjusted come?" but "What types of home environments produce behavior problems or good adjustment?" There are two regression lines, which are not identical. Scientific information is obtained from both, and, lacking the second, we can use the first. It is much more difficult to interpret, however, and, from the point of view of experimental design, less effective, since it goes from an end result in behavior to context rather than from context to behavior.

Normative Cross-section Approach. The normative cross-section approach involves the presentation to comparable samples of children of various age, grade, and other levels, of constant situations, problems, tests, experiments, etc., in order to determine for each level measures of central tendency and dispersion on the basis of which trends can be plotted and standards prepared with which individual children can be compared. As the child moves from infancy to adulthood, growth takes place. The adult is essentially at a maintenance level. For both practical and theoretical purposes it is necessary to determine the rate and manner of change with time and the internal and external conditions which determine their nature. Furthermore, because human beings—whatever their developmental level—show much variability, the data obtained at various levels will furnish norms or standards with which individuals can be compared. When plotted against level, norms describe or picture the developmental process itself. Much of the literature in child psychology is concerned with picturing development, for example, the many studies of motor, linguistic, intellectual, and social skills. The value of norms for practical application should not obscure the fact that for child psychology, since all problems are complicated by developmental level, normative studies are essential.

Although at present there is a substantial shift to longitudinal studies, nevertheless the cross-section study has particular advantages, since the new samples drawn from the population at each age level cross-check upon the data at other age levels. Uniform sampling criteria can be set up and applied from the beginning to the end of the age series studied, a fact which is not true of longitudinal data in which unforeseen and uncontrollable selective elimination inevitably occurs. In using norms obtained by the cross-section method, an answer is sought to the question, "How, at this particular moment, does this child compare in performance with other children of the same age level, grade level, sex, etc.?"

Although many norms are based on chronological age, because of its definiteness and ready comparability, norms are often based on other factors, or some combination of them, such as sex-age-height for weight or sex-age for motor development. In psychological studies relatively little smoothing is done for either the means or the standard deviations, in contrast with physical-growth studies where smoothing is more common. Since the sample at each age level can be regarded as new and independent, smoothing is a justifiable process for increasing the precision of the norms.

In designing normative studies, the chief problem is to obtain a random sample within each classification used for stratifying the population in order to secure results that will be typical. Terman and Merrill (1937), restandardizing the Binet tests, used paternal occupation, geographical location, and rural-urban residence, in addition to sex.

Genetic-Longitudinal Approach. As child research progressed, it became clear that a type of data different from that obtained in the cross-section would add significantly to our understanding, since curves based on averages at successive cross-sections did not necessarily represent the growth pattern in an individual child. Children grow at different rates and reach similar developmental levels at different times. Thus a cross-section study on an age basis groups together at the thirteen-year age level girls who are well past puberty and girls who are months away from puberty.

As a result, longitudinal studies involving the measurement of the same children at successive periods came into existence. Whereas means and standard deviations at each age level can be obtained as in the cross-section study, the longitudinal study permits, in addition, (1) the analysis of curves showing the development and characteristic growth of each individual child, (2) a detailed study of the increments of growth, both for the individual and the group as a whole, and (3) a detailed analysis of the interrelationships between growth processes, because all data have been obtained on the same children. But it, too, has some disadvantages. No matter how carefully a sample is selected at the beginning, because it is drawn but once the limiting characteristics inherent in the original sample will affect all the data subsequently obtained. Also, there will be casualties because of death, illness, families moving out of the area in which the study is done, and changes in the cooperation of children and parents with the investigator. Since these factors are both selective and differential in some functions, the final sample may depart quite far from the original group with which the study started. In some studies, the effect of losses is minimized by selecting families of stable position in the community, such as home owners, or by selecting a community known to have little mobility. The investigator will also find it necessary to throw away data for the incomplete cases, since by their use he not only loses the advantages gained through the longitudinal method but also may actually distort his results (Anderson and Cohen, 1939).

Immediately longitudinal data become available, new methodological problems appear. A cross-section method lumps all individuals together at a particular age level, irrespective of their stage of development. To do this with longitudinal data would give no advantage. How, then, are longitudinal data to be treated? Shuttleworth (1939) superimposed the period of maximal rate of physical growth for early- and late-maturing groups, irrespective of chronological age, and then plotted curves and made an analysis. A basic similarity in the growth pattern is revealed which was not apparent prior to this treatment. Markey's (1928) individual curves for vocabulary growth from the baby biographies differ markedly from the usual growth curves worked out by cross-section methods. Gulliksen (1934) and Wiley and Wiley (1937a, 1937b), attacking a similar problem in the field of animal learning, have shown that the course of learning is predictable when equations are plotted for individuals rather than for groups. All of this suggests that the statistical methods centering about measures of status, that is, means, standard deviations, correlation coefficients, etc., appropriate for cross-section studies, have more limited use in longitudinal data, where the mathematical processes concerned with progression, rates, increments, and velocity are more appropriate. Courtis (1932), who has applied the Gompertz curve to cross-section data, feels that even with that type of data statistical methods for studying growth and prediction can be much improved. Honzik (1938) and Anderson (1939b) have shown that measures of intelligence vary in predictive value for terminal status with separation of the measures in time and the overlap of the functions measured. Since substantial masses of longitudinal data have become available to investigators only recently, the statistical techniques for their analysis, especially in the psychological field, are in process of development.

The design of longitudinal studies is simple unless a control group runs parallel to the longitudinal group. The cases must be selected in far larger numbers than are expected at the termination of the study because of the large amount of selective elimination. Once children are selected, emphasis passes to the choice of various measures and observational techniques to be used and the arrangement of the time sequences for giving them. Precision is increased by using fixed intervals with reference to the child's birthday. In planning longitudinal studies, particular care must be taken to anticipate the data that will be needed at the termination of the study in order to interpret later material. Early records should be extraordinarily complete (Macfarlane, 1938), as, once the study has gone on, it is almost impossible to make up deficiencies.

Included under the longitudinal-genetic approach are a number of methods for studying children. The classical baby biography describes the development of a single child. A number of detailed studies of the successive drawings of the same children over a long span of years have been made. There have been descriptive accounts of the development of peculiar or abnormal children. More recently we find extensive and well-planned programs in which the same children are followed for long terms of years with the use of virtually every available technique for their study. With the development of cumulative recording systems in schools and the preservation of folders containing all accessible information about particular children in clinics, a type of record keeping is developing which should give us many of the advantages of the longitudinal technique in future studies, as well as permit a substantial amount of checking and evaluation of the end products of behavior in terms of its antecedents. It should also be noted that the genetic-longitudinal approach overlaps with the earlier-described approaches which seek generalizations, and that out of such studies may come insight into both the growth process and the mechanics of the organism.

The Assessment of the Individual, or the Horizontal Inventory. If we view an individual at any level, we can speak of him as a combination of skills, knowledges, attitudes, emergency reaction mechanisms, etc. For many practical purposes—educational, clinical, guidance, etc.—a horizontal inventory of the child's skills and attitudes is of importance. The scientifically most satisfactory technique is plotting his position in terms of well-established norms and standards on a psychograph. Examples are found in the clinical use of standard intelligence and achievement tests. In the absence of standardized instruments and norms, descriptive accounts and ratings are sometimes used. Because of the wide practical value of the horizontal inventory, child psychologists could well give attention to the establishing of norms and standards for a wide variety of behavioral patterns. Unfortunately, many norms in the literature are for rather unusual performances of a laboratory type not related directly to any life situation. Norms or standards for such everyday things as dressing habits, ordinary motor performances, and almost all practical skills, except the school skills represented in the achievement tests, are strikingly lacking. In spite of this lack, the assessment function constantly devolves upon the child psychologist.

One outcome of assessment is its possible use for predicting future development. The intelligence test has been demonstrated to have substantial predictive value. For any other assessment procedure the limits and possibilities of prediction can be worked out. Although actual achievement at any moment is probably more significant for an adult than is a test, for the child the problem of potentiality is one of constant concern.

Genetic Account of the Individual in Terms of the Whole Setting. By this unwieldy phrase are meant those studies which attempt to represent the unique character and quality of the individual.

They differ from the assessment at any one level in that they seek to present the background and genesis of present behavior. In its search for generalizations applicable to many, traditional psychology pulls the individual apart. Each person, however, is a unique combination, with his own history and his own particular patterns of behavior. Is the problem of uniqueness rather than commonality a problem for the child psychologist? Allport (1937, 1940) says that it is and devotes much space to pointing out our ineffectiveness in studying personality. In this classification to a greater or less degree fall the many studies of individual children by the case history, clinical, and psychoanalytic methods that bulk so large in the literature, in so far as they seek to describe the individual rather than generalize about all individuals. Two points may be made: first, although we have developed rather effective methods for describing the individual in terms of single measurements, because of technical difficulties so little work has been done on combinations and patterns that no one knows how far we can go in a scientific attack on the problem of uniqueness; and second, when achieved, the representation of a pattern may be more accurate, in spite of inaccuracies in single measurements and observations, than any representation in terms of isolated and single characteristics, for it is itself a generalization in which errors may cancel out.

Central Problems of Method

From the recent literature on child psychology three central problems of method emerge. Two grow out of the impact of Gestalt psychology and the third comes simultaneously from several sources. The attack is threefold: first, upon the misuse of descriptive and statistical procedures to set up phenotypes rather than genotypes; second, upon the use of actuarial rather than individual prediction; and third, upon the limitations of the classical experiment which studies a single factor in isolation instead of studying phenomena in their contexts and working out a theoretical system into which the experiment fits.

Phenotype and Genotype. Lewin (1935, 1936), in his important discussion of Aristotelian and Galilean modes of thought, criticizes many of the studies of children on the ground that acts are grouped together on the basis of similarities in appearance and then treated as though they were distinct and discrete phenomena. Thus he (1935) says:

> Present-day child psychology and affect psychology also exemplify clearly the Aristotelian habit of considering the abstractly defined classes as the essential nature of the particular object and hence as an explanation of its behavior. Whatever is common to children of a given age is set up as the fundamental character of that age. The fact that three-year-old children are quite often negative is considered evidence that negativism is inherent in the nature of three-year-olds, and the concept of a negativistic age or stage is then regarded as an explanation (though perhaps not a complete one) for the appearance of negativism in a given particular case. [And goes on] The statistical procedure, at least in its commonest application in psychology, is the most striking expression of this Aristotelian mode of thinking (pp. 15, 16).

Lewin calls such a mode of classification a *phenotype* and distinguishes it sharply from the *genotype,* in which the causal or antecedent phenomena that lead to these appearances are studied. A genotype is a homogeneous context of factors, either simple or complex, that produces effects which may differ widely; a phenotype is a classification in terms of the homogeneity of end results, which may have arisen from very different origins. For Lewin the central problem of child psychology becomes the study of genotypes. The genotype preserves the natural setting (even though artificially set up); the phenotype takes events out of their setting and puts them off by themselves. In actual practice, Lewin's experimental procedures conform to his principle, for he systematically modifies the environmental context and observes the effects on behavior.

The Lewin view has its critics. A clear statement is found in Thurstone (1935):

> The constructs in terms of which natural phenomena are comprehended are man-made inventions. To discover a scientific law is merely to discover that a man-made scheme serves to unify, and thereby to simplify, comprehension of a certain class of natural phenomena. A scientific law is not to be thought of as having an independent existence which some scientist is fortunate to stumble upon. A scientific law is not a part of nature. It is only a way of comprehending nature (p. 44). [And further] Some social scientists have objected because two individuals may have the same attitude score toward, say, pacifism, and yet be totally different in their backgrounds and in the causes of their similar social views. If such critics were consistent, they would object also to the statement that two men have identical incomes, for one of them earns when the other one steals. They should also object to the statement that two men are of the same height. The comparison should be held invalid because one of the men is fat and the other is thin. This is again the resistance against invading with the generalizing and simplifying constructs of science a realm which is habitually comprehended only in terms of innumerable and individualized detail. . . . What is not generally understood, even by many scientists, is that no scientific law is ever intended to represent any event pictorially. The

law is only an abstraction from the experimental situation. No experiment is ever completely repeated. . . . There is an unlimited number of ways in which nature can be comprehended in terms of fundamental scientific concepts (p. 47).

Individual and Actuarial Prediction. Another and closely related problem arises when a question as to the nature of prediction is raised. The Gestaltists consistently emphasize the lawfulness of behavior in the individual. Allport (1940) feels that most of our past psychological generalizations are actuarial in nature, that is, they are statements of probability for groups rather than principles that will enable us to predict in the individual case. If we say that delinquency occurs five times as frequently among children from broken homes as among children from normal homes, we state a probability. For an individual child from a particular broken home, however, with knowledge of all the attendant circumstances, the chances of delinquency may be zero or one hundred or anywhere between.

Two points may be made in criticism of this view. First, prediction in individual cases depends upon the completeness of knowledge. Thus, if we know the income level of the broken home, whether it was broken by desertion, divorce, or death, the character of the spouse remaining with the child, etc., the accuracy of our prediction increases. As we learn more about the combination of factors, and especially more about "genotypes," the possibilities of prediction will increase. There have been significant advances in modern statistical method centering about the design of experiments to analyze the weight and contribution of combinations of factors. These developments have come mainly in the field of agricultural statistics—Fisher (1936, 1937), Tippett (1937), Snedecor (1938), Treloar (1939), etc.—but are being made available to psychologists and educators (Rider, 1939; Lindquist, 1940; Peters and Van Voorhis, 1940).

Second, although individual prediction is always an ideal, it is not completely reached even in the physical and natural sciences. Instead we have prediction only within limits which can themselves be statistically defined. Prediction becomes a matter of the number of decimal places to which one wishes to carry his data and the confidence (in the statistical sense) which he can place in the prediction. Thus the result of developing an emulsion of known constitution in a developer of known constitution for a definite period of time at a constant temperature seems to the naïve person to be perfectly predicted. It is, however, accurate only within a certain number of decimal places, and with more precise measurement variations will be discovered. For my practical purposes of developing a print the prediction is perfect; for the research worker interested in the fundamental relations of emulsion and developer it is far from perfect. In the sense that the limits within which prediction is possible can be defined, the data available to the psychologist differ only in degree from those in other scientific fields.

There are two viewpoints from which we may regard science, one as an explanatory system of concepts that gives us understanding, the other in terms of prediction and control in a world of affairs. The child psychologist finds himself shifting from one viewpoint to the other because he is in a field of wide practical, as well as theoretical, relations. One of his difficulties centers about the word "cause."

In explanatory science we deal with a system of relations which we describe in terms of the correlation of and interdependence of variables. In this framework we think of *cause* not as efficient cause but only as antecedence, and *relationship* only as association. In the field of practical relations, cause is quite properly used in another sense. Thus, if the photographic print turns black after development and drying, with perfect appropriateness I can say that it has turned black because of the absence of a fixing bath. If a second print is placed in a fixing bath and does not turn black, I can say, "The first print was spoiled because it was not placed in a fixing bath." Note here that our concern is with obviously practical relations in which by changing the complex of factors present a specific, particular, and predictable result is produced. Similarly, when I recommend a tutor for a child of high IQ and normal vision who is doing poorly in reading, and I find that his reading improves, I can speak of the improvement as the result of the tutoring. This result, moreover, has been produced by introducing a specific and describable factor, or complex of factors, into the boy's environment. Although prediction in this sense has meaning, it is never literally perfect, nor is it to be confused with the explanatory function of science—even though that function is often tested by verifying predictions.

Theoretical Systems. In the psychological and social sciences there are many investigations, both experimental and statistical, that are isolated from all context and so little related to one another that both the student and the scientist are bewildered and feel that the task of integration is almost hopeless. Child psychology and educational research are among the worst offenders. We are justified in seeking methods by means of which our results can be integrated in orderly and systematic fashion.

The traditional approach is to urge upon all scientific workers the obligation and responsibility of so presenting their material by giving such precise descriptions

of sampling, experimental design, procedure, and results that other workers can use the data and generalizations. A study is not done for the immediate moment, or for a particular set of children, but to advance our knowledge and understanding of all children. When an attempt is made to reproduce earlier studies or to fit together data on similar problems, the deficiencies of our own and other investigations become painfully apparent.

Modern discussions of scientific method stress the importance of considering integration in the planning and design of a study. Many think of an experiment or study as a simple and single determination of a relation. Actually, however, both in the laboratory and in science as a whole a particular study is only an incident in a long sequence. Ebbinghaus's work on memory consists of a series of single experiments in which, one after another, various factors are controlled, that is, length of list, time interval, etc.—and these experiments, though done in sequence, make an orderly whole.

The modern contribution to the problem is twofold: (1) Fisher (1937) raises the question of designing experiments in such a way that for a given expenditure of time and energy they will yield maximum returns and at the same time systematically, through the design itself, explore all the essential relations which previously were done by single experiments; and (2) Hull and his students (Hull, Hovland, Ross, *et al.*, 1940), working with memory, concern themselves with the logical derivatives and implications of the postulates growing out of our present information, and then lay out a whole system of experiments that will give us the entire web of relations in the area under consideration, or permit the keying-in of crucial experiments that will test and verify. By this process the postulates and principles will be checked, eliminated, modified, or enlarged and an entire system of explanation substituted for the isolated experiment.

In the past the approaches to these far-reaching problems of method have been, on the whole, haphazard, with each investigator building to some extent on the work of his predecessors, but following individual leads rather than deliberately setting up an ideal of elegance and completeness of design for an area. Although Hull's work has not been directly concerned with child psychology, the forward-looking student of method should be familiar with his approach. Lewin (1936), who is causing reorganization of much of our thinking along methodological lines, has worked out a theoretical system in the field of child psychology, not quite, however, in such formal terms as those of Hull. It represents a major attempt to put meaning into an entire area and to work out the experiments that follow from the basic postulates of the system. In any event, it is becoming clear that we are enlarging the principle so often repeated of clearly formulating the single study by preliminary conceptualization to include whole areas of relations and whole series of experiments.

Sources of Material for Child Study

As the child moves on his course, he leaves behind him more or less complete records of his performance and adjustment, in addition to the specific behavior which can be elicited at any moment under controlled conditions. Following is a list of the sources for material for the study of children:

(1) *The present behavior of the child, including his verbal output.* This, the primary and best source, includes the observations, measurements, and records of behavior as obtained in test or experimental situations designed to elicit responses for specific research purposes. Included also are direct observations of behavior in play and social situations, the value of which increases for scientific purposes as systematic and planned recording is done.

(2) *Products of the child left behind as permanent records.* This includes such permanent products as drawings, letters written by the child, compositions, etc., which often yield significant data. The value of such products increases as accessory information is available, such as the date or age at which the product was made and the conditions which occasioned it.

(3) *Records on file at home, school, governmental agencies, health versus social agencies, etc.* Included are all types of records which are presented by a variety of agencies dealing with children, such as birth certificates and health records. Of particular value are school records, especially the more recent cumulative records that include many data. Often investigators can save themselves effort and secure much better sampling, as well as important accessory information, by checking with schools in the areas in which their studies are undertaken.

(4) *Introspections of the child.* Modern investigators pay relatively little attention to this source. They prefer to look upon the verbal output as behavior; this is the case, for example, in the studies of children's thought processes as revealed in their language (Piaget, 1923).

(5) *Memories of the child, or of the adult, of his own earlier life.* Once almost the only source of information on child life, these are now of rather minor importance. They vary as to completeness and accuracy in relation to events and are subject to many errors, both systematic and unsystematic. Modern literature distinguishes two techniques for tapping them, one the recording of conscious memories, and the other getting at more deeply buried memories by a free-association process, or projective methods. But even here modern emphasis is much more upon the child's present reactions than upon his past behavior.

(6) *Memories of the child's life as retained by those who have been associated with him.* Here are included the many effects which are left behind by the child in his relations with others and which are more or less adequately retained by them. These have little scientific value because they are likely to be very incomplete, haphazard, and biased. Sometimes, however, they are used. As the distance in time between contact with the child and reproduction increases, the data become less and less valuable.

(7) *Measures of the parents, siblings, and other relatives of the child or of the environment, culture, or background in which he develops.* Strictly speaking, this source does not furnish direct information on the child. It does, however, supply the data by means of which the results of observations on the child's behavior can be analyzed or broken down. It is necessary both for sampling and for the determination of many significant relations. Examples of the use of such accessory data are to be found in the studies of heredity and environment, such as those of Freeman, Holzinger, and Mitchell (1928), Burks (1928), and Leahy (1935); in the various community studies, in which such matters as the relation of delinquency and city area (Shaw *et al.*, 1929) or intelligence and rural or urban residence (Baldwin, Fillmore, and Hadley, 1930) are analyzed; and in the many studies of the relation of linguistic development to social level, such as those of Hetzer and Reindorf (1928) and McCarthy (1930).

Techniques for Securing Data

It has long been recognized that two characteristics of the scientific method are the *careful observation of phenomena as they occur* and the *accurate recording of these observations* in order that they may be tabulated, analyzed, and checked later. The scientist does not depend upon his memory, but records events as they occur in order to obtain complete reports and to eliminate bias and retrospective falsifi-

cation. He devises situations in which the individual responds directly to stimulation, and makes permanent records of the performance, as when a test blank is filled out, a polygraph is used, or a motion picture record made. Where direct observations or recorded responses cannot be made, he uses ratings made by other persons and reports from his subjects based on interviews, questionnaires, and inventories. We can then divide the techniques for securing data into (1) observations, (2) tests and measurements, (3) ratings, and (4) reports.

Observation. Incidental observations without any attempt to control the conditions or deliberately to produce the event observed are made by everyone who relates anecdotes, makes statements, or speculates about children or adults. Such observations are of little scientific value, whether or not they are made by a scientifically trained person, since the precision of the observations is not known, the sampling is inadequate, and there is no control of conditions or factors. This does not mean that they may not be accurate; it does mean that they have little value as a basis for generalization and that little confidence can be placed in them.

By systematic observation we refer to a technique in which the observer either selects beforehand from the mass of events occurring around the child particular situations which recur and develops a way of recording them systematically or presents the child with a deliberately set-up situation, and then records his responses. The situation presented may be very completely controlled, as in the experiment, or it may be loosely structured, as in the situations used to elicit language responses or in the projective techniques. In the experiment, however, tests, measurements, and mechanically recorded behavior usually take the place of observation.

Some situations recur in ordinary life and can be grouped in similar categories and the behavior occurring in them compared. Thus behavior at home may be compared with that at school, free-play periods may be compared with teacher-guided periods, social reactions when only one companion is present with those when three or four companions are present (Jersild and Meigs, 1939). Many kinds of behavior difficult or impossible to produce under laboratory conditions occur with fair frequency in life. In the large, psychology has neglected these. Within recent years, however, methods of observing them have been much used in a variety of fields, for example, in studies of reactions to museum exhibits, advertising on streetcars, and conversations on trains and at concerts. They have been much used in the study of emotional and social behavior in young children. It is but a step from the utilization of these situations which occur naturally to the setting up of a relatively simple situation, partially controlled and uniformly presented to a large number of children.

In order to permit quantification of observations, *the technique of time sampling* as developed by Olson (1929; Olson and Cunningham, 1934), Goodenough (1928a, 1930), Thomas *et al.* (1929), and others came into wide use. For a comprehensive review, see Arrington, 1943. It introduces no control in the natural situations except recording the frequency of definite events during a constant time interval, which is systematically spaced. By taking a series of such observations on the same day or on successive days, a score is obtained for each child which shows the frequency of the particular phenomena under observation during each period and during the total number of periods. These scores lend themselves readily to statistical treatment. Reliability can be determined by correlat-

ing scores for odd and even periods, and the number of observations necessary to secure stable results can be determined. The scores can also be correlated with other factors. These sampling techniques work well with behavior that occurs frequently. The length of the individual period of observation and the number of observations necessary to achieve stable results vary with the type of behavior studied.

Projective Techniques. Another variant of the observational method is found in the projective techniques used by psychoanalysts and clinical workers for diagnosis and therapy in child adjustment problems. Since many children cannot verbalize their conflicts or hesitate to do so, play and other materials freely available may lead them to express their anxieties, conflicts, insecurities, and wishes in play. Many materials have been used—dolls, knives, drawing and painting (finger) materials, puppets, etc. (Fries, 1937; Frank, 1939; Despert, 1940; Shalloo, 1940). Children have also been encouraged to engage in dramatic play. Sometimes the play itself, sometimes the stimulated conversation, is regarded as the significant outcome.

Our concern is not with the use of these methods for diagnosis or therapy but as a source of generalizations that will give insight into the nature of children. Little or no work has yet been done on the consistency or reliability of the play structures developed by the child over a substantial period of time. In spite of the high value with which their proponents regard them, careful studies of their adequacy in picturing the child's own situation, that is, studies of validity, do not exist. They do, however, represent a very promising area for the study of personality and emotion.

Not so far distant from these techniques are those in which the child is presented with a series of pictures showing various degrees of emotional response. Such pictures have been used to measure social intelligence (Gates, 1923) and sympathy responses (Murphy, 1937). The Rorschach method, about which a substantial literature is developing (Hertz, 1936, 1942), is probably better classified here than with tests.

The use of the motion picture as a source of stimulation for personality and emotional reactions has been only partially explored. In the studies of the Motion Picture Research Council, children at all age levels were found to give significant reactions. In the Clarke School (1940) study of deaf children, a motion picture showing a single dramatic incident was found to be very effective in securing compositions which could be used for analyzing language structure. The measurements in these studies, however, were made in terms of attitude scales, expressive movements, and language form and structure, rather than fantasy, play, or social behavior.

Measurement. Under this heading are included the many direct measures based on time, movement, amount accomplished or retained, errors, simple tests, etc., and the many indirect measures and tests of complex functions that have been developed over many years by many research workers. Basically, all record in some fashion a characteristic or response pattern in quantities that can be measured or classified and subjected to statistical manipulation. Because of their wide variety the specific limitations of each cannot be discussed here. The general principles underlying their use will be discussed in the next section. Whipple (1924) and Greulich, Day, Lachman, *et al.* (1938) present the procedures for many such measurements, and Shuttleworth's (1938) *Atlas* contains many curves based on measurements.

Ratings. In the present state of our knowledge, and possibly permanently, many complex phases of behavior cannot readily be measured either directly or indirectly. For their analysis we depend on rating or ranking methods in which an observer—another person—expresses in some form his estimate of the degree or amount of a particular characteristic or pattern of behavior manifested by the subject. The techniques involved are of two main types. The first compares stimuli, situations, individuals, or products by assigning each to a relative position or rank-order with reference to every other. The second technique involves categorizing several aspects of the life or behavior of the individual, each of which makes up a continuum, and then placing the child in question in his approximate position within each category by marking off his distance either graphically or numerically from the bottom or top of the group with respect to the particular characteristic in question. The variants of the method in the types of items used, the general form of scales, and the method of summating items into a single score are many. Ratings increase in value with the number of raters used. Self-rating scales are also in use. The technique has also been applied to children's products, such as drawings, writing, and the like. Extensive discussions of the methodology of ratings are found in Hull (1928), Symonds (1931), Weiss (1933), etc.

Conrad (1933), in an extensive study, found that the reliability of ratings of young children by nursery school teachers and the agreement between judges vary significantly with (1) the trait being judged, (2) the child being judged, (3) the estimated significance of the particular trait for the child in question, and (4) the confidence with which the judge rates the particular trait for the child in question. The fact that the figures tended to be somewhat higher than those usually published for older children suggests that some unreliability in ratings can be traced to the unequal acquaintance under different circumstances of the raters with those rated. For these teachers were in close contact with the children for long periods. One method for improving ratings is to insure equal amounts of observation under similar external conditions. This partially explains why the observational methods, which often use categories and descriptions similar to ratings, show such high reliabilities.

Report. Under this heading are included a number of techniques which have in common the fact that reports by individuals as to their own status, opinions, facts, etc., or the status and facts of other persons are made. These include the face-to-face interview, the questionnaire, and the inventory. There is some overlapping with other techniques, such as ratings, since the reporter may be asked to rate himself or compare his performance with that of others. And the results, especially of the inventory and occasionally those of a questionnaire, may be pooled into subscores or a total score to be used for indirect measurement of personality or general traits. Great variation in the manner in which data are secured is found; it may vary from a simple series of questions answered *in extenso* to a highly structured list of questions in which the reporter or interviewer merely checks or underlines appropriate responses.

Interview. The interview has been used for obtaining data for many years. Originally merely a conversation on the basis of which a summary or report was written, it has become a careful procedure based upon a blank on which data are systematically entered and complete responses recorded. Usually the blanks begin with a face-sheet for recording essential sampling and evaluative data, such as name, address, telephone, age, education, occupation, other members of the family, etc. The remaining blank seeks information concerning the particular area or problem in hand. The advantages of schedules prepared in advance and given systematically are many, especially since data gathered by haphazard and unplanned interviews are difficult to use for scientific purposes. Thus on a prepared blank the fact that the individual refused to answer, did not have the information, etc., can be checked and appropriate interpretations made in the analysis. Unless this is done a refusal, a negative answer, or the failure of the interviewer to give the question cannot be distinguished.

In interviewing for scientific purposes some record should be made for every question asked. Attention must also be paid to the form of the question and the order in which questions are given. An example of an extensive series of interviews laid out by a national committee and obtained from every area of the United States, by a planned sampling procedure, is found in the White House Conference reports (Burgess, 1934; Anderson, 1936). The public opinion polls, developments in the field of social work, and the development of guidance are turning the interview technique into a valuable scientific instrument. The newer practice of recording interviews by electrical means will permit further study and analysis of the technique.

Questionnaire. There are two types of questionnaires: (1) those which seek the opinion of a group with reference to particular situations, modes of behavior, individual characteristics, matters of policy, training, etc.; and (2) those which seek facts which the person filling out the questionnaire is in a position to know on the basis of direct observation, available figures, tests, etc.

Much of the distrust of the questionnaire arises from confusion between matters of opinion and matters of fact. Thus, if a group of experts are asked to give an opinion as to the value of motion pictures for young children, their expression of opinion is of value only in so far as the particular persons asked to contribute are qualified to express an opinion. Neither the individual opinions nor the group opinion is the equivalent of scientific data based on observation, measurement, or experiment unless the scientist is engaged in a study of opinion and uses the material itself as data. When, however, the questionnaire deals with facts collected from those in a position to know, it may have much scientific value. In a sense, every report on a prepared blank, such as a financial report, can be looked upon as a questionnaire. A questionnaire which enlists the cooperation of mothers in recording the sleep of their children may be of value scientifically, whereas a collection of opinions about sleep would be of relatively little scientific value. A questionnaire of this type sets up conditions which result in systematic observation.

The questionnaire method aims to obtain from large numbers of individuals observations which could not be made by a single individual. Its accuracy depends upon the skill with which it is made out, that is, the definiteness, specificity, and practicality of the questions, the capacity of the persons answering, the length of time that has elapsed since the occurrence of the events to be recorded, and the sampling of persons to whom the blanks are sent—and, what is even more important, within that sampling, upon the sampling characteristics of those that reply. It is subject to errors of memory, misunderstanding of terms, and mental sets imposed by the questions. In general, verification by other methods is necessary.

Inventory. Within the classification, "questionnaire," Symonds (1931), who presents a very complete analysis of the methods available for the study of personality and conduct, places adjustment questionnaires, such as the psychoneurotic inventory in its various forms, measures of introversion-extroversion and of ascendance and submission; attitude questionnaires, such as measures of social attitudes, fair-mindedness tests, and the Thurstone attitude scales; and interest questionnaires, such as the Strong tests for vocational interest, and other measuring devices for determining the permanence of interests, or specific types of interests. All these devices have a common characteristic, namely, the individual himself is engaged in answering questions about his own attitudes, interests, etc. The purpose of the inventory is usually not so much an analysis of the individual responses, in and for themselves, as deriving a general measure which can be used for various theoretical and practical purposes. Many of these devices are susceptible of administration to groups and are often loosely spoken of as tests. Actually, however, there is no right or wrong answer to the questions put and, irrespective of their direction or value, responses may be included because of a demonstrated relation to the function measured.

The Development of Measuring Instruments and the Determination of Their Precision

In the first approach to psychological problems, measures were used which had an obvious and direct relation to the phenomena studied. Thus, the speed of reaction was measured in units of time, memory or retention in terms of the amount retained or the reduction in time or errors on succeeding trials, and the height and weight of children in inches or pounds. In a sense these are simple measures as well as direct measures. Later, "indirect" measures, sometimes called the measures of complex functions, appeared. Because of the functional unity of the organism which prevents its physical separation into discrete parts, and because few functions can be isolated easily, psychologists were forced, if their science was to progress, to develop indirect measures by means of which some quality or aspect of functioning could be separated out of the total mass that makes up the person.

The classical instance is furnished by the measurement of intelligence, in which difficulties are encountered both in defining the term and in demonstrating that test items which superficially bear little resemblance to one another measure a common factor. Actually, intelligence can be defined only in terms of the criteria by means of which a leverage or foothold has been obtained in the total mass of functioning. These criteria are age progression, teachers' rankings or ratings, academic grades, and success in life adjustment. Intelligence is not perfectly correlated with any one of these. It is assumed, however, that by using these criteria and selecting for the components of a test those positively correlated with each—those on which the scores increase with chronological age, school grades, ratings of brightness, and ratings or performance in life adjustment—and combining the components into a single measuring instrument, a factor common to all but not identical with any of the criteria will be measured. Moreover, the value of the component parts is increased if their interrelations with one another are lower than the cor-

relations of each with the criteria, since that means commonality of measurement in terms of the criterion without identity or great similarity in the components. If different criteria are used, a different complex will be measured. Indirect measurement then begins with a series of assumptions which may be explicit and clearly recognized, but often are implicit and not recognized, and ends with an instrument which gains its meaning from those assumptions, however the instrument may be labeled. Failure to recognize this very fundamental point has caused much confusion in the literature and no end of argument and controversy.

In the development of many measures, another procedure of a somewhat different order, called the *criterion of internal consistency*, is added. It is assumed that the total score, that is, a summation of the scores on the various parts, measures more of the psychological function than does any individual component. Hence, by correlating the components with this total score by some technique of item analysis, those items or components which show little or no relation with the total score can be eliminated and the remainder used. Thus the length of the instrument is reduced to an effective minimum, and a purer measure of whatever is measured is obtained. It is possible also to use factor analysis (Spearman, 1927; Kelley, 1928; Thurstone, 1935, 1940; Guilford, 1936; Thomson, 1939), a primary tool for the analysis of human abilities, also for a similar purpose, namely, to determine which test components carry particular loadings, to eliminate and purify, and to show the need for devising and adding more components.

With the actual details of the measuring devices, both direct and indirect, for the many problems and areas in child psychology, we cannot here concern ourselves. Their number is legion.

There are, however, two interrelated but fundamental problems which arise in the use of all types of measurement. One of them has come to be known as the problem of *validity*, which is the extent or degree to which the measuring device measures what it purports to measure; the other is the problem of *reliability*, which refers to the consistency of results obtained by a measuring device over a short period of time.

Validity. The problem of validity is of minor concern when we deal with direct measures. It is obvious that height is measured by distance on a scale of inches or centimeters, or that reaction time is measured in units of time—in fact, for many types of direct measures the very terms used to describe the measure characterize its type. Often, however, direct measures are teamed together for purposes of indirect measurement, in which case our interest is not in the direct measure itself but in its contribution to the team.

An arithmetic test given to measure the children's knowledge of the material taught the preceding week is an example of direct measurement. If, however, the children are given a standardized achievement test in arithmetic, our purpose is not so much to discover what the child knows of what has just been taught as to determine his level of arithmetical functioning. Here is the borderline between direct and indirect measurement. The particular questions are considered indicators or samples of a more generalized capacity which manifests itself irrespective of the particular questions used; two alternative standardized forms of the achievement test with different questions may yield the same result. If the arithmetic test is used as a member of a team of tests in an intelligence battery, however, we are concerned neither with the particular problems as such, nor with arithmetical ability, but with intel-

lectual level—a still more generalized capacity. It is clear, then, that the purpose of measurement, rather than the particular items used, determines the difference between direct and indirect measurement. Similarly, we may measure height and weight directly, or we may, as has been done, use weight in relation to age and height as an index of nutrition or health. Although psychologists are sometimes criticized for their extensive use of indirect measures, in actual practice the use of indirect measures, tracers, or indicators is common to many sciences.

With indirect measures, however, the problem of validity—the relation between the indicator or tracer and the process of which it is an indicator—becomes of central importance. After such a device has been developed by some method of selecting parts in terms of their correlation with pooled criteria, the total scores can be correlated with each of the criteria or with the pooled criteria, or a new group of individuals on which the criteria are available can be given the measure, and the correlations obtained. The latter is the sounder procedure. When the scores of a group used for item selection are totaled and correlated with the criteria, a spuriously high figure is obtained. It is a generally accepted principle that the data from the group used for item selection shall not be used for validation or standardization. Both item selection and validation may be done in a variety of ways by using the entire distribution of the criteria, by using extreme or contrasting groups of various degrees of separation in terms of the criterion, or even, in those cases where a measuring instrument of known value is already available, by direct correlation with it. Thus some group intelligence tests have been validated by correlation with the results of Stanford-Binet individual examinations. In some instances cleverly devised experimental or social situations have been used to validate portions of personality scales (Marston, 1925).

Scaling and Standardization. A second problem in the development of a measuring device is scaling or standardizing it in terms of the criteria. With direct measures, the unit of measurement is reasonably clear or definite—the child reacts in so many thousandths of a second, is so many inches tall, remembers so many words after a lapse of time, etc. With indirect measures, units of various meanings and of differing values have to be combined. In the age scaling of the intelligence test this problem is met in terms of the known performance of the child at various age levels; in many instruments definite reference is made to the validation process, either through percentiles or standard scores, points above or below which the individual is classed as neurotic, introverted, defective, etc. In many cases these limits are set in terms of what may be called a practical or social criterion.

Reliability. The consistency with which a measuring instrument functions is known as reliability. The child's height today is so slightly different from what it was yesterday that the same results should be obtained in measuring it, unless an extraordinarily delicate device were available for its measurement. Over long periods of time we expect significant changes. Hence, by repeating measures on the same group of children after a short interval, the correlation coefficient obtained between them should approximate unity, and its size give a measure of reliability.

The three methods commonly used for determining the self-correlation of measures are: (1) the correlation between repetitions of the same measure, (2) the correlation between two similar and comparable but not identical forms, and (3) the division of the items or parts of the measure on a definite plan into equivalent parts (usually by summing the scores on odd and even items separately) and determining the correlations between those parts. The first method is sometimes vitiated by the differential carry-over of practice effects; the second method corrects for this, but necessitates two or more measures demonstrated to be equivalent; the third is much used since no practice effects are involved and no second form is necessary. The determination of reliability is especially important for any measure that is used for the prediction or evaluation of the performance of individuals.

The reliability of a scaled and standardized measuring instrument can be readily determined. But many of the data available in child psychology are based not upon such tests, but upon observations made on the basis of carefully worked out schedules divided into defined categories. For these a reliability measure (perhaps not strictly comparable with that of tests but nevertheless of great value) is obtained by having two observers, usually trained in advance, record the behavior of the same children or groups and obtain the correlation between their observations. This has also been used with recorded language responses that are to be classified. Or, when rating scales are used, the correlation between independent raters, or between successive ratings by the same individual, may be used. Some investigators use the percentage of agreement between two raters or observers, or between two successive observations or ratings, as measures of reliability. Since no consistent procedures are followed in calculating these percentages, it is difficult to interpret them. More care should be taken to quantify such data in order to permit the use of established correlational procedures. In any event, the use of such reliability measures often results in substantial improvement in observational techniques.

There is one very serious problem in the interpretation of reliability coefficients obtained on children. Since the size of a correlation coefficient is a function of the homogeneity or heterogeneity of the population on which it is calculated, and since almost every function in children changes in some degree with chronological age, spuriously high coefficients can be obtained by using a wide age range. Hence in the determination of validity and reliability coefficients the careful worker calculates these coefficients for a narrow age range—usually a single year—in order to eliminate the heterogeneity due to age. When reliability coefficients are compared, corrections for range have to be made, or comparisons avoided unless the range is known. Both readers of the experimental literature and investigators should watch this problem with some care.

Heterogeneity also affects the intercorrelations of separate measures. Intercorrelations for different motor performance over a range of four or five years, particularly at younger age levels, are exceptionally high, and indicate the possibility of developing a scale for general motor skill. When calculated over a one-year range, however, the reliabilities are so low as to indicate that such a scale cannot be developed. Moreover, since these reliability coefficients decrease rapidly with age, whereas those obtained for intelligence items increase, it is clear that the effect of age varies with the function studied.

The construction of a good measuring instrument is a technical job that requires ingenuity, skill, and an understanding of basic principles and of appropriate statistical techniques. A good instrument opens up areas of research that previously were inaccessible. It is unfortunate that so many haphazard, poorly standardized, inadequately evaluated, and inappropriately named devices are put forward. Nowhere is this more evident than in the fields of child psychology and educational measurement, where such a host of devices is available that an annual volume is necessary merely to catalogue them (Buros, 1938). Excellent discussions of the principles, statistical procedures, and techniques for validating, scaling, standardizing, and determining the reliability of measuring instruments are found in a number of texts (Hull, 1928; Symonds, 1931; Guilford, 1936, 1942; Peters and Van Voorhis, 1940) and in an extensive literature of articles.

Sampling

Recently it has become clear that some of the inconsistencies and the contradictions in published research grow out of variations in the selection of the cases studied. Whereas a decade ago psychologists were much concerned with the precision of measures, the past decade has shown a great interest in sampling problems. In a scientific investigation the subjects studied are looked upon as representatives of a larger population. In practical relations, on the other hand, concern is with a finite population. Thus a test of reading proficiency is given to a fifth grade. If interest is only in that grade's performance, the test results have no significance except as a measure of that limited population. If it is given to establish norms or as a phase of a study of the value of one method of instruction as compared with another, however, its significance is extended. For this fifth grade has now become the representative of the fifth-grade population. The question of its representativeness and the significance of the conclusions reached for all fifth-grade children become of paramount importance.

This distinction is not always recognized. Some authors carefully and almost apologetically limit their conclusions to the particular sample studied. One may ask, then, why publish at all? Others go to the opposite extreme and make generalizations on samples that are neither representative nor adequate in size. If all conclusions were examined in the light of sampling, many inconsequential studies would not be published.

Implicit in any discussion of sampling is the problem of statistical significance. Since the purpose of most research is to generalize from a sample to a population, the question whether or not the results obtained from the sample arise by chance or are truly the outcome of the relations or phenomena in question is pertinent. In modern treatments, the *null hypothesis* is assumed, namely, that whatever results comes by chance in the particular sample. The obligation is, then, placed upon the investigator to prove that *this is not so,* which he does by the tests of significance, showing the degree of confidence to be placed in the results obtained, or the likelihood that they would not occur by chance alone.

Sampling problems first arose in normative studies, since the value of a standard is clearly a function of the sample. Height-weight tables and intelligence test scales are standards against which thousands of individual children are checked for diagnostic and practical purposes. If they are inaccurate, the usefulness of the instrument is reduced and injustice done to many innocent children.

At first thought it would seem possible to select children at random. With animals it is possible to select random samples, the essential condition for which is *that each individual is as likely as any other to appear in the sample drawn.* Human beings, however, are social and live in a context that is shot through with selective processes. In cities, families of the same income level tend to live in the same neighborhoods. Each occupation and profession is itself selective. A church, a political group, a social club, a leisure time activity is selective. Often children in the public school are thought of as a typical or complete population. Since some children do not enter public school because of mental and physical defects, and others go to private schools, even the kindergarten or first grade is somewhat selective. After school entrance some children progress more and others less rapidly. In a short time children of a given chronological age are spread out over a number of grades. If one were to study all first-grade children in an area which has compulsory education, a better sample would be secured from the standpoint of representativeness than if seventh- or eighth-graders in the same schools were tested. Since many children never go to high school and only relatively few get to college, high school and college populations are far from representative. Even the schools and areas within a city are highly selective. Table 1, taken from Maller (1933), shows the mean IQ's of fifth-grade children in 273 health areas in New York City. The mean IQ for the areas varied from 74 to 120. If a school selected for study happened to be one with a mean IQ of 74, or with a mean IQ of 118, how typical or valid would be the generalizations arrived at?

To meet the problem imposed by the differential selection of human beings in their social environments, various techniques have been evolved for drawing systematic or stratified samples from the total population. [See Yule and Kendall (1937) for principles and McNemar (1940) for a detailed discussion and extensive bibliography on the problems of sampling.] These procedures involve the use of sam-

TABLE 1

DISTRIBUTION OF MEAN IQ'S IN 273 HEALTH
AREAS IN NEW YORK CITY

(Based on the examination of 100,153 fifth-
grade children)

Scale	Frequency
118	2
114	11
110	18
106	42
102	46
98	57
94	40
90	29
86	14
82	7
78	6
74	1
Total	273
Mean	100.43
SD	8.28

pling criteria which can be laid down in advance in order to select a sample that conforms to the characteristics of the population.

Age and Sex. Many earlier studies used unequal numbers of cases and of the sexes at different age levels. In modern studies the problem of age and sex sampling is solved by using the same number of children at each age level, say 100 at two, 100 at three years, and so on. Within each age group the children are distributed equally with respect to sex, say 50 boys and 50 girls at each age level. Actually, an equal sex division is not quite representative of the true proportion of the sexes in the population, but it is so close to it that no serious error is introduced. Age sampling can be further controlled by testing on birthdays, or selecting children within one month of their birth date, instead of selecting over a range of a whole year within the age classification. This determines the points on the age curve more precisely and increases accuracy.

Cultural or Socioeconomic Level. The problem of sampling in terms of cultural level is difficult. Various proposals have been made for its solution. The most common involve selection either in terms of a single factor, such as paternal occupation or income level, or in terms of a series of questions covering occupation, income, possessions, etc., as in the Sims scale (1928) or the very complete scale of Leahy (1936). Many modern studies in child psychology control selection in terms of paternal occupation, which has a distinct advantage since the occupational distribution for any particular area or section or for the country as a whole can be determined from the census data. Occupation is one of the few cultural facts for which we have universal figures. One of the most widely used socioeconomic devices is the Minnesota Scale of Paternal Occupation (Goodenough and Anderson, 1931), which divides adult males into seven classifications according to their occupations, as shown in Table 2.

To set up a sample of 100 children at any age level, knowing the occupation of their fathers, we can match proportions by rounding the percentages or, by rounding to even numbers, split the sample in half to permit control of sex as well as occupation. The third and fourth columns show such samples for 100 and 50 cases, respectively. It should be noted, however, that this sampling is concerned with increasing the accuracy of the mean and standard deviation of the whole distribution, not with determining the differences between occupational groups.

If published data are checked in terms of representative sampling, much sampling is found to be far from typical. Children from the extremes are more readily accessible than in the middle ranges. Parents

TABLE 2

CLASSIFICATION OF OCCUPATIONS OF EMPLOYED MALES IN THE UNITED STATES

	1940 Census		Sample	
	Total	Percentage	100	50
Class I. Professional	922,156	2.71	3	2
Class II. Semi-professional and managerial	2,436,397	7.16	7	4
Class III. Clerical, skilled trades, and retail business	4,808,143	14.13	14	7
Class IV. Farmers	5,192,658	15.26	15	7
Class V. Semi-skilled occupations, minor clerical positions, and minor business	8,129,266	23.89	24	12
Class VI. Slightly skilled trades and occupations requiring little training or ability	4,954,463	14.56	15	7
Class VII. Day laborers of all classes (including agriculture)	7,584,820	22.29	22	11

in the upper three occupational groups, which contain 23 per cent of the population, tend to be more cooperative, more easily reached, more interested in programs of measurement, and more likely to volunteer or take advantage of an agency set up for children. Some parents in Classes VI and VII are in close contact with social agencies, day nurseries, etc. A private school with tuition draws its population almost entirely from Classes I and II. A day nursery or a settlement house draws its population from Classes VI and VII. Thus Classes III and V in the urban areas tend to be neglected, and only very few studies contain representatives of the rural groups in Classes IV and VII.

The necessity of controlling occupational background depends upon the correlation of the particular characteristics which are being studied with occupational status. But studies show that a very substantial number of traits, environmental conditions, etc., with which the student of child behavior is concerned are correlated in some degree with occupational status (Anderson, chairman, 1936). Failing control of sampling, it is important, especially from the standpoint of subsequent integration and interpretation of research findings, to give such complete descriptions of the sampling used in any investigation that the reader will be able to interpret the results and compare them with others. The minimum is chronological age, sex, socioeconomic status, and school grade. Often additional material is presented in terms of mental age, urban and rural residence, etc.

A second sampling problem involved concerns the size of the sample necessary to obtain significant results for the particular problem at hand. Two decades ago it was assumed that the more cases used the more significant were the results. Although this principle is still sound, most workers undertaking investigations are under practical limitations of time, money, and the availability of subjects. Hence it is desirable so to design and arrange an experiment that the results will be significant without the necessity of doing a great amount of unnecessary experimentation. From modern discussions the principle emerges that a small sample selected in accordance with criteria rigidly laid down in advance gives more significant and meaningful results than a much larger sample the characteristics of which are unknown. The better public opinion polls and the sampling techniques used in modern industry are based on this principle.

It should be noted, however, that the importance and the necessity of adequate sampling procedure vary somewhat with the type of problem under investigation. For instance, reaction time can be determined with a high degree of accuracy on a relatively small number of cases, whereas measures of more complex processes need a larger number of cases. Furthermore, the size of the sample necessary depends also upon the number of relationships involved in the data. Where the relationship of two variables is to be studied and extraneous factors have been rigorously controlled by the experimental set-up, a smaller sample is necessary than when the weight and pattern of many factors contributing to a complex area of behavior are to be determined without control. Furthermore, the precision of a study depends both upon the number of cases used and the reliability and validity of the measuring instruments. When the measuring instrument is coarse, a larger number of cases is necessary to establish whatever trends or relations exist.

Again the reader is referred to Mc-Nemar's (1940) bibliography and article, which closes with this statement:

Perhaps the confidence to be placed in the results of a study should vary directly with the amount of information concerning the sampling and experimental techniques rather than inversely with the square root of the number of cases (p. 363).

The Organization and Design of Studies

In discussing the organization of research projects, we may speak of experimental design. Fisher (1936, 1937) has used the term for a procedure which begins with a definition of a population and a description of the sample drawn from it at random, and moves on so to arrange the observations in terms of single and multiple factors that maximum information will be obtained. An essential element is the deliberate consideration of the number of cases, the number of samples, and the arrangement of observations in order to secure the information wanted and establish the significance or lack of significance of the results obtained. This implies that the methods of measurement, the sampling procedures, and the methods of control are laid out in advance and are interrelated. Serial and isolated experiments are consolidated into single studies to obtain more information with a smaller number of cases and to evaluate the interaction of factors statistically.

The problem of design is an old one. In laboratories systematic arrangements for control have always been used. See, for instance, Melton's (1936) extensive discussion of experimental methodology in learning. Although many of these designs have neglected sampling criteria for subjects, concern with the number of observations necessary for generalization has been shown. Fisher and his co-workers have also given us new tools for determining statistical significance which permit the use of smaller samples and new techniques, such as Latin and Graeco Latin Squares, for the analysis of complex relations.

The term *design* may be broadened to cover every schema for investigations, laboratory experiments, control group studies. The studies using the sampling controls set up by Fisher may be regarded as particular instances. Immediately, past and projected investigations can be examined with respect to their design, and questions regarding their quality or adequacy can be raised. Is the design such that scientific information will be obtained? Is it such that the maximum information for the amount of time, money, energy, and number of cases available will be obtained? Of these questions, the second is the more important, because it implies a type of planning that will enable the investigator to know in advance what he may expect from his efforts and assumes some knowledge of the variables under investigation and of the specific hypotheses.

The plan or schema of published or projected studies may be represented in diagrammatic form, as in the chart showing the technique of the control group on page 28. The Latin square is a diagram of an investigation in algebraic form. The implications of postulates for a system of experiments may be put in terms of symbolic logic, as in Hull, Hovland, Ross, *et al.* (1940), or in topological diagrams, as in Lewin (1936). Methods of representing design in generalized symbolic form or schema are of great value in the planning of studies and in thinking through their outcomes, since they abstract in some degree from the particular material of the investigation and lead the student to the essential features underlying many different types of scientific study. One can hardly engage in this symbolic process without improvement in the specific study undertaken.

Experiment. The phenomena of interest to science seldom occur in isolation, nor with such high frequency that observations can readily be made. No matter how careful the recording or how unbiased the observation, little progress is made when science has to await natural occurrences.

Experiment, then, becomes a primary and basic scientific method which finds its rationale in a deliberate attempt to isolate phenomena and reproduce them frequently enough under controlled conditions to determine their characteristic relations. Two methods are used to eliminate or isolate the effect of various factors: one is making factors constant in order that they may not affect the particular factors under observation, and the other is purifying a factor or substance by stimulating all extraneous material and then studying its nature and effects. In either case, the experiment takes the complex phenomena of nature, breaks them up into segments, studies the action and relation of these segments, either singly or in combination, and arrives at appropriate generalizations. Thus, every experiment is an abstraction, since material is pulled out of its individual and characteristic context. Whatever the method used, the control is deliberate and in a sense artificial. Thus children similarly motivated and free from distracting influences in a special room throw a ball at a target from a known distance in order that their learning may be studied. Or a series of difficult tasks may be set before children working individually, in groups without team structure, in groups as members of teams, and praise may be given to half the children in these varied tasks and withheld from the other half. Thus the effects of individual effort and of effort under social facilitation and under competition may be compared both with and without the special incentive of praise.

The simple experiment seeks to keep as many factors constant as possible and then systematically to vary the particular one under study. And in the complex experiment there is a systematic arrangement, with rotation of groups, stimulation, etc., in order that the weight and nature of various factors may be determined and compared. In most experiments on children, however, a major difficulty is soon encountered. If an attempt is made to use the same subjects over again with the same or different stimulation, the children will have changed because of growth and the incidental and formal learning which constantly goes forward. With adults the growth factor is of such slight moment

absence of this condition by dash lines. The lighter solid lines indicate the accessory measurements which may have been used for sampling or to cover functions which might show transfer or spread because of the introduced condition. The differences in the change between first tests and end tests determine the immediate effect of the condition introduced, and the

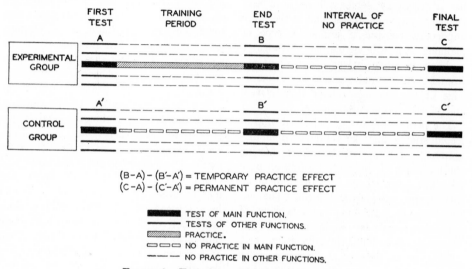

$$(B-A) - (B'-A') = \text{TEMPORARY PRACTICE EFFECT}$$
$$(C-A) - (C'-A') = \text{PERMANENT PRACTICE EFFECT}$$

TEST OF MAIN FUNCTION.
TESTS OF OTHER FUNCTIONS.
PRACTICE.
NO PRACTICE IN MAIN FUNCTION.
NO PRACTICE IN OTHER FUNCTIONS.

FIGURE 1. Technique of the control group.

that it can be ignored, and the practice factor can be met by appropriate design. *The Technique of the Control Group.* Hence in actual practice many experiments are enlarged to include a second group of subjects in which the particular factors under observation are not introduced except in so far as periodic measurement is necessary, thus permitting comparison between groups subject to an experimental condition and groups lacking it. Thus the method of the control group has many ramifications and many modifications. Figure 1 shows the essential features of the control group. In this diagram tests are indicated by solid lines, the experimental condition by crosshatched lines, and the

difference between first tests and the final test indicates the permanency of that effect.

This schema can be extended vertically by the addition of other groups subjected to different conditions, and longitudinally over such periods of time as meet the needs of the particular experiment. The number of cases used may vary through wide ranges—from two cases, as in the method of co-twin control, to large populations. The separations of the original groups can be made on the basis of factors which inhere in the individual or in the context or environment as indicated in an earlier section. Thus the experimental group may consist of very bright children and the control group of normal children, or of children of high musical capacity, and of low musical capacity, etc. Here the investigator is primarily concerned with the types of behavior at subsequent periods of development that grow out of these differences. Or the capacities of the children may be kept constant in so far as measured, and variations introduced into the environment or context. Thus the experimental group may be exposed to typewriters while the control group lacks such access in order to determine the effect of typewriters upon spelling, reading, and writing. Or the experimental group may have geography lessons plus motion pictures and the control group geography lessons without motion pictures. The experimental group may have one type of instruction in reading, and the control group another. The experimental group may be given intensive training in motor, intellectual, or linguistic skills, while the control group moves ahead in its ordinary environment.

The use of the control technique represents an attempt to secure a base or reference line from which comparisons can be made. Logically, it seeks to avoid generalizations based upon mere concomitance by definitely taking account of exceptions, that is, by determining whether or not the changes occur in the absence of the particular factor under consideration. To the naïve observer concomitance often seems of high importance; to the scientist the determination of whether the concomitance is genuine or is an accident of observation or sampling is much more important. In an only child with a behavior problem, no doubt exists as to the presence of the problem in the particular child; and someone may make a generalization that "onliness" and "behavior problems" are related. For the scientist, however, the critical question concerns the amount of con-

fidence to be placed in this generalization, not the fact that the two events occurred together and came under observation. Additional cases in which only children and behavior problems went together would not eliminate the possibility of bias, sampling errors, or misinterpretations. The additional information necessary for the scientist is the proportion of only children who do not show behavior problems, and the proportion of non-only children who show behavior problems and who do not show behavior problems. With this fourfold table and a sufficient number of subjects, the association between being a behavior problem and being an only child can be measured and a generalization made in which the scientist can repose a measurable degree of confidence.

Whether control is achieved by laboratory methods, parallel groups, or statistical devices, all of which seek to determine *net* relations, there are three distinct methodological problems. The *first*, which is the determination of the relations or associations between the variables under consideration, is essentially a matter of descriptive statistics. The *second*, which is the determination of the confidence to be placed in the relations as determined, is a matter of the statistics of inference. Confidence, expressed as a measure of significance or as a fiducial limit, involves disproving the null hypothesis by showing the likelihood that similar results could not have occurred by chance. The *third* is the matter of the psychological significance or the meaningfulness of the relations found. This should not be confused with statistical significance. Essentially psychological significance is a matter of the fit of the generalizations discovered with the framework of our existing knowledge, their capacity to reorganize and make meaningful data that previously did not fit, and the insight they give into new relations and phenomena.

The Matched Control Group. In this variation of the control group technique, the children within a defined group are divided into two groups as alike as possible. Through preliminary measurements their status is determined and the best possible matches made within the framework of the group. With one variable involved, the matching is very simple. By putting the top child on the matching variable in the experimental, the second in the control, the third in the control, and the fourth in the experimental group, and so on throughout the population, the means and the standard deviations of the two groups are equalized. As the number of variables on which matching is done increases, the possibilities of matching within narrow limits are reduced and a much larger population is necessary in order to secure precise matches. In the best applications of this technique the criteria for matching are laid down in advance and then adhered to rigidly. Thus, for example, where matching is done on more than one variable the sexes can be equalized between the two groups, socioeconomic status precisely matched in terms of parents' occupation, a variation of three months in chronological age and a variation of ten points of IQ permitted between pairs. Usually the matching on the variable to be studied—that in which the experimental condition is to be introduced—is very precise.

The choice of matching factors depends upon this variable. If it is positively correlated with any other factor it should be controlled; if there is no correlation, its control is not necessary. For instance, in studying motor skills it is usually not necessary, except with very young children, to control the intelligence or the socioeconomic factor since the correlation of intelligence or socioeconomic status with motor skill for a group homogeneous for age and sex is very low. In a study of language, however, with which both socioeconomic status and intelligence are positively correlated, both should be controlled. It might appear that, since the means and dispersions for both groups on the original measurements are known, a correction could be applied to take care of differences in intelligence and socioeconomic status. This is partly true, but it is likely that any gain in language ability in the course of the experiment would be differential with respect to both intelligence or socioeconomic level. Hence a spurious difference would be obtained even though a correction had been applied.

There is always a possibility of controlling the variables so completely that little or no variation with the experimental condition is permitted. Sometimes more is held constant than should be. This is not so likely to happen with the matching variables as with the materials or procedures used for the experimentally introduced condition. Thus in an educational experiment, materials, texts, and exercises were so closely parallel for two groups compared for two different methods of instruction that no differences were obtained. In the actual practical use of these methods of instruction, however, the materials, texts, and exercises vary with the method of instruction. In experiments evaluating laboratory instruction in science matching was done on a preliminary examination, but the final testing was done on the lecture material common to both groups and not on the laboratory content. Gates and Taylor (1926) found little or no difference between an experimental and a control group as a result of training in a simple motor skill, whereas Mattson (1933), working with skills of three levels of complexity, found that the results obtained in a controlled experiment varied with complexity. Jersild (1932) found little change with motor skills of a simple type and much change in ability to reproduce pitches and intervals. Since these studies suggest that the results obtained in control group experiments vary with the measures used to test the effects, the complexity of the process itself, and the type or modality of the process, great care must be exercised in interpreting the results.

One source of statistical misinterpretation is found in the use of measures for evaluating the differences between experimental and control groups. Many investigators have used the formula for significance in which the correlational term is absent. When the phenomena studied are positively correlated with the factors by means of which the matching is done, that formula for the standard error of the difference, or a modification of it, should be used in which the correlation term is present:

$$\sigma_D{}^2 = \sigma_{\overline{X}_1}{}^2 + \sigma_{\overline{X}_2}{}^2 - 2r_{12}\sigma_{\overline{X}_1}\sigma_{\overline{X}_2}$$

Guilford (1936, 1942), McNemar (1940), and Peters and Van Voorhis (1940) discuss the appropriate statistical formulae.

Furthermore, in pairing, the control of a factor such as intelligence also partially controls socioeconomic status and vice versa, because they are positively correlated with each other. McNemar points out that, as one increases the number of variables over which control is exercised, the returns obtained diminish much as do weights in a regression equation where many overlapping variables are used. The question of the number of variables necessary for control for the particular study at hand should be carefully considered in advance, as no rule can be laid down to cover all studies. In most modern studies the variables used for matching are: (1) sex, (2) chronological age (or school grade in educational studies), (3) intelligence, (4) socioeconomic status, and (5) initial status on the factor investigated.

Controls Drawn from a Supply. In many studies the individuals in a finite population are paired with children drawn from a supply of cases in the general population. If the supply from which the control group is drawn is large, very precise matching can be done to meet very narrow criteria. Thus the investigator may be able to match chronological age within ten days on either side of the birthday, IQ's within five points, and socioeconomic status, sex, and other factors rigidly. The number of cases necessary to secure pairs increases with the number of matching variables used. Thus in a study by Goodenough (1928b), in which children were paired with respect to sex, age, IQ, education of father, education of mother, socioeconomic status of the father, and the nativity of parents, a supply of over three hundred children was necessary in order to secure matches for an experimental group of twenty-eight children.

Matching After Exposure to Experimental Conditions. Sometimes in a minor variant of the control group technique, one segment of a fairly large population is exposed to experimental conditions and another is used as control, with matching done after the collection of data for both segments. It is often more convenient to test and experiment with all the children in a school in order not to interrupt the class routine by drawing out the special cases needed for a particular study. Later matching can be done and irrelevant cases thrown out. Although loath to do this, the experimenter secures a more complete and precise answer to the question with which he is concerned than if all the data were used. Here, too, the criteria laid down for matching must be clearly stated, rigidly adhered to, and the matching done on the first measures obtained, not on the end results. Often by selection and matching of this type on data already collected important problems can be attacked and significant generalizations made.

Co-twin Control. Because nature does an excellent job of pairing in identical twins, the method of co-twin control offers an unusual opportunity for attacking many scientific problems. One or more pairs of identical twins are selected; one member of each pair is exposed to a particular condition, while the other child is not so exposed. Pretests, followed by exposure, end tests, and final tests after an interval, are given. Gesell and Thompson (1929), Strayer (1930), and Hilgard (1933) furnish good examples of such studies carried on for short periods. In these investigations the twins used in the separate parts of the studies were reversed. In one, Twin A was given the experimentally introduced condition, while Twin B was held as control; in the next, Twin B was given the experimental condition, and Twin A held as control. In the McGraw (1935) study of Johnny and Jimmy, Johnny was given intensive training in motor skills over many months, while Jimmy was not. Periodically, both twins were given standard developmental tests, as well as tests in the specific functions in which training was given. Later on the twins were reversed for some training, and still later entirely new test and training situations were given to both. The method of co-twin control also permits many variations, not only in setting up parallel groups, but also in setting up contrasting groups, as in the study of identical twins reared apart and the many studies of twin resemblances.

An interesting variation of the control group technique is found in Kellogg and Kellogg (1933), who reared an infant chimpanzee and a human infant under similar conditions and made comparative tests and observations of performance at various intervals.

Control by Groups Rather than by Individuals. Pairing may be done on the basis of groups rather than individuals. For example, a school in a middle economic district in one city will be paired with a similar school in another city of the same size, and so on. In one half the schools instruction of one type is given, while in the other half instruction of another type is given or a particular experimental condition is introduced. An excellent example is found in the Wood and Freeman (1932) study of the influence of the typewriter in the elementary school, in which 21 public schools in 8 cities were used as controls and 22 public schools in 8 cities as experimentals, together with 3 private schools for controls and 8 for experimentals. Some 15,000 children participated in the experiment. In this type of study comparisons may be made in terms of schools, grades, and the individual child's performance. It is a question whether or not results of equal statistical and psychological significance might have been obtained with much less expense, time, and effort by using smaller numbers of children matched for individual performance.

Although the trend of modern statistics is away from large numbers of cases toward small numbers selected in accordance with rigorously defined criteria, there is some difference of opinion in the field of educational research, where large populations are available. Peters and Van Voorhis (1940), in a chapter on controlled experimentation, stress precise matching of individuals, whereas Lindquist (1940), in an extensive discussion of a variety of control designs for groups, favors the use of schools.

Control by Statistical Devices. In the experiment an attempt is made to isolate or make constant the effect of factors by artificial control of conditions, selection of subjects, etc. By the use of partial correlation, a statistical technique, a somewhat similar result can be secured. Suppose that the relations between three variables —intelligence, time spent in study, and scholastic success—are investigated. After measurements on each of the three variables are obtained for a group of children, time of study can be held constant in a partial correlation and the relation between intelligence and scholastic success determined. Or two groups of children, one of high, the other of low, intelligence, can be paired with respect to time spent in study, and their scholastic performance compared. Or a group of children who vary with respect to intelligence may be placed under such conditions that all study equal amounts of time, and the relation between intelligence and scholastic success determined.

Although the fact that time spent in study is not a perfect measure because of variation in motivation and energy is common to all these approaches, nevertheless it is clear that the same problem is attacked in three different ways. These attacks range from one involving very complex statistical treatment to one in which the statistical treatment is relatively simple, since, by deliberate control of one factor, much of the subsequent need for complex analysis is eliminated. This is a very important point on method: In general, control of conditions in advance is to be preferred to many measurements accumulated without control. Good experimental design may make complex statistical procedures unnecessary. Statistics, which supplies the most valuable tools for handling of data, never becomes a complete substitute for more precise methods of collecting data.

The Behavior Survey. A type of study made upon children at all age levels, but especially upon infants, can be character-ized as the behavior survey. Usually its design is simple in that it seeks to record as much and as wide a range of behavior as can be observed within the time and space available. It may be either cross-sectional or longitudinal in type. An early example is found in the Blanton (1917) study of infants with its rather informal descriptions of behavior in many infants. If compared with the Gesell (1928) surveys, which led to the normative schedules, then with the Shirley (1931, 1933a, 1933b) studies, and with the more recent studies of Bayley (1933) and Gesell and Thompson (1934, 1938), the improvement in the descriptions of the procedures and tests, in the use of standard statistical procedures for analyzing data, and in describing the sampling will be clear. Behavior surveys supplement, and are themselves supplemented by, the more intensive studies of limited areas of behavior. With older children comprehensive surveys are seldom made except in the longitudinal studies, of which that at California is a good example. Behavior surveys should not be confused with the questionnaire surveys, with which the term survey is often identified. In the infant behavior surveys, measurements, ratings, systematic observations, experiments, interviews and reports, measures of home background, etc., are utilized.

Individual Case Study. The collection of all available information about a single case is of great practical value in guiding and treating children. When, however, such material is published and conclusions are drawn for a universe of children, the individual case is to be regarded as a design at the lower limit of possible design. As such, it is to be treated in the light of the scientific information it yields, which is obviously very little since N in every formula is 1. The concept of the lawfulness of the individual's own history is not to be confused with the use of the single case as a basis for generalization to wide populations. McNemar (1940) says:

> Surely psychologists have learned that very little light is thrown on, say, delinquent behavior by a minute clinical study of one case, yet we are expected by some to believe that the mysteries of human personality will somewhere be unraveled by an intensive study of just one case (p. 362)

There is, however, one type of prediction in the individual case in which confidence in the statistical sense can be measured. If observations are available on the behavior of an individual in a situation that is repeated again and again, predictions of future performance for that individual in that situation can be made. Upon this principle rest the handicap systems used for athletic performances. Here N becomes the number of observations made on the case. More study should be made of the possibilities of this type of individual prediction.

Recently two very significant methodological discussions of the possibilities and limitations of the case study have appeared. The Allport (1942) study refers more particularly to the use of personal documents as sources of psychological material, whereas the Horst study (1941) not only deals with the case study, but also devotes substantial attention to prediction in any individual case.

Several types of individual study are found in the literature. *Case history* refers to a collection of such facts about a child who has been referred to an agency for one reason or another as can be obtained from official records, his own story, the accounts of relatives, teachers, and others, and the results of any examinations or interviews. Although such histories are of much practical value for guidance, their scientific value is limited by the fact that the data being collected after the fact are subject to many errors of interpretation and that those that are available are dependent upon accidental circumstances.

In modern practice many agencies keep a cumulative record of each child, sometimes called a *case study*, with the measurements and observations recorded at various times as the child develops. This type of case record is superior to the case history, both because of its greater completeness and because it avoids the errors of interpretation arising when working back from an end result. With the wide extension of the testing movement, the improved cumulative records kept in school systems, and the cumulative folders which various agencies maintain, data collected before the event that gives the child social visibility are increasingly available. In time, with more complete records and successive observations of the same children, a wealth of research material will be available that will make possible the solutions of problems previously impossible of attack. Because of the long life span of the human being and his slow progress in a short period of time, the need for the preservation of data is great. The Glueck and Glueck (1934) and Baller (1936) studies are examples. It should, however, be noted that the follow-up should be very complete, as has been shown in the later study which reverses many earlier generalizations. Otherwise incorrect conclusions may be drawn because the cases easily contacted are more likely to be those with which success has been achieved.

Clinical studies refer ordinarily to descriptions of pathological or abnormal cases. They usually consist of notes on the progress of the particular abnormality and are often supplemented by objective data.

As the term *personality study* is used in the literature, it refers to two rather distinct modes of approach. One is really a case study, as illustrated in Woolley's (1925, 1926) on-going developmental record of several children with unusual experiences. The other is found in the *psychoanalytic studies*, which vary greatly in completeness. The analyst, after establishing rapport with another, attempts to tap underlying memories and secure information regarding the origin of complexes and conflicts, etc. (See the discussion of projective methods on p. 15.) Through this process the analyst seeks to re-educate the patient in order that he may achieve a balance or integration of his instinctual drives and the demands the world makes upon him. Although his primary purpose is therapeutic, sweeping generalizations and a whole system of explanations have been erected on such case studies.

The books on child analysis (Anna Freud, 1925; Klein, 1932) present some cases in great detail and others briefly. To one who knows normal young children, it is clear that the child is approached from and his responses are fitted to a particular theoretical point of view. Little attempt is made to evaluate, no statistical or quantitative material is presented, no complete statements or records of the analyst's speech and actions and of the child's responses are given. Some content seems to be directly or indirectly suggested to the child. And younger children are very suggestible. No control is exercised over the sampling of children subjected to analysis, nor are precise data over a span of years made available to show the success or failure of the therapy.

Sears (1942), who has recently published an extensive survey of the objective studies of psychoanalytic concepts, finds that few observers accept Freud's statements at their face value, because of the reliance of psychoanalysis upon techniques that do not admit of the repetition of observation, that have no self-evident or denotative validity, and that are tinctured to an unknown degree with the observer's own suggestions. Although these difficulties do not interfere with therapy and do not necessarily mean that all the findings are false, the method fails when used to uncover psychological facts required to have objective validity. Hence, Sears concludes that other methods must be sought for the critical evaluation and validation of the findings of psychoanalysis.

Variations of Techniques with Age

Prenatal Behavior. Knowledge of prenatal behavior comes from experimental and laboratory techniques with animal fetuses, together with limited experiments and extensive observations on premature human infants. The difficulties in research are tremendous, and the methods in use constitute almost a science in themselves.

Infants. With infants, experiments, direct measurements, and observations constitute the chief source of data. Little indirect measurement is done. Because of the lack of structuring of response systems and the absence of language, most functions, including the sensory and perceptual, are difficult of study. Numerous ingenious techniques have been developed, such as one-way vision screens, cinema recording, the Gesell observation dome, and the stabilimeter. A disproportionate number of studies are made on neonates because of their availability in large numbers in maternity hospitals. More than with older children there is a tendency to ignore sampling and take whatever group of children is available for study.

One particular methodological problem deserves special attention. Watson (1919), in his precise description of the emotional patterns of infants, projected his knowledge of the well-structured patterns of older individuals upon them. Sherman (1927) has shown the inadequacy of these descriptions and demonstrated that the investigator is likely to pick out of the behavior manifold that which meets his purpose. In earlier studies of reflexes, the particular activity of segments was noted to the neglect of other simultaneous activity. Recent investigators, Pratt, Nelson, and Sun (1930), Irwin (1930), Jensen (1932), etc., who describe the complete behavior of the infant to stimulation, give a very different picture. Most psychologists take some pains to avoid crude anthropomorphic interpretations. Another type of projection, however, is equally dangerous, namely, the unconscious assumption that the highly organized and precise patterns characteristic of older children and adults are found in infants and very young children. Hence for scientific purposes, especial care must be taken to give complete descriptions of the behavior manifold.

Preschool Children. With preschool children methods involving direct observation and experiments occupy a prominent place. Because of the child's limited language responses and his inability to read and write, many tests and measurements available for older children cannot be used. Moreover, there is some difficulty in obtaining cooperation and motivation, and, because of the lack of complete structuring, particular difficulty in setting instructions and restrictions that will limit the child's responses to the matter in hand. Hence many ingenious methods involving setting the stage or situation and then observing "natural" behavior have been developed. These are best illustrated in the studies on social behavior in which children have been observed in free-play periods, in experimentally modified social settings, etc. For summaries and discussions of method see Jones and Burks (1936), Murphy, Murphy,

and Newcomb (1937), and Anderson (1939a).

Older Children and Adolescents. With older children, paper-and-pencil tests and indirect-measurement techniques supplant direct observation. Opportunities for free play are more limited, and time and activities of the child are more definitely scheduled. The child knows how to read and write, is more easily motivated, more docile, and better acquainted with test or experimental situations. But he is also more self-conscious and may be clever at concealing his thoughts and feelings. Hartshorne and May (1928) developed ingenious methods to offer possibilities of deceptive and honest behavior within the pencil-paper framework. In recent years methods of observation in "natural" or controlled situations have spread from the preschool field to the older child and offer an antidote to the somewhat excessive concern with paper and tests. In the studies by Lewin and his co-workers of social atmospheres (Lippitt, 1940) we find an excellent example of the use of one-way vision screens and careful recording of direct observations of the group structure and individual behavior as it changes within that structure. The sociometric technique of Moreno (1934), a combination of interviews, statements of choices, of playmates, dramatic-play situations, observations in groups, etc., coupled with a method of diagraming relations, is of promise since it furnishes a method of studying the evolution of group structures and the interrelations of individuals at all age levels.

The Evaluation of a Study

Following is an outline that has proved of use both in evaluating studies and checking on planned researches. In a sense, it summarizes much of what has been said in earlier pages. Although it could be extended to include many more details, it has here been kept as brief and schematic as possible.

(1) *Problem.* Is a significant problem attacked? Is an hypothesis set up and clearly stated that may be supported or refuted by the data collected? Or, if a normative or survey study, have adequate precautions been taken to insure that the final results will be of value in understanding children? Is sufficient account taken of the results of past studies and of the interrelation of scientific principles to permit the fitting of the results of this study into the framework of scientific understanding?

(2) *Design and Sampling.* Is the study planned so that it will give an answer to the problem proposed? Can the design be graphed or represented in other symbolic form? Is the number of cases adequate? How are they selected from the total population? Of what universe are they the representatives? Within the limits of sampling set up, is their allocation randomized or subject to bias? Are the sampling and design planned with reference to the later statistical treatment and analysis of the data? If the sampling is not representative, is it described so completely that the results may be compared and integrated with other studies? Does the description of the sample include chronological age, mental age, sex, grade location, socioeconomic status, and any other sampling criteria that are important? Can trends with sampling criteria or their combination be determined?

Are the factors which are controlled described? How are control and isolation achieved? In investigations with control groups, is the sampling in control and experimental groups adequately described, and similar or identical? How is matching or pairing done? Is the motivation constant for both groups? If not, is motivation checked on another group? Are the effects of incidental practice and indirect stimulation upon the function known? Are valid and reliable measurements of proficiency level

for the primary function and for related variables available for the beginning, the end, and after a period of elapsed time?

(3) *Measurement.* Are the variables studied described in specific terms and clearly differentiated? Are they subject to quantitative treatment, either directly or indirectly? What are the units of measurement and how are they scaled? How are the primary measures obtained? Are they valid, reliable, suitable?

(4) *Procedure.* Are the procedures used—apparatus, tests, measuring devices, observational records, etc.—clearly and accurately described? Can the study be repeated from the descriptions of the sampling, design, and measurement procedure? Are data systematically collected? Are adequate and permanent records kept? Is the method of recording uniform throughout? Are omissions and negative instances recorded?

(5) *Results.* Are the statistical procedures sound? Are they adapted to the problem? Are all the essential relations studied? Are all the necessary statistical procedures—number of cases, means, dispersion, percentages, measures of significance, correlation coefficients, etc.—used and presented? Is the null hypothesis rejected? Are tests of significance made? Are the sources and direction of error ascertained and reported, or reduced to a minimum by appropriate procedures? Have the sources and direction of constant error been checked? Is the quantitative material presented so as to bring out essential relationships? Are the results clearly and succinctly presented? Do the verbal statements agree with the tabular and quantitative findings?

(6) *Conclusions and Interpretations.* Are the conclusions warranted by the data? Are they too limited in scope or do they transcend the data widely? Is statistical significance confused with psychological significance? Are spurious relations or artifacts detected? Are significant trends overlooked? Are the results integrated in the general scientific field? Is the significance of the findings for related fields pointed out?

Conclusion

In child psychology problems are being attacked in a variety of ways by scientific workers who are increasingly concerned with the technique and methodology of investigation. Child psychology has passed through the first enthusiastic rush toward children as subjects of investigation in which results at any cost were sought, and has moved on to that more mature attitude which is concerned with a critical examination of results in terms of method and with deliberate attempts to devise new methods and techniques for attacking the very complex phenomena before it. It would be unfortunate if too much preoccupation with a particular method or a narrow preconception of what child psychology *should be* were to cut off a manifold approach. From today's studies, however inadequate they may be, come the highly developed techniques of tomorrow. Science crawls before it walks, and walks before it runs. And science learns, even though it progresses more slowly than we would wish. Methods and techniques do not fall into mid-Victorian classifications of right or wrong, of all or nothing. They are the tools which the scientist forges as he goes along. Scientific sin consists not so much in the use of a particular method as in the failure to use a more adequate method for the problem in hand when such a method is available.

Bibliography

ALLPORT, G. W. 1937. *Personality: A psychological interpretation.* New York: Holt.

——. 1940. The psychologist's frame of reference. *Psychol. Bull., 37,* 1–28.

——. 1942. *The use of the personal document in psychological science.* New York: Social Science Research Council.

ANDERSON, J. E. 1931, 1933. The methods of child psychology. In C. MURCHISON (Ed.), *A handbook of child psychology.* Worcester: Clark University Press. 1st ed., pp. 1–27, 2d ed., rev., pp. 3–28.

ANDERSON, J. E. 1939a. The development of social behavior. *Amer. J. Sociol., 44,* 839–857.

——. 1939b. The limitations of infant and preschool tests in the measurement of intelligence. *J. Psychol., 8,* 351–379.

——. 1944. Freedom and constraint or potentiality and environment. *Psychol. Bull., 41,* 1–29.

ANDERSON, J. E. (Chairman). 1936. *The young child in the home.* (White House Conference on Child Health and Protection.) New York: Appleton-Century.

ANDERSON, J. E., and J. T. COHEN. 1939. The effect of including incomplete series in the statistical analysis of longitudinal measurements of children's dental arches. *Child Develpm., 10,* 145–149.

ARRINGTON, R. E. 1943. Time sampling in studies of social behavior: A critical review of techniques and results with research suggestions. *Psychol. Bull., 40,* 81–124.

BALDWIN, B. T., E. A. FILLMORE, and L. HADLEY. 1930. *Farm children: An investigation of rural child life in selected areas of Iowa.* New York: Appleton.

BALLER, W. R. 1936. A study of the present social status of a group of adults who, when they were in elementary schools, were classified as mentally deficient. *Genet. Psychol. Monogr., 18,* 165–244.

BAYLEY, N. 1933. Mental growth during the first three years: A developmental study of sixty-one children by repeated tests. *Genet. Psychol. Monogr., 14,* 1–92.

BINET, A., and T. SIMON. 1905. Méthodes nouvelles pour le diagnostic du niveau intellectual des anormaux. *Année psychol., 11,* 191–244.

BLANTON, M. G. 1917. The behavior of the human infant during the first thirty days of life. *Psychol. Rev., 24,* 456–483.

BOLTON, T. L. 1892. The growth of memory in school children. *Amer. J. Psychol., 4,* 362–380.

BRADBURY, D. E. 1937. The contribution of the child study movement in child psychology. *Psychol. Bull., 34,* 21–38.

BÜHLER, C. 1937. Theoretische Grundprobleme der Kinderpsychologie. *Z. Psychol., 140,* 140–164.

BURGESS, E. W. (Chairman). 1934. *The adolescent in the family.* (White House Conference on Child Health and Protection.) New York: Appleton-Century.

BURKS, B. S. 1928. The relative influence of nature and nurture upon mental development: A comparative study of foster parent-foster child resemblance and true parent-true child resemblance. *Yearb. Nat. Soc. Stud. Educ., 27*(I), 219–316.

BUROS, O. K. (Ed.) 1938. *The 1938 mental measurements yearbook.* New Brunswick: Rutgers University Press.

CLARKE SCHOOL FOR THE DEAF. 1940. Studies in the psychology of the deaf: No. 1. *Psychol. Monogr.*, **52**, 42–103.

CONRAD, H. S. 1933. *The California behavior inventory for nursery school children*. Berkeley: University of California Press.

COURTIS, S. A. 1932. *The measurement of growth*. Ann Arbor: Brumfield and Brumfield.

DARWIN, C. 1877. A biographical sketch of an infant. *Mind*, **2**, 285–294.

DESPERT, J. L. 1940. A method for the study of personality reactions in preschool age children by means of analysis of their play. *J. Psychol.*, **9**, 17–29.

FISHER, R. A. 1936. *Statistical methods for research workers*. 6th ed. (1st ed., 1925.) Edinburgh: Oliver and Boyd.

——. 1937. *The design of experiments*. 2d ed. Edinburgh: Oliver and Boyd.

FRANK, L. K. 1939. Projective methods for the study of personality. *J. Psychol.*, **8**, 389–413.

FREEMAN, F. N., K. J. HOLZINGER, and B. C. MITCHELL. 1928. The influence of environment on the intelligence, school achievement, and conduct of foster children. *Yearb. Nat. Soc. Stud. Educ.*, **27**(I), 103–218.

FREUD, A. 1925. *Einführung in die Technik der Kinderanalyse*. Leipzig, Vienna, and Zurich: Internationale Psychoanalytische Verlag. (*Introduction to the technique of child analysis*. Trans. by L. P. CLARK, 1928. *Nerv. Ment. Dis. Monogr. Ser.*, No. 48. Pp. 62.)

FRIES, M. E. 1937. Play techniques in the analysis of young children. *Psychoanal. Rev.*, **24**, 233–245.

GATES, A. I., and G. A. TAYLOR. 1926. An experimental study of the nature of improvement resulting from practice in a motor function. *J. Educ. Psychol.*, **17**, 226–236.

GATES, G. S. 1923. An experimental study of the growth of social perception. *J. Educ. Psychol.*, **14**, 449–462.

GESELL, A. 1928. *Infancy and human growth*. New York: Macmillan.

GESELL, A., and H. THOMPSON. 1929. Learning and growth in identical infant twins: an experimental study by the method of co-twin control. *Genet. Psychol. Monogr.*, **6**, 1–124.

GESELL, A., and H. THOMPSON, assisted by C. S. AMATRUDA. 1934. *Infant behavior: Its genesis and growth*. New York: McGraw-Hill.

——. 1938. *The psychology of early growth*. New York: Macmillan.

GILBERT, J. A. 1894. Researches on the mental and physical development of school children. *Stud. Yale Psychol. Lab.*, **2**, 40–100.

GLUECK, S., and E. T. GLUECK. 1934. *One thousand juvenile delinquents*. Cambridge: Harvard University Press.

GOODENOUGH, F. L. 1928a. Measuring behavior traits by means of repeated short samples. *J. Juv. Res.*, **12**, 230–235.

GOODENOUGH, F. L. 1928b. A preliminary report on the effect of nursery school training upon the intelligence test scores of young children. *Yearb. Nat. Soc. Stud. Educ.*, **27**(I), 261–269.

——. 1930. Inter-relationships in the behavior of young children. *Child Develpm.*, **1**, 29–47.

GOODENOUGH, F. L., and J. E. ANDERSON. 1931. *Experimental child study*. New York: Century.

GRUELICH, W. W., H. G. DAY, S. E. LACHMAN, J. B. WOLFE, and F. K. SHUTTLEWORTH. 1938. A handbook of methods for the study of adolescent children. *Monogr. Soc. Res. Child Develpm.*, **3**, No. 2. Pp. 406.

GUILFORD, J. P. 1936. *Psychometric methods*. New York: McGraw-Hill.

——. 1942. *Statistics for students of psychology and education*. New York: McGraw-Hill.

GULLIKSEN, H. 1934. Rational equation of the learning curve based on Thorndike's law of effect. *J. Gen. Psychol.*, **11**, 395–434.

HALL, G. S. 1891. The contents of children's minds on entering school. *Ped. Sem.*, **1**, 139–173.

HARTSHORNE, H., and M. A. MAY. 1928. *Studies in deceit*: Book 1: *General methods and results*; Book 2: *Statistical methods and results*. New York: Macmillan.

HERTZ, M. R. 1936. The method of administration of the Rorschach ink-blot test. *Child Develpm.*, **7**, 237–254.

——. 1942. Rorschach: Twenty years after. *Psychol. Bull.*, **39**, 529–572.

HETZER, H., and B. REINDORF. 1928. Sprachentwicklung und soziales Milieu. *Z. angew. Psychol.*, **29**, 449–462.

HILGARD, J. R. 1933. The effect of early and delayed practice on memory and motor performances studied by the method of co-twin control. *Genet. Psychol. Monogr.*, **14**, 493–567.

HONZIK, M. P. 1938. The constancy of mental test performance during the preschool period. *J. Genet. Psychol.*, **52**, 265–302.

HORST, P. 1941. *The prediction of personal adjustment*. New York: Social Science Research Council.

HULL, C. L. 1928. *Aptitude testing*. Yonkers-on-Hudson: World Book.

HULL, C. L., C. I. HOVLAND, R. T. ROSS, M. HALL, D. T. PERKINS, and F. B. FITCH. 1940. *Mathematico-deductive theory of rote learning*. New Haven: Yale University Press.

IRWIN, O. C. 1930. The amount and nature of activities of newborn infants under constant external stimulating conditions during the first ten days of life. *Genet. Psychol. Monogr.*, **8**, 1–92.

JENSEN, K. 1932. Differential reactions to taste and temperature stimuli in newborn infants. *Genet. Psychol. Monogr.*, **12**, 361–476.

JERSILD, A. T. 1932. Training and growth in the development of children. *Child Develpm. Monogr.*, No. 10. Pp. 73.

JERSILD, A. T., and M. F. MEIGS. December, 1939. Direct observation as a research method. *Rev. Educ.*, 1–14.

JONES, M. C., and B. S. BURKS. 1936. Personality development in childhood. *Monogr. Soc. Res. Child Develpm.*, **1**, No. 4. Pp. vi + 205.

KELLEY, T. L. 1928. *Crossroads in the mind of man: A study of differentiable mental abilities.* Stanford University, Calif.: Stanford University Press.

KELLOGG, W. N., and L. A. KELLOGG. 1933. *The ape and the child: A study of environmental influence upon early behavior.* New York: McGraw-Hill.

KLEIN, M. 1932. *The psycho-analysis of children.* (Trans. by A. STRACHEY.) New York: Norton.

KOFFKA, K. 1924. *The growth of the mind: An introduction to child psychology.* (Trans. by R. M. OGDEN. New York: Harcourt, Brace; London: Kegan Paul.

LEAHY, A. M. 1935. Nature, nurture and intelligence. *Genet. Psychol. Monogr.*, **17**, 236–308.

——. 1936. *The measurement of urban home environment.* (*Inst. Child Welfare Monogr. Ser.*, No. 11.) Minneapolis: University of Minnesota Press. Pp. 10.

LEWIN, K. 1935. *A dynamic theory of personality.* New York: McGraw-Hill.

——. 1936. *Principles of topological psychology.* New York: McGraw-Hill.

LINDQUIST, E. F. 1940. *Statistical analysis in educational research.* Boston: Houghton Mifflin.

LIPPITT, R. 1940. An experimental study of the effect of democratic and authoritarian group atmospheres. Iowa City: *Univ. Iowa Stud. in Child Welfare,* University of Iowa, **16**, No. 3, 45–195.

MACFARLANE, J. W. 1938. Studies in child guidance: I. Methodology of data collection and organization. *Monogr. Soc. Res. Child Develpm.*, **3**, No. 6. Pp. 254.

MALLER, J. B. 1933. Vital indices and their relation to psychological and social factors. *Human Biol.*, **5**, 94–121.

MARKEY, J. F. 1928. *The symbolic process.* New York: Harcourt, Brace.

MARSTON, L. R. 1925. The emotions of young children. *Univ. Iowa Stud. Child Welfare*, **3**, No. 3. Pp. 99.

MATTSON, M. L. 1933. The relation between the complexity of the habit to be acquired and the form of the learning curve in young children. *Genet. Psychol. Monogr.*, **13**, 299–398.

MCCARTHY, D. 1930. *The language development of the preschool child.* (*Inst. Child Welfare Monogr. Ser.*, No. 4.) Minneapolis:

University of Minnesota Press. Pp. xiii + 174.

MCGRAW, M. B. 1935. *Growth: A study of Johnny and Jimmy.* New York: Appleton-Century.

MCNEMAR, Q. 1940. Sampling in psychological research. *Psychol. Bull.*, **37**, 331–365.

MELTON, A. W. 1936. The methodology of experimental studies of human learning and retention: 1. The functions of a methodology and the available criteria for evaluating different experimental methods. *Psychol. Bull.*, **33**, 305–394.

MONROE, W. S. (Ed.) 1941. *Encyclopedia of educational research.* New York: Macmillan.

MORENO, J. L. 1934. *Who shall survive? A new approach to the problem of human interrelations.* Washington: Nervous and Mental Disease Publishing Co.

MURPHY, G., L. B. MURPHY, and T. M. NEWCOMB. 1937. *Experimental social psychology.* (Rev. ed.) New York: Harper.

MURPHY, L. B. 1937. *Social behavior and child personality.* New York: Columbia University Press.

NATIONAL SOCIETY FOR THE STUDY OF EDUCATION. 1938. The scientific movement in education. *Yearb. Nat. Soc. Studies Educ.*, 37(II).

——. 1939. Child development and the curriculum. *Yearb. Nat. Soc. Studies Educ.*, 38(I).

OLSON, W. C. 1929. *The measurement of nervous habits in normal children.* (*Inst. Child Welfare Monogr. Ser.*, No. 3.) Minneapolis: University of Minnesota Press. Pp. 97.

OLSON, W. C., and E. M. CUNNINGHAM. 1934. Time-sampling techniques. *Child Develpm.*, **5**, 41–58.

PETERS, C. C., and W. R. VAN VOORHIS. 1940. *Statistical procedures and their mathematical bases.* New York: McGraw-Hill.

PIAGET, J. 1923. *Le langage et la pensée chez l'enfant.* Neuchâtel and Paris: Delachaux and Nestle. (*The language and thought of the child.* Trans. by M. WARDEN, 1936. New York: Harcourt, Brace.)

PRATT, K. C., A. K. NELSON, and K. H. SUN. 1930 *The behavior of the newborn infant. Ohio State Univ. Stud. Contr. Psychol.*, No. 10. Pp. 237.

PREYER, W. 1882. *Die Seele des Kindes.* Leipzig: Fernau. (5th ed., 1900.)

——. 1888, 1889. *The mind of the child:* Pt. 1. *The senses and the will;* Pt. 2. *The development of the intellect.* (Trans. by H. W. BROWN.) New York: Appleton.

RIDER, P. R. 1939. *An introduction to modern statistical methods.* New York: Wiley.

SCUPIN, E., and G. SCUPIN. 1907. *Bubi's erste kindheit.* Leipzig: Grieben.

SEARS, R. R. 1942. *Survey of objective studies of psychoanalytic concepts.* New York: Social Science Research Council.

SHALLOO, P. J. 1940. Understanding behavior problems of children. *Ann. Amer. Acad. Pol. Soc. Sci.*, **212**, 194–201.

SHAW, C. R., *et al.* 1929. *Delinquency areas: A study of the geographic distribution of school truants, juvenile delinquents, and adult offenders in Chicago.* (*Behav. Res. Monogr.*) Chicago: University of Chicago Press. Pp. xxi + 214.

SHERMAN, M. 1927. The differentiation of emotional responses in infants. I. Judgments of emotional responses from motion picture views and from actual observation. II. The ability of observers to judge the emotional characteristics of the crying of infants and the voice of an adult. *J. Comp. Psychol.*, **7**, 265–284; 335–351.

SHERMAN, M., and T. R. HENRY. 1933. *Hollow folk.* New York: Crowell.

SHINN, M. W. 1893–1899. Notes on the development of a child. *Univ. Calif. Publ.*, **1**, 1–178; 179–424.

———. 1900. *Biography of a baby.* Boston: Houghton Mifflin.

SHIRLEY, M. M. 1931. *The first two years, a study of twenty-five babies:* Vol. I. *Postural and locomotor development.* (*Inst. Child Welfare Monogr. Ser.*, No. 6.) Minneapolis: University of Minnesota Press. Pp. vi + 227.

———. 1933*a*. *The first two years, a study of twenty-five babies:* Vol. II. *Intellectual development.* (*Inst. Child Welfare Monogr. Ser.*, No. 7.) Minneapolis: University of Minnesota Press. Pp. xvi + 513.

———. 1933*b*. *The first two years, a study of twenty-five babies:* Vol. III. *Personality manifestations.* (*Inst. Child Welfare Monogr. Ser.*, No. 8.) Minneapolis: University of Minnesota Press. Pp. xi + 228.

SHUTTLEWORTH, F. K. 1938. The adolescent period: Graphic and pictorial atlas. *Monogr. Soc. Res. Child Develpm.*, **3**, No. 3. Pp. 246.

———. 1939. The physical and mental growth of girls and boys age six to nineteen in relation to age at maximum growth. *Monogr. Soc. Res. Child Develpm.*, **4**, No. 3. Pp. vi + 291.

SIMS, V. M. 1928. *The measurement of socioeconomic status.* Bloomington, Ill. Public School Publishing Co.

SNEDECOR, G. W. 1938. *Statistical methods.* Ames, Iowa: Collegiate Press.

SPEARMAN, C. 1927. *The abilities of man: Their nature and measurement.* New York and London: Macmillan.

STERN, C., and W. STERN. 1907. *Die Kindersprache: Eine psychologische und sprachtheoretische Untersuchung.* (*Monogr. secl. Etwick. Kindes,* Vol. 1.) Leipzig: Barth. Pp. 394. (3d ed., rev., 1922. Pp. xii + 434.)

———. 1909. *Erinnerung, Aussage und Lüge in der ersten Kindheit.* (*Monogr. seel. Entwick. Kindes,* Vol. 2.) Leipzig: Barth. Pp. x + 160.

STRAYER, L. C. 1930. Language and growth: The relative efficiency of early and deferred vocabulary training studied by the method of co-twin control. *Genet. Psychol. Monogr.*, **8**, 215–326.

SYMONDS, P. M. 1931. *Diagnosing personality and conduct.* New York: Century.

TERMAN, L. M., *et al.* 1925. *Genetic studies of genius:* Vol. 1. *Mental and physical traits of a thousand gifted children.* Stanford University, Calif.: Stanford University Press.

TERMAN, L. M., and M. A. MERRILL. 1937. *Measuring intelligence.* Boston: Houghton Mifflin.

TERMAN, L. M., and M. ODEN. 1940*a*. Status of the California gifted group at the end of sixteen years. *Yearb. Nat. Soc. Stud. Educ.*, 39(I), 67–74.

———. 1940*b*. Correlates of adult achievement in the California gifted group. *Yearb. Nat. Soc. Stud. Educ.*, 39(I), 74–89.

THOMAS, D. S., *et al.* 1929. Some new techniques for studying social behavior. *Child Develpm. Monogr.*, No. 1. Pp. 213.

THOMAS, W. I., and D. S. THOMAS. 1928. *The child in America.* New York: Knopf.

THOMSON, G. H. 1939. *The factorial analysis of human ability.* Boston: Houghton Mifflin.

THORNDIKE, E. L. 1904. *An introduction to the theory of mental and social measurements.* New York: Teachers College, Columbia University.

———. 1913*a*. *Educational psychology:* Vol. 1. *The original nature of man.* New York: Teachers College, Columbia University.

———. 1913*b*. *Educational psychology:* Vol. 2. *The learning process.* New York: Teachers College, Columbia University.

———. 1914. *Educational psychology:* Vol. 3. *Mental work and fatigue and individual differences.* New York: Teachers College, Columbia University.

THURSTONE, L. L. 1935. *The vectors of mind.* Chicago: University of Chicago Press.

———. 1940. Current issues in factor analysis. *Psychol. Bull.*, **37**, 189–236.

TIEDEMANN, D. 1787. *Beobachtungen über die Entwickelung der Seelenfähigkeiten bei Kindern.* (New ed., ed. by C. UFER. 1897.) Altenburg: Bonde.

TIPPETT, L. H. 1937. *The methods of statistics.* (2d ed.) London: Williams & Norgate.

TRELOAR, A. E. 1939. *Elements of statistical reasoning.* New York: Wiley.

WATSON, J. B. 1919. *Psychology from the standpoint of a behaviorist.* New York: Lippincott.

WEISS, L. A. 1933. Rating scales: with special reference to the field of child development. *Psychol. Bull.*, **30**, 185–208.

WHIPPLE, G. M. 1924. *Manual of mental and*

physical tests: Vol. 1. *Simple processes;* Vol. 2. *Complex processes.* Baltimore: Warwick and York.

WILEY, L. E., and A. M. WILEY. 1937a. Studies in the learning function: I. An empirical test of Thurstone's theoretical learning curve. *Psychometrika,* **2,** 1–19.

———. 1937b. Studies in the learning function: II. Critical values of the learning curve. *Psychometrika,* **2,** 107–120.

WOOD, B. D., and F. N. FREEMAN. 1932. *An experimental study of the educational influences of the typewriter in the elementary school classroom.* New York: Macmillan.

WOOLLEY, H. T. 1925. Agnes: A dominant personality in the making. *Ped. Sem.,* **32,** 569–598.

———. 1926. Peter: The beginnings of a juvenile court problem. *Ped. Sem.,* **33,** 9–29.

YULE, G. U., and M. G. KENDALL. 1937. *An introduction to the theory of statistics.* (11th ed.) London: Griffin.

CHAPTER 2

THE ONSET AND EARLY DEVELOPMENT OF BEHAVIOR [1]

LEONARD CARMICHAEL

Yes,—the history of a man for the nine months preceding his birth, would, probably, be far more interesting, and contain events of greater moment, than all the threescore and ten years that follow it.
—COLERIDGE (1885, p. 301)

The Importance for Psychology of an Understanding of the Early Development of Behavior Patterns

In any complete discussion of child, developmental, or genetic psychology two questions must be asked: When does behavior begin? How does behavior develop during the early weeks and months of life? These two questions may be phrased as one: What is the origin and what is the embryology of the behavior patterns which are significant in an understanding of human mental life?

This chapter is written in an effort to deal with these questions. The material brought together here concerns itself not only with facts about early human development but also with relevant facts about the development of infrahuman animals. Much more is known in certain respects concerning the early development of life in the animals below man than in man himself, and much of this information has direct bearing upon an understanding of human development.

A knowledge of behavior in prenatal life throws light upon many traditional psychological problems. For example, some of the old questions concerning the relative importance of heredity and environment in the determination of adult human mental life are answered by this study. The contest between empiristic and nativistic theories of perception, the question of whether development is continuous or saltatory, the problem of whether behavior is first general and later specific or first specific and later general, and even the question of the fundamental nature of human learning itself are all illuminated by the facts disclosed in a study of prenatal behavior.

In the investigation of the early growth of behavior, it is important to remember that at every stage the scientist is essentially describing some reaction of an organism then living in an environment. At every level of development one must think of the organism as maintaining itself in its present environment. This last statement sounds like a truism. Actually, however, a great many errors have been made in the study of the early development of behavior by assuming that later performance is somehow implicit or hidden in earlier types of response. This has been called classically "the error of potentiality" (Lange, 1925, pp. 198–200). For example, one who wishes to describe the linguistic performance of a five-year-old child must describe that performance as it appears at five. It is not possible to infer the full character of that performance in any given individual from any study of linguistic

[1] This chapter is an extensive revision of a chapter in this same field previously published (Carmichael, 1933). See preface.

43

performance, for example, in the first year of life. The five-year-old performance is not implicit in the two-year-old performance. The environment of the third and fourth years is all-important in determining, for example, whether the child at five will speak Spanish or English.

The error of potentiality may be avoided quite simply. It is necessary only to remember that the scientist who is dealing with development must study a series of temporally separated stages of growth. These are his facts. The tendencies or "growth processes" which give meaning to the relationship of these various stages are the scientific inferences that he draws. The question thus becomes not: What adult trait is mysteriously hidden in this or that early behavior pattern? but rather: What is the nature of the many developmental stages which actually were preliminary to the particular adult characteristic which is being studied? In the investigation of the prenatal growth of response, this distinction becomes especially important. The older workers in this field almost always wrote on the basis of a preconceived theory. One such view was the "doctrine of recapitulation." This theory saw in every action of the growing individual a complete parallelism with the action in adult life of an evolutionary ancestor of the individual being studied. This view is now discredited as a universal theory, and so are many other alleged explanations of behavior.

In this chapter an effort is made to deal with growth as the histologist deals with the wax reconstruction of the structure which he is studying. This wax-reconstruction method in microscopical anatomy involves the cutting, mounting, and staining of a series of very thin sections of tissue, and then by appropriate techniques the cutting-out of particular details from each one of these sections in layers of wax of proportional thickness. As these cut-out wax sections are put together, a magnified and truly three-dimensional object emerges. In the dynamic field of behavior a similar procedure is in many cases valuable. Thus behavior as a series of temporal stages can be fully described, and then when these stages are viewed in relation to time a real reconstruction of the growth of behavior may be made. Whenever possible in this chapter, behavioral development will be considered in this way.

When Does Behavior Begin?

Many of the older writers on child psychology, such as Compayré (1896, p. 44), allege that the study of child psychology begins at birth. Throughout the history of biological science, however, the incompleteness of this answer has been obvious to certain writers. Today all agree that we must move into the prenatal period in order to determine what Gesell (1928, pp. 303–306; 1929a, p. 631) has called the "ontogenetic zero." The term ontogenetic as used here means development in the individual as contrasted with phylogenetic or development in the race, or evolutionary series, of the human and prehuman ancestors of man. Ordinarily, in biology, ontogenetic development is taken as beginning at the time of individual fertilization. Of course, in order that fertilization may take place there is antecedent life in both the ovum and the sperm (at least always in the ovum) before fertilization. Scientifically we must still accept the dictum "Omne vivum e vivo." The new individual as such, then, may best be considered as beginning from the processes which are initiated at fertilization.

As just suggested, it is impossible to say that fertilization is in all senses the beginning of the new individual, because the reproductive cells trace themselves back through countless generations. Similarly, it is difficult to distinguish between the dynamic processes of structural development and the processes of the organism which may be called true behavior. Such distinctions can be made only by the use of commonly agreed-upon definitions. Ordinarily the beginning of behavior, and hence the starting point of behavioral psychology, is placed at the point where true neuromuscular activity begins. It is assumed that this point is the one at which activities of the organism take place which involve sense organs and nervous system as well as muscles. Some writers hold that behavior, instead of beginning at the time of the first sensory neuromuscular response, really *emerges* at this time. The word "emergence" is used by many writers on developmental psychology. Sometimes this word is given an almost mystical definition, but when it is used in this chapter its meaning will be a simple one. Here the word emergence will be used to describe a relationship between events antecedent in time and a new and different event which is itself also described. For a critique of the definition of the word emergence, see Lovejoy (1926).

It is easy to deal with the emergent or novel creation of behavior in the abstract, but when one turns to specific experimental studies of this emergence, the difficulty of the problem becomes clearer. The writer has studied in some detail, as will be noted below, the very first responses of many organisms. For example, let us take the guinea pig fetus. Logically, it is clear that there must be a time in growth when stimulation of this organism's receptors will not be effective. Then, at an immediately subsequent time, say, one second later, when such stimulation is given, behavior results. At time A this response is not possible, but after added growth—that is, at subsequent time B—it is possible.

The possibility of this first response is considered as dependent upon elaborate changes which we call growth and which are taking place in the organism under consideration. Let us trace these changes back in the history of the individual. The processes basic to behavior involve the development of the germ cells in the parents and in the parents' parents. The growth and maturation of the germ cells in the parents are necessary, as are the so-called reduction divisions of the nuclear substance of the germ cells, fertilization, cell division, cell differentiation, cell migration, organ formation, and a whole series of other dynamic changes.

As a result of all this growth, a structure capable of making this first behavioral reaction *emerges*. Without these countless antecedent cellular and subcellular processes, the first external response of an appendage or of the trunk of the living organism could not occur. These processes, moreover, must not be thought of as a simple unfolding of preformed organs. This old "preformism view" is no longer held. Rather, at each stage the living organism is now considered to be maintaining itself in a dynamic relationship with the energies and the foodstuffs of its environment. This is not to say that the organism is being formed wholly by its environment, as the other old view, that of "epigenesis," held. Indeed, today it is clear that inheritance and environment always cooperate in development. The old quarrel between preformism and epigenesis is now seen to have been largely a battle of words engaged in before the relevant facts were known.

The processes basic to the reproduction of living animals are brought about in a number of different ways. In some animals the egg, after fertilization, continues to develop in protective coverings still within the maternal body. In other animals the egg leaves the body and continues development outside. In many animals the growth of all the fundamental organ systems is complete before hatching or birth. This condition may be considered as characteristic of many vertebrates, some worms, and certain arthropods. In the coelenterates, insects, and vertebrate amphibians, varying stages of growth after the new organism emerges from the egg are the rule. Common usage seems to have established the fact that the first stage of the development of any organism is to be described as *germinal*, the next stage as *embryonic*, and the latest stage preliminary to birth as *fetal*. The word *larval* is used to characterize independent, living, but organically immature organisms.

In describing larval development, two classes of such growth, direct and indirect, have been set up. In the first of these, development is linear—that is, each developmental stage produces an organism which is in most respects more like the adult than was the organism in its preceding stage. In the case of indirect larval development, however, organs often of a high order of complexity are produced which are later destroyed before maturity is reached. The term *metamorphosis* is applied to development of this latter sort. The terms *larval* and *pupal* are applied to describe stages in indirect development. Too little is known concerning the effect of environmental modification during the larval stage upon adult animals. This is a field in which more experimental investigation is almost certain to be done. For example, what influence will certain experimentally induced forms of activity in the wormlike larva have upon the fully developed *imago*, such as an adult butterfly? It is interesting in this connection to notice that among the older writers even on so-called inherited human instinct many examples were taken from types which pass through larval

stages. (Cf. Bergson, 1911, pp. 172–176, and McDougall, 1923, pp. 69–71.)

The degree of maturity reached before the new organism begins an independent existence varies markedly from type to type. In so-called *oviparous* species, such as most fish and certain amphibians, eggs are laid as single cells and are subsequently fertilized after they have left the mother's body. In *viviparous* animals, such as certain fish and most mammals, on the other hand, all the early developmental stages are normally passed within the mother's body. Between these two extremes are the so-called *ovoviviparous* organisms, in which fertilization takes place before the egg is laid. Birds are good examples of this type. It is interesting to note that the so-called evolutionary level does not give a clear indication of the sort of reproduction which may be expected of an animal. The common dogfish bears its young inside the body until they are developed so that they may have an independent existence. On the other hand, the monotremes among the primitive mammals lay eggs. There are, moreover, certain forms in which favorable or unfavorable environmental conditions seem to determine the fact of the hatching of eggs inside or outside the mother's body (Hertwig, 1912, p. 151).

Among the mammals it is also interesting to note that there is a great diversity in the degree of development that has been reached at the time of normal birth. Thus, as will be noted in more detail below, the young of the opossum are born in many respects as relatively early embryos, as contrasted with the newborn guinea pig, in which almost full-grown characteristics are observed (Hartman, 1920; Avery, 1928, pp. 258–265). This fact should be kept in mind at all times as these pages are read. To put this in another way, it may be said that the behavioral age or even the "mental age" of different species of mammals is very different at the time of birth.

The Development of Behavior in the Lower Vertebrates

There are stages in the morphological development of the fish, amphibian, reptile, bird, infrahuman mammal, and man which are so similar as to make the study of one form important for a complete understanding of the development of other forms. This fact has long been recognized in anatomical embryology. By analogy, the same may be held to be true of behavior. Care must be taken, however, not to pretend to see homologies of behavior until by direct observation such homologies can be shown to exist. Figure 1 gives a somewhat too idealized picture of some of these relationships. For example, in certain forms nourishment during the entire fetal period is provided by the yolk of the egg in which the developing organism originated. This means that behavior in connection with alimentation is less important in such types than in others in which at an early developmental stage the ingestion of food is necessary. In spite of this difficulty, the study of fish and amphibians has provided much information of importance to one who would understand the gradual development of behavior. Swenson (1928a) has courageously attempted to set up seven fundamental acts of behavior as basic to the responses of lower vertebrates, mammals, and even man. These forms of behavior are progression, respiration, ingestion, expression, excretion, phonation, and reproduction. The fact that these processes can be studied in the amphibian larva as well as in the human infant makes the complete understanding of the simple organism especially important. Coghill (1929c, pp. 1004–1009) and others (Windle

and Griffin, 1931, pp. 180–184) have developed this point of view in various papers.

The best history of the development of the study of vertebrate embryos is given by the scientist who did so much for the study of behavior that he may be considered the founder of the experimental study of early behavior. This man is William Preyer, late professor of physiology at Jena. His book, *Specielle Physiologie des Embryo. Untersuchungen über die Lebenserscheinungen vor der Geburt*, published in 1885, may be taken as the starting point for all subsequent investigation in this field. Part of this fundamental work has been translated by Coghill and Legner (1937).

In this basic work Preyer summarizes and reviews a good many observations made on the early movements of fish embryos. Some of these studies were based on the observations of fish embryos growing after definitely dated periods of fertilization. Slow rotary movements characterize the early behavior of many fish embryos. Fillipi is quoted by Preyer as finding in *Alosa finta* such movements soon after fertilization. In a species of trout Preyer found movement of trunk at a definite number of days subsequent to fertilization. In general, on the day following the first trunk movement the first head movement is noted. Then, in a few days, energetic movements of the whole tiny fish body may be observed. After the liberation of such organisms from their egg coverings, it is found that pressure stimulation on the body surface is followed by responses involving apparently the entire musculature of the trunk. Preyer points out that these movements involve fully developed reflexes (p. 397). He makes this conclusion because the movements described consist in the total organism's drawing together of the head and tail.

This same response occurs no matter what the locus may be of the point of pressure stimulation. As growth goes on, however, the strength of movement increases, and gills as development progresses (pp. 398–399).

Paton (1907, 1911) more recently studied the development of behavior in selachian

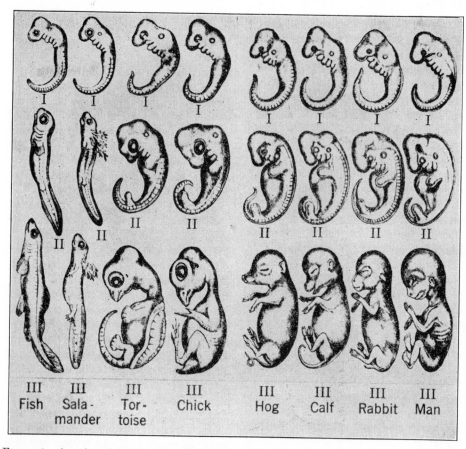

FIGURE 1. A series of drawings constructed to emphasize similarities in structure in various embryos at three comparable and progressive stages of development (marked I, II, and III). (From *Darwin, and After Darwin.* Vol. I. *The Darwinian Theory,* by G. J. Romanes. Chicago: Open Court, 1896, 152–153. By permission of the publisher.)

This old diagram is presented here as a schematic device only. Research since it was drawn has made some alteration in the relationships demonstrated here.

the movements become more and more regular and specific in relation to the exact locus of the area stimulated. Preyer gives quantitative tables of the increase in rapidity of the movements of the heart and the embryos. He demonstrated the possibility of movement in fish embryos only nine or ten millimeters in length. For a study of teleost morphogenesis, see Oppenheimer (1934).

White (1915) describes the development of behavior in brook trout embryos. His observations cover the period from hatching until the yolk sac is absorbed. He notes that "the hatching is initiated by movements starting at the head and later extending through the whole length of the body . . ." (p. 46). After hatching, the swimming reaction is gradually made more nearly perfect. Touch and mechanical jars are effective stimuli immediately after hatching, and, interestingly enough, at this time the head is found to be the region least sensitive to pressure stimuli. Rheotropism, or response to water flow in currents, negative phototaxis, or the avoidance of light, and photokinetic responses, or responses initiated but not necessarily directed by light, are also present at this time. Excess carbon dioxide in the water in which fish are studied is activating up to a point, and then depressing on bodily functions. The dependence of the fish upon the chemical make-up of its external watery environment presents many analogies with the dependence of the higher animal upon the chemical make-up of the liquid internal environment of its own blood stream in which its own central nervous system maintains itself. Or, to put this in another way, the internal environment of the fish embryo is seen to be most closely related to its external environment. Before the nourishment-supplying yolk sac disappears at about two months, the reaction of the fish to stimuli seems to be away from the point of contact. After this, the fish embryo becomes quite suddenly exploratory and aggressive, and hence it moves toward the point stimulated (Preyer, 1885, p. 59). This striking observation may remind the reader that an intimate relationship exists between the degree of maturation of an organism and the "drive" which the organism shows in relation to external stimulation. Nicholas

(1927) has applied experimental methods to the development of *Fundulus* embryos.

From the general standpoint of the development of behavior, however, the work of Tracy (1926) is especially worthy of study. This investigator has studied fish embryos, especially those of the toadfish. He has carefully observed and recorded the growth of activity in this form from its first movement to a final free-swimming condition. The first activity of the embryo in this form as in so many others is what may be termed in Parker's sense the preneural and "independent effector" action of the heart (Parker, 1919, pp. 53–63). The first behavioral movement of the fish is the bending of the trunk in the anterior region. At times this movement is to the right, at times to the left. It is probable that the afferent proprioceptor or muscle-sense system is not functional at first. At an early point a spontaneous flutter movement develops. This movement probably is important in freeing the organism from the remaining egg membranes. In general, toadfish larvae when hatched lie at the bottom of the containing vessel in a quiescent state. Then suddenly they move. On the basis of careful study, Tracy concludes that this "spontaneous" behavior is related to cumulative changes in the blood of the organism such that at a certain point the central nervous system is directly stimulated or the threshold of the central nervous system is so altered that previously inoperative sensory impulses break over into motor outlets. Thus he concludes that spontaneous movements are the result of metabolites and oxygen deficiency in the blood stream (p. 345). Soon after the onset of such responses, the organism becomes very sensitive to exteroceptive stimuli. The mucous membrane area about the mouth is the first to be sensitized. In general, the spread of sensitivity is from this point toward the tail or possibly to the region that has just become most active. The "cephalocaudal progression" of sensory and motor development which some writers propose as a law is certainly far from regular in this organism, as will be seen in Figure 2. Receptors for light, vibration, chemicals, and body movement (proprioceptors) soon become effective. The be-

the beginning, and more or less continuously during its whole existence, the animal is driven through its environment as a result of stimuli which arise periodically in connection with its metabolic processes" (p. 345). The nature of later behavior may be thought of, he further suggests, as dependent upon neural development and

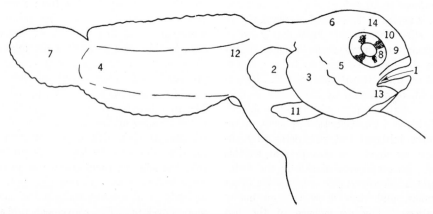

FIGURE 2. Diagram of toadfish larva to show by numbered areas the approximate temporal order of development of tactile reactions from various regions. (From "The Development of Motility and Behavior Reactions in the Toadfish [*Opsanus tau*]," by H. C. Tracy. *Journal of Comparative Neurology*, 1926, **40**, 295. By permission of The Wistar Institute, publisher.)

It will be noted that, with some exceptions, this course of development of sensitivity is cephalocaudal, that is, from the head to the tail.

havior initiated by stimulation of these receptors involves jaw movements, trunk movements, and, interestingly enough, rotational and postrotational nystagmus of the eyes.

Tracy draws some fundamental conclusions from these studies. He holds that if external conditions could be kept constant the activities of the organism would be determined by its own life processes or metabolism. This would mean that all behavior would be rhythmic, like that of an excised muscle in a balanced salt solution (p. 345). At a later point we shall note that T. G. Brown (1915) holds that early mammalian reflexes may be of this nature. In conclusion, Tracy says: "From

the interference in the intrinsic rhythms of behavior brought about by the stimulation of the special exteroceptors of the organism by external energies. The basic relevance of this observation even for adult human behavior is worthy of full consideration.

We now turn to the study of the development of behavior in amphibians. Swammerdam, in his *Bibel der Natur* (1752), written prior to 1685, makes observations on the behavior of frog embryos five days after fertilization and at other periods (Preyer, 1885, p. 392; Swammerdam, edited, 1907). Swammerdam has also recorded observations concerning the development of behavior in snails and other invertebrates. Leeuwenhoek (1697, p. 792) made observations in this same field. Among other early students of behavior in invertebrates may be mentioned Stiebel (1815), Grant (1827), and Home (1827). Bischoff (1842) published a confirmation of the description of movements previously observed by Swammerdam in amphibians. He added a notation of the fact that the rate of these movements is a function of the temperature of the water in which the animals are maintaining themselves. Preyer (1885, pp. 392 ff.) reviewed all this work as well as that of Perschir and Cramer on the amphibian embryo. Preyer himself made elaborate observations on the early movements of frog and salamander embryos. He noted that stimulating the embryo led first to a slight twitch in the anterior portion of the organism. Following this movement in time he noted that the body was bent so as to bring the head and tail nearer together. Reference to Preyer's original drawings, reproduced as Figure 3, as well as to the text of his book, shows that he considered these C or reverse C movements very important. It is also clear from his drawings that he observed the fundamental S or sigmoid form of reaction. The importance of this S movement in freeing the organism from the egg is pointed out. That this movement is also related to the activity of swimming is an important consideration (pp. 393–394).

Other students have worked on the relationship between temperature and embryonic movements in larval amphibians (Preyer, 1885, p. 395). Many others have used this convenient laboratory type in work in experimental embryology. Much of this experimental embryology has direct bearing on the problems of this chapter. (See Detwiler, 1920, 1921, 1922, 1923a, 1923b, and the bibliographies given by him.)

If Preyer may be called the father of the scientific study of the development of behavior, the late G. E. Coghill (see references in the bibliography) must always be remembered as the investigator who first charted the relationship between the detailed growth of the nervous system and the consequent alterations which occur in behavior. This investigator is notable also

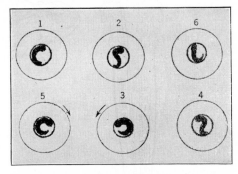

FIGURE 3. Diagram of various positions of frog embryos (*Rana temporaria*) just before emergence from the egg. Note especially the C and S reactions. (From *Specielle Physiologie des Embryo. Untersuchungen über die Lebenserscheinungen vor der Geburt,* by W. Preyer. Leipzig: Grieben, 1885.)

because of the completeness of his work on the salamander *Amblystoma*, as well as on other types. A brief summary of the life of Coghill and his complete bibliography were published by C. J. Herrick (1943) in the Biographical Memoirs of the National Academy of Sciences. Coghill's first paper in this field was written in 1902, and from that time until his death he published a most important series of papers on the development of behavior in relation to the anatomy of structure. In the course of his many papers, Coghill reported detailed studies of the neural mechanism underlying the first movement and the later sequences of movements as they develop in *Amblystoma*. The first response results from the contraction of muscles just behind the head. As the embryo advances in age, this contraction becomes, after a period of gradual transition lasting for about thirty-six hours, one which involves the whole

hill (1929a) notes that at this time: "Nothing really new has yet been introduced into the behaviour pattern of the animal since its first movement was performed, and the coil reaction gives the animal no locomotor

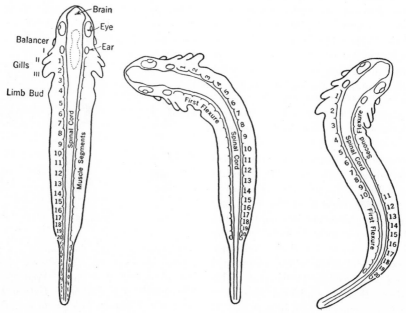

FIGURE 4. Three diagrams of *Amblystoma*. (From *Anatomy and the Problem of Behaviour*, by G. E. Coghill. Cambridge: University Press. New York: Macmillan, 1929, 7–8. By permission of The Macmillan Company.)

The diagram at the left shows the organism in an early swimming stage but without indication of muscle contraction. The diagram in the middle illustrates the beginning of a swimming movement as a first flexure by contraction of a number of anterior muscle segments, indicated by cross-hatching. The diagram on the right illustrates the swimming movement in which the first flexure has passed tailward and the second flexure is beginning in the anterior region.

animal. The result of this reaction, as pointed out by Coghill, is that the organism assumes a position which may be described as that of a tight coil. This C or exaggerated C coil is sometimes oriented to the right and sometimes to the left. It may reverse instantly. At this point in development, all behavioral activities are initiated in the head region and progress toward the tail.

In commenting upon this sequence, Cog-

power. Nevertheless the coil has in it the primary locomotor factor: cephalocaudal progression of muscular contraction" (p. 6). The transition from this behavioral level to the S reaction is amazingly simple. One C contraction begins, for example, on the left, but before it has reached the tail another contraction to the right begins.

The components of this movement may be made clearer by consulting Figure 4. As this reaction gains speed, its performance exerts pressure upon the water and thus drives the organism forward. Thus the S reaction becomes the basis of swimming or aquatic locomotion. This fundamental pattern of behavior may well be a peculiarly significant stage in many other types of growing organisms. This same stage is seen clearly in the swimming of the lower vertebrates. It is somewhat obscured in the four-legged mammals and still more obscured in man, but that this S reaction plays its part in the growth of behavior in these higher organisms seems to be an established fact. Five stages in the development of this basic swimming activity have been made out by Coghill (1929a, p. 9). They may be presented as follows: (1) the nonmotile stage, in which direct muscle stimulation by mechanical or electrical means leads to muscular contraction and hence to externally observable response; (2) the early C flexure stage, in which light touch on the skin of any portion of the body leads to a response; (3) the tight-coil stage, in which the contractions noted in stage 2 become more pronounced and the extent of the contraction greater; (4) the S reaction, which is characterized by a reversal of flexure before the previous flexure has been completely executed as a coil, thus leading to the sinuous behavior of the total organism; (5) the speeding-up of the S reaction so as to produce the typical swimming movement of the amphibian larva.

Youngstrom (1937) in studies upon *Anura* (frogs, toads, etc.) concludes that the Coghillian sequence of developing behavior applies with only slight variations to the *Anura* studied. Wang and Lu (1940, 1941), too, have shown that the stages through which the frog passes are similar to those described by Coghill. These investigators have also shown that severance of the spinal cord arrests the development of swimming at about Coghill's stage 4.

Coghill studied in great detail the neural structure characteristic of the salamander in each of the five stages noted above. On the basis of these investigations he shows how the known structure of the nervous system may make possible the behavior which has previously been described. It is important to recognize that for the most part Coghill (1929a, p. 13) believed that in young organisms movement is typically away from the point of stimulation.

As already noted, the salamander has, besides aquatic locomotion, other significant behavior systems. Of these, walking or terrestrial locomotion and feeding require special consideration. The *Amblystoma* swims before its anatomical development has progressed to the point where it has true limbs. Structurally and functionally the forelimbs are in advance of the developing hindlimbs. In this organism, however, at first both sets of limbs, when they appear, move only in relation to the larger trunk movements described above as those of swimming. Coghill shows why this must be so because of the developing nervous system. Gradually, however, independence of limb action or *individuation* of limb behavior over the dominance of the trunk movements begins (1930e, p. 638). First the forelimbs gain a certain autonomy, and later the hindlimbs also. "It is obvious, therefore," observes Coghill (1929a), "that the first limb movement is an integral part of the total reaction of the animal, and that it is only later that the limb acquires an individuality of its own in behaviour" (p. 19). He then suggests that the forelimb itself may be considered to possess a pattern of development which is comparable to that of the total organism. At first, if movement occurs at all, the whole limb moves. Later, elbow flexion and wrist and digit movement in turn gain independence of the total member. It is important to recognize that during this developmental sequence the time relations of the swimming reaction may be considered as in a way superimposed upon limb activity. Thus one may, if he wishes to, think of the alternate movements of walking in a four-legged organism as a growth out of the basic trunk movements of swimming previously described. Coghill (1929a), indeed, says: "Movement of the trunk in walking is nothing more nor less than the swimming movement with greatly reduced speed" (p. 25). Gradually the sinuous movement of the trunk is reduced as walking becomes more independent, and eventually the characteristic land locomotion of the salamander appears.

The development of the feeding reaction in this same organism has been similarly studied by Coghill (1929a). This response begins with a movement of the trunk; then comes a reaction which involves a sudden lunge of the whole organism; after this there is a gradual correlation between this lunge movement and the activity of the jaws and the muscles of the esophagus. In summarizing this whole development, Coghill (1929a) says: "Behaviour develops from the beginning through the progressive expansion of a perfectly integrated total pattern and the individuation within it of partial patterns which acquire various degrees of discreteness" (p. 38). It should also be noted that as this development continues new senses become important in relation to behavior. Coghill (1930a) believes that ". . . the individual acts on its environment before it reacts to its environment" (p. 345). In considering these beautifully elaborated generalizations of Coghill's, it is important to remember that a different sequence in the development of behavior may well characterize the growth of a mammal and a salamander. In the guinea pig, for example, the limbs are quite fully formed before the first behavioral re-

sponse or reflex takes place, but in the salamander behavior begins before there is any real morphological forelimb at all.

In a series of papers the writer has presented the results of his studies of the development of behavior in *Amblystoma* and the frog under conditions such that experimental groups of animals were raised under unusual environmental circumstances (Carmichael, 1926a, 1927, 1928, 1929). A technique devised by Randolph (1900) and developed by Harrison (1904) was employed. For a consideration of the effect of the anesthetic chloretone on the organism in question, a paper by Matthews and Detwiler (1926) should be consulted. At a period before motility had begun, a large number of developing *Amblystoma* were divided into two groups. The first of these groups was used as a control. The second was used as an experimental group. The experimental group was placed in water containing the anesthetic—a solution of chloretone. The control group was allowed to develop normally in water. Later, at a developmental point previously described by Herrick and Coghill (1915), vigorous responses began in the control group. At this time the experimental group showed morphological development but otherwise remained absolutely inert because of the action of the anesthetic. However, in a short time—often only a minute or two—after the drugged embryos were placed in fresh water, they began to swim well. "In fact, a number of the eighteen *Amblystoma* embryos swam so well in less than one half hour after they had shown the first sign of movement that they could with difficulty, if at all, be distinguished from the members of the control group who had been free swimmers for five days" (Carmichael, 1926a, p. 55).

In later experiments efforts were made to control stimulation in other ways (Carmichael, 1928). As a result of these investigations, the conclusion is drawn that the development of the neural and other mechanisms upon which behavior depends does take place in these organisms whether or not they are as individuals responding to external stimulation. This seems to have a negative implication concerning an extreme interpretation of Child's (1921) environmentalist theory of the causation of growth in the nervous system. Nothing in these experiments is to be taken, however, as invalidating the idea that the growth of the nervous system itself involves activity. Studies such as those of Burr (1932) and P. Weiss (1926, 1939) on this same organism emphasize the dynamic character of such growth processes.

Nicholas and a number of collaborators have studied the development of *Amblystoma*, especially in regard to the development of motility in relation to the nervous system. Some of their results show that the sensory component is exceedingly important in coordinating the activity of groups of muscles (Nicholas and Barron, 1935). Nicholas has also carried out a series of studies on limbs of amphibians developed after experimental embryological manipulations so that they have foreign innervation (1924, 1933a). Some of the results obtained in these studies are interpreted as dependent upon the coordination of nerve responses in the central nervous system rather than upon peripheral selection as suggested in the "resonance theory" of P. Weiss (1926, 1939). Nicholas (1929a) published an extensive study of the analysis of the responses of isolated parts of the amphibian nervous system. In this paper an excellent historical summary of the whole field of the innervation of the limbs in developing *Amblystoma* is presented.

In the reptile class comparatively little work has been done, although Preyer (1885, p. 404) reports some occasional observations on snakes. Tuge (1931) also has done some very interesting work upon the growth of behavior in the turtle. In this work the sequence of Coghill is seen as modified by the existence of the shell which especially characterizes this form.

The Development of Behavior in the Embryos of Birds

From an evolutionary point of view, the bird may be thought of as presenting an interesting comparison with the lower vertebrate and the mammal. The amphibian embryo provides unusually favorable material for developmental study. The growing salamander or frog embryo may be observed, without interference of any sort, through its translucent egg covering and in free life after leaving these coverings. Its egg yolk provides food during a long part of the early developmental period. On the other hand, the study of the development of behavior in the mammal involves relatively complex surgery and, at present at any rate, a certain disturbance of the normal environment of the growing organism. The bird embryo is harder to study than the amphibian but easier than the mammal. It may be studied in a relatively normal environment, but a special technique is necessary to render the development of the bird embryo continuously observable. Down through the years, however, the chicken's egg has been the subject of embryological study. Needham (1931) reviews the use that has been made of the hen's egg in embryology since earliest times. This writer describes the history of the artificial incubation of hens' eggs. He notes also the beginning of systematic observation of embryos taken from eggs in various periods of incubation at the time of Hippocrates (about 460 B.C.). From that time on, the hen's egg has been extensively used in morphological studies of development. Among those who have contributed to this development are Aristotle, Aelian, Pliny, Plutarch, Albertus Magnus, Leonardo da Vinci, Aldrovandus, Fabricius (who made beautiful illustrations of a series of chick embryos), Highmore, Sir Thomas Browne, Harvey, and Malpighi. Today the many admirable manuals on the embryology of the chick, such as those by Patten (1929) and F. R. Lillie (1919), present a large amount of evidence in regard to the structural development of the chick.

Preyer (1885), reviewing certain of these facts more than fifty years ago, noted that, whereas the structural development of the chick is comparatively well known, its behavioral development is not. Although advances have been made since that time, this observation is still true. A few casual observations on this development, nevertheless, were made at an early time. Harvey as long ago as 1651 noted that the chick in the sixth day of development showed a bending and stretching of the head (Preyer, 1885, p. 405). About a century later Béguelin noted the heart beat of the small embryo on the third day, and on the sixth day the oscillation of the whole body, and from that point on he records elaborate changes in movement. He records the fact that he was able to observe the development for fifteen days in the same living and developing embryo (Preyer, 1885, p. 405). Home, in 1822, was probably the first to note the movement of the extremities on the sixth day (Preyer, 1885, p. 405). Von Baer, in 1828, published rather extensive studies on the development of behavior in the chick, in which he noted the inception of the pendular movement of the whole embryo as a result of amnion contractions (Preyer, 1885, p. 405). Amnion contractions, he noted, were most marked on the eighth day and were successively less on the succeeding days. This same investigator reported

general activity of the embryo on the eleventh, twelfth, and thirteenth days. The amnion contractions of the bird's egg have no complete parallel in other forms. The growing chick seems, as it were, to be tossed in a blanket as it grows. Von Baer also saw what he considered to be the beginning of breathing movements in the 14- to 16-day embryo. Several other investigators are quoted by Preyer as having also made observations upon the development of behavior in the chick. By far the most extensive study up to his time on the development of the bird embryo, however, was made by Preyer himself. The extent of his study may be indicated by the fact that he used some five hundred eggs in his experiments.

In this work Preyer gave much attention to the movements of the amnion which have been referred to above. Preyer pointed out that the rhythmic movement of the amnion when at its maximum extent, between the seventh and ninth days, leads to such an agitation of the fetus that no study of fetal activity can be made without taking these contractions into account. The amnion contractions are generally described as independent muscle reactions. They are non-neural. Preyer also describes the gradual development of behavior of the chick embryo from its earliest head movement to the behavior necessary for hatching (pp. 408–416, 555–585). Since the time of Preyer there have been a number of special studies on particular aspects of the fetal and hatching behavior of the bird, such as those by Breed (1911), W. Craig (1912), Clark and Clark (1914), and Patten and Kramer (1933). For the purposes of this chapter by far the most important work is Kuo's, which is presented in a series of papers (1932a, 1932b, 1932c, 1932d, 1932e, 1938, 1939a), and Orr and Windle's (1934).

To collect material for the study of the morphological development of the egg, it is necessary only to open the shells at known periods of incubation. Opening of eggs without special precaution leads to the early death of the embryo, but this is not important if the organism to be studied is placed at once in a fixative to prepare it for the histologist. A number of techniques, however, have been devised to open the shell and still allow the continuous observation of the early development of behavior in the bird. One of these methods, devised by Kuo (1932a), has yielded excellent results. Kuo's method makes possible an uninterrupted study of the developing fetus without interfering in any essential way with the natural membranes of the egg, or, more important, with respiration of the embryo. Kuo's operation may be described as follows: The shell of the blunt end of the egg is cut off with a fine pair of scissors as far as the inner membrane. The whole inner membrane, however, is allowed to remain intact. A very small amount of melted vaseline is immediately and rapidly applied to this membrane with a Chinese writing brush. At the temperature of the incubator the vaseline remains liquid but, when applied by an expert, does not spread. This treatment produces a transparent membranous window through which the embryo and the extraembryonic structures and functions can be observed. This technique renders the membrane so transparent that it is almost as satisfactory as removing the membrane. In the course of observations Kuo uses three incubators, one in which the eggs are kept before they are experimented upon, another in which the operation is performed, and the third a special observation incubator fitted with appropriate glass plates through which a microscope may be used. For a criticism of Kuo's technique, see Becker (1940, 1942).

Kuo has also devised a transparent dial graded in fractions of a millimeter which may be put over the cut end of the egg, thus making the quantitative measurement of fetal movements possible. The writer has collaborated with Kuo in making a moving picture film of the typical stages of development of the chick embryo. For the most part these pictures were taken through the membrane treated as described above. This procedure has been described (Kuo and Carmichael, 1937). In connection with this technique a consideration of the air space of the hen's egg and its changes during incubation is interesting. (See Romijn and Roos, 1938.)

Using his special technique, Kuo has studied many thousands of eggs, and on the basis of this study he has made definite statements in regard to the developmental sequence of behavior in the chick embryo. This work deserves special consideration in this chapter because it is the work of a scientist who is interested in the psychological significance of behavior and because it places emphasis on the part played by the environment in the determination of the course of behavioral development. The results are also presented in such a way that they are peculiarly applicable to psychological problems.

Kuo has traced the chronology and general nature of behavior in the chick embryo (1932a), the mechanical factors in the various stages leading to hatching (1932b), the influence of prenatal behavior upon postnatal life (1932d), and many other special topics such as the relationship between acetylcholine and the onset of behavior (1939a). In the last-named study Kuo shows that the first true neurally determined responses do not appear until after this substance may be detected. This suggests that there may be a chemical mediation of the first response of the chick. For a review of the general importance of acetylcholine, see Cannon and Rosenblueth (1937). A reference to Figure 1 will show that at one typical stage the embryo of the chick is very similar to the fetus of the reptile and, indeed, to the fetus of man. It must, however, be remembered that the arrangement of the embryo of the bird in relation to its extrafetal membranes is, as suggested above, in a number of ways peculiar. A description of this anatomical relationship may be found in Patten (1929).

Kuo's work on the chick may possibly best be given in summary by indicating briefly something of the observed movement and the time at which the movement was *first* observed. It should be noticed that the writer, by using the time at which the movement was first observed, may do an injustice in certain cases to the facts as presented by Kuo, because that investigator shows that in many cases the movement does not, on the average, arise until some hours or even days after it was first observed in peculiarly favorable specimens. A summary of the commencement of the passive and active movements characterizing the developmental behavior of the chick may, however, give the best generalized picture of the development of the chick that is possible in the compass of this chapter. The following activities are among those noted: heartbeat, at 36 hours; head vibration, 66 hours; body vibration, 66 hours; head lifting, 68 hours; head bending, 70 hours; trunk movement, 84 hours; amnion contraction, 86 hours; yolk sac movement, 86 hours; swinging, 86 hours; head turning, 90 hours; movement of forelimbs, 90 hours; movement of hindlimbs, 90 hours; movement of tail, 92 hours; movement of toes, 5 days; response to electricity (in an embryo removed from the shell and placed in a physiological salt

solution), 6 days; eyelid movement, 6 days; response to pressure, 6 days; movement of eyeball, 7 days; swallowing, 8 days; leg folding, 9 days; fixation of body position, 9 days; bill clapping, 9 days; response to touch (in physiological salt solution), 9 days; first wriggling, 11 days; turning of body, 12 days; protrusion of neck, 16 days; respiratory movement, 16 days; response to rotation, 17 days; tearing of membrane, 17 days; peeping, 17 days; response to light, 17 days; response to sound, 18 days; response to vibration, 18 days; hatching, 19 days. Final leaving of the shell does not typically occur, however, until the twentieth or the twenty-first day (Kuo, 1932a).

Kuo has not been content with a mere passive description of the movements indicated above in their time sequences, but in every case he has attempted to give a description of the mechanical and environmental factors which are important in determining the special movements and the special modifications of movements that he notes. Thus, for example, he points out that the beating of the heart leads to a general rhythmic vibration of the inert fetal body which starts the head into passive mechanical movement. In connection with the heart beat of the chick, it may be noted that the structural and functional change of this organ during growth has been intensively studied by Patten and Kramer (1933). Almost from the first appearance of the cells which are to form the organ, beating may be noted. This passive mechanical movement continues until at length it gives place on the fourth or fifth day to a true active movement. Head movement in the chick begins as an up-and-down bowing. Gradually, as a result of the change of the weight of the head and of associated structures in the egg, this up-and-down movement is changed to a sidewise movement, which is eventually inhibited by the altered relationship between the fetus and the yolk sac.

Kuo makes similar observations in regard to the movement of the appendages and to other special behavioral functions. He notes that during the period of the most forceful amnion activity, from the seventh to the ninth day, the mechanical movement of the fetus so stimulates it that there is a large increase in the active movements of the embryo. These movements are considered significant in the development of further movement. It is also observed that an active movement originating in the embryo may incite further activity of contraction in the temporarily relatively quiescent amnion. Indeed, possibly as a result of this reciprocal activation during the period of vigorous amnion contractions, the movements of the developing chick in this period are almost ceaseless. It thus comes about that every part of the musculature of the embryo has been exercised before half its incubation period is over. This fact led Kuo (1932b) to point out that any correlation which it is desired to make between the development of behavior and the development of the nervous system in the chick must take into especial consideration the changing conditions of response due to morphological growth and increase in weight of the body parts themselves and especially to the changing relationships between these growing body parts and the environment in which the growth is taking place.

It is interesting to note that the specialized movements of the eye and of the eyeball occur as early as the eighth or ninth day but that the first light response of the organism does not ordinarily appear until the seventeenth to the nineteenth day under experimental conditions. Thus the eye reflexes are present in the absence of effective visual stimuli. These early eye movements, indeed, have been found by Kuo to occur in conjunction with movement of the body in space instead of in response to visual stimuli. A similar temporal sequence in mammals and its probable mechanisms as worked out by the writer will be discussed below. Only in the later periods of development do the eyes begin to acquire a relative degree of independence from the rest of the organism. Kuo reports that in general the responses to touch, pressure, and electricity, which may be elicited from at least the tenth day onward, are similar to the normally excited responses which he has observed. In conclusion, Kuo asserts that practically every physiological effector mechanism is thus shown to be in a functional condition long before hatching. Thus the organs begin to function in many cases before they reach adult form; indeed, many function in rudimentary form. He feels that, as is true in the development of structure, too much stress cannot be laid on the fact that the development of behavior is gradual and continual. In Kuo's opinion, the early embryonic movements may be thought of as the elements out of which every later response of the adult bird is built. In this connection he points out that certain of the typical postural attitudes of the adult fowl are but returns to the tonus condition of the attitudes of prehatching life (1932d, p. 113). This same observation, incidentally, although too infrequently presented, can be made in the case of mammals and man, and as such will do much to explain the maturation of many allegedly saltatory behavior patterns of postnatal life.

In the carrier pigeon Tuge (1934) has shown that active movements as opposed to passive movements begin at about 105 hours after the beginning of incubation. The first movements observed are extensions and flexions of the head. In 10 additional hours muscles of the neck, trunk, rump, and tail are also involved. "Spontaneous" movements begin before response to chemical or tactile stimuli can be evoked. At about 125 hours in the incubation period the first flexion of the head and neck to tactile stimulation is called out. The reflexogenous zone spreads from the cephalic to the caudal region as development proceeds. Local reflexes of the wings and legs appear at about 155 hours.

Orr and Windle and their collaborators (Orr and Windle, 1934; Windle and Orr, 1934a; Windle and Barcroft, 1938; Windle and Nelson, 1938; Windle, Scharpenberg, and Steele, 1938) have studied in detail the development of the bird. In 1934 Orr and Windle reported that the first response to a blunt vegetable fiber needle takes place in the embryonic chick at 6½ to 7 days after the onset of incubation. This first response is a quick movement of the wing away from the trunk, a lateral flipperlike extension. This movement remains localized. The local reflexes of the embryo do not seem to develop from a generalized behavior pattern but rather arise independently. In another paper (Windle and Orr, 1934a) these two investigators show that the flexion of the chick fetus which takes place on the fifth day is of a sort which cannot be explained by the spinal cord structure at that time. Probably the mechanism which sets off this behavior is chemical in nature. The motor and sensory sides of the nervous system develop in independence of each other, and the motor side is functional first. For a detailed report of the neural structure of the chick as its behavior develops, the reader should consult Windle and Orr's paper (1934a). Windle and his collaborators (Windle and Barcroft, 1938; Windle and Nelson, 1938; Windle, Scharpenberg, and Steele, 1938) have also published a series of papers upon the initiation of res-

piration and the development of respiration in the duck and the chick.

Kuo has also developed an elaborate theory of the growth of behavior in relation to environmental factors. He points out that the intensity of stimulation must be controlled if one is to make any statement concerning the generality or specificity of an organism's response. In a rather recent study (1938) he has pointed out that the physiological *and* behavioral growth of the organism may be summarized in ten stages: (1) cardiac movement, (2) active head movement, (3) trunk movement and response to electric currents, (4) first limb and tail movements and first amnion contraction, (5) head turning and lateral flexion, (6) the hyperactive period from six to nine days, (7) reduction of bodily activities, (8) period of relative quiet (fifteen to eighteen days), (9) prehatching stage, (10) hatching behavior. This is a descriptive procedure much to be preferred to any too easy generalization attempting to summarize the whole course of behavioral growth. Kuo (1939b, 1939c) has also given an interesting review of the whole question of which comes first, total patterns or local reflexes.

As suggested above, the possible importance of chemical mediation in the determination of the onset of behavior requires study. Kuo (1939a) published a paper summarizing his investigations in this field. He found that acetylcholine, the chemical whose presence would most likely be correlated with the onset of activity, was detectable in the embryonic tissues as early as 2½ days after the onset of incubation. Between the fourth and the twelfth days the production of acetylcholine produced per gram of body tissue fluctuates. This substance thus appears before any synapses are present, and it is present in easily detectable quantities before any somatic movement occurs. Kuo has not found any relationship between the acetylcholine development and the development of reflexes.

In considering chemical mediation, it is important not to lose sight of the parallel development of the nervous elements themselves. Windle and Austin (1936) showed in some detail the anatomical growth of the central nervous system of the chick up to five days' incubation.

The Development of Prenatal Behavior in the Infrahuman Mammal

The development of behavior in the infrahuman mammal is in a number of respects more significant for one who would understand the growth of behavior and psychological functions in man than is the consideration of the amphibian or bird presented above. There are peculiar difficulties, however, in studying the development of fetal behavior in mammals. These difficulties can be made clear only by a brief review of the bodily structures and functions involved in the prenatal development of typical placental mammals, including man. In barest outline, disregarding many differences between various species of such mammals and many consequent qualifications, this process of development may be reviewed as follows:

The tiny fertilized mammalian egg is not at first attached but, probably as a result of ciliary action and the muscular contraction of the tubes, moves from the oviduct where it has been fertilized to the uterus. Parker (1931) has summarized the evidence in this field. During the process of movement, which occupies four to ten days, depending on the type of mammal under consideration, the processes of development have begun which are to form the embryo and its membranes. Two embryonic folds are early formed which join to make up the then enclosing amniotic

sac. This sac gradually enlarges. It is filled with a special liquid, the so-called amniotic fluid, which has a very definite chemical make-up and a specific gravity of 1006–1081 (Feldman, 1920, p. 139). The specific gravity of this liquid is thus not far from that of the developing embryo, a fact of great importance in understanding the mechanics of certain forms of receptor-nervous-system–effector action in the fetus at a later period. As growth continues, the sac more and more completely surrounds the embryo.

The embryo thus immersed and supported is relatively independent of most direct mechanical surface contacts. Coincident with this development the other fetal sacs are formed. One of these, the vitelline sac, corresponds to the yolk sac of lower forms, although of course in the higher mammalian types it contains virtually no yolk. In later development of the fetus this sac is relatively much reduced in size, and at the time of birth is known as the umbilical vesicle. The allantois also makes its appearance as an outgrowth of the developing digestive tract of the embryo. This saclike structure comes in contact with the previously formed primitive chorion, with which it fuses to make up the true chorion. This doubly derived chorion now rapidly becomes a completely enclosing membranous wall outside the amniotic sac. The chorion continues to be attached to the embryo proper, however, by means of the allantoic stalk, which comes to conduct as well the two allantoic arteries and the two allantoic veins.

As this development has progressed, therefore, the egg has become attached to the wall of the maternal uterus. As the very complex morphological changes, some of which have been suggested above, take place, the circulatory system of the fetus and its membranes continues to develop. This fetal circulatory system is mechanically completely separated from the maternal blood system, but the separation is, in certain areas, only that of a cell wall. By interchange through living membranes, therefore, oxygen and food materials pass capsulating the developing embryo and its membranes, which have just been described. This true maternal membrane, as distinguished from the previously considered fetal membranes, is called the *decidua capsularis*. In human development, as the fetus grows this decidua capsularis comes

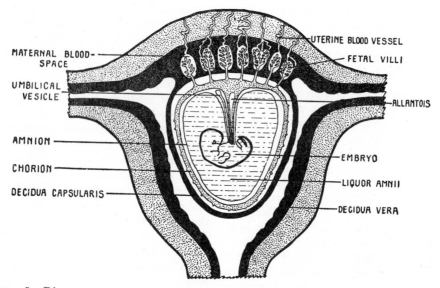

FIGURE 5. Diagram representing the relationship between the uterus, the membranes, and the embryo during early pregnancy. (From "Origin and Prenatal Growth of Behavior," by L. Carmichael. In C. Murchison [Ed.], *A Handbook of Child Psychology*. 2d ed., rev. Worcester: Clark University Press, 1933, 50. By permission of the publisher.)

from the maternal blood system into the independent embryonic blood system; similarly, carbon dioxide and other metabolites pass in the opposite direction into the maternal blood stream. Typically, in the higher mammals only part of the chorion is thus directly attached to the maternal uterus. This area of attachment is called the placenta. The placenta may best be thought of as involving two parts, one of which is derived from the embryo and the other from the maternal uterus. The part which is derived from the maternal uterus becomes larger and larger, eventually en-

to be in contact with the mucous membrane lining of the rest of the uterine cavity, the so-called *decidua vera*. Thus as it grows the fetus is enveloped in an elaborate series of membranes. Figure 5 shows these relationships in very schematic form in the human organism. These developed membranes serve an important function. They provide within the mother's body a strong, many-layered sac in which is maintained an aquatic environment of very constant temperature and remarkably constant physical and chemical constitution. For an elaborate consideration of this development made clear by excellent diagrams, see Spee (1915).

By means of the association at the placenta, as just noted, the independently developing embryo is able, parasitically as it were, to receive food materials, oxygen, and other needful substances from the maternal blood supply and to send back into that system the waste products of its own organic life. The extremely important and technical topic of fetal respiration has been intensively studied in recent years by Barcroft and his associates and by many other workers. For a review of this literature see Barcroft (1938) and Windle (1940). The mechanism of the fetal membranes, therefore, makes possible fetal respiration, nutrition, and excretion. It is in a physical world of this sort that we must consider the fetal mammal as developing and in its later stages as actively responding. The nature of this very special environment must not be forgotten in considering every evidence of sensory or behavioral life which the fetus shows. It must be emphasized, however, that there are great differences in detail in the relationship between fetus and maternal organism in different mammals. As Windle (1940) has pointed out, "Time and again in the study of prenatal physiology it will appear that species variations in the intimacy between maternal and fetal blood streams may explain differences in experimental results" (p. 5).

Birth consists in the rupture of these membranes, often produced by the contractions of the muscular walls of the uterus. The physiology of birth is complex and important. (See Barron, 1940.) A short time after the birth of the young mammal or the child there follows the expulsion of the now discarded enveloping membranes. This "afterbirth" consists largely of the remains of the decidua, the chorion, and the amnion. In infrahuman mammals this afterbirth is customarily eaten by the mother (Tinklepaugh and Hartman, 1930). This is an interesting observation in relation to the problem of the special hungers of the organism.

From what has been said, it is obvious that the developing mammal is so well protected that it is difficult to study its growth at different periods, and nearly impossible—although the "impossible" has been accomplished, as will be pointed out below—to observe continuously the development of the same mammalian fetus. A whole series of papers by Nicholas (1925, 1926, 1927, 1929a) demonstrates the possibility of experimental manipulation of the mammalian egg and growing embryo. This work has fundamental implications not only for the "new" embryology but for the whole study of the growth of behavior.

It may still be said that it is "impossible" to study the mammalian fetus under as nearly normal conditions as those under which Kuo has studied the chick. There is real danger in generalizing upon the nature of fetal development on the basis of observations made under abnormal conditions, as Kuo himself (1932c, p. 265) has said. Observations on the mammalian fetus must ordinarily be abnormal because the very protection which is provided by the fetal membranes just considered must be destroyed if direct observation is to be possible.

It will, of course, be unnecessary here to give an account of the development of behavior in all classes and orders of mammals. Indeed, no special studies have been made of most mammalian forms in this connection. For example, so far as the writer is aware, no special study has been made of the development of behavior in the fetal monotremes. The study of the development of behavior in these primitive Australian egg-laying mammals would probably provide fundamentally significant facts that might be applied to higher truly viviparous forms. In both the ornithorhynchus and the echidna, eggs with soft shells, rich in yolk, undergo segmentation in the uterus and are then laid and incubated. The incubation by the ornithorhynchus is in a nest; by the echidna, in a pouch. When hatched, the young of this subclass are nourished by the secretion of great glands possibly more like sweat glands than like the true mammary structures of higher mammals. But a detailed description of behavioral growth in these forms is not, so far as the writer can discover, available.

Study of the development of behavior in what is generally considered the next higher subclass above the monotremes—namely, the marsupials—has been carried on. Indeed, the marsupials are found to be very favorable material for developmental studies. The young of animals in this subclass are born in a condition which can be considered only that of a relatively immature fetus (Langworthy, 1928). In the marsupials, although early development occurs in the maternal uterus, and although the fetus is nourished by secretions from the uterine wall, no true placenta is formed. Possibly for this reason these true mammalian fetuses are born while still at an early period of development and are as yet open to easy continual external observation during most of the important growth stages in which behavior change may be noted. This fact has made this form a favorite one for studies of neurological development by such students as Weed and Langworthy (1925a, 1925b) and Langworthy (1928). After birth the young are cared for by the mother for many weeks in a pouch, the marsupium, into which the mammary nipples open (Hartman, 1920). In certain of the marsupials, indeed, the once independent fetus again becomes functionally but not structurally attached to the mother, as for a long period after the maternal nipple is taken into the mouth the nipple is never removed until the animal is ready to enter upon truly free life (Hartman, 1920, p. 260).

From the standpoint of the student of the development of behavior, the most adequately studied form of this subclass is the Virginia opossum. In a series of complete and brilliant papers, Hartman (1916a, 1916b, 1919a, 1919b, 1920) has brought together the knowledge in regard to the development of the fetus in the opossum and related types. Until his own work was begun, Hartman points out that the birth of the opossum and the behaviorally significant journey of the newborn organisms to the pouch had been observed and described by but one man, Middleton Michel. Michel's observations, which are reprinted by Hartman (1920, p. 252), led to a belief that the mother transferred the newborn animals to the pouch. Hartman's work, however, has shown that the newborn organisms travel directly from the vulva to the maternal pouch without the aid of the mother. He says:

Unerringly the embryo traveled by its own efforts; without any assistance on the mother's part, other than to free it of liquid on its first emergence into the world, this ten-day-old embryo, in appearance more like a worm than a mammal, is able, immediately upon release from its liquid medium, to crawl a full three inches over a difficult terrain. Indeed, it can do more: after it has arrived at the pouch it is able to find the nipple amid a forest of hair. This it must find—or perish (p. 255).

Hartman has further shown that this essential journey is to be considered a negative geotropism, because under experimental conditions embryos can be made to travel away from the pouch if only the skin upon which they are moving is tilted upward. The locomotion of the embryo is described as a kind of overhand swimming stroke in which the head sways as far as possible to the side opposite the hand which is taking the propelling stroke. It is further noted that "With each turn of the head the snout is touched to the mother's skin . . . and if the teat is touched, the embryo stops and at once takes hold" (p. 256).

The conclusion may be suggested, therefore, that this young mammalian organism, less than two weeks removed from an unfertilized ovum, has already developed to a point of independent ability so far as air respiration, alimentary canal digestion, and the receptor-neuromuscular mechanism of geotropically orientated simple progression are concerned. McCrady (1938) has recently devoted a book to the description of the development of the opossum, a notable book in many respects but especially because of its beautiful drawings.

McCrady, Wever, and Bray (1937) have studied by electrical techniques the onset of hearing in the postnatal pouch-young opossum. They find a gradual growth in electrical output by the developing cochlea during the period studied, namely, 59 to 82 days after birth.

Goerling, in an article also reprinted by Hartman (1920, p. 259), gives an account of the birth of the kangaroo, an animal of the same subclass as the opossum. It has been observed that in the kangaroo the young animal moves through the fur from the opening of the urogenital canal to the pouch. The following observation is recorded in regard to the fetus: "It moved about slowly, very slowly, through the fur upwards, using the arms in its progress, and continually moving the head from side to side . . ." (Hartman, 1920, p. 260). Thirty minutes were required for the passage, but during this time the mother gave no assistance whatsoever. Goerling further notes that the arms of the newborn kanga-

roo are strongly developed. The small hands open and close like a cat's paws. He says: "By these strong little arms and hands the young one is enabled to labour its way to the pouch, the place of safety and nourishment" (Hartman, 1920, p. 260). It is further pointed out that, so far as the sucking reflex is concerned, once a young

FIGURE 6. A so-called mammary fetus of the kangaroo attached to the maternal teat. (From *A Text-Book of Zoology*, by T. J. Parker and W. A. Haswell. London: Macmillan, 1921, Vol. II, 577. By permission of The Macmillan Company.)

kangaroo is removed from the teat which it has taken in its mouth it is apparently unable to reattach itself. Figure 6 shows the early fetal appearance of the pouch-young kangaroo (Parker and Haswell, 1921, p. 577).

In the series of papers referred to above, Hartman reports his studies of the early embryology of the opossum but without any detailed reference to the onset and development of behavior before the early motility stage in which it is found at birth. It is interesting to note, however, on the basis of the evidence given above, that in the marsupials young organisms which might even still be called embryos are born in what is in many respects a very early fetal condition. Their behavior, as indicated above, is significant at any rate in a number of ways for the general student of the development of response. Once in the pouch these organisms can be studied without the usual difficulties of disturbed respiration and digestion of higher mammalian fetuses of comparable developmental age which still depend upon the placental attachment. The reports just given suggest that in this organism there is a general conformity with the pattern of development of the amphibian larvae considered above. As in the case of *Amblystoma*, the young opossum moves with a wriggling movement which from the description, "the head swaying as far as possible to the side opposite the hand which is taking the propelling stroke" (Hartman, 1920, p. 256), suggests the double S movement elaborated by Coghill and others as a characteristic of the onset of aquatic locomotion in larval amphibians. It is also significant to note that it is the forelimbs, both in the opossum and even in that characteristically hindlimbed organism, the kangaroo, which are mentioned as the effective agents of locomotion.

This again at least does not contradict the view that behavior typically develops from the anterior to the posterior segments of the organism. This generalization may be said to be essentially true of behavior growth in invertebrates, amphibians, and bird embryos. Moreover, there is nothing in the development of the feeding reaction which is presented that shows its essential sequence to be different from that already noted in lower types. Langworthy (1925, 1928) and Weed and Langworthy (1925a, 1925b) have studied the development of progression and body posture in pouch-young opossums. They find that decerebration of young opossums does not lead to decerebrate rigidity, but rather to an increase in progression movements.

This suggests that at this period the cortex has as yet established little dominance over the other neural determinants of behavior. Similarly, they note, after giving a complete review of the work on the nervous system of the opossum, that electrical stimulation of the brains of pouch-young opossums gives contralateral leg responses but no other responses for over 50 developmental days (Weed and Langworthy, 1925b, p. 23). These observations are important in regard to the part played by myelinization of the nervous system in behavior and, incidentally, seem to confirm the priority of forelimb progression in the early behavioral repertory of this form. Larsell, McCrady, and Zimmerman (1935) have studied the morphological and functional development of the membranous labyrinth of the inner ear of the opossum. Nerve endings are present around the hair cells before the ear is functional. Vestibular reflexes appear at about 43 days after insemination; acoustic reflexes appear at 50 days. Myelin appears on the vestibular nerve fibers at the time reflexes first appear. It increases as the reflexes become more pronounced. (See also the study on electrical phenomena of the cochlea in the young opossum by McCrady, Wever, and Bray, 1937.)

Of all orders of infrahuman mammals, the rodents have probably been most completely studied, so far as the development of behavior is concerned. It is difficult to say when the study of behavioral growth in rodent fetuses began. They are convenient animals to work upon, and it is highly probable that some member of this order was used by the classic embryologists, whose work will be historically reviewed below when a discussion of the specific development of behavior in man is given. It is known, at any rate, that the dead embryos of typical rodents—namely, the rabbit, guinea pig, and mouse—besides many other animal forms, were discussed by Hieronymus Fabricius in his monumental work *De Formato Foetu* in 1604 (Needham, 1931, p. 115). It is highly probable that this writer or some of the other great embryologists of the Renaissance observed the behavior of fetal rodents, because at this time embryology was still much concerned with the Aristotelian problem of the development of the vegetable, sensible, and rational souls in all the forms which were studied.

The first important experimental studies of the development of behavior in this order, however, that the writer has been able to find are those of Bichat (1819, 1827). This eminent early experimental physiologist studied the living embryos of a number of animals, particularly investigating the relationship between the blood stream of the mother and of the fetus. In this work he used the guinea pig extensively. As a result of his studies, Bichat came to a number of interesting, although to some extent unsound, conclusions in regard to the development of behavior in the fetus. He presents a generalized thesis, possibly growing out of the speculations of the Renaissance, that the organism at all stages combines what he calls two lives, one of which is that of sensibility, involving the brain and the senses, and the other that of the vegetative life, involving digestion, circulation, and the like. On the basis of his researches on fetal behavior he concludes that the life of sensibility does not begin before birth, although surprisingly enough he notes and describes in some detail the nature of fetal movements. He alleges that the fetus must be thought of as living in a world virtually devoid of stimulation, as he holds, correctly enough, that an energy, in order to be a stimulus, must change. As the fetus is held in a liquid of constant temperature and properties, he contends that it is virtually un-

stimulated. He does admit that the sense of touch may be stimulated before birth, but it is not, he further contends, really touch, as every true sensation supposes a comparison between a present and a past state of being.

For this conclusion he is roundly criticized by another eminent French physiologist, Magendie, who later edited Bichat's work. Magendie says in a footnote to Bichat's statements on touch: "Whatever Bichat may say, it exists in the fetus before birth." Bichat himself (1827), however, points out that touch is to be considered as the most fundamental of the senses and suggests that "philosophers say it is the only one of the senses which always is the agent of truth" (p. 136). Against this sweeping generalization, Magendie, in another footnote, quotes the old experiment of Aristotle upon the illusory localization of the crossed fingers (p. 137). Partly on the basis of his work on guinea pigs, Bichat concludes that the responses of the fetal organism develop continuously from zero to a point of greatest activity just before birth. He supports this conclusion by much anatomical evidence, which includes a discussion of the musculature of the limbs, the brain, the nerves, and the sense organs. He then attempts, it almost seems, to explain away the observations which he has just made, in the light of his own theory. For he at once asserts that the existence of the fetus is not that of an animal but virtually that of a vegetable. This conclusion is based upon the dichotomy which he attempts to establish even in the adult life of man between movements which are dependent upon the will, and hence "animal," as contrasted with such movements as those occurring in sleep, which he alleges are not animal but merely "living."

It is a long step from these early theories and observations to the present knowledge of the development of behavior in rodents, and indeed this step was not taken in a single jump. In 1818 Emmert, an embryologist, published certain incidental observations on the behavioral activity of field mouse embryos (Emmert and Bugätzy, 1818). Zuntz (1877) used fetal rodent material in a series of scientific observations. His work was devoted for the most part to a consideration of the chest movements of the newborn fetus of the rabbit, which was used in part of his study of the development of fetal respiration in mammals.

It was not, however, until Preyer began his series of experiments on fetal guinea pigs and other animals that the modern period of the study of the behavioral growth of the rodent began. In his great summarizing work of 1885, Preyer gives an elaborate history of the study of the development of behavior in each form which he considers. Significantly enough, however, in this treatise, when he deals with the development of mammalian behavior, he begins almost without historical references.

Preyer (1885, pp. 416–428), in his own experiments, however, used a number of different types of mammals and a number of different techniques in his study of the development of behavior. His most significant work was done on the guinea pig. In studying this rodent he used at least six methods:

(1) The animal was placed on its back, and the movements of the external abdominal wall of the pregnant mother were observed without interference. He also made such observations on pregnant females on which so-called animal hypnosis or tonic immobility had been induced by an appropriate posture and pressure manipulation. As a result of these types of direct observation he concluded that there are periods of quiescence, lasting sometimes for more than an hour, interspersed with periods of great

activity in fetal behavior, at least during the latter part of the pregnancy.

(2) In another experiment he placed a long, thin needle directly through the abdominal wall and the fetal sacs of the pregnant female and pressed it into the fetus. This needle was inserted so that, when the fetus moved, the needle, forming a sort of lever, could be observed to change its position. As a result of these investigations, the frequency of fetal activity was noted. It is all too clear to the modern investigator accustomed to the use of anesthetics in animal experiments that the fetus and the mother could hardly be considered "normal" during these studies.

(3) He listened to the fetal movements through a stethoscope and recorded that in the latter stages of pregnancy they made a peculiar *Knistern* and *Knacken.*

(4) By operation he found it possible to allow a single limb to extrude from the sac in such a way that its movement could be observed.

(5) By experimental surgery it proved possible to observe the movements of the fetus still in the mother's body. In this situation he was able to note the effect of changing the blood supply upon fetal behavior and to come to the conclusion that, although deprivation of oxygen did at times lead to general fetal movements, such deprivation was not an essential cause of such movements.

(6) He also removed guinea pig fetuses in the air-breathing stage and studied them when supported by blood-warm physiological salt solution and in a warm chamber. In observing the movements of such fetuses he characterized their responses as *"sehr manigfaltig, ungeregelt, asymmetrisch, arhythmisch"* (p. 418).

It is interesting to note below that these are virtually the same words used by Minkowski and many others later in describing early human fetal movements. Preyer also observed certain movements of stretching and of reflex contraction and extension which would be difficult for the fetus while confined in the sac. This phenomenon has been seen many times by the writer, who knows of no evidence that Preyer used any anesthetics in employing any of the methods noted above. The criticism of the more humane work of later investigators, that possibly the fetal material was anesthetized, cannot therefore be urged against this pioneer work of Preyer, which may, however, be criticized on humanitarian grounds.

In one case Preyer (1882) notes that, when his observations were made on a guinea pig in the still intact sac, touching the skin of the face led to a localized brushing movement on the part of the forelimb of the fetus as if to wipe away the offending stimulus which was touching the pad of the vibrissae (p. 212). We shall see that the study of the development of this ability in the fetus may throw light upon certain aspects of the old question as to whether or not the perception of space is natively or empirically determined.

Preyer gives a rather general description of development in the fetal guinea pig. In a fetus 20 to 21 mm. in length no movement was seen, but he adds that this may not be interpreted as assurance that no movement had previously occurred while the organism was in the uterus. In one of 81 to 83 mm., however, opened under blood-warm salt solution, the heart was seen to beat strongly and chest movements were noted. In much larger fetuses, 105 to 111 mm. long, a complete repertory of action almost like that seen in the adult animal was recorded. Many other observations are given on fetuses the lengths of which are not recorded. On the basis of these observations on fetuses, often approximately dated by statements in regard to the hair and teeth condition of

the organism, it is possible to say that Preyer noted in the development of behavior in the guinea pig a gradual change in response with growth. The very early movements changed by gradual development until elaborate adaptive responses appeared. Concerning a series of carefully weighed litters in later stages he gives a detailed account of definite responses. These activities include the pinna reflex to sound, now often called *Preyer's reflex*, the pupillary reflex to light, and even the cerebral inhibition of reflexes as a result of antagonistic stimuli (1885, pp. 587–595). He points out that in a 173-gram guinea pig the teeth of the organism were so well developed that they bit his fingernail sharply (p. 423). On the basis of all this observational and experimental work, Preyer turns to his consideration of the development of behavior in the human fetus, to which reference is made below.

The first systematic study of the development of fetal behavior in guinea pigs, from the point of view of genetic psychology, is Avery's (1928), carried out in the Psychological Laboratory of Stanford University. As a background for the study of prenatal development, Avery carefully investigated the responses to stimulation shown by newborn guinea pigs. As contrasted with the naked and almost helpless neonatal marsupials described above, the guinea pig is at birth in many respects structurally and functionally a mature animal. It is born with a sleek coat of fur. Its teeth are well erupted. Its eyes and ears are open. Its heart pulsations and breathing may be quite continuous and regular. It is able to roll from back to side, side to back, and side to haunches. It can crawl, stand, and walk.

To the pinch stimulus applied to the foot it responds by kick or withdrawal of foot. The electrical stimulus elicits a muscular twitch, respiratory gasp, and jump. It can execute the scratch reflex spontaneously or when stimulated in the facial region. Although muscular weakness is evident the patterns of response show good coordination (Avery, 1928, p. 264).

The sensory control of behavior, this investigator points out, has also progressed to a remarkable degree. Lid and pupillary reflexes are present. The newborn animal avoids objects without touching them as it moves about. The ears are functional, and total bodily movements and pinna twitches are elicited by appropriate auditory stimulation. Needle pricks and heated objects lead to quick response. Olfactory stimuli evoke movement of the head. The complex movements of swallowing are well developed. So far as more integrated behavior is concerned, Avery reports that the young run together when separated from each other and run to the mother when separated from her. Somewhat similar observations were also made by Preyer (1882, p. 93). The young lick themselves, swim when placed in deep water, chew shavings, and attempt to disengage a foot held by an observer. No retreat responses were noticed when young guinea pigs were placed with an adult white rat. The prenatal development of behavior of this Minerva-like organism is therefore peculiarly interesting because it is such a complete story.

Avery's work on prenatal development must be strictly evaluated, however, in terms of the rather special conditions which he employed in his experimental study. Abandoning the techniques used by some of the earlier investigators in mammalian behavioral development, Avery removed from the mother each fetus that he studied. He thus, of course, intercepted placental circulation and therefore brought about all the changes which have been found to result from oxygen deprivation and an increasing concentration of metabolites in the fetal blood stream. That is, he often worked with dying fetuses. Thus his work is strictly comparable to most of the work on human fetuses reviewed below. Observations were most often made on a large metal tray placed on a well-lighted observation table. "An electric heater, reflector type, was placed nearby. It served to dry the young and to keep them warm. A temperature of 98° F. was maintained on the observation table" (Avery, 1928, p. 258). This technique provided that, so far as early embryos were concerned, they were studied not only without normal respiration but in what was apparently a continually drying condition.

The results of Avery's pioneer study, therefore, must be considered as a function of these special conditions, because previous studies had shown, and some of the writer's experimental observations adequately demonstrate, that many responses are possible in an aquatic environment which are quite impossible when the organism is placed upon a solid surface in the air. Avery studied animals of gestation ages of 45 to 68 days. The lower point was chosen because, in Avery's opinion, "Prior to this time responses are so slight as to be of little importance for this problem" (p. 270). This decision is in some respects surprising, because Preyer reported movement in fetal guinea pigs of much younger gestation age. Indeed, according to Draper's tables (1920) and Preyer's own estimate (1885, p. 588), the first of Preyer's fetuses moved when they were 26 to 29 gestation days old. The writer has seen movement in a 25-day fetus. Avery's work, therefore, from the standpoint of the general problem of development, must be taken as significant of the development of behavior in the later stages of gestation. Indeed, it is probably most significant in regard to fetuses which have developed to the point that they can, under appropriate conditions, breathe and move without difficulty in an air environment.

This same investigator also considered the question of whether or not there is a distinction between the responses of fetuses taken from young and old mothers. He came to the conclusion that there is no significant difference in the maturity of response elicited from the fetuses of young and of fully adult mothers (p. 311). This conclusion is unlike that of King (1915) and of Angulo y González (1932b) in regard to the white rat, in which various parental conditions were found to influence fetal development.

By the use of X-rays Avery also most ingeniously studied the orientation of the fetuses in the uterus of the guinea pig. This study convinced him that gravitation is apparently not very significant in determining rapid changes in the orientation of the fetus in the uterus. He concludes: "The shifts of the foetuses in utero are inadequate to explain their activity after experimental delivery" (p. 324). As a final conclusion to his study Avery says: "These results substantiate the belief that certain congenital response mechanisms exist in foetal and newborn guinea pigs. Some of these are subject to early modification through experience" (p. 329). For an interesting early study in this field, see Virey (1833).

The writer (Carmichael, 1934a) studied a large number of fetal guinea pigs in a series of experiments in which as many factors as possible were controlled. This study involved more than two years of work and the typing of more than two thousand pages of protocols dictated at the time of the experiments. In most cases photographic records of behavior were also made. A picture of the apparatus used is shown in Figure 7. A summary of results may be given (pp. 422–466):

(1) Heartbeat was the only activity observable in the youngest fetuses studied in this investigation. . . .

(2) Before any behavior was observed the skeletal muscles of the still immobile fetus could be made to respond by direct electrical stimulation. . . .

(3) In a 28-day fetus behavior involving skeletal muscle response without electrical stimulation was observed for the first time. . . .

(4) The first observed responses occurred "spontaneously," that is, as a result of unknown causes. . . .

(5) The first "spontaneous" movement observed was a lateral flexion of the neck and a synchronous and possibly independent movement of the forelimbs. . . .

(6) The first sensory area from which behavior was released in the present study was . . . the concha of the ear. . . .

(7) In general, responses at every stage are a function of what were called . . . (a) modes of stimulation and (b) variable conditions of the organism.

(8) The first stimulus-released response noted in the study may be characterized, at its first appearance, as a pattern of behavior, which involves a relationship between neck flexion and forelimb movement. . . .

(9) Many of the points indicated . . . when stimulated, release behavior from the first which in spite of very great variability could always be considered as a special "pattern of behavior." . . .

(10) Each behavior pattern released by the stimulation of a particular area may be said to undergo a series of changes during fetal life. . . .

(11) Photic stimulation of the eye may lead to motor responses of the limbs, etc., before the eyes are normally open in the fetus, when such stimulation is made possible by an operative exposure of the eye. . . .

(12) Auditory stimuli released behavior in a 63-day fetus after the liquid had been removed from the external meatus. . . .

(13) Needle stimulation ("pain stimuli") in general released responses which were quite comparable to responses

(15) In late fetuses compensatory movements during rotation and in the immediate post-rotational period were demonstrated. . . .

(16) There is evidence that in late fetal life higher brain centers influence responses

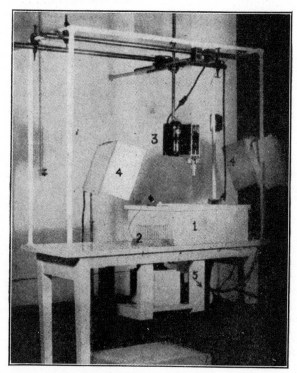

FIGURE 7. Photograph of apparatus. (From "Quantified Pressure Stimulation and the Specificity and Generality of Response in Fetal Life," by L. Carmichael and M. F. Smith. *Journal of Genetic Psychology*, 1939, **54,** 427. By permission of The Journal Press, publisher.)

(1) Constant temperature tank in which is inserted a tray filled with physiological saline solution. Maternal animal is held in this bath by suitable supports and fetal organisms are then exposed for study. (2) Holder and graded series of esthesiometers. (3) Electrically driven motion picture camera for recording. (4) Reflectors for two 1000-watt lamps used to illuminate the field. (5) Foot-operated switch to start and stop the recording motion picture camera.

leased by pressure stimuli rather than to the vigorous responses characteristic of the adult animal when subjected to pain stimulation. . . .

(14) Temperature stimuli well above and well below the temperature of the fetus, when applied to the skin, release behavior. . . .

which are characteristically called "spinal reflexes." . . .

(17) As development progresses, the amount of "motor diffusion resulting from specific receptor stimulation" decreases, at least in certain areas and under certain stimulus conditions. . . .

(18) The present study does not confirm

in detail the specific laws of development, alleging that development is in all respects cephalo-caudal, proximo-distal, or from "fundamental" to "accessory" muscles. . . .

(19) It is possible to view most of the typical patterns of behavior released by the stimulation of given areas as capable of securing some end or ends, which during fetal life itself or during subsequent independent life may serve adaptive needs of the organism. . . .

(20) The present study does not give unqualified support to any of the more general theories of the development of behavior, such as those summarized by the words "individuation" or "integration," but suggests rather that the formulation of such generalizations is at present premature. . . .

After this general study it became apparent that a more detailed study of certain aspects of fetal behavior in the guinea pig was important. Bridgman and Carmichael (1935) studied forty-seven fetal litters *at just about the time that behavior first begins*. As a result of this study the following conclusions were drawn (pp. 262–265):

(1) Prior to the onset of behavior in the fetal guinea-pig, myogenic contractions can be elicited from certain muscles. That these early responses are truly myogenic, and not sensory-motor responses, there is little doubt, because of their character, particularly as compared to later movements.

(2) Active behavior in the fetal guinea-pig begins in the last hours of the twenty-fifth day. Previous observers had placed the onset at least one day later than this.

(3) True behavior, that is, response that results from stimulation, and which is secondarily induced by nervous discharge, can be elicited 10 to 14 hours before "spontaneous" behavior appears. These stimulated responses are of a sufficiently different character from the earlier myogenic contractions to be classified as active; i.e., involving neural activity. . . .

(4) The first active responses of the fetal guinea-pig are definite in character, and involve movements of the head, brought about by contraction of the neck muscles, and of the fore leg. The evidence is as yet inconclusive concerning which of these components arises first.

(5) It is seen that, from the earliest period, the neck and limb responses occur sometimes together, and sometimes independently, and that throughout the developmental period studied, independent elements of behavior are present at all times. That is, no gradual progressive "individuation" of the specific responses out of a total pattern is seen. . . .

(6) Because of the simple and specific nature of much of the earliest behavior of the fetal guinea-pig, it is thought that these responses may advantageously be described as reflexes. Moreover, no need to use such words as "generalized," "totally integrated," or "non-specific" in the description of this behavior has arisen. . . .

The development of temperature sensitivity in the fetal guinea pig has been studied by Carmichael and Lehner (1937). The results of this study are summarized in Figure 8. This figure shows that in fetuses of all ages there is an increase in released behavior as stimuli (drops of water) are used which are either warmer or cooler than the physiological zero (about 37.5° C.) of the organism. The conclusions of this study (pp. 224–226) may be summarized in the following statements:

(1) Temperature stimuli . . . are effective in releasing responses during most of the motile fetal period of the guinea-pig.

(2) At each of three fetal development periods, as these periods were established for the purposes of this study—young, mid, and old—the greater the difference between the temperature of the stimulus and the physiological zero of the organism, the

greater the relative number of responses released by that stimulus.

(3) At the youngest ages studied, there appears to be a slight tendency for cold stimuli to be relatively more effective than warm stimuli if certain assumptions of equality are made concerning units of measurement.

(4) During the "young" period of fetal life, as defined above, there appears to be

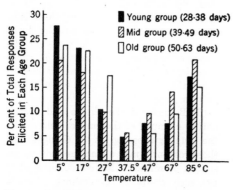

FIGURE 8. Responses of guinea pig fetuses to thermal stimuli. (From "The Development of Temperature Sensitivity during the Fetal Period," by L. Carmichael and G. F. J. Lehner. *Journal of Genetic Psychology,* 1937, **50,** 222. By permission of the publisher.)

development of temperature sensitivity. Sensitivity is greater, that is, in the mid period studied than in the initial period. There is no corresponding increase during the other periods studied. In the last period, the growth of the insulating hair coat unquestionably modifies the effectiveness of the stimuli as applied in this investigation.

(5) There is no great change in the percentage of specific and general responses released by the stimuli used at any of the three periods studied, nor does the effective intensity of stimulation (as measured by the greater degree of difference from physiological zero) change in a definite manner as development progresses in its efficacy in releasing either general or specific responses. There is a slight preponderance

of specific over general responses, as these two words are defined in this paper in each period, but this finding can hardly be considered as statistically significant.

(6) There is some shift in the relative sensitivity of the six areas stimulated during fetal development. These data may be considered as supporting the generalization made by previous investigators that the development of sensitivity spreads from the cephalic to the caudal regions of the body and from the proximal to the distal regions of limbs.

Hooker and other investigators have emphasized the importance of the use of quantified pressure stimuli in working upon fetal material. Carmichael and Smith

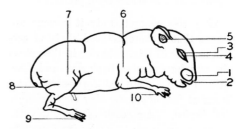

FIGURE 9. Typical reflexogenous zones. (From "Quantified Pressure Stimulation and the Specificity and Generality of Response in Fetal Life," by L. Carmichael and M. F. Smith. *Journal of Genetic Psychology,* 1939, **54,** 428. By permission of the publisher.)

(1) Midpoint of the vibrissae pad on the snout. (2) Inner surface of the vestibule of one external naris (nostril). (3) Midpoint of the upper eyelid. (4) Midpoint of the lower eyelid. (5) Midpoint of the concha of the ear. (6) Skin over the shoulder joint of the pectoral girdle. (7) Skin over the hip bone joint of the pelvic girdle. (8) Anus. (9) Point in medial plantar surface of one hindpaw. (10) Point in medial palmar surface of one forepaw.

(1939) attempted to study this question in detail. (See also Carmichael, 1937.) First they decided to use certain well-established reflexogenous zones as shown in Figure 9. They then prepared a series of calibrated von Frey esthesiometers. In each case the lightest esthesiometer that would elicit a response was used, as well as one seven to nine points higher in the scale of esthesiometers. The quantitative conclusions of this study are shown in Figure 10. An example of the difference in re-

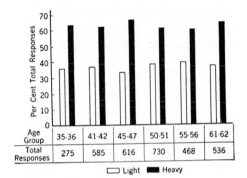

Age Group	35-36	41-42	45-47	50-51	55-56	61-62
Total Responses	275	585	616	730	468	536

☐ Light ■ Heavy

FIGURE 10. Percentage of responses at each fetal age group studied. (Normal gestation period is 68 days.) (From "Quantified Pressure Stimulation and the Specificity and Generality of Response in Fetal Life," by L. Carmichael and M. F. Smith. *Journal of Genetic Psychology*, 1939, **54**, 431. By permission of the publisher.)

Group 35–36 days		
Total responses 275	Light 36.5%	Heavy 63.5%
Group 41–42 days		
Total responses 585	Light 37.5%	Heavy 62.5%
Group 45–47 days		
Total responses 616	Light 33.6%	Heavy 66.4%
Group 50–51 days		
Total responses 730	Light 38.4%	Heavy 61.6%
Group 55–56 days		
Total responses 468	Light 39.7%	Heavy 60.3%
Group 61–62 days		
Total responses 536	Light 35.4%	Heavy 64.6%

sponse to the light and heavy stimuli is shown in Figure 11. In summary of this study it may be said that pressure stimuli are like temperature stimuli in the importance of intensity upon resulting response.

Moreover, the present results show that the same relative proportion of general and specific responses seems to be released at all of the typical fetal ages studied. This finding adds further confirmation to the view that specific responses are early developed in fetal life. Thus it becomes more than ever clear that the widely accepted formula that all specific behavior develops from the individuation of previously more general patterns of behavior needs revision. Such revision can come only from continued study of fetal behavior as released by stimuli of quantitatively known character (Carmichael and Smith, 1939, p. 434)

Jasper, Bridgman, and Carmichael (1937) have studied the electrical brain potentials of the fetal guinea pig. Their conclusions (pp. 70–71) are:

(1) The brain potentials of the guinea pig first appear when the age of 48–56 days of gestation has been attained.

(2) No quantitative ontogenetic trend in the characteristic frequency of potential variation, nor in the total range of frequencies, has been discovered. The appearance of secondary groupings of characteristic frequencies is found more often as age increases.

(3) The average amplitude of the characteristic frequencies at any age shows an irregular yet definite increase with age.

(4) Definite though not invariable effects of stimulation on the character of the cortical electrogram have been noted, occurring as early as the 60th day of gestation.

(5) The guinea pig brain first exhibits electrical activity at a time when behavioral indications also point to maturation of higher nervous centers.

In connection with this study it was noted that tying off the umbilical cord abolished cortical activity but did not for some time abolish the lower reflexes of the fetus.

In another study, using high-gain electrical amplification of bioelectric phenomena in the fetal guinea pig, Rawdon-Smith, Carmichael, and Wellman (1938) have demonstrated that the cochlear electrical response (the so-called Wever-Bray effect) is present in a guinea pig fetus of 52 post-insemination days. The electrical response secured at 52 days had a peak voltage of 1 to 2 microvolts to a stimulus of 600 cycles per second at an intensity of 100 decibels above human threshold. Declin-

this sort is reported in an unpublished thesis by Swenson (1926). The experimental work for this thesis was done under the direction of Coghill. The thesis is entitled *The Development of Movement of the Albino Rat before Birth*. The operation by which the female is rendered immobile is described by Swenson in a special article (1925). The mother is deeply anesthetized, the neck is opened, and the

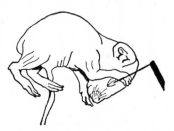

FIGURE 11. Outline tracings from moving picture film of two postures of 51-day guinea pig fetus. (From "Quantified Pressure Stimulation and the Specificity and Generality of Response in Fetal Life," by L. Carmichael and M. F. Smith. *Journal of Genetic Psychology,* 1939, **54**, 432. By permission of the publisher.)

Picture at left shows resting posture of the fetus as stimulated with light esthesiometer. Only response in this case was an eye wink. Picture at right shows one phase of movement elicited by a heavier esthesiometer. In this case, the entire trunk and all limbs are involved in the reaction. Note the precise localization of the stimulated spot by the forepaw.

ing responses were noted to tones below this and above 2000 cycles per second. The rise in electrical output was rapid as development progressed, for by 62 days 100 microvolts was recorded. It is interesting to note that the time of onset of the electrical response of the fetal ear—namely, 52 days—is exactly the same time at which the first overt behavior released by auditory stimuli can be observed in the fetal guinea pig.

Of all rodents, however, not the guinea pig but the white rat seems to be the most generally studied laboratory mammal. It is not surprising, therefore, that in recent years an increasing amount of attention has been given to the prenatal development of behavior in this convenient organism. One of the most elaborate studies of

carotid arteries are ligated as close to their origin as possible. The large left and right external jugular veins are also secured and ligated. Ether is now discontinued and the skin incision is closed. After the anesthesia has been allowed to pass off, the mother is immersed in physiological salt solution. Each fetus is then in turn shelled out and studied.

Swenson's observation began with fetuses showing absolutely no movement save heart beat and continued at convenient stages to birth. It is difficult to generalize about any such developmental sequence because the omission of any of the details of the onset of behavior is likely to give a prejudiced picture of the total process. It is possible in review here, however, to give a few of the salient points of the growth of behavior in the rat as found by Swenson. The first movement noticed was a slight lateral bending of the head. This same movement, differently interpreted, may be characterized as a slight cephalic trunk-bending movement. From this early action to the precise adaptive movements of tongue and paws in late fetuses, there is found a continuous quantitative and qualitative change in the movements as observed in litters of increasing gestation age. In the general theoretical discussion of the causal factors concerned in the development of behavior, we shall again refer to the work of Swenson, particularly to the observations which he made upon fetuses with clamped umbilical cords. Clamping of the cord he found to lead to an increase of metabolites in the fetal system and certain characteristic behavioral changes. Abstracts of the thesis noted above, and additional observations, have been published by Swenson (1928b, 1929).

Angulo y González (see references in bibliography), also associated with Coghill, has published some very important studies of the development of behavior in the fetal albino rat. He used much the same technique as Swenson in operating on the mother rat and in preparing the fetal material for observation. He selected his material with unusual care. Of the 643 fetuses used in one study, all came from healthy female rats of known stock 110 to 190 days of age, his previous work having indicated that these precautions were necessary in order to obtain scientifically comparable results at various gestation ages. In his work moving picture records were taken to supplement the written protocols. Angulo y González in his experimental report gives the percentages of fetuses showing each movement at each age. For these detailed conclusions the reader is advised to consult the original papers (1929a, 1930b, 1932a, 1939). This same author,

after using the drug *curare*, which alters the physiological relationship of motor nerves and muscles, was able to stimulate muscles directly in young fetuses. This indicates that the first responses of the rat fetus may be purely myogenic.

It is interesting to note that both Swenson and Angulo y González independently first observed movement in the rat fetus in the three hundred and seventy-eighth hour after insemination. Angulo y González' general description of the developmental process, particularly so far as the process of "individuation" of behavior is concerned, may best be given in his own words:

During the early stages of development the appendages move only with the trunk. Thus, upon stimulation of the snout the reaction more frequently obtained is a total mass reaction which involves the trunk and appendages. This total mass reaction we called a total pattern. This total-pattern reaction consists of a primary or basic movement, lateral flexion of the trunk, and a series of secondary movements. Similarly, there develops later a total pattern consisting of a basic movement of head extension and a series of secondary movements. The basic movements, during the early period of behavioral development, assert their sovereignty upon the secondary movements. During the later period of the development of fetal behavior, we find a number of specific reflexes showing what at first seems to be a breaking up of the total patterns into individual and specific reflexes. But close study has convinced me that the process by means of which the individuation and specificity of certain reflexes is attained is not a disintegration or breaking up of the established pattern, but, rather, is due to an inhibitory action by means of which the primary or basic movements are in a large measure arrested. In other words, the total-pattern reaction is never abolished completely, nor is the dominance of the primary over the secondary movements lost (1932a, p. 442).

This same investigator (1933a) has suggested that there are three phases in the development of somatic activity in albino rat fetuses: (1) a myogenic phase in which behavior can be elicited only by direct muscle stimulation; (2) a neuromotor stage in which internal stimuli acting upon the nervous system initiate behavior; (3) a sensory-motor phase in which true reflex action begins.

Angulo y González (1934a) has also shown that the dissolution of the behavioral systems of the fetal rat is in inverse order to its evolution, which is in general cephalocaudal and proximodistal. The relationship of this observation to Hughlings Jackson's generalizations (1884) should be noted. Angulo y González (1934b, 1939, 1940) has studied in detail the change in neural mechanisms which are correlated with behavioral development.

Besides these studies of the whole developmental sequence in the rat there have been a number of investigations devoted to certain aspects of the growth of the activity of the response mechanism in the rat. Lane (1917) has studied the development of the correlation between structure and function of the special senses in the white rat. His method of preparing fetal material consisted in killing the pregnant mother and studying the excised fetuses in a warm chamber. This method is open to the limitations pointed out in the evaluation of Avery's work given above. During the observation period the fetus was bathed in a warm physiological salt solution.

Lane's (1917) observations on the development of the senses in the white rat may be summarized as follows:

Touch. He found no evidence of this sense in 7½-mm. embryos, which are generally agreed to be immobile. Neurologically, at this stage he found both sensory and motor fibers developed. The sensory fibers, however, had not as yet reached the periphery. In 16-mm. embryos, that is, in organisms approximately 17 gestation days old, the tactual sense is reported as present on the flanks and snout, as evidenced by motor response to needle pricks. Lane reports no response to stimulation with a sable brush at this time. This is contrary to the findings of all subsequent investigators and is probably a function of the special condition of the embryos used. In 23- to 28-mm. embryos, that is, embryos approximately 19 to 20 gestation days old, he reports response to stimulation with a fine sable brush as well as with a needle prick. The snout region is most sensitive, although stimulation about the shoulder, upper arm, hip, rump, and thighs also evokes motor responses. He reports that there is a noticeable increase in the number of vibrissae as well as a greater complexity in the neural fiber basket of the vibrissae follicle. In very late fetuses and newborn rats a still better development of the tactual sense is found, responses being elicited by stimulation of any point on the entire body, including the tail. Pain as the result of needle stimulation is at this period shown by squeaks. The fibrillae baskets in the vibrissae follicles are now elongated cylinders, from the base of which neural fibrils in comparatively large bundles are seen to emerge, distad to the base of the follicle itself. In later stages there is no particular advance noted in tactual sensitivity, although the snout region continues to be superior to the rest of the surface in sensitivity.

Equilibrium. In regard to this sense, this investigator found in 7½-mm. embryos that stimulation leads to no behavioral trace whatsoever. Histologically, he reports the semicircular canals to be as yet undeveloped. In the 16-mm. embryo, Lane again found no experimental evidence of the sense of equilibrium, although the semicircular canals are now well developed. In 23- to 28-mm. embryos, Lane still finds no experimental evidence of a sense of equilibrium. Histologically, the differentiation of the cells of the cristae is at this time further advanced than in the previous stage, although the sensory and supporting elements are not yet distinguishable. Slight indications of central connection with the cerebrum are noted. In a 35-mm. fetus the sense of equilibrium was first observed, as seen in the righting responses of the organism when in contact with a surface. Structurally, the semicircular canals are now virtually complete. On the first day after birth, however, the righting responses were better developed, as were the histological and neural connections seen in the semicircular canals. In later stages there was manifested a greater perfection of the sense of equilibrium accompanying an increasing power of coordinated movement. Lane makes no reference to the part possibly played by neck proprioceptors or by other receptor fields in determining these righting responses, nor is any reference made to the analysis of postural reactions suggested by the school of Magnus, to which reference will be made below.

Smell. Lane reports no satisfactory method of smell stimulation in rat embryos from 7½ mm. to 28 mm. in length. Histologically, he says: "During these stages the olfactory apparatus is being gradually laid down, both as regards its sensory and peripheral portions. The histological differentiation of the olfactory epithelium has not advanced sufficiently far to enable the sensory cells proper to be identified" (p. 51). Using a brush placed in an odoriferous substance, Lane obtained no certain response to olfactory stimuli in 35-mm. fetuses. Histological development, however, is noted as continuing. Small's work

(1899) on smell in the newborn rat is quoted, and the statement is made by Lane that "there is on the whole a gradual perfecting of the olfactory sense from day to day" (p. 52). No experimental proof is given of this statement, and it is hard to understand its basis in view of the difficulty reported by Liggett (1928) in dealing with this sense in the white rat.

Taste. In this sense, Lane reports that the 35-mm. fetuses were able to swallow, but neither in these nor in those of any preceding stage were any true evidences of a sense of taste discovered. At no time previous to birth could taste buds or other fully differentiated organs of taste be demonstrated. On the first day after birth, however, he notes that sugar solutions were received with less objection than salt or acid solutions. Lane again makes a generalized statement that in postnatal life this sense is gradually perfected, although no experimental evidence is given to support the view.

Hearing. Here Lane reports that "absolutely no response to sound was noted before the twelfth day after birth," and that "from that day to the sixteenth or seventeenth day there is a gradual increase in the ability to perceive sound" (p. 63). No evidence is given for this conclusion in the monograph, however, save that change is inferred from structure. In his conclusions he says:

Previous to the twelfth day the portions of the ear concerned with the perception of sound have been undergoing a gradual development, but have not yet reached that degree of differentiation of the organ of Corti necessary for the perception of sound. By the twelfth or thirteenth day the organ of Corti is apparently differentiated for at least part of its extent, though the lumen of the external auditory meatus is not fully opened. The next few days witness the completion of the differentiation of the apparatus of hearing (p. 63).

For a study of the early growth of the inner ear of the rat, see Wada (1923).

Vision. As far as this sense is concerned, the report of Lane is: "Absolutely no response to light was obtained before the opening of the eyes on the sixteenth or seventeenth postnatal day" (p. 69). This was determined by the use of an electric flashlight. The objection may be raised, on the basis of a good deal of other experimental work, that this stimulus was possibly not strong enough to bring about response. No record is given of the pupillary response which might have been obtained had the eyelids been opened by operation. Histological evidence, however, is given to suggest that there is a neural and receptor development paralleling the reported functional development.

Lane's theoretical conclusions concerning the anatomical basis of early development in the rat fetus and the function of the receptor in the development of the reflex arc will be given at the close of this chapter.

From the report just given of Lane's work, as well as from the incidental observations in the work of Swenson and Angulo y González, it becomes obvious that, of all the sensory fields in the white rat, that of skin sensitivity is apparently earliest and most completely developed during prenatal life. The development of this sense in the fetal rat was quite extensively investigated by Raney, working with the writer (Raney and Carmichael, 1934). In this work the pregnant female was deeply anesthetized and the spinal cord completely transected between the sixth and seventh cervical vertebrae. The result of this operation was to provide an effectively immobilized and, so far as the field of the operation is concerned, a completely desensitized adult organism in which, however, circulation and respiration continue in a virtually normal condition. After a period of one and a half to two hours, the fetuses were shelled out, with placental circulation maintained, into physiological salt solution held at 37.5° C. by thermostatic control. Raney and Carmichael's work was conducted not only in an effort to study the effect of change of skin sensitivity at various fetal developmental ages, but also to consider the origin of what may be called "local sign," at least in so far as such local sign may be demonstrated in the progress of localizing movements of the limbs of the fetus resulting from punctiform stimulation.

Klemm (1914), in his history of space perception, has referred to the development of the view that space is perceived in relation to body movement. James (1890, Vol. II, pp. 170–282) also has considered the factors leading to this view, and more recently Peterson's experimental work (1926) on local signs as orientation tendencies has again emphasized this conception. Raney and Carmichael's work shows that with increasing gestation age the fetus first becomes sensitive to areal stimulation, as, for example, to stimulation with a camel's-hair brush approximately 5 mm. in diameter. Response to punctiform stimulation by a single light hair is observed to begin some time later. The first appearance of sensitivity is in the head region and is observed to pass gradually caudad (that is, toward the tail). The first responses to stimulation are slight movements of the trunk occurring during the sixteenth day, as noted by previous investigators. As development continues, stimulation at any sensitive point may elicit much more complicated behavior, often involving neck, trunk, forelimb, hindlimb, and other muscle movements. The peculiar sensitivity to tactual stimulation of the region from which the vibrissae issue is noted throughout this developmental sequence. The early function of this tactual organ, as it may be called, is particularly interesting in reference to the full innervation of this area as shown by Lane and in the behavioral observations on the function of the vibrissae in young rats by Small (1899), and especially in the special study of this receptor field by Vincent (1912).

Raney and Carmichael (1934) have found, however, where the mechanical possibility of movement is present, that is, where the limb may touch the surface, that the responses may gradually become more and more precisely related to the point of stimulation. Thus at an early gestation age stimulation of the region of the vibrissae may lead to slight trunk movements. Later such stimulation may lead to the movement of many muscle groups of the fetus, including the limbs. At a still later time, the principal response may be merely that of the forepaw moved ever so slightly toward the point stimulated. If the point touched is on the body wall, the movement may be toward that point. If it is on the nose, it may be toward that point. It must be noted, however, that, even at the best time for such differentiated response in late gestation periods, the stimulation of any point may also bring out very general activity. It is possible that such generalized response is due to interruption of some "spontaneous" movement, or that it is related to the strength of stimulation. The frequency of stimulation or the immediate past activity of the organism may also be important in inducing such activity. The significance of intensity of stimulation in this connection in the guinea pig fetus is explained above. This is not the place for a full consideration of the theoretical implications of Raney and Carmichael's study as it bears on space perception, but the results suggest a certain reformulation of one form of a modi-

fied genetic theory of the perception of extension as considered by Boring (1929, pp. 250–262).

Lincoln (1932), also working in collaboration with the writer, was able to show in the rat fetus something of the elaborate sensory and behavioral sequences which are antecedent to the sucking reflex as that reflex is seen at birth. The report of this investigation is recorded in library copies of a thesis. This work is especially interesting in relation to Lane's work on the correlation between structure and function in the nursing reflex of the young rat and guinea pig. In Lane's work (1924) especial attention is given to the development of the tongue both as a locus of taste receptors and as a prehensile organ. Further references to the sucking reflex are given below.

Angulo y González (1937) has shown that the sensory system follows the motor system in development. The earliest functional sensory endings develop in the region of the snout as tactile receptors. The receptors in the forelimbs, for example, are later in development than those in the snout. The total arc connections seem to be formed by the growth of collateral fibers which establish functional connections after the sensory and motor systems are complete.

Windle (1934b) has demonstrated that all the spinal reflex arcs are present at 11 mm. but they are incomplete because sensory collaterals are just beginning to enter the mantle layer of the spinal cord. The main difference between the nervous system of motile and nonmotile fetuses lies in the number and length of these elements.

Besides the special studies noted above, there have been a number of other investigations dealing with particular muscle groups or special behavioral characteristics of the white rat fetus. Corey (1931) has studied the causative factors of the initial inspiration of mammalian fetuses, using the white rat as material. In this study it is concluded that the initial respiration of the fetus is normally brought about by a change in the relationship between carbon dioxide and oxygen in the blood in cooperation with the stimulating effect of the drying of the skin. Blincoe (1928*a*, 1928*b*) has worked on the development of behavior in the motor system of the forelimb of the rat. He has elaborately studied the anatomy of the limb before the fifteenth day, that is, just before the onset of motility. An effort has also been made to present a correlation between this stage of development in the rat and in man. In the later study he points out that it seems that the arm of the rat shows "the static assembling of many bodily components which await some complementary addition to render them a dynamic whole" (p. 293). It is suggested that this addition is to be found in functional innervation. In this connection see also a paper by Barron (1934) on the results of his experiments on the peripheral anastomoses between the fore- and hindlimb nerves of albino rats.

Also working with the rat fetus, Windle, Minear, Austin, and Orr (1935) have shown that physiological muscular development may be summarized in the course which it takes. In general this development proceeds from the head to the tail region and distad and ventrad from the dorsal part of the trunk. (See also Windle and Baxter, 1935, 1936.)

Bors (1925), Nicholas (1925, 1926, 1929*c*), Hooker and Nicholas (1927, 1930), Nicholas and Hooker (1928), and others have performed experimental operations on rat fetuses. Following a very elaborate technique, these students have been able to operate on mammalian fetuses without interrupting pregnancy. In the course of this work they have made a number of incidental observations on the development of motility, and Hooker and Nicholas (1930) particularly have pointed out the fact that during intrauterine existence "movements are restricted to a large degree and there is also a greater degree of independence of the individual cord segments than is found in later postnatal stages" (p. 431). These observations are significant, for they were made under conditions more nearly approaching those of normal development than any other studies of the development of mammals.

Straus and Weddell (1940) have shown that the earliest visible contractions of the forelimb muscles of the rat appear during the latter half of the fifteenth or the first half of the sixteenth postinsemination day. The extensor muscles are more readily stimulated than the flexor muscles, and if a nerve trunk can be stimulated the response is greater than if the muscle must be directly stimulated. (See also Straus, 1939.)

Corey (1934) has shown that in the fetal rat the cortex is not extensively involved in the production of fetal movements.

A number of studies of special aspects of the development of behavior have been made on the rabbit, to a few of which reference has been made above. Preyer (1885, pp. 418 ff.) makes some observations on fetal organisms of this type. Langworthy (1926) has worked on progression in very young rabbits. He points out that in such animals decerebration does not lead to extensor rigidity but to prolonged progression movements. In the more mature newborn guinea pig, however, rigidity follows decerebration. This difference is attributed to the degree of myelinization in the central nervous system. The importance of myelinization, or the formation of the myelin sheaths, on neurons is discussed below. Zuntz (1877) also used the rabbit fetus in his work on respiration. Richter (1925) has observed sucking movements in rabbit fetuses about 20 days old. Pankratz (1931*b*) has adapted Swenson's technique to the study of the rabbit. Mechanical stimulation of nose, head, and neck led to response of simple lateral flexion of neck and trunk in 15- to 16-day rabbit fetuses. In a 17-day fetus there was a marked ventrolateral flexion of head and upper trunk, with some movement of the forelimbs. In 20-day-old fetuses, opening and closing of the mouth, active movements of the forelimbs, flexion of the hindlimbs, and lateral flexion of the whole trunk were observed. As the gestation period advanced the movements became more complex.

The cat has proved itself to be an eminently suitable animal for the laboratory study of the development of fetal behavior. Its neuromuscular system is quite highly organized. Its gestation age of over sixty days allows for the development of an organism at birth that is relatively mature. Much is also known as a result of past research concerning its structural development (Hill and Tribe, 1924; Latimer, 1931; Latimer and Aikman, 1931), anatomy, and certain of its adult behavioral characteristics, such as the righting response (Camis, 1930). These factors combine to make the animal peculiarly satisfactory for research upon the development of fetal behavior. The general purposes of this chapter, therefore, demand a rather complete summary of the investigations of fetal behavior in the cat.

Windle and Griffin (1931) reported a study in which a large number of cat fetuses of precisely known or accurately estimated gestation age were experimentally studied. The technique employed by these investigators involved an operation on the brain of the mother cat such that later, without anesthesia, it was possible to study the fetal organisms under warm physiological salt solution with fully main-tained placental circulation. The methods of studying the fetuses varied more or less according to age. In all, 34 pregnant cats were used, giving 125 living embryos and fetuses for study. Of the litters of the 34 cats thus employed, 19 were of known age since copulation. The ages of the other fetuses were calculated from their body measurements, a procedure that is not in all respects satisfactory.

These investigators reported that no movement was seen in the 23-day stage or on any day previous to that. In later studies, however, it has been established that movement does take place on the twenty-third day (Windle and Becker, 1940*a*). In the 24- and 25-day stage, what the reader may now begin to consider as the characteristic response of young fetuses, namely, the very slightest slow ventral lateral head flexion, was observed in a number of embryos. This has also been independently confirmed by Windle (1930*a*). The earliest limb reflexes are well-localized movements occurring on the side of stimulation at the twenty-fourth day (Windle, 1934*a*). In the 26- to 27-day stage, movements were in general more complex and of greater amplitude or duration and strength than those noted in the previous case. Generalized trunk undulations, however, still formed the permanent background of activity, but forelimb flexion had also begun. The investigators have pointed out that, at this stage, rotation of head and trunk appears to be coordinated with older components, but that this activity results in movements which strikingly resemble the righting reflexes seen in later fetal life. At this stage the fetuses seem unresponsive to brush or probe. At 28 days slight flexion of the hindlegs was noticed, and at this time also the first responses to touch, particularly in the head region, were observed. Stimulation of this sort was followed by typical apparently "random" head-trunk-limb undulations. At 30 days the activity recorded was still more complex. Active flexion of the hind-limbs was noted, and at the same time definite, although sluggish, mouth movements appeared. From this time until birth, continued and progressive increase in the specificity of behavior was noted by these observers.

So far as the development of sensory capacity in these animals is concerned, it has already been noted that no external response to stimulation is found in fetuses of less than 26 mm., that is, of approximately 28 gestation days. These investigators hold that there is evidence, however, of exteroceptive and proprioceptive function even in the first animals that show spontaneous movements. "The fact that the unilateral trunk or neck flexions seemed always to be executed toward the observer and away from the surface on which they rested may indicate that the earliest sensation is one of deep pressure" (Windle and Griffin, 1931, p. 175). So far as behavior at the 26-mm. stage is concerned, it is held that the activity noted may be the result of a "primitive type of proprioception" (p. 175). This would explain the spread of motor response, although there is some possibility that the wavelike progression of muscular contraction noted is due to the function of long association pathways in the central nervous system.

The first so-called cutaneous reflexogenous zone, that is, cutaneous area, in which stimulation can be shown to lead to response included the nose areas and in general most of the head. Pronounced response in the fetuses at 28 days followed stimulation of the nose. Gradually, as fetuses of later ages were considered, the area spread caudally to the neck, pectoral region, forelimbs, trunk, hindlimbs, and finally to the tail. Windle and Griffin point out: "It is interesting to note that spon-taneous motor activity always involved a part of the body before responses could be elicited either locally or at a distance from the point stimulated" (p. 175). The strength of stimulation was also reported as significant in determining the nature of response. Usually the light touch of a brush was found to be ineffective in specimens less than 60 mm. long. In a few fetuses a little longer than this a response was secured when the brush was applied to the nose. It was noticed that a light stimulus which caused no response if once applied was sometimes adequate if repeated several times. Very little difference could be observed between strong innocuous stimulation and stimulation producing observable protoplasmic damage. The authors believe that the primitive type of pressure-touch sensitivity, which they postulate as the characteristic state of the receptor surface of early fetuses, was not replaced by definite touch and pain until relatively late in fetal life. In fetuses of 75 to 80 mm. marked differences between the responses to light and to strong stimuli were observed, and pain responses were thought to be definitely present.

In the cat, vestibular function probably appears in prenatal life. No absolute evidence of its presence is found until very shortly before birth. It should be borne in mind in all considerations of this sense in fetal life that there are great difficulties in testing it accurately in a squirming fetus. In a later study, however, Windle and Fish (1932) demonstrated by the use of several techniques, including the operative interference with the vestibular apparatus, that the true vestibular righting reflex elicited in animals in contact with a surface probably appears in fetal kittens of 100- to 115-mm. crown-rump length, that is, on the fifty-fourth day of gestation. These same investigators (Fish and Windle,

1932) have considered the onset of rotary and postrotary nystagmus in the eyes of newborn cats.

For an important early study of the developing of the "falling reflex," see Muller and Weed (1916). Carmichael (1934*b*) and later Warkentin and Carmichael (1939) studied the genetic devel-

fore the total pattern in time can be accomplished in the short period allowed by a free fall.

From study of the vestibular sense, Windle and Griffin (1931) turn to a consideration of the development of posture and progression in general. In this study they follow in part the analysis of Hinsey,

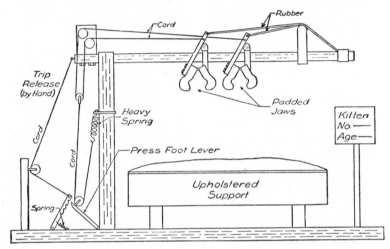

FIGURE 12. Apparatus used in the study of the development of the air-righting reflex in small mammals. (From "A Study of the Development of the Air-Righting Reflex in Cats and Rabbits," by J. Warkentin and L. Carmichael. *Journal of Genetic Psychology*, 1939, **55,** 68. By permission of the publisher.)

opment of the kitten's capacity to right itself when falling through the air. Rabbits were also used in the second study. The apparatus used to release the animals is shown in Figure 12, and a typical sequence as drawn from high-speed moving picture films is shown in Figure 13. These studies were correlated with studies on the development of vision in kittens (Warkentin, 1938). They show that there is a genetic relationship between the time sequence of the partial responses making up air righting and the performance of the act. Thus an animal may be able to perform all the behavioral acts needed in air righting be-

Ranson, and McNattin (1930). Walking can be shown to require the coordination of several behavioral patterns, including the ability to maintain an erect posture. In this connection the analysis of Magnus (1924, pp. 357 ff.), which shows that posture may depend on impulses from the various receptor groups of the nonauditory labyrinth, from the proprioceptors of the muscles and associated structures, and from the exteroceptors including touch and the distance receptors, is distinctly relevant. In view of the facts it becomes obvious that the maintenance of erect posture may demand quite elaborate stimulation and the establishment of postural tonus by the proper neurological balance between flexor and extensor muscle groups. This complex mechanism makes possible successful opposition to gravity and behavioral acts dependent upon such opposition. For an

changed in such a way that stepping movements may be accomplished.

Windle and Griffin report that these mechanisms, which are essential to locomotion, develop at different times during fetal growth. The onset of the righting

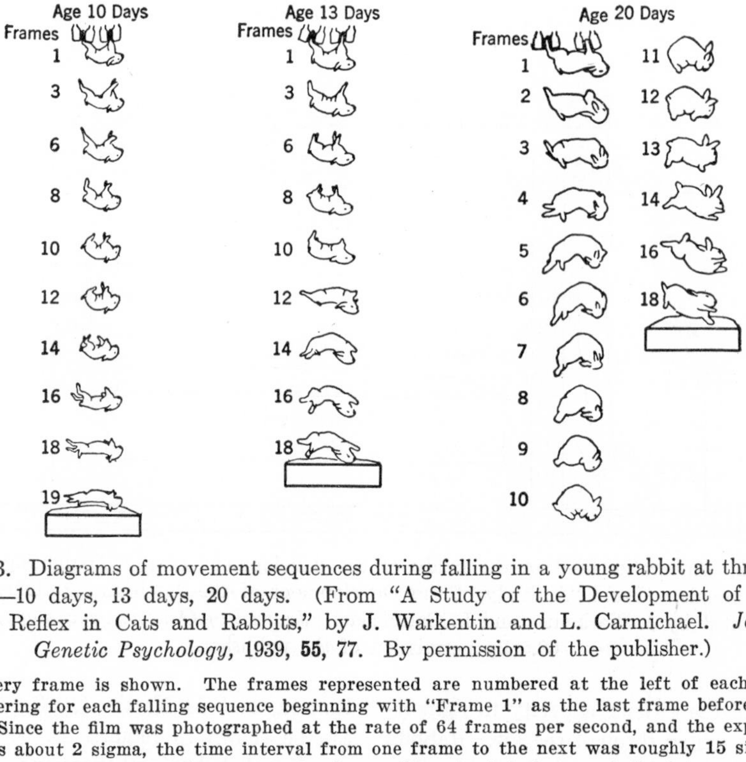

FIGURE 13. Diagrams of movement sequences during falling in a young rabbit at three different ages—10 days, 13 days, 20 days. (From "A Study of the Development of the Air-Righting Reflex in Cats and Rabbits," by J. Warkentin and L. Carmichael. *Journal of Genetic Psychology*, 1939, **55**, 77. By permission of the publisher.)

Not every frame is shown. The frames represented are numbered at the left of each diagram, the numbering for each falling sequence beginning with "Frame 1" as the last frame before the jaws opened. Since the film was photographed at the rate of 64 frames per second, and the exposure per frame was about 2 sigma, the time interval from one frame to the next was roughly 15 sigma. All the diagrams are drawn to the same scale; hence the animal is larger at the later ages because of normal gain in size and weight during the days represented.

illuminating evaluation of the effect of gravity on the development of behavior in mammals, the reader should consult a treatment of this subject by Holt (1931, pp. 62–72). Windle and Griffin (1931) further show that the essential receptor and effector mechanisms necessary for progression involve an added condition, by means of which alternate and rhythmic changes in the limbs are brought about. This last component is necessary if balance is to be

reflex has just been reviewed. The first positive evidence of rhythmic movement of the forelimbs, involving flexion and extension movements, was seen in a 58- to 60-mm. fetus. At this time the hindleg movements were less rhythmical. Occasionally in a 100-mm. fetus complete stepping movements were observed. In this connection the study of Laughton (1924) on the nervous mechanism of progression in mammals should also be consulted. It is further suggested by Windle and his associates that the unilateral rhythmic flexion-extension of the limb as seen in the scratching reflex may have a relationship to the occurrence of the alternate rhythms of locomotion. The first indication of the scratch phenomenon was thought to have been observed at the 75- to 80-mm. stage, following ear stimulation. These observations show that the walking movement even as seen in prenatal life involves a complex series of factors which are concerned with virtually the entire receptive field and the entire muscular system of the organism.

Besides this characteristic behavior pattern, these same investigators have also studied the development of the sucking reaction, a response which, like that of locomotion, is characteristic of early vertebrate behavior and to which reference has been made above. The first head raising and lowering of the jaw were noted in 27- to 28-mm. fetuses. This early prefeeding response was followed in the 45- to 50-mm. organisms by tongue reflexes which were so amplified in the 70- to 80-mm. organisms as possibly to be characterized as sucking. In the 95- to 103-mm. organisms, this response had developed so much farther that it was present in virtually its adult form (Windle and Griffin, 1931; Windle and Minear, 1934). Windle and Minear have also shown that the response to faradic shock given to the snout changes with age. At first the reaction is dominantly away from the stimulus (that is, on the opposite side); later, homolateral responses appear. Windle (1937) and his collaborators (Windle, O'Donnell, and Glasshagle, 1933) have also studied the detailed neurology related to the first forelimb responses. At 14 mm., or about 23 days, true reflexes are elicited. At this time the sensory collaterals of the cord are just complete. Windle emphasizes the fact that these responses are not part of a total mass re-

action pattern when they first appear. He had previously (1935) shown that the simplest forms of reflex pathways are laid down in the central nervous system before higher integration systems are functional. (See also Windle, Orr, and Minear, 1934.) This same investigator (Windle, 1939) suggests that calcium and potassium deficiencies may account for certain delays observed in the onset of fetal movements.

Another elaborate study of the development of behavior in the fetal cat was undertaken in 1928 by Coronios, working in collaboration with the writer and other investigators (Coronios, 1930, 1931, 1933; Coronios, Schlosberg, and Carmichael, 1932). Unlike Windle and Griffin, Coronios used only fetuses from litters whose insemination age he accurately knew. In Coronios' work the pregnant female was prepared for observation under deep ether anesthesia. While the animal was anesthetized the carotid arteries were ligated, a cannula inserted in the trachea, and a complete midbrain section carefully performed. After this section, the anesthetic was immediately discontinued. The decerebrate adult cat was then allowed to remain quiet for an hour and a half or two hours before the fetuses were exposed for observation by an operative technique. Before the observations began, the cat was placed in a specially devised bath apparatus in which physiological salt solution was maintained thermostatically at 37.5° ± 0.5° C. Into this blood-warm liquid the fetuses were shelled out one by one. A summary of the behavior observed at various copulation ages may be found in Figure 14. In a supplement to this chart Coronios (1933) offers the following conclusions:

In the early stages the behavior is diffuse, variable, relatively uncoordinated, and weak. With the increase in gestation age, the reactions become more vigorous, more

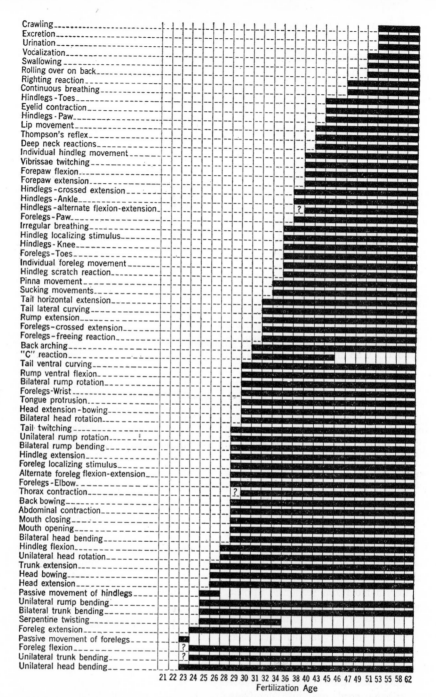

FIGURE 14. A chart constructed to show the development of behavior in cat fetuses of various gestation ages. (From "Development of Behavior in the Fetal Cat," by J. D. Coronios. *Genetic Psychology Monographs*, 1933, **14**, 362. By permission of The Journal Press publisher.)

regular in their appearance, less variable, individualized, and better coordinated. These qualitative changes do not occur abruptly but are continuously progressive modifications in the quality of the observed reactions. Moreover, these qualitative changes do not, as it were, "invade" the total organism at once. Rather they seem to follow a general course in their development, beginning at the head region and progressing toward the tail (p. 363).

It is interesting to note in this description of the development of behavior in a highly organized mammalian fetus a marked similarity to the description of the development of behavior noted in *Amblystoma* and virtually all other forms considered above. It must be emphasized, however, that there is danger in making too sweeping generalizations about fetal behavior, but it is impossible to deny that there are certain descriptive forms which accurately characterize the development of behavior in many forms.

As a conclusion to his work, Coronios (1933) makes the following points:

(1) Before birth there is a rapid, progressive, and continuous development of behavior in the fetus of the cat.

(2) The development of behavior progresses from a diffuse, massive, variable, relatively unorganized state to a condition where many of the reactions are more regular in their appearance, less variable, better organized, and relatively individualized.

(3) In the early stages of prenatal development the behavior appears to be progressing along a cephalocaudal course.

(4) The development of the sensitivity of the reflexogenous zones passes through a continuous and transitional development from a time when rather vigorous stimulation of any "spot" of the body within a large area serves to elicit variable, diffuse, uncoordinated patterns of behavior to a later time when a weak stimulus becomes adequate, within a much more circumscribed area for precise, well-coordinated,

uniform, and less variable patterns of behavior. The direction of such development is cephalocaudal.

(5) The "primitive" reactions of breathing, righting, locomotion, and feeding are the products of a long and continuously progressive course of prenatal development.

(6) Behavior development appears first in the gross musculature, and in the fine musculature later.

(7) Behavior develops in each of the limbs from a proximal to a distal point; that is, the entire limb is first involved in the response and then gradually the more distal joints become, as it were, independent of the total movement (pp. 377–378).

Each of these generalizations is to be taken as a statement of a typical course of development and not as a specific formula that can be applied to other mammals or man in advance of observation. For example, from the time of Aristotle the anteroposterior course of development has been noted (Needham, 1931, p. 75). This apparently holds true in the primitive gradients of the organism and in the weight of different organs of its developing structure, as well as in the development of "individuated" behavior. This generalization must, of course, be considered descriptive and not explanatory. For further discussion, see Kingsbury (1924, 1926) and Child (1925).

Besides these two elaborate studies of the development of behavior in the fetal cat, there have been a number of incidental studies calculated to investigate some special problem in fetal behavioral growth. T. G. Brown (1914, 1915) reports an experiment on the development of the mechanism of progression in the fetal cat. He used four fetuses of unknown gestation age, the placental circulation being maintained and the observations made in a warm salt solution. The fetuses were studied both before and after decerebration. On the basis of this work he asserts that blood stimulation is very important in eliciting the rhythmic movements seen before birth. He concludes:

It is possible that the "quickening" movements which are a symptom of human pregnancy may be due to similar progression movements in man; and if they are thus evoked by some such accidental asphyxia as that conditioned by pressure upon the umbilical cord they may tend, in an indiscriminate manner it is true, to relieve that pressure (1915, p. 214).

He also suggests on the basis of other observations a phylogenetic theory of the development of locomotion based on Sherrington's view of motor half-centers in the central nervous system.

Langworthy (1929) has also studied the development of behavior in the fetus of the cat. He reported a study on six fetuses near term and a number of kittens of varying ages after natural birth. In these fetuses after decerebration he found behavior that is characteristic of the late cat fetus, although less well-defined hindleg movements were observed than those reported by Brown. The behavior of the fetal and young organisms was then correlated with structural studies of the nervous system. He reported in summary of this work:

Bilateral movements of the extremities begin to coordinate when the ventral commissural fibers of the cord receive their myelin sheath. The animals turn the body at a time when myelinated vestibular fibers reach the spinal cord. The hind-leg movements become better coordinated when myelinization becomes marked in the lumbar portion of the cord (p. 169).

The general significance of this correlation of behavior and myelinization will be considered below.

Tilney has prepared a chart showing the stream of behavior reaction in the cat similar to the chart concerning the development of behavior in the guinea pig cited above (Woodworth, 1929, p. 204). In this chart many behavioral acts are shown as appearing in postnatal life which the studies given above show in prenatal life. This is true of "primitive escape," "snatching," and, indeed, virtually all the reactions shown in the chart. The "sudden emergence" of some of these behavior patterns noted below the chart, as in most "saltatory maturation," may seem therefore to involve the reactivation under different environmental conditions of behavior which has had a prenatal developmental history. Similar facts of human fetal development are significant in interpreting the conclusions of Gesell (1929b) and Shirley (1931a, 1931b) concerning human behavioral maturation. Windle and Orr (1934b) have shown that when the fetus is dying there is likely to be a vermiform contraction. These general reactions may appear after the heart has ceased to beat.

A number of special studies have been made on other mammals. Erasmus Darwin (1796, p. 101) quotes an account from Galen of the fetal development of the goat. The fetus, after removal, got to its feet and walked, shook itself, scratched, smelled of objects, and then drank milk. Huggett (1927, 1930) has used this same ungulate in elaborate studies of the onset of breathing reflexes in the fetus, which will be considered below. He used animals one or two months before full term. The size of the animal made it convenient for operative purposes, but some difficulties which experimenters with small animals are spared may be noted since a "domestic bath" had to be used to hold the saline solution into which the fetus was delivered (1927).

Scharpenberg and Windle (1938) have now shown that, in the sheep, myogenic responses precede neurogenic ones. Some sensory collateral fibers have grown out from the dorsal funiculus and have reached the internuncial neurones of the cord at the time the first true reflex arcs are established. The most elaborate studies of the fetus of the sheep, however, have been made by Barcroft and Barron (1939). In this paper they outline the results of an elaborate series of investigations upon this large fetus. In this animal the first spontaneous movements appear on the thirty-fifth day after insemination. These responses involve forelimb, neck, and trunk movements. By the thirty-eighth day the observed movements are more "definite" and the movements are larger and more numerous. Such spontaneous movements are quite transient. Even in a forty-day fetus they may last only five minutes after delivery. Maintained posture following movement is seen by the forty-second day. In their study of responses these investigators stimulated by various means the fields related to some of the important peripheral nerves of the body. As a conclusion of the study of the maxillary nerve, for example, they state that the motor response to specific stimulation is at first confined to a few muscles, then more muscles become involved, but at length only those are activated which respond in the adult sheep. Again, in regard to the sensory nerves distributed to the trunk and limbs they conclude that local muscular reactions are first evoked, but with increasing development more and more muscles may be brought into play.

Barcroft and Barron (1936) have also studied the genesis of respiratory movements in the fetus of the sheep. Barcroft, Barron, and Windle (1936) have shown in the same large embryo localized responses to mechanical and electrical stimulation. These writers conclude that behavior may be considered to have its genesis in localized patterns of response. This conclusion is qualified, however, in a later paper by Barcroft and Barron (1937a), in which a neurological distinction is drawn between reflexes and local contractions, for example, of the neck. These same investigators in another paper (1937b) give an excellent description of the movements of the fetal sheep in midfetal life. Barcroft himself gives a more general description of this work in a paper entitled "The Mammal Before and After Birth" (1935).

Barcroft's best summary of much of this work appears in his volume of Terry Lectures entitled *The Brain and Its Environment* (1938). In this volume brain activity in relation to its internal environment in fetal and neonatal life is brilliantly described. In all of Barcroft's work the importance of the changing internal environment of the fetus subjected to experimental study is emphasized.

Bolk (1926) has made a comparative morphological study of fetuses of the gorilla, chimpanzee, and man in relation to a theory of development. Tinklepaugh, Hartman, and Squier (1930) have studied fetal heart rate in the monkey. Hines and Straus (1934) have studied the motor cortex of fetal and infant rhesus monkeys. The gestation period of the macaques used was taken as 168 days. Fetuses 85 days old showed good contralateral responses of shoulder and head on cortical stimulation. The fingers gained cortical representation during the first week after birth, as did also the facial areas and lower extremities. It seems that the muscles innervated by the dorsal strata of the limb plexus (extensor system) are the first muscles of the extremities to gain representation in the motor cortex.

Incidental observations on other animal fetuses are given by J. F. Craig (1930) in his revision of Fleming's *Veterinary Ob-*

stetrics. Needham (1931, pp. 484–489) gives tables of the gestation times of hundreds of animals which are valuable for comparative purposes.

General Aspects of Human Fetal Development

PRESCIENTIFIC STUDY

From one point of view at any rate, all that has gone before in this chapter has been intended to prepare the reader for the consideration of the prenatal development of behavior in human beings. Behavioral development before birth has long been the subject of notice in the human race, but only comparatively recently has it been studied in a systematic and scientific manner.

That the fetus moves before birth is knowledge as old as mankind. Certainly there are references to this phenomenon in the folklore of primitive peoples (Ploss and Bartels, 1927). It is interesting to notice also, so far as the anthropomorphic theory of primitive deities is concerned, that the process of making gods in the image of man even included speculations about god embryos. For a consideration of this topic, see Briffault's work *The Mothers* (1927) and Witkowski (1887). There are references to prenatal development of behavior in Biblical literature and in ancient Indian and Chinese writings. The Egyptians early began the consideration of this matter, as is shown in a hymn to the sun god attributed to Amenophis IV (about 1400 B.C.):

Creator of the germ in woman,
Maker of seed in man,
Giving life to the son in the body of his
    mother,
Soothing him that he may not weep,
Nurse (even) in the womb.
Giver of breath to animate everyone that he
    maketh

When he cometh forth from the womb on the day of his birth.

(Needham, 1931, p. 49) [1]

In pre-Socratic Greek antiquity, among the many who speculated on almost all aspects of nature were those who considered embryology and, apparently, also the beginnings of fetal activity. It was at this time, the very beginning of recorded scientific history, that some of the notions arose in what has been called "theological embryology" which have come down to our own period. At this time some held that the general form of the body is completed in males many days before it is completed in females (Needham, 1931, pp. 51–53). Similarly, Empedocles (about 450 B.C.) began the speculation, which was long to continue, as to whether or not the "life" of the embryo was like the "life" of the independent individual (Needham, p. 51). Plutarch says that Plato (circa 429–347 B.C.) directly asserts that the fetus is a living creature that moves and is fed within the body cavities of the mother (Needham, p. 60).

It was not, however, until the time of Aristotle (384–322 B.C.) that the life and soul of the embryo were considered in detail. In the third chapter of Aristotle's remarkable treatise on embryology, the entrance of the various souls into the embryo is considered. The views there expressed

[1] For much of the historical material given in various parts of this chapter, including the quotation at the head of the chapter, the writer is indebted for actual references and for many interpretations to Needham's illuminating history of embryology (1931). The writer had begun the collection of material in this field before Needham's book was published, but when it appeared it proved to be so fruitful in suggestion that it has been used extensively in this chapter. Whenever possible, specific references are given. For a study of the ideas of primitive peoples concerning generation as they have evolved into modern scientific understanding, the reader is urged to consult Meyer's *The Rise of Embryology* (1939).

have possibly influenced the laws of abortion which have appeared since Aristotle's time in canon and civil codes. In transmuted form these ideas appear in both patristic and scholastic philosophy. It is possible that this Aristotelian doctrine is basic to the rules of the church in regard to prenatal baptism, which is considered historically by Witkowski (1887, pp. 133–152). Aristotle taught that the vegetative or nutritive soul existed in the unfertilized material of the embryo. In summary, Aristotle, in the following quotation given by Needham (p. 69), says:

> . . . for nobody . . . would put down the unfertilised embryo as soulless or in every sense bereft of life (since both the semen and the embryo of an animal have every bit as much life as a plant). . . . As it develops it also acquires the sensitive soul in virtue of which an animal is an animal. . . . For first of all such embryos seem to live the life of a plant, and it is clear that we must be guided by this in speaking of the sensitive and the rational soul. For all three kinds of soul, not only the nutritive, must be possessed potentially before they are possessed actually.

During the third century B.C., Herophilus, according to Plutarch, attributes to newborn babies a natural movement, but not respiration. The sinews are the instrumental cause of this movement. Afterward the baby becomes a perfect living animal, and when it is taken forth from the mother's body it inhales air (Needham, pp. 78–80).

Galen is also credited with writing much between A.D. 150 and A.D. 180 upon the subject of developmental embryology. He has especially considered the question of whether the embryo may be described as an animal. A reference to Galen's observations on a goat fetus has already been made.

In the years sometimes called, because of the dominance of the church fathers, the Patristic Period, interest continued in the movements of the fetus. Tertullian (born A.D. 160) held that the soul was fully present in the embryo through uterine life. In his *De Anima* he says:

> Reply . . . O ye Mothers, and say whether you do not feel the movements of the child within you. How then can it have no soul? (Needham, 1931, p. 91).

Saint Augustine, Bishop of Hippo, apparently did not wholly agree with this, but held that the soul entered the fetus in the second gestation month and sex in the fourth month. Other church authorities followed Saint Augustine in this matter. The council of the church held at Byzantium in 692, however, declared that no distinction could be made so far as infanticide is concerned as to whether the fetus was "formed" or "unformed." Canon law for a time came to recognize the fortieth day for males and the eightieth day for females as the moment of animation, but later the fortieth day was accepted for both sexes (Goeckel, 1911, p. 5). The reader who may wish a modern view of sex differences in development as an exercise in contrasts may well consult Riddle (1927).

In the Talmudic writings of the learned Jews between the second and sixth centuries are found a number of views concerning the possibility of stimulating the fetus in the uterus. It is possible that the cutaneous sensitivity of the fetus was understood by these writers (Needham, p. 93). Needham gives a reproduction of a picture from the *Liber Scivias* of Saint Hildegard of Bingen, approximately A.D. 1150, which shows a pictorial representation of the soul passing down from heaven and entering the body of a pregnant woman and then entering the embryo (p. 96). It is not difficult to believe that the basis for this picture is to be found not only in such embryological knowledge as had come down to this time from antiquity, but also in the direct observations current in all times concerning the quickening of the embryo (Needham, p. 102). The greatest of the Schoolmen, however, Saint Thomas Aquinas (1227–1274), often called "the Angelic Doctor," developed a more elaborate theory of embryonic animation. Needham interprets his views as follows:

> He had a notion that the foetus was first endowed with a vegetative soul, which in due course perished, at which moment the embryo came into the possession of a sensitive soul, which died in its turn, only to be replaced by a rational soul provided directly by God (Needham, p. 104).

On the other hand, Duns Scotus (1266–1308), here as in so many other speculations a worthy opponent of Saint Thomas, considered that the embryo contained only a rational soul, which was infused directly into the organism. The views of both these scholastic teachers led to certain theological difficulties. It was difficult to say how the errors intrinsic in man since Adam's fall could be transmitted to each generation if the soul entered the fetus directly from heaven in each generation (Needham, p. 105). This really profound scholastic argument may in certain ways be considered the foreshadowing of some of the present-day arguments concerning the rôles of heredity and environment as determiners of development.

In Dante (1893 edition) it is interesting to note that a neurological theory of the animation of the fetus comes into play. He says:

> . . . but how from being an animal it becomes a child, thou seest not yet, moreover this is so difficult a point that formerly it led astray one more wise than thou . . . so that in his teaching he separated the active "intellect" from the soul

because he could not see any organ definitely appropriated by it. Open thy heart to the truth and know that as soon as the brain of the foetus is perfectly organised, the Prime Mover, rejoicing in this display of skill on the part of Nature, turns him towards it and infuses a new spirit replete with power into it which subsumes into its own essence the active elements which it finds already there, and so forms one single soul which lives and feels and is conscious of its own existence (Needham, p. 106).

After the Renaissance, books on midwifery began to appear, and in these practical treatises there are a number of observations on fetal movements. For information on these views, see Spencer's *History of British Midwifery from 1650–1800* (1927).

The great William Harvey (Spencer, 1921) combined in himself a knowledge of classical Renaissance embryology, a practical knowledge of midwifery, and a truly scientific ability in observation. A combination of these various advantages makes his writing peculiarly important in this field. He says in one place, according to Needham (p. 139):

> I saw long since a foetus . . . the magnitude of a peasecod cut out of the uterus of a doe, which was complete in all its members & I showed this pretty spectacle to our late King and Queen. It did swim, trim and perfect, in such a kinde of white, most transparent and crystalline moysture . . . about the bignesse of a pigeon's egge. . . .

In all his work Harvey maintained that growth was a process of continual epigenetic development and not the unfolding of something preformed in the eggs of the organisms considered. Harvey also gave a rather elaborate picture of the activity of the human fetus in which he said, in a quotation from Spencer (1921, p. 35):

For he swimmeth in a water and moveth himself to and fro, he stretcheth himself now this way, and now that, and so is variously inflected and tumbled up and down, in so much that sometimes, being entangled in his own navel string, he is strangely ensnared.

Harvey noted the fact that the mother can feel the kicks of the unborn child in such a way as to assure her that the fetus does not always lie in the same position.

In 1664, Gregorius Nymmanus wrote in support of the proposition that the fetus in the uterus lives a life of its own, evincing its own vital actions, and if the mother dies it not uncommonly survives for a certain period, so that it can sometimes be taken alive from the dead body of its mother. The fetus, he continued, prepared its own vital spirits and the instruments of its own soul, there being no nerve between it and the mother. This is demonstrated by the fact that the fetus in utero moves during the mother's sleep (Needham, p. 160).

In the citation just given is seen a combination of the old speculation and the new statement of observation that had become so characteristic of the rebirth of science. This combination of attitudes toward fetal development comes down almost to our own day, but increasingly as the years have passed the problems of embryology have become questions of observation and not of fancy. For a consideration of certain aspects of the triumph of science over superstition in these matters, see Spencer's lecture entitled *The Renaissance of Midwifery* (1924). In the opinion of the writer there is, however, real significance in the fact that during the long centuries of speculation concerning the "besouling" of the fetus, the point of quickening was often considered most important. There is good reason for this. The writer is as convinced as was Tertullian that the quickening of the fetus is significant in the story of the onset of man's most distinctive characteristic—his mental life. Common sense and vulgar tradition are not sure scientific guides, but the observational basis of nonscientific speculation sometimes points to a truth neglected.

One of the problems that grow out of the view that the fetus early comes to have an independent existence is the value placed upon human fetal life. This problem of evaluation is essentially ethical rather than scientific. As such, it continues down to the present time to be significant. It is not, however, a topic within the scope of this chapter. Among the numerous treatments of this topic, the monograph by Goeckel (1911) dealing with the changes that have taken place in the evaluation of the life of the unborn human fetus is important. In this monograph the author reviews primitive opinion and the statements of Roman and old Germanic law in regard to the fetus. He presents an excellent bibliography of Catholic theological pronouncements and of civil legal opinions on the value of the life of the fetus. The legal aspect of prenatal life is also given especial consideration in a paper by Morache (1904). As already noticed, the earlier history of the evaluation of fetal life is fully considered in Witkowski's detailed *Histoire des accouchements chez tous les peuples* (1887). Much of this work, however, seems to be based upon Cangiamila's *Embryologia Sacra* of 1775, which the writer has not seen.

Modern thinking about the value of the fetus is reviewed in such papers as those of Hughes (1905), Arendt (1910), and Glenn (1911), which treat of various aspects of the ethics of dealing with the life of the unborn child.

From early times the belief has been current that the mother's thoughts and experiences directly influence the fetus.

For many years, however, this view of prenatal influence has existed in the popular rather than in the scientific tradition. That "thought transference" or some mysterious nervous relationship exists between mother and fetus is not, in general, held today by scientific investigators. Save in the chemical interchange between the two blood streams or in mechanical or infectious transmissions, biology and psychology offer no basis for this view. Compayré (1896, pp. 32–33) gives a brief history of this superstition. He describes the now amusing assertions of Malebranche in regard to the complete intercerebral sharing of all mental processes between fetus and mother and then carries the subject on to the speculations current in nonscientific writings at the end of the nineteenth century. Compayré does not, however, refer to the remarkable assertions of the philosopher Hegel (1894, pp. 28–29) concerning psychological embryology, in which mother and fetus are said to be in undivided "psychic unity." This magic relationship is held to be of the nature of animal magnetism, by which the character and talent of the mother are communicated to the child.

That superstitious views of prenatal influence are still discussed may be discovered by reading articles by the following writers: Coughlin (1905), Walton (1910), Christenbery (1910–1911), Tompkins (1911–1912), Barham (1915–1916), and R. L. Brown (1918). An example of such an observation is the following case described by Morrison (1920). A mother of five healthy children had two teeth removed during pregnancy. She feared that the child would have a harelip. She became obsessed with the idea. The child was born with a harelip. It proved difficult to convince the mother that maternal impressions were not an accepted scientific cause. In this case just given, one is

apparently dealing with an unusual coincidence which seems very like a causal connection to those who participate in it emotionally. To the parent such a conclusion may thus be psychologically if not scientifically pardoned. Until new evidence is presented, however, such cases cannot be considered as having scientific significance. We may still say with some assurance that "prenatal influence" in the sense discussed is a superstition.

Scientific study

We must now turn back in our consideration to the scientific study of the fetus in order to consider what is known about the actual behavioral development of the unborn child. For the purpose of understanding this prenatal development of human behavior some general idea of morphological development will be found to provide a useful baseline upon which to represent the changing continuum of behavior. Figure 15, taken from Keibel and Elze (1908), shows a selected series of human embryos and fetuses 2.1 mm. to 23 mm. in length. The length of each specimen is given in the legend below the figure.

Many efforts have been made to compile a table from which the ages of fetal human organisms can be estimated on the basis of known physical measurements. Scammon (1927), indeed, estimated that there were seventy-five hundred titles on the growth and physical development of the fetus, infant, and child. The construction of satisfactory norms of growth in prenatal life has proved to be a very hard scientific task because of the difficulties that must be overcome in evaluating the material to be measured. In the first place, even if organisms of truly known age were plentifully available, each age norm would necessarily be stated in terms of some statistical average, because of the

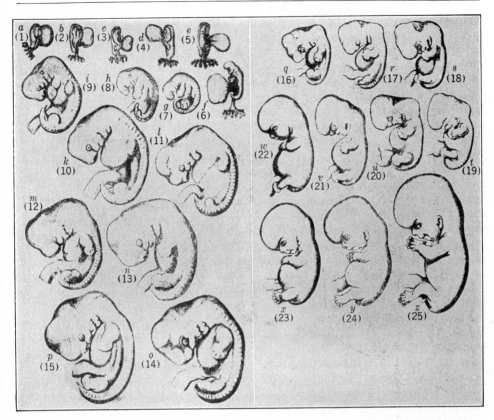

FIGURE 15. The human embryo of His's *Normentafel* as given by Keibel and Elze. (From *Normentafel zur Entwicklungsgeschichte des Menschen,* by F. Keibel and C. Elze. Jena: Fischer, 1908.)

The letter designating each fetus, its size in millimeters, and its estimated age in days are: *a,* 2.1, 12–15; *b,* 2.12, 12–15; *c,* 2.15, 12–15; *d,* 2.2, 12–15; *e,* 2.6, 18–21; *f,* 4.2, 18–21; *g,* 4.0, 23; *h,* 5.5, 24–25; *i,* 7.5, 27–30; *k,* 10.0, 27–30; *l,* 9.1, 27–30; *m,* 9.1, 27–30; *n,* 10.5, 31–34; *o,* 11.0, 31–34; *p,* 11.5, 31–34; *q,* 12.5, 31–34; *r,* 13.7, 31–34; *s,* 13.8, about 35; *t,* 13.6, about 35; *u,* 14.5, about 37–38; *v,* 15.5, about 39–40; *w,* 16.0, about 42–45; *x,* 17.5, 47–51; *y,* 18.5, 52–54; *z,* 23.0, 60.

many factors such as genetic stock, nourishment, and specific pathology which influence fetal size. For a consideration of some of these factors in infrahuman mammals, see the work of Bluhm (1929).

A greater stumbling block than this variability of size at any true age, however, is found in the fact that it is peculiarly difficult in the human individual to place correctly the starting point of de-

velopment, even though, in the light of the discussion given at the beginning of this chapter, such point be taken as the moment of fusion of the nuclei of the two parent cells. As a matter of fact, this moment can never be absolutely accurately determined, and therefore many different ways of approximating the zero point of development have been used in the history of human embryology. Even now no complete agreement has been reached as to the most desirable procedure in arriving at this calculation. Of these methods the following are probably most important:

(1) *Menstruation age.* In this scale the age of the fetus is calculated from the first day of the last period of menstruation prior to the onset of pregnancy (Mall, 1918).

(2) *Mean menstruation age.* This age is similar to the above, except that it is based on the average calculated from many cases. Thus if 51 days is taken as a mean, there is a possible deviation from 40 to 62 days, so far as the relationship to morphological measurement is concerned (Mall, 1918).

(3) *Conception age.* The age of the fetus is calculated from the last day of the last menstrual period prior to pregnancy. This is the age used by His and adopted by Minot (1892).

(4) *Copulation, or insemination, age.* This age, based upon calculation and upon trustworthy cases of known copulation time, is found to be approximately 10 days shorter than the mean menstrual age defined above (Mall, 1918).

(5) *Ovulation age.* This age is calculated from the time of ovulation. It is at present extremely difficult to determine directly the time of ovulation. Determinations are complicated by many factors, such as the observation that it is difficult to know how long spermatozoa may live after entering the female genital tract, and by many other considerations. A complete and critical study of the time of ovulation and the fertile period of the menstrual cycle is given by Hartman (1936) in a book devoted to a consideration of recent data and theories in this field.

(6) *Fertilization, or true, age.* This age cannot at present be directly determined, but must be calculated from (1), (2), or (4) above. In general it may be said that the present evidence points to the fact that fertilization occurs in less than 48 hours after copulation (Mall, 1918).

A standard table of age-length equivalents during the prenatal period of development is still further complicated by the fact that the linear measurements of the specimens have been obtained by different methods. The measurements commonly used include the crown-rump length and crown-heel length or standing height. The second of these is really related to the first, that is, it is crown-rump length added to the rump-heel length (Minot, 1903). Besides these two usual measurements, there is the *Näckenlange* of His, that is, the length measured from a particular point in the caudal bend to a particular point in the neck bend of the specimen (His, 1880, 1882, 1885).

Of these measurements the crown-rump measurement is possibly best for embryological purposes (Minot, 1903), but in most of the work on the development of behavior the crown-heel length has been employed (Minkowski, 1923, p. 477, 1928a, p. 531; cf. also Scammon and Calkins, 1929).

In a subject so full of possible divergences of opinion, therefore, it is little wonder that many apparently conflicting tables of age-length relationships have been produced. Among the tables frequently referred to are those of C. M. Jackson (1909), Preyer (and the other embryologists summarized by him) given in Minot (1892, p. 381), and the summarizing table from Keith (1913). Instead of giving all these tables and many others to which reference might be made, or of attempting any averaging of the results, it has seemed wise to present Mall's (1910) table, which seems to the writer to be based on excellent evidence. This table, based on Mall's own work and upon the collection of material by ISSMER, is given as Table 1. Mall (1918) has reviewed his

TABLE 1

ABBREVIATED DATA FROM MALL TO SHOW RE-
LATIONSHIP BETWEEN VARIOUS AGE DETERMI-
NATIONS OF THE FETUS AND *CH* (CROWN-HEEL)
AND *CR* (CROWN-RUMP) MEASUREMENTS OF
HEIGHT IN MILLIMETERS *

Probable Age in Weeks	Probable Age in Days	Mean Menstrual Age	Mean Length of Embryo (*CH*)	Mean Length of Embryo (*CR*)
1	7			
2	14			
3	21	31	.5	.5
4	28	37	2.5	2.5
5	35	43	5.5	5.5
6	42	51	11	11
7	49	59	19	17
8	56	65	30	25
9	63	72	41	32
10	70	79	57	43
11	77	86	76	53
12	84	94	98	68
13	91	100	117	81
14	98	108	145	100
15	105	114	161	111
16	112	121	180	121
17	119	128	198	134
18	126	136	215	145
19	133	143	233	157
20	140	150	250	167
21	147	157	268	180
22	154	165	286	192
23	161	171	302	202
24	168	177	315	210
25	175	185	331	220
26	182	192	345	230
27	189	199	358	237
28	196	205	371	245
29	203	212	384	252
30	210	219	400	265
31	217	228	415	276
32	224	234	425	284
33	231	241	436	293
34	238	248	448	301
35	245	256	460	310
36	252	262	470	316
37	259	271	484	325
38	266	276	494	332
38½	270	280	500	336

* From *Manual of Human Embryology*, by F. Keibel and F. P. Mall. Philadelphia: Lippincott, 1910, Vol. II, p. 199. By permission of J. B. Lippincott Company, publishers.

work subsequent to the publication of this table and finds the table still accurate. It should be noted, however, that particularly so far as the younger stages are concerned there is a possibility of great variability in judging age from such a table as that given. Weight is probably a better index but is seldom given (Minot, 1892, p. 381). Therefore, in all age determinations given in this chapter, it should be borne in mind that the word "approximate" should really be placed in front of almost any statement of fetal age. Streeter (1920) has prepared a series of growth curves of the human fetus based upon most carefully computed data. In his tables and graphs the relationships of weight, sitting height, head size, foot length, and menstrual age of the human embryo are presented. Gesell (1928, pp. 315 ff.) has considered the problem of human age in relation to infancy.

Growing immediately out of the relationship between growth and age of the fetus is a whole series of studies on the morphological development of the fetus, which of course cannot be reviewed in this chapter. Figure 16 shows graphically the significance of such knowledge for one who thinks of the fetus as a "smaller infant." The literature on general fetal development has several times been summarized, the early work having been brought together in an excellent summary by Pinard (1877). In this summary, the work on the morphology, physiology, and pathology of the fetus is treated separately. A bibliography of eight hundred and seventy titles is appended to this treatise. Next to Pinard's summary in importance is Wertheimer's (1904), which brings together the general literature on the fetus to 1904. Probably the most complete summary in English of the anatomical and physiological aspects of fetal development is Feldman's (1920), which, in spite of certain lacunae, should be read by all who are interested in the fetus.

As pointed out above, it may almost be said to be necessary, in order to understand the development of behavior, to have some reference line in terms of measurements of anatomical development. It has become a convention by following such a temporal

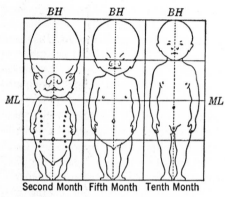

Second Month Fifth Month Tenth Month

FIGURE 16. Changes in body proportions in fetal life. *BH*—body height; *ML*—midline. (From *Premature and Congenitally Diseased Infants,* by J. H. Hess. Philadelphia: Lea & Febiger, 1922, 36. By permission of the publisher.)

line to divide the prenatal life of the human being into three periods (Feldman, 1920, p. 61; Williams, 1931, p. 163). The first period of one or sometimes two weeks is spoken of as the *germinal* period. From the third to fifth or sixth week is the *embryonic* period. From the sixth week to birth is the *fetal* period. The normal term of pregnancy is usually placed at 280 days (Williams, 1931, p. 163), although estimates varying between 270 and 284 days have been given by various investigators and summarized by Needham (1931, p. 486). It must be obvious, however, that such figures are meaningless unless the method of calculating true fertilization time is given. The normal length at birth is ordinarily given as 500 mm. in crown-heel, or 320 mm. in crown-rump, length. Sometimes, however, premature infants are born and successfully reared who have passed less than 180 days in the mother's body; but 180 or 181 days is usually taken as the average lower limit below which viability cannot be maintained (Hess, 1922). Claims have been made that much younger fetuses have been raised, but as, for example, in the case of Rodman's fetus which was alleged to have been but 4 months old, there is much doubt of the accuracy of the age estimation (Rodman, 1815; Baker, 1825).

At the other end of the scale the terminal point of postmaturity is also open to great difficulty of estimate. In considering this matter, Ballantyne and Browne (1922) hold that no single index such as fetal length, weight, ossification of the skeleton, placental structure, or cord structural condition is sufficient to date the fetus. They state that the best estimate is obtained by combining a knowledge of the last menstrual period, the date of copulation, the date of the onset of morning sickness, the date of the quickening of the fetus, the size of the uterus, the difficulty of delivery, as well as the evidences of postmaturity such as measurements of length, weight, and ossification. Probably 334 days is the longest period legally considered during which a fetus may be thought possibly to have lived in the mother's body and still be delivered alive (Ballantyne and Browne, 1922, p. 198). Thus, from one point of view at any rate, the human fetal life span that will be dealt with in this chapter must be taken as lasting from fertilization until birth, a time which in the extremest possible cases may vary by as much as 154 days!

In this chapter most of the references to fetal behavior are made to unborn fetuses. It should be kept in mind, however, that the study of correctly dated premature infants may throw light upon the later fetal period. In interpreting the sensory ability or response activity of a prematurely born infant, it is not safe to attribute the same abilities to the unborn fetus of the same age. As suggested in the first part of this chapter, the greatest errors in genetic science are made by suggesting that because environmental conditions of one sort produce behavior of a particular kind in one individual, therefore these same abilities must be "implicit" in an organism living under wholly dissimilar conditions. A normal fetus of the same age as a successfully air-breathing premature infant may act in a very different way from the comparison organism. This is true not only because of mechanical differences of bodily make-up, such as the presence or absence of liquid in the ear, but because of the gross differences brought about by the change from placental respiration to pulmonary respiration and from placental nourishment to alimentary canal nourishment. The sheer mechanical change from life in a liquid with the specific gravity of the amniotic fluid to life in air is most important. Similarly, the effectiveness of external stimulation is vastly changed in the transition from a relatively constant stimulus world before birth to a continually changing and varied set of physical energies after birth. An excellent brief summary of the development of the fetus week by week is given by Williams (1931, p. 163). In this chapter, save for the tables of fetal length and age, and save for the reproduction of the famous Keibel and Elze series of embryos and fetuses given above, no detailed consideration can be given to gross structural change which occurs during prenatal growth.

An interesting graphic representation of prenatal physical development is that in Figure 17, reproduced from Scammon and Calkins and redrawn by Needham (1931, p. 382), in which the age, height, or weight can, to the limits of accuracy of the original data, be read off if any one of these measurements is known. (See also Streeter, 1920.)

In a paper entitled "Physical Fitness in Terms of Physique, Development and Basal Metabolism" Wetzel (1941) presents a critique of a new method of evaluating individual progress from birth to maturity which suggests that there are types of physique which influence all growth tables. A similar observation could undoubtedly be made of fetal life as well. In this connection a recent study of body build by Sheldon and his collaborators (Sheldon, Stevens, and Tucker, 1940) should be consulted. For a convenient graphic age conversion scale, see McCarthy (1936).

In the paragraphs below a review of the development of behavior in human fetal life without detailed reference to morphology is presented. In this presentation brief consideration will be given to clinical observations on fetal movements observed without operation on the mother or the interruption of pregnancy. After this discussion, as accurate and complete a summary as possible will be given of the experimental studies on the development of behavior in operatively exposed human embryos. After these lines of evidence of fetal behavior have been summarized, a review of the knowledge concerning human fetal sensory life will be presented. A knowledge of sensory development will at once lead to a consideration of the theories that have been proposed to account for the development and control of fetal behavior, and an evaluation of all these observations for human psychology will then be presented.

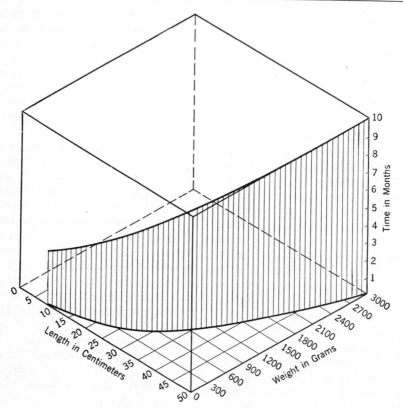

FIGURE 17. Three-dimensional isometric projection from which height, weight, and age of human embryos may be read off if one is known. (From "The Relation between the Body-Weight and Age of the Human Fetus," by R. E. Scammon and L. A. Calkins. *Proceedings of the Society for Experimental Biology and Medicine*, 1924, **22**, 3. By permission of the publisher.)

Nonoperative Studies of Behavioral Development in the Human Fetus

A number of different methods have been used for the scientific study of the development of the human fetus without disturbing its normal course of development. The simplest of these methods involves the direct recording of reports of the mother concerning the movements of the fetus as she experiences such movements. A mother can sometimes perceive the "quickening of the fetus" by the seventeenth week (Feldman, 1920, p. 204). At times the physician may by the use of the stethoscope hear fetal movements as early as the fourteenth week (Mailliot, 1856, p. 258; Neu, 1915, p. 292). It is customary, however, to say that the first time at which such movements can be detected by the physician is in the fifteenth or sixteenth week (Feldman, p. 204). Feldman points out that in fetuses of eight weeks the umbilical cord shows regular spiral twists (p. 204). Since such twists are not characteristic of animals that carry many young and therefore have little room for the fetus to turn in, it is assumed that the movements of the fetus even at such an early age determine the twisting of the cord. The writer, however, can see no reason why such twisting might not result from passive as well as from active movements.

In later periods of pregnancy, mothers give reports of movement involving part of the body. Sometimes the movements of the extremities or of the trunk alone are noted. Mermann (1887, p. 623), for example, reports a case of rhythmic movement of the fetal back palpated through the mother's abdominal wall in a fetus of seven months. Whitehead (1867) gives an extended report of a case of violent convulsion of the fetus while still in the uterus. This convulsive condition occurred during the ninth month of pregnancy. The activity of the fetus caused the mother great pain. By palpation and by direct observation it was found that the fetus was in a state of marked hyperactivity. Both the head and limbs of the fetus were moved so violently as to cause active disturbances of the mother's body wall. The child, born twenty-one days later, was in all respects healthy and vigorous.

Palpation and various instruments for magnifying or recording various fetal movements observed through the intact body wall of the mother have long been in use. MacKeever (1833) pointed out that the stethoscope was a valuable instrument in this connection. The direct hearing and registering of fetal heartbeat also have long been a subject that has attracted the attention of clinicians. Feldman (1920, p. 157) says that this phenomenon was discovered by a Swiss physician, but its importance was first brought out by de Kergaradec (1822, 1823). This student concluded that the fetal heartbeat could be heard from the eighteenth week of pregnancy on. Mailliot (1856, p. 258)

thought that it could be heard much earlier. Later, among others, DeLee (1927, 1928) and Hyman (1930) made special studies of the fetal heartbeat, including such phenomena as irregularities in its rhythm.

In 1891 Pestalozza succeeded in taking a cardiograph of the second twin after the first twin had been born (Feldman, 1920, p. 159). In this he was more successful than Hicks (1880), who by the use of an instrument like a cardiograph obtained certain records which were, however, so badly obscured by the rhythmic activities of the mother that they could scarcely be identified. Krumbhaar and Jenks are reported by Feldman (1920, p. 162) as having obtained typical electrocardiographic tracings of the fetal heart. (See also Sachs, 1922). Maekawa and Toyoshima (1930) have, by the use of amplifiers and a string galvanometer with electrodes placed on the front abdominal wall of the mother, secured excellent electrographic tracings of the fetal heart. After birth the beat of the same heart is also recorded for purposes of comparison.

Stimulated by this work, the author in 1935 attempted, with equivocal results, to record normal fetal heart activity by high-gain amplification. More recently, Mann and Bernstein (1941) and Geiger, Monroe, and Goodyer (1941) have published in this field, and the physiological psychologist, D. B. Lindsley (1942), has published a most interesting paper on the heart and brain potentials of human fetuses *in utero*. In this paper a reliable method of recording maternal and fetal electrocardiograms is given. What is even more interesting, however, is the fact that this investigator has also been able to record fetal electroencephalograms. In the latter case, during the seventh and eighth months of human pregnancy electrodes were at times placed on the maternal abdominal wall over the palpated head of the fetus. By suitable amplification and recording, fetal electro-encephalograms were secured by this means. The records were typical of those from the precentral region of the brain in the newborn. In all work upon fetal or neo-natal heart rate the effect of asphyxia must be considered (Barcroft, 1938). A fall in heart rate that is nonvagal has been demonstrated in fetal rabbits by tying off the umbilical cord (Bauer, 1938).

Among the other early movements of the fetus which are often directly recorded are the so-called *Ahlfeld breathing movements*, or the rhythmic contractions of the fetal thorax felt through the mother's body. These movements should not be confused with uterine contractions occurring after the third month, sometimes called *Ahlfeld's sign*, which incidentally may have something to do with the onset of behavior, if an analogy with the amnion contraction of the chick noted above may be suggested (Kuo, 1932c, p. 263). In spite of the difficulty of the ancients concerning fetal respiration that involves the intake of no air into the lungs, it has of course long been understood, as Leonardo da Vinci knew, that the fetus does not breathe water (Needham, 1931, p. 108). The gaseous interchange of the mammalian fetus occurs in the placenta between the blood stream of the mother and that of the fetus. The general significance of this process and its detailed consideration have been studied by many physiologists. The history of the early advance of knowledge on this matter is summarized by Starling (1900), and the generally accepted facts about the fetus are brought together by Sarwey (1915) and more recently by Bar-croft and Mason (1938). (See also By-licki, 1921.)

The liquid environment, of course, com-pletely precludes true lung breathing, but at least since 1798 movements of the chest and thorax of the fetus similar to breathing movements have been occasionally noticed. Béclard (1815) observed such movements in various mammalian embryos without re-moving the amniotic sac through which they were observed. Ahlfeld (1890) has devel-oped a view on the nature and significance of certain irregular but vaguely rhythmic movements of the fetus which seem to be caused by the contraction of the same mus-cles which will make respiration possible in postnatal life. (See also Kouwer, 1919, and Kellogg, 1930.) Ahlfeld has made graphic records of these movements, which in typical cases vary from thirty-eight to seventy-six per minute.

Teleologically, it has been suggested that these movements may be thought of as preparation for the act of breathing which comes at birth. In the fetus such move-ments are considered to lead only to the ebbing and flowing of the amniotic fluid in the trachea, but, as movements, they exercise and strengthen the neuromuscular mechanism of breathing. It is possible that this behavior is related to the func-tional establishment of the rhythmic ac-tion of the respiratory centers of the cen-tral nervous system. The theory has been proposed, therefore, that birth is not to be considered the point at which the onset of rhythmic respiration occurs. In carry-ing this idea further, it has been suggested that these prenatal chest movements are initiated, like adult breathing movements, by a change in the concentration of me-tabolites in the blood stream acting upon the breathing centers of the central nerv-ous system (T. G. Brown, 1915).

In combining the views in regard to fetal breathing movements and their cause, it has been suggested that the active or passive general bodily movements of the fetus may occasionally be such as to im-pede circulation in the umbilical cord. This mechanical obstruction of the umbilical cord, therefore, leads to an increase in carbon dioxide tension in the blood. This in turn may lead to a facilitation of activity or the activation of appropriate centers in the brain and thus initiate movements whereby the mechanical relationship of fetus and cord is changed in such a manner as to re-establish placental circulation (T. G. Brown, 1915). It has been suggested even more speculatively that not only are the chest movements of the fetus part of the general movements which bring about a change in the position of the organism, but also they act as a supplement to the fetal heart. They thus may act, it is suggested, as a sort of auxiliary pump brought into play as a result of a change in gas tension in the blood acting upon the breathing center (Walz, 1922, p. 334).

If these speculations are in any sense correct, therefore, the so-called first breath of the child may be considered to be just a change in the way in which the same neuromuscular mechanism determines the oxygenation of the blood (Walz, 1922, p. 341). For an excellent popular statement concerning the onset of breathing, see Henderson (1937).

A number of investigators have severely criticized the Ahlfeld concept of prenatal breathing movements. Walz (1922) attributed these objections to the fact that the initial statement of Ahlfeld's view was unfavorably received by the two leading obstetricians of Germany at the time, and that the weight of authority long kept this phenomenon from being correctly evaluated. It should be noted, however, that Huggett (1930) in an experimental study of fetal respiratory reflexes referred to above says: "The exact mechanism suggested by Ahlfeld is not in every sense confirmed."

A good many speculations have been made as to the causes involved in the first intake of air breath. As noted above, many students have held that the increase of metabolites, and especially of carbon dioxide tension in the blood, is one of the essential causes of the first gasp (Corey, 1931). Cohnstein and Zuntz (1884) observed that in a fetal lamb clamping of the umbilical cord led to the first intake of air. The writer has noticed this same result in fetal cats, rats, and guinea pigs. Indeed, the procedure of clamping the umbilical cord to study the effect of the blood stimulus on general bodily movements has been part of the experimental technique of several recent investigators and notably so of Swenson (1926) in his study of the fetal rat. Angulo y González (1933b) reports that in fetuses of nineteen postinsemination days in which tactile stimulation of the hindleg aroused no response there was immediate response after ligation of the umbilical cord. The general result of this procedure seems to be an increase in amount and vividness of activity for a time. Pflüger (1877), however, held that some external stimulus, such as cold air, was necessary besides blood change to bring about the first breathing act (cf. Huggett, 1930). Preyer (1885, p. 452) also suggested a relationship between cutaneous stimulation of some sort and the onset of breathing. Corey (1931) holds that an increase in the metabolites of the blood stream and some external stimulus, such as drying of the skin, seem to be in most cases antecedent to the initial respiratory gasp.

Snyder and Rosenfeld (1937) have made direct studies of the onset of respiratory movements. They have studied the fetuses of the cat, rabbit, guinea pig, and man. Rhythmic respiratory movements are initiated in all these types in the uterus. Oxygen and carbon dioxide affect fetal breathing movements; a certain level of carbon dioxide, for example, is essential to the maintenance of fetal respiration.

Windle, Monnier, and Steele (1938) and Abel and Windle (1939) show that there are no respiratory movements in cat fetuses less than 13 mm. in length. But in the middle third of the gestation period delicate and rapid rhythms of respiration may begin. Under certain conditions carbon dioxide breathed in by the mother starts such movements. There is no significant increase in blood volume at birth in the pulmonary system. There is a circulation in the lungs during the last part of pregnancy capable of caring for oxygenation when air breathing is established. For a more detailed consideration of the blood gases of the cat fetus, see Steele and Windle (1939), and for a consideration of the physiology and anatomy of the respiratory system in the fetus and newborn infant, see Windle (1941b).

Besides "breathing movements" there are other movements of the fetus which are indirectly significant in behavior. The movements of the organs of the digestive tract as seen in fetal organisms have been studied by a number of investigators. Yanase (1907a, 1907b) has studied peristaltic intestinal movements in fetal guinea pigs, cats, rabbits, and men. As a result of these studies, he concludes that peristaltic movements may begin long before birth. The status of gastrointestinal activity *in utero* has also been studied, especially in the cat and guinea pig, by Becker, Windle, Barth, and Schulz (1940), Becker (1941), and Becker and Windle (1941). In man such movements are possible in the seventh week. So far as hunger contractions are concerned, Patterson (1914) has shown that hunger contractions are practically continuous in young dogs. As age advances these contractions decrease in magnitude. Carlson and Ginsburg (1915), working on fetal dogs and newborn children, have written: "The empty stomach at birth and in the prematurely born exhibits the typical periods of tonus and hunger contractions of the adult, the only difference between infant and adult being the greater frequency and relatively greater vigor of these periods in the young" (p. 29). For other aspects of the function of the stomach before birth, see Sutherland (1921).

Certainly, in view of the large amount of work on the "hunger drive" as a determiner of activity, part of which is summarized by Warden (1931), the possibility that these stomach and intestinal contractions are stimuli to "random" and "spontaneous" skeletal muscle movement, and indeed to much of the behavior of the premature or full-term infant, cannot be neglected by one who would understand fetal behavior. Such behavior initiated by internal stimulation may well be considered merely the setting into action of inborn neural mechanisms. In this connection, see De Snoo (1937).

The question has often been raised as to whether or not gross external fetal movements of the various sorts considered above have any part in the rearrangement of the fetus in the uterus in the normal position for delivery at birth. As is so often the case when a phenomenon is difficult to explain, it has been alleged that the position of the fetus is governed by instinct (Dubois, 1833). Mechanical and physical explanations have been advanced by Paramore (1909), Barnum (1915), Griffith (1915), McIlroy and Leverkus (1924), and others. Possibly it may be said that no absolutely positive proof has been advanced to show that active fetal movements are essential in determining the normal position of the fetus at the time of delivery.

In the study of the changes of fetal position before birth, much has been learned by the use of the X-ray. We have already seen that Avery attempted to study the changes in position of guinea pigs by the use of roentgenograms. This work of

Avery's was directly adapted from human clinical procedures used in the study of the fetus. The use of the X-ray in the study of the fetus has given a new clue to the determination of fetal age by the study of the ossification of the fetal skeleton, although it is by no means an absolute clue. Hess (1918) has brought together much of the literature on this subject and suggests approximate norms of ossification at certain periods. (See also Mall, 1906, and Adair, 1918.) The recent study by Rudolph and Ivy (1933) on the rotation of the fetal head shows that uterine contractions and the movement of the fetus both contribute to this change in posture. Danforth and Ivy (1938) have shown that uterine activity is in part at any rate a function of calcium. Augmentation of uterine activity is brought about by increasing the calcium present; by decreasing the calcium the action is depressed. In this connection it is interesting to note that Good (1924) has shown that a patient may have the spinal cord completely severed and still give birth to a baby normally and painlessly.

A phenomenon of prenatal and immediately postnatal behavior which has long attracted attention is the first cry of the human organism. Kant (1799) found significance in the first sound uttered by the human infant. Preyer (1893, p. 213), indeed, quotes Kant as saying:

> The outcry that is heard from a child scarcely born has not the tone of lamentation, but of indignation and of aroused wrath; not because anything gives him pain, but because something frets him; presumably because he wants to move, and feels his inability to do it as a fetter that deprives him of his freedom.

Both Preyer (1893, p. 213) and Compayré (1896, p. 89) have pointed out the futility of such verbal fancies. Such speculation, however, is not as yet entirely dead. An analytical psychiatrist who is quoted by Blanton (1917, p. 458) has written of the cry of the human infant at birth: "It is an expression of its overwhelming sense of inferiority on thus suddenly being confronted by reality, without ever having had to deal with its problems." By operative technique Minkowski (1922, p. 754) has found that crying occurs as early as the sixth month in the prematurely delivered fetus. In clinical practice many cases of *vagitus uterinus*, or fetal crying, have been reported. A typical case is that reported by M. Graham (1919), in which in a difficult delivery, the fetal sac having been ruptured by operative means to assist delivery, the crying of the still unborn fetus could be distinctly heard. Many such cases are reported, but they need not be reviewed here. (See also Feldman, 1920, p. 207.) Fetal hiccup has also been reported by a number of observers. These cases are summarized by DeLee (1928). (See also a more recent study by Norman, 1942.)

All cases of fetal crying reported above seem to be the result of appropriately activated muscles, which bring about the expulsion of air in such a way as to cause it to vibrate. There seems to be no reason to assume that this phonation has any greater mechanistic significance than many of the other random acts of the child. It catches the notice of the observer, however, because from such behavior language develops in later life. This function is, of course, one of the most important aspects of adult human behavior, and an aspect which will in itself come to be, at least in the subvocal stage of "verbal thought," peculiarly important even in strictly introspective psychology.

This concludes the consideration of human fetal behavior of the sort that can for the most part be studied during the normal course of development. In the next pages the study of the development of human fetal behavior in fetuses removed from the uterus before the end of the normal term of gestation will be considered.

The Study of Behavior in Operatively Removed Human Fetuses

Most of the living human fetuses to which reference will be made in the next paragraphs were removed while still alive from the mother's body because some disease of the mother rendered the artificial termination of pregnancy medically necessary. Minkowski's technique (1928a, pp. 518–532) is typical. This investigator and a collaborator removed each fetus that was to be studied by a Caesarean section, usually performing the operation under a local anesthetic. The fetus, placenta, and amnion were removed. The fetus was then placed in a bath of physiological salt solution at normal blood temperature. This meant that such fetuses were cut off from their oxygen supply, and the movements which resulted must be thought of as the movements of increasingly asphyxiated organisms. This is important in the evaluation of the behavior reported, for, as pointed out above, increased metabolites in the blood at first lead to hyperactivity and then to hypoactivity.

The behavioral development of the human fetus as determined in operatively removed cases will be considered here in one series. This has its disadvantages because in certain reports estimated age is given; in others only measurements are presented; but certainly for an understanding of development it is most important to give estimated age. The writer has attempted to make a summarizing table of human fetal development, but he does not feel that such a table gives a correct impression. One who wishes to see this material expressed as well as possible in tabular form should consult Coghill (1929c, pp. 993–996).

The development, then, of human fetal behavior as observed by various investigators in relation to estimated postinsemination age or menstrual age may be given as follows:

FETUSES LESS THAN NINE WEEKS OLD

In very young human fetuses operatively removed from the mother, the first movement observed is that of the beating heart. For several centuries there has been a scientific controversy as to whether or not the heartbeat of the adult individual is to be thought of as essentially determined by direct muscle or by neural stimulation. It now seems that the early embryonic heartbeat must be thought of as essentially an independent muscle contraction (Parker, 1919, pp. 50–63). Therefore, in most of the work on the development of behavior the beating of the heart is not considered to mark the onset of "true behavioral life." Pflüger (1877) has demonstrated the beginning of heartbeat in the fetus as being in the third week, that is, in a fetus of approximately 4 mm. (See also Strassmann, 1903, p. 951.)

For a consideration of the mechanism of the initiation of contraction in different parts of the heart of a typical vertebrate, see Goss (1937, 1938, 1940) and Copenhaver (1939).

Williams (1931, p. 163) gives an excellent summary of development in this early period. The germinal stage of the human being may be considered to be the first week or two of life. The third week is thought of as the onset of the true embryonic period. At this period the medullary groove begins to be formed. A little later cell structures which make up the primitive heart are laid down and, as just noted, these cells begin the lifelong beat of the heart. At about this time, also, cerebral and optic vesicles begin to be differentiated and limb buds first appear. The muscles also develop rapidly in fine structure during this period.

In the second month there is continued morphological growth both in total height and weight and in the fine structure of the organs of the growing individual. Windle and Fitzgerald (1937) in a paper on the development of the spinal reflex show that all the elements needed for a reflex arc in the central nervous system are laid down during the sixth week but no spinal arcs are complete before the eighth week. Bolaffio and Artom (1924, p. 472) note in this period that isolated limbs torn during delivery can be stimulated directly.

Minkowski (1920b, p. 1202) reports that at the end of the second month cutaneous stimulation elicits response. This finding is not confirmed by Bolaffio and Artom (1924, p. 473), for they point out that at this time the skin is very thin and may involve in its stimulation the activation of receptors in underlying tissues.

Much is known of the structural and minute functional development of the receptors, nervous system, and effectors in this as in all later embryonic and fetal stages. It is not, however, until the fetus reaches the length of 15 mm., or is about 4 weeks old, so far as the writer can discover, that any direct statement can be made in regard to the activity of any part of the response mechanism, and this is a negative statement. In a fetus of this length, Minkowski (1928b, p. 66) reports that it was impossible to bring about muscular response even to an electric current of 40 milliamperes. He made observations on two fetuses of this length, with the same conclusion.

This is not entirely unexpected, as Hewer (1927) has shown that histologically the musculature of the fetus develops at uneven rates, the unstriped musculature, which is the first to develop, being clearly formed in an embryo 1 mm. in length. Striped musculature could not be detected in a fetus smaller than 2.5 mm. long, and it did not take on its definitive characteristics in fetuses less than 22 weeks old. Special changes of structure are also noted by this same investigator in regard to heart musculature.

Possibly the youngest human fetus to be observed to move is one reported by Yanase (1907b) in his studies of the development of intestinal movement noted above. In a fetus 20 mm. long and of an estimated age of 6 weeks, one movement involving the right arm is rather casually noted (p. 455). The next youngest human fetus to be reported moving is a fetus 22 mm. long and probably about 6 weeks old described by Strassmann (1903) in a case of extrauterine pregnancy. He observed through a rupture in the tube wall slow movements, backward and forward, of the arms and legs of the fetus (p. 963). In evaluating this observation it should be noted that Strassmann's report is given in such a manner as possibly to lead to a questioning of his observations, since apparently the fetus was observed in such a way that rhythmic mechanical movement of the adult body was possible. Certainly all observers of fetal behavior have had difficulty in deciding whether or not they were seeing something which was not the result of passive external mechanical movement. It should be borne in mind, therefore, that possibly these two earliest observations should be substantiated before they are finally accepted. In a fetus of 30 mm., or an estimated age of 8 weeks, Minkowski (1923, p. 477) observed a wormlike movement of the arms, legs, and trunk.

In Hooker's (1939b) description of his carefully controlled recent work the statement is made that no response to tactile stimulation has been observed before the eighth week of menstrual age (p. 8). In a 25-mm. fetus of a menstrual age of 8 to 8½ weeks, however, response to tactile stimulation has been recorded. This same investigator has repeated this observation on two other fetuses of approximately the same age. At this stage tactile stimulation is effective only in the area over the mouth and immediately adjacent to that supplied by the mandibular and maxillary divisions of the fifth nerve (p. 9). Hogg (1941) points out that the cutaneous nerves and nerve endings are very immature when responses are first elicited. No encapsulated endings are seen. Excitation is probably dependent upon deformation of the growing tips of the fibers by displacement of the surrounding tissue at this time, according to this author. Stimulation in this area in a fetus of this age led to contraction of the long muscles of the body and neck to produce body flexion. Limb girdle muscles related to both upper extremities were also activated. Rotation of the rump, caused by activation of the pelvic girdle muscles, was observed in very slight degree. Hooker notes that at this period stimulation by a hair capable of exerting a pressure greater than 25 mg. may cause direct mechanical stimulation. Faradic stimulation at this time is also effective. No spontaneous movements were noted by Hooker at or before this age.

Fitzgerald and Windle (1942) report that in a study of fifteen fetuses 7 weeks to a little over 8 weeks old, fetal movement was seen in only three organisms. These responses were individual reflexes of trunk, arms, or legs when oxygenated blood was still supplied to them. For an excellent summary of the early development of human behavior, see Hooker (1943).

FETUSES NINE THROUGH TWELVE WEEKS OLD

In a fetus of 35 mm. (estimated age 8 or 9 weeks) Minkowski (1928b, p. 65) reports muscle contraction to galvanic current. Minkowski's work shows that fetuses of 40 to 50 mm. (9 to 10 weeks) sometimes still show this characteristic muscle response possibly without neural activation. This observation coincides with the observations noted above on the fetuses of lower mammals, in which the musculature comes to respond to direct stimulation before true neuromuscular action begins. The most elaborate studies of this sort of muscular response have been made by Wintrebert (1904, 1920). (See also Minkowski, 1924, p. 244.)

Among the many significant observations that might be made at this period, it is interesting to note that the vestibular apparatus seems to be anatomically developed to its full (Minkowski, 1922, p. 753).

A fetus of 42 mm. was removed under operation by Woyciechowski (1928) to interrupt a pathological pregnancy. At the operation a mass was removed from the uterus. As soon as the mass was taken out, a fetus of 42 mm. dropped from the excised sphere of tissue. This fetus, estimated by the operator to be of approximately two months' gestation age, was seen to move both arms and legs spontaneously. When it was touched by a finger an energetic "protective movement" began which involved a much stronger moving of the arms and hands and the opening of the mouth. The observations made upon the movement of this fetus were checked by another observer. In spite of cooling, the movements of the fetus lasted in an active form for more than five minutes (p. 410).

In fetuses of the 9- to 10-week age period, Minkowski (1921b, p. 148; 1922, p.

753) noticed slow, asymmetrical, arrhythmic, noncoordinated movements. He also noted (1922, p. 753) that at this time neurologically the elements of the spinal reflex arc are developed anatomically.

Bolaffio and Artom (1924) studied a fetus of about this same age. They report that dropping the fetus from a height of a few centimeters to a table led to active contractions of the flexor muscles of the limbs. Further, they noted that tapping the table lightly with the fingers elicited responses of energetic movements involving the elevation of the scapulas, movement of the arms, and flexion of the thighs and legs. These movements were elicited for about three minutes, after which time they rapidly diminished in intensity and ceased. During the active period, stimulation by a blunt metal rod of the skin of the breast and of the abdomen led to no response. After the cessation of activity, direct brain stimulation led to no muscle response (p. 465).

In a fetus less than eight weeks old, Minkowski (1922) reports that percussion of the patellar tendon resulted in contraction of the quadriceps muscle. After this contraction had taken place, irradiation followed to other muscles. In this fetus the heartbeat was relatively constant at 80 beats per minute, but covering the fetus with normal salt solution at 40° C. led to an increase in the beat of the heart from a basal beat of 80 to 100 beats per minute (p. 752). Extirpation of the cerebral hemispheres in this fetus did not change the reflexes described. Sectioning the medulla just above the cord region, however, abolished the reflexes due to change in the position of the body.

In a fetus about two months old, Bolaffio and Artom report that stroking and tapping elicited slow local contractions of all the muscles of the limbs. For example, if these stimuli were applied to the palm of the hand, adduction and internal rotation of the corresponding arm were noted; if to the leg, flexion of the corresponding thigh. These investigators state, moreover, that mechanical stimulation of the cortex in this fetus gave a constant movement of elevation of the left shoulder, but no contraction of either of the lower limbs or of the right shoulder. After this same fetus was decerebrated they note a greater vividness (*vivacità*) of the local contractions referred to above and the reappearance of diffusion of movement at a distance from the stimuli which had ceased. In this experiment mechanical stimulation of the medulla led to respiratory movements. They further suggest that even in a fetus of this age removal of the cerebral cortex does remove some inhibition from the lower reflexes. It is interesting to note that during this period the neural and muscular mechanisms basic to sucking are developed so that they may function. A study of the evolution of this mechanism throughout the rest of the fetal period is instructive. For suggestions, see Feldman (1920, pp. 448 ff.) and, for the later period, Irwin (1930).

Bolaffio and Artom report in regard to another fetus about two months of age that gentle stimulation of the skin of the whole body was followed by no response, but percussion led to definite responses. Definite percussion blows on the forearm sometimes led to flexion, adduction, and slight internal rotation of the arm. Percussion on any part of the lower limb led to flexion and adduction of the thighs with slight flexion of the legs. If the percussion is rather light, the contractions are limited to the homolateral limbs; if somewhat more energetic, contractions also of the heterolateral limbs are reported. Percussion on the breast and abdomen gave homolateral responses about the pectoral muscles and bilateral responses about the abdominal muscles (pp. 465–466).

It is generally thought that even during the third month the cerebral cortex has as yet assumed no functions in relation to the general bodily activity. Bolaffio and Artom, however, report that removal of the cortex in a fetus of this age seems to remove inhibition from the reflexes of the lower limbs. This result is difficult for the writer to interpret. During this period sucking is theoretically possible; that is, the neuromuscular mechanisms necessary to bring about this response have probably already been determined. The reader who wishes a complete consideration of this earliest feeding reaction of the human individual should read the specific references given above to this reaction and then should refer to the summary of the knowledge of the reaction given by Feldman (1920, pp. 448–455). (See also Irwin, 1930.)

After superficial and deep stimulation of numerous points on the body of a decerebrate fetus of 90 mm., Bolaffio and Artom at first recorded very vivid contractions of apparently all muscles. After about three minutes, however, the contractions were still bilateral, but limited now to segments and homologous regions of the body. As time passed, the contractions became more and more circumscribed, and after about three minutes they were limited to the muscles corresponding to the stimulated point. After 15 minutes every reaction had ceased (p. 466).

During the third month Minkowski (1922, p. 724; 1928a, p. 565) reports labyrinthine reflexes, but Bolaffio and Artom (1924, p. 471), obtaining the same responses that Minkowski reports, interpret them rather as responses elicited as the result of the stimulation of proprioceptors in the neck. Minkowski (1922, p. 723) reports tendon reflexes at this age, but

Bolaffio and Artom (p. 473) do not find them until the sixth month. Here once more the decision must be a very difficult one to make, if the writer may judge from his own observations on infrahuman fetuses. Stimulation at the locus of a tendon may lead to a response, but this may be due to several possible forms of stimuli, such as (1) cutaneous stimulation, (2) direct muscle stimulation, or (3) a true tendon-stretch muscle stimulation. Mere observation of the response makes very difficult the decision as to which of these forms of stimulation has been effective. Bolaffio and Artom's careful work, however, seems to indicate that at first muscle sensitivity dominates when the tendons are stimulated, but in later fetuses true tendon reflexes begin gradually to arise.

Hooker (1939a) in summarizing development during this period says that by 9½ weeks of menstrual age the reflexogenous area has been restricted to the nose-mouth region but responses include rotation of rump and body flexion. The neck-trunk reactions are usually contralateral. At this period "spontaneous" human responses were first observed. This same investigator notes that from 9½ to 12 weeks a "total pattern" of response is dominant. At 11 weeks palmar stimulation causes a quick but incomplete finger closure which marks the onset of the grasping reflex. Hooker (1938) has studied the development of this reflex in great detail. He (1939a) also notes the onset of the plantar reflex during this period.

FETUSES THIRTEEN THROUGH SIXTEEN WEEKS OLD

Minkowski (1922), studying a fetus in the early part of this period (110 mm.), records the fact that touching the lower lip or tongue with a blunt probe led to a closing of the mouth, brought about through the lowering and lifting of the jaw (p. 723). He also noticed in the same fetus that reflexes of the trunk and extremities were seen prominently, but after the transection of the cord in the dorsal region the lower reflexes were discontinued at once. This seemed to prove that conduction of activation in this case, at any rate, was through the cord. After this operation, moreover, he noticed that the short reflexes remained unchanged but were themselves abolished after total extirpation of the cord. Destruction of the lumbar and sacral cord abolished the hindlimb reflexes, whereas similar destruction of the cervical cord abolished those of the forelimbs.

The so-called spontaneous movements observed by Hooker at 14 weeks include the activity of most body parts as well as of the "organism as a whole." For the first time these movements, like those at about the same period elicited by tactual stimulation, may be characterized as "graceful" and "delicate."

In a fetus of 135 mm. Minkowski (1922, p. 723) notes that a touch on the skin, using a blunt stimulus, led to reactions of diverse parts of the body. Characteristic of such stimulation were the flexion of both arms, the repeated opening and closing of the mouth, and simultaneous retraction of the head. He notes that at this stage of fetal development every part of the skin can act as a reflexogenous zone for various reactions. These reactions, however, tend to spread more or less over the entire fetal organism. Direct muscle excitability still remained at this stage one hour after the cord had been extirpated. Total removal of the cerebral cortex did not change the observable responses noted above. Transection at the midbrain, however, seemed to weaken the responses, although they still continued.

In a fetus 160 mm. long Minkowski (1922, p. 723) reports spontaneous dorsal flexion of the great toe, although he could secure no direct response to the touch of the sole of the foot. Distinct contractions of the abdominal walls were evoked in this fetus by brushing. Touching the closed eyelid in this fetus evoked a contraction of the orbicularis muscle.

Erbkam (1837) reports a study of a fetus, accidentally delivered, approximately 170 mm. long. He noted the contraction of both arms and legs and the movement of the head from side to side, "as if to breathe." In this fetus the heart beat for 10 minutes. After that time the water in which the fetus was lying became cool and the heartbeat became slower. When more warm water was poured in, however, the heartbeat became lively. The eyes of this fetus were closed. The great physiologist Johannes Müller saw the fetus and agreed with the author that it was of approximately four months' fetal age.

In a fetus of 180 mm. Minkowski (1923) noted spontaneous movements of all the extremities and the head. These were noted before the umbilical cord was ligated. In this fetus, touching the sole just at the time of delivery led to the dorsal extension of the big toe, the Babinski reflex. Later the plantar flexion followed (1923, p. 486; 1928a, p. 551).

In a fetus 190 mm. long Minkowski (1924, p. 250) obtained definite indication of reciprocal muscle innervation. He also reports at this stage that diagonal reflexes were established; that is, stimulating one foot of the fetus would lead to the movement of the arm on the opposite side. In certain instances the stimulation of the sole of the foot on one side even led to the movement of one finger, the little finger, on the hand of the opposite side of the body. These diagonal reflexes are considered by Minkowski (1922, p. 723) as significant in relation to the trotting reflex noted by a number of students of the genetic development of locomotion.

During this period the sole of the foot reflexes are thought by Minkowski (1928) to have their connection in the spinal cord and the tegmentum. In terms of response this involves the domination of the response of extension over flexion (p. 551). (See also Dewey, 1935.) For a photographic sequence of the foot reflexes of a 14-week fetus, see Figure 18, from Hooker (1939*b*).

FETUSES FROM SEVENTEEN WEEKS TO NOR-
MAL BIRTH TIME

In several fetuses approximately 200 mm. long, that is, about 17 weeks old, Minkowski found that brushing the sole of the foot led to plantar flexion of the toes, except the big toe, which did not move. This was directly related to Minkowski's elaborate study of the reflexes of the sole of the foot. (See 1922, p. 723; 1923, pp. 478–480; 1928*a*, pp. 550–556.) Direct mechanical stimulation of the motor roots of the spinal nerve at this stage showed that intersegmental spinal conduction is well established (1922, p. 752). Mechanical stimulation of the cranial nerves at the level of the medulla led to the opening and closing of the mouth. It is presumed by Minkowski that this reaction resulted from the direct stimulation of the facial nerve (p. 752). At this period direct stimulation of the cortex does not lead to response (Bolaffio and Artom, 1924, p. 477), but breathing changes do result from stimulation of the medulla.

In a fetus of 210 mm. Minkowski (1922, p. 723) observed opening and closing of the mouth accompanied by arm movements. The duration of such movements at this period was limited. Maximum responsiveness seldom lasted more than one minute at the most. In a fetus of 230 mm. Minkowski (p. 723) noted for the first time continued rhythmic contractions of the sort often described as Ahlfeld's breathing movements.

In a fetus of this same length Bolaffio and Artom (1924) noted that by employing superficial stimulation they were able to elicit localized muscular contractions in the limbs and other specialized muscle groups. By using strong and deep stimulation on a single segment of one limb, it is possible to elicit flexion of the whole contralateral limb. They also noted that stroking the ridge of the tibia gave vivid adduction of the homolateral thigh. In regard to the development of cortical dominance at this time it is interesting to note that mechanical stimulation of the Rolandic zone of the brain, either through the cranial cap or after its removal, did not call forth any reaction. Nevertheless, removal of the hemispheres did lead to more vivid local responses than in preceding excitations when the brain was intact. Stroking the pectoral muscles called forth adduction of the contralateral limb. In this case also these investigators reported that, if the intensity of the stimuli was increased somewhat, they got contraction of the whole corresponding limb. By stimulating the medulla they were able to call forth violent respiratory movements with active participation of the cervical, thoracic, and abdominal muscles, and those of the diaphragm. These movements were so violent they also led to elevation of the shoulder and adduction of the arms. It is further significant to realize that these investigators found, after repeated successive experiments and as the vitality of the fetus became less, that the muscular contractions disappeared first in the lower limbs and then later in the upper limbs (p. 466).

In a fetus of 240 mm. Krabbe (1912) reported slow movement of the limbs and

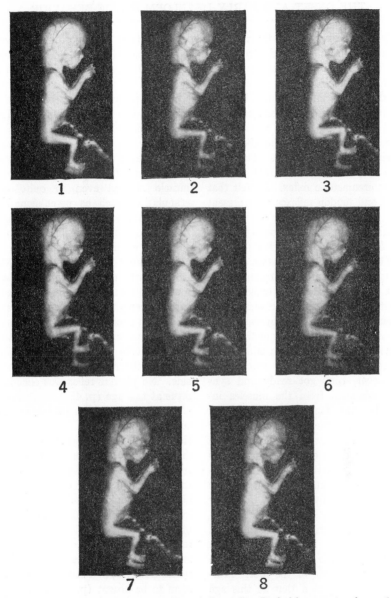

Figure 18. Response to tactile stimulation of the sole. Probable menstrual age 14 weeks. (From *A Preliminary Atlas of Early Human Fetal Activity*, by D. Hooker, page 91. Privately published, 1939. By permission of the author.)

Stimulation was applied by stroking the sole of the right foot with a 2-gram hair (1). The response consisted of the following elements: (*a*) Extreme dorsiflexion of the hallux (2 to 4) and "fanning" of the other toes (3 to 6). The toes, other than the hallux, ultimately show slight plantar flexion (6 and 7). (*b*) Flexion at the hip (2 to 4), slight flexion at the knee (3 to 5), and slight dorsiflexion of the foot (2 to 4). (*c*) Return to normal posture (5 to 8).

contraction of the muscles as the result of percussion. He also obtained strong abdominal reflexes as the result of light blows. The plantar reflex occurred without involving the participation of the big toe. In the fetus which he investigated the heartbeat was strong and he was able to elicit a number of reflexes, the abdominal reflex being especially strong. The fetus was a female, but he was unable to elicit the female cremasteric reflex. He felt that both bone and tendon reflexes were present and was able to demonstrate that direct muscle stimulation was possible (p. 434).

In a fetus of 260 mm. Bolaffio and Artom (1924) attempted certain specific neurological experiments. By means of appropriate electric stimuli they explored the cortex but did not obtain any reaction even with intense stimulation. By operation the internal capsule and peduncles of the brain were exposed, but still electric stimulation gave no response. When they reached the pons, however, they got ready and synchronous responses from the muscles innervated by the facial nerve. Finally, stimulation of the medulla gave energetic respiratory movements. Stimulation of the cervical cord led to energetic movements of elevation of the shoulder with flexion of the upper limbs, and stimulation of the lumbar cord gave movements of the lower limbs (p. 466).

In a fetus 270 mm. long Minkowski (1922) noted that from the first the plantar flexion of the toes was present to stimulation of the sole of the foot. Minkowski is of the opinion that at this age the plantar flexion must still be considered as a pure spinal reflex (p. 754).

In a fetus of 280 mm. Minkowski was able to bring about rather elaborate but quite well-differentiated muscular responses to a single electric stimulus. For example, the muscles of the eyelid could be activated with great specificity. After exposure in air this fetus is reported to have made faint sounds (p. 754). These sounds are possibly the earliest observed in a human organism. They may be taken by those who are interested in zero points as the onset of functional activity in the great mechanism which makes human speech possible.

In a fetus of the same length Bolaffio and Artom (1924) observed that every muscle reacted even to quite energetic stimulation, such as percussion, by local contraction. This specificity is more marked in the head region than in the leg region of the fetus. Percussion in front of the ear led to a movement of closing of the eye with elevation of the angle of the mouth and chin. Strangely enough, however, it seems that the deep reflexes are not easily obtained at this age in the arms. Stimulation of the legs shows that the patellar reflex can be called forth bilaterally and the Achilles tendon reflex on one side. No plantar reflex was elicited in one fetus at this age (p. 467).

In a fetus of 310 mm. Bolaffio and Artom further reported the observation of periodic respiration. Breathing was "by fits and starts." The heartbeat was regular. At this period all the muscles of the limbs can be excited one by one with percussion, obtaining vivid reaction. Appropriate local stimulation serves to bring out most of the typical percussion reflexes, including minor responses of the fingers, of the toes, and of the sole of the foot. The plantar reflex, however, and some of the others still seem to be absent (p. 467).

In general in the sixth month there is an increased tendency of various receptor-neuromuscular mechanisms to act independently, and this independent contraction is part of the greater vividness of response which characterizes this period as contrasted with earlier periods. Bolaffio and Artom (p. 472) find in this month for the first time tendon reflexes which seem to be assuredly not the result of cutaneous or muscle stimulation. Their judgment on this matter is based on the facts that the specific responses given at this period are not found before this time, but they continue to increase in strength during the later fetal periods, and that they are the same responses which are elicited in early infancy as true tendon reflexes. Direct stimulation of the mouth and tongue at this age elicited the sucking reflex, according to Bolaffio and Artom. In older fetuses stimulation of the lips alone leads to sucking movements which may or may not be accompanied by the protrusion of the tongue (p. 477). As noted above, Minkowski found this reflex at an earlier period.

These same investigators, using a slightly larger fetus (330 mm.), again reported superficial respiratory movements. These breathing reactions ceased after a minute or two. They reappeared when pressure and percussion of the thorax were used. In this fetus they noted also that with percussion the muscles gave powerful and localized contractions. The tendon reflexes which could be elicited included those of the biceps and triceps and the Achilles reflex. Direct stimulation of the cortex still brought no response. In this fetus it seems that no true cutaneous reflexes could be called forth either before or after the removal of the brain. In another fetus of exactly the same size these same investigators report that the fetus cried weakly and moved about spontaneously but with less strong movements than those characteristic of a fetus at term (p. 468). When death seemed imminent in this fetus the top of the skull was removed and the cortex directly stimulated electrically. The various zones of the cerebral cortex were all stimulated with negative results. Stimulation of lower brain centers, however, led

to specific results such as increased breathing rate, shoulder, arm, and finger movements.

Bolaffio and Artom also reported the behavior of a fetus of 340 mm. which appeared to be slightly undernourished. This fetus made weak crying sounds and breathed weakly. After about two hours it stopped breathing. During the period before breathing stopped they elicited contractions by tapping one by one the muscles and groups of muscles of the body. In this specimen by stroking the sole of the foot the plantar flexion of the toes was brought out. All these reactions became more vivid just before the death of the fetus (p. 469). This suggests a change in the higher brain centers as a result of a lack of oxygen.

Certain responses noted in the seventh month, while definite, nevertheless are seen to involve synergic muscle groups (Bolaffio and Artom, 1924, p. 481). This finding must be taken into consideration in evaluating statements given in regard to the randomness of activity in the newborn child. It may well be that much of the apparent "mass activity" of the newborn child (Irwin and Weiss, 1930) is not truly diffuse response of the sort found in the early fetus, but rather the activation of groups of synergic muscles in the sense of the term as used by Sherrington and his associates (Creed, Denny-Brown, Eccles, Liddell, and Sherrington, 1932, p. 129). Krabbe, Minkowski, and Bolaffio and Artom all report abdominal reflexes at this period. A number of other specific reflexes are also clearly brought out at this time. The knee jerk is definitely elicited. The plantar reflex, according to Minkowski, now probably involves not only the centers concerned during previous months, but also part of the lenticular nucleus and the red nucleus. Bolaffio and Artom feel that at this period the plantar reflex in its typical form is much like that of adult life but that it is still much more variable than it will be at a later period. This leads them to be critical of statistical work on reflexes, such as that of De Angelis (1922). (Cf. also Cesana, 1911.) The corneal reflexes are seen in the seventh month. Direct stimulation of the cornea of the eye leads from this time on to an increasingly strong response. Decerebration in this month was found to lead to increased vividness of most reflexes, but also to a tendency to reflex spread.

In a still larger fetus Bolaffio and Artom reported that with slight percussion of all the muscles of the limbs they observed vivid responses not limited to single muscles. Such responses spread to synergic muscle groups. With percussion of the pectoral muscles they obtained adduction and internal rotation of the arm and flexion of the forearm. They obtained bilaterally the patellar reflex and an extension of the leg, sometimes associated with flexion of the thigh. Associated with this pattern of response was the dorsal flexion of the foot. The Achilles tendon reflexes, however, were not always obtained even in a fetus as old as this one. These investigators also failed to get abdominal reflexes in fetuses of this age. However, the slight excitation of the sole called forth a definite unified toe phenomenon, and then a more energetic stimulation called forth flexion of the toes. The sucking reflex was secured only by stimulating the tongue. They reported that the movement of grasping which they got by applying pressure to the palm of the hand was energetic. These same investigators reported that from the seventh month to birth they investigated 13 fetuses of 7 months, 3 of 8 months, and a large number of mature fetuses. In this study they have not considered protocols of any fetuses which, because of condition of nutrition or on account of the presence

of disease, did not present normal situations. They assert that from the end of the sixth month the movements of the fetus became so powerful and complex as to render very difficult and sometimes impossible detailed and specific report of behavior (pp. 470–487).

During the last two months of pregnancy the muscular reflexes decreasingly tend to prevail over the tendon reflexes, according to Bolaffio and Artom (p. 472). By the end of the ninth month the tendon reflexes are so well established that they prevail over special muscular reflexes. All the tendon reflexes are found to be present during this period of fetal life, with the exception of those of certain of the upper limbs which are elicited with difficulty because of the small size of the member. Contralateral adductor reflexes are sometimes called out in this period. Even in the fetuses nearest term, the cremasteric reflex was difficult to elicit (Bolaffio and Artom, 1924, p. 474).

At any prenatal age, including this last period, however, it is noticed that very light stimulation of the hand gives variable and inconstant movements, whereas strong stimulation, possibly involving the muscle or other underlying tissue, leads uniformly to grasping (Bolaffio and Artom, 1924, p. 476). Bolaffio and Artom, therefore, believe that the grasping reflex is not to be thought of as a purely cutaneous reflex in prenatal life. Minkowski (1928a, p. 545) finds this reflex at an earlier period. Iris reflexes are present during the prenatal period (Bolaffio and Artom, 1924, p. 477). The reaction of the iris, however, is slow, and very strong light is needed to call out the response. (See also Minkowski, 1928a, p. 558.) It is difficult to say when the response would begin if stimuli as strong as direct sunlight could always be used. Bolaffio and Artom do not note the fact, but it seems obvious that with such strong stimulation as that they recommend, the danger of independent muscle effector action of the sort described by Parker (1919, p. 53) must be guarded against.

There is some evidence that the cerebral cortex is directly stimulable at this period, although as yet the evidence is not conclusive (Bolaffio and Artom, 1924, p. 480), as will be pointed out below in considering the possibility of fetal learning.

It is possible to add to this consideration of fetal development month by month, therefore, some general statements that have been made by those who have been most directly concerned in these investigations. Thus Minkowski holds that one may say that every part of the skin can, as its receptivity is progressively established, serve as a reflexogenous zone for quite variable reactions which tend to spread more or less over the whole fetal organism. In the whole developmental process the gradual acquisition of postural responses and muscle tone is peculiarly important. The development of these responses will be considered below in the section in which the origin and development of the proprioceptive and static senses are considered. Minkowski offers in part explanation of the spread of reflexes during the early periods the fact that the spinal cord tracts as well as the nerve trunks have no medullary sheaths before the fourth month of fetal life. Illustrations of Minkowski's anatomical work on the nervous system are given in several places (1921a, 1928a). There is a suggestion that from this time onward there is an anatomical increase in specificity correlated with the differentiation of the nervous elements in ways possibly involving the nature of protoplasm, neurofibrils, medullary sheaths, synapses, long conduction paths, and other cell changes (Minkowski, 1922, p. 753). These gradual alterations in the nervous system, it is suggested, lead progressively to the possibility of more and more circumscribed and definite response. Compared with the diffuse character of early fetal response, therefore, in the late fetus, Minkowski (1920a) feels that all the well-known special reflexes have more or less been established. The discussion above, however, has shown that the process of development of these reflexes is a complex one and later in adult life injury to the nervous system may bring about reactions which were characteristic of a previous period, even of a fetal period (Minkowski, 1922, p. 754). For the historical breaking of ground in this connection, see H. Jackson's essay (1884) on the evolution and dissolution of the nervous system.

It must be impossible to read what has gone before in this chapter without realizing that there is a general relationship in sequence of development of behavioral capacities from fish to man. It must be noted, however, that there are peculiar dangers in generalizing from, for example, the amphibian development of behavior, or even the rodent or cat development of behavior, to the growth of adaptive actions in man. For example, it has been shown clearly in the case of fish, amphibians, and lower mammals that the first responses involve a unilateral bending of the trunk. This stage may or may not exist in the human individual, but at any rate no observations have so far been made in which trunk movements unaccompanied by arm movements are observed in early fetuses.

The basic pattern for the development of locomotion and other "individuated" responses, as suggested by Coghill and his students, may be seen in a less typical form in human development than might be supposed, although Coghill (1929c, p. 1009) himself has called attention to the attractive possibilities of the analogy. Little evidence of rhythm in the limbs of the human fetus has been determined. It may well be, therefore, that locomotorlike movements of the limbs do not appear until very late in the human fetal period. Windle and Griffin (1931) have summarized this comparative evidence, and they suggest that the movements observed in the kitten fetuses with which they have worked possibly should not be compared directly to human fetal movements because of the differences between the two in the type of adult locomotion. In a similar way the locomotor mechanisms in fish and amphibians which require a high degree of trunk-muscle integration may be difficult to compare with the conditions obtaining in a mammal that stands erect. Such considerations as this bring up the old problem of the recapitulation in ontogeny of the phylogeny of behavior. This problem is as old as Aristotle (Needham, 1931, p. 69), and yet there seems to be nothing in the present evidence to make this view seem anything but a generalized, and in many details an inaccurate description, and certainly not an explanation, of development. (See Davidson, 1914; Needham, 1931, pp. 1632–1638.)

Too much emphasis cannot be placed upon the fact that easy generalizations, such as the assertion that all behavioral development occurs from a generalized total pattern of the organism to the specific responses of adult life, must be taken with great caution. While this description may be true in many respects, particularly if the word "pattern" is given an unambiguous meaning, it seems certain on the basis of the specific responses considered above that it cannot be indiscriminately applied. Before generalizations can be made with assurance, there must be a large amount of accurate measurement and the determination of a series of statistical norms in regard to the development of each of the specific developmental stages in each form considered. Typical cross-sections in development in every form and in all responses from significant receptor surfaces must be considered before such a generalization can be made. Certainly the late fetus has an elaborately organized and in some respects quite specific response mechanism. To some stimuli the relatively early fetus makes quite definite responses.

It seems hard to believe that anyone who knows anything of the structure and function of the tracts and centers of the central nervous system can read the report of fetal activity at various developmental levels given above and still feel that there is much to be gained by saying that before birth the organism reacts as a whole, as certain psychologists, possibly under the influence of one form of the *Gestalttheorie*, have suggested. Much of the nervous system may, in some sense, be involved in any partial activity of the system, but this does not mean that the system is not in many respects sharply differentiated. Certain essential relationships between diffuseness and specificity and between individuation and integration of behavior will become clearer after the parts played by the specific senses in fetal life have been considered.

The account presented above from the reports of several investigators gives a picture of the development of behavior in human fetal organisms of estimated ages. No effort has been made to include all known fetuses but only those in which behavior significant for the general problem of this chapter was noted. Minkowski (1923, pp. 486–489) refers to at least eleven fetuses not considered here in which primarily the only reflexes studied were those released by stimulation of the sole of the foot. In the study of this response Bersot (1918, 1919; 1920, 1921) has also considered fetal activity in detail in relation to a study of the development of the clinically significant plantar reflex. This same response has been considered from a scientific and theoretical point of view by Feldman (1922) and by Minkowski (1926) in work that has been referred to above. For an account of a fetus investigated by Winterstein, see Minkowski (1928a, p. 517).

In a personal letter to the author Hooker has given permission to refer to his *Preliminary Atlas of Early Human Fetal Activity* (1939b), which was in the first instance issued for restricted use only. Reference has been made above to this work, but the author wishes to call especial attention to it because it contains very beautiful reproductions of photographs of human fetal material 8½ to 14 weeks of menstrual age. A careful study of this atlas may give a more adequate picture of early human fetal behavior than any other single reference.

The Special Senses in Human Prenatal Life

Historically there has been much speculation in regard to the rôle of the senses before birth. In earlier psychology these speculations centered largely about the question of whether or not some sort of dim conscious awareness exists in the infant before birth. More recently this essentially nonexperimental question has given place to one that may be studied. The question now asked is: How and when does the stimulus control of fetal behavior determined by the activation of the various receptor systems begin before birth, and how do behavior capacities develop? Objective techniques for study of the senses in the premature or newborn infant have been devised, of which those of Canestrini (1913) and A. P. Weiss (1929) are significant examples. These techniques have not only made quantitative study of the senses possible in a new way, but they have also added to the general knowledge of the part that stimulation plays in the subtle alterations of bodily activity. In this chapter, therefore, the various specific senses will be considered in turn in relation to fetal behavioral or mental life when such behavioral or mental life is considered as including not only experience but also specific receptor-controlled behavior.

After all the senses have been treated, some generalizations will be made by the author on the significance for psychology of receptor-aroused activity in the fetus. The reader should be reminded that the material presented above on the development of the senses in lower animals and especially the elaborate work on the guinea pig has much relevance in a consideration of the growth of the human senses. In this section, however, the whole emphasis is placed upon human development except where specific reference to infrahuman forms is considered necessary for strictly comparative purposes.

THE CUTANEOUS RECEPTORS

In a consideration of the senses of touch, an effort is made to suggest such differences as have been made in fetal life between light and deep pressure, temperature, and cutaneous pain. The development of skin in the human fetus has been anatomically described by a number of writers. This work is summarized by Feldman (1920, pp. 233–236). In appearance the skin of the late fetus or early premature infant is very red, owing to the visibility of the vascular system just beneath it. At two or three months before birth the skin is still very thin and is covered with *lanugo hairs*, which appear at about the fifth month of pregnancy. The skin of the fetus during midpregnancy is typically much wrinkled, because of the comparative absence of subcutaneous fat. The hair on the scalp at this period is short and poorly pigmented. The nails grow gradually during late fetal life (Hess, 1922, pp. 74–77).

There has been much speculation on the skin as a sensory surface during the uterine life of the fetus. Cabanis is quoted by Genzmer (1882, p. 10) as holding the skin to be a peculiarly important receptor field at this period. Bichat (1827, p. 137) and Magendie, as noted above, discussed the skin sensibility of the fetus. Some casual observations are also reported in relation to the material summarized on a previous page of this chapter concerning the possibility of stimulating the fetus by pressing on the abdominal wall of the mother. Of course, stimulation of this sort may well activate the deep-lying proprioceptors as well as the true tactile receptors. In the review of the literature in the experimental study of the development of fetal behavior in infrahuman organisms, many references have already been made to tactual stimulation. In the human field alone, Minkowski, Bolaffio and Artom, Krabbe, Hooker, and others have considered fetal responses that are released by cutaneous stimulation as indicated above. Hooker has been especially careful to use quantified stimuli. The part played by the sense of touch in animals and man in discrimination and even in responses of equilibration is considered by Kidd (1907).

A. Pressure. In summarizing the work that has been done on human and infrahuman fetuses, the following factors may possibly be isolated as important in a consideration of the pressure sense before birth:

(1) *Place stimulated.* In general, cutaneous sensitivity seems to begin in the oral-nasal region, that is, the region involving the mucous membrane of the nostrils and the red of the lips (Genzmer, 1882, p. 6; Windle and Griffin, 1931, p. 179). In rodents the pads of the vibrissae also very

early become sensitive (Lane, 1917, p. 34; Raney and Carmichael, 1934; Carmichael, 1934a), and in many animals the regions about the eyes and the openings of the ears are also very early sensitive, as is the anal region (Coronios, 1931). In the human infant Kussmaul (1859, p. 23) found the eyelashes very sensitive, but this was not confirmed by Genzmer (1882, p. 6). Most studies seem to suggest that, with individual variations, skin sensitivity develops by spreading out over the head region and then progressively over the surface of the body. In this development in certain organisms, such as the toadfish, the salamander, the rat, and the cat, a fairly well-worked-out course of temporal difference in the arrival of sensitivity in increasingly caudal segments of the body may be observed. In animals with tails this even goes on out to the end of the tail.

In this general course of development, however, certain exceptions have been made out, as noted above, by the writer, in a study of the development of the receptive zones of the fetal guinea pig. Sensory development in general has been treated by Minkowski and other investigators as the spreading of what they have termed reflexogenous zones. This term has much to recommend it because at present almost the only method used in the study of fetal sensory capacity of the skin is the recognition of behavior correlated with the experimental stimulation. Windle and Griffin (1931, p. 175) suggest in general that motility precedes the ability of a part to be stimulated. In his consideration of the "reflex circle," Holt (1931, pp. 37–43) has suggested the large part that self-stimulation may possibly play in the development of specific forms of behavior as organisms develop. Certainly no one who has watched an active mammalian fetus can help being struck by the fact that in its movements it stimulates almost its entire body surface by its own moving paws and head. It is peculiarly striking to watch a forty-eight-day guinea pig fetus, for example, stimulate its head and face by appropriately cupped "hands." These scrubbing movements, performed not once but over and over again, are such that the surface must certainly be irritated by the friction.

(2) *Areal versus punctiform stimuli.* Minkowski (1922, p. 723), Coronios (1931), Windle and Griffin (1931, p. 175), Carmichael (1934a), Raney and Carmichael (1934), and Hooker (1936) have all apparently noticed that stroking produces stimulation when single punctate stimulation does not bring about response. Following this suggestion, Raney has been able to show that stimulation of a point on the skin by a single hair may not bring about response, but stimulating the same area immediately around such a point with a brush made up of comparable hairs will sometimes bring about response. (In this connection, see also Kuo, 1932e, p. 507.)

(3) *Summation of stimuli.* The writer (1934a) and others have noted that a single touch with a light hair may fail to bring out response, but several touches apparently of the same intensity at the same point may be effective in eliciting response.

(4) *Weak and strong stimulation.* Genzmer (1882, p. 10) long ago noted that entirely different responses might be elicited in a premature infant to weak and strong cutaneous stimulation. The distinction in terms of the strength of cutaneous pressure is one that has too infrequently been made in studies of fetal development. Thus, as noted above, Bolaffio and Artom disagree with Minkowski as to the point at which cutaneous reflexes begin in the developing fetus. This disagreement may be based on the fact that Bolaffio and Artom (1924, p. 473) indicate the possibility that Minkowski was unwittingly stimulating the underlying musculature and thus that the massive responses which he reports in young fetuses are not cutaneous but are due to the stimulation of deep receptors. The possibility of direct muscle stimulation in such cases must also be remembered. Holt (1931, pp. 40–43) considers that the distinction between strong and weak stimulation is a peculiarly important one in the development of the functional activity of the growing organism. He believes that in most cases light stimulation will lead to response moving toward the stimulus, or *adiently*, whereas only secondarily does strong stimulation of the same receptor field lead to *abient*, or withdrawal and avoidance, responses. Richter (1925) and others have confirmed this observation. Indeed, Coronios, Schlosberg, and the writer (1932) have been able to take moving pictures showing exactly this response as the result of stimulating the paw of a fetal kitten.

Under other circumstances, however, observations have not been such as to confirm this generalization. Thus Coghill (1929a, p. 13) asserts that the first responses of *Amblystoma* are all away from the region stimulated. Windle and Griffin (1931, p. 175) point out that the unilateral trunk or neck flexions of the earliest fetuses seem to be executed toward the observer and away from the surface on which the animal is resting. Kuo (1932e, p. 507) also uses the strength of the stimulus as a peculiarly important part of the theory of development which he has proposed. It seems possible that in responses in which apparently the same receptor field is stimulated first lightly and then more strongly two distinct neural mechanisms may sometimes be brought into play. It might be suggested speculatively that the facts behind the differentiation between the allegedly developmental epicritic and protopathic sensitivity, as proposed by Head and Rivers and especially as explained by Boring (1916) and more recently by Sharpey-Schäfer (1928), will ultimately provide some clue in the explanation of this diversity of response to different stimulus intensity.

Windle and Griffin (1931, p. 176) also discuss a developmental system of cutaneous receptor mechanisms. This difference in responses to light and heavy tactile stimulation makes peculiarly uncertain the interpretation of results of investigators who do not indicate that they have considered the strength of the stimulus as important in describing the fetal responses which they have elicited in experimental work. It is all the more peculiar that this distinction should not have been continuously made, because of the statement in regard to the difference in responses to weak and strong stimuli made, as noted above, many years ago by Genzmer. As previously reported, Smith and the writer (Carmichael and Smith, 1939) have demonstrated a quantitative relationship between the extent and spread of response and the intensity of punctiform stimulation when calibrated esthesiometers were used.

(5) *Localization.* Preyer (1882, p. 110) believes that the first localization response to tactile stimuli is the seeking of the nipple by means of the cutaneous stimulation of the lips. Many specific references have been given above to the motor responses of various fetuses set off by tactual stimulation. It has been suggested in connection with the work of Raney and the writer (1934) that such responses possibly develop greater accuracy in localization as age progresses.

(6) *Cutaneous reflexes.* As suggested in the preceding paragraphs, the skin may be thought of as a mosaic of points, each spot of which is the locus of stimulation for a more or less specific behavioral response.

Many writers have discussed the significance of cutaneous reflexes in adult life. Givler (1921) has suggested the wide significance of the development of one such reflex, that of grasping. Hooker's (1938) careful observations on the grasping reflex show that it develops during fetal life in two phases: finger closing and gripping. Finger closing appears as a quick flexion of the digits except the thumb at about eleven weeks of menstrual age. Gripping is first observed in the eighteenth week. It is still weak in the twenty-fifth week of menstrual age. In the first twenty-five weeks of fetal life the thumb seems to play no rôle in fetal grasping.

Minkowski, as noted above, considers in detail the variations in the pattern of the reflexes elicited by the stimulation of the skin of the sole of the foot. Sucking, in its later stages, is possibly conditioned by a number of exteroceptive and interoceptive stimuli, such as the stomach contraction of hunger, but it is in essentials always a cutaneous and mucous membrane reflex. The cremasteric reflex and certain of the abdominal reflexes also result from stimulation of the cutaneous field.

In general, then, it may be pointed out that many of the specific acts of the fetus are induced by stimulation of cutaneous pressure receptors. Mucous membrane reflexes (Minkowski, 1928a, pp. 556–558) are also probably best thought of as involving receptor mechanisms, so far as pressure is concerned, that are similar to cutaneous reflexes. Peiper (1928, p. 92) has tabulated the cutaneous responses seen in newborn children. The writer must here again emphasize his belief that, given a stimulus just above the lower threshold and a quiescent fetus in a standard posture, there is typically *one behavior act* or *reflex* set off by the stimulation of each cutaneous area. These cutaneous "push buttons" are remarkably specific in their behavioral relations when the complexity of the central nervous system is considered.

B. *Temperature.* Warmth is one of the skin senses attributed by the philosopher John Locke (1849 edition) to the fetus. In spite of this early sanction it is difficult to understand how marked differences in temperature can normally be present in prenatal life. In the study of the temperature sense in the prematurely delivered infant the matter is further complicated by the great variability of body temperature which characterizes the premature infant (Hess, 1922, p. 151; Evensen, 1931, pp. 11–15). Currently accepted views in regard to the mechanism of temperature stimulation start with the assumption that the temperature to which the skin is adapted must be taken as the physiological zero point. From this zero other stimuli are to be considered as above or below; therefore quantified work in regard to temperature in the premature infant is rendered difficult when only absolute temperatures of stimuli are recorded.

Some indications, however, of responses to both warm and cool stimuli in premature infants are given by both Kussmaul (1859, p. 23) and Genzmer (1882, p. 11). For the most part these observations agree with those of the following investigators of the temperature sense of newborn children: Preyer (1882, pp. 111–116), Canestrini (1913, pp. 76–85), Blanton (1917), and Peiper (1928, pp. 28–29). These opinions are criticized by Pratt, Nelson, and Sun (1930, pp. 144–167), who also add their own controlled experimental observations. These three collaborators report that newborn infants react much less strongly to stimuli warmer than the body than to stimuli that are cooler. The writer has described above a study of fetal temperature sensitivity (Carmichael and Lehner, 1937) in which some observations

on the temperature responses of guinea pigs were made. In this study unmistakable reactions to temperature both of warm and cool stimuli were obtained under controlled conditions. Drops of blood-warm water call out no response save as they arouse tactile receptors, but cold- or hot-water drops do call out such activities. This sensitivity has appeared by approximately the middle of the gestation period. Here again the "more intense" stimulus (warm *or* cold) calls out more active responses than does the "less intense" stimulus.

C. *Pain.* Locke (1849 edition) also attributed the experience of pain to the fetus. Since his speculation there has been little direct experimentation upon the fetal pain sense. A number of casual observations show, however, that the application of stimuli that must have caused gross destruction of skin and protoplasm has not called out very pronounced movements on the part of the fetus. Genzmer (1882, p. 12), on the basis of such observations, holds that the pain sense is very poorly developed in the fetus. On the first day of a premature infant's neonatal life he stimulated it until blood came and got no response. It is certainly true that increase in pressure over that necessary to bring out the typical responses to deep pressure does not always seem in the guinea pig fetus, at any rate, to increase the extent or intensity of response. Thus in certain cases the light pressure of a fine hair may lead to extension and stronger pressure of a heavier hair to retraction, but very strong and even obviously destructive stimulation of the same point may or may not make any observable difference in the elicited response over that noted to strong pressure stimulation. Similar observations have been made on the cat fetus (Windle and Griffin, 1931, p. 176). There can be no doubt that protoplasm-destroying stimuli sometimes bring about violent responses in late fetuses, but even this reaction does not always occur. Speculations on the part played by pain in relation to unpleasantness and discomfort will be referred to in the consideration of the organic senses.

The foregoing paragraphs may be summarized by the statement that there is much evidence that the specialized skin senses have developed to an active functional state long before birth and are able when appropriately stimulated to initiate the release of behavior that is typically precisely related to the point stimulated.

THE PROPRIOCEPTIVE SENSES

The neuromuscular spindles may be taken as typical of the many classes of proprioceptors. They are found in the fourth month of fetal life in practically all muscles, including the extrinsic muscles of the tongue and the external eye muscles (Elwyn, 1929, p. 248). Historically it was not until quite recently that the kinesthetic senses came to be distinguished at all from touch. The writer (Carmichael, 1926b, pp. 204–209) has described the history of knowledge concerning the "muscle sense." Much that Bichat (1819) wrote about the active touch of the fetus probably referred to the proprioceptive rather than to the cutaneous sense. Kussmaul (1859, p. 32) and Genzmer (1882, p. 8) both refer to responses which must have involved muscle-sense stimulation. Preyer (1885, p. 547) makes similar references. Peterson and Rainey (1910) also hold that not only touch but also the activity of the muscles of the fetus must lay the foundation "under the threshold of consciousness for a sense of equilibrium and vague spatial relationships" (p. 122). In his study of the relationship between local reflexes and posture, Coghill (1929a) comes to the conclusion

that ". . . the limb is able to respond very precisely to stimuli arising within the body (proprioceptive) as the result of a particular posture before it can respond to stimuli that arise exclusively from the outside world (exteroceptive) . . ." (p. 21).

In experimental work on operatively exposed human and infrahuman fetal material during the active period, the proprioceptive senses are always much in evidence. Indeed, in the responses in fetal rats both Swenson (1926) and Angulo y González (1932a) find evidence of this sense in a sixteen-day fetus. Coronios (1933) and Windle and Griffin (1931, p. 177) deal with this sense in detail. (See also Windle, 1940.) As noted above in the consideration of the cutaneous senses, these investigators report activities that show that the posture of the cat fetus at the time of stimulation seems in certain cases to determine the response that will be elicited. This point is substantiated by many protocols of the experimental studies of fetal behavior that the present writer has recorded. It is possible that this fact alone may be taken as indicating an early onset of proprioceptive control of behavior.

In this connection one must remember the differential gravitational action on the limb and body in air and in the liquid of the amniotic sac. In one of the studies of a very young human fetus—by Strassmann (1903), noted above—it is recorded that the observer pressed against, in a manner which apparently means moved, the limb of the fetus. As a result of this stimulation the experimenter could feel the foot press down on his hand. The writer has noticed this same response in young guinea pig fetuses. Even when very gentle or even relatively strong tactual stimulation would not release a response in the forelimb of the fetus, it not infrequently has happened that a forcible movement of the limb itself by the experimenter gave a specific and direct response. As the skin was not anesthetized in the cases reported, this may not of course be thought of as a wholly proprioceptive stimulus, but, as cutaneous stimulation was ineffective in producing the same response, the facts seem to favor the view that the responses noted were proprioceptively aroused. This conclusion must be taken with reservations because the bending and stretching of the skin which result from the bending of a limb are a very strong pressure stimulus.

There is still other evidence that the proprioceptors are effective very early in fetal development. Hooker and Nicholas (1930) have reported experiments on fetal rats in which the spinal cords were completely sectioned at various levels. After some of these experiments it was found that stimulation above or below the sectioned point of the cord might lead to responses in parts of the body innervated by segments of the cord above or below the cut. The question at once arose as to how these impulses were transmitted. As one of the possible explanations of this transmission, these investigators have suggested the following course of events. An exteroceptive stimulus leads to afferent conduction over peripheral nerves to the cord above the region of the section. From this still intact segment of the cord impulses pass out over efferent peripheral nerves to trunk muscles leading to this response. This response mechanically moves the adjoining musculature and thus directly stimulates the proprioceptors in it. These newly activated proprioceptors then initiate afferent impulses which pass into the cord below or above the region of the cut, as the case may be, and thus in turn activate arcs in the intact region of the cord above or below the section, which in turn lead to responses obviously in-

nervated by connections in the cord beyond the section. (See also Hooker, 1911.)

Windle and Griffin (1931) report many evidences of movement that may be considered on the basis of the analysis of Sherrington and his school of reflex physiologists as at least in part proprioceptively innervated. These investigators report (p. 186) that a quiescent embryo held in the cramped condition of the sac will, on the cutting of the sac, sometimes at once assume an exaggeratedly stretched position. It seems as though it were attempting to exercise itself after the close confinement of its entire previous existence. It may be remarked that the writer has seen and photographed similar responses. These maintained "extensor thrusts" are in many respects similar to the tonus of decerebrate rigidity as seen in the adult animal and may possibly involve proprioceptive stimulation. The experiments of Weed (1917), Weed and Langworthy (1926), and Langworthy (1928, 1929) give very clear evidence of other reactions involving this receptor system. The writer has sometimes noted when dealing with a late guinea pig fetus that if the fetus, still wholly immersed in the bath, is held by its own forepaws on a submerged projection, the animal will seem to try to crawl up onto the projection. Correlated movements are here used which seem, to superficial observation, similar to those employed by a swimmer lifting himself out of the water onto a diving raft. This well-integrated and apparently purposeful activity seems to involve complex proprioceptively directed responses.

Most students of the development of fetal behavior agree that locomotion, as, for example, in the first crawling movements of the fetal opossum considered above, sucking, and breathing are three of the earliest essential behavior systems of the newborn animal. It is interesting to note that each of these in its developed form may involve marked proprioceptive stimulation. The geotropic responses of the opossum fetus considered above, occurring less than two weeks after copulation, seem, in the light of Crozier's work (1929, pp. 83–98) on geotropism in the rodent, to represent a response in which proprioceptive stimulation plays a part. Hunter (1931) has pointed out in a similar study that the vestibular apparatus and other stimulus factors are probably also important in determining such responses.

As noted above, Minkowski (1922, p. 723; 1928a, pp. 559–560) reports that there are true tendon reflexes in the early fetus. This is questioned, however, by Bolaffio and Artom (1924, p. 472). These latter observers suggest that the responses seen by Minkowski in very early fetuses may have been the result of other forms of stimulation. The mechanism of deep stimulation which they suggest and true tendon-stretch stimulation both involve proprioceptive activity. Indeed, it may be said that the whole study of prenatal behavior in man and in the lower mammals indicates that the proprioceptors in muscles and tendons, and possibly joints, are functional well before birth. By the time of birth these mechanisms have undergone such development that they are among the best-organized receptor fields so far as the initiation and control of behavior are concerned. Much of the "movement of the organism as a whole" which so many writers refer to seems to be the result of rather specific proprioceptive stimulation. Such stimulation often leads to the "spread" of what are really quite delicately timed families of specific responses which can easily be mistaken for "vague" or "diffuse" behavior.

THE RECEPTORS IN THE NONAUDITORY LABYRINTH

Adult posture, righting responses, and other reactions to gravity, tonus changes due to rotation, and other alterations of the body in space are often held to result from stimulation of receptors in the nonauditory labyrinth and associated receptor fields (Camis, 1930, pp. 262–268). As suggested above in a consideration of the development of behavior in the fetal cat, the change of body posture in space has been shown sometimes to involve various combinations of nonauditory labyrinthine, kinesthetic, and exteroceptive stimuli. In the fetus it is peculiarly difficult to isolate the part played by the body exteroceptors and muscle proprioceptors from the part played by the receptors in the nonauditory labyrinth. It should be noted that there is some evidence also that in certain types there is an auditory function subsumed by receptors in this *non*-auditory receptor complex.

Historically, comparatively little reference has been made to the static senses in connection with fetal mental life as this life was considered in the older speculative child psychology. Some reference, however, has been made to the part played by these receptors in determining the position of the fetus in relation to gravity. Lane (1917) has noted in his study of the development of the senses in the fetal rat considered above that there is an apparent correlation between the histological development of the semicircular canals and the acquisition of postural righting responses on the part of the fetus. In Lane's work, however, no effort to differentiate between proprioceptive and static stimuli is reported.

The development of the labyrinth has been considered by many writers, including Streeter (1906) and Larsell (1929).

(Cf. also Bowen, 1932, and McCrady, Wever, and Bray, 1937.) Minkowski (1922, p. 753), as noted above, has demonstrated from neurological studies that the labyrinth is fully differentiated in a human fetus of 40 mm. As noted above also, Windle and Griffin (1931) report that in very early cat embryos of twenty-six or twenty-seven days ". . . rotation of head and trunk appeared to be indefinitely coordinated with the older components, namely, lateral and ventral head and trunk flexion. This activity resulted in motions that strikingly resembled the righting reflexes seen in late fetal life" (p. 156). Windle and Fish (1932, p. 95) show that in cat fetuses several days before normal birth true labyrinthine reflexes do appear. These reactions make possible what has been called the first "purposeful" movement of the cat, that is, successful locomotion (Windle and Griffin, 1931, p. 171). This complex behavior act, as already suggested, is held to be a combination of equilibration, body-righting responses, general postural tonus, and rhythmic movement of the limbs.

Coronios and the writer have both noticed that, in late cat and guinea pig fetuses, turning the animal over while it is completely immersed in the warm bath does not always lead to righting movements. If the cord is ligated and the same fetus is placed on its side on the experimental table, righting may begin at once. This is possibly to be interpreted as indicating that at this period righting still, at any rate, involves exteroceptive and proprioceptive as well as vestibular functions.

Similarly, Coronios and the writer have both been able to elicit typical Magnus reflexes of limb extension as the fetal mammal's neck is turned to the right or the left. These responses are strikingly similar to those of decerebrate mammals and tend to confirm the observation agreed

upon by all other investigators that for the most part the young fetus is not under the active control of the cerebral hemispheres. Minkowski (1922, p. 724) reports labyrinthine reflexes in early human fetuses. He suggests that it is not only possible to elicit responses from general labyrinthine stimulation but also possible to distinguish between the reflexes attributed by Magnus and his colleagues to the utriculus-sacculus complex of receptors as contrasted with those attributed to the complex of semicircular-canal receptors. His analysis leads him to believe that most of the fetal responses to nonauditory labyrinthine stimulation are the result of semicircular-canal receptor action.

Minkowski (1922, p. 753) states further that in his opinion the early anatomical development and functional use of the vestibular apparatus in the fetus are probably related to the fact that the fetus is living in a fluid medium the specific gravity of which is almost equal to its own specific gravity. Therefore it is "weightless," a condition in which he believes the labyrinthine reflexes may be seen to operate to excellent advantage (p. 753). Minkowski (1928a, pp. 565–568) is careful, however, not to disregard the possibility that the phenomena noted as the basis for attributing labyrinthine function to the fetus may be the result of the stimulation of proprioceptors in the neck and related receptors. Magnus (1924, p. 113), in reviewing this work, seems to emphasize the part of the tonic neck reflexes in such activities.

There is some reason to believe that the first eye movements of the fetus are in response to changes of the bodily position of the fetus in space; that is, the first eye movements are occasioned not by retinal stimulation but as part of the general tonus changes of the body brought about by gross movements in space. This fact is brought out very clearly in Kuo's work

(1932a, p. 426). Early eye muscle movements, indeed, may be thought of as part of a generalized pattern of muscular responses out of which later specific movements of the body are in certain respects differentiated (Minkowski, 1924, p. 253; 1928a, p. 568; Tracy, 1926, p. 283).

There is no reason to believe, however, that these early "postural" responses of the eye muscles are as definitely related to specific aspects of semicircular-canal stimulation as they are in the adult condition so well summarized by Maxwell (1923), Favill (1929), and Holsopple (1929).

Eye movements in adult life that are determined by vestibular function may be modified in various ways (Dodge, 1923). Wellman and the writer have made preliminary and as yet unpublished studies of the origin and development of eye movements in the fetal guinea pig. Although these results are still tentative, the following statements may be made, based upon the electrical recording of eye movements in living fetuses: (1) Vestibular stimulation brings about responses before light stimulation is effective in causing eye movements. (2) Optokinetic (that is, light-induced) responses which have some of the same characteristics as such responses in older animals can be called out in the fetal guinea pig. In these experiments a moving field of bars of light and shade gradients is passed near the eyes of the fetus. The resulting reactions show the slow and fast photic responses typical of such stimuli in adult animals.

In conclusion, then, it is difficult to say with assurance the exact part which the labyrinthine senses play in determining behavior before birth, but it is certain that the tonus adjustments of the body muscles in postural responses, including precise adjustments of eye muscles, are among significant prenatal activities. An understanding of these responses in fetal and adult life is important (Magnus, 1925). One of the points, however, at which a knowledge of the development of proprioceptive responses in the fetus is most important is the evaluation of the studies of postnatal life in which the alleged saltatory character of certain responses there noted is observed in the light of the knowledge of prenatal postural responses. Popularly speaking, the postural actions of the fetus may be considered a fundamental preparation for a diversity of actions in postnatal life. Walking and localizing responses of arms, trunk, and legs can take place only in an organism in which postural mechanisms are developed. It is almost as if these senses provide the essential "gyro-control" necessary before a reaction can be made, just as gyro-apparatus on a warship is necessary if the guns are to be pointed effectively in a heavy sea.

THE ORGANIC SENSES

Historically there has been some speculation in regard to the organic senses in the fetus. Some have held that the fetus lives in a perfect world in which hunger, thirst, and all other needs are cared for before they arise (Bichat, 1827, p. 133). Locke (1849 edition), on the contrary, held at an early period in the total story of speculation about fetal life that the unborn child has "perhaps some faint ideas of hunger and thirst." Kussmaul (1859, p. 31) agrees with this view. As noted above, Yanase (1907a, 1907b) has studied the movement of the fetal intestines. In the rhythmic nature of these movements is found a basis for possible organic experience and, indeed, for the indirect activation of the skeletal musculature.

The work of Patterson (1914) and Carlson and Ginsburg (1915) on newborn infants and on dogs delivered before normal time indicates something of the nature of the tonus changes of the stomach which may occur in late fetal life. These changes in these organisms are found under appropriate conditions to be rapid and active. This coincides with the observations of Preyer (1893, pp. 152–158) and of Peterson and Rainey (1910, p. 121) on the hunger of newborn full-term or even premature infants. Some suggestion of the developmental course of hunger activities and stimulation may be obtained from an observation of Hess (1922, pp. 177–180) that very early premature fetuses are much less able than later premature infants to show the usual signs of needing to be fed. Jensen (1932, pp. 368–375) notes the dependence in the infant of the reflex of sucking, a reflex incidentally too often considered merely tactual, on the concomitance of hunger stimuli and tactual stimuli. Preyer (1893, p. 153) notes the whole sequence of bodily changes, even including those of the eye muscles, which come to be related to the hunger activities of the newborn child.

The theory of "drive" or motivation held by many modern comparative psychologists, which correlates such activities to some extent with organic stimulation, finds support in the observations of the "random" activity of the fetus which is shown by Irwin (1930) and others to accompany hunger stimuli. As noted above, this activity may not be "random" in the ordinary sense of the word but rather the consecutive or concomitant release of a series of already described patterns of behavior. (See Carmichael, 1941.)

This concept of "drive" is closely related to phenomena considered by certain of the older descriptive psychologists as characterizing the motivating power of the affective processes. That is, "drive" is related to the bodily basis of pleasantness and unpleasantness. Thus Preyer (1882, pp. 140–176; 1885, pp. 486–487) and others have discussed reaction related to pleasantness and unpleasantness as apparent before birth or immediately after birth. These conclusions are inferences based on unaided observation of facial expression and on instrumentally recorded bodily changes, such as breathing and directly measured cerebral volume (Canestrini, 1913). Facial expression is reported by Minkowski as beginning in the relatively early weeks of active fetal life, and so it seems that this expressive pattern of so much significance in pleasant and unpleasant situations of later life has had ample opportunity for exercise during the prenatal period.

It may be noted in passing that the rate of fetal heartbeat can be modified by external stimulation, thus possibly leading to vascular stimuli of the sort often considered to fall under the heading of "organic experience." The possibility of respiratory experiences, or "feelings of suffocation," is certainly present, so far as may be judged from a knowledge of stimulation and response. But there is, of course, no evidence that any introspective state actually follows such stimulation.

In conclusion, it may be said that there are possibly certain organic changes in the stomach, intestines, heart, and vascular and respiratory systems which occur before birth which may be important in receptor stimulation. It is possible that the stimulation of these receptor systems may lead to fetal activity which does not, of course, have any specific external end in view until, as a result of external stimulation and learning, such stimulation in postnatal life comes to initiate adaptive responses which some wish to characterize as "end-seeking." It may also be noted that no one who has worked with fetal material has failed to see that, after repeated responses, "fatigue" sets in, and for a time stimulation is difficult or impossible (Peiper, 1925).

The question as to whether or not fetal quiescence is to be considered as fetal sleep has also been debated (Preyer, 1885, p. 488).

Taste. The histological work on the development of the taste mechanism in the embryo is summarized by Keibel and Mall (1910). Taste buds are said by Parker (1922) to begin to appear in man during the third fetal month. The taste receptors are also found to be much more widely distributed in fetal life than in adult life. Parker thus points out that there is evidence of a real retraction of the sensory field in man from the late fetal period to the adult state. At first, taste buds are found on the tonsils, hard palate, and parts of the esophagus. Later, functional taste cells are almost always limited to the tongue (1922, p. 110). Here is a striking example of a "reflexogenous" or receptor zone which changes as a function of developmental time.

Historically, there have been several different speculative opinions concerning this sense in prenatal life. The early opinions are summarized by Bichat (1827, p. 136). It is undoubtedly true that the amniotic fluid might serve as a taste stimulus. As change is ordinarily thought of as essential to real external stimulation, however, the question may be debated as to whether or not the change in the amniotic fluid as pregnancy progresses is enough to make it at any point a taste stimulus (Feldman, 1920, p. 139). To the writer this seems unlikely. A safe conclusion seems to be that, although the mechanism for taste is present before birth, there is no adequate stimulation of this sense until after birth.

Experiments on the sense of taste in newborn children have been carried out by Kussmaul (1859, pp. 16–21), Genzmer (1882, p. 15), and Peterson and Rainey (1910, p. 120), using the method of general observation of facial expression after stimulation. The conclusion of these writers is that sweet is distinguished, even by premature infants, from salt, sour, and bitter. It is difficult to be sure, however, that salt, sour, and bitter are stimuli for behavior that is specific. Canestrini (1913) and Jensen (1932) have worked out a method of experimentally recording bodily changes which result from taste. Pratt, Nelson, and Sun (1930) find that under the conditions of their experiment, involving very dilute concentrations, there is not as strong evidence in regard to taste differentiation at birth as had previously been supposed. These later experimenters conclude that the stimulating efficiency of various sapid substances in early life is not only quantitatively but also qualitatively different from the condition in adult life (p. 124). (See Pfaffman, 1936, in this connection.)

In conclusion, it may be said that the receptors for taste are probably never normally activated before birth. The receptor-neuromuscular mechanism, however, has been shown, by work on premature infants, to be ready to function in late fetal life whenever appropriate stimulating conditions are brought to bear upon it. Most experimenters seem to conclude that sweet stands in a class by itself so far as the infant is concerned. Salt, sour, and bitter are apparently distinguishable with greater difficulty. References to the sense of taste in infrahuman fetuses have been given above.

Smell. Bedford and Disse and others quoted by Parker (1922, pp. 23–41) have considered the embryonic development of the receptor cells of the nervous fibers of the olfactory epithelium. Lane (1917, pp. 51–52), as noted above, has studied the development of the olfactory structures in the rat. Feldman (1920, p. 237) points out that the olfactory and tactual parts of the brain were found by Flechsig to be the earliest to be myelinated in the fetus. Historically, save where taste and smell have been grouped together, there seems to have been general agreement, in the early period at least, that while the nasal cavity is filled with the amniotic liquid there can be no *adequate* olfactory stimulation. Preyer (1885, p. 478) specifically defends this conclusion, basing his statement on Weber's assertion (1847) that substances that could be smelled when vaporized were quite unable to arouse the sense of smell when introduced into the nose as liquids.

A great deal of relevant work in this field has been critically summarized by Parker (1922). This work shows that there is excellent reason to believe "that the olfactory organs of an air-inhabiting vertebrate can be stimulated by ordinary solutions, though this form of stimulation cannot be looked upon as normal" (p. 59). Even though this is true, however, the same difficulty as that met with in the sense of taste must be remembered to exist. Even though the amniotic fluid may be an effective inadequate stimulus for the olfactory receptors, there is little reason to suppose that there would be sufficient change in the liquid to effect significant stimulation during prenatal life.

In this sense field, therefore, the study of smell reactions of prematurely delivered infants will again be very significant in any determination of how the functional development of the olfactory mechanism progresses during late fetal life. Kussmaul (1859, p. 23) found that asafetida and certain other odors, but not irritating substances, led to responses in a one-month premature infant. He is not sure that he was able to secure responses in earlier premature infants. Peterson and Rainey (1910, p. 121) also found smell reactions in premature infants.

Historically, there has long been a belief that the newborn child could distinguish odors effectively. Feldman (1920, p. 237) asserts that the Jewish sages in the time of the Talmud believed that a blind baby could tell his mother's milk by smell and taste. Rousseau also commented on the sense of smell in newborn infants (Feldman, 1920, p. 237). Preyer (1882, p. 134) reports that an eighteen-day infant refused a breast nipple on which kerosene had been placed but eagerly took the other odorless breast immediately after the refusal. Preyer (1882, p. 134) also demonstrated that newborn guinea pigs apparently select their food by the sense of smell. He asserted, moreover, that in young animals, including man, the sense of smell in general is most important in determining behavior. Indeed, in infrahuman animals it is suggested that this significant aspect of behavior determination by smell does not come to be neglected to the extent that it is by civilized man.

Experimental work on the sense of smell in newborn infants, which is probably also in general applicable to late premature infants, has been summarized by Canestrini (1913, pp. 86–87), Peiper (1928, p. 27), and Pratt, Nelson, and Sun (1930, p. 143). Canestrini concludes that there has been some exaggeration in regard to the effectiveness of the sense of smell in young animals. He feels that most of the work on smell has been concerned with stimuli which act on the receptors related to the trigeminal cranial nerve components of the nasal receptor surfaces. These trigeminal components are probably best considered as the "common chemical sense" (Parker, 1922, pp. 103 ff.) and not in the usual sense of the term "tactual" as suggested by Pratt, Nelson, and Sun (1930, p. 127). Certainly the trigeminal endings are not "olfactory" in the ordinary sense. Stimulation of the common chemical sense receptors typically sets off violent reactions, such as sneezing. A characteristic irritant of this sort is ammonia. It is significant in this connection to notice that Pratt, Nelson, and Sun found ammonia to be a peculiarly effective "smell" stimulus. Probably the responses of a newborn infant to ammonia should be considered as responses to the common chemical sense rather than to true olfactory stimulation.

In summary: The neural mechanism for olfaction—that is, the mechanism related to the so-called first cranial nerve—is developed before birth, and the possibility of inadequate stimulation exists before birth. It is probably true, however, that olfaction does not generally occur in its normal form until the nasal cavity comes to be filled with air. Premature infants, at least in the last month, are able to smell substances when air enters the olfactory cavity. Much work on smell, however, has probably been vitiated by the fact that the free nerve endings of the trigeminal nerve (the fifth cranial nerve), the receptors for the common chemical sense, have been stimulated rather than the true olfactory spindles.

Hearing. Anatomically the development of the ear in the individual has been extensively studied. This work is summarized by Keibel and Mall (1910, pp. 264–290). Hess (1922, p. 76) shows an original drawing of a section through the ear of a late fetus. Stevens and Davis (1938) have summarized much of the recent experimental work upon the adult auditory mechanism.

Historical opinion on the sense of hearing in the human fetus is probably best summarized in the words of Kussmaul (1859, p. 27): "Von allen Sinnen schlummert das Gehör am tiefsten." The history of experiment on the sound response of full-term and prematurely born infants is excellently summarized by Pratt, Nelson,

and Sun (1930, pp. 78–85). The general conclusion of these authors is in harmony with that of the later investigators, that hearing becomes effective only in the very early part of postnatal life.

Most of the early investigators of the development of audition concluded that the auditory mechanism was developed to a point at which it could be functional before birth but that the infant remained deaf until by breathing, crying, and possibly yawning the Eustachian tube was opened. Only in this way, they suggested, could the somewhat gelatinous liquid of the fetal middle ear be drained out (Preyer, 1882, pp. 72–96). Peterson and Rainey (1910, p. 118) specifically secured evidence of auditory response in a prematurely delivered infant as soon as there had been an opportunity for the draining of the middle ear. More modern work seems to have offered no reason to differ with this conclusion so far as stimuli of normal intensity are concerned. Preyer (1882, p. 92) also reports that newborn guinea pigs are deaf for one-half hour after birth and are then sensitive to tonal stimuli of a great variety of frequencies (C of third octave to E of eighth). Avery (1928, p. 265) has secured comparable results on late guinea pig fetuses prematurely delivered, as noted above. The experiment of Rawdon-Smith, Carmichael, and Wellman (1938), which shows by electrical methods of recording the onset of functional activity in the cochlea, has already been referred to. This experiment shows that the guinea pig fetus can hear before birth, judging by both electrical and behavioral criteria.

Although there has been some speculation on the fact that the sounds inside the mother's body might act as sound stimuli to the fetus, little evidence has been brought forward to make this seem certain (Preyer, 1885, p. 480). There are experimental findings which suggest that loud auditory stimuli may activate the human fetus. Peiper (1925, p. 237) was led to this study because he noted that in six neonates, very soon after birth, changes in the breathing curve were found in response to a special sound stimulus. The change in the breathing curve is reported as marked. He therefore decided to try to find out whether or not any indication of hearing before birth could be secured. It had been discovered that auditory and other sudden stimuli give two sorts of responses in the newborn—one, a change in breathing rhythm, and the second, a change in the level of general movements. Peiper felt that there was no sure reason to believe that the unborn child would respond differently if it could be stimulated in its auditory receptors. The breathing center in the brain is open to stimulation before birth. He therefore thought of the possibility of using the prenatal "breathing movements" of Ahlfeld as an indicator of sound response. The disadvantage was found, however, that these movements were not always present, and so the number of subjects was limited. But with proper recording apparatus he was able to take records of the general movement of the fetus through the body wall of the mother.

It was obvious that sounds would be much muffled on their way to the fetus. Therefore a very loud sound was chosen as a stimulus, an automobile horn being used. The experimenter waited until the fetus was absolutely quiet and the mother had been prepared so that she would not herself respond to the stimulus. Incidentally, it proved impossible to train all mothers in this way. The stimulus was given in a quiescent interval. In more than a third of the subjects studied, definite fetal reactions were secured to stimulation of this sort. There were, however, individual differences in responsiveness.

Sometimes the response was given on one day and not on the next. The movements which the fetus made in response to the stimuli also showed individual differences. Most often, however, the fetus seemed to draw its whole body together. Peiper (1925) comments that it might seem to one who had not been present at the experiments that the movement was a response of the mother and not of the fetus. He is certain, however, that one who had actually observed the experiment would be convinced that the response was fetal and not maternal. As an additional safeguard, a pneumograph was placed on the mother's chest and her breathing curve taken during the experiment. After a good deal of practice it was possible to train some mothers so that they made practically no response, and thus the fetal response could be recorded. Continued stimulation led to a diminution of the effect. This corresponds to a frequently observed phenomenon of fetuses and neonates, namely, that their responses are easily fatigued or exhausted. Peiper even goes so far as to suggest that this change in response may be thought of as a simple kind of attention. He also states that one mother remarked that she had noticed definite movements of the fetus while attending a concert.

Forbes and Forbes (1927, pp. 353–355) have reported a case of apparent fetal hearing. Thirty-one days before her baby was born a pregnant woman was lying in a metal bathtub full of warm water. A two-year-old child was playing on the floor beside the tub. Accidentally the child struck the side of the tub with a small glass jar, and at once a sudden jump of the fetus was felt by the mother, which gave a sensation quite unlike the usual kicks or limb movements. A few days later an observer struck the side of the tub below the water line a quick rap with a small metallic object, meanwhile watching the mother's abdomen. A fraction of a second after the rap, a single quick rise of the anterior abdominal wall was clearly visible. The mother at this moment felt the same jump inside her abdomen as previously reported. Her own muscles were entirely relaxed, and she was not at all startled by the noise, nor was she conscious of perceiving any vibration through the skin. The mother's tactual sense later tested showed that the same intensity of vibration could be perceived only by those portions of the skin coming in contact with the tub. In the infant in question, eight days after birth, it is interesting to note that while the baby was nursing an auditory stimulus occurred which resulted in the flattening of the baby's ear against the side of the head for a few seconds, after which the ear relaxed again. These same investigators also report another case in which concerts attended toward the end of pregnancy resulted in troublesome activity on the part of the fetus. The conclusion of these writers (1927, p. 355) is:

> Good evidence exists that the human fetus four or five weeks before birth can respond with sudden movements to a loud sound originating outside the body of the mother. It seems probable that this is a true auditory-muscular reflex but the possibility of reception through tactile organs in the skin cannot be excluded.

The response of the fetus to auditory stimulation has been made the basis of several studies of fetal learning, to which reference is made below.

In summary: It may be said that the auditory mechanism seems to be well developed structurally during later fetal life, but in general, possibly because of the closure of the external ear or because of the gelatinous liquid which fills the middle ear, the fetus is probably deaf to sounds

of normal intensity before birth and during a short period immediately after birth. Strong sounds, however, especially those which can directly pass through the mechanical blocks noted, seem to be able to bring about auditory stimulation before birth, although it is still possible that such responses are tactual rather than truly auditory.

Vision. The specific morphological cellular changes which are the essential antecedents to the development of the function of the human eye begin in the second or third week of development of the embryonic period, and from that time on an elaborate series of events occurs until, in the normal human individual, binocular convergence and the elaborate activities associated with visual space perception and stereoperception develop in the young child. The anatomical aspects of this growth have been summarized by Keibel and Mall (1910, pp. 218–258) and by Mann (1928). Hess (1922, p. 75) has described in some detail the eye of an early premature infant.

So far as the function of sight in normal prenatal life is concerned, there has been general agreement that the absence of radiation of the sort that typically activates the retina makes true sight all but impossible in prenatal life (Preyer, 1885, p. 483). The possibility does exist that under very strong light stimulation, if the head were in just the right place, radiation falling on the mother's abdomen might stimulate the fetal retina, but this seems most unlikely. There is evidence, however, given by Kussmaul (1859, p. 26) that pronounced differences between light and dark bring about specific reactions in an infant born two months before term. Peterson and Rainey (1910, p. 118) also found light reactions in premature infants. Genzmer (1882, p. 21) does not confirm this observation. Preyer (1885, p. 485) agrees that adequate stimuli are impossible during fetal life, but he considers the possibility that inadequate stimuli of pressure similar to the stimuli which bring about phosphenes might be effective in prenatal life.

There is evidence that even at normal birth the optic nerve and related structures have not fully developed anatomically (Pratt, Nelson, and Sun, 1930, pp. 44–51). This knowledge has led to speculation in regard to the neural basis of the development of eye muscle function in neonatal life. This whole question has been considered by Preyer (1882, p. 71) in relation to the nativistic and empiristic theories of the visual spatial world, with the conclusion that the evidence is conflicting.

The writer has taken a few records of the eye movements of human babies, using the electrical recording method. The movements in these cases were induced by placing the baby's head in a large rotating drum on which there were striations. The results of these experiments showed that it was possible to elicit optokinetic nystagmus in early infants. This technique may also be used as an objective means of determining lower brightness and color vision thresholds in normal or premature newborn infants.

One of the best indices of the sensitivity of the fetus to light, although possibly not to the full neural mechanism involved in true visual responses, is thought to be the onset of the light-stimulated pupillary reflex. Portal (1818) alleged that responses of the iris diaphragm did not appear during fetal life. Hess (1922, p. 75) and others, however, have recently shown that in premature infants strong light stimulus leads to contraction of the pupil, followed in two or three seconds by dilation again. Bolaffio and Artom (1924, p. 476) and Minkowski (1928a, p. 558), as noted above, have been unable to make unequivocal statements about light reflexes in late fetuses. As pointed out in another part of this chapter, care must be exercised, especially when strong light is used, not to confuse the independent non-neurally determined muscular response of the iris to light with the true iris reflex. The development of the pupillary response in postnatal life has been summarized by Peiper (1928, pp. 11–13).

Much of the evidence in regard to the general muscular movements of the eyes in the first days of life has been summarized by Pratt, Nelson, and Sun (1930, pp. 44 ff.). Early eye movements have been carefully studied in the newborn child by Sherman and Sherman (1925). As already noted above, however, there is excellent evidence to show that during fetal life eye movements occur as part of the general tonus change of the body musculature resulting from the spatial reorientation of the entire fetal body. (See Carmichael, 1940b.) Preyer (1882) and many students since his time have discussed the development of function in the auxiliary musculature of the eye, including the mechanism of winking. In general, great differences are noted in the tonus and general behavior of the lids in the newborn child as contrasted with those of the older child. Some hints of the beginning of this development are to be found in the reports on fetal development given by Minkowski. In a fetus of only 160 mm. he found that touching the closed eyelid led to a contraction of the orbicularis muscle (1922, p. 723).

So far as infrahuman organisms are concerned, there is the greatest divergence from type to type in respect to the time of the opening of the eyes. The subject was early investigated, Emmert, one of the first students of fetal mammals, having studied this phenomenon in the mouse (Emmert and Burgätzy, 1818). Certainly no generalizations can be made from form to form in regard to eyelid activities at the time of birth. The guinea pig is born with eyes open and apparently in an adult functional condition, whereas the lids of the rat do not gain their adult condition until the sixteenth or seventeenth postnatal day (Lane, 1917, p. 69). Warkentin and Smith (1937) and Warkentin (1938) have studied the development of a number of visual functions by various techniques in developing animals. (See also Mowrer, 1936, for a general consideration of learning versus maturation in this field.)

In conclusion: Concerning vision in the fetus it can be said that the specific morphological changes that lie behind the development of the visual mechanism occur from possibly the second week after fertilization until well after birth. Light stimuli at intense levels ordinarily do not affect the retina before birth, but in the case of premature infants it can be shown that the eye is probably sufficiently structurally developed before birth to make possible the light or iris reflex and the differentiation between light and dark. The functional development of the neuromuscular apparatus of the eye is also gradual. Indications have been obtained in regard to the relationship between vestibular stimulation and eye movements before birth which suggest that vestibular control is more primitive than visual control. Eyelid reactions are also found to undergo a progressive series of changes before normal birth.

The Senses in General Relationship to the Onset of Mental Life in the Prenatal Period

For the psychologist there are at least two major problems connected with the study of the senses. The first of these is the classic problem of the relationship between the senses and what the philosophers have long called conscious experience. The second is the relationship between receptor activity and the initiation, modification, and control of behavior. Many psychologists, on the basis of some excellent reasons, hold that ultimately these two problems reduce to one, as Langfeld (1931) and others have urged in the interpretation of consciousness in terms of response. Historically, however, and indeed at the present time, the two problems are ordinarily treated as separate, or at any rate as separable. Some prefer to say that consciousness and behavior are aspects of the total functional description of the relationship between the adult or immature human organism and its environment. Here, although no attempt will be made to find an ultimate answer to the question as to whether these problems are really one or two, they will be treated as independent.

A study of the fetal senses contributes little to our knowledge of the so-called introspective psychology of consciousness. There has been some speculation concerning sensory experience before birth, but little of scientific validity has been written. As incidentally noted above, several of the empiristic philosophers concerned themselves with prenatal life. John Locke (1849 edition) did not neglect the possibility that some dim ideas were present before birth. Cabanis (Genzmer, 1882) held that quite elaborate sensory experiences were present in the fetus, even to the consciousness of self. (Cf. Compayré, 1896, p. 40.) Kussmaul (1859, p. 36) held that the child came into the world with a dim perception of an outer world. Preyer (1882, p. 177) also attributed experience of a sort to the fetus. Peterson and Rainey (1910, p. 121) say, "The newborn comes into the world with a small store of experience and associated feelings and a shadowy consciousness."

Such observations could be added to by other excerpts from early psychologists, but on the whole they seem profitless. Compayré (1896, p. 44), almost fifty years ago, summarized the scientific arguments against such speculations as well as against the fancies of the Neo-Platonists that "our birth is but a sleep and a forgetting." The gist of his argument is that there can be no evidence on the matter. With this point of view the writer is in accord.

James (1890) and, more recently, Koffka (1924) and his associates have made much of the fact that in early postnatal life specific experiences, like specific acts of behavior, become individuated out of totalities rather than at first synthesized out of discrete elements. Thus James (1890, Vol. I, p. 488) says: "The baby, assailed by eyes, ears, nose, skin, and entrails at once, feels it all as one great blooming, buzzing confusion." And again (p. 487): "Our original sensible totals are, on the one hand, subdivided by discriminative attention, and, on the other, united with other totals." Koffka (1924, p. 131) similarly asserts: "From an unlimited and ill-defined background there has arisen a limited and somewhat definite phenomenon, a quality." Certainly if these descriptions are adequate to the experiential life of the neonate, there is no reason to suppose that they may not also be adequate, although possibly in a still vaguer form, to conscious fetal life. If the writer were asked to make a guess in regard to the matter, he would say that he feels that the description given above by Koffka is probably relatively adequate as a description of the development of fetal conscious experience.

It must be noted, however, that so far as the writer is able to determine, there is no way to prove or disprove such a surmise. Consciousness of a particular sort must in such cases be assumed from the external observation of the structure and function of an organism in a particular setting. The fetus is of course quite unable itself to give linguistic introspective reports. The general method of introspection as a scientific tool has been severely criticized during the last quarter of a century, and certainly, if the general method is open to objection, the so-called method of indirect introspection is even more vulnerable. But it is only the latter method which may be used in fetal life. As Washburn (1926), one of the ablest exponents of the use of indirect introspection in animal psychology, has said:

> We know not where consciousness begins in the animal world. We know where it surely resides—in ourselves; we know where it exists beyond a reasonable doubt —in those animals of structure resembling ourselves which rapidly adapt themselves to the lessons of experience. Beyond this point, for all we know, it may exist in simpler and simpler forms until we reach the very lowest of living beings (p. 33).

So far as the writer is concerned, there is no objection to applying to ontogeny, that is, growth in the individual, a point of view similar to that expressed above in regard to the growth of consciousness in the development of the animal series. Such judgments must be treated as complex inferences, however, and not as facts of observation.

The second large problem which concerns the psychologist in relation to receptor activity has grown out of the approach to the study of mental life which deals explicitly with the processes of behavior. The problem of the receptor or, possibly better, of stimulus control of behavior is, however, much older than the so-called school of behaviorism. Kussmaul (1859, p. 6) explicitly defended this view in undertaking his study of premature and normal newborn infants. It is related to a much more general position, as is the view expressed by Forel and quoted by Canestrini (1913, p. 100): "Das wahre Baumateriel der Organismen liefern die Reize der Aussenwelt."

It certainly seems more and more certain that, whatever else scientific psychology may do, it must concern itself increasingly with the relationship between the environment external to the receptors, be they exteroceptors, interoceptors, or proprioceptors, and to the responses of the organism to such stimulation. In any consideration of fetal psychology, therefore, especial attention should be given to the facts of the stimulus control of behavior. In order to understand this relationship, it will be necessary to review the current status of fact and theory in regard to the causes underlying the beginning and differentiation of activity in the fetal organism. This consideration may well serve as a conclusion to this chapter, because any such discussion will necessarily involve a review of many of those processes of fetal life which are even inferentially significant for general psychology. For an excellent consideration of this general field see Hooker (1942).

In the beginning of this chapter, something was said of the early processes of morphogenesis in the developing organism. It was suggested that the point should be kept continually in view by one who is interested in behavioral development, that the general growth of structure and function always occurs in an organism that is in an environment. Organisms do not live or grow in a physical or biological vacuum. From the first cell division in the developing individual, each process of structural and functional modification is, moreover, to be considered as a complex resultant of activities. Some of these determinants are intrinsic in the cell and are, indeed, in the correct sense of the term hereditary, but such intrinsic determinants always act in a dynamic system which is also subjected to extrinsic influences. Development is apparently always a resultant of these two sets of forces working *interdependently*. For some of the evidence on this matter, see earlier papers by the writer (1925, 1938). Sharp (1926) summarizes this point of view when he says in his consideration of general cytology:

> The cell should not be thought of as a static . . . structure. It is rather a dynamic system in a constantly changing state of molecular flux, its constitution at any given moment being dependent upon antecedent states and upon environmental conditions (p. 58).

If space permitted a review of the present status of that part of scientific embryology which is devoted to developmental mechanics, it would become apparent that the process of growth in the organism involves a most complex series of energy relationships, some of which, it seems probable, have as yet only begun to be unraveled. It is certainly true, however, that, at least since the work in the latter part of the last century by Roux (1896), the older static view of development based on the study of dead histological material has gradually given way to the modern notion of an *Entwicklungsmechanik*. For an evaluation of this change, consult Morgan (1927) and Holt (1931, pp. 8–23). As suggested above in regard to the cell, this study has shown that the process of development in one sense, at any rate, must apparently be considered a dynamic organization of a system of energies. This view of the development of an active organism makes it apparent that growth is not to be thought of as a mere unfolding of preformed materials, but rather as the construction of a new pattern of organized systems and subsystems in protoplasm.

Each such system is to be understood only in its particular environment. As Dürken (1929, pp. 109–113) has well said: "Die Entwicklung ist keine einfache Entfaltung, sondern eine wirkliche Neubildung. . . ." And again: "Kurz gesagt, ist daher an der Allgemeingültigkeit des epigenetischen Charakters des Entwicklungsprozesses nicht zu zweifeln."

Many similar statements, and the elaborate evidence upon which they are based, could be found in the rich experimental work of the modern students of developmental mechanics. In such a view, however, it is of course possible, starting with the energy relationships between the organism and its environment, to go beyond the established facts. Whether or not this has been done by Child is difficult for the writer to judge. The following quotation from that student of the physiological development of the nervous system, however, indicates that it is possible for an experimental biologist to consider the external energy relationships of the organism as of the greatest significance in determining development. Child (1921) makes this very definite when he says:

> The organism represents an order and unity in protoplasm which is related at every point to the external world. The development and evolution of organismic integration are essentially the evolution of mechanisms and methods of response and adjustment to environmental conditions (p. 7).

This investigator has developed, on the basis of much experimental work, a concept of various sorts of gradients in the living and developing organism. In certain respects these gradients may in the last analysis be thought of as energy relationships, which are embryologically often precursors of definite organ systems. In so far as the nervous system is concerned, he says:

. . . the reflex strictly speaking is a specialized behavior pattern depending on the presence of certain morphological mechanisms; but it is physiologically a development from the primary organismic behavior mechanism, the excitation gradient (1924, p. 235).

It may well be, of course, that the relationships between the series of events occurring in the organism and the series of events occurring outside the organism are more elaborate than would be suggested by a relationship "at every point"; that is, that some such view as the "organizer" of Spemann (1927) may supplement the simple intrinsic-extrinsic relationship by what may be essentially a chemical process or other process occurring in time and intrinsic in the organism. Whatever the details of this development may be, however, it seems relatively sure, as the work of many investigators seems to demonstrate, that there is, antecedent to the possibility of functional action in the differentiated nervous system, an elaborate series of processes in the organism some of which involve what are, to the elements of the system, environmental forces. An hypothesis concerning the relationship between a primitive gradient of activity and the beginning and development of true nervous structures and functions has been made especially clear by Coghill (1929a, pp. 39–78). This point of view emphasizes, as Burnham (1917) has well pointed out, that environmental stimulation which is basic in an understanding of adult psychological phenomena is itself in certain respects, at any rate, significant in determining the mechanisms which make such adult responses possible.

In this connection the work of Kappers (1917) and Bok (1917) on the functional activity of neuroblasts in the development of the elements and the relationships of the central nervous system may be mentioned. The theory of neurobiotaxis developed by these writers, which suggests that the growth and arrangements of the nervous components are tropistically determined responses of the elements of the nervous system, has proved to be one of the valuable hypotheses in describing the experimental embryology of the nervous system. The contributions of Ingvar (1920) and others to this point of view are summarized by Child (1921, 1924) and Herrick (1924, pp. 111–112). The brilliant work of Detwiler (1920, 1921, 1922, 1923a, 1923b) and other experimental embryologists on the morphology and energetics of neural development also presents specific evidence on the relationship between external and intrinsic factors in the development of the functional nervous system. For a whole picture of cell activity in the living organism, the reader should consult Gerard (1940).

There seems, therefore, to be excellent evidence for the view elsewhere discussed by the writer (1925) at greater length that, from the moment that growth has begun in the fertilized ovum until senescence or death, development consists in the alteration of existing structures and functions in an organism living in a continually changing environment. It cannot be overemphasized that there is both an external and an internal environment. As elsewhere noted in this chapter, the alterations which take place in the chemistry of the blood stream which supplies the central nervous system are fundamental in altering the way in which this system responds to the afferent neural impulses which come in from its receptors.

In the question of behavior change, it is not possible save for pragmatic reasons to say at any point that growth has stopped and learning has begun, but that the environment plays a part in all "maturation," and maturation plays a part in all learning. The course of this development, however, is apparently almost infinitely complex. It cannot be summarized by any catchword phrase. It does seem, however, that the suggestion made in the introduction to this chapter that even the first receptor-neuromuscular response of the organism is not to be considered in all respects a novel event follows directly from the knowledge that the organism develops in relation to an environment of energies. The processes which have gone on in the organism in order that the first response can occur apparently themselves involve elaborate stimulus-response relationships in narrower environments. Thorndike (1931) has picturesquely said that the life processes of a neuron include (1) eating, (2) excreting waste, (3) growing, (4) being sensitive, conducting, and discharging, and (5) movement. "The neuron thus lives much as would an amoeba or paramecium which had been differentiated to make conduction its special trade and which had become fixed immovably save for a few extremities here and there" (p. 57).

A similar portrait could be drawn of the other cells of the developing response mechanism. Thus it seems probable that the first activity of the total neural arc must be thought of as both old and new. The processes of change that are involved are similar to the processes of its growth in certain respects, but when total activity results, new time relations, if not new polarities, are involved. Thus in a sense an "organismic" response emerges from more discrete and primitive activities. But the function is to be understood completely only if described in terms of the past history of the total mechanism concerned and of the present stimulating situation.

This distinction between *part function* and *total function* which causes so much confusion in biology and psychology is clearly illustrated in the known facts of

peripheral nerve regeneration. Sherrington (1922) points out that, when a previously cut nerve is regenerated, what is developed in the nerve, so far as the adaptive
function of the total arc is concerned, is
useless until total regeneration and end
organ attachment are completed. But of
course the processes of development are
themselves functions of the growing cells
and the specific environment of these re-
generating cells. Thus the eventual emergence of the so-called property of total
arc conduction is in one sense not a saltatory change. So far as the functions of
the protoplasmic patterns are concerned,
it may be said that they involve a novel
temporal and spatial organization of processes that have occurred in other energy
relationships during previously described
stages, but, from another point of view,
with the completed nerve comes a most
important and wholly novel emergence of
total function. For a suggestion of some
of the many factors involved in such development, see Goldstein (1904, 1939).

It seems to the writer, therefore, that
the fact that cells and tissues do not develop in isolation, as Irwin (1932b, p. 194)
points out in an excellent summary of the
so-called *organismic hypothesis* of development, does not necessarily mean, as the
same writer asserts, that the "nervous system is a complex dynamic organization
which operates as a whole." On the contrary, it seems to suggest that the story
of the development of behavior must be
written not in any generalized formulae
but in terms of the development of minute
specific processes, no matter how diffuse
or particularized, occurring in individual
organisms under definitely described environmental conditions.

The discussion in the last few paragraphs
has been presented to prepare the way for
the consideration of the psychological aspects of the stimulus control of behavior.

In the course of the study of the onset of
receptor-neuroeffector behavior, many suggestions have been made for the cause of
these first acts. The writer can see no
reason to believe that all the diverse causal
factors suggested are necessarily mutually
exclusive, in spite of some assertions to that
effect. Indeed, it seems that so far as the
onset of behavior in the fetus is concerned,
the *fallacy of the single cause* has been
peculiarly in evidence. As Jennings (1930)
well says:

> This fallacy is the commonest error of
> science, making unsound a considerable
> proportion of its conclusions. Everywhere
> there is a search for "the" cause of this
> or that phenomenon; the investigator is
> not content until he has found "it." Yet
> natural phenomena—and most emphati-
> cally is this true of biological phenomena—
> merely arise out of the complex situation
> in which they occur. Many elements of
> that situation affect them; and all that ex-
> perimental science can do is to determine
> what difference is made by altering one or
> more of these elements; none is "the"
> cause to the exclusion of the others (p.
> 208).

In this chapter, therefore, an effort is
made to summarize some of the many scientific facts and some of the theories which
relate to the onset and development of
early behavior in organisms. Here no attempt is made to arrive at one single conclusion, unless that conclusion is that the
onset of behavior is most complexly determined.

Fundamental in the writings of most
students who have concerned themselves
with early development of behavior is the
view that the nervous system is basic to
the observed responses of the organism.
As we have seen above, this view was implicit even in Dante's speculation on the
onset of behavior in the fetus. Each advance in the knowledge of the true func-

tion of the nervous system has indirectly influenced the thought of those who are concerned with the early development of function in the fetus.

The details of the specific neural changes necessary for the onset and development of behavior have, however, been diversely dealt with. Some students, such as Coghill, although not neglecting other factors, emphasize above all else the anatomical relationships in the nervous system of the organisms under consideration as the determiner of behavior. The following quotation from Coghill (1929a) in regard to the neural basis of behavior in *Amblystoma* may be considered typical of this anatomical tendency. It also gives a fair picture of what is at once one of the simplest and one of the most adequately studied of all the neural mechanisms subtending behavior:

> There are therefore in this non-motile *Amblystoma* both sensory and motor nerves in contact with their respective organs, the sensory field on the one hand and the muscles on the other, but the anatomical relations between these systems are such that an excitation cannot pass from the sensory to the motor mechanism. The muscles, while contracting in response to a mechanical stimulus applied directly to them, do not respond to stimuli from the skin, either tactile or chemical. Even when dropped into slowly-acting fixing solution, embryos of this stage do not give any evidence of muscular excitation.
>
> With the ability to respond to tactile or chemical stimulation of the skin there appears a third series of cells. They bridge the gap between the sensory system of one side and the motor system of the other. . . . Their bodies lie in the floor plate of the medulla oblongata and upper part of the spinal cord. . . . In the nonmotile stage these cells are unipolar. The one pole of the cell extends either to the right or to the left into close relation with the motor tract on one side only. When

they become bipolar they complete the path from the sensory field to the muscle; and this path leads to the muscles of the opposite side from the stimulus because the conductors from the sensory field pass across the motor path of the same side to establish synapses with the dendrites of the commissural cells in the floor plate . . . (pp. 11–13).

A similar but usually much less completely worked out neural picture could be presented for many of the organisms the development of whose behavior has been considered above. For example, the anatomy of the nervous system of the fetal rat in relation to its behavior has been studied in quite elaborate detail by Angulo y González (1927, 1928, 1929b, 1930c), and this type and many others by Windle (1940) and his associates. But the development of neural structure alone may not explain fully the onset of behavior in any type.

Minkowski (1923; 1928a, pp. 548–556), himself primarily a neurologist, has given in great detail the neural mechanisms which he believes underlie the changes he has observed in the clinically significant reflexes initiated in human fetuses by the stimulation of the sole of the foot.

Although there is almost complete agreement that the nervous system is significant in the onset and development of mammalian behavior, it must be admitted that there is not complete agreement as to the detailed factors of this development. One of the most commonly held views in regard to the basis of functional activity in the nervous system asserts that there is a differing threshold at the synaptic junctures existing between neurons. Sherrington and his associates (Creed, Denny-Brown, Eccles, Liddell, and Sherrington, 1932, pp. 14–15) have reviewed the evidence for such a view, and both Herrick (1924, pp. 103–111) and R. S. Lillie (1932) have dealt with special phenomena basic to an understanding of the synapse. Holt (1931, pp. 24–29) has shown that, in his view at any rate, this theory is adequate, when correctly understood, to explain the complexities of neural-embryonic development, particularly when it is supported by a correct understanding of the functional development summarized in the theory of neurobiotaxis. Lashley (1924) and Irwin (1932a), on the contrary, have raised a number of objections to the synapse, particularly as *the* one and only explanatory factor in the change of behavior. Certainly one must always remember that, in attributing anything to the synapse, one is referring to a *concept* which has been elaborated in part from behavioral data. The danger of a circular argument in "explaining" behavior by the synapse should be remembered. Other views, such as that of nerve fiber density in the spinal gray matter in relation to behavior, have been suggested. (See Windle, 1930b.)

Since the time of Flechsig, there has been a tendency on the part of many neuroanatomists to link myelinogeny, that is, the development of the myelin sheath of neurons, with the onset of differentiated behavior. Flechsig in his later publications even attempted to correlate the degree of myelinization with increase in the complexity of behavior and indeed with psychic life. Tilney and Casamajor (1924), Langworthy (1929), and other students have attempted to show the correlation between myelinization in the central nervous system and the onset of behavior in the newborn and fetal cat, opossum, and other forms. For the most part these investigators point out that this theory must be taken as specific to the particular function and to the particular type considered. Tilney, however, once made the statement in very general terms: "I think there can be no doubt as to the coincidence in the

time of myelinization and the establishment of function." (See also Tilney and Kubie, 1931.)

There is, however, evidence of exceptions to this generalization. Probably it is no longer safe, however, to say of this "myelinogenetic law," as Thorndike did (1913, p. 229) on the basis of the experiments of Watson (1903) and others, that it seems "gratuitous and improbable." The evidence for the relationship of myelin and function does not show it as the only cause of the onset of behavior. As Angulo y González (1929a) has shown: "From the point of view of myelinogeny, our studies have proved that myelination is not necessary for function, since all the movements described by Doctor Swenson and by myself in the rat fetus occur many days before myelination could be observed" (p. 461). This same author objects to the observations on behavior made by Tilney and Casamajor, believing that the movements which they observed were really established long before the time at which they were described and hence well before the myelinization which they report. Angulo y González (1929a), moreover, finds that a rat fetus, nineteen days after insemination, is capable of discrete reflexes and of showing the inhibitory action of higher centers.

These discrete reflexes, which are specific to a given stimulation, demonstrate a selectivity in the conducting mechanism. Since myelination does not take place until several days after birth, this observation proves that physiological insulation of the conduction path occurs without myelination, and, therefore, that myelination is not a criterion of functional insulation (p. 461).

Windle, Fish, and O'Donnell (1934) have studied the relationship between myelinogeny and the onset of behavior in cat fetuses. They conclude that myelinization in the animals studied is not cor related with function. Myelinization may be considered a consequence of the order of appearance of neurons in the embryo. (See also Langworthy, 1927, 1932.) There are other theories of development besides that of myelinization. For example, following the lead of Paton (1907, 1911) and other investigators, Lane (1917, pp. 15–21) held that the onset of behavior is specifically related to the anatomical development of the neurofibrillae. This investigator advances an elaborate series of arguments to show that the neurofibrillae are possibly to be thought of as the essential basis of functional activity in the nervous system.

> If therefore an absolutely conclusive answer cannot now be given to the question of the function of the neurofibrillae, it is most probable, in the light of our present knowledge in this field, that the power of conducting nerve-impulses lies rather in the neurofibrillae than elsewhere. At any rate, the presence of neurofibrillae may be taken as an indicator, a criterion of the functional state of the neurons . . . (p. 21).

After definitely accepting this view, Lane explains the fact that after the neurofibrillae have developed, before the are can become functional, it is necessary that the receptor develop (pp. 14, 79). In each of the senses he believes that function must wait for the development of the end organ, and that this is the last link to be connected up in the chain between effective environmental stimulation and response. In all the explanations which he offers for the development of this system, he emphasizes intrinsic rather than extrinsic factors (p. 84). In this he is seconded by Avery (1928), who concludes, without further explaining the matter, that fetal behavior is, in part at any rate, caused by and dependent upon "certain response mecha-

nisms which are definitely congenital or innate" (p. 324). Certainly in the general sense of these terms few today will disagree with this conclusion, but it is not an observation which advances "functional knowledge."

Windle (1930a), in studying the spinal cord development of cat embryos 17.5 mm. to 18.5 mm. long in which the first movement—"wormlike, total waves proceeding caudad from an indefinite point in the neck region"—had been observed, notes:

> Pyridine-silver preparations of these embryos demonstrate the neurofibrillar structure of the central nervous system. Primitive reflex arcs are distinguishable, afferent, association, commissural, and efferent neurons appearing in proper relationship to each other. . . .
> The earliest movements appear in regions where primitive reflex arcs were first distinguishable and not until some time after these have formed (p. 249).

(See also Windle, 1931, 1932.) Herrick (1924), in referring to neurofibrils, says: "They are commonly regarded as the essential conductors of the nervous impulse, but of this there is no direct evidence" (p. 108).

Certain physiologists assert that neural functions and indeed the capacities of the adult organism are related primarily to the time relationships of the neuron (Lapicque, 1926). Or, even more generally, it has been suggested that the facts of the activity of the peripheral nerve fiber, as developed by Adrian, his predecessors, and his associates, may be basic to some aspects of the differentiation and specificity of behavior. For a brilliant exposition of this view, see Erlanger and Gasser (1937). Forbes wrote an article, "The Interpretation of Spinal Reflexes in Terms of the Present Knowledge of Nerve Conduction" (1922), in which the suggestion is tentatively made that specificity of behavior and "the evolution of the dominant activities of man" (p. 414) may be thought of as being determined in a system the essential characteristics of which are to be found in a knowledge of the facts of the nervous impulse as it is seen in peripheral nerve fibers. P. Weiss (1926) has studied this relationship from a different and more revolutionary physiological point of view which may well contain within it basic suggestions concerning the onset of those neural activities which make behavior possible.

It is clear that the increasingly detailed knowledge of the specific structure and function of the receptors, the peripheral nervous system, and the various levels of the central nervous system, particularly in regard to the relationships between these processes as brought out by Sherrington and his pupils (Creed, Denny-Brown, Eccles, Liddell, and Sherrington, 1932), must be ultimately taken into consideration in an explanation of the onset and early development of behavior. As indicated many times above, however, this view is almost certainly to be considered in relation to the changes of the chemical make-up of the whole internal environment of the organism.

Pankratz (1930) has suggested that the onset of behavior is in time, at any rate, related to the beginning of functional action of the secretion of the suprarenal medulla, which possibly causes "an increase in the irritability of the muscular or neuromuscular system, and thus facilitates the beginning of foetal movements" (p. 235). He (1931a) believes that he has experimentally demonstrated in newborn organisms, including man, that there is a temporal correlation between the onset of functional activity in this gland and the first responses of the growing organism.

Possibly more fundamental than this speculation is the now widely accepted view of the chemical mediation of nerve impulses. Certain aspects of this work have been summarized by Cannon and Rosenblueth (1937). According to this point of view, synaptic function may in certain reflex systems be mediated by acetylcholine or in other systems by an adrenaline-like substance. Kuo (1939a) has demonstrated the presence of acetylcholine in the chick embryo at the time of the onset of motility, and others have also suggested its significance in the mammalian fetus. Nachmansohn (1940) has shown that in the sheep high concentration of choline esterase appears in different parts of the central nervous system at different periods of development. Choline esterase is an enzyme which rapidly alters acetylcholine. Choline esterase is present in the spinal cord in high concentrations between the sixtieth and the eightieth days of gestation, but at that time its concentration in the brain is low. It rises rapidly in the higher centers just before birth, however. These results are in agreement with the activity of the centers involved. Youngstrom (1941) has determined the acetylcholine esterase concentration in typical fetal organisms. This study shows a significant relationship between developing motility and the concentration of choline esterase. A fully satisfactory explanation has not yet, however, been found for the occurrence of greater concentrations of choline esterase in fetal than in adult tissues.

The results just referred to are but a few indications of the modern emphasis on various forms of internal environmental change as related to the onset of activity in the organism. It has become obvious to many investigators that the movements of respiration, as well as other rhythmic movements known to be brought about or facilitated by a "blood stimulus," are important in a total understanding of behavior. For example, it has been reported that the asphyxia of the mother brought about definite movements in a very early fetus (Kussmaul, 1859, p. 31). Preyer (1885) was before his time in considering this problem, as in so many other ways. He considers the importance of the blood condition in connection with fetal movements on the basis of experiments in which he interfered with the normal respiration of the adult animal (p. 417). As already indicated, Ahlfeld and most of the other students of premature breathing movements have considered the "blood stimulus" to be significant. This sort of activation is also especially considered in the work of Zuntz (1877), T. G. Brown (1915), E. A. Graham (1913–1915), Walz (1922), and Tracy (1926), most of which has been previously reviewed.

Tracy (1926), as explained above, well combines the views of the importance of stimulation and the importance of the development of the nervous system in the determination of the onset of behavior in larval organisms. Thus he says:

> . . . The behavior reactions displayed by embryos and larvae of different species at different stages of development are dependent upon the relative time at which efficient connections are established between the various elements of the early nervous system (primitive bilateral motor system, commissural elements, spinal-ganglion cells, Rohn-Beard cells, and receptors) (p. 357).

But he also points out, as noted above, that:

> From the beginning, and more or less continuously during its whole existence, the animal is driven through its environment as a result of stimuli which arise periodically in connection with its metabolic processes (p. 345).

Barcroft (1938) shows on the basis of elaborate experimental work that, as Claude Bernard said, the constancy of the environment is the condition of the free life. The work of Barcroft and his school, indeed, throws doubt upon many experiments in fetal behavior which have been done without continually checking the oxygen tension and other characteristics of the fetal blood. In spite of this vast store of information upon the nature of fetal and maternal blood, it is interesting to note that Barcroft does not make a final judgment concerning the part of the internal environment in the initiation of behavior (1936). He points out that in a typical reflex the external stimulus is important, and because of the changing cortical oxygenation of blood the center is also important. Thus the two sets of factors should be considered together. Barcroft (1938) does point out, however, that:

> The higher centers await investigation on modern lines; at present there is nothing to be said about them except what is rather obvious, namely, that the foetus of the sheep even up to birth presents few if any signs of consciousness. Within a few minutes of birth . . . the lamb lifts its head and tries to get up. It is plainly awake, and may be sent to sleep once more either by cold or by reducing the amount of oxygen in the blood. These matters must await further investigation; but it is evident that the higher faculties need a higher tension oxygen supply than those of a more vegetative nature (p. 67).

Changes in temperature, oxygen, carbon dioxide, glucose, water, sodium, calcium, and other substances are known as they alter the internal environment to have a part in the changes which result in behavior. These all no doubt contribute to alterations in fetal behavior. (See Carmichael, 1940a, p. 136, and Barcroft and Mason, 1938.)

Sontag (1941) has suggested some important considerations on the significance of fetal environmental differences. He believes that drugs used by women during pregnancy, their nutrition, endocrine status, and even emotional life, may be important in the postnatal life of the children they bear.

Newbery, Pyle, and Champnëy (1943) have attempted a quantitative study of the ability of mothers to rate the fetal environment in respect to thirteen factors during pregnancy.

Besides such students as Barcroft, who emphasize both the internal and external environment, there are some who emphasize the rôle of the intensity of external stimulation in the onset and development of behavior without much reference to the neural basis of such behavior. Kuo is in certain respects an exponent of such a view. He says:

> . . . As has been previously stated, I am inclined to think that to explain the total behavior pattern in terms of neural anatomy (that is, in terms of certain special connections between neurons) seems unnecessary or far-fetched, since all the neurons in the nervous system are interconnected in some way, and since body parts without direct neural connections may also move together, as in the case of the synchronous movement of the tail with the beak and eyes (1932e, p. 511).

The neurological-minded reader of the above paragraph is probably struck at first by the question of how, if the assertion is true, the observed differentiation in behavior is to be explained. Kuo offers the explanation that local reflexes are determined in part by external environmental influences. In the case of the chick he has ingeniously made many observations, some of which have been presented above, to show that in the fetal organism, growing in a rigidly shell-defined environment, cer-

tain mechanical influences interfere with the ease of general movement. For example, as development goes on, head movements come to be interfered with mechanically by the yolk sac, and thus he explains the fact that partial head movements, such as those of the beak, occur in the head region. Kuo (1939a, 1939b) has, as noted above, more recently emphasized other concomitant functions such as the part of acetylcholine in the onset and early development of behavior.

On the basis of elaborate experiments, Lashley (1929) and his predecessors have shown that there was much misunderstanding in regard to the absolute specificity of central nervous system elements which subtend behavior, particularly in the higher centers. (See also bibliography cited by Lashley, 1929.) Lashley's work and the work of many other students make clear that no single brain neuron is probably ever functionally absolutely isolated and that the reflex arc is never so simple as the elementary textbooks a generation ago showed it to be. Indeed, Lashley's brilliant experimental work has revolutionized many of the older conceptions of the specificity of the arcs in the higher centers of mammals.

From these discoveries, however, there is much question as to whether or not such writers as Irwin (1932b) are justified in suggesting that "the early form of activity, with its lack of mature specificity and the presence of so few effective coordinations or reaction patterns, probably points to an organismic rather than to a reflex chain theory of behavior." The writer has no wish to disagree with this statement, save only to point out that the "cell theory" and the "reflex theory" that are usually attacked by "organismic" writers are in most such criticisms truly "men of straw." All that has gone before in this chapter seems to suggest that the explanation of behavior will hardly be advanced by saying that the nervous system "operates as a whole." Unquestionably, in the human fetus as in the human adult there are functions which can never be understood in isolation, but only by looking at the *totality* of processes, but totality alone does not explain the specific long, short, homolateral, and heterolateral skin reflexes, the face, hand, and foot reflexes, the mucous membrane and tendon reflexes, the proprioceptor and static reflexes, and the many other specific responses of the fetus. The fact that an early concept of the reflex arc was inadequate is no reason to assert that there is no truth in the general view that behavior involves discoverable relationships both temporal and anatomical between stimulation and response. Some such responses are more variable and some are more specific than others, but still there are specific patterns of behavior in the growing organism. As Skinner (1931) has effectively said in summary of a paper in which he criticizes current attacks upon the reflex hypothesis:

> The essence of the description of behavior is held to be the determination of functional laws describing the relationship between the forces acting upon, and the movement of, a given system. The reflex is, by definition, the precise instrument for this description (p. 455).

From the paragraphs just given, it is clear that there have been many efforts to explain in simple terms the mechanism which makes the onset of behavior possible. External stimulation is not *alone* important in the development of behavior; nor probably is the change in the synapses, the onset of acetylcholine, or any other factor *alone* the one determinant of all new responses in all organisms at all times. It does seem at present, nevertheless, that so far as the fetus is concerned there can be

little doubt that an adequate explanation of its behavior at every stage in its development must be given in terms of the dynamics of its organization in each specific environment. Such dynamics, however, can be expressed only in terms of as detailed a knowledge of the structures and functions of the organism as possible. Any response can be understood only if it is recognized that it may not be the result alone of the most obvious stimulus that is apparently calling it out, but rather that it may be a resultant of the total interoceptive, proprioceptive, and exteroceptive stimulation of the moment in an organism the chemistry of whose internal environment is known in its often rapidly changing characteristics.

In a final understanding of the sensory control of behavior in fetal life, as complete a knowledge of all such relevant factors as possible is important. Seldom apparently during late fetal life can an exteroceptor be stimulated so as to bring about a response that may not be conditioned also by other internal stimuli which may at the same time be tending to drive the organism "at random." This is particularly true of fetuses such as those studied by Minkowski, Bolaffio and Artom, and Hooker, which during observation are always undergoing more and more complete asphyxiation. As suggested above, it must not be forgotten that it may be that at certain periods of development and in certain physiological states the exteroceptors are best thought of as interrupting and directing behavior that is internally aroused. At such times the "drive" of the fetus may be said to be more important than its "knowledge of the external world." In any case, in a situation of this sort, gradually more and more adaptive behavior develops, which means that the exteroceptors play an increasingly important rôle.

Coghill's well-known formula for behavioral growth is possibly an adaptation of Spencer's famous definition which held evolution to be a passage from "a relatively indefinite incoherent homogeneity to a relatively definite coherent heterogeneity." Coghill taught that his formula has wide if not universal application in the development of behavior in all vertebrates. He (1929c) states it as follows:

> The behavior pattern from the beginning expands throughout the growing normal animal as a perfectly integrated unit, whereas partial patterns arise within the total patterns and, by a process of individuation, acquire secondarily varying degrees of independence. . . . Complexity of behavior is not derived by progressive integration of more and more originally discrete units (p. 989).

On the basis of what has gone before in this chapter, it seems that this process of *individuation* is certainly *one* important means of describing the process of development, but not the only means of describing such development. On the other hand, concomitantly but not necessarily temporally concomitantly, *integration* has long been recognized as a mechanism of behavior development. As Pavlov (1932) has put it in another context, one must consider the "initial decomposition of the whole into its parts or units, and then the gradual reconstruction of the whole from these units or elements" (p. 102).

In terms of a very broad generalization, the writer believes that an excellent case can be made out for the view that *individuation* is the pattern of all development, including all learning, but certainly in the experimental situation the concept of the *integration* or the combination of responses also provides, at times, a convenient working hypothesis. James (1890, Vol. I, p. 487) said that "psychology must be writ *both* in synthetic and in analytic terms." To the writer this seems to give a satisfactory clue to the expedient way of considering the changes in behavior that occur as fetal and neonatal behavior progresses. As we have seen above, certain responses are early individuated, while others are still quite nonspecific.

New relationships between specific responses, as in the development of the plantar reflex, begin to develop before specification has gone far in certain other bodily acts. Each process must be considered at each level if a false generalization is to be avoided. Hooker (1937) has recently analyzed this problem and suggested three possible sequences of development: (1) At first reflexes are nonspecific. (2) At first reflexes are specific. (3) Specific and total reflexes develop simultaneously. He urges the detailed study of behavior to answer these questions. This chapter suggests that all three are possible descriptions of certain responses, but the writer's own experimental work leads him to believe that (2) above should be emphasized much more than has recently been "fashionable." For a consideration of a generalized story of functional development of mammalian neuromuscular mechanisms, see Barron (1941).

Genzmer (1882, p. 28), after reviewing the debated question as to whether or not the newborn child has intelligence, suggests that the observed movements of the early infant are not the result of intelligence but are rather the material out of which the later intelligence is to be built. If the process of development is one of sheer individuation out of a totality, it would seem that statistical studies of early infancy might well show a high degree of what Spearman calls a "general factor." If the techniques used in the studies of Furfey, Bonham, and Sargent (1930) are satisfactory, however, it seems that the opposite is the case. In a study of seventeen responses, such as the plantar and grasping reflexes in newborn children, corrected intercorrelations proved to be zero. These investigators conclude: "These results suggest that there is no mental integration in the newborn child. Integration takes place during the first postnatal month. . . ." Although there are technical questions that may be raised in regard to this study, it certainly seems that, with the use of the same techniques, there is no reason to suppose that the responses of the fetus would show a more general factor than would those of the newborn child.

Minkowski (1924) has considered the part played by the conditioning of reflexes in later development, and certainly the question of the relationship between individuation and integration will be made clearer when it can be said at what ontogenetic level of development true conditioning of responses is possible. Ray (1932) has attempted to condition fetal responses. Spelt (1938), using the auditory response of the fetus described above, has worked on the conditioning of human responses. Marquis (1931), however, has brought about in the newborn child conditioning of the food-taking reaction to the sound of a buzzer. She holds that this may be conditioning at the subcortical level, but in any case it involves what is commonly considered combination rather than individuation of responses. Carmichael (1936) has elsewhere reviewed the work that has been done on early learning in young animals. Here the work of Kasatkin and Levikova (1935a, 1935b) on early conditioning and other studies are reviewed. It is possibly true that at a verbal level all conditioning can be described as individuation, but in such a formulation a generalization of the concept of individuation beyond the point at which it is pragmatically most useful seems required.

It may even be suggested that so-called learning itself always depends upon *maturation* or *growth*. In a trial-and-error sequence the animal must always be able to perform the successful act before learning, that is, the later elimination of maladaptive acts, begins. This same view may even be applied, but less directly, to so-called conditioned response learning. In this connection, see Guthrie (1942).

In general conclusion, then, in regard to the sensory control of behavior in the fetus and in regard to the related processes of the individuation and integration of behavior, it seems that as yet, at any rate, it is better to record as unambiguously as possible the responses that can be made by a fetus at any stage rather than to attempt to fit all developmental change into one formula. It seems to the writer, nevertheless, that the actually recorded facts of this development of behavior in infrahuman and human fetuses have been shown to throw important light upon certain of the insistent problems of psychology. It has been impossible to consider each of these processes in detail in this chapter. It seems, however, that in the later chapters of this book when, in postnatal life, problems of the development of behavior patterns, heredity and environment, the nature of instinct, the development of perception, the continuity or saltatoriness of development, and the nature of learning are considered, it will be obvious that the facts presented in this chapter will always have a bearing on certain aspects of the answers that are given to such problems. As Tracy (1926, p. 253) has suggested, a study of adult behavior without a consideration of its origin before birth is as incomplete as would be the at present unthinkable study of adult anatomy without reference to the embryology of the structures considered.

The student who wishes further study in this field should consult, besides the detailed references given, papers by Hooker (1936, 1939a, 1942, 1943), which summarize much of the work in this field, the summary of the development of behavior by Dewey (1935), and the recent and important book *Physiology of the Fetus: Origin and Extent of Function in Prenatal Life* by Windle (1940).

Bibliography

ABEL, S., and W. F. WINDLE. 1939. Relation of the volume of pulmonary circulation to respiration at birth. *Anat. Rec.*, **75**, 451–464.

ADAIR, F. L. 1918. The ossification centers of the fetal pelvis. *Amer. J. Obstet.*, **78**, 175–199.

AHLFELD, J. F. 1890. Beiträge zur Lehre vom Uebergange der intrauterinen Athmung zur extrauterinen. In *Beiträge zur Physiologie, Festschrift zu Carl Ludwig, zu seinem 70. Geburtstage gewidmet von seinen Schülern*, pp. 1–32. Leipzig: Vogel.

ANGULO Y GONZÁLEZ, A. W. 1927. The motor nuclei in the cervical cord of the albino rat at birth. *J. Comp. Neurol.*, **43**, 115–142.

——. 1928. Preliminary report on the motor-cell columns in the cervical region of the albino rat before birth. *Anat. Rec.*, **38**, 46–47.

——. 1929a. Is myelinogeny an absolute index of behavioral capability? *J. Comp. Neurol.*, **48**, 459–464.

——. 1929b. Neurological interpretation of fetal behavior: The motor-cell columns of the albino rat before birth. (Abs.) *Anat. Rec.*, **42**, 17.

——. 1930a. Endogenous stimulation of albino rat fetuses. *Proc. Soc. Exp. Biol. Med.*, **27**, 579.

——. 1930b. Motion-picture records showing the typical stages in the development of muscular activity in albino-rat fetuses which are used in connection with the corresponding changes in the nervous system. *Anat. Rec.*, **45**, 284.

——. 1930c. Neurological interpretation of fetal behavior: The progressive increase of muscular activity in albino-rat fetuses. (Abs.) *Anat. Rec.*, **45**, 254.

——. 1932a. The prenatal development of behavior in the albino rat. *J. Comp. Neurol.*, **55**, 395–442.

——. 1932b. The prenatal growth of the albino rat. *Anat. Rec.*, **52**, 117–138.

——. 1933a. Development of somatic activity in the albino rat fetuses. *Proc. Soc. Exp. Biol. Med.*, **31**, 111–112.

ANGULO Y GONZÁLEZ, A. W. 1933b. Endogenous stimulation of albino rat fetuses. *Anat. Rec.*, Suppl., **55**, 3.

——. 1934a. Functional dissolution of the nervous system in albino rat fetuses induced by means of asphyxia. *Anat. Rec.*, Suppl., **58**, 45.

——. 1934b. Neurological interpretation of fetal behavior: Structural changes in the nervous system of the albino rat and their relation to behavioral development. *Anat. Rec.*, Suppl., **58**, 2.

——. 1935. Further studies upon development of somatic activity in albino rat fetuses. *Proc. Soc. Exp. Biol. Med.*, **32**, 621–622.

——. 1937. Neurological interpretation of fetal behavior: The development of the sensory system in albino rat. *Anat. Rec.*, Suppl., **67**, 4.

——. 1939. Histogenesis of the monopolar neuroblast and the ventral longitudinal path in the albino rat. *J. Comp. Neurol.*, **71**, 325–359.

——. 1940. The differentiation of the motor-cell columns in the cervical cord of albino rat fetuses. *J. Comp. Neurol.*, **73**, 469–488.

ARENDT. 1910. Wann ist die Perforation des lebenden Kindes notwendig? *Dtsch. med. Presse*, **14**, 167–168.

AVERY, G. T. 1928. Responses of foetal guinea pigs prematurely delivered. *Genet. Psychol. Monogr.*, **3**, 245–331.

BAKER, T. E. 1825. Description of a singularly small child. *Trans. Med. Phys. Soc.*, Calcutta, **1**, 364–365. Also in *Edinburgh New Phil. J.* 1826, October, 398.

——. 1827. Nachricht von einem ausserordentlich kleines Kind. *Z. organ. Physik*, **1**, 260–261.

BALLANTYNE, J. W., and F. J. BROWNE. 1922. The problem of foetal post-maturity and prolongation of pregnancy. *J. Obstet. Gynaec. Brit. Emp.*, **29** (New ser.), 177–238.

BARCROFT, J. 1935. The mammal before and after birth. *Irish J. Med. Sci.*, **1**, 289–301.

——. 1936. Fetal circulation and respiration. *Physiol. Rev.*, **16**, 103–128.

——. 1938. *The brain and its environment.* New Haven: Yale University Press.

BARCROFT, J., and D. H. BARRON. 1936. The genesis of respiratory movements in the foetus of the sheep. *J. Physiol.*, **88**, 56–61.

——. 1937a. The establishment of certain reflex arcs in foetal sheep. *Proc. Soc. Exp. Biol. Med.*, **36**, 86–87.

——. 1937b. Movements in midfoetal life in the sheep embryo. *J. Physiol.*, **91**, 329–351.

——. 1939. The development of behavior in foetal sheep. *J. Comp. Neurol.*, **70**, 477–502.

BARCROFT, J., D. H. BARRON, and W. F. WINDLE. 1936. Some observations on genesis of somatic movements in sheep embryos. *J. Physiol.*, **87**, 73–78.

BARCROFT, J., and M. F. MASON. 1938. The atmosphere in which the foetus lives. *J. Physiol.*, **93**, 22.

BARHAM, W. B. 1915–1916. Maternal impressions. *Va. Med. Semi-mo.*, **20**, 454–459.

BARNUM, C. G. 1915. The effect of gravitation on the presentation and position of the fetus. *J. Amer. Med. Ass.*, **64**, 498–502.

BARRON, D. H. 1934. The results of peripheral anastomoses between the fore and hind limb nerves of albino rats. *J. Comp. Neurol.*, **59**, 301–323.

——. 1940. Recent contributions to the physiology of birth. *Sigma Xi Quart.*, **28**, 127–133.

——. 1941. The functional development of some mammalian neuromuscular mechanisms. *Biol. Rev.*, **16**, 1–33.

BAUER, D. J. 1938. The effect of asphyxia upon the heart rate of rabbits at different ages. *J. Physiol.*, **93**, 90–103.

BECKER, R. F. 1940. Experimental analysis of Kuo vaseline technique for studying behavior development in chick embryos. *Proc. Soc. Exp. Biol. Med.*, **45**, 689–691.

——. 1941. The status of gastro-intestinal activity in utero. *Quart. Bull. Northwestern Univ. Med. School*, **15**, 85 ff.

——. 1942. Experimental analysis of the vaseline technique of Kuo for studying behavioral development in chick embryos. *J. Genet. Psychol.*, **60**, 153–165.

BECKER, R. F., and W. F. WINDLE. 1941. Origin and extent of gastro-intestinal motility in the cat and guinea pig. *Amer. J. Physiol.*, **132**, 297–304.

BECKER, R. F., W. F. WINDLE, E. E. BARTH, and M. D. SCHULZ. 1940. Fetal swallowing, gastro-intestinal activity and defecation in amnio. *Surg. Gynec. Obstet.*, **70**, 603–614.

BÉCLARD, P. A. 1815. Untersuchungen, welche zu beweisen scheinen, das der Fötus das Schafwasser athmet. *Dtsch. Arch. Physiol.*, **2**, 154–155.

BERGSON, H. 1911. *Creative evolution.* (Trans. by A. MITCHELL.) New York: Holt.

BERSOT, H. 1918, 1919. Variabilité et corrélations organiques. Nouvelle étude du réflexe plantaire. *Schweiz. Arch. Neurol. Psychiat.*, **4**, 277–323; **5**, 305–324.

——. 1920, 1921. Développement réactionnel et réflexe plantaire du bébé né avant terme à celui de deux ans. *Schweiz. Arch. Neurol. Psychiat.*, **7**, 212–239; **8**, 47–74.

BICHAT, M. F. X. 1819. *Anatomie générale précédée des récherches physiologiques.* Paris: Brosson, Gabon. 1822. *General anatomy applied to physiology and medicine.* (Trans. by G. HAYWARD.) Boston: Richardson and Lord.

——. 1827. *Physiological researches upon life and death.* (2d Amer. ed., including notes by F. MAGENDIE. Trans. by F. GOLD.) Boston: Richardson and Lord. 1829. *Récherches*

physiologiques sur la vie et le mort. (5th ed.) Paris: Gabon.

BISCHOFF, T. L. W. 1842. *Entwicklungsgeschichte des Kaninchen-Eies.* Brunswick: Vieweg.

BLANTON, M. G. 1917. The behavior of the human infant during the first thirty days of life. *Psychol. Rev.*, **24**, 456–483.

BLINCOE, H. 1928a. Anatomy of the fore limb of the albino rat at approximately the time in fetal life when muscular movements begin. *Anat. Rec.*, **38**, 40.

——. 1928b. The anatomy of the fore limb of the albino rat at approximately the time in fetal life when somatic movement begins. *Anat. Rec.*, **40**, 277–295.

BLUHM, A. 1929. Über einige das Geburtsgewicht der Säugetiere beeinflussende Faktoren. *Arch. Entwicklungsmech. Organ.*, **116**, 348–381.

BOK, S. T. 1917. The development of reflexes and reflex tracts. *Psychiat. Neurol. Bl. Amst.*, **21**, 281–303.

BOLAFFIO, M., and G. ARTOM. 1924. Ricerche sulla fisiologia del sistema nervosa del feto umano. *Arch. sci. biol.*, **5**, 457–487.

BOLK, L. 1926. Vergleichende Untersuchungen an einem Fetus eines Gorillas und eines Schimpansen. *Z. Anat. Entwicklungsgeschichte.*, **81**, 1–89.

BORING, E. G. 1916. Cutaneous sensation after nerve-division. *Quart. J. Exp. Physiol.*, **10**, 1–95.

——. 1929. *A history of experimental psychology.* New York: Century.

BORS, E. 1925. Die Methodik der intrauterinen Operation am überlebenden Säugetierfoetus. *Arch. Entwicklungsmech. Organ.*, **105**, 655–666.

BOWEN, R. E. 1932. The ampullar organs of the ear. *J. Comp. Neurol.*, **55**, 273–313.

BREED, F. S. 1911. The development of certain instincts and habits in chicks. *Behav. Monogr.*, **1**, No. 1. Pp. vi + 178.

BRIDGMAN, C. S., and L. CARMICHAEL. 1935. An experimental study of the onset of behavior in the fetal guinea-pig. *J. Genet. Psychol.*, **47**, 247–267.

BRIFFAULT, R. 1927. *The mothers.* Vol. 1. New York: Macmillan.

BROWN, R. L. 1918. Maternal impressions. *W. Va. Med. J.*, **13**, 86.

BROWN, T. G. 1914. On the nature of the fundamental activity of the nervous centers; together with an analysis of the conditioning of rhythmic activity in progression, and a theory of the evolution of function in the nervous system. *J. Physiol.*, **48**, 18–46.

——. 1915. On the activities of the central nervous system of the unborn foetus of the cat; with a discussion of the question whether progression (walking, etc.) is a "learnt" complex. *J. Physiol.*, **49**, 208–215.

BURNHAM, W. H. 1917. The significance of stimulation in the development of the nervous system. *Amer. J. Psychol.*, **28**, 38–56.

BURR, H. S. 1932. An electro-dynamic theory of development suggested by studies of proliferation rates in the brain of *Amblystoma*. *J. Comp. Neurol.*, **56**, 347–371.

BYLICKI, L. 1921. À la biologie du foetus. *Gynécol. obstet.*, **4**, 541–543.

CAMIS, M. 1930. *The physiology of the vestibular apparatus.* (Trans. by R. S. CREED.) Oxford: Clarendon Press.

CANESTRINI, S. 1913. Über das Sinnesleben des Neugeborenen. (*Monograph Gesamtgeb. Neurol. Psychiat.*, No. 5.) Berlin: Springer. Pp. 104.

CANNON, W. B., and A. ROSENBLUETH. 1937. *Autonomic neuro-effector systems.* New York: Macmillan.

CARLSON, A. J., and H. GINSBURG. 1915. Contributions to the physiology of the stomach: XXIV. The tonus and hunger contractions of the stomach of the new-born. *Amer. J. Physiol.*, **38**, 29–32.

CARMICHAEL, L. 1925. Heredity and environment: Are they antithetical? *J. Abnorm. Soc. Psychol.*, **20**, 245–260.

———. 1926a. The development of behavior in vertebrates experimentally removed from the influence of external stimulation. *Psychol. Rev.*, **33**, 51–58.

———. 1926b. Sir Charles Bell: A contribution to the history of physiological psychology. *Psychol. Rev.*, **33**, 188–217.

———. 1927. A further study of the development of behavior in vertebrates experimentally removed from the influence of external stimulation. *Psychol. Rev.*, **34**, 34–47.

———. 1928. A further experimental study of the development of behavior. *Psychol. Rev.*, **35**, 253–260.

———. 1929. The experimental study of the development of behavior in vertebrates. *Proc. Papers 9th Int. Congr. Psychol.*, New Haven, 114–115.

———. 1933. Origin and prenatal growth of behavior. In C. MURCHISON (Ed.), *A handbook of child psychology.* (2d. ed., rev.), pp. 31–159. Worcester: Clark University Press.

———. 1934a. An experimental study in the prenatal guinea-pig of the origin and development of reflexes and patterns of behavior in relation to the stimulation of specific receptor areas during the period of active fetal life. *Genet. Psychol. Monogr.*, **16**, 337–491.

———. 1934b. The genetic development of the kitten's capacity to right itself in the air when falling. *J. Genet. Psychol.*, **44**, 453–458.

———. 1936. A re-evaluation of the concepts of maturation and learning as applied to the early development of behavior. *Psychol. Rev.*, **43**, 450–470.

———. 1937. Stimulus intensity as a determiner of the characteristics of behavior in the fetal guinea pig. (Abs.) *Science*, **86**, 409.

CARMICHAEL, L. 1938. Fetal behavior and developmental psychology. *Rapp. et C. R. onzième congr. int. psychol.*, Paris. 108–123.

———. 1940a. The physiological correlates of intelligence. *Yearb. Nat. Soc. Stud. Educ.*, **39**(I), 93–155.

———. 1940b. A technique for the electrical recording of eye movements in adult and fetal guinea pigs. (By title.) *Psychol. Bull.*, **37**, 563.

———. 1941. The experimental embryology of mind. *Psychol. Bull.*, **38**, 1–28.

CARMICHAEL, L., and G. F. J. LEHNER. 1937. The development of temperature sensitivity during the fetal period. *J. Genet. Psychol.*, **50**, 217–227.

CARMICHAEL, L., and M. F. SMITH. 1939. Quantified pressure stimulation and the specificity and generality of response in fetal life. *J. Genet. Psychol.*, **54**, 425–434.

CESANA, G. 1911. Lo sviluppo ontogenico degli atti riflessi. *Arch. Fisiol.*, **9**, 1–120.

CHILD, C. M. 1921. *The origin and development of the nervous system from a physiological viewpoint.* Chicago: University of Chicago Press.

———. 1924. *Physiological foundations of behavior.* New York: Holt.

———. 1925. The physiological significance of the cephalocaudal differential in vertebrate development. *Anat. Rec.*, **31**, 369–383.

CHRISTENBERRY, H. E. 1910–1911. Maternal impressions. *J. Tenn. Med. Ass.*, **3**, 274–277.

CLARK, E. L., and E. R. CLARK. 1914. On the early pulsations of the posterior lymph hearts in chick embryos: Their relation to the body movements. *J. Exp. Zoöl.*, **17**, 373–394.

COGHILL, G. E. 1902. The cranial nerves of *Amblystoma tigrinum*. *J. Comp. Neurol.*, **12**, 205–289.

———. 1906. The cranial nerves of *Triton taeniatus*. *J. Comp. Neurol.*, **16**, 247–264.

———. 1908. The development of the swimming movement in amphibian embryos. (Abs.) *Anat. Rec.*, **2**, 148.

———. 1909. The reaction to tactile stimuli and the development of the swimming movement in embryos of *Diemyetylus torosus*, Eschscholtz. *J. Comp. Neurol.*, **19**, 83–105.

———. 1913a. The correlation of structural development and function in the growth of the vertebrate nervous system. *Science*, **37**, 722–723.

———. 1913b. The primary ventral roots and somatic motor column of *Amblystoma*. *J. Comp. Neurol.*, **23**, 121–143.

———. 1914. Correlated anatomical and physiological studies of the growth of the nervous system of Amphibia: I. The afferent system of the trunk of *Amblystoma*. *J. Comp. Neurol.*, **24**, 161–233.

COGHILL, G. E. 1916. Correlated anatomical and physiological studies of the growth of the nervous system of Amphibia: II. The afferent system of the head of *Amblystoma*. *J. Comp. Neurol.*, 26, 247–340.

——. 1924a. Correlated anatomical and physiological studies of the growth of the nervous system in Amphibia: III. The floor plate of *Amblystoma*. *J. Comp. Neurol.*, 37, 37–69.

——. 1924b. Correlated anatomical and physiological studies of the growth of the nervous system of Amphibia: IV. Rates of proliferation and differentiation in the central nervous system of *Amblystoma*. *J. Comp. Neurol.*, 37, 71–120.

——. 1926a. Correlated anatomical and physiological studies of the growth of the nervous system of Amphibia: V. The growth of the pattern of the motor mechanism of *Amblystoma punctatum*. *J. Comp. Neurol.*, 40, 47–94.

——. 1926b. Correlated anatomical and physiological studies of the growth of the nervous system in Amphibia: VI. The mechanism of integration in *Amblystoma punctatum*. *J. Comp. Neurol.*, 41, 95–152.

——. 1926c. Correlated anatomical and physiological studies of the growth of the nervous system of Amphibia: VII. The growth of the pattern of the association mechanism of the rhombencephalon and spinal cord of *Amblystoma punctatum*. *J. Comp. Neurol.*, 42, 1–16.

——. 1926d. The growth of functional neurones and its relation to the development of behavior. *Proc. Amer. Phil. Soc.*, 65, 51–55.

——. 1928. Correlated anatomical and physiological studies of the growth of the nervous system of Amphibia: VIII. The development of the pattern of differentiation in the cerebrum of *Amblystoma punctatum*. *J. Comp. Neurol.*, 45, 227–247.

——. 1929a. Anatomy and the problem of behaviour. Cambridge: University Press. New York: Macmillan.

——. 1929b. The development of movement of the hind leg of *Amblystoma*. *Proc. Soc. Exp. Biol. Med.*, 27, 74–75.

——. 1929c. The early development of behavior in *Amblystoma* and in man. *Arch. Neurol. Psychiat.*, 21, 989–1009.

——. 1930a. Correlated anatomical and physiological studies of the growth of the nervous system of Amphibia: IX. The mechanism of association of *Amblystoma punctatum*. *J. Comp. Neurol.*, 51, 311–375.

——. 1930b. The development of half centers in relation to the question of antagonism in reflexes. *J. Gen. Psychol.*, 4, 335–337.

——. 1930c. The genetic interrelation of instinctive behavior and reflexes. *Psychol. Rev.*, 37, 264–266.

——. 1930d. Individuation versus integration in the development of behavior. *J. Gen. Psychol.*, 3, 431–435.

COGHILL, G. E. 1930e. The structural basis of the integration of behavior. *Proc. Nat. Acad. Sci.*, 16, 637–643.

——. 1931. Correlated anatomical and physiological studies of the growth of the nervous system of Amphibia: X. Corollaries of the anatomical and physiological study of *Amblystoma* from the age of the earliest movement to swimming. *J. Comp. Neurol.*, 53, 147–168.

——. 1936. Integration and motivation of behavior as problems of growth. *J. Genet. Psychol.*, 48, 3–19.

COGHILL, G. E., and W. K. LEGNER. 1937. Embryonic motility and sensitivity. (Trans. of W. PREYER. *Specielle Physiologie des Embryo*.) *Monogr. Soc. Res. Child Develpm.*, 2, 1–115.

COHNSTEIN, J., and N. ZUNTZ. 1884. Untersuchungen über das Blut, den Kreislauf und die Athmung beim Säugetierfötus. *Pflüg. Arch. ges. Physiol.*, 34, 173–233.

COLERIDGE, S. T. 1885. *Miscellanies, aesthetic and literary*. (Bohn's Standard Library ed.) London: Bell and Sons.

COMPAYRÉ, G. 1896. *The intellectual and moral development of the child*. Pt. 1. (Trans. by M. E. WILSON.) New York: Appleton.

COPENHAVER, W. M. 1939. Initiation of beat and intrinsic contraction rates in the different parts of the *Amblystoma* heart. *J. Exp. Zoöl.* 80, 193–224.

COREY, E. L. 1931. Causative factors of the initial inspiration of the mammalian fetus. (Abs.) *Anat. Rec.*, Suppl., 48, 41.

——. 1934. Effects of brain cautery on fetal development in the rat. *Proc. Soc. Exp. Biol. Med.*, 31, 951–953.

CORONIOS, J. D. 1930. Preliminary note: Technique for observing and motion-picture recording of fetal behavior (cat). *J. Genet. Psychol.*, 37, 544–545.

——. 1931. The development of behavior in the fetal cat. (Abs.) *Psychol. Bull.*, 28, 696–697.

——. 1933. Development of behavior in the fetal cat. *Genet. Psychol. Monogr.*, 14, 283–386.

CORONIOS, J. D., H. SCHLOSBERG, and L. CARMICHAEL. 1932. Moving-picture film showing the development of fetal behavior in the cat. (With accompanying booklet.) Chicago: Stoelting.

COUGHLIN, R. E. 1905. Report of two cases of maternal impression. *Brooklyn Med. J.*, 19, 199–200.

CRAIG, J. F. 1930. *Fleming's veterinary obstetrics*. (4th ed.) London: Baillière.

CRAIG, W. 1912. Behavior of the young bird in breaking out of the egg. *J. Anim. Behav.*, 2, 296–298.

CREED, R. S., D. DENNY-BROWN, J. C. ECCLES,

E. G. T. LIDDELL, and C. S. SHERRINGTON. 1932. *Reflex activity of the spinal cord.* Oxford: Clarendon Press.

CROZIER, W. J. 1929. The study of living organisms. In C. MURCHISON (Ed.), *The foundations of experimental psychology,* pp. 45–127. Worcester: Clark University Press. London: Oxford University Press.

DANFORTH, D. N., and A. C. IVY. 1938. Effect of calcium upon uterine activity and reactivity. *Proc. Soc. Exp. Biol. Med.,* 38, 550–551.

DANTE. 1893. *The divine comedy: II. Purgatory.* (Trans. by C. E. NORTON.) Boston: Houghton Mifflin.

DARWIN, E. 1796. *Zoonomia; or the laws of organic life.* New York: T. and J. Swords.

DAVIDSON, P. E. 1914. The recapitulation theory and human infancy. *Teachers College Contr. Educ.,* No. 65. Pp. 105.

DE ANGELIS, F. 1922. I riflessi nel neonato. *Pediatria,* 30, 1107–1113.

DE KERGARADEC, L. 1822, 1823. Ueber die Ausculation, angewandt auf das Studium der Schwangerschaft. *Notizen Geb. Natur Heilk.,* 2, 191, 202–207; 3, 159.

DELEE, J. B. 1927. Counting fetal heart beat. *J. Amer. Med. Ass.,* 88, 1000.

———. 1928. *The principles and practice of obstetrics.* (5th ed.) Philadelphia: Saunders.

DEMARSH, Q. B., H. L. ALT, W. F. WINDLE, and D. S. HILLIS. 1941. The effect of depriving the infant of its placental blood. *J. Amer. Med. Ass.,* 116, 2568–2573.

DEMARSH, Q. B., W. F. WINDLE, and H. L. ALT. 1940. Effect of depriving newborn of placental blood upon early postnatal blood picture. *Proc. Soc. Exp. Biol. Med.,* 44, 662–664.

DE SNOO, K. 1937. Das trinkende Kind im Uterus. *Mschr. Geburtsh. Gynäk.,* 105, 88–97.

DETWILER, S. R. 1920. Functional regulations in animals with composite spinal cords. *Proc. Nat. Acad. Sci.,* 6, 695–700.

———. 1921. Experiments on the hyperplasia of nerve centers. *China Med. J.,* 35, 95–107.

———. 1922. Experiments on the transplantation of limbs in *Amblystoma:* Further observations on peripheral nerve connections. *J. Exp. Zoöl.,* 35, 115–161.

———. 1923a. Experiments on the reversal of the spinal cord in *Amblystoma* embryos at the level of the anterior limb. *J. Exp. Zoöl.,* 38, 293–321.

———. 1923b. Experiments on the transplantation of the spinal cord in *Amblystoma,* and their bearing upon the stimuli involved in the differentiation of nerve cells. *J. Exp. Zoöl.,* 37, 339–393.

DEWEY, E. 1935. *Behavior development in infants: A survey of the literature on prenatal and postnatal activity, 1920–1934.* New York: Columbia University Press.

DODGE, R. 1923. Habituation to rotation. *J. Exp. Psychol.,* 6, 1–35.

DRAPER, R. L. 1920. The prenatal growth of the guinea-pig. *Anat. Rec.,* 18, 369–392.

DUBOIS, P. 1833. Causes de la présentation de la tête, dans l'accouchement. *Arch. gén. méd.,* 1 (2d ser.), 292–295.

DÜRKEN, B. 1929. *Grundriss der Entwicklungsmechanik.* Berlin: Borntraeger.

ELWYN, A. 1929. The structure and development of the proprioceptors. In F. TILNEY et al. (Eds.), *The cerebellum: An investigation of recent advances,* pp. 244–280. (*Proc. Ass. Res. Nerv. Ment. Dis.,* 1926.) Baltimore: Williams and Wilkins.

EMMERT, A. G. F., and BURGÄTZY. 1818. Beobachtungen über einige schwangere Fledermäuse und ihre Eihüllen. *Dtsch. Arch. Physiol.,* 4, 1–33.

ERBKAM. 1837. Lebhafte Bewegung eines viermonatlichen Fötus. *Neue Z. Geburtsk.,* 5, 324–326.

ERLANGER, J., and H. S. GASSER. 1937. *Electrical signs of nervous activity.* Philadelphia: University of Pennsylvania Press.

EVENSEN, H. 1931. *Entwicklung und Schicksal der zu früh geborenen Kinder.* (Dissertation.) Berlin: Friedrich-Wilhelms-Universität.

FAVILL, J. 1929. The relationship of eye muscles to semicircular canal currents in rotationally induced nystagmus. In F. TILNEY et al. (Eds.), *The cerebellum: An investigation of recent advances,* pp. 530–546. (*Proc. Ass. Res. Nerv. Ment. Dis.,* 1926.) Baltimore: Williams and Wilkins.

FELDMAN, W. M. 1920. *Principles of antenatal and post-natal child physiology, pure and applied.* London and New York: Longmans, Green.

———. 1922. The nature of the plantar reflex in early life and the causes of its variations. *Amer. J. Dis. Child.,* 23, 1–40.

FISH, M. W., and W. F. WINDLE. 1932. The effect of rotatory stimulation on the movements of the head and eyes in newborn and young kittens. *J. Comp. Neurol.,* 54, 103–107.

FITZGERALD, J. E., and W. F. WINDLE. 1942. Some observations on early human fetal movements. *J. Comp. Neurol.,* 76, 159–167.

FORBES, A. 1922. The interpretation of spinal reflexes in terms of present knowledge of nerve conduction. *Physiol. Rev.,* 2, 361–414.

FORBES, H. S., and H. B. FORBES. 1927. Fetal sense reaction: Hearing. *J. Comp. Psychol.,* 7, 353–355.

FURFEY, P. H., M. A. BONHAM, and M. K. SARGENT. 1930. The mental organization of the newborn. *Child Develpm.,* 1, 48–51.

GEIGER, A. J., W. M. MONROE, and A. V. N. GOODYER. 1941. Clinical fetal electrocardiography: Its practical accomplishment. *Proc. Soc. Exp. Biol. Med.,* 48, 646–648.

GENZMER, A. 1882. *Untersuchungen über die*

Sinneswahrnehmungen des neugeborenen Menschen. (Dissertation, 1873.) Halle: Niemeyer.

GERARD, R. W. 1940. *Unresting cells.* New York: Harper.

GESELL, A. 1928. *Infancy and human growth.* New York: Macmillan.

——. 1929a. The individual in infancy. In C. MURCHISON (Ed.), *The foundations of experimental psychology,* pp. 628–660. Worcester: Clark University Press. London: Oxford University Press.

——. 1929b. Maturation and infant behavior pattern. *Psychol. Rev.,* 36, 307–319.

GIVLER, R. C. 1921. The intellectual significance of the grasping reflex. *J. Phil.,* 18, 617–628.

GLENN, W. F. 1911. Is a foetus a person? *South. Pract.,* 33, 117–120.

GOECKEL, H. 1911. *Die Wandlungen in der Bewertung des ungeborenen Kindes.* (Dissertation.) Heidelberg.

GOLDSTEIN, K. 1904. Kritische und experimentelle Beiträge zur Frage nach dem Einfluss des Zentralnervensystems auf die embryonale Entwicklung und die Regeneration. *Arch. Entwicklungsmech. Organ.,* 18, 57–110.

——. 1939. *The organism.* New York: American Book.

GOOD, F. L. 1924. Pregnancy and labor complicated by diseases and injuries of the spinal cord. *J. Amer. Med. Ass.,* 83, 416–418.

GOSS, C. M. 1937. Early development of the rat heart in vitro. *Anat. Rec.,* Suppl., 67, 20.

——. 1938. The first contractions of the heart in rat embryos. *Anat. Rec.,* 70, 505–524.

——. 1940. First contractions of the heart without cytological differentiation. *Anat. Rec.,* 76, 19–27.

GRAHAM, E. A. 1913–1915. The origin and nature of fetal movements. *Trans. Chicago Path. Soc.,* 9, 123–124.

GRAHAM, M. 1919. Intrauterine crying. *Brit. Med. J.,* 1, 675.

GRANT, R. E. 1827. Beobachtungen über den Bau und das Wesen der *Flustrae. Z. organ. Physik,* 1, 401–418.

GRIFFITH, W. S. A. 1915. An investigation of the causes which determine the lie of the foetus in utero. *Lancet,* 2, 319–325.

GUTHRIE, E. R. 1942. Conditioning: A theory of learning in terms of stimulus, response, and association. *Yearb. Nat. Soc. Stud. Educ.,* 41(II), 17–60.

HARRISON, R. G. 1904. An experimental study of the relation of the nervous system to the developing musculature in the embryo of the frog. *Amer. J. Anat.,* 3, 197–220.

HARTMAN, C. G. 1916a. Studies in the development of the opossum *Didelphys virginiana* L.: I. History of the early cleavage. *J. Morphol.,* 27, 1–41.

HARTMAN, C. G. 1916b. Studies in the development of the opossum *Didelphys virginiana* L.: II. Formation of the blastocyst. *J. Morphol.,* 27, 42–83.

——. 1919a. Studies in the development of the opossum *Didelphys virginiana* L.: III. Description of new material on maturation, cleavage and entoderm formation. *J. Morphol.,* 32, 1–73.

——. 1919b. Studies in the development of the opossum *Didelphys virginiana* L.: IV. The bilaminar blastocyst. *J. Morphol.,* 32, 73–142.

——. 1920. Studies in the development of the opossum *Didelphys virginiana* L.: V. The phenomena of parturition. *Anat. Rec.,* 19, 251–261.

——. 1936. *Time of ovulation in women.* Baltimore: Williams and Wilkins.

HEGEL, G. W. F. 1894. *Philosophy of mind.* (Trans. by W. WALLACE.) Oxford: Clarendon Press.

HENDERSON, Y. 1937. How breathing begins at birth. *Science,* 85, 89–91.

HERRICK, C. J. 1924. *Neurological foundations of animal behavior.* New York: Holt.

——. 1943. *Biographical memoir of George Ellett Coghill: 1872–1941.* Washington: National Academy of Sciences.

HERRICK, C. J., and G. E. COGHILL. 1915. The development of reflex mechanisms in *Amblystoma. J. Comp. Neurol.,* 25, 65–85.

HERTWIG, R. 1912. *A manual of zoology.* (Trans. by J. S. KINGSLEY.) New York: Holt.

HESS, J. H. 1918. The diagnosis of the age of the fetus by the use of roentgenograms. *Ill. Med. J.,* 33, 73–88.

——. 1922. *Premature and congenitally diseased infants.* Philadelphia: Lea and Febiger.

HEWER, E. E. 1927. The development of muscle in the human foetus. *J. Anat.,* 62, 72–78.

HICKS, J. B. 1880. On recording the fetal movements by means of a gastrograph. *Trans. Obstet. Soc. London,* 22, 134.

HILL, J. P., and M. TRIBE. 1924. The early development of the cat (*Felis domestica*). *Quart. J. Micro. Sci.,* 68, 513–602.

HINES, M., and W. L. STRAUS. 1934. The motor cortex of fetal and infant rhesus monkeys (*Macaca mulatta*). *Anat. Rec.,* Suppl., 58, 18.

HINSEY, J. C., S. W. RANSON, and R. F. MCNATTIN. 1930. The role of the hypothalamus and mesencephalon in locomotion. *Arch. Neurol. Psychiat.,* 23, 1–42.

HIS, W. 1880, 1882, 1885. *Anatomie menschlicher Embryonen.* (3 vols.) Leipzig: Vogel.

HOGG, I. D. 1941. Sensory nerves and associated structures in the skin of human fetuses of 8 to 14 weeks of menstrual age correlated with functional capability. *J. Comp. Neurol.,* 75, 371–410.

HOLSOPPLE, J. Q. 1929. Space and the nonauditory labyrinth. In C. MURCHISON (Ed.), *The foundations of experimental psychology*, pp. 414–433. Worcester: Clark University Press. London: ꭓford University Press.

HOLT, E. B. 1931. *Animal drive and the learning process.* Vol. I. New York: Holt.

HOME, E. 1827. Über die Fortpflanzung der Auster und der Flussmuschel. (Croonian Lecture, 1826.) *Z. organ. Physik*, **1**, 391–396. (See also *Phil. Trans. Roy. Soc. London*, Pt. 1, 1827, 39.)

HOOKER, D. 1911. The development and function of voluntary and cardiac muscle in embryos without nerves. *J. Exp. Zoöl.*, **11**, 159–186.

——. 1936. Early fetal activity in mammals. *Yale J. Biol. Med.*, **8**, 579–602.

——. 1937. The development of reflexes in the mammalian fetus. *Anat. Rec.*, Suppl., **70**, 55.

——. 1938. The origin of the grasping movement man. *Proc. Amer. Phil. Soc.*, **79**, 597–606.

——. 1939a. Fetal behavior. *Res. Publ. Ass. Nerv. Ment. Dis.*, **19**, 237–243.

——. 1939b. A preliminary atlas of early human fetal activity. Privately published.

——. 1942. Fetal reflexes and instinctual processes. *Psychosomatic Med.*, **4**, 199–205.

——. 1943. Reflex activities in the human fetus. In R. G. BARKER, J. S. KOUNIN, and H. F. WRIGHT (Eds.), *Child behavior and development*, pp. 17–28. New York: McGraw-Hill.

HOOKER, D., and J. S. NICHOLAS. 1927. The effect of injury to the spinal cord of rats in prenatal stages. (Abs.) *Anat. Rec.*, **35**, 14–15.

——. 1930. Spinal cord section in rat fetuses. *J. Comp. Neurol.*, **50**, 413–467.

HUGGETT, A. ST. G. 1927. Foetal blood-gas tensions and gas transfusions through the placenta of the goat. *J. Physiol.*, **62**, 373–384.

——. 1930. Foetal respiratory reflexes. *J. Physiol.*, **69**, 144–152.

HUGHES, H. 1905. Status of the foetus in utero. *N. Y. Med. J.*, **82**, 963.

HUNTER, W. S. 1931. The mechanisms involved in the behavior of white rats on the inclined plane. *J. Gen. Psychol.*, **5**, 295–310.

HYMAN, A. S. 1930. Irregularities: Phonocardiographic study of the fetal heart sounds from fifth to eighth months of pregnancy. *Amer. J. Obstet. Gynec.*, **20**, 332–347.

INGVAR, S. 1920. Reaction of cells to the galvanic current in tissue cultures. *Proc. Soc. Exp. Biol. Med.*, **17**, 198–199.

IRWIN, O. C. 1930. The amount and nature of activities of new-born infants under constant external stimulating conditions during the first ten days of life. *Genet. Psychol. Monogr.*, **8**, 1–92.

IRWIN, O. C. 1932a. The organismic hypothesis and differentiation of behavior: I. The cell theory and the neurone doctrine. *Psychol. Rev.*, **39**, 128–146.

——. 1932b. The organismic hypothesis and differentiation of behavior: II. The reflex arc concept. *Psychol. Rev.*, **39**, 189–202.

IRWIN, O. C., and A. P. WEISS. 1930. A note on mass activity in newborn infants. *J. Genet. Psychol.*, **38**, 20–30.

JACKSON, C. M. 1909. On the prenatal growth of the human body and the relative growth of the various organs and parts. *Amer. J. Anat.*, **9**, 119–165.

JACKSON, H. 1884. Evolution and dissolution of the nervous system. *Lancet*, **1**, 555–558, 649–652, 739–744.

JAMES, W. 1890. *The principles of psychology.* (2 vols.) New York: Holt.

JASPER, H. H., C. S. BRIDGMAN, and L. CARMICHAEL. 1937. An ontogenetic study of cerebral electrical potentials in the guinea pig. *J. Exp. Psychol.*, **21**, 63–71.

JENNINGS, H. S. 1930. *The biological basis of human nature.* New York: Norton.

JENSEN, K. 1932. Differential reactions to taste and temperature stimuli in newborn infants. *Genet. Psychol. Monogr.*, **12**, 363–479.

KANT, I. 1799. *Anthropologie.* Leipzig.

KAPPERS, C. U. A. 1917. Further contributions on neurobiotaxis: IX. An attempt to compare the phenomena of neurobiotaxis with other phenomena of taxis and tropism. The dynamic polarization of the neurone. *J. Comp. Neurol.*, **27**, 261–298.

KASATKIN, N. I., and A. M. LEVIKOVA. 1935a. The formation of visual conditioned reflexes and their differentiation in infants. *J. Gen. Psychol.*, **12**, 416–435.

——. 1935b. On the development of early conditioned reflexes and differentiations of auditory stimuli in infants. *J. Exp. Psychol.*, **18**, 1–19.

KEIBEL, F., and C. ELZE. 1908. *Normentafel zur Entwicklungsgeschichte des Menschen.* Jena: Fischer.

KEIBEL, F., and F. P. MALL. 1910. *Manual of human embryology.* Vol. II. Philadelphia: Lippincott.

KEITH, A. 1913. *Human embryology and morphology.* London: Arnold.

KELLOGG, H. B. 1930. Studies on fetal circulation of mammals. *Amer. J. Physiol.*, **91**, 637–648.

KIDD, W. 1907. *The sense of touch in mammals and birds, with special reference to the papillary ridges.* London: Adam and Charles Black.

KING, H. D. 1915. On the weight of the albino rat at birth and the factors that influence it. *Anat. Rec.*, **9**, 213–231.

KINGSBURY, B. F. 1924. The significance of

the so-called law of cephalocaudal differential growth. *Anat. Rec.*, **27**, 305–321.

KINGSBURY, B. F. 1926. On the so-called law of antero-posterior development. *Anat. Rec.*, **33**, 73–87.

KLEMM, G. O. 1914. *A history of psychology.* (Trans. by E. C. WILM and R. PINTNER.) New York: Scribner's.

KOFFKA, K. 1924. *The growth of the mind: An introduction to child psychology.* (Trans. by R. M. OGDEN.) New York: Harcourt, Brace. London: Kegan Paul.

KOUWER, B. J. 1919. Adembewegingen van de vrucht voor en na de geboorte. *Ned. Tijdschr. Geneesk.*, **11**, 815–822.

KRABBE, K. 1912. Les réflexes chez le foetus. *Rev. neurol.*, **24**, 434–435.

KUO, Z. Y. 1932a. Ontogeny of embryonic behavior in Aves: I. The chronology and general nature of the behavior of the chick embryo. *J. Exp. Zoöl.*, **61**, 395–430.

——. 1932b. Ontogeny of embryonic behavior in Aves: II. The mechanical factors in the various stages leading to hatching. *J. Exp. Zoöl.*, **62**, 453–487.

——. 1932c. Ontogeny of embryonic behavior in Aves: III. The structure and environmental factors in embryonic behavior. *J. Comp. Psychol.*, **13**, 245–272.

——. 1932d. Ontogeny of embryonic behavior in Aves: IV. The influence of embryonic movements upon the behavior after hatching. *J. Comp. Psychol.*, **14**, 109–122.

——. 1932e. Ontogeny of embryonic behavior in Aves: V. The reflex concept in the light of embryonic behavior in birds. *Psychol. Rev.*, **39**, 499–515.

——. 1938. Ontogeny of embryonic behavior in Aves: XII. Stages in the development of physiological activities in the chick embryo. *Amer. J. Psychol.*, **51**, 361–378.

——. 1939a. Development of acetylcholine in the chick embryo. *J. Neurophysiol.*, **2**, 488–493.

——. 1939b. Studies in the physiology of the embryonic nervous system. *J. Comp. Neurol.*, **70**, 437–459.

——. 1939c. Total pattern or local reflexes? *Psychol. Rev.*, **46**, 93–122.

KUO, Z. Y., and L. CARMICHAEL. 1937. A technique for the motion-picture recording of the development of behavior in the chick embryo. *J. Psychol.*, **4**, 343–348.

KUSSMAUL, A. 1859. *Untersuchungen über das Seelenleben des neugeborenen Menschen.* Leipzig: Winter.

LANE, H. H. 1917. The correlation between structure and function in the development of the special senses of the white rat. *Univ. Okla. Bull.* (New ser. No. 140) (*Univ. Stud.*, No. 8), 1–88.

——. 1924. A mechanism showing a remarkable correlation between structure and func-

tion in connection with the nursing reflex in the young mammal. *Kan. Univ. Sci. Bull.*, **15** (Whole ser. 26), 247–253.

LANGE, F. A. 1925. *History of materialism.* (1873.) (Trans. by E. C. THOMAS.) New York: Harcourt, Brace. London: Kegan Paul.

LANGFELD, H. S. 1931. A response interpretation of consciousness. *Psychol. Rev.*, **38**, 87–108.

LANGWORTHY, O. R. 1925. The development of progression and posture in young opossums. *Amer. J. Physiol.*, **74**, 1–13.

——. 1926. Relation of onset of decerebrate rigidity to the time of myelinization of tracts in the brain-stem and spinal cord of young animals. *Contr. Embryol., Carnegie Inst. Wash.*, **17**, No. 89, 125–140.

——. 1927. The histological development of cerebral motor areas in young kittens correlated with their physiological reaction to electrical stimulation. *Contr. Embryol., Carnegie Inst. Wash.*, **19**, No. 104, 177–208.

——. 1928. The behavior of pouch-young opossums correlated with the myelinization of tracts in the nervous system. *J. Comp. Neurol.*, **46**, 201–247.

——. 1929. A correlated study of the development of reflex activity in fetal and young kittens and the myelinization of tracts in the nervous system. *Contr. Embryol., Carnegie Inst. Wash.*, **20**, No. 114, 127–171.

——. 1932. The differentiation of behaviour patterns in the foetus and infant. *Brain*, **55**, 265–277.

LAPICQUE, L. 1926. *L'excitabilité en fonction du temps.* Paris: Presses Université de France.

LARSELL, O. 1929. The comparative morphology of the membranous labyrinth and the lateral line organs in their relation to the development of the cerebellum. In F. TILNEY et al. (Eds.), *The cerebellum: An investigation of recent advances.* (*Proc. Ass. Res. Nerv. Ment. Dis.*, 1926.) Baltimore: Williams and Wilkins.

LARSELL, O., E. MCCRADY, and A. ZIMMERMAN. 1935. Morphological and functional development of the membranous labyrinth in the opossum. *J. Comp. Neurol.*, **63**, 95–118.

LASHLEY, K. S. 1924. Studies of cerebral function in learning. VI. The theory that synaptic resistance is reduced by the passage of the nerve impulse. *Psychol. Rev.*, **31**, 369–375.

——. 1929. Brain mechanisms and intelligence. (*Behav. Res. Fund Monogr.*) Chicago: University of Chicago Press.

LATIMER, H. B. 1931. The prenatal growth of the cat: II. The growth of the dimensions of the head and trunk. *Anat. Rec.*, **50**, 311–332.

LATIMER, H. B., and J. M. AIKMAN. 1931. The prenatal growth of the cat: I. The growth in weight of the head, trunk, forelimbs, and hind-limbs. *Anat. Rec.*, **48**, 1–26.

LAUGHTON, N. B. 1924. Studies on the nervous regulation of progression in mammals. *Amer. J. Physiol.*, **70**, 358–384.

LEEUWENHOEK, A. 1697. Part of a letter dated Delft, September 10, 1697, concerning the eggs of snails, the roots of vegetables, teeth, and young oysters. *Phil. Trans.*, **19**, 790–799.

LIGGETT, J. R. 1928. An experimental study of the olfactory sensitivity of the white rat. *Genet. Psychol. Monogr.*, **3**, 1–64.

LILLIE, F. R. 1919. *The development of the chick.* New York: Holt.

LILLIE, R. S. 1932. *Protoplasmic action and nervous system.* (2d ed.) Chicago: University of Chicago Press.

LINCOLN, A. W. 1932. *The behavioral development of the feeding reaction in the white rat.* Unpublished master's thesis, Brown University.

LINDSLEY, D. B. 1942. Heart and brain potentials of human fetuses in utero. *Amer. J. Psychol.*, **55**, 412–416.

LOCKE, J. 1849. *Essay concerning human understanding.* (1690.) Philadelphia: Kay and Troutman.

LOVEJOY, A. O. 1926. The meanings of "emergence" and its modes. *Proc. 6th Int. Congr. Philadelphia*, 20–33.

MACKEEVER, T. 1833. On the information afforded by the stethoscope in detecting the presence of foetal life. *Lancet*, **24**, 715.

MAEKAWA, M., and J. TOYOSHIMA. 1930. The fetal electro-cardiogram of the human subject. *Acta Scholae Med. Univ. Imp., Kioto*, **12**, 519–520.

MAGENDIE, F. (*See* BICHAT, 1827.)

MAGNUS, R. 1924. *Körperstellung.* Berlin: Springer.

——. 1925. Animal posture. (Croonian Lecture.) *Proc. Roy. Soc. London*, **98B**, 339–353.

MAILLIOT, L. 1856. *L'auscultation appliquée à l'étude de la grossesse.* Paris: Baillière. (German summary by Sickel in *Schmidt's Jb. ges. Med.*, 1857, **93**, 258–260.)

MALL, F. P. 1906. On ossification centers in human embryos less than one hundred days old. *Amer. J. Anat.*, **5**, 433–458.

——. 1910. Determination of the ages of human embryos and fetuses. In KEIBEL, F., and F. P. MALL. *Manual of human embryology*, Vol. 1, pp. 180–201. Philadelphia: Lippincott.

——. 1918. On the age of human embryos. *Amer. J. Anat.*, **23**, 397–422.

MANN, H., and P. BERNSTEIN. 1941. Fetal electrocardiography. *Amer. Heart J.*, **22**, 390–400.

MANN, I. C. 1928. *The development of the human eye.* Cambridge: University Press.

MARQUIS, D. P. 1931. Can conditioned responses be established in the newborn infant? *J. Genet. Psychol.*, **39**, 479–492.

MATTHEWS, S. A., and S. R. DETWILER. 1926.

The reactions of *Amblystoma* embryos following prolonged treatment with chloretone. *J. Exp. Zoöl.*, **45**, 279–292.

MAXWELL, S. S. 1923. *Labyrinth and equilibrium.* Philadelphia: Lippincott.

MCCARTHY, D. 1936. A graphic age conversion scale. *Child Develpm.*, **7**, 74.

MCCRADY, E. 1938. *The embryology of the opossum.* Philadelphia: Wistar Institute of Anatomy and Biology.

MCCRADY, E., E. G. WEVER, and C. W. BRAY. 1937. The development of hearing in the opossum. *J. Exp. Zoöl.*, **75**, 503–517.

MCDOUGALL, W. 1923. *Outline of psychology.* New York: Scribner's.

MCILROY, A. L., and D. LEVERKUS. 1924. Changes in polarity of the foetus during the later weeks of pregnancy. *Lancet*, **2**, 267–271. Also in *Proc. Roy. Soc. Med.* (*Sect. Obstet. Gynec.*), 1924, **17**, 89–99.

MERMANN. 1887. Ueber eigenthümliche rhythmische Fötalbewegungen. *Cbl. Gynäk.*, **11**, 622–624.

MEYER, A. W. 1939. *The rise of embryology.* Stanford University, California: Stanford University Press.

MINKOWSKI, M. 1920a. Movimientos y reflejos del feto humano durante la primera mitad del embarazo. *Trabojos del Laboratorio de Investigaciones Biologicas, Univ. Madrid*, **18**, 269–273.

——. 1920b. Réflexes et mouvements de la tête, du tronc et des extrémités du foetus humain pendant la première moitié de la grossesse. *C. R. Soc. Biol., Paris*, **83**, 1202–1204.

——. 1921a. Sur les mouvements, les réflexes, et les réactions musculaires du foetus humain de 2 à 5 mois et leurs rélations avec le système nerveux foetal. *Rev. neurol.*, **37**, 1105–1118, 1235–1250.

——. 1921b. Ueber Bewegungen und Reflexe des menschlichen Foetus während der ersten Hälfte seiner Entwicklung. *Schweiz. Arch. Neurol. Psychiat.*, **8**, 148–151.

——. 1922. Ueber frühzeitige Bewegungen. Reflexe und muskuläre Reaktionen beim menschlichen Fötus und ihre Beziehungen zum fötalen Nerven- und Muskelsystem. *Schweiz. med. Wschr.*, **52**, 721–724, 751–755.

——. 1923. Zur Entwicklungsgeschichte, Lokalisation und Klinik des Fussohlenreflexes. *Schweiz. Arch. Neurol. Psychiat.*, **13**, 475–514.

——. 1924, 1925. Zum gegenwärtigen Stand der Lehre von den Reflexen in entwicklungsgeschichtlicher und der anatomisch-physiologischer Beziehung. *Schweiz. Arch. Neurol. Psychiat.*, **15**, 239–259; **16**, 133–152, 266–284.

——. 1926. Sur les modalités et la localisation du réflexe plantaire au cours de son évolution du foetus à l'adulte. *C. R. Congr. Médecins, Aliénistes et Neurologistes de France*, Geneva, **30**, 301–308.

——. 1928a. Neurobiologische Studien am

menschlichen Foetus. *Handb. Biol. ArbMeth.*, Pt. V, **5B,** 511–618.

MINKOWSKI, M. 1928*b*. Ueber die elektrische Erregbarkeit der fötalen Muskulatur. *Schweiz. Arch. Neurol. Psychiat.*, **22,** 64–71.

MINOT, C. S. 1892. *Human embryology.* New York: William Wood.

——. 1903. *A laboratory text-book of embryology.* Philadelphia: Blakiston.

MORACHE, G. 1904. La vie intra-utrine et sa durée. *J. méd. Paris*, **2,** 14–16.

MORGAN, T. H. 1927. *Experimental embryology.* New York: Columbia University Press.

MORRISON, F. J. 1920. Maternal impressions. *Va. Med. Mo.*, **47,** 127.

MOWRER, O. H. 1936. "Maturation" vs. "learning" in the development of vestibular and optokinetic nystagmus. *J. Genet. Psychol.*, **48,** 383–404.

MULLER, H. R., and L. H. WEED. 1916. Notes on the falling reflex in cats. *Amer. J. Physiol.*, **40,** 373–379.

NACHMANSOHN, D. 1940. Choline esterase in brain and spinal cord of sheep embryos. *J. Neurophysiol.*, **3,** 396–402.

NEEDHAM, J. 1931. *Chemical embryology.* (3 vols.) Cambridge: University Press.

NEU, M. 1915. Die Diagnose der Schwangerschaft. In A. DÖDERLEIN (Ed.), *Handbuch der Geburtshilfe*, pp. 246–328. Wiesbaden: Bergmann.

NEWBERY, H., I. PYLE, and H. CHAMPNEY. 1943. Can mothers rate fetal environment? *J. Psychol.*, **15,** 197–221.

NICHOLAS, J. S. 1924. Regulation of posture in the fore limb of *Amblystoma punctatum. J. Exp. Zoöl.*, **40,** 113–159.

——. 1925. Notes on the application of experimental methods upon mammalian embryos. *Anat. Rec.*, **31,** 385–394.

——. 1926. Extirpation experiments upon the embryonic forelimb of the rat. *Proc. Soc. Exp. Biol. Med.*, **23,** 436–439.

——. 1927. The application of experimental methods to the study of developing *Fundulus* embryos. *Proc. Nat. Acad. Sci.*, **13,** 695–698.

——. 1929*a*. An analysis of the responses of isolated portions of the Amphibian nervous system. *Roux' Arch. Entwicklungsmech. Organ.*, **118,** 78–120.

——. 1929*b*. Movements in transplanted limbs. *Proc. Soc. Exp. Biol. Med.*, **26,** 729–731.

——. 1929*c*. Transplantations of tissues in fetal rats. *Proc. Soc. Exp. Biol., Med.*, **26,** 731–732.

——. 1933*a*. The correlation of movement and nerve supply in transplanted limbs of *Amblystoma. J. Comp. Neurol.*, **57,** 253–283.

——. 1933*b*. Development of transplanted rat eggs. *Proc. Soc. Exp. Biol., Med.*, **30,** 1111–1113.

NICHOLAS, J. S., and D. H. BARRON. 1935.

Limb movements studied by electrical stimulation of nerve roots and trunks in *Amblystoma. J. Comp. Neurol.*, **61,** 413–431.

NICHOLAS, J. S., and D. HOOKER. 1928. Progressive cord degeneration and collateral transmission of spinal impulses following section of the spinal cord in albino rat fetuses. *Anat. Rec.*, **38,** 24.

NICHOLAS, J. S., and D. RUDNICK. 1934. The development of rat embryos in tissue culture. *Proc. Nat. Acad. Sci.*, **20,** 656–658.

NORMAN, H. N. 1942. Fetal hiccups. *J. Comp. Psychol.*, **34,** 65–73.

OPPENHEIMER, J. M. 1934. Experimental studies on the developing perch (*Perca flavescens* Mitchill). *Proc. Soc. Exp. Biol., Med.*, **31,** 1123–1124.

ORR, D. W., and W. F. WINDLE. 1934. The development of behavior in chick embryos: The appearance of somatic movements. *J. Comp. Neurol.*, **60,** 271–283.

PANKRATZ, D. S. 1930. The possible relations of the development of the suprarenal gland to the origin of foetal movements in the albino rat. *Anat. Rec.*, **45,** 235.

——. 1931*a*. The development of the suprarenal gland in the albino rat, with a consideration of its possible relation to the origin of foetal movements. *Anat. Rec.*, **49,** 31–49.

——. 1931*b*. A preliminary report on the fetal movements in the rabbit. (Abs.) *Anat. Rec.*, Suppl., **48,** 58–59.

PARAMORE, R. H. 1909. A critical inquiry into the causes of the internal rotation of the foetal head. *J. Obstet. Gynec., London*, **16,** 213–232.

PARKER, G. H. 1919. *The elementary nervous system.* Philadelphia: Lippincott.

——. 1922. *Smell, taste, and allied senses in the vertebrates.* Philadelphia: Lippincott.

——. 1931. The passage of sperms and of eggs through the oviducts in terrestrial vertebrates. *Phil. Trans. Roy. Soc., London*, **219,** 381–419.

PARKER, T. J., and W. A. HASWELL. 1921. *A text-book of zoology.* Vol. II. London: Macmillan.

PATON, S. 1907. The reactions of the vertebrate embryo and the associated changes in the nervous system. *Mitt. Zoöl. Stat. Neap.*, **18,** 535–581.

——. 1911. The reactions of the vertebrate embryo and associated changes in the nervous system. *J. Comp. Neurol.*, **21,** 345–372.

PATTEN, B. M. 1929. *The early embryology of the chick.* (3d ed.) Philadelphia: Blakiston.

PATTEN, B. M., and T. C. KRAMER. 1933. The initiation of contraction in the embryonic chick heart. *Amer. J. Anat.*, **53,** 349–375.

PATTERSON, T. L. 1914. Contributions to the physiology of the stomach: XIII. The variations in the hunger contractions of the empty stomach with age. *Amer. J. Physiol.*, **33**, 423–429.

PAVLOV, I. P. 1932. The reply of a physiologist to psychologists. *Psychol. Rev.*, **39**, 91–127.

PEIPER, A. 1925. Sinnesempfindungen des Kindes vor seiner Geburt. *Mschr. Kinderheilk.*, **29**, 236–241.

——. 1928. *Die Hirntätigkeit des Säuglings.* Berlin : Springer.

PETERSON, F., and L. H. RAINEY. 1910. The beginnings of mind in the newborn. *Bull. Lying-In Hosp. City of N. Y.*, **7**. 99–122.

PETERSON, J. 1926. Local signs as orientation tendencies. *Psychol. Rev.*, **33**, 218–236.

PFAFFMAN, C. 1936. Differential responses of the new-born cat to gustatory stimuli. *J. Genet. Psychol.*, **49**, 61–67.

PFLÜGER, E. 1877. Die Lebensfähigkeit des menschlichen Foetus. *Pflüg. Arch. ges. Physiol.*, **14**, 628–629.

PINARD. 1877. Fétus, anatomie et physiologie. Fétus, pathologie. *Dictionnaire encyclopedique des sciences médicales.* (Ser. 4.) Vol. II, pp. 472–556. Paris.

PLOSS, H., and M. BARTELS. 1927. *Das Weib in der Natur- und Völkerkunde.* (3 vols.) (11th ed.) Berlin : Neufeld.

PORTAL. 1818. Ueber die Pupillarmembran. *Dtsch. Arch. Physiol.*, **4**, 640–641.

PRATT, K. C., A. K. NELSON, and K. H. SUN. 1930. The behavior of the newborn infant. *Ohio State Univ. Stud., Contr. Psychol.*, No. 10.

PREYER, W. 1882. *Die Seele des Kindes.* Leipzig : Fernau. (5th ed, 1900.) 1888, 1889. *The mind of the child:* Pt. 1. *The senses and the will;* Pt. 2. *The development of the intellect.* (Trans. by H. W. BROWN.) New York : Appleton.

——. 1885. *Specielle Physiologie des Embryo. Untersuchungen über die Lebenserscheinungen vor der Geburt.* Leipzig : Grieben.

——. 1893. *Die geistige Entwicklung in der ersten Kindheit.* Stuttgart : Union. 1893. *Mental development in the child.* (Trans. by H. W. BROWN.) New York : Appleton.

RANDOLPH, H. 1900. Chloretone (acelonchloroform) : An anesthetic and mascerating agent for lower animals. *Zoöl. Anz.*, **23**, 436–439.

RANEY, E. T., and L. CARMICHAEL. 1934. Localizing responses to tactual stimuli in the fetal rat in relation to the psychological problem of space perception. *J. Genet. Psychol.*, **45**, 3–21.

RAWDON-SMITH, A. F., L. CARMICHAEL, and B. WELLMAN. 1938. Electrical responses from the cochlea of the fetal guinea pig. *J. Exp. Psychol.*, **23**, 531–535.

RAY, W. S. 1932. A preliminary report on a study of fetal conditioning. *Child Develpm.*, **3**, 175–177.

RICHTER, C. P. 1925. Some observations on the self-stimulation habits of young wild animals. *Arch. Neurol. Psychiat.*, **13**, 724–728.

RIDDLE, O. 1927. Sexual difference in prenatal growth and death. *Amer. Nat.*, **61**, 97–112.

RODMAN, J. 1815. Case of a child born between the fourth and fifth month and brought up. *Edinburgh Med. Surg. J.*, **11**, 455–458.

ROMANES, G. J. 1896. *Darwin, and After Darwin:* Vol. I. *The Darwinian theory.* Chicago : Open Court.

ROMIJN, C., and J. ROOS. 1938. The air space of the hen's egg and its changes during the period of incubation. *J. Physiol.*, **94**, 365–379.

ROUX, W. 1896. The problems, methods, and scope of developmental mechanics. (*Wood's Hole Biol. Lectures,* pp. 149–190.) Boston : Ginn.

RUDOLPH, L., and A. C. IVY. 1933. Internal rotation of the fetal head. *Amer. J. Obstet. Gynec.*, **25**, 74–94.

SACHS, H. 1922. Elektrokardiogrammstudien am Foetus in utero. *Arch. ges. Physiol.*, **197**, 536–542.

SARWEY, O. 1915. Anatomie und Physiologie der Schwangerschaft. Pt. 2. In A. DÖDERLEIN (Ed.), *Handbuch der Geburtshilfe,* pp. 153–245. Wiesbaden : Bergmann.

SCAMMON, R. E. 1927. The literature on the growth and physical development of the fetus, infant, and child : A quantitative summary. *Anat. Rec.*, **35**, 241–267.

SCAMMON, R. E., and L. A. CALKINS. 1924. The relation between the body-weight and age of the human fetus. *Proc. Soc. Exp. Biol. Med.*, **22**, 157–161.

——. 1929. *The development and growth of the external dimensions of the human body in the fetal period.* Minneapolis : University of Minnesota Press.

SCHARPENBERG, L. G., and W. F. WINDLE. 1938. A study of spinal cord development in silver-stained sheep embryos correlated with early somatic movements. *J. Anat.*, **72**, 344–351.

SHARP, L. W. 1926. *An introduction to cytology.* New York : McGraw-Hill.

SHARPEY-SCHÄFER, E. 1928. The effects of denervation of a cutaneous area. *Quart. J. Exp. Physiol.*, **19**, 85–107.

SHELDON, W. H., S. S. STEVENS, and W. B. TUCKER. 1940. *The varieties of human physique.* New York : Harper.

SHERMAN, M., and I. C. SHERMAN. 1925. Sensori-motor responses in infants. *J. Comp. Psychol.*, **5**, 53–68.

SHERRINGTON, C. S. 1922. Some aspects of animal mechanism. *Science*, **56**, 345–355.

SHIRLEY, M. M. 1931*a*. A motor sequence favors the maturation theory. *Psychol. Bull.*, **28**, 204–205.

——. 1931*b*. Is development saltatory as well as continuous? *Psychol. Bull.*, **28**, 664–665.

SKINNER, B. F. 1931. The concept of the reflex in the description of behavior. *J. Gen. Psychol.,* **5,** 427–458.

SMALL, W. S. 1899. Notes on the psychic development of the young white rat. *Amer. J. Psychol.,* **11,** 80–100.

SNYDER, F. F., and M. ROSENFELD. 1937. Direct observation of intrauterine respiratory movements of the fetus and the role of carbon dioxide and oxygen in their regulation. *Amer. J. Physiol.,* **119,** 153–166.

SONTAG, L. W. 1941. The significance of fetal environmental differences. *Amer. J. Obstet. Gynec.,* **42,** 996–1003.

SPEE, F. 1915. Anatomie und Physiologie der Schwangerschaft. Pt. 1. In A. DÖDERLEIN (Ed.), *Handbuch der Geburtshilfe,* pp. 1–152. Wiesbaden : Bergmann.

SPELT, D. K. 1938. Conditioned responses in the human fetus in utero. *Psychol. Bull.,* **35,** 712–713.

SPEMANN, H. 1927. Organizers in animal development. (Croonian Lecture.) *Proc. Roy. Soc. London,* **102B,** 177–187.

SPENCER, H. R. 1921. *William Harvey, obstetric physician and gynaecologist.* (The Harveian Oration, 1921.) London : Harrison and Sons.

———. 1924. The renaissance of midwifery. (Lloyd Roberts Lecture, 1924.) *Lancet,* **2,** 1049–1056.

———. 1927. *The history of British midwifery from 1650–1800.* London : Bale and Danielsson.

STARLING, E. H. 1900. The muscular and nervous mechanisms of the respiratory movements. In E. SHARPEY-SCHÄFER (Ed.), *Textbook of physiology.* Vol. 2, pp. 274–312. Edinburgh : Pentland.

STEELE, A. G., and W. F. WINDLE. 1939. Some correlations between respiratory movements and blood gases in cat foetuses. *J. Physiol.,* **94,** 531–538.

STEVENS, S. S., and H. DAVIS. 1938. *Hearing: Its psychology and physiology.* New York : Wiley.

STIEBEL, F. 1815. Ueber die Entwicklung der Teichhornschnecken (*Limneus slagnalis*). *Dtsch. Arch. Physiol.,* **1,** 423–426.

STRASSMANN, P. 1903. Das Leben vor der Geburt. *Samml. klin. Vortr., N. F., Gynäk.,* No. 353, 947–968.

STRAUS, W. L. 1939. Changes in the structure of skeletal muscle at the time of its first visible contraction in living rat embryos. *Anat. Rec.,* Suppl., **73,** 50.

STRAUS, W. L., and G. WEDDELL. 1940. Nature of the first visible contractions of the forelimb musculature in rat fetuses. *J. Neurophysiol.,* **3,** 358–369.

STREETER, G. L. 1906. On the development of the membranous labyrinth and the acoustic and facial nerves in the human embryo. *Amer. J. Anat.,* **6,** 139–165.

STREETER, G. L. 1920. Weight, sitting height, head size, foot length, and menstrual age of the human embryo. *Contr. Embryol., Carnegie Inst. Wash.,* **11,** No. 55, 143–170.

SUTHERLAND, G. F. 1921. Contributions to the physiology of the stomach: LVII. The response of the stomach glands to gastrin before and shortly after birth. *Amer. J. Physiol.,* **55,** 398–403.

SWAMMERDAM, J. 1752. *Bibel der Natur.* Leipzig.

———. (Edited.) 1907. Versuche, die besondere Bewegung der Fleischstränge am Frosche betreffend. In *Opuscula selecta neerlandecorrim de arte medica,* Fasc. 1, 82–135. Amsterdam.

SWENSON, E. A. 1925. The use of cerebral anemia in experimental embryological studies upon mammals. *Anat. Rec.,* **30,** 147–151.

———. 1926. *The development of movement of the albino rat before birth.* Unpublished Doctor's Thesis, University of Kansas.

———. 1928a. Motion pictures of activities of living albino-rat fetuses. (Abs.) *Anat. Rec.,* **38,** 63.

———. 1928b. The simple movements of the trunk of the albino-rat fetus. *Anat. Rec.,* **38,** 31.

———. 1929. The active simple movements of the albino-rat fetus: The order of their appearance, their qualities, and their significance. (Abs.) *Anat. Rec.,* **42,** 40.

THORNDIKE, E. L. 1913. *Educational psychology:* Vol. I. *The original nature of man.* New York : Teachers College, Columbia University.

———. 1931. *Human learning.* New York : Century.

TILNEY, F., and L. CASAMAJOR. 1924. Myelinogeny as applied to the study of behavior. *Arch. Neurol. Psychiat.,* **12,** 1–66.

TILNEY, F., and L. S. KUBIE. 1931. Behavior in its relation to the development of the brain. *Bull. Neurol. Inst. N. Y.,* **1,** 229–313.

TINKLEPAUGH, O. L., and C. G. HARTMAN. 1930. Behavioral aspects of parturition in the monkey (*Macacus rhesus*). *J. Comp. Psychol.,* **11,** 63–98.

TINKLEPAUGH, O. L., C. G. HARTMAN, and R. R. SQUIER. 1930. The fetal heart rate in the monkey (*Macacus rhesus*). *Proc. Soc. Exp. Biol. Med.,* **28,** 285–288.

TOMPKINS, J. McC. 1911–1912. Influences during pregnancy upon the unborn child. *Old Dominion J. Med. Surg., Richmond,* **13,** 219–224.

TRACY, H. C. 1926. The development of motility and behavior reactions in the toadfish (*Opsanus tau*). *J. Comp. Neurol.,* **40,** 253–369.

TUGE, H. 1931. Early behavior of embryos of the turtle, *Terrapene carolina* (L). *Proc. Soc. Exp. Biol. Med.,* **29,** 52–53.

TUGE, H. 1934. Early behavior of the embryos of carrier-pigeons. *Proc. Soc. Exp. Biol. Med.*, **31**, 462–463.

VINCENT, S. B. 1912. The function of the vibrissae in the behavior of the white rat. *Behav. Monogr.*, **1**, No. 5. Pp. 81.

VIREY. 1833. Rémarques sur la position du foetus dans l'utérus dans les diverses séries des animaux. *Arch. gén. méd.* (2d ser.), **1**, 295–298.

WADA, T. 1923. Anatomical and physiological studies on the growth of the inner ear of the albino rat. *Amer. Anat. Memoirs, Wistar Inst. Anat. Biol.*, **10**, 174.

WALTON, C. E. 1910. Maternal impressions. *J. Surg. Gynec. Obstet., New York*, **32**, 27–29.

WALZ, W. 1922. Ueber die Bedeutung der intrauterinen Atembewegungen. *Mschr. Geburtsh. Gynäk.*, **60**, 331–341.

WANG, G. H., and T. W. LU. 1940. Spontaneous activity of the spinal tadpoles of the frog and the toad. *Science*, **92**, 148.

———. 1941. Development of swimming and righting reflexes in frog (*Rana guetheri*): Effects thereon of transection of central nervous system before hatching. *J. Neurophysiol.*, **4**, 137–146.

WARDEN, C. J., *et al.* 1931. *Animal motivation: Experimental studies on the albino rat.* New York: Columbia University Press.

WARKENTIN, J. 1938. *A genetic study of vision in animals.* Unpublished Doctor's Thesis, University of Rochester.

WARKENTIN, J., and L. CARMICHAEL. 1939. A study of the development of the air-righting reflex in cats and rabbits. *J. Genet. Psychol.*, **55**, 67–80.

WARKENTIN, J., and K. U. SMITH. 1937. The development of visual acuity in the cat. *J. Genet. Psychol.*, **50**, 371–399.

WASHBURN, M. F. 1926. *The animal mind.* New York: Macmillan.

WATSON, J. B. 1903. *Animal education: The psychical development of the white rat.* Chicago: University of Chicago Press.

WEBER, E. H. 1847. Ueber den Einfluss der Erwärmung und Erkältung der Nerven auf ihr Leitungsvermögen. *Arch. Anat. Physiol.*, 342–356.

WEED, L. H. 1917. The reactions of kittens after decerebration. *Amer. J. Physiol.*, **43**, 131–157.

WEED, L. H., and O. R. LANGWORTHY. 1925a. Decerebrate rigidity in the opossum. *Amer. J. Physiol.*, **72**, 25–38.

———. 1925b. Developmental study of excitatory areas in the cerebral cortex of the opossum. *Amer. J. Physiol.*, **72**, 8–24.

———. 1926. Physiological study of cortical motor areas in young kittens and in adult cats. *Contr. Embryol., Carnegie Inst. Wash.*, **17**, No. 87, 89–106.

WEISS, A. P. 1929. The measurement of infant behavior. *Psychol. Rev.*, **36**, 453–471.

WEISS, P. 1926. The relations between central and peripheral coordination. *J. Comp. Neurol.*, **40**, 241–252.

———. 1939. *Principles of development.* New York: Holt.

WERTHEIMER, E. 1904. Foetus. In C. RICHET (Ed.), *Dictionnaire de physiologie,* Vol. VI, pp. 499–634. Paris: Alcan.

WETZEL, N. C. 1941. Physical fitness in terms of physique, development and basal metabolism. *J. Amer. Med. Ass.*, **116**, 1187–1195.

WHITE, G. M. 1915. The behavior of brook trout embryos from the time of hatching to the absorption of the yolk sac. *J. Anim. Behav.*, **5**, 44–60.

WHITEHEAD, J. 1867. Convulsions in utero. *Brit. Med. J.*, 59–60.

WILLIAMS, J. W. 1931. *Obstetrics.* New York: Appleton.

WILSON, E. E., W. F. WINDLE, and H. L. ALT. 1941. Deprivation of placental blood as a cause of iron deficiency in infants. *Amer. J. Dis. Child.*, **62**, 320–327.

WILSON, E. E., W. F. WINDLE, and J. E. FITZGERALD. 1941. Development of the tractus solitarius. *J. Comp. Neurol.*, **74**, 287–307.

WINDLE, W. F. 1930a. The earliest fetal movements in the cat correlated with the neurofibrillar development of the spinal cord. (Abs.) *Anat. Rec.*, **45**, 249.

———. 1930b. Normal behavioral reactions of kittens correlated with the postnatal development of nerve-fiber density in the spinal gray matter. *J. Comp. Neurol.*, **50**, 479–503.

———. 1931. The neurofibrillar structure of the spinal cord of cat embryos correlated with the appearance of early somatic movements. *J. Comp. Neurol.*, **53**, 71–113.

———. 1932. The neurofibrillar structure of the five-and-one-half-millimeter cat embryo. *J. Comp. Neurol.*, **55**, 315–331.

———. 1934a. Correlation between the development of local reflexes and reflex arcs in the spinal cord of cat embryos. *J. Comp. Neurol.*, **59**, 487–505.

———. 1934b. Correlation between the development of spinal reflexes and reflex arcs in albino-rat embryos. (Abs.) *Anat. Rec.*, Suppl., **58**, 42.

———. 1935. Neurofibrillar development of cat embryos: Extent of development in the telencephalon and diencephalon up to 15 mm. *J. Comp. Neurol.*, **63**, 139–172.

———. 1937. On the nature of the first forelimb movements of mammalian embryos. *Proc. Soc. Exp. Biol. Med.*, **36**, 640–642.

———. 1939. Calcium and potassium deficiency as possible causes of certain delayed fetal movements. *Physiol. Zoöl.*, **12**, 39–41.

———. 1940. *Physiology of the fetus: Origin*

and extent of function in prenatal life. Philadelphia : Saunders.

WINDLE, W. F. 1941a. Development of the blood and changes in the blood picture at birth. *J. Pediat.*, 18, 538–563.

——. 1941b. Physiology and anatomy of the respiratory system in the fetus and newborn infant. *J. Pediat.*, 19, 437–444.

WINDLE, W. F., and M. F. AUSTIN. 1936. Neurofibrillar development in the central nervous system of chick embryos up to 5 days' incubation. *J. Comp. Neurol.*, 63, 431–463.

WINDLE, W. F., and J. BARCROFT. 1938. Some factors governing the initiation of respiration in the chick. *Amer. J. Physiol.*, 121, 684–691.

WINDLE, W. F., and R. E. BAXTER. 1935. Development of reflex mechanisms in the spinal cord of albino rat embryos. Correlations between structure and function and comparisons with the cat and the chick. *J. Comp. Neurol.*, 63, 189–209.

——. 1936. The first neurofibrillar development in albino rat embryos. *J. Comp. Neurol.*, 63, 173–185.

WINDLE, W. F., and R. F. BECKER. 1940a. The course of the blood through the fetal heart. An experimental study in the cat and guinea pig. *Anat. Rec.*, 77, 417–426.

——. 1940b. The relation of anoxemia to early activity in the fetal nervous system. *Arch. Neurol. Psychiat.*, 43, 90–101.

WINDLE, W. F., and W. M. FISH. 1932. The development of the vestibular righting reflex in the cat. *J. Comp. Neurol.*, 54, 85–96.

WINDLE, W. F., M. W. FISH, and J. E. O'DONNELL. 1934. Myelogeny of the cat as related to development of fiber tracts and prenatal behavior patterns. *J. Comp. Neurol.*, 59, 139–166.

WINDLE, W. F., and J. E. FITZGERALD. 1937. Development of the spinal reflex mechanism in human embryos. *J. Comp. Neurol.*, 67, 493–509.

WINDLE, W. F., and A. M. GRIFFIN. 1931. Observations on embryonic and fetal movements of the cat. *J. Comp. Neurol.*, 52, 149–188.

WINDLE, W. F., and W. L. MINEAR. 1934. Reversal of reaction pattern in the course of development of the snout reflex of the cat embryo. (Abs.) *Anat. Rec.*, Suppl., 58, 92.

WINDLE, W. F., W. L. MINEAR, M. F. AUSTIN, and D. W. ORR. 1935. The origin and early development of somatic behavior in the albino rat. *Physiol. Zoöl.*, 8, 156–175.

WINDLE, W. F., M. MONNIER, and A. G. STEELE. 1938. Fetal respiratory movements in the cat. *Physiol. Zoöl.*, 11, 425–433.

WINDLE, W. F., and D. NELSON. 1938. Development of respiration in the duck. *Amer. J. Physiol.*, 121, 700–707.

WINDLE, W. F., J. E. O'DONNELL, and E. E.

GLASSHAGLE. 1933. The early development of spontaneous and reflex behavior in cat embryos and fetuses. *Physiol. Zoöl.*, 6, 521–541.

WINDLE, W. F., and D. W. ORR. 1934a. The development of behavior in chick embryos : Spinal cord structure correlated with early somatic motility. *J. Comp. Neurol.*, 60, 287–308.

——. 1934b. Vermiform contractions of the musculature of cat embryos at death. *Anat. Rec.*, Suppl., 58, 92.

WINDLE, W. F., D. W. ORR, and W. L. MINEAR. 1934. The origin and development of reflexes in the cat during the third fetal week. *Physiol. Zoöl.*, 7, 600–617.

WINDLE, W. F., L. G. SCHARPENBERG, and A. G. STEELE. 1938. Influence of carbon dioxide and anoxemia upon respiration in the chick at hatching. *Amer. J. Physiol.*, 121, 692–699.

WINDLE, W. F., M. SWEET, and W. H. WHITEHEAD. 1940. Some aspects of prenatal and postnatal development of the blood in the cat. *Anat. Rec.*, 78, 321–332.

WINTREBERT, M. P. 1904. Sur l'existence d'une irritabilité excito-motrice primitive, indépendante des voies nerveuses chez les embryons ciliés de Batraciens. *C. R. Soc. Biol., Paris,* 57, 645.

——. 1920. La contraction rhythmée aneurale des myotomes chez les embryons de selaciens : I. Observation de Scylliorhinus canicula L. *Gill. Arch. zoöl. expér.,* 60, 221.

WITKOWSKI, G. J. 1887. *Histoire des accouchements chez tous les peuples.* Paris : Steinheil.

WOODWORTH, R. S. 1929. *Psychology.* (Rev. ed.) New York : Holt.

WOYCIECHOWSKI, B. 1928. Ruchy zarodka ludzkiego 42 mm. *Polsk. Gazeta Lekarska,* 7, 409–411.

YANASE, J. 1907a. Beiträge zur Physiologie der peristaltischen Bewegungen des embryonalen Darmes : I. Mitteilung. *Pflüg. Arch. ges. Physiol.,* 117, 345–383.

——. 1907b. Beiträge zur Physiologie der peristaltischen Bewegungen des embryonalen Darmes : II. Mitteilung. *Pflüg. Arch. ges. Physiol.,* 119, 451–464.

YOUNGSTROM, K. A. 1937. Studies on the developing behavior of *Anura. J. Comp. Neurol.,* 68, 351–379.

——. 1938. On the relationship between the acetylcholine esterase content and the development of motility in *Amblystoma punctatum.* (Abs.) *Anat. Rec.*, Suppl., 70, 85.

——. 1941. Acetylcholine esterase concentration during the development of the human fetus. *J. Neurophysiol.*, 4, 473–477.

ZUNTZ, N. 1877. Ueber die Respiration des Säugethier-Foetus. *Pflüg. Arch. ges. Physiol.,* 14, 605–637.

CHAPTER 3

ANIMAL INFANCY

RUTH M. CRUIKSHANK

Historical Introduction

The study of the genetic development of human behavior would not be complete without some reference to and comparison with the ontogeny of behavior in sub-human forms. Accordingly, this chapter has been included in this manual. An analysis of the development of young animals should show in clearly defined ways the general similarities and differences in the development of behavior in man and animals from which general principles can be drawn. Gesell (1928) has very tersely stated this:

The study of infancy in its broadest sense must therefore be a comparative science. The more general laws of development in the very nature of things will be applicable to all vertebrates not excluding either fish or man. In spite of the bewildering diversity of the behavior traits of the young of widely varying species, it is not improbable that there are certain orders of emergence and sequences of pattern which are common to all. It is conceivable moreover that certain pervading correspondences may even yield to quantitative and qualitative gradations when the infancies of a large array of species are systematically studied from the standpoint of developmental economy (p. 336).

More than this, however, such studies make the contribution of supplying information on problems which may not be readily accessible or even possible for observational and experimental study in the human being. A survey of the preceding chapter by Carmichael as well as of this chapter will suffice to point out certain problems to which studies of the development of the young animal have contributed, or may in the future contribute, additional crucial data. Until complete descriptive accounts of the normal development of young animals have been made, however, progress in the studies whose aim is more than descriptive must remain limited.

Although the young of groups other than the mammals are of interest for any complete survey of this topic, this review is restricted to a consideration of mammalian infancy. Lack of space and, indeed, lack of sufficiently correlated detail make this limitation seem advisable at this time. However, the reader interested in the inclusion of other animals is referred to the accounts of Mitchell (1912) and Pycraft (1913).

That the young as well as the adult of a given species must be observed has probably been considered for some time, although careful and accurate observational studies of young animals in the field or laboratory have not been carried out until comparatively recent times. A statement by Rennie in 1838, quoted by Yerkes and Yerkes (1929), expresses this idea:

The great interest attached to the chimpanzee, as approaching so nearly to ourselves in the scale of animal life, has induced us to dwell longer upon this part of his history than we had originally intended, but we hope without either wearying the patience or exhausting the curiosity of our readers. A thorough acquaintance with the manners and intelligence of the young animal, as accurately observed and related by zoologists accustomed to such investigations, was besides necessary to enable us to form a just estimate of the habits and economy attributed to the adult in his native forests, and of the degree of credit to which the accounts of different travellers are entitled (p. 209).

John Fiske states the case for an understanding of animal infancy as it is probably most familiar to a student of genetic psychology. His essay, *The Meaning of Infancy,* written in 1883 and republished several times, brought attention to this problem, although post-Darwinian workers in biology, physiology, and psychology had already begun to investigate it. This is Fiske's informal report of how he became interested in the problem:

Well, in the spring of 1871, when Darwin's "Descent of Man" came out, just about the same time I happened to be reading Wallace's account of his experiences in the Malay Archipelago, and how at one time he caught a female orang-outang with a new-born baby, and the mother died, and Wallace brought up the baby orang-outang by hand; and this baby orang-outang had a kind of infancy which was a great deal longer than that of a cow or a sheep, but it was nothing compared to human infancy in length. This little orang-outang could not get up and march around, as mammals of less intelligence do, when he was first born, or within three or four days; but after three or four weeks or so he would get up, and begin taking hold of something and pushing it around, just as children push a chair; and he went through a period of staring at his hands, as human babies do, and altogether was a good deal slower in getting to the point where he could take care of himself. And while I was reading of that I thought,

Dear me! if there is any one thing in which the human race is signally distinguished from other mammals, it is in the enormous duration of their infancy; but it is a point that I do not recollect ever seeing any naturalist so much as allude to (1911 ed., pp. 25–26).

Although at this time a complete historical account of the early studies on the development of behavior in young animals will not be given, it might be well to mention just a few of the more important contributions which have led to our present interest in the subject.

One of the early studies of animal infancy was made by Spalding (1873, 1875), who stressed the necessity for an understanding of the development of young organisms in order to answer certain theoretical questions then prevalent. Spalding's observations were carried out to establish evidence regarding the existence of instincts in the young animal.

Preyer's work (1882) may be taken as pioneer in the experimental study of the psychological aspects of infancy considered in the broad comparative sense. Preyer refers to various behavior items of young animals, comparing them with those of the human infant. His work also includes observations of fetal behavior so that, notwithstanding the fact that his studies are among the first to treat of behavioral development, they do not fall into the error of considering it as a strictly postnatal phenomenon.

Mills (1898) likewise appears to be among the first to attempt a description of the behavior of young animals. Mills enlarges the significance of the study by pointing out the necessity of such a study as part of the total field of psychology. His position is clearly stated:

It must be equally clear to those who, guided by facts alone, untrammelled by tradition and dogma of every kind, compare the psychic status of the young with that of the mature animal, that psychogenesis is a fact; that the mind does unfold, evolve, develop equally with the body. And as with the body so with the mind, each stage in this development can only be understood in the light of all the previous stages.

This truth is apparently as yet only dimly comprehended, for, till recently, studies on psychic history, development or psychogenesis have been all but unknown, and as yet, even in the case of man, are very few and confessedly imperfect (pp. 113–114).

The next important work concerning the young mammal is Small's (1899). Taking his lead from Mills, Small made a detailed study of the development of the white rat. Small, distinctly recognizing his problem as one in genetic psychology, introduced his study as follows:

A study of the psychic development of any young animal needs no apology. Apart from the fascination and the self-education of watching the development of any form of life from its early protoplasmic simplicity into complex maturity, there is the solid scientific reason that Genetic Psychology has much to hope from minute and accurate records of the developmental periods of young animals of all species. It may never be possible to reconstruct a complete psychic organism from the evidence of a single trait—an ideal borrowed from morphology—but something surely may be accomplished towards a *comparative embryology* of the soul. What Preyer and others have done for the human infant, needs to be done also for the babyanimal of every species (p. 80).

In 1903, Watson published an experimental study of the psychological development of the white rat correlated with the growth of its nervous system. Watson did not repeat Small's work but, testing the

rat in simple learning situations, endeavored to ascertain the age of psychological maturity for the rodent. This he placed at approximately twenty-four days, although the animal learned in simpler situations at an earlier age.

Allen's work (1904) on the behavior of the guinea pig was published the next year. Allen's study was comparable to Watson's in aim, an examination of another member of the rodent group.

Yerkes' work (1907) on the dancing mouse contains reference to the development of the young mouse, but it is primarily a study of the mature animal.

More recent work on the development of behavior in young animals is treated topically rather than chronologically in other sections of this chapter.

Behavior of the Newborn Animal

Several references to the behavior of the newborn animal are to be found in the literature. These studies derive their significance from the fact that birth represents a stage of transition from one type of environment to another. When such observations are interpreted in light of the longer developmental history of the organism, they offer valuable data; but when they are interpreted without reference to the preceding behavioral development of the animal, they are extremely misleading. When the literature on certain topics of psychological interest such as that of "instinct" is reviewed, the reader is indeed impressed with this fact.

The developmental levels which mammals have reached in intrauterine life have been reviewed for the reader in the preceding chapter by Carmichael. Descriptions of the functional development of the animal at birth are found in succeeding parts of this chapter. For further discussions of the development of specific animals at or soon after birth the reader is referred to the accounts of: Small (1899), rat; Allen (1904), guinea pig; Goerling (1913), kangaroo; Lashley and Watson (1913), monkey; Blair (1920), chimpanzee; Hartman (1920, 1921, 1928a), opossum; Allesch (1921), chimpanzee; Tilney and Casamajor (1924), cat; Robinson (1925), gibbon; Shaw (1925), Columbian ground squirrel; Johnson (1927), prairie dog; Kao (1927), rabbit; Wade (1927), striped ground squirrel; Avery (1928), guinea pig; Hartman (1928b), monkey; Struthers (1928), Canadian porcupine; Fox (1929), chimpanzee and orangutan; Sturman-Hulbe and Stone (1929), rat; White (1929), chimpanzee; Brown (1930), chimpanzee; Kuroda (1930), monkey; Sherman (1930), bat; Windle (1930), cat; Enders (1931), agouti; Jacobsen, Jacobsen, and Yoshioka (1932), chimpanzee; Tinklepaugh (1932), chimpanzee; Tinklepaugh and Hartman (1932), monkey; Coolidge (1933), gibbon; Coronios (1933), cat; Huestis (1933), deermouse; Foley (1934), monkey; Svihla (1934), deermouse; Tomilin and Yerkes (1935), chimpanzee; Yerkes and Tomilin (1935), chimpanzee; Errington (1939), muskrat; Fisher (1940), sea otter; Yerkes (1940), chimpanzee; and Cooper (1942), lion.

Sensory Development of Young Animals

Vision. The ages at which certain visual responses are observed after birth can be seen by reference to Table 1. A survey of certain studies of the development of visual acuity is made by Warkentin and Smith (1937). They also report the best evidence concerning the development of visual acuity for the young kitten. They give average ages for eye opening (9 days), nystagmus (14 days), visual placing (25 days), acuity of 360-minute visual angle (14 days), acuity of 180-minute visual

angle (16 days), acuity of 43-minute visual angle (21 days), and acuity of 11-minute visual angle (25 days). There was no relationship noted between the age of eye opening and the appearance of nystagmus, but a high degree of visual acuity preceded visual placing responses. Concerning the visual acuity of the young chimpanzee and the young child, the Kelloggs (1933) point out that the animal seems to possess very great acuity and notices many finer details than does the child (pp. 89–90). The point needs experimental study.

Turner (1935) has investigated the visual responses of young rats allowed to orient toward a black door in a brightly lighted field. Animals with eyes open perform more efficiently than animals with eyes still closed, and the older animals orient with a greater degree of accuracy, indicating some genetic development of this type of response. This development seems to be correlated with the increased efficiency of the eye mechanism and possibly also with increased learning in the situation. Food deprivation does not seem to have any large effect upon the young rat's orientation to light (Biel, 1939). For a discussion of phototropisms in rats, see Crozier and Pincus (1927a).

Investigations of the genetic development of color vision in those mammals which might be expected to have such vision are practically nonexistent. There are to be found investigations of sensitivity to red in the rabbit (Washburn and Abbott, 1912) and in the calf (Kittredge, 1923), a few comments such as those of the Kelloggs (1933, p. 92) concerning the infant chimpanzee, and a study of methods suitable for such work by A. W. Yerkes (1935).

The development of distance perception in young animals, it would seem, might be investigated experimentally with profitable results. Foley (1934) comments that during the early days for the young monkey he observed "misjudged distances were the rule rather than the exception" (p. 76). The reactions of the older animal, however, were swift and accurate (Foley, 1935). Kuckuk (1936) reports a number of interesting observations of young bears' regognition of a familiar figure at a distance. In contrast with these observations are those of Lashley and Russell (1934), who found that adult rats reared in total darkness during their earlier life can, without training, discriminate distances and jump with a force well adapted to the distances involved.

We also have some evidence concerning the genetic development of such functions as pattern vision, size discrimination, and brightness discrimination. Hebb's experimental investigations (1937a, 1937b) of the adult rat's discrimination of these variables after being reared in darkness from the age of six or eight days to maturity indicate that for this animal the proficiency of performance does not depend upon previous visual stimulation. When tested at maturity, pattern vision of rats from which the visual cortex had been removed in infancy is lost according to Tsang (1937b), although discrimination of brightness and relative size persists as it does in adult operates. Tsang notes a few cases which be believes suggest a primitive type of pattern vision in young operates, which, however, is by no means as delicate as that of the normal animals.

Audition. Observational evidence concerning audition in young animals is given in Table 1. Data of this sort are subject to considerable error, but until further evidence is offered they must suffice. Pitch discrimination and intensity discrimination have not been satisfactorily tested. Biel (1939) notes that young animals deprived of food respond to sound stimulation at a significantly later age than do normally fed rats.

Interesting comparisons of auditory localization in the young chimpanzee and the child were obtained by the Kelloggs (1933), who required the blindfolded subject to find the experimenter, whose position could be determined only by his voice. The child at 16 to 17 months made an average error of 40.2 degrees in localizing the sound, whereas the chimpanzee at 13½ to 14½ months made an average error of 25.9 degrees. An 8-year-old child tested in the same way made an average error of 15 degrees. Observations by Kuckuk (1936) on auditory distance perception in young bears are of note.

Olfaction and Gustation. Evidence concerning olfactory and gustatory sensitivity in young animals is given in Table 1 under the appropriate headings. Techniques adequate for measuring olfaction in young animals unable to make decisive motor responses have not been worked out. Pfaffman's technique (1936) for studying gustatory sensitivity in young animals deserves special mention. The number of sucking responses which a young animal makes to various solutions is recorded graphically. Using young kittens, Pfaffman reports differential sensitivity to salt and milk at one day. The 10-day-old animal discriminates solutions of salt and bitter and shows some sensitivity to solutions of sweet and sour. Comments upon the responses of the young chimpanzee to gustatory and olfactory stimuli are given by the Kelloggs (1933).

Touch, Pain, Temperature, and Kinesthesis. Since nearly all young animals observed seem to be sensitive to tactile stimulation (see Table 1), a study of the ontogeny of such responses must deal with the fetal organism. It is probable that thigmotactic responses play a large part in the huddling behavior of young animals, although to what extent this occurs has not been experimentally demonstrated.

TABLE 1

Typical Results from Observations of the Development of Behavior in Young Mammals *

Response	Rat	Guinea Pig	Rabbit	Cat	Dog	Monkey	Chimpanzee
Pupillary response			12 days K † 14th day M	7 days TC 12th day M 7–10 days Wi		(3) days F 2 days LW 2, 3 days HT	1st week JJY
Winking, nonvisual		1 day P	2 days K 14th day M	9 days M	13 days M	(3) days F 1 day LW 1 day HT	1 day JJY
Winking, visual	17 days S	2 days M		11 days M	3d week M	10 days F 8 days HT	10th week JJY
Visual pursuit		2 days M	22 days K 22 days M	14 days TC 14 days M 15 days Wi	18th day M	7 days F 3 days LW 5, 11 days HT	1–2 weeks JJY 1 mo. W
Reaching, visually directed						6 days F 5 days LW	8th week JJY
Responds to sound	17 days S	1 day M 1 day P	11 days K 10 days M	8 days M ?1 day Wi	17th day M	(3) days F 2 days LW 2, 4 days HT	1 day JJY early weeks W
Auditory localization		1 day P		26 days TC 9 days M 21 days Wi	3d–4th week M	12 days LW	
Olfactory responses	1 day S	1 day M 1 day P	4 days K 1st week M	?1 day M	1–2 weeks M	(3) days F 2, 3 days HT	
Gustatory response	1 day S	1 day M 1 day P	2d week M	?9 days M	1 week M		2 days JJY
Tactual responses	?1 day S		1 day M	1 day M	?1 day M	(3) days F 1 day LW	1 day JJY early weeks W
Pain responses	1 day S		1 day K 1 day M	?1 day M	1st week M	(3) days F 1 day LW	1 day JJY

Temperature	1 day S		1 day K ?1 day M	1 day M	1st week M	(3) days F 1 day HT	1 day JJY
Surface righting	1–4 days S		1 day K	1 day Wi			
Air righting				28–30 days Wi			
Scratching	14 days S		1 day K 2nd day M	23 days TC 1 day Wi 16 days M	17th day M	9 days F 12 days LW 7, 14 days HT	3½ mo. W
Crawling	4 days S	1 day M	1 day K 1 day M	1 day TC 1 day M 1 day Wi	1 day M		7–11th week JJY
Swimming				1 day TC 1 day Wi			
Sitting				20 days TC 21 days Wi			12th week JJY
Standing	12–14 days S	1 day M	17 days K 15th day M	14 days Wi 15 days M	?2 weeks M	13 days F 13 days LW 1, 3 days HT	12th week four limb 27th week erect JJY
Walking	12 days S	1 day M 1 day P	6 days K 12 days Hopping 10 days Hopping M	22 days TC 20 days M	2 weeks M	13 days F 13 days LW 1, 5 days HT	13th week four limb 29th week erect JJY
Running	14 days S	1 day M 1 day P		26 days TC 28 days Wi	5th week M		23rd week JJY
Climbing	12–14 days S			31 days TC 4th week Wi 18 days M		(3) days F 24 days LW 1, 2, 4 days HT	25th week JJY

* The chart should be read with recognition of its many sources of error, including (1) observation of the neonatal animal without reference to the fetal animal, (2) casual rather than systematic observations, and (3) variability of developmental ages. Reference for more accurate data for animals whose fetal development has been studied should be made to the preceding chapter by Carmichael.

† Abbreviations: F—Foley (1934); HT—Hartman and Tinklepaugh (1932); JJY—Jacobsen, Jacobsen, and Yoshioka (1932); K—Kao (1927); LW—Lashley and Watson (1913); M—Mills (1898); P—Preyer (1882); S—Small (1899); TC—Tilney and Casamajor (1924); W—White (1929); Wi—Windle (1930).

Almost nothing concerning tactual localization in the neonatal animal appears in the literature. The Kelloggs' (1933) tests, in which a blunt pencil was touched to the body of the young chimpanzee at ten months, show that the animal makes almost perfect localizing responses. The animal appeared to be very sensitive to tickling (pp. 112–114).

Young animals show definite response to pain stimulation. (See Table 1 and also Anderson and Patrick, 1934.) The chimpanzee examined by the Kelloggs (1933) gave evidence of ability to localize the source of pain when tested at ten months (p. 118).

Numerous investigators report that they believe temperature variations play a dominant part in the activities of young animals. Huddling in young rats, for example, is considered by Small (1899) to be a manifestation of the need for warmth, and he suggests, as do others, that the need for warmth may be basic in socialization. That variations in temperature influence the amount of spontaneous activity of young animals has been shown by Stier (1930).

Orientation of young animals on an inclined plane has been studied in the rat by Crozier and Pincus (1926, 1927b, 1928, 1929a, 1929b, 1931a, 1931b, 1932a, 1932b, 1933) and by Pincus (1927); in mice by Crozier and Oxnard (1927); in the guinea pig by Upton (1930, 1932) and Elliott and Stavsky (1933); and in the kitten by Stavsky (1932).

Motor Development

A number of observations on the motor development of young animals are summarized in Table 1. For detailed descriptions of the motor development of specific animals the reader is referred to the investigations listed in the section on the behavior of the newborn animal. See also the description of reflexes in puppies (Bahrs, 1927), other discussions of locomotion in young animals (Hatt, 1931; Kennard, 1938; Beach, 1939), placing reactions in young animals (Tang, 1935; Warkentin and Smith, 1937), air-righting reflexes (Carmichael, 1934; Anderson and Patrick, 1934; Warkentin and Carmichael, 1939), grasping in young animals (Richter, 1931), handedness in rats (Wentworth, 1938), general activity of young rats (Slonaker, 1907, 1912), and persistence of sucking behavior (Lashley, 1914; Richter, 1925; Courthial, 1929).

A comparison of the development of motor functions in the infant chimpanzee and the human infant may be made by referring to the table compiled by Shirley (1931), to which Jacobsen, Jacobsen, and Yoshioka (1932) have appended the age of appearance of the behavior item in question for the young chimpanzee they observed. The first number refers to the age of appearance for the human infant, and the second to the age for the chimpanzee. (See Table 2.)

The young chimpanzee raised by the Kelloggs (1933) had passed through the stages of locomotion noted by the Jacobsens and Yoshioka except the final one of erect walking when she was first observed by them at 7½ months of age (pp. 71 ff.). Further development of climbing, jumping, and skipping occurred, and from the descriptions of these activities it appears that they reached a high level of proficiency comparable with the maturation and strength of the young chimpanzee.

The observations of the Jacobsens and Yoshioka (1932) on the development of manipulation in the young chimpanzee are worthy of more elaborate description, for they present a direct comparison with one of the more complex motor developments of the human infant. The young chim-

TABLE 2

Motor Development of Human Infant and Young Chimpanzee

(From Jacobsen Jacobsen, and Yoshioka, 1932, a adapted from Shirley 1931)

1. Progress toward creeping goes through the following stages:
   a. Lifting th head, chin free, when on the stomach; (3/3).
   b. Lifting the head, chest free, when on the stomach; (9/5).
   c. Knee pushing or swimming; (25/7).
   d. Rolling; (29/8–10).
   e. Rocking, pivoting, worming along; some method of making progress; (37/11).
   f. Scooting backward by using the hands.*
   g. Creeping forward.*
2. Progress assuming an upright posture goes through the following stages:
   a. Lifting the head when lying on the back; (15/5).
   b. Sitting along momentarily; (25/12).
   c. Sitting alone; (31/13).
   d. Standing, holding to furniture; (42/15).
   e. Pulling self to standing position by means of furniture; (47/15)
   f. Sitting from standing position.*
3. Progress toward walking goes through the following stages:
   a. An early period of stepping.†
   b. Standing with support of a person.†
   c. Walking with help, led by a person; (45/17).
   d. Standing alone; (62/20).
   e. Walking alone; (64/25–29).

* Did not appear for the chimpanzee
† Adequate tests not made for chimpanzee.

panzee shows reflex grasping at birth, continuation of the ability to hang by one arm (in contrast with its waning in the human infant), reaching without grasp during the fifth week, hand play and thumb and toe sucking in the seventh week, reaching and grasping during the eighth week, and further development of reaching and grasping during the succeeding weeks.

The animal's use of its mouth and its feet in reaching and grasping is noted by the authors. The descriptions of these authors and the comments by the Kelloggs (1933) concerning the very fine manipulations made with the lips by the chimpanzee Gua (p. 59) and the loss of certain skills in foot grasping by Gua after she had worn shoes (p. 237) indicate that under normal conditions the use of these members is more persistent and reaches a higher level of development in the chimpanzee than in the child, although mouth grasping and foot reaching do occur in the human infant. Significant in the manipulations of the chimpanzee is the level of proficiency to which they attain so that the animal is able to perform such skilled acts as guiding a spoon to the mouth (twenty-first week), removing a lid from a small can (twenty-eighth week), holding a nursing-bottle in each hand (thirtieth week), and walking erectly while carrying two small objects (forty-fourth week).

In the series of tests with common objects which the Kelloggs used in comparing the prehension of the child and the chimpanzee, the child excelled the chimpanzee in all but the handling of the envelope, which they both were able to do satisfactorily (pp. 61–62).

Considerable interest has been attached to the development of motor reactions in young animals through correlative neurological studies. It is not intended to treat this topic in detail here, but a few of the studies will be mentioned.

The study of the "electrically excitable" motor areas of the cortex has led to some observations with regard to the correlation of excitability and genetic development of certain motor reactions. The reader is referred to Huber (1934) for an historical review of this problem in which reference is made to the work of Soltmann (1876), Tarchanoff (1878), Ferrier (1880), Paneth

(1885), Mills (1898), Michailow (1910), Bechterew (1911), Weed and Langworthy (1925, 1926), and Langworthy (1927), among others. Most of these studies have indicated that excitability of the cortex occurs some days after birth with the areas associated with the hindlimbs and facial regions excitable later than those areas associated with the forelimbs. The conclusions listed below are ones to be found in the literature, but there is reason to believe that some of the data upon which they are based will be found to be inexact when techniques embodying improved apparatus and more specific knowledge of cortical anatomy are employed.[1]

1. There is a tendency for the appearance of excitability of forelimb areas before hindlimb areas.
2. There is an increase in the number of excitable points with age.
3. The threshold of excitability is higher for younger animals and decreases with age.
4. First movements so elicited are of the whole limb, and movement of discrete segments occurs later.
5. Correlation of development of function with "electrical excitability" of the cortex is difficult to appraise at present.

Attempts at correlating behavioral development with the myelinization of the nervous system have not given conclusive results. Watson (1903) and Angulo y González (1929), for example, have not found such a correlation. Tilney and Casamajor (1924) and Langworthy (1929), on the other hand, suggest that myeliniza-

tion occurs before the functional development of the parts.

Windle (1930) reports an increase in the density of nerve fibers in the spinal cord with increasing motor performance of the kitten.

Studies of the bioelectric phenomena of the central nervous system may in time give additional evidence concerning relationships between behavioral and neural development. Kornmüller's (1935) work and that of Jasper, Bridgman, and Carmichael (1937) are pioneer in this field.

Recent studies of the effect of brain lesions upon the behavior of the young animal and its subsequent behavior have extended the correlation between neurological and behavioral developments still further. Brooks and Peck (1940), removing the cortex of young rats during the first five days of postnatal life, found that ablation of the area of the cortex which for adult rats is the sensory motor area renders the placing and hopping reactions of these animals, when tested several months later, deficient to the same extent that it does those of the adult animal. Kennard (1936, 1938) has observed the effect of lesions made in the motor and premotor areas of the cortex in young monkeys upon their later motor performances. The age of the animal is one of the most important factors determining the deficiencies resulting from the lesion, inasmuch as the loss is not as severe in young animals.

Learning and Memory

As yet the work on the modifiability of response and the permanence of this change in the young animal is somewhat fragmentary, but there are a few problems such as the relationship of maze learning and age which have received more attention, al-

---

[1] Henry and Woolsey (1943), for example, have repeated the work on the kitten, using 60-cycle sine wave stimulation and exploring the cortex of the kitten in greater detail. They find, contrary to results of previous workers, that electrical stimulation elicits responses in the newborn animal from all the principal motor foci which are identifiable for the adult animal. It would seem that crucial data should be sought for the fetal animal.

though the results are not completely conclusive.

Incidental Observations. A number of incidental observations of learning in young animals can be found in the literature, but only a few items will be reported here. The feeding situation often provides interesting observations concerning the learning ability of young animals. Dove (1935) notes that the young of animals learn early in life to follow the mother and to eat the same type of food. Foley (1935) comments that, when he entered the laboratory in the morning before feeding time, the sound of his footsteps and the closing of the icebox door would elicit the "hunger-anticipation" cry of the young monkey he observed. The reader will profit from the discussions of the Kelloggs (1933) concerning the incidental learning of Gua in the human environment (pp. 188 ff.).

Maze Learning. There are a number of reports of maze-learning studies in animals of varying ages. Watson (1903) reports that young rats learn a maze more readily than do adult animals. Yerkes (1909) found that 1- to 2-month-old mice learned less readily than 10-month-old animals. Hubbert's (1915) results indicate that younger rats learn better than do older animals. Liu's (1928) animals 30 and 45 days old made the poorest scores, whereas animals 75 days old made the best scores. Animals older than 75 days performed less well. Stone (1929a, 1929b) reports that young animals 30 to 75 days old make superior scores. Biel (1939, 1940) found in a study of maze learning in young rats 16 to 29 days old that the older animals' performance is significantly superior to that of the younger ones. In an unpublished study of the writer it was found that no large differences in the ability of guinea pigs to run a maze are correlated with age. The younger animals were more active

than the older ones, but they did not make consistently superior performances.

Comparing the maze-learning ability of normal adult rats, adult rats hemidecorticated at 21 days of age, and animals decorticated in adulthood, Tsang (1937a) reports that greater deficiencies exist for the animals older at the time of operation than for the ones which were younger. He reports that a loss of less than 10 per cent of the cortex in the adult animal is as serious as that of 40 per cent in the young animal. Hemidecortication in which a diagonal decortication (that is, anterior and posterior quadrants of different hemispheres) was made had a greater detrimental effect than a unilateral decortication.

Other Problems. Golubeva (1939) was able to condition motor responses to acoustic stimuli in newborn guinea pigs.

Yerkes (1909) reports that young dancing mice 1 month old learn to make a white-black discrimination in fewer trials than do animals 4, 7, and 10 months old. Learning of a light-dark discrimination by kittens given differing amount of electrical shock for incorrect choice has been investigated by Dodson (1915). From his results it is indicated that the relationship of strength of stimulus to speed of learning depends upon the difficulty of the problem, so that with a difficult problem a medium shock is superior to a strong one, whereas with a simple problem a strong shock is definitely superior to a medium or a weak one.

Shuey (1932) found little evidence that kittens between 11 and 12 weeks old at the beginning of training can perform a simple alternation problem consisting of pressing two plates of the Jenkins problem box, although one of the nine animals tested seemed to have established a fairly consistent habit. All the kittens tested by Shuey (1931) in the Jenkins problem box learned three steps. A number of other steps were learned by some of the animals, but too few animals were used to show how significant the scores are.

For other observations of learning see Kinnaman (1902), Allen (1904), Hamilton (1911), and Kuckuk (1936).

Some reference is made in the literature to studies of immediate or delayed memory in young animals. The Kelloggs (1933) carried out a delayed-reaction experiment with their son and the young chimpanzee when the subjects were at the approximate ages of 10½ to 12 months and 8 to 10 months, respectively. Under the circumstances of their test situation, they found that the child could delay for 5 minutes, but that at 10 minutes he made errors in about half the trials. The animal, on the other hand, satisfactorily responded to the shorter time intervals and responded correctly in 7 out of 10 trials for an interval of 30 minutes. It appears that the chimpanzee could delay longer than the child in these circumstances. It would be interesting to know the whole course of development for the animal and the child.

Jacobsen, Taylor, and Haslerud (1936) investigated the question of immediate recall after frontal lesions in young monkeys. They found this to be permanently abolished with lesions in the young animal as well as in the older animals.

Effect of Food Deprivation on Learning. The question as to whether food deprivation in the very young animal has any deleterious effects upon subsequent learning has been studied recently by several investigators. Biel (1938) examined the effects upon the maze-learning behavior of young animals of severe inanition brought about by subjecting them to reduced food intake. He found no deleterious effect in their learning of the Warden U-maze or the Stone multiple-T maze. Using a multiple-T water maze, he found that rats subjected to food deprivation performed less efficiently at a later age than normally fed rats (1939).

Deprivation of vitamin B is shown by several workers to be detrimental to subsequent maze learning (Maurer and Tsai, 1929, 1930; Bernhardt, 1934; Maurer, 1935a; Poe, Poe, and Muenzinger, 1936, 1937; and Bernhardt and Herbert, 1937). Vitamin B_2 deficiency beginning at two weeks gives less retardation than B_1 or B complex deficit according to Muenzinger, Poe, and Poe (1937), although Maurer (1935b) showed retardation when the deprivation is begun earlier than at two weeks of age. The animals show greater deprivation when they are given a diet lacking vitamin B during the nursing period than at a later age.

Acute vitamin A shortage does not lead to as severe retardation in nursing rats as does a vitamin B deficiency. The number of trials for learning a maze is not significantly different from the learning of normals, although the time scores are reliably different, indicating loss of speed (Maurer, 1935c). The maze performance of young rats fed a diet of whole pasteurized cow's milk is not different from that of normally fed controls (Maurer, 1935d).

Emotional Behavior

Evidence for the development of emotion in young animals will be limited in this review almost entirely to a discussion of emotional development in subhuman primates. Avoidance responses and aggressive responses are, of course, to be noted in other animals. Small (1899), for example, notes that fear in young rats develops considerably after the onset of visual and auditory functions, and he believes that the young give evidence of pleasurable emotions, for they "show signs of satisfaction when hunger and the desire for warmth are satisfied" (p. 98). Kellogg (1931), however, did not find evidence of fear of a moving stimulus in young rats (four to five weeks old).

The aggressive behavior of cats toward rats has often been cited as an instance of instinctive behavior. Early observations showed that kittens do kill rats (Yerkes and Bloomfield, 1910), but more recent studies have shown certain variations in rat-killing behavior in young kittens. Rogers (1932) noted that the young kitten reacts differently to the rat, depending upon whether olfactory, visual, or tactual cues are dominant and whether or not the animal is hungry. The five-week-old kitten observed by McDougall and McDougall (1927) did kill wild mice, but it did not in the time of the observations kill several white rats with which it was caged from time to time. Kuo (1930) showed that animals reared in isolation killed less frequently than those reared with an adult in a rat-killing environment. Some animals which had previously not killed rats did so after they had seen this done, whereas animals reared with rats did not kill a rat like their cage-mate and, when allowed to watch another cat kill a rat, still failed to make frequent responses of this nature. More recent studies by Kuo (1938) show that, when kittens were reared together and with two cage-mate rats, they very seldom killed a cage-mate although they frequently ate a shaved rat or the young of the cage-mate rats (as did the adult rats themselves at times).

The monkey observed by Lashley and Watson (1913) showed avoidance responses to such noises as rustling paper at three weeks of age. Tinklepaugh and Hartman (1932) observed that, as long as the young monkeys under two weeks of age were clinging to some object, loud noises or stimuli which might lead to fear behavior were not effective. If the animal was pre- vented from clinging or grasping, however, it showed some fear. Thwarting of the movement of the animal resulted in anger responses. Bingham (1927) reports that one young chimpanzee which he observed gave evidence of fear of the male parent by running to the female parent and cling- ing to her when the adult male was excited.

Several studies are reported from the Yale laboratories with regard to the de- velopment of emotional behavior in the chimpanzee. Jacobsen, Jacobsen, and Yoshioka (1932) report that patterns of fear, anger, mild fear, timidity, and mild excitement may be distinguished for the young chimpanzee. Patterns of fear and anger, although not well differentiated at first, could be observed from birth. The early fear responses were indicated by "clenching of feet and hands, drawing up of the arms and legs, and a tendency to cling to objects; by wrinkling of the face and retraction of the lips; and by a high- pitched crescendo scream" (p. 63). This behavior was elicited according to the au- thors in several situations: "(1) picking up the infant from the crib, a sudden light touch on various parts of the body, and sudden jarring of the crib; (2) complete removal of support when the infant was held in the arms; and (3) sudden intense noises" (p. 63). Some modifications of the response occurred during the first three months, and later, with the development of progression, the animal was able to re- treat from the situation.

Anger as a response during the first six months was difficult to distinguish from fear. What the authors consider a clear- cut instance of anger was observed during the twelfth week when the animal rejected a nursing-bottle after she had eaten. Thereafter on several occasions the chim- panzee screamed angrily when left alone. Later, anger was often set up by some activity of the animal which was interrupted or forced upon her.

The Jacobsens and Yoshioka differentiate fear from mild fear in that:

(1) Mild fear or timidity did not appear until the fourth or .fifth month, when the infant showed marked disturbance if a stranger approached her crib or attempted to handle her; (2) there was whimpering rather than screaming; (3) while the animal retreated under both conditions, in timidity the retreat was less rapid and less intense; the object was observed more or less continuously during withdrawal in contrast to the headlong flight in fear; (4) timidity was more readily overcome than fear (pp. 69–70).

Mild excitement is described by the Jacobsens and Yoshioka as indicated by

(1) approach toward or manipulation of the stimulating object or person, in contrast to withdrawal in timidity; (2) marked freedom of movement in contrast to the tension of fear and anger; and (3) usually vocalization of a distinctive type, namely, the soft bark which later was replaced upon occasion by rapid inspiration and expiration without laryngeal sound production (p. 70).

Yerkes and Yerkes (1936) observed the behavior of chimpanzees of different ages when a series of animate and inanimate objects were placed before them. The youngest chimpanzees, ranging in age from one to two years, were in general less responsive than were slightly older or adult animals. These workers point out the importance of perceptual development and experience in the genesis of the avoidance response, and they suggest as possible stimulus characteristics predominant in the response: visual movement, intensity, suddenness, and rapidity of change in stimulus. Haslerud's study (1938) of the effect of animate and inanimate objects in a food-securing situation upon the animals pre-

viously observed by Yerkes and Yerkes (1936) indicates that the younger animals showed less avoidance of an inanimate object than they did of an animate object, but the adults showed only slightly less avoidance of the inanimate object than of its animate counterpart.

McCulloch and Haslerud (1939) observed a chimpanzee, reared in isolation, in the food-approach situation. At the first test, at seven months of age, it was found that only moving objects elicited avoidance responses. Definite avoidance responses were made to a live alligator and a bouncing ball. Some aggression was shown toward a bouncing ball, but on the whole very little response was of the aggressive type. Some months later, at the age of fifteen months, the chimpanzee showed more avoidance behavior and more aggressive behavior to a wider range of stimuli. The animal no longer avoided objects on the basis of movement alone, however.

The emotional behavior of the infant ape, Gua, is described by the Kelloggs (1933) as being predominantly fear behavior, but including also evidence of anger, mild anger, jealousy, anxiety, and pleasant emotions. At first the principal conditions for eliciting fear behavior were loss of support and being alone, but later the suddenness or abruptness of occurrence of strange objects or persons presented visually, auditorially, or tactually called forth an avoidance response. Often the animal retreated toward the human person in her environment.

Yerkes and Tomilin (1935) report relatively little behavior of sexual significance on the part of infant chimpanzees. They state that "there are instances, but the surprising limitation in variety as well as in frequency suggests that they are exceptions" (p. 339).

Social Behavior

The study of the development of social behavior in young animals presents a very fertile field for investigations inasmuch as in mammals so many different patterns of adult social behavior seem to exist. To what extent these patterns are modifiable is an interesting question. Since the possibility of many mammals' existing apart from the female adult during the neonatal period is very slight—although a large and well-developed animal such as the guinea pig might occasionally live [1]—complete isolation is not likely. Many mammalian young, however, can be almost completely isolated so that an exact study of the development of the animal under known conditions of social stimulation can be made.

The complexity of social relationships between young and adult animals varies considerably. There are some mammals where the main "social" factors seem to be need for warmth and food on the part of the young, the guinea pig representing this level of development. Still other animals are born in such a weak state that additional "social" factors must be sought in the behavior of the maternal animal, for the offspring are too immature to react in any fashion completely adequate for maintenance of life. On the other hand, some animals, such as the opossum, are extremely immature at birth but are able to make certain adequate adjustments without the aid of the adult (Hartman, 1920). At later ages the young too give evidence of certain reactions to the adult which are social in character, although, as soon as self-sufficiency is reached and weaning occurs, there may be no longer any special social bonds between the animals. Still other animals, extremely im-

[1] The writer has raised several guinea pigs in isolation without forced feedings of any sort although food was left within the cage. Mortality is high.

mature at birth, are cared for by the female until the young are weaned and sometimes longer, but reciprocal social relationships exist for a period of time after this.

Little behavior of the paternal sort has ordinarily been observed in accounts of social behavior, but it must be noted that many of our studies of those animals where such behavior might be expected have been made under conditions of isolation or under laboratory conditions where natural grouping of the animals could not occur. It is well to remember these limitations in interpreting our knowledge of the normal social development of the young animal. For a discussion of the relationship between parent and offspring in which a wide survey of animal groups is made, see Mitchell (1912), and, for a classification of social groupings, see Alverdes (1927).

Instances of maternal care of the young in various species may be found in the surveys by Mitchell (1912), Lang (1925), Yerkes and Yerkes (1929), and Causey and Waters (1936). For the typical laboratory animals a number of observations concerning certain aspects of maternal care of the young have been made. The adult female rat makes certain preparations in the form of nest building before parturition, collects the young into the nest, and hovers over them, allowing them to suckle (Kinder, 1927; Sturman-Hulbe and Stone, 1929; Wiesner and Sheard, 1933). Retrieving behavior occurs for a period of several weeks until the animals start crawling in and out of the nest at about 17 to 20 days of age (Sturman-Hulbe and Stone, 1929). Maternal behavior of rats with cortical lesions is inferior to that of normal animals, according to Beach (1938), but animals operated upon in infancy are usually superior to adult operates.

Other animals, such as the guinea pig, clean the young after birth in a more or less haphazard fashion, allow the young to suckle, but seem to make no attempts to gather the young about them although the young are usually to be found in the near vicinity of the adult. Seward and Seward (1940), in a study of the maternal drive of adult guinea pigs, found that the animal crosses to a litter in a shorter time just after parturition than it does several weeks later. Seward (1940), attempting to analyze more systematically the many factors which go to make up filial behavior in the guinea pig, found that the average time for crossing to the incentive compartment decreases after the animals are one week old with little difference in the number of crossings in a period of ten minutes for either the unfed or the fed group. The difference in time of running to an empty compartment and to the mother is in favor of the adult guinea pig as an incentive. Seward suggests two factors as playing the major part in filial behavior: (1) a biological factor, the need for warmth in addition to food, and (2) a social factor, the result of conditioning to the mother. Evidence fully supporting the theory is not given, but the study is a further step in applying adequate techniques to developmental problems.

Most complete details concerning the social relationships of young and adult subhuman primates come from the work of the Yale laboratories (see, for example, Yerkes and Tomilin, 1935). Carpenter's (1934) observations of young and female howling monkeys in their native habitat show that the young animals cling to and climb upon the adult and that the adult orients the infant toward her and prevents it from climbing too far, retrieves the infant when it falls, and seems to give it a certain amount of tuition as it grows older. The young react fairly specifically to their mothers after they are a few days old. Carpenter suggests that the strength of the

social bonds between the adult and young reach their maximum at about 8 to 10 months and decline thereafter. (See also, for descriptions of the young primate, Lashley and Watson, 1913; Allesch, 1921; Bingham, 1927; and Tinklepaugh and Hartman, 1932.)

Evidences of maternal tuition in certain activities of the infant, such as Carpenter (1934) mentions, have been cited by other investigators. Yerkes and Tomilin (1935) comment with regard to this that "effects are achieved, whether or not intentionally, as result of example, request, command, prohibition, prevention" (p. 342).

Very little is known about the relationships among the adult male, adult female, juveniles, and young subhuman primates. Bingham (1927) observed a family of male, female, and infant chimpanzee in its second year. He comments that the male animal neither interfered with the female and the child nor did he assume responsibility for the child. Carpenter's (1934) account of monkeys in their native habitat gives evidence of the concern of all animals in the group at the cries of a fallen young animal. (See also Yerkes, 1936.)

Likewise, little is known about the relationships of young animals to each other in a naturalistic situation. Carpenter (1934) comments upon the attempts of the juveniles in a group of howling monkeys to pull an infant away or to wedge themselves in a position near the adult. Tomilin and Yerkes (1935) report the activities of two infant chimpanzee twins.

The social behavior of animals reared in isolation for a large part of their life is commented upon by Jacobsen, Jacobsen, and Yoshioka (1932) and by Foley (1935).

Grooming behavior is probably very infrequent for the subhuman primate infant (Yerkes, 1933), but an instance of such is reported by the Jacobsens and Yoshioka

(1932) for the chimpanzee in the thirty-ninth week.

Play. Considerable interest in the play of young animals has been evidenced since the publication in 1896 of Groos' *The Play of Animals.* General comments on the subject can be found in Mitchell (1912), and a number of observations are reported below. Many young animals give evidence of play behavior of the running, jumping, climbing, biting sort. (See, for example, Mills, 1898; Small, 1899; and Allen, 1904.) This type of activity becomes more easily identifiable in the more developed animals. Foley (1935) reports play behavior in the young monkey consisting of running, jumping, and leaping upon objects. An increase in play behavior occurred after eighteen months when the animal was placed with other animals. Instead of a self-directed play which had previously seemed to be the rule, the animal's activity now seemed to be externally directed. There may be some question as to whether this transfer resulted from the termination of the isolation of the animal, for Lashley and Watson (1913) noted behavior which Foley considers comparable in a young monkey before fifteen weeks.

Carpenter (1934), in his observations of young howling monkeys, notes that the young animals may play alone or with small objects and at a later age may play with other animals in wrestling or chasing types of play. The play activity "rises to a maximum by the time the animal is classed as a juvenile 1, and following a period of development there is a rather sharp decline in the amount of play" (p. 79).

The Jacobsens and Yoshioka (1932) suggest the following analysis of play behavior in the chimpanzee they observed. They note *exploration, manipulation, and simple play,* which occurred infrequently during the first two months and developed into a tactile examination of objects during the third month. *Organized play,* "in which the animal organized diverse activities in relationship to a central point" (p. 72), was observed first during the sixth month. A third type of play, *bodily activity as play,* seems to have developed with the motor development of the animal. A fourth type, classed as *play and manipulation essentially social,* was evidenced in such behavior as the threatening and attacking responses with which the animal approached the human observers, a pet dog, and other infant chimpanzees.

By far the richest account of the play of the young chimpanzee is by the Kelloggs (1933). To be sure, the account lacks the details of the early development of play before seven and one-half months, but it is illuminating with regard to the type of play activities entered into by a chimpanzee infant and a human infant. The large numbers of objects which the ape appropriated for play, the way these plays were carried out, and the evidence of activities resembling such games as tag, peek-a-boo, reciprocal giving and taking of objects make it seem clear that in an environment where it is possible to do so the young chimpanzee will show decidedly advanced play behavior.

For other descriptions of play activities, see Bingham (1927) and Yerkes and Tomilin (1935).

Vocalization. Most of the references to the behavior of young animals include some descriptions of the vocalizations of the animal—the birth cry, the cries of the young when not sucking, the cries occurring during play, startle cries, hunger cries, etc. Descriptions of the vocalizations of monkeys and chimpanzees, with some comment on the possible function of such vocalizations, are to be found in Jacobsen, Jacobsen, and Yoshioka (1932), Kellogg and Kellogg (1933), Carpenter (1934), Foley

(1935), and Yerkes and Tomilin (1935). According to Yerkes and Tomilin, the infant chimpanzee's vocalizations include a shrill birth cry, cries of *uh-uh*, barks of *oo-oo*, whimpering, whining, shouting, and screaming. They believe the adult recognizes these cries not so much in terms of the kind of vocalization as in their pitch, volume, and abruptness. The young animal seems to learn very slowly to react to the sounds and gestures of the adult, but it finally responds differentially to a great many sounds. The observations of the Kelloggs agree with those of Yerkes and Tomilin. Their observations further indicate that the young ape gives no evidence of learning the vocalizations of human beings but that the animal does respond quite definitely to some of the words of the human being.

Effect of Isolation. In one study on the effect of isolation upon social behavior Bayroff (1936) reared rats in isolation from the twentieth day to approximately the one hundred and fifteenth day. Using a technique designed to test whether the animal displayed any behavior indicating social preference, he found none indicated in his results. The technique used, however, while allowing a response of a social nature, also permitted the establishment of a positional habit on the part of the animal. Accordingly, Bayroff (1940) used another technique which made it necessary for rats swimming under water to reach the escape compartment first in order to be released. No significant differences appeared in the speed of swimming of animals reared in isolation after weaning from that of animals reared together. The experimenter concludes that "the nature of the early life is not the principal determiner of success in the competition" (p. 306).

Descriptive accounts of young primates reared in isolation are given by Jacobsen, Jacobsen, and Yoshioka (1932) and by Foley (1934).

Need for Further Work

The reader who has followed the course of this chapter has probably been impressed by several facts: (1) the accumulation of observations regarding the ontogenetic development of behavior in numerous mammalian groups, (2) the incompleteness of data and possible inaccuracy of some conclusions, and (3) the importance of knowledge in this field to the ultimate solution of certain insistent problems in genetic psychology. Considerable work remains yet to be done. Descriptive studies are by no means complete, and experimental studies undertaken to examine a special problem are very few in number.

Probably most adequately treated up to now is the development of motor responses in young animals. Here the responses are less difficult to observe, and several groups of scientific workers other than psychologists have been interested in the problem. Relatively lacking in experimental work, but yet providing richly provocative material for research, is the question of the analysis of the perceptual responses of the young animal. Additional work is needed on the problems of learning, memory, and intelligence; and recent increased interest and use of more adequate techniques for observation should contribute further work upon the problems of emotional and social development.

Bibliography

ALLEN, J. 1904. The associative process of the guinea pig. *J. Comp. Neurol.,* **14,** 293–359.

ALLESCH, G. I. 1921. Geburt und erste Lebensmonate eines Schimpansen. *Naturwiss.,* **9,** 774–776.

ALVERDES, F. 1927. *Social life in the animal world.* New York: Harcourt, Brace.

ANDERSON, A. C., and J. R. PATRICK. 1934. Some early behavior patterns in the white rat. *Psychol. Rev.,* **41,** 480–496.

ANGULO Y GONZÁLEZ, A. W. 1929. Is myelinogeny an absolute index of behavioral capability? *J. Comp. Neurol.*, 48, 459–464.

AVERY, G. T. 1928. Responses of foetal guinea pigs prematurely delivered. *Genet. Psychol. Monogr.*, 3, 245–331.

BAHRS, A. M. 1927. Notes on the reflexes of puppies in the first six weeks after birth. *Amer. J. Physiol.*, 82, 51–55.

BAYROFF, A. G. 1936. The experimental social behavior of animals: I. The effect of early isolation of white rats on their later reactions to other white rats as measured by two periods of free choices. *J. Comp. Psychol.*, 21, 67–81.

———. 1940. The experimental social behavior of animals: II. The effect of early isolation of white rats on their competition in swimming. *J. Comp. Psychol.*, 29, 293–306.

BEACH, F. A., JR. 1938. The neural basis of innate behavior: II. Relative effects of partial decortication in adulthood and infancy upon the maternal behavior of the primiparous rat. *J. Genet. Psychol.*, 53, 109–148.

———. 1939. Maternal behavior of the pouchless marsupial *Marmosa cinerea*. *J. Mammal.*, 20, 315–322.

BECHTEREW, W. VON. 1911. *Die Funktionen der Nervencentra*. Jena: Fischer.

BERNHARDT, K. S. 1934. The effect of vitamin B deficiency during nursing on subsequent learning in the rat. *J. Comp. Psychol.*, 17, 123–148.

BERNHARDT, K. S., and R. HERBERT. 1937. A further study of vitamin B deficiency and learning with rats. *J. Comp. Psychol.*, 24, 263–267.

BIEL, W. C. 1938. The effect of early inanition upon maze learning in the albino rat. *Comp. Psychol. Monogr.*, 15, No. 2. Pp. 33.

———. 1939. The effects of early inanition on a developmental schedule in the albino rat. *J. Comp. Psychol.*, 28, 1–15.

———. 1940. Early age differences in maze performance in the albino rat. *J. Genet. Psychol.*, 56, 439–453.

BINGHAM, H. C. 1927. Parental play of chimpanzees. *J. Mammal.*, 8, 77–89.

BLAIR, W. R. 1920. Notes on the birth of a chimpanzee. *Bull. N. Y. Zool. Soc.*, 23, 105–111.

BROOKS, C. M., and M. E. PECK. 1940. Effect of various cortical lesions on development of placing and hopping reactions in rats. *J. Neurophysiol.*, 3, 66–73.

BROWN, C. E. 1930. Birth of a second chimpanzee in the Philadelphia Zoölogical Garden. *J. Mammal.*, 11, 303–305.

CARMICHAEL, L. 1934. The genetic development of the kitten's capacity to right itself in the air when falling. *J. Genet. Psychol.*, 44, 453–458.

CARPENTER, C. R. 1934. A field study of the behavior and social relations of howling monkeys (*Alouatta palliata*). *Comp. Psychol. Monogr.*, 10, No. 48. Pp. 168.

CAUSEY, D., and R. H. WATERS. 1936. Parental care in mammals with especial reference to the carrying of young by the albino rat. *J. Comp. Psychol.*, 22, 241–254.

COOLIDGE, H. J., JR. 1933. Notes on a family of breeding gibbons. *Human Biol.*, 5, 288–294.

COOPER, J. B. 1942. An exploratory study on African lions. *Comp. Psychol. Monogr.*, 17, No. 7. Pp. 48.

CORONIOS, J. D. 1933. Development of behavior in the fetal cat. *Genet. Psychol. Monogr.*, 14, 283–386.

COURTHIAL, A. S. 1929. The persistence of infantile behavior in a cat. *J. Genet. Psychol.*, 36, 349–350.

CROZIER, W. J., and T. T. OXNARD. 1927. Geotropic orientation of young mice. *J. Gen. Physiol.*, 11, 141–146.

CROZIER, W. J., and G. PINCUS. 1926. The geotropic conduct of young rats. *J. Gen. Physiol.*, 10, 257–269.

———. 1927a. Phototropism in young rats. *J. Gen. Physiol.*, 10, 407–417.

———. 1927b. Geotropic orientation of young rats. *J. Gen. Physiol.*, 10, 519–524.

———. 1928. On the geotropic orientation of young mammals. *J. Gen. Physiol.*, 11, 789–802.

———. 1929a. Analysis of the geotropic orientation of young rats: I. *J. Gen. Physiol.*, 13, 57–80.

———. 1929b. Analysis of the geotropic orientation of young rats: II. *J. Gen. Physiol.*, 13, 81–120.

———. 1931a. Analysis of the geotropic orientation of young rats: III. *J. Gen. Physiol.*, 15, 201–242.

———. 1931b. Analysis of the geotropic orientation of young rats: IV. *J. Gen. Physiol.*, 15, 243–256.

———. 1932a. Analysis of the geotropic orientation of young rats: V. *J. Gen. Physiol.*, 15, 421–436.

———. 1932b. Analysis of the geotropic orientation of young rats: VI. *J. Gen. Physiol.*, 15, 437–462.

———. 1933. Analysis of the geotropic orientation of young rats: VII. *J. Gen. Physiol.*, 16, 801–813.

DODSON, J. D. 1915. The relation of strength of stimulus to rapidity of habit-formation in the kitten. *J. Anim. Behav.*, 5, 330–336.

DOVE, W. F. 1935. A study of individuality in the nutritive instincts and of the causes and effect of variations in the selection of food. *Amer. Nat.*, 69, 468–544.

EDGE, E. R. 1931. Seasonal activity and growth in the Douglas ground squirrel. *J. Mammal.*, 12, 194–200.

ELLIOTT, M. H., and W. H. STAVSKY. 1933. The effect of an upward stress upon the geotropic orientation of young guinea pigs. *J. Gen. Psychol.,* **9,** 216–220.

ENDERS, R. K. 1931. Parturition in the agouti, with notes on several pregnant uteri. *J. Mammal.,* **12,** 390–396.

ERRINGTON, P. L. 1939. Observations on young muskrats in Iowa. *J. Mammal.,* **20,** 465–478.

FERRIER, D. 1880. *The functions of the brain.* New York: Putnam's.

FISHER, E. M. 1940. Early life of a sea otter pup. *J. Mammal.,* **23,** 132–137.

FISKE, J. 1883. *The meaning of infancy:* I. *The part played by infancy in the evolution of man:* II. Boston: Houghton Mifflin. (New ed., 1911.)

FOLEY, J. P., JR. 1934. First year development of a rhesus monkey (*Macaca mulatta*) reared in isolation. *J. Genet. Psychol.,* **45,** 39–105.

———. 1935. Second year development of a rhesus monkey (*Macaca mulatta*) reared in isolation during the first eighteen months. *J. Genet. Psychol.,* **47,** 73–97.

FOX, H. 1929. The birth of two anthropoid apes. *J. Mammal.,* **10,** 37–51.

GESELL, A. 1928. *Infancy and human growth.* New York: Macmillan.

GOERLING, A. 1913. *Observations on the kangaroo,* reprinted in C. G. HARTMAN (1920).

GOLUBEVA, E. L. 1939. [Conditioned reflexes of the newborn guinea pig.] *Ankh Biol. Nauk,* **54,** 132–142. (*Psychol. Abstr.,* 1939, No. 6113.)

GROOS, K. 1915. *The play of animals.* (Trans. by E. L. BALDWIN.) (1st German ed., 1896.) New York: Appleton.

HAMILTON, G. V. 1911. A study of trial and error reactions in mammals. *J. Anim. Behav.,* **1,** 33–66.

HARTMAN, C. G. 1920. Studies in the development of the opossum (*Didelphis virginiana* L.): V. The phenomena of parturition. *Anat. Rec.,* **19,** 251–261.

———. 1921. Breeding habits, development, and birth of the opossum. *Smithsonian Rep.,* Publ. 2689, 347–363.

———. 1928a. The breeding season of the opossum (*Didelphis virginiana*) and the rate of intra-uterine and postnatal development. *J. Morphol.,* **46,** 143–216.

———. 1928b. The period of gestation in the monkey (*Macacus rhesus*), first description of parturition in monkeys, size, and behavior of the young. *J. Mammal.,* **9,** 181–194.

HASLERUD, G. M. 1938. The effect of movement of stimulus objects upon avoidance reactions in chimpanzees. *J. Comp. Psychol.,* **25,** 507–528.

HATT, R. T. 1931. Habits of a young flying squirrel (*Glaucomys volans*). *J. Mammal.,* **12,** 233–238.

HEBB, D. O. 1937a. The innate organization of visual activity: I. Perception of figures by rats reared in total darkness. *J. Genet. Psychol.,* **51,** 101–126.

———. 1937b. The innate organization of visual activity: II. Transfer of response in the discrimination of brightness and size by rats reared in total darkness. *J. Comp. Psychol.,* 1937b, **24,** 277–299.

HENRY, E. W., and C. N. WOOLSEY. 1943. Somatic motor responses produced by electrical stimulation of the cerebral cortex of new-born and young kittens. *Fed. Proc. Amer. Soc. Exp. Biol.,* **2,** 21.

HOWELL, A. B., and L. LITTLE. 1924. Additional notes on California bats; with observations upon the young of *Eumops. J. Mammal.,* **5,** 261–263.

HUBBERT, H. B. 1915. The effect of age on habit formation in the albino rat. *Behav. Monogr.,* **2,** No. 6. Pp. 55.

HUBER, E. 1934. A phylogenetic aspect of the motor cortex of mammals. *Quart. Rev. Biol.,* **9,** 55–91.

HUESTIS, R. R. 1933. Maternal behavior in the deermouse. *J. Mammal.,* **14,** 47–49.

JACOBSEN, C. F., M. M. JACOBSEN, and J. G. YOSHIOKA. 1932. Development of an infant chimpanzee during her first year. *Comp. Psychol. Monogr.,* **9,** No. 41. Pp. 94.

JACOBSEN, C. F., F. V. TAYLOR, and G. M. HASLERUD. 1936. Restitution of function after cortical injury in monkeys. *Amer. J. Physiol.,* **116,** 85–86.

JASPER, H. H., C. S. BRIDGMAN, and L. CARMICHAEL. 1937. An ontogenetic study of cerebral electrical potentials in the guinea pig. *J. Exp. Psychol.,* **20,** 63–71.

JOHNSON, G. E. 1927. Observations on young prairie-dogs (*Cynomys ludovicianus*) born in the laboratory. *J. Mammal.,* **8,** 110–115.

KAO, H. 1927. *Notes on the congenital behavior of rabbits.* Unpublished Master's Thesis, Stanford University.

KELLOGG, W. N. 1931. A note on fear behavior in young rats, mice and birds. *J. Comp. Psychol.,* **12,** 117–121.

KELLOGG, W. N., and L. A. KELLOGG. 1933. *The ape and the child: A study of environmental influence upon early behavior.* New York: McGraw-Hill.

KENNARD, M. A. 1936. Age and other factors in motor recovery from precentral lesions in monkeys. *Amer. J. Physiol.,* **115,** 138–146.

———. 1938. Reorganization of motor function in the cerebral cortex of monkeys deprived of motor and premotor areas in infancy. *J. Neurophysiol.,* **1,** 477–496.

KINDER, E. F. 1927. A study of the nest building activity of the albino rat. *J. Exper. Zool.,* **47,** 117–161.

KINNAMAN, A. J. 1902. Mental life of two *Macacus rhesus* monkeys in captivity : I ; II. *Amer. J. Psychol.*, **13**, 98–148 ; 173–218.

KITTREDGE, E. 1923. Some experiments on the brightness value of red for the light adapted eye of the calf. *J. Comp. Psychol.*, **3**, 141–145.

KOHTS, N. 1935. [*Infant ape and human child: Instincts, emotions, play, habits.*] *Scientific Memoirs of the Museum Darwinianum in Moscow.* Vol. III. Pp. xvi + 596, c. 145 plates. (Review by A. GESELL, *J. Genet. Psychol.*, 1937, **50**, 465–467.)

KORNMÜLLER, A. E. 1935. Die bioelektrischen Erscheinungen architektonischer Felder der Grosshirnrinde. *Biol. Rev.*, **10**, 383–426.

KUCKUK, E. 1936. Tierpsychologische Beobachtungen an zwei jungen Brunbären. *Z. vergl. Physiol.*, **24**, 14–41.

KUO, Z. Y. 1930. The genesis of the cat's responses to the rat. *J. Comp. Psychol.*, **11**, 1–35.

——. 1938. Further study on the behavior of the cat toward the rat. *J. Comp. Psychol.*, **25**, 1–8.

KURODA, R. 1930. Untersuchungen über die körperliche und sinnesphysiologische Organisation eines neugeborenen Affen (*Macacus cynomologus*). *Acta Psychol. Keijo*, **1**, 3–16.

LANG, H. 1925. How squirrels and other rodents carry their young. *J. Mammal.*, **6**, 18–24.

LANGWORTHY, O. R. 1925. The development of progression and posture in young opossums. *Amer. J. Physiol.*, **74**, 1–13.

——. 1927. Histological development of cerebral motor areas in young kittens correlated with their physiological reaction to electrical stimulation. *Contr. Embryol., Carnegie Inst. Wash.*, No. 104, pp. 177–208.

——. 1928. The behavior of pouch-young opossums correlated with the myelinization of tracts in the nervous system. *J. Comp. Neurol.*, 1928, **46**, 201–248.

——. 1929. A correlated study of the development of reflex activity in fetal and young kittens and the myelinization of tracts in the nervous system. *Contr. Embryol., Carnegie Inst. Wash.*, No. 114, pp. 127–171.

LASHLEY, K. S. 1914. A note on the persistence of an instinct. *J. Anim. Behav.*, **4**, 293–294.

LASHLEY, K. S., and J. T. RUSSELL. 1934. The mechanism of vision : XI. A preliminary test of innate organization. *J. Genet. Psychol.*, **45**, 136–144.

LASHLEY, K. S., and J. B. WATSON. 1913. Notes on the development of a young monkey. *J. Anim. Behav.*, **3**, 114–139.

LIU, S. Y. 1928. The relation of age to the learning ability of the white rat. *J. Comp. Psychol.*, **8**, 75–85.

MAURER, S. 1935a. The effect of partial depletion of vitamin B (B₁) upon performance in rats : III. *J. Comp. Psychol.*, **20**, 309–317.

——. 1935b. The effect of early depletion of vitamin B₂ upon performance in rats : IV. *J. Comp. Psychol.*, **20**, 385–387.

——. 1935c. The effect of acute vitamin A depletion upon performance in rats : V. *J. Comp. Psychol.*, **20**, 389–391.

——. 1935d. The effect of a diet of pasteurized milk upon performance in rats : VI. *J. Comp. Psychol.*, **20**, 393–395.

MAURER, S., and L. S. TSAI. 1929. Vitamin B deficiency in nursing young rats and learning ability. *Science*, **70**, 456–458.

——. 1930. Vitamin B deficiency and learning ability. *J. Comp. Psychol.*, **11**, 51–62.

McCULLOCH, T. L., and G. M. HASLERUD. 1939. Affective responses of an infant chimpanzee reared in isolation from its kind. *J. Comp. Psychol.*, 1939, **28**, 437–445.

McDOUGALL, W., and K. McDOUGALL. 1927. Notes on instinct and intelligence in rats and cats. *J. Comp. Psychol.*, **7**, 145–175.

MICHAILOW, S. 1910. Zur Frage über die Erregbarkeit der motorischen Zentra in der Hirnrinde neugeborener Säugetiere. *Pflüg. Arch. ges. Physiol.*, **133**, 45–70.

MILLS, W. 1898. *The nature and development of animal intelligence.* London : Unwin.

MITCHELL, P. C. 1912. *The childhood of animals.* New York : Stokes.

MUENZINGER, K. F., E. POE, and C. F. POE. 1937. The effect of vitamin deficiency upon the acquisition and retention of the maze habit in the white rat : II. Vitamin B₂(G). *J. Comp. Psychol.*, **23**, 59–66.

NISSEN, H. W. 1931. A field study of the chimpanzee. *Comp. Psychol. Monogr.*, **8**, No. 36. Pp. 122.

PANETH, J. 1885. Über die Erregbarkeit der Hirnrinde neugeborener Hunde. *Pflüg. Arch. ges. Physiol.*, **37**, 202–208.

PFAFFMAN, C. 1936. Differential responses of the new-born cat to gustatory stimuli. *J. Genet. Psychol.*, **49**, 61–67.

PINCUS, G. 1927. Geotropic creeping of young rats. *J. Gen. Physiol.*, **10**, 525–532.

POE, C. F., E. POE, and K. F. MUENZINGER. 1937. The effect of vitamin deficiency upon the acquisition and retention of the maze habit in the white rat : III. Vitamin B₁. *J. Comp. Psychol.*, **23**, 67–76.

POE, E., C. F. POE, and K. F. MUENZINGER. 1936. The effect of vitamin deficiency upon the acquisition and retention of the maze habit in the white rat : I. The vitamin B-complex. *J. Comp. Psychol.*, **22**, 69–77.

——. 1938. The effect of vitamin deficiency upon the acquisition and retention of the maze habit in the white rat : IV. Vitamin B-complex, B₁, and B₂(G). *J. Comp. Psychol.*, **27**, 211–214.

PREYER, W. 1882. *Die Seele des Kindes.* Leipzig: Fernau. (2d ed., 1884.)

——. 1888. *The mind of the child:* Pt. 1. *The senses and the will.* (Trans. by H. W. BROWN.) New York: Appleton.

PYCRAFT, W. P. 1913. *The infancy of animals.* New York: Holt.

RENNIE, J. 1838. The menageries. The natural history of monkeys, opossums, and lemurs. In *The library of entertaining knowledge.* London. (From YERKES and YERKES, 1929.)

RICHTER, C. P. 1925. Some observations on the self-stimulation habits of young wild animals. *Arch. Neurol. Psychiat.,* Chicago, **13,** 724–728.

——. 1931. The grasping reflex in the newborn monkey. *Arch. Neurol. Psychiat., Chicago,* **26,** 784–790.

ROBINSON, S. M. 1925. Birth of a white-handed gibbon (*Hylobates lar*) in captivity. *J. Bombay Nat. Hist. Soc.,* **30,** 456–458. (From YERKES and YERKES, 1929.)

ROGERS, W. W. 1932. Controlled observations on the behavior of kittens toward rats from birth to five months of age. *J. Comp. Psychol.,* **13,** 107–125.

SEWARD, G. H. 1940. Studies on the reproductive activities of the guinea pig: II. The rôle of hunger in filial behavior. *J. Comp. Psychol.,* **29,** 25–41.

SEWARD, J. P., and G. H. SEWARD. 1940. Studies on the reproductive activities of the guinea pig: I. Factors in maternal behavior. *J. Comp. Psychol.,* **29,** 1–24.

SHAW, W. T. 1925. Breeding and development of the Columbian ground squirrel. *J. Mammal.,* **6,** 106–113.

SHERMAN, H. B. 1930. Birth of the young of *Myotis austroriparius. J. Mammal.,* **11,** 495–503.

SHIRLEY, M. M. 1931. *The first two years. A study of twenty-five babies:* I. *Postural and locomotor development.* (Inst. Child Welf. Res. Monogr. Ser., No. 6.) Minneapolis: University of Minnesota Press. Pp. vi + 227.

SHUEY, A. M. 1931. The limits of learning ability in kittens. *Genet. Psychol. Monogr.,* **10,** 287–378.

——. 1932. Some experiments with kittens on the simple alternation problem. *J. Genet. Psychol.,* **41,** 393–405.

SLONAKER, J. R. 1907. The normal activity of the white rat at different ages. *J. Comp. Neurol. and Psychol.,* **17,** 342–359.

——. 1912. The normal activity of the albino rat from birth to natural death. *J. Anim. Behav.,* **2,** 20–42.

SMALL, W. S. 1899. Notes on the psychic development of the young white rat. *Amer. J. Psychol.,* **11,** 80–100.

SOLTMANN, O. 1876. Experimentelle Studien über die Funktionen des Grosshirns der Neugeborenen. *Jb. Kinderheilk.,* **9.** 106.

SPALDING, D. A. 1873. Instinct with original observations on young animals. *Macmillan's Mag.,* **27,** 282–293. Reprinted in *Pop. Sci. Mo.,* 1902, **61,** 126–142.

——. 1875. Instinct and acquisition. *Nature,* **12,** 507–508.

STAVSKY, W. H. 1932. The geotropic conduct of young kittens. *J. Gen. Psychol.,* **6,** 441–446.

STIER, T. J. B. 1930. "Spontaneous activity" of mice. *J. Gen. Psychol.,* **4,** 67–101.

STONE, C. P. 1929a. The age factor in animal learning: I. Rats in the problem box and the maze. *Genet. Psychol. Monogr.,* **5,** 1–130.

——. 1929b. The age factor in animal learning: II. Rats on a multiple light discrimination box and a difficult maze. *Genet. Psychol. Monogr.,* **6,** 125–202.

STRUTHERS, P. H. 1928. Breeding habits of the Canadian porcupine (*Erethizon dorsatum*). *J. Mammal.,* **9,** 300–308.

STURMAN-HULBE, M., and C. P. STONE. 1929. Maternal behavior in the albino rat. *J. Comp. Psychol.,* **9,** 203–237.

SVIHLA, A. 1934. Development and growth of deermice (*Peromyscus maniculatus artemisiae*). *J. Mammal.,* **15,** 99–104.

TANG, Y. 1935. On the development of different placing reactions in the albino rat. *Chin. J. Physiol.,* **9,** 339–346.

TARCHANOFF, J. DE. 1878. Sur les centres psychomoteurs des animaux nouveau-nés (lapin, chien, cochon d'Inde). *Rev. mens. méd. chir.,* **2,** 826.

TILNEY, F., and L. CASAMAJOR. 1924. Myelinogeny as applied to the study of behavior. *Arch. Neurol. Psychiat., Chicago,* **12,** 1–66.

TINKLEPAUGH, O. L. 1932. Parturition and puerperal sepsis in a chimpanzee. *Anat. Rec.,* **53,** 193–205.

TINKLEPAUGH, O. L., and C. G. HARTMAN. 1932. Behavior and maternal care of the newborn monkey (*Macaca mulatta*—"*M. rhesus*"). *J. Genet. Psychol.,* **40,** 257–286.

TOMILIN, M. I., and R. M. YERKES. 1935. Chimpanzee twins: behavioral relations and development. *J. Genet. Psychol.,* **46,** 239–263.

TSANG, Y. C. 1937a. Maze learning in rats hemidecorticated in infancy. *J. Comp. Psychol.,* **24,** 221–253.

——. 1937b. Visual sensitivity in rats deprived of visual cortex in infancy. *J. Comp. Psychol.,* **24,** 255–262.

TURNER, W. D. 1935. The development of perception: I. Visual direction; the first eidoscopic orientations of the albino rat. *J. Genet. Psychol.,* **47,** 121–140.

UPTON, M. 1930. The geotropic conduct of young guinea pigs. *J. Gen. Physiol.,* **13,** 647–655.

——. 1932. The effect of added loads upon the geotropic orientation of young guinea pigs. *J. Gen. Physiol.,* **15,** 333–340.

WADE, O. 1927. Breeding habits and early life of the thirteen-striped ground squirrel, *Citellus tridecemlineatus* (Mitchill). *J. Mammal.*, **8**, 269–276.

WARDEN, C. J., and T. A. JACKSON. 1938. *Development and behavior of the white rat* (Film). 350 ft. 16 mm. New York: Columbia University.

WARKENTIN, J., and L. CARMICHAEL. 1939. A study of the development of the air-righting reflex in cats and rabbits. *J. Genet. Psychol.*, **55**, 67–80.

WARKENTIN, J., and K. U. SMITH. 1937. The development of visual acuity in the cat. *J. Genet. Psychol.*, **50**, 371–399.

WASHBURN, M. F., and E. ABBOTT. 1912. Experiments on the brightness value of red for the light-adapted eye of the rabbit. *J. Anim. Behav.*, **2**, 145–180.

WATSON, J. B. 1903. *Animal education: The psychical development of the white rat.* Chicago: University of Chicago Press.

WEED, L. H., and O. R. LANGWORTHY. 1925. Developmental study of excitation areas in the cerebral cortex of the opossum. *Amer. J. Physiol.*, **72**, 8–24.

——. 1926. Physiological study of cortical motor areas in young kittens and in adult cats. *Contr. Embryol., Carnegie Inst. Wash.*, **17**, No. 87, pp. 89–106.

WENTWORTH, K. L. 1938. The effect of early reaches on handedness in the rat: A preliminary study. *J. Genet. Psychol.*, **52**, 429–432.

WHITE, B. A. 1929. A captive-born chimpanzee. *Sci. Mo., N. Y.*, **29**, 558–565.

WIESNER, B. P., and N. M. SHEARD. 1933. *Maternal behavior in the rat.* London: Oliver and Boyd.

WINDLE, W. F. 1930. Normal behavioral reactions of kittens correlated with the postnatal development of nerve-fiber density in the spinal gray matter. *J. Comp. Neurol.*, **50**, 479–503.

YERKES, A. W. 1935. Experiments with an infant chimpanzee. *J. Genet. Psychol.*, **46**, 171–181.

YERKES, R. M. 1907. *The dancing mouse.* New York: Macmillan.

——. 1909. Modifiability of behavior in its relations to the age and sex of the dancing mouse. *J. Comp. Neurol. and Psychol.*, **19**, 237–271.

——. 1933. Genetic aspects of grooming, a socially important primate behavior pattern. *J. Soc. Psychol.*, **4**, 3–25.

——. 1936. A chimpanzee family. *J. Genet. Psychol.*, **48**, 362–370.

——. 1939. The life history and personality of the chimpanzee. *Amer. Nat.*, **73**, 97–112.

——. 1940. Laboratory chimpanzees. *Science*, **91**, 336–337.

YERKES, R. M., and D. BLOOMFIELD. 1910. Do kittens instinctively kill mice? *Psychol. Bull.*, **7**, 253–263.

YERKES, R. M., and M. I. TOMILIN. 1935. Mother-infant relations in chimpanzee. *J. Comp. Psychol.*, **20**, 321–359.

YERKES, R. M., and A. W. YERKES. 1929. *The great apes: A study of anthropoid life.* New Haven: Yale University Press.

——. 1936. Nature and condition of avoidance (fear) response in chimpanzee. *J. Comp. Psychol.*, **21**, 53–66.

CHAPTER 4

THE NEONATE [1]

KARL C. PRATT

Birth

Nature and Significance. Birth is the term applied to the transfer of the developing child from the uterine environment to that of the external world. It is accomplished by contractions of the uterus which, by exerting pressure, rupture the fetal membranes and expel the child through the birth canal. This event severs the parasitic connections with the mother and necessitates an autonomy of vegetative functions if the child is to survive. The effects of birth on the infant may be inconsequential and transitory or they may greatly affect the course of subsequent development.

Organismic Changes. In the fetal environment the child leads a parasitic existence. It is dependent upon the maternal organism for external respiration, for digestion of food and the preparation of nutrient materials, for excretory functions, for thermal regulation, and for protection.

During the birth process the circulatory relations with the maternal organism (by way of the umbilical cord and the placenta) are at first disturbed and then broken off. At about this time the crucial vegetative function, external respiration, must appear or the child will be asphyxiated. Up to the onset of the birth cry the lungs have been uninflated and nonfunctional.

According to Fernandez (1918) and Feldman (1920), two major theories have been advanced to account for the initiation of pulmonary respiration: (1) that the process is started by external stimuli; (2) that it is brought about by a critical concentration of CO_2 in the blood stream of the infant.

According to the first theory, cutaneous stimuli (contact and thermal) serve to bring about an innervation of the musculature of the thorax while atmospheric pressure inflates the lungs. Relaxation of the muscles produces exhalation. The process is repeated with succeeding inhalations brought about by neural discharges proceeding from the respiratory center. In support of the theory of the excitatory rôle of cutaneous stimuli it is pointed out that the attending physician employs still more intense cutaneous stimuli if the infant has not begun to breathe. The effects of thermal stimuli below physiological zero upon the breathing of newborn infants have been observed by Pratt, Nelson, and Sun (1930), and are a matter of common experience at later age periods.

According to the second theory, pulmonary respiration is started when the CO_2 content of the blood attains the critical concentration which acts directly upon the respiratory center to arouse it to activity. It is said that the birth process, by disturbing the circulatory relations between the maternal organism and the child, in-

[1] The writer is indebted to Doctor O. C. Irwin and to Doctor D. M. Trout for suggestions and for criticism in the preparation of this chapter.

creases the CO_2 content of the child's blood stream and that breathing starts as soon as the respiratory center is activated. This theory accounts for the Ahlfeld "breathing movements" of the fetus. Doubtless both cutaneous stimuli and those provided by the blood stream cooperate in establishing pulmonary respiration.

Coincidental with the onset of breathing, valves in the heart operate to alter the circulation from the fetal to the natal type. Instead of passing to the placenta for aeration the blood now flows to the lungs.

The interruption and cessation of circulatory relations with the maternal organism mean that no more nutrient materials ready for assimilation are available to the child. Henceforth it must take food, digest it, excrete, egest, and maintain a relatively uniform body temperature despite variations in its thermal environment.

Environmental Changes. Birth transfers the developing child from an environment of relatively few to one of many stimuli; from one in which the conditions for learning are unfavorable or restricted to one presenting manifold possibilities; from one devoid of the social factor to one in which it is operative. From the observations of Bersot (1920, 1921) and Langworthy (1933) it seems probable that this postnatal environment not only provides richer opportunities for learning but also stimulates the continuing development of the nervous system.

Birth Trauma. The pressures produced in the birth process sometimes give rise to fractures of bones during passage through the birth canal, but the more common consequences are hemorrhages. They may be of slight extent and quickly absorbed; they may involve vital nerve centers and result in death; or they may permanently affect parts of the nervous system with consequent impairment of function.

The relation of defective intelligence to birth injuries is discussed by Doctor Doll in this book (Chapter 17). In addition to their effects upon general intelligence, birth injuries have transitory or permanent consequences for sense organs such as the ear and the eye. Kutvirt (1912) and Vosz (1923) have correlated lack of auditory sensitivity with prolonged and difficult labor; Sicherer (1907) and Edgerton (1934) have discussed the effect of retinal hemorrhages and other optic disturbances in the neonate.

The psychoanalytical school postulates psychic trauma resulting from the rupture of the fetal relations with the mother. According to Stirnimann (1933), this school holds to the existence of a primal anxiety (*Urangst*) during birth, of which subsequent anxiety states are a repetition. In general, psychoanalytic interpretations of the experience of the child at birth show a kinship with the antecedent literary and philosophical treatments of Lucretius, Kant, and others.

Definitions

Derivation. The term *neonate* is a Graeco-Latin derivative. Its respective Italian, French, German, and English equivalents are *neonato, nouveau-né, Neugeborener,* and *newborn.* The Spanish *recién nacido* has a slightly different but scarcely less indefinite connotation.

Further ambiguity for indices and bibliographies is created by the use of such terms as *child, infant, Säugling, nourrisson, enfant, bambino, lattante,* etc., without restricting adjectives or statements of the age range of the studies.

Duration of the Period. According to McGraw (1932), the child is not a *neonate* until the "umbilical cord is dressed and the baby is taken to the maternity nursery." Prior to this the just-born child for a period of "about the first fifteen minutes of life" is a *partunate*. This is the period "during and immediately following parturition." In terms of the latter statement the time stated for this period must be grossly inaccurate. Furthermore, it would appear doubtful whether McGraw, in terms of her own definition, is actually reporting the behavior characteristics of *partunates*.

A few authorities hold that the neonatal period extends to approximately the end of the first postnatal week; for others it comprises the first two weeks. Still others extend the period to one month, with Vinay (1897) going further to an extreme of three months. Gundobin (1907) rejects a fixed chronological terminus and instead considers it as ending when complete regularity of assimilation indicates the general integrated functioning of all organs.

Valentine and Dockeray (1936) would differentiate between *newborn infant* ("the first ten days of life") and *neonate* ("the first thirty days"). There is nothing, however, in the etymology of the terms or in historical usage to warrant such a distinction.

The prevailing usage in the field of infant behavior follows Feldman (1920) and Gesell (1925) in defining the *neonatal* period as extending from birth at full term to the end of the first postnatal month.

General Characteristics. The duration of the period is determined by physiological, medical, and psychological criteria. It is a period of adjustment and perfection of newly acquired vegetative functions. It is marked by the obsolescence of such structures as the ductus Botalli, the umbilical vein, etc., and by the recovery from injuries such as asphyxia, umbilical infections, tetanus, obstetrical paralyses, hemorrhages, and so on, incurred during the birth process. It is likewise a period during which certain sensory-motor structures are first activated by adequate stimuli, such stimula-

tion helping to bring about further maturation of the nervous system. This reactivity reveals the effects of fetal maturation but in itself induces no pronounced developmental events, nor does it afford a basis for more than the mere beginnings of learning. In brief, the most important developmental events of the period appear to be those immediately consequent to the incident of birth which ushers in the period.

History of the Study of Neonate Behavior

The Longitudinal Approach. The first more or less systematic attempts to describe the behavior of the newborn infant appeared in the *baby biographies*. Of the fifty or more published during the preceding century and the first decade of this one, the following may be cited as outstanding in content or influence: Tiedemann (1787), Darwin (1877), Champneys (1881), Preyer (1882), Binet (1890), Hall (1891), Shinn (1893–1899), Lowden (1895), and Major (1906). Of these, the biographies by Preyer and by Shinn have had most significance and enduring value for child psychology. Dennis (1936) has compiled a bibliography of baby biographies and Dennis and Dennis (1937) have made a tabular organization of the temporal incidence of the more important items of behavior as reported in forty such studies.

The serious limitations of the biographical approach to problems of development are well known: a paucity of cases, a probable nonrepresentative selection, and bias because of family ties. Furthermore, the lack of systematically introduced and controlled stimuli together with inadequate provisions for controlling the conditions of observation must result in the inevitable errors of the anecdotal method. The virtue of the "naturalness" of observation as opposed to the "artificiality" of experimentation has, however, been championed by Bridges (1935).

In recent years the longitudinal approach to behavioral development has been revived, but with modifications which distinguish it in several respects from the biographical procedure. The investigator pursues the development of a number of children with respect to specific problems. The children are not related to the biographer and are probably not so select a population as that described in the early baby biographies. The observations may be made at fixed time intervals and frequently refer to the performance of children under specific *test* conditions. Notable among investigations of this type are those undertaken by Shirley (1931a, 1931b, 1933a, 1933b), Bayley (1933), Gesell, Thompson, and Amatruda (1938), and other collaborators.

McGraw (1935) and John Dewey, in the introduction to the former's account of the nonidentical twins (Johnny and Jimmy), have been inclined to characterize all other studies as presenting merely a series of cross-sectional *achievements* and to claim that only her investigations are truly longitudinal. McGraw's conclusions in regard to normal development are, however, not supposed to rest solely upon observations of the one set of twins, but also to depend upon the results of an average of 38 examinations of 68 infants over a period of 2 years. It would thus appear that there is no fundamental distinction in respect to the frequency of sampling of behavioral development, aside from the twins, between McGraw's work and the studies which she has criticized. In a review of McGraw's book, the writer (1936b) has pointed out that all such studies of behavioral development represent time samplings of behavior and that the pursuit of a particular mode of behavior from time section to

time section may be described as a longitudinal study, but such usage in no way alters the fact that the pursuit is discontinuous; and hence everything observed in a given time sampling is an "achievement" at the moment regardless of the size of the interval separating the samples.

The Cross-sectional Approach. The ontogenetic progression of behavior may likewise be explored by investigating the response repertory in cross-sections of the population at successive age levels. Because it is difficult to pursue sequential development in a large constant population, most of the data of child development have been obtained from researches of the cross-sectional type, which provide more stable norms and more information regarding individual variation. Almost all investigations of the neonate represent this approach.

Population Controls in Experimentation. In longitudinal studies of development the same population is followed through succeeding age periods. The co-twin control method, devised by Gesell and Thompson (1929) to provide populations with the same hereditary potentialities for the purpose of contrasting the effects of exercise or learning with those due to maturation alone, has as yet not been employed during the neonatal stage. Instead, recourse has been had to the familiar device of control and experimental groups. This is illustrated in Marquis' (1931) attempt to establish conditioned sucking responses in the neonate to auditory stimuli.

In cross-sectional studies which aim to establish the effect of specific stimuli upon the behavior or activity of the infant, as in the researches of Pratt, Nelson, and Sun (1930) and Pratt (1934b), a populational control is in effect when the activity of a given infant is observed and measured not only during an experimental period in which specific stimuli are introduced but also during a control period in which there are no experimental stimuli.

The need for population controls is emphasized further by the fact that the character of a response is influenced by the physiological state of the infant at the time of stimulation. A sampling control may attempt to meet this by varying the position and the order of control and experimental periods. The effects of specific stimuli upon the child must be allowed to subside before other stimuli are applied. When all this is done, however, differences in physiological state remain which seem to necessitate the description and measurement of behavior according to differing physiological conditions. In the field of neonate study Pratt, Nelson, and Sun (1930), Pratt (1934*f*), Irwin and his students—Weiss (1934), Stubbs (1934), and others—and Wagner (1937) have made beginnings in this direction.

Experimentation. Control and measurement are the essence of the experimental method and they apply to the stimulating conditions, to the nature of the populations studied, and to the responses of the individual organisms.

The rudimentary beginnings of experimental methods may be seen in a few of the baby biographies and in the cross-sectional investigations of Kussmaul (1859), Genzmer (1873), and Kroner (1881) during the past century, and in the studies of Peterson and Rainey (1910) and of Blanton (1917) in the early years of this century. These sometimes involved sizable neonate populations and an extensive survey of the behavior equipment but comprised merely the introduction, without control or measurement, of experimental stimuli, and a more or less uncontrolled observation of the responses elicited. Studies of this type, but confined to some particular response, are illustrated by Eng-

stler's (1905) observations of the plantar responses of one thousand children.

Bechterew (1908) was one of the first students of human behavior to urge that quantitative registration and measurement of responses be substituted for qualitative observation and description. Canestrini (1913) realized this objective by using a pneumograph and a polygraph to register the effect of various stimuli upon respiration. In a similar fashion he recorded circulatory responses by employing a Marey pneumograph attached at the infant's fontanelle. He did not, however, achieve any appreciable control or measurement of his experimental stimuli nor did he provide an expression, in quantitative terms, of his kymograph records so that central tendency and individual variation might be determined. At about the time of Canestrini's researches, Benedict and Talbot (1914) were using a crib-recorder to afford a continuous registration of the "spontaneous" movements of newborn infants, even for periods of twenty-four hours.

Peiper, whose researches encompass all aspects of early human behavior (see a partial list of his contributions in the bibliography), employed a modified Morse apparatus to measure reaction times (1925*b*, 1926*a*) and devised stimulus controls (1924*b*, 1926*a*) for the investigation of thermal and of pain sensitivity. Eckstein and Rominger (1921) measured respiration by means of a facial mask and pneumatic system, Eckstein (1927) improved the earlier crudely instrumentalized study of the sucking response, and Eckstein and Paffrath (1928) employed apparatus to measure the general activity of the neonate. Carlson and Ginsburg (1915) first measured the stomach contractions of the newborn infant.

The problem of emotional patterns of behavior was explored by Sherman (1927*a*) through the medium of motion picture photography. At the Yale laboratory Gesell made use of the photographic dome in obtaining motion pictures from different angles, and the subsequent frame analysis of such records provided a remarkable normative series (1934). The production of instructional films of child development, likewise under his direction, is, as Beck's (1938) list indicates, an outstanding contribution.

The comprehensive researches upon neonate behavior undertaken at Ohio State University by Doctor A. P. Weiss (1929) and his students established the groundwork in general technique for many subsequent studies. Objective and automatic recording of the activity of the newborn infant was accomplished by an adaptation of the stabilimeter-polygraph apparatus originally designed by Renshaw and Weiss (1926) for the study of postural responses in adults. Pratt, Nelson, and Sun (1930) designed and described an experimental cabinet [1] which would effect some control of the stimuli impinging upon the child. The work of Pratt, Nelson, and Sun likewise represented an advance in the direction of control and measurement or evaluation of many of the stimuli employed. Irwin (1930) made the most extensive studies of neonate activity through twenty-four-hour periods so far attempted. Other major contributions by Weiss and his students are illustrated by Jensen's (1932) remarkably instrumentalized research upon the sucking response, and the first attempt by an American, Marquis (1931), to establish conditioned responses in newborn infants.

[1] The Pratt experimental cabinet was first modified and improved by Irwin and his students with the introduction of facilities for motion picture photography, including a "cold" light (1931). Dockeray and Valentine (1939) have redesigned it to meet the original aims more adequately as well as to incorporate the improvements introduced by Irwin.

After the untimely death of Doctor Weiss the center of significant research upon neonate behavior shifted to Iowa State University, where Irwin and his students not only made the innovations already mentioned but also, in addition to undertaking the solution of new and important problems of neonate behavior, pressed steadily forward in the setting-up of the best control of all aspects of experimentation that has so far been attained in this field. With Richards (1936), Irwin has demonstrated that the era of uncritical reliance upon the "clinical method" in the investigation of behavioral development must come to an end with realization not only of the inadequacy but also of the personal distortion inherent in the purely observational recording of behavior.

The latest research tool to be employed in investigating the responses of the newborn infant (Hunt, Clarke, and Hunt, 1936) is ultrarapid motion picture photography as developed by Hunt and Landis (1936). Prior to their work ordinary motion pictures had been employed for record purposes, for frame analysis of some responses, and for a rough measurement of certain reaction times. With ultrafast motion pictures, however, Landis and Hunt have been able to overcome the limitations of our sensory-motor mechanisms and to differentiate responses temporally which heretofore appeared to be overlapping and confused. As Landis and Hunt (1937) point out, what one observes depends in part upon the temporal relations of events, and hence it may become necessary in the future to state the temporal conditions of observation according to which the description of behavior applies.

In the statistical expression of data on infant behavior Bersot (1920, 1921) has been a pioneer. He stressed the need for noting and evaluating the variability of responses. Correlational procedures have been employed by the Shermans (1925) to follow maturational changes or improvement in responses with increasing age; by Furfey, Bonham, and Sargent (1930) to determine whether any general factor runs through all neonate responses; by Pratt (1930) to study the relation of activity to environmental temperatures; and by Irwin (1932*f*) to pursue the change in activity from one nursing period to another. The standard error of percentage has been employed by Richards and Irwin (1934*c*) to determine the prevailing type of toe movements in the plantar response.

Richards and Irwin (1934*a*) have written the best account of experimental methods in the investigation of neonate behavior, and reviews of the behavior repertory of the infant have been furnished by Peiper (1928, 1930), Pratt (1933), Hurlock (1933), Dennis (1934), Dewey (1935), Munn (1938), and Stirnimann (1940).

Physiology

Circulation. With the beginning of pulmonary respiration the course of fetal circulation changes to the postnatal type. With increase in age the cardiac rhythm decreases while the blood pressure increases (according to Feldman, 1920, the latter is 60 in the newborn infant and 120 in the adult). Sontag and Wallace (1935*a*) found that the heart rate averaged 144 beats per minute during the latter part of the fetal period. Murlin, Conklin, and Marsh (1925), as reported by Richards (1935), obtained a basal pulse rate of 117 per minute in the neonate. Halverson's (1941) most comprehensive investigation of the pulse rate under different situations indicates great variation. In *profound sleep* the mean rate was 123.5; during *crying* it was 94.7 beats greater. The velocity of the pulse wave is said by Rominger and Meyer (1932) to increase

with age. Bernfeld (1931) has confirmed the Yllpö thesis that the capillary resistance is less at first, particularly among prematures, and that this may be related to a high incidence of hemorrhages during the birth process.

Both rate of heart beat and blood pressure are modified by the various stimuli acting upon the organism. Sontag and Wallace (1935*b*, 1936) have shown that in the last month before birth vibratory stimuli applied to the mother's abdomen increase the average heart rate by 14.3 ± 0.74 beats per minute. The effects are first demonstrated during the third month before birth. They have also shown that 8 to 12 minutes after the expectant mother begins smoking the fetal heart rate increases 5 ± 0.19 beats per minute.

Canestrini (1913) proved the sensitivity of the neonate to stimuli of different modalities by registering the changes in rate and volume of the pulsations at the fontanelle. Although differentiation of modalities in terms of brain curves is impossible, some stimuli result in a slower pulse rate and others in a faster rate. These are interpreted as indicating, respectively, pleasant and unpleasant feeling tones.

Respiration. According to one view, pulmonary respiration is initiated by intense cutaneous stimulation. Runge (1895) is an exponent of this view. A second theory states that breathing is precipitated by a critical concentration of CO_2 acting upon the respiratory center. Other writers believe that both factors are operative. Peiper (1933*a*) adheres to the second theory. For him the viability of the premature infant depends upon the level or critical maturation of the respiratory center. In a number of researches he (1933*a*) and collaborators such as Good (1934) have discovered that the breathing movements of prematures have the characteristics of those which are physiological rather than pathological in lower animals. Creutzfeldt and Peiper (1932) have shown that death from respiratory failure depends upon immaturity of the respiratory center rather than upon its impairment by hemorrhages.

According to Peiper (1933a, 1933b), among the types of breathing indicative of immaturity of the respiratory center are periodic breathing (Cheyne-Stokes), which is sometimes seen in the full-term infant and which is characteristic of the premature, and gasping respiration (*Schnappatmung*), which reveals a still greater immaturity. Breathing of the neonate is of the abdominal type with the thorax becoming more involved when the child assumes an upright posture and begins to walk.

Ahlfeld (1905) registered "breathing movements" of the fetus *in utero* of a rate similar to that of the neonate. In the latter, Vormittag (1933) reports the average to be 35 per minute during the first week after birth, and 37.7 per minute during the remainder of the neonatal period. By the end of the first year it has declined to 27.8, and from 10 to 15 years, to 19.1 per minute. Murphy and Thorpe (1931) found an average of 43.1 per minute in the newborn infant, and Peiper (1933a) places it between 35 and 45 per minute. Halverson (1941) reported that the breathing rate alters markedly from one situation to another and from one infant to another. In *sleep before awakening* the mean rate was 32.3; in *crying* it was 133.3 respirations per minute.

Employing a Krogh spirometer, Murphy and Thorpe (1931) found an average minute volume of 721.4 cc. and a mean tidal air of 16.7 cc.

A number of responses deeply involve or are intimately associated with the respiratory mechanisms. Among them are sneezing and coughing, reported as occurring shortly after birth. The birth cry itself is interpreted as a concomitant of the initiation of pulmonary respiration. Peiper (1933a, 1933b) interprets yawning, found even in young prematures, as a breathing movement of a primitive type, but having no pathological significance in its persistence. Peiper (1933a) has likewise demonstrated that during the suckling period a relation exists between the respiratory and sucking centers which enables the child to suck, swallow, and breathe at the same time, an ability not present in the adult. Crying must be considered a breathing response also.

The rate and amplitude of breathing movements in the newborn are, as Canestrini (1913) proved, modifiable by stimuli of various types and manifest great differences according to the physiological state of the child. As in circulation, the effects of stimuli upon respiration are general and nondifferentiating. Slow and regular breathing movements following certain stimuli are interpreted as revealing a pleasant feeling tone, whereas the heightened respiratory activity consequent to other stimuli is said to indicate unpleasant feeling tones. The effects of specific stimuli are mentioned in other sections of this chapter. Peiper (1933a) emphasizes the contrast in respiratory activity and regularity between sleeping and waking states.

Alimentation. Prior to birth nutrient materials ready for assimilation by the fetus are furnished by the maternal organism. The alimentary tract, whose function it is to ingest food, to undertake its digestion, and to egest the indigestible materials, is not functional in the accepted sense of the term. But this does not mean that it is wholly inactive. Bersot (1920, 1921) has emphasized that here, as in respiration, there is preliminary activity during the fetal period. Examination of the contents of the alimentary canal reveals the presence of amniotic fluid which has been swallowed.

From the nutritional point of view it is to be noted that the transition to autonomy in digestion is accompanied by a loss of birth weight until about the middle of the first week, when the child begins to increase in weight and achieves birth weight by the seventh to tenth day. Various and conflicting theories have been developed to account for this loss in birth weight. According to one theory it is caused by scanty milk production. As a general explanation this seems untenable because supplementary feeding does not prevent some loss. This leads to the supposition that imperfect assimilation is responsible. A part of the loss may be mechanical as, for example, a loss of water. Talbot (1917a), however, believes that it arises because colostrum does not meet the energy requirements of the newborn infant.

In most mammals the process of alimentation is served by mouth orientation responses which, elicited by tactual stimulation of the face and lip areas of the young, operate to bring the opened mouth to the nipple. When contact or coupling is thus effected sucking starts, and ingestion of food follows. Salivation takes place and swallowing responses are coordinated with sucking and breathing. Gastric secretion likewise follows. When the stomach fills, the child ceases to nurse and contact is broken. Frequently there is regurgitation, often followed by hiccuping.

The stomach empties in 4 to 5 hours at most; the small intestines in 7 to 8 hours; and the large intestine within 2 to 14 hours. Kahn (1921) has noted that the young suckling differs most in this respect from the adult, who requires 20 to 40 hours for movement of materials through the colon. Defecation or egestion completes the sequence of activities in the alimentary tract. Halverson (1940) has found that defeca-

tion occurs most frequently during the first half hour after feeding. On the basis of 8½ hours of daytime observation he places the median number of defecations in 24 hours at 4.7. Most of the defecations occurred during wakefulness, but, contrary to other observers, he reports that the infants are usually quiet during and after the act.

Aside from the fact that alimentation is a vital process, it is of interest to the student of behavior because it appears to be intimately associated with the two "drives" of "thirst" and "hunger." Simsarian and McLendon (1942) have stated that on a self-demand schedule of nursings an infant had greater frequency of feedings and spent more time nursing during the first ten days after birth than occur under the customarily imposed schedule. The relation of general activity or motility in the neonate to "hunger" has been the object of a number of investigations.

Having correlated the subjective "hunger" in adults with certain muscular contractions of the stomach, henceforth termed "hunger contractions," Carlson and Ginsburg (1915) have demonstrated their presence by means of the balloon technique in infants that have not yet nursed. These contractions differ from those of the adult only in the shortness of periods of quiescence between periods of contraction. According to these investigators awakening and crying had some relation to the vigor of the contractions.

In more extensive studies Taylor (1917) found that the "hunger" contractions of the neonate were more vigorous than those of the adult. In the latter they may be inhibited when taste substances are introduced in the mouth; in the newborn infant no such effects follow. Small quantities of water or of milk introduced into the stomach, however, do produce temporary inhibition of the contractions.

Taylor (1917) describes the sequence of events as follows:

> The first contraction period is apt to be short. After a wait of perhaps twenty minutes a longer and more intense hunger period arrives; then another and another. The infant's sleep becomes lighter. He is more easily awakened by external stimuli or by gastric discomfort. He is put to the breast, nurses vigorously, becomes fatigued or experiences satiety from distention and again goes to sleep.

According to Taylor (1917), increase in reflex excitability is synchronous with the periods of these stomach contractions. Often the latter are accompanied by automatic sucking movements. In normal full-term infants "hunger" contractions begin about 2 hours and 50 minutes after nursing, during the first 2 weeks; from 2 to 8 weeks they start in about 3 hours and 40 minutes after nursing. This demonstrates that they arise before the stomach has emptied and are therefore not ascribable to an empty stomach. This particular study offered no evidence that "hunger" is the immediate cause of crying.

These studies, as well as those made of other animals, seemed to indicate that some of the general activity of such organisms is related to events in the alimentary tract. Pratt, Nelson, and Sun (1930) observed the difficulty of obtaining infants who were not crying and were not excessively active as a nursing period approached. They measured general activity in control periods set up to provide a basis for comparison of activity during periods of experimental stimulation.

The most thorough studies of general motility in the neonate are those made by Irwin (1930, 1932c, 1932f) and by Richards (1936a, 1936b). From his 24-hour studies of activity Irwin came to the following conclusion:

The fact that activity usually is greatest toward the end of the observation period, that is, just before nursing, and usually is least at the beginning of the period, just after nursing, suggests that the activity is stimulated probably by hunger contractions. This inference is best illustrated by the exceptional rise of the curve during the long night period when the nursings were eight hours apart. Since the external stimuli were constant, the conclusion seems justified that the activity of these infants is due largely to internal factors, presumably of the alimentary canal.

In a later research involving 73 infants, but with sampling of activity from 2:30 to 5:45 P.M. only, Irwin (1932e) substantiated his earlier findings and demonstrated that there is a significant increase in motility by the fourth to fifth day. Irwin (1932f) also found that general motility correlates $.97 \pm .04$ with lapse of time from one nursing period to another. Contrary to usual belief, he found that more infants were awake during the first 15 minutes than during the last 15 minutes and that more were asleep during the middle 15 minutes of the period. Activity during the first 15 minutes amounted to 17.0 oscillations per minute; during the last 15-minute period it soared to 45.0 oscillations per minute.

Pursuing these studies of motility, Irwin (1933d) found that general motility correlated $-.13 \pm .008$ with Pirquet's index of nutritional status, and $.007 \pm .08$ with Finlay's index. Irwin (1932d) likewise found no significant relations to exist between intestinal area and motility.

Richards (1936c) has attempted to review the evidence bearing upon the nature and origin of the stimuli producing general activity in the newborn infant. He (1936a, 1936b) has conducted experimental researches to determine the relations between motility and muscular activity of the stomach. From the results he has concluded that peristaltic activity increases with the time since feeding. Bodily activity increases similarly but does not result from peristalsis because there is no more bodily activity during strong peristalsis than during gastric quiescence. Furthermore, the presence of the balloon in the infant's stomach inhibits general activity but not peristalsis. This investigator's conclusion, "It is likely that in hunger gastric activity is a specific reaction to the general nutritional state of the organism as expressed, perhaps, by constituents of the blood," leaves the problem of the direct excitant of motility still unsolved.

Excretion. Halverson (1940), on the basis of 8½-hour periods of observation of male infants, has estimated the average number of voidings per 24 hours to be 18.6. The greatest number of micturitions occurred during the first hour after feeding. A wide variation (ranging from 5 to 285 minutes) in the intervals between micturitions was observed. Most voidings took place during wakefulness and while the infant was quiet. The relation of micturition to bathing and to auditory or to other external stimuli appears as yet to have had no systematic study.

Secretion: Duct Glands. Most of the duct glands are functional at birth, although secretion may be limited in amount and restricted to specific stimuli.

Jacobi and Demuth (1923) reported that salivary secretion is difficult to elicit, occurring only during the feeding act. Stirnimann (1936c) also has commented upon the infrequency of salivation of newborn infants to gustatory stimulation. When it does occur to the experimental stimuli he views it as a protective reflex. The ferment concentration of the saliva is greater in the full-term infant than in the adult, according to Hensel (1933).

Nothmann (1909) obtained gastric juice

when infants that had not yet nursed were allowed to suck upon an empty bottle. This would seem to indicate innate reflex connections between the sucking act and gastric secretion, but Schmidt (1927) was unable to confirm Nothmann's findings. The premature, as compared with the full-term, infant has a less acid and less stable gastric secretion, according to Schmitt and Móritz (1933).

Sweat and tear glands secrete during the neonatal period, but tears are not an accompaniment of crying. In relation to the protective effects of tear gland secretion Ködding (1940) reported about two spontaneous winks per minute in the neonate as contrasted with six appearing at the end of childhood. The histological studies of Becker (1921) indicate increased tempo of development of the structures in the skin during the neonatal period.

Feldman (1920) accounts for obliteration of the meatus of the ear by the presence of numerous sebaceous glands.

Mammary secretion (witch's milk) of the neonate has long excited popular interest, and an extensive literature has developed on the subject. It is found, regardless of sex, in the majority of newborn infants and is regarded by most investigators as a part of the physiological picture commonly described as the "genital crisis of the newborn." A few, including Feldman (1920), view such secretion as a pathological phenomenon.

Apert (1914), Arteaga (1918), Hoeland (1927), Lorenz (1929), Joseph (1929), and others hold that it first makes its appearance 3 to 4 days after birth. Apert (1914) maintains that it begins to decrease from the eighth day; Jaroschka (1929) that it disappears between 30 and 100 days; and Joseph (1929) that it stops in 3 to 4 weeks. Apert (1914), Hoeland (1927), and Lorenz (1929) report that all stages from colostrum to milk resembling mother's milk are secreted by the mammary glands of the neonate. Apert (1914) has stated the view of those who hold that the phenomenon is produced by placental hormones, whereas Zaharescu-Karaman and Nastase (1931) have demonstrated that intramuscular injection of ovarian sex hormone in female infants is followed by hypertrophy of the mammary glands. Arteaga (1918) found no relation of the dropping-off of the umbilical cord to mammary secretion. Hoeland (1927) and Lorenz (1929) have noted that manual expression of secretion from the glands plays the same rôle in developing and prolonging the period of secretion as nursing does to the maternal breast. Castro (1930) found such prolongation occurred in only one breast of the infant whom he studied. The hormonal stimulation of mammary secretion has been minimized and criticized by Lorenz (1929). He believes that the times of incidence and maximum secretion are not compatible with theories that such secretion is caused by the presence or by the disappearance of placental or ovarian hormones from the infant's system.

Secretion: Ductless Glands. Indirect evidence indicates the functioning of endocrine glands fairly early in the fetal period. The thymus has been termed the gland of infancy and is said to have an inhibitory effect upon growth, particularly upon sexual development.

The Genital Crisis. During the early part of the neonatal period the infant manifests phenomena which are considered characteristic of puberty. In addition to mammary secretion in both sexes, female infants have enlargement of the uterus, secretion from its mucous membrane, growing follicles and blood spots, according to Hartmann (1932) and other investigators. Hartmann (1932) and Moore (1936) found evidence of stimulation or enlargement of the prostate, and the former investigator

reported activity in the testes of male infants. He also held that these phenomena are produced by ovarian hormones and by those of the hypophysis. Litzka (1933) demonstrated that in pregnant guinea pigs these hormones pass through the placenta.

The phenomena of the genital crisis are not, however, to be interpreted as having the sexual significance of puberty. Not only are they transitory but they are also not accompanied by differentiation of receptor organs to make the genital zones highly sensitive to external stimuli. The histological researches of Becker (1933) reveal a marked contrast to the richly endowed oral areas of the neonate.

Similarly, Halverson (1940) found tumescence of the penis in male infants to have neither a sexual significance nor to be ascribable to the factors producing the genital crisis. Studying the time and incidence of the response in relation to micturition and to defecation, he concluded that tumescence was caused by pressure stimulation of the bladder. It is accompanied usually by restlessness and has a frequency of 3 to 11 per day with durations ranging from one-half minute to 66 minutes.

Metabolism. Birth represents an increase in the rate of living of the infant. The neonate's metabolism, in terms of unit surface, is not, according to Carpenter and Murlin (1911), above that of the nursing mother but is above "that of a woman in complete sexual rest."

Talbot (1917a) affirms that the *basal* energy requirement increases with age from 44 calories per kilogram at 1½ to 6 days to 55 calories at 4 to 5 months. Talbot (1917b) estimates that to maintain normal activity and growth 100 calories per kilogram of body weight is needed as a *total* energy requirement.

Schlossman and Murschhauser (1933) report the basic exchange of newborn infants involves an oxygen consumption of 27.9 cc. per minute with a respiratory quotient of 0.828.

The interrelations of metabolic rates, heat production, body temperatures, pulse rate, specific food, etc., have all received attention.

Benedict and Talbot (1914, 1915) and Talbot (1917a, 1917b) attempted to determine the relation of metabolism and pulse rate and to ascertain what proportions of the food energy are expended to produce activity and growth of infants.

Benedict and Talbot's standards for determining basal metabolism in infants have been confirmed by Levine and Marples (1931), that referring to stature being most reliable. In itself, age has slight relation to metabolism.

The creatinine coefficient is suggested by Paffrath and Ohm (1933) as an index of the level of muscular activity.

Rectal temperatures of newborn infants were discovered by Irwin (1933c) to range from 96 to 101.6° F. Correlation with activity expressed in stabilimeter oscillations per minute was $-.02 \pm .08$. Bayley and Stoltz (1937) found a mean rectal temperature of 98.96 ($PE_m = .08$) at one month, and at two months one of 99.13 ($PE_m = .03$). Imperfect temperature regulatory mechanisms may make the infant slightly poikilothermic for a few hours, according to Herzfeld (1922). Talbot (1917a) maintains that healthy newborn infants tend to maintain their body temperature through increased muscular activity and crying. Levy (1928) indicates that temperature maintenance may be a serious problem in the premature infant.

In a critical survey of the relation of activity in the neonate to metabolic indices, Richards (1935) has concluded that no one index of physiological function correlates highly with bodily activity.

Neuromuscular Physiology. The first responses of the fetus, according to Minkowski (1928), may be idiomuscular rather than neurally aroused. The pioneer researches of Soltmann (1876, 1878), C. Westphal (1886), and A. Westphal (1894) showed that nerve and muscle tissues of newborn mammals are not as irritable as those of adult animals. This view as applied to human neonates is supported by Banu and Bourguignon (1921), by Banu, Bourguignon, and Laugier (1921), and by Rothe (1929). Rothe has stated that irritability is greater to mechanical than to electrical stimulation.

Banu and Bourguignon (1921), Banu, Bourguignon, and Laugier (1921), and Rothe (1929) found that muscle chronaxies in the newborn infant are greater (2 to 10 times) than those of the adult. In the latter the chronaxies of different muscle groups are sharply differentiated; in the neonate there is little differentiation. In the neonate, proximal chronaxies are greater than distal chronaxies. Banu, Bourguignon, and Laugier (1921) associate this with an alleged greater movement of distal segments of extremities. These observations of movement run counter to those of Irwin (1930) and Shirley (1931a) regarding the order of development of movement.

Muscle chronaxies of neonates differ more than do nerve chronaxies from those of adults. The former approach adult values in 7 to 20 months, the latter in about 2 months.

Reaction times are stated in those sections of this chapter which deal with the different types of stimuli.

Hazard (1936) found the slowest reflex conduction rate for the patellar reflex in the newborn infant. The rate increases throughout childhood.

In Smith's (1938a, 1938b, 1939) electroencephalograms of the neonate the pattern derived from the occipital electrodes is a "straight line," but from either post- or precentral regions there are "recurrent, brief, ill-defined series of rhythmic waves of various frequencies." They are present only in sleep and disappear when the child wakes.

Flechsig's myelinogenetic law, function following myelinization, has been widely accepted even to modern times, as represented by Tilney and Casamajor (1924). Among workers in the field of infant development, Bersot (1920, 1921), Minkowski (1922), Peiper (1925a), and Langworthy (1933) have maintained that function may precede myelinization.

Reactions to Visual Stimuli

Sensitivity. The ready arousal of various visual reflexes has obviated any serious doubt regarding the existence of visual sensitivity in the newborn infant. The functioning of mechanisms essential to sensory discriminations and to perception is not granted so readily. Thus the presence of retinal hemorrhages, the shape of the eyeball, the alleged nonfunction of accommodatory mechanisms, and so on would seem to preclude the focusing of clear images upon the retinae, whereas the relative lack of fixation and coordination of the eyes would likewise deprive the child of binocular criteria for depth perception.

Relation to Stimuli. For the adult, visual discriminations vary according to the wave length, wave amplitude, wave composition, and the duration of the visual stimulus.

At present, according to Munn (1938), there are no unequivocal data indicating the possession by the neonate of differential responses to the wave length characteristic of visual stimuli. Peiper (1926b), after his discovery of an ocular-neck reflex which is dependent upon the intensity of the visual stimulus, was the first to attack the problem of color vision experimentally in premature infants. According to Peiper, the totally color blind adult does not manifest the Purkinje phenomenon. Hence, if the infant under dark adaptation can be shown to have the Purkinje shift in brightness, there is good reason to believe that the child reacts differently to different wave lengths of the visual stimulus. From his study of the four prematures Peiper concluded that the Purkinje phenomenon is present at this stage of development, the brightness values of the hues corresponding to those of the adult and thus implying color vision in the young infant.

Smith (1936) showed that even after dark adaptation the long-wave end remained brighter than or as bright as the short-wave end of the spectrum for Peiper's subjects. Hence the Purkinje shift of greatest brightness to the short-wave end is not demonstrated. In her own investigation of the brightness values of hues for twenty newborn infants Smith employed three hues (blue, green, and red) of equal energy as transmitted by Wratten filters. Before subjecting the infants to the five-minute illumination period they were dark-adapted for five minutes. The respiration and the activity during the two periods were automatically registered and observers recorded responses and crying. The percentage of immediate overt responses and the respiratory responses failed to discriminate between the hues. Activity and crying were inhibited most by blue and least by red. Whether the infant's eyes were closed or open did not seem to affect this discrimination. In terms of the means, blue and green—but not red—inhibit crying and activity in males, whereas all three hues are effective for females. This student of the problem concludes that the reactions of the male infants conform to the picture presented by the totally color blind adult, whereas those of female infants are compatible with dichromatic vision of the protanopic type. Hence the brightness values for hues of the same physical energy are not the same for infants as for adults with complete color vision.

Peiper (1937b), in commenting upon Smith's criticism, states that the Purkinje phenomenon refers to a change in brightness of the hues relative to each other rather than to white light. He likewise points out that Smith's subjects were not completely dark-adapted, and he questions whether a difference between the means for the sexes warrants the conclusion that *one* sex is color blind and the *other* partially color blind. Smith (1937), in reply, notes that the crux of the disagreement rests in conflicting interpretations of what constitutes the Purkinje phenomenon.

Chase (1937), employing a small moving spot of color within a larger field of another color but of the same luminosity value for the adult, found that infants as young as fifteen days showed pursuit movements for all the hues studied but did not pursue a colorless spot within a colorless field of a different brightness. This is taken to mean that the infant has differential reactions to the wave length characteristics of the visual stimulus.

In regard to these major researches, Munn (1938)[1] maintains that the sex differences and brightness values for the different colors found by Smith are not statistically reliable, but that her criticism of the inadequacy of Peiper's data in demonstrating *equivalent* brightness values of

hues for infants and adults is valid. He says:

> If the brightness value of hues is alike for infant and adult, the results of these experiments indicate color differentiation in very young infants. If the brightness value of the various hues is not the same for infant and adult, most of the data on color vision in infants are equivocal.

This fundamental difficulty in the investigation of color vision in infants had been anticipated by Pratt, Nelson, and Sun (1930) as follows:

> It seems that the structure and function of the adult eye must be regarded as one factor in our definition of luminosity. When we speak of the eye of the infant, the problem becomes more complex still.

Aside from the factor of duration, the visible and measurable activity of the neonate seems to depend primarily upon the intensity characteristic of the visual stimulus. Thus Peiper (1926c) determined the threshold for the ocular-neck response, whereas Sherman, Sherman, and Flory (1936) observed that the rapidity of the pupillary reflexes depends upon the intensity of the stimulus. Greater sensitivity with increase in age is shown by a decrease in the intensity required to elicit the responses. Irwin[2] has repeated certain aspects of Peiper's experiment showing the effects of different intensities of light upon the ocular-neck reflex. The percentage of infants responding and the percentage of responses to stimulation of brief duration (one second) and ranging in intensity from 5 to 200 foot-candles were recorded. He concluded "that when a brief stimulus is used with a specific reflex the relation is directly proportional, but when a stimulus of continued duration is used with general activity, the effect is inverse."

---

[1] Munn, however, errs in saying that the differences under discussion are less than three times the PE. Some are less than three times the standard error of the difference, but one may well ask whether this is not primarily a reflection of the small size of the sample.

[2] Personal communication to the writer upon the results of unpublished research.

Greater general activity, according to Irwin and Weiss (1934c), occurs neither under moderate intensities of visual stimulation nor in complete darkness, but under minimal light conditions (0.002 foot-candle). The same investigators, using three intensities of light stimulation (3.9, 0.02, and 0.002 foot-candles), found that activity was greatest under minimal and least under moderate light. Observational records of activity and of crying for the most part corroborated the polygraph recording of the stabilimeter oscillations. Weiss (1934), in the preliminary study of this series using the intensities mentioned, had found that the immediate effects, if any, were excitatory but nondifferential of different intensities. With prolongation of the illumination, however, activity decreased with increase in the intensity of the visual stimulus. The maximal inhibitory effects occurred 2 to 4 minutes after the onset of the stimulus. Maximum differentials occurred when the infants were not close to a feeding period or younger than the fourth day. Females appear to be more sensitive to differences in intensity than males. Irwin (1941a), employing visual stimuli of 5, 25, and 50 foot-candles, demonstrated that general activity is decreased by these higher intensities also. It was further shown that passage of the infant from an illumination period of 5 minutes' duration and at 5 foot-candles to a period of darkness is followed by an increase in activity.

The relation of intensity and adaptation is discussed in a subsequent section and the effects upon activity of combining visual and auditory stimuli of some duration are reviewed in the section on the reactions to auditory stimuli.

With the demonstrated uncertainty regarding differential responses in the neonate to the wave length characteristic of light, it is of course understandable that no investigations of possible reactions to wave composition have been undertaken.

Peiper (1926c), Pratt, Nelson, and Sun (1930), Pratt (1934c), and others have reported that visual stimuli of short duration evoke limited reflexes such as the palpebral and the pupillary, or more extensive responses such as the Moro or the "startle." Stimuli of longer duration, as Weiss (1934) has shown, may at the outset produce similar results, but as they persist activity and crying decrease under dim and moderate illuminations.

Infants under low illumination approaching deep twilight conditions do not manifest any appreciable increase in bodily activity during experimental periods of repeated visual stimulation furnished by flashes of light at various time intervals, as contrasted with the activity in control periods.

Visual spot illumination moving within the general visual field may elicit eye and head pursuit movements.

Relation to State of Organism. The general effect of a period of dark adaptation is to increase sensitivity to visual stimuli. Under these conditions Peiper (1926b) found that stimuli of an intensity inadequate for the light-adapted eye are effective in releasing the ocular-neck reflex. Similarly, according to Irwin and Weiss (1934c), there is decreased activity during periods of continuous dim or moderate stimulation, when such periods have been preceded by periods of darkness. Under subsequent minimal intensity of illumination, however, activity is increased. The dark adaptation process from beginning to final stages cannot be differentiated in terms of activity differences. Redfield (1937), employing dark adaptation periods of 1, 5, 10, and 20 minutes and intensities, in the later more extensive study (1939), of 0.5, 1.1, and 4.7 foot-candles in one series, and in another series of 0.04,

0.09, and 0.4 foot-candle, concluded that "increasing sensitivity to light after long as opposed to short periods of dark adaptation is indicated throughout the range of experimental intensities."

The possible alteration of the brightness values of hues and the question whether under dark adaptation the Purkinje phenomenon is produced have been considered in the review of the Peiper-Smith controversy.

In the activity differentials, from minimal to moderate intensities of visual stimulation, Weiss (1934) reported a greater decrease under waking conditions than when infants were asleep. Smith (1936), on the other hand, found no evidence of significant differences in the discrimination of the brightness of hues under these states of the infant.

The palpebral and most other overt responses are elicitable in both waking and sleeping states, but coordinated eye movements in pursuit of a moving light occur apparently only when the infant is awake.

Reaction Times. According to Canestrini (1913) the latent time of the circulatory and respiratory responses to visual stimulation is one-half to two seconds.

Types of Response. The responses range from the limited involvement of the accessory muscles of the visual sense organs to the greater involvement of the organism in circulatory and respiratory changes, in movements of the head and eyes, and more rarely of activity of most of the larger segments of the body. Inhibition of general activity appears when stimulation continues.

The *visuopalpebral reflex* (a closing of the eyes or a further tightening or twitch of the eyelids to a flash of light if they are already closed) had been described by Kroner (1881). Preyer (1882) was careful to distinguish this, as he termed it, innate blinking from the protective wink reflex to an approaching object, the latter not being elicitable until about the end of the second month. Pratt, Nelson, and Sun (1930) found that, in point of occurrence to discontinuous stimulation, the visuopalpebral response was the most invariable of those aroused by visual stimuli.

According to the early investigators, Kussmaul (1859), Genzmer (1873), and Kroner (1881), even premature babies manifest a lively *pupillary reflex.* Later investigators such as Guernsey (1929), Beasley (1933b), and Sherman, Sherman, and Flory (1936) seem to have demonstrated that the reflex, although sluggish at birth, rapidly perfects itself during the early part of the first postnatal week. Preyer (1882) and Feldman (1920) reported a consensual pupillary reflex. Gudden (1910) has noted that the pupil of the neonate is smaller than that of the adult during sleep and that there is no sudden dilatation to a maximum upon awakening. The continual play of movement of the margin of the iris, which increases upon external stimulation, was not found by Peiper (1926d) to occur in the neonate.

It is not known whether the ciliary muscle provides any *accommodation* in the early part of the neonatal period. The diameter of the eye, however, according to Peiper (1928), makes it myopic, and retinal hemorrhages would make it even less likely that clear-cut images can be focused upon the retina.

The convergence of the two eyes to produce *fixation* upon a bright light was observed by Genzmer (1873) and Preyer (1882) in infants shortly after birth. The Shermans (1925, 1936) find improvement in the response during the first three days. Even after coordination has been demonstrated, however, *strabismus* may be observed. Gutmann (1924) had obtained similar results. Peiper (1928) maintains that there is no real fixation during the neonatal period, and Guernsey (1929) states that it is lacking until well into the second month. Beasley (1933b), on the other hand, finds coordination in fixation rather than incoordination to be the general rule.

Kussmaul (1859), Kroner (1881), Preyer (1882), Blanton (1917), and later investigators had observed that a slowly moving light arouses *pursuit movements* of the eye and head. Jones (1926) did not obtain true visual pursuit movements until after the neonatal period. The most completely instrumentalized study of these responses was undertaken by McGinnis (1930). Moving visual stimuli were furnished by a rotating visual field and motion pictures were made of the eye movements. Under these conditions, successful pursuit (eye movements in the same direction without frequent movements in the opposite direction and with head movements decreasing in frequency) appeared after the second week. Beasley (1933a) and Chase (1937) report that visual pursuit occurs within the first week. The former found that vertical and circular pursuit movements appear later than the horizontal, thus confirming the order though not the age of occurrence of these responses as stated by Jones (1926). According to Beasley (1933a), the optimum rate of movement and distance of the moving light from the eyes varies from infant to infant. This, if confirmed, reveals methodological weaknesses in those experimental techniques wherein these factors were constant from infant to infant. Visual pursuit movements of eye and head are analogous to those observed in young kittens and termed by Tilney and Casamajor (1924) the "oculocephalo-gyric" response.

Optic nystagmus, of the same type found in adults, was observed by McGinnis (1930) to be present in infants a few hours after birth. Catel (1932) reports "physiological" nystagmus in the newborn infant, whereas Bartels (1932) holds that such eye movements resemble those of the blind.

The *ocular-neck reflex,* a bending backward of the head to a flash of light, was shown by Peiper (1926c) to depend upon the intensity of the visual stimulus.

A bright, intense flash of light may evoke, as Peiper (1926c) has noted, a response which some have designated *fear* and others *Moro's Umklammerungs reflex.* From the tables of Pratt, Nelson, and Sun (1930) it seems that either this or the "startle" have a higher incidence during the first days of the neonatal period. Dupérié and Bargues (1932), however, were unable to elicit the Moro response by visual stimulation.

According to Canestrini (1913), the respiratory and circulatory responses of the neonate resemble those of the frightened adult.

Weiss (1934), Irwin and Weiss (1934a), and Richards (1936b) have demonstrated that, within certain intensity ranges, general activity decreases as the intensity of the visual stimulus increases.

Learning. According to Denisova and Figurin (1929), visual CR's [1] appear later than auditory CR's and are not set up within the neonatal period. Wenger (1936), pairing visual and electrotactual stimuli for two infants, found some indication of conditioning by the sixth day.

Technique of Investigation. The earlier investigators of the problem of color vision had little or no control over their stimuli and were in no position to determine which aspects of the visual stimulus were related to the observed responses of the infant. The later investigators, employing Wratten filters, have presented visual

[1] CR is here used as an abbreviation for conditioned reflexes (or responses).

stimuli of known wave length, physical energy, and luminosity value for the human adult.

The problem of the presence or absence of color vision in newborn infants has been approached by attempting to discover whether, under dark adaptation, there is a Purkinje shift in the brightness values of the hues similar to that found in the adult with normal color vision. The ocular-neck reflex has been used as an indicator of change in intensity to stimuli of short duration, and the effects of stimuli of long duration upon general activity have also been determined. Another attempt to solve the problem consists in the movement of a colored spot within a visual field of the same luminosity for the adult, but of a different hue.

Pursuit movements have been studied in relation to manually produced moving visual stimuli and in relation to control of movement within a given plane.

Respiratory and circulatory responses have been recorded through pneumograph-kymograph systems, whereas general activity has been recorded through stabilimeter oscillations registered upon a polygraph or through electrical counters. Eye movements have been photographed.

Summary. The newborn infant reacts to light, but it is not certain whether any differential responses are made to the wave length or to the complexity characteristic of visual stimuli. Responses do depend upon the duration and the intensity of the stimuli. Those which are sufficiently intense and of short duration release lid responses, circulatory and respiratory responses, the ocular-neck reflex, and probably the Moro and "startle" responses. If moving spot illumination within the visual field is provided there is some evidence of fixation, of pursuit movements, and of nystagmus. If the stimulus is of sufficient duration the pupillary reflex may be observed, and with continued illumination there is a decrease in general activity. Increasing the intensity, within certain limits, decreases the activity. The effect of a given stimulus intensity is profoundly influenced by the previous conditions of stimulation, that is, as in dark adaptation. Whether newborn infants manifest the Purkinje phenomenon is a matter of controversy.

Reactions to Auditory Stimuli

Sensitivity. From the earliest days of neonate study down to the present there has been a certain amount of controversy regarding the auditory sensitivity of newborn infants. Kussmaul (1859) was convinced that they were insensitive to auditory stimuli, whereas Genzmer (1873) claimed that not only did they possess such sensitivity on the first or second day after birth but that in all probability also the fetus received auditory stimulation from the heartbeats and aortic pulse and from the activities in the digestive tract of the maternal organism.

Kroner (1881) and Moldenhauer—according to Preyer (1882)—reported the early presence of sensitivity but commented upon its great variability. Moldenhauer observed the following reactions to auditory stimuli: quivering of the eyelids, wrinkling of the forehead, head movements, screaming, and awakening from sleep. Repetition of the stimulus either produced no effects or else was quieting. Poli (1893) and Sachs (1893) considered sensitivity to be evidenced by the palpebral reflex, and Sachs also noted the "fear" (*Schreck*) reaction.

Since these early investigations the existence of auditory sensitivity in the neonate has been confirmed by the researches of Koellreutter (1907), Peterson and Rainey (1910), Canestrini (1913), Blanton (1917), Waltan (1921), Peiper (1924c), Pratt, Nelson, and Sun (1930), Irwin (1932g), Pratt (1934b), Weiss (1934), and Stubbs (1934). A few writers during this period, namely, Feldman (1920), Löwenfeld (1927), Bryan (1930), and Haller (1932), maintain that there is relative insensitivity during the early postnatal days.

The discovery by Peiper (1924c), later confirmed by the observations and researches of Forbes and Forbes (1927), Ray (1932), and Sontag and Wallace (1934, 1935b, 1936), that the fetus *in utero* reacts to vibratory stimuli of a rate affecting the auditory receptors of adults would seem to indicate a similar stimulation of the fetal auditory receptors. This may, however, take place through bone conduction, whereas postnatal insensitivity, if present, may depend upon the condition or state of structures normally responsive to air vibrations.

Various explanations have been offered for such alleged insensitivity: (1) mucus in the middle ear (Preyer, 1882); (2) occlusion of the external auditory meatus (Preyer, 1882; Feldman, 1920); (3) tympanic membrane not in a state to respond easily to air vibrations (Feldman, 1920); (4) fixity of auditory ossicles (Compayré, 1896); (5) transitory or permanent birth injuries (Kutvirt, 1912; Vosz, 1923); (6) imperfectly developed auditory nerve (Shinn, 1893–1899; Stern, 1914).

Relation to Stimuli. Auditory stimuli present certain variable characteristics of which the more important are frequency, amplitude, and complexity. As in other stimulus modalities, the duration of the stimulus is likewise of great significance.

There is no indubitable evidence that infants possess either differential responses to varying frequencies of vibration or the possibility of acquiring them during the neonatal period. Moldenhauer claimed that easily observed responses are more likely to occur to high-pitched sounds. This observation has been supported by Sachs (1893), who produced stimuli with tuning forks and Galton whistle; by Waltan (1921), who employed whistles and tuning forks; by Haller (1932), who used an audiometer; and by Muzio (1933) with tuning forks (according to this investigator females react quicker than males). In none of these investigations was there instrumentalized recording of responses.

Stubbs (1934) appears to have been the first to obtain adequate control of the auditory stimulus and at the same time to secure objective records of the responses of infants to it. The effects upon overt activity, recorded by the stabilimeter-polygraph unit, and upon implicit respiratory activity pneumographically registered, were compared when the stimuli were four different frequencies (128, 256, 1024, and 4096 cycles) produced by an audiometer at constant intensity levels in terms of sensation units and with a duration of 10 seconds. Observations were made by two observers, and their reliability was statistically determined. In this research the stabilimeter record disclosed no differences in overt responses to differences in frequency. Nor do the respiratory records reveal any effect of varying frequencies upon respiratory rate, but they do show significantly fewer cases of no response at the lowest as compared with the highest frequency. Of the responses observed, only eyelid opening and decrease in body activity appeared to occur more often at the lower than at the higher frequencies.

In view of Kasatkin and Levikova's (1935a) lack of success in establishing conditioned sucking responses to auditory stimuli before the first half of the second month, it seems unlikely that the conditioned reflex technique will demonstrate any capacity for pitch discrimination in the newborn infant.

The degree of organismic involvement in a response is related to the amplitude of the auditory stimulus. The correlation has been widely noted, but few have carefully investigated it. In the studies by Pratt, Nelson, and Sun (1930) the amount of measurable and observable activity of the neonate did not seem to correspond with the adult ratings of intensity or loudness of the experimental stimuli. The lack of control of the stimulus variables and the undetermined reliability of observations and of measurements render their evidence inadequate for determining the exact relationship of overt activity to the amplitude of auditory stimuli.

Stubbs (1934), who controlled the stimulus by means of audiometer and oscillator, found that with a 10-second duration for each frequency studied the percentage of responses increased as the stimulus intensities ranged upward from 30 through 50, 70 to 85 sensation units. The louder stimuli produced more bodily movements, greater frequency of eyelid closing and respiratory action, and a decrease in crying.

Weiss (1934) investigated the effects of two intensities (50 ± 5 and 75 ± 5 decibels) of a tone with a frequency of 420 cycles for durations of 5 minutes. She measured activity by stabilimeter oscillations and found that under sound-dark conditions the infant exhibited "a significant tendency toward lessened activity with increased sound intensity." In the sound-light experiment visual stimulation reinforced the auditory to bring about an even greater lessening of activity.

The possibility of variation of responses according to variation in the complexity of the auditory stimulus does not seem to have received any experimental study.

Early observations, such as those by Sachs (1893), and all later studies show that overt responses are greater if the stimulus duration is short (as in noises), whereas there may be inhibition of activity or complete lack of response if the stimulus is of longer duration (as in musical tones). These pacifying or inhibiting effects of stimuli of longer duration have been reported by Pratt, Nelson, and Sun (1930). These latter observations should be accepted with caution because the intensities of the stimuli employed were not adequately controlled. Haller (1932) reported that even with a stimulus duration of only 10 seconds the response began with the onset of stimulation and declined or disappeared by the time the stimulus had ceased. Stubbs (1934) used durations of 1, 3, 5, and 15 seconds. The percentage of responses to the longest duration was significantly greater than to the shortest duration of the stimulus. The longer durations operated also to evoke greater bodily activity, increases in rate, and corresponding decreases in amplitude of respiratory responses. The longer durations, such as the 5-minute periods given by Weiss (1934), decrease bodily activity significantly as compared with periods during which no stimuli are presented.

These experiments seem to indicate that the auditory stimulus first releases certain overt responses and thereafter, if the stimulus persists, overt activity subsides and there is less movement than would occur in a period of no experimental stimulation. The continuous stimuli may inhibit the activity which ordinarily results from internal stimuli, or possibly the situation is analogous to the "listening" posture of the adult.

Discontinuous, repeated auditory stimuli produce rapid decreases in the circulatory and respiratory responses, according to the researches of Canestrini (1913). And Peiper (1924c) found that the "fear" response of the fetus *in utero* usually followed upon only the first stimulus. They ascribe this decline to inhibition rather than to fatigue. Pratt (1934*b*) used relatively constant but unmeasured auditory stimuli to demonstrate that during a period of discontinuous auditory stimulation activity is confined to movements following the discrete stimuli, that the response declines with successive repetitions of the stimuli, and that the amount of activity per stimulation decreases as their frequency is increased within a given period of time.

Relation to State of Organism. Aside from the transitory residual effects of previous stimulation it is known that the response evoked by a given stimulus is also dependent upon the physiological state of the organism. Poli (1893) observed that the cochlear-palpebral reflex (principally closing of the eyes if they are open or further tightening of the lids if they are closed) was most easily elicited during sleep but was most difficult to activate when the child was nursing. Canestrini (1913) noted that the nature of respiratory and circulatory responses depended somewhat upon whether the infant was asleep or awake. Peiper (1925*b*) obtained a longer reaction time for the "fear" reaction during sleep than during waking, and a number of investigators have affirmed that this "fear" response is best detected in the sleeping infant. That it is invariably followed by awakening is not supported by the data of Pratt, Nelson, and Sun (1930). Stubbs (1934) found that the smallest percentage of responses to auditory stimuli occurred when infants were crying, and the largest when they were awake and inactive.

Reaction Times. Peiper (1925*b*) reported a longer reaction time for premature infants than for a 2-month-old infant (0.25 second for the latter). Irwin (1932*g*), with an auditory stimulus of 581 cycles, a duration of 0.07 second, and a constant unmeasured intensity, found that the mean "body startle" reaction time of twelve infants, measured by stabilimeter-polygraph records, was 0.18 ± 0.03. The reaction time of respiratory responses was found by Stubbs and Irwin (1934) to be 0.09 second, with a standard error of the mean of 0.025.

Types of Responses. The overt responses elicited by discontinuous auditory stimuli, according to the intensity of the stimuli and the previous stimulating conditions, range from the minimum involvement of the palpebral reflexes on through to the maximum involvement of most of the large behavior segments. When auditory stimuli are continuous for some appreciable duration, decrease in activity sets in after the initial overt responses.

The *cochlear-palpebral reflexes* may occur in relative isolation when the stimuli are of slight intensity or when the infant has been repeatedly stimulated, as Pratt (1933, 1934*b*) has shown. Moldenhauer was one of the first to observe these in the complex of responses, and Cemach (1920), who gave them particular attention, emphasized their persistence beyond the neonatal period. Irwin (1932*g*) has noted that they are more invariable in occurrence than the "body startle," whereas Landis and Hunt (1939) have maintained that blinking is a component of the "startle" pattern.

Bartels (1910) and Peiper (1928) state that auditory stimuli produce pupillary dilatation in newborn infants, but the latter observes that there is great irregularity in its occurrence.

When infants are asleep, according to Canestrini (1913), auditory stimuli of some duration, such as musical tones, make breathing slower and shallower and decrease the pulse rate. If the stimuli are intense enough to wake the child the rates of respiration and pulse are increased. Intense stimuli of short duration (such as a pistol shot) result in an immediate increase in the amplitude of respiration, followed by irregular breathing. Stubbs (1934) found that increase in intensity and duration had measurable consequences in respiratory responses and that "respiratory responses were found less often to higher than lower pitches."

The earlier investigators of neonate behavior were impressed with the gross muscular response of the infant to auditory stimuli. Sachs (1893) was one of the first to term these reactions the "fear" (*Schreck*) response, and Watson (1919) made the alleged emotional pattern one of the corner stones in his theory of three primary emotions. Peiper (1925a) was one of the first to liken the fear response, as elicited by auditory stimuli, to the "Moro" response, while granting that there was a difference in latent time. Schaltenbrand (1925) maintained that the Moro response was elicited by sudden sounds. Following these, Irwin (1932g), Pratt (1934b), Dennis (1934), Richards (1936a), and Wenger (1936) have held that the terms "fear," "body jerk," "body startle," etc., are merely different names for a general but variable response which may be elicited by stimuli of various modalities.

Other research workers have insisted that the fear response and the Moro response are distinct, for, according to Dupérié and Bargues (1932), the Moro cannot be evoked by auditory stimuli. They and Gordon (1929) maintain that the responses merely simulate each other and they agree with Peiper (1925a) that in a given stimulus situation the fear reaction precedes the Moro.

Strauss (1929), as reported by Hunt, Clarke, and Hunt (1936), ascribed a "startle" response to intense auditory stimuli which differed not only in pattern but in age of appearance from the Moro

response. According to this view, the Moro, but not the startle, is present during the neonatal period. In regard to arm movements, Hunt and Landis (1938) have stressed the extensor characteristic of the Moro as compared with the flexor characteristic of the startle.

Pratt (1937) viewed all these as variants of the Moro, and Wagner (1938a) has proposed that they all be called "body jerks." Hunt and Landis (1938) and Hunt (1939) point out that the evidence from ultrarapid motion pictures reveals two patterns of response, one commonly known as the Moro and the other which they, following Strauss, call the startle. They (Landis and Hunt, 1939) assert that both patterns are clearly present at six weeks and that after a few months the Moro disappears but the startle remains. They cautiously favor the view that both responses may be present from birth, with the startle somewhat masked by the Moro (for segmental comparison of these see the section on the Moro and startle responses).

Pratt (1933) described variable plantar responses as part of the response to auditory stimuli, and Clarke, Hunt, and Hunt (1937) have photographed them. Pratt, using less intense stimuli than those employed by the three later investigators, noted that toe movements and the palpebral reflexes in many instances persist as other components of the response drop out with successive repetitions of the stimulus.

Learning. The conditioned reflex technique, as a means of studying auditory sensitivity, was suggested by Aldrich (1928). Kasatkin and Levikova (1935a), however, were unable to establish conditioned sucking responses during the neonatal period. Denisova and Figurin (1929), according to Razran (1933), established conditioned food-seeking responses to auditory stimuli during the second month, although natural as opposed to laboratory CR's appeared during the first month. Marquis (1931) stated that conditioned sucking and quietening to auditory stimuli were established during the first ten days after birth. Wenger (1936), despite some masking of the conditioning auditory stimulus by other auditory stimuli, obtained some indication of unstable leg withdrawal and respiratory "gasp" CR's with electrotactual unconditioned stimuli. The Wickenses (1940) attempted, with inconclusive results, to set up auditory-leg movement CR's, with electric shock as the unconditioned stimulus.

Technique of Investigation. Auditory stimuli have been produced with varying degrees of control by tuning forks, Galton whistles, devices providing constant but unmeasured stimuli, and instruments of precise control such as the audiometer. Circulatory and respiratory responses to auditory stimuli have been recorded by means of pneumatic systems (pneumograph and tambour), the kymograph, and the polygraph. Gross movements and increase or decrease of bodily activity have been recorded by means of stabilimeter-polygraph systems or by stabilimeter oscillations through electrical counters. Reaction times have been measured by a modified Morse apparatus, by the stabilimeter-polygraph apparatus, and by ultrarapid motion picture photography. The patterning of responses and the incidence of responses not registered by mechanical systems have been recorded by some observers and photographed by others.

Summary. The neonate is not deaf, but there is little evidence that it makes pitch discriminations or differential responses correlated with the complexity characteristic of auditory stimuli. Its responses are, however, modified according to the duration and the intensity of the stimuli. If they are of short duration and sufficiently intense, responses such as lid reflexes, circulatory and respiratory changes, and gross muscular patterns of response, such as the Moro and possibly the startle, appear. With successive repetitions of the auditory stimuli the gross muscular components decline in extent of involvement and disappear, leaving the more invariant palpebral reflexes, and frequently responses of the toes. If the stimuli are of long duration their effect is to lessen the activity which would normally occur during the period, and the decrease becomes greater as the intensity of the stimulus is increased.

Reactions to Olfactory Stimuli

Sensitivity. The demonstration of the presence or absence of olfactory sensitivity in the neonate presents such methodological difficulties that the lack of agreement of different investigators is not surprising. Some have held that the sense of smell is important and well developed. Among them are Darwin (1877), Kroner (1881), and Peterson and Rainey (1910). Somewhat less certain of the importance and of the maturity of this sensory field are Ciurlo (1934) and Stirnimann (1936b, 1936c), whereas Disher (1934) is willing to grant that the neonate at least discriminates between odorous and nonodorous substances. Most of the workers in this field, however, have been extremely doubtful whether newborn infants react to olfactory stimuli. Kussmaul (1859), although subscribing to the view that the infant possesses olfactory sensitivity, was one of the first to note that ammonia and acetic acid fumes were most effective in eliciting reactions and to decide that such substances produce their effects as tactile rather than as olfactory stimuli. Preyer (1882) supported this view by saying that such substances irritate the mucous membrane of the nose. Canestrini (1913) found that only such substances affected respiration and circulation. He ascribed these effects to stimulation which set up impulses in the trigeminal nerve. Watson (1919) and Peiper (1928) accept this interpretation, and Tanner (1915), Blanton (1917), Drummond (1921), and Pratt, Nelson, and Sun (1930) likewise hold that olfactory sensitivity is not present or else is poorly developed.

Relation to Stimuli. In the first researches to introduce the principle of a nonodorous air control, a duration control by means of an olfactory pump, and a high degree of saturation of a given volume of air at room temperatures, Pratt, Nelson, and Sun (1930) used acetic acid, ammonia, oil of cloves, and valerian as stimuli. The observers noted the number of responses to stimuli, recorded in code the movements of different segments of the body, and afterward measured the stabilimeter-polygraph records of activity. Although they did not determine the statistical reliability of their observations and measurements, there seems little doubt that of the substances employed only ammonia and acetic acid, as evaluated by the air control, produced unquestionable results. Analysis of the percentage of specific movements of body segments in the responses that did occur to the different stimuli shows that with the air control the body extremities and eyes were most often involved, whereas there were scarcely any head or facial movements. Vocalizations and facial responses had greater incidence to ammonia and acetic acid. Sucking was more conspicuous in the responses to valerian. The infants reacted about as vigorously to acetic acid as to ammonia, whereas adults considered acetic acid much less irritating than the ammonia.

Disher (1934) devised a thermal control and used gas-collecting tubes for her reservoirs of odors. Three different degrees of saturation were obtained by drawing from these and from a pure air source by hypodermic syringes. Stimulation was effected by pushing on the plunger of the syringe, while the experimenter counted to 25. Besides the nonodorous air control, odorous substances following Henning's classification, such as violet, asafetida, sassafras, citronella, turpentine, pyridine, and lemon, were employed. Responses were recorded by two observers, and a set of motion picture records was made. According to this investigator, newborn infants respond significantly in terms of percentage response to stimulation by the odor stimuli as compared with the percentage response to stimulation by pure air. Observation and segmental analysis of the responses, however, disclose no evidence of differential odor discriminations, and the pattern of responses to air alone, when there are responses, is apparently no different from that aroused by olfactory stimuli. Percentage of response and extent of organismic involvement appear to depend upon the degree of saturation of the olfactory stimulus.

Ciurlo (1934), using essence of lavender, valerian, and mint, which, it is supposed, do not stimulate the trigeminal nerve, is reported to have demonstrated by means of graphic records of respiration that the newborn infant differentiates odors as pleasant or unpleasant.

Stirnimann (1936b, 1936c) is of the opinion that volatile substances stimulate not only the olfactory and trigeminal nerves but also the glossopharyngeal nerve. The absence of the olfactory nerve does not lead to lack of response to stimuli which are ordinarily supposed to stimulate the olfactory nerve and to be pleasant. Hence the interpretation that the trigeminal, when activated, gives only unpleasant experiences is unwarranted. Stirnimann holds that differential responses to odorous stimuli are revealed by facial or mimetic responses.

Anise oil involves nasal taste (*gout nasale*) and gives rise to expressions of pleasure and to sucking and licking responses. Oil of chenopodium leads to grimaces of discontent; ammonium carbonate produces grimaces and pronounced turning-away of the head from the test tube containing the substance.

Types of Response. The overt responses elicited by ammonia, acetic acid, and so on consist of a throwing-back or turning-away of the head, wrinkling or grimacing of the face, squirming of the trunk, movements of the extremities, and frequently sneezing and crying. Such substances likewise affect respiration and circulation. Other substances, such as anise oil, essence of lavender, valerian, mint, and oil of chenopodium, generally held to be purely odorous stimuli, may give rise to *mimetic* and respiratory responses, supporting a classification into agreeable or disagreeable odors, according to Ciurlo (1934) and Stirnimann (1936b, 1936c). The "pleasant" odors may be accompanied by sucking and licking movements.

Technique of Investigation. The duration, saturation, and temperature of the air in which olfactory stimuli are presented have been controlled by various devices such as the olfactory pump, reservoirs of fully saturated vapor, and pure air source. Responses have been recorded by observers, photographed with the motion picture camera, and registered by the stabilimeter-polygraph unit. Respiratory and circulatory responses have been graphically recorded by pneumograph-kymograph combinations.

Summary. It seems to be well established that newborn infants react vigorously to such stimuli as ammonia and acetic acid, but whether these rather general reactions of the body musculature are to be ascribed

to the sense of smell or of pain is uncertain. According to some investigators, other substances, which are purely odorous for adults, are responded to by infants with mimetic responses indicating "pleasant" or "unpleasant" experiences. Some stimuli lead to avoiding movements; others are followed by sucking and licking responses.

Reactions to Gustatory Stimuli

Sensitivity. Taste was considered by Kussmaul (1859), Preyer (1882), and Peterson and Rainey (1910) to be highly developed in the neonate. Shinn (1893–1899) believed it to be dormant, and Blanton (1917) maintained that taste, smell, and touch are not differentiated at this time. Canestrini (1913) obtained prompt circulatory and respiratory responses to gustatory stimuli but no reactions which would indicate differential responses or discrimination between "sour" and "bitter" stimuli. Pratt, Nelson, and Sun (1930) observed little differentiation, particularly when the percentage of responses evoked was compared with the percentage elicited by distilled water. With increase in age it appears that sucking responses to sugar solutions increase, whereas facial reactions become more pronounced to "salt," "sour," and "bitter" stimuli. Stirnimann (1936b, 1936c) holds that the neonate demonstrates taste discriminations of all four qualities, largely in terms of facial or mimetic reactions. Eckstein (1927) and Jensen (1932) have demonstrated that certain taste substances modify the sucking response.

Relation to Stimuli. The problem of taste sensitivity in the neonate resolves itself into several questions. Does the child make differential responses to taste substances? Are these of the same order or nature as those of the adult? Does the response alter as the strength of the stimulus is changed? The problem is complicated, as in the case of olfactory stimuli, by the fact that other than taste receptors are being stimulated. Also, the area of stimulation is not easily controlled. The arousal of a response may, again, depend upon the intensity rather than upon its specific modality. And, unfortunately, the effective strength of gustatory stimuli cannot be established in terms of equally concentrated solutions. Nor, as Pratt, Nelson, and Sun (1930) found, can it be said that the effective intensity of a taste substance is the same for the infant as for the adult.

Introduction of gustatory stimuli by means of applicator sticks dipped in solutions of salt, sugar, citric acid, and quinine in Pratt, Nelson, and Sun's investigation did not, when compared with similar introduction of distilled water, provide impressive evidence for taste differentiation in infants. Quinine and citric acid solutions appeared to be more effective than salt and sugar solutions. Jensen (1932), using the sucking reflex as an indicator, found differential responses (changes in the sucking response as compared with the control of mother's milk) to air and salt solutions. The approximate limen for the latter is a solution of 0.300 per cent. These differential reactions do not appear until the infant has sucked a few seconds, and therefore the reactions may depend upon the stimulation of other areas than those involved in experiments wherein the taste substance makes immediate contact with tongue areas.

Stirnimann (1936b, 1936c) applied taste solutions to the newborn infant's tongue by means of a nipple-shaped piece of cotton. In his opinion the neonate discriminates all four of the taste qualities, although there are no responses which may be said to be characteristic of each one. The differentiation is evidenced in part by differences in mimetic responses and in part by the sequential order of these in relation to responses of withdrawal, repulsion of the stimulating device, or in relation to sucking responses. The same investigator found that infants reacted more vigorously to a 7 per cent solution of saccharine than to a 7 per cent lactose solution, and again more vigorously to a 16 per cent solution of the latter than to the weaker solution of the same substance. No clear-cut differentiation was made between 0.9, 1.5, and 2.0 per cent salt solutions.

Relation to State of Organism. Jensen (1932) states that the "moderately full baby is a better discriminator than the very hungry infant."

Reaction Times. The responses to gustatory stimuli are varied in nature. From Canestrini's (1913) curves it seems that circulatory and respiratory responses follow quickly upon stimulation. Other responses apparently have a longer latent time.

Types of Response. According to Stirnimann (1936b, 1936c), taste as well as tactual stimuli frequently release a *vasomotor reflex* which produces a tumefaction of the inner surface of the lips. *Sucking responses,* as reported by Pratt, Nelson, and Sun (1930), occur to all taste stimuli They are more pronounced to sugar solutions and become increasingly so with age Stirnimann (1936b, 1936c) found these responses to be greatest to lactose, with citric acid a close second, but only of feeble occurrence to stimulation by quinine. Sonohara (1934a) found, as had Stirnimann, that saccharine arouses sucking responses. Jensen (1932) discovered that only salt solutions, among gustatory stimuli, impaired the sucking responses or caused them to cease. This confirms Canestrini's observation.

Movements of the tongue and lips, sometimes termed *defense* or *rejection,* have been observed by Pratt, Nelson, and Sun

(1930) and by Stirnimann (1936*b*, 1936*c*). Stirnimann noted that muscles of the pharynx are innervated, as in vomiting. Allied to these responses are general activity and even crying. Sonohara (1934*b*) disagrees with most investigators, who hold that "bitter" stimuli evoke reactions of rejection.

Some have held that facial responses or mimetic reactions—the "wry" face, for example—are rather characteristic to "bitter" stimuli.

The *salivary reflex*, as Stirnimann (1936*b*, 1936*c*) and others have noted, is not well established in the neonate.

According to Canestrini (1913), "sweet" stimulation calms the child, salt solutions produce a slight disturbance, and "sour" and "bitter" solutions initiate pronounced irregularity of the *respiratory* and *circulatory* curves.

Technique of Investigation. In most of the investigations the concentrations of the taste solutions have been stated. Responses to these have been compared with those evoked by distilled water and mother's milk as controls. These substances have been introduced into the infant's mouth by applicator sticks or other devices, or have been sucked from a special nursing bottle. The mimetic and other responses have been recorded by observers, while circulatory, respiratory, and sucking responses have been automatically registered by kymographs and polygraphs.

Summary. It is uncertain whether the neonate differentiates all four taste qualities. It appears, however, that in terms of the sucking response salt solutions tend to break up the response, whereas sugar solutions elicit and maintain it. Acid solutions to a lesser extent evoke sucking; quinine solutions seldom do. Facial responses mimetic of "disagreeable" affects are conspicuous responses to the latter. In general, respiration and circulation are least influenced by "sweet," slightly disturbed by "salt," and considerably affected by "sour" and "bitter" solutions. Sucking mounts with age to sugar solutions as do facial responses to quinine. There is some evidence that, beyond the threshold point, responses may be altered by differences in concentration of the taste solution.

Reactions to Thermal Stimuli

Sensitivity. The presence of thermal sensitivity in the newborn infant was noted by the early experimenters, Genzmer and Kroner, and has not been questioned in subsequent studies.

The researches which have been undertaken involve either limited areal stimulations (but not punctiform exploration in newborn infants) or activity under different environmental temperatures. There has been no really systematic exploration of the cutaneous surface or other parts of the body to ascertain the differential sensitivity of the various areas. Canestrini (1913) demonstrated that "cold" stimuli applied to the forehead produced prompt and vigorous circulatory and respiratory responses. Pratt, Nelson, and Sun (1930), stimulating the same area with a temperature cylinder (50 sq. mm. application area) at an average temperature of 11 to 12° C., obtained observable responses to 73 per cent of the stimulations. Stirnimann (1939), applying water-filled glass tubes (18 mm. diameter) to the infant's cheeks, found 89 per cent response to temperatures of 43 to 45° C. and 96 per cent response to temperatures of 15 to 17° C. Peiper (1924*b*), holding constant the contact while changing the thermal stimulation, stimulated the chest with "cold" stimuli and obtained pronounced responses. Stirnimann (1939) stimulated hand areas (hollow of the hand or ball of the thumb) with the temperatures previously mentioned and received no response in 74 per cent of the cases. Application by Pratt, Nelson, and Sun (1930) of the temperature cylinder to the inner surface of the leg at the knee yielded reactions to 91 per cent of the stimulations. Crudden (1937), employing stimuli of ±5° C. or more from the initial neutral (33 to 34° C.) and applying them by Peiper's technique to the dorsal surface of the leg midway between foot and knee, reported some degree of response, as shown by examination of cinema records, to all stimulations. Stirnimann (1939) obtained 94 per cent response to stimulations of the sole of the foot by stimuli of 43 to 45° C. and 100 per cent to those of 15 to 17° C. Although the size of cutaneous areas stimulated and the duration of the stimulation varies in the researches mentioned, they suggest the possibility that leg and foot are more sensitive to thermal stimuli than hand and head areas.

Thermal sensitivity has likewise been demonstrated in the oral cavity. Pratt, Nelson, and Sun (1930) introduced small amounts of distilled water at temperatures ranging from 8 to 53° C. and observed the movements which were elicited. Jensen (1932) measured the alterations produced in the sucking response by milk at temperatures above and below 40° C.

Environmental temperatures likewise give evidence of the thermal sensitivity of the newborn infant. If they are atmospheric, activity tends, as Pratt (1930) has shown, to be negatively correlated with them. Excitatory effects of lowering the temperature of the bath have been noted by Preyer (1882).

The thermal sensitivity of the neonate has not been compared with that of children in later developmental stages, nor are we able from the work of Peiper (1924b) and Stirnimann (1939) to compare with any certainty the premature with the full-term infant.

Relation to the Stimuli. Temperatures present continuous series, but the "cold" spots respond when some critical point below physiological zero (skin or other body temperature) is reached and again, paradoxically, when a critical point above physiological zero is attained, whereas the "warm" spots respond when a critical point above physiological zero is reached.

Physiological zero in infants has been given various values by different investigators and according to the area stimulated. It seems clear that oral and anal temperatures will differ from cutaneous temperatures. It is also evident that any thoroughgoing investigation of thermal sensitivity will require the determination of the skin or body area temperature for each neonate prior to the application of the thermal stimulus.

Pratt, Nelson, and Sun (1930) did not ascertain the temperatures of the areas stimulated. Stimulation of head and leg areas with the temperature cylinder at 33 to 45° C. did not seem to produce appreciable responses, whereas at 11 to 12° C. vigorous responses were aroused. Crudden (1937), on the basis of lack of response in preliminary trials, decided that 33 to 34° ± 5° C. was neutral for the area of the leg which he studied.

To oral stimulation, by distilled water applied with a medicine dropper, Pratt, Nelson, and Sun (1930) observed least response at 43° C. among temperatures of 8, 13, 18, 23, 33, 48, and 53° C. From these studies it would appear that the point of least stimulation for this area must lie between 33 and 43° C. Jensen (1932) found no disturbances in the sucking response to mother's milk at 40° C. The higher thresholds or critical points ranged from 50 to 65° C. (median approximately 52° C.); the lower thresholds ranged from 23 to 5° C. (median approximately 19° C.). Physiological zero for mouth areas seems to be within the range 35 to 36° ± 16 to 17° C., and Crudden's (1937) figures show it to be 33 to 34° ± 5° C. for leg areas.

Among early investigators, Preyer (1882), Canestrini (1913), and Peiper (1924b) were impressed with the potency of temperatures below physiological zero as compared with temperatures correspondingly higher. Pratt, Nelson, and Sun (1930) and Crudden (1937) have drawn similar conclusions. Jensen (1932), however, has pointed out that in terms of critical points for the sucking response the lower temperatures employed by Pratt, Nelson, and Sun represent greater deviations than do the higher temperatures. Pratt, Nelson, and Sun and Jensen have reported that the incidence and extent of the response depend upon the degree of deviation from the critical thresholds. Crudden found no consistent relationship.

Purely thermal stimulation is difficult if not impossible to set up. In the case of stimuli applied through thermal conduction the only control available is to make the contact stimuli constant while varying the thermal. According to Peiper (1928), Sikorski (1908) reported a turning of the head toward the side stimulated by thermal radiation. Peiper (1928) was unable to confirm this, but Stirnimann (1939), using a *Goldscheiderlampe aus Rubinglas*, found reactions in 85 per cent of the stimulations, with movements toward the stimulus.

Relation to State of Organism. The effect of previous stimulation is illustrated by Crudden's (1937) demonstration of the setting-up of temporary neutral temperatures, in other words, the rapid onset of adaptation.

Pratt, Nelson, and Sun (1930) did not find any clear difference between thermal sensitivity during sleep and waking states, but Crudden (1937) and Stirnimann (1939) are inclined to the view that the threshold is raised in sleep.

The enormous range between the high and low thresholds for thermal effects upon the sucking response, reported by Jensen (1932), may reflect the physiological state of the infant when nursing. Under different conditions the range of thermal neutrality might be considerably reduced.

Reaction Times. According to one of Canestrini's figures (1913), the reaction time of circulatory and respiratory responses to stimulation of the forehead with a cold piece of metal is not more than 0.5 second. Effects upon sucking are shown by Jensen (1932) to be delayed several seconds and to vary with the temperature deviation. Possibly this indicates the dominance of the stimuli producing the sucking response, or it may simply mean that changes in the sucking response await stimulation of other portions of the alimentary tract. With the capsule technique, Crudden (1937) reports reaction times of 2.5 to 11 seconds, with an average of 6.8 seconds to stimulation of the leg area.

Types of Response. Acceleration of breathing, throwing the head backward, gasping, shuddering, increase in brain volume, and irregular pulse follow the application of "cold" stimuli to the infant's forehead. Stimulation of the cheeks with temperatures of 15 to 17° C. leads to a turning-away of the head, whereas those of 43 to 45° C. generally evoke a turning-toward, seeking, or mouth orientation.

Stimulation of leg areas near the knee by the "cold" temperature cylinder produces most commonly flexion of the leg at the hip, with extension occurring only about one third as often. Stimulation of the calf of the leg produces most frequently general patterns of response with most of the activity confined to the legs and with extension more frequent than flexion. Also, according to Crudden (1937), there is evidence of a "scratch"-localizing reflex.

Stirnimann (1939) reports that stimulation of the sole of the foot with "warm" stimuli leads to "seeking" movements of the other foot, whereas "cold" stimuli lead to withdrawal movements.

Thermal stimulation of the oral cavity elicits mimetic reactions, mouth movements, head movements, and squirming. It makes the sucking response irregular, and, with sufficient intensity, leads to disorganization and cessation of the response.

General environmental temperatures may give rise to shivering, as related by Blanton (1917), and general activity is correlated $-.205 \pm .024$ with temperature through a range of 74 to 88° F., according to Pratt (1930). Pilomotor reflexes (gooseflesh) to the normal combination of mechanical and thermal stimuli are very fleeting and slight in the newborn but are brought forth by adrenalin according to Hartmann-Karplus (1931).

Technique of Investigation. Cutaneous areas have been explored by thermal stimuli produced by temperature cylinders, evaporation of alcohol, etc. Tactual stimulation has been kept constant through use of a metal capsule attached to some portion of the body, the temperature being varied by changing the water in the capsule by means of inlet and outlet tubes. Radiant heat likewise makes possible a limited study of thermal sensitivity without any tactual accompaniment. The oral cavity has been stimulated with fixed amounts of distilled water at constant temperature, administered with medicine droppers, and by having the baby suck milk at different temperatures.

Jensen (1932) has used a manometer-polygraph combination to record the effects of thermal stimuli on sucking responses. Crudden (1937) has made cinema records and others have provided verbal descriptions of the responses.

Summary. The newborn infant is sensitive to temperatures that fall below the lower and above the higher thresholds, which appear to vary according to the part of the body stimulated and probably according to certain physiological states. They produce vigorous movements of the parts stimulated by the stimuli deviating most from the thresholds. Respiration and circulation are affected, and the sucking response becomes irregular or even ceases. The response involves more than the segment stimulated although greatest frequency of reaction occurs in the stimulated member. There may be a localizing reflex of a "scratch" nature. Mild thermal stimuli above the higher threshold may lead to movement toward the stimulus, whereas those below the lower threshold lead to withdrawal movements.

Environmental temperatures appear to be correlated negatively with activity in the newborn infant.

Reactions to Contact or Pressure Stimuli

Sensitivity. A great variety of responses elicitable by contact or pressure stimuli upon the cutaneous areas or within the external cavities of the body leave, as Pratt (1937) has emphasized, no doubt regarding the presence and importance of such sensitivity in the neonate. Phylogenetically and ontogenetically, as Carmichael (1933) has pointed out, this type of sensitivity is the first to appear. It arises first in the oral-nasal region, but the sensitivity is widely distributed by the time the neonatal stage is attained.

There have been no systematic investigations of differences in tactual sensitivity of the cutaneous surfaces of the body. Genzmer (1873) and Preyer (1882), as reported by Peiper (1928), maintain that the face, the hand, and the sole of the foot have greatest sensitivity, whereas the shoulders, the breast, the abdomen, and the back have least sensitivity.

Differentiation of the effects of pressure or contact stimuli from the effects of other stimuli is difficult. The confusion with the effects of thermal, pain, gustatory, and other stimuli presents a difficult problem of control in studying the behavior of the newborn infant.

Another source of uncertainty arises from inadequate control of stimulus intensity so that cutaneous reflexes are confused with those due to deep pressure.

Stimuli which give rise to tickle in the older child produce no analogous vocalization, motility, or facial expression in the young infant, according to Nassau (1938). If it reacts at all it manifests expressions of "unpleasantness" and of withdrawal.

Hartmann-Karplus (1931) asserts that the position of itch as contrasted with pain, thermal, and tactual sensations is not clear. The stimuli producing it are such that perhaps it should be classified by itself, or with pain. Using a commercial itch powder composed of little plant hairs, this investigator reports that during the first two weeks there is little or no reaction. When a response does occur its reaction time is about two to three minutes compared with the one minute of older sucklings. The crying and restlessness which are elicited quickly subside. Neither at this time nor during most of the first six months is there evidence of localized scratching, although the general activity becomes more pronounced with age. This confirms the basic finding of Szymanski.

Watson (1919), the Shermans (1925, 1936), Peiper (1928), and Crudden (1937) have all reported "defense movements" to continued pressure upon certain body areas.

Relation to Stimuli. The responses evoked from a given body surface by tactual stimuli depend upon their intensity, duration, and whether they are of punctiform or stroking contact application. Summation effects have been noted.

Relation to State of Organism. The nature of the toe movements in the plantar response seems to be altered somewhat in sleep. The mouth orientation and sucking movements are not elicitable after the infant has completed nursing. The plantar response may vary according to postures, possibly determined by preceding stimulation. These are illustrative of various modifications of response which depend upon the condition of the infant at the time of stimulation.

Responses. They range from localized reflexes like the tactuopalpebral to responses which involve much of the body musculature. Many of the responses evoked are commonly described as defense movements. Some are viewed as withdrawal movements; others are supposed to localize and to ward off the stimuli which are being applied. Or they provide a fundamental orientation of the organism, as in the mouth orientation response to contact stimuli of certain facial areas (see section on responses for further description).

Summary. The newborn infant manifests widespread sensitivity to pressure or contact stimuli. The responses aroused constitute much of the neonate repertory and are interpreted by some writers as having a protective utility.

Reactions to Noxious (Pain) Stimuli

Sensitivity. The problem of pain sensitivity in the neonate is twofold: (1) the differences in sensitivity from one body area to another; (2) the degree of sensitivity as compared with later age periods.

In regard to the problem of differential areal sensitivity, Preyer (1882) considered the sole of the foot to be most sensitive, and the Shermans (1925) reported a differential between head and leg areas from birth on, the head areas being more sensitive to repeated needle jabs than the leg areas. Dockeray and Rice (1934), employing one needle jab with one-sixteenth-inch maximum penetration, found that in terms of vigor and quickness of response head areas were least sensitive, arm areas more sensitive than head areas, and leg areas most sensitive. The Shermans and Flory (1936) in further experiments with minimal intensities of stimuli have confirmed their earlier findings in regard to a cephalocaudal differential in sensitivity. They point out that sensitivity is shown by responsiveness of the organism and not by the amount of activity in the part stimulated.

Whether there is a marked pain insensitivity in the neonate, as compared with later periods, has long been an unsettled question. Genzmer (1873), applying needle pricks to the nose, lips, and hands of premature infants, reported little effect. Newborn infants on the first day manifested similar reactivity, with sensitivity slowly increasing during the first week. Canestrini (1913) noted relative insensitivity to needle pricks and also to faradic and galvanic stimulation. The Shermans (1925) found that an average of 6.5 needle jabs in the head areas was required to arouse a response at 0.5 to 5.5 hours, whereas at 35.5 to 40.5 hours 1.7 stimuli were needed, with one stimulation sufficing after 41 hours. The increase in the sensitivity of leg areas is shown by a decrease in necessary needle jabs from ten at 0.5 to 5.5 hours to two at 70.5 to 75.5 hours, with only one stimulation required after 76 hours. Peiper (1926a), on the basis of controlled needle stimulation of arm areas, is convinced that there is no marked insensitivity of the premature and the neonate as compared with older sucklings. The sensitivity of normal newborn infants as contrasted with the marked insensitivity of some idiots suggests pain insensitivity as a possible criterion of serious defect. Within the neonatal period Dockeray and Rice (1934) could discover no change in responses with increase in age.

Relation to Stimuli. In studying this field of sensitivity the stimuli commonly employed have been pricks administered with a needle to different cutaneous areas of the body. Whether stimuli usually thought of as falling within some other field, such as those provided by application of ammonia or acetic acid fumes to the nostrils, should be classified as pain or noxious stimuli is not certain. Likewise, whether intense stimuli in such sensory fields as the thermal, the auditory, and the visual, or those involved in holding an infant's nose for a number of seconds, are to be interpreted as pain stimuli is also undetermined.

Relation to State of Organism. Wolowik (1927) observed in a two-month-old infant that much more intense electrical stimulation was required to evoke crying during nursing than at other times.

Reaction Times. The reaction time (2 seconds) to stimulation of the sole of the foot is longer than that of adults, according to Preyer (1882). Peiper (1926a), applying needle jabs to the volar surface of the arm and measuring reaction times by a modified Morse apparatus, found the reaction time of body movements to range from 0.12 to 0.70 second, and of crying from 2 to 5 seconds.

Types of Response. In general, the responses, if the stimuli are not too intense, consist of withdrawal movements of the part stimulated and facial reflexes of "discomfort." Dockeray and Rice (1934), however, found only a general mass form of movements regardless of the area stimulated. Crying is a common feature of many of these responses.

Technique of Investigation. Needle jabs administered by the experimenter with more or less control of the penetration provide the stimuli in most investigations. Peiper (1926a) appears to have made this stimulation most constant and automatic. The responses have been recorded by observers, photographed, and their time relations obtained from the records of a Morse apparatus.

Summary. The presence in the neonate of sensitivity to pain stimuli has been demonstrated. Differential sensitivity of the cutaneous areas of the body has not been carefully explored and there is disagreement regarding the relative sensitivity of the areas which have been investigated. Similarly, there is lack of agreement regarding the degree of pain sensitivity in the just-born infant as compared with that found at later age periods.

Reactions to Movement or Change in Position

Sensitivity. This sensitivity is demonstrated when spatial movements of the body stimulate the static receptors and thus give rise to postural responses. It is likewise manifested by responses aroused by active or passive movement of a part of the body. The sequences in coordinated movements are also said to illustrate the presence of sensitivity of this type.

Some have held that the generalized responses of newborn infants to stimuli may not be touched off directly by the experimental stimulus but that the part first responding produces kinesthetic stimuli which in turn evoke responses in other parts. Givler (1921) has suggested that learning in relation to kinesthetic and tactual stimuli during the fetal period may determine some of the characteristics of the grasping reflex.

Movements of hands and legs toward contact, or other stimuli upon the body, may include kinesthetic stimulation as an essential element in producing the necessary coordinations.

Relation to Stimuli. Peiper and Isbert (1927) and Peiper (1928) provided experimental stimuli by supporting the body in various positions. The postural and other consequences of such positions have also been studied by McGraw (1935). The movements of the infant's head when the child is placed in a prone position constitute the initial step in Shirley's (1931a) schema of sequential development. Jarring of the infant, used by Moro (1918), the withdrawal of support, mentioned by Watson (1919), and the vertical movements produced by Irwin (1932h) provide static stimuli. The effects of turning the head upon the body and limb postures, and of the body upon the head posture, have been investigated by Peiper and Isbert (1927). The effects of rotation upon eye movements (rotational nystagmus) and head movements, with the child in either a horizontal or vertical position, have been reviewed by Peiper (1928), as have the studies of caloric nystagmus.

Relation to State of Organism. Information on this point is very casual or lacking in the studies reviewed.

Responses. According to Peiper and Isbert (1927) and Peiper (1928), support of the newborn infant at the abdomen only, or at the back on the buttocks, or at the side at the hip shows such complete dominance of gravity that the child is unable to hold its head and trunk upright or in alignment. When placed in a prone position on a table, however, the neonate partially lifts its head. This has also been confirmed by Bryan (1930) and Shirley (1931a).

McGraw (1935, 1941b) has described the process of falling over when the child is placed in a sitting position.

Peiper (1929) demonstrated that, when the newborn infant is held in an erect position with its feet resting upon a surface, alternate or "stepping" movements are made. Peiper made photographs of these and obtained footprint records. Possibly static and kinesthetic, as well as tactual, stimuli are involved in this response. McGraw (1932) has confirmed Peiper's findings.

Inverted suspension (holding the child by the feet, head downward) occasionally produces in the neonate a bending-back of the head as reported by Peiper and Isbert (1927). According to McGraw (1935, 1940b), a flexion of the legs at knee and hip occurs, resulting in an up-and-down movement of the body. Body and head are in general alignment in the vertical plane with arms maintained more or less in the usual flexed position. Irwin's (1936) motion pictures showed that inverted suspension produces in the neonate a momentary backward bending of the head. The reaction, occurring in the cervical region, is designated by him as opisthotonoid.

Jarring or the sudden dropping or raising of the infant evokes, as Irwin (1932h) has shown, the *Moro's Umklammerungs reflex*, which is described in greater detail elsewhere in this chapter.

According to Peiper (1928), it is uncertain whether the *Brudzinski phenomenon* (a drawing-up of the legs when the head is bent forward) is a tonic neck reflex. Peiper and Isbert (1927) found it to be of rare occurrence in the neonatal period. Turning the infant's head to one side with a sudden jerk results in a "fencing" posture of the limbs. Other postural reflexes involving head and trunk consist of movements of the trunk if the head is moved and movements of the head if the body is moved. Mesina (1936) reports that if one leg of a baby resting upon its back is flexed, the other automatically flexes.

Rotation of the body produces nystagmus and sometimes compensatory head movements arising from stimulation of the static rather than of the visual receptors. Bartels (1910) found that the latter were in opposite direction when the child was rotated in horizontal positions; Alexander (1911), that they were in the same direction during rotation, and in the opposite after rotation had ceased. The latter finds no rotation nystagmus, but an after-nystagmus for about fifteen seconds. McGraw's (1941a) study appears to support Alexander rather than Bartels. Other investigations reviewed by Peiper (1928) present similar contradictory findings. The presence of caloric nystagmus is likewise uncertain.

Summary. Static-kinesthetic sensitivity is demonstrated in the neonate by a variety of responses elicited by movement of the body as a whole, or in part. Beginnings of responses which will lead to upright postures and to walking are discernible.

Reactions to Internal (Organic) Stimuli

Sensitivity. The nature of internal stimuli and the sites of their operation are not well defined or known. But the general motility of the infant, when other stimuli are brought under control or reduced, is accepted by many as evidence that such sensitivity is present in the newborn infant. Indeed, the work of Pratt, Nelson, and Sun (1930), Pratt (1934b), and especially that of Irwin (1930), interpreted from this point of view, indicate that internal stimuli are responsible for most of its activity. As stated elsewhere in this chapter, external stimuli of short duration, although releasing responses which have present or future significance in the life of the child, add little to its total motility. External stimuli of longer duration inhibit activity which otherwise would be aroused by internal stimuli.

The functioning of respiratory and circulatory organs and of other parts of the viscera doubtless do contribute internal stimuli, but the preponderant number are apparently associated with the activities of the alimentary canal and of the excretory systems.

Conditions within or associated with the activities of the digestive tract are known to determine whether contact stimulation will arouse mouth orientation and sucking movements.

Nursing may be followed by *regurgitation* and this, in turn, by *hiccuping*. Pendleton (1927), studying 40 newborn infants, found that hiccuping started about 10 minutes after regurgitation, lasted 5 to 15 minutes, and had a rate of about 18 per minute. Treatment by rapid administration of fluids soon stopped hiccuping in 72.5 per cent of the cases, immediately in 57.5 per cent of these. This suggests that gastric contents carried into the esophagus by regurgitation provide the stimuli for hiccuping.

Recently, Wagner (1938b) has affirmed that

> the hiccough, generally attributed to pressure of a full stomach upon the diaphragm, has frequently been observed in the infant shortly after birth. However, no attempt has been made to proceed further and study the hiccough as an isolated behavior item.

From pneumographic records of 17 neonates she found a duration ranging from 35 seconds to 18 minutes and 20 seconds (mean = 6 minutes, 34 seconds). The mean interval between hiccups ranged from 2.6 seconds to 7.9 seconds (mean of all = 4.5 seconds). This would be at the rate of little more than 13 hiccups per minute as contrasted with Pendleton's (1927) rate of 18. Wagner also found that the number of hiccups per minute tended to decrease throughout the period.

The relations of general motility to content and pressure stimuli as well as to the muscular activity of the stomach have received careful study by Carlson and Ginsburg (1915), Taylor (1917), Irwin (1930, 1932f), and Richards (1936a, 1936b, 1936c). It is probable that a great deal of the child's total motility is in some way dependent upon alimentary processes, but whether it is directly related to activity of the stomach or more indirectly produced by some nutritional state is not known (the researches bearing upon these problems are given detailed consideration in the section on physiology).

In the final sequences of alimentation and assimilation, excretion and egestion occur. The excretory aspects of perspiration have no visible connection with general motility. Micturition may, as Pratt (1933) has elsewhere suggested, be preceded by slight activity with quiescence after the act. More activity precedes egestion or defecation. According to Dennis (1932a), the latter presents the following pattern response:

> With each . . . abdominal contraction the legs and toes are extended and raised and the forearms are held to the upper chest. At the same time the infant may grunt and his face often reddens.

Summary. Internal stimuli on the whole are of fairly long duration, and the responses, excepting those involving sphincter muscles, are of rhythmical or periodic incidence. The transition from fetal to postnatal life probably involves an even greater stepping-up of internal than of external stimuli. It is the internal stimuli which account for most of the motility of the infant. The rôle of external stimuli according to type, intensity, or duration is to add variable but negligible amounts to the total activity, or actually to reduce the total which would occur were they not present.

Responses

The Feeding Responses. The responses which orient the newborn mammal to the nipple of the mother's breast and effect an ingestion of milk are among the most fundamental in the young mammal's repertory.

First in the series of these responses are the *head-mouth orientation* movements. The prerequisite condition for their arousal by contact stimulation is that the infant be approaching a nursing period rather than having just nursed. Pepys (1667) was one of the first to observe that if an infant's cheek is touched the head turns and the mouth opens to grasp the finger. This *"search reflex"* was described very carefully by Kussmaul (1859) and mentioned by Preyer (1882). According to Popper (1921), stroking contact of the cheek may evoke head turning, mouth opening, and snapping movements. The reflexogenous zone of the *oral* responses has been shown by Minkowski (1928) to be quite extensive early in the fetal period, and Pratt, Nelson, and Sun (1930) have confirmed its extensiveness in the neonatal period. In terms of sucking or mouth responses to contact stimulation they found sensitivity ranging in decreasing order in the following areas: lips, above lips, below lips, cheek. Sensitivity was greater in the waking state and appeared to decrease with age in the cheek areas. Jensen (1932) found the head movements

to increase with age upon stimulation of this area.

The nature and the extent of the response depend upon the area which is stimulated. When the cheek is touched the head turns toward the side stimulated and the mouth opens. If the area above the lips is stimulated the head is thrown back and the mouth opens to its widest extent. If contact is maintained, the head may shake vigorously from side to side. Similarly, if the area below the lips is touched the chin drops, the mouth flies open, and the head may bend forward.

These responses have been confirmed by Baliassnikowa and Model (1931–1932) and by Stirnimann (1937a). According to the latter the child must be awake for any except simple reflexes to appear. Halverson (1938) interprets the significance of the responses as follows:

> At birth the mouth is superior to the hand in what might be called directed activity and definiteness of function. Upon proper stimulation the mouth can both open and close and with the aid of head and neck movements institute a strenuous search for the stimulating object.

Certainly such coordinations are among the most effective made by the neonate, although in human beings the head and neck or "searching" movements must be regarded as atavistic survivals.

Lip reflexes are coordinated with head-mouth orientation and are more specific to the act of coupling and sucking. This limitation of response progresses as one moves from stimulation of the periphery of the reflexogenous zone toward the lip areas. Head movement decreases or changes character according to the locus of excitation.

Thompson's (1903) lip reflex, consisting of pursing or pouting, is released by tapping the surface of the upper lip. Its relation to the contact-aroused erection of the mother's nipple has been noted. This reflex has been confirmed by Lambanzi and Pianetta (1906), Blanton (1917), Popper (1921), Baliassnikowa and Model (1931–1932), and Stirnimann (1937a), who has found it elicited most frequently by stimulation of the corners of the mouth. Stirnimann (1936a) has also observed a tumescence of the inner surface of the lips.

Sucking and *swallowing* constitute the crucial elements of the feeding responses. Although present at birth, the sucking response increases in vigor during the neonatal period. The response has a long history of objective instrumentalized study from the early researches of Basch (1893), Lifschitz as reported by Bechterew (1908), Pfaundler (1909), and Barth (1914), in which the infant sucked upon a bottle or the mother's breast through special types of nipple shield, or in which a pneumatic system recorded movements of the chin, to apparatus which measured the changes in pressure set up by the infant's sucking in a closed system such as Kashara's (1916), or manometric set-ups such as those devised by Jensen (1932) and Halverson (1938). The Roentgen kymograph studies of sucking, swallowing, and breathing made by Peiper (1931, 1935b) are likewise a contribution in methodology.

When sucking starts, general activity, according to Jensen (1932), begins to disappear. Salt solutions cause the response to deteriorate or cease, as do certain critical temperatures of milk. Wolowik (1927) has shown that when the two-month-old child is nursing it requires electrical stimulation over three times as intense to cause crying as at other times. When the infant has stopped sucking, but while contact is yet maintained, other stimuli such as visual stimuli or those afforded by pulling the hair or pinching the big toe will, according to Jensen (1932), again initiate

sucking. Under these conditions the organism is, he states, "set" to respond only in this way. Peiper (1938) terms this the dominance of the sucking center and holds (1937a) that this center shows two levels of excitation, one giving periodic sucking and the other regular and rhythmic sucking. The analogy to breathing as well as a developmental relationship are suggested (1939). The sustained character of the orientation in sucking is striking.

Halverson (1938) considers sucking as arising from pronounced muscle tension. Simultaneous records of sucking pressure, gripping pressure of the hand, and observation of general activity show their maxima at the beginning of sucking and they decrease together during the course of the feeding period. When the nursing process is hampered there is incidence of penial tumescence which is ascribed to marked abdominal pressure. Peiper (1931, 1935b) and Hofmann and Peiper (1937) found that in the hungry suckling there were between 60 and 80 sucking movements, or 1 or 2 for every inspiration. Neither sucking nor breathing is interrupted by swallowing. The latter occurs during the phases between inspiration-expiration or expiration-inspiration.

Some have held that swallowing, as Baliassnikowa and Model (1931–1932) express it, is part of a chain reflex appearing when sucking fills the mouth. Jensen (1932) has observed that sucking, as upon air, may occur without swallowing. And sucking of some substances may be followed by rejection rather than continued swallowing.

Finger sucking is a common response in the neonate, appearing shortly after birth, according to Blanton (1917). Dennis (1932a) has described the nursing posture of the child.

Peiper's review (1936b) is probably the

most comprehensive treatment of the feeding responses which has appeared.

Defense or Protective Reflexes. This classification, although in common usage, is not entirely satisfactory. The terms are usually ill defined and bear the connotation of either conscious intent or unconscious purpose, whereas further study of the responses may disclose that the organism's response is determined by its structure rather than by the precise end which is to be accomplished. Here, as elsewhere, the need is for accurate and comprehensive description of behavior and of the conditions under which it appears and is modified.

There have been attempts to classify responses in terms of movement away from or movement toward the stimulus. Carmichael (1933) has reported the observations of various writers to the effect that the intensity of the stimulus determines the direction of movement. In terms of the life economy of the infant, however, movement of the part of the organism toward the stimulus or site of stimulation may lead, as in mouth orientation, to continued contact with the stimulus, or it may result in active pushing-away or rejection of the stimulus. Thus it is possible, without any implication of conscious purpose on the part of the infant, to term those responses "protective" which remove it or any part of the infant from stimuli, or those in which some part moves toward and pushes away a stimulus object applied to some part of the body. These latter responses are particularly significant because they demonstrate a certain amount of ability to orient in the environment and to localize the sources of excitation.

With this broad definition, the classification of responses such as the palpebral, pupillary, mouth rejection, and so on as "protective" seems justifiable. The claim that other responses such as the Moro and the grasping reflex are defensive, in terms of the arboreal past of man, should be received with considerable skepticism. Similarly, Babinski's (1922) attempt to classify both extensor and flexor plantar responses as defense movements, the first by virtue of withdrawal of the toes and the latter in terms of "attack," has contributed little toward the understanding of the plantar responses. The purposive interpretation of these movements becomes somewhat difficult in the light of Pratt's (1934d, 1936a) demonstration that stimulation of the upper surface of the foot produces the *same types of movements* of the foot and toes as does stimulation of the plantar surface, so that whether it is defense by withdrawal or defense by attack depends upon the location of the stimulus. Considerations such as these should lead to caution in interpreting the purpose of a response.

Among the withdrawal responses not cited elsewhere in this chapter are the spinal and abdominal reflexes described by Galant (1917). In all essentials these consist in a concave bowing or bending-away of the side of the body from stroking contact stimulation. Others, including Peiper, have differentiated between Galant's "spinal reflex" and the abdominal reflexes, but Galant (1930) is of the opinion that they are not different responses but rather the same response released from an extensive reflexogenous zone.

Of even more significance for future development of the infant are those responses in which continuous contact stimulation of some part of the body surface is followed by movement of hand, arm, or leg toward the locus of stimulation. When the infant's nose was held by the experimenter's fingers, Watson (1919) reported defense arm movements. Pratt, Nelson, and Sun (1930), Taylor (1934), and

Daniels and Maudry (1935) were unable to confirm this.

The Shermans (1925) and the Shermans and Flory (1936) have reported similar defense movements, improving rapidly during the first few days after birth, to pressure exerted upon the infant's chin. Although Daniels and Maudry (1935) and others have not confirmed the Shermans' findings, the experimental controls of the latter in their later research seem to indicate that some coordinations of this type are present. Indeed such coordinations may mark the early beginning of the hand-mouth movements which play such an important rôle in the subsequent development of the child.

On the other hand, Hartmann-Karplus (1931) found no localizing movements when itch powder was applied to other parts of the body surface.

Crudden (1937) reported a localizing scratch reflex of the contralateral leg to the capsule in his investigations of thermal sensitivity. Peiper (1936a) also, applying curtain clamps to various parts of the body, found, at first, local reactions, followed frequently by movements of hand or foot to the part stimulated. When the infant's hands are each encased in cloths tied at the wrists they move against each other or against the sheet until, according to Stirnimann (1937b), the hands frequently become disengaged. He considers this impulsion toward freedom to be second only to that toward nourishment.

The Oculo-Cephalo-Gyric Response. The visual pursuit movements described in the section on reactions to visual stimuli constitute further evidence that the newborn infant possesses responses which enable it to orient to some aspects of its environment. These orientations, unlike mouth orientation, have increasing importance among the activities of the organism. Indeed here is an early manifestation of what has been termed attention.

Palmar Response and Arm Movements. The response of the fingers in the palmar response is homologous to that of the toes in the plantar response, save for the variability between extension and flexion of the latter. From the first descriptions given, writers have differentiated between the early neonatal and the later grasping by terming the grasping of the newborn infant involuntary while the adult form is voluntary, except in pathological cases. The voluntary type is said to appear when the involuntary type wanes. Halverson (1937) questions this and argues that there is chronological overlapping of the two. The earlier writers state that involuntary grasping disappears between four and six months, and Wagoner (1924) considers its persistence a sign of retardation.

Robinson (1891), Buchman (1895, 1900), and Mumford (1897) believed that neonatal grasping proved that, in the past, man or his ancestors lived in trees.

Givler (1921) was one of the first to suggest that the response might be perfected by exercise during the prenatal life and not result entirely from maturation.

The response was described as simian in nature—that is, palm and finger flexion without thumb opposition—by Buchman (1895, 1900). McGraw (1935, 1940a) likewise emphasizes its digital character when the child is partially or completely suspended. Halverson (1937), who has given this response most careful study, reports that the neonatal grasping reflex has two phases: first, closure to light pressure upon the palm; second, gripping or clinging as a proprioceptive response to pull upon the finger tendons. Closure disappears in 16 to 24 weeks, whereas the proprioceptive gripping or clinging disappears after 24 weeks. Closure is a specific or limited response; gripping has associated with it many other movements.

The strength of the infant's grasp has been expressed most frequently in terms of the time the infant can sustain its own weight with one or both hands. The pioneers, Robinson (1891) and Buchman (1895, 1900), reported times as long as 2½ minutes using both hands, and a few seconds using one hand. Blanton (1917) found the child could support its weight for only a few seconds employing both hands. Richter (1934) suspended infants by both hands from parallel rods and obtained in different infants average suspension times ranging up to 60 seconds, with 128 seconds the longest time obtained. Valentine and Wagner (1934) employed the handle of a dynamometer as a lifting device, and, neglecting the fact that pulling to suspension is not the same situation as suspension of the infant, drew the following conclusion:

It has been generally accepted as a fact that newborn infants are capable of supporting their own weight when grasping with one hand a rod of about the diameter of a lead pencil. The use of the dynamometer in this experiment, where the dynamometer was lifted vertically until the infant released the handle, emphatically disproved such an assumption, for the maximum grasping strength of the strongest subject was 2200 g., less than the weight of the smallest subject.

The Shermans and Flory (1936) measured the strength of the grasp by the Chatillon Balance and found it to average 1732 grams in the right and 1765 grams in the left hand. A little over 10 per cent of the infants could lift themselves with one hand. Halverson (1937) found the clinging strength of the left hand to be slightly superior to that of the right. At birth the mean strength of the latter is 1952 grams. Halverson found that infants support more

than 70 per cent of their weight with both hands when pulled toward suspension. Of 97 infants less than 24 weeks old, 27, under these circumstances, supported their own weights with both hands, and one at 4 weeks did it with the right hand alone. Halverson states that "it was evident that some of them could have supported considerably more weight than their own mass." The relative strength of the different fingers was also determined by this investigator. Richter (1934) and Halverson (1937) both indicate that the response, measured in terms of suspension time and by the dynamometer, is not so great during the early part of the neonatal period.

The Shermans and Flory (1936) noted, as had earlier investigators, that the grasping reflex is weakest when the infant is asleep, and strongest when the infant is crying. Halverson (1937), testing the gripping pressure upon a small sensitive rubber capsule, found that the strength of the grasp was greatest at the beginning of nursing, decreasing as the infant approached satiety. Thus the grasping response reflects the degree of muscle tension.

The study of handedness in newborn infants has been approached, as we have seen, by measuring the relative strength of the grasping reflex in the right and left hands. The latter appears at this stage to be stronger. Watson (1919) attempted to determine whether there was preferential motility in arm movements but could discover none. Stubbs and Irwin (1933) reported a significant difference, and Valentine and Wagner (1934) found greater motility in the right arm. This did not appear to be correlated with the later preferential reaching of some of the same subjects.

Reaching toward stimuli acting upon the visual sense organs does not occur during the neonatal period, but, as described in defense movements, there are rather direct movements toward the site of contact stimulation of some areas of the body.

Locomotor Movements. The newborn infant possesses no effective means of movement from place to place. From its normal supine, prone, or lateral postures it may shift its position by various responses, but this involves little translation of the body in the horizontal plane.

Bauer (1926) obtained a "creeping phenomenon" when the neonate was placed on its abdomen and contact or resistance offered the soles of the feet. Under these circumstances the infant responds by thrusts of one or both feet, followed by alternate arm movements which tend to raise the body from the supporting surface. At the same time the body bends from side to side. These creeping responses are elicitable during the first four months and, according to Bauer, are second only to sucking in their complexity.

Peiper (1928) and Stirnimann (1938) have confirmed Bauer's observations and the latter, finding it present in an anencephalic subject, decided that it was a subcortical reflex. The creeping phenomenon of the neonate bears some relation to its stepping movements but neither, according to this writer, has any relation to later creeping or walking.

Peiper (1929) discovered that when the newborn infant is supported in an erect posture with the soles of the feet resting upon a table top, the legs extend upon contact and make alternate stepping movements, the length of the double step being about 20 cm. Frequently the leg, on being set forward, crosses in front of the other, preventing further progression. These stepping movements differ from later walking in that the activity in the neonate is confined to the lower extremities. The stepping movements are highly variable and uncertain of appearance. In a few months they disappear and under the same

conditions the suckling withdraws its feet. Peiper photographed the stepping movements and obtained footprints by having the infant step upon soot-blackened glazed paper. The discovery of stepping movements of the newborn infant was reported by McGraw (1932). She held that genuine "upright ambulation" is impossible at this period because of an undeveloped equilibratory apparatus. Stepping movements have greater incidence from 9 to 14 days than during the first 24 hours, according to Stirnimann (1938). The response disappears in 4 to 5 months.

The Plantar Responses. The literature upon these responses is probably more extensive than upon all other aspects of neonate behavior combined. This is, of course, no indication of a correspondingly important rôle in the life economy of the child, nor are these studies as significant for child psychology as for neurology. Indeed apt is the statement by Richards and Irwin (1934c) that "the popularity which this problem has been accorded may possibly be due to a seeming necessity for the student of infant reactions at some time in his career to do an experiment on infantile plantar phenomena."

In this section no attempt will be made to review the literature in detail. Those who wish to study the problems presented by the plantar responses should consult the following researches and reviews: Bersot (1920, 1921), Minkowski (1926, 1928), Pratt, Nelson, and Sun (1930), Fulton and Keller (1932), Pratt (1934d), and especially the review by Richards and Irwin (1934c).

Historically, major interest and attention to these responses date from Babinski's (1896, 1898) correlation of extension of the big toe, and sometimes extension and fanning of the toes (1903), with pyramidal tract disturbances in adults and the prediction that such responses would be physiological in infants. Although Leri (1903–1904), Engstler (1905), and many others have reported the Babinski complex to prevail during the neonatal period, others, such as Feldman (1921) and the Shermans (1925), have found a higher percentage of flexion of the toes during this period. Burr (1921) and Wolff (1930) have reported variability so great as to make it seem inadvisable to speak of a "plantar reflex."

In the narrowest sense the term "Babinski" has applied to the limited extension of the big toe alone but, as already stated, Babinski himself recognized that frequently the other toes were involved in the *signe d'éventail*, and that there was triple retraction of foot, leg, and thigh. Bersot (1920, 1921) and Minkowski (1932–1933) have recognized the necessity of reporting all the behavior segments which are activated by plantar stimulation, and also the necessity for exploring the extent of the reflexogenous zone from which the responses may be evoked.

The work of Richards and Irwin (1934c) indicates that toe extensions occur more frequently than flexions during the neonatal period. This research has additional importance because it demonstrates that one may not place too great reliance in the reliability of the clinical method. Indeed, the lack of agreement in many studies is probably the result as much of errors of observation as of differences in methods or of variability in stimulation. These same considerations have led Pratt (1934d, 1934e), in his studies of the reflexogenous zone and of the patterning of responses, to the belief that no further contributions can be made to the knowledge of plantar responses until frame analysis of motion picture records is made.

Exploration of the reflexogenous zone tentatively indicates that plantar areas of the leg have greatest sensitivity and that

their stimulation results in the greatest generalization of response, whereas stimulation of the hallux results in the most specific response. Leg and thigh segments are more likely and toe and foot segments less likely to be involved when the mesial surface of the leg is stimulated. When toe segments are viewed as one, they are about equally involved in responses, but leg and thigh are less frequently represented. About two-thirds of the toe movements are movements of extension and one-third of flexion. The foot, leg, and thigh manifest mostly flexor movements. Analysis of the responses observed revealed less than 200 different patterns of which 4, or 2 per cent, accounted for 29 per cent of the observed responses, 6 per cent of the patterns accounted for 50 per cent of the responses, and 15 per cent of the patterns for 75 per cent of the responses. From this it is concluded that no one response pattern may be termed the plantar response. The five most frequent patterns are: foot flexion; extension of toes and foot flexion; extension of the hallux; toes extended, fanning, and foot flexion; hallux extension and foot flexion.

Ontogenetically, the work of Minkowski (1922) and others shows that during the latter part of the fetal period the prevailing response of the toes is flexion. Engstler (1905) and Bersot (1920, 1921) report that this is likewise true in prematures. Babinski (1922) and his associates and Lantuejoul and Hartmann (1923) find flexion the rule during the first few hours after birth.

According to the Shermans (1925), the nature of the response depends upon the previous posture of the toes; repetition of the stimulus will change toe extension to flexion. This dependence upon the posture at the time of stimulation is also affirmed by Richards and Irwin (1934b, 1934c).

In sleep, according to Richards and

Irwin's (1934c) research, and as reported by them in other studies, extension of the toe is not so great as when the infant is judged to be awake.

The movements of the segments of the leg in the plantar responses have been viewed by Babinski (1915, 1922) as defense movements. Their alteration with age has usually been correlated with myelinization of the pyramidal tracts.

The Foot-Grasping Response. The Stirnimanns (1940) have reviewed previous reports of a foot-grasping reflex in the newborn infant to light pressure upon the plantar surface near the toes. They report the presence of this tonic reflex in 98 per cent of 800 neonates which they investigated with a special esthesiometer. The toes flex and grasp at a minimal pressure between 40 and 70 grams. Galant (1931) has interpreted plantar flexion of the toes as a rudimentary foot-grasping reflex.

The Moro and "Startle" Responses. The relation or the differentiation of these responses, as noted in the section on reactions to auditory stimuli, is difficult. Moro (1918) himself was aware that stimuli other than jarring would release the response which he described, and that it was suggestive of fear. This identification of responses or at least common elements has come on down through Peiper (1925a), Irwin (1932g), Pratt (1934b), Dennis (1934), and others. Strauss (1929), however, followed by Hunt, Clarke, and Hunt (1936), Hunt and Landis (1938), and Landis and Hunt (1939), has differentiated a startle response from the Moro, even though both may be released by the same stimulus or the same types of stimuli.

According to Moro (1918), the clasping response to jarring consists of an extension of the arms followed by their bowing and return toward the body. The response is symmetrical and the legs undergo much the same kind of movement. Freudenberg (1921) states that the arms extend, spread, and are adducted to the middle line of the body with the fingers spread and half flexed. The legs are extended, the toes spread and bent. Schaltenbrand (1925, 1928) has furnished essentially the same description with the further notation that it may be elicited not only by jarring but by sudden noises, rotating the head on the body, or tapping the abdomen. According to Gordon (1929), the Moro simulates the fear response. He observed tremor of the hands in the clasping movement and less participation of the lower extremities. The response is symmetrical except in case of birth injuries. It disappears by the fourth month. Sanford (1931) confined his attention only to arm movements and found that fracture of the child's clavicle resulted in an asymmetrical response. Dupérié and Bargues (1932) have pointed out that the leg responses are highly variable. They were unable to evoke the response by auditory stimuli. McGraw (1937) has described the movement of the trunk as follows:

> Simultaneously there is an extension of the spine, often involving a retraction of the head toward the interscapular part of the spine and a rolling of the body slightly to one side.

Whether the movement of the legs is flexor or extensor depends upon their position at the time of stimulation. She also claims that the response is usually followed by crying. Against this must be set Irwin's (1932h) studies on the effect of vertical elevation of the infant—this did not result in crying. Finally, Richards (1936a) has observed these responses to occur without the application of any experimental stimuli. Dennis (1935) doubts that the response actually disappears at four months.

Landis and Hunt (1939) have shown that Peiper's earlier observation of the more rapid fear response preceding the Moro is descriptive of the startle. The primary difference in the two patterns is:

The startle pattern is primarily a flexion response, while the Moro reflex is primarily an extension response. In the latter the arms are extended straight out at the sides at right angles to the trunk, fingers extended, the trunk is arched backward, and the head is extended. Following the primary extension in the Moro reflex there is a secondary flexion response which has been described as a "clasping" response, but it is doubtful whether this is a true clasping response or merely a slow return to normal posture. The primary extension movement seems to be the genuinely significant portion of the response. Despite this gross difference in the two reactions, both Moro reflex and startle pattern may be called forth by many situations involving sudden unexpected stimulation.

Clarke's (1939) genetic studies of the response to auditory stimuli show that first they are typically Moro, then some elements of the response disappear and the character of movements changes from extension to flexion, giving the "startle."

Vocalization. The birth cry represents the first vocally produced sounds from the newborn infant, but it seems best to regard this as a respiratory response and not a true precursor of speech. Subsequent crying either in response to external or internal stimuli is, according to Schachter (1932a), a part of the generalized behavior which is characteristic of the neonate. It is also closely related to breathing and partakes of its rhythm in continuous crying. As we have seen, activity of this type ceases when auditory stimuli are presented, when the child is swung or rocked, and of course is terminated by sucking.

Although Sherman (1927b) has demonstrated that emotional patterns are not differentiated by differences in crying, it is none the less true that this type of activity is the infant's most powerful tool in acting upon its social environment and in thereby obtaining attention and care.

Irwin (1941c) and Irwin and Curry (1941) have reviewed previous studies of the vocalization of neonates and, as a result of their analysis of the differentiation of vocal content in forty neonates, report that during the first ten days front vowels predominate, with scarcely any middle, and no back, vowels. Consonant sounds are infrequent, the most common being *h*, with occasionally a *w* or a *k*. Irwin and Chen (1941) checked the reliability of observers for frequency of speech elements and their patterning. Irwin (1941b) has employed the profile to indicate central tendencies in the vowel elements of newborn infants.

Facial Responses. "Mimetic" responses of the musculature of the face and head play an important rôle in the anthropomorphism of neonate behavior and in this way serve to control or elicit differential responses from adults. The basis for conditioning of facial expressions is thereby provided.

Peiper (1935a), who has made the most detailed study of the origin, types, and significance of facial expressions in early infancy, has divided the responses into those which facilitate further stimulation of the sense organs and those which close or withdraw them from stimulation. Many of the responses are intimately associated with breathing movements.

Miscellaneous. There are many reflexes of interest to the neurologist which have not been reviewed in this chapter. Among them are the tendon reflexes and the cremasteric reflex. The galvanic skin reflex, reported present during the first year by Jones (1930) and denied by Peiper (1924a), has not seemed to offer sufficient data for a detailed inclusion. For a listing of some of the more obscure responses the reader should consult Dennis (1934).

Emotions

Many have inferred, on the basis of "expressive" movements or "mimetic" responses to auditory, olfactory, gustatory, tactual, and other stimuli, that the newborn infant experiences emotions or other affective psychic states.

The gross muscular responses evoked by intense auditory stimuli have been called *fear* from the time of Sachs (1893) on, but it remained for Watson (1919) to elevate the observed pattern into a primary emotion. Other stimuli releasing these responses are those provided by removal of support and by shaking or jarring. Moro (1918) had shown that the latter arouses a characteristic clasping response, and later writers, such as Peiper (1925a), Irwin (1932g), and Pratt (1933, 1934b), came to the conclusion that the Moro response is elicitable by a variety of stimuli, including the auditory. Whether the fear response and the Moro, despite variations, are one and the same response occurring to any sudden stimulus, or whether some of the early responses of the neonate form another pattern, the *startle*, which is an element in adult fears, is not as yet definitely established.

Furthermore, the quick reflexive nature of the responses to auditory stimuli followed by immediate return to quiescence, demonstrated in the researches of Peiper (1924c) and Pratt (1934b), does not conform to the temporal durations implied in the prevailing definitions of emotional responses. Also, movement in the vertical plane, dropping, or quick elevation did not produce crying or long-continued activity in the infants studied by Irwin (1932h).

In Watson's (1919) words, the emotion of fear consists of "a sudden catching of the breath, clutching randomly with the hands (the grasping reflex invariably appearing when the child is dropped), sudden closing of the eyelids, puckering of the lips, then crying." (This should be compared with the descriptions of the Moro and the startle responses.)

Rage is another of the emotions termed primary by Watson (1919). The pattern comprises crying, screaming, stiffening the body, slashing or striking movements of hands and arms, and holding the breath so that the infant's face becomes flushed. These responses are said to come in consequence of hampering or restricting the infant's movements. Pratt, Nelson, and Sun (1930) repeated the experiment of restraining or holding the child's arms —claimed by Watson to be a potent stimulus for rage. Such a pattern of responses not only failed to appear but also in most instances no effects followed or else restraint actually served to quiet the infant. Taylor (1934), who made the most careful attempt to reproduce Watson's experiments, was unable to obtain the patterns described by Watson. Dennis (1940), however, holds that these experimenters failed to elicit rage because they did not employ as intense and prolonged stimulation as Watson.

The third primary emotion postulated by Watson (1919) is *love*. This consists of a "cessation of crying, smiling, attempts at gurgling and cooing released by stimulation of some erogenous zone, tickling, shaking, gentle rocking, patting and turning upon the stomach across the attendant's knee."

According to Watson, all other emotions appear in consequence of the conditioning of the original innate patterns to other stimuli. This theory has had great vogue because of its simplicity but overlooked, as Valentine (1930) was quick to point out, the possibility that some emotional reactions might not be elicitable at birth and yet appear later on as a result of maturation rather than as a product of conditioning.

The validity of the theory suffered most from Sherman's (1927a) demonstration that observers, presumably acquainted with infant behavior, were unable to agree in naming emotional patterns of behavior as observed in motion pictures unless the stimuli were likewise shown.

These researches have resulted in the abandonment of the theory of differentiated emotional patterns in the neonate. Indeed they have led Irwin (1932h), Pratt (1933), Dennis (1934), and Taylor (1934) to abandon the term "emotion" as applying to infant behavior. In its place they advocate a purely descriptive account of the extent of organismic involvement in a response under definite conditions of stimulation, age of the organism, and so on.

Bridges (1932, 1935, 1936), as a result of observational studies, has likewise concluded that the newborn infant does not have differentiated emotional responses but instead an agitation or general excitement from which, partly through maturation and partly through experience, different emotions become differentiated.

In general, students of early infantile behavior are inclined to the view that emotional behavior is represented by generalized rather than specific responses and that upon the acquisition of the latter depends the adequacy of the adjustment to the stimulating situation. This is in marked contrast with the position of certain educators who hold that one of the objectives of education is to develop the emotions.

Sleep

Criteria of Sleep and Depth of Sleep. The criteria of sleep in newborn infants are neither well defined nor universally ac-

cepted. The oldest and most widely employed, though perhaps naïve, is closure of the eyes. Supporting it is the criterion of decreased irritability and activity. Study of both adults and infants shows that neither is lacking during sleep.

The term *sleep* is usually defined by psychologists in terms of continuous gradations of irritability or of motility rather than in terms of the *either-or* of the two categories, *asleep* and *awake*.

Using this scientific criterion of sleep, Czerny (1892) differentiated gradations of sleep in terms of the strength of electrical stimuli necessary to awaken the infant. Depth of sleep, so expressed, is variable from infant to infant according to the antecedent condition or activities of the child.

Richter (1930) reported that palmar skin resistance increases with the depth of sleep in the neonate. Wenger and Irwin (1935, 1936) suggest that such resistance is basically correlated with muscular relaxation.

The most elaborate attempt to redefine sleep in terms of the degree of motility and of irritability of the newborn infant has been made by Wagner (1937). For her, sleep is a relative term, not antagonistic to the waking state, but applying to different degrees of reactivity which express different degrees or depths of sleep. Thus:

> Now if an infant merely flexes its toes in response to one stimulus and moves its entire body in response to another, should we say it is equally asleep to both stimuli? It seems logical to consider it less deeply asleep to the stimulus to which it makes the greatest response. Taking an infant in any condition whatsoever, then, we can apply various stimuli and observe the responses made, judging the infant as being less deeply asleep to those stimuli to which it responds more.

Relating degree of reactivity (as expressed by extent and duration of responses to pain, tactual, olfactory, and auditory stimuli) to motility patterns, Wagner has set up seven stages of sleep ranging from the most profound, in which the infant is generally quiet, breathing is regular, and there are no eyelid or mouth movements, to the shallowest, in which the infant is generally active, with eyes open and with mouth movement. According to her report the extent and duration of responses to the experimental stimuli increase as sleep becomes shallower.

Irwin's (1932f) measurement of motility from one nursing period to another shows, however, that Wagner's motility pattern of least depth of sleep actually is found in the period of least motility, but increased motility is demonstrated in periods manifesting some of Wagner's motility pattern of deeper sleep.

Temporal Incidence of Sleep and Location of Greatest Depth. Canestrini (1913), employing the technique developed by Czerny, placed the greatest depth of sleep at 45 to 60 minutes after falling asleep. In infants 2 months or older Marquis (1933) reported greatest depth (in terms of least temporal periods of activity) of sleep during the first half hour in daytime naps, and during the second hour in nighttime naps. Irwin's (1930, 1932f) studies show that activity is least after nursing, increasing as the next nursing period approaches. Greatest incidence of sleep (eyes closed) occurs about midway between the nursing periods.

The limited time samplings (90 minutes on the average) of Wagner (1937, 1939) and of Reynard and Dockeray (1939) provide an insufficient basis for determining the time of incidence of greatest depth of sleep in either diurnal periods or from one nursing period to another. Irwin (1930) in his 24-hour studies of activity has found greatest motility from 5 to 6 A.M. and least about noon. Similarly, in the measurement of motility between nursing periods least motility is shown immediately after nursing, with increasing activity up to the next nursing period, but Wagner's (1937) seven motility patterns do not agree with the observations made by Irwin. If the fundamental physiological state is most accurately described by actual measurement of general motility, then the duration and disposition of control periods in the researches of Pratt, Nelson, and Sun (1930) and of Pratt (1934b, 1934c) have greater validity than the alleged motility patterns which do not appear to be very well correlated with motility.

Amount of Sleep and Its Periodicity. Among the earlier writers, according to Peiper (1928), it was estimated that the neonate sleeps 20 hours of a day, but that the duration of each period of sleep is no more than 3 hours and is usually less. Pratt, Nelson, and Sun's (1930) records of control periods confirm these earlier estimates.

Wagner (1939) studied the sleep of newborn infants between 2 and 3:30 P.M., and in terms of her own criteria of sleep affirmed that infants are awake 40.3 per cent and sound asleep 12.7 per cent of the time. On the basis of 90 minutes of continuous observation in each 24 hours and with no time samplings at any other part of the day, the author concludes that "Such findings contradict the layman's casual assumption that the newborn infant spends most of its time sleeping."

Age and Sleep. Czerny (1892) found that at later age periods, as contrasted with the neonatal, weaker electrical stimulation awakened the child. According to some writers, as the child grows older the total hours of sleep decrease but the length of sleep periods increases.

Reactivity during Sleep. It is generally believed that during sleep irritability is decreased, reaction times are lengthened, certain responses may not be evoked, and others may be altered. According to Wagner (1937), responses decrease in extent and duration as the depth of sleep increases. Despite the lessened irritability just mentioned, it should be noted that most investigations have taken place under the condition of sleep as expressed by the simplest criterion. In other words, quiescent infants have been selected so that the effects of experimental stimuli would not be masked by activity aroused by internal stimuli.

The postural responses during sleep have evoked considerable interest. Peiper (1928) found a rather well-defined sleep or resting posture in the arms, hands, and legs of the suckling. The legs were flexed upon the body, the fists clenched, and the arms extended so that in the most extreme form the upper arms were at right angles to the body and the forearms parallel to the head. Marquis (1933) reported that during the first year the dorsal posture of the body with the head turned to the right was most frequent among body and head postures. There was likewise bilateral, symmetrical flexion at the elbows. Irwin (1930) also gave a description of postures in the neonate which resemble those found at slightly older age periods. This picture, in all major essentials, was confirmed by Wagner (1938c). She emphasized that there were many variations of the pattern and that other postures are to be observed.

Canestrini (1913) found it difficult to distinguish waking from sleeping states in terms of curves of respiration and circulation. In his opinion respiratory intervals are longer in sleep and the brain pulsations are decreased.

The effects of sleep on specific responses are discussed in sections dealing with such responses and in those relating sensitivity to different stimulus modes.

Summary. The criteria of sleep, stated in terms of motility, postural or other response patterns, are unsatisfactory so far as the accurate and consistent expression of the physiological state of the organism is concerned. The latter is best revealed by the minimal intensity of a given stimulus, typically electrical, necessary to elicit a particular response, and by the amount of measurable motility. The degree of reactivity and the level of motility will define the state of the infant but will not, of course, describe the effects of particular postures or of immediately preceding stimulation upon the responses to experimental stimuli.

In general, reactivity is less during sleep. Some responses are diminished or may not be evoked; others are viewed most easily against a background of lowered general motility. The newborn infant spends the greater part of the day in sleep, in the commonly accepted sense of the term. The child is not, however, immobile most of the time.

Learning

General observations of the neonate in the feeding situation disclose changes in behavior suggestive of learning during the course of the first month. Illustrative of these are the adjustments cited by Feldman (1920) whereby the infant after elimination of a night feeding begins to sleep during most of the night. Denisova and Figurin (1929), Ripin and Hetzer (1930), and Marquis (1941) have all reported evidence of early learning in relation to the feeding situation.

The first investigations of the Russian school of physiologists seemed to indicate that conditioned reflexes could not be established before the fifth month. The later research by Denisova and Figurin

(1929) revealed that natural CR's of food-seeking movements to originally inadequate stimuli appeared in 23 to 27 days. Experimental CR's, however, were not established until the second month. Then auditory CR's began to appear but visual CR's followed later in the second month.

Marquis (1931) reported the establishment of conditioned sucking and other responses to auditory stimuli by the fourth to fifth day. The auditory stimuli were produced by a buzzer and had a duration of five seconds before insertion of the nipple of the nursing bottle in the infant's mouth and the same duration after the insertion. The infant's responses were recorded by an observer and the chin movements were registered upon the polygraph tape by means of a pneumatic system under the infant's chin. Conditioning to auditory stimuli in seven out of eight of the experimental group was said to be demonstrated by increase in mouth opening and by a decrease in general activity and crying, as contrasted with the non-appearance of such responses in a control group of four infants regularly stimulated by the buzzer at feeding times but not with access to the bottle immediately afterward. Near the end of the period of investigation the experimental group was subjected to auditory stimuli produced by a fall hammer striking a tin can, but general activity was not decreased nor was mouth opening elicited. Pratt (1933) has pointed out that this procedure is invalid because, without any conditioning at all, the neonate responds in a different fashion to stimuli of very short duration from those of longer duration—the latter acting to cause decreased activity. This criticism is reinforced by the results of researches reported by Weiss (1934) and Stubbs (1934).

Marinesco and Kreindler (1933), employing electric shock as the unconditioned stimulus and visual and auditory as the conditioning stimuli, did not establish any CR's during the neonatal period.

Kasatkin (1935) and Kasatkin and Levikova (1935a, 1935b) did not succeed in conditioning sucking or feeding responses to auditory or to visual stimuli in newborn infants. When CR's did appear at a later time the auditory preceded the visual.

Probably, in point of techniques and scope, Wenger's (1936) study of conditioning in the first half of the neonatal period is the most important investigation so far attempted. In some of the experiments, however, the number of infants was very small. Stimuli in the various experiments were well controlled and responses were recorded by observers and registered by photography or by the polygraph. In one of the experiments eyelid closure conditioned to tactual vibratory stimuli applied to the plantar surface of the foot appeared on the fifth postnatal day, on three of which experimentation involving 124 paired stimulations was carried on. In another set of experiments the unconditioned stimuli were electric shocks, applied through an electrode at the plantar surface of the left big toe. This type of stimulus evoked a withdrawal movement described as a flexor twitch of the toes accompanied sometimes by other responses. When tactual vibratory stimuli were used, there was no unequivocal evidence of conditioning in the infant studied. Three out of five infants gave clear indication of the conditioning of the flexor twitch and respiratory gasp in response to a pure tone stimulus. Withdrawal responses conditioned to visual stimuli appeared on the sixth postnatal day after 120 paired stimulations had been given. In a third type of experiment regularly intermittent auditory stimulation (buzzer) during feeding gave no evidence of conditioning during eight weeks of stimulation. Wenger (1936) concluded that conditioning of certain types is possible in some newborn infants but that it is highly unstable.

The Wickenses (1940) applied an electric shock to the sole of the foot as the unconditioned stimulus releasing withdrawal movements, and a buzzer as the conditioning stimulus. Their experimental group of twelve infants received 12 paired stimulations a day for three consecutive days, and a control group of twelve infants received 12 shocks alone per day for three consecutive days. Both groups manifested the usual evidence of conditioning, but a second control group tested on the first day by the buzzer and again on the third day showed no response.

Summary. There is some evidence that certain responses may be conditioned to experimental stimuli during the neonatal period. The responses are difficult to establish, highly unstable, and cannot be set up in all infants.

Sex and Race Differences

Sex. In the "genital crisis," and under other physiological conditions of the newborn infant, reactions characteristic of each sex are observed, although differentiation of these phenomena is not complete because both sexes exhibit mammary secretion. Aside from the studies relating to the genital organs there are few dealing with sex differences in the behavior of neonates.

In terms of bodily and segmental movements reported in observational protocols, Gatewood and Weiss (1930) found that males were less active and had less vocalization than females. Pratt's (1932) comparisons of the activity of these same subjects in terms of percentage of time active, according to the stabilimeter-polygraph records, revealed that males were unreliably less active than females. Halverson

(1941) states that "in *Profound Sleep* the boys had a significantly lower pulse rate and a correspondingly lower breathing rate than had girls."

Smith (1936), on the other hand, has found more activity and crying in males. She holds that the brightness values of hues, as determined by their effect upon activity, for males are similar to those of color blind adults, whereas for females they are similar to those of partially color blind adults. The sex differences with respect to auditory stimulation discovered by Stubbs (1934) were statistically unreliable.

Feldman (1921) and Richards and Irwin (1934c) have reported conflicting results regarding sex differences in the incidence and nature of toe movements in the plantar response. The differences found are apparently not statistically significant.

Race. Gatewood and Weiss (1930), in their tabulation of observed responses, came to the conclusion that Negro infants are less active than white infants. In terms of percentage of time the infants were active, Pratt (1932) found no significant race differences among these subjects. Bryan (1930) asserted that the Babinski is delayed longer in making its appearance in Negro than in white infants. Beasley (1933a) found a higher percentage of superior visual pursuit movements in Negroes on the first day and reported that these movements improved more rapidly than in the whites.

In summary, there is little unequivocal evidence of sex and race differences in newborn infants.

The Nature of the Neonate Organism

The Neonate as a Man in Miniature. The layman and the literary writer alike regard the newborn infant as a kind of man in miniature or a tabloid version of the adult. It is conceded that the infant is rather helpless, that it cannot talk, get about, or appreciably manipulate its surroundings. Its behavior, however, is anthropomorphized to the emotional, perceptional, and ideational levels of the adult.

The literary man is prone to fix upon quite common items of neonate behavior as symbolically betokening distinguishing idiosyncrasies in later life. Or, waxing poetic in a pessimistic way, the birth cry becomes a wail of anguish at being expelled from the paradise of prenatal life into the terrors of postnatal existence. And, if the poetic philosopher be both disillusioned and sentimental, he may describe all goodness, virtue, and insight as indwelling in the innocence of the babe.

The literary man and the layman err in anthropomorphisms which recognize only a difference in size between the newborn infant and the adult. Their conception of the nature of the neonate is only a popular counterpart of the discarded speculations concerning the homunculus.

The Neonate as a Recapitulation. The extension by G. Stanley Hall of the doctrine of biological recapitulation in the form of a cultural recapitulation, manifesting itself in childhood, is no longer acceptable to psychologists even though occasionally entertained by the layman.

As we have seen, Buchman (1895, 1900) and Mumford (1897) have cited the neonatal grasping reflex, and Moro (1918) the clasping or embrace reflex, as evidence that man's ancestors led an arboreal existence. McGraw (1939) considers the behavior of the newborn infant to consist in part of atavistic reflexes.

Davidson (1914), in a critical review of the doctrine, has shown that the notion of a precise or complete biological recapitulation of the phylogenetic past is not supported by the data of embryology. This is in no sense a denial that vertebrate animals resemble each other more in early than in later developmental periods.

The Neonate as an Organism Developing Autonomy. From the time of implantation of the fertilized ovum in the uterus until birth the organism leads a parasitic type of existence. At birth the infant achieves autonomy of respiration, digestion, excretion, and the maintenance of body temperature. These are all vital activities which the child must undertake if it is to live.

In the postnatal environment it has greater freedom of movement and the opportunity, by virtue of orienting responses, to react with some selectivity to aspects of a more complicated universe. It responds to some stimuli by movements which prolong stimulation, to others by withdrawal or rejection, and to some it at first responds and thereafter inhibits further motility.

The neonate cannot effectively manipulate its physical environment to provide food, care, and requisite protection. It is possessed of the ability to act upon its social environment by crying and by mimetic responses so that adults minister to its needs. In this manner the environment is effectively manipulated by proxy until the development of voluntary movements, particularly successful reaching to visually perceived objects and directed forms of locomotion, provides still further autonomy of action.

The Neonate as a System of Reflexes. Some neurologists have viewed the behavior of the newborn infant as that of a purely spinal being. Cruchet (1911, 1930), who represents this point of view, states that Virchow was the first to liken the reactions of the newborn infant to those of the decerebrate frog. De Crinis (1932), also, believes that the neonate is a reflex being of a lower type because the cerebral cortex is not functional. Peiper (1925a) holds that a part of the optic thalamus is functional at birth, and that athetoid movements are due to lack of inhibition from the corpus striatum. Langworthy (1933) maintains that "the behavior of the newborn is essentially that of a brain-stem preparation although medullation may extend as high as the upper end of the mid-brain." Diffusiveness and lack of coordination of movements are interpreted as due to a lack of cerebral inhibition. Minkowski (1932–1933) views the newborn infant as a cortical and subcortical spinal being, with emphasis upon the subcortical spinal. Marquis (1931) advanced the idea that conditioning occurs at subcortical levels. The ability of the infant to inhibit responses to successive auditory stimuli is proof, according to Peiper (1930), that it is not a purely "spinal being." Kroh (1926) concurs in this judgment because of persistence of a set or disposition for the few hours elapsing from one feeding period to another.

The theory of simple, discrete reflexes as the primary origin of behavior, with the complex responses to be derived from environmental integration of separate, part activities to form coordinated wholes, was championed by Watson (1919). The only exceptions to this process were those patterns of responses termed "primary emotions." This conception of the nature of the neonate organism seems not to be supported by the studies of Bersot (1920, 1921), Minkowski (1928, 1932–1933), Pratt, Nelson, and Sun (1930), Coghill (1930a, 1930b, 1933), Irwin (1932a, 1932b, 1932c), Pratt (1934a), and Delman (1935).

Recently Carmichael and his collaborators, Lehner (1937) and Smith (1939), have demonstrated that the generalization or specificity of a response depends in a given age period of the guinea pig upon the intensity of the stimuli. Coghill (1940), in a summary of basic studies upon the origin

and nature of early movements in birds and mammals, states that Carmichael and Smith (1939) did not undertake their experiments during the period of earliest movement.

Although not denying a relation between organismic involvement in a response and the intensity of the stimulus, it is still possible to affirm a genetic sequence from generalization to specificity, particularly in view of the fact that there is no good reason to believe that the various researches upon the developing child have been ranged in decreasing order of intensity of the stimuli.

The Neonate as a Developing Organism. In contrast with the view which regards the behavior of the newborn infant as completely describable in terms of simple, discrete reflexes, there is an organismic approach which attempts to describe and to pursue behavioral development ontogenetically. The neonate is considered to be a generalized organism because few of its responses are called forth by just one type of stimuli, few are limited to stimulation of just one sense organ or receptor area, and the responses are not sharply localized in a limited number of effector segments. In its most extreme form the organismic view would appear to neglect the observation of the varying participation of the parts of the neonate and to be content with affirmation that the organism was or was not responding.

From the stage of greatest generalization during the late fetal and the neonatal period the infant for the most part develops in the direction of increasing specificity of response: stimuli, unless conditioning occurs to effect a generalization, become more "adequate"; the reflexogenous zones for a given response shrink; and there is progressively less involvement of the organism in the response.

Development or maturation does not

take place at the same rate in all parts of an organism. Axial trends in the development of behavior are discernible.

Pratt (1937), in analyzing the behavior of the neonate from the stimulus-receptor angle, has shown that many responses such as the circulatory, respiratory, Moro, plantar, and palpebral are released by several types of stimuli acting upon different sense organs. Stimuli which are originally effective for some sense organ may become temporarily or more permanently ineffective; others, because of conditioning, become effective. Learning, as Pratt (1934a) has indicated, may produce a generalization of responses to stimuli which were originally inadequate. Initial generalization of the conditioning stimulus before it becomes specifically restricted in releasing the response was demonstrated in Pavlov's (1928) classic experiments.

Bersot (1920, 1921) and Minkowski (1928) have noted the extremes in extent of reflexogenous zones of various responses during the fetal and neonatal stages of development, and have followed their subsequent restriction, especially in the case of the plantar response. Similarly, Galant (1930) has pointed out the extent of the reflexogenous zone of the spinal reflexes. Reduction of the reflexogenous zone of the sucking response during the first ten days was observed by Pratt, Nelson, and Sun (1930). Stirnimann (1937a) has determined differences in reactivity of the facial areas from which the mouth orientation response may be elicited. Pratt (1934d, 1934e, 1934f) has explored several areas within the reflexogenous zone of the plantar response to determine differences in sensitivity and specificity. Although certain of the reflexogenous zones appear to shrink as time goes on, they do not, according to Bersot (1920, 1921), completely disappear. If the intensity of the stimulus is increased,

the responses may continue to be elicited from beyond the standard clinical areas.

The behavior of the newborn infant has frequently been described as random, uncoordinated, or diffuse. This impression has arisen because even without external stimulation the infant is not only active much of the time but that activity seems to involve most of the body. This general motility has been described and commented upon by Irwin (1930), Schachter (1932b), and many others. It is usually assumed that the basic cause of this play of activity is a lack of inhibition from the cerebrum. The principal exciting cause is probably organic and appears to be in some way related to events occurring in the alimentary tract.

The earliest movements of neurogenic origin in the animals studied by Coghill (1929a, 1929b, 1930b) are not simple reflexes but rather movements which initially start with the head and trunk and which apparently involve the grosser musculature. This is followed by differentiation so that movement of smaller segments, such as the extremities, occurs within the larger total pattern. When individuation is complete, specific responses may appear in relative localization when the total pattern is inhibited.

According to Minkowski's (1928, 1932–1933) analysis of fetal development, stimulation of a given area does not at first result in an active and extensive involvement of the organism. As maturation of the nervous system proceeds, crossed, long, and diagonal reflexes appear. Maximum generalization of response, in the sense of active participation of behavior segments, is then attained.

Irwin and Weiss (1930) set up the descriptive categories of "specific movements" and "mass activity" for neonate behavior. The former are those which are somewhat localized and which occur at a rate slow enough to be noted and recorded by an observer; the latter applies to activity which involves the whole organism at a rate too rapid for analysis. They state that either external or internal stimuli may release such mass activity and that the distinction between such activity and specific movements is quite arbitrary. Following this, Irwin (1932c) has considered "mass behavior" the matrix from which specific responses are later individuated. Dennis (1932b) and Pratt (1934a) have held that "mass activity" is the result of stimuli operating upon an organism at a time when the development of the nervous system has brought about the functional connection of almost all receptors with almost all effectors, and that, antedating this phase, as indicated by the work of Bersot (1920, 1921) and Minkowski (1928), some of those responses exist in relative isolation and hence should not be considered as individuating from "mass behavior" as the matrix. Irwin (1933a), in reply to Dennis, advances the idea that there are a succession of "mass" patterns, with individuation proceeding from each one.

Carmichael (1934) and Coghill (1940) have also been critical of the concept of "mass behavior," the latter holding that the term is inappropriate because of its implication of lack of differentiation and lack of organization, whereas organization is implied in the term "total pattern."

Recently Bridgman and Carmichael (1935), Carmichael and his collaborators, Lehner (1937), and Smith (1939), as a result of researches upon the fetal guinea pig, have come to the conclusion that some of the earliest neurogenic responses of the organism are reflex in nature. For this reason they are inclined to question both the concept of an initial total pattern from which reflexes become individuated and the

view that the entire course of behavioral development may be summarized as from-generalization-to-specificity.

The principal axial trends of development are the cephalocaudad and the proximodistal. The doctrine of development from fundamental to accessory movements, as expounded by Buck (1898), Moore (1901), and Shepardson (1907), is the forerunner of the idea that development proceeds proximodistally. In the present day Irwin (1930), Shirley (1931a), and Marquis (1933) have all contributed evidence supporting this principle. Bersot (1920, 1921) has reported that some aspects of the plantar response run counter to this conception, and McGraw (1933) has asserted that, so far as the elements of the grasping reflex are concerned, it is the distal segments which show prior anatomical and functional differentiation. Irwin (1933b), in reviewing the literature, says:

> It would seem that the evidence in regard to the differentiation of vertebrate limbs including morphological structure as well as behavior is convincingly in favor of the proximodistal principle.

The work of the Shermans (1925) and the Shermans and Flory (1936) on pain sensitivity illustrates a cephalocaudad gradient in sensitivity and in rapidity of development. The researches of Irwin (1930) and Shirley (1931a) also lend support to this principle of development in human infants.

The important need in the study of neonatal behavior and development is to obtain increasingly accurate and detailed descriptions of the infant's responses and the stimulating conditions under which they are obtained. The generalizations regarding principles of organization and of development of behavior serve a legitimate end just as long as they do not impede further research or constrain the student to force all observations to fit these frames of reference.

Bibliography

AHLFELD, F. 1905. Die intrauterine Tätigkeit der Thorax- und Zwerchfellmuskulatur. Intrauterine Atmung. *Mschr. Geburtsh. Gynäk.*, 21, 143–163.

ALDRICH, C. A. 1928. A new test for hearing in the newborn, the conditioned reflex. *Amer. J. Dis. Child.*, 35, 36–37.

ALEXANDER, G. 1911. Die Reflexerregbarkeit des Ohrlabyrinthes an menschlicher Neugeborener. *Z. Psychol. Physiol. Sinnesorg.*, 45, 153–196.

APERT, E. 1914. La tuméfaction mammaire et la sécrétion lactée chez le nouveau-né. *Le nourrisson*, 2, 293–299.

ARTEAGA, J. F. 1918. El liquido mamario del recién nacido. *Rev. med. cirug. Habana*, 23, 321–343.

BABINSKI, J. 1896. Sur le réflexe cutané-plantaire dans certains affections organiques du système nerveux central. *C. R. Soc. Biol., Paris*, 48, 207–208.

——. 1898. Du phénomène des orteils et sa valeur sémiologique. *Semaine méd.*, 18, 321.

——. 1903. De l'abduction des orteils (signe de l'éventail). *Rev. neurol.*, 11, 1205–1206.

——. 1915. Réflexes de défense. *Rev. neurol.*, 27, 145–155.

——. 1922. Réflexes de défense. *Rev. neurol.*, 38, 1049–1082.

BALIASSNIKOWA, N. J., and M. M. MODEL. 1931–1932. Zur Neurologie des Saugens. *Z. Kinderforsch.*, 39, 1–16.

BANU, G., and G. BOURGUIGNON. 1921. Évolution de la chronaxie des nerfs et muscles du membre superieur des nouveau-nés. *C. R. Soc. Biol., Paris*, 85, 349–352.

BANU, G., G. BOURGUIGNON, and H. LAUGIER. 1921. La chronaxie chez le nouveau-né. *C. R. Soc. Biol., Paris*, 85, 49–51.

BARTELS, M. 1910. Ueber Regulierung der Augenstellung durch den Ohrenapparat. *v. Graefes Arch. Ophthal.*, 76, 1–79.

——. 1932. Ueber Augenbewegungen bei Neugeborenen. *Dtsch. med. Wschr.*, 58, 1477–1478.

BARTH, H. 1914. Untersuchungen zur Physiologie des Saugens bei normalen und pathologischen Brustkindern. *Z. Kinderheilk.*, 10, 129.

BASCH, K. 1893. Beiträge zur Kenntnis des menschlichen Milchapparats. *Arch. Gynäk.*, 44, 15–54.

BAUER, J. 1926. Das Kriechphänomen des Neugeboren. *Klin. Wschr.*, 5, 1468–1469.

BAYLEY, N. 1933. Mental growth during the first three years: A developmental study of sixty-one children by repeated tests. *Genet. Psychol. Monogr.*, 14, No. 1.

BAYLEY, N., and H. R. STOLZ. 1937. Maturational changes in rectal temperatures of 61 infants from 1 to 36 months. *Child Develpm.*, 8, 195–206.

BEASLEY, W. C. 1933a. Visual pursuit in 109 white and 142 negro newborn infants. *Child Develpm.*, 4, 106–120.

——. 1933b. An investigation of related problems in the vision of newborn infants. *Psychol. Bull.*, 30, 626.

BECHTEREW, W. M. 1908. Ueber die objektive Untersuchung der kindlichen Psyche. *Russki Wratsch*, No. 16. (Abstract in *Folia neurobiol.*, 2, 362–366.)

BECK, L. F. 1938. A review of sixteen-millimeter films in psychology and allied sciences. *Psychol. Bull.*, 35, 127–169.

BECKER, J. 1921. Ueber Haut und Schweissdrüsen bei Foeten und Neugeborenen. *Z. Kinderheilk.*, 30, 3–20.

——. 1933. Ueber periphere Nervenendigungen in den äuszeren Genitalien von Neugeborenen. *Z. Kinderheilk.*, 55, 264–268.

BENEDICT, F. G., and F. B. TALBOT. 1914. The gaseous metabolism of infants with special reference to its relation to pulse-rate and muscular activity. *Carnegie Inst. Wash.*, Publ. 201.

——. 1915. The physiology of the new-born infant. Character and amount of katabolism. *Carnegie Inst. Wash.*, Publ. 223.

BERNFELD, W. 1931. Experimentelle Untersuchungen über die Capillarresistenz junger, insbesondere frühgeborener Säuglinge (Saugglockenmethode). *Mschr. Kinderheilk.*, 51, 1–14.

BERSOT, H. 1918, 1919. Variabilité et corrélations organiques. Nouvelle étude du réflexe plantaire. *Schweiz. Arch. Neurol. Psychiat.*, 4, 277–323; 5, 305–324.

——. 1920, 1921. Développement réactionnel et réflexe plantaire du bébé né avant terme à celui de deux ans. *Schweiz. Arch. Neurol. Psychiat.*, 7, 212–239; 8, 47–74.

BINET, A. 1890. Recherches sur les mouvements chez quelques jeunes enfants. *Rev. phil.*, 29, 297–309.

BLANTON, M. G. 1917. The behavior of the human infant during the first thirty days of life. *Psychol. Rev.*, 24, 456–483.

BRIDGES, K. M. B. 1932. Emotional development in early infancy. *Child Develpm.*, 3, 324–341.

——. 1935. Le développement des émotions chez le jeune enfant. *L'Union méd. Canada*, 64, 15–19; 130–139.

——. 1936. Le développement des émotions chez le jeune enfant. *J. psychol. norm. path.*, 33, 40–87.

BRIDGMAN, C. S., and L. CARMICHAEL. 1935. An experimental study of the onset of behavior in the fetal guinea-pig. *J. Genet. Psychol.*, **47**, 247–267.

BRYAN, E. S. 1930. Variations in the responses of infants during first ten days of postnatal life. *Child Develpm.*, **1**, 56–77.

BUCHMAN, S. S. 1895. Babies and monkeys. *Pop. Sci. Mo.*, **46**, 371–388.

——. 1900. Babies and monkeys. *Nineteenth Cent.*, **36**, 727–743.

BUCK, F. 1898. From fundamental to accessory in the development of the nervous system and of movements. *Ped. Sem.*, **6**, 5–64.

BURR, C. W. 1921. The reflexes of early infancy. *Brit. J. Child. Dis.*, **18**, 152–153.

CANESTRINI, S. 1913. Ueber das Sinnesleben des Neugeborenen. (*Monogr. Gesamtgeb. Neurol. Psychiat.*, No. 5) Berlin: Springer. Pp. 104.

CARLSON, A. J., and H. GINSBURG. 1915. Contributions to the physiology of the stomach: XXIV. The tonus and hunger contractions of the stomach of the new-born. *Amer. J. Physiol.*, **38**, 29–32.

CARMICHAEL, L. 1933. Origin and prenatal growth of behavior. In C. MURCHISON (Ed.), *A handbook of child psychology* (2d ed., rev.), pp. 31–159. Worcester: Clark University Press.

——. 1934. An experimental study in the prenatal guinea-pig of the origin and development of reflexes and patterns of behavior in relation to stimulation of specific receptor areas during the period of active fetal life. *Genet. Psychol. Monogr.*, **16**, 337–491.

CARMICHAEL, L., and G. F. J. LEHNER. 1937. The development of temperature sensitivity during the fetal period. *J. Genet. Psychol.*, **50**, 217–227.

CARMICHAEL, L., and M. F. SMITH. 1939. Quantified pressure stimulation and the specificity and generality of response in fetal life. *J. Genet. Psychol.*, **54**, 425–434.

CARPENTER, T. M., and J. R. MURLIN. 1911. The energy metabolism of mother and child just before and just after birth. *Arch. Intern. Med.*, **7**, 184–222.

E CASTRO, F. 1930. Sécrétion lactée du nouveau-né prolongée jusqu'au onzième mois. *C. R. Soc. Biol., Paris*, **105**, 485–486.

CATEL, W. 1932. Zum Spontannystagmus des Neugeborenen. *Dtsch. med. Wschr.*, **58**, 1478–1479.

CEMACH, A. I. 1920. Beiträge zur Kenntnis der kochlearen Reflexe. *Beitr. Anat., Physiol., Pathol., Therap. Ohres, Nase, Halses*, **14**, 1–82.

CHAMPNEYS, F. H. 1881. Notes on an infant. *Mind*, **6**, 104–107.

CHASE, W. P. 1937. Color vision in infants. *J. Exp. Psychol.*, **20**, 203–222.

CIURLO, L. 1934. Sulla funzione olfattoria nel neonato. *Valsalva*, **10**, 22–34. (Abstract in *Zbl. ges. Kinderheilk.*, 1934, **29**, 134.)

CLARKE, F. M. 1939. A developmental study of the bodily reaction of infants to an auditory startle stimulus. *J. Genet. Psychol.*, **55**, 415–427.

CLARKE, F. M., W. A. HUNT, and E. B. HUNT. 1937. Plantar responses in infants following a startle stimulus. *J. Genet. Psychol.*, **50**, 458–461.

COGHILL, G. E. 1929a. The development of movement of the hind leg of *Amblystoma*. *Proc. Soc. Exp. Biol. Med.*, **27**, 74–75.

——. 1929b. The early development of behavior in *Amblystoma* and in man. *Arch. Neurol. Psychiat., Chicago*, **21**, 989–1009.

——. 1930a. Individuation versus integration in the development of behavior. *J. Gen. Psychol.*, **3**, 431–435.

——. 1930b. The structural basis of the integration of behavior. *Proc. Nat. Acad. Sci., Wash.*, **16**, 637–643.

——. 1933. The neuro-embryologic study of behavior: principles, perspective and aim. *Science*, **78**, 131–138.

——. 1940. Early embryonic somatic movements in birds and in mammals other than man. *Monogr. Soc. Res. Child Develpm.*, **5**, 1–48.

COMPAYRÈ, G. 1896. *The intellectual and moral development of the child.* Pt. 1. (Trans. by M. E. WILSON.) New York: Appleton.

CREUTZFELDT, H. G., and A. PEIPER. 1932. Untersuchungen über die Todesursache der Frühgeburten. *Mschr. Kinderheilk.*, **52**, 24–36.

CRUCHET, R. 1911. Évolution psycho-physiologique de l'enfant, du jour de sa naissance à l'âge de deux ans. *Année psychol.*, **17**, 48–63.

——. 1930. La mésure de l'intelligence chez l'enfant de la naissance. *J. méd. Bordeaux*, **107**, 951–960.

CRUDDEN, C. H. 1937. Reactions of newborn infants to thermal stimuli under constant tactual conditions. *J. Exp. Psychol.*, **20**, 350–370.

CZERNY, A. 1892. Beobachtungen über den Schlaf im Kindesalter unter physiologischen Verhältnissen. *Jb. Kinderheilk.*, **22**, 1–28.

DANIELS, E. E., and M. MAUDRY. 1935. Die Entwicklung der Abwehrreaktionen auf Storungsreize. *Z. Psychol.*, **135**, 259–287.

DARWIN, C. 1877. A biographical sketch of an infant. *Mind*, **2**, 285–294.

DAVIDSON, P. E. 1914. The recapitulation theory and human infancy. *Teach. Coll. Contr. Educ.*, No. 65.

DE CRINIS, M. 1932. Die Entwicklung der Grosshirnrinde nach der Geburt in ihren Beziehungen zur intellektuellen Ausreifung des Kindes. *Wien. klin. Wschr.*, **45**, 1161–1165.

DELMAN, L. 1935. The order of participation of limbs in responses to tactual stimulation of the newborn infant. *Child Develpm.*, **6**, 98–109.

DENISOVA, M. P., and N. L. FIGURIN. 1929. [The problem of the first associated food reflexes in infants.] *Voprosy Geneticheskoy Reflexologii i Pedologii Mladenchestva.*, **1**, 81–88. (Cited in RAZRAN, 1933.)

DENNIS, W. 1932a. Two new responses of infants. *Child Develpm.*, **3**, 362–363.

——. 1932b. Discussion: The rôle of mass activity in the development of infant behavior. *Psychol. Rev.*, **39**, 593–595.

——. 1934. A description and classification of the responses of the newborn infant. *Psychol. Bull.*, **31**, 5–22.

——. 1935. A psychologic interpretation of the persistence of the so-called Moro reflex. *Amer. J. Dis. Child.*, **50**, 888–893.

——. 1936. A bibliography of baby biographies. *Child Develpm.*, **7**, 71–73.

——. 1940. Infant reaction to restraint: An evaluation of Watson's theory. *Trans. N. Y. Acad. Sci.*, **2**, 202–218.

DENNIS, W., and M. G. DENNIS. 1937. Behavioral development in the first year as shown by forty biographies. *Psychol. Rec.*, **1**, 349–361.

DEWEY, E. 1935. *Behavior development in infants: A survey of the literature on prenatal and postnatal activity, 1920–1934.* New York: Columbia University Press.

DISHER, D. R. 1934. The reactions of newborn infants to chemical stimuli administered nasally. *Ohio State Univ. Stud., Contr. Psychol.*, No. 12, pp. 1–52.

DOCKERAY, F. C., and C. RICE. 1934. Responses of newborn infants to pain stimulation. *Ohio State Univ. Stud., Contrib. Psychol.*, No. 12, pp. 82–93.

DOCKERAY, F. C., and W. L. VALENTINE. 1939. A new isolation cabinet for infant research. *J. Exp. Psychol.*, **24**, 211–214.

DRUMMOND, M. 1921. *The dawn of mind: An introduction to child psychology.* London: Arnold.

DUPÉRIÉ, R., and R. BARGUES. 1932. À propos des réflexes inconditionnels du nourrison: le réflexe de l'étreinte de Moro. *Gaz. hebd. sci. méd. Bordeaux*, **53**, 66–70.

ECKSTEIN, A. 1927. Zur Physiologie der Geschmacksempfindung und des Saugreflexes bei Säuglingen. *Z. Kinderheilk.*, **45**, 1–18.

ECKSTEIN, A., and H. PAFFRATH. 1928. Bewegungsstudien bei frühgeborenen und jungen Säuglingen. *Z. Kinderheilk.*, **46**, 595–610.

ECKSTEIN, A., and E. ROMINGER. 1921. Beiträge zur Physiologie und Pathologie der Atmung. Die Atmung des Säuglings. *Z. Kinderheilk.*, **28**, 1–37.

EDGERTON, A. E. 1934. Ocular observations and studies of the newborn; with a review of the literature. *Arch. Ophthal., N. Y.*, **11**, 838–867.

ENGSTLER, G. 1905. Ueber den fussohlen Reflex und das Babinski-phänomen bei tausend Kindern der ersten Lebensjahre. *Wien. klin. Wschr.*, **18**, 567–570.

FELDMAN, W. M. 1920. *The principles of antenatal and post-natal child physiology, pure and applied.* London and New York: Longmans, Green.

——. 1921. The nature of the plantar reflex in early life and the causes of its variations. *Brit. J. Child. Dis.*, **18**, 24–27.

——. 1927. *The principles of ante-natal and post-natal child hygiene.* London: Bale & Danielsson.

FERNANDEZ, U. 1918. Puericultura post-natal. El recién nacido. Algunos fenómenos fisiológicos inmediatos al nacimento. *Semana med.*, **25**, 115–118.

FORBES, H. S., and H. B. FORBES. 1927. Fetal sense reaction: Hearing. *J. Comp. Psychol.*, **7**, 353–355.

FREUDENBERG, E. 1921. Der Morosche Umklammerungsreflex und das Brudzinskische Nackenzeichen als Reflexe des Säuglingsalters. *Münch. med. Wschr.*, **68**, 1646–1647.

FULTON, J. F., and A. D. KELLER. 1932. *The sign of Babinski: A study of the evolution of cortical dominance in primates.* Springfield, Ill.: Thomas.

FURFEY, P. H., M. A. BONHAM, and M. K. SARGENT. 1930. The mental organization of the newborn. *Child Develpm.*, **1**, 48–51.

GALANT, J. S. 1917. *Der Rückgratreflex.* Dissertation, Basel. (Abstracted in Peiper, 1928.)

——. 1930. Über die abdominale Variation des Galant'schen Rückgratreflexes (der "abdominale Rückgratreflex") und über die Ausbreitung der reflexogen Zone des Rückgratreflexes bei Säuglingen überhaupt. *Jb. Kinderheilk.*, **129**, 239–241.

——. 1931. Über die rudimentären neuropsychischen Funktionen der Säuglinge. *Jb. Kinderheilk.*, **133**, 104–108.

GATEWOOD, M. C., and A. P. WEISS. 1930. Race and sex differences in newborn infants. *J. Genet. Psychol.*, **38**, 31–49.

GENZMER, A. 1873. *Untersuchungen über die Sinneswahrnehmungen des neugeborenen Menschen.* (Dissertation, 1873.) Halle: Niemeyer, 1882. (Abstracted by PETERSON and RAINEY, 1910; CANESTRINI, 1913; and PEIPER, 1928.)

GESELL, A. 1925. *The mental growth of the preschool child: A psychological outline of normal development from birth to the sixth year, including a system of developmental diagnosis.* New York: Macmillan.

——. 1934. *An atlas of infant behavior: A systematic delineation of the forms and early growth of human behavior patterns:* Vol. I. *Normative series* (with H. THOMPSON and C. S. AMATRUDA); Vol. II. *Naturalistic series* (with A. V. KELIHER, F. L. ILG, and J. J. CARLSON). New Haven: Yale University Press.

GESELL, A., and H. THOMPSON. 1929. Learning and growth in identical infant twins: An experimental study by the method of co-twin control. *Genet. Psychol. Monogr., 6*, 1–124.

GESELL, A., H. THOMPSON, and C. AMATRUDA. 1938. *The psychology of early growth.* New York: Macmillan.

GIVLER, R. C. 1921. The intellectual significance of the grasping reflex. *J. Phil., 18*, 617–628.

GORDON, M. B. 1929. The Moro embrace reflex in infancy: Its incidence and significance. *Amer. J. Dis. Child., 38*, 26–34.

GUDDEN, H. 1910. Das Verhalten der Pupillen beim Neugeborenen. *Münch. med. Wschr., 57*, 405–406.

GUERNSEY, M. 1929. A quantitative study of eye reflexes in infants. *Psychol. Bull., 26*, 160–161.

GUNDOBIN, N. 1907. Die Eigentümlichkeiten des Kindesalters. *Jb. Kinderheilk., 65*, 720–732.

GUTMANN, M. I. 1924. Ueber Augenbewegungen der Neugeborenen und ihre theoretische Bedeutung. *Arch. ges. Psychol., 47*, 108–121.

HALL, G. S. 1891. Notes on the study of infants. *Ped. Sem., 1*, 127–138.

HALLER, M. W. 1932. The reactions of infants to changes in the intensity and pitch of pure tone. *J. Genet. Psychol., 40*, 162–180.

HALVERSON, H. M. 1936. Complications of the early grasping reactions. *Psychol. Monogr., 47*, 47–63.

——. 1937. Studies of the grasping responses of early infancy: I, II, III. *J. Genet. Psychol., 51*, 371–449.

——. 1938. Infant sucking and tensional behavior. *J. Genet. Psychol., 53*, 365–430.

——. 1940. Genital and sphincter behavior of the male infant. *J. Genet. Psychol., 56*, 95–136.

——. 1941. Variations in pulse and respiration during different phases of infant behavior. *J. Genet. Psychol., 59*, 259–330.

HARTMANN, H. 1932. Zur Anatomie der Geschlechtsorgane Neugeborener. *Arch. Gynäk., 148*, 708–723.

HARTMANN-KARPLUS, D. 1931. Untersuchungen über Juckempfindung, Kratzen und Pilomotorenreflex im Säuglingsalter. *Jb. Kinderheilk., 132*, 140–158.

HAZARD, C. 1936. The relation of reflex conduction rate in the patellar reflex to age in human beings. *Univ. Iowa Stud. Child Welfare, 12*, 183–197.

HENSEL, G. 1933. Untersuchungen über den Diastasegehalt des Speichels bei Frühgeborenen. *Z. Kinderheilk., 54*, 367–376.

HERZFELD, B. 1922. Das neugeborene Kind und seine Eigentümlichkeiten. *Jb. Kinderheilk., 99*, 75–85.

HOELAND, H. 1927. Über die Hexenmilch und die histologischen Veränderungen in den Brüsten des Neugeborenen. *Mschr. Geburtsh. Gynäk., 77*, 114–120.

HOFMANN, E., and A. PEIPER. 1937. Der Schluckvorgang. *Mschr. Kinderheilk., 70*, 54–56.

HUNT, W. A. 1939. "Body jerk" as a concept in describing infant behavior. *J. Genet. Psychol., 55*, 215–220.

HUNT, W. A., F. M. CLARKE, and E. B. HUNT. 1936. Studies of the startle pattern: IV. Infants. *J. Psychol., 2*, 339–352.

HUNT, W. A., and C. LANDIS. 1936. Studies of the startle pattern: I. Introduction. *J. Psychol., 2*, 201–205.

——. 1938. A note on the difference between the Moro reflex and the startle pattern. *Psychol. Rev., 45*, 267–269.

HURLOCK, E. B. 1933. Experimental studies of the newborn. *Child Develpm., 4*, 148–163.

IRWIN, O. C. 1930. The amount and nature of activities of new-born infants under constant external stimulating conditions during the first ten days of life. *Genet. Psychol. Monogr., 8*, 1–92.

——. 1931. A cold light for photographing infant reactions with the high-speed camera. *Child Develpm., 2*, 153–155.

——. 1932a. The organismic hypothesis and differentiation of behavior: I. The cell theory and the neurone doctrine. *Psychol. Rev., 39*, 128–146.

——. 1932b. The organismic hypothesis and differentiation of behavior: II. The reflex-arc concept. *Psychol. Rev., 39*, 189–202.

——. 1932c. The organismic hypothesis and differentiation of behavior: III. The differentiation of human behavior. *Psychol. Rev., 39*, 387–393.

——. 1932d. The relation of body motility in young infants to some physical traits. *J. Exp. Educ., 1*, 140–143.

——. 1932e. The amount of motility of seventy-three newborn infants. *J. Comp. Psychol., 14*, 415–428.

——. 1932f. The distribution of the amount of motility in young infants between two nursing periods. *J. Comp. Psychol., 14*, 429–445.

——. 1932g. The latent time of the body startle in infants. *Child Develpm., 3*, 104–107.

——. 1932h. Infant responses to vertical movements. *Child Develpm., 3*, 167–169.

——. 1933a. Dennis on mass activity: A reply. *Psychol. Rev., 40*, 215–219.

——. 1933b. Proximo-distal differentiation of limbs in young organisms. *Psychol. Rev., 40*, 467–477.

——. 1933c. Motility in young infants: I. Relation to body temperature. *Amer. J. Dis. Child., 45*, 531–533.

——. 1933d. Motility in young infants: II.

Relation to two indexes of nutritional status. *Amer. J. Dis. Child.*, 45, 534–537.

IRWIN, O. C. 1936. Qualitative changes in a vertebral reaction pattern during infancy: A motion-picture study. *Univ. Iowa Stud. Child Welfare*, 12, 201–207.

———. 1941a. Effect of strong light on the body activity of newborns. *J. Comp. Psychol.*, 32, 233–236.

———. 1941b. The profile as a visual device for indicating central tendencies in speech data. *Child Develpm.*, 12, 111–120.

———. 1941c. Research on speech sounds for the first six months of life. *Psychol. Bull.*, 38, 277–285.

IRWIN, O. C., and H. P. CHEN. 1941. A reliability study of speech sounds observed in the crying of newborn infants. *Child Develpm.*, 12, 351–368; *Psychol. Abstr.*, No. 1738, 1942, 16, 194.

IRWIN, O. C., and T. CURRY. 1941. Vowel elements in the crying vocalization of infants under ten days of age. *Child Develpm.*, 12, 99–109.

IRWIN, O. C., and A. P. WEISS. 1930. A note on mass activity in newborn infants. *J. Genet. Psychol.*, 38, 20–30.

IRWIN, O. C., and L. A. WEISS. 1934a. Differential variations in the activity and crying of the newborn infant under different intensities of light: A comparison of observational with polygraph findings. *Univ. Iowa Stud. Child Welfare*, 9, 137–147.

———. 1934b. The effect of clothing on the general and vocal activity of the newborn infant. *Univ. Iowa Stud. Child Welfare*, 9, 149–162.

———. 1934c. The effect of darkness on the activity of newborn infants. *Univ. Iowa Stud. Child Welfare*, 9, 163–175.

JACOBI, W., and F. DEMUTH. 1923. Die wahre Acidität der Mundflüssigkeit beim Säugling und Neugeborenen. *Z. Kinderheilk.*, 34, 293–296.

JAROSCHKA, K. 1929. Ein Beitrag zur Kenntnis der Sekretionsvorgänge der Brustdrüse von Säuglingen. *Mschr. Kinderheilk.*, 42, 523–527.

JENSEN, K. 1932. Differential reactions to taste and temperature stimuli in newborn infants. *Genet. Psychol. Monogr.*, 12, 363–479.

JONES, H. E. 1930. The galvanic skin reflex in infancy. *Child Develpm.*, 1, 106–110.

JONES, M. C. 1926. The development of early behavior patterns in young children. *J. Genet. Psychol.*, 33, 537–585.

JOSEPH, S. 1929. Zur Biologie der Brustdrüse beim Neugeborenen. *Mschr. Geburtsh. Gynäk.*, 83, 219–224.

KAHN, W. 1921. Über die Dauer der Darmpassage im Säuglingsalter. *Z. Kinderheilk.*, 29, 321–330.

KASATKIN, N. I. 1935. [The development of visual and acoustic conditioned reflexes and

their differentiation in infants.] *Sovetsk. Pediat.*, 8, 127–137. (Abstract 1756, *Psychol. Abstr.*, 1936.)

KASATKIN, N. I., and A. M. LEVIKOVA. 1935a. On the development of early conditioned reflexes and differentiations of auditory stimuli in infants. *J. Exp. Psychol.*, 18, 1–19.

———. 1935b. The formation of visual conditioned reflexes and their differentiation in infants. *J. Gen. Psychol.*, 12, 416–435.

KASHARA, M. 1916. The curved lines of suction. *Amer. J. Dis. Child.*, 12, 73–87.

KÖDDING, I. 1940. Der Lidschlag im Kindesalter. *Mschr. Kinderheilk.*, 84, 212–223; *Psychol. Abstr.*, No. 5429, 1941, 15, 590.

KOELLREUTTER, W. 1907. Schwerhörigkeit der Neugeborenen als reine Störung im schallzuleitenden Teile des Ohres. *Z. Ohrenheilk. Krankh. Luftwege*, 53, 123–138.

KROH, O. 1926. Die Anfänge der psychischen Entwicklung des Kindes in allgemeinpsychologischer Beleuchtung. *Z. Psychol.*, 100, 325–343.

KRONER, T. 1881. *Ueber die Sinnesempfindungen der Neugeborenen.* Breslau: Grass, Barth. (Abstracted in PETERSON and RAINEY, 1910; PREYER, 1882; and PEIPER, 1928.) Pp. 14.

KUSSMAUL, A. 1859. *Untersuchungen über das Seelenleben des neugeborenen Menschen.* Tübingen: Moser. (Abstracted in PETERSON and RAINEY, 1910; PREYER, 1882; and PEIPER, 1928.) Pp. 32.

KUTVIRT, O. 1912. Ueber das Gehör der Neugeborenen und Säuglinge. *Beitr. Anat., Physiol., Pathol., Therap. Ohres, Nase, Halses*, 5, 249–257.

LAMBANZI, R., and C. PIANETTA. 1906. Recherches sur le réflexe buccal. *Rev. psychiat. psychol. exp.*, 10, 148–154.

LANDIS, C., and W. A. HUNT. 1937. Magnification of time as a research technique in the study of behavior. *Science*, 85, 384–385.

———. 1939. *The startle pattern.* New York: Farrar and Rinehart.

LANGWORTHY, O. R. 1933. Development of behavior patterns and myelinization of the nervous system in the human fetus and infant. *Contr. Embryol., Carnegie Inst. Wash.*, 24, No. 139.

LANTUEJOUL, P., and E. HARTMANN. 1923. Note sur le réflexe cutané-plantaire chez le jeune enfant, notamment au moment de la naissance. *Rev. neurol.* 39, 387–399.

LERI, A. 1903–1904. Le réflexe de Babinski chez les enfants. *Gaz. malad. inf.*, 5, 277.

LEVINE, S. Z., and E. MARPLES. 1931. The respiratory metabolism in infancy and in childhood: XII. A biometric study of basal metabolism in normal infants. *Amer. J. Dis. Child.*, 41, 1332–1346.

LEVY, S. 1928. Ueber die körperliche und

geistige Entwicklung von Frühgeborenen. *Jb. Kinderheilk.*, **121**, 51–85.

LITZKA, G. 1933. Experimentelle Untersuchungen über den Einfluss der Schwangerschaftshormone auf den Organismus des Fetus und Neugeborenen. *Z. Kinderheilk.*, **54**, 742–757.

LORENZ, E. 1929. Ueber des Brustdrüsensekret des Neugeborenen. *Jb. Kinderheilk.*, **124**, 268–274.

LOWDEN, T. S. 1895. The first half year of an infant's life. *Post-grad. and Wooster Quart.*

LÖWENFELD, B. 1927. Systematisches Studium der Reaktionen der Säuglinge auf Klänge und Geräusche. *Z. Psychol.*, **104**, 62–96.

MAJOR, D. R. 1906. *First steps in mental growth: A series of studies in the psychology of infancy.* New York: Macmillan.

MARINESCO, G., and A. KREINDLER. 1933. Des réflexes conditionnels: I. L'organisation des réflexes conditionnels chez l'enfant. *J. Psychol. norm path.*, **30**, 855–886.

MARQUIS, D. P. 1931. Can conditioned responses be established in the newborn infant? *J. Genet. Psychol.*, **39**, 479–492.

——. 1933. A study of activity and postures in infants' sleep. *J. Genet. Psychol.*, **42**, 51–69.

——. 1941. Learning in the neonate: The modification of behavior under three feeding schedules. *J. Exp. Psychol.*, **29**, 263–282.

MCGINNIS, J. M. 1930. Eye-movements and optic nystagmus in early infancy. *Genet. Psychol. Monogr.*, **8**, 321–430.

MCGRAW, M. B. 1932. From reflex to muscular control in the assumption of an erect posture and ambulation in the human infant. *Child Develpm.*, **3**, 291–297.

——. 1933. Discussion: Grasping in infants and the proximo-distal course of growth. *Psychol. Rev.*, **40**, 301–302.

——. 1935. *Growth: A study of Johnny and Jimmy.* New York: Appleton-Century.

——. 1937. The Moro reflex. *Amer. J. Dis. Child.*, **54**, 240–251.

——. 1939. Behavior of the newborn infant and early neuromuscular development. *Res. Publ. Ass. Nerv. Ment. Dis.*, **19**, 244–246; *Psychol. Abstr.*, No. 3816, 1940, **14**, 390.

——. 1940a. Suspension grasp behavior of the human infant. *Amer. J. Dis. Child.*, **60**, 799–811; *Psychol. Abstr.*, No. 3635, 1941, **15**, 398.

——. 1940b. Neuromuscular mechanism of the infant. Development reflected by postural adjustments to an inverted position. *Amer. J. Dis. Child.*, **60**, 1031–1042; *Psychol. Abstr.*, No. 3636, 1941, **15**, 399.

——. 1941a. Development of rotary-vestibular reactions of the human infant. *Child Develpm.*, **12**, 17–19; *Psychol. Abstr.*, No. 3637, **15**, 399.

——. 1941b. Neuro-motor maturation of antigravity functions as reflected in the development of a sitting posture. *J. Genet. Psychol.*, **59**, 155–175.

MESINA, R. 1936. [The tonic reactions of the normal child due to position and movement.] *Riv. Clin. Pediat.*, **34**, 510. (Abstract 2694 *Psychol. Abstr.*, 1938.)

MINKOWSKI, M. 1922. Über frühzeitige Bewegungen. Reflexe und muskuläre Reaktionen beim menschlichen Fötus, und ihre Beziehungen zum fötalen Nerven- und Muskelsystem. *Schweiz. med. Wschr.*, **52**, 721–724; 751–755.

——. 1923. Zur Entwicklungsgeschichte, Localisation und Klinik des Fussohlenreflexes. *Schweiz. Arch. Neurol. Psychiat.*, **13**, 475–514. (Summarized in MINKOWSKI, 1926.)

——. 1926. Sur les modalités et la localisation du réflexe plantaire au cours de son évolution du foetus à l'adulte. *C. R. Congr. Médecins, Aliénistes et Neurologistes, Geneva*, **30**, 301–308.

——. 1928. Neurobiologische Studien am menschlichen Foetus. *Handb. Biol. ArbMeth.*, Pt. V, **5B**. No. 5, 511–618.

——. 1932–1933. Sur le développement, la localisation et la clinique des réflexes. *Bull. soc. roy. méd. Égypte*, **10**, 1–20.

MOORE, K. C. 1901. Comparative observations on the development of movements. *Ped. Sem.*, **8**, 231–238.

MOORE, R. 1936. The histology of the newborn and prepuberal prostate gland. *Anat. Rec.*, **66**, 1–9.

MORO, E. 1918. Das erste Trimenon. *Münch. med. Wschr.*, **65**, 1147–1150.

MUMFORD, A. A. 1897. Survival movements of human infancy. *Brain*, **20**, 290–307.

MUNN, N. L. 1938. *Psychological development: An introduction to genetic psychology.* Boston: Houghton Mifflin.

MURCHISON, C., and S. LANGER. 1927. Tiedemann's observations on the development of the mental faculties of children. *J. Genet. Psychol.*, **34**, 205–230. (See TIEDEMANN, 1787.)

MURLIN, J. R., R. E. CONKLIN, and M. E. MARSH. 1925. Energy metabolism of normal newborn babies: With special reference to the influence of food and of crying. *Amer. J. Dis. Child.*, **29**, 1–28. (Reviewed in RICHARDS, 1935.)

MURPHY, D., and E. THORPE, JR. 1931. Breathing measurements on normal newborn infants. *J. Clin. Invest.*, **10**, 545–558.

MUZIO, O. 1933. Sulla audizione dei neonati. *Ann. Laring. ecc.*, **33**, 105–110. (Abstracted in *Zbl. ges. Kinderheilk.*, 1934, **29**, 134.)

NASSAU, E. 1938. Die Kitzelreaktion beim Säugling. *Jb. Kinderheilk.*, **151**, 46–49.

NOTHMANN, H. 1909. Zur Frage der "psychischen" Magensaftsekretion beim Säugling. *Arch. Kinderheilk.*, **51**, 123–138.

PAFFRATH, H., and W. OHM. 1933. Zur Frage der Kreatinurie des Frühgeborenen. *Z. Kinderheilk.*, **54**, 377–379.

PAVLOV, I. 1928. *Lectures on conditioned re-*

flexes. (Trans. by W. H. GANTT.) New York : International Publishers.

PEIPER, A. 1924*a*. Untersuchungen über den galvanischen Hautreflex im Kindesalter. *Jb. Kinderheilk.,* **107,** 139–150.

——. 1924*b*. Beiträge zur Sinnesphysiologie der Frühgeburt. *Jb. Kinderheilk.,* **104,** 195–200.

——. 1924*c*. Sinnesempfindungen des Kindes vor seiner Geburt. *Mschr. Kinderheilk.,* **29,** 236–241.

——. 1925*a*. Die Hirntätigkeit des Neugeborenen. *Jb. Kinderheilk.,* **111,** 290–314.

——. 1925*b*. Untersuchungen über die Reaktionzeit im Säuglingsalter : I. Reaktionzeit auf Schallreiz. *Mschr. Kinderheilk.,* **31,** 491–506.

——. 1926*a*. Untersuchungen über die Reaktionzeit im Säuglingsalter : II. Reaktionzeit auf Schmerzreiz. *Mschr. Kinderheilk.,* **32,** 136–143.

——. 1926*b*. Ueber die Helligkeits und Farbenempfindungen der Frühgeburten. *Arch. Kinderheilk.,* **80,** 1–20.

——. 1926*c*. Über einen Augenreflex auf den Hals im frühem Säuglingsalter. *Jb. Kinderheilk.,* **113,** 87–89.

——. 1926*d*. Ueber das Pupillenspiel des Säuglings. *Jb. Kinderheilk.,* **112,** 179–183.

——. 1928. *Die Hirntätigkeit des Säuglings.* Berlin : Springer.

——. 1929. Die Schreitbewegungen der Neugeborenen. *Mschr. Kinderheilk.,* **45,** 444–448.

——. 1930. Sinnesreaktionen des Neugeborenen. *Z. Psychol.,* **114,** 363–370.

——. 1931. Die Nahrungsaufnahme des Säuglings. *Mschr. Kinderheilk.,* **50,** 20–28.

——. 1933*a*. Die Atmung des Neugeborenen. *Jahreskurse ärztl. Fortbild.,* **24,** 21–25.

——. 1933*b*. Die Atembewegungen des Unterkiefers. (Ein weiterer Beitrag zum Zerfall des Atemzentrums.) *Jb. Kinderheilk.,* **139,** 117–123.

——. 1935*a*. Die Entwicklung des Mienenspiels. *Mschr. Kinderheilk.,* **63,** 39–91.

——. 1935*b*. Röntgenkymographie des Saugvorganges. *Klin. Wschr.,* **14,** 1723–1725.

——. 1936*a*. Hautschutzreflexe. *Jb. Kinderheilk.,* **146,** 233–239.

——. 1936*b*. Der Saugvorgang. *Ergeb. inn. Med. Kinderheilk.,* **50,** 527–567.

——. 1937*a*. Die Erscheinung der Dominanz und die Erregungsstufen des Saugzentrums. *Jb. Kinderheilk.,* **149,** 201–206.

——. 1937*b*. Comments upon J. M. SMITH'S work, "The relative brightness values of three hues for newborn infants." *Child Develpm.,* **8,** 299–300.

——. 1938. Die Erscheinung der Dominanz bei Reizlöschung. *Jb. Kinderheilk.,* **151,** 1–2.

——. 1939. Die Saugstörung. *Mschr. Kinderheilk.,* **79,** 241–255.

PEIPER, A., and C. F. GOOD. 1934. Die Herztätigkeit während des Zerfalles des Atemzentrums. *Jb. Kinderheilk.,* **143,** 1–10.

PEIPER, A., and H. ISBERT. 1927. Über die Körperstellung des Säuglings. *Jb. Kinderheilk.,* **115,** 142–176.

PENDLETON, W. R. 1927. Hiccups among infants. *Amer. J. Dis. Child.,* **34,** 207–210.

PEPYS, S. 1667. *Diary.*

PETERSON, F., and L. H. RAINEY. 1910. The beginnings of mind in the newborn. *Bull. Lying-In Hosp. City of N. Y.,* **7,** 99–122.

PFAUNDLER, M. 1909. Chapter in *Handbuch der Milchkunde,* ed. by P. SOMMERFELD. Wiesbaden : Bergmann. (Abstracted in ECKSTEIN, 1927.)

POLI, C. 1893. L'udito nei neonati. *Arch. ital. Otol.,* **1,** 358–364. (Abstracted in *Arch. Ohrenheilk.,* 1896, **41,** 82.)

POPPER, E. 1921. Studien ueber Saugphänomene. *Arch. Psychiat. Nervenkr.,* **63,** 231–246.

PRATT, K. C. 1930. Note on the relation of temperature and humidity to the activity of young infants. *J. Genet. Psychol.,* **38,** 480–484.

——. 1932. A note upon the relation of activity to sex and race in young infants. *J. Soc. Psychol.,* **3,** 118–120.

——. 1933. The neonate. In C. MURCHISON (Ed.), *A handbook of child psychology* (2d ed., rev.), pp. 163–208. Worcester : Clark University Press.

——. 1934*a*. Specificity and generalization of behavior in new-born infants : A critique. *Psychol. Rev.,* **41,** 265–284.

——. 1934*b*. The effects of repeated auditory stimulation upon the general activity of newborn infants. *J. Genet. Psychol.,* **44,** 96–116.

——. 1934*c*. The effects of repeated visual stimulation upon the activity of newborn infants. *J. Genet. Psychol.,* **44,** 117–126.

——. 1934*d*. Generalization and specificity of the plantar responses in newborn infants. The reflexogenous zone : I. Differential sensitivity and effector-segment participation according to the area of stimulation. *J. Genet. Psychol.,* **44,** 265–300.

——. 1934*e*. Generalization and specificity of the plantar responses in newborn infants. The reflexogenous zone : II. Segmental patterning of response. *J. Genet. Psychol.,* **45,** 22–38.

——. 1934*f*. Generalization and specificity of the plantar responses in newborn infants. The reflexogenous zone : III. The effects of the physiological state upon sensitivity, segmental participation, and segmental patterning. *J. Genet. Psychol.,* **45,** 371–389.

——. 1936*a*. Problems in the classification of neonate activities. *Quart. Rev. Biol.,* **11,** 70–80.

——. 1936*b*. Review of MCGRAW'S *Growth: A study of Johnny and Jimmy. J. Educ. Res.,* November.

PRATT, K. C. 1937. The organization of behavior in the newborn infant. *Psychol. Rev.*, **44**, 470–490.

PRATT, K. C., A. K. NELSON, and K. H. SUN. 1930. The behavior of the newborn infant. *Ohio State Univ. Stud., Contr. Psychol.*, No. 10.

PREYER, W. 1882, 1888, 1889. *Die Seele des Kindes.* Leipzig: Fernau. (5th ed., 1900.) *The mind of the child:* Pt. 1. *The senses and the will;* Pt. 2. *The development of the intellect.* (Trans. by H. W. BROWN.) New York: Appleton. (Reprinted ed., 1901.)

RAY, W. S. 1932. A preliminary report on a study of fetal conditioning. *Child Develpm.*, **3**, 175–177.

RAZRAN, G. H. S. 1933. Conditioned responses in children. A behavioral and quantitative critical review of experimental studies. *Arch. Psychol., N. Y.*, **23**, No. 148.

REDFIELD, J. E. 1937. A preliminary report of dark adaptation in young infants. *Child Develpm.*, **8**, 263–269.

——. 1939. The light sense in newborn infants. *Univ. Iowa Stud. Child Welfare*, **16**, 107–145.

RENSHAW, S., and A. P. WEISS. 1926. Apparatus for measuring changes in bodily posture. *Amer. J. Psychol.*, **37**, 261–267.

REYNARD, M. C., and F. C. DOCKERAY. 1939. The comparison of temporal intervals in judging depth of sleep in newborn infants. *J. Genet. Psychol.*, **55**, 103–120.

RICHARDS, T. W. 1935. Gross metabolic changes characteristic of the activity of the neonate. *Child Develpm.*, **6**, 231–241.

——. 1936a. The relationship between bodily and gastric activity of newborn infants: I. Correlation and influence of time since feeding. *Human Biol.*, **8**, 368–380.

——. 1936b. The relationship between bodily and gastric activity of newborn infants: II. Simultaneous variations in the bodily and gastric activity of newborn infants under long-continued light stimulation. *Human Biol.*, **8**, 381–386.

——. 1936c. The importance of hunger in the bodily activity of the neonate. *Psychol. Bull.*, **33**, 817–835.

RICHARDS, T. W., and O. C. IRWIN. 1934a. Experimental methods used in studies on infant reactions since 1900. *Psychol. Bull.*, **31**, 23–46.

——. 1934b. Die Veränderung der Fuszsohlenreaktion bei Neugeborenen unter der Einwirken von Reizung und anderen Einflüssen. *Z. Kinderheilk.*, **57**, 16–20.

——. 1934c. Plantar responses of infants and young children: An examination of the literature and reports of new experiments. *Univ. Iowa Stud. Child Welfare*, **11**. Pp. 146.

——. 1936. The use of the clinical method in experimental studies of behavior. *J. Abnorm. Soc. Psychol.*, **30**, 455–461.

RICHTER, C. P. 1930. High electrical skin resistance of newborn infants and its significance. *Amer. J. Dis. Child.*, **40**, 18–26.

——. 1934. The grasp reflex of the newborn infant. *Amer. J. Dis. Child.*, **48**, 327–332.

RIPIN, R., and H. HETZER. 1930. Früheste Lernen des Säuglings in der Ernährungssituation. *Z. Psychol.*, **118**, 83–127.

ROBINSON, L. 1891. Darwinism in the nursery. *Nineteenth Cent.*, **30**, 831–842. (Cited by HALVERSON, 1937.)

ROMINGER, E., and H. MEYER. 1932. Klinisch-experimentelle Untersuchungen zur Kreislaufphysiologie im Kindesalter. *Mschr. Kinderheilk.*, **52**, 421–423.

ROTHE, H. 1929. Untersuchungen über die elektrische Erregbarkeit bei frühgeborenen Kindern. *Jb. Kinderheilk.*, **125**, 285–299.

RUNGE, M. 1895. Der erste Schrei und der erste Athemzug. *Berlin. klin. Wschr.*, **32**, 93–95.

SACHS, R. 1893. Beobachtungen über das physiologische Verhalten des Gehörorgans Neugeborener. *Arch. Ohrenheilk.*, **35**, 28–38.

SANFORD, H. N. 1931. The Moro reflex as a diagnostic aid in fracture of the clavicle in the newborn infant. *Amer. J. Dis. Child.*, **41**, 1304–1306.

SCHACHTER, M. 1932a. Les cris des nourrissons et des petits enfants. *Bull. méd.*, **46**, 637–642.

——. 1932b. Le comportement neuropsychique du nourrisson. *Rev. méd. de l'Est*, **60**, 808–819.

SCHALTENBRAND, G. 1925. Normale Bewegungs- und Lage-reaktionen bei Kindern. *Dtsch. Z. Nervenheilk.*, **87**, 23–59.

——. 1928. The development of human motility and motor disturbance. *Arch. Neurol. Psychiat., Chicago*, **20**, 720–730.

SCHLOSSMAN, A., and H. MURSCHHAUSER. 1933. Gasstoffwechseluntersuchungen bei Neugeborenen und Frühgeborenen. *Z. Kinderheilk.*, **54**, 301–316.

SCHMIDT, A. 1927. Über die Beziehungen des Saugreflexes zur Magentätigkeit. *Z. Kinderheilk.*, **45**, 19–27.

SCHMITT, A., and D. v. MÓRITZ. 1933. Magenfunktionsprüfungen bei Frühgeborenen. *Arch. Kinderheilk.*, **99**, 23–27.

SHEPARDSON, E. 1907. A preliminary critique of the doctrine of fundamental and accessory movements. *Ped. Sem.*, **14**, 101–116.

SHERMAN, M. 1927a. The differentiation of emotional responses in infants: I. Judgments of emotional response from motion-picture views and from actual observation. *J. Comp. Psychol.*, **7**, 265–284.

——. 1927b. The differentiation of emotional responses in infants: II. The ability of observers to judge the emotional characteristics of the crying of infants, and of the voice of the adult. *J. Comp. Psychol.*, **7**, 335–351.

SHERMAN, M., and I. C. SHERMAN. 1925. Sensori-motor responses in infants. *J. Comp. Psychol.*, **5**, 53–68.

SHERMAN, M., I. C. SHERMAN, and C. D. FLORY. 1936. Infant behavior. *Comp. Psychol. Monogr.*, **12**, No. 4.

SHINN, M. W. 1893–1899. Notes on the development of a child. *Univ. Calif. Publ.*, **1**. Pp. 424.

SHIRLEY, M. M. 1931a. The sequential method for the study of maturing behavior patterns. *Psychol. Rev.*, **38**, 507–528.

——. 1931b. *The first two years, a study of twenty-five babies: Vol. I. Postural and locomotor development.* (*Inst. Child Welfare Monogr. Ser.*, No. 6.) Minneapolis: University of Minnesota Press. Pp. vi + 227.

——. 1933a. *The first two years, a study of twenty-five babies: Vol. II. Intellectual development.* (*Inst. Child Welfare Monogr. Ser.*, No. 7.) Minneapolis: University of Minnesota Press. Pp. xvi + 513.

——. 1933b. *The first two years, a study of twenty-five babies: Vol. III. Personality manifestations.* (*Inst. Child Welfare Monogr. Ser.*, No. 8.) Minneapolis: University of Minnesota Press. Pp. xi + 228.

SICHERER, O. v. 1907. Ophthalmoskopische Untersuchung Neugeborener. *Dtsch. med. Wschr.*, **33**, 1564.

SIKORSKI, I. A. 1908. *Die seelische Entwicklung des Kindes.* (2d ed.) Leipzig. (As reported by PEIPER, 1928.)

SIMSARIAN, F. P., and P. A. McLENDON. 1942. Feeding behavior of an infant during the first twelve weeks of life on a self-demand schedule. *J. Pediat.*, **20**, 93–103; *Psychol. Abstr.*, No. 2521, **16**, 284.

SMITH, J. M. 1936. The relative brightness values of three hues for newborn infants. *Univ. Iowa Stud. Child Welfare*, **12**, No. 1, 91–140.

——. 1937. Reply to Peiper. *Child Develpm.*, **8**, 301–304.

SMITH, J. R. 1938a. The electroencephalogram during normal infancy and childhood: I. Rhythmic activities present in the neonate and their subsequent development. *J. Genet. Psychol.*, **53**, 431–453.

——. 1938b. The electroencephalogram during normal infancy and childhood: III. Preliminary observations on the pattern sequences during sleep. *J. Genet. Psychol.*, **53**, 471–482.

——. 1939. The "occipital" and "pre-central" alpha rhythms during the first two years. *J. Psychol.*, **7**, 223–226.

SOLTMANN, O. 1876. Experimentelle Studien über die Funktionen des Grosshirns der Neugeborenen. *Jb. Kinderheilk.*, **9**, 106.

——. 1878. Ueber einige physiologische Eigentümlichkeiten der Muskeln und Nerven des Neugeborenen. *Jb. Kinderheilk.*, **12**, 1–20. (Abstracted by PEIPER, 1928, and ECKSTEIN, 1927.)

SONOHARA, T. 1934a. Ueber den Einfluss der Saccharinreizungen auf die Leersaugbewegungen bei den Neugeborenen. Eine systematische psychologische Untersuchung von Neugeborenen. 1, 2. *Jap. J. Exp. Psychol.*, **1**, 1–18. (Abstract 1503, *Psychol. Abstr.*, 1935.)

——. 1934b. (Systematic studies on psychology of human neonates. [1, 3] Reactions to bitter stimuli.) *Jap. J. Exp. Psychol.*, **1**, 127–141. (Abstract 3798, *Psychol. Abstr.*, 1936.)

SONTAG, L. W., and R. F. WALLACE. 1934. Preliminary report of the Fels fund. *Amer. J. Dis. Child.*, **48**, 1050–1057.

——. 1935a. The effect of cigaret smoking during pregnancy upon the fetal heart rate. *Amer. J. Obstet. Gynec.*, **29**, 77–82.

——. 1935b. The movement response of the human fetus to sound stimuli. *Child Develpm.*, **6**, 253–258.

——. 1936. Changes in the rate of the human fetal heart in response to vibratory stimuli. *Amer. J. Dis. Child.*, **51**, 583–589.

STERN, W. 1914. *Psychologie der frühen Kindheit, bis zum sechsten Lebensjahre.* Leipzig: Quelle & Meyer. (4th ed., 1927.)

STIRNIMANN, F. 1933. *Das erste Erleben des Kindes.* Leipzig: Huber.

——. 1936a. Der Saugwulst der Neugeborenen. *Kinderärztl. Prax.*, **7**, 210–212.

——. 1936b. Versuche über Geschmack und Geruch am ersten Lebenstag. *Jb. Kinderheilk.*, **146**, 211–227.

——. 1936c. Le goût et l'odorat du nouveau-né. Une contribution à la connaissance des réactions du nouveau-né. *Rev. franç. pédiat.*, **12**, 453–485.

——. 1937a. Die Einstellreaktion beim Neugeborenen. *Jb. Kinderheilk.*, **149**, 326–329.

——. 1937b. Les réactions du nouveau-né contre l'enchaînement. *Rev. franç. pédiat.*, **13**, 496–502.

——. 1938. Das Kriech- und Schreitphänomen der Neugeborenen. *Schweiz. med. Wschr.*, **19**, 1374–1376.

——. 1939. Versuche über die Reaktionen Neugeborener auf Wärme- und Kältereize. *Z. Kinderpsychiat.*, **5**, 143–150.

——. 1940. *Psychologie des neugeborenen Kindes.* Zürich: Rascher.

STIRNIMANN, F., and W. STIRNIMANN. 1940. Der Fussgreifreflex bei Neugeborenen und Säuglingen. Seine diagnostische Verwendbarkeit. *Ann. Paediat.*, **154**, 249–264.

STRAUSS, H. 1929. Das Zusammenschrecken. *J. Psychol. Neurol., Lpz.*, **39**, 111–231. (Cited by LANDIS and HUNT, 1939.)

STUBBS, E. M. 1934. The effect of the factors of duration, intensity, and pitch of sound stimuli on the responses of newborn infants.

Univ. Iowa Stud. Child Welfare, 9, No. 4, pp. 75–135.

STUBBS, E. M., and O. C. IRWIN. 1933. Laterality of limb movements of four newborn infants. *Child Develpm.,* 4, 358–359.

——. 1934. A note on reaction times in infants. *Child Develpm.,* 5, 291–292.

TALBOT, F. B. 1917a. Physiology of the newborn infant. *Amer. J. Dis. Child.,* 13, 495–500.

——. 1917b. Twenty-four hour metabolism of two normal infants with special reference to the total energy requirements of infants. *Amer. J. Dis. Child.,* 14, 25–33.

TANNER, A. E. 1915. The new-born child. *Ped. Sem.,* 22, 487–501.

TAYLOR, J. H. 1934. Innate emotional responses in infants. *Ohio State Univ. Stud., Contrib. Psychol.,* No. 12, pp. 69–81.

TAYLOR, R. 1917. Hunger in the infant. *Amer. J. Dis. Child.,* 14, 233–257.

THOMPSON, J. 1903. On the lip reflex (mouth phenomenon) of new-born children. *Rev. Neurol. Psychiat.,* 1, 145–148.

TIEDEMANN, D. 1787. *Beobachtungen über die Entwicklung der Seelenfähigkeiten bei Kindern.* (First published in 1787.) Altenburg: Bonde, 1897. (See MURCHISON and LANGER, 1927.)

TILNEY, F., and L. CASAMAJOR. 1924. Myelinogeny as applied to the study of behavior. *Arch. Neurol. Psychiat. Chicago,* 12, 1–66.

VALENTINE, C. W. 1930. The innate bases of fear. *J. Genet. Psychol.,* 37, 394–420.

VALENTINE, W. L., and F. C. DOCKERAY. 1936. The experimental study of the newborn, 1926–36. *Educ. Res. Bull., Ohio State Univ.,* 15, 127–133.

VALENTINE, W. L., and I. WAGNER. 1934. Relative arm motility in the newborn infant. *Ohio State Univ. Stud.,* No. 12, 53–68.

VINAY, C. 1897. La psychologie du nouveau-né. *La semaine méd.,* 17, 33–36.

VORMITTAG, S. 1933. Untersuchungen über die Atmung des Kindes: I. Atemzahl und Atemform des gesunden Kindes. *Mschr. Kinderheilk.,* 58, 249–265.

VOSZ, O. 1923. Geburtstrauma und Gehörorgan. *Z. Hals- Nasen- u. Ohrenheilk.,* 6, 182–219.

WAGNER, I. F. 1937. The establishment of a criterion of depth of sleep in the newborn infant. *J. Genet. Psychol.,* 51, 17–59.

——. 1938a. The body jerk of the neonate. *J. Genet. Psychol.,* 52, 65–77.

WAGNER, I. F. 1938b. A note on the hiccough of the neonate. *J. Genet. Psychol.,* 52, 233–234.

——. 1938c. The sleeping posture of the neonate. *J. Genet. Psychol.,* 52, 235–239.

——. 1939. Curves of sleep depth in newborn infants. *J. Genet. Psychol.,* 55, 121–135.

WAGONER, L. C. 1924. A note on the grasping reflex. *Ped. Sem.,* 31, 333–336.

WALTAN, O. 1921. L'audizione nei neonati. *Il policlinico (sezione pratica),* 28, 1010–1011.

WATSON, J. B. 1919. *Psychology from the standpoint of a behaviorist.* Philadelphia: Lippincott.

WEISS, A. P. 1929. The measurement of infant behavior. *Psychol. Rev.,* 36, 453–471.

WEISS, L. A. 1934. Differential variations in the amount of activity of newborn infants under continuous light and sound stimulation. *Univ. Iowa Stud. Child Welfare,* 9, 1–74.

WENGER, M. A. 1936. An investigation of conditioned responses in human infants. *Univ. Iowa Stud. Child Welfare,* 12, 1–90.

WENGER, M. A., and O. C. IRWIN. 1935. Variations in electrical resistance of the skin in newborn infants. *Proc. Iowa Acad. Sci.,* 42, 167–168.

——. 1936. Fluctuations in skin resistance of infants and adults and their relation to muscular processes. *Univ. Iowa Stud. Child Welfare,* 12, 141–179.

WESTPHAL, A. 1894. Die elektrischen Erregbarkeitsverhältnisse des peripherischen Nervensystems des Menschen im jugendlichen Zustand und ihre Beziehungen zu dem anatomischen Bau. *Arch. Psychiat. Nervenkr.,* 26, 1–98. (Abstracted by PEIPER, 1928, and ECKSTEIN, 1927.)

WESTPHAL, C. 1886. Die elektrische Erregbarkeit der Nerven und Muskeln Neugeborener. *Neurol. Zentbl.,* 5, 361–363. (Abstracted by PEIPER, 1928.)

WICKENS, D. D., and C. WICKENS. 1940. A study of conditioning in the neonate. *J. Exp. Psychol.,* 26, 94–102.

WOLFF, L. V. 1930. The response to plantar stimulation in infancy. *Amer. J. Dis. Child.,* 39, 1176–1185.

WOLOWIK, A. B. 1927. Ueber die gegenseitige Wirkung der Schmerz und Nahrungsreflexe bei Kindern. *Jb. Kinderheilk.,* 115, 185–193.

ZAHARESCU-KARAMAN, N., and A. NASTASE. 1931. La crise génitale des nouveau-nés provoquée par l'hormone sexuelle ovarienne. *C. R. Soc. Biol., Paris,* 107, 396.

CHAPTER 5

PHYSICAL GROWTH

HELEN THOMPSON

There are important reasons why child psychology must be concerned with the physical changes which a child undergoes in his progress toward maturity. In the first place, it is through his physical self that a child receives his impressions. A toddler whose eyes are at the level of an adult's knees sees a far different world from that visioned by an adult; a child whose center of gravity is relatively low, other factors being equal, will have less difficulty in balance than one whose center of gravity is relatively high. The mechanics of picking up an inch cube presents a different problem to the tiny hand of the one-year-old from the one presented to the larger hand of the five-year-old. The fact that the brain at the age of four years has achieved about 80 per cent of its weight at maturity makes the feats of the child prodigy more understandable. The child psychologist, as an intelligent teacher, researcher, or clinician, must know the outstanding facts of physical growth at least to the extent that they pertain to behavior.

In the conduct of experimental studies in child psychology the problem of equating groups for the purposes of control is a highly important part of the experiment. Should one use chronological age, or anatomical age, or physiological age, or some composite of these? How can the ages be measured? What is the relationship between them? Is it necessary to equate for physical fitness? How can it be judged? And what is the consensus as to body type?

The relationships between physical and mental growth are not always apparent. It is possible that studies of mental and physical relationships have been largely negative because consideration has not been given to the truly significant traits. Interaction between the mental and the physical often occurs. The undersized child may be a malnourished child who is whiny and fretful. The whining and fretting are likely to be accompanied by personality and social percussions and repercussions, which, although they may not alter independent mental performance, may be of sufficient social handicap to destroy permanently the effectiveness or even the actual development of potential mentality. It may even be a fair prophecy that, in investigations of individual physical and mental life histories, studies of social behavior and personality may find their fullest realization in the genetic analysis of physical individuality.

Furthermore, the student of mental growth may learn much from a study of physical growth with respect to methods and techniques of study. It is comforting as well as instructive to know that behavior changes from age to age complicate even such an objective determination as height or length. The six-month-old infant cannot stand, whereas the two-year-old resists being placed supine and the three-year-old assumes distorted and fairly rigid postures in his effort to cooperate. To the student of physical growth these behavior changes are as important to cope with as the changes in physical growth are important to the student of child psychology. Techniques in the one field are suggestive of possible techniques in the other field of study. To secure measures of size comparable from one age to another it is frequently necessary to take two measurements, using the two methods adapted to the younger and older child. Allowance for the change in method can then be made. A similar scheme may be employed to advantage in studies of behavior growth.

Growth is the most pervasive problem of child psychology. It is by envisaging mental growth in relation to the laws of growth in other fields that knowledge can be systematized and generalized. One example of this is the law of cephalocaudal development, noted first in physical growth, and later studied and confirmed in relation to behavior development.

The Literature

The literature on the subject of physical growth is vast. In 1927 the Children's Bureau of the United States Department of Labor compiled an annotated list of references on the *Physical Growth and Development of the Normal Child*. It contained 2567 citations, which represented a selection from "approximately 10,000 books and articles" available up to July 1, 1926. Only articles reporting original research were annotated. Between July, 1926, and August, 1938, there were over 700 publications on physical growth from the United States and Canada alone.

Publications on physical growth are discovered in obscure references frequently not covered by the usual bibliographic abstracts. Scammon (1927b) found that the most complete bibliographic source listed less than 50 per cent of the references for the years 1910 through 1912. The reason for the wide scattering of the literature is the variety of professional and business interests in the subject. From a purely scientific point of view it is the anatomist, the physical anthropologist, the biometrician, and the psychologist who are led to research in the field of physical growth, but obstetricians, pediatricians, dentists, educators, public health officials, life insurance companies, criminologists, eugenicists, and clinical child psychologists all contribute to our knowledge of the subject.

Fortunately the literature through 1926 has been most adequately summarized. Particularly useful are the summaries of Baldwin (1921), Children's Bureau (1927), Scammon (1927a, 1927b), Martin (1928), and Meredith (1936a). Since 1926 the American literature on growth from birth to maturity has been systematically reviewed by Brooks (1933), Dawson and Stoddard (1933), Jones (1933, 1936, 1939), Meredith and Stoddard (1936), and Meredith (1939a, 1939b). Krogman's recent extensive bibliography (1941b) includes foreign publications. *Child Development Abstracts,* begun in 1927, and *Biological Abstracts,* begun in 1926, now remedy the condition deplored by Scammon in 1927.

In view of the scope of physical growth, a comprehensive summary of the literature cannot be given in the following pages. Instead, references will be selected on the basis of their importance to the child psychologist. Recent studies will be emphasized. No attempt at comprehensiveness and inclusiveness will be made. The subject is too extensive.

Historical Summary

Although the first interest in mental development arose in relation to education, the first interest in bodily growth was the concern of the artist. The practical problem of realistically portraying the child led artists to study size and proportion in relation to age. In that early era, beauty values were considered in the absolute sense, and the artist searched for the perfect proportions of youth (Baldwin, 1921). Prior to 1799, measuring instruments in different centers of learning varied considerably in calibration, as a visit to any museum of physical science will demonstrate. The standard meter bar, constructed in 1799, gradually introduced uniformity. Its construction reflected a deep interest in measurement and served to stimulate further measurement. The human body was a natural subject. Quetelet (1871) was the first to systematize the study of physical growth. He is credited with originating the word *anthropometry*. His figures on body dimensions from birth to maturity are still quoted. Shortly before 1760 there were scientific studies of the weight and physical proportions of the newborn, but it was not until 1779 that the first seriatim study of physical growth was published (Buffon, 1837). This preceded Tiedemann's publication on mental development by only eight years (Murchison and Langer, 1927).

It was practically one hundred years later (Hall, 1896) that physical and mental growth were studied simultaneously, and even then the data were uncorrelated. In the last decade of the nineteenth century and the first decade of the twentieth century, however, there was general interest among psychologists in the relationship between mental and physical traits. Binet (1900, 1910) was concerned with head and face measurements. He attempted to find in them an index of mentality. His failure to establish a close relationship was followed by similar results from the laboratories in London. In this country Porter (1893), Gilbert (1895, 1897), and others were concerned with the relationship between mental and physical traits. Dull children tended to be smaller for their age; bright children tended to be larger. Crampton (1908), studying boys at adolescence, concluded that boys who matured early were better scholars. Goddard (1912), Binet and Simon (1914), and Doll (1916) were among those who studied the physical growth of the feeble-minded and found them physically inferior to the normal. Baldwin in 1921 stated:

> Another experimental study just completed shows that the mental age of the individual bears a direct relationship to the physiological age as indicated by height and weight. The results show that at each chronological age the physiologically accelerated boys and girls have a higher mental age than those of the average or below the average physiological age (pp. 196–197).

His results were typical of others.

It was generally conceded that physical defects were likely to be associated with mental defects and physical acceleration and well-being associated with accelerated mental growth. Nevertheless, the correlation of mental and physical traits was found to be small, and general interest in the relationship waned. Clinical psychologists routinely noted height and weight but made little use of the data. Researchers in child psychology, to a large extent, lost interest in physical correlates. Two notable exceptions to this generalization are of course the Harvard Growth Study by Dearborn and the Iowa Child Welfare Research Station studies initiated by Baldwin.

Interest in physical development was revived in the middle 1920's with the advent of the various research centers for child development. The whole child, physical, mental, and emotional, as well as his environment and nutrition, became the subject for investigation (Krogman, 1940).

Data thus accumulated have by no means been completely studied and published. It will probably be many years yet before the fruits of these researches are realized. It can be safely predicted, however, that if and when such studies are completed the subtle reciprocal influence of mental and physical growth will be greatly illuminated and students of child psychology will find their subject matter greatly increased and their professional scope greatly broadened. In the meantime, it behooves the child psychologist to recognize the facts of physical development in so far as they are known.

Techniques of Measurement

Physical anthropometry is the science particularly concerned with the techniques and instruments for the study of physical growth. Measuring, weighing, and comparing with standard scales might seem at first thought to be routine, mechanical procedures which anyone with general scientific training might easily perform. The problem is not so simple as that, however, if the collected data are to have value. For instance, Meredith and Goodman (1941) have shown that routine hospital records of length at birth are seriously unreliable when compared with records made by trained anthropometrists. Also, landmarks should be selected with reference to possible interpretation of the data. The value of data is greatly enhanced if they conform with existing correlated data. Measurements with greater probable error than the growth increment to be measured are valueless. Meredith (1936b) and Knott (1941) show that in studying growth it is futile to make all measurements with equal frequency. Instead, time of remeasurement should depend on the magnitude of the growth increment and its measured reliability.

The personal error of the novice in anthropometry is great. Even among trained workers there is marked individual variation. Lincoln (1930) concludes: "It is apparent that when exact anthropometric measurements on individuals are desired, they must be obtained by methods which include the most careful checking" (p. 450).

The human body is surprisingly elastic and plastic. Boyd (1929) notes:

In spite of common agreement in technique and practice, the human body cannot be measured with a high degree of precision; that height is more reliable than other dimensions; that the living is measured with less precision than the dead; that the degree of precision is different for different dimensions and for different measurements of the same dimension; and that daily physiological linear reduction affects both stature and body stem. . . . [She notes further that error results from] the inaccuracy of the examiner, his instruments and methods; the character of the endpoints of a given measurement; the amount of physiological linear reduction; and the degree to which the child's attitude affects the prescribed position (p. 396).

Davenport (1937) and Baum and Vickers (1941) give further specific discussion of sources of error in anthropometric work with children.

Maresch and Deming (1939) have reported studies which show that roentgenographic rather than anthropometric methods are to be favored for measuring long bones, whereas Francis (1939) found no evidence that in measuring the tibia roentgenography was superior to anthropometry. Obviously, each method has its sources of error. Stuart, Hill, and Shaw (1940), however, have had considerable success in studying the growth of bone, muscle, and overlying tissue of the leg by means of roentgenograms. Direct measurements of tissue thickness have been shown to be the least reliable of twenty-eight dimensions (Knott, 1941).

An appropriate selection of the following references should be consulted *prior* to initiating a study of physical growth.

Fetal period
  Schultz (1929); Scammon and Calkins (1929).
General techniques
  Baldwin (1921); Davenport (1927); Sullivan (1928); Martin (1928); Franzen (1929); McCloy (1936, 1938); Hrdlička (1939).
Infancy and early childhood
  Baldwin (1921); Thompson (1929); Bakwin and Bakwin (1931a); Davenport (1937, 1938); Gesell and Thompson (1938); Baum and Vickers (1941).
Skin and subcutaneous fat
  Franzen (1929); McCloy (1938).
Bone, muscle, and overlying tissue by roentgenography
  Stuart, Hill, and Shaw (1940).
Surface area
  Boyd (1935).
Hair
  Trotter (1939).
Palm and fingerprints
  Wilder and Wentworth (1918).

Norms of Physical Growth

In recent years there has been confusion about the value and purpose of norms. Norms are not criteria for optimal growth. They are statistics for basic comparisons. They are mathematical devices to avoid the error of generalization from isolated cases. They are conclusions of scientific surveys and as such they are indispensable scientific data which should be groundwork for the systematization and analysis of other data. Norms may be used as control group data. By comparing experimental data, individual or group, with the norms, conclusions can be reached which will be valid to the extent that the norms and the experimental data have

common attributes, except with respect to the variable in question.

Obviously, comparison with norms is valid only when similar techniques have been used in measurement. Theoretically this is so obvious that to mention it seems unnecessary. Practically, however, even psychologists trained in the importance of scientific control will use their own measurement techniques and then search through the literature for comparative norms, using the first figures they find which are measures of the dimension they have taken, forgetting entirely that techniques of measurement may make the comparisons completely invalid.

The more heterogeneous the composition of the group with respect to traits related to the normative trait, the greater will be the number of cases necessary to determine the norm, and the greater will be the variability of the trait as measured. The more highly selective the group on which norms are based, the more precise will be their scientific usefulness. We know that, for physical growth norms, it is generally important to consider race, sex, and locale. Socioeconomic status is important but not always easy to define. Individuals obviously atypical should be excluded. Factors which are operating at particular ages must be considered. The inclusion of premature children in a normative study of infancy will shift all values downward.

It was noted above that norms are not criteria for optimal growth. It should be noted also that what is normal for one individual is not normal for another. It is valid to compare an individual with the normal in order to analyze his particular growth pattern, but interpretation of any divergence must recognize individual growth differences. Appraisal of individual growth is most helpful in terms of past growth. A dwarf whose increment in stature is normal for a given period is growing relatively very rapidly considering his growth tempo in the past.

Norms of growth may be in terms of the central tendency and variability of groups, at regularly spaced chronological or other maturity age intervals, or in terms of the statistics of individual growth increments at these ages. Instead of using chronological age as a basis, Boas (1930) and Shuttleworth (1937, 1939) particularly give reasons for evaluating growth according to age at the time of maximum growth. Although this procedure may be highly desirable in the analysis of growth data, it cannot be applied practically at the time of measurement. The same comment applies to appraising growth in terms of size at maturity. It is possible to evaluate growth in terms of some maturity age measurable at the time, such as skeletal age or dental age, but the probable error of these ages is large compared with the probable error of birth age, even considering the variability of conception age at birth. The use of norms, on any basis, must be tempered with the understanding and judgment required of all interpretive analysis.

It is not practical to give tables of growth norms in this handbook. A few selected norms would tend to emphasize their use when other growth data might be more pertinent. The following list of references will direct the researcher to the more outstanding source material.

NORMS: SELECTED REFERENCES

Body Growth

Fetal period
Streeter (1920); Schultz (1926); Scammon and Calkins (1929).

Neonatal period
Taylor (1919); Freeman and Platt (1932); Bakwin and Bakwin (1934a, 1934b); Hess, Mohr, and Bartelme (1934); Meredith and Brown (1939).

Infancy and early childhood
Woodbury (1921); Freeman (1933); Bayley and Davis (1935); Bayley (1936): Bakwin and Bakwin (1936); Gesell and Thompson (1938); Peatman and Higgons (1938); Davenport (1938); Boyd (1941); Robinow (1942).

Infancy and late childhood
Freeman (1933); Simmons and Todd (1938); Vickers and Stuart (1943).

Infancy to maturity
Bardeen (1920); Baldwin (1921); Baldwin, Wood, and Woodbury (1923); Englebach (1932); White House Conference (1933); Meredith (1935); Boynton (1936); McCloy (1938); Pryor (1941).

Childhood
Johnson (1925); Wilson, Sweeny, Stutsman, *et al.* (1930); Wallis (1931).

School age to maturity
Baldwin (1925); Franzen (1929); Gray and Ayres (1931); Palmer and Reed (1935); Goldstein (1936); Palmer, Riiti, and Reed (1937); Dearborn, Rothney, and Shuttleworth (1938).

Adolescence
Pryor (1936); Richey (1937); Shuttleworth (1937, 1938, 1939); Stone and Barker (1937); Greulich, Day, Lachman, *et al.* (1938); Greulich, Dorfman, Catchpole, *et al.* (1942).

Head and Face Growth

Wallis (1931); Bakwin and Bakwin (1931a, 1936); Fleming (1933); Bayley (1936); Boynton (1936); Goldstein (1936, 1939); Broadbent (1937); Klein, Palmer, and Kramer (1937); McCloy (1938); Davenport (1940).

Dentition

Boas (1927); Cattell (1928); Hellman (1933); Klein, Palmer, and Kramer (1937); Klein, Palmer, and Knutson (1938).

Skeletal Development

Graves (1921); Stevenson (1924); Pryor (1925); Baldwin, Busby, and Garside (1928); Sawtell (1929); Camp and Cilley

(1931); Hodges (1933); Flory (1936); Kelly (1937); Todd (1937); Shuttleworth (1938); Francis and Werle (1939); Hill (1939); Sontag, Snell, and Anderson (1939).

Miscellaneous

Surface area

Boyd (1935); since measurement of surface area is so difficult, formulae have been developed for its estimation—Weinbach (1938).

Vital capacity

Baldwin (1928); McCloy (1938).

Racial differences

Weissenberg (1911); Shirokogoroff (1925); Appleton (1927); Godin (1935); Martin (1928); Wissler (1930); Fleming (1933); Steggerda and Densen (1936); Meredith (1939*a*); Krogman (1941*a*).

Weight (nutrition)

Baldwin, Wood, and Woodbury (1923); Pryor and Stolz (1933); Franzen and Palmer (1934); Royster (1936); Richey (1937); Daniels, Hutton, and Neil (1938); Dearborn and Rothney (1938); McCloy (1938); Peatman and Higgons (1938); Metheny (1939); Stuart, Hill, and Shaw (1940); Pryor (1941); Wetzel (1941); Stuart and Dwinell (1942).

Growth Trends

The physical growth of the child to be fully appreciated must be considered in relation to growth in general, but that subject would lead us too far astray. Robertson (1923), Davenport (1926*b*, 1934), Pearl (1928), Robbins, Brody, Hogan, *et al.* (1928), Huxley (1932), Courtis (1932, 1937), the Cold Spring Harbor *Symposium on Quantitative Biology* (1934, Vol. II), and Hammett (1936) are among the best sources treating the subject of growth comprehensively and from a theoretical point of view. The search for a theoretical curve of growth generally applicable over any but a relatively short period has not been fruitful (Davenport, 1926*a*, 1926*b*,

1934, 1938; Davenport and Drager, 1936). There are, however, certain mathematical equations which, for certain periods of growth or for general growth trends, are fair approximations, such as the autocatalytic curve suggested by Robertson (1923), the Gompertz curve recommended by Courtis (1932), the exponential curve of Huxley (1932), and the more complicated exponential curve of Jenss and Bayley (1937).

The body does not grow as a whole and in all directions at once. Each part must be considered separately. In general, embryonic and fetal growth proceed cephalocaudally and proximodistally. That is, with few exceptions, head development precedes neck development, neck development precedes chest growth, chest growth precedes pelvic growth, and arm growth precedes leg growth; also upper-arm growth precedes lower-arm growth, which in turn precedes hand growth; and likewise for the lower extremities. Jackson (1914, 1928), who was the first to formulate this law with respect to human growth, concisely describes human morphogenesis from its initial differentiation to the adult body. The changes are pictured in Figure 1. Schultz (1926) and Scammon and Calkins (1929) have investigated the changes in body dimensions for the fetal period, that is, from about two months after conception to birth. Both authors note that during this period of growth the changes in bodily dimensions are proportional to the changes in total fetal length. In other words, although there is considerable change in body form during this period, the changes are those initiated in embryonic rather than in fetal life.

The complicated transformations occurring in prenatal life are simply and skillfully described by Gilbert (1938). She ends by describing the anomalies of development as misfortunes of growth at a critical stage. An analogy between physical and behavior growth processes suggests itself to the psychologist.

Racial characteristics appear even in fetal life. Schultz (1926) found distinct racial characteristics in the five-month-old fetus when he compared the white and type, followed by the body as a whole, external dimensions excepting head and neck, respiratory and digestive organs, kidneys, aorta and pulmonary trunks, spleen, musculature as a whole, and skeleton as a whole; and (4) the *genital type*, characteristic of testes, ovaries, epididymis, uterine tubes, prostatic urethra, and seminal ves-

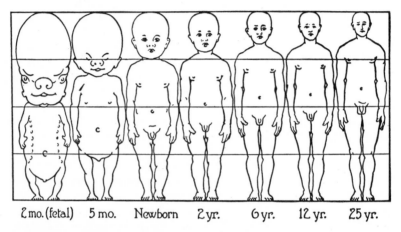

2 mo. (fetal)   5 mo.   Newborn   2 yr.   6 yr.   12 yr.   25 yr.

FIGURE 1. Changes in form and proportion of the human body during fetal and postnatal life. (From "Some Aspects of Form and Growth," by C. M. Jackson. In *Growth*, by W. J. Robbins, S. Brody, A. G. Hogan, C. M. Jackson, and C. W. Green. New Haven: Yale University Press, 1928, 118.)

Negro specimens, but he noted no racial distinction in the fetus which was not present in adults of the same race; and, furthermore, the racial distinctions were found to increase rather than diminish with age.

Scammon (1930) has shown that in prenatal life the various parts of the body follow a similar growth trend, but after birth their course diverges (see Figure 2). He has grouped the various growth trends under four types: (1) the *lymphoid type*, which includes the thymus, lymph nodes, and intestinal lymphoid masses; (2) the *neural type*, that is, the brain and its parts, the dura, spinal cord, optic apparatus, and many head dimensions; (3) the *general* icles. Nature, however, is never as invariable as man-conceived laws, and Scammon notes divergences from the four types, such as neck circumference, which follows the neural growth curve through early childhood and then follows the curve for general body growth. The suprarenals are even more irregular and atypical. After birth they rapidly diminish in size and then grow slowly until prior to puberty, when they increase relatively rapidly. Other glands have their characteristic curves.

It is the consensus that postnatal growth changes are brought about by a multitude of determining factors, the understanding of which requires carefully controlled and analyzed studies.

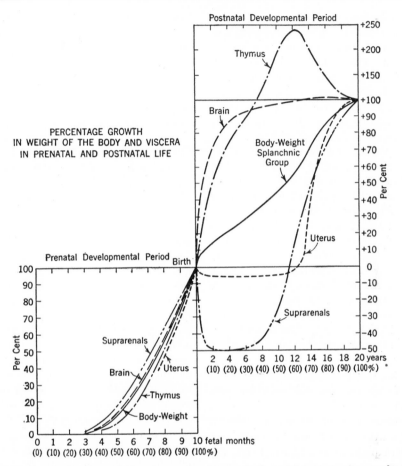

FIGURE 2. Graph showing relative (percentage) growth in weight of the human body and viscera during fetal and postnatal life. (From "Some Aspects of Form and Growth," by C. M. Jackson. In *Growth*, by W. J. Robbins, S. Brody, A. G. Hogan, C. M. Jackson, and C. W. Green. New Haven: Yale University Press, 1928, 132.)

The horizontal base line (abscissa) indicates age; vertical distance (ordinate) indicates the percentage of the weight at the end of the period, prenatal or postnatal, which has been reached at the corresponding age. (Graph by R. E. Scammon.)

Recently, several investigators have used factor analysis techniques to study the underlying principles of growth. Carter and Krause (1936), analyzing the data of Bakwin and Bakwin (1934a) on newborns, find that, although all body measures show some correlation, "no two parts are highly intercorrelated" and "no single factor can account for a major part of the measured variance when widely different parts of human bodies are measured." They also find that "anthropometric data show greater complexity, lesser importance of each component, greater number of components, and greater specificity" than when mental test data are similarly analyzed. Since data from males and females separately yield these conclusions, the statistics do not result from unreliability of measurements.

Marshall (1936) has used this method to study the growth factors of 18 measurements for the age period from birth to 6 years. He has found four group factors and a number of specific factors. One group factor is identified with subcutaneous fatty tissue, but the other three group factors are not identified in biological terms.

Mullen (1940), using Holzinger's method of factor analysis which assumes a general factor plus group factors, studied data on girls between 7 and 17 years old. She identified a general size factor related to sexual maturation and two group factors. One factor was concerned with height, span, length of forearm, and lower-leg length. The other factor related to weight, bi-iliac and bi-trochanteric diameters, chest girth, width, and depth. These two factors were considered significant with respect to body type.

McCloy (1940), using Thurstone's method of factor analysis, and analyzing data on both sexes from birth to maturity, found four subdivisions of Scammon's general body growth: (1) fat growth which may be superimposed on any type of build; (2) general growth seen in the tall, long-limbed, excessively slender; (3) cross-section type seen in short, very stocky, broad-headed, short-limbed, lateral, or pyknic build; and (4) "Type IV," not definitely identified but most prominent in chest measurement and shoulder width. He concludes: "This would seem to leave us with at least seven types of growth instead of four" (as shown by Scammon).

The Newborn

Usually birth occurs between 270 and 290 days after the beginning of the last menstrual period prior to conception. If birth takes place earlier, the child is considered prematurely born; if later, postmaturely born. When, as frequently happens, the menstrual history indicates irregularity, or when birth weight is less than 5 pounds, an estimation of the length of term is based on clinical evaluation. Measurements of the body help in this determination; total length gives an approximation. Cates and Goodwin (1936) note that total length is a better criterion of maturity than chronological age even in full-term infants. Table 1, adapted from Kjölseth (1913), gives the average body weight, length, and head circumference according to pregnancy duration. Scammon (1922) finds that the "growth tendency of prematures is in general that of fetuses of the same size and age rather than of full-term children." This finding emphasizes ontogenetic age.

It is a well-established fact that the full-term male infant is larger in all body measurements and weighs more than the full-term female infant. The closest approximation of the sexes is in pelvic width. Cates and Goodwin (1936) report that the weight of the male exceeds the weight of the female by 4 per cent and that the height of the male exceeds the height of the female by 2 per cent. Bakwin and Bakwin (1934b) find that newborns from a poverty-stricken environment are smaller in all dimensions measured than newborns from a more favorable environment, but that the infants from different environments are similarly proportioned. The sex difference finding is consistent with the conclusions of both Schultz (1926) and Scammon and Calkins (1929), who report no sex differences when fetuses are compared in relation to total length rather than age.

Although there are racial differences in birth weight, seasonal variation in temperature has not been found to influence it (Brenton, 1922). Meredith and Brown (1939) have reviewed the literature on the

TABLE 1 *

SIZE OF FETUS OR NEWBORN IN TERMS OF PREGNANCY DURATION

Number of Cases	Pregnancy Duration (Weeks)	Body Weight (Grams)		Total Length (Centimeters)		Head Girth (Centimeters)	
		Males	Females	Males	Females	Males	Females
4	28–29	1255.00	2020.00	38.50	43.25	27.00	31.25
5	30–31	1690.00	1630.00	42.17	40.50	30.00	29.25
11	32–33	2178.63	1906.67	44.88	42.00	31.79	30.00
23	34–35	2477.80	2308.46	46.35	45.96	32.89	31.95
22	36	2837.69	2778.89	48.42	47.28	34.29	33.38
28	37	3146.47	3097.27	49.44	48.41	34.41	34.00
77	38	3201.66	3064.44	49.82	49.21	34.86	34.53
124	39	3445.54	3191.19	50.79	49.38	35.44	34.57
180	40	3477.13	3413.95	50.84	50.40	35.63	35.13
	Full term (days)						
239	284–299	3601.25	3482.81	52.45	50.89	35.82	35.42
52	over 300	3927.86	3513.60	52.84	50.90	36.65	35.47

* Adapted from Kjölseth (1913).

effect of various factors on birth weight and weight gain during the first ten days of postnatal life and present further data from Iowa. They conclude that throughout the period "mean weight is least for first borns, intermediate for infants of second to fourth birth order, and greatest for infants of fifth and higher birth order." They, like Brenton, report no seasonal differences.

Postnatal Growth

The three composite measures of body growth commonly studied are weight, a three-dimensional measure; surface area, a two-dimensional measure; and height, a linear measure. Scammon (1930) notes that these three functions have the same growth trend except that the curve for surface area has less accentuated inflection points than the curve for weight, and more points than the curve for length (see Figure 3). The general growth trend of the body as pictured by these curves is characterized by rapid increase in infancy, a slowing-down followed by steady increase in childhood, an increased growth rate beginning between eight and ten years and continuing to adolescence, followed by a fairly abrupt tapering-off of growth to maturity.

There is a characteristic sex difference in attaining maturity. Girls are generally more mature than boys of the same age. In early childhood, although girls are more mature, they are smaller. The preadolescent spurt starts earlier in girls than in boys, and, owing to this earlier spurt in growth, the girls temporarily surpass the boys in total size. But the girls' growth spurt is less intense and lasts for a shorter period than the boys' adolescent spurt.

Finally, at maturity there is a greater discrepancy in measurements than existed earlier. The characteristic difference is exemplified by the height curve pictured in Figure 4.

follows a relatively rapid growth of the trunk. Growth in trunk girth continues longer than growth in length. In females, from puberty to maturity, the trunk elongates in the lumbar region and the pelvis

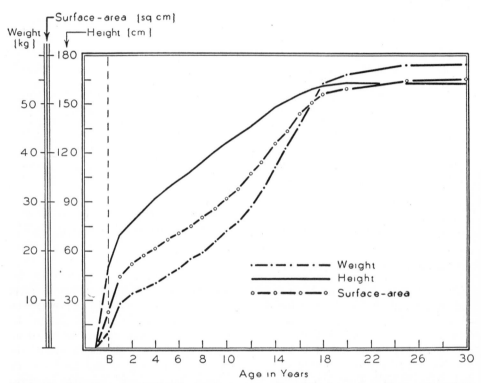

FIGURE 3. Growth curves for height, surface area, and weight drawn according to Quetelet's figures. (Given by E. Boyd in "Growth of the Surface Area of the Human Body," *Institute of Child Welfare Monographs.* Minneapolis: University of Minnesota Press, 1935, No. 10, 114.)

The changes in body proportions from birth to maturity are summarized in Section I of the White House Conference publication (1932). It is noted there that, although growth in the first half year after birth is rapid, changes in body proportion are relatively slight. From then to puberty head growth is slow, limb growth rapid, and trunk growth intermediate. In males, from puberty to maturity, growth of the trunk and limbs is at first equal, then there

enlarges while the lower extremities cease to grow in proportion to the trunk. As noted previously, growth in stature ceases earlier in girls and their increase in trunk width, except in the pelvic region, is less marked during the later part of adolescence.

Other sex differences have been noted: Boynton (1936), comparing her study on girls with that of Meredith's on boys (1935), finds that boys are larger than girls in thoracic circumference and girth of fore-arm throughout the growth years; that girls have a larger thigh than boys from 3 stature, boys exceed girls in girth of fore-arm and bicondylar diameter of left hu-merus from 11 to 18 years, whereas at this

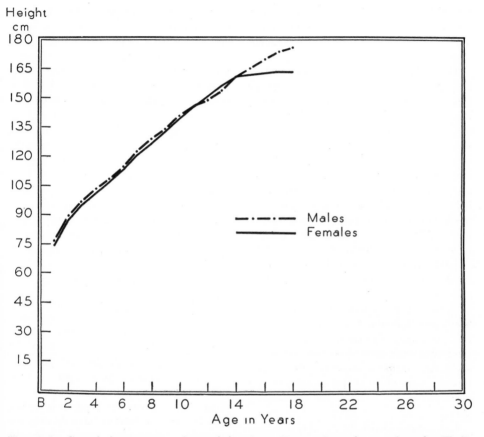

FIGURE 4. Growth in stature, males and females. (Drawn from figures given by H. V. Meredith in "The Rhythm of Physical Growth: A Study of Eighteen Anthropometric Measurements on Iowa City White Males Ranging in Age between Birth and Eighteen Years," *University of Iowa Studies in Child Welfare,* 1935, **11,** 44, and B. Boynton in "The Physical Growth of Girls: A Study of the Rhythm of Physical Growth from Anthropometric Measurements on Girls between Birth and Eighteen Years," *University of Iowa Studies in Child Welfare,* 1936, **12, 12.)**

to 18 years; that subcutaneous tissue measurements show a similar pattern for the sexes below 6 years, but from 13 to 18 years girls show a steady increase in this measurement, whereas this same measure-ment for boys decreases; that, relative to time girls surpass boys in growth of thigh; and that the bicondylar diameter of the left femur is larger in boys from 11 to 15 years, and larger in girls from 16 to 18 years. Relatively longer leg length of fe-males, noted by Bardeen (1920), has been found in childhood (Wallis, 1931) and even in infancy (Thompson, 1938).

The relatively longer leg length of the females may be ascribed to their greater maturity. Wallis (1931) also finds more mature proportions of the female between 2 and 8 years with respect to hand-radius, trunk-arm, and arm-leg indices.

The male child not only is less mature and grows more rapidly than the female child of the same age, but also his chances for survival are less. In fetal life the ratio of male to female abortions in the third to the fifth month is from 1.07 to 1.22. According to Schultz (1921), Greulich (1931), and Holmes and Mentzer (1931), the ratio starts at a fairly high point, declines to between the sixth and seventh month of pregnancy, and then rises to the period of birth. Bakwin (1929) gives the mortality ratio at birth as between 1.30 and 1.40. On the third day after birth the ratio reaches its peak, between 1.45 and 1.50, and then declines sharply to a low point of 1.20 to 1.30 between 2 and 3 weeks; rises again between 1 and 2 months and then gradually decreases with age until the fourth year, when it is near unity. A slight rise occurs in the fifth year. After this the ratio may fall below unity in the teens and in the most active childbearing period.

The findings of Schultz (1921), who concludes that 1.08 to 1.09 males are conceived for every female, would not account for the greater disparity in mortality. Bakwin (1929) points out that there are seasonal and regional differences in the mortality sex ratio which suggest that the ratio depends on the amount of sunlight reaching the infant and that the male has greater need for this sunlight since he is growing faster and his calcium-regulatory mechanism is highly taxed.

These sex differences in growth are particularly important for the child psychol-ogist. Since the differences in physical growth are pervasive, any well-controlled study must recognize and appraise a possible sex factor.

No seasonal influence has been found on growth in height, but the majority of investigators have found seasonal changes in postnatal body weight growth (Marshall, 1937). Summer and autumn are most conducive to weight gain for the preschool child; school children, likewise, have been shown to gain weight most rapidly in the fall, less rapidly in the summer, and least rapidly in the winter and spring months. The seasonal changes in weight growth have not been found to be related to food, colds, or minor illnesses. Since seasonal growth changes are confined to body weight, perhaps they reflect merely a seasonal difference in the water content of the body rather than a true growth trend.

Infancy

The rapidity of growth in infancy makes that period a particularly significant and important one. Bakwin and Bakwin (1931b) reported a general tendency for dimensional growth in the first postnatal year to progress in proportion to total length as in prenatal life. Nevertheless, when infant growth is studied in detail, modifications in relative growth rate are apparent. Davenport (1938) finds the curve for neck and thigh growth to be highly aberrant and the shoulder and thoracic index changes to indicate special growth adaptations in infancy. Thompson (1938) reports that between 8 and 56 weeks of age the head and thorax circumferences show a gradually decreasing relative growth rate and lower limb length shows a definitely increasing relative growth rate.

Between birth and 3 years, Bayley and Davis (1935) note that the growth rate in all dimensions is decreasing; the decrease is more rapid at first and then occurs more slowly. They also report that, during the first year, growth ratios show a proportionately increasing width. Thompson (1938) notes that the soles-pubes length relative to total length reaches a critical minimum sometime after birth, but prior to 8 weeks, and thereafter increases rapidly. This finding is in accord with that of Meredith and Knott (1938) with respect to the skelic index, or the ratio of lower limb to stem length. The ratio between lower limb length and total length is an important one because it differentiates the sexes. The females, relatively more mature than the males, have relatively longer lower limbs even as early as 8 weeks.

Cephalic and facial changes in infancy are discussed in the section devoted to face and head growth.

Ponderal growth in infancy follows the general course of growth. Pediatricians rely heavily and probably too exclusively on weight gain as evidence of adequate nutrition. Weight, however, is a sensitive indication of nutrition. Bakwin and Bakwin (1931b) report that infants from poor homes weigh less and are shorter in stature than infants from good homes and that the retardation in bodily dimensions accompanying retardation in weight is greater for the transverse than for the vertical dimensions. They also report (1936) that supervision of a group of infants from poor homes in a pediatric clinic raised the height and weight of these infants to that of the normal group and likewise changed the relative proportions from relative "linearity" to the normal of the control group.

Although male infants are larger than female infants of the same age (Bakwin and Bakwin, 1931b; Bayley and Davis, 1935; Thompson, 1938; Peatman and Higgons,

1938; and others) and although the growth increment tends to be larger for the male infant, the percentage rate of growth does not in general differ significantly in the two sexes (Thompson, 1938). Dunham, Jenss, and Christie (1939) emphasize the importance of considering both sex and race in studying the growth of infants. Colored infants have long been known to be smaller and to weigh less than white infants (Children's Bureau, 1927; and others). Dodge (1927) finds the growth of colored infants definitely slower than the growth of white infants and concludes that the difference is probably due to race rather than to any other factor. He also emphasizes the use of separate norms for colored infants and children.

Childhood

During childhood, height and weight progress at a fairly uniform rate (Wallis, 1931). Rate of weight gain is nearly twice the rate of height gain. The lower limbs grow rapidly in proportion to the stem length (Meredith and Knott, 1938). Neither shoulder breadth nor pelvic breadth is increasing as rapidly as trunk length, but the pelvis is broadening more rapidly than the shoulders. The total configurational change is a longer-legged, longer-bodied, and more rectilinear and flatter-bodied child.

Sex difference with respect to skelic index, that is, the ratio between lower extremities and stem lengths, disappears between 5 and 6 years and reappears at 7 years. Females then have the relatively longer legs, despite the fact that they are shorter. This difference continues through the ninth year (Meredith and Knott, 1938).

Other sex differences during childhood have been noted on previous pages.

Adolescence

Recently, adolescence, the second period of rapid postnatal growth, has received special attention. Greulich, Day, Lachman, *et al.* (1938) have made a well-rounded survey of the methods for studying physical, mental, and social adolescent growth. Shuttleworth (1937, 1939), Greulich, Dorfman, Catchpole, *et al.* (1942), Bayley (1943*a*, 1943*b*), and Simmons and Greulich (1943) have made special studies of the body and skeletal changes occurring at this period. The period is a truly metamorphic one, as shown by the actual growth curve (Davenport, 1926*b*) and by the marked body changes which complete the differentiation of the sexes.

Girls enter the period of acceleration in height growth, on the average, at about 9 years of age, about two years earlier than boys (Boynton, 1936). Girls reach the maximum phase of growth at an average age of about 12.5 years, boys at about 14.8 years (Shuttleworth, 1939). Puberty is demarcated in girls by the menarche and in boys by active spermatozoa which may be found in the morning urine. Puberty is closely related to the age of maximum growth (Shuttleworth, 1939; Simmons and Greulich, 1943). The maximum increase in standing height never occurs after the menarche, and the interval between the time of maximum growth increment and the menarche is greater in late-maturing girls than in those who mature early (Simmons and Greulich, 1943). Girls of early, average, or late menarche can be differentiated by assessment of their skeletal maturity in advance of their acceleration in height and weight (Simmons and Greulich, 1943).

The menarche normally occurs between 12 and 14 years of age and is preceded by a series of bodily changes. First the breasts enlarge, then pubic hair appears, and a little later axillary hair.

In boys, puberty is preceded by increased growth of the testes and penis, and perhaps a slight swelling of the breasts, then the appearance of pubic hair, followed by the appearance of axillary and facial hair. Voice change usually occurs after the appearance of pubic hair but prior to its lateral spread. Since the determination of spermatozoa in the urine requires laboratory analysis, the appearance of axillary hair has been used by some as an indication of puberty (Richey, 1937). Greulich, Dorfman, Catchpole, *et al.* (1942) have defined five stages of somatic sex characteristic in puberal and adolescent boys, giving actual photographs of breasts and genitals, as well as full-length pictures by which individual maturity may be appraised.

Boas and Wissler (1906) have noted that the average growth curve minimizes the decline in growth rate in childhood and the increase at adolescence owing to the individual variation in age of growth rate change. Boas (1930, 1932) has found that in some individuals physiological development, so far as it is expressed by stature, is rapid, energetic, and short; whereas in others it is sluggish and occupies a much longer period. His statistics for boys show that the earlier the maximum growth, the greater the maximum growth rate; and the taller the initial stature, the earlier the maximum growth rate.

With respect to the individual growth of girls at adolescence, Boas (1932) has found that the interval between the moment of maximum rate of growth and the first menses is greater the earlier the maximum rate of growth; and that the earlier the maximum rate of growth, the shorter the total period of growth. He has found also that the type of growth curve characteristic of an individual is more closely related to the age of maximum growth than to the date of the first menses; and that individuals who have the same stature at an early age are, as adults, shorter the earlier the age of maximum growth rate.

Richey (1937), investigating growth rates before and after puberty in both sexes, has found growth in height and weight slightly accelerated before puberty but more markedly decelerated after puberty. Although the prepubertal spurt in growth increases the disparity in size for children of early, average, and late puberty, the disparity is still more influenced by differences in growth rate after puberty.

The findings of Boas (1932), as well as Shuttleworth's own investigations, led Shuttleworth (1939) to make an extensive study of adolescence in terms of growth increments, relating them to the period of maximum growth. Comparing the growth curves of boys and girls with the same maximum growth age, he finds no crossing of the growth curves, but, instead, he finds that at every age the boys are taller than the girls. Also, the growth increments of the boys are greater at every age than those of the girls, but the difference is particularly marked at the age of maximum growth. Analyzing the actual stature difference in terms of accelerating phase, initial decelerating phase, and final decelerating phase, Shuttleworth (1939) finds they contribute 3.67 cm., 5.88 cm., and 3.28 cm., respectively, making a total difference at maturity of 12.85 cm. When he compares children of the same sex but with different ages of maximum growth, he finds that those with later maximum growth ages are only slightly taller at maturity since they have a smaller initial decelerating increment, and a smaller final decelerating increment although their initial decelerating is of longer duration though of less intensity. In other words, the effect of the longer period of growth is canceled by generally less intense growth.

Because of the variability in growth rates associated with the time of maximum growth rate, stature can be predicted more accurately from stature at 6 to 10 years than it can at the following years. In general, Shuttleworth (1939, p. 61) concludes that girls who are tall at any age tend to be tall at maturity; but girls who are tall at 6 to 9 years are more likely to be taller at maturity (correlation .73 to .83) than girls who are tall at ages 11 and 12 years (correlation .64 to .71). Similarly, correlation in height of boys 6 to 10 years with their adult stature is .72 to .80, whereas the correlation in height of boys 13 to 14 years old with their mature stature is .56 to .61.

Puberty appears to be related to body build. Pryor (1936) finds that girls of broad body build menstruate earlier than girls of slender body build, and Bayley's data (1943b) show that early-maturing boys and girls tend to have broad hips and narrow shoulders. Bayer (1940b) finds that disturbances in weight and menstruation are associated with deviations from normal build. Bruch (1941b), however, in a study of more than 200 children, finds that mere obesity is not related to delayed puberty in either boys or girls. Godin (1935) concludes that puberty is a germinal affair, and the maturity of the germ itself is an affair of nutrition. Pryor (1936) suggests that possibly the glandular balance of the broad-built child brings about an optimum nutritional state for pubescence sooner than in the underweight, narrow-built child. Shuttleworth (1937, 1939) tends to emphasize endocrine factors in activating adolescent changes. Greulich, Dorfman, Catchpole, et al. (1942, p. 62) from the study of gonadotrophic hormone excretion in adolescent boys conclude, "A likely mechanism for the initiation of puberty is a gradual increase in pituitary secretion, combined probably with an increasing sensitivity of the gonads to the hormone."

Body Types

Mankind tends naturally to order knowledge by generalization. Marked deviations from normal are impressive and foster categorical classifications and artificial pigeonholing. Thus many attempts have been made to separate individuals into physical types. Differences in skin color, shape of head, hair form, ear form, shape of nose (Bean, 1926), stature, span, and weight are commonly recognized as distinctive racial traits. Jackson (1930) points out that these differences do persist from generation to generation and, although there may be some modification, the traits tend to persist even in new environments. He shows, however, by comparing distribution curves of races, that overlapping of the races with respect to any trait is almost complete. Whether the extremes do represent true biotypes is uncertain.

In clinical medicine, abnormal body types are diagnostic of such conditions as acromegaly, acondroplastic dwarfism, mongolism, and cretinism, but even here there are borderline cases which confuse diagnosis. Nevertheless, the concept of type is useful if kept within bounds and not allowed to dominate the analysis and interpretation of data.

Among normal individuals the stout and thin types have long been recognized. Davenport (1923, 1927), particularly, suggests that these are truly types since he finds their distribution bimodal, that they have concomitant differential characteristic, and that they are inheritable traits.

Other suggestions for body type distinctions are Naccarati's (1921) macro- and microplanchnic types, in which the trunk is respectively proportionately larger or smaller than the extremities; Kretschmer's (1925) pyknic type, with round trunk and short extremities; asthenic type, with small trunk and long extremities; athletic type, moderately proportioned; and dysplastic (mixed) type; and Bayer's (1940a) 4 types of adolescent girls, hypofeminine (Diana), feminine (Venus), hyperfeminine (Rubens), and virile (Amazon) according to their skeletal proportions and covering tissue.

Sheldon, Stevens, and Tucker (1940) have developed a promising system of typing somatic adult characteristics according to three components and four second-order variables. The three components are related to the three embryonic tissues, the endo-, the meso-, and the ectoderm. Thus endomorphy is the characteristic of the visceral-dominated body as shown by soft, rounded body regions; mesomorphy is characteristic of the bone-, muscle-, and connective-tissue-dominated body, as shown by a heavy, hard, and rectangularly outlined body; and ectomorphy is characteristically dominated by the central nervous system, as shown by a linear, fragile body with a relatively large surface area. The four second-order variables are: dysplasia, or disharmony between various parts of the body; gynandromorphy, or degree of bisexuality; texture, or the fineness or coarseness of structure; and hirsutism, or amount of body hair. All the above traits are rated on a seven-point scale by anthropometric and anthroposcopic methods. The method has not yet been applied to studies of growth.

Many complicated formulae have been devised to classify adults objectively according to type, but without notable success (McCloy, 1936). When the problem of types is extended to childhood, it is further complicated by the changing proportions associated with growth. Certain indices, such as the stem length: recumbent length ratio (Hejinian and Hatt, 1929)

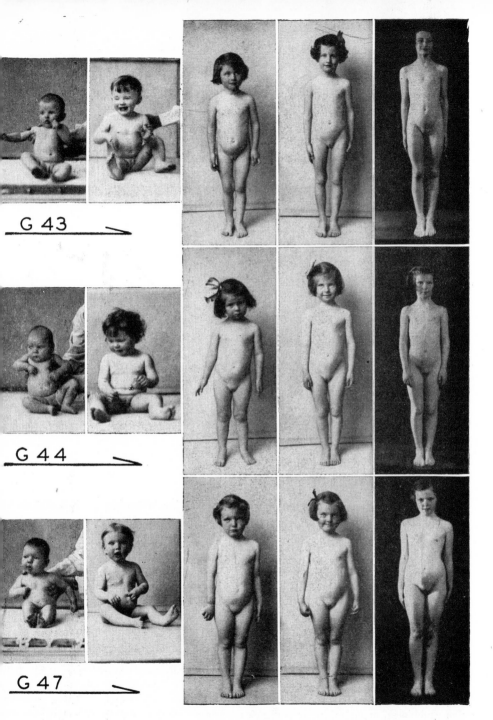

G 43

G 44

G 47

8 WEEKS 1 YEAR   3 YEARS 5 YEARS 9 YEARS

FIGURE 5. Changing body proportions of three girls all taller than average but of different body "types." (Thompson, The Clinic of Child Development, Yale University.)

have proved valid for certain periods of growth, but lose their significance at other ages.

McCloy (1936), investigating the whole period of physical growth from birth to dividual's body build will be later. The pictures in Figure 5 show clearly the vagaries of growth. Three girls, all taller than average, but of distinct body types, are pictured at various stages of growth.

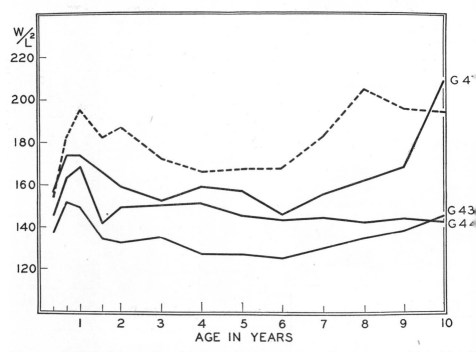

Figure 6. Individual changes in weight/length[2] index with age. (Thompson, unpublished data.)

Girls G43, G44, and G47 are taller than average but of different body build. G43 is underweight for age and height; legs proportionately long. G44 approximates normal proportions. G47 is overweight for height; pelvis wide for body length. (See Figure 5, p. 273.) Dotted line represents index changes for short stocky girl.

maturity by Thurstone's (1935) method of factor analysis, concludes that the two indices most useful in appraising body type are weight $1/3$: height; and chest girth : height. But even these ratios are unsatisfactory in infancy.

Bayley and Davis (1935), in their study of the first three years of life, find weight : length[2] the most valid measure of relative chubbiness, or lateral-linear tendencies in build. But they are unable to predict from indices at an early age what an in-

The ratios weight : length[2] for these three children between the ages of 10 weeks and 10 years are plotted in Figure 6. From 28 weeks to 9 years the curves do not cross, but G43 at 28 weeks is more chubby then than G44 at 5 years; and G44 is decidedly more chubby at 28 weeks than G47 is at 5 years. Chubbiness, as Bayley and Davis (1935) find, reaches a peak between 9 and 12 months of age.

It should be emphasized again that great caution must be exercised in the use of the

type concept. Individual variations in any one bodily measurement are great, and the permutations of the combinations of bodily dimensions are legion. To be sure, the dimensions are not wholly independent, but there is sufficient independence to bring about a variety of body forms too numerous to fit logical classificatory formulae.

Weight and Nutritional Status

Weight increase is a correlate of growth, but weight increase is not necessarily indicative of growth. Weight changes may be merely the result of changes in fatty deposits or in water content, both of which may be transitory modifications (Hammett, 1937; Simmons and Todd, 1938). Weight is more variable and more indicative of nutritional status than other physical measurements. Franzen (1929) has devised an instrument for measuring skin and subcutaneous tissue to indicate quantitatively the fatty deposits affecting weight. He and McCloy (1938) have established age and sex norms for this measure on various parts of the body. The norms are useful for transmuting body dimensions to skeletal dimensions and for thus determining body build more explicitly. Stuart, Hill, and Shaw (1940) have developed a technique for measuring the muscle and overlying tissues of the leg area by roentgenography. Norms for children from birth through 10 years are available (Stuart, Hill, and Shaw, 1940; Stuart and Dwinell, 1942).

Although weight is an acknowledged indication of nutritional status, optimum weight is an individual requirement, since it depends on age, stature, and body build as well as on nutrition. Age norms for weight, which even today are sometimes used, fail to consider that tall children of a given age should generally weigh more than short children of that age. Height-weight norms, which are widely used, account for differences in height but not in body build. Thus height-weight tables have received much criticism from Pryor and Stolz (1933), Royster (1936), Dearborn and Rothney (1938), Simmons and Todd (1938), and others.

Constructive suggestions for more valid nutritional appraisal methods are many. Pryor and Stolz (1933) express the index of nutrition in terms of the percentage deviation of the obtained weight from the weight norm for age, sex, height, and bi-iliac width to this weight norm. They furnish standard tables for ages 6 to 16 years. Franzen and Palmer's (1934) index of nutritional status for children between 7 and 12 years old employs the sum of arm girth with arm flexed, plus arm girth with arm extended, plus chest depth on inspiration, plus chest depth on expiration in terms of age, and bitrochanteric width. Individuals below a certain value are considered undernourished. Royster (1936) has established weight norms for Negro children between 5 and 15 years of age based on age, stature, and bi-iliac diameter. He emphasizes that the Negro child is of a more slender build than the white child and should therefore be appraised only in terms of his own race. McCloy (1938) finds that normal weight is best predicted by four measurements: height, chest circumference corrected for fat, hip width corrected for fat, and knee width. From thirty regression equations, one for each sex and year for ages 4 through 18 years, he has computed tables from which normal weight may be derived. Dearborn and Rothney (1938) have derived a formula for normal weight which is a simple function of chest width, chest depth, standing height, and bi-iliac width, useful for both sexes between 14 and 18 years of age. Wetzel (1941, 1943) has devised a grid by which a child's position may be determined in terms of his height, weight, and age. This grid carries seven channels. A child's growth curve normally progresses in a particular channel; deviation from this channel is indicative of change in health status. On a supplementary chart are five representative growth curves which include 76 per cent of those of each standard. A child's growth course may be evaluated, thus, in terms of his own standard. It should be noted, however, that this evaluation, no matter how individual, is fundamentally based only on height, weight, and age. Only to that extent, therefore, can it assess an individual child.

Daniels, Hutton, and Neil (1938) advocate the use of the creatinine-height index for nutritional appraisal. The determined ratio is the urinary creatinine in milligrams in proportion to height cubed. They claim that this index accounts for poor skeletal development which other indices of nutrition do not measure.

The question of appropriate weight for any child of adolescent age is particularly difficult because of the great variability associated with accelerated, normal, and retarded puberty. At this age, Richey (1937) points out, no statement of overweight or underweight should be made without a consideration of maturity factors.

The underweight and overweight children present special problems for investigation by the child psychologist (McHale, 1926). Recently, Bruch (1939, 1940, 1941b) has made highly significant studies showing that obesity, even in severe cases, is commonly a dietary rather than an endocrine problem; that obesity is related to parental overprotection and overfeeding, and to deprivation of satisfying outlets and contacts so that, for the child, food intake assumes inordinate importance. Similarly, Bronstein, Wexler, Brown, and Halpern (1942) conclude that for thirty-five children whom they studied no endocrine reason could be found for their obesity. Instead, it appeared to be related to sedentary habits, abnormal appetites, parental attitudes, and other environmental factors.

There is the further question of the degree of deviation which a child may show from a method of assessment without being considered under- or overweight. Metheny (1939) concludes that any child found to be 3 per cent underweight or 10 per cent overweight, in terms of the normal weight predicted by McCloy's formula, should be examined fully. It is the consensus, that, in addition to any standard of underweight or overweight, clinical judgment also should be used in appraising any individual child.

Head and Face Growth

Head and face growth has had and will probably continue to have particular interest for the psychologist. It is therefore treated here more extensively than would otherwise be the case.

The most recent study of head and face growth has been made by Davenport (1940), who gives longitudinal data on the growth trends and analyzes causes for the irregularities which he finds. He lists an extensive bibliography on the subject and discusses the findings of others in relation to his study. He concludes that a multitude of factors operate to modify the growth trend and that any simple expression of the growth of these parts is inadequate. Some of the factors which influence the external cranial and facial dimensions are uterine pressure in fetal life, gravity at the age of sitting and walking, growth of sinuses and tooth alveoli, possibly masticatory pull, sex, race, and other inherited traits, nutrition, and glandular activities.

The growth centers of the head and face, like those of the rest of the body, have different periods of maximum activity. Todd (1935) comments that:

> Brain-case growth is characteristic of infancy and early childhood and with it go the antero-posterior and transverse dimensions of the face, including the zygamota or malar arches. Vertical or respiratory growth of the face attains maximum velocity in later childhood. Vertical growth of the jaws between floor of the nose and chin reaches its most vigorous phase at and after puberty (p. 262).

He comments further that, since the head and face are sensitive to any factors which affect growth at these ages, defective cranial size must date from infancy, deficient upper facial growth from childhood, and inadequate jaw growth from adolescence. In any individual instance, however, it is difficult to separate growth disturbances from inherited growth tendencies.

THE HEAD

The five most commonly studied head dimensions are length, antero-posterior diameter; breadth, maximum transverse diameter; frontal diameter from temporal bridge to temporal bridge; height, the projected vertical distance from ear to the vertex; and circumference. Landmarks to define these and other dimensions of the head and face are detailed by Sullivan (1928) and Hrdlička (1939) and by other authors who discuss method. The cephalic index, the ratio of head breadth to head length, is used to distinguish long from round heads. The following conventional terms are given by Hrdlička (1939) for making the distinctions. He points out

Term	Cephalic Index
Hyperdolichocephaly	Below 70
Dolichocephaly	70–74.9
Mesocephaly	75–79.9
Brachycephaly	80–84.9
Hyperbrachycephaly	85 and above

that these are arbitrary rather than determined by nature.

The head and face differentiate early in prenatal life. Even in fetal life they are growing more slowly than the body as a whole. Scammon and Calkins (1929) report that at 3 fetal months the total head and face height is nearly one-third of the total fetal length; at 6 fetal months, about one-fourth; and at birth a little less than one-fourth. Absolutely, however, the cranial dimensions all increase rapidly in intrauterine life. Postnatally the head length and breadth continue to increase rapidly for two years and then slow down quickly, with a slight spurt at adolescence. Head circumference likewise follows this trend. Meredith (1935) points out that this type of growth characterizes neural growth as described by Scammon (1930). Although head growth has the same growth trend as the brain, it does not follow that cranial measurements are correlated with brain function.

Davenport (1940) expresses the rapid early head growth in terms of percentage of adult head length (190 mm.) at various ages: birth, 63 per cent; end of 6 months, 76 per cent; 1 year, 82 per cent; 2 years, 87 per cent; 3 years, 89 per cent; 5 years, 91 per cent; 10 years, 95 per cent; and 15 years, 98 per cent.

Bayley (1936) reports that head width increases more rapidly in the first 7 months, whereas head length increases more rapidly after 8 months. She found infants relatively dolichocephalic at birth. From birth to 7 months they rapidly become brachycephalic and after 10 months they again become dolichocephalic. According to Davenport (1940), the head has practically finished its width growth at 3 years, whereas the head continues to grow in length, but at a greatly reduced rate. Goldstein (1939), reporting on head growth of the same individuals between 2 and 16 years, finds for length a relatively high annual increment between 2 and 5 years, a sharp drop in the increment until 7 years, followed by pulsations of growth until adolescence. For width, he finds a comparatively high annual increase between 2 and 4 years, with a gradual decline, less steep than for length. Goldstein also finds the most common individual change in cephalic index to be a drop. Some individuals, however, showed no change and some even increased. Davenport (1940), reporting similarly on individual growth trends, finds that after the first year growth in length was much greater than in width in dolichocephalics, though the reverse was true for brachycephalics.

Absolute cephalic and facial measurements are less in the female than in the male (Davenport, 1940). Bayley (1936) states that the breadth difference tends to increase with age. The cephalic index of the sexes, according to Bayley, does not differentiate them until 11 months of age. Then the mean of the boys is higher than the mean of the girls. Between 5 and 6 years of age, this difference, according to Wallis (1931), diminishes until from 6 to 9 years of age the sexes are equal. Between 9 and 12 years the girls again have longer heads, but at 16 years boys equal and then surpass girls in cephalic index. Bayley (1936) concludes that the cephalic index is unrelated to body build as measured by weight/length^2 or stem length/total length, but that cephalic indices of the same children at different ages are fairly consistent.

Head height, particularly after 2 years of age, has a slower growth tempo than head length or breadth. Davenport (1940) reports that its growth is irregular and that decrease in head height is accompanied by increase in head width. Goldstein (1936) notes that head height is definitely greater in man than in the anthropoids.

The frontal breadth of the head grows irregularly. Davenport (1940) reports that it is near its final size at the age of one year. He also concludes that "Up to 4 years as the breadth is increasing, the transverse frontal index decreases; but after that, as the forehead widens, the index increases." The relative forehead width [1] tends to increase with age in all individuals studied.

Head circumference increases more regularly than other head dimensions. It is not a very reliable measure, however, since it is affected by different degrees of hair growth.

Intelligence and Cranial Dimensions. Psychologists have long sought a relationship between head measurements and intelligence. Hamilton (1936), in a review of the literature, finds a fairly consistently reported correlation of intelligence and cranial measurements of +.05 to +.10. He concludes that a true correlation would not exceed +.15.

Fernald and Southard (1918, 1921), in their macroscopic and microscopic study of the brains of feeble-minded, found a direct relationship with intelligence in only the extreme cases. It is not to be expected then that the external dimensions of the skull would be indicative of intellect. Ashby and Stewart (1933) did report a falling-off in size of the head measurements of the mentally deficient. The smaller measurements were most marked in the idiot region and affected equally head length, breadth, height, and ear-to-ear measurements, but they also found a more marked relationship between body size and IQ than between head size and IQ. Head growth, occurring genetically earlier than body growth, suffered less. This finding Ashby and Stewart point out, tends to reinforce the notion that feeble-mindedness is an arrest or retardation in intelligence

[1] Head width/total length.

At the other extreme, the large head of a hydrocephalic may be associated with feeble-mindedness or normal intelligence.

Head Size and Race. Head length, particularly, varies with race. At 14 years of age the average head length of Negroes is 184.0 mm.; United States Nordics, 180.5 mm.; Jews, 177 mm.; and Italians, 175.0 mm. Although Negroes have the longest heads, the Nordics have the largest postauricular head segment and the largest ratio of height/length, and the relatively widest foreheads (Davenport, 1940).

THE FACE

Psychologists have not been as interested in face growth as they have been in cranial growth, but, with the present shift in emphasis from intelligence to personality and social behavior, greater interest in facial growth may develop, particularly as far as child psychology is concerned. Study of the face should be encouraged as a potentially profitable field of investigation in relation to behavior-growth studies. The face is easily measured and photographed; its measurement does not involve disrobing as does measurement of the body.

Dimensions of the face are either taken by direct measurement or from roentgenological records. Some of the commonly studied dimensions are *total height:* the vertical distance from the nasion, which is a point near the depression at the upper part of the nose, to the menton, or anterior lower margin of the chin; *nasal height:* from the nasion to the point where the nasal septum joins the upper lip; *bizygomatic breadth:* the distance between the most lateral aspects of the upper jawbone; *bigonial breadth:* the distance between the lower points at the posterior angle of the lower jawbone; *upper face length:* from the auditory meatus to the nasion; and *lower face length:* from the auditory meatus to the menton. Other landmarks and diameters are used according to the interest of the investigator.

Krogman (1939) points out that normal growth of the face is continuous but not uniform; that different parts alternate in their velocity and intensity of growth. He reports that between birth and six years growth is vigorous in all directions, as shown by the figures in Table 2.

TABLE 2

Percentage of Growth at Various Ages

Facial Dimension	Age		
	Birth	2 Years	5 Years
Height	40	70	80
Breadth	60	80	85
Length	70	75	85

Davenport (1940) shows that, in relation to total face height, height of the nose increases most rapidly after birth and height of the chin next. After 8 or 9 months postpartum he finds that the lower jaw builds up more rapidly than the upper until 2 or 3 years of age. From 6 to 12 years of age, according to Krogman (1939), growth occurs principally in height, least in length; from 12 to 20 years the increase is principally in length, and growth in breadth exceeds growth in height. Krogman states further that, in general, length and breadth growth precede dentition and growth in height, and follows tooth eruption. Hellman (1933) notes that width is the largest dimension, height next, and length or depth least, and that between 5 and 22 years of age the largest dimension increases least and the smallest increases most. Hellman uses the gonion-menton diameter to measure length. He also comments that growth in height and length alternate and that increase in facial depth and width is more in the mandibular than in the zygomatic region and that increase in height is greatest in the ramus or posterior aspect of the lower jaw. Quoting

Hellman (1933): "As children grow up . . . there is considerable loss of subcutaneous tissue and an increase in bony increment beneath it. In females the bony increment seems insufficient to make up for attenuation of the skin" (p. 1123). As a result girls beyond 16 or 17 years show no increase or an actual decrease in facial dimension. In boys the bony growth is greater and the growth trend is progressive.

Davenport (1940) finds that the interpupillary distance increases absolutely as the head enlarges but decreases relatively to bizygomatic width. He also notes that chin height increases differently in different individuals, probably under the influence of special glandular activities, and that the other elements of facial height also vary with individual differences in tooth and sinus development. Todd (1935) notes that generally growth of the female practically ceases at puberty but the male continues to grow for several years following puberty and that hence the majority of women have relatively smaller jaw growth. Although, absolutely, female facial dimensions are all smaller than those of the male, Hellman (1933) reports that the female face is relatively longer and that the male face is relatively deeper.

Many studies have noted the sensitivity of the transverse diameters of the face to disturbances of growth in early childhood. Boas (1911) finds a change in bizygomatic width of children transferred from Europe to the Lower East Side in New York. Bakwin and Bakwin (1931c) find that, relative to body length, infants with such diseases as eczema, tetany, and acute intestinal intoxication are smaller in bimolar and bigonial face widths than healthy infants from the same social environment. Broadbent (1937) also finds face growth affected by nutritional disturbances in childhood. In any individual instance, however, disturbances of growth are not easy to identify except by repeated measurements. The disturbances are imposed on inherited growth tendencies, and to distinguish one from the other is not simple. It is not justifiable to conclude, for instance, that just because a child has a relatively narrow face he is suffering from malnutrition. With repeated measurements, abnormal growth trends can be recognized and, if it seems wise, remedial measures may be employed.

The relationship between facial growth and dentition is discussed under the section on dentition.

Skeletal Growth

Measurements of the external dimensions of the body, using skeletal landmarks, are gross measures of skeletal growth as far as size is concerned. Bone size and maturity, however, are not perfectly correlated. A child may be relatively small yet relatively mature; another child may be relatively large yet relatively immature. It is the differentiation and integration of the bony parts which reveal the maturity aspect of growth. To understand the distinction it is necessary to review briefly the facts of bone growth.

Bony structure is originated by osteoblasts in either connective tissue or cartilage. The membrane bones of the face and cranium develop directly within the connective tissue, whereas the skeletal bones generally develop in the cartilage. Most bones, especially those formed in cartilage, have more than one center of ossification. In the human body there are over 800 centers of ossification, but half of them do not appear until after birth and centers continue to appear throughout the teens. Fusion begins as early as the eighth lunar month of fetal life and continues to middle age. At birth the infant has about 270 bones. The number increases to about

350 at puberty. This number increases, sometimes beyond the twenties, yet because of the fusion the final mature skeleton has only 206 bones (Arey, 1934). Certain long bones increase in size in the following manner: The cartilage increases in length while progress in ossification takes place from the center, forming the diaphysis. Secondary ossification centers at the ends of the bone activate to form the epiphyses. When adult length is attained, cartilage proliferation ceases, but ossification continues, epiphyses and diaphysis unite and merge. Maturity is then reached (Arey, 1934, p. 339).

In 1896 the discovery of X-rays and their properties by Roentgen offered a means of studying the growth of the bony structure of the body in the living. Since then great advance has been made in standardization of the techniques of roentgenology and in the appraisal of bone growth. Hodges (1933) has published a most graphic and concise chart depicting the development of the human skeleton in general.

Psychologists have been most concerned with the hand-and-wrist ossification as an index of anatomical maturity. In normal development growth of the bones of the wrist and hand closely parallels general skeletal growth. Pryor (1925) and others find sufficient lateral symmetry so that in general one hand only need be examined.

The literature up to 1935 is well reviewed by Flory (1936). The first methods of appraisal were naturally inspectional. Then, in an attempt at greater precision, measurement was resorted to. Baldwin, Busby, and Garside (1928) and others published figures for changes in area of the wrist bones from birth to 16 years and also computed anatomical indices which discounted for differences in wrist size. Flory (1936) and Todd (1937) each published an atlas of the osseous development of the hand with age standards. Wallis (1931) measured the width of the diaphysis and epiphysis of ulna and radius and used the ratio of the two measures as an index of anatomical maturity. Both of the above-cited publications noted great variability differences in time of first ossification of the carpal bones and warned against using this manifestation as an index of maturity. It is the consensus that matching with a standard series is the most reliable and predictive method of assessing maturity of ossification. According to Todd (1937),

Maturity determinations in the skeleton are successional changes in outline of shaft ends and in contour of epiphysial ossification centers which mark the progress in skeletal maturation to its final adult form. Dates of appearance of ossification centers, whether in epiphyses or in short bones of wrist and ankle, are not maturity determinators. Like the features of the growing ends they are related to Vitamin D activity (p. 40).

It is the different vulnerability of the different centers which causes different patterns of development. More specifically, Todd states:

The principle of assessment is therefore the utilization of the most advanced centers, not the average of all, as a guide to actual bodily maturity. . . . In the hand it results in reservations on carpal bones and epiphysis of radius, eliminates epiphysis of ulna, and places greatest reliance upon metacarpal and phalangeal epiphyses (p. 15).

Flory (1936) gives very convincing figures to show that a skeletal age rating based on "bone appearance and development, epiphyseal appearance and development, and general developmental characteristics" in terms of a standard age scale is decidedly superior to evaluation in terms of total carpal area or in terms of ossification ratio (p. 105). If the age at which ossification in the hand is complete is used as a criterion of skeletal maturity, correlations with the criteria and carpal area are approximately .42 at 9 years, .48 at 11 years, .23 at 13 years, and .04 at 15 years, with PE's ranging between .06 and .08; correlations of ossification ratio (the area ossified in relation to a defined area of the wrist) with the criterion are approximately .52 at 9 years, .62 at 11 years, .40 at 13 years, and .33 at 15 years, with PE's between .04 and .08; correlations of skeletal months rating with the criterion are approximately .68 at 9 years, .75 at 11 years, .84 at 13 years, and .86 at 15 years, with a PE between .02 and .06. The greatest advantage of the skeletal age rating is at puberty. Skeletal age is comparable in many respects to mental age, and as such it is of value both in research and practice.

Todd (1937) gives 40 male standards and 35 female standards, spaced at not less than 6-month intervals, from birth up to 19 years. Flory's standards are 20 for each sex at yearly intervals from birth through 19 years. Both Flory and Todd accompany each standard with notes concerning the significance of its various characteristics.

Todd (1930) was enthusiastic in his evaluation of the skeletal appraisal. He said:

> Wisely used record of differential maturity, combined with that of differential growth, throws light on vagaries of emotion, on problems of social adjustment, on failure in promotion and a host of problems that beset the teacher of the pre-adolescent grades 4–6.
> . . . Determinations of progress in physical maturation qualifying those of growth in stature and weight differentiate the out-sized child, the subnormal child, the superior child of advanced physical develop-

ment, the physical impress of malnutrition, of respiratory disorders such as hay fever and asthma, of the disharmonically progressing child who is a problem to himself as well as to those responsible for his guidance and health.

Pyle and Menino (1939) have recently compared the Todd and Flory standards. They find a correlation of +.87 ±.03 between ratings based on the two standards for 50 unselected 3-year-old children. Skeletal age ratings according to Todd's atlas are more delayed in bone growth than according to Flory's atlas. The more frequent standard intervals of Todd's atlas are considered by Pyle and Menino "clearly advantageous for skeletal age assessments at all age levels below six years of age" (p. 34).

Although the appearance of ossification centers cannot be relied upon to judge maturity, they are sensitive indicators of nutrition. As such they must not be discarded in enthusiasm for the more stable growth phenomena. It is highly important from a psychological point of view to know of environmental disturbances. There is the possibility that they are related to fluctuations in behavior. Variability and probable age of appearance of the carpal bone and the radial and ulnar epiphyses as given by Flory (1936, p. 35) are reproduced in Table 3. The location of these bones in the wrist is shown graphically in Figure 7.

In spite of the general correlation between hand growth and body growth, Sontag, Snell, and Anderson (1939) claim that appraisal of the wrist and hand alone is not sufficient. Using roentgenograms of the left shoulder, elbow, wrist, hand, hip, knee, ankle, and foot, Sontag and his associates have established norms for thirteen ages from 1 month to 5 years. Their method reduces technical and subjective errors to a minimum.

TABLE 3 *

PERCENTAGE OF CHILDREN AT VARIOUS AGES WHOSE CARPAL BONES AND RADIAL AND ULNAR EPIPHYSES HAVE APPEARED

(Based on more than 6500 records)

Bone	Sex	B	1	2	3	4	5	6	7	8	9	10	11	12	13	14	15	16	Probable Age of Appearance in Months
Capitate	F	8	96	100															6
	M	2	98	100															6
Hamate	F	8	96	100															6
	M	2	98	100															6
Radial epiphysis †	F	0	78	100															9
	M	0	34	98	100														15
Triquetrum	F	0	20	52	79	100													23
	M	0	22	50	57	92	84	93	100										24
Lunate	F	0	0	32	50	80	91	99	100										36
	M	0	8	18	36	64	64	87	98	99	100								42
Naviculare	F	0	0	0	12	30	61	95	99	100									56
	M	0	0	0	4	17	34	51	75	92	99	100							72
M. majus	F	0	0	4	18	53	74	94	99	100									50
	M	0	0	0	4	14	33	51	72	88	96	97	100						72
M. minus	F	0	0	0	15	40	65	95	100										53
	M	0	0	0	4	22	9	48	81	95	100								73
Ulnar epiphysis †	F	0	0	0	0	0	16	60	99	100									68
	M	0	0	0	0	0	7	27	59	82	98	100							80
Pisiforme	F	0	0	0	0	0	0	0	1	19	50	79	96	100					108
	M	0	0	0	0	0	0	0	0	2	6	22	28	66	95	99	99	100	140

* From Flory (1936, p. 35).

† The radial and ulnar epiphyses have been included here because Carter used both in determining the ossification ratio.

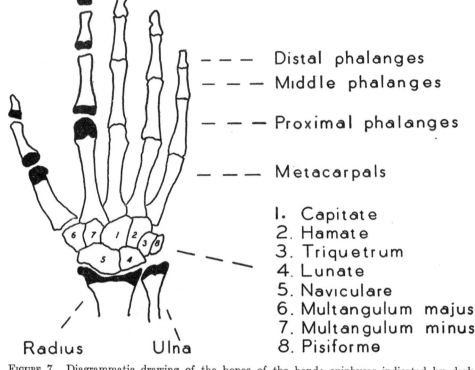

- - - Distal phalanges

- - - Middle phalanges

- - - Proximal phalanges

- - - Metacarpals

1. Capitate
2. Hamate
3. Triquetrum
4. Lunate
5. Naviculare
6. Multangulum majus
7. Multangulum minus
8. Pisiforme

Radius   Ulna

FIGURE 7. Diagrammatic drawing of the bones of the hand; epiphyses indicated by dark areas. (Adapted from H. Gray, in *Anatomy of the Human Body*. 21st ed., revised by W. H. Lewis. Philadelphia: Lea and Febiger, 1924, 230.)

Also recently Francis and Werle (1939) have charted the appearance of ossification centers for the skeleton in general from birth to 5 years. They give percentages of incidences of ossification separately for the sexes at birth, at 3, 6, 9, and 12 months of age, and at 6-month intervals thereafter. Age standards based on the 80 percentile are given for each ossification center. They conclude that

> The reason for variation in date of commencement of ossification and in its progressive development is not some obscure cause inherent in the germ plasm but the result of metabolic disturbance. . . . The centers of ossification appear in sheaves of miscellaneous composition but primary

centers are more apt to be delayed in commencement of ossification than are centers appearing in epiphyses (p. 298).

Hill (1939) points out that

> In fetal life the record of maturity must depend largely on the appearance of centers since subepiphyseal surfaces are not yet defined and therefore cannot assist identification. . . . [But he also notes that] Because of the protection against nutritional maladies afforded by prenatal existence it may be expected that variability in date of appearance will not be as marked as in infancy (p. 251).

Using crown-rump length as a basis for classification and the 50 percentile as standard, Hill has charted the ossification of bone in fetal life, giving percentages of incidences of ossification for the ten lunar month ages. He also gives a list of standard degrees of ossification for these ages, basing his standard on the 50 percentile.

Sex Differences in Skeletal Growth

There is a well-defined sex difference in skeletal maturity which according to Flory's data gradually increases with age. There is a readily perceptible difference at birth, practically a year's difference at beginning elementary school age, and approximately a two-year difference at high school entrance. This is consistent with sex differences in other aspects of physical growth. Female children, although smaller than male children of the same chronological age, are more mature and reach puberty earlier.

Hereditary factors may play a certain part in determining ossification rate. The correlation between deviations from the norm in ossification ratios are for brothers .62, for sisters .27, and for brothers and sisters .39 (Flory [1936]). Minor fluctuations in ossification rate tend to correct themselves in a year or two and should not be regarded too seriously. Variability in ossification maturity of children in general increases up to late adolescence, after which it decreases to the adult variability. Todd (1937) states that children from privileged homes are approximately twelve months advanced in ossification maturity and children from underprivileged homes are often twelve months retarded (p. 22). He also expresses the opinion that:

A child retarded in maturity rating 12 months or more on our standards below his chronological age has experienced a setback in constitution from which he has not yet recovered even though he shows no signs of ill-health and neither parents nor physician can recall anything in the past history which would lead one to suspect constitutional disturbances (p. 15).

Child psychologists might profitably compare methods of bone maturity appraisal with methods of mental maturity appraisal. Can it be that a matching method such as the Gesell technique for appraising the preschool child is really a more reliable and valid technique in terms of prediction than a more exact and rigid measuremental method? Is the reason that Gesell has found a higher correlation between infant tests and mental development at later ages perhaps due to the superiority of his apparently less objective scale? Certainly the findings in the realm of skeletal growth should give child psychologists cause to reconsider more carefully the problem of behavior-maturity appraisal.

Dentition

The skeleton differentiates from the mesoderm, whereas the teeth develop from both mesoderm and ectoderm: enamel from the mesoderm; and dentine, pulp, and cement from the ectoderm. Teeth, hair, and nails are similar in that they all develop from skin tissue. Deciduous teeth are formed early in fetal life. The twenty enamel organs and their associated dental papilla of the deciduous teeth are present in the 10-week fetus; those for permanent molars are present at birth; those for the second molars at 6 months; those for the wisdom teeth or third molars are not found until the fifth year.

Eruption of deciduous teeth begins at about the age of 6 months; of the permanent teeth at about 6 years. There is great variability in the time of eruption of deciduous teeth. Infants have been born with a tooth erupted, whereas children of one year of age may not yet have even a single tooth. Because of the great variability, authors do not agree very precisely on the normal age of eruption. The ages given in Table 4 are approximations.

TABLE 4

DECIDUOUS TEETH: AGE OF ERUPTING AND SHEDDING *

Tooth	Age of Erupting (Months)	Age of Shedding (Years)
Median incisor	6–8	7
Lateral incisor	7–10	8
Canine	17–20	12
First molar	12–16	10
Second molar	18–24	11–12

* Modified from Arey (1934).

Teeth in the lower jaw usually erupt before the corresponding teeth in the upper jaw. There are very few data in the literature regarding sex difference in eruption age for the deciduous teeth. Boas (1927) in his study of Hebrew children finds no characteristic sex difference in time of eruption except that the second deciduous molars of the boys erupted later than the corresponding teeth of the girls. Wallis (1931) finds the average time of eruption of the first tooth, according to mothers' reports, 7.6 months for both boys and girls. At 22 to 27 months she finds that 56 per cent of the boys have 16 teeth, whereas only 40 per cent of the girls have this number. Gesell and Thompson (1938) also find no sex difference in time of eruption of the first tooth, but after 28 weeks through 56 weeks of age male infants are in general more advanced than female infants (Table 5).

Girls, however, are more precocious in shedding their deciduous teeth than boys, perhaps because the permanent dentition of females is more advanced at each age than the permanent dentition of males. Klein, Palmer, and Kramer (1937) give figures based on 4416 boys and girls at Hagerstown, Maryland, which are reproduced in Table 6.

TABLE 6

SHEDDING OF TEETH: NUMBER OF DECIDUOUS TEETH PRESENT

Age in years	6½	8½	10½	12½
Boys: Average number	16.9	11.4	6.0	1.3
Girls: Average number	16.0	10.6	4.3	0.8

Psychologists have been particularly concerned with the effect of thumb sucking on the primary teeth and the dental arch. Lewis (1937), from a study of models made yearly, finds that the type of thumb sucking most damaging to the shape of the arch is that in which the child holds the volar

TABLE 5

ERUPTION OF DECIDUOUS TEETH: 16–56 WEEKS OF AGE

Age in weeks	16	20	24	28	32	36	40	44	48	52	56
Boys: Average number teeth	0	0.1	0.3	1.0	2.0	3.4	4.6	5.5	6.3	6.4	7.3
Range	..	0–2	0–2	0–4	0–5	0–8	0–8	0–8	0–10	0–12	4–12
Girls: Average number teeth	0	0.1	0.3	0.8	1.5	2.1	3.3	4.3	4.5	5.9	7.0
Range	..	0–2	0–3	0–6	0–6	0–7	0–7	0–8	0–8	1–10	2–9

surface toward the palate. A child who persisted in thumb sucking until 3 years old, with resulting deformity, experienced a full correction of the deformity a year and a half after the habit was broken. Another child who broke the habit of sucking the right thumb at 9½ years showed subsequent improvement of the displacement and open bite. Cases where the habit was continued showed no self-correction. There were instances of thumb sucking with no resulting deformity; all such cases broke the habit between the first and second year.

The eruption of permanent teeth begins with the eruption of the six-year molar. The figures given by Klein, Palmer, and Kramer (1937) (Table 7) are derived from the percentage of children at successive ages who have the designated teeth erupted at the time of examination.

With the exception of the first and second premolars, the teeth of the lower jaw erupt prior to the corresponding teeth of the upper jaw.

The White House Conference data (1932, 1933) complete the story by giving the average age at which the third molars are beginning to erupt as follows:

Third molars:
  boys, average age, 18.59 years
  girls, average age, 20.10 years

Thus, with respect to permanent teeth, females are more precocious at least up to the teen ages, but by the end of the teens males are again more precocious.

The use of dental age has been suggested as an indication of anatomical maturity (Bean, 1914; Cattell, 1928). The wide variability in time of eruption of the teeth makes an assessment on that basis undesirable. Clinically, however, it is most important to include such an assessment as part of the total examination.

There are certain ages when the teeth are particularly susceptible to metabolic and cellular disturbances, namely, the neonatal period, about 10 months of age, about 2½ years, and about 5 years of age (Massler, Schour, and Poncher, 1941).

TABLE 7

AVERAGE ERUPTION AGE FOR THE PERMANENT TEETH *

Tooth	Upper Jaw (Years)		Lower Jaw (Years)	
	Boys	Girls	Boys	Girls
Central incisor	7.49	7.20	6.50	6.19
Lateral incisor	8.62	8.15	7.64	7.31
Canine	11.80	11.05	10.70	9.85
First premolar	10.42	10.00	10.75	10.20
Second premolar	11.18	10.82	11.45	11.00
First molar	6.64	6.54	6.44	6.12
Second molar	12.70	12.40	12.20	11.90

* Standard deviations range between 0.70 and 1.77.

The cause of dental caries is still questioned. Some relate caries to the presence of *Bacillus acidophilus* in the mouth; others blame dietary deficiencies. Recently significant familial relationships have been found to exist in the level of caries experience of children as well as in the time characteristics of tooth eruption (Klein, Palmer, and Knutson, 1938).

Naturally there is an intimate relationship between the growth of the face and dentition. The White House Conference (1932, 1933) summarizes three corresponding periods of development as follows:

The first five years of life, during which the deciduous dentition is completed, and the most intensive antero-posterior growth of the face is taking place. The ten years following, from five to fifteen, during which the deciduous dentition is shed, all but the third molars are erupted, and the most intensive lateral and vertical growth of the face is taking place. The five years following, from fifteen to twenty, during which the third molars erupt and residual vertical growth is still taking place in females and more intensive growth in males (Part 2, p. 143).

With the eruption and shedding of the first twenty teeth and the eruption of the thirty-two permanent teeth, together with the accompanying growth of the jaw, there are bound to be associated changes in occlusion. Hellman (1932, 1933) notes that the percentage of normal occlusion in a group of children drops from 70 per cent at four years to 22 per cent at nine years and then gradually increases with age. However, some types of malocclusion are not self-corrective and need orthodontic care.

Conclusion

The physical-growth changes discussed in this chapter relate principally to morphological changes. This is a reflection of research interests which have been a result of available techniques for measurement, plus lack of basic data on somatic changes. The immediate future will undoubtedly reflect the already current and growing interest in the more physiological, the biochemical, and the electropotential changes associated with age. These aspects of growth are more intimately related to functional changes and thence to behavior phenomena. Studied in this way, physical characteristics become as integral a part of an individual's personality as are behavior traits. With this point of view the problem of mental and physical relationships changes from an interest in a one-to-one relationship to an interest in a more analytic growth association. As Paterson (1930) suggests, there is need for research emphasizing factors in mental and physical growth rather than mass correlations.

Bibliography

APPLETON, V. B. 1927. Growth of Chinese children in Hawaii and in China. *Amer. J. Phys. Anthrop.*, **10**, 237–252.

AREY, L. B. 1934. *Developmental anatomy.* Philadelphia: Saunders.

ASHBY, W. R., and R. M. STEWART. 1933. Size in mental deficiency. *J. Neurol. Psychopath.*, **13**, 303–329.

BAKWIN, H. 1929. The sex factor in infant mortality. *Human Biol.*, **1**, 90–116.

BAKWIN, H., and R. M. BAKWIN. 1931a. Body build in infants: I. The technique of measuring the external dimensions of the body in infants. *J. Clin. Invest.*, **10**, 369–375.

——. 1931b. Body build in infants: II. The proportions of the external dimensions of the healthy infant during the first year of life. *J. Clin. Invest.*, **10**, 377–394.

——. 1931c. Body build in infants: III. Body build in disease. *J. Clin. Invest.*, **10**, 395–403.

——. 1934a. Body build in infants: V. Anthropometry in the newborn. *Human Biol.*, **6**, 612–626.

——. 1934b. External dimensions of the newborn. *Amer. J. Dis. Child.*, **48**, 1234–1236.

——. 1936. Growth of thirty-two external dimensions during the first year of life. *J. Pediat.*, **8**, 177–183.

——. 1939. Body build in infants: IX. Body build in eczema. *Human Biol.*, **11**, 269–276.

BAKWIN, H., R. M. BAKWIN, and L. MILGRAM. 1934. Body build in infants: IV. Influence of retarded growth. *Amer. J. Dis. Child.*, **48**, 1030–1040.

BALDWIN, B. T. 1921. The physical growth of children from birth to maturity. *Univ. Iowa Stud. Child Welfare*, **1**, No. 1.

——. 1925. Weight-height-age standards in metric units for American-born children. *Amer. J. Phys. Anthrop.*, **8**, 1–10.

——. 1928. Breathing capacity according to height and age of American-born boys and girls of school age. *Amer. J. Phys. Anthrop.*, **12**, 257–267.

BALDWIN, B. T., L. M. BUSBY, and H. GARSIDE. 1928. Anatomic growth of children: A study of some bones of the hand, wrist, and lower forearm by means of roentgenograms. *Univ. Iowa Stud. Child Welfare*, **4**, No. 1.

BALDWIN, B. T., T. D. WOOD, and R. M. WOODBURY. 1923. Weight-height-age tables. Supplement to July issue *Mother and Child.* Washington: American Child Health Association.

BARDEEN, C. R. 1920. The height-weight index of build in relation to linear and volumetric proportions and surface-area of the body during post-natal development. *Contr. Embryol., Carnegie Inst. Wash.*, No. 46, 483–554.

BAUM, M. P., and V. S. VICKERS. 1941. Anthropometric and orthopedic examinations. *Child Develpm.*, **12**, 339–345.

BAYER, L. M. 1940*a*. Build variations in adolescent girls. *J. Pediat.*, **17**, 331–344.

——. 1940*b*. Weight and menses in adolescent girls with special reference to build. *J. Pediat.*, **17**, 345–354.

BAYLEY, N. 1936. Growth changes in the cephalic index during the first five years of life. *Human Biol.*, **8**, 1–18.

——. 1943*a*. Skeletal maturing in adolescence as a basis for determining percentage of completed growth. *Child Develpm.*, **14**, 1–46.

——. 1943*b*. Size and body build of adolescents in relation to rate of skeletal maturing. *Child Develpm.*, **14**, 47–89.

BAYLEY, N., and F. C. DAVIS. 1935. Growth changes in bodily size and proportions during the first three years: A developmental study of sixty-one children by repeated measurements. *Biometrika*, **27**, 26–87.

BEAN, R. B. 1914. The eruption of the teeth as a physiological standard for testing development. *Ped. Sem.*, **21**, 596–614.

——. 1926. Human types. *Quart. Rev. Biol.*, **1**, 360–392.

BINET, A. 1900. Recherches complémentaires de céphalométrie sur 100 enfants d'intelligence inégale, choisis, dans les écoles primaires du département de Seine et Marne. *Année psychol.*, **7**, 375–428.

——. 1910. Les signes physiques de l'intelligence chez les enfants. *Année psychol.*, **16**, 1–30.

BINET, A., and T. SIMON. 1914. *Mentally defective children*. (Trans.) New York: Longmans, Green.

BOAS, F. 1911. *Changes in bodily form of descendants of immigrants*. (*U. S. Senate Document 208.*) Washington, D. C.: Government Printing Office.

——. 1927. The eruption of deciduous teeth among Hebrew infants. *J. Dent. Res.*, **7**, 245–253.

——. 1930. Observations on the growth of children. *Science*, **72**, 44–48.

——. 1932. Studies in growth. *Human Biol.*, **4**, 307–350.

BOAS, F., and C. WISSLER. 1906. Statistics of Growth. *Rep. U. S. Comm. Educ. for 1904*, **1**, 25–132.

BOYD, E. 1929. The experimental error in measuring the growing human body. *Amer. J. Phys. Anthrop.*, **13**, 389–432.

——. 1935. Growth of the surface area of the human body. *Inst. Child Welfare Monogr.*, No. 10. Minneapolis: University of Minnesota Press. Pp. 145.

——. 1941. *Outline of physical growth and development*. Minneapolis: Burgess.

BOYNTON, B. 1936. The physical growth of girls: A study of the rhythm of physical growth from anthropometric measurements on girls between birth and eighteen years. *Univ. Iowa Stud. Child Welfare*, **12**, No. 4. Pp. 105.

BRENTON, H. 1922. Climate and race as factors influencing the weight of the newborn. *Amer. J. Phys. Anthrop.*, **5**, 237–249.

BROADBENT, B. H. 1937. The face of the normal child. Bolton standards and technique in orthodontic practice. *Angle Orthod.*, **7**, 183–208.

BRONSTEIN, I. P., S. WEXLER, A. W. BROWN, and L. J. HALPERN. 1942. Obesity in childhood. *Amer. J. Dis. Child.*, **63**, 238–251.

BROOKS, F. D. 1933. Mental and physical development in adolescence. *Rev. Educ. Res.*, **3**, 108–129.

BRUCH, H. Studies in obesity in childhood. I. 1939. Physical growth and development of obese children. *Amer. J. Dis. Child.*, **58**, 457–484. III. 1940. Physiologic and psychologic aspects of the food intake of obese children. *Amer. J. Dis. Child.*, **59**, 739–781.

——. 1941*a*. Obesity in childhood and personality development. *Amer. Orthopsychiat.*, **11**, 467–474.

——. 1941*b*. Obesity in relation to puberty. *J. Pediat.*, **19**, 365–375.

BRUCH, H., and G. V. TOURAINE. 1941. The family frame of obese children. *Psychosom. Med.*, **2**, 141–206.

BUFFON, COUNT DE. 1837. Sur l'accroissement successif des enfants; Guéneau de Montbeillard mesure de 1759 à 1776. In *Œuvres complètes*, Vol. III, pp. 174–176. Paris: Furne and Pie.

CAMP, J. D., and E. I. L. CILLEY. 1931. Diagrammatic chart showing time of appearance of the various centers of ossification and period of union. *Amer. J. Roentg.*, **26**, No. 6, p. 105.

CARTER, H. D., and R. H. KRAUSE. 1936. Physical proportions of the human infant. *Child Develpm.*, **7**, 60–68.

CATES, H. A., and J. C. GOODWIN. 1936. The twelve-day-old baby. *Human Biol.*, **8**, 433–450.

CATTELL, P. 1928. Dentition as a measure of maturity. *Monogr. Harv. Stud. Educ. Psychol.* Pp. viii + 91.

CHILDREN'S BUREAU. 1927. References on the physical growth and development of the normal child. *U. S. Child. Bur. Publ.*, No. 179.

COLD SPRING HARBOR, NEW YORK, BIOLOGICAL LABORATORY. 1934. *Symposium on quantitative biology.* Vol. II.

COURTIS, S. A. 1932. *The measurement of growth*. Ann Arbor: Brumfield and Brumfield.

——. 1937. What is a growth cycle? *Growth*, **1**, 155–174.

CRAMPTON, C. W. 1908. Physiological age: a fundamental principle. *Phys. Educ. Rev.*, **13**, 141–151; 214–227.

DANIELS, A. L., M. K. HUTTON, and B. NEIL. 1938. Relation of the creatinine-height coefficient to various indexes of nutrition. *Amer. J. Dis. Child.*, **55**, 532–543.

DAVENPORT, C. B. 1923. Body build and its inheritance. *Carnegie Inst. Wash. Publ.*, No. 329.

——. 1926a. Human metamorphosis. *Amer. J. Phys. Anthrop.*, **9**, 205–232.

——. 1926b. Human growth curve. *J. Gen. Physiol.*, **10**, 205–216.

——. 1927. *Guide to anthropometry and anthroposcopy.* Baltimore: Waverly Press.

——. 1934. Critique of curves of growth and of relative growth. *Cold Spring Harbor Symposium Quant. Biol.*, **2**, 203–208.

——. 1937. Some principles of anthropometry. *Amer. J. Phys. Anthrop.*, **23**, 91–99.

——. 1938. Bodily growth of babies during the first postnatal year. *Contr. Embryol., Carnegie Inst. Wash.*, No. 169.

——. 1940. Post-natal development of the head. *Proc. Amer. Phil. Soc.*, **83**.

DAVENPORT, C. B., and W. DRAGER. 1936. Growth curve of infants. *Proc. Nat. Acad. Sci. Wash.*, **22**, 639–645.

DAWSON, H. L., and G. D. STODDARD. 1933. Physical growth from birth to puberty. *Rev. Educ. Res.*, **3**, 130–149.

DEARBORN, W. F., and J. W. M. ROTHNEY. 1938. Basing weight standards upon linear bodily dimensions. *Growth*, **2**, 197–212.

DEARBORN, W. F., J. W. M. ROTHNEY, and F. K. SHUTTLEWORTH. 1938. Data on the growth of public school children. *Monogr. Soc. Res. Child Develpm.*, **3**, No. 1. Pp. 136.

DODGE, C. T. J. 1927. Weight of colored infants. *Amer. J. Phys. Anthrop.*, **10**, 337–345.

DOLL, E. A. 1916. *Anthropometry as an aid to mental diagnosis.* Vineland, N. J.: Training School.

DUNHAM, E. C., R. M. JENSS, and A. U. CHRISTIE. 1939. A consideration of race and sex in relation to the growth and development of infants. *J. Pediat.*, **14**, 156–160.

ENGLEBACH, W. 1932. *Endocrine medicine: I. General considerations.* Springfield, Ill.; Thomas.

FERNALD, W. E., and E. E. SOUTHARD. 1921. Waverly researches in the pathology of the feebleminded. Cases XI–XX. *Mem. Amer. Acad. Arts Sci.*, pp. 133–207. 32 plates.

FERNALD, W. E., and E. E. SOUTHARD, with the collaboration of A. E. TAFT. 1918. Waverly researches in the pathology of the feebleminded. Cases I–X. *Mem. Amer. Acad. Arts Sci.*, pp. 20–128. 20 plates.

FLEMING, R. M. 1933. *A study of growth and development.* London: Medical Research Council.

FLORY, C. D. 1936. Osseous development in the hand as an index of skeletal development.

Monogr. Soc. Res. Child Develpm., **1**, No. 3. Pp. 141.

FRANCIS, C. C. 1939. Growth of the human tibia. *Amer. J. Phys. Anthrop.*, **25**, 323–331.

FRANCIS, C. C., and P. P. WERLE. 1939. The appearance of centers of ossification from birth to 5 years. *Amer. J. Phys. Anthrop.*, **24**, 273–300.

FRANZEN, R. 1929. *Physical measures of growth and nutrition.* New York: American Child Health Association.

FRANZEN, R., and G. T. PALMER. 1934. *The A C H index of nutritional status.* New York: American Child Health Association.

FREEMAN, R. G., JR. 1933. Skeletentwicklung und Wachstum im Alter von 2 bis 18 Monaten, von 2 bis 7½ Jahren und von 8 bis 14½ Jahren. *Anthrop. Anz.*, **10**, 185–208.

FREEMAN, R. G., JR., and V. PLATT. 1932. Skeletentwicklung und Wachstum der Säuglinge von der Geburt bis zu einem Monat. *Anthrop. Anz.*, **9**, 68–78.

GESELL, A., and H. THOMPSON. 1938. *The psychology of early growth.* New York: Macmillan.

GILBERT, J. A. 1895. Researches on the mental and physical development of school children. *Stud. Yale Psychol. Lab.*, **2**, 40–100.

——. 1897. Researches on school children and college students. *Univ. Iowa Stud. Psychol.*, **1**, 1–39.

GILBERT, M. S. 1938. *Biography of the unborn.* Baltimore: Williams and Wilkins.

GODDARD, H. H. 1912. The height and weight of feebleminded children in American institutions. *J. Nerv. Ment. Dis.*, **39**, 217–235.

GODIN, P. 1913. *La croissance pendant l'âge scolaire.* Neuchâtel: Delachaux et Niestle.

——. 1935. *Recherches anthropometriques sur la croissance des diverses parties du corps.* Paris: Legrand.

GOLDSTEIN, M. S. 1936. Changes in dimensions and form of the face and head with age. *Amer. J. Phys. Anthrop.*, **22**, 37–89.

——. 1939. Development of the head in the same individuals. *Human Biol.*, **11**, 195–219.

GRAVES, W. W. 1921. The types of scapulae: A comparative study of some correlated characters in human scapulae. *Amer. J. Phys. Anthrop.*, **4**, 111–128.

GRAY, H. 1924. *Anatomy of the human body.* (21st ed., rev. by W. H. LEWIS.) Philadelphia: Lea and Febiger.

GRAY, H., and J. G. AYRES. 1931. *Growth in private school children.* Chicago: University of Chicago Press.

GREULICH, W. W. 1931. The sex ratio among human still births. *Science*, **75**, 53–54.

GREULICH, W. W., H. G. DAY, S. E. LACHMAN, J. B. WOLFE, and F. K. SHUTTLEWORTH. 1938. A handbook of methods for the study of adolescent children. *Monogr. Soc. Res. Child Develpm.*, **3**, No. 2. Pp. xvii + 406.

GREULICH, W. W., R. I. DORFMAN, H. R. CATCHPOLE, C. I. SOLOMON, and C. S. CULOTTA. 1942. Somatic and endocrine studies of puberal and adolescent boys. *Monogr. Soc. Res. Child Develpm.*, **7**, No. 3. Pp. 65 + 9 plates.

HALL, W. S. 1896. The first five hundred days of a child's life. *Child Study Monthly*, **2**, Nos. 6 and 7, pp. 332–342; 394–407.

HAMILTON, J. A. 1936. Intelligence and the human brain. *Psychol. Rev.*, **43**, 308–321.

HAMMETT, F. S. 1936. *The nature of growth.* Lancaster, Pa.: Science Press.

——. 1937. Nutrition vs. growth. *Science*, **86**, 560–561.

HEJINIAN, L., and E. HATT. 1929. The stem-length: Recumbent-length ratio as an index of body type in young children. *Amer. J. Phys. Anthrop.*, **13**, 287–307.

HELLMAN, M. 1932. Malocclusion as a phase of growth. *Mouth Health Quart.*, **1**, No. 2, pp. 20–21.

——. 1933. Growth of the face and occlusion of the teeth in relation to orthodontic treatment. *Int. J. Orthod., Oral Surg. and Radiog.*, **19**, 1116–1146.

HESS, J. H., G. J. MOHR, and P. E. BARTELME. 1934. *The physical and mental growth of prematurely born children.* Chicago: University of Chicago Press.

HILL, A. H. 1939. Fetal age assessment by centers of ossification. *Amer. J. Phys. Anthrop.*, **24**, 251–272.

HODGES, P. C. 1933. *Development of the human skeleton: I. Trunk and extremities.* Chicago: University of Chicago Press.

HOLMES, S. J., and V. P. MENTZER. 1931. Changes in the sex ratio in infant mortality according to age. *Human Biol.*, **3**, 560–575.

HRDLIČKA, A. 1939. *Practical anthropometry.* (2d ed.) Philadelphia: Wistar Institute of Anatomy and Biology.

HUXLEY, J. S. 1932. *Problems of relative growth.* London: Dial Press.

JACKSON, C. M. 1914. Morphogenesis, in *Morris' human anatomy.* (5th ed.) Philadelphia: Blakiston.

——. 1928. Some aspects of form and growth. In W. J. ROBBINS, S. BRODY, A. G. HOGAN, C. M. JACKSON, and C. W. GREEN, *Growth*, pp. 111–140. New Haven: Yale University Press.

——. 1930. Normal and abnormal human types. In J. A. HARRIS, C. M. JACKSON, D. G. PATERSON, and R. E. SCAMMON, *The measurement of man*, pp. 79–113. Minneapolis: University of Minnesota Press.

JENSS, R. M., and N. BAYLEY. 1937. A mathematical method for studying the growth of a child. *Human Biol.*, **9**, 556–563.

JOHNSON, B. J. 1925. *Mental growth of children in relation to the rate of growth in bodily development.* New York: Dutton.

JONES, H. E. 1933. Relationships in physical and mental development. *Rev. Educ. Res.*, **3**, 150–162.

——. 1936. Relationships in physical and mental development. *Rev. Educ. Res.*, **4**, 102–123.

——. 1939. Relationships in physical and mental development. *Rev. Educ. Res.*, **9**, 91–102.

KELLY, H. J. 1937. Anatomic age and its relation to stature. *Univ. Iowa Stud. Child Welfare*, **12**, No. 5. Pp. 38.

KJÖLSETH, M. 1913. Untersuchungen über die Reifezeichen des neugeborenen Kindes. *Mschr. Geburtsh Gynäk.*, **38**, 216–298.

KLEIN, H., C. E. PALMER, and J. W. KNUTSON. 1938. Studies on dental caries: I. Dental status and dental needs of elementary school children. *Publ. Health Rep., Wash.*, **53**, 751–765.

KLEIN, H., C. E. PALMER, and M. KRAMER. 1937. Studies on dental caries: II. The use of the normal probability curve for expressing the age distribution of eruption of the permanent teeth. *Growth*, **1**, 385–394.

KNOTT, V. B. 1941. Physical measurement of young children: A study of anthropometric reliabilities for children three to six years of age. *Univ. Iowa Stud. Child Welfare*, **18**, No. 3. Pp. 99.

KRETSCHMER, E. 1925. *Physique and character.* (Trans. by W. J. H. SPROUT.) New York: Harcourt, Brace; London: Kegan Paul.

KROGMAN, W. M. 1939. Facing facts of face growth. *Amer. J. Orthod. Oral Surg.*, **25**, 724–731.

——. 1940. Trend in the study of physical growth in children. *Child Develpm.*, **11**, 279–284.

——. 1941a. *Growth of man. Tabulae Biologicae.* Den Haag, Nederlands: Junk.

——. 1941b. *Bibliography of human morphology, 1914–1939.* Chicago: University of Chicago Press.

LEWIS, S. J. 1937. The effect of thumb and finger sucking on the primary teeth and dental arches. *Child Develpm.*, **8**, 93–98.

LINCOLN, E. A. 1930. The reliability of anthropometric measurements. *J. Genet. Psychol.*, **38**, 445–450.

MARESCH, M. M., and J. DEMING. 1939. The growth of the long bones in 80 infants. Roentgenograms versus anthropometry. *Child Develpm.*, **10**, 91–106.

MARSHALL, E. I. 1936. A multiple factor study of eighteen anthropometric measurements of Iowa City boys aged nine days to six years. *J. Exp. Educ.*, **5**, 212–228.

——. 1937. A review of American research on seasonal variation in stature and body weight. *J. Pediat.*, **10**, 819–831.

MARTIN, R. 1928. *Lehrbuch der Anthropologie:* Vol. I, *Somotologie;* Vol. II, *Kraniologie, osteologie;* Vol. III, *Bibliographie, literaturver-*

zeichnis, sachregister, autorenregister. Jena: Fischer.

MASSLER, M., I. SCHOUR, and H. G. PONCHER. 1941. Developmental patterns of the child as reflected in the calcification pattern of the teeth. *Amer. J. Dis. Child.*, 62, 33–67.

McCLOY, C. H. 1936. Appraising physical status: The selection of measurements. *Univ. Iowa Stud. Child Welfare*, 12, No. 2. Pp. 126.

——. 1938. Appraising physical status: Methods and norms. *Univ. Iowa Stud. Child Welfare*, 15, No. 2. Pp. 260.

——. 1940. An analysis for multiple factors of physical growth at different age levels. *Child Develpm.*, 11, 249–277.

McHALE, K. 1926. Comparative psychology and hygiene of the over-weight child. *Teach. Coll. Contr. Educ.*, No. 221.

MEREDITH, H. V. 1935. The rhythm of physical growth: A study of eighteen anthropometric measurements on Iowa City white males ranging in age between birth and eighteen years. *Univ. Iowa Stud. Child Welfare*, 11, No. 3. Pp. 128.

——. 1936a. Physical growth of white children: A review of American research prior to 1900. *Monogr. Soc. Res. Child Develpm.*, 1, No. 2. Pp. 83.

——. 1936b. The reliability of anthropometric measurements taken on eight- and nine-year-old white males. *Child Develpm.*, 7, 262–272.

——. 1939a. Stature of Massachusetts children of North European and Italian ancestry. *Amer. J. Phys. Anthrop.*, 24, 301–346.

——. 1939b. Physical growth from birth to maturity. *Rev. Educ. Res.*, 9, 47–79.

——. 1939c. Techniques of research in physical growth and anthropometry. *Rev. Educ. Res.*, 9, 80–90.

MEREDITH, H. V., and A. W. BROWN. 1939. Growth in body weight during the first ten days of postnatal life. *Human Biol.*, 11, 24–77.

MEREDITH, H. V., and J. L. GOODMAN. 1941. A comparison of routine hospital records of birth stature with measurements of birth stature obtained for longitudinal research. *Child Develpm.*, 12, 175–181.

MEREDITH, H. V., and V. B. KNOTT. 1938. Changes in body proportions during infancy and the preschool years: III. The skelic index. *Child Develpm.*, 9, 49–62.

MEREDITH, H. V., and G. STODDARD. 1936. Physical growth from birth to maturity. *Rev. Educ. Res.*, 6, 54–84.

METHENY, E. 1939. The variability of the percentage index of build as applied to the prediction of normal weight. *Human Biol.*, 11, 473–484.

MULLEN, F. A. 1940. Factors in the growth of girls. *Child Develpm.*, 11, 27–42.

MURCHISON, C., and S. LANGER. 1927. Tiedemann's observations on the development of the mental faculties of children. *J. Genet. Psychol.*, 34, 205–230.

NACCARATI, S. 1921. The morphological aspect of intelligence. *Arch. Psychol.*, No. 45.

PALMER, C. E., and L. J. REED. 1935. Anthropometric studies of individual growth: I. Age, height, and growth in height, elementary school children. *Human Biol.*, 7, 319–324.

PALMER, C. E., K. RIITI, and L. J. REED. 1937. Anthropometric studies of individual growth: II. Age, weight, and rate of growth, elementary school children. *Child Develpm.*, 8, 47–61.

PATERSON, D. G. 1930. *Physique and intellect.* New York: Century.

PEARL, R. 1928. *The rate of living.* New York: Knopf.

PEATMAN, J. G., and R. A. HIGGONS. 1938. Growth norms from birth to the age of five years: A study of children reared with optimal pediatric and home care. *Amer. J. Dis. Child.*, 55, 1233–1247.

PORTER, W. T. 1893. Physical basis of precocity and dullness. *Trans. Acad. Sci. St. Louis*, 6, 161–181.

PRYOR, H. B. 1923. Differences in time of development of centers of ossification in the male and female skeleton. *Anat. Rec.*, 25, 252–273.

——. 1925. Time of ossification of bones of the hand of the male and female and union of epiphyses with the diaphyses. *Amer. J. Phys. Anthrop.*, 8, 401–410.

——. 1936. Certain physical and physiological aspects of adolescent development in girls. *J. Pediat.*, 8, 52–62.

——. 1941. Width-weight tables (Revised). *Amer. J. Dis. Child.*, 61, 300–304.

PRYOR, H. B., and H. R. STOLZ. 1933. Determining appropriate weight for body build. *J. Pediat.*, 3, 608–622.

PYLE, S. I., and C. MENINO. 1939. Observations on estimating skeletal age from the Todd and the Flory bone atlases. *Child Develpm.*, 10, 27–34.

QUETELET, A. 1871. *Anthropometrie.* Bruxelles: Muquardt.

RICHEY, H. G. 1937. The relation of accelerated, normal and retarded puberty to the height and weight of school children. *Monogr. Soc. Res. Child Develpm.*, 2, No. 1. Pp. vi + 67.

ROBBINS, W. J., S. BRODY, A. G. HOGAN, C. M. JACKSON, and C. W. GREEN. 1928. *Growth.* New Haven: Yale University Press.

ROBERTSON, T. S. 1923. *The chemical basis of growth and senescence.* Philadelphia: Lippincott.

ROBINOW, M. 1942. The variability of weight and height increments from birth to six years. *Child Develpm.*, 13, 159–164.

ROYSTER, L. T. 1936. Body type of Negro children. *Arch. Pediat.*, 53, 259–262.

SAWTELL, R. O. 1929. Ossification and growth of children from one to eight years of age. *Amer. J. Dis. Child.*, **37**, 61–87.

SCAMMON, R. E. 1922. On the weight increments of premature infants compared with those of the same gestation age and those of full-term children. *Proc. Soc. Exp. Biol. Med.*, **19**, 133–136.

——. 1927*a*. The first seriation study of human growth. *Amer. J. Phys. Anthrop.*, **10**, 329–336.

——. 1927*b*. The literature on the growth and physical development of the fetus, infant, and child: A quantitative summary. *Anat. Rec.*, **5**, 241–267.

——. 1930. The measurement of the body in childhood. In J. A. HARRIS, C. M. JACKSON, D. G. PATERSON, and R. E. SCAMMON. *The measurement of man*, pp. 173–215. Minneapolis: University of Minnesota Press.

SCAMMON, R. E., and L. A. CALKINS. 1929. *The development and growth of the external dimensions of the human body in the fetal period.* Minneapolis: University of Minnesota Press.

SCHULTZ, A. H. 1921. Sex incidence in abortions. *Carnegie Inst. Wash. Publ.*, No. 275, 177–191.

——. 1926. Fetal growth of man and other primates. *Quart. Rev. Biol.*, **1**, 465–521.

——. 1929. The technique of measuring the outer body of human fetuses and of primates in general. *Contr. Embryol. Carnegie Inst. Wash. Publ.*, No. 394, pp. 213–257.

SECOND CONFERENCE ON RESEARCH IN CHILD DEVELOPMENT. 1927. Session 6: *Constitution and mental types.* Washington, D. C.: National Research Council.

SHELDON, W. H., S. S. STEVENS, and W. B. TUCKER. 1940. *The varieties of human physique.* New York: Harper.

SHIROKOGOROFF, S. M. 1925. *Process of physical growth among the Chinese.* Shanghai: Commercial Press.

SHUTTLEWORTH, F. K. 1937. Sexual maturation and physical growth of girls age six to nineteen. *Monogr. Soc. Res. Child Develpm.*, **2**, No. 5. Pp. xx + 253.

——. 1938. The adolescent period: A graphic and pictorial atlas. *Monogr. Soc. Res. Child Develpm.*, **3**, No. 3. Pp. 246.

——. 1939. The physical and mental growth of girls and boys age six to nineteen in relation to age at maximum growth. *Monogr. Soc. Res. Child Develpm.*, **4**, No. 3. Pp. vi + 291.

SIMMONS, K., and T. W. TODD. 1938. Growth of well children: Analysis of stature and weight, 3 months to 13 years. *Growth,* **2**, 93–143.

SIMMONS, K., and W. W. GREULICH. 1943. Menarcheal age and the height, weight and skeletal age of girls 4 to 17 years. *J. Pediat.*, **22**, 518–548.

SONTAG, L. W., D. SNELL, and M. ANDERSON. 1939. Rate of appearance of ossification centers from birth to the age of five years. *Amer. J. Dis. Child.*, **58**, 949–957.

STEGGERDA, M., and P. DENSEN. 1936. Height, weight and age tables for homogeneous groups with particular reference to Navajo Indians and Dutch Whites. *Child Develpm.*, **7,** 115–120.

STEVENSON, P. H. 1924. Age order of epiphyseal union in man. *Amer. J. Phys. Anthrop.*, **7**, 53–93.

STONE, C. P., and R. G. BARKER. 1937. On the relationship between menarcheal age and certain measurements of physique in girls of the ages 9 to 16 years. *Human Biol.*, **9**, 1–28.

STREETER, G. L. 1920. Weight, sitting height, head size, foot length and menstrual age of the human embryo. *Contr. Embryol. Carnegie Inst. Wash. Publ.*, No. 274, pp. 143–170.

STUART, H. C., and P. H. DWINELL. 1942. The growth of bone, muscle and overlying tissues in children six to ten years of age as measured by studies of roentgenograms of the leg area. *Child Develpm.*, **13**, 195–213.

STUART, H. C., P. HILL, and C. SHAW. 1940. Studies from the Center for Research in Child Health and Development, School of Public Health, Harvard University: III. The growth of bone, muscle and overlying tissues as revealed by studies of roentgenograms of the leg area. *Monogr. Soc. Res. Child Develpm.*, **5**, No. 3. Pp. 190 + 23 tables.

SULLIVAN, L. R. 1928. *Essentials of anthropometry.* (Rev. by H. L. SHAPIRO.) New York: American Museum of Natural History.

TAYLOR, R. 1919. The proportionate measurements of 250 full term newborn infants. *Amer. J. Dis. Child.*, **17**, 353–362.

THOMPSON, D. W. 1917. *On growth and form.* Cambridge: University Press.

THOMPSON, H. 1929. A measuring board for infants. *Amer. J. Phys. Anthrop.*, **13**, 281–286.

——. 1938. Body proportions in the growing infant. *Growth,* **2**, 1–12.

THURSTONE, L. L. 1935. *The vectors of mind.* Chicago: University of Chicago Press.

TODD, T. W. 1930. The roentgenographic appraisement of skeletal differentiation. *Child Develpm.*, **1**, 298–310.

——. 1933. *Roentgenographic appraisement of developmental growth in the skeleton,* pp. 258–279. (White House Conference on Child Health and Protection, Growth and Development of the Child.) New York: Century.

——. 1935. Anthropology and growth. *Science,* **81**, 260–263.

——. 1937. *Atlas of skeletal maturation (hand).* St. Louis: Mosby.

TROTTER, M. 1939. Classifications of hair color. *Amer. J. Phys. Anthrop.*, **25**, 237–260.

VICKERS, V. S., and H. C. STUART. 1943. Anthropometry in the pediatrician's office. *J. Pediat.*, **22**, 155–170.

WALLIS, R. W. 1931. How children grow: An anthropometric study of private school children from two to eight years of age. *Univ. Iowa Stud. Child Welfare*, **5**, No. 1.

WEINBACH, A. P. 1938. A simple method for estimating the surface area of the human body from birth to maturity. *Growth*, **2**, 303–317.

WEISSENBERG, S. 1911. *Das Wachstum des Menschen nach Alter, Geschlecht und Rasse.* Stuttgart: Strecker and Schröder.

WETZEL, N. C. 1941. Physical fitness in terms of physique, development and basal metabolism. *J. Amer. Med. Assoc.*, **116**, 1187–1195.

——. 1943. Assessing the physical condition of children: I. Case demonstration of failing growth and the determination of "par" by the grid method. II. Simple malnutrition: A problem of failing growth and development. III. The components of physical status and physical progress and their evaluation. *J. Pediat.*, **22**, 82–110, 208–225, 329–361.

WHITE HOUSE CONFERENCE ON CHILD HEALTH AND PROTECTION. 1932, 1933. *Growth and development of the child: 1, General considerations; 2, Anatomy and physiology; 3, Nutrition; 4, Appraisement of the child.* New York: Century.

WILDER, H. H., and B. WENTWORTH. 1918. *Personal identification.* Boston: Gorham Press.

WILSON, C. A., M. E. SWEENY, R. STUTSMAN, L. E. CHESIRE, and E. HATT. 1930. *The Merrill-Palmer standards of physical and mental growth.* Detroit: Merrill-Palmer.

WISSLER, C. 1930. *Growth of children in Hawaii: Based on observations by Louis R. Sullivan.* Honolulu: Memoirs of the Bernice P. Bishop Museum.

WOODBURY, R. M. 1921. Statures and weights of children under six years of age. *U. S. Child. Bur. Publ.*, No. 87.

CHAPTER 6

THE ONTOGENESIS OF INFANT BEHAVIOR

ARNOLD GESELL

Introduction

Ontogeny is the life history or development of an individual organism. This chapter will concern itself mainly with the first two postnatal years of the human life cycle and with that outward aspect of life which goes by the familiar name of *behavior*. Behavior is in a sense more than an aspect; it is the very essence and a culminating manifestation of the life processes of the individual, including the all-pervading process of growth. Biologically —or shall we say semantically—the infant is a growing action system. He comes by his "mind" in the same way that he comes by his body; namely, through the mechanisms of development. Our task is to formulate some of the general principles which underlie the developmental patterning of his total action system.

Comparative Considerations

The individual is a member of a species. His most fundamental behavior characteristics are those which are common to the species as a whole. Less fundamental are those which are peculiar to a breed or stock, differentiated within the species. Some patterns of behavior are so primitive that they are common to a wide range of species. The startle reflex, universal among infants and children, is also found in primates and among lower mammals in types as widely separated as bear and badger. The tonic neck reflex, which plays such a

prominent rôle in the early ontogenesis of infant behavior, has been investigated in the rabbit as well as in man (Magnus, 1924). The lowly *Amblystoma* embodies generic patterns of terrestrial locomotion. This primitive vertebrate in the hands of Coghill (1929) has become a touchstone for elucidating problems of human behavior.

Infancy is the period in which the individual realizes his racial inheritance. This inheritance is the end product of evolutionary processes which trace back to an extremely remote antiquity. But infancy itself is a product of evolution. It was evolved not only to perpetuate a groundwork of racial inheritance, but also to add thereto a contingent margin of specific modifiability. In the more complex orders of life, such as fish, amphibian, reptile, bird, and mammal, the postnatal period of immaturity has become a recognizable part of the individual life cycle and plays an important part in the economy of that cycle. Infancy was evolved to subserve the needs of individual growth. It lengthens as the organism becomes more complex. It varies significantly among different species.

The study of infancy in its broadest sense must therefore be a comparative science. The most general laws of development will prove to be applicable to all vertebrates, not excluding either fish or man. In spite of the bewildering diversity of the behavior characteristics of widely varying species, certain developmental sequences must be common to large groups and orders. Differences in gestation, longevity, size, and growth cycle yield to quantitative comparative study of correlated behavior characteristics. The findings of chemical embryology and of electrochemistry suggest that there is a general physiology of development. There are far-reaching implications in the fact that the thyroid substance of ox or sheep will profoundly influence the ontogenesis of the behavior of a cretinous infant (Gesell, Amatruda, and Culotta, 1936).

It would take a lengthy syllabus to list and classify resemblances in the behavior of human and infrahuman species. Lashley and Watson (1913) made a valuable pioneering study on the development of a young monkey, reporting the age of appearance in a macaque of such behavior items as creeping, winking, eye following, walking, running, thumb opposition, and grasping. Boutan in 1914 compared adaptation in problem-solving situations of a gibbon and young child, whereas Yerkes in 1916 contrasted the behavior of a 4-year-old orangutan and a 3-year-old child in a problem-solving situation.

Jacobsen, Jacobsen, and Yoshioka (1932) and Kellogg and Kellogg (1933) each reported on the behavioral development of a young chimpanzee and compared responses to infant tests in the four fields of behavior—motor, adaptive, language, and personal-social—with those of normal infants at the same ages. Experimental studies of form discrimination (Gellermann, 1933) and responses to problem-solving situations (Brainard, 1930) make direct comparisons between chimpanzees and preschool children. A. W. Yerkes (1935) has recently explored the possibility of investigating problems of behavior in chimpanzee infancy.

Madam Kohts (1935) compared the behavior of a male chimpanzee during the age period of 1½ to 4 years with that of her son from birth to 4 years of age. She sums up her observations as follows:

(1) In the functional biological field: the chimpanzee totally ignores the possibility of walking erect and of freeing his hands for carrying weights. (2) In the sphere of imitation: the chimpanzee is devoid of imitation in so far as human sounds are concerned and generally fails to extend or improve his imitatory behavior. (3) In respect of emotional, altruistic and social behavior: the chimpanzee fails to understand the advantages of friendly sympathetic intercourse with creatures standing on a lower biological level than himself. (4) With regard to habit-forming: the chimpanzee does not improve in the motor habits connected with the use of tools and household implements. (5) In the sphere of playful behavior: he does not indulge in creative constructional play.

On the basis of the foregoing evidence, Madam Kohts concludes: "It is impossible to say that he [the chimpanzee] is 'almost human'; we must go even further and state quite definitely that he is 'by no means human.'"

The comparative study of interspecies resemblances must be approached with critical caution, because many of the similarities are offset by important contextual differences. Similarities often are apparent when differences are hidden and profound. On evolutionary grounds one may expect the highest degree of resemblance in the ontogenesis of anthropoid and of human species. At no phase of the entire life cycle, however, are *homo* and *anthropos* the same. Human characteristics are not superadded as a late installment upon a lower primitive stage. They inhere in the very beginnings of fetal and postnatal behavior.

The pre-eminence of human infancy lies in the scope, the depth, and the duration of plasticity. There is a maturation of basic motor patterns as in subhuman species; but this proceeds less rigidly and the total behavior complex is suspended in a state of greater formativeness. This increased modifiability is extremely sensitive to social milieu. In the impersonal aspects of adaptive behavior of the nonlanguage type (practical intelligence) there is a high degree of early correspondence between man and other primates. Some of this correspondence is so consistent as to justify a phyletic and even recapitulatory explanation. Transcending and pervading the interspecies similarities, however, is a generalized conditionability or responsiveness to other personalities which is distinctively human.

Principles of Developmental Morphology

In the comparative study of behavior one cannot escape problems of pattern and form. When Goethe coined the word *Morphologie*, he was interested in the forms of flowers and skulls. To this day the term carries physical connotations. But the concepts of morphology can be extended to the phenomena of behavior. Morphology is the science of form. The dictionary reminds us that form is the shape of anything as distinguished from the substance of that thing. Behavior has shape.

The shapes which behaviors assume can be investigated in their own scientific right. A morphological approach leads to the description and measurement of specific forms, the systematic study of topographic relations and correlations of such forms, their ontogenetic progression and involution, their comparative features among individuals and among species.

"Structure is only the intimate expression of function" was a leading maxim of John Hunter. In a monistic (but not mystic) sense, "the mind" may be regarded as a living, growing "structure" even though it lacks corporeal tangibility. It is a complex, organized, and organizing action system which manifests itself in characteristic forms of behavior—in patterns of posture, locomotion, prehension, manipulation, of perception, communication, and social response. The action systems of embryo, fetus, infant, and child undergo pattern changes which are so sequential and orderly that we may be certain that the patterning process is governed by mechanisms of form regulation—the same mechanisms which are being established by the science of embryology.

Experimental embryology is now one of the most active and flourishing of all the life sciences. It has undertaken the analysis of development, particularly as it affects the anatomy of the organism. Investigators, however, are using functional and behavior criteria increasingly to define the somatic anatomy. This is natural, for, by the principle of hierarchical continuity, there is but one physiology of development. The growth of tissues, of organs, and of behavior is obedient to identical laws of developmental morphology.

It cannot, therefore, be doubted that the general physiology of mental development will find its deeper roots in the same scientific soil which is now intensively cultivated in laboratories of experimental embryology. Already many of the current morphogenetic concepts have more than vague analogy to psychical processes: embryonic field, gradient theory, regional determination, autonomous induction, complementary induction, potency, polarity, symmetry, time correlation, etc. Associationism as a psychological tradition has come down from Aristotle and still has considerable vitality, as shown by a prodigious preoccupation with problems of learning and the conditioned reflex. The laws of association deal with the factors of contiguity, assimilation, frequency, primacy, intensity, duration, context, acquaintance, maturity. Needless to say, these laws will some day be reformulated in terms of the biology and physiology of development. The full coordination of animal and child psychology will depend upon such reformulations.

Psychological growth, like somatic growth, is a morphogenetic process. It produces a progressive organization of behavior forms. Our scientific knowledge of this process is still very meager. We lack the grammar and the lexicon for defining form characteristics. We need morphographic as well as mathematical methods which will simplify and generalize form phenomena.

It is possible, however, to define several principles of development which have psychomorphological implications. These principles concern the shaping of the action system and its trends in oriented space and oriented time. The principle of *developmental direction*, for example, recognizes that the action system of the infant does not increase symmetrically like an expanding balloon but is subject to the far-reaching consequences of the biological factor of anteroposterior differentiation.

The very architectonics of the neuromuscular system determines not only a cephalocaudal course but also the relationships between paired and opposed motor organs. We shall propose a principle of *reciprocal interweaving* to characterize this aspect of behavior organization.

Laterality is distinctly a morphological phenomenon, in that it represents a form of dynamic asymmetry. It represents a significant principle of *functional asymmetry*.

During ontogenesis the total action system undergoes specific differentiation in restricted spheres. This orderly specification is governed by a principle of *individuating maturation*.

The growing organism is of necessity in a state of unstable and shifting equilibrium. Also, of necessity, it must restrict the modes and degrees of instability. The oscillations of the organism are self-limited by a principle of *regulatory fluctuation*.

A brief discussion of these five principles may serve to delineate some of the general features of the ontogeny of infant behavior. The several principles are not entirely absolute, and they certainly do not operate independently or in isolation. They overlap and modify each other in interesting and significant ways.

General Sequences of Early Behavior Growth

As a background for the discussion of the several principles of development it will be profitable to take a panoramic glance at the whole domain of behavior development in the first five years of life. This domain can be envisaged as four major fields of functional organization: (1) motor behavior, (2) adaptive behavior, (3) language behavior, (4) personal-social behavior.

(1) Motor characteristics include postural reactions, prehension, locomotion, general bodily coordination, and specific motor skills.

(2) Adaptive behavior is a convenient category for those varied adjustments—perceptual, orientational, manual, and verbal—which reflect the child's capacity to initiate new experience and to profit by past experience. This adaptivity includes alertness, intelligence, and various forms of constructiveness and exploitation.

(3) Language embraces all behavior which has to do with soliloquy, dramatic

expression, communication, and comprehension.

(4) Personal-social behavior embraces the child's personal reactions to other persons and to the impacts of culture; his adjustments to domestic life, to property, to social groups, and to community conventions.

These four major fields of behavior comprise most of the visible patterns of child behavior. They do not, of course, fall neatly into separate compartments. The child always reacts as an integer.

Elsewhere the writer and his collaborators have summarized the ontogenetic trends of development in the four behavior fields at ten age levels from 4 weeks to 5 years (Gesell, Halverson, Thompson, *et al.*, 1940, Chapters III, IV).

The accompanying chart (Figure 1) depicts the trends and sequences of early behavior growth. The chart includes the fetal period to indicate the continuity of the growth cycle. The ontogenetic organization of behavior begins long before birth. The general direction of this organization is from head to foot, from proximal to distal segments, and from fundamental to accessory control. Lips and tongue lead, eye muscles follow, then neck, shoulder, arms, hands, fingers, trunk, legs, feet. The chart reflects this law of developmental direction; it also suggests that the four distinguishable fields of behavior develop conjointly in close coordination. The motor field of development presents the most evident and extrinsic continuity between the prenatal and postnatal periods (Gesell and Amatruda, 1941).

In terse terms the trends of behavior development are:

In the *first quarter* (4–16 weeks) of the first year the infant gains control of his twelve oculomotor muscles.

In the *second quarter* (16–28 weeks) he comes into command of the muscles which support his head and move his arms. He reaches out for things.

In the *third quarter* (28–40 weeks) he gains command of his trunk and hands. He sits. He grasps, transfers, and manipulates objects.

In the *fourth quarter* (40–52 weeks) he extends command to his legs and feet; to his forefinger and thumb. He pokes and plucks. He stands upright.

In the *second year* he walks and runs; articulates words and phrases; acquires bowel and bladder control; attains a rudimentary sense of personal identity and of personal possession.

In the *third year* he speaks in sentences, using words as tools of thought. He shows a positive propensity to understand his environment and to comply with cultural demands. He is no longer a "mere" infant.

In the *fourth year* he asks innumerable questions, perceives analogies, displays an active tendency to conceptualize and generalize. He is nearly self-dependent in routines of home life.

At *five* he is well matured in motor control. He hops and skips. He talks without infantile articulation. He can narrate a long tale. He prefers associative play; he feels socialized pride in clothes and accomplishment. He is a self-assured, conforming citizen in his small world.

The Principle of Developmental Direction

The principle of developmental direction is reflected in the foregoing summary of developmental trends. The phenomena of polarity and of gradients (electrochemical and otherwise) underlie this principle. The direction of early embryonic growth is determined by the longitudinal gradient of the mesoderm. This gradient governs alike the course of somatic organization and that of behavioral organization. In the growth of the fetus there is an unmistakable precocity in the development of the anterior

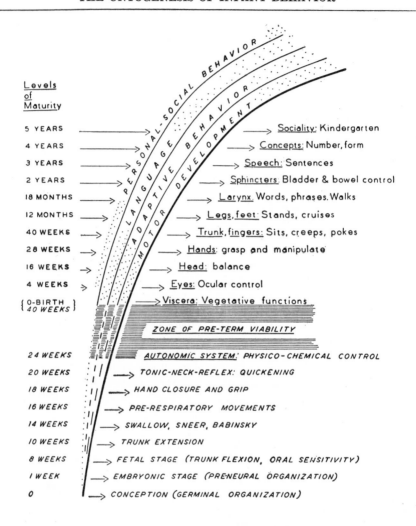

Levels
of
Maturity

5 YEARS ——————————→ ——→ Sociality: Kindergarten

4 YEARS ——————————→ ——→ Concepts: Number, form

3 YEARS ——————————→ ——→ Speech: Sentences

2 YEARS ——————————→ ——→ Sphincters: Bladder & bowel control

18 MONTHS ————————→ ——→ Larynx: Words, phrases. Walks

12 MONTHS —————————→ ——→ Legs, feet: Stands, cruises

40 WEEKS ——————————→ ——→ Trunk, fingers: Sits, creeps, pokes

28 WEEKS ——————————→ ——→ Hands: grasp and manipulate

16 WEEKS ——————————→ ——→ Head: balance

4 WEEKS ———————————→ ——→ Eyes: Ocular control

{ 0-BIRTH }   ——→ Viscera: Vegetative functions
{ 40 WEEKS }

ZONE OF PRE-TERM VIABILITY

24 WEEKS   *AUTONOMIC SYSTEM: PHYSICO-CHEMICAL CONTROL*

20 WEEKS   ——→ *TONIC-NECK-REFLEX: QUICKENING*

18 WEEKS   ——→ *HAND CLOSURE AND GRIP*

16 WEEKS   ——→ *PRE-RESPIRATORY MOVEMENTS*

14 WEEKS   ——→ *SWALLOW, SNEER, BABINSKY*

10 WEEKS   ——→ *TRUNK EXTENSION*

8 WEEKS   ——→ *FETAL STAGE (TRUNK FLEXION, ORAL SENSITIVITY)*

1 WEEK   ——→ *EMBRYONIC STAGE (PRENEURAL ORGANIZATION)*

0   ——→ *CONCEPTION (GERMINAL ORGANIZATION)*

ONTOGENETIC TRENDS AND SEQUENCES

FIGURE 1. Ontogenetic trends and sequences of behavior growth. (From *Developmental Diagnosis: Normal and Abnormal Child Development*, by A. Gesell and C. S. Amatruda. New York: Paul B. Hoeber, Inc., 1941, page 9.)

end of the organism. At the close of the second fetal month the height of the head rivals the length of the trunk, and the umbilicus is at the level of the cervical vertebrae. The posteriorward migration of the umbilicus is a reflection of the cephalo-caudad trend. This trend, however, must not be taken too literally, for the caudad appendage of the embryo, which was prominent in the middle of the second month, is already beginning to regress at the end of that month.

There are many apparent exceptions to the directional rule which do not, however, impair the validity of the general principle. Some of the exceptions arise out of the fact that there are successive head-to-foot sweeps of development so that the trend repeats itself at certain periods appropriate to the ascending levels of organization. We thus expect to find cyclical evidence of the trend in the preneural as well as in the neural stage and in late as well as early stages of infancy.

The principle is well illustrated in the behavior characteristics of the 20-week-old infant. His trunk is still so flaccid that he must be propped or strapped in a chair to maintain a sitting posture. When he is so secured, however, his eyes, head, and shoulders exhibit heightened activity and intensified tonus. The pelvic zone and the lower extremities at 20 weeks are, in comparison, very immature.

Evidence of the cephalocaudad trend will be seen in a later summary of the ontogenetic sequences of prone behavior patterns. The very fact that this sequence converges toward and culminates in the assumption of the erect posture suggests the presence of a unidirectional principle. The principle does not operate with complete simplicity, however, because the mastery of the erect posture depends in turn upon the development of the functions of equilibrium which have a cephalic as well as a caudad status.

Just as neuromotor organization proceeds from head to foot in the direction of the longitudinal axis, so it tends to proceed from the central to peripheral segments. The fundamental axial muscles are among the first to react in a coordinated manner, as shown by the primitive body flexion of the fetus. There is a progressive advance of motor control from the larger, fundamental muscles to the smaller muscles which execute the more refined movements.

This trend from fundamental or proximal to accessory and distal control is illustrated in the ontogenesis of postural attitudes, of prehensory approach, manipulation, and prone locomotion.

During the earlier periods of development the arms and also the legs tend to react as wholes, the impulses arising mainly from the shoulder and the pelvic girdles. With advancing maturity, mobility asserts itself at the elbow and wrist joints and at the knee and ankle joints. Forearm, foreleg, hand, and foot show specific segmental activity. The cephalocaudad and the proximal-distal trends overlap and correlate. For this reason, independent activity of the distal segments becomes apparent in the upper extremities before the lower extremities. In the field of prehension, as Halverson (1933) has pointed out, from 16 weeks on, the elbow and digits participate in reaching movements with increasing effectiveness, until at 40 weeks they closely approximate the shoulder in efficiency, whereas trunk and wrist remain functionally retarded.

In the ontogenesis of prehension there is not only a proximal-distal trend but there is an ulnar-radial shift. This shift is closely bound up with the growth of thumb opposition. At 20 weeks a crude palmar grasp, often favoring the ulnar aspect of the palm, is evident; but after 28 weeks there is an obvious preference for radial as opposed to ulnar grasp and manipulation. The developmental shift from ulnar to radial grasp is so strong that the infant actually displays a well-defined intolerance as well as motor rejection when an object is pressed against the ulnar aspect of the palm. At 40 weeks he extends his index finger and makes oblique radial approach upon objects which require precise prehension. He brings the volar pad of the thumb against the volar pad of the index (Gesell and Halverson, 1936).

The operation of the cephalocaudad principle in relation to other developmental principles is further illustrated in the summary of the ontogenetic sequence of the prone behavior of the human infant, summarized in Table 1.

The Principle of Reciprocal Interweaving

It is natural that the metaphor of the loom should constantly reappear in the description and interpretation of the developmental process. The products of growth are envisaged as a fabric in which threads and designs are visible. Even at the molecular level the analogy of warp and woof becomes helpful. Wrinch conceives the chromosome as a structure constituted of two elements: long filaments of identical protein molecules in parallel and a set of ringlike nucleic acid molecules surrounding these filaments and holding them together in a wooflike manner. From such an arrangement and the asymmetric constitution of biomolecules, fabric issues.

The bilateral nature of the anatomy of the human physique and of its musculature suggests that the balance and opposition of its paired organs need to be interrelated in an orderly manner during the long period of ontogenesis. Even single members are bilateral or bivalent in the sense that they have both flexor and extensor activators. Accordingly, in the four-limbed infant there are many double aspect structures (and functions) to be coordinately interwoven: anterior bilateral, posterior bilateral, ipsilateral, crossed lateral, flexor, and extensor.

Flexion and extension are the most fundamental components of muscular movement. Sherrington (1906) has formulated a law of "reciprocal innervation" which shows the functional relationships of these components in the counteraction of antagonistic muscles. The inhibition of one set of muscles while the opposing muscles are in excitation is a condition for effective movement. Reciprocal innervation is a mode of coordination, a physiological mechanism.

In the ontogenesis of the neuromotor system a complicated integration must likewise be achieved between antagonistic muscles. Appropriate structures for subserving inhibition must be progressively provided. There is a mode of growth which asserts itself in a developmental fluctuation of dominance in flexors versus extensors and also in unilateral and crossed lateral versus bilateral muscle groups. Inasmuch as behavior patterning and structural growth are intimately correlated, we shall describe this developmental principle or mechanism as a reciprocal interweaving process.

Neurologically, this process implies an intricate cross-stitching or involuted interlacing which organizes opposing muscle systems into reciprocal and increasingly mature relationships. Functionally, such a process results in a progressive spiral kind of reincorporation of sequential forms of behavior.

These phenomena of fluctuating dominance and of progressive reintegration can be advantageously studied in the development of prone behavior in the human infant, because the prolongation of human infancy widens the scope and lengthens the cycle of observable motor development. It takes the average infant a full year to acquire the upright posture. We have distinguished at least twenty-three stages in the patterning of the prone behavior which eventuates in standing and walking (Gesell and Ames, 1940). From the standpoint of ontogenesis these stages may be envisaged as a series of postural transformations

TABLE 1

DEVELOPMENTAL STAGES OF PRONE BEHAVIOR IN THE HUMAN INFANT

(The age at which a given action pattern typically makes its appearance is indicated in parentheses.)

FLEXOR DOMINANCE	EXTENSOR DOMINANCE
1. *Passive kneel* (1 week) Both arms and both legs are *symmetrically* and sharply *flexed*. Cheek contacts platform, or head may be everted.	
	2A. *Passive leg extension* (4 weeks) The legs passively assume a *symmetric extended* posture. Arms still *flex*, fists at shoulders. Head lifts slightly less than 45°.
2B. *Active kneel* (about 4 weeks) Infant spontaneously draws up one knee at a time by (*unilateral*) *flexion*.	
	3A. *Active leg extension* (8 weeks) Legs actively assume a *symmetric extended* posture. Arms *flex* slightly forward.
3B. *One-knee thrust* (about 8 weeks) Infant draws up one knee by *flexion* with an abducted thrust (*unilateral*). Head lifts from 45 to 90°.	
	4A. *Alternate extensor kick* (12 weeks) Infant lies with legs well *extended* and kicks in *alternation*. Fists at temples. Head lifts slightly.
4B. *Abducted one-knee thrust* (about 12 weeks) Infant draws up one knee by *flexion* with increased abduction (*unilateral*). Head lifts 45 to 90°.	
	5. *Swimming* (16 weeks) Back arches so that infant's weight rests only on abdomen and lower chest. Arms lift, *flexed symmetrically*. Legs lift, in *symmetric extension*. Head lifts 90°.
6. *Simultaneous low creep* (20 weeks) Both arms and both legs are *flexed symmetrically*. Face and chest contact the supporting surface but abdomen is lifted.	
	7. *Frogging* (24 weeks) Arms are *flexed* **or** *extended symmetrically*. Legs are *extended symmetrically* in abduction. feet everted. Head lifts 90°.

303

TABLE 1 (*Continued*)

FLEXOR DOMINANCE

EXTENSOR DOMINANCE

8 *Advanced unilateral knee thrust*

9. *Same with foot eversion* (28 weeks)
Both arms *extend symmetrically*, or one *extends* and one *flexes*. Infant draws up one knee by *flexion* with an abducted thrust. (9) Same except that foot is everted. Head lifts 90° or more.

10. *Pivoting* (29 weeks)
Arms alternately *flex and extend*, one after the other, causing trunk to pivot on abdomen. *Symmetrical* leg extension is followed by forward *flexion* of one knee, in abduction. Head lifts 90° or more.

11A. *Inferior low creep* (30 weeks)
Arms *flex symmetrically*. One knee flexes forward in adduction. Other knee then *flexes* forward after heel has rotated outward. Weight rests on side of body. Head everted, cheek on platform.

11B. *Backward crawl* (31 weeks)
Legs *extend symmetrically* and passively and abdomen rests on the supporting surface. Infant pushes body backward from *symmetrically flexed* arms which come to extension as body pushes away from them. Head lifts less than 90°.

12. *Low creep* (32 weeks)
Both arms are *flexed symmetrically*. Legs *flex* forward in adduction, *one at a time*. Face and chest contact supporting surface but abdomen is lifted.

13A. *Crawling* (34 weeks)
Legs *extend symmetrically* and are dragged forward passively. Infant pulls trunk forward by *extending*, then *simultaneously flexing* both forearms. Head lifts 90° or more.

13B. Later (34½ weeks) pulls weight forward by *extending* and then *flexing* forearms *one at a time*.

14. *High creep* (35 weeks)
Both arms are *extended* and both legs are *flexed symmetrically*. Knees are forward under trunk in adduction, lifting abdomen and chest from supporting surface. Head is well up from floor and eyes look ahead.

15. *Backward creep* (36 weeks)
Infant is in the high creep position. *Extends* first one leg then the other, lowering abdomen and falling backward. Arms are *flexed symmetrically*.

TABLE 1 (*Continued*)

FLEXOR DOMINANCE	EXTENSOR DOMINANCE

16. *Rocking* (about 36 weeks)

Arms *extend symmetrically* and both legs are *flexed symmetrically*. Knees are forward under trunk, lifting abdomen and chest from supporting surface. Infant rocks back and forth, remaining in one location.

17. *Creep-crawl* (37 weeks)

In high creep position, both arms *extended* and both legs *flexed*. Falls forward, both legs coming to *extension*. Arms *extend* forward and infant attains high creep position again. Progresses in this fashion.

18. *Creeps* (40 weeks)

19. *Creeps, near step one foot* (42 weeks)

Both arms extend downward from shoulder, then *extend* forward, *alternately*. Legs *flex* forward, *alternately*. Arm and leg on opposite sides of body move simultaneously.

20. *Creeps, step with one foot* (45 weeks)

Arms *extend* forward *alternately*. Legs move forward *alternately*, one flexed, one extended.

21A. *Plantigrade position* (49 weeks)

Arms and legs both *extend* downward.

21B. *Plantigrade progression* (49½ weeks)

Arms and legs *extend* forward, *alternately;* left hand and right foot moving at same time.

22. *Standing* (56 weeks)

Trunk upright. Arms and legs *extend bilaterally.*

23. *Walking* (60 weeks)

Arms and legs both *extended*, move *alternately.*

whereby the infant by slow but sure sequence finally achieves the upright posture. None of the stages or patterns can be dismissed as being merely recapitulatory or vestigial. Each stage, however transient, appears to be a necessary feature of developmental mechanics, because of the numerous motor relationships which must be coordinated, that is, reciprocally interwoven. The upright posture ultimately involves a permanent preponderance of the extensor systems, but it is attained only

after a long series of preparatory coordinations.

Table 1 [1] summarizes the distinguishing

1 This tabulation outlines what may be regarded as an ideal sequence of stages. Every one of the stages has been observed in a number of children but not all the stages have been observed in all the children. For example, in 20 cases under observation from 6 months to 1 year, 93.5 per cent of all possible stages were observed, that is, 262 stages out of a possible 280 (Ames, 1937). A few of the stages listed in the table are almost evanescent, but they cannot be excluded from a complete outline of the ontogenetic sequence.

features of twenty-three developmental stages, with special reference to abduction, adduction, bilaterality, unilaterality, ipsilaterality, and crossed laterality. The left-hand column lists the stages in which flexor characteristics predominate; the right-hand column lists "extensor" stages. The distinctions are based on a careful cinemanalysis of research records. The entire gamut of stages is depicted in a silent film entitled *Prone Progression in the Human Infant* (Gesell, 1938a).

spiral kind of neuromotor organization characteristic of reciprocal interweaving. When the movements of arms and legs are charted on a maturity grid, the significance of this "spiral" recurrence becomes apparent (Figure 2).

The infant's prone behavior progresses from an immature to a more mature state,

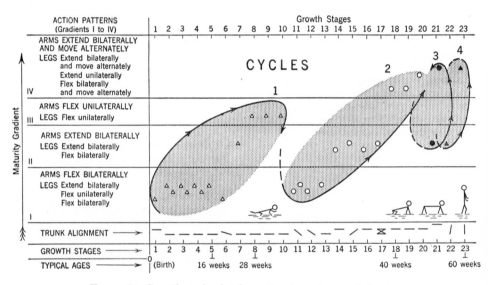

FIGURE 2. Growth cycles in the patterning of prone behavior.

ysis of research records. The entire gamut of stages is depicted in a silent film entitled *Prone Progression in the Human Infant* (Gesell, 1938a).

The Total Developmental Sweep. Inasmuch as the patterning of prone behavior affords us a slowed motion glimpse into the very ordering of development, it is profitable to take a panoramic view of the entire pageant of stages. The nature of this developmental flow can be best appreciated when contemplated in its totality. The infant has four extremities. Viewed in ample perspective, the action patterns of these extremities do not assume a straight-line seriation. The course of development turns on itself in a manner to suggest a

but three or four times it partially reverts to a less mature state. In the first ten stages the infant advances from a primitive bilateral flexion of arms and legs to unilateral flexion of arms and legs, unilaterality signifying greater maturity. The trunk remains throughout in primordial contact with the ground surface. But in the last of these ten stages (pivoting), the infant is able to use his upper extremities for circular locomotion and extrication. This terminates the first of four developmental cycles.

The second cycle entails the elevation of the trunk above its prostrate position. In accomplishing this new adjustment, the arms revert temporarily to their primitive posture of bilateral flexion, but the developmental patterning proceeds unabated even though in the crawling stage (stage 13) the trunk relapses to a groveling level. At stage 18, arms are extended forward bilaterally, legs are flexed bilaterally, and each pair of limbs moves alternately. This is classic creeping which all but terminates the ontogenetic sequence. Stages 19 and 20 are transitional to upright posture.

To achieve the exalted status of bipedal locomotion the developmental spiral takes two more short turns at ascending levels, constituting the third and fourth cycles. In both these short cycles there is a partial reversion to immobile bilateral extension, namely, in the plantigrade stance and in standing. Each cycle, however, culminates in locomotion; the third cycle, in plantigrade progression; the fourth, in walking.

It takes the average human infant about sixty weeks to attain independent walking. For a half year he is virtually immobile in the prone position. Before he acquires the upright posture he exhibits a number of primitive and abortive modes of locomotion: rolling, pivoting, forward crawl, backward crawl, regression, rocking, creep-crawling, creeping, and cruising. The very diversity of these activities testifies to the complexity of the process of developmental patterning. Some of the patterns have a recapitulatory suggestion, but they may be mainly regarded as functional expressions of transient but necessary stages in the organization of the neuromotor system.

The general direction of this ontogenetic organization is unmistakably cephalocaudal. The infant can lift his head in the first week of life; not until the end of the first year does he stand on his feet. The expansion of his neuromotor coordination also proceeds in general from proximal to distal segments. Upper arm and upper leg come into postural integration before forearm, foreleg, hands, and feet. The foot is both a caudal and distal terminus, the final fulcrum for locomotion. These directional trends are simple when compared with the intricate interweaving which is essential for functional organization.

The Principle of Functional Asymmetry

The principle of functional asymmetry is a special inflection of the principle of reciprocal interweaving and is inseparable therefrom. Bilateral and ipsilateral members must be brought into parallel and diagonal coordination. This takes an enormous amount of dovetailing, which is accounted for by the principle and process of neuromotor interweaving.

But man, in spite of his bilateral construction, does not face the world on a frontal plane of symmetry. He confronts it at an angle and he makes his escapes, also, obliquely. He develops monolateral aptitudes and preferences in handedness, eyedness, footedness, and other forms of unidexterity. Perfect ambidexterity, if it exists, would seem to be almost an abnormality, because effective attentional adjustments require an asymmetric focalization of motor set. The behavioral center of gravity always tends to shift to an eccentric position. Unidexterity of hand, foot, or eye does not so much represent an absolute difference in skill as a predilection for stabilized psychomotor orientations.

These orientations are fundamentally postural sets; and they are asymmetric. Ideally reciprocal interweaving operates to preserve harmony and balance; but in actuality there is a superadded ontogenetic deflection to insure the greater efficiency of functional asymmetry.

The tonic neck reflex (t.n.r.) is an asymmetric pattern of behavior, common to man and beast. Magnus, in his classic work on *Körperstellung*, reported an analysis of the postural reaction of decerebrate quadrupeds when their heads were experimentally turned to an extreme right or left position. He found a characteristic response: (1) extension of the forelimb on the side toward which the head was turned; (2) flexion of the opposite forelimb. The

sponse a ubiquitous, indeed a dominating, characteristic of normal infancy in the first three months of life. In a clinical sense the response should be regarded as abnormal only when it occurs in children of more advanced age who are suffering from arrest or damage of the central nervous

BEHAVIOR ITEMS plotted to show the ontogenetic trends of reactions involving the manifestations and decline of the TONIC NECK REFLEX (TNR).

The infants were observed at lunar month intervals (26 to 49 at each age), in controlled and repeated situations:

I Spontaneous behavior, in the supine position.
II Reactions to a dangling ring, in the supine position.

I   SPONTANEOUS
    SUPINE
    BEHAVIOR

· Su 1 Head predominantly rotated
⊘ Su 2 Head predominantly rotated to one given side (right or left)
△ Su 4 Head maintains midposition
▲ Su 7 Rotates head from one side to the other
× Su 9 Arms predominantly in TNR position
▢ Su 26 Arms in windmill motion
▣ Su 30 Hands predominantly open
▨ Su 35 Hands active in mutual fingering

II REACTIONS TO
    DANGLING
    RING

● RD8 Regards ring in midplane (long head)
○ RD29 Approaches ring with both hands
▲ RD42 Transfers ring from hand to hand

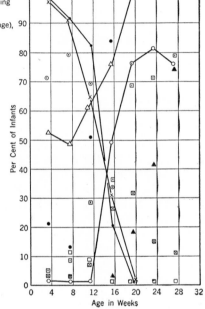

FIGURE. 3. Ontogenetic trends underlying tonic neck reflex.

reflex occurred in pure form when the labyrinths were extirpated, and it was ascribed to proprioceptive impulses arising in the neck from torsion.

Magnus (1924, 1925) demonstrated the existence of the tonic neck reflex in idiots and patients suffering from extrapyramidal tract lesions; he was unable to induce the reflex in 26 normal infants a few hours to 16 weeks of age. He came to the conclusion that in man the tonic neck reflex is a pathologic phenomenon.

This conclusion is somewhat amazing because we have found the tonic neck re-

system. In our normative survey of the ontogenetic sequences of behavior pattern, 26 to 49 infants were examined at lunar-month intervals up to the age of 56 weeks (Gesell and Thompson, 1934, 1938). It is a remarkable fact that 100 per cent of the infants at 4 weeks of age, when observed in a free supine posture, spontaneously maintained the head predominantly rotated to one side; 100 per cent likewise held their arms in characteristic t.n.r. attitudes. We conclude that the tonic neck reflex is a normal and virtually universal feature of neonatal infancy. Indeed, for 8 weeks the t.n.r. holds strong sway; at 12 weeks it is less conspicuous; at 16 weeks it is in transition; at 20 weeks in eclipse, for at 20 weeks 100 per cent of our normative infants maintained the head in midposition. And when the head is predominantly held in midposition, at least one-half of each t.n.r. subsides, and tonic cephalic symmetry dis-

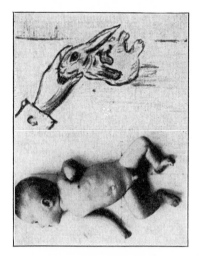

FIGURE 4. Right tonic neck reflex in rabbit and child.

places tonic neck asymmetry. The ontogenetic trends which underlie these transformations of postural pattern are plotted in Figure 3.

The accompanying illustrations show that this attitudinal pattern is clearly evident in the spontaneous waking postures of the normal infant, whether he lies quiescent or active. Figure 4 illustrates t.n.r. in a rabbit and in a normal infant. The rabbit is adapted from Magnus; the infant is a healthy 8-week-old subject basking in the soft light of the photographic dome. Both are in the right t.n.r. Figure 5 pictures two normal infants, both 6 weeks of age. One is in right t.n.r. and the other in left t.n.r. In each instance the face-arm

and face-leg are in extension, the contralateral extremities in flexion. Note the striking semblance to a fencing stance. Figure 6 shows a normal infant who at 1, 6, 8, and 12 weeks of age spontaneously and consistently exhibited a right t.n.r.

Figure 7 pictures the same infant at 24 weeks of age. The spontaneous asymmetry of the earlier ages has been superseded by a symmetric attitude in which both arms flex and the hands engage above the chest in the midline. This is a lawful developmental sequence. The t.n.r. mechanisms are not extinguished at 24 weeks; they are simply submerged by symmetric bilateral patterns. In another month the bilateral

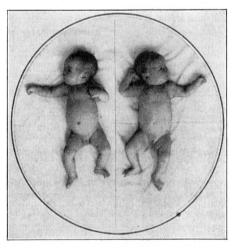

FIGURE 5. Right and left tonic neck reflex in 6-week-old infants.

in turn will give way to new unilateral patterns: one-hand reaching, one-handed manipulation, and hand-to-hand transfer, and ultimately to well-defined dextrality or sinistrality. Throughout early human development there is an almost periodic interweaving maturation, now of symmetric and then of asymmetric behavior forms, with corresponding shifts in postural manifestations.

When a large number of normal infants are examined at intervals during the first three months, we find that at least one-third consistently assume a right t.n.r.; possibly a third, the left t.n.r.; and the remainder adopt either right or left in a somewhat ambivalent manner. These figures are crude (the problem needs refined defined and elaborated in the latter half of the prenatal period. Fifteen minutes after the birth of a normal infant, I recently detected a greater tonicity in the right as opposed to the left arm (the legs were in equal relaxation). This discrepancy was predictive of a left t.n.r., in which the right or occiput arm tends to show the

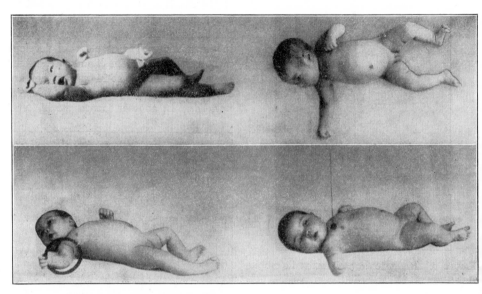

FIGURE 6. Right tonic neck reflex spontaneously and consistently exhibited in infant V. W. at 1, 6, 8, and 12 weeks of age.

study), but they suggest important trends and individual differences in the genesis of laterality. Handedness is a partial and sometimes a misleading index of physiologic unilaterality. It is probable, however, that emphatic, constitutional left-handedness is correlated with a strong infantile left t.n.r.

Morphogenetically, the human t.n.r. should not be envisaged as a stereotyped reflex but as a growing pattern, changing with the maturity and the economy of the organism. Torsion of the head to one side in a living fetus 20 weeks old arouses a movement of the arm on that side. This is a rudimentary t.n.r. which becomes better greater tonus. The infant was kept under continuous observation for 14 days and nights, and, although he was placed in varying postures, he consistently displayed a waxing left t.n.r. Another infant, belonging to the right wing, was photographed daily in a standard supine position, from the fifteenth day throughout most of the first year of life. This infant spent approximately one-half of the 834 seconds of cinematically recorded behavior up to the eighty-second day in t.n.r. Sixty-five separate t.n.r.'s were observed; only one of these was leftward.

Figure 8 graphs the incidence of these

t.n.r.'s, which fell to zero on the ninetieth day, when the head preferred a midposition and the arms assumed more symmetric and versatile attitudes.

The submergence of the naïve t.n.r. of early infancy is the result of the ascendancy

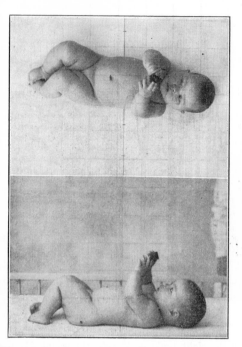

FIGURE 7. Symmetric prehensory and postural patterns at 24 weeks. Simultaneous photographs taken with one camera at zenith and the other at the horizon of the photographic dome.

of cortical controls, probably in the motor and premotor regions, if Bieber and Fulton's (1938) data, regarding ablation, for monkeys and baboons apply to man. This probability is strengthened by our findings in a case of cerebral palsy, in which necropsy (at the age of 14 years) revealed a severe but uncomplicated birth lesion of the basal ganglia (status marmoratus). The boy in question, A.C., was afflicted with extreme double athetosis and, although

intelligent, could not sit, walk, talk, grasp, or even hold up his head sustainedly. Cinema records of his spontaneous behavior in the supine position were made at the age of 7 years. Subjected to frame-by-frame analysis, these records revealed temporal and spatial patterns remarkably similar to those of the activated t.n.r. of normal infancy. Figure 9 portrays eleven comparable phases in the arm and head movements of the palsied boy, aged 7 years, and of a normal infant, 4 weeks old.

These phases may be envisaged as a slashing windmill reaction emerging out of and returning to a basic t.n.r. attitude. The presence of the t.n.r. was obscured by lively athetotic movements, but, when the cinema films were quantitatively studied, it was found that this boy was in a t.n.r. posture 41 to 56 per cent of the recorded time at 7, 10, and 13 years of age. The head generally took the lead in initiating the t.n.r. attitude. In no instance was a reversed t.n.r. attitude (head averted to one side with the arm of that side flexed) assumed even momentarily. All this suggests that the proprioceptive stimulus in the neck was operating to bring about the natural reflex.

The process of transformation from t.n.r. to symmetric postures is extremely complex. It is not a process of simple substitution but one of progressive interlocking so that neither symmetry nor asymmetry gains permanent or complete ascendancy. The addiction of the young infant to t.n.r. postures is both a symptom and a condition of his behavior growth. The infantile t.n.r. represents a morphogenetic stage in which fundamental neurological coordinations are laid down to form the framework for later postural, manual, locomotor, and psychomotor reactions. Indeed, the t.n.r. is part of the ground plan of the organism pervasively identified with its unitary, total action system.

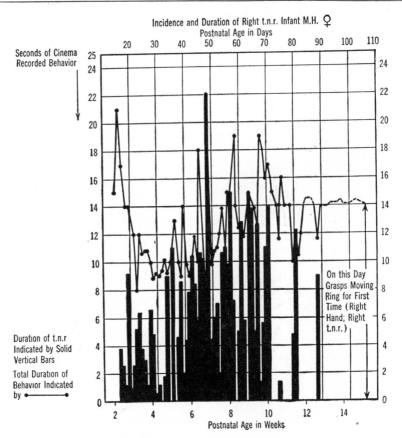

FIGURE 8. Duration and incidence by ages of the right tonic neck reflex in infant M. H. between 2 and 16 weeks of age.

The t.n.r. accordingly has an ecology. More or less directly it subserves adaptations to the environment, prior to birth as well as later. The t.n.r. helps the fetus to accommodate to the conformation of the uterine cavity, and it may even facilitate the longitudinal presentation and orientation of the fetus at the entrance of the birth canal. The t.n.r. of the neonatal infant is well suited to postural attitudes which the child needs to assume when suckled at the breast. The activated windmill t.n.r. of the early weeks with its intensification of grasp responses suggests vestiges of arboreal groping and gripping. The future and formative references of the t.n.r., however, are more significant. The t.n.r. attitude promotes and channelizes visual fixation by the infant on his extended hand; it leads to hand inspection, to eye-hand coordinations, to prehensory approach, and eventually to unidextrality. It contributes to the organization of the diagonal reflexes of prone locomotion. It reduces the hazard of suffocation to the infant and is well adapted to acts of rejection, extrication, and withdrawal. Elaborated and inflected, it finally figures in

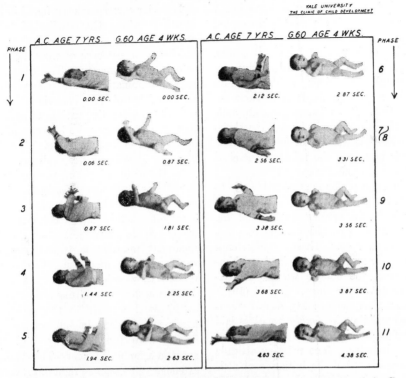

FIGURE 9. Comparable consecutive phases of the athetotic action pattern of A. C., aged 7 years, and of the spontaneous supine action pattern of a normal infant, G60, aged 4 weeks. (From "Correlations of Behavior and Neuro-pathology in a Case of Cerebral Palsy from Birth Injury," by A. Gesell and H. M. Zimmerman. *American Journal of Psychiatry,* 1937, **94,** Plate 3.)

Eleven phases, with the elapsed time indicated in seconds, are shown side by side in vertical columns. These phases may be envisaged as a slashing windmill reaction emerging out of and returning to a basic tonic neck reflex attitude.

innumerable adult acts of skill, aggression, and extrication. Attitudinal asymmetry always remains in reflex reserve, as well as subject to voluntary mobilization.

The Principle of Individuating Maturation

This principle may help us to recognize the mechanism by means of which the behavioral organism achieves its species characteristicness and yet at the same time makes specific adaptations within its environmental field. From the moment of fertilization, intrinsic and extrinsic factors cooperate in a unitary manner; but the original impulse of growth and the matrix of morphogenesis are endogenous rather than exogenous. The so-called environment, whether internal or external, does not generate the progressions of development. Environmental factors support, inflect, and specify; but they do not engender the basic forms and sequences of ontogenesis.

Even before the human embryo has a nervous system it is a perfectly integrated organism. It changes in shape and dimensions with each passing hour. It grows. This process of growth which derives its fundamental impulsions and directions from the zygote produces continuous reconfiguration. It configures the embryonic vesicle, the blastodermic layers, the skeleton, the skull, the profile of fetal, infantile, and adult nose, and the primary organization of the neuromotor system.

The function of the nervous system is to maintain the integrity of the organism and to anticipate the specific demands of the environment with provisional and preparatory arrangements. These forereference arrangements are not determined by stimulation from the outside world. Experience does not create them. Coghill (1929) has shown that the primary neural mechanism of walking (in *Amblystoma*) is laid down before the animal can at all respond to its environment. The primary attitude of the organism and the initiative of attitude are thus intrinsically determined. We apply the term "maturation" to this intrinsic and prospective aspect of ontogenetic patterning. It has been abundantly illustrated in the sequential series of motor attitudes which characterize the development of prone and upright postures. The pervasive and steady influence of maturation has also been demonstrated with the aid of daily cinema records of behavior in a study of 220 consecutive recordings of diurnal changes in behavior reported by Gesell and Halverson (1942).

The sequential patterning expresses itself in progressive differentiations within a total action system. The basic order and the general modality if not the specific outline of these differentiations are determined by intrinsic factors. The intrinsic nature of this determination is most strikingly demonstrated in the marked degree of behavior correspondence found in highly identical twins. Our studies of twins T and C showed that the resemblances in the behavior patterns of these twins were astonishingly numerous. Thirteen developmental examinations were analyzed and inventoried for discrete behavior items; 612 separate comparative ratings of such items were made. There were 99 items of minor disparity and 513 items of identical or virtually identical correspondence.

In the field of pellet prehension, this parity was very neatly disclosed. A small pellet, 8 mm. in diameter, was placed on a tabletop before each child, within easy reach. At 28 weeks both the twins, being somewhat retarded in their development, were visually unheedful of the pellet, though they definitely regarded a cube. At 38 weeks they addressed themselves in an identical manner to the pellet. The hands were placed in full pronation, the fingers were fully extended and spread apart in a fanlike manner. The thumb was extended almost at right angles. The photographic record of their attack upon the pellet in the motion pictures shows an almost uncanny degree of identity in the details of postural attitude, hand attitude, approach, and mechanism of grasp. At 40 weeks there was a crude raking attack upon the pellet; at 42 weeks this raking approach was replaced by a poking with the tip of the index finger. These changes in prehensory pattern occurred contemporaneously in both children.

Such changes may be regarded as manifestations of the individuating aspect of maturation. The maturational mechanisms are so firmly entrenched that they are not readily transcended by training, as shown by experimental studies by the method of co-twin control (Gesell and Thompson, 1929; Strayer, 1930; Hilgard, 1933).

Maturation and Learning. The intimate relationships between maturation and learning also are revealed in the behavior of identical twins. Simultaneous comparative observations of T and C disclosed a fundamental identity of behavior responses in the pellet and bottle situation at the age of 48 weeks. The twins were in the same crib, seated back to back, and each confronting her own examining table. Two examiners simultaneously held a small 4-ounce glass bottle in view and dropped an 8-mm. pellet into the bottle. Three trials were made with each child. The examiner, having dropped the pellet into the bottle, gave the bottle to the child.

Both children watched this dropping of the pellet with the same transfixed attention. Both children on the first trial, and again on the second trial, seized the bottle, apparently heedless of the contained pellet; but both children on the third trial (without, of course, any influence of imitation) pursued the pellet by poking at it against the glass—identical capacity to profit by experience.

In this instance we find that the correspondence of behavior patternings extends into the minute fields of specific adaptation or of learning. It may be readily granted that maturational factors primarily account for the similarity in capacity and general maturity displayed by these twins. Perhaps these same maturational factors also account for the more detailed correspondences, such as the mode of visual attention, the primary preoccupation with the bottle, and the secondary interest in the pellet. Within a brief span of time we see the spontaneous behavior patterns undergo a specific adaptation and call this adaptation learning. The distinctive criteria of maturation and learning, however, are not easily applied.

Let us assume that on the morrow, in the pellet-and-bottle situation, both children poke immediately with extended forefinger against the side of the bottle. Is this fixation of behavior due to the experience of the previous day? Shall the assimilative processes of the intervening night be regarded as maturation because the modification did not occur in immediate response to the situation; or shall it be called learning because it is virtually a specific adaptation to stimuli recently in the external environment? The fixation of the poking pattern, however, proves to be temporary, because in another lunar month, without specific experience, these same twins adaptively tilt both bottle and hand, and thrust the extended index finger into the open mouth of the bottle in pursuit of the pellet. Is this incremental differentiation of behavior pattern to be attributed to maturation or to learning?

The concept of maturation emphasizes the unity of the organism and the priority of the total pattern of response. The unity of the organism is not to be regarded as a mystical abstraction, but as a reality, namely, the functional unity of the total reaction system. Herrick (1929) identifies it particularly with the diffuse nervous network of

> . . . neuropil which pervades the brain substance and binds it all together as a functional unit. Into this neuropil there is a continuous discharge from every sensory surface of the body, fluctuating from moment to moment but always acting. Here growth is going on as long as learning is possible, here the total pattern expands, and here partial patterns are individuated.

Here also is the anatomic basis for conditioning of the Pavlovian type.

The basic ontogenetic forms of individuation are the result of maturation. Conditioning is superimposed, as it were, upon a maturational substrate. As conceived by Coghill,

Conditioning of reaction is accompanied by restriction (narrowing) of the zone of adequate stimulation and concomitant restriction in the field of action. The primacy of structural basis for this is in the mechanism of the total pattern.

Which pattern, be it remembered, "is a growing thing."

For this reason all learning involves growth. According to Herrick:

It involves a change, more or less stable in the anatomical structure of the body, and the neuropil as the most labile part of the nervous system plays the most significant part in this reorganization of the mechanisms of behavior (1929).

Maturation and Acculturation. The individual comes into his racial (and ancestral) inheritance through the processes of *maturation.* He comes into his social inheritance through processes of *acculturation.* These two processes operate and interact in close conjunction. Only through systematic studies of child development, naturalistic, biometric, and experimental, can we gain an insight into the relationship of maturation and acculturation. Here indeed is one of the most comprehensive and crucial problems of the life sciences. In this problem genetic psychology and cultural anthropology have a common stake.

The distinction between maturation and acculturation must not be drawn too sharply, but it must be made. Malinowski (1937) has characterized culture as "a large-scale molding matrix." His meaning is, of course, clear and up to a certain point incontrovertible; but in the interpretation of child development I should prefer to reserve the term "matrix" for the maturational mechanisms which literally establish the basic patterns of behavior and of growth career. A matrix is that which gives form and foundation to something which is incorporated, in this instance, through growth. By growth we do not mean a mystical essence, but a physiological process of organization which is registered in the structural and functional unity of the individual. In this sense the maturational matrix is the primary determinant of child behavior.

Growth is a unifying concept which resolves the dualism of heredity and environment. Environmental factors support, inflect, and modify; but they do not generate the progressions of development. Growth is an impulsion and as a cycle of morphogenetic events is uniquely a character of the living organism. Neither physical nor cultural environment contains any architectonic arrangements like the mechanisms of growth. Culture accumulates; it does not grow. The glove goes on the hand; the hand determines the glove. And the hand, by the way, is a primitive survival, shockingly similar to the hand of the ancient tortoise who swam the seas and walked the earth millions of years before the advent of man.

The Principle of Self-Regulatory Fluctuation

Every living organism is a storer and distributor of energy. The human infant is no exception. His daily cycle of activity and rest reflects the way in which he husbands and expends his energies; it also reflects a method of growth. "Aging and death may be considered to result from the gradual degradation of the original energy which caused the formation of an organism in the environmental field" (Eulenberg-Wiener, 1938).

The living system during the period of active growth is in a state of formative instability combined with a progressive movement toward stability. The so-called growth gains represent consolidations of stability. This opposition between two apparently opposing tendencies results in seesaw fluctuations. The maturing organism does not advance in a straight line but oscillates along a "spiral" course between two self-limited poles.

A spiral kind of organization was also suggested in the phenomenon of reciprocal interweaving. The concept of spirality is not mystical if, in spite of its vagueness, we simply let it denote metaphorically the devious but progressive involutions by which structure and function are jointly matured. The organism at times seems to retreat from a locus of maturity which it had already attained. Temporarily such a retreat may look like an abandonment. It would be abandonment if it continued on one tangent. The course of development, however, being spiral, turns back toward the point of departure; and it does not return precisely to this point. It returns to the same region but at a higher level. The neurological result is an interwoven texture which expresses itself in progressive patterns of behavior. The unity of the ground plan of the organism is preserved. It is a process of reincorporation and consolidation, rather than one of hierarchical stratification.

Many of the ephemeral variabilities of human functioning may be due to fluctuations or inconstancies of internal milieu. On the other hand, advanced forms of adaptive variability may be dependent upon a highly stable milieu and a consolidated developmental organization. Productive modifiability implies stability as well as a certain degree of instability. Stability and variability coexist not as contradictory opposites, but as mutual complements. The relationships are extremely complicated and specific. They may be studied in a dynamic aspect in narrow fields restricted to small periods of duration. They may be studied in a developmental aspect against the broader time frame of the ontogenetic cycle.

Fluctuation is therefore a normal expression of the self-regulatory mechanisms of development. Elsewhere we have presented objective data illustrating the operation of this principle in the development of feeding behavior (Gesell and Ilg, 1937). Detailed observations were made on the spontaneous self-demand schedule of a healthy infant throughout the first year of life. This infant, child J, was fed on the basis of her own carefully observed demands, and with minor exceptions her sleep was not disturbed. Accurate records of times of feeding, food intake, naps, and sleeping were made daily by a physician and a full-time nurse. This undertaking proved to be a long-range experiment which revealed the capacities of self-regulation in an infant who was literally allowed to shape her own behavior day.

Each behavior day was recorded and charted. The entire chart for the period of a year spreads, on ordinary plotting paper, to a formidable length of seven feet. In the accompanying graphs we reproduce sections of this chart. Figure 10 covers 49 successive days for the age period of 3 to 10 weeks. Figure 11 condenses the total record by plotting 60 successive Thursdays from 3 to 63 weeks. The charts may be read both horizontally and vertically. The shaded areas, read across, show the sleeping periods for a 24-hour cycle. The open circles indicate bottle feedings; a figure in the circle designates ounces of intake.

Lines drawn vertically or obliquely connect these circles and show shifts in the times of feeding. Ages in weeks are ranged in the vertical column at the left. When the chart is examined as a whole, and is scanned from top to bottom, it reveals the process of adjustment by which an infant accomplishes revisions in a schedule of feedings and sleepings.

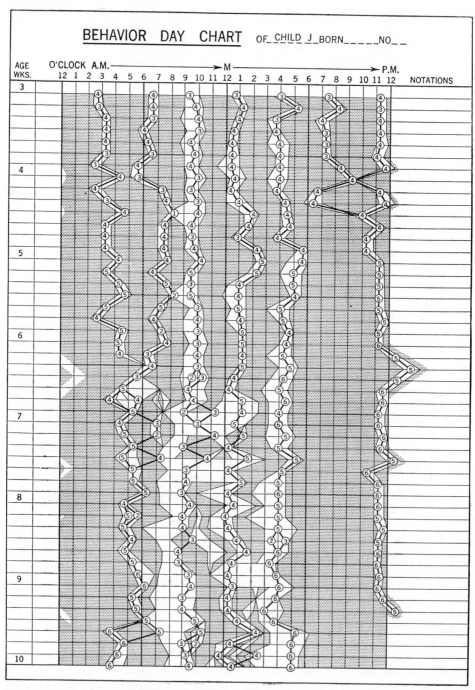

FIGURE 10. Child J. Feeding schedule from 3 to 10 weeks. (From *The Feeding Behavior of Infants: A Pediatric Approach to the Mental Hygiene of Early Life,* by A. Gesell and F. L. Ilg. Philadelphia: J. B. Lippincott Co., 1937, page 95.)

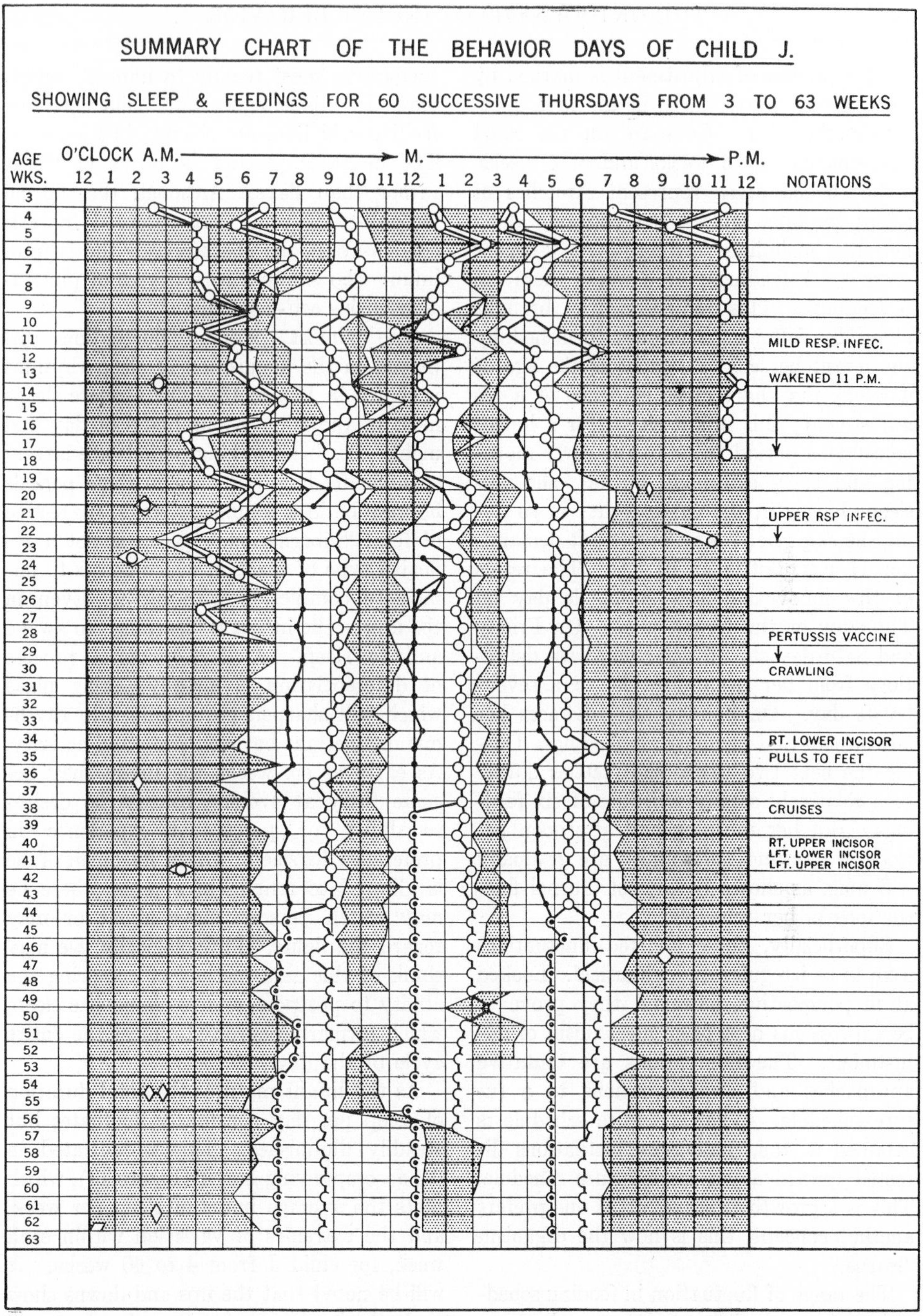

FIGURE 11. Child J. Sleep and feeding for 60 successive Thursdays from 3 to 63 weeks. (From *The Feeding Behavior of Infants: A Pediatric Approach to the Mental Hygiene of Early Life,* by A. Gesell and F. L. Ilg. Philadelphia: J. B. Lippincott Co., 1937, page 97.)

This process of adjustment is marked by fluctuations, particularly in the first quarter of the year. Compare on the chart the schedules at 3 weeks and at 8 weeks. (The shaded areas represent stretches of sleep; the open spaces, stretches of waking activity, including feeding.) At 3 weeks there are 7 feedings; at 8 weeks there are 5 feedings. This reduction was brought about by following the cues furnished by the infant herself. As early as the age of 4 weeks the chart gives evidence of a readjustment; this infant sleeps for a longer continuous period prior to the early morning and early afternoon bottles; she also sleeps longer in the early night; in so doing she skips her 7 P.M. bottle but demands her 11 P.M. bottle at 10 P.M. The result of this innovation is a six-bottle day on Thursday of the fourth week. On Friday and Saturday she swings back, with deflections from her usual routine, to a seven-bottle day. On Sunday she advances her adjustment and has only six feedings. During the next two weeks she "settles down" to a relatively steady schedule of six feedings. But her morning and afternoon periods of daytime wakefulness are gradually widening, as shown by almost diurnal fluctuations in her schedule.

Superficially, these charted fluctuations seem to be irregular and whimsical. Looked at in perspective, however, they prove to be expressions of a basic mechanism of adjustment. The fluctuations are tentative approaches and approximations to a future schedule. When a future schedule is attained it, too, undergoes fluctuations directed toward a yet more future schedule. This is a growth process; or, if one prefers another concept, this is how the organism "learns."

The range of fluctuation in feeding schedules varies with different infants. In some the coefficient of fluctuation is high; in others it is low. The latter accommodate themselves most readily to imposed schedules. In this category falls child C, whose feeding schedules are charted in Figure 12. The chart is plotted in terms of weeks rather than days. Although the diurnal variability is somewhat obscured by this condensation, the chart reveals the type of infant who shows a high degree of punctuality in his self-demands.

The almost periodic fluctuation displayed in the acquisition of sleep rhythms is shown in Figure 13. The neonate sleeps most of the twenty-four hours of day and night. His brief waking periods are largely spent in feeding, but even in these periods he may be in a somnolent stage, suggestive of fetal "hibernation." Sleep is not a reflexive type of reaction which comes to immediate completion with birth. Even in the uterus the infant is "learning" to awake and to sleep. A developmental process of differentiation is already taking place which will sharpen postnatally into rhythmic distinctions between sleep and activity. As early as six weeks the infant may become fussy at evening because he desires sociability or perceptual experience in preference to sleep. Often he quiets if he is allowed to remain in a room where he may watch persons move about or may regard the lights. Physiologically, we may think of this as a method of acquiring the ability to postpone and to channelize sleep, which formerly engrossed almost the entire cycle of the day.

As the infant matures the total duration of sleep per day constantly fluctuates but steadily diminishes. This is indicated in the accompanying graph (Figure 13), which plots the average hours of sleep per week, and the extremes of variation within each week, for child J from 4 to 40 weeks. It will be noted that the ups and downs show a rhythmic character. But the downs in the end exceed the ups, so that the average amount of diurnal sleep falls from 19

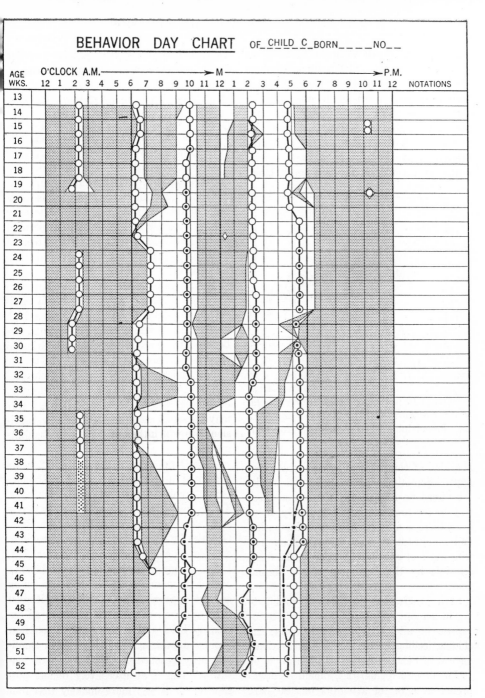

FIGURE 12. Child C. Sleep and feeding from 13 to 25 weeks. (From *The Feeding Behavior of Infants: A Pediatric Approach to the Mental Hygiene of Early Life,* by A. Gesell and F. L. Ilg. Philadelphia: J. B. Lippincott Co., 1937, page 101.)

hours in the fourth week to 13 hours in the fortieth week. The number of naps likewise may rise and fall repeatedly but with a trend toward reduction. Usually the early morning and evening naps are the first to shorten and to disappear by merging with the night sleep. The later morning and the afternoon naps persist ordinarily throughout the first year. There

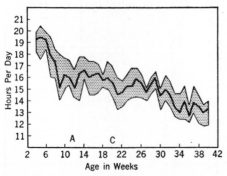

FIGURE 13. Child J. Sleep chart from 4 to 40 weeks. (From *The Feeding Behavior of Infants: A Pediatric Approach to the Mental Hygiene of Early Life,* by A. Gesell and F. L. Ilg. Philadelphia: J. B. Lippincott Co., 1937, page 99.)

is a kind of competition between these two naps. Sometimes as early as 28 weeks the afternoon nap shortens and soon gives way to the morning nap. Typically, however, there is a longer period of fluctuation and readjustment, and the afternoon nap wins out and gains ascendancy in the daily schedule by the beginning of the second year.

Such progressive fluctuations, culminating in a more stable response, are characteristic of all behavior development, including feeding behavior. The fluctuations, instead of being regarded as undesirable or as fortuitous irregularities, should be interpreted as effortful attempts on the part of the organism to accomplish increasingly mature adjustments. From this point of

view, fluctuations have a positive function in the economy of growth and learning.

The Individuality of Growth Careers

By virtue of the foregoing principles the human infant shows a strong tendency to develop along well-defined morphogenetic lines characteristic of the species. Inherited engrams, or comparable regulators, not only determine behavior forms common to the race, but they also determine behavior modes and idiosyncrasies peculiar to the individual. The growth career of each individual infant assumes a distinctive pattern.

The range of individual differentiation is wide and diverse. Only in extremely similar monozygotic twins do we find a high degree of developmental correspondence between two individuals. In such twinship the resemblance may extend even to the timing and the minute details of physical and behavioral patterning. A recent study of twins A and B (Gesell and Blake, 1936) may be cited here to indicate the precision with which the ontogenetic mechanisms operate.

These twin girls at the age of 12 years presented a duplication of bilateral coloboma involving each of their four eyes. These colobomas were amazingly alike in size, shape, position, and pigmentation. Genetically each coloboma traced back to a defective closure of the fetal ocular cleft. If a single "environmental" adversity caused the notching of the optic cup (in an embryo approximately 7 mm. long) it must have operated coincidentally within an extremely brief and critical interval on four rapidly organizing structures which simultaneously reached identical levels of maturity. This is an excessively remote possibility. It is still more unlikely that four defects of as many choroids, so similar in size, outline, position, and pigmentation, could have occurred at different times in consequence of four separate moments of infection, of irritation, or of damage neatly directed at each of the four eyes. It is, however, conceivable that the original single zygote or the constitutive factors in the twin embryos, which already held the hereditary determiners of all four eyes, held also the specific factors (or mutations) which delimited the development of the choroid. Similar specific factors would likewise account for the persisting remnant of the left hyaloid artery and for the correspondences of the shape and refraction of the four eyes. These eyes were derived from a single cell with one genetic constitution. Similar specific factors must also account for the striking resemblance in the emotional, intellectual, and motor make-up of these twins, including even their handwriting and the spellings and comparable misspellings of simple dictated words, such as *day, eat, sit, let, box, belong, door, yes, low, soft.*

Numerous studies of twins are now available for further analysis of the influence of genetic and epigenetic factors in the production of individuality (Carter, 1940). The medical literature on the pathological correspondences in twins is particularly suggestive with respect to the intrinsic developmental factors involved.

We have studied one highly identical pair of twins at the Yale Clinic of Child Development over a period of fourteen years. By repeated physical and mental measurements, by systematic motion picture records of behavior and experimental observations using the method of co-twin control, we have followed the life careers of these twin girls from infancy to adolescence (Gesell and Thompson, 1941). In the co-twin control studies, we trained one twin (T) and reserved the other twin (C) as a comparative control, to determine the effects of intensive training in such

sample functions as stair-climbing, block-building, vocabulary, and manual coordination. These effects proved to be relatively impermanent: the untrained twin attained the equivalent skill as soon as she reached the requisite maturity. Numerous tests at advancing ages revealed an amazing parallelism in their physical and mental growth.

On close analysis, however, even this remarkably similar pair of twins presented consistent individual differences, many of which could be traced back to infancy. The differences are slight but they are durable. Here are some of them. T is quicker, more direct, more decisive; C is more deliberate, more inclusive, more relaxed. T is a bit brighter; but C is more sociable, more communicative. T shows a predilection for straight and angular lines in her drawings of a house, of smoke, of curtains, and of balloon strings. C favors curves. Her curtains are flounced, her smoke curls. In attentional characteristics, T's pick-up is more prompt, she focalizes more sharply, is more alert for details. C's attention is more generally alert, more imaginative, more roving. These differences are slight in degree; but they are permanent in the perspective of fourteen years. They are permanent because they are constitutional.

The remarkable correspondences in many instances of twinship serve to emphasize the frequency and diversity of developmental variability among ordinary siblings. Some of the variations can be interpreted in terms of the ontogenetic principles which have just been outlined. Motor ineptitudes, for example, may arise out of exaggerations or defects in the process of reciprocal interweaving; many so-called regressions, likewise. The different modes by which children learn to walk and to run are impressive for variety of style. And often a style of acquiring motor control pervades other fields of behavioral adaptation. It is increasingly clear that many behavior difficulties with accompanying personality manifestations are based upon confused laterality or faulty functional asymmetry. Many forms of abnormality in mental life can be construed, following Coghill's suggestion, as due to excessive individuation. We have already called attention to the wide range of individual differences with respect to the amplitude of self-regulatory fluctuations. A thoroughly healthy individual is not likely to display any extreme deviations or deficiencies in the physiology of development represented by the five ontogenetic principles which have been described.

Nature is infinite in variety and variability. Even identical twins are not perfectly identical. The popular impression that all babies are much alike, especially young babies, cannot be confirmed. This impression has received some scientific support from psychologists who hold that the behavior of infants is chiefly patterned through conditioning processes and through specific learning.

On the basis of the conditioning theory of development, individual differences at birth are slight and increase with age. The investigations at Yale, including the detailed biogenetic studies of twins T and C, of the normative infants and selected subjects of the naturalistic survey all point in a different direction. One study (Gesell, assisted by Ames, 1937) was based upon an analysis of the cinema records of five different infants. The children were photographed under homelike conditions at lunar month intervals throughout the first year of life. These extensive cinema records embraced the major events of the infant's day—sleeping, waking, bath, dressing and undressing, feeding, play, and social behavior at advancing age levels. Additional cinema records and psychological

observations of the same children were made at the age of five.

A trained and unbiased observer (L.B.A.), *who had never seen the infants*, made a detailed analysis of the cinema records covering the first year of life. On the basis of the objective evidence of the films alone, an estimate of fifteen behavior traits was made and the children were arranged in rank order for each trait. The same children were again studied at the age of five and were again rated with respect to the fifteen behavior traits which they had displayed in infancy. The two appraisals were made independently.

Is the strength of a behavior trait in the first year of life predictive of a similar strength in the fifth year? The fifteen traits of behavior individuality which were considered were: (1) energy output, (2) motor demeanor, (3) self-dependence, (4) social responsiveness, (5) family attachment, (6) communicativeness, (7) adaptivity, (8) exploitation of environment, (9) "humor" sense, (10) emotional maladjustment, (11) emotional expressiveness, (12) reaction to success, (13) reaction to restriction, (14) readiness of smiling, (15) readiness of crying.

For each child and for each trait at 1 year and again at 5 years a comparative judgment was made. Out of the 75 comparative judgments, 48 coincided; 21 showed a displacement of one rank order only; 5, a displacement of 2; and 1, a displacement of 3 (Figure 14).

Every infant seems to have what may be called a motor habitude or characteristicness which expresses itself in postural demeanor and modes of movement. This characteristicness is difficult of description because it is the compound result of numerous factors, including skeletal frame, disposition of musculature, speed, synergy, smoothness and precision of action. Some of these factors, however, yield to quantitative study. One of the most accessible of these is laterality. A consistent laterality in both handedness and footedness showed itself in all the children.

normative situations. The interval consumed between the zero moment of reaching to the moment of grasp of the test object was computed by counting cinema

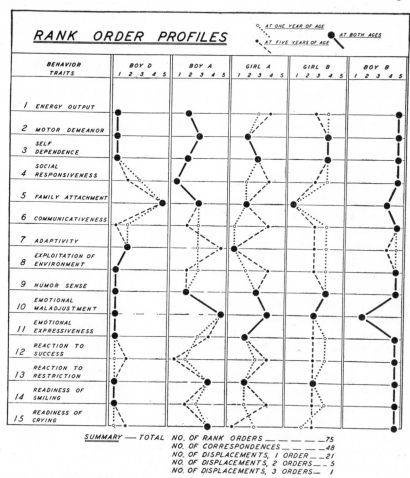

FIGURE 14. Rank order profiles for individuality traits in infancy and at 5 years.

In general bodily control and also in manual dexterity, the four children for whom quantitative data were secured readily fell into the following rank order: 1, boy D; 2, boy A; 3, girl B; and 4, boy B. Several hundred feet of cinema records were available for measuring the prehension time of these children in controlled

frames. Each frame has a time value of 0.05 second. The prehension time (that is, the reach-grasp time) increased with the rank order as follows: boy D (rank order 1), 40 seconds; boy A (rank order 2), 47 seconds; girl B (rank order 3), 50 seconds; and boy B (rank order 4), 60 seconds.

In these time values we apparently have a rather basic trait of motor individuality, for this rank order held up with consistency when the patterns of prone progression were measured in detail. For these measurements over a thousand feet of film depicting creeping behavior were available.

Creeping speed, like prehension time, was measured by counting frames, in this instance the number of frames which recorded a forward movement of a hand or of a leg. A *creep advance* represents a single cycle of progression accomplished by a single forward placement of each of the four members. The total time required for one creep advance was determined for each of the subjects in turn. The time values ranged from 0.7 to 1.6 seconds for such a single creep advance. Once more the resulting rank order was identical with that just given in the preceding paragraph.

In other stages of prone behavior— namely, the *near-step advance* and the *one-step advance*—as well as in simple hands-and-knees creeping, the time values for the four children retained their characteristic motor rank order.

Another individual difference asserted itself with respect to the age at which the various stages of prone locomotion were attained. For example, the ages when the near-step stage was attained were: boy D, 36 weeks; boy A, 40 weeks; girl B, 48 weeks; boy B, 48 weeks. When the nascent ages for the entire sequence of 23 stages in the ontogenesis of progression are expressed in terms of summated rank for each of the four children, we get a significant series of values: boy D, 38; boy A, 43; girl B, 70; boy B, 78. Again the rank order remains true to the characteristic order established by the measurement of specific motor traits.

Another recent cinema study (Ames, 1940) on the constancy of individual differences analyzed the locomotor and manual behavior of eight infants over a three-year period. When the eight subjects were arranged in rank order with regard to speed of combining pellet with bottle and cup with spoon, creeping speed, and time of attaining successive stages of prone behavior, six retained the same relative rank order for each type of behavior. Only two subjects varied in position. Such psychomotor constancy bespeaks a persisting factor in the make-up of individuality.

The Stability of Mental Growth Careers

In illustrating the principles of development, we have most frequently referred to motor and psychomotor characteristics. This is natural because these so-called motor phenomena are the most objective and measurable. It must not be thought, however, that the ontogenetic principles operate only in the motor sphere. It will be well to inquire whether they do not pervade the total domain of psychological growth, including language, adaptive, and personal-social behavior.

Growth is a morphogenetic process of progressive individuation and integration which leads to specific ends. To a considerable extent these ends are inherent in the organism. The organism also displays a prodigious capacity to adapt to circumstances, exigencies, and adversities. In this sense the growth of the individual is plastic and labile. But the individual retains durable characteristicness, and this is the stable aspect of growth.

The writer, in 1928, published the mental growth curves of thirty-three infants and young children, whose behavior development had been repeatedly appraised by clinical examinations. We have followed the subsequent careers of thirty of these children, who are now in their teens or older. By comparing the early with the later findings, we can in retrospect determine the predictiveness of the first appraisals, many of which were made during the first year of life.

The group of thirty cases comprised a wide variety of developmental conditions: normal, retarded, mentally defective, superior, premature and postmature infants, a case of cerebral palsy with approximations to normal mentality, cases of cretinism, mongolism, hemihypertrophy, and *pubertas praecox*.

How consistent over a decade and more have been these mental growth careers? In no instance did the course of growth prove whimsical or erratic. In only one case within the period of ten years was there a marked alteration of trend, namely, from a low average to a high average level (child B.D.). In a few defectives there was a progressive retardation without deterioration. For all others there was a maintenance of the general trend which was ascertained by the early examinations.

Graphs were plotted for DQ and IQ, but the detailed case records also incorporated after each examination our clinical appraisals, which were by no means always identical with the psychometric quotients. These interpretive clinical judgments, we believe, have more significance than the raw quotients in investigating the consistency and stability of mental growth careers.

Our clinical evidence based on normative determinations demonstrates a high degree of consistency in the trends of early and later growth. Take, for example, the six siblings reported elsewhere (Gesell, 1928) as children D.E., E.F., F.G., G.H., H.I., and I.J. Three of these children over a period of ten years have clung unmistakably to a normal course of behavior development; the other three, as decisively, to a subnormal course. It took no diagnostic subtlety to distinguish between these two kinds of growth potentiality on the basis of one behavior examination in infancy. The point is that these infant behavior pictures were unambiguously prophetic of the later careers. The predictions, therefore, were accurate. They were safe, also, because nature is never so whimsical as to mix up sectors of the growth curves of two sets of individuals as differently endowed as D.E. and I.J. (Figure 15).

In a similar way the predictive estimates of three distinctively superior children in our group did not miss the mark. The estimates were made before the children could read or write, which means that there was a high degree of indicativeness in the early behavior symptoms.

In less well-defined behavior pictures, equally confident predictions are not forthcoming because we do not have the techniques or acumen to identify and assess the indicators; but a comparable latent predictiveness resides in these pictures as well.

When there is a fairly even balance between the endogenous and the sustaining or exogenous factors, the trends of mental growth, whether subnormal, superior, or mediocre, are likely to be most consistent. Developmental diagnosis and prognosis then come nearest to their mark. When, however, the organism is under stress of distortion because of unfavorable conditions, its ultimate adjustments as expressed in growth characteristics become least predictable. There are too many variables to appraise. External environment can be estimated with some shrewdness; but not so readily the internal developmental reserves.

These hidden reserves are the intrinsic insurance factors with which we have had to reckon repeatedly in cases of atypical and irregular behavior development. The concept of insurance factors is not mystical. It is derived from experimental embryology and from clinical observation. The surgical excisions, transplantations, and other interferences with the growing tissues of laboratory embryos have demonstrated that the organism is protected with a remarkable fund of reserve mechanisms which promptly or gradually move into

cue when development is retarded or impaired. As a poison stimulates the formation of antibodies, so certain errors or depressions of development stimulate a regulatory self-correction. These reserve factors, however, are not a single generalized capacity. They are specific biochemical

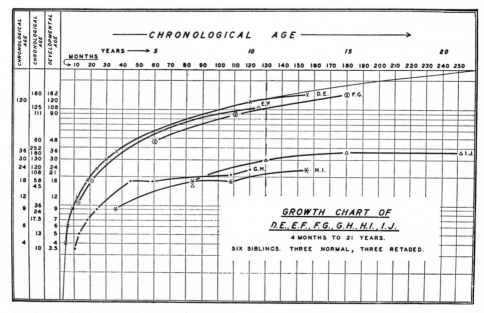

FIGURE 15. Growth graphs of D. E., E. F., F. G., G. H., H. I., I. J. (From *Biographies of Child Development: The Mental Growth Careers of Eighty-four Infants and Children*, by A Gesell, B. M. Castner, H. Thompson, and C. S. Amatruda. New York: Paul B. Hoeber, Inc. 1939, page 26.)

every breach and fill it in some way, either through regeneration or compensatory and substitutive growth. If the lesion is too great, the organism dies. If the lesion is not too severe, and the organism not too old, growth may continue in a more or less normal manner.

In the development of the nervous system and in the ontogenesis of behavior, the human organism displays comparable insurance mechanisms. Locked in inner recesses beyond diagnostic scrutiny are reserve factors which may come to the res-

and somatic structures almost infinite in number and variety, and of many degrees of availability. They are present in defective as well as normal individuals. They are probably most abundant in the most vital and best endowed. Vitality is an index of the plenitude and vigor of these very insurance factors. In spheres of behavior they operate not only during the period of growth, but also in old age, at least in the most "vital" individuals.

If there is a principle of uncertainty in the physiology of development it is a biological principle which rests upon important individual differences with respect to these insurance factors. Since they vary in amount, it is difficult to ascertain their strength in those inscrutable infants who present an inadequate and yet not decisively defective behavior picture. Here diagnosis must be wary, sometimes for a whole year or more, because sometimes the insurance factors come tardily and slowly into full force. But if they are present, and if the attendant conditions permit, they will ultimately assert themselves. When there is no counteracting deteriorating process, the tendency of growth will be toward something better and toward an optimal organization of the available equipment.

General Conclusion

Behavior at all stages of development is patterned. Patterning is displayed in the phase of the moment, in the dynamic sequence of specific behavior events, and in the progressive differentiations of the ontogenetic cycle.

The forms of behavior are governed by laws of developmental morphology, and these forms can be analyzed in terms of time and space.

The basic configurations, correlations, and successions of behavior pattern are determined by a process of maturation. The tenacity of this process has been demonstrated by developmental studies of both premature and full-term infants and by experimental studies of monozygotic twins.

The rôle of maturation is most conspicuous in the fetus and infant, but it persists throughout the life cycle until the growth potential completely subsides.

A psychic constitution is more than a general diathesis. It is a structured product of growth. It endures, but it also changes during the life cycle.

The psychic individual is a distinctive entity by virtue of a certain characteristicness in his manifold behavior tendencies and in his secular pattern of growth. Such characteristicness can be investigated from the standpoint of form and can be formulated by morphographic methods. A systematic study of the ontogenesis of behavior thus becomes a psychomorphological approach to the ancient problem of constitution and type.

Bibliography

AMES, L. B. 1937. The sequential patterning of prone progression in the human infant. *Genet. Psychol. Monogr.*, **19**, 409–460.

——. 1940. The constancy of psycho-motor tempo in individual infants. *J. Genet. Psychol.*, **57**, 445–450.

——. 1942. Supine leg and foot postures in the human infant in the first year of life. *J. Genet. Psychol.*, **61**, 87–107.

BERTALANFFY, L. VON. 1933. *Modern theories of development: An introduction to theoretical biology.* (Trans. by J. H. WOODGER.) London: Oxford University Press.

BIEBER, I., and J. F. FULTON. 1938. Relation of the cerebral cortex to the grasp reflex and to postural and righting reflexes. *Arch. Neurol. Psychiat.*, **39**, 433–454.

BOUTAN, L. 1914. Les deux méthodes de l'enfant. *Act. Soc. linn. Bordeaux*, **68**, 3–146.

BRAINARD, P. P. 1930. The mentality of a child compared with that of apes. *J. Genet. Psychol.*, **37**, 268–293.

CARMICHAEL, L. 1933. Origin and prenatal growth of behavior. In C. MURCHISON (Ed.), *A handbook of child psychology* (2d ed., rev.), pp. 31–159. Worcester: Clark University Press.

CARTER, H. D. 1940. Ten years of research on twins: contributions to the nature-nurture problem. *Yearb. Nat. Soc. Stud. Educ.*, 39(I), 235–255.

COGHILL, G. E. 1929. *Anatomy and the problem of behaviour.* Cambridge: University Press; New York: Macmillan.

DÜRKEN, B. 1932. *Experimental analysis of development.* (Trans. by H. G. and A. M. NEWTH.) New York: Norton.

EULENBERG-WIENER, R. VON. 1938. *Fearfully and wonderfully made: The human organism in the light of modern science.* New York: Macmillan.

GELLERMANN, L. W. 1933. Form discrimination in chimpanzee and two-year-old children: I. Form (triangularity) *per se*. II. Form versus background. *J. Genet. Psychol.*, **42**, 3–27, 28–50.

GESELL, A. 1928. *Infancy and human growth.* New York: Macmillan.

——. 1938*a. Prone progression in the human infant.* (Film.) New Haven: Photographic Library, Yale Clinic of Child Development. 1000 ft. 35 mm.; 400 ft. 16 mm.

——. 1938*b.* The tonic neck reflex in the human infant: Its morphogenetic and clinical significance. *J. Pediat.*, **13**, 455–464.

——. 1938*c. The tonic neck reflex* (t.n.r.) *in the human infant.* (Film.) New Haven: Photographic Library, Yale Clinic of Child Development. 130 ft. 16 mm.

——. 1939*a.* The appraisal of mental growth careers. *J. Consult. Psychol.*, **3**, 73–75.

——. 1939*b.* Reciprocal neuromotor interweaving: A principle of development evidenced in the patterning of infant behavior. *J. Comp. Neurol.*, **70**, 161–180.

——. 1940. The stability of mental-growth careers. *Yearb. Nat. Soc. Stud. Educ.*, 39(II), 149–160. See also A. GESELL, Some observations of developmental stability, in W. R. MILES (Ed.), *Psychological Studies of Human Variability. Psychol. Monogr.*, 1936, **47**, No. 212, pp. 35–46.

GESELL, A., and C. S. AMATRUDA. 1941. *Developmental diagnosis: normal and abnormal child development.* New York: Hoeber.

GESELL, A., C. S. AMATRUDA, and C. S. CULOTTA. 1936. Effect of thyroid therapy on the mental and physical growth of cretinous infants. *Amer. J. Dis. Child.*, **52**, 1117–1138.

GESELL, A., in collaboration with C. S. AMATRUDA. 1945. *The embryology of behavior: The beginnings of the human mind.* New York: Harper.

GESELL, A., assisted by L. B. AMES. 1937. Early evidences of individuality in the human infant. *J. Genet. Psychol.*, **47**, 339–361.

GESELL, A., and L. B. AMES. 1940. The ontogenetic organization of prone behavior in human infancy. *J. Genet. Psychol.*, **56**, 247–263.

GESELL, A., and E. M. BLAKE. 1936. Twinning and ocular pathology. With a report of bilateral macular coloboma in monozygotic twins. *Arch. Opthal., N. Y.*, **15**, 1050–1071.

GESELL, A., B. M. CASTNER, H. THOMPSON, and C. S. AMATRUDA. 1939. *Biographies of child development: The mental growth careers of eighty-four infants and children.* New York: Hoeber.

GESELL, A., and H. M. HALVERSON. 1936. The development of thumb opposition in the human infant. *J. Genet. Psychol.*, **47**, 339–361.

——. 1942. The daily maturation of infant behavior. A cinema study of postures, movements and laterality. *J. Genet. Psychol.*, **61**, 3–32.

GESELL, A., H. M. HALVERSON, H. THOMPSON, F. L. ILG, B. M. CASTNER, L. B. AMES, and C. S. AMATRUDA. 1940. *The first five years of life: A guide to the study of the preschool child.* New York: Harper.

GESELL, A., and F. L. ILG. 1937. *The feeding behavior of infants: A pediatric approach to the mental hygiene of early life.* Philadelphia: Lippincott.

GESELL, A., and F. L. ILG, assisted by J. LEARNED and L. B. AMES. 1942. *Infant and child in the culture of today. The guidance of development in home and nursery school.* New York: Harper.

GESELL, A., and H. THOMPSON. 1929. Learning and growth in identical infant twins: An experimental study by the method of co-twin control. *Genet. Psychol. Monogr.*, **6**, 1–124.

——. 1941. Twins T and C from infancy to adolescence. A biogenetic study of individual differences by the method of co-twin control. *Genet. Psychol. Monogr.*, **24**, 3–121.

GESELL, A., and H. THOMPSON, assisted by C. S. AMATRUDA. 1934. *Infant behavior: Its genesis and growth.* New York: McGraw-Hill.

——. 1938. *The psychology of early growth.* New York: Macmillan.

GESELL, A., and H. M. ZIMMERMAN. 1937. Correlations of behavior and neuro-pathology in a case of cerebral palsy from birth injury. *Amer. J. Psychiat.*, **94**, 505–536.

HALVERSON, H. M. 1931. An experimental study of prehension in infants by means of systematic cinema records. *Genet. Psychol. Monogr.*, **10**, 107–286.

——. 1932. A further study of grasping. *J. Gen. Psychol.*, **7**, 34–64.

——. 1933. The acquisition of skill in infancy. *J. Genet. Psychol.*, **43**, 3–48.

HERRICK, C. J. 1929. Anatomical patterns and behavior patterns. *Physiol. Zoöl.*, **2**, 439–448.

HILGARD, J. R. 1933. The effect of early and delayed practice on memory and motor performances studied by the method of co-twin control. *Genet. Psychol. Monogr.*, **14**, 493–567.

JACOBSEN, C. F., M. M. JACOBSEN, and J. G. YOSHIOKA. 1932. Development of an infant chimpanzee during her first year. *Comp. Psychol. Monogr.*, **9**, 1–94.

KELLOGG, W. N., and L. A. KELLOGG. 1933. *The ape and the child: A study of environmental influence upon early behavior.* New York: McGraw-Hill.

KLÜVER, H. 1933. *Behavior mechanisms in monkeys.* Chicago: University of Chicago Press.

KÖHLER, W. 1924. *The mentality of apes.* (Trans. by E. WINTER.) London: Kegan Paul; New York: Harcourt, Brace (1925).

KOHTS, N. 1935. *Infant ape and human child: Instincts, emotions, play, habits.* (Scientific *memoirs of the museum darwinianum in Moscow,* Vol. III, pp. xvi + 596, c. 145 plates.)

LANDIS, C., and W. A. HUNT. 1939. *The startle pattern.* New York: Farrar and Rinehart.

LASHLEY, K. S., and J. B. WATSON. 1913. Notes on the development of a young monkey. *J. Anim. Behav.,* **3,** 114.

MAGNUS, R. 1924. *Körperstellung.* Berlin: Springer.

——. 1925. Animal posture. Croonian Lecture, *Proc. Roy. Soc.,* **89B,** 339–353.

MALINOWSKI, B. 1937. Culture as a determinant of behavior, pp. 133–168. In *Harvard Tercentenary Publication: Factors determining human behavior.* Cambridge: Harvard University Press.

MUNN, N. L. 1938. *Psychological development: An introduction to genetic psychology.* Boston: Houghton Mifflin.

NEEDHAM, J. 1936. *Order and life.* New Haven: Yale University Press.

SHERRINGTON, C. S. 1906. *The integrative action of the nervous system.* New York: Scribner's.

STRAYER, L. C. 1930. Language and growth: The relative efficacy of early and deferred vocabulary training studied by the method of co-twin control. *Genet. Psychol. Monogr.,* **8,** 209–319.

SWAN, C. 1934. *Postural patterning of the resting infant hand.* Unpublished Master's Essay, Yale University.

YERKES, A. W. 1935. Experiments with an infant chimpanzee. *J. Genet. Psychol.,* **46,** 171–181.

YERKES, R. M. 1916. The mental life of monkeys and apes: A study of ideational behavior. *Behav. Monogr.,* **3,** No. 1. Pp. 145.

Chapter 7

MATURATION OF BEHAVIOR

Myrtle B. McGraw [1]

Introduction

Early interest in structure and function was concerned not directly with behavior but with specific organs and their use. It harks back to the days when Lamarck (1773), emphasizing the development of *soma* through exercise, formulated a theory which has come to be known as the inheritance of acquired traits. Lamarck not only contended that individuals improved in function through exercise of somatic muscles but that it was the protracted use of muscle groups which effected the creation of new organs and new species. Amid these propositions are found quaint ideas to the effect that the giraffe gained his long neck by reaching into the trees for food; that the snake lost his legs by creeping through narrow crevices. When one considers the abundance of evidence in everyday life showing the increase in muscle strength through exercise it is no wonder that the Lamarckian theory gained credence. As an explanation for the mechanism of heredity, however, the theory was dealt a severe blow when Weismann (1889) pointed out the distinction between *germ plasm* and *somatoplasm,* the continuity of germ plasm from generation to generation, and its comparative insulation from other tissues of the body. Weismann's conten-

tions also served to crystallize the dichotomy of heredity and environment.

Following the work of Weismann and the resurrection of Mendel's (see Castle, 1921) papers in 1900, investigators in the field of behavior as well as morphology were laboring under the conviction that the nucleus of the germ plasm was the sole agent of hereditary factors, and that the germ was impervious to modification by environmental stimuli. As a result of this dichotomy the bulk of psychological literature during the early part of the twentieth century was concerned with the determination of those aspects of human behavior which are hereditary in origin as contrasted with other types of behavior which are acquired individually. Textbooks (Angell, 1908; McDougall, 1914; Thorndike, 1919; Perrin and Klein, 1926) of the time customarily classified behavior into (1) reflexes, (2) instincts, and (3) acquired traits. Such classifications were based upon a consideration of the complexity, variability, origin, and modifiability of the activity concerned. The labeling of human behaviors in categories of this order was for the sole purpose of facilitating ratiocination about the nature of man. The vast amount of literature accumulated within a decade on the .subject of instincts and acquired characteristics bears testimony to the assertion that the system defeated its own end. Soon the various compilations of instincts became so diverse and some so expansive that they were intellectually unwieldy.

---

[1] The writer acknowledges the valuable assistance of Vera Dammann in assembling the list of references and in the translation of foreign articles. Illustrations were drawn by Kenneth Breeze.

The influence of these controversies, however, was at least twofold. On the one hand they served to emphasize the distinction between innate and acquired characteristics, and on the other hand they stimulated extensive experimentation for the purpose of determining those traits which are predominantly hereditary in origin. The complexities which arose from such categories made it evident, however, that the conceptual framework in which the workers of the time were operating was in need of revision.

The revolution came with the birth of *behaviorism,* when instincts and consciousness were swept aside. Actually, the foundation of the heredity-environment dichotomy was left standing and a new structure was built on the old foundation. The essential difference between the new and the old structure was a matter of degree. The behaviorist (Watson, 1919; A. P. Weiss, 1929) readily admitted that there was a distinct difference in the development and function of traits transmitted through the germ plasm and those individually acquired, but they greatly restricted the number of characteristics which could be so transmitted. As a result of this shift in emphasis they have gone down in history as ardent environmentalists. In 1914 Watson, the chief protagonist of behaviorism, asserted:

> The student of behavior has come to look upon instinct as a combination of congenital responses unfolding serially under appropriate stimulation; the series as a whole may be "adaptive" in character (always adaptive from the Darwinian standpoint) or it may be wholly lacking in adaptiveness. Each element in the combination may be looked upon as a reflex. An instinct is thus a series of concatenated reflexes. The order of the unfolding of the separate elements is a strictly heritable character. Instincts are thus rightly said

to be phylogenetic modes of response (as contrasted with habit, which is acquired during the lifetime of the individual).

In making this statement, Watson not only reduced instincts to a series of reflexes, but also suggested a new theory of behavior development. The theory might be reduced to simple terms in the statement that the hereditary endowment of the individual is limited and the hereditary units of behavior can be identified by structural or physiological correlates. These innate units of behavior are conveniently termed "reflexes," and by a system of concatenation, association, conditioning, etc., more complex activities are constructed from these simple behavior units. There were several existing conditions which helped the theory to flame. In the first place the popular scientific mood at the time was to reduce each phenomenon to its smallest unit; the simple reflex was the psychologist's answer to this urge. Furthermore, the work of Pavlov (1927) had suggested the means whereby the simple reflex units of behavior might become complex constructs; so the business of the psychologist was to determine how, by a process of "conditioning," and "reconditioning," extraordinarily complex behavior mechanisms could be effected. Genetics (Lock, 1916; Conklin, 1916; Castle, 1921; Morgan, 1932) at the time not only burdened the ultramicroscopic gene with the hereditary load but also postulated that within the germ plasm there were definite determinants for every heritable character. This theory has come to be known as the inheritance of unit characters. Naturally, if the ultramicroscopic gene was to carry the load for every heritable trait, the limitation of heritable characters to a minimum seemed more reasonable. Furthermore, the theory of the environmentalists gained credence because of its simplicity, and it achieved great popularity because of its hopeful outlook.

On the other hand, theories of the behaviorists stimulated other lines of approach in the search for a better understanding of the complexities of behavior development. Their emphasis upon physio-

psychology, especially child psychology, even though the early infant studies by Watson (1919) were primarily to determine the repertoire of innate endowment. But as soon as attention shifted from inventories of behavior traits to developmental changes in activities it became evi-

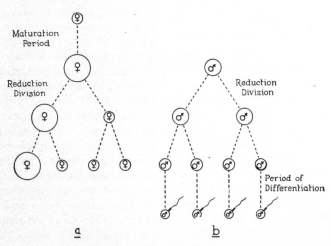

FIGURE 1. Diagram showing the maturational process of germ cells: (*a*) female, (*b*) male. (Adapted from *How Animals Develop*, by C. H. Waddington. New York: Norton, 1936, 31. By permission of the publisher.)

The egg mother-cell is built up and furnished with yolk during the maturation period, and then undergoes two divisions, giving four cells of which three are very small and die. The sperm mother-cell divides twice, and all four resulting cells are transformd into sperms during the period of differentiation.

logical correlates of behavior activities certainly enhanced, though it would not be claimed to have activated, the more recent investigations concerning the correlation of neurostructural development and behavior. Indeed, so extensive has been the work along these lines that the phrase "structure and function" has practically lost its original connotation of organ and use and has come to refer essentially to the relationship between cytological structures of the nervous system and behavior. Moreover, the behaviorist group, and particularly Watson, can justly lay claim to some credit for the current vogue of genetic

dent that the mechanistic theory, ascribing complex behavior to a concatenation of simple reflex units, was an inadequate explanation of the intricate process involved in development. Hence another term and another dichotomy have gained prominence in more recent literature. The term is *maturation,* and the dichotomy is *maturation and learning.*

Definitions of Maturation

Opposing the rigidity of the environmentalists' viewpoint, Gesell (1929) has been particularly active in popularizing the term *maturation* through the literature on child psychology. In its original application as a scientific term the word was used by geneticists and embryologists to denote that period of development prior to fertilization which converts an immature germ cell into a mature one. The significant change that takes place during this phase is the reduction of chromosomes, so that the mature germ cells (ovum or sperm) have only half as many chromosomes as the immature germ cell or other body cells. A simple diagram of this maturational process, reproduced from Waddington (1936), is shown in Figure 1. For a clear presentation of this process the reader is referred to Jennings (1935). The accompanying figure (Figure 2) adapted from Jennings shows the relation of germ cells to body cells. Clearly the original biological meaning of the term

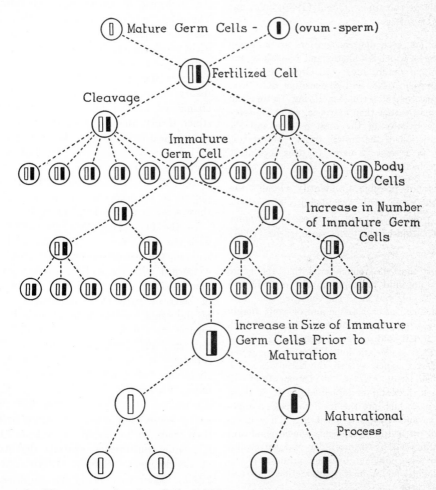

FIGURE 2. Diagram showing the relationship between germ cells and body cells. (Adapted from *Genetics*, by H. S. Jennings. New York: Norton, 1935, 46. By permission of the publisher.)

maturation has specific reference to the organization of chromosomes in the germ cells, although it has acquired a more general application in biological as well as psychological literature.

In his observation of infant behavior development, Gesell (1925) had repeatedly observed phenomena which could not be adequately explained in terms of the conditioning theories of the behaviorists in vogue at the time. Gesell (1933) felt that such theories

> do not give due recognition to the inner checks which set metes and bounds to the area of conditioning. . . . Growth is a process so intricate and so sensitive that there must be powerful stabilizing factors, intrinsic rather than extrinsic, which preserve the balance of the total pattern and the direction of the growth trend. Maturation is, in a sense, a name for this regulatory mechanism.

It is not possible to identify Gesell's use of the term with any definite physiological process, but he justifies his broader application of the term, since, as he (1933) says:

> It must be remembered that the genes do not find lodgment in the reproductive cells only but in all the somatic cells. Into each cell of each tissue and of every bodily organ go appropriate subdivisions of both paternal and maternal genes. These ancestral genes are found in every neurone. They produce, as well, the hormones which secondarily regulate development at all ages, prenatal and postnatal. It is these genes which are the focal sources of directive and constructive energy. They interact with the cytoplasm, which is always influenced by intracellular and extracellular environment; but the primary physiological factor in this interaction traces to the gene.

It is evident that Gesell does not use the term *maturation* to indicate any particular rearrangement or reduction process of the chromosomes within the somatic cells as the individual grows. These quotations in isolation sound as if he considered the genes sitting, like censors, within the organism telling environment when to stop. Actually, such an interpretation would be most unfair. Gesell was seeking an expression for those phenomena which develop in an orderly fashion without direct influence of known external stimuli. The older term *instinct*, having fallen into scientific disgrace, was a feeble instrument with which to combat the tenets of the radical environmentalists. In a real sense, however, the sponsors of the maturation theory have taken up the battle front abandoned by the contenders for the instinct theory and are reasserting the rôle of biological inheritance in the development of behavior performances. In that sense they are confronted with the same problems, and the criteria and methods employed in experimentation are not unlike those used in the study of instinct.

In the first place, they are concerned with the appearance of particular abilities without the benefit of practice; they are concerned with the sudden appearance of new behavior items; with the consistency of behavior patterns in different subjects of the same species; with an orderly sequence in the manifestation of different patterns; and, finally, with the gradual or saltatory course of growth. The facts that most babies are able to reach for an object within the visual field before they can maintain the sitting position, that they sit up before they stand, and creep before they walk are presented as evidence that a genetic constituency controls the order of development. Shirley (1931b, 1933a, 1933b, 1933c) particularly has emphasized the consistency in a sequential order of development and the sudden emergence of new behavior items as criteria of maturational development. Some of the points at issue in discussions of ontogenetic development are reminiscent of similar issues raised in controversies of the evolutionary process. For example, the question as to whether development is gradual or social, and the mature state may be either that of the organism as a whole or that of any of its parts or functions (Courtis, 1935).

The term had not found its way into psychological textbooks of twenty years ago,

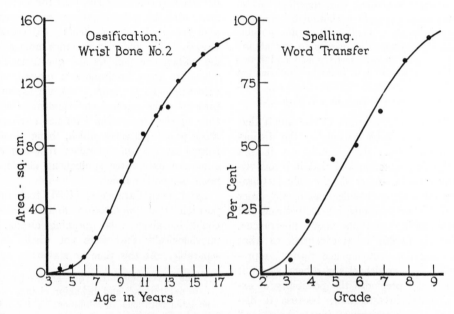

FIGURE 3. Curves showing the development of two different types of phenomena, namely, increasing ossification of wrist bone and development as represented by the increasing ability of children in different grades to spell the word "transfer." (From "Maturation as a Factor in Diagnosis," by S. A. Courtis. *Yearbook of the National Society for the Study of Education*, 1935, **34**, 173. By permission of the Society.)

saltatory (Shirley, 1931c) harks back to old disputes over continuous and discontinuous variation.

Other writers apply the term more loosely as referring to any phenomenon in the process of completion without reference to physiological or genetic correlates.

Maturation may be defined precisely as the progress of an immature organism toward a mature, or terminal, state—a progress produced by constant forces acting under constant conditions. The organism itself may be either individual or but the complexity of the concept is reflected in the definition proposed in a recent textbook (Boring, Langfeld, and Weld, 1939):

Maturation consists in structural changes which are mainly hereditary—i.e., which have their origin in the chromosomes of the fertilized ovum—but which are also in part a product of the interaction of the organism with its environment.

Indeed, the concept is so difficult to manipulate that some writers have taken the position that any attempt to separate the maturational and learning processes only adds to intellectual confusion. Carmichael (1933) emphasizes that

> from the moment growth has begun in the fertilized ovum until senescence or death, development consists in the alteration of existing structures and functions in an organism living in a continually changing environment. That is, it is not possible save for pragmatic reasons to say at any point that growth has stopped and learning has begun, but that the environment plays a part in all "maturation" and maturation plays a part in all learning.

Gesell and Thompson (1934) admit that it is not desirable to belabor the distinction, but assert that scientifically it is a desirable distinction and that it is analytically feasible. After all, the only justification for making classifications of any order is that they facilitate intellectualizing and manipulating concepts about phenomena. Marquis (1930) takes exception to what he calls the "convergence theory" represented by Carmichael and others, since "it practically precludes the possibility of experimental investigation; because it dismisses the problem of innate behavior." He further points out what he believes to be a valid distinction between a maturational process and learning:

> Both processes represent an interaction of organism and environment, but learning is distinguished from maturation by this fact: It represents a modification of the organismic pattern in response to specific stimuli present in the external environment at the time of the modification. Maturation, on the other hand, is a modification of the organismic pattern in response to stimuli present in the inter-cellular and intra-cellular environments which at the given moment are independent of external influences.

He also emphasized that intracellular and intercellular environments are hereditary

components, derived from the parent in a manner comparable to the inheritance of the germ plasm.

Marquis's definition at first glance appears to denote valid and workable distinctions. On examination, however, the definition is confusing and calls for a clarification of the terms *organism* and *internal and external environments* (McGraw, 1940a). This confusion becomes more evident when one ponders the question: To what are these environments *internal* or *external?* Furthermore, "specific stimuli present in the external environment *at the time of the modification*" do not envisage those past experiences which, though ineffectual at the time, become functionally operative only after subsequent development of another order.

Later, even Carmichael (1936) took the position that *maturation* and *learning* could be given valid meaning although physiologically they were not wholly inseparable. At this time he stated:

> The development of "our knowledge of external things," and behavior change associated with such development, is dependent upon the fact that certain receptor mechanisms are specialized to be stimulated by one sort and only one sort of energy. . . . From this point of view, the development of adaptive behavior associated with receptor stimulation in ontogeny becomes the account of the gradual evolution and change in the organism of anatomically specialized receptor-neuro-motor systems of such a sort that their so-called resting activity may easily be affected only by very definite changes of a limited kind in the external world of stimuli.

He defines external environment as "the sum total of all the physico-chemical energies releasing neural activity as a result of action on *exteroceptors*," and internal environment as the "sum of energy changes acting on *interoceptors* and *pro-*

rioceptors, even though they involve de-
forming pressures or chemical or electri-
al stimulation brought about by the
body's own active movement." He suggests that the term *learning,* in contrast to
maturation, "may be used to characterize
the development of responses which can
be demonstrated to be changed because
of certain antecedent stimulus-released
processes." Despite his admission that a
valid distinction may be drawn between
the two concepts, he still contends that
such words add little to the study of behavior development and as a final proposal he suggests that

> the facts of developmental change in be-
> havior can best be represented as empirical
> curves and that generalizations derived
> from such curves, together with the prop-
> erties which they represent, would not be
> appreciably enriched by labelling them
> under a less specific nomenclature.

Digressing for the time being from the
problem of genetics in the process of maturation, let us consider the practical issues involved in ontogenetic development.
Specifically the issues are two, viz.: (1)
What are the physiological changes in
neurosomatic tissues—structural changes
and changes in chemical and electrical
function—which correlate with developmental changes in overt behavior? (2) In
what way and to what extent does the
change (increase or decrease) in practice
or exercise of a function accelerate or re-
ard its development? As a corollary of
his question, one is prompted to speculate
whether or not the practice affects the
changes in neurosomatic structures, or
whether the modification of overt behavior
must await organic changes in the neuromuscular system. Evidence brought to
bear on these subjects is generally in the
nature of (1) investigations which have in
some way attempted to alter or measure

the factor of practice and to determine
practice-effects by measurement of overt
behavior and (2) investigations which have
aimed at altering the neural organization
or otherwise at determining the neural
status at the onset of behavior function.

Methods of Investigation

*Practice or Exercise the Experimental
Variable.* In general, those investigations
which have operated within a framework
of overt behavior only may, for convenience, be considered in the following categories: (1) those which base their criteria
of maturation primarily upon the accuracy or precision of a given function at
the time of or immediately after its emergence; (2) experiments where function has
been experimentally restricted beyond the
expected period of its manifestation; (3)
experiments where practice or repetition
of performance has been experimentally induced for the purpose of determining the
effect of practice *per se* upon performance;
and (4) experimental situations where the
effects of both repetition and restriction of
performance might be ascertained with respect to the same developing phenomenon.

Some of the early familiar studies on
the subject of instincts bear repetition lest
they be forgotten and their contributions
in the study of maturation be lost. That
the concepts of *instincts* and *maturation*
are kindred in nature is evidenced by the
frequent similarity in experimental methods employed and the criteria proposed as
a basis for analysis. So close is this relationship that Witty and Lehman (1933)
contend that the term maturation refers
merely to phenomena previously known as
delayed instincts. A familiar criterion of
instincts was the sudden appearance of a
particular behavior pattern and the precision of its function. These same arguments are set forth in current distinctions

between maturation and learning. In 1911, Breed pointed out that the pecking of chicks was not a function which burst forth in the full bloom of perfection. Even Shirley (1931a, 1933a, 1933b, 1933c), who lays great stress upon the sudden manifestation of new motor activities in the growing infant, does not claim that they emerge at a peak of perfection. Certainly it seems that in the higher organism no adaptive behavior function is at its optimum from the moment of inception. For that reason the perfection or efficiency criterion alone seems to be an inadequate basis upon which to determine innate phenomena or the fundamentals of the maturational process.

The technique of restricting function beyond the inception period has been more fruitful. As early as 1873 Spalding had employed a method of hooding young chicks to prevent their seeing or pecking at food for several days. Spalding made many observations on the behavior of chicks and other fowls, and among some of his interesting observations he noted that young chicks who had been hooded and kept from the hen for a day or two would, when released, run immediately to her in response to her call, but if the chicken had been kept from the mother for a period of ten days it could not be induced to follow her. The moment of "ripeness" for that particular behavior had apparently been exceeded, and presumably some other method would have to be introduced in order for the chick to achieve a type of behavior which would have been simple a few days earlier. Spalding (1875) also used the restraint method in preventing flight of young swallows beyond the time when they would ordinarily begin to fly. He reports varying degrees of efficiency with which different birds made their first flight, although they all exhibited flight movements.

Recently Dennis (1941) used buzzard in a repetition of Spalding's flight experiments. Dennis caged two young bird just beginning to feather and prior to the normal manifestation of flight behavior Ten weeks later, after unrestrained immature buzzards had been soaring with adult skill, the flight behavior of the caged birds was examined. At this time the birds sometimes spread their wings as they ran and in so doing on one or two occasions raised themselves off the ground for a distance of two feet only. Even when the birds were placed on the perch they not only exhibited poor balancing ability but fell, instead of trying to fly, from the perch to the ground. Experimental observations were continued on these birds for a period of several weeks. The evidence is strong that the impaired flight ability of the birds was a result of their prolonged captivity

Shepard and Breed (1913) fed chicks artificially while they were kept in a dark room and prevented them from pecking at food for periods of three, four, or five days. On testing, they found that it required about two days for the chicks to gain normal efficiency in pecking and swallowing. The rapid improvement which occurred during those two days they attribute to practice, and subsequent improvement to maturation.

Yerkes and Bloomfield (1910) utilized the prevention method in studying the tendency for kittens to catch mice. They observed that "suddenly" during the second month the behavior of the kittens changed so materially when the mouse was introduced into the cage as to justify the conclusion that kittens instinctively kill mice. They pointed out, somewhat incidentally, that this type of behavior was increasingly difficult to evoke as the animal grew older. This observation, along with the responses of Spalding's chickens to the mother hen, suggests that there may be a avorable maturational status for the elici-ation of any particular type of behavior, but if it is not afforded external stimulation the original tendencies become less sensi-tive. Attention is called to these incidental observations because they were, in both instances, passed off as of small conse-quence, but, as a matter of fact, they may be of greater significance in elucidating the meaning of maturation than were the cen-tral data of these studies.

Kuo (1930) did a more elaborate study on the rat-killing tendencies of kittens, one aspect of which was to keep 20 kittens in isolation so that they would have no chance to observe rat-killing behavior of other rats. Of these 20, 9 did at some time dur-ing the first four months of life kill the rat, and 11 did not. Kuo offers no satis-factory explanation for the predatory be-havior of the 9 kittens except to disclaim the usefulness of a term such as *instinct* to identify such a phenomenon.

Carmichael (1926) showed considerable ingenuity in his use of the restriction method in studying the swimming move-ments of the young frog and salamander. Taking embryos at an early stage of de-velopment before any bodily movements appeared, he divided them into two groups. One group he allowed to develop in ordi-nary tap water; the other group he placed in a solution of chloretone, of just sufficient concentration to anesthetize the animal but not concentrated enough to impair its physical growth. The larvae in tap water grew more rapidly in size than did the experimental group, but there was no dis-tinction in organ differentiation. Bodily movement in response to external stimu-lation was absent in the experimental group so long as they were in the chloretone solu-tion. After the control embryos had begun to display swimming movements, the ex-perimental ones were taken from the

chloretone solution and placed in ordinary tap water. It was found that, on the average, within less than twelve minutes they began to respond to external stimu-lation and within thirty minutes these previously drugged embryos were engaging in swimming movements. The salamanders swam so well within that time that it was only with difficulty that they could be dis-tinguished from the controls.

Subsequently, Carmichael (1927, 1928) followed up the original study by checking the influence of the anesthesia, or the time of recovery. He reanesthetized the ani-mals after they had been for a period of twenty-four hours in tap water. On re-moving them from the chloretone solution the second time he found that the time interval between removal from the chlore-tone solution and the onset of swimming movements was just as long as on the pre-vious occasion. This period, therefore, was considered as representing the time neces-sary to recover from the anesthesia, and not a period of rapid learning. Later he grew salamanders in isolation, free from light and vibration. When light was flashed on them after the period when swimming might have been established it was observed that they swam freely, in no wise different from the controls who had been brought up under ordinary labora-tory conditions. Despite these extraordi-nary findings Carmichael (1928) concludes that:

A knowledge of the developmental me-chanics of the nervous system precludes the use of these results as a final confirma-tion of the theory that the development of behavior is merely a maturation of the native factors. On the contrary, viewed in its largest aspects, the development of behavior seems to be the result of the *in-terdependent* influence of the action of both environmental and hereditary factors.

In his presidential address Carmichael (1941) took occasion to retract some of the implications of his earlier statements.

> When I wrote my first papers in this field . . . I was so under the domination of a universal conditioned reflex theory of the development of adaptive responses that I denied categorically the truth of the statement just made. [The growing animal functions in a way that is in general adaptive at every stage.] But every experiment that I have done in the field of the early growth of behavior has forced me to retreat from this environmentalist hypothesis. Now, literally almost nothing seems to me to be left of this hypothesis so far as the very early development of behavior is concerned (p. 17).

Matthews and Detwiler (1926), also using the chloretone technique to restrict the activity of *Amblystoma* embryos, varied the concentration of solution as well as the duration of immersion. They found that the onset of neuromuscular movement after the embryos were returned to tap water was contingent upon the strength of the chloretone solution and the duration of immersion. Normal reactions were exhibited by embryos immersed only seven or eight days, but an atypical response followed prolonged use of chloretone. Exposure to anesthesia for more than thirteen days generally resulted in atypical and feeble responses, though the animals continued to live. These findings seem to indicate that restriction of function is effective if the restriction is enforced beyond a critical period. So again we are reminded that the issue is not a simple one of restriction of activity versus practice, but that the stage of development at the inception of the experimental factor (restriction or exercise) and the duration of such factors are of major importance.

Mowrer (1936), who sutured the eyelids of young squabs until they were five or six weeks old, points to a distinction in the developmental processes involved in vestibular nystagmus and optokinetic nystagmus. Vestibular nystagmus in these birds deprived of normal vision, was both quantitatively and qualitatively indistinguishable from that of birds with normal vision whereas optokinetic nystagmus was not established until three days after vision had been restored. This rapid development after the restoration of vision he attributed to learning, or, in any event, the maturational factors involved were not alone sufficient to bring these responses to functional maturity. Metfessel (1940) kept roller canaries in soundproof cages so they could not be exposed to the songs of other birds. Selected tones were introduced into some of the cages. Subsequently, all the birds were placed in flight cages where the songs of other birds could be heard. He found that the isolated birds developed rudimentary elements of a species song. The birds exposed to experimental tones showed modification of song elements in accordance with the environmental factor, and the songs of all the birds underwent alteration after they were placed in flight cages.

Dennis (1934a) made a survey of case reports on patients whose sight, either during late childhood or adulthood, had been restored by surgery, for the purpose of culling any information available as to the presence of unlearned behavior as a result of the sudden restoration of vision. Although the results were inconclusive, the author felt that there was no evidence of an unlearned control of behavior by vision. Dennis (1935, 1938) utilized the restriction method in an experimental study of the development of infants. Twin girls were reared from the first until the end of the fourteenth month under nursery conditions which provided the minimum social and motor stimulation. When the development of these infants was from time to time compared with standard norms, it was found that in certain motor achievements they were retarded beyond the upper age period for the appearance of these items in normal groups. The writer was of the opinion that this retardation should be attributed to the restriction of motor practice; on the other hand, he did not find the customary social stimulation indispensable to normal behavioral development.

According to Danzinger and Frankl (1934), extraordinary restrictions are imposed during the first year upon infants reared in Albanian culture. It is reported that the babies, bound to small wooden cradles, are released only for cleansing, not even for nursing. These investigators tried to rate Albanian infants according to the Viennese baby tests. Measured by these standards, the Albanian infants showed retardation in motor development, especially during the third year. In social reactions they showed no retardation. It was in this sphere that they received the greatest amount of stimulation.

Dennis (1940) studied among the Hopi and Navaho Indians the effects of differences in culture upon the development of infants. One striking difference between Indians and Americans is the relative amount of cradle binding or restriction of general motor activity during the first six or twelve months. During the first three months the Hopi child is bound to the cradle all the time except for approximately one hour daily. After that time the periods of freedom increase. Despite these physical restrictions Dennis found that the fundamental development of Indian babies during the first year was not in any appreciable degree different from that of American infants.

The study of maturation has been attacked not only by the restriction of activity beyond the supposed ripening period but also by the introduction of selected environmental factors, particularly increased exercise or practice of a function, into the experimental situation. The overall increase in performance above the norm is usually attributed to the special factor of practice or training. The number of studies bearing upon the effect of specific training is voluminous. In this chapter only a few of those which have particular bearing upon the maturational theory can be mentioned. A common method of study in investigations of this type is known as the equivalent-group method. Groups are equated according to accepted standards—chronological age, mental age, initial achievement, etc.—and then the experimental group is given special exercise in selected activities for a period of time. At the end of the practice periods the achievements of the two groups are again compared, and the superiority (if such is found) of the experimental group over the control group is attributed to the special factor of exercise. Jersild (1932) used this method in testing practice-effect on mental, motor, and musical performances of over 200 children ranging in age between 2 and 10 years. Practice extended over a period of 6 months. Both groups at the end of that time showed an improvement over their initial tests, but the experimental group showed greater improvement than the control. Innate endowment seemed to be reflected by individual differences in the ability to profit from training. Hilgard (1932) trained an experimental group of young children in such activities as buttoning, cutting with scissors, and climbing a ladder. After 12 weeks of practice the experimental group exceeded the control group on all tests, but one week of practice of the control group at the later age period was sufficient to bring their scores to the level of the experimental group after 12 weeks of practice. The greater profit from training in a shorter period of time by the control group led to the conclusion that other factors than training (partly maturational factors and partly practice in related skills) contributed to the development of these three skills.

Gesell and Thompson (1929) introduced the co-twin method in their famous study of identical twins in stair climbing and cube building behavior. When the twins were 46 months old both infants were at the threshold of stair climbing and cube building behavior. At that time training of twin T was initiated. For 10 minutes each day over a period of 6 weeks she was stimulated to climb stairs and build a tower with cubes. At the end of this 6-week period of training twin T, twin C was started on a 2-weeks training course in the same activities. Although twin T was more agile in these performances, the investigators were much impressed by the fact that twin C on this first occasion actually climbed the four nursery steps which figured in the experiment, and after 2 weeks of practice twin C was performing these activities as well as her sister had done at the end of 6 weeks of similar training at a slightly earlier age. On the basis of these findings, the authors claim that "There is no conclusive evidence that practice and exercise even hasten the actual appearance of types of reactions like climbing and tower building. The time of appearance is fundamentally determined by the ripeness of the neural structures."

It might be noted in this connection that, since the infants were at the threshold of their climbing and tower building behavior at the inception of the training period, the experimental practice had nothing whatever to do with the "actual appearance" or emergence of these types of reactions. It dealt rather with the effect of practice on the *expansion* of these activities. This difference is an important one in a discussion of the nature of maturation. Furthermore, when the protocols submitted in the synopsis of the monograph are reviewed, the effect of practice in stair climbing is more evident than the writers' conclusions imply. At the inception of twin C's training period, twin T is admittedly more skillful; 10 weeks later she is still noted as more skillful; 16 weeks later she is reported as more agile, walks faster, and is less afraid of falling; and even as late as 26 weeks after the onset of twin C's training period twin T is reported to be more mobile than twin C, traverses more ground in play, and generally shows more abandon in her motor activities. The issue involved in this study really is not whether practice had any effect upon the emergence of these activities, but rather the relative effect of practice if it is introduced at one time or 6 weeks later. This investigation not only introduced the co-twin technique but also served to stimulate the maturation-versus-learning controversy.

Subsequently these same twins were used as subjects by Strayer (1930) and Hilgard (1933) in studies of different behavior phenomenon. In general, both investigators support the maturational thesis.

Influenced by these conclusions of the co-twin studies, especially the inference that motor behavior of infants was not subject to appreciable improvement through practice, but at the same time recognizing that older children and adults do improve in performance through exercise, McGraw (1935) undertook a study with the idea of determining the age when children would begin to show improvement from practice influences in motor performances. From the age of 21 days until he was 22 months old, Johnny, one member of a set of twin boys, was exercised in those motor activities of which he was somewhat capable, whereas his twin, Jimmy, was kept in a crib during the days at the laboratory so that, comparatively, his exercise was restricted. As the children grew, additional behavior items were added to the practice repertory. From time to time the behavior development of these two children was compared to that of a group of 68 children in whom the same activities were being observed. In discussing the effect of increased and restricted exercise upon the development of the various activities considered, it was found convenient to group the activities into two types according to their susceptibility to practice influences. Phylogenetic activities, or those behavior patterns which every child must acquire in order to function biologically as a normal human being (not necessarily as a civilized human being), are more fixed and subject to less modification through mere repetition of performance than are ontogenetic activities, that is, those activities which an individual may or may not acquire.

The extent to which exercise of an activity may alter the development of a particular behavior course in infancy is contingent upon the following conditions: (1) the neuro-structural level at which the activity is controlled; (2) the state of plasticity or fixity of the behavior course at the time increased exercise or use is introduced; (3) the state of fixity attained by the behavior pattern at the time the factor of special exercise is withdrawn; and (4) the phylogenetic origin and importance of the behavior pattern.

Those behavior-patterns which have achieved a high degree of fixity and are controlled at an infracortical level are subject to no appreciable alteration through mere repetition of the activity during the post-natal development of the subject. Also phyletic rudiments of behavior patterns controlled at an infracortical level are resistant to influence or alteration of any

significance by increased exercise of the activity. Those phylogenetic activities which succeed these infracortical rudiments, that is, the kindred activities which are governed at a higher structural level, can be modified in minor details through individual exercise of the function. . . . Activities of ontogenetic origin can be greatly accelerated through exercise of the performance, but the degree to which they can be modified is dependent upon the state of maturation or plasticity of the behavior pattern at the time the factor of exercise is introduced (McGraw, 1935).

The writer emphasizes that there are critical periods when any given activity is most susceptible to modification through repetition of performance. Repeated observations (McGraw, 1939b) on these two boys over a period of years have revealed that the child given greater opportunity for motor activity during the first two years still exhibits superior motor coordination.

McGraw (1940b) also used the co-twin technique in studying the effect of training in the achievement of voluntary micturition. Two sets of identical twin boys were used as subjects. After the first few weeks of life one member of each pair was placed on the chamber for voiding at hourly intervals during seven hours of the day until they were 17 and 26 months of age respectively. Their brothers were not permitted to use the vessel until they were 14 months of age in one instance and 24 months in the other. From the achievement curves of these four children (Figure 4) it can be seen that the experimental subjects did not profit by the long and systematic training program. It was pointed out that during the early months the reflex mechanism controlling micturition was so hypersensitive that any mild handling or disturbance of position might initiate voiding. The slight elevation in the achievement curve at this time was attributed to the hypersensitivity of the reflex mechanism. As the reflex became less sensitive to vicarious stimuli, a decline in the achievement curve was noted. Later a rapid rise in the percentage of successful responses to the vessel paral-

the achievement curve, after which the performance is stabilized at a fairly high level.

It is evident from the discussions of these studies of practice effects upon behavior development that there are two

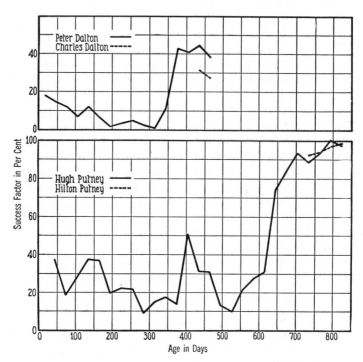

FIGURE 4. Curves obtained from the records of two sets of identical twin boys showing their achievement of bladder control. (From "Neural Maturation as Exemplified in Achievement of Bladder Control," by M. B. McGraw. *Journal of Pediatrics*, 1940, **16**, 584. By permission of The C. V. Mosby Company, publisher.)

leled the onset of cortical participation in the act of micturition, the cortical participation being reflected in the child's behavior by unmistakable signs of awareness of the act and the result. As the cortical influence shifts from simple association to more complex discrimination and generalization a second decline in the achievement curve is evident. The functional integration of complex cortical processes is reflected in a second rapid rise of

fundamental problems involved in the maturational theory. The first concerns the genetic components of behavior development and its corollary, the modifiability of behavior through environmental influences; and the second concerns the relationship between developmental changes of the nervous system and behavior as it is manifested during ontogeny.

Determination of Neural Status and Associated Behavior. It is safe to say that those who think of maturation as a term for describing certain changes taking place within the nervous system before function can be detected do not presuppose that these changes are in the nature of chromosomal rearrangements. In this application, the term refers generally to some other type of anatomical or chemical change which develops without reference to neuromuscular functioning. And the real issue of the maturational theory is whether or not the neurostructural changes are prefunctional or whether the structural changes are molded by somatic function out of a rather homogeneous neural mass. That is, does function determine the neural organization or does the neural organization form the framework within which function takes place?

Investigations bearing upon these problems are in general of the following order: (1) studies in neurogenesis which reflect in a general way the developmental character of embryonic nerve tissues; (2) observation upon the development of overt behavior; and (3) determination of a relationship between specific somatic activities and certain anatomical and physiological constructs in a time-space framework.

In embryological studies of the ontogeny of the nervous system there are some impressive observations the interpretations of which are basic to an understanding of neuromuscular functioning. In the first place, developmental changes in neural morphology—subdivisions, bulges, folds, fissures, etc.—are strikingly constant in all normal individuals of a species. Not only is it well substantiated that nerve cells of a given structure, location, and organization demonstrate functional peculiarities, but, furthermore, it is possible to detect certain morphological and histological differentiation in an early embryonic stage. It is possible to know as soon as the medullary plate is laid down those divisions that

will develop into brain and those that will ultimately develop into spinal cord. The question of intrinsic and extrinsic factors is aroused as soon as the medullary plate assumes more definite form. Development at this stage is indicated by an increase in thickness and mechanical rigidity, attributed to an increased height of the cells. Embryologists ask whether the cells possess some intrinsic power to grow in height or whether they are compressed into elongation by the surrounding ectoderm. Similarly, does the medullary plate possess an independent power to form a neural tube, or is it dependent upon the adjacent ectoderm? Experiments in this connection lead to the conclusion that "the medullary plate and non-neural ectoderm are both taking an active, cooperative, part in the movements of neurulation. Although capable of manifesting their individual abilities independently they normally do team work by assisting and reinforcing each other" (Weiss, 1939). It is evident that the problem of neurostructural development and its relations to surrounding environment is one that arises early in embryology. It is also evident from the citations of Weiss that conflicting results may be obtained.

Many of the transplantation and extraplantation experiments of embryonic neural systems provoke thought concerning the growth qualities of nerve tissues. There is considerable evidence too that the problem is not simply a matter of determining a relationship between neural cells and their environment. The element of time is highly significant. The exciting experiments of Spemann (1925) brought out the point that there is a critical period when the presumptive neural plate becomes determined and will continue to develop into neural tissue despite its transplanted location. Transplantation at an earlier stage, however, showed differentiation in accordance with the new environment.

Detwiler (1920, 1928, 1931) showed that during later stages of embryonic development of the *Amblystoma* a transplant of a limb bud caudad would attract the brachial nerves away from their normal pathways in order to innervate the displaced limb bud. It was also shown that the force of attraction which a transplanted limb may exert upon the brachial nerves operates only through a relatively short period of time. Furthermore, the influence appeared to be nonspecific, as transplants of nasal placode or eye grafts would exert an attractive force upon spinal nerves with which they normally had no connection. Apparently it is the state of rapid differentiation which influences the direction of spinal innervation. It has been suggested that an electrical field may be set up as a result of the high physiological activity at the focus of rapid differentiation.

Gilchrist (1933) also points out that there is a crucial stage in the development of amphibian embryos when the neural fold is responsive to thermal changes. He found that if eggs were warmed on the right side during the *blastular* stage they developed a larger neural fold, whereas a comparable increase of the neural fold was not educed by warming during the period of early *gastrulation*. He points out that the period of increased susceptibility to thermal stimulation corresponds to the time at which the determination of neural plate material was most actively under way.

Dürken (1932) has shown that at the end of the process of gastrulation of *Triton* embryos presumptive epidermis and medullary material are no longer interchangeable. If they are interchanged after this stage, they develop not in accordance with their position but in accordance with their origin. These studies of the embryonic nervous system bring up several considerations which are pertinent to an understanding of the process of maturation and development. They suggest that presumptive neural tissue is first in an indeterminate state when it is more or less susceptible to particular environmental forces. They suggest further that there are critical periods in the development of any phenomenon when it is most responsive to extrinsic stimulation, and there is some indication that these crucial periods correspond to periods of rapid differentiation and development.

Other writers have felt that the type or quality of early neurosomatic movements is of special significance to the maturation theory, and that the relationships between neural structures and functions are reflected in the quality of these embryonic movements. The central issue concerning these early fetal movements seems to revolve around a controversy as to their localization or specificity in contradistinction to a total body or mass response. The controversy has reference to theories of development as a process. If the earliest detectable fetal movements are in the nature of localized specific reflex activities, development presumably proceeds from the simple to the complex. On the other hand, if the initial neurogenic movement is of the nature of mass or "total body" response, the process of early development is one wherein the local or discrete response gains specificity out of the general mass matrix.

Such controversies on the nature of the developmental process have served to stimulate intensive observations on the primary embryonic and fetal movements of many different species. Some have based their interpretations entirely upon the nature of behavior response without essaying to determine the developmental state of neural counterparts. Bridgman and Carmichael (1935), who worked with fetal guinea pigs, report that the order of neuromuscular reactions is (1) myogenic, (2) local response to external stimuli, and (3) spontaneous activities. Tuge (1937), utilizing the saline solution technique in studying embryonic movements of carrier pigeons, also reports myogenic prior to neurogenic movements. The earliest neuromuscular action appears to be a lateral flexion of the neck, a reaction which expands until it embraces the entire axial musculature. Kuo (1939), from his observations of chick embryos, says that so-called local reflexes may appear during any stage of development, though there is a steady increase in the percentage of local responses as the fetus develops. Tracy (1926) also reports discrete muscular activity as primary in the toadfish. According to Swenson (1929), the first movements of the fetal rat consist of a lateral flexion of the head, trunk, and rump; and essentially the same type of movement is reported by Pankratz (1931) as characteristic of the fetal rabbit. The same type of unilateral head and upper-trunk flexion is reported by Coronios (1933) as the primary neuromuscular movement of the fetal cat. Indeed, one is again and again impressed when descriptions of embryonic movements of different species—birds, fishes, and mammals—are presented that the unilateral flexion of the cervical axis is such a common occurrence.

Other investigators have supported their observations of overt behavior by cytological analysis of the nervous system of the experimental fetuses. The now classical researches of Coghill (1929) are demonstrative of the knowledge which may be gained by such colossal and tedious methods. Coghill has not only determined the neural status of the nervous system in *Amblystoma* embryos at the onset of neurogenic behavior but also has followed it through all the progressive stages to adulthood. Angulo y González (1930, 1935) has applied essentially the same methods in studying structural and functional correlation as evidenced in the fetal rat. According to Tuge (1931), early embryonic movements of the turtle are essentially of the same nature as those of other embryonic vertebrates although in adulthood the vertebral axis of this animal is attached to his shell. Windle and his collaborators (1930, 1931, 1933, 1934), in their studies of fetal chicks and fetal cats, have been concerned with the nature of the first neurogenic movements of embryos as well as with the structural counterparts of fetal behavior. Tilney, giving particular attention to the structural maturation of the rat brain, has shown parallel changes in behavior and cerebral maturation not only during the fetal period but also during postnatal development until the rat achieves adulthood. He (1933) interprets his findings in the light of phylogenetic as well as ontogenetic development. There have been a few studies of the primary neuromuscular movements of the human fetus. The early reports (Strassmann, 1903; Yanase, 1907; Krabbe, 1912; Minkowski, 1922; Bolaffio and Artom, 1924) antedate the current interests in the quality of primary behavior responses, though Coghill (1933) has interpreted Minkowski's observations in terms of his own theory of "individuation." Current work on the human fetus will be discussed more fully later. Since the discussion of fetal behavior will be more amply reviewed in another chapter of this book, only those implications concerning the nature of maturation and development will be mentioned here.

As indicated above, the writers on the subject of primary embryonic movements seem to be divided into two schools of thought. Since the classical challenge of Coghill, there has been one group, including Coghill, Angulo y González, Tuge, and, more recently, Hooker (1936, 1937), who assert that neurogenic behavior in its origin is in the nature of a total pattern which, from the beginning, is integrated; [1] local reflexes, or independent limb movements, are "individuated" out of this dominant pattern. Windle, Carmichael, Tracy, and Kuo claim that local reflexes may be primary, or at least that local reflexes occur as early as the total body response. The issue is not merely an academic one but one which is basic to an understanding of the process of development.

According to Coghill (1933):

An action is regarded as total when it involves all the muscles of a functional system that are capable of responding at the time. . . . Action appears first in the anterior part of the axial musculature, and spreads thence tailward through the axial system, and then into the appendicular system, so that before an appendage can act on its own it acts only as an integral part of a whole, which is axial and appendicular.

Individuation is the process whereby appendages or local muscular groups achieve motility somewhat independent of the axial system. He points out that individuation is not the same as specialization or specification, which involve an adjustment of the organism to the environment, but it represents rather a "definite and peculiar relation of a part of the organism to the

organism itself as a whole." Windle and Orr (1934) draw a distinction between responses to mechanical stimulation and spontaneous motility. They state that the first response of the chick embryo to mechanical stimulation is a local reflex but that at the same time spontaneous motility in the form of well-coordinated swimming movements is present. Coghill (1940) has recently summarized the principal contributions of various investigators concerning the nature of primary embryonic movements.

The descriptive protocols of the embryonic behavior of various species by different observers show striking consistency in the manner in which certain types of embryonic movements become organized. Movements begin by flexion in the cervical region, gradually expand until the trunk is involved, then a contralateral movement is initiated in the cervical region. The two movements become synthesized and finally consummate in a swimming movement. Subsequently, the movements of the appendages achieve independent action. These fundamental movements are basic to the development of progression. In addition to the priority of spontaneous or stimulated reactions, the issue seems to be whether mechanical or electrical stimulation activates the basic pattern or whether such stimulation elicits a local response. Basically, the question at stake is whether reactions to exogenous stimulation develop in a manner different from the organic, phyletic, neuromuscular activities.

These investigations of embryonic and fetal behavior (particularly those of Coghill and Windle and their collaborators) are of further significance because in some instances they represent monumental efforts toward the determination of the relationship between overt behavior development and neural structures. Coghill (1933) has emphasized the importance of determin-

[1] Coghill apparently uses the term "integration" as referring to the unification of movement, although groups of muscles are involved. Other authors, including the writer, apply the term to the smoothness and articulation of various movements which constitute an activity. In this sense, particular muscles may be capable of independent action but they function as an integral part of the larger activity under consideration, whereas, in Coghill's analysis of early embryonic movements, local muscle groups are incapable of independent action.

ing the neural structures correlative with the observed behavior but adds:

Argument as to whether structure precedes function or function precedes structure, or in other terms, whether structure *causes* function or function *causes* structure, is beside the mark, for neither can exist without the other at any point in space or time; they merge, in fact, into a space-time relation. . . . If we think structure *in* function as a space-time relation, as we must in a purely scientific discipline, we may hope to attain to all the understanding of behavior that science has to offer. . . . The embryological method . . . has transformed anatomy into a science, in so far as it has correlated time relations with space relations which constituted the anatomy of other days. Also, it is now engaged in a similar transformation of physiology through the contribution of such concepts as totipotence, pleuripotence, organizers, gradients, all of which have meaning only as the organism is regarded, not as a static pattern in space, but as a dynamic pattern in time.

It is fitting that these new concepts of *organizers, gradients, electrodynamic fields,* etc., should be given at least passing consideration, especially as they have reference to an understanding of the meaning of maturation of behavior. According to the old theories of heredity there was, strictly speaking, no problem of development distinct from the problem of heredity. Modern theories of heredity contend that every cell inherits a complete set of chromosomes from the germ plasm, but they do not explain how, during the course of ontogenetic development, cells differentiate and become distinct both structurally and functionally. At the present time the solution of this problem has scarcely advanced beyond the stage of postulates. The most we can hope for is an evaluation of the various hypotheses, an interpretation of experimental results in terms of the most

acceptable logical system. Spemann (1925) has applied the term *organizer* in reference to embryonic cells capable of inducing the formation of new *Anlagen;* other writers have made more general application of the concept as referring to chemical constituents which operate in effecting cellular and organ differentiation. Child (1924) proposes the term *physiological gradients,* with the explanation that the primary factors in determining organization and differentiation are regional differences in the rates of metabolism. Furthermore, these differences in rates of metabolism are organized along an axis pattern in a gradient system and centers of high metabolism are centers of dominance, influencing and determining the rate of more remote regions. In discussing the concept, Child (1939) says:

The gradient conception in its relation to development is a working hypothesis which, though based on many lines of evidence, is, like other conceptions of development, subject to modification as experiment progresses. It is essentially a conception of the living organism as primarily not a mosaic of chemical substances, but a dynamic system in which the fundamental activities of the species protoplasm concerned are the ordering, determining and integrating factors. . . . Moreover, the primary dynamic system is regarded, not as autonomous, but as directly or indirectly a product of environmental factors as well as of heredity; in short, as a behavior pattern of a protoplasm of specific constitution.

Burr and Hovland (1937) and Northrop and Burr (1937) have formulated a theory of biological organization which is based primarily upon the bioelectric properties of living protoplasm.

The fundamental thesis of this theory is that physical, philosophical, and biological considerations warrant the extension to biology of the hypothesis that "The pattern of organization of any biological system is established by a complex electrodynamic field, which is in part determined by its atomic physico-chemical components and which in part determines the behavior and orientation of those components." This field is electrical in the physical sense (Northrop and Burr, 1937).

Weiss (1939), in discussing the field concept, admits that it is an abstraction but since practically all developmental phenomena exhibit fieldlike characters there is reason to believe that it is an expression of physical reality. This is scarcely the place to embark upon a discussion of the shades of differences in the concept of biological fields as presented by various experimenters, or of the polemics which have arisen over the merits of the various concepts, gradients, field, organizers, etc. Weiss (1939) and Child (1940) have each ably criticized the points of view of the other. These references serve here merely to indicate that the conceptual frameworks for interpreting biological phenomena are becoming progressively dynamic, and that the concepts of biological differentiation are pertinent to an interpretation of data concerning complex human behavior. In the last chapters of his book Child (1924) has called attention to the parallel between the simpler biological processes and social integration.

In the meantime the study of ontogenetic development is aided by the introduction of more dynamic concepts into modern theories of genetics. Current ideas as to the rôle of genes in ontogenesis have been lucidly appraised by both Stern (1939) and Waddington (1939). It has been pointed out that no single formula, such as the chromosome theory, is adequate to envisage all recent observations on the connection between the gene and the individual character with which it is asso-

ciated. Obviously the gene is no longer accredited the specificity of its early days. It is now recognized that specific characters (phenotypes) are determined by the interaction of many genes, and that any one gene may affect many characters. There have been many studies (Stadler, 1939; Dunn, 1940) which show the genes themselves and their chromosomal arrangement to be subject to alteration through external agents, such as the roentgen ray. Furthermore, it has been demonstrated (Danzinger and Frankl, 1934; Dunn, 1940) that the introduction of certain environmental factors (temperature changes) at critical periods can produce changes in a developmental process in the same way that gene changes or other mutations do. Whatever the gene produces is contingent upon the gene combinations and the conditions under which the organism develops. Goldschmidt (1938) has reported studies which seem to indicate that various characteristics are the result of changes in growth rates and that the genes exercise a controlling influence upon the rates of development. In studying the family of Cucurbitaceae, Sinnott (1937b, 1939) has observed that the relationship between width and length remained constant despite the great variety of forms which they finally display. He (1937a) thereupon concludes:

> What is inherited, and therefore what genes control, seem to be these constant growth relationships. As growth proceeds, the proportions of parts change, complexity increases, and the familiar developmental story unfolds. Running through all this complexity, however, is a basic constancy, the inherited growth relationship, established from the beginning. It should be possible to determine for any organic pattern a series of constants of this sort. If genes control relationships between rates of growth in various dimensions, they may perhaps control relationships between rates

of other developmental processes which are not spatially arranged, notably the complex series of chemical changes concerned in the development of many traits. This is opposed to the view that the gene initiates only the first step in such a series, the later ones bearing no resemblance to the original genic impetus.

At the present time one of the most promising methods of approach in attacking problems of development seems to be the analysis of the interrelation of the rates of growth manifested by the various aspects of development. Huxley (1931) has shown that, although different parts of an organism may grow at different rates, the ratio between them is a constant, and Sinnott and Dunn (1939), as well as Goldschmidt (1938), seem to regard growth rates as the primary domain of the gene. These suggestions are especially promising, as the determination of growth constants may provide a common denominator whereby evidence assembled in the various disciplines may be comparably interpreted. It is conceivable that determinations of the relative growth rates of various aspects of behavior development may provide a technique for comparing activities which are predominantly *maturational* in their process of development with those which are the result of training, or distinctly ontogenetic in origin.

These speculations, however, are far ahead of the game. At the present time ontogenetic studies of both architectonics of the central nervous system and overt behavior of the human being are still in an exploratory stage. Before much can be accomplished toward determining the correlation of structure of nerve tissues and overt behavior additional descriptions of both aspects of behavior must be accumulated, and accumulated in such a manner that they can be subjected to symbolic manipulation.

Neural Maturation of the Central Nervous System of the Human Being

INFANT

The paucity of data on the structural maturation of the human nervous system is understandable. In the first place, it is impossible beyond the fetal period to obtain functional or behavior data and analysis of the neural structures of the same subjects. Since human beings are not born in litters it is impossible to secure comparable data on different subjects, as has been done with lower animals. Moreover, the technical labor involved in analyzing one brain or one segment of the nervous system is colossal. Despite the promise of modern electrophysiological techniques, the best evidence of neural maturation is still obtained from histological sections. The methods employed in such studies are well known, though the criteria used as evidence of structural maturation vary and some of these criteria have been the subject of controversy.

One of the earliest reports of structural studies of the human cortex is that of Bolton and Moyes (1912), who made a cytological analysis of the cortex of a human fetus of eighteen weeks. After being hardened in formalin, the sections of the brain were stained both by the polychrome and iron-alum-haematoxylin methods. It was found that at this stage there was sufficient cellular differentiation to distinguish five local areas. An area of pyramidal cells (Betz cells) was mapped out in the frontoparietal region. Even at this early stage the area of Betz cells, which corresponds roughly to the precentral motor area of the mature brain, shows the most advanced development. The presence of Betz cells and well-defined cortical areas at a time when the fissure of Rolando and the *sulcus cinguli* are barely perceptible led to the conclusion that histological differentiation precedes fissuration.

Langworthy (1930, 1933) used the Weigert-Pal method of staining postmortem sections to bring out the medullation of nerve tracts in a study of the brain stem of fetuses between 6 months of age and birth. One 2-month brain was in-

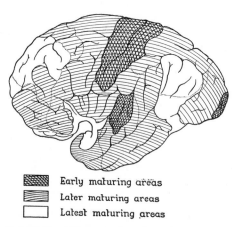

▨ Early maturing areas
▧ Later maturing areas
☐ Latest maturing areas

FIGURE 5. Diagram showing the order in which different areas of the human cortex mature. (Adapted from "Die Entwicklung der Grosshirnrinde nach der Geburt in ihren Beziehungen zur intellektuellen Ausreifung des Kindes," by M. de Crinis. *Wiener klinische Wochenschrift*, 1932, **45**, 1163.)

cluded in the series. Langworthy notes that in general tracts become medullated in the order of their phylogenetic development, but reflex activity may be elicited prior to myelinization. A rapid increase in myelinization occurs in the brain stem between birth and the second postnatal month. Langworthy is of the opinion that the inception of function advances the medullary process. Even in the seventh-month fetus the pathways concerned with the fundamental processes of living are well medullated. From these studies of myelinated pathways it seems clearly evident that the infracortical centers are the

ones prepared to govern neuromuscular activities of the maturing fetus and the newborn infant.

Realizing that postnatal maturation of the brain cannot be attributed to multiplication or subdivision of the cells, de Crinis (1932) used the Golgi method of staining so as to determine advancement in dendritic processes, and he considered cell proliferation as a fundamental criterion of structural maturation. He reports analysis of 68 human brains, varying in age from 5 days to 13 years. In the 5-day-old infant's brain preparations from the motor region did not reveal dendritic processes, but in preparations from the brain of a 10-week-old child such processes were clearly discernible. Sections from the motor region of an 11-month-old infant's brain give a picture of advanced development. Pyramidal cells have become strikingly long, the processes are well matured, and the dendrites are clearly impregnated. The onset of rapid maturation in Broca's area occurs later. Although development in this region is from the beginning behind that of the motor area, during the first year this disparity becomes even greater. At 14 months cellular maturation in Broca's area has not attained the stage of maturation reached by the motor region at 11 months, and it does not achieve a comparable stage of development until about the age of 17 postnatal months. Other frontal lobe areas lag behind even more. Although some evidence of maturation in the frontal region occurs at about 11 months, it is not until approximately the fourth year that the apical processes develop to a stage comparable to those of the motor area at 11 months. De Crinis further points out that the area of muscle sense (sensiblen) and the sensory projection areas are the first to mature. He postulates that these early-maturing centers are the cornerstones of intellectual development.

For some time Tilney was interested not only in the ontogenetic relationship between the structure of the nervous system and behavior but also in the phylogenetic evolvement of the brain. To this end he launched an extensive investigation to delineate the structural and functional maturation in six different species (opossum, rat, guinea pig, pig, cat, and man). (Tilney and Kubie, 1931.) The basic assumption in these investigations was that a structural adequacy in the nervous system is essential before specialized reactions can be elicited. The neocortex is a common heritage of all mammals, including man. For this reason Tilney focused much of his attention upon the development of this organ. Three methods were employed in the analysis of structural maturation: (1) organogenetic studies by means of the Born method of reconstruction, which discloses the chief features in the organic differentiation of the brain; (2) histogenic studies which reveal the maturing processes of nerve cells and their fibers; and (3) the myelinogenetic studies which indicate the final ripening processes of the nerve cells. Much of his work on the structural maturation of the brain of lower animals has been published, and in many of these reports references are made to the basic maturational processes of the human cortex. Structural studies, at monthly intervals, of the human brain had been completed for the fetal period, including the brain of the infant at birth.

In unpublished reports of this phase of his investigation Tilney has found it convenient, both on the basis of structural differentiation and qualities of behavior, to draw a distinction between two major types of behavior, namely, nuclear activities and cortical behavior. On the structural side nuclear regions are recognized by the way in which the cells are clustered together without much distinction or order in arrangement and also by cytological distinctions in the size, shape, and dendritic processes of the nerve cells. The nuclear regions are much older phylogenetically than the cortical areas, in fact as ancient as the beginning of vertebrate life. During ontogeny they mature earlier than the cortical areas do. Behavior controlled at a nuclear level exhibits a sudden turnover of impulses without much latency in the period of delivery. Structurally, the cortex shows an orderly arrangement of cells, and cortical behavior discloses a planned element in the reaction, a latency and variety of response.

According to Tilney (1937) there are three major phases in the development of the cerebral cortex:

(1) General cortical differentiation is characterized by a series of migratory laminations, resulting in a six-layered neocortex.

(2) Divisional cortical differentiation denotes the time when four major cortical divisions can be delineated, namely, the bulbar cortex, the paleocortex, the archicortex, and the neocortex. Of them the first to appear is the archicortex which, Tilney believes, governs vital functions having to do with such behavior activities as hunger and thirst, elimination, sex behavior, and such cortical activity as may be involved in breathing and pulsation of the heart.

(3) Local cortical differentiation, the third major phase, is distinguished by the rearrangement and disposition of cells which produce such local areas at the motor, auditory, sensory, and visual, recognized in the mature brain. During this period there is marked alteration in cellular structures. There is a tendency for the cells to become pyriform or pyramidal in

outline and to show a relative reduction in granular elements.

General cortical differentiation is indicated in the brain of the 6-week-old embryo; by 7 weeks there is the beginning of primary migratory lamination; by 9 weeks primary migratory lamination has become well defined; 10 weeks marks the onset of secondary migratory lamination; and the 13-week-old embryo shows the beginning of tertiary migratory lamination. This process of lamination continues until in the 4-month fetus the six cortical layers are laid down, though at this time they are probably contributing nothing to behavior. Not until the seventh month is the migratory process completed. Fissuration can be detected earlier, and, although the 6-month fetal cortex is almost homogeneous, it is approaching the inception of local differentiation. At 8 months increased development in depth and richness of fissuration is indicated. Although there are incipient signs of local cortical differentiation during the last stages of fetal development, even in the cortex of the newborn infant there is not sufficient local cortical differentiation to indicate that particular areas are concerned with function. Apparently the cells are all there in readiness for final ripening.

About the same time that Tilney extended his structural functional investigations to include the human, Conel (1939a, 1939b) independently began a program of studies on the development of cytological structures of the human brain, using the cortex of the newborn infant as the point of departure. Conel utilized several staining methods in order to educe developmental changes in cell bodies and fibers. Structural features which were accepted as criteria in estimating advancing development were: (1) size of cell body, presence of neurofibrils, size and length of cell processes, (2) number, size, and length of horizontal and vertical fibers in the cortex, (3) the density of the neuropil in the various horizontal laminae, and (4) the quantity of myelin present. So far Conel has published reports on the newborn brain only, though analyses of more advanced stages are under way. Even in the newborn cortex the cells have achieved their adult arrangement, which is in agreement with the observations of Tilney that the cellular division and migratory processes are complete at birth. According to all criteria, the cells in the most advanced stage of development at the time of birth are those in the anterior-central gyrus. More specifically, that part of the anterior-central gyrus which mediates movements of the neck and shoulder is more advanced than any other part of this area. The most immature area is localized in the anterior half of each of the three frontal gyri.

Conel has recently been able to extend his publications on the development of the cerebral cortex to include that of the one-month infant. He has noted the difference between the newborn and one-month brain and points out that the greatest change has taken place in the region of the hand of the motor area of the *gyrus centralis*. In all functional areas, however, the development of the cortex during the first month is but slight, and whether the neurons of the cortex are functioning with respect to conducting nerve impulses is still questionable.

Behavior Development of the Infant

The abundance of evidence gleaned from the several studies of the structural maturation of the newborn infant's brain renders functional participation of the cortex problematical at this stage of development. Recently Hooker (1939) has been conducting extensive investigations of fetal behavior and has obtained data on 41 specimens ranging in age from 7 to 28 weeks of menstrual age. Hooker reports that he has elicited movements in response to tactile stimulation shortly after 8 weeks of age. At this age response is elicited only when the area supplied by the mandibular and maxillary divisions of the fifth cranial nerve is stimulated. Although the nature of the response was somewhat diffused, involving all neuromuscular mechanisms capable of function at the time, the response to external or mechanical stimulation apparently preceded overt response to endogenous stimulation. Spontaneous movements were first observed in a fetus of 9 weeks of menstrual age. By the end of 14 weeks most of the neonatal reflexes could be elicited. Hooker (1937) has presented an evaluation of Minkowski's findings in the light of his own work. He believes that both Minkowski's and his observations support the Coghillian theory of individuation as to the process whereby local reflexes emerge. Determination of the neurostructural maturation of the nervous system of the fetuses in Hooker's investigation has not been reported, though the plan of investigation embraces this aspect of the behavior as well as function. Endocrine status and electrocardiograms are being made upon the same specimen. For a more complete summary of the various reports upon fetal behavior, the reader is referred to Munn (1938).

In many respects the neonatal period is the one most available to investigators prior to school age. There have been many studies appraising the behavior repertoire of the newborn infant. An extensive bibliography of such investigations was presented by Dennis (1934b), as well as a classification of the responses reported. Selected bibliographies on behavior at this stage of development have also been assembled by Pratt (1933) and Dewey (1935). In general most of these studies are in the nature of inventories listing the types of reactions with which the newborn infant is equipped.

During the past quarter of a century volumes have been accumulated on the behavior development of the infant and growing child. Much of the earlier work consisted of biographical reports of the achievements of individual children, of which Preyer (1888), Shinn (1900), and Fenton (1925) are familiar references.

The general arousal of interest in the behavior of the infant and preschool child found expression in the psychological and educational laboratories throughout the country. The prevailing thought operating in most of the early investigations was that individual difference in the development of children is so great that only norms or averages of achievement, based upon the study of large groups of children within given chronological periods, would be of scientific value. The period saw the production of a number of standardized tests or scales for the purpose of measuring developmental achievements. Gesell (1925) was a pioneer in applying this technique to the study of infant development. Application and modifications of the Gesell tests have been presented by other investigators, notably Bühler (1930) and Bayley (1939). Stutsman (1931) and the Minnesota group (Goodenough, Maurer, and Van Wagenen, 1940) published standardized scales for the measurement of behavior development during the preschool period. Most of these tests consisted of listing in order selected items of behavior, the order being determined by the chronological age at which the "average" child would presumably achieve that particular behavior. There was no reason to assume that the achievement of items listed in one chronological period was directly related to the achievement of behavior items listed in a subsequent chronological interval. Such standardized measures provide information as to *when* particular behavior items are achieved, but they do not disclose *how* a function undergoes change as it progresses from inception toward optimum efficiency. It is also recognized that since children do not grow uniformly the average norms do not reflect the actual course of growth as represented by any one individual. A child may be advanced in one aspect of development and retarded in another.

Recognition of this aspect of normative scales aroused interest in the longitudinal, as distinct from the cross-sectional, methods of collecting data on behavior development. Shirley's study (1931a, 1933a, 1933b) of twenty-five infants over a period of two years reflects both these methodological influences. Although she presents descriptive reports of behavior changes in individual infants, the actual treatment of the data is the same as that customarily utilized in purely cross-sectional studies. A further refinement of the longitudinal method was introduced with the realization that in order to analyze behavior development as a process of change not only the child subjects but sequential changes in specific behavior phenomena would have to become the subject matter of investigation. The method of analysis calls for an appraisal of behavior, not as it deviates from some reputed average but as it compares to its own functioning at an earlier time. In other words, the behavior phenomenon becomes the subject of inquiry and the reference base is determined by the points of origin and termination. Focusing inquiry upon definite behavior phenomena rather than inventorying mass achievements of the individual is both reasonable and practical; and, logically, the experimental problem is not different from the study of the individual.

Socially speaking, an individual represents merely nodal points of activity within a society. . . . In much the same way that arbitrary limits can be prescribed around nodal points within a society to signify a particular individual, so may arbitrary limits, for experimental and observational reasons, be set around nodal points of a psycho-motor activity (McGraw, 1940a).

Halverson's (1931, 1932) analysis of progressive changes exhibited by the child in prehending various objects is illustrative of the method. Applying this method intensively over a period of years, McGraw (1942) has been able to delineate significant features in the neuromuscular development of a series of activities common to the growing infant. In general the technique employed and the objectives in all these studies have been essentially the same. In the main the studies focus upon development of the motor activities of the infant during the first two years of life. The investigations were launched under the altogether reasonable assumption that changes in the nature or qualities of muscular movements reflect maturation of the central nervous system.

Inventories of the behavior repertoire of the newborn infant indicate that certain types of somatic activity attain a mature stage of development during the fetal period. A newborn infant coughs, sneezes, yawns, etc., about as efficiently as the adult, and qualitatively there is little difference in the somatic aspect of these performances when expressed by individuals of differing degrees of maturation. Although it is quite true that the motor aspect of such reflexes is mature at the time of birth, it is equally obvious that even these typically reflex functions gain a degree of voluntary or deliberate control as the individual matures. A cough or yawn may become organized as a part of one's social behavior, but the motor aspect of that cough or yawn remains essentially the same. For example, at a prolonged social gathering a husband, catching the eye of his wife far across the room, may yawn to indicate he would like to leave, but after the initial deliberate start the yawn is a yawn so far as the motor performance goes (McGraw, 1939a). This simple instance of a deliberate quality being superimposed or incorporated into a reflex mechanism illustrates the problem of behavior development as exhibited in the neuromuscular maturation of the growing infant.

McGraw observed and recorded descriptively those changes in motor performances of infants which lead to the consummation of behaviors such as creeping, erect locomotion, the assumption of erect and sitting postures, swimming, adjustment to an inverted position, suspension-grasp behavior, and responses to sudden startle stimuli. In appraising the data, those qualities of each behavior function were selected which reflected the course or trend of development without regard to individual differences or peculiarities. Although the data were recorded originally without interpretative rationale, it became evident in the course of investigation that certain qualities of movement signify grossly the level of neural organization involved. Ratings of the original observations were made with these thoughts in mind. In interpreting the data, it seemed reasonable, especially in the light of cytological evidence cited above, to embark with the assumption that the cerebral cortex is not functioning appreciably at the time of birth. Without being specific or attempting to allocate a given function to a particular neural counterpart, it was found both feasible and practical to think of behavior as of two major centers of control, namely, (1) cortical and (2) subcortical or nuclear. It was also recognized that

the cerebral cortex is twofold in function. It not only exercises an activating or governing influence upon neuromotor behavior but also exerts an inhibitory influence upon behavior controlled at an infracortical level. In evaluating the observations on changing behavior patterns an attempt was made to point out those qualities which indicate when an activity is (1) under infracortical dominance, (2) when inhibitory influences from the cortex become apparent, (3) when cortical participation in muscular movements is involved, and (4) when the activity attains a comparatively mature state of cortical functioning.

The early reflex patterns of behavior, such as the Moro or body startle and the suspension grasp reflex, are of subcortical dominance. The diminution of such behaviors reflects the development of cortical inhibition. When the startle reaction is followed through its entire course, an increase in the manifestation of the subcortical activity is observed during the first three or four weeks (McGraw, 1937). This period is followed by a period of decline, representing cortical inhibitory influences, until finally the characteristic response is merely a body jerk. This is an activity in which the subcortical centers continue to play an active rôle even during adulthood. After ultimate development is achieved, however, the cortex is definitely engaged practically at the instant of the startling stimulation, and cortical inquiry as to the meaning of the startling stimulus serves to restrict the nuclear aspect of the reaction. It has been asserted that the reflex is of phyletic origin, reminiscent of the "clasping reflex" of primates. The suspension grasp reflex also shows a decline after the first few weeks of life (McGraw, 1940c). The period of cortical inhibition extends over several weeks or months and the onset of voluntary suspension is evident when the child exercises his own choice in the mat-'ter of suspension.

Many of the typically newborn behavior patterns appear to be of phyletic origin. It has been demonstrated in a study of aquatic behavior that when newborn infants (as early as eleven days) are submerged in water they engage in rhythmical swimming movements simulating those of

In following developmental changes of behavior patterns which lead to deliberate progression it is possible to determine grossly those periods when the movements are predominantly nuclear, when the cortex begins to suppress or inhibit the nuclear activities, and when the cortex takes a dominant rôle in activating or controlling the muscular movements involved (Mc-

FIGURE 6. Three phases in the development of aquatic behavior of the infant: (*A*) reflex swimming movements, (*B*) disorganized behavior, and (*C*) voluntary or deliberate movements. (From "Swimming Behavior of the Human Infant," by M. B. McGraw. *Journal of Pediatrics*, 1939, **15**, 488. By permission of The C. V. Mosby Company, publisher.)

other vertebrates (McGraw, 1939c). The presence of swimming movements in the newborn of many species, including the human, suggests functional evidence of the phylogeny of man. Swimming is probably one of the oldest phylogenetic activities of which there is a residual in infant behavior. Swimming movements of the newborn are controlled at an infracortical level. The onset of an inhibitory influence from the cortex is expressed by disintegration of the swimming movements and the substitution of disorganized struggling activities. Basically, the neuromuscular mechanisms which mediate the reflex swimming movements may be essentially the same as those activated in the reflex crawling and stepping movements of the infant.

Graw, 1941a). The course of development as manifested in these various activities seems to indicate that subcortical movements show their maximum manifestation at about the end of the first month, and between the first and the fourth month, approximately, there occurs a progressive decline in subcortical movements. The onset of cortical inhibitory influences is observed in the muscles of the upper part of the body earlier than in the region of the pelvis and lower extremities. Likewise, the development of cortical control over neuromuscular activity proceeds essentially in a cephalocaudal trend. One who has observed the development of prone progression in infants cannot fail to be struck by the similarity in the infant's development of progression and the progression of the salamander, as described by Coghill (1929). At the inception of cortical participation in a given activity the

repertoire of the newborn infant (McGraw, 1941b). This activity is of recent phylogenetic origin and probably was never organized at a nuclear level. In most in-

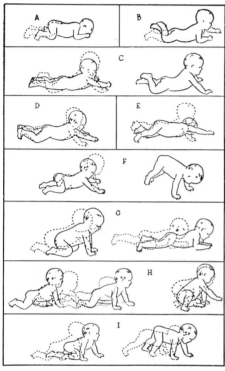

FIGURE 7. Line drawings showing the sequence of neuromuscular development in the achievement of an integrated creeping pattern. (From "Development of Neuro-muscular Mechanisms as Reflected in the Crawling and Creeping Behavior of the Human Infant," by M. B. McGraw. *Journal of Genetic Psychology,* 1941, **58**, 86. By permission of The Journal Press, publisher.)

movements are ordinarily staccato and poorly coordinated. Further development is reflected more by increasing integration of the movements involved than by any actual changes in motor pattern.

Unlike the activities of progression, there is no reflex sitting posture in the behavior

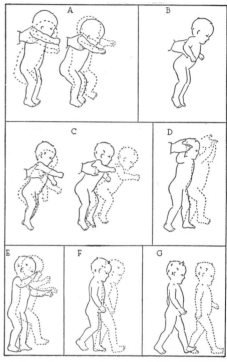

FIGURE 8. Line drawings showing infant neuromuscular development in the achievement of erect locomotion. (From "Neuromuscular Development of the Human Infant as Exemplified in the Achievement of Erect Locomotion," by M. B. McGraw. *Journal of Pediatrics,* 1940, **17**, 750. By permission of The C. V. Mosby Company, publisher.)

(*A*) Newborn or reflex stepping. (*B*) Inception of cortical inhibition. (*C*) Transition from infracortical to cortical control. (*D*) Inception of deliberate stepping. (*E*) Inception of independent walking. (*F*) Heel-toe progression. (*G*) An integrated gait.

fants cortical control over the function precedes complete cortical participation in the progressive activities. Maturation of the central nervous system is also indicated in the postural adjustments of the infant to an inverted position (McGraw, 1940*d*). The situation has the advantage of being simple, and, at the same time, it

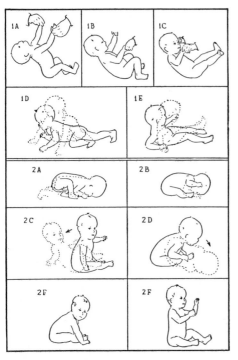

FIGURE 9. Sequential phases showing the development of anti-gravity muscles involved in the development of a sitting posture. (From "Neuro-motor Maturation of Anti-gravity Functions as Reflected in the Development of a Sitting Posture," by M. B. McGraw. *Journal of Genetic Psychology*, 1941, **59**, 158. By permission of The Journal Press, publisher.)

is not one which the child would experience through "spontaneous" exercise. The predominant adjustment of the newborn infant is one of general flexion. The flexor movements are under subcortical control. After the first few months the development of extensor muscles becomes evident, as is shown in the arched spine during in-

version. Cortical participation in the adjustment is indicated when the child makes a deliberate effort to right himself, and complete integration of the various centers stimulated is evident when the child's understanding of the situation is such that he displays an acquiescent or playful attitude.

Although studies of infant behavior development as presented by McGraw are

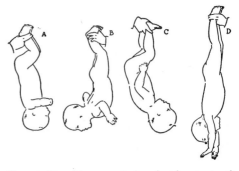

FIGURE 10. Neuromuscular development of the infant as reflected in postural adjustments to an inverted position. (From *Growth: A Study of Johnny and Jimmy*, by M. B. McGraw. New York: D. Appleton-Century, 1935, 63. By permission of the publisher.)

confined largely to functioning of the motor mechanism, it has also been pointed out that during the first two years of life there are four outstanding periods which may be classified roughly in terms of the type of development taking place most rapidly at the time.

The first period covers approximately four months and is marked by a diminution of the atavistic reflexes and rhythmical movements characteristic of the newborn. The second period ranges from about four to eight or nine months and is characterized by the development of deliberate or voluntary movements in the superior spinal region and by comparatively reduced activity in the region of the pelvic girdle and lower extremities. The third period is characterized by increasing control of activities in the inferior spinal region and represents the age range from eight to fourteen months. The fourth period covers the remaining ten months and is marked by rapid development in associational processes, simple or direct, conditional, and symbolic associations, including language (McGraw, 1939a).

These broad categories are of practical value, but analyses of behavior development must be explored intensively with respect to both the structural and functional components before the underlying principles involved can be ascertained or formulated. Both theoretically and empirically there is every reason to believe that behavior development moves according to law and order. The determination of these laws of growth awaits improvement in the concepts and techniques of investigation in subject matter of this type. McGraw's studies demonstrate an attempt to order observational data according to a symbolic system, and Weinbach (1937, 1940; McGraw and Weinbach, 1936) has shown how data, even observational data of different physiological phenomena, may be fitted to growth equations. These equations yield constants which are descriptive of the phenomenon of change which characterizes all growth; by means of such equations and constants, features of growth which are qualitatively different can be compared. In view of the propositions set forth by Huxley (1931), Goldschmidt (1938), and Sinnott (1939) concerning the relative rates of growth, it is conceivable that the determination of constants representing the rates of particular types of behavior development and the ratios between such constants may open the way to a new approach in investigating the process of development in behavior.

Discussion

Certainly among psychologists the term *maturation* has acquired a somewhat specific meaning, referring essentially to changes in behavior as a result of anatomical or physiological development in the nervous system, and in distinction to changes brought about by exercise or use of the function. It seems fairly evident that certain structural changes take place prior to the onset of overt function; it seems equally evident that cessation of neurostructural development does not coincide with the onset of function. There is every reason to believe that when conditions are favorable function makes some contribution to further advancement in structural development of the nervous system. An influential factor in determining the structural development of one component may be the functioning of other structures which are interrelated. Whereas structural growth in such instances is not the product of function directly, neither is it free from or opposed to function as such. Obviously, rigid demarcation between structure and function as two distinct processes of development is not possible. The two are interrelated, and at one time one aspect may have greater weight than the other.

Limited as our knowledge of these two aspects of development is, an understanding of the process of development must embrace studies not only of neural structures and their related functions but also other aspects of the growing organism. In some instances alterations in behavior pattern may be definitely influenced by changes in bone and muscle structures, by hormonal or vascular maturation. For example, not only neural innervation but also the size of the child's hand, the size of the object to be seized, and its mobility will affect his mode of prehension. Changes in static equilibrium, as a result of relative growth in leg length to body height, are factors which affect a child's manner of performance in activities such as climbing and roller skating (McGraw and Weinbach, 1936; McGraw, 1939b; Weinbach, 1940). There are periods in individual development when emotional adaptability is more easily accredited to a process of physiological maturation than to increased familiarity through repetitive experience (McGraw, 1939b).

Maturation is not a process peculiar to certain activities, nor is it restricted to early stages of life. Both from embryological studies and from studies of infant behavior developmental evidence has accumulated which suggests that critical periods occur in the growth of any phenomenon when it is most susceptible to definite kinds of stimulation. The critical period for one activity may occur at one time in the life of the individual and at another time for a different activity. The major factor contributing to an alteration in behavior may at one time be the status of neurostructural components, at another time variations in anatomical dimensions, and at another time personal or individual experience. In fact, it probably is the interrelationship of a multitude of factors which determines the course of behavior development at any time. Determination of the direction of growth in specific behavioral activities, the rate of improvement, and the fluctuations, not so much among individuals, but in the phenomenon per se, constitutes a primary step in investigations of behavior development.

Observations of development in these various disciplines provoke the thought that the "maturation-versus-learning" dichotomy is a cumbersome conceptual framework. In the present state of knowledge a more profitable approach lies in the systematic determination of the chang-ing interrelationships between the various aspects of a growing phenomenon. It has been suggested that relative rates of growth may afford a common symbol by means of which the underlying principles of development may be formulated. Once the laws of development have been determined the maturation concept may fade into insignificance.

Bibliography

ANGELL, J. R. 1908. *Psychology: An introductory study of the structure and function of human consciousness.* New York: Holt.

ANGULO Y GONZÁLEZ, A. W. 1930. Neurological interpretation of fetal behavior: the progressive increase of muscular activity in albino rat fetuses. *Anat. Rec., 45,* 254.

———. 1935. Further studies upon development of somatic activity in albino rat fetuses. *Proc. Soc. Exp. Biol., N. Y., 32,* 621–622.

BAYLEY, N. 1939. Mental and motor development from two to twelve years. *Rev. Educ. Res., 9,* 18–37.

BOLAFFIO, M., and G. ARTOM. 1924. Ricerche sulla fisiologia del sistema nervosa del feto umano. *Arch. di sci. biol., 5,* 457–487.

BOLTON, J. S., and J. M. MOYES. 1912. The cyto-architecture of the cerebral cortex of the human fetus of eighteen weeks. *Brain,* 35(I), 1–25.

BORING, E. G., H. S. LANGFELD, and H. P. WELD. 1939. *Introduction to psychology.* New York: Wiley.

BREED, F. S. 1911. The development of certain instincts and habits in chicks. *Behav. Monogr., 1,* No. 1. Pp. vi + 178.

BRIDGMAN, C. S., and L. CARMICHAEL. 1935. An experimental study of the onset of behavior in the fetal guinea-pig. *J. Genet. Psychol., 47,* 247–267.

BÜHLER, C. 1930. *The first year of life.* New York: Day.

BURR, H. S., and C. I. HOVLAND. 1937. Bioelectric correlates of development in *Amblystoma. Yale J. Biol. Med., 9,* 541–549.

CARMICHAEL, L. 1926. The development of behavior in vertebrates experimentally removed from the influence of external stimulation. *Psychol. Rev., 33,* 51–58.

———. 1927. A further study of the development of behavior in vertebrates experimentally removed from the influence of external stimulation. *Psychol. Rev., 34,* 34–47.

———. 1928. A further experimental study of the development of behavior. *Psychol. Rev., 35,* 253–260.

———. 1933. Origin and prenatal growth of behavior. In C. MURCHISON (Ed.), *A hand-*

book of child psychology. (2d ed., rev.), pp. 31–159. Worcester: Clark University Press.

CARMICHAEL, L. 1936. A re-evaluation of the concepts of maturation and learning as applied to the early development of behavior. *Psychol. Rev., 43,* 450–470.

——. 1941. The experimental embryology of mind. *Psychol. Bull., 38,* 1–28.

CASTLE, W. E. 1921. *Genetics and eugenics.* Cambridge: Harvard University Press. (See Appendix for Mendel's Papers.)

CHILD, C. M. 1924. *Physiological foundations of behavior.* New York: Holt.

——. 1939. Physiological gradients in relation to development. *Current Science* (Special number, "Organisers in animal development"), 51–57.

——. 1940. Lithium and echinoderm exogastrulation. *Physiol. Zoöl., 13,* 4–41.

COGHILL, G. E. 1929. *Anatomy and the problem of behaviour.* Cambridge: University Press; New York: Macmillan.

——. 1933. The neuro-embryologic study of behavior: Principles, perspective and aim. *Science, 78,* 131–138.

——. 1940. Early embryonic somatic movements in birds and in mammals other than man. *Child Develpm. Monogr., 5,* No. 2. Pp. 48.

CONEL, J. LeR. 1939*a. The postnatal development of the human cerebral cortex:* Vol. I. *Cortex of the newborn.* Cambridge: Harvard University Press.

——. 1939*b.* The brain structure of the newborn infant and consideration of the senile brain. *Res. Publ. Ass. Nerv. Ment. Dis., 19,* 247–255.

——. 1941. *The postnatal development of the human cerebral cortex:* Vol. II. *Cortex of the one-month infant.* Cambridge: Harvard University Press.

CONKLIN, E. G. 1916. *Heredity and environment in the development of man.* Princeton: Princeton University Press. (Chaps. 1 and 2.)

CORONIOS, J. D. 1933. Development of behavior in the fetal cat. *Genet. Psychol. Monogr., 14,* 283–386.

COURTIS, S. A. 1935. Maturation as a factor in diagnosis. *Yearb. Nat. Soc. Stud. Educ., 34,* 169–187.

DANFORTH, C. H. 1932. Artificial and hereditary suppression of sacral vertebrae in the fowl. *Proc. Soc. Exp. Biol., N. Y., 30,* 437–438.

DANZINGER, L., and L. FRANKL. 1934. Zum Problem der Funktionsreifung. *Z. Kinderforsch., 43,* 219–254.

DE CRINIS, M. 1932. Die Entwicklung der Grosshirnrinde nach der Geburt in ihren Beziehungen zur intellektuellen Ausreifung des Kindes. *Wien. klin. Wschr., 45,* 1161–1165.

DENNIS, W. 1934*a.* Congenital cataract and unlearned behavior. *J. Genet. Psychol., 44,* 340–351.

DENNIS, W. 1934*b.* A description and classification of the responses of the newborn infant. *Psychol. Bull., 31,* 5–22.

——. 1935. The effect of restricted practice upon the reaching, sitting and standing of two infants. *J. Genet. Psychol., 47,* 17–32.

——. 1938. Infant development under conditions of restricted practice and of minimum social stimulation: A preliminary report. *J. Genet. Psychol., 53,* 149–158.

——. 1940. Does culture appreciably affect patterns of infant behavior? *J. Soc. Psychol., 12,* 305–317.

——. 1941. Spalding's experiment on the flight of birds repeated with another species. *J. Comp. Psychol., 31,* 337–348.

DETWILER, S. R. 1920. Experiments on the transplantation of limbs in *Amblystoma. J. Exp. Zool., 31,* 117–120.

——. 1928. Further experiments upon the alteration of the direction of growth in amphibian spinal nerves. *Proc. J. Exp. Soc., 51,* 8.

——. 1931. Problems in the development of the nervous system. *J. Nerv. Ment. Dis., 73.*

DEWEY, E. 1935. *Behavior development in infants: A survey of the literature on prenatal and postnatal activity, 1920–1934.* New York: Columbia University Press.

DOBZANSKY, T. 1936. *Biological effects of radiation.* (Edited by B. M. DUGGAR.) Vol. 2. New York: McGraw-Hill.

DUNN, L. C. 1939–1940. Heredity and the development of early abnormalities in vertebrates. In *Harvey lectures, New York Academy of Medicine,* pp. 135–165. Lancaster: Science Press.

DÜRKEN, B. 1932. *Experimental analysis of development.* New York: Norton.

FENTON, J. 1925. *A practical psychology of babyhood.* Boston: Houghton Mifflin.

GESELL, A. 1925. *The mental growth of the pre-school child: A psychological outline of normal development from birth to the sixth year, including a system of developmental diagnosis.* New York: Macmillan.

——. 1929. Maturation and infant behavior pattern. *Psychol. Rev., 36,* 307–319.

——. 1933. Maturation and the patterning of behavior. In C. MURCHISON (Ed.), *A handbook of child psychology.* (2d ed., rev.), pp. 209–235. Worcester: Clark University Press.

GESELL, A., and H. THOMPSON. 1929. Learning and growth in identical infant twins: An experimental study of the method of co-twin control. *Genet. Psychol. Monogr., 6,* 1–124.

GESELL, A., and H. THOMPSON, assisted by C. S. AMATRUDA. 1934. *Infant behavior: Its genesis and growth.* New York: McGraw-Hill.

GILCHRIST, F. G. 1933. The time relations of determinations in early amphibian development. *J. Exp. Zool.*, **66**, 15–49.

GOLDSCHMIDT, R. 1938. *Physiological genetics.* New York: McGraw-Hill.

GOODENOUGH, F. L., K. M. MAURER, and M. J. VAN WAGENEN. 1940. *Minnesota preschool scale.* Minneapolis: Educational Test Bureau.

HALVERSON, H. M. 1931. An experimental study of prehension in infants by means of systematic cinema records. *Genet. Psychol. Monogr.*, **10**, 107–286.

——. 1932. A further study of grasping. *J. Gen. Psychol.*, **7**, 34–64.

HILGARD, J. R. 1932. Learning and maturation in preschool children. *J. Genet. Psychol.*, **41**, 36–56.

——. 1933. The effect of early and delayed practice on memory and motor performances studied by the method of co-twin control. *Genet. Psychol. Monogr.*, **14**, 493–567.

HOLMES, J. S. 1922. A tentative classification of the forms of animal behavior. *J. Comp. Psychol.*, **2**, 173–186.

HOOKER, D. 1936. Early fetal activity in mammals. *Yale J. Biol. Med.*, **8**, 579–602.

——. 1937. The development of reflexes in the mammalian fetus. *Anat. Rec.*, Suppl., **70**, 55.

——. 1939. Fetal behavior. *Res. Publ. Ass. Nerv. Ment. Dis.*, **19**, 237–243.

HUXLEY, J. 1931. *Problems of relative growth.* New York: Dial Press.

JENNINGS, H. S. 1935. *Genetics.* New York: Norton.

JERSILD, A. T. 1932. Training and growth in the development of children: A study of the relative influence of learning and maturation. *Child Develpm. Monogr.*, No. 10. Pp. 73.

KRABBE, K. 1912. Les réflexes chez le foetus. *Rev. neurol.*, **24**, 434–435.

KUO, Z. Y. 1930. The genesis of cats' responses to the rat. *J. Comp. Psychol.*, **11**, 1–35.

——. 1939. Total pattern or local reflexes? *Psychol. Rev.*, **46**, 93–122.

LAMARCK, J. B. 1773. *Philosophie zoologique.* Paris.

LANGWORTHY, O. R. 1930. Medullated tracts in the brain stem of a seven-month human fetus. *Contr. Embryol., Carnegie Inst. Wash.*, **21**, No. 120, pp. 37–52.

——. 1933. Development of behavior patterns and myelinization of the nervous system in the human fetus and infant. *Contr. Embryol., Carnegie Inst. Wash.*, **24**, No. 139.

LOCK, R. H. 1916. *Recent progress in the study of variation, heredity and evolution.* New York: Dutton.

MARQUIS, D. G. 1930. The criterion of innate behavior. *Psychol. Rev.*, **37**, 334–349.

MATTHEWS, S. A., and S. R. DETWILER. 1926. The reactions of *Amblystoma* embryos following prolonged treatment with chloretone. *J. Exp. Zool.*, **45**, 279–292.

McDOUGALL, W. 1914. *An introduction to social psychology.* Boston: Luce.

McGRAW, M. B. 1935. *Growth: A study of Johnny and Jimmy.* New York: Appleton-Century.

——. 1937. The Moro reflex. *Amer. J. Dis. Child.*, **54**, 240–251.

——. 1939a. Behavior of the newborn infant and early neuro-muscular development. *Res. Publ. Ass. Nerv. Ment. Dis.*, **19**, 244–246.

——. 1939b. Later development of children specially trained during infancy. *Child Develpm.*, **10**, 1–19.

——. 1939c. Swimming behavior of the human infant. *J. Pediat.*, **15**, 485–490.

——. 1940a. Basic concepts and procedures in a study of behavior development. *Psychol. Rev.*, **47**, 79–89.

——. 1940b. Neural maturation as exemplified in achievement of bladder control. *J. Pediat.*, **16**, 580–590.

——. 1940c. Suspension grasp behavior of the human infant. *Amer. J. Dis. Child.*, **60**, 799–811.

——. 1940d. Neuromuscular mechanism of the infant. Development reflected by postural adjustments to an inverted position. *Amer. J. Dis. Child.*, **60**, 1031–1042.

——. 1940e. Neuromuscular development of the human infant as exemplified in the achievement of erect locomotion. *J. Pediat.*, **17**, 747–771.

——. 1941a. Development of neuro-muscular mechanisms as reflected in the crawling and creeping behavior of the human infant. *J. Genet. Psychol.*, **58**, 83–111.

——. 1941b. Neuro-motor maturation of anti-gravity functions as reflected in the development of a sitting posture. *J. Genet. Psychol.*, **59**, 155–175.

——. 1942. *The neuro-muscular maturation of the human infant.* New York: Columbia University Press.

McGRAW, M. B., and A. P. WEINBACH. 1936. Quantitative measures in studying development of behavior patterns (erect locomotion). *Bull. Neurol. Inst. N. Y.*, **4**, 563–571.

METFESSEL, M. 1940. Relationships in heredity and environment in behavior. *J. Psychol.*, **10**, 177–198.

MINKOWSKI, M. 1922. Über frühzeitige Bewegungen. Reflexe und muskuläre Reaktionen beim menschlichen Fötus und ihre Beziehungen zum fötalen Nerven- und Muskelsystem. *Schweiz. med. Wschr.*, **52**, 721–724; 751–755.

MORGAN, T. H. 1932. *The scientific basis of evolution.* New York: Norton.

MOWRER, O. H. 1936. "Maturation" vs. "learning" in the development of vestibular and optokinetic nystagmus. *J. Genet. Psychol.*, **48**, 383–404.

MUNN, N. L. 1938. *Psychological development:*

An introduction to genetic psychology. Boston : Houghton Mifflin.

NORTHROP, F. S. C., and H. S. BURR. 1937. Experimental findings concerning the eletrodynamic theory of life and an analysis of their physical meaning. *Growth,* 1, 78–88.

PANKRATZ, D. S. 1931. A preliminary report on the foetal movements in the rabbit. *Anat. Rec.,* Suppl., 48, 58–59.

PAVLOV, I. P. 1927. *Conditioned reflexes: An investigation of the physiological activity of the cerebral cortex.* (Trans. by G. V. ANREP.) London : Oxford University Press.

PERRIN, F. A. C., and D. B. KLEIN. 1926. *Psychology: Its methods and principles.* New York : Holt.

PRATT, K. C. 1933. The neonate. In C. MURCHISON (Ed.), *A handbook of child psychology.* (2d ed., rev.), pp. 163–208. Worcester : Clark University Press.

PREYER, W. 1888. *The mind of the child: Pt. 1. The senses and the will.* (Trans. by H. W. BROWN.) New York : Appleton.

SHEPARD, J. F., and F. S. BREED. 1913. Maturation and use in the development of instinct. *J. Anim. Behav.,* 3, 274–285.

SHINN, M. W. 1900. *The biography of a baby.* Boston : Houghton Mifflin.

SHIRLEY, M. M. 1931a. *The first two years, a study of twenty-five babies:* Vol. I. *Postural and locomotor development.* (Inst. Child Welfare Monogr. Ser., No. 6.) Minneapolis : University of Minnesota Press. Pp. vi + 227.

———. 1931b. The sequential method for the study of maturing behavior patterns. *Psychol. Rev.,* 38, 507–528.

———. 1931c. Is development saltatory as well as continuous? *Psychol. Bull.,* 28, 664–665.

———. 1933a. *The first two years, a study of twenty-five babies:* Vol. II. *Intellectual development.* (Inst. Child Welfare Monogr. Ser., No. 7.) Minneapolis : University of Minnesota Press. Pp. xvi + 513.

———. 1933b. *The first two years, a study of twenty-five babies:* Vol. III. *Personality manifestations.* (Inst. Child Welfare Monogr. Ser., No. 8.) Minneapolis : University of Minnesota Press. Pp. xi + 228.

———. 1933c. Locomotor and visual-manual functions in the first two years. In C. MURCHISON (Ed.). *A handbook of child psychology.* (2d ed., rev.), pp. 236–270. Worcester : Clark University Press.

SINNOTT, E. W. 1937a. The genetic control of developmental relationships. *Amer. Nat.,* 71, 113–119.

———. 1937b. The relation of gene to character in quantitative inheritance. *Proc. Nat. Acad. Sci., Wash.,* 23, 224–227.

———. 1939. A developmental analysis of the relation between cell size and fruit size in cucurbits. *Amer. J. Bot.,* 26, 179–189.

SINNOTT, E. W., and L. C. DUNN. 1939. *Principles of genetics.* New York : McGraw-Hill.

SPALDING, D. A. 1873. Instinct ; with original observations on young animals. *Macmillan's Mag.,* 27, 282–293.

———. 1875. Instinct and acquisition. *Nature,* 12, 507–508.

SPEMANN, H. 1925. Some factors of animal development. *Brit. J. Exp. Biol.,* 2, 493.

STADLER, L. J. 1939. The experimental alteration of heredity. *Growth,* 3, 321–322.

STERN, C. 1939. Recent work on the relation between genes and developmental processes. *Growth* (Supplement: First Symposium on Development and Growth), 3, 19–36.

STRASSMANN, P. 1903. Das Leben vor der Geburt. *Samml. klin. Vortr., N. F., Gynäk.,* No. 353, pp. 947–968.

STRAYER, L. C. 1930. Language and growth : The relative efficacy of early and deferred vocabulary training, studied by the method of co-twin control. *Genet. Psychol. Monogr.,* 8, 209–319.

STUTSMAN, R. 1931. *Mental measurement of preschool children.* Yonkers-on-Hudson : World Book.

SWENSON, E. A. 1929. The active simple movements of the albino-rat fetus : The order of their appearance, their qualities, and their significance. *Anat. Rec.,* 42, 40.

THORNDIKE, E. L. 1919. *Educational psychology:* Vol. I. *The original nature of man.* New York : Teachers College, Columbia University.

TILNEY, F. 1933. Behavior in its relation to the development of the brain : II. Correlation between the development of the brain and behavior in the albino rat from embryonic states to maturity. *Bull. Neurol. Inst. N. Y.,* 3, 252–358.

———. 1937. *The structure and development of the brain.* Unpublished lecture, New York.

TILNEY, F., and L. S. KUBIE. 1931. Behavior in its relation to the development of the brain. *Bull. Neurol. Inst. N. Y.,* 1, 229–313.

TRACY, H. C. 1926. The development of motility and behavior reactions in the toadfish (*Opsanus tau*). *J. Comp. Neurol.,* 40, 253–369.

TUGE, H. 1931. Early behavior of embryos of the turtle, *Terrapene carolina* (L). *Proc. Soc. Exp. Biol., N. Y.,* 29, 52–53.

———. 1937. The development of behavior in avian embryos. *J. Comp. Neurol.,* 66, 157–175.

WADDINGTON, C. H. 1936. *How animals develop.* New York : Norton.

———. 1939. *An introduction to modern genetics.* London : Allen and Unwin.

WATSON, J. B. 1914. *Behavior: An introduction to comparative psychology.* New York : Holt.

———. 1919. *Psychology from the standpoint of a behaviorist.* Philadelphia : Lippincott.

WEINBACH, A. P. 1937. Some physiological phenomena fitted to growth equations: I. Moro reflex. *Human Biol.*, 9, 549–555.

——. 1940. Some physiological phenomena fitted to growth equations: IV. Time and power relations for a human infant climbing inclines of various slopes. *Growth*, 4, 123–134.

WEISMANN, A. 1889. *Essays upon heredity and kindred biological problems.* (Chap. 4.) Oxford: Clarendon Press.

WEISS, A. P. 1929. *A theoretical basis of human behavior,* pp. 132–134. Columbus: Adams.

WEISS, P. 1939. *Principles of development.* New York: Holt.

WINDLE, W. F. 1930. Normal behavioral reactions of kittens correlated with the postnatal development of nerve-fiber density in the spinal gray matter. *J. Comp. Neurol.*, 50, 479–503.

WINDLE, W. F., and A. M. GRIFFIN. 1931. Observations on embryonic and fetal movements of the cat. *J. Comp. Neurol.*, 52, 149–188.

WINDLE, W. F., J. E. O'DONNELL, and E. E. GLASSHAGLE. 1933. The early development of spontaneous and reflex behavior in cat embryos and fetuses. *Physiol. Zoöl.*, 6, 521–541.

WINDLE, W. F., and D. W. ORR. 1934. The development of behavior in chick embryos: Spinal cord structure correlated with early somatic motility. *J. Comp. Neurol.*, 60, 287–308.

WITTY, P. A., and H. C. LEHMAN. 1933. The instinct hypothesis versus the maturation hypothesis. *Psychol. Rev.*, 40, 33–59.

YANASE, J. 1907. Beiträge zur Physiologie des peristaltischen Bewegungen des embryonalen Darmes. *Pflüg. Arch. ges. Physiol.*, 117, 345–382; 119, 451–464.

YERKES, R. M., and D. BLOOMFIELD. 1910. Do kittens instinctively kill mice? *Psychol. Bull.*, 7, 253–263.

Additional References Which the Writer Has Found Helpful in the Preparation of This Chapter

ADRIAN, E. D. 1937. *The nervous system: Factors determining human behavior.* (In *Harvard Tercentenary Publications.*) Cambridge: Harvard University Press.

ANDERSON, J. E. 1936. Child development and the interpretation of behavior. *Science*, 83, 245–252.

ANGULO Y GONZÁLEZ, A. W. 1927. The motor nuclei in the cervical cord of the albino rat at birth. *J. Comp. Neurol.*, 43, 115–142.

——. 1929. Is myelinogeny an absolute index of behavioral capability? *J. Comp. Neurol.*, 48, 459–464.

——. 1939. Histogenesis of the monopolar neuroblast and the ventral longitudinal path in the albino rat. *J. Comp. Neurol.*, 71, 325–359.

BENTLEY, A. F. 1939. Situational vs. psychological theories of behavior. *J. Phil.*, 36, 405–413.

——. 1940. Observable behaviors. *Psychol. Rev.*, 47, 230–253.

BENTLEY, M. 1909. Mental inheritance. *Pop. Sci. Mo.*, 75, 458–468.

BRAINARD, P. P. 1927. Some observations of infant learning and instincts. *J. Genet. Psychol.*, 34, 231–254.

BRIDGES, C. B. 1935. Salivary chromosome maps. *J. Hered.*, 26, 60–64.

——. 1938. Revised map of the salivary gland X-chromosomes of *Drosophila melanogaster.* *J. Hered.*, 29, 11–13.

BROWN, T. G. 1914. On the nature of the fundamental activity of the nervous centers; together with an analysis of the conditioning of rhythmic activity in progression, and a theory of the evolution of function in the nervous system. *J. Physiol.*, 48, 18–46.

BÜHLER, C. 1937. Theoretische Grundprobleme des Kinderpsychologie. *Z. Psychol.*, 140, 140–164.

CARMICHAEL, L. 1934. An experimental study in the prenatal guinea-pig of the origin and development of reflexes and patterns of behavior in relation to the stimulation of specific receptor areas during the period of active fetal life. *Genet. Psychol. Monogr.*, 16, 337–491.

CASTLE, W. E. 1912. The inconstancy of unit-characters. *Amer. Nat.*, 46, 352–362.

CHILD, C. M. 1924. Modification of development in relation to differential susceptibility. *Amer. Nat.*, 58, 237–253.

——. 1925. The physiological significance of the cephalo-caudal differential in vertebrate development. *Anat. Rec.*, 31, 369–383.

CONKLIN, E. G. 1929. Problems of development. *Amer. Nat.*, 63, 5–36.

DARBY, H. H. 1934. The mechanism of asymmetry in the alpheidae. *Carnegie Inst. Wash., Publ.* 435, pp. 347–361.

DARWIN, C. 1869. *On the origin of species by means of natural selection.* London: Murray.

——. 1871. *The descent of man.* London: Murray.

DEMOLL, R. 1932. *Über den Instinkt.* (*Münch. Universitätsreden.*) Munich: Hueber.

DOLL, E. A. 1938. Social maturation. *Proc. 5th Conf. Child Res. Clin. Woods Sch.*, 3–7.

FURFEY, P. H. 1935. Maturation. *Cath. Educ. Rev.*, 33, 88–99.

GESELL, A. 1939. Reciprocal interweaving in neuro-muscular development: A principle of spiral organization shown in the patterning of infant behavior. *J. Comp. Neurol.*, 70, 161–180.

GESELL, A., H. M. HALVERSON, H. THOMPSON, F. L. ILG, B. M. CASTNER, L. B. AMES, and C. S. AMATRUDA. 1940. *The first five years of life: A guide to the study of the preschool child.* New York : Harper.

HARLOW, H. F. 1936. The neuro-physiological correlates of learning and intelligence. *Psychol. Bull.*, **33**, 479.

HUNTER, W. S. 1920. Modification of instinct from the standpoint of social psychology. *Psychol. Rev.*, **27**, 247–269.

IRWIN, O. C. 1932. The organismic hypothesis and differentiation of behavior : I. The cell theory and the neurone doctrine. *Psychol. Rev.*, **39**, 128–146.

IRWIN, O. C., and A. P. WEISS. 1930. A note on mass activity in newborn infants. *J. Genet. Psychol.*, **38**, 20–30.

KINGSBURY, B. F. 1924. The significance of the so-called law of cephalocaudal differential growth. *Anat. Rec.*, **27**, 305–321.

——. 1926. The so-called law of anteroposterior development. *Anat. Rec.*, **33**, 73–87.

KOSSIKOV, R. V., and H. J. MULLER. 1935. Invalidation of the genetic evidence for branched chromonemas. *J. Hered.*, **26**, 305–317.

LANGWORTHY, O. R. 1929. A correlated study of the development of reflex activity in fetal and young kittens and the myelinization of tracts in the nervous system. *Contr. Embryol., Carnegie Inst. Wash.*, **20**, No. 114, pp. 127–171.

LILLIE, F. R. 1927. The gene and the ontogenetic process. *Science*, **66**, 361.

LOEB, J. 1916. *The organism as a whole.* New York : Putnam.

MEYER, A. W. 1939. *The rise of embryology.* Stanford University, Calif. : Stanford University Press.

MORGAN, C. L. 1913. *Instinct and experience.* (Chaps. 3 and 4.) London : Methuen.

MULLER, H. J., and T. S. PAINTER. 1926. The cytological expression of changes in gene alignment produced by X-rays in *Drosophila. Amer. Nat.*, **63**, 193–200.

MYERSON, A. 1939. The relationship of hereditary factors to mental processes. *Res. Publ. Ass. Nerv. Ment. Dis.*, **19**, 16–49.

NEWMAN, H. H. 1921. *Readings in evolution and genetics.* Chicago : University of Chicago Press.

NOBLE, G. K. 1939. The experimental animal from the naturalist's point of view. *Amer. Nat.*, **73**, 113–126.

PAINTER, T. S. 1934. Salivary chromosomes and the attack on the gene. *J. Hered.*, **25**, 465–476.

RANEY, E. T., and L. CARMICHAEL. 1934. Localizing responses to tactual stimuli in the fetal rat in relation to the psychological problem of space perception. *J. Genet. Psychol.*, **45**, 3–21.

ROMANES, G. J. 1892. *Darwin, and after Darwin.* (Chaps. 1, 2, and 9.) Chicago : Open Court.

SEWARD, A. C. (Ed.). 1909. *Darwin and modern science.* (Chaps. 1–9 and 21.) Cambridge : University Press.

SINNOTT, E. W. 1939. The cell and the problem of organization. *Science*, **89**, 41–46.

THOMPSON, H. 1932. The growth and significance of daily variations in infant behavior. *J. Genet. Psychol.*, **40**, 16–36.

TILNEY, F., and L. CASAMAJOR. 1924. Myelinogeny as applied to the study of behavior. *Arch. Neurol. Psychiat., Chicago*, **12**, 1–66.

WHITMAN, C. O. 1893. The inadequacy of the cell-theory of development. *J. Morphol.*, **8**, 639–658.

YOUNGSTROM, K. A. 1938. On the relationship between choline esterase and the development of behavior in *Amphibia. J. Neurophysiol.*, **1**, 357–363.

CHAPTER 8

LEARNING IN CHILDREN

NORMAN L. MUNN

Introduction

Learning may be said to occur whenever behavior undergoes incremental modification of a more or less permanent nature as a result of activity, special training, or observation. To say that learning involves an *incremental* modification is to distinguish it from fatigue, which is also due to activity, but with which a performance decrement is associated. By indicating that the learning process involves a more or less *permanent* modification, we differentiate it from sensory adaptation, which disappears soon after removal of the stimulating circumstances. Finally, by including the statement that learning depends upon *activity, special training,* or *observation,* we point to the fact that it differs from modification which depends upon maturation *per se.*

In order to approximate complete coverage of experimental investigations on learning in children, one must take cognizance of conditioning, acquisition of motor skill, memorizing and related mnemonic functions, and problem solving.

Investigations of learning in children, rather than introducing new problems and essentially novel techniques, have followed the leads of animal and adult human psychology. The first investigation of conditioned responses in children (Krasnogorski, 1909) involved modification of the technique of Pavlov, who more than a decade earlier had begun his pioneer investigations on conditioned salivary response in dogs. Researches on learning of motor skills in children began to appear some time after the experiments of Thorndike (1898) and Small (1899) on animals and those of Bryan and Harter (1897), Swift (1903), and Book (1908) on learning of skills by human adults. The earliest published experiments on learning of motor skills which involved children as subjects are those of Judd (1908) on dart throwing and those of Hicks and Carr (1912) on maze learning. In researches carried out since 1912 the maze technique has figured prominently.

Investigations of mnemonic processes in children began shortly after Ebbinghaus's pioneer study on himself. Jacobs (1887) devised the memory-span test and used it with children. Binet and Henri (1894) worked with the memory span and included memory-span tests in their intelligence scales. Several of the early memorizing experiments (Steffens, 1900; Pentschew, 1903; Radossawljewitsch, 1907) involved children incidentally.

Problem solving, apart from that incidentally involved in the school subjects, has been extensively investigated only in recent years. Nevertheless, Lindley (1897) studied how children and adults solve various unicursal puzzles. He also, as we shall indicate more fully later, made some pertinent observations on differences in the way in which children and adults attack such problems. Widespread interest in the experimental investigation of problem solving by children has, however, appeared only since publication of Köhler's (1925) researches on problem solving in apes. Investigations of the rôle of incentives and of various other factors relating to economical learning have also followed leads given by animal and adult human psychology.

In many investigations of learning, inclusion of children has been merely incidental. Early students of child development, although they investigated many other problems with children directly, tended, as far as learning was concerned, to accept and apply results obtained with animals and human adults. This accounts, in part at least, for a long delay in the appearance of researches aimed at determining how *children* learn.

The Conditioned Response

During his study of gastric secretion in dogs, Pavlov (1889–1890) observed that stimuli frequently associated with the presence of food become, in themselves, adequate to arouse secretory responses such as salivation. Salivation in response to hitherto neutral stimuli, such as sounds and skin irritation, was later referred to by Pavlov (1903) as a *psychic secretion.* Bekhterev, another Russian investigator, began in 1906 to develop what he termed *associative reflexes* in dogs. In response to shock on the foot or leg, withdrawal or *protective* reflexes were aroused. Bekhterev observed elicitation of similar reflexes by previously *neutral* stimuli after such had been presented in association with shock. Numerous researches based upon the above observations were soon carried out by Pavlov, Bekhterev, and their students.

That conditioned responses are relatively simple habits is doubted by no psychologist. Much of the controversy concerning

them hinges upon the claim of Pavlov, Watson, and others that all learning, no matter how complex, results from conditioning. Habits are referred to by these investigators as chains of conditioned reflexes, or as compound conditioned responses. Our present discussion will avoid theoretical issues by describing the conditioned response in children merely as a type of habit formation. Whether or not all learning may adequately be envisaged in terms of conditioning will be determined only after more data are available. For an excellent discussion of the present status of this controversy the reader is referred to a book by Hilgard and Marquis (1940).

Prenatal Conditioning. The possibility that certain "reflexes" of the newborn are responses conditioned prior to birth (Holt, 1931) has led several investigators to attempt conditioning of fetuses. The two earliest attempts (Ray, 1932; Sontag and Wallace, 1934) were either unsuccessful or ambiguous in result. However, Spelt (1938) has reported success. Fetuses between the ages of 6½ and 8½ months responded vigorously to the sound of a clapper but made no response to tactile vibration of the maternal abdomen. After X-rays had indicated the position of the head, arms, and legs of the fetus, activity was recorded with tambours placed at appropriate places on the mother's abdomen. Within 100 paired presentations of tactile vibration, followed 5 seconds later by the loud noise, there were movements in response to the tactile vibration alone. Spelt claims that conditioning was thus demonstrated. Since only a brief abstract is available, critical evaluation of these results is not possible.

Conditioning in Newborn Infants. The most extensive conditioning experiments on infants in the first week of life have been reported by Marquis (1931) and Wenger (1936). In the investigation by Marquis,

10 infants between the ages of 2 and 9 days were stimulated with a buzzer for 5 seconds prior to each feeding period. Within 5 days of training, 8 of these infants began to exhibit sucking and mouth-opening responses to the buzzer. Correlated diminution of crying and of general activity also appeared. Four control infants stimulated with the buzzer, but without associated food, failed to exhibit conditioned responses.

This experiment is criticized by Wenger (1936) on the basis that controls were inadequate and observation of responses too subjective. He failed to obtain conditioned feeding reactions in two newborn infants. That newborn infants may be conditioned, however, is shown by results obtained in his experiments involving eyelid, limb withdrawal, and respiratory responses. In conditioning of eyelid responses the unconditioned stimulus was a flash of light and the conditioned stimulus a tactile vibration of the foot. Tactile vibration preceded light by three seconds. During control tests, six 9-day-old infants exhibited lid responses to a tactile stimulation of the foot in 29 per cent of the presentations. The range was from 23 to 34 per cent. Infants with whom conditioning began on the second day of life, however, reached percentages of 58 to 74 by the ninth day. Acquisition curves showed much daily fluctuation and Wenger therefore concluded that, although conditioning is undoubtedly present, it is quite unstable. Conditioning of one infant was continued for 6 months. The percentage of eyelid responses to tactile stimulation rose as high as 89 on one daily test involving 40 stimulations. The acquisition curve, however, exhibited large fluctuations with no evident trend toward greater stability.

Wenger also obtained conditioning when the unconditioned stimulus comprised an electric shock which elicited foot withdrawal and respiratory changes. Tactile vibration at the sternum served as the conditioned stimulus. One infant which exhibited no flexion responses to tactile stimulation 2 days after birth was, by the ninth day, making such responses to 50 per cent of the stimulations.

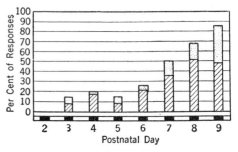

FIGURE 1. Conditioning of withdrawal responses to tone. (From "An Investigation of Conditioned Responses in Human Infants," by M. A. Wenger. *University of Iowa Studies in Child Welfare*, 1936, **12**, 52. By permission of The Iowa Child Welfare Research Station, publisher.)

The shaded area of each bar indicates the percentage of full leg retractions in response to the auditory stimulus; the unshaded area represents slight retraction.

More acceptable evidence of conditioning than could be obtained with tactile vibration at the sternum was disclosed when a tone of 1084 cycles, and having a loudness of 50 decibels above the adult threshold, was substituted. Three infants exhibited conditioned flexion and respiratory responses. Figure 1 summarizes the flexion results obtained with the infant whose conditioned reactions were most stable. Stability of conditioning was almost as great in one but very much poorer in the other of the two remaining subjects. One notes that auditory stimulation on the second day elicited no withdrawal reactions. In successive daily conditioning sessions, each involving 23 to

45 observations, the percentages of complete and incomplete retractions of the leg gradually increased. Observations on seven 9-day-old infants stimulated with tone but not with electric shock indicated flexion responses averaging 28 per cent, with a range of 9 to 61 per cent under these conditions. Most of the responses were slight. The mean percentage of withdrawals for 3 conditioned infants was 63 on the ninth day. It is thus assumed that conditioning was present.

Two infants trained with a flash of light as the conditioned stimulus also manifested conditioned withdrawal in response to light. They reached a mean percentage of 46 withdrawals. The percentage for controls of the same age was 13. In this, as in all the earlier experiments, conditioning was not stable.[1]

[1] Wickens and Wickens (1939) question whether the ordinary type of conditioning appears in neonates. Their research, published only in a brief abstract as yet, involved 24 infants below 10 days of age. The conditioned stimulus was a buzzer and the unconditioned stimulus a shock administered to the sole of the foot. None of the infants used in this experiment made withdrawal responses to the initial presentation of the buzzer. A control group of 12 subjects received 12 stimulations with the *shock alone* for 3 consecutive days. An experimental group was given the same shock stimulations as the control group, but *with the buzzer*. It is reported that both groups evidenced similar responses in subsequent tests with the buzzer alone. Continued presentation of the buzzer led to results which simulated extinction and spontaneous recovery. Such "pseudo-conditioning" has also been observed in experiments with animals (see especially Grether, 1938). It is likely that this phenomenon is related to that of irradiation. Shock represents a change in the usual stimulus complex and at the same time elicits reflex withdrawal. The sound of a buzzer, especially when presented in the same context as the shock, also represents a change in the same stimulus complex. It does not seem strange, therefore, that withdrawal should occur to the buzzer, even though it has not been paired with shock. The above experiment does, of course, raise the question as to whether or not other studies, in which this type of control is not made, involve the same conditioning phenomenon. Where controls like those of Wenger are used, however, one

Other Investigations of Conditioned Responses in Infants. Conditioned feeding reactions in infants between the second and fourth months of life have been investigated by Denisova and Figurin (1929)[2] and Kantrow (1937). All but one of Denisova and Figurin's 11 infants were between the ages of 10 and 23 days at the beginning of the experiment. Natural conditioned responses, consisting of food-getting reactions to previously neutral stimuli, but occurring without experimental training, appeared between the ages of 21 and 27 days. For some of the infants, experimental training consisted of presentation of a bell for 15 seconds before and 30 seconds after feeding began. In other cases, the conditioned stimulus was a bell or a bell and light. Feeding reactions to these stimuli appeared at ages ranging from 33 to 77 days, and after 132 to 350 trials.

A more comprehensive and carefully conducted investigation than the one just described is Kantrow's (1937). Sixteen infants aged 44 to 117 days at the beginning of the experiment rapidly developed conditioned feeding reactions to the sound of a buzzer. Sucking movements were recorded by placing over each infant's chin a harness attached to the pen of a polygraph. Other responses, such as crying and general activity, were noted. A control period of variable length (to avoid conditioning to a temporal sequence) preceded onset of the buzzer, which was sounded for 20 seconds. At the end of 5 seconds of stimulation with the buzzer, a bottle, which had been kept outside the visual field, was inserted in the infant's

does at least have evidence as to whether or not the unconditioned infants manifest as frequent a response to the conditioned stimulus as do the conditioned infants.

[2] This research has been published only in Russian. The present summary is based upon Razran's (1933).

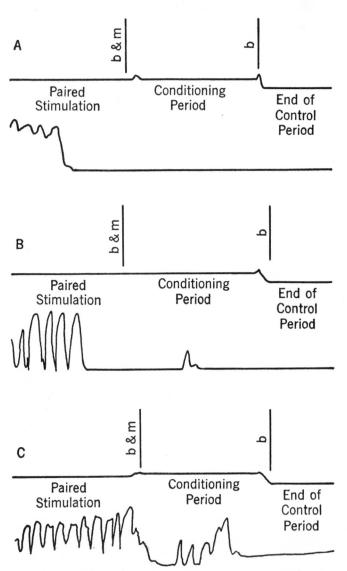

FIGURE 2. Sample sucking records of an infant before and after conditioning to the sound of a buzzer. (From "An Investigation of Conditioned Feeding Responses and Concomitant Adaptive Behavior in Young Infants," by R. W. Kantrow. *University of Iowa Studies in Child Welfare*, 1937, **13**, 11. By permission of the publisher.)

Read from right to left. At the end of a control period of variable duration, a buzzer *b* was sounded for 5 seconds, the conditioning period. At the end of this period, the nipple was placed in the infant's mouth and the buzzer continued for another 15 seconds, *b & m*. The lower line in each part of the figure is a record of sucking activity. It was obtained by means of a chin harness attached to the pen of a polygraph. *A*. First experimental feeding, fifth paired stimulation. *B*. Fifth experimental feeding, thirty-second paired stimulation. Note anticipatory feeding reaction. *C*. Eighth experimental feeding, fifty-fourth paired stimulation. Note conditioned sucking activity.

mouth. Stimulation with the buzzer continued for 15 seconds after feeding began. The stimulating sequence and the nature of responses at different stages of conditioning are indicated in Figure 2. Stable conditioned sucking responses appeared within 1 to 5 days, after 3 to 9 experi-

pearance of the sucking decrement mentioned above. Analysis of the data in terms of degree of hunger at the time of the tests indicated that, unless the infant was hungry, little conditioning appeared. Curves based upon sucking activity during experimental extinction, produced by suc-

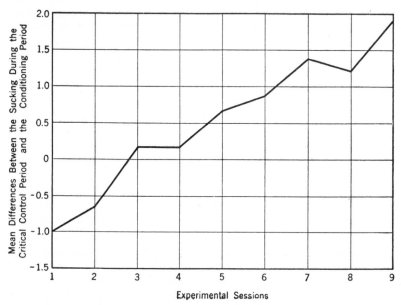

FIGURE 3. Acquisition curve of conditioned sucking in fifteen infants for nine consecutive experimental feedings. (From "An Investigation of Conditioned Feeding Responses and Concomitant Adaptive Behavior in Young Infants," by R. W. Kantrow. *University of Iowa Studies in Child Welfare*, 1937, **13**, 32. By permission of the publisher.)

mental feedings and 16 to 72 paired stimulations. An acquisition curve based upon the difference in the means for sucking during successive groups of control and conditioning periods is shown in Figure 3. Continued presentation of paired stimulations beyond the ninth experimental session led to a plateau and, finally, to a drop in the acquisition curves. Crying and general activity at first showed a gradual decrease as a function of experimental pairing of the buzzer and feeding. They then increased at about the same time as ap-

cessive stimulations with the buzzer alone, represent what approximates a mirror image of the curve shown in Figure 3. An increase in general activity and in the amount of time spent in crying was also noted during extinction experiments.

Conditioned differential sucking activity to tones and to intensities of light has been developed by Kasatkin and Levikova (1935a, 1935b) in infants between 1 and 2 months of age.

Conditioning of emotional responses in infants has been studied by several investigators. Since emotional behavior is the subject of another chapter in this book, however, we shall not undertake a detailed discussion of these studies. It is sufficient to say, at this point, that Watson and Rayner (1920) and H. E. Jones (1930*a*, 1930*b*) have succeeded in conditioning fear reactions and galvanic skin responses, respectively, to previously neutral stimuli. Retention of the conditioned responses over periods ranging up to 7 months was noted by Jones. Moss (1924) conditioned two children, the younger of whom was 2 years old, to dislike the sound of a snapper which was associated with squirting of vinegar into the mouth. Bregman (1934) was unsuccessful in her attempt to condition emotional attitudes of 15 infants between the ages of 8 and 16 months. Sounds assumed to be disagreeable were associated with some objects while supposedly agreeable sounds were associated with others. Negative and positive reactions to these objects which might be expected from the nature of associated stimuli did not appear. Although there were no consistent changes in attitude as a result of the conditioning procedure, some infants at times evidenced negative reactions to stimuli associated with the noise. As Wenger (1936) has pointed out, there is no proof of the agreeableness and disagreeableness, for infants, of the sounds used in this investigation. Bregman's claim that conditioning *per se* cannot account for changes in the emotional attitudes of infants seems unwarranted in the light of her results.

Although the restricted data so far available do not justify any extensive generalizations, one may, in summary, say that investigations of conditioning in infants have shown that: (1) sucking, blinking, limb withdrawal, respiration, crying, general activity, galvanic skin responses, and **fear reactions** may be conditioned to tac-

tual, visual, and auditory stimuli during infancy; (2) although newborn infants may be conditioned, the reactions are often lacking in stability; (3) older infants tend to evidence more stability of conditioned reactions than the newborn; (4) conditioning of the sucking reaction is dependent upon existence of hunger; (5) retention of conditioned responses developed in infancy has in some instances been observed over periods ranging up to 7 months; (6) spontaneous recovery following extinction training has been observed; (7) continued presentation of the paired stimuli may, after conditioning has developed, lead to a decrement in the frequency of conditioned reactions; and (8) the curve of extinction for conditioned feeding reactions approximates a mirror image of the curve of acquisition.

Conditioned-Response Studies with Older Children. Investigations of conditioned responses in children beyond the period of infancy have been numerous. Razran (1933) has summarized more than thirty researches from the Russian laboratories alone. In the following discussion we shall consider only a few studies which are more or less representative of those with children beyond infancy.

As indicated earlier, the pioneer research on conditioned responses in children was Krasnogorski's (1909). In Krasnogorski's initial experiment a child of 3½ years was conditioned so that salivation first elicited only by food occurred in response to a bell. The index of salivary response was swallowing. In later experiments with other children, Krasnogorski placed a tambour over the thyroid cartilage and recorded the swallowing reactions on a kymograph. He also used mouth opening as the response to be conditioned. Later still, saliva was collected by means of suction cups (saliometers) placed over the salivary glands. As Razran's review indicates, the experiments from Krasnogorski's laboratory have, in general procedure, results, and interpretation, closely paralleled those of Pavlov on dogs. Krasnogorski (1925) has reviewed in English some of his investigations of conditioning in normal and neu-

general experimental situation is illustrated in Figure 4. The child is seated before the apparatus with a rubber bulb in his hand. As the experimenter, who is in an adjoining room, presses his bulb, food is released and slides down a tube toward

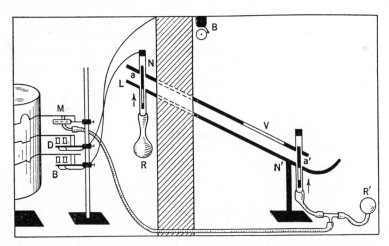

FIGURE 4. Ivanov-Smolensky's method of conditioning. (From "On the Methods of Examining the Conditioned Food Reflexes in Children and in Mental Disorders," by A. G. Ivanov-Smolensky. *Brain*, 1927, **50**, 139. By permission of the publisher.)

The experimenter, seated in the room at the left, presses the bulb R and causes a piece of chocolate, a, on the shelf, L, to slide down the tube N-N'. As the chocolate passes the window, V, in the adjoining room it may be seen by the child, who sits with his hand over the bulb R'. By pressing this bulb and thus causing a photographic shutter to move upwards, the child releases the chocolate, which falls into the position a'. A Marey tambour, M, records the child's grasping response on a kymograph drum. The signal marker, D, likewise records release of the chocolate by the experimenter. In conditioning experiments a bell, B, or some other stimulus, is presented just before release of the food and its presentation recorded by the signal marker, B. Conditioning is evidenced by grasping at the sound of the bell or prior to observation of food.

rotic children. Mateer (1918), whose research on 50 normal and 14 subnormal children will be mentioned again later, utilized Krasnogorski's general technique. The unconditioned stimulus, which elicited mouth opening and swallowing, was chocolate placed in the mouth. Pulling a bandage over the child's eyes just prior to presentation of the chocolate served as the conditioned stimulus.

Ivanov-Smolensky (1927a, 1927b) has devised a technique markedly different from that of previous investigators. His

the child. Just prior to release of the food, a bell or other conditioned stimulus is activated. The child observes the food through a small window on the tube and, by pressing his bulb, is able to obtain it. Presentation of the conditioned and unconditioned stimuli and pressing of the child's bulb are recorded objectively by kymographic or other means. Children between the ages of 4 and 15 years have been conditioned in 2 to 88 trials to make stable grasping reactions upon presentation of such conditioned stimuli as the sound of a bell and the flash of a light. Investigations from Ivanov-Smolensky's laboratory are reviewed by Razran (1933). They demonstrate individual differences in susceptibility to conditioning, higher-order conditioning, statistically unreliable differences in the speed with which conditioned grasping and withdrawal responses are developed, and development of reflexes to chains of stimuli. There has also been an attempt to classify children into excitable, inhibitable, labile, and inert types upon

is the sounding of a metronome for 50 seconds prior to onset of the shock, which lasts for 20 seconds. A tracing from part of the record obtained in conditioning a child of 26 months is shown in Figure 5. One will note that there is, in this case, no evidence of conditioning at the tenth trial. At the eleventh trial, however, the foot is partially withdrawn in response to the metronome. A more marked withdrawal appears at the twelfth presentation of the metronome.

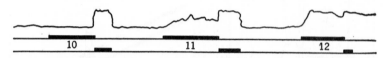

FIGURE 5. Conditioned withdrawal in a child of 26 months. (From "Des réflexes conditionnels: I. L'organisation des réflexes conditionnels chez l'enfant," by G. Marinesco and A. Kreindler. *Journal de Psychologie*, 1933, **30**, 873.)

Bottom line: duration of electric shock. *Second line from bottom:* duration of metronome. *Top line:* foot withdrawal.

the basis of their conditioning behavior. However, only 13 children were used in this study. Bayne, Winsor, and Winters (1929), using the Ivanov-Smolensky technique, found that conditioning to red light was obtained in 8 to 10 trials in two 6-year-old children. A 4-year-old child, however, required over 200 trials to develop grasping responses to the sound of a metronome.

Still another technique used to develop conditioned responses in children is that of Marinesco and Kreindler (1933). It involves a modification of Bekhterev's general procedure in that the reaction conditioned is withdrawal of a limb from weak electrical stimulation. An electrode is attached to the child's abdomen and another to the foot or hand. The arrangement is such that shock is felt in the limb. A thread attached to the limb and, through a pulley system, to the marker on a kymograph drum serves to record retraction of the arm or leg. The conditioned stimulus

Use of this technique has enabled Marinesco and Kreindler to demonstrate clearly, in children between the ages of 15 and 30 months, many of the phenomena of conditioning disclosed in experiments with animals. The chief phenomena observed in this study were:

1. *Conditioned differentiation of movements.* At first all limbs responded despite the fact that only one was stimulated. During the course of conditioning, however, retraction of limbs other than the one stimulated decreased in amplitude and finally ceased.

2. *External inhibition.* Presentation of a second stimulus, such as light, while the metronome was sounding reduced the amplitude of movements previously made to the metronome.

3. *Trace responses.* When stimulation with shock followed cessation of the metronome by several seconds, the conditioned retraction was delayed for a corresponding interval of time.

4. *Experimental extinction.* Continued presentation of the metronome, without following it with shock, led to diminished conditioned responses and, finally, to their disappearance.

5. *Spontaneous recovery.* After conditioned responses had disappeared as a result of extinction training, they reappeared without further training.

6. *Higher-order conditioning.* After the metronome aroused withdrawal responses it was, with occasional further reinforcement, used as the conditioning stimulus in training with other stimuli to be conditioned.

Speed of Conditioning as a Function of Age and Intelligence. Mateer's (1918) investigation (see page 377) involved 50 normal and 14 subnormal children between the ages of 12 and 90 months. For normal children the correlation between CA and the number of trials required to produce two successive anticipatory responses was .571 ± .06. The approximate average number of trials required at successive yearly age levels, for the normal group aged 1 to 7 years, was 8, 7, 5, 4, 4, 5, and 4, respectively. These results suggest that, within the age range of 1 to 4 years, and for the type of response involved, susceptibility to conditioning increases with chronological age. The other extensive investigations, however, show results not in agreement with the above. Osipova (1926) conditioned withdrawal reactions in children between the ages of 7 and 19 years. He found that the average number of trials increased with age. The correlation between CA and speed of formation of the conditioned withdrawal response was −.358 ± .033. A biserial correlation based upon 144 cases between 14 and 19 years was −.716 ± .06. Osipova's findings are supported by those of Dernowa-Yarmolenko (1933), who conditioned 1000 subjects between the ages of 8 and 19 years. Each subject was told to raise his hand

when the examiner did so. The examiner then tapped on the table with a pencil. Two seconds later he raised his left hand. Ten such paired presentations of the tap and hand raising were presented. Anticipatory hand raising was noted, that is, raising the hand after a tap but before the examiner raised his hand. The percentage of subjects exhibiting anticipatory conditioned reactions within ten trials was 90 at 8 years. In successive yearly age levels the percentage gradually decreased until, at the upper levels, very few were responding. With increasing age, furthermore, the number of associations of the two stimuli required to produce conditioned reactions increased and the number of conditioned reactions in ten trials decreased.

In considering the results of Osipova and Mateer, Razran (1935) suggests that conditioning of the laboratory type may be rendered more difficult as an individual grows beyond the early years of childhood, not because of decreased susceptibility to conditioning *per se* but because "instrumental mastery of verbal and conscious processes," with an associated decrease in naïveté, makes him *less willing to submit to the procedure.* Recent researches by Razran (1936) on adults conditioned indirectly, while they were engaged in other activities, lend support to this view. Mitrano (1939) has attempted to overcome deleterious attitudinal factors by using feeble-minded children and adults as subjects.

Mateer found a correlation of .588 ± .06 between speed of conditioning and MA. Osipova (1926), on the other hand, obtained a biserial correlation of −.540 ± .08 between intelligence and speed of forming the conditioned withdrawal reaction. On the basis of the results so far available, therefore, it would be hazardous to make any generalizations about the relation between speed of conditioning and intelligence. If Razran's view is correct, one might expect a negative correlation between intelligence and the speed of laboratory conditioning.

Solution of Behavior Problems by Conditioned-Response Procedures. Krasnogorski (1925, 1933), Ivanov-Smolensky (1927a, 1927b), Seham (1932), and Gesell (1938) have reviewed applications of conditioned-response procedure to child psychiatry. From the standpoint of indicating actual accomplishment, however, these reviews are quite disappointing. They merely describe general techniques and what these *promise* for solution of behavior problems. Nevertheless, a few specific applications of conditioned-response principles have been made in this field.

Aldrich (1928) and Marinesco, Sager, and Kreindler (1931) have used conditioned-response procedures to determine the presence of hearing in, respectively, a 3-month-old infant thought to be deaf and a 9-year-old functionally mute child.

Jones's (1924a) elimination of a child's fear response by conditioning is well known. Reference to this experiment is made in Chapter 15.

Morgan (1938), Mowrer and Mowrer (1938), and Morgan and Witmer (1939) have been highly successful in eliminating enuresis by a conditioned-response procedure. The problem involved in enuresis is very well stated by Mowrer and Mowrer (1938):

> Learning to awaken to the relatively vague and not very intense pressure created by a filling bladder, while successfully ignoring many other potentially disturbing stimuli, must be for the young child something of a feat, especially in view of the pre-existence of a strictly reflex, subcortical neural mechanism for the autonomic relief of this need (p. 437).

Use of conditioned-reflex procedure here has as its aims, (1) causing the child to associate *getting up* with bladder tension and (2) making the child responsive to bladder tension in its earlier stages, that is, lowering his threshold for this stimulus.

All the above studies have involved essentially the same technique for producing these effects. The child was required to sleep on a mat which, when urination began, short-circuited and rang a bell. Each child was instructed to get up as soon as the bell rang, to open a switch disconnecting the bell, and then to go to the bathroom and finish urinating. All of Mowrer and Mowrer's 30 cases between the ages of 3 and 13 years were cured of enuresis within 4 to 8 weeks. They learned, in other words, to anticipate the ringing of the bell by arising before bladder tension became so great as to cause reflex urination. Morgan and Witmer report that 4 of their 5 subjects were cured of enuresis by this method in 4 to 14 nights. Morgan says that all children who cooperate are readily cured by application of this technique.

Learning of Sensorimotor Skills

Acquisition of sensorimotor skills is of singular importance during early childhood. The chief problems of adjustment which confront the infant concern acquisition of skills necessary for manipulation of and orientation with respect to its environment. Some of these skills, such as crawling, walking, and finger-thumb opposition, are probably functions more of maturation than of learning. Even when learning is shown to be involved in the acquisition of such skills, it is, as Dennis (1935) has so aptly pointed out, frequently autogenous. Such learning results from the child's own untutored activities rather than from specific training. On the other hand, there are many skills, such as talking, writing, and buttoning clothes, which fail to develop unless specific training or opportunities for imitation are provided. These skills and the various factors which influence their acquisition will be our prime concern in the following discussions.

The Relative Influence of Maturation and Learning. Acquisition of skill which results from learning is our chief concern, yet we cannot ignore the fact that learning and maturation are concomitant factors in child development. Although some skills develop primarily as a result of maturation and others primarily as a result of learning, the two processes are reciprocally related. This relationship is of especial importance during early childhood when the neuromuscular system is undergoing rapid growth and when, at the same time, there are numerous influences to encourage learning. With increasing age there is a relative decrease in the importance of new maturational factors.

These considerations indicate that investigation of the learning process *per se* in young children must take cognizance of maturation. Failure to control maturational influences has greatly lessened the value of many early, and even some recent, studies on learning in children. In some instances a loose use of the term *learning* has been involved. Thus Kirkpatrick (1899) describes how a child "learns" to walk. Ketterlinus (1931) presents a study which illustrates the ambiguity of interpretation which results when the possible improvement in skill resulting from maturation is ignored. The problem was to determine whether children between 2 and 5 years of age are able to adjust to mirror reversal. The experiment covered a period of 4 weeks, with two trials on a certain day each week. One problem was to pick up objects and put them in a cup. The objects and cup were seen only

in a mirror. Age groups of 2, 3, and 4 years were used. Each age group began the experiment with a lower time score than did the preceding one. This may be interpreted as due to the effect of maturation or perhaps to general training which preceded the experiment. Acquisition curves show a decrease in time during the course of the experiment. The *rate* at which a curve dropped, however, was greatest for the youngest group and least for the oldest. This is what one might expect were maturation an important factor. If learning were the chief factor, would one not expect the older, more mature group, to learn faster than the younger group? It might be claimed, on the other hand, that since the 4-year-old group began with the lowest time score it was closer to the physiological limit and thus could not be expected to improve as much as the younger groups.

Such ambiguity of interpretation could have been prevented by using a control group matched with the experimental group in terms of age, sex, intelligence, and initial ability on the tests in question. The same criticism applies to Beebe's (1933, 1934) investigations of *motor learning* in children. Since no control groups were used, the curves obtained cannot be interpreted with any degree of certainty.

Several investigations of learning at the early age levels have used the method of co-twin control or have utilized a trained and an untrained group matched in terms of age, sex, intelligence, and initial performance. The co-twin control investigations of Gesell and Thompson (1929) on climbing and cube manipulation, Strayer (1930) on speech, Hilgard (1933) on walking boards, cutting, and ring tossing, McGraw (1935) on a variety of motor activities, and Mirenva (1935) on jumping, throwing at a target, and rolling a ball toward a target have been considered in the chapter on maturation (Chapter 7). These studies all indicate the strong influence of maturation at early age levels.

Hilgard's (1932) investigation of climbing, cutting, and buttoning activities involved trained and untrained groups of approximately equivalent initial ability. The average time score for a group given 12 weeks of practice in climbing dropped from 18 to 8½ seconds, approximately. Tests at the end of the experimental periods indicated that the average time score of the untrained group had dropped to 13 seconds. Within one week of further training, however, the score for this group approximated that of the trained group. Both groups improved in cutting and buttoning, but the untrained group was not able to reach the level of the trained group within an additional week of practice.

Acquisition of skills more complex than the above is also markedly influenced by maturation and nonexperimental training. Hicks (1930a) found that 8 weeks of throwing at a moving target yielded no greater gains than were produced in the control group by "structural growth and general practice which had a direct bearing on the specific skill." The children had an age range of 2½ to 6½ years. In a further report concerning such skills as tracing between two lines and making perforations, Hicks (1930b) obtained similar results. Hicks and Ralph (1931) found that children ranging in age from 24 to 40 months thread the Porteus diamond maze as well without training as they do after 7 weeks of training. The trained and untrained groups began the experiment with a score of 23 points. Two trials per week for 7 weeks yielded the following successive average scores: 27.2, 24.4, 27.9, 26.2, 27.7, 29.7, 29.4. Tests at the eighth week yielded an average score of 31.8 for the trained group. The group which had received no training since the initial tests

made an average score of 32.1. Hence the improvement of the trained group was matched by that of the untrained group. Maturation, and perhaps to a certain degree nonexperimental training, produced as much improvement in skill as did specific training.

Mattson's (1933) investigation with a rolling-ball maze yielded results somewhat like the above when the maze pattern was simple. With more complicated patterns, however, the trained group gave a significantly better performance than the untrained, and the advantage possessed by the trained group increased as the complexity of the maze pattern increased. Since Mattson's is the most thorough investigation of the relative influence of maturation and specific practice in acquisition of a complex skill, we shall consider it in some detail.

The maze patterns used by Mattson are illustrated in Figure 6. Instruction in how to manipulate the maze—that is, press it down in various directions upon its supports so as to make the ball roll in different directions—was given each child at the beginning of the experiment. The goal was then shown and the experimenter said:

This is the house where the marble lives, and this is where we put it [putting the ball at the starting point of the labyrinth]. Do you think you can find the path right down to the little house? Press very hard every time so that the bell rings, and if the gate is shut, and the marble can't go any farther, try another way. Now begin.

The subjects were 24 boys and 26 girls ranging in age from 58 to 72 months. Their average age was 64.7 months and average IQ, 103.4. Practice and control groups were matched for age, sex, IQ, and maze scores for the initial four days of training. Training was given on all three patterns each day. The order of presentation

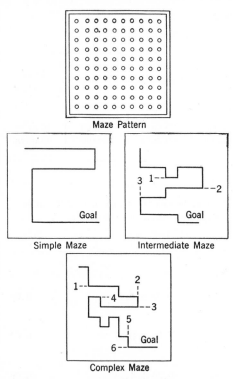

Maze Pattern

Simple Maze   Intermediate Maze

Complex Maze

FIGURE 6. Three maze patterns used to investigate the influence of maturation and learning in acquisition of a complex skill. (From "The Relation between the Complexity of the Habit to Be Acquired and the Form of the Learning Curve in Young Children," by M. L. Mattson. *Genetic Psychology Monographs*, 1933, **13**, 332. By permission of The Journal Press, publisher.)

The top view illustrates the rows of screws which made an invisible pathway, through which the ball rolled as the maze was tilted in different directions. Small gates placed at appropriate positions blocked further progress of the ball in certain directions. These gates were placed so that the ball could reach the exit only by rolling along the paths indicated in the remaining diagrams, which show the three degrees of complexity involved.

was such that, in 9 daily trials, each pattern came once as first, once as second, and once as third. Distribution of practice for the two groups is indicated in Table 1.

The two groups, it will be observed from the table, differed only in that the practice group had 26 more days of tests than the control group.

Progress was measured in time and errors. The means, differences, and reliability of the differences for the two groups on each of the mazes are given in Tables 2 and 3. From the data in these tables it is apparent that, although the practice and control groups began the experiment with approximately equal performances, the subjects who had 26 days of additional practice manifested superior performances on each of the three mazes. This was true in the test at the end of training and also in the retest given 60 days later. It held true for both time and error scores. All these differences except those for time scores on the simple maze in the test period and on the two simpler mazes in the retest were statistically reliable. It is also clearly apparent from the data summarized in Tables 2 and 3 that the advantage of the trained group over the untrained was greater as the complexity of the task increased. A study of relative differences based upon ratios of gain and percentages of gain or loss supported the above conclusions.

This study suggests that earlier investigations in which there was as much gain from maturation and possibly general practice as from specific practice derived their result from the simplicity of the tasks involved. Comparison of learning curves from these studies with those of Mattson for the two complex mazes shows relatively little gain even in the practice groups. One might conclude that, when large gains are made by the practice group, the group left to depend upon maturation will be shown to suffer a disadvantage in later tests.

Learning of Sensorimotor Skills as a Function of Age. Investigations of the

TABLE 1

Distribution of Practice for Subjects

Group	Initial	Practice	Test	Forgetting	Retest	Total Practice
Experimental	4 days	26 days	8 days	60 days	8 days	46 days
Control	4 days	none	8 days	60 days	8 days	20 days

TABLE 2

Means and Differences of Time Scores for Experimental and Control Groups

Pattern	Mean	Difference	$D/\sigma_{diff.}$
	Initial		
Pattern I			
Experimental	17.83 ± 2.17	0.02 ± 0.72	0.03
Control	17.81 ± 2.90		
Pattern II			
Experimental	47.08 ± 8.70	1.52 ± 2.27	0.67
Control	48.60 ± 7.30		
Pattern III			
Experimental	84.98 ± 14.24	0.36 ± 4.11	0.09
Control	85.34 ± 14.78		
	Test		
Pattern I			
Experimental	10.84 ± 0.62	2.71 ± 0.40	6.73
Control	13.55 ± 5.12		
Pattern II			
Experimental	18.82 ± 2.85	15.00 ± 1.17	12.80
Control	33.82 ± 5.12		
Pattern III			
Experimental	30.86 ± 6.16	32.94 ± 0.30	14.34
Control	63.80 ± 9.70		
	Retest		
Pattern I			
Experimental	11.07 ± 0.71	1.37 ± 0.37	3.73
Control	12.44 ± 1.56		
Pattern II			
Experimental	20.18 ± 7.55	7.09 ± 1.29	5.51
Control	27.27 ± 5.08		
Pattern III			
Experimental	34.00 ± 7.55	20.68 ± 3.08	6.71
Control	54.68 ± 12.32		

TABLE 3

MEANS AND DIFFERENCES OF ERROR SCORES FOR EXPERIMENTAL AND CONTROL GROUPS

Pattern	Mean	Difference	$D/\sigma_{\text{diff.}}$
	Initial		
Pattern I			
Experimental	2.43 ± 1.47	0.63 ± 0.355	1.78
Control	1.80 ± 1.01		
Pattern II			
Experimental	10.90 ± 3.48	0.01 ± 0.804	0.01
Control	10.89 ± 2.03		
Pattern III			
Experimental	21.15 ± 5.35	2.30 ± 1.247	1.84
Control	18.85 ± 3.12		
	Test		
Pattern I			
Experimental	0.29 ± 0.16	0.19 ± 0.07	2.65
Control	0.48 ± 0.30		
Pattern II			
Experimental	3.14 ± 1.51	4.80 ± 0.584	8.21
Control	7.93 ± 2.50		
Pattern III			
Experimental	7.54 ± 3.04	10.21 ± 1.008	10.13
Control	1.7.74 ± 4.02		
	Retest		
Pattern I			
Experimental	0.37 ± 0.28	0.06 ± 0.096	0.67
Control	0.44 ± 0.36		
Pattern II			
Experimental	3.89 ± 1.96	1.11 ± 0.698	1.60
Control	5.00 ± 2.62		
Pattern III			
Experimental	9.55 ± 3.04	5.82 ± 1.38	4.27
Control	15.36 ± 5.71		

relative influence of maturation and learning in acquisition of motor skills have demonstrated that *at early age levels and for skills that are simple or which show little short-time improvement from either maturation or practice,* the effect of increasing maturation is to make given amounts of practice increasingly effective.

When skills as complicated as manipulating Mattson's mazes II and III are concerned, little if any improvement occurs in the absence of practice. Would older children, however, learn such skills more readily than younger ones? One might expect an affirmative answer for two reasons. In the first place, it seems reasonable to suppose that the older child, having a sensory, neural, and muscular system of greater maturity, should profit more from given amounts of practice than a younger child.

In the second place, the older child has a wider previous experience upon which to draw in acquiring new skills and this might be expected to give him an advantage over the younger child.

Since previous experience is a variable and an uncontrollable factor when human beings are concerned, students of the age effect in learning would do well to eliminate the differential effect of experience as much as possible. This was accomplished in Stone's (1929–1930) experiments by using rats which were reared in a relatively constant environment prior to the tests. If human subjects are used, experiential advantages of the older individual can be reduced to a minimum only by studying the acquisition of skills far removed from those of everyday life. Certain maze problems call for approximately such skills.

The most comprehensive and thorough investigation of the age function in maze learning by children is McGinnis's (1929). Young's (1922) slot maze was used. Each child was required to push a stylus in the form of a shoe along a grooved pathway until the figure of a boy was reached. The subject was instructed to "take the shoe to the boy" as quickly as possible. There were 20 children, 10 boys and 10 girls, in each of three age groups. The average ages were approximately 3, 4, and 5 years. Average IQ's were, respectively, 107.9, 117.5, and 103.8. Each child was given 5 trials daily 5 days per week until a total of 50 trials had been completed. Learning curves based upon median time and error scores are shown in Figure 7. One will observe that the median time and error scores for the first 5 trials decreased with age. Final levels of performance, however, were similar. The average number of errors for successive age groups beginning with the youngest was: 153.7 ± 19.7, 108.9 ± 10.5, and 78.6 ± 16.4. The difference of 75.1 between average error scores

of the 3- and 5-year groups alone approximated statistical reliability, its critical ratio being 2.9. The average time in seconds for successively older groups was: 2071.2 ± 68.7, 1954.3 ± 51.8, and 1211.4 ± 38.8. Differences between the time scores of the groups showed the older to be superior. However, only the differences between the 4- and 5-year and 3- and 5-year groups were statistically reliable.

Despite better maze performance of the successively older groups, *learning during the course of the experiment* was similar regardless of age. McGinnis (1929) calculated the differences in time between the initial and final trials for each of the groups. The percentage of gain was similar (91 to 93) for each age group. When averages for the first five trials were compared with those for the last five, the percentage gain was slightly greater for the 3- and 4-year groups (85) than for the 5-year group (75). Analysis of initial and final error scores shows that the *younger* the group the greater the absolute gains.

The older groups, since they began the maze performance at a greater level of efficiency than the younger, were initially closer to their physiological limit in time and closer to perfection in terms of error scores. It is quite possible, therefore, that the actual degree of improvement is not shown by data indicating gain in final over initial scores.

Another approach to this problem is through analysis of changes in variability. Coefficients of variation were larger for the initial than for the last trial, suggesting that intragroup individual differences had been decreased by training. The decrease was greatest for the oldest and least for the youngest group. This suggests that practice reduced the variability of the oldest more than it reduced the variability of the youngest group. Apart from this suggestion, there is no clear evidence of

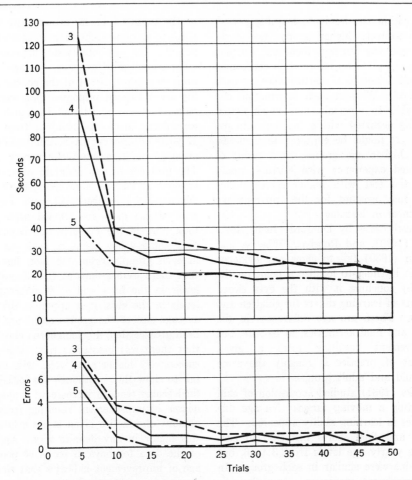

FIGURE 7. Learning curves for time and errors for three age groups. (From "The Acquisition and Interference of Motor-Habits in Young Children," by E. McGinnis. *Genetic Psychology Monographs,* 1929, **6,** 241, 244. By permission of the publisher.)

differential *learning ability* at the three age levels studied.

Other investigations of maze learning at different age levels have been performed by Hicks and Carr (1912), Gould and Perrin (1916), Wieg (1932), and Wenger (1933). Analysis of the results of these investigations fails to reveal any consistent evidence of age changes in maze-learning ability.

Studies of the effect of age on acquisition of skills other than maze performance also yield results which are either negative or equivocal. Clinton's (1930) study of mirror drawing at yearly age levels from 6 to 17 shows that the average number of lines drawn within a 5-minute learning period increases from 4.7 at 6 years to 30.8 at 17 years for boys and from 2.9 at 6 years to 38.6 at 17 years for girls. On the surface it would appear that there is greater adaptation to the mirror distortion, within the 5-minute learning period, at successively higher yearly age levels. Although the author mentions learning curves, he gives no information concerning the initial and final performance at each age level. Without such information one is unable to ascertain how much actual learning occurred within the 5-minute periods. It might be expected that successively higher age groups, as a result of increased experience with mirrors, would start the test with higher scores. This alone may account for the apparent age differences in learning.

Investigations by Dunford (1930), Renshaw (1930), and Renshaw, Wherry, and Newlin (1930) fail to show any evidence that in learning to localize a point on the skin by touching it with the eyes closed the rate of learning differs for children and adults. There are age differences in the initial and final accuracies, to be sure, but improvement resulting from a given amount of practice is roughly the same for child and adult groups.

Hicks (1931) studied acquisition of skill in hitting a moving target. No age differences in learning ability appeared. The initial and final scores increased in successive yearly age levels from 3 to 6, but the gains were similar in each group. In this experiment, moreover, a control group to test the influence of maturation gained as much as the trained group.

The only remaining experiments on the influence of age in learning of motor skills by children are those of Eigler (1932) and Langhorne (1933). Eigler studied the problem of learning to synchronize a finger reaction with a recurring flash of light. Twenty-two children between 2 and 6 years and 20 adults were subjects. Age differences in favor of the older groups are suggested. It is apparent, however, that there were differences in the motivation and in the fundamental coordinating ability

of the groups. These, rather than differences in learning ability *per se*, could easily account for the observed differences in adaptation. For example, younger children were more afraid of the shocks given for asynchronized responses than were the older children and adults. In Langhorne's experiment groups of children from 7 to 17 years of age were given training in operation of the Renshaw-Weiss pursuitmeter. The problem was to maintain contact between a stylus and a revolving lever arm. Seventy-eight subjects, 45 boys and 33 girls, whose data are treated separately, took part in the experiment. Langhorne does not say how many of each sex were in each group. From the fact, however, that there were groups at 10 different age levels in the boys and at 9 different age levels in the girls, it is apparent that the average size of the groups could not have been greater than 4. Langhorne concludes that there was greater learning ability at successively higher age levels. His results fail to show this. Although the initial and final scores tend to increase with age, the degree of improvement resulting from the amount of practice given is not related to this factor in any definite way. Analysis of the data for boys in terms of percentage of improvement indicates that the age groups from 14 to 17 have higher percentages of gain than the lower age groups. Below 14, however, there is no consistent variation with age. Even less evidence of improved learning ability with age was found in the female groups. In any event, such data are meaningless unless the size of the groups is such as to warrant comparisons.

One is forced to conclude that, if the learning of such motor skills as have so far been studied improves with age, the results fail to show clear evidence of it. Although children of increasing age usually evidence an increasingly high initial level of performance, which may be accounted for on the basis of greater maturity, greater experience, or both, the gross amount and percentage of improvement resulting from given amounts of practice do not appear to change in any consistent way as a function of age. It may be said, of course, that since the older children begin with a higher level of performance (closer to the upper limit) than younger ones, the actual relative accomplishment within the same range of practice is not measured by gross gains. McGinnis (1929) reported decreasing intragroup variability as a function of given amounts of practice at successively higher age levels. This may be an index of the relative gains from training if the groups are sufficiently large to warrant use of the statistical procedures involved. As one will recall, however, the largest single age group comprised only 20 children.

Sex Differences in Learning of Sensorimotor Skills. Several problems discussed in the preceding section have been used to investigate the influence of sex on learning of sensorimotor skills. In reporting standardization data on his slot maze, Young (1922) mentioned that girls have greater difficulty than boys in completing two trials within the time limit of 5 minutes each. Easby-Grave (1924), using the same test with 6-year-old children, 256 boys and 244 girls, found that of those who failed to complete both tests, 75 per cent were girls. Since only two trials were given, these studies are measures more of initial ability than of learning. The previously mentioned investigation of McGinnis (1929), in which 30 boys and 30 girls were used, showed the same sort of initial advantage for boys as was found in the above studies with the Young slot maze. With continued training, however, this difference disappeared and the girls' final performance approximated that of the boys. In terms of gross improvement as a result of a given amount of training, the girls were thus ahead. We have already mentioned the dubious nature of such comparisons.

Wieg (1932) found no difference between the performances of boys and girls in learning her grooved finger and toe mazes. Using a maze through which the subjects walked, Batalla (1936) investigated the learning ability of 58 boys and 50 girls having an average age of approximately 12 years. Boys began the problem with better scores than the girls and their final performance was still superior, although the gross difference became increasingly smaller as a function of practice. Batalla says that girls required more trials than boys to satisfy the criterion of learning, but he reports no figures to support this observation. The problem is said to be more interesting to boys than to girls, hence there existed a difference in motivation which may have influenced learning.

Mattson (1933), whose study has already received some consideration in this chapter, reports data concerning sex differences in maze performance. Sex comparisons are somewhat questionable due to the fact that there were only 12 to 13 children of each sex on each of the three mazes. Mattson believes, however, that if sex differences in maze learning existed she should have found at least some suggestion of their presence. The learning curves for time and errors are shown in Figure 8. They are almost identical for the two sexes.

Investigations of other motor skills also reveal little or no evidence of a sex difference in learning *per se*. Hicks (1931) found that, in throwing balls at a moving target, the average initial score of 13 boys was 14, whereas that of 17 girls was 9.9. The average final score for boys was 14.6 and that for girls, 12.9. On the basis of such

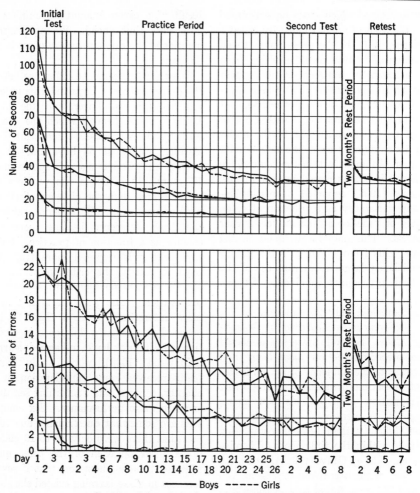

FIGURE 8. Learning curves for time and errors for boys and girls who learned rolling ball mazes of three degrees of complexity. (From "The Relation between the Complexity of the Habit to Be Acquired and the Form of the Learning Curve in Young Children," by M. L. Mattson. *Genetic Psychology Monographs,* 1933, **13**, 369. By permission of the publisher.)

For a description of the problem, see page 382 of the present discussion.

data, one might conclude that girls had learned more than boys as a result of an equal amount of practice. Such a conclusion, however, can hardly be justified when it is recalled that so few subjects are involved, that little learning is evident in either group, and that an untrained con-

trol group to measure maturational effects improves as much as trained children.

Clinton's (1930) investigation of mirror drawing demonstrated that, although girls make poorer scores than boys at lower age levels, at higher age levels the girls surpass the boys. Learning curves are reported to be more regular for girls than for boys, but they or the data on which they are based do not appear in the article. In her motor-coordination study, Eigler (1932) found no evidence for a difference in favor of either sex. Langhorne (1933) found no consistent sex difference in his investigation with the Renshaw-Weiss polygraph. At the lower age levels the initial scores of the girls were poorer than those of the boys. At higher age levels, however, there was no difference. The validity of comparisons at any age level in this investigation is, as mentioned earlier, very doubtful because of the smallness of the groups.

Perl (1933) found no significant sex difference in the learning of a simple motor skill, which comprised making small gates (ⲘⲎⲮ) as fast as possible. Good learning curves were obtained for 20 one-minute periods of practice. The learning curves for 46 fourth-grade boys and 53 fourth-grade girls of approximately the same IQ were similar in shape and, where they did not overlap, were quite close together. Both raw and T scores yielded similar curves. A slight apparent superiority of the boys was unreliable statistically.

On the basis of these investigations one must conclude that a differential influence of sex in the learning of simple motor skills such as those investigated has not been disclosed. Although the initial scores of boys have in several studies been higher than for girls, perhaps as a result of previous differences in experience, the gross amount of progress resulting from given amounts of training has been similar for both sexes.

Learning of Sensorimotor Skills as a Function of Intelligence. Investigations of the relation between intelligence test performance and learning of sensorimotor skills in young children agree in forcing the conclusion that, at early ages at least, there

is no significant correlation.[1] One study with adolescents has yielded results not in agreement with those at early and later age levels, hence we shall discuss this last.

McGinnis (1929), training children between 3 and 5 years of age on a stylus maze, found rank-order correlations ranging from $-.280 \pm .291$ to $.600 \pm .202$ between IQ and total time scores. Correlations between IQ and total errors ranged from $.100 \pm .221$ to $.660 \pm .178$. Owing to their large probable errors, few of the correlations for the different groups of subjects can be regarded as reliable. Initial scores and IQ also yielded insignificant correlations. McGinnis concluded that maze performance is not "related very highly to the function which is measured by scores on an intelligence test."

Performance on Mattson's (1933) rolling-ball mazes (see page 383) by children averaging 65 months was likewise unrelated to intelligence test performance. Mean time for 38 days of training yielded correlations with IQ of $-.66 \pm .28$ to $-.28 \pm .12$. Mean errors for the 38 days of training gave correlations with IQ of $-.04 \pm .09$ to $-.06 \pm 09$.

Learning by young children of sensorimotor skills other than maze performance also has little or no relation to intelligence test scores. Goodenough and Brian (1929) trained children in their fourth year to toss quoits over a ring. Rank-order correlation of the number of ringers with results on a battery of intelligence tests was $-.349$. The PE is not reported, but the authors say that this correlation is probably without significance. Hicks (1930a)

[1] Ruch (1925) presents data for card sorting which indicate a small correlation between intelligence and learning. The correlation decreased in successive practice periods. Correlations between time to sort 100 cards and MA (with CA partialed out) went from $.329 \pm .083$ on the first trial to $.107 \pm .092$ on the fifth. Fifty-two seventh- to ninth-grade children were subjects.

found a correlation of only .05 between performance in throwing at a moving target and mental age, with CA held constant. The age of the subjects was between 2½ and 6½ years.

Another skill the learning of which has been studied in relation to intelligence is mirror drawing. Wilson (1928) gave 20 boys 20 trials each on a six-pointed star. The ages ran from 8½ to 12¾ years. IQ's ranged from 76 to 148. Separate learning curves were constructed for each boy. These curves indicate no differential influence of intelligence in the acquiring of this skill.

Against all these results suggesting no relation between learning of motor skills and intelligence test scores must be placed data obtained by Knotts and Miles (1929). Two mazes of the Warden multiple-U pattern, one stylus and one raised, were learned by groups of blind and seeing adolescents. For both groups and both mazes, time scores yielded small and unreliable correlations with MA. Insignificant correlations between trials and errors and MA were found on the stylus maze for *blind* and on the raised finger maze for seeing subjects. However, the correlations between MA and, respectively, trials and errors were $-.75 \pm .07$ and $-.75 \pm .07$ for *seeing* subjects on the stylus maze. Data for blind subjects learning the raised finger maze yielded correlations almost as large as these, the correlations being $-.61 \pm .09$ and $-.62 \pm .09$. All four correlations are statistically significant. They therefore suggest that the more intelligent the individual the fewer the trials and errors likely to be involved in mastery of the respective mazes.

The above-mentioned studies force upon us the conclusion that, as far as young children are concerned, learning to thread mazes, to hit a moving target, to throw quoits over a peg, and to overcome effects of mirror distortion in drawing star patterns is unrelated to scores on intelligence tests. The experiment with adolescents is out of line with these findings for younger children and with findings obtained on similar problems with adults. The reason for this discrepancy is not apparent.

Incentives and the Learning of Sensorimotor Skills. Investigations of learning in animals and human adults have shown that the efficiency with which problems are mastered, and in some cases whether or not they are mastered at all, is a function of incentives. Similar investigations on learning in children have been few. Studies by Chapman and Feder (1917) on addition, cancellation, and substitution, Hurlock (1924) on intelligence test performance, Flügel (1928) on addition, Chase (1932) and Anderson and Smith (1933) on squeezing a dynamometer, and Mast (1937) on time required to open a box, although they deal with other factors than learning of motor skills *per se,* show that special incentives such as material rewards, praise, and reproof lead children to increase their effort in the performance of a task.[1]

Abel (1936) has reported the only thorough investigation of the rôle of motivation in learning of a sensorimotor skill by children. She used a raised finger maze of the pattern shown in Figure 9. The subjects were 100 boys between the ages of 9 and 10 years. Their IQ's ranged from 100 to 129. Each child was shown how to proceed from the entrance to the exit of a simple maze by running his index finger along the raised pathway. The subjects were separated into five groups equivalent in CA and MA. They were given thirty trials at a single sitting. Group I received no reward other than that which might be inherent in the situation. The members

[1] For comprehensive reviews of the rôle of incentives in child behavior, see Hurlock (1931) and Abel (1936).

of Group II received a material reward, a penny, at the end of each trial. A verbal reward, "Good," "Very good," and "Let me see if you can make even fewer mistakes

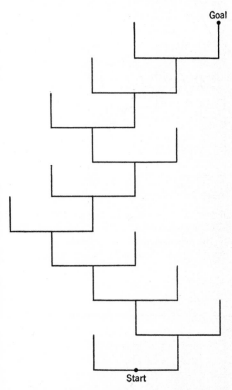

Goal

Start

FIGURE 9. The Warden U maze which was used to investigate the influence of different incentives. (From "The Effects of Shift in Motivation upon the Learning of a Sensorimotor Task," by L. B. Abel. *Archives of Psychology*, 1936, **29**, 16. By permission of the publisher.)

this time," was given Group III. Group IV received no special reward for the first fifteen trials. Beginning with the sixteenth trial, however, each child was given a penny per trial. Members of Group V received the above-mentioned verbal reward until the sixteenth trial, at which time the material reward was substituted. Abel's

aim in adding and in changing incentives at the middle of the training period was to determine whether children, like the rats tested by Tolman (1932) and his students, would show a sharp change in performance following introduction of the different incentives.

As the error curves in Figure 10 indicate, Groups I to III improved. However, the group with no special reward showed least, and, that with the material reward most improvement. In Figure 11 are represented data for the two change-of-incentive groups (IV and V). One will observe that introduction of a different incentive beginning with the sixteenth trial led to no obvious change in the rate of learning such as was found in experiments of a somewhat comparable nature with rats. Comparison of the mean number of errors in the first fifteen as compared with the last fifteen trials, however, suggests an increased rate of learning subsequent to the change. When equations for the curves before and after the change were determined and the slope lines compared, it was also apparent that introduction of new incentives had effected a greater rate of learning.

In order to determine whether the change in mean errors and in slope was greater than could be expected in terms of sampling errors, Abel used a method suggested by Fisher (1930, pp. 75–139). She determined the $P/2$ of the differences in the respective means and slopes. Since fifteen trials were involved, a $P/2$ of 0.05 or less would indicate a reliable difference. The $P/2$ of the difference between the means of the first and second halves of both the curves in Figure 11 was 0.00. Change from a verbal to a material reward yielded a $P/2$ of 0.00 for the difference between the respective slopes. However, the two slopes for, respectively, no reward and material reward had a $P/2$ for the

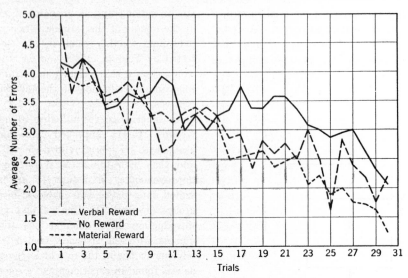

FIGURE 10. Learning curves for children provided with different incentives. (From "The Effects of Shift in Motivation upon the Learning of a Sensori-motor Task," by L. B. Abel. *Archives of Psychology*, 1936, **29**, 22, 23. By permission of the publisher.)

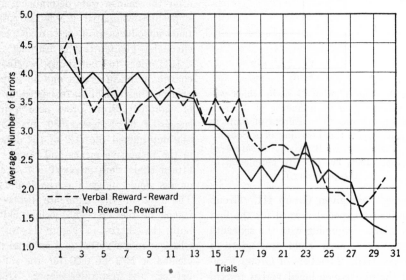

FIGURE 11. The effect of changing incentives. (From "The Effects of Shift in Motivation upon the Learning of a Sensori-motor Task," by L. B. Abel. *Archives of Psychology*, 1936, **29**, 23, 24. By permission of the publisher.)

difference in slope of 0.39, suggesting un-reliability of this difference.

Another method of analyzing the data was to compare the final levels of per-formance in terms of the mean number of errors in the last five trials. The means were: *no reward–reward*, 1.675; *material reward*, 1.675; *verbal reward–material re-ward*, 1.875; *verbal reward*, 2.325; and *no reward*, 2.625. The differences between the first and third and second and third means are not statistically reliable. The difference between the *verbal and material reward* groups, however, has a critical ratio $(D/\sigma_{diff.})$ of 3.110, indicating that there are approximately 100 chances in 100 of a difference greater than zero. The differ-ence between the means for the *verbal re-ward* and *no reward–reward* groups is equally reliable. There are, however, only 99.7 chances out of 100 that the difference in the means of the *verbal reward* and *verbal reward–material reward* groups is also greater than zero. One must conclude, therefore, that *material reward, no reward–reward,* and *verbal reward–material reward* are of approximately equal value as in-centives to learning the present maze and that their incentive value is greater than a *verbal reward* or *no special reward*. The latter condition, although it produced learning, was least effective.

Abel points out that it makes no signifi-cant difference whether a material reward is given throughout learning or whether it is given only in the last fifteen trials. In other words, 15 pennies in the last half of training elicited as much in terms of final achievement as 30 pennies, one per trial throughout training. She also sug-gests that a verbal reward, while stimulat-ing for the first ten trials or so, gradually loses effectiveness.

In a second experiment with the same maze and following the same method of scoring and analysis, but involving chil-dren with lower than average IQ's, Abel determined the effect of giving rewards *only when a certain amount of progress had been achieved*. Whereas the children of the experiment described above received a reward at the end of each trial, regard-less of whether or not they had progressed, those of the present experiment were prom-ised the rewards for improvement and were given them only when they improved. Five groups paralleled those of the ex-periment discussed above. There was, however, an additional group (maximum material reward), the members of which were promised a quarter for every trial without an error. Few of them received the reward; nevertheless, this group mani-fested more improvement than any other group in either experiment. The differ-ence, however, is clearly apparent only in the last five trials, when the curve, which has continually crossed the others, shows a precipitous drop.

Despite the lower intelligence of the children and the changed nature of the incentives, the results for the other five groups of the second experiment did not differ greatly from those of the first experi-ment. The only statistically significant difference between the results of the two experiments was for the *material reward* group. The average number of errors in the last five trials for this group in the first experiment was 1.675; in the second experiment it was 2.260. The difference is 3.4 times its standard error. Abel con-cludes, therefore, that "The effect of re-ward dependent upon improvement with a group of average intelligence does not seem to be as great as that of reward, admin-istered at every trial, with a group of superior intelligence" (p. 50).

An interesting outcome of the present experiments is Abel's failure to find clear evidence of the so-called *latent* learning disclosed in experiments with rats. The unrewarded rats, it will be recalled, failed to show consistent signs of learning before being given a special incentive, such as food or water. When the incentive was introduced there was an extremely rapid drop in the learning curves. This was interpreted as application of learning which had been taking place, but which had not been utilized before an incentive was introduced. As far as children are concerned, learning of the above sensorimotor skill despite the absence of special incentives may be attributed to inherent interest of the task, to desire to finish the experiment and get out to play, to desire to please the experimenter, or perhaps to competitive factors such as desire of the subject to better his own performance or to do as well as or better than others. The fact that children evidenced so much learning without presence of material or verbal rewards perhaps also explains the absence of a precipitous drop in the learning curves after the introduction of these special incentives. In any event, the rats were hungry or thirsty, and such factors are undoubtedly of much greater motivating value than the relatively artificial incentives which can be offered children.

Learning of Sensorimotor Skills as a Function of the Training Procedure. Many skills which depend upon specific training for their acquisition will develop regardless of the precise method of training adopted. It is obvious, however, that some methods of training may be more effective than others. We have already indicated that training which involves certain incentives is more effective than that which involves others. In the present section we are interested in the relative efficacy of different training procedures used under constant conditions of motivation. For example, given a certain motivation, does more or less improvement result when the skill to be acquired is demonstrated frequently?

What advantages, if any, will accrue if the child is given manual guidance in the task to be performed? Does faster learning or a higher level of achievement result when the correct procedure is enforced from the start, or is it better to allow the child, by random trial and error, to find the correct procedure for himself?

Gates and Taylor (1923) have made one approach to this problem. These investigators were interested in determining whether motor control in writing is facilitated by "putting the child through" the various movements to be made. One group, consisting of 21 kindergarten children, was given an opportunity to learn to write the letters *a b c d e* by tracing them through tissue paper.[1] A group of comparable age, motor ability, and intelligence, but consisting of only 14 children, *copied* the letters throughout the learning period. This group was thus free to make many mistakes which the tracing group would not be very likely to make. Five minutes of daily practice for 5 days were given the *tracing* group. In terms of the number of strokes required to write each letter, the mean scores on the 5 successive days were 11.4, 20.6, 20.8, 24.2, and 29.8. In a 5-minute *copying* test, given on the sixth day, the mean score for this group was 8.2. During the 5 days of training in *copying* the same letters freehand, the other group gained in their mean score as follows: 3.7, 7.2, 13.5, 17.6, and 19.5. On the sixth day their copying score was 21.1. In other words, the copying skill of this group, a skill which approximates that called for in everyday life, and which is the aim of training, was more than twice as good as that of the group which was,

[1] This is comparable to the "putting-through" technique used by Carr and his students with white rats. The procedure was not effective as a training technique with rats. See Munn (1933, pp. 342–343) for a brief review of these studies.

as it were, put through the appropriate movement with little chance of making errors.

In further training with the letters *e–g* and, later, with the letters *f–j*, both groups continued to improve. When called upon to *copy* letters that they had neither traced nor copied before, both groups had low scores. The mean score of the *tracing* group, however, was only 0.77, as compared with 4.6 for the *copying* group. Thus the transfer value was also greater for the copying than for the tracing procedure.

Melcher's (1934) investigation of stylus maze learning in preschool children who were given visual, manual, and visual and manual guidance indicated that very little learning occurs with such guidance. The learning which did appear may be attributed to the test trials (two out of every six guided trials), during which the children were free to learn by trial and error.

On the basis of the above investigations and those with rats and human adults, one must conclude that more rapid learning of such motor skills as writing and threading a stylus maze occurs when the individual is free to initiate his own movements and to make incorrect as well as correct responses than when he is manually guided in the correct performance.

Goodenough and Brian (1929) determined the relative efficacy of different kinds and amounts of *verbal guidance* upon the learning by 4-year-old children of a ring-toss skill. Although two of the three groups were very small and no statistical analysis of differences is therefore warranted, marked differences in the effectiveness of the methods are clearly suggested. All children, regardless of verbal guidance or its absence, were similarly motivated. They were given praise and encouragement for "ringers" and **also received** stickers,

which changed in nature from day to day, to paste on the wall.

Group A, consisting of 4 boys and 6 girls, was given the following instructions:

> This is a game where we try to throw rings over a post. You stand here on this base—be sure both of your feet are in the base all the time—and I'll hand you the rings. Try to throw them on the post over there. Do you see what I mean? All right, go ahead.

No criticism or verbal guidance was given this group.

Group B, comprising 2 boys and 4 girls, was shown how to throw the ring and was given critical verbal guidance throughout the experiment. The initial instructions were like those for the above group except that the experimenter said, "I'll show you how it is done," and then demonstrated. Whenever the child failed to get a "ringer" the experimenter pointed out the source of error, saying, for example, "Not quite so far next time," "A little bit higher so it won't hit the post," etc. These children were also told to hold the ring at the point of juncture of the rope so as to insure better balance. Each chose his own general procedure, some throwing overhand and others underhand, some throwing the ring down onto the peg and some squatting and throwing it up. Within this group the method was changed by the child from time to time, often without adequate test of a given procedure.

Group C, consisting of 2 boys and 2 girls, was required to adhere to a constant method of holding and throwing the ring. Members of this group were instructed to grasp the ring at the point of juncture, to hold it horizontally before them, and, after swinging it a few times, to pitch it forward and upward toward the post. Furthermore, they were given verbal guidance which matched that of Group B.

Twenty trials per day for 50 days were given each child. Scoring was in terms of the number of "ringers" in each 20 tosses. Two children in Group A and one in Group B failed to gain. All other children manifested absolute gains ranging from 4 to 56 in Group A, 5 to 47 in Group B, and 21 to 70 in Group C. The corresponding percentage gains ranged from 5 to 287, 24 to 147, and 53 to 175. The median gains for Groups A to C, respectively, were 11.5, or 36 per cent; 17.5, or 66 per cent; and 42.5, or 92 per cent. Until the thirtieth day of the experiment, learning curves overlapped considerably. The highest curve was that of Group C, the next that of Group A, and the lowest that of Group B. If the groups were not so small, we should be justified in concluding that, for this game and for children of this age and intelligence, the best procedure is to enforce from the start a given effective method and to combine this with verbal guidance. In terms of the percentage of gain, if not on the basis of the latter part of the learning curves, we might also be justified in concluding that verbal guidance, even without a standardized throwing procedure, is more effective than leaving the child entirely to his own resources. As the situation stands, however, what might have been a very significant experimental test of the efficacy of verbal guidance is ruined by the fact that groups are too small to warrant any definite conclusions concerning this aspect of the investigation.

In good learners there was a marked tendency for successes to be grouped. This suggests that these children continued to use those responses which they observed to be associated with success. Poor learners showed little evidence of such observation and application. Errors immediately following success were usually due to throws beyond the post. Analysis of individual learning data indicated the following factors to be significant in determining success or failure: overconfidence and undue caution; setting-up of stereotyped undesirable reactions; false association of cause and effect; peculiar associations of meaning with verbal expressions, as when "trying hard" was assumed to be synonymous with "throwing with great violence"; incorrect focusing of attention, such as looking at arm instead of goal; and random changes in procedure.

Another approach to this problem is Cox's (1933). Thirty-eight boys from the two upper classes of an English elementary school practiced assembling, wiring, and stripping an electric-lamp holder. They were merely told to repeat the operations at top speed until each day's series had been completed. Time required to perform the operations was recorded. Under these conditions no significantly greater progress occurred than was exhibited by a control group of 32 boys given only initial and final tests. Similar results were obtained with adult subjects trained by this technique. In a further investigation with experimental and control groups of adults, initial tests on assembling and stripping were followed, in the experimental group, by 11 days of special instruction and performance of supervised exercises. Under these conditions the experimental group made gains significantly greater than did the control group. The author points out that much more rapid and efficient learning of such operations occurs when, rather than being left to their own resources, individuals are given special exercises and verbal guidance. Undoubtedly the effectiveness of such training would differ for different skills and for individuals of different levels of maturity.

Transfer of Motor Skill.[1] We have already mentioned the fact that Gates and Taylor (1923) found greater transfer from copying the letters *a–e* to copying the letters *f–j* than when the letters *a–e* were merely traced. Since we do not know what success entirely untrained children would have in copying the letters *f–j* under identical conditions, it is impossible to determine the actual transfer in the two cases. McGinnis (1929) investigated transfer in maze performance. The maze was of the stylus type (McGinnis, 1928), apparently with open alleys. Invisible stops placed at appropriate points limited the movements of the stylus. Four patterns, the paths of which covered the same distance but went in different directions, were used. Since the patterns were not of equal difficulty, scores were equated in terms of their relative difficulty. Four groups, each of which consisted of six 4-year-old children equated in intelligence, received training on the maze patterns in the order AB, BA, ABCD, BADC, respectively. Scoring was in terms of time and errors for 40 trials, in the case of the first two groups, and 50 trials in the case of the others. Positive transfer occurred in every group regardless of the fact that some patterns,

[1] Judd's (1908) study of transfer involved dart throwing, but transfer comprised application of principles to motor skill rather than transfer of skill *per se.* One group of fifth- and sixth-grade boys received instruction in principles of refraction while another, comparable, group received no such instruction. Both groups were then required to hit a target placed 12 inches under water. They were equally successful. Thus knowledge of principles failed to aid the instructed group. When the target was shifted to 4 inches of water, however, boys with a knowledge of the principles of refraction made a much more rapid adjustment than did those without such knowledge. As the result of this and other researches, Judd came to the conclusion that "generalization" plays a large part in determining the magnitude and direction (positive or negative) of transfer when such occurs. For a further discussion of transfer, see pages 416–418.

by changes in the direction of the goal, were calculated to produce negative transfer. The percentage saved in transferring from one maze pattern to the other ranged from 12.6 to 41.8 seconds and 9.4 to 35.8 errors.

Wieg (1932) investigated bilateral transfer, using a grooved multiple-T maze through which the index finger or big toe could be run. Her aim was to measure transfer from right hand to left hand, from left hand to right hand, from left hand to left foot, from right foot to left foot, from right foot to right hand, and from left foot to left hand. Twenty-four boys and 20 girls, ranging in age from 66 to 78 months, were grouped in sets of four. These were equated in terms of IQ, CA, socioeconomic status, sex, and initial maze-learning ability. All subjects were first given 3 successive trials with each hand and each foot for 2 days. They were then divided into different groups and given 3 daily trials until they had reached a criterion of not more than 2 errors in 3 successive trials. Time and errors were the bases of comparison. There was, in most cases, a saving in speed and in errors during learning with the transfer limb. The number of cases was too small to allow determination of the reliability of transfer scores. There was, however, a suggestion of greater transfer effects going from a less efficient to a more efficient limb, as from foot to hand or from left to right hand. A greater transfer was apparent in going from the right foot to each of the other limbs than from any one of these limbs to another. A group of adults showed larger transfer scores than children. The reliability of this difference, like that between the various directions of transfer, cannot be determined; hence the results can be regarded merely as suggestive.

Significant transfer from one stylus maze pattern to another was obtained by Jones and Yoshioka (1938) in an investigation with 81 boys and 71 girls, each approximately 13½ years of age. The groups learned different patterns and used different procedures. When these differences

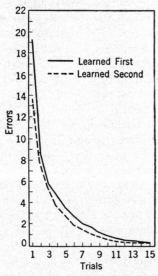

FIGURE 12. Transfer in learning of stylus mazes. (From "Differential Errors in Children's Learning on a Stylus Maze," by H. E. Jones and J. B. Yoshioka. *Journal of Comparative Psychology,* 1938, **25,** 470. By permission of the publisher, The Williams and Wilkins Co.)

were balanced, however, there were lower error scores for the learning of the second than for the learning of the first maze. In different groups the critical ratio ranged from 1.62 to 3.68.

The error curves are shown in Figure 12. One will note that there is an average advantage of 5½ errors in the initial trial with the second maze and that, although this advantage decreases considerably, the two curves remain separated until the fifteenth trial. In accounting for transfer, Jones and Yoshioka say:

Factors in this transfer probably include an increase in effort to observe and remember the results of maze exploration, although it may be pointed out that the second order shows fewer errors even on the first trial. The subject is acquainted with both his time and error record on the first test, and commonly seeks to improve his record (pp. 471–472).

The existence of transfer in this experiment is made all the more interesting when it is pointed out that all the subjects had received previous training on stylus and body mazes from time to time. Without such previous training the present transfer would probably have been greater.

In this connection one will recall Cox's experiment (1933) which was discussed earlier (page 398). Practice in assembling and stripping electric light holders did not enable a group of 38 boys to do any better in a final test than a control group given only the initial and final tests. The result was similar to that obtained with adults. Specific training, verbal instructions alone and combined with exercises designed to bring important aspects to the learner's attention, did have a transfer value for adults. No children were used under the latter conditions.[1]

[1] Transfer in the perceptual field has been studied in children by Jackson, Stonex, Lane, and Dominguez (1938), Jackson (1939), and Jackson and Dominguez (1939). The problem investigated is that of relative and absolute response in test trials following mastery of size, weight, and other discriminations. It is the transpositional problem emphasized by Gestalt psychologists. The first of this series of researches demonstrates that the amount of practice following mastery of the discrimination is an important factor in determining whether an absolute or relative response occurs in the critical transposition tests. A small amount of practice is followed by confusion, a greater amount by response on a relational basis, and a still greater amount, in some children, by response on an absolute basis. The other studies in the series are concerned with the transpositional response as a function of stimulus factors.

Memory

Most experiments in memory deal with learning, recall, recognition, or relearning of symbolic materials such as numbers, words, nonsense syllables, poems, prose passages, and figures. The chief emphasis is upon retention of the effects of previous stimulation. Retention may be measured in terms of ability to make appropriate responses in the absence of stimuli which originally elicited them (delayed reaction and reproduction), in terms of ability to differentiate old and new stimuli (recognition), or in terms of ability to relearn previous material with a saving of time and effort.

The earliest measurable evidence of a child's ability to respond in terms of absent stimuli comes from tests of the delayed-reaction type. These yield a measure of retentivity prior to the time when conventionalized symbols such as are used in most memory tests have been acquired. Hence we shall begin our discussion of memory in children by considering delayed reaction. This discussion will be followed by a summary of other researches on memory.

Delayed Reaction. The principle underlying delayed-reaction tests is that of presenting stimuli toward which differential responses are required and then removing the stimuli prior to response. In the original Carr-Hunter (Hunter, 1913) method, for instance, the animal was confronted by three compartments, only one of which was lighted in a given trial. The lighted compartment, which offered the only means of escape, varied in position from trial to trial. At first the subject had to learn that escape was possible only through the lighted compartment. The delayed-reaction tests were those in which a differential response to the compartments was required *after the light had been turned off.* The interval between removal of the external differentiating stimulus and the time of response was gradually increased until the subject could no longer remember which door had been lighted.

Instead of escaping through the lighted or previously lighted door, Hunter's child subjects pressed a button corresponding to the position of the door. Since the animals and children in this experiment first had to *learn* that the lighted door was the correct one, this has been called the *indirect* method of testing delayed reaction. The *direct* method, also first used by Hunter (1917), does not require specific training by the experimenter before delay tests are instituted. Hunter and later investigators obtained the child's attention while hiding a toy or some other desirable object in or under one of two or more devices such as boxes, plates, or cups. After an interval, they determined whether the child could locate the hidden object.

In Hunter's investigation, for example, a girl of 13 months was confronted with three similar boxes having hinged covers. A toy with which she had been playing was placed in one of the boxes. When he ascertained that the infant had seen in which box the toy was placed, Hunter disoriented her and, after given intervals, offered an opportunity to find the toy. She located the toy with a high degree of accuracy after intervals between 8 and 12 seconds. At 16 months of age she responded with high accuracy after 24 seconds.

All investigations of delayed reaction in children, except Hunter's first one with animals and children, have involved modifications of the *direct* method just described. Some of these studies have been carried out as routine clinical tests; others have involved intensive experimental investigation.

The most extensive clinical tests of memory in infants are described by Bühler (1930). The earliest test is for infants of 3 months. In this test, the face of the tester appears and then disappears. If it looks for the face or seems disturbed by its absence, the infant is credited with memory. Bühler claims that the 3-month-old infant characteristically searches for, or is disturbed by disappearance of, the tester's face.[1] In a test at the 5-month level, a toy is presented and then removed. The infant is credited with memory if it looks "searchingly" in the direction in which the toy has disappeared.

One of the best delayed-reaction tests of this general type is that devised by Bühler (1930) and Hetzer and Wislitzky (1930) for use with children ranging in age from 10 to 24 months. A ball containing a chicken which pops out is placed in the child's hand. The child plays with the ball, making the chicken appear and disappear. Then the ball is removed and other activity is encouraged. Some time later a ball which looks like the previous one, but does not contain a chicken, is presented. The child is credited with memory if, upon squeezing the new ball, it shows "astonishment," looks "questioningly" at the tester, or puts its finger in the hole when a chicken fails to appear. The maximum delay followed by evidence of memory is about 1 minute at 10 to 11 months, 8 minutes at 15 to 17 months, 15 minutes at 19 to 20 months, and 17 minutes at 21 to 24 months.

[1] Hurlock and Schwartz (1932) have summarized many biographical reports of this type of response in infants. Preyer mentions an infant of 3 months who cried and looked around the room when his nurse disappeared. Shinn reports such behavior in a child of 4 months. Fact and interpretation are so interwoven in such studies that one cannot be sure of their validity. A chance response, occurring once, may be taken as an indication of memory.

Allen (1931) has investigated delayed reaction in 50 boys and 50 girls approximately one year old. Each child sat on its mother's lap during the experiment. Three boxes which looked exactly alike were placed on a card table at equal distances from the subject, as shown in Figure 13. Various toys were used as lures. While the mother's eyes were closed (to

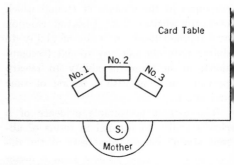

FIGURE 13. Arrangement for measuring delayed reaction in infants. (From "Individual Differences in Delayed Reaction of Infants," by C. N. Allen. *Archives of Psychology,* 1931, **19**, 14. By permission of the publisher.)

prevent helpful attitudes), but while the infant was watching, a toy was tapped on a box three times and dropped in, where it was out of sight. The table was then pulled out of the infant's reach for periods ranging from 10 to 165 seconds. At the end of a delay period, the table was pushed toward the child, who was thus given an opportunity to respond. Three tests in rapid succession, with the toy in a different box each time, were given after 10-, 20-, and 30-second delay periods. For longer delays there were fewer tests, the exact number differing somewhat from one subject to another. Loss of interest during the longer delays was one reason for this variation.

Since there were three possible locations for the toy, chance accuracy would approximate 33 per cent. Accuracy after a

MEMORY **403**

10-second delay was 61 per cent for boys and 66 per cent for girls. After a 20-second delay, it was 65 per cent for boys and 57 per cent for girls. A 30-second delay was followed by accuracy, respectively, of 50 and 48 per cent. With a 45-second delay the percentages were 19 and 36, respectively. The number of cases at longer delays was too small to make the results worthy of consideration. Sex differences were insignificant.

The experiments of Hunter, Bühler, Hetzer and Wislitzky, and Allen all agree in demonstrating that memory of the delayed-reaction type (that is, recall memory) is present during the first year of life. These experiments differ, however, in their findings with respect to the maximum correct delays. The discrepancies with respect to this factor may be attributed to different test situations and to different criteria of successful delay. Bühler and her co-workers, it will be recalled, report maximum delays of *one minute* as occurring in the first year. Hunter and Allen, however, report maximum delays no longer than *30 seconds*. The "naturalness" and interest value of Bühler's tests perhaps contribute to the longer delays in her studies. Another factor of possible importance, however, is the criterion of response. In Hunter and Allen's experiments, the child was required to make a clear-cut overt differential response, whereas in Bühler's tests facial expression and fingering of the ball were accepted as indicative of memory.

The most extensive investigation of delayed reaction in preschool children is Skalet's (1931). Sixty children between 2 and 5½ years were given tests similar in principle to those discussed above. In the first group of experiments, a child was confronted with three plates under one of which a cooky was placed. After seeing the cooky hidden under a given plate, the

subject was taken out of the room. Upon his return to the original situation, the child was required to locate the hidden cooky. If it was located without error, he was allowed to eat it. In successive trials the cooky varied in position in a random manner. Average accuracy of response was 64.8 per cent after delays of 1 to 3 days. After delays of 21 to 29 days, accuracy dropped to 46.2 per cent. Longer delays were followed by merely chance accuracy. The correlation between age and maximum correct delay was .478 ± .077. Skalet points out that verbal symbols enabled the preschool children to make correct delays after long periods. The great difference in maximum correct delays between the ages of 1 and 2 years may be accounted for partly on the ground that the older child has acquired linguistic substitutes for absent stimuli.

The response required in Skalet's second group of experiments was to select from a random array of figures the one observed in isolation some time previously. She thus obtained a measure of delayed reaction in terms of recognition. In one set of tests, familiar animals were involved. In another, Skalet used geometrical figures of various kinds. Familiar animals gave the best results. For these tests the correlation between maximum correct delay and age was .669 ± .093. Tests with geometrical figures were too difficult for most children.

Two investigations of how certain stimulus factors influence correct delayed reactions in children have been reported. The first deals with the position of the subject and the second with the position and color of the stimuli. In his original delayed-reaction experiment, Hunter (1913) found that some animals did not perform correctly unless allowed to maintain a fixed bodily orientation during delay. He supposed that a continuing kinesthetic cue was being used. Hunter's findings suggested to Emerson (1931) that the delayed reactions of children might be affected differentially by introducing variations in the degree of bodily orientation during delay. Thirty-two children, ranging in age from 27 to 59 months, were each shown an easel which contained a board with 42 pegs arranged in 7 rows of 6 each. While a child was watching, the experimenter placed a ring over one peg. The child was then required to turn to a similar easel and place a ring over the corresponding peg. In each test the delay was approximately 5 seconds. Nine degrees of orientation were involved. They ranged from stepping to an easel at the side of the stimulus easel to going round to an easel facing in the opposite direction. Scores for correct placement were low throughout. With no disorientation, the average number of correct responses was 17.82. With the first degree of disorientation indicated above, the average score dropped to 6.45. When the positions of the stimulus and the response easels were back to back, the average score was only 1.81. There was an increase in scores with age. The average number of correct placements throughout the experiment correlated .77 ± .05 with CA and .758 ± .05 with MA.

Miller's (1934) investigation concerns the question of how certain exteroceptive stimulus relations affect accuracy of delayed response. His problem may be framed in the following question: When the child makes a delayed response, does the implicit symbol represent the *absolute* position, color, or other aspect of the box in which the lure has been hidden or does it represent some *relation* between this and other boxes? Miller refers to his test situations as involving "critical choice delayed reaction." A 10-second delay was used in each situation. Ninety-eight children between 11½ and 162 months of age

served as subjects. The first experiment was conducted as follows: A child was seated opposite the experimenter and was asked, "Do you like to play games?" Two boxes of the same size, but one red and the other yellow, were placed in front of the child. The experimenter said: "See the boxes. Now I'm going to hide the dog under a box. Look!" The toy was hidden. A screen was then interposed between the boxes and the child for 10 seconds. At the end of this interval, the experimenter said, "See if you can find the dog." After each response he said, "Fine!," and again hid the toy. The child was then asked, "Can you find it this time?" Various lures besides the toy dog were used.

As soon as the child completed two successive correct responses, critical tests to determine the cues utilized were introduced. The nature of these tests can best be grasped by referring to Figure 14. Three critical tests are represented. The idea was to see whether, in these tests, the child would select a box of the same color as that under which he had seen the lure placed, whether he would select the box having the same relation with respect to his own position, whether he would select the one having the same position relative to the other box, whether he would select on the basis of two of these cues combined, or whether he would select on the basis of some other possible combination of cues. In the critical tests each box contained the toy, although the subject had seen it placed in only one box.

The 11½- to 24-month-old children, of which there were 4, all responded in terms of *position relative to the other box*. In successive age groups, however, there was a gradual decrease in the frequency of this type of response. Response in terms of *color* began, with a frequency of 20 per cent, in the age group of 25 to 36 months.

The group contained 11 subjects. Color was an increasingly frequent basis of response until the 5-year level, after which its frequency decreased. *Position relative to the subject* was not a very frequent cue at any age level. Response in terms of the *box with two cues in its favor* was also quite infrequent at all ages. *Unclassified responses* increased with age, reaching a

these experiments show that the child below 2 years of age has some representation of the *position of one box relative to another*. This symbol serves as the chief basis of response when he is required to remember under which box he has previously seen a toy placed. Older children, on the other hand, frequently retain a representation of *color*, which symbol en-

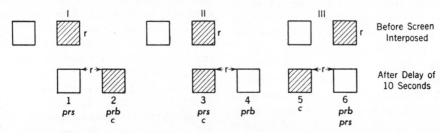

FIGURE 14. Critical tests of cues used in delayed reaction. (From "The Perception of Children: A Genetic Study Employing the Critical Choice Delayed Reaction," by N. E. Miller. *Journal of Genetic Psychology*, 1934, **44**, 327. By permission of The Journal Press, publisher.)

The top line represents the original position of the boxes in each of the three tests. The lower line represents the critical choice positions. Each box is designated by a number for purposes of reference. *c*, choice on the basis of color; *prs*, response to position of box with respect to the child's own position; *prb*, response in terms of the position of one box in relation to the position of the other box. If the cue were color, boxes 2, 3, and 5 would be selected. Should the cue be position of the box with respect to himself, the subject would respond to boxes 1, 3, and 6. However, if the box presenting two cues were selected, the child would respond to 2, 3, and 6. There are four other theoretically possible cues.

frequency of about 30 per cent at the 120- to 162-month level.

When the distance between the two boxes was doubled, the youngest age group responded 66 per cent in terms of *position relative to the other box* and 33 per cent in terms of *position relative to the subject*. Under these conditions, however, color again became an increasingly important cue in successively older groups.

In a number of further experiments involving principles similar to those of the above tests, use of such cues as position relative to a group of other boxes, different color from a group of boxes alike in color, and combinations of color and position cues was tested. In general, the results of

ables them to remember the box containing a toy.

Retention after a Single Presentation. Retention of materials seen or heard a single time has been investigated extensively in children. The problem is usually stated more specifically as one of immediate memory or memory span. It was first investigated by Jacobs (1887).[1] Special

1 Materials used to test the memory span of children have included *digits:* Jacobs (1887), Bolton (1892), Henri (1902), Smedley (1902), Humpstone (1917), Pintner and Paterson (1917), Ide (1920), Town (1921), Starr (1923), Easby-Grave (1924), Gesell (1925), Young (1928), Hallowell (1928), McCaulley (1928), Hurlock and Newmark (1931), Wilson and Fleming (1937), and Terman and Merrill (1937); *letters:* Jacobs (1887); *words:* Kirkpatrick (1894), Henri (1902), Burt (1909), Whipple

studies have had as their aims (1) to ascertain how differences in age, intelligence, and sex affect the memory span; (2) to compare the memory span for different kinds of material; (3) to determine the relative efficacy of visual and auditory means of presentation; (4) to observe differences in results obtained when recall or recognition tests of retention are used; and (5), especially in the case of narratives, figures, and pictures, to determine the nature of differences between the original and "recalled" material.

That the memory span of children increases with age has been shown for all kinds of material investigated. The auditory-vocal memory span for digits, as indicated by Starr's (1923) investigation with 2000 children between the ages of 4 and 15 years, is 4 between the fourth and fifth years, 5 between the sixth and eighth years, 6° between the ninth and twelfth years, and 7 beyond the twelfth year. Other studies on auditory-vocal digit span summarized by Hurlock and Newmark (1931), as well as the Terman-Merrill (1937) norms, are in close agreement with these. Although the memory span for words, letters, objects, figures, and ideas in a narrative also increases with age, the

particular span is dependent upon the meaning of the materials involved.

Most investigations have shown a positive, but medium, correlation between intelligence and memory span for various types of material. In Bayley's (1926) study, which involved 100 subjects between approximately 3 and 6 years old, correlations between MA and memory span for digits ranged from .40 at the third year to .67 at the sixth year. Correlations between memory span for objects and MA ranged from .44 to .58. Hurlock and Newmark (1931) report the following correlations between the IQ and memory spans of 20 preschool children: *digits* .59 ± .11; *syllables*, .72 ± .08; *concrete words*, .52 ± .11; *abstract words*, .55 ± .11; *pictures*, .61 ± .09; *movements*, .59 ± .11; *ideas in a narrative*, .76 ± .07; and *commands*, .64 ± .09. Clark's (1924) investigation suggests that, although there is a positive correlation between intelligence and digit span at early age levels, the correlation is negligible at the high school level.

It is generally claimed that memory spans for boys and girls show a difference in favor of the latter. This view is based, primarily, upon the researches of Kirkpatrick (1894) and Pyle (1920), both of whom measured memory span for words. The developmental range in both studies combined was from about the third grade to the high school level. That a sex difference exists in the memory span for digits is doubtful. Several studies involving both sexes fail to mention a difference, and Pintner and Paterson (1917) and Bryan (1934) found none. Some investigations involving pictures (Shimidu, 1934) and narratives (Shaw, 1896; Bassett, 1929; Dietze, 1932) have disclosed slight superiority of boys. It is of course quite possible that, where meaningful materials of this nature are involved, a sex

(1915), Achilles (1920), Stutsman (1926), Hurlock and Newmark (1931), Lumley and Calhoun (1934), and Wilson and Fleming (1937); *objects:* Dewey, Child, and Ruml (1920), Bronner, Healy, Lowe, and Shimberg (1927), and McElwee (1933); *movements:* Baldwin and Stecher (1924), Hurlock and Newmark (1931), and Mallay (1935); *figures:* Achilles (1920), Allport (1930), Komatsu (1931), Shimidu (1934), Hall (1936); *pictures:* Stern (1904), Squire (1912), Carpenter (1913), Myers (1913), Winch (1914), Town (1921), Baldwin and Stecher (1924), J. A. McGeoch (1925, 1928), Bayley (1926), Conrad and Jones (1929), and Holaday and Stoddard (1933); and *narratives:* Shaw (1896), Yoakum (1921), Bassett (1929), Dietze (1931, 1932), Hurlock and Newmark (1931), Dietze and Jones (1931), Northway (1936), Terman and Merrill (1937), and Loder (1937).

difference indicates differential acquaintance with the material rather than differences in retentivity.

As reported by Hurlock and Newmark (1931), the average memory span of preschool children for digits is 5 ± 1.00; for concrete words, 4.3 ± 0.65; for abstract words, 3.0 ± 0.30; for syllables in a sentence, 15.1 ± 1.20; for pictures, 1.2 ± 0.35; for movements, 4.3 ± 0.65; for ideas in a narrative, 4.3 ± 0.00; and for commands, 5.3 ± 0.50. Whipple (1915) reports that meaning greatly affects the size of the memory span for words.

Smedley's (1902) results show that the memory span for digits does not differ for auditory and visual methods of presentation until the age of approximately 9 years. After this age the visual span exceeds the auditory. Jones (1927) likewise finds no difference in the digit memory span for visual and auditory presentation. All his subjects were under 9 years of age.

Recognition is apparently easier than recall. Achilles (1920) found that children between 8½ and 11½ years of age recognized an average of 23.95 words and recalled an average of only 5.22 words. For forms, the recognition and recall scores were, respectively, 9.61 and 3.97. Syllables yielded scores of 9.41 and 1.86. An older group exhibited higher scores than these, but the relative difference in favor of recognition as compared with recall scores was similar. In Hurlock and Newmark's (1931) study the memory span for pictures was 1.2 by the recall and 6.1 by the recognition method. Shimidu (1934) reports similar results.

Recall of pictures observed a single time was first investigated extensively by Stern (1904), who framed the problem as one of aussage or testimony. He found that children not only fail to report items in the picture but they also add details of their own and, when questioned, respond to suggestions given. The test is thus not one of memory per se. Nevertheless, when items fall within the individual's range of experience and vocabulary and when fictitious details are ignored, the number of items reported is fundamentally a measure of recall memory. Winch (1914) tested 200 children, most of whom were between the ages of 3 and 8 years. Stern's picture was used. At successive age levels the average number of items reported was 8.3, 16.1, 26.5, 30.0, and 35.6. The items involved (boy, woman, bread, knife, etc.) were represented in the previous experience of even the youngest child. It is possible, however, that differences in ability to observe and differences in vocabulary, as well as in memory per se, contributed to the increments in score at successively higher age levels. Similar experiments have been reported by McGeoch (1925, 1928) with, respectively, normal versus subnormal children and normal children between the ages of 9 and 14 years. Beyond the level of intelligence requisite to observation, intelligence did not affect the number of items reported. Recall scores of normal children increased with age, but increments became small and statistically insignificant at the upper age levels. Conrad and Jones (1929), who tested recall of the contents of three entertaining motion pictures by means of completion and multiple-choice tests involving a simple vocabulary, found that scores increased rapidly between the ages of 10 and 20 years. These studies lead to the conclusion, therefore, that recall of pictures witnessed a single time improves as a function of age. How much of the improved recall is based upon increased adequacy of observation and how much upon increased retentivity per se is not apparent.

Allport (1930) and Hall (1936) have investigated changes in reproductions of pictures observed a single time. In Allport's study, 275 children between the ages of 10 and 13 years were shown a simple drawing and then required to reproduce it. Further reproductions were drawn after intervals of 2 weeks and 4 months. Few perfect reproductions appeared. The figures did not, however, lose their identifiability in reproduction. Alterations from the original were chiefly in size, symmetry, and simplicity. Allport

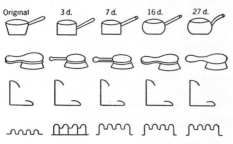

FIGURE 15. Examples of successive changes of diagrams and pictures. (From "The Effects of a Time Interval on Recall," by V. Hall. *British Journal of Psychology*, 1936, **27**, 44. By permission of the publisher.)

suggests that dynamic brain processes "force memory traces into typical lines of change." Hall showed pictures and diagrams to over 200 children between the ages of 9 and 15 years. Each child was told that he would be required to reproduce the picture or diagram after seeing it for a short period (20 seconds). As shown in Figure 15, the general characteristics of the pictures and diagrams were retained while details differed. Naming of the object was a factor in determining the nature of reproductions. A given picture, for example, was referred to by different subjects as "tents," "mountains," "pyramids," and "blades of grass." When called upon to reproduce what they had observed, the subjects were markedly influenced by such verbalizations. Familiar objects tended to change gradually and

diagrams suddenly in repeated reproduction.

Studies somewhat comparable to the above, but utilizing narratives instead of visual materials, have been made by Northway (1936) and Wees and Line (1937). Northway's subjects, ranging in age from 10 to 15 years and coming from private and public schools, read a story once and immediately after doing so, attempted a written reproduction. This reproduction was read by another child who, in turn, attempted to reproduce it. Some reproductions were made after a week's interval. Three stories, each having 250 words, were used. Older children tended to retain the story in its own form more accurately and for a longer time than younger ones. Changes, additions, and omissions were usually such as to recast the story in familiar phraseology and settings. The more unfamiliar the material, the greater was the tendency to recast it. In some instances the story "reproduced" was almost entirely of the child's invention. As one might expect, however, the theme was usually retained with greater accuracy than the details. In Wees and Line's research sixth-grade children read a story and attempted to reproduce it. The same story was presented to different children in changed form. Wees and Line's chief finding is that the nature of the reproduction is determined by the form in which the story is presented.

Memorizing. When materials such as those discussed above are presented repeatedly and retention is measured after each repetition, we have a typical learning experiment. This type of experiment and those considered earlier in the present chapter differ chiefly in that the child is here required to learn symbols rather than movements as such.

The first reported experiment in memorizing in which children were subjects is Steffens's (1900). Children were used only incidentally.[1] In this, as in most of the early memorizing experiments with adults and children, nonsense syllables and poems were learned.

Foster (1928) investigated memorizing of narratives by nursery school children varying in CA from 2 years and 7 months to 4 years and 9 months and in MA from 3 years and 2 months to 5 years and 8 months. Fifteen boys and 16 girls were involved. Stories containing 388 to 472 words were each read to a child 10 times. After the first reading of a story, pauses were introduced at predetermined intervals and the subject was encouraged to continue the narrative as far as possible. His score per repetition was the number of words correctly recalled. Whenever a correct reproduction was made, the experimenter said, "Good." Incorrect reproductions were corrected. After 10 repetitions (9 recall tests) had been given a new story was begun. One repetition was given daily. Twenty-two of the children learned 8 stories in this manner while the rest learned 3 to 4.

A learning curve based upon the mean number of words per child per story for the 8 stories is presented in Figure 16. One notes that the curve is approximately linear, and that the limit of achievement was not reached during the 9 tests. Simi-

larly plotted curves for subjects below a CA of 3 years and 4 months and an MA of 3 years and 10 months, however, show a decided flattening after the eighth repetition. Mean scores of the lowest CA group went from approximately 1 on the first repetition to 8 on the last, whereas the comparable scores of the five oldest children went from 9 to 73. Similarly, the scores of the lowest MA group went

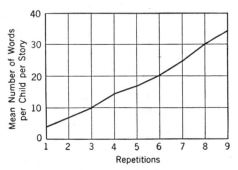

FIGURE 16. Curve for memorizing of stories. (From "Verbal Memory in the Pre-school Child," by J. C. Foster. *Journal of Genetic Psychology*, 1928, **35**, 31. By permission of the publisher.)

from 1 to 8, whereas those of the highest went from 5 to 64. The correlation between CA and total score for all stories was .74; that between MA and total score for all stories, .65. Although the number of subjects was small, the above data all agree in suggesting that the memorizing of narratives by young children increases with age and intelligence. Whether this increase is in mnemonic ability *per se* or in attitudes, previous experience, or the like, cannot be determined. Although girls were slightly higher than boys in MA, their average scores were lower than those of boys on 7 of the 9 stories. Since the groups were so small, this may not represent a true sex difference.

Several investigators of memorizing in children have used variations of the paired-

[1] Other early studies with children are by Pentschew (1903), Radossawljewitsch (1907), Busemann (1911), and Meumann (1913). The number of children included in these investigations was too small to warrant comparison of their memorizing ability with that of the adults involved. In any event, comparison of child and adult learning of symbolic materials may be invalidated by the fact that the symbols have different degrees of meaning for children and adults. Motivation is another possible differentiating factor. Nevertheless, Meumann (1913) discusses alleged differences between the memorizing ability of children and adults. Studies in which memorizing by a single child has been intensively investigated are reported by Winch (1904), Guillet (1909), and Hildreth (1935).

associates method. The color-naming studies of Lund (1927) and Jersild (1932) are of this variety. Children were shown colors and required to recall the appropriate names as quickly as possible. Lund's 5-year-old child and Jersild's 7- to 8-year-old children exhibited an initial rapid increase in speed of naming. This was followed by slow improvement. Jersild used a control group which, despite the fact that it performed only an initial and a final test, also improved. The improvement of this group was less than one half that shown by the trained group. After an interval of 4 months without intervening experimental practice, however, the speed of naming in both groups was approximately equal. Only the control group showed improvement during the interval. It appears that the maturation and/or incidental learning of this group enabled it to approximate what the other group had achieved by experimental practice.

Experiments by Meek (1925) and Kirkwood (1926) also involved paired associates. Meek required 68 children between the ages of 4 and 6 years to associate names of objects with the objects when confusing words (having the first, last, two middle letters, etc., of the key word) were presented simultaneously. Thus the word *ball* appeared on a box containing a ball but, associated with this box were other, empty boxes containing the words *burr, feel, sale, bake,* and *kill.* The other words to be learned in this way were *flag, doll, lion, duck,* and *rose.* Improvement was measured in terms of time, number of corrections, and number of false recognitions in each practice period. Six practice periods separated by intervals of 1 to 30 days were given. Each period was terminated after a specified number of correct recognitions, the number depending upon differences in the training procedure for different groups. Meek's results indicate

no conclusive evidence of improvement in memorizing as a function of age. This is perhaps due to the fact that her procedure was not comparable at different age levels. The correlation between MA and time required to learn *ball* to the point of two recognitions ranged, for the age groups of 4 to 6 years, between .302 ± .101 and .456 ± .142. When corrections made in learning all words were correlated with MA the correlations ranged from —.011 ± .189 to .583 ± .128. Correlations increased at each successive age group. The last correlation, based upon data from only 14 children, however, is alone statistically significant. Most of the learning curves show a sharp improvement in the first few periods, followed by little or no improvement. One of the most interesting aspects of this investigation is the analysis of individual cases. This analysis shows that temporary excitement, boredom, worry over a scolding from the mother given prior to the experiment, daydreaming, etc., lead to marked variations in memorizing.

Kirkwood (1926) investigated association of pictures and blocks having a vague resemblance to each other. Her subjects were 180 preschool children. Twenty blocks and 20 pictures were used. At each practice period the experimenter picked up pictures in random order and asked the child to hand her "the block that goes with this picture." In some instances the block was handed to the child and he was required to select the correct picture. Learning curves based upon the number of correct associations exhibited a rapid rise and then flattened upon approaching the upper limit of 20.

The relation of age and intelligence to memorizing has been the subject of special investigations by Wilson (1931a, 1931b, 1931c) and Stroud and Maul (1933). Wilson found that dull children were, on the average, inferior to bright children in memorizing shorthand characters and descriptive selections. In some individual cases, however, bright children were surpassed by dull children. In Stroud and Maul's study, 172 subjects between the ages of 7 and 11 years, 26 subjects aged 14 years, and 28 subjects aged 18 years were given 10 minutes' practice with nonsense syllables and, on a different occasion, 15 minutes' practice with poems. The number of nonsense syllables and the number of lines of the poems recalled increased with age. Correlations between CA and recall scores, however, decreased from .61 for poems and .49 for nonsense syllables to approximately zero when MA was partialed out. The correlation between MA and recall scores was $.67 \pm .024$ for poetry and $.61 \pm .028$ for nonsense syllables. Stroud and Maul therefore conclude that memorizing ability is significantly related to intelligence, a conclusion supported, it will be recalled, by the data of Meek (1925) and Foster (1928).

The Relative Efficacy of Different Memorizing Procedures. If certain memorizing procedures result in faster learning and in better retention than others, it is important that these procedures be discovered and applied in classroom teaching. A few approaches to this problem have been made in the laboratory and the classroom and with both adults and children as subjects. Use of children in such research was at first incidental. There has been a tendency in recent years, however, to investigate the relative efficacy of different procedures with large groups of children as subjects and, at the same time, to approximate schoolroom conditions as closely as possible.

Several investigators have attempted to determine the relative merits of *whole versus part procedures*. Steffens (1900) was the first to investigate this problem. She found that her adult subjects and two children learned poems more rapidly when the poems were read from beginning to end than when verses were learned separately and later connected. Neumann (1907), who required 6 children between the ages of 9½ and 10½ years to associate German and foreign words by whole and part procedures, also found the whole procedure to be superior. He observed, however, that the effectiveness of this procedure increased with increasing intelligence.

Winch (1924) did not find the whole to be superior to the part procedure. He worked under classroom conditions with large groups of children. The children were paired on the basis of age and memory ability as determined by a preliminary test. One child of a pair learned poems by the whole method, whereas his partner learned the same poems by the pure part procedure. Three separate experiments were performed, involving groups of 26 to 38 children ranging in age from 11 years and 8 months to 13 years and 1 month. With the exception of the results for one poem at one age level all data were in favor of the part procedure. Pechstein (1926) found no reliable evidence in favor of either whole or part methods in his investigation with bright and dull children.

The equivocal nature of the above findings led McGeoch (1931) to carry out a further investigation, which appears to be the most thorough yet performed on this problem with children as subjects. Her subjects were 33 gifted and 35 normal children, all approximately ten years old. The IQ of the gifted group averaged 151 and that of the normal group, 99. The groups were divided equally with respect to sex. Turkish-English vocabularies, nonsense syllable–English pairs, and poems were memorized by whole or part methods. In learning of the last two types of material a progressive part procedure, as well as whole and pure part procedures, was used.

The same number of repetitions, in the case of paired associates, and the same time, in the case of poems, were given with each procedure. Scores for paired associates comprised the number of associates recalled upon presentation, singly and in changed order, of the initial members of the pairs. Memorizing of poems was scored in terms of the number of lines recalled.

Data obtained with the Turkish-English vocabulary yielded unequivocal evidence of the superiority of the whole procedure both for gifted and average children. Furthermore, the superiority of this procedure was greater for gifted than for average children. The means, SD's, differences, and standard errors of the differences are given in Table 4. One will observe that all differences between the whole and part procedures for both learning and retention are statistically significant. Nonsense syllable-English pairs yielded results in the same direction, but few of the differences were found to be statistically significant. The progressive part procedure gave ambiguous results, in some instances being more effective and in others less effective than the whole method. None of the differences was significant statistically. Poems were learned better by gifted than by average children. However, slight differences between the scores for whole, progressive part, and pure part methods were statistically insignificant. McGeoch concluded that the effectiveness of the whole and part methods depends upon the intelligence of the subjects and the type of material to be memorized.

TABLE 4

COMPARISON OF METHODS

Group	No.	Whole		Part		Whole Minus Part		P/W
		Mean	SD	Mean	SD	Diff.	$SD_{diff.}$	
Learning								
Gifted	31	5.06	1.55	2.53	1.27	2.53	0.29	50%
Normal	32	2.42	1.32	1.48	.87	.94	.20	61%
Normal/Gifted		48%		58%				
Retention								
Gifted	31	4.12	1.49	2.17	1.36	1.95	0.26	52%
Normal	32	1.76	1.21	.78	.74	.98	.18	44%
Normal/Gifted		43%		36%				

In a study reported briefly by Northway (1937), poems of varying difficulty, as determined by their "thought content," were memorized by school children. There was no clear superiority of the whole or part procedure. The relative effectiveness of the two procedures differed from one poem to another, and there was no clear relation between the efficiency of the procedure and the difficulty of the poem. It is suggested, however, that poems of intermediate difficulty were learned best by the whole method, whereas those of lesser and greater difficulty were learned about as effectively by either method. Griffiths (1938), as the result of a study involving 14-year-old boys, claims that simple materials are learned with equal efficiency by either part or whole methods but that difficult material should be approached in terms of the whole method at first and then in parts.

The results of researches on whole versus part methods of learning in adults are also conflicting. On the basis of findings so far reported one must conclude that, even for memorizing of a given type of material— for example, poems—findings differ concerning the relative effectiveness of the whole and part procedures. One investigator finds the whole procedure most effective, another the part procedure, and still another finds no difference. Woodworth (1938), after critically evaluating all the literature on whole versus part learning, says that the net result is somewhat as follows:

> The parts are easier to learn than the whole and the learner is often happier and better adjusted to the problem when beginning with the parts. He carries over some of the skill and knowledge gained in learning the parts into the subsequent learning of the whole performance. But he finds that putting together the parts is a serious problem requiring much further work. In the end he may have saved time and energy by commencing with the parts —or he may not—much depending on the size and difficulty of the total task and the learner's poise and technique. If he can adjust himself to the whole method and handle it properly, he can learn quite complex performances effectively by the whole method. In a practical situation it is probably best to start with the whole method while feeling free to concentrate at any time on a part where something special is to be learned (p. 223).

The relative efficacy of *massed and distributed practice* has been investigated extensively with animals and adults. Such researches have shown some form of distribution to be more efficient than massing of practice periods. Similar experiments with children have been few and inadequate.

Munn (1909), in her study of the learning curve, found that short frequent practice periods led to faster learning of a substitution problem by both children and adults than long practice periods. With the exception of this study and a master's thesis, the results of which are summarized by Peterson (1933, pp. 428–430), all reported work with children on this problem has involved memorizing.[1]

Kirkwood (1926) required two matched groups of eleven children each to associate pictures and blocks which were vaguely similar (see page 410). Upon being presented with each of twenty blocks the child was required to select its associated picture. Each day's score was the number of correct associations. One group practiced every day; the other practiced

[1] This thesis, by Long, deals with distribution of practice in dart throwing. There were only 10 boys in each group, the initial ability of the two groups was markedly different, and only a minute statistical analysis, which seems unwarranted in the light of the small number of subjects, discloses any difference in the effectiveness of the two procedures.

on alternate days. The results are summarized in Table 5. One will observe that the group with a greater distribution of practice not only achieved the criterion of three successive correct trials five practice periods earlier than the other group, but also attained higher scores at every trial.

inhibitory than of facilitory association during an interval. Any or all of these factors may operate in a given instance The phenomenon under discussion is also possibly related to better retention of incomplete than of completed tasks (Zeigarnik, 1927) and reminiscence (Hovland

TABLE 5

AVERAGE SCORES OBTAINED BY TWENTY-TWO PAIRED CHILDREN IN ASSOCIATING PICTURES WITH BLOCKS

Practice Periods

1	2	3	4	5	6	7	8	9	10	11	12	13	14
						Practice Once Daily							
10.2	14.9	16.5	18.8	19.1	19.0	19.8	19.6	19.3	20.0	19.7	20.0	20.0	20.0
						Practice on Alternate Days							
11.3	15.2	18.9	19.6	20.0	19.8	20.0	20.0	20.0					

Foster (1928) found distributed practice to yield better results than massed practice in the learning of narratives by 29 nursery school children. After one story had been given a single repetition daily for ten days, another story, assumed to be of approximately equal difficulty, was given five daily repetitions for two days. The average number of words recalled per repetition was consistently higher for distributed than for massed practice. A few individuals, however, had higher scores for massed than for distributed practice. Although the trend of Foster's results is in line with that of other researches on distribution of practice, her experiment lacks conclusiveness owing to the fact that a different poem was memorized under each of the conditions.

The advantage of rests between practice periods has been attributed to decreased fatigue, to preservation of neural traces following removal of the stimuli which aroused them, to opportunities for recitation or rehearsal, and to more rapid dropping-out of

1938a). For a discussion of this, see pages 418–423.

Another problem concerns the relative efficacy of *recitation and passive reading* of materials to be recalled. It has long been known that retention is poor unless the individual intends to memorize.[1] Myers (1913), for example, found that children and adults fail to remember many items from everyday experience when there has been no intention of recalling them later. On the basis of such facts one should expect recitation to facilitate learning and retention. A specific investigation of this problem was undertaken by Gates (1917), whose experiments were carried out under classroom conditions. Forty to 45 children, from Grades I, III, IV, V, VI, and VIII, were used. The materials to be memorized were lists of nonsense syllables and brief biographies. Each group memorized under each of the conditions of the experiment in such order that all factors other

[1] See especially the case cited by Radossawljewitsch (1907, p. 127).

than the relative amounts of recitation and reading were equated. The total time given to memorizing nonsense syllables was divided between reading and recitation so that the percentages of reading were as follows: 100, 80, 60, 40, and 20. Reading comprised going over the material from the beginning to the end without repeating any unit except while looking at it. When recitation was called for, the child was instructed to look over the top of the card and repeat as many units as possible. Only when a unit could not be remembered was he to glance at the card while reciting. More material was given in a lesson than could be memorized in the time limit. A written recall was made after this limit had expired. The results obtained for memorizing of nonsense syllables appear in Table 6.[1] Scores are relative, be-

TABLE 6

THE RELATIVE EFFICACY OF DIFFERENT PROPORTIONS OF READING AND RECITATION IN MEMORIZING NONSENSE SYLLABLES

Percentage Reading	100	80	60	40	30
Grade VIII					
Relative score	65.40	92.23	99.69	105.45	137.26
PE	2.37	2.69	2.53	2.57	3.35
Grade VI					
Relative score	59.13	88.35	101.34	112.57	136.61
PE	2.74	3.78	2.70	4.09	4.81
Grade IV					
Relative score	63.42	80.53	108.05	113.75	134.42
PE	3.42	2.76	3.36	4.50	4.74

ing derived from average scores by considering the average of each class for all five methods as 100.

The same general procedure was followed in memorizing of short biographies. Grade III was allowed a total of 7 min-

[1] Results for Grade I are not included because, owing to differences in technique, they were not comparable with those of other grades.

utes and 30 seconds per biography, whereas Grades IV, V, VI, and VIII were allowed 9 minutes. Added to the proportions of reading and recitation used with nonsense syllables was a 10 reading–90 recitation percentage. Recall scores reduced to a relative basis are given in Table 7. Statistical analysis of these scores discloses that, for all grades, some degree of recitation is significantly superior to reading alone. Taking the average of all scores into consideration, Gates obtained the following relative scores for, respectively, no recitation to 90 per cent recitation: 83.71, 95.32, 101.63, 110.35, 106.67, and 102.30. Considering these data as a whole, it appears that 40 per cent reading and 60 per cent recitation give the best results for this type of material under these conditions.

Tests of retention given three to four hours after original learning showed trends similar to those found for immediate recall. Relative retention scores for nonsense syllables, averaged for all grades, were, for the successively greater amounts of recitation, as follows: 45.34, 72.96, 93.53, 119.13, and 169.17. Thus an increasing proportion of recitation, within the limits of zero and 80 per cent, led to increasingly better retention of nonsense syllables. For biographical material the comparable scores were: 73.31, 85.44, 110.23, 122.98, 115.65, and 110.82. As in the case of immediate recall, retention scores were highest with 60 per cent recitation.

In repeating these experiments with adults, Gates obtained results essentially similar to those mentioned. His analysis of the process of memorizing suggests that recitation enables the individual to develop with greater facility than is possible in reading alone the requisite "bonds" between items. Where these bonds must be built up by the learner himself, as in learn-

TABLE 7

THE RELATIVE EFFICACY OF DIFFERENT PROPORTIONS OF READING AND RECITATION IN
MEMORIZING SHORT BIOGRAPHIES

Percentage Reading	100	80	60	40	20	10
Grade VIII						
Relative score	87.78	94.62	104.98	105.45	106.80	100.03
PE	3.01	3.64	2.93	2.89	2.09	3.43
Grade VI						
Relative score	89.21	97.58	106.19	104.36	104.77	98.06
PE	4.42	3.48	4.09	4.01	4.83	4.01
Grade V						
Relative score	80.42	95.15	103.75	108.86	104.57	107.36
PE	2.72	2.93	3.27	3.81	3.41	3.75
Grade IV						
Relative score	86.34	99.94	96.69	111.17	104.13	101.65
PE	4.54	4.60	5.07	4.54	4.13	4.18
Grade III						
Relative score	74.78	89.29	96.54	121.93	113.12	104.40
PE	3.35	4.21	4.21	3.95	4.81	4.64

ing nonsense materials, recitation seems of most value. In general:

> Recitation leads to greater certainty of one's knowledge. It enables the learner not only to know but to be aware of how well he knows. Fewer blunders and erroneous recalls are made. The material is better organized; it is in more usable form (p. 101).[1]

Transfer of Improvement in Memorizing. Does memorizing a particular kind of material increase a child's *ability*

[1] Investigations concerning other aspects of economical memorizing in children have been carried out by Dell (1912), on position of items in a series and the relation of this position to ease of learning and recall; by Sullivan (1924), on development of attitudes concerning success and failure; by Meek (1925), on the most effective number of repetitions at different stages of learning; by Jensen and Schrodt (1936), on wording materials so as to bring them within the child's range of comprehension; by Forlano and Hoffman (1937), on the relative adequacy of guessing and telling methods in learning foreign words; and by Adams (1938), on the effect of correcting and repeating errors in serial rote learning.

to memorize? Several investigators have sought an answer to this question.[2]

Winch (1908) had school children between 10 and 13 years of age memorize poetry on one day per week for 3 weeks, after which they memorized history and

[2] Although they do not concern memorizing *per se,* the following studies are somewhat relevant. Thorndike (1924) and Brolyer, Thorndike, and Woodyard (1927) investigated the transfer value of various high school subjects. Transfer was measured in terms of improvement in mental-test performance. The small apparent transfer of some subjects, such as mathematics, could be attributed to similarities between subject and mental-test material. The investigators claim that no general transfer occurred. Gordon's (1938) experiment on transfer of training within verbal tests is of interest in this connection. She found that a group of children trained on analogies for eight weeks following initial tests had significantly higher final analogy scores than did a comparable group given only the initial and final tests. Transfer was probably in terms of an acquired "feeling" for analogy material and perhaps a technique. There is no implication that reasoning ability *per se* had been improved by the training with analogies. On tests which did not include analogies, both groups performed with equal skill.

geography lessons. A control group, equated with the former in terms of initial tests and in terms of teachers' judgments of mnemonic ability, memorized the same lessons after doing sums for 3 weeks. The experiment was repeated with several different groups of children. As an example of the results obtained in these studies we shall cite the data of the initial one, which involved experimental and control groups of 17 children each. The average initial score of each group for memorizing history was 88. The average final score in memorizing history (another lesson of greater length than the first) was 121 for the experimental and 111 for the control group. All experiments yielded results in the same direction. Winch concluded that: "Improvement, gained by practice in memorizing one subject of instruction, is transferred to memory work in other subjects whose nature is certainly diverse from that in which the improvement was gained" (p. 293).

In a further experiment of the same general nature, Winch (1910) found that training in rote memory led to improvement in substance memory. Sleight (1911), who worked with both school children and adults, questioned Winch's techniques and the reliability of his data on transfer from rote to substance memory. Children averaging 12.8 years of age were divided into four groups of equal mnemonic ability as determined by a series of tests. One group learned poetry in rote fashion, one memorized tables, one learned the substance of prose selections, and the fourth, during the same period, did arithmetic problems involving no memorization. These activities occurred 30 minutes daily, 4 days per week, for 3 weeks. All four groups were finally required to memorize nonsense syllables, prose selections, the data of maps, and other materials. In two instances there was a statistically significant difference in favor of the trained group. In memorizing nonsense syllables, the groups which learned poetry and tables gained, respectively, 66 and 85 more points than their controls. The differences had a PE of 11. There was a statistically insignificant drop of 32 points in memorizing prose after learning nonsense syllables and a statistically insignificant increase of 21 to 31 points in going from training with prose to, respectively, literal and substance memorization of prose. Sleight concluded that, where transfer occurs, it is in terms of specific techniques. Subjects developed a procedure which served as well in memorizing one type of material as in memorizing another.

Winch (1911) presents data which seem to indicate transfer from memorizing to inventing stories having a different content. In each case there is a small, but probably insignificant, difference in favor of the trained group. Correlations between memory and invention scores run as high as .623, which is statistically significant.

Gates and Taylor (1925) and Gates (1928) report a transfer experiment involving digit span. Their subjects were 82 children separated into experimental and control groups on the basis of sex, age, intelligence, scholastic maturity, grade, initial memory span for digits, and other mnemonic performances. Children of the experimental group were given 78 days of practice in memorizing series of digits of differing length. The control group was tested for digit span only on the initial and final days of the experiment. The initial digit span of both groups was 4.33. During 78 days of practice the experimental group increased its average digit span to 6.40, a gain of 2.07. The control group had a final score of 5.06, a gain of 0.73. It is apparent that practice in memorizing digits increased the digit span. In a further test 4½ months later, however, both groups exhibited approximately equal spans. Gates assumes, therefore, that "the improvement brought about by training in this case is due to subtle techniques rather than to increased fundamental capacities" (p. 455). An interval of only 4½ months was apparently too long for the techniques to be retained. Both groups were given further practice 8 months after the final tests. On the first day of this practice period the scores of the experimental and control groups were, respectively, 4.73 and 4.83. Twenty-one days of training increased these scores to 5.73 and 5.92. It is again apparent that the 78 days of training 8 months earlier gave the experimental group no superiority over the control group at this later period.

On the basis of the above-mentioned experiments one must conclude that training in memorizing aids further memorizing only in so far as techniques acquired in one situation are applied to further situations. There is no evidence, in other words, that *memorizing ability per se* is improved by training.

Forgetting. Ebbinghaus (1885), who was his own subject, found that forgetting of nonsense syllables and poems learned to the point of one perfect repetition is at first rapid and then slow. Radossawljewitsch (1907), the first investigator to study forgetting in children, used 11 subjects whose ages ranged from 7 to 13 years. Nonsense syllables and poems were learned to the point of two perfect repetitions. These were relearned after intervals ranging from 5 minutes to 60 days. Comparison of the number of repetitions required to learn and to relearn gave an indication of the amount forgotten after each interval.[1] Adults learned and relearned the

same materials. Radossawljewitsch found that both children and adults forgot much more slowly than Ebbinghaus. Results for children and adults did not differ in any consistent manner. Data obtained with children are summarized in Table 8. Some variation from interval to interval is probably due to the fact that relearning took place at different times during the day.

It is obvious that, when material is completely learned, as in the above experiments, either retention will be perfect after an interval or there will be decreased retention. Henderson (1903), Ballard (1913), Huguenin (1914), and several later investigators whose subjects memorized material to a point short of perfection found *better* retention after an interval during which there was no experimental training than immediately after learning. Ballard called this phenomenon *reminiscence.* His research has precipitated many further studies and much discussion.

Since reminiscence has been regarded as peculiar to children, and since most of the research has involved child subjects, it warrants careful consideration in any discussion on learning in children.

Ballard's subjects had an age range of 6 to 21 years. In one investigation, involving over 5000 school children, lines of poetry and lists of nonsense syllables were studied for shorter periods than would allow complete learning. A recall was given immediately after the study period and, as far as the subjects knew, there would be no further recall. The amount recalled immediately was taken to be 100 per cent.

been 17 per cent (Vertes, 1931). Experiments by Charles (1929) and Burtt (1932, 1937) have shown that material presented before the second year of life, although beyond recall 6 months (Charles) and 8 to 14 years later, is relearned with large savings in the number of repetitions required for new material. In Burtt's study the savings at 8 years was 30 per cent and at 14 years 8 per cent.

[1] Forgetting in children has also been measured in terms of recall. Under these circumstances, forgetting after only 10 seconds has

TABLE 8

PERCENTAGE OF NONSENSE SYLLABLES AND POEMS FORGOTTEN

Intervals	5 minutes	20 minutes	60 minutes	8 hours	24 hours	2 days	6 days	30 days	60 days
Syllables	9	15	23	37	28	32	43	66	94
Poems	3	11	23	39	21	29	42	75	85

Different groups gave a further recall after intervals of, respectively, 1 to 7 days. Recall of poetry by 6-year-olds improved 38 per cent after the first day, 57 per cent after the second day, 60 per cent after the third day, and then began to decline. Only relatively slight improvement (10 to 20 per cent) was evidenced by 12-year-olds. Adults showed decreased rather than increased retention. The scores so far mentioned are based upon *averages* for the various age groups. Ballard also analyzed his data in terms of the *percentage of individuals* showing reminiscence at each age level. Reminiscence was present in 90 per cent at the 6-year level, 75 per cent at the 12-year level, and 30 per cent at the adult level. It is thus apparent that, although average scores indicated improved retention for children alone, some adults also improved. Henderson (1903) likewise found improved retention in adults but greater relative improvement in children. Nevertheless, Ballard's results have been taken as evidence that reminiscence is peculiar to children and more evident in younger than in older children. His results suggest, furthermore, that reminiscence is more apparent for poetry than for nonsense material.

Williams (1926) undertook to check Ballard's findings. Four groups, the average ages of which were 9, 12, 16, and 21, studied 40 lines of "The Spider and the Fly" for 5 minutes. They then recalled as much as possible immediately and after periods ranging, for different groups of 100 subjects each, from 1 to 7 days. Disconnected words were also partially learned

and recalled. Recall was scored in terms of correct verbal reproduction, reproduction of sense, and reproduction of sense or partial sense. As in Ballard's research, immediate reproduction was scored as 100 per cent. Comparisons were entirely in terms of group averages. Data for retention of poetry by the four age groups after intervals of 1, 2, 3, 5, and 7 days are reproduced in Figure 17. It is apparent that, in terms of averages, reminiscence was exhibited only by the two younger groups. Also apparent is the fact that, even for the older groups, forgetting was initially less rapid than in the experiments of Ebbinghaus and Radossawljewitsch. Data reproduced in the table are for correct verbal reproduction. Other methods of scoring yielded essentially similar results. Scores for retention of disconnected words are reproduced in Figure 18. They indicate no reminiscence and no consistent differences in the retention curves of the different age groups.

Recent studies of reminiscence have attempted to answer questions raised by the researches of Ballard and Williams. One question concerns the claim that reminiscence is more prevalent in children than in adults. Luh and Liang (1933) and McGeoch (1935a) found no satisfactory evidence in support of this claim. The former investigators used 11-year-old children and college students. Chinese poetry was studied, then recalled immediately and after an interval. There was no difference in the average amount of reminiscence exhibited by each group. However, a larger percentage of children than of students had scores indicating reminiscence. Mc-Geoch analyzed the original data and found

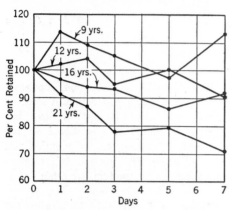

FIGURE 17. Retention of poetry after intervals of 1, 2, 3, 5, and 7 days. (From "A Study of the Phenomenon of Reminiscence," by O. Williams. *Journal of Experimental Psychology*, 1926, **9**, 373. By permission of The American Psychological Association, publisher.)

Scores are for correct verbal reproduction of lines from "The Spider and the Fly."

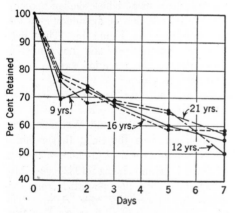

FIGURE 18. Retention of disconnected words after intervals of 1, 2, 3, 5, and 7 days. (From "A Study of the Phenomenon of Reminiscence," by O. Williams. *Journal of Experimental Psychology*, 1926, **9**, 374. By permission of the publisher.)

Scores are in terms of correct verbal reproduction.

this difference to be unreliable statistically. Her own investigation involved 100 preschool children and 100 college students. Toy animals and common objects were exposed for 30 seconds and then covered.[1] Recall was given immediately and after 24 hours. Small differences in the number of each group reminiscing and in the number of items reminisced were in favor of adults. These differences, however, were not statistically reliable. Adults learned a greater amount of the material than did children; hence McGeoch (1935b) decided to determine whether the amount of material learned is in any way related to the degree of reminiscence. Materials comparable with those of the above-mentioned experiment were used. Adults and three groups of children learned, respectively, to the point where they could recall 71, 53, 42, and 29 per cent of the material. In a recall 24 hours later the following percentages of subjects showed reminiscence: 94, 89, 85, and 92. Thus the factor of initial learning did not appear to affect the frequency of reminiscence.

These investigations, and others in which adults have been used exclusively, show that the phenomenon of reminiscence is not more prevalent in children than in adults.[2] It will be recalled, in this connection, that some of Ballard's adults exhibited reminiscence but group averages obscure this fact. The same may be said of Williams's experiment. For this reason, McGeoch (1935a) claimed that the only valid measures of age differences in reminiscence are the percentage of subjects reminiscing and the amount reminisced by these.

---

[1] This method was earlier used with children by Nicolai (1922), who found it to yield higher scores in later than in immediate recall.

[2] See the experiments of Ward (1937) and Hovland (1938a, 1938b) with adult subjects. Reminiscence (of nonsense syllables) was clearly evident in these studies.

May reminiscence be attributed to the effects of intentional review during the interval between immediate and delayed recall?[1] Ballard (1913) claimed that, although reviewing aids reminiscence, it does not account for the phenomenon. McGeoch (1935c) investigated this problem in a partial repetition of Williams's study. She used over 400 third- and fourth-grade children. They studied lines of poetry for 5 minutes. Recall was immediate and after 24 hours. After the final recall had been completed, each child was asked whether, before doing the experiment, he had ever heard or read the poem. Seventy-three per cent denied previous knowledge of the poem. They were asked whether they had thought of, or talked about, the poem between the first and second recall. It was made clear that such review was quite permissible and that they should not hesitate to tell about it. Data were then analyzed separately for those who did and those who did not report having reviewed. The percentage of subjects who exhibited reminiscence and the amount of material reproduced on the second recall did not differ significantly for the two groups. Scores for verbatim recall of lines were slightly in favor of the review group, whereas these scores combined with those for recall of substance favored nonreviewers. Thus McGeoch concluded that review between the first and second recall does

not account for reminiscence or even influence significantly the degree exhibited.

A further question concerns the possibility that reminiscence is due to improvement resulting from the immediate recall. Recall constitutes a review of what has been learned. Even material not recalled immediately may be revived later as a result of an effort to recall it earlier.[2] In her study on maze learning in kindergarten children, McGeoch (1937) controlled this factor by equating the two groups on the basis of initial scores and requiring each to take only one further trial. One group had a further trial immediately; the other group waited for 24 hours. Scores on the last trial were compared to ascertain whether reminiscence had occurred. Reminiscence did not occur. This may be due to factors other than the control instituted, however, for Ward (1937) and Hovland (1938a, 1938b), using nonsense syllables and adult subjects, found reminiscence when similar controls were instituted.[3]

[1] Other approaches to the problem of review are (1) use of material which cannot easily be reviewed (e.g., a maze pattern); (2) use of organisms which, presumably, cannot review; and (3) interpolating activity which interferes with review. McGeoch (1937) found no evidence of reminiscence in maze learning by kindergarten children. On the other hand, Bunch and Magdsick (1933) found reminiscence in maze learning by rats. These studies differed markedly in technique; hence the discrepancy should not be attributed to a difference in subjects. Ward (1937) and Hovland (1938a), who used adult subjects, interpolated activity (color naming) between recalls, yet observed reminiscence.

[2] On this point see Woodworth's (1938, pp. 66–68) discussion of research with adults.

[3] Bunch (1938), who stresses the need for matched groups and only one recall by each, believes that the influence of an immediate recall is too small to account for all the improvement found in earlier experiments on reminiscence. In a study with adults, he found only 11 per cent improvement when a second recall was given immediately. A recent study by Gray (1940) is relevant but inconclusive. Matched groups of children studied words, sentences, and a narrative. One group gave an immediate recall, whereas the other did easy problems in addition to control review. Both groups recalled 24 hours after learning. The first group evidenced an insignificant improvement in recall of the narrative after 24 hours. Otherwise all data for both groups indicated a loss in retention during the interval. Gray regards as important, however, the fact that there was a significantly greater loss in the group which had no immediate recall. This finding perhaps loses significance because the group in question did addition immediately after learning. Although the addition problems were easy, they may have inhibited to some degree what the children had just learned.

The phenomenon of reminiscence has been related to the fact that incompleted tasks are recalled more easily than completed tasks. Zeigarnik (1927) required 47 adults and 45 children to perform a series of 18 tasks. They were allowed to complete only one-half the tasks, which were distributed in random order among tasks the completion of which was prevented. Finally, the subjects were asked to recall tasks which they had performed. Significantly more interrupted than completed tasks were recalled. The memorial advantage of interrupted over completed tasks was 90 per cent for adults and 110 per cent for children. Thirty-seven adults and 36 children remembered the interrupted tasks better than the completed. Zeigarnik's results have been verified with children in studies by Pachauri (1935a, 1935b, 1936) and Abel (1938).[1] Martin (1940) reports, moreover, that interrupted tasks yield a greater degree of reminiscence than completed tasks. His subjects were all adults.

The phenomenon of reminiscence has as yet received no satisfactory explanation. Most commonly expressed is the view, first suggested by Ballard, that removal of stimulating circumstances allows neural activity to continue and bring about further consolidation of what has been learned. Hovland (1938a), who presents an excellent critical examination of several theories, points out that reminiscence appears even when subjects are required to name colors during the period between learning and recall (in his experiment only

two minutes). Color naming should, he claims, prevent continued activity (perseveration) of the neural traces involved in original learning. Ward (1937) and Hovland (1938a) both favor the view that a rest period after learning weakens "negative excitatory processes" (inhibition), thus facilitating recall. Referring to an apparent relation between reminiscence and distributed learning, Ward says:

> It may be that both phenomena are mediated by some more fundamental process or processes. For example, it would theoretically be possible that the different rates of dying out of correct responses or associations on the one hand, and of inhibiting or interfering associations and tendencies on the other hand, could account not only for reminiscence at very short intervals of time, but also for the greater relative economy of practice sessions distributed at intervals of one or two days. This type of explanation would require the additional assumption that once the interfering associations or tendencies are dropped out they will not return as rapidly with a continuation of learning as do correct responses and associations (p. 56).

It is of course not yet certain that all reported reminiscence phenomena have the same basis, since investigators have used different materials, methods, intervals, criteria, and age levels. Further research will be needed before many points mentioned in the above discussion can be clarified and a satisfactory explanation reached.

Other investigations on retention and forgetting in children have concerned the relation between quickness of learning and retention (Lyon, 1916; Gillette, 1936) and relative retention for pleasant and unpleasant associations (Rosenzweig and Mason, 1934; Carter, 1935, 1936, 1937; and Gilbert, 1937). The first-mentioned studies have shown that quickness of learning is

---

[1] Related to this research are studies in which the relative retention of complete and incomplete words and figures has been investigated. A study from Nanking (1935) shows that children retain completed words and pictures better than incomplete ones. Tiernan (1938), on the other hand, finds a slight, but not statistically reliable, advantage for incomplete figures. This tendency was more marked between the ages of 7 and 11 than later.

positively related to retention. Quick learners are not, as has often been supposed, quick forgetters. In general, results from the second group of experiments have shown that pleasant associations and words are retained somewhat better than unpleasant ones. Carter found, however, that unpleasant words are retained better than indifferent ones. In Gilbert's study children retained pleasant and unpleasant words equally well.

Problem Solving

Every learning situation presents a problem of one sort or another. Escaping from a maze, buttoning a coat, hitting the correct keys of a typewriter, and memorizing nonsense syllables or poems are *problems* when confronted initially. As psychologists use the term, however, problem solving refers to activity as a somewhat higher psychological level than is necessitated in learning of sensorimotor and mnemonic skills such as those mentioned. The type of learning designated as problem solving involves attainment of some more or less specific goal under such conditions that observing relations, reasoning, generalizing, "getting the idea," or what the Gestalt psychologists call "insight," greatly facilitate the learning process. Solution of some problems may be achieved only after discovery of an underlying principle, relation, or system of relations. Discovery of a principle is frequently the only immediate goal of the learning process.

Investigators of problem solving in children have utilized materials ranging in complexity from puzzle boxes to tasks calling for abstract reasoning. Many of the relatively simple materials have been patterned after those used in experiments with animals. The puzzle box tests of Healy and Fernald (1911), for example, are similar in principle to those used by Thorn-dike (1898) and Small (1900) to investigate problem solving in cats, monkeys, rats, and other animals. A large number of researches on problem solving in children take as their point of departure the similar experiments of Hobhouse (1901) and of Köhler (1925) on the use of tools by animals. In these studies the problem is to discover that tools may be used to attain otherwise inaccessible goals. More complicated still are the puzzles used by Lindley (1897) and Ruger (1910) to investigate problem solving in children and adults. J. Peterson's (1918, 1920) rational-learning and mental-maze tests represent another type of problem solving used in investigations with children as well as adults. These devices and several others which involve generalizing are of a predominantly verbal character.

How Children Attack a Problem Situation. Before discussing the solution of problems like those mentioned above it will be enlightening to consider Hamilton's (1911, 1916) observations on how children and other organisms attack insoluble problems. Children and adults were confronted by four doors, only one of which was unlocked. If a given door had been unlocked in one trial it was locked in the next. The problem was to escape from the enclosure. If the unlocked door had always been on the extreme right, on the extreme left, the second from the right or left, or the right on one trial and the left on the next, the problem could have been solved. Hamilton, however, purposely avoided following such principles. Which door would be unlocked from trial to trial was determined by chance. All subjects exhibited a variety of reactions which he designated as trial and error. Nevertheless, some exhibited a more "logical" trial and error than others. It seemed that they were using *hypotheses* as to the nature of the problem confronting them.[1] From the most to the least logical, the methods of attack were as follows: (A) trying the three inferentially possible doors—that is, those locked in the preceding trial—and avoiding the one previously unlocked; (B) trying all four doors once each in irregular order; (C) trying all four doors in regular order from left to right or right to left; (D) trying a given door more than once with intervening attempts to open some other door; (E) trying on two or more occasions to open a given door without intervening attempts at other doors, or persistent avoidance of a given door while trying all others. An infant of 26 months exhibited 15 per cent A reactions, 5 per cent B reactions, 20 per cent C reactions, 25 per cent D reactions, and 35 per cent E reactions. With subjects of increasing age, however, there was an increase in A and a decrease in E and similarly "illogical" reactions. Human adults exhibited 76 to 85 per cent A reactions and very seldom gave any C, D, or E reactions. The trial and error of young children was quite similar to that of infrahuman animals.

In his experiment with unicursal puzzles —that is, those in which a figure must be traced without lifting the pencil, retracing, or crossing lines—Lindley (1897) also found that younger children exhibit a quite inadequate mode of attack. His subjects were from grades 3 to 8. The reactions of children in the lowest grade were, according to Lindley, characterized by lack of circumspection, conventional beginnings, slight and inconsequential variations from one attempt to another, frequent relapses into a former routine, and tardiness in profiting from errors. In older children, these characteristics slowly made way for

"greater prevision, more adequate analysis of the design, less conventionality and automatism in procedure, more radical reconstruction of plan in successive trials, all of which led to greater promptness in profiting by mistakes" (p. 469). L. W. Gates (1938), using a multiple-choice situation, likewise observed increasing deliberateness of exploration with increasing age. The ages ranged from 5 to 10 years.

Other investigators of problem solving whose studies will be considered in the following discussions have also noted increasing appropriateness of attack as a function of age.

Puzzle Problems. A puzzle box frequently used to investigate problem solving in older children was devised by Healy and Fernald (1911). The nature of the problem is illustrated in the diagram and legend of Figure 19. Healy and Fernald used the following instructions:

> *You see that this box opens by the lid lifting up. The glass is put in so that you can see the way to open it. You can work through the holes and use the buttonhook. Study the box, and if you do the right things in the right order, it can readily be opened. Do not break the string or glass. Open it as quickly as you can.*

The problem is made more difficult by merely telling the child to open it, using the buttonhook. He then has to *discover* that the holes are his only approach to the rings and cords. After the box has been opened, the subject may be asked to close it.

The typical mode of attack is by overt trial and error. Occasionally, however, an older subject surveys the internal mechanism carefully and, after some delay, opens the box with no overt trial and error. When questioned he says that he "figured out the correct moves." This probably means that implicit trial and error was the basis of solution.

---

[1] Hamilton did not use the term *hypothesis* in this connection. It was later (1932) used by Krechevsky in reporting his observations of similar trial-and-error behavior in rats.

Norms for the above problem are reported by Woolley (1926) and Bronner, Healy, Lowe, and Shimberg (1927). Woolley, who had over 400 subjects in each of her groups, gives the median time on the initial trial as 251 seconds at 15 and 153 seconds at 16 years for boys and 436 seconds at 15 and 212 seconds at 16 years for girls. These results indicate a differ-

chologists claim that such sudden learning results from a more or less sudden grasping of relations, or *insight*. Where relations are not apparent, as in the usual maze problem, an individual is obliged to use overt trial and error, perhaps supplemented by implicit processes such as counting or other verbalization.[1] In situations like the present one, however, an

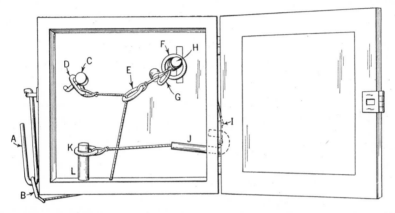

FIGURE 19. The Healy-Fernald puzzle box. (After W. Healy and G. Fernald.)

Seven distinct steps must be followed if the box is to be opened. They are: (1) removing ring *K* from post *L;* (2) pulling out staple *J;* (3) removing ring *I;* (4) removing ring *F* from post *H;* (5) removing ring *D* from arm of post *C;* (6) removing ring *B* from hook *A;* and (7) removing hook *A* and opening box.

ence in favor of the older individuals and the boys. Differences in mechanical skill rather than in problem-solving ability *per se* may underlie these differences. After the initial success, time curves drop precipitously and, within a few further trials, the box is opened in approximately the minimum time required for sheer manipulation. Time scores for closing the box are much higher than for opening it. Healy and Fernald report that the initial closing time is approximately twice that required to open the box.

The sudden drop in the learning curve for this problem is rather characteristic of problems, the various aspects of which are all apparent to the subject. Gestalt psy-

individual may attack the problem as he would a maze or he may, since opportunities are offered, observe the internal relations, and so reach a quick solution with perhaps no overt trial and error.[2]

The ability of preschool children to solve puzzle situations without overt trial and error has been studied by Harter (1930). Each problem involved a solution requir-

1 Some investigators have used mazes, the entire paths of which are observable. In such instances insight may be apparent. See especially the study by de Sanctis (1931) of observational maze learning in normal and feeble-minded children.

2 For other studies of insight in puzzle solving by children, see Ruger (1910), whose research was primarily on adults but involved four boys, and Wunderling (1935), who used children from the first to eighth grades.

ing that one step be completed before the next. Overt trial and error would involve moving one part of the apparatus or another until the solution appeared. It was possible, however, to "figure out" the moves beforehand and thus to respond without error. A diagram of one of Harter's puzzle devices is shown in Figure 20. The nature of the problem is described in the legend of this figure.

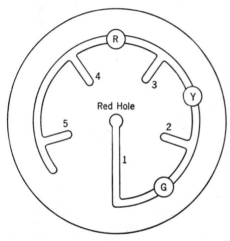

Red Hole

FIGURE 20. Obstacle peg test used to measure problem solving with or without overt trial and error. (From "Overt Trial and Error in the Problem Solving of Pre-school Children," by G. L. Harter. *Journal of Genetic Psychology*, 1930, **38**, 362. By permission of the publisher.)

A grooved path with side alleys 2, 3, 4, and 5 had red, yellow, and green pegs at the positions marked *R, Y,* and *G*. The pegs were modified styluses with a round knob at the top. They could be slid along the groove but not removed from the apparatus. The experimenter pointed to the red ball between 3 and 4 and told the child to put it in the red hole. If the child pulled at the red knob, he was told to push, not pull. Those who solved the problem used either of the following methods: (1) placing *G* and *Y* in the side grooves and then sliding *R* around to the red hole; or (2) moving the red peg into a side groove, pushing *Y* and *G* back to the blind end of the pathway, and then moving the red peg around to the hole. Ninety per cent of 40 adults and 74 per cent of 53 children used the first method.

Ability to solve such puzzles increased with CA and MA. Biserial r's ranged from $.54 \pm .08$ to $.73 \pm .06$ for success and CA and between $.49 \pm .09$ and $.57 \pm .08$ for success and MA. The amount of overt trial and error, as indicated by the average number of moves, decreased with age. Four yearly age groups from 3 to 6 made the following average number of moves, respectively, on the obstacle peg test: 36.0, 24.7, 20.4, and 17.6. Children who failed to solve the problems made more moves than did successful ones. Only 1 child out of 75, given the obstacle peg test solved it without making any error. Eighteen out of 75 solved a similar type of problem without error. In each case, the average age of the children achieving errorless solutions was much higher than that of those who solved with overt trial and error. On a repetition of the problems, solution was achieved with a marked decrease in moves and an increase in the number of errorless reactions. For instance, 32 out of 50 children given a second trial on the obstacle peg test solved it without overt trial and error as compared to 1 child out of 75 for the first trial. Adults who succeeded on the tests reacted like children who succeeded, but time was greatly reduced.

Problems Involving Utilization of Tools. Tool problems were used by Hobhouse (1901) with animals. Köhler (1925) revived and greatly extended the use of the method in his researches on learning in chimpanzees. It consists, essentially, of confronting the subject with some *lure*, such as food or a toy, which is inaccessible unless certain tools are utilized. These tools may comprise attached strings, a lever with lure attached, a stick sufficiently long to reach the lure if fitted together, a box or number of boxes to be stacked, or some other indirect means of obtaining the lure. The task which confronts the subject is chiefly to learn that the given objects may be used as a means of obtaining the lure.

Richardson's (1932, 1934) investigations dealt with infants between the ages of 28 and 52 weeks. Kellogg and Kellogg (1933) used tool problems with an infant ape and an infant human subject. Researches by Alpert (1928), Brainard (1930), Matheson (1931), Moriya (1937a, 1937b), Sawa (1937), Tagawa (1937), and Sobel (1939) involved preschool children. Comparative

lay. In others the barrier was removed since, until the age of 44 weeks, it appeared to hinder solution of the problems. Representative string situations are illustrated in Figure 21. Each setting was arranged behind a screen. As soon as this was removed, the experimenter tapped the toy on the table, squeaked it, rocked it, or rattled it, depending on its nature. The reactions of the subject were then observed. If he pulled in the lure, he was

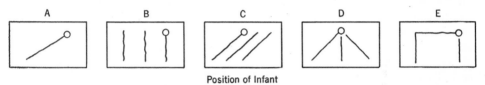

Position of Infant

FIGURE 21. Representative string problems used with infants. (From "The Growth of Adaptive Behavior in Infants: An Experimental Study of Seven Age Levels," by H. M. Richardson. *Genetic Psychology Monographs*, 1932, **12**, 230. By permission of the publisher.)

In other situations the position of the correct string was the reverse of that shown in these diagrams. The child sat in one half of a crib, and the top of the other half was covered to form a table top on which the settings of the strings were arranged. In some tests a barrier was between the child and the table top; in other tests there was no barrier.

investigations of normal and feeble-minded children have been carried out by Aldrich (1931), Aldrich and Doll (1931a, 1931b), and Gottschaldt (1933). Since several of these investigations have much in common, we shall describe in detail only the most representative ones. Results of related studies will then be summarized briefly.

Since Richardson's investigations deal with infants, they will be discussed first. The two studies were carried out concurrently and on the same infants. In the 1932 article are reported the reactions of 10 boys and 6 girls to string problems given at monthly intervals between the twenty-eighth and fifty-second weeks. The lure was a toy attached to a string. Although the end of the string was within reach, the lure was not. In some tests a barrier prevented the infant from reaching the table top on which the lure and string

allowed to play with it a short time before it was removed. Only settings such as that shown in Figure 21A were used at the earliest age level. Type B was added at 32 weeks. At 36 weeks, type C was added to the tests. From 40 to 52 weeks, all types were used.

The reactions of infants to the above situations suggested five types of *perceptive attitude*. They were: (a) interest in the string rather than in the lure, (b) interest in the lure and apparently accidental contact with the string, (c) awareness of both lure and string without evident purposive utilization of the string, (d) experimentation, and (e) definite utilization of the string as a means to bring the lure into reach. Richardson claims that a and b represent success without insight; c and d, success with incomplete insight; and e, success with insight. The last type was associated with a marked drop in time. Types of response said to involve insight increased in frequency with age. The other types decreased as a function of age. Relative difficulty of the various situations appeared to be determined by the directness with which the dummy string or strings led to the lure. In terms of the percentage of children making initial correct choices, the relative difficulty was in the order shown from *A* to *E* in Figure 21.

Richardson's second report describes lever experiments carried out with the same infants and under the same general conditions. The experimenter rang a small bell and, while the infant watched, placed the bell on the end of a lever, the short arm of which was within the infant's reach. Turning the short arm of the lever a sufficient number of degrees brought the bell within grasping distance. Two positions of the lever, straight out in the median plane or oblique to the right, were used. A counterclockwise turn of, respectively, 90 to 45 degrees was thus required. If the child failed, a demonstration was given. This was followed by further tests and, if necessary, demonstrations. Between 40 and 44 weeks the percentage of infants succeeding at least once in securing the lure increased from 20 to 67. By the fifty-second week, the percentage had increased to 83. Other criteria likewise indicated increasing ability to perform the problem as a function of age. Part of the improvement was undoubtedly due to greater mechanical ability and better motivation at the higher age levels. As in the string problems, several degrees of "perceptive attitude" or insight could be discerned, and the degree increased with age. Demonstrations failed to influence the infants' grasp of the nature of the situation although, after 44 weeks, they appeared to increase motivation.

In problem-solving situations the behavior of individual subjects is frequently more enlightening than group trends. The following protocol is presented by Richardson as representing development of insight in a 44-month infant.[1]

As soon as the lever board is in place, B gets her hand on the short arm of the lever and tries to tug it toward her. She rotates it about 40 degrees in the counterclockwise direction.

The lever is returned to its former position by E. The bell is rung. B reaches for it with her left hand as E moves it to the far side of the grill and sets it on the tray. Right hand is also active. B has turned the tray about 20 degrees before the bell is put on the tray. Left and right hands alternately approach short arm, turning it. She does not yet turn it more than 40 degrees in the counterclockwise direction, and occasionally turns it clockwise. As she rotates it back and forth with her right hand, she eagerly watches the bell in the tray. Once she turns the lever as much as 90 degrees, so that the stick is parallel to the grill. After *80 seconds* the tray, following trial rotations, is brought into contact with the grill, and B secures the bell.

E returns the bell to the lever in original position. B, with her right hand, turns the short arm about 40 degrees in the counterclockwise direction. She brings up her left hand. With her right, in a steady movement, she rotates the lever so that *20 seconds* after the beginning of the situation the tray is near the grill. She secures the bell. The bell is removed and set again on the tray. This time the first turn of the short arm is greater. *Five seconds* after the beginning of the situation B has secured the bell and carried it through the grill.

Alpert's (1928) research is representative of those on preschool children. It is

---

[1] Paraphrased from Richardson's (1934) protocols, p. 368.

a repetition of several situations presented by Köhler to chimpanzees. Forty-four nursery school children 19 to 49 months old were confronted with situations like the following: An object suspended from the ceiling could be reached only by placing a near-by block beneath it in an appropriate position; an attractive toy too far from the play pen to be reached by hand could be obtained if a near-by stick was used to pull it in; a toy placed at a greater distance from the bars of the pen than was the former one became accessible only when two sticks were fitted together and used to angle for it.

The initial responses to such situations were usually of what might be called a trial-and-error nature. There was no grasping of the fact that the otherwise inaccessible lure could be obtained by the tools lying at hand, even when these were observed and, in some instances, played with. A good example is the behavior of Case 20, a girl of 42 months, in response to the suspended lure.

First exposure. S went up to objective, stared at it, and waveringly raised her left arm halfway up, looking at E; remained thus for 2 minutes, then indicated that she wished her coat taken off. While adjusting her sweater sleeves, caught sight of block, looked long and hard at it, then again partly outstretched her arm toward objective, looking at E, began to chew her nails, still staring at E.

Second exposure. S walked slowly up to objective and tried to reach it with her right hand, looking at E. S remained thus, with arm partly outstretched, gazing around, for 2 minutes. S looked at the block and took a few steps toward it, looking at E; alternated between a step toward block and attempt to reach up for objective; walked off, past the block, looking back at objective several times.

Third exposure. S looked at objective and at E, advanced slowly toward former,

arm outstretched, reaching for object in an ineffectual manner as she gazed all around; saw block but continued to reach up. S began to amuse herself with the woodwork on the nearest wall.

Even with two further presentations of this situation, the subject failed to observe that the problem could be solved by using the block. Most children eventually solved the problem. A few solved it very quickly. An example is Case 15, a boy aged 39 months. Only one exposure of 30 seconds' duration was required.

S was much distressed when asked to come with E, but at sight of balloon—objective—he rushed at it trying to reach it with both hands. S turned around to complain to E, spied the block, and announced tearfully that he would get on it; dragged block under objective, got on, and reached up for it but found it rather a hard stretch; jumped off, turned block on its perpendicular side, got on, and swung objective with glee.

A good example of apparent trial and error followed by sudden solution is that of a girl of 38 months reacting to the two-stick problem.

First exposure. S examined one of the sticks and tried to reach objective with it over the top of pen; examined the other stick and used it in the same way, repeating, "I can't" over and over; tried out the stick between the bars, over the top of pen, finally striking it viciously against the floor; complained bitterly, and tried again to reach as before, stretching and straining; tried to climb out and whined, "I can't." E terminated exposure to avoid fatigue.

Second exposure. S reached for objective as above and in 10 seconds said, "Look, I can't," but continued her efforts; fitted sticks up against bars of pen, banged them together, etc. S tried to reach objective with her hand through the spaces, to force her way out, to shake the pen, etc.; said, "Dolly does not want me to get him."

Third exposure. As above, complaining intermittently and finally giving up.

Fourth exposure. S stretched for objective over top of pen, striking out angrily with stick, complaining and asking E to move object closer. S said, "Let's try big stick on little one," picked up the other stick, examined ends carefully and succeeded in fitting them, with a shout of "Bang!" S angled for objective, reached it exultantly, and repeated stunt several times.

Alpert found "exploration and elimination" to be the most frequent behavior of preschool children in responding to the problem situations. Where insight occurred, it tended to be immediate rather than gradual. It was apparent in varying degrees. Chance operated by bringing about "an optimum constellation of the elements" required for solution. The presence of an optimum constellation, however, did not guarantee that insight would appear. Brainard (1930) carried out similar experiments on a child of 2 years and 7 months whose IQ was 141. Insight was present for some situations but not for others.

Matheson's (1931) investigation differed from Alpert's and Brainard's in certain respects. The subjects were 28 children between the ages of 2 and 4½ years. One problem involved taking a ring off a hook in order to lower a basket containing the lure. Another was of the crossed-string variety, the child being required to pull in a longer string, alone of adequate length. A stick and a box-stacking problem somewhat like those used by Alpert were also involved. Matheson noted 15 types of reaction to these situations, all of which were called out to some extent by each problem. The most frequent of these were "manipulation" and "pointing and reaching," also designated as "trial and error." The rarest responses were "solution without previous manipulation" and "solution for the sake of solution." Only 14 per cent of the children exhibited such responses.

The percentage of children solving the problems went from zero at 2, to 62 at 4 years. The correlation between solution and CA was .464 ± .10; that between solution and MA, .422 ± .107.

Aldrich (1931) and Aldrich and Doll (1931a, 1931b) extended problems like the above to the idiot level of intelligence. The degree of insight attained in stacking boxes, combining sticks, using single sticks, and using a rake to reach a lure is reported to be somewhere between that attained by Köhler's apes and Alpert's preschool children. The importance of strong incentives as a factor in achievement of insight is especially noted in these studies and in one by Sawa (1937) on normal children. Gottschaldt's (1933) investigation involved normal, moron, imbecile, and idiot children. Stick, string, and block-stacking situations were used. The chief contribution of this research is analysis of the behavior in terms of level of aspiration and in terms of field forces, following the lead of Lewin. Gottschaldt found a lower level of aspiration with decreasing intelligence. Feeble-minded children were satisfied with various substitute "solutions." The influence of vectors was brought out in stick problems of the following nature: A short stick lay near at hand and a long one was more distant. The long stick was alone adequate for reaching the lure. In some instances the short stick was secured and played with, the child seeming to forget the long stick and the lure. The presence of a toy near the short stick had a still greater influence upon the "attractiveness" of this inadequate instrument. Whenever an apparently easy, yet inadequate, solution appeared possible, the difficulty of the problem was greatly increased. Such "distraction" was more apparent in feeble-minded than in normal children. Similar principles are involved in detour problems used by Lewin (1935), Sawa (1937), and Tagawa (1937). Theoretical discussions of such problems have been presented by Lewin (1935), in terms of vector analysis, and Hull (1938), in terms of the goal-gradient hypothesis.

Moriya (1937a, 1937b) wished to determine whether preschool children achieve insight into the solution of problems involving the principle of a lever. Only the older of 29 kindergarten children evidenced insight in balancing objects on the flattened top of a pyramid. In a further problem involving removal of strings from a lever arm in such a manner as to leave it still balanced in the horizontal direction, no insight was evidenced. The author concludes that preschool children use trial and error predominantly in solving problems involving the principle of a lever. Lack of previous experience with levers is, however, probably the real explanation. G. M. Peterson (1932) used somewhat similar lever problems, but on a verbal basis. His subjects were children between the ages of 132 and 168 months. In these, as in many other problems, insight may involve transfer to the new situation of what has been learned previously in somewhat similar situations. The results of a preliminary investigation by Sobel (1939) is of interest here. Sobel found that some children between the ages of 18 and 48 months achieved immediate solution of tool problems. Others solved a given problem only after previous training which involved use of similar implements. The "insight" evidenced in the latter instances was thus known to be based upon transfer.

Solution of Problems by Learning a Principle. To the degree to which problems are solved as a result of implicit rather than readily observed overt activities, the solution is said to result from rea-soning. The implicit activity involves "manipulation" of symbols, or substitutes for past stimulation. Such manipulation is often of a trial-and-error nature.[1] When solution of a problem involves learning a principle, we usually speak of the reasoning process as *generalizing.* Several investigations on learning in children have involved problems demanding generalization. Such problems will be considered in the present section.

Heidbreder (1927, 1928) used three problem situations to investigate generalizing in 30 children between 2½ and 10 years and in 10 adults. Each problem involved a principle, the discovery of which was the chief task confronting the subjects. In Problem I the child was presented with two boxes, one of which contained a doll. The *right-hand box* always contained the doll, yet it might be closer than the left in one trial and farther away in the next. Problem II utilized plain and flowered boxes. Regardless of its position (right-left, near-far) with respect to the other box, the *flowered* one always contained the toy. Problem III involved boxes with plain figures and boxes with figures, having perimeters with red dots. Two boxes of a given kind were used at each trial. If both had plain figures, the doll was in the farther box. On the other hand, if both had dotted figures, *the nearer box* contained the doll. Table 9 shows the number of solutions and number of reactions per problem for subjects at different age levels. One will note that children above the sixth year solved all three problems, and in relatively few trials. The first problem was solved by one 3-year-old and by six 4-year-olds. Whereas only two 3-year-olds solved Problem II, it was solved by all above this age. The young-

---

[1] For a more extensive discussion of the nature of implicit activity such as involved in reasoning, see Munn (1938), pp. 333 ff.

TABLE 9

GENERALIZING AS A FUNCTION OF AGE *

Age	No.	Problem I		Problem II		Problem III	
		Solutions	Reactions	Solutions	Reactions	Solutions	Reactions
3	10	1	219	2	230	0	216
4	10	6	178	10	23	1	348
6–10	10	10	174	10	23	10	81
Adult	10	10	34	10	16	10	40

* From Heidbreder (1928), p. 525.

est individual to solve Problem III was a 4-year-old. No children of the youngest age group gave a satisfactory reason for selecting a given box. When questioned, they sometimes said that the box was selected because they like it. Only 5 per cent of the next age group verbalized their solutions. Above the age of 6 years, however, almost every solution was given an adequate verbal formulation.

More difficult of solution than the above is the double-alternation problem used by Gellermann (1931) with 38 children between 3 and 13 years of age. The apparatus was a modification of one used by Hunter with rats and raccoons. Its main features are shown in Figure 22. This is called a "temporal maze" by Hunter to distinguish it from mazes of the spatial variety, that is, those in which the turn in each part may be elicited by stimuli peculiar to this part. The problem which confronted each of Gellermann's subjects was learning to turn *right, right, left, left,* in successive trials, upon reaching the point X. Since the stimuli in the central alley were always alike, and hence could not give differential cues for right or left turns, the subjects were called upon to "figure

out" the correct order of turns. They were given no instructions which would in any way suggest the solution. Unless they guessed it, as a matter of fact, the subjects did not at first know that a problem confronted them. They were merely invited

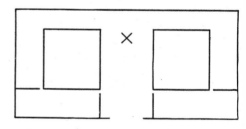

FIGURE 22. A double alternation maze.

to enter the apparatus and to keep moving. Incorrect responses were followed by the closing of a door which prevented progress in the incorrect direction. The subject was, on such occasions, required to retrace and take the correct turn. As soon as the *rrll* response had been made the child was allowed to leave the apparatus. It was readmitted after completion of a trial. This continued until three trials in succession without error had been completed. Finally, and without previous intimation, each child was required to give the response *rrllrrll*, that is, to repeat the series without leaving the apparatus. No questions were asked by the experimenter or answered by him while learning was in progress. After completion of the extended series, however, he asked these questions: "What did you think of it?" "How did you learn that [the solution]?"

Whereas adults learned this problem in an average of 6, children required an average of 15 trials. Trials to learn ranged from 4 to 37. The average number of errors (incorrect turns) made by children was 30, almost twice that made by adults. The rank-difference correlation between CA and trials was only .28 ± .11. The two youngest (3- and 4-year-old) children, however, failed to master the problem. From 5 years on, the number of trials and the number of errors decreased with age. The two 5-year-olds failed to extend the series, even after 10 to 12 extension tests. Older children extended the series in 2 to 3 tests.

The nature of the problem which confronts the subjects is perhaps best indicated by their verbal reports. A 10-year-old boy who learned in 14 trials gave the following report:

> First I thought all the walls would close in, and you were going to test my nerve or something like that. Then I found the doors were open, and I kept on walking. I thought there was something to it, because sometimes the doors were closed. After awhile I found you must go around each place twice.

Other reports were of a somewhat similar nature. At first there was no idea concerning what was to be expected, then came the idea that a *problem* was to be learned. Finally, the subjects formulated the problem in some such manner as *"twice to the right and twice to the left."*

The rôle of verbalization in develop-ment of generalizations by children has been demonstrated in a multiple-choice type of experiment reported by Pyles (1932). Eighty children ranging in age from 2 to 7 years were confronted with 5 figures under one of which a toy was hidden. The instructions were: *"One of these shapes has a toy under it. See if you can find which shape has a toy."* The child tried this shape and that until the toy was discovered. Then the experimenter said, *"Where did you find the toy?"* The child indicated. The experimenter then said, *"Yes, that one had it."* Such comments were made on the first three and subsequently on every third trial, the aim being to maintain interest and to stress the importance of having the first selection correct. Three series of experiments were used, with rotation of matched groups to equate for order of presentation. One series had nonsense figures which were unnamed. A second series involved the same figures, but now given a name, "Bokie," or the like. In a third series, well-known animal forms were used. These were named spontaneously by the children. A series was regarded as learned when the child selected the correct figure four times in succession.

The results are summarized in Table 10. They indicate that verbalization is an aid to this kind of learning and that the more familiar the material, the more rapid the learning. The correlation between trials and CA ranged from −.19 to −.72; that between trials and MA from −.21 to −.62. The highest correlations were for series *B*, involving the named nonsense figures.

Investigation of ability to respond to different situations in terms of a common principle was made by Roberts (1932) with 43 children between 2 and 5 years of age. The children were confronted by three doors above each of which a colored toy aeroplane was visible. The experimenter

TABLE 10

COMPARISONS OF SCORES MADE ON THE THREE SERIES WITH ORDER OF PRESENTATION EQUATED

Groups	1-6	1-6	1-6
Series	A. Unnamed	B. Named	C. Animals
Mean number of trials *	21.3 ± 1.95	14.2 ± 1.6	5.3 ± .4
Median number of trials	16.5	7.5	4.0
SD number of trials	22.6	18.1	4.8
Range	1-91	1-76	1-25
Percentage complete failure	15	10	3
Percentage succeeding in 25 trials or less	54	72	96

* Omitting cases of complete failure. From Pyles (1932), p. 111.

said, *"This house has three doors; all of them open, but only one makes an aeroplane fall."* Doors and aeroplanes differed in color. There was, however, always one door with an aeroplane of the same color above it. This was the correct door. All children solved this problem, but the youngest child giving a statement as to the principle involved was 3 years and 4 months old. At higher age levels there was an increasing frequency of generalizing. All but the 2-year-old subjects reacted appropriately to new situations involving the same principle.

In a second study which was similar, in general principles, to that described, Roberts (1933) used figures of various shapes or sizes instead of colors. In one situation, six lower doors contained squares. Above them, in order, were a triangle, crescent, square, semicircle, octagon, and figure with parallel sides and concave ends. The toy was always hidden behind the figure which matched that above, in this case the square. In some situations, both upper and lower figures differed, but there was always one above which matched the door below. The subjects were 21 children who were aged 4 years and 19 orphanage children between 4 and 8 years of age. These were separated into three matched groups which learned the problems in different orders. Learning of an initial problem was fol-

lowed by learning of other problems involving different colors, figures, or sizes. The criterion of learning comprised four trials without error. In this study the chief aim was to discover whether a principle learned in one situation would be applied in others. Complete application of the principle would result in absence of errors in the solution of the next problem in the series. When the groups were equated in terms of MA, there was no difference in the learning ability of preschool and orphanage children. The correlation between trials to learn the initial problem and CA was −.40 ± .089. The correlation with MA was −.47 ± .083. With CA held constant, the correlation between trials and MA was reduced to −.30. The percentage of subjects making no errors in achieving the criterion increased with successive problems. On the first problem, for example, no subjects learned without errors; on the second problem, 71 per cent made no errors; on the third problem, 81 per cent made no errors. When the ninth problem was presented, 95 per cent performed without error. Although the children could solve these problems and thus make an overt generalizing response, they were unable to state the principle involved.[1]

[1] This difficulty is perhaps merely linguistic. Hazlitt (1930), in her investigation of concepts

J. J. Ray (1936) investigated generalizing in 6 dull, 6 average, and 6 bright 12-year-old children. Pictures were exposed, two at a time, in the aperture of a small apparatus which was operated manually by the subject. Whenever a key under the *correct* picture was pressed, a green light went on. Pressure on a key under the *incorrect* picture lit a red light. Pressure of either key, in addition to connecting a light, also exposed the next pair of pictures. The child's task was to get a green light every time as soon as possible. Twenty series of problems were used and each involved twenty pairs of pictures. The pictures of a series were repeated until the child responded correctly to the whole series or verbalized the solution. In the simplest problem, the key under the *curved* figure ($\rightarrow\!\!\!\prec$, $\sim\!\!\sim\!\!\sim$, $\wedge$,) etc., always lit the green light while that under the straight figure

$\longmapsto$, $\triangle$, $\longrightarrow\!\!\wedge\!\!\longrightarrow$,

etc., always lit the red light.

Other series involved animate versus inanimate objects, tools versus playthings, quadrupeds versus nonquadrupeds, and the like. Ability to solve these problems was correlated with intelligence, the dull children solving few and the bright children many series. The nature of the problem

such as "exception," found that children between 3 and 7 years of age could *make an exception* in behavior although they did not understand what they were to do when *asked* to make an exception. A child was given a large egg into which various smaller colored eggs fitted. The series of eggs was opened before him and he was asked to put all back into the big egg except the *green* one. The younger subjects either failed to respond or put back all the eggs. When they were asked to put back all eggs *but* the red one, many more children responded correctly. See also Kreezer and Dallenbach (1939), on learning the relation of opposition, Hicks and Stewart (1930), on concepts of size, and Lacey and Dallenbach (1939), on the cause-effect relation.

confronting the child and some insight into the mode of solution are shown by verbalizations. The verbal responses of only two subjects can be presented here. Subject R responded to the quadruped versus nonquadruped situation, beginning with the eighth pair, as follows:

"Animal." Next pair, "Wait a minute—might be animal with a tail." Second presentation of series, first pair, "I think—wait, let me go through one more time to make sure." Twelve pairs later, "If it's animal it's right, but I think something's wrong." Four series later, "If I'm not mistaken it's an animal that has legs." One pair later, "It's either the largest or a mammal. Wait a minute, let me go through once more." Two pairs later, "I think it's an animal with four legs. The thing that got me puzzled was the snake and the turtle. Couldn't see any difference hardly."

Thus an implicit trial and error is apparent. Subject K, responding to the animate versus inanimate series, gave evidence of trial and error punctuated with sudden insight. After five pairs had been presented he said:

"I can't get this one." Ten pairs later he said, "I never get this one—I know." After the eleventh pair of the fourth presentation he said, "I believe I've caught on! (Great relief.) It's the animal. Easy as pie when I caught on." [1]

[1] Welch (1938, 1939a, 1939b, 1939c, 1940a, 1940b) and Welch and Long (1940a, 1940b) present a series of studies on development of concepts and generalizations in children. In some respects they are extensions of the early and much more limited studies of Munn and Steining (1931) and Gellermann (1933) on "form" discrimination in children. Limitations of space do not permit an adequate discussion of such investigations in the present chapter, where emphasis must be placed upon learning *per se*. The reader interested in development of concepts and generalizations will find the papers by Welch and by Welch and Long of great value. He should see Welch (1940a) also for an extensive bibliography of related studies.

Rational Learning. In solving J. Peterson's (1918) "rational learning" problem the subject is required to associate with each of a group of words a number which has been arbitrarily assigned to it. For instance, the letters *A, B,* and *C* may be numbered, respectively, 2, 3, and 1. The child is told that the letters *A, B,* and *C* are numbered from 1 to 3, but the *A* may not be 1, *B* may not be 2, and *C* may not be 3. He is then asked, *"What number do you think A has?"* He guesses numbers from 1 to 3 until the number 2 is given. Then he is asked to guess the number for *B.* When he says that it is 3, he is asked the number that goes with *C.* When he guesses this, the letters are repeated. When he repeats each number correctly as the letters are called, the child is given a longer list of letters.

This problem is believed to involve "rational" learning because, if the subject notes that a number which is correct earlier in the series cannot be used again in the same series, his learning is greatly facilitated. Repetition of an earlier correct number is designated a *logical error.* Likewise, learning will be facilitated if the subject does not repeat a given incorrect number while guessing the numbers which go with a given letter. Such repetitions are designated *perseverative errors.* In Peterson and Harrelson's (1923) study of rational learning in white and Negro children between 7 and 10 years of age, the letters *A* to *E* were used with the numbers 4, 2, 5, 1, and 3, respectively. Learning curves based upon data for 299 white and 314 Negro children were negatively accelerated and very similar to those obtained in learning of sensorimotor skills. As shown in Table 11, which contains the data for a 10-year-old white girl, the process involved is of a trial-and-error nature. Nelson (1936) presents several learning curves for problems involving rational learning of the above-mentioned type.

There was no sex difference for the learning of this problem. The mean score of white children was 1.69 PE units above that of the Negro children. A somewhat similar problem was later used by J. Peterson (1926) to investigate the limits of learning by trial and error in high school subjects.

Maier's Reasoning Problem Adapted for Children. In addition to those problems which involve solution of puzzles, use of tools, learning and application of a principle, and so-called rational learning, there are others not easily classified; Maier's reasoning problem is one of these.

Maier's (1936) investigation is based upon the view that the essence of reasoning is combination of past experiences in solution of a problem. He used the apparatus diagrammatically represented in Figure 23. The child was first made familiar with the entire apparatus. Then the experiment proper was conducted as follows: After another brief exploration of the apparatus the child was allowed to emerge through a door of one of the exit booths. This comprised *Experience I.* The child was then led around the apparatus by a devious route until another booth was reached. In this booth it was shown a toy house. When a penny was dropped into the house a tune played. This experience in a specific booth was *Experience II.* Both experimenter and child then left the booth to go in search of a penny by means of which the child could again play the tune. After the penny had been found and the child had been disoriented in the process, he was placed in a third booth and told to go and play the tune. In order to do this without trial and error he would have to utilize Experiences I and II. In other words, if the first experience had been in *Y* (see Figure 23), the second one

TABLE 11

RATIONAL LEARNING IN A TEN-YEAR-OLD GIRL

Repetitions	A 4	B 2	C 5	D 1	E 3	Total Errors	Logical Errors	Perseverative Errors
1	1 5 4	5 3 1 (6) 2	3 5	1	3	7	1	0
2	4	5 2	1 3 5	1	3	3	0	0
3	4	5 3 2	5	1	2 4 1 2 4 5 3	8	6	2
4	4	5 2	4 5	1	3	2	1	0
5	4	2	3 1 4 2 5	1	3	4	2	0
6	4	5 2	3 2 4 5	1	3	4	2	0
7	4	2	3 5	1	3	1	0	0
8	4	2	5	1	3	0	0	0
9	4	2	5	1	3	0	0	0

Time: 5 minutes.
After Peterson and Harrelson (1923), p. 97.

in *X*, and the entrance from which he was to reach *X* in *W*, the child would have to think of the fact that *W* had a given position with respect to *X*. He could react in

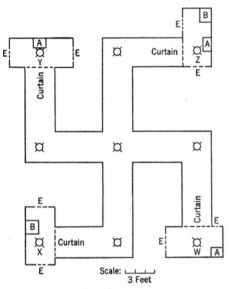

FIGURE 23. Ground plan of an apparatus for testing the ability of children to reason. (From "Reasoning in Children," by N. R. F. Maier. *Journal of Comparative Psychology*, 1936, **21**, 356. By permission of the publisher.)

W, X, Y, and *Z* represent booths placed at the end of the pathways. *E* represents entrances to the booths. These entrances are covered by drop curtains. Similar curtains also separate the booths from the pathways. *A* represents an adult chair and *B* a nursery school chair. The position of 25-watt electric lights is indicated in the diagram. The apparatus is built of a wooden framework covered with black cloth.

such terms only on the basis of his original exploration and the two specific experiences. The starting booth in each test was always the goal booth of the preceding test. Since the child had three possible goals in each trial, chance accuracy would approximate 33 per cent.

The subjects ranged in age from 42 to 112 months. They were arranged into groups having average ages of 47.6, 62.3, 70.1, 84.3, and 92.5 months. The size of the groups ranged from 4 to 12. There was an increase in the accuracy of response at successive age levels, the percentages being, respectively, 32.0, 43.6, 58.6, 73.3, and 82.5. The percentage of subjects giving five or more correct responses in 10 trials was, respectively, 20.0, 36.3, 71.4, 83.3, and 100. One will note that it was not until the age approximated 70 months that accuracy went far above what would be expected on the basis of chance. Maier says: "The ability to combine the essentials of two isolated experiences in such manner as to reach a goal is rather late in maturing. It is rarely developed in a marked extent in children below six years of age." When the data were arranged in terms of mental age groups, greater than chance accuracy was not apparent below a mental age of six years. Scores increased with mental age, as did the percentage of subjects making better than five correct responses out of ten.

Problem Solving in the Schoolroom Situation with School Materials.[1] Several investigators have studied problem solving under school conditions and in so doing have utilized arithmetic, geometry, and civics. Donovan and Thorndike (1913) report learning data on addition. Stevenson (1925) outlines some of the difficulties met by children from various grades in solving arithmetical problems. Monroe's (1928) investigation, which also deals with arithmetic, is more analytical than earlier studies. He stated the same arithmetical problems in technical terms, in everyday terms, or in relation to irrelevant material. Equated groups from the seventh grade were tested. Greatest success was achieved when the problems were framed in terms

[1] For a review of literature on factors which influence learning in school situations, see Stroud (1940).

of everyday life. Monroe concludes, however, that a large percentage of seventh-grade children fail to reason in solving arithmetic problems. He claims that they depend upon habit for solution. Some corroboration for this view comes from Henry's (1934) investigation with geometric problems. Only 32 per cent of his group of college students gave evidence of insight in solution of such problems. In 285 test situations, responses of the "Oh, I see" type occurred but seventeen times. Brownell (1938) reports that both repetition and insight are involved in learning arithmetic. Stump (1927) plotted curves for the learning of civics problems in terms of the number of "elements" learned. The subjects were high school seniors. Learning curves had a very gradual rise. Although the problems were logical ones, involving development and application of principles, there was little evidence of higher processes than those involved in sheer memorizing. This may be due to the method of presenting the problems rather than to lack of insight in the students.

Learning in Children and Adults

Comparison of learning in children and adults appears especially relevant here, for at the beginning of the present chapter we noted the fact that educators and other students of child development have, until relatively recent years, treated children as though their learning process were in no fundamental way different from that of animals and adults. Were they correct in supposing that principles worked out with animals and adults are also applicable to children? Has the research on learning in children disclosed anything not already apparent?

It should be evident, in the first place, that in so far as investigations on learning

in children have been carried out in the classroom, or under similar conditions, they have disclosed the adequacy or inadequacy of given procedures in such situations, something which could not with any degree of assurance have been prognosticated from work with adults in the laboratory. To mention one example, the whole method has not worked nearly so well with children in classroom situations as with adults in the psychological laboratory. In the second place, conditions which serve to motivate adults and children, although alike in certain respects, are sufficiently different to warrant separate investigation. In the third place, so little is known about learning, despite the large amount of research, that we need information from as many sources and from as many levels of development as possible. Finally, it must be acknowledged that learning is dependent upon modification of neuromuscular mechanisms, mechanisms the development of which continues at a rapid pace during the early years of childhood. It is in terms of the growth of these mechanisms that we may expect the learning process in children and adults to differ most fundamentally.

The learning of infants is inferior to that of older children and adults chiefly because of neuromuscular immaturity. There is, of course, no sudden transition at any age level. The growth of learning ability is gradual, and one stage, if we may speak of stages, merges imperceptibly with the next. Nevertheless, when we compare the learning of an infant with that of a school child, the inferiority of the former is glaringly apparent. We see this inferiority in tardiness of development and instability of conditioned responses; in inability to acquire motor skills readily learned by the older child; in poor retentivity, especially in situations of the delayed-reaction variety; and in lack of ability to attack problems with sufficient effectiveness to allow solution. Not only is the infant handicapped by neuromuscular immaturity, but he is also devoid of the motives which are most effective in impelling the older child to learn, of the background of experience which may be applied to new situations calling for adjustment, and of an effective repertoire of words and other symbols with which external situations can, as it were, be implicitly manipulated.

As a child grows older we are confronted not so much by neuromuscular immaturity as we are by what might, for want of a better term, be called recalcitrance. It is clearly apparent in the conditioned-response experiment. From about the fifth year and thereafter the ease with which conditioned responses may be developed shows a continued decrease despite the fact that the child's nervous system is undergoing further development. As Razran has pointed out, although the child is more capable of modification than at an earlier age he *resists* such modification. He is no longer as docile as formerly. His naïveté has decreased, he has become increasingly critical of his surroundings, he has developed interests and attitudes of which those who would modify his behavior must take cognizance. After the relatively passive stage of infancy is passed, therefore, the psychology of incentives becomes increasingly important. Several investigations mentioned in this chapter have indicated the effectiveness of rivalry and of verbal and material rewards of various kinds in channelizing the efforts of children in learning situations. Lewin's concept of valences may yield fruitful results in this field.

In most of the learning situations considered in this chapter very little difference has been discovered in the modifiability of adequately motivated children and adults. Beyond the early years of childhood, when the handicaps of neuromuscular immaturity have largely been overcome, practically all differences in the learning of children and adults may be attributed to differences in motivation and in previous experience. Our discussion of motor skills, for example, demonstrated that, although older children and adults may begin with higher scores than younger children, the percentage of improvement resulting from a given amount of practice is alike regardless of age. Mnemonic processes show large differences in the ability of children and adults. The writer doubts, however, whether this represents true differences in modifiability and retentivity. In the first place, there is no way, even by use of nonsense syllables, to avoid the fact that increasing age brings increasing acquaintance with symbols and their manipulation. This is a factor of experience, not of neural growth. In the second place, it is difficult, if not impossible, to equate motivation in individuals at different age levels, especially when the levels are as widely separated as those between the first-grade child and the adult. Finally—and this is related to the two previously mentioned factors—mnemonic ability demands good observation as well as good modifiability and retentivity. Because of their wide range of interests and experience, adults are likely to be much better observers than children. Even reminiscence, which was once thought to differentiate child from adult forgetting, has been demonstrated to be prevalent at both levels.

The clearest case of a difference in the learning ability of children and adults could perhaps be made out in the field of problem solving. Even here, however, differences in motivation and in past experience, including familiarity with symbols and their use, rather than in problem-solving ability *per se,* may be the chief differentiating factors. Hazlitt (1930) has particularly challenged the view that a fundamental difference exists between child and adult reasoning. She attributes apparent differences to the type of factors just mentioned.

It seems apparent to the writer that the chief problems relating to learning in children are those of discovering the most adequate motivating conditions and the most effective procedures for the situations in which children must develop. The practical outcome of researches on learning in children will lie in these directions.

So far as discovering anything fundamentally new concerning the learning process is concerned, the investigations on learning in children have failed. One possible reason for this is that such investigations have from the first been patterned too much after the lines of earlier research with animals and adults in the laboratory. A more likely reason, however, is that the phenomenon of learning is fundamentally the same whether studied in the animal, child, or adult. Differences may be attributed to variations in neuromuscular maturation, in motivation, and in previous experience but not, apparently, to a different kind of learning process in each.

Bibliography

ABEL, L. B. 1936. The effects of shift in motivation upon the learning of a sensori-motor task. *Arch. Psychol., N. Y.*, **29**, No. 205.

ABEL, T. M. 1938. Neuro-circulatory reaction and the recall of unfinished and completed tasks. *J. Psychol.*, **6**, 377–383.

ACHILLES, E. M. 1920. Experimental studies in recall and recognition. *Arch. Psychol., N. Y.*, **6**, No. 44.

ADAMS, L. 1938. Five methods of serial rote learning: A comparative study. *Arch. Psychol., N. Y.*, **31**, No. 221.

ALDRICH, C. A. 1928. A new test for hearing in the newborn, the conditioned reflex. *Amer. J. Dis. Child.*, **35**, 36–37.

ALDRICH, C. G. 1931. Experimental studies of idiot behavior. *Train. Sch. Bull.*, **28**, 151–159.

ALDRICH, C. G., and E. A. DOLL. 1931a. Problem solving among idiots: The use of implements. *J. Soc. Psychol.*, **2**, 306–336.

ALDRICH, C. G., and E. A. DOLL. 1931b. Problem solving among idiots. *J. Soc. Psychol.*, **12**, 137–169.

ALLEN, C. N. 1931. Individual differences in delayed reaction of infants. *Arch. Psychol., N. Y.*, **19**, No. 127.

ALLPORT, G. W. 1930. Change and decay in the visual memory image. *Brit. J. Psychol.*, **21**, 133–148.

ALPERT, A. 1928. The solving of problem-situations by preschool children. *Teach. Coll. Contr. Educ.*, No. 323.

ANDERSON, H. H. 1936. Motivation of young children: Further studies in success and failure, praise and blame. *Child Develpm.*, **7**, 125–143.

ANDERSON, H. H., and R. S. SMITH. 1933. Motivation of young children: The constancy of certain behavior patterns. *J. Exp. Educ.*, **2**, 138–160.

ARPS, G. F., and H. E. CONARD. 1916. An experimental study of economical learning. *Amer. J. Psychol.*, **27**, 507–529.

BALDWIN, B. T., and L. I. STECHER. 1924. *The psychology of the preschool child.* New York: Appleton.

BALLARD, P. B. 1913. Obliviscence and reminiscence. *Brit. J. Psychol. Monogr. Suppl.*, **1**, No. 2. Pp. 82.

BASSETT, S. J. 1928. Retention of history in the sixth, seventh, and eighth grades with special reference to the factors that influence retention. *J. Hopkins Stud. Educ.*, **12**.

———. 1929. Factors influencing retention of history in sixth, seventh, and eighth grades. *J. Educ. Psychol.*, **20**, 683–690.

BATALLA, M. B. 1934. An experimental study of children's behavior in a spatial complex. *J. Genet. Psychol.*, **44**, 127–138.

———. 1936. The learning curve and the reliability of learning scores in a body maze. *Univ. Calif. Publ. Psychol.*, **6**, 153–162.

BAYLEY, N. 1926. Performance tests for three, four and five year old children. *Ped. Sem.*, **33**, 435–454.

BAYNE, T. L., A. L. WINSOR, and E. S. WINTERS. 1929. Conditioned motor responses in children. *Proc. Soc. Exp. Biol. Med.*, **26**, No. 4.

BEEBE, E. L. 1933. Motor learning of children in hand and eye coordination with introduction of prismatic deflection. *Child Develpm.*, **4**, 6–25.

———. 1934. Motor learning of children in equilibrium in relation to nutrition. *Genet. Psychol. Monogr.*, **15**, 99–243.

BINET, A., and V. HENRI. 1894. La mémoire des mots et la mémoire des phrases. *Année psychol.*, **1**, 1–23; 24–59.

BOGGS, L. P. 1905. How children learn to read: An experimental study. *Ped. Sem.*, **12**, 496–502.

BOLTON, T. L. 1892. The growth of memory

in school children. *Amer. J. Psychol., 4,* 362–380.

BOOK, W. F. 1908. The psychology of skill. *Univ. Mont. Publ. Psychol.,* No. 1. Reprinted under same title in 1925, New York: Gregg.

BOTT, E. A., W. E. BLATZ, N. CHANT, and H. BOTT. 1928. Observation and training of fundamental habits in young children. *Genet. Psychol. Monogr., 4,* 1–61.

BRAINARD, P. P. 1927. Some observations of infant learning and instincts. *Ped. Sem., 34,* 231–254.

———. 1930. The mentality of a child compared with that of apes. *J. Genet. Psychol., 37,* 268–293.

BREGMAN, E. O. 1934. An attempt to modify the emotional attitudes of infants by the conditioned response technique. *J. Genet. Psychol., 45,* 169–198.

BROLYER, C. R., E. L. THORNDIKE, and E. WOODYARD. 1927. A second study of mental discipline in high school studies. *J. Educ. Psychol., 18,* 377–404.

BRONNER, A. F., W. HEALY, G. M. LOWE, and M. E. SHIMBERG. 1927. *A manual of individual mental tests and testing.* Boston: Little, Brown.

BROWNELL, W. A. 1938. Two kinds of learning in arithmetic. *J. Educ. Res., 31,* 656–664.

BRYAN, A. I. 1934. Organization of memory in young children. *Arch. Psychol., N. Y., 24,* No. 162.

BRYAN, W. L., and N. HARTER. 1897. Studies in the physiology and psychology of the telegraphic language. *Psychol. Rev., 4,* 27–53.

BÜHLER, C. 1930. *The first year of life.* New York: Day.

BUNCH, M. E. 1938. The measurement of reminiscence. *Psychol. Rev., 45,* 525–531.

BUNCH, M. E., and W. K. MAGDSICK. 1933. The retention in rats of an incompletely learned maze solution for short intervals of time. *J. Comp. Psychol., 16,* 385–409.

BURT, C. 1909. Experimental tests of general intelligence. *Brit. J. Psychol., 3,* 94–177.

BURTT, H. E. 1932. An experimental study of early childhood memory. *J. Genet. Psychol., 40,* 287–295.

———. 1937. A further study of early childhood memory. *J. Genet. Psychol., 50,* 187–192.

BUSEMANN, A. 1911. Lernen und Behalten. *Z. angew. Psychol., 5,* 211–271.

CARPENTER, D. F. 1913. Mental age tests. *J. Educ. Psychol., 4,* 538–544.

CARTER, H. D. 1935. Effects of emotional factors upon recall. *J. Psychol., 1,* 49–59.

———. 1936. Emotional correlates of errors in learning. *J. Educ. Psychol., 27,* 55–67.

———. 1937. Emotional factors in verbal learning: IV. Evidence from reaction times. *J. Educ. Psychol., 28,* 101–108.

CHAPMAN, J. C., and R. B. FEDER. 1917. The effect of external incentive on improvement technique in addition. *J. Educ. Psychol., 11,* 469–475.

CHARLES, J. W. 1929. An experiment in teaching reading. *J. Genet. Psychol., 36,* 591–594.

CHASE, L. 1932. Motivation of young children: An experimental study of the influence of certain types of external incentives upon the performance of a task. *Univ. Iowa Stud. Child Welfare, 5,* No. 3.

CLARK, A. S. 1924. Correlation of the auditory digit memory span with general intelligence. *Psychol. Clin., 15,* 259–260.

CLINTON, R. J. 1930. Nature of mirror drawing ability: norms on mirror drawing for white children by age and sex. *J. Educ. Psychol., 21,* 221–228.

CONRAD, H. S., and H. E. JONES. 1929. Psychological studies of motion pictures: III. Fidelity of report as a measure of adult intelligence. *Univ. Calif. Publ. Psychol., 3,* No. 7, pp. 245–276.

COWAN, E. A. 1928. Results of motor reconditioning methods used in training a backward child. *J. Genet. Psychol., 35,* 98–104.

COWAN, E. A., and M. FOULKE. 1934. Variation in susceptibility to the conditioning of inhibition as an index of constitutional type. *Child Develpm., 5,* 201–236.

COX, J. W. 1933. Some experiments on formal training in the acquisition of skill. *Brit. J. Psychol., 24,* 67–87.

DAVIDSON, H. P. 1931. An experimental study of bright, average, and dull children at the four-year mental level. *Genet. Psychol. Monogr., 9,* 119–289.

DAVIS, F., and M. B. BATALLA. 1932. A life-size alley maze for children. *J. Genet. Psychol., 41,* 235–239.

DELL, J. A. 1912. Some observations on the learning of sensible material. *J. Educ. Psychol., 3,* 401–406.

DENISOVA, M. P., and N. L. FIGURIN. 1929. The problem of the first associated food reflexes in infants. *Vopr. Genet. Refl. Pedol. Mladen., 1,* 81–88. (*See* RAZRAN, 1933.)

DENNIS, W. 1935. The effect of restricted practice upon the teaching, sitting, and standing of two infants. *J. Genet. Psychol., 47,* 17–32.

DERNOWA-YARMOLENKO, A. A. 1933. The fundamentals of a method of investigating the function of the nervous system as revealed in overt behavior. *J. Genet. Psychol., 42,* 319–338.

DE SANCTIS, S. 1931. Visual apprehension in the maze behavior of normal and feeble-minded children. *J. Genet. Psychol., 39,* 463–468.

DEWEY, E., E. CHILD, and B. RUML. 1920. *Methods and results of testing school children.* New York: Dutton.

DIETZE, A. G. 1931. The relation of several factors to factual memory. *J. Appl. Psychol., 15,* 563–574.

DIETZE, A. G. 1932. Some sex differences in factual memory. *Amer. J. Psychol.*, 44, 319–321.

DIETZE, A. G., and G. E. JONES. 1931. Factual memory of secondary school pupils for a short article which they read a single time. *J. Educ. Psychol.*, 22, 586–598; 667–676.

DONOVAN, M. E., and E. L. THORNDIKE. 1913. Improvement in a practice experiment under school conditions. *Amer. J. Psychol.*, 24, 426–428.

DUNFORD, R. E. 1930. The genetic development of cutaneous localization. *J. Genet. Psychol.*, 37, 499–513.

EASBY-GRAVE, C. 1924. Tests and norms at the six year old performance level. *Psychol. Clin.*, 15, 261–300.

EBBINGHAUS, H. 1885. *Über das Gedächtnis.* Leipzig. 1913. *Memory: A contribution to experimental psychology.* (Trans. by H. A. RUGER and C. E. BUSSENIUS.) (*Teach. Coll., Educ. Reprints*, No. 3.) New York: Teachers College, Columbia University.

EIGLER, P. 1932. The effect of unusual stimulation on motor coordination in children. *Child Develpm.*, 3, 207–229.

EMERSON, L. L. 1931. The effect of bodily orientation upon the young child's memory for position of objects. *Child Develpm.*, 2, 125–142.

FISHER, R. A. 1930. *Statistical methods for research workers.* (3d ed.) London: Oliver and Boyd.

FLÜGEL, J. C. 1928. Practice, fatigue, and oscillation. *Brit. J. Psychol. Monogr. Suppl.*, No. 13. Pp. 92.

FORLANO, G., and M. N. H. HOFFMAN. 1937. Guessing and telling methods in learning words of a foreign language. *J. Educ. Psychol.*, 28, 632–636.

FOSTER, J. C. 1928. Verbal memory in the preschool child. *J. Genet. Psychol.*, 35, 26–44.

FREELAND, G. E. 1921. A year's study of the daily learning of six children. *Ped. Sem.*, 28, 97–115.

GATES, A. I. 1917. Recitation as a factor in memorizing. *Arch. Psychol., N. Y.*, 6, No. 40.

———. 1928. The nature and limits of improvement due to training. *Yearb. Nat. Soc. Stud. Educ.*, 27(I), 444–461.

GATES, A. I., and G. A. TAYLOR. 1923. The acquisition of motor control in writing by preschool children. *Teach. Coll. Rec.*, 24, 459–468.

———. 1925. An experimental study of the nature of improvement resulting from practice in a mental function. *J. Educ. Psychol.*, 16, 583–592.

GATES, L. W. 1938. The genetic development of rational learning in children. *Psychol. Bull.*, 35, 713.

GELLERMANN, L. W. 1931. The double alternation problem: II. The behavior of children and human adults in a double alternation temporal maze. *J. Genet. Psychol.*, 39, 359–392.

GELLERMANN, L. W. 1933. Form discrimination in chimpanzees and two-year-old children. *J. Genet. Psychol.*, 42, 3–27.

GESELL, A. 1925. *The mental growth of the pre-school child.* New York: Macmillan.

———. 1938. The conditioned reflex and the psychiatry of infancy. *Amer. J. Orthopsychiat.*, 8, 19–30.

GESELL, A., and H. THOMPSON. 1929. Learning and growth in identical infant twins: An experimental study by the method of co-twin control. *Genet. Psychol. Monogr.*, 6, 1–124.

GILBERT, G. M. 1937. Age differences in the hedonistic tendency in memory. *J. Exp. Psychol.*, 21, 433–441.

GILLETTE, A. L. 1936. Learning and retention: A comparison of three experimental procedures. *Arch. Psychol., N. Y.*, 28, No. 198.

GOODENOUGH, F. L., and C. R. BRIAN. 1929. Certain factors underlying the acquisition of motor skill in pre-school children. *J. Exp. Psychol.*, 12, 127–155.

GORDON, M. A. 1938. General and specific factors in transfer of training within verbal tests. *Arch. Psychol., N. Y.*, No. 227.

GOTTSCHALDT, K. 1933. Der Aufbau des kindlichen Handelns. *Z. angew. Psychol., Beih.*, No. 68.

GOULD, M. C., and F. A. C. PERRIN. 1916. A comparison of factors involved in the maze learning of human adults and children. *J. Exp. Psychol.*, 1, 122–154.

GRAY, S. 1940. The influence of methodology upon the measurement of reminiscence. *J. Exp. Psychol.*, 27, 37–44.

GRETHER, W. F. 1938. Pseudo-conditioning without paired stimulation encountered in attempted backward conditioning. *J. Comp. Psychol.*, 25, 91–96.

GRIFFITHS, M. M. 1938. *Part and whole methods of presentation.* (*Aust. Comm. Educ. Res. Ser.*, No. 52.) Melbourne: Melbourne University Press.

GUILLET, C. 1909. Retentiveness in child and adult. *Amer. J. Psychol.*, 20, 318–352.

HALL, V. 1936. The effects of a time interval on recall. *Brit. J. Psychol.*, 27, 41–50.

HALLOWELL, D. K. 1928. Mental tests for preschool children. *Psychol. Clin.*, 16, 235–276.

HAMILTON, G. V. N. 1911. A study of trial and error reactions in mammals. *J. Anim. Behav.*, 1, 33–66.

———. 1916. A study of perseverance reactions in primates and rodents. *Behav. Monogr.*, 3, No. 2. Pp. 65.

HARTER, G. L. 1930. Overt trial and error in the problem solving of pre-school children. *J. Genet. Psychol.*, 38, 361–372.

HAZLITT, V. 1930. Children's thinking. *Brit. J. Psychol.*, 20, 354–361.

HEALY, W., and G. M. FERNALD. 1911. Tests

for practical mental classification. *Psychol. Monogr.*, **13**, No. 54. Pp. 54.

HEIDBREDER, E. F. 1927. Reasons used in solving problems. *J. Exp. Psychol.*, **10**, 397–414.

——. 1928. Problem solving in children and adults. *J. Genet. Psychol.*, **35**, 522–545.

HENDERSON, E. N. 1903. A study of memory for connected trains of thought. *Psychol. Monogr.*, **5**, No. 23. Pp. 94.

HENRI, V. 1902. Education de la mémoire. *Année psychol.*, **8**, 1–48.

HENRY, L. K. 1934. The ôle of insight in the analytical thinking of adolescents. *Univ. Iowa Stud. Educ.*, **9**, No. 5, pp. 65–102.

HETZER, H., and S. WISLITZKY. 1930. Experimente über Erwartung und Erinnerung beim Kleinkind. *Z. Psychol.*, **118**, 128–141.

HICKS, J. A. 1930a. The acquisition of motor skill in young children. *Child Develpm.*, **1**, 90–105.

——. 1930b. The acquisition of motor skill in young children: II. The influence of specific and of general practice on motor skill. *Child Develpm.*, **1**, 292–297.

——. 1931. The acquisition of motor skill in young children: An experimental study of the effect of practice in throwing at a moving target. *Univ. Iowa Stud. Child Welfare*, **4**, No. 5.

HICKS, J. A., and D. W. RALPH. 1931. The effects of practice in tracing the Porteus diamond maze. *Child Develpm.*, **2**, 156–158.

HICKS, J. A., and F. D. STEWART. 1930. The learning of abstract concepts of size. *Child Develpm.*, **1**, 195–203.

HICKS, V. C., and H. A. CARR. 1912. Human reactions in a maze. *J. Anim. Psychol.*, **2**, 98–125.

HILDRETH, G. 1935. An individual study in word recognition. *Elem. Sch. J.*, **35**, 606–619.

HILGARD, E. R., and D. G. MARQUIS. 1940. *Conditioning and learning.* New York: Appleton-Century.

HILGARD, J. R. 1932. Learning and maturation in preschool children. *J. Genet. Psychol.*, **41**, 31–56.

——. 1933. The effect of early and delayed practice on memory and motor performances studied by the method of co-twin control. *Genet. Psychol. Monogr.*, **14**, 493–567.

HOBHOUSE, L. T. 1901. *Mind in evolution.* New York: Macmillan.

HOLADAY, P. W., and G. D. STODDARD. 1933. Getting ideas from the movies. In W. W. CHARTERS, P. W. HOLADAY, and G. D. STODDARD. *Motion pictures and youth.* New York: Macmillan.

HOLT, E. B. 1931. *Animal drive and the learning process: An essay toward radical empiricism.* Vol. I. New York: Holt.

HOVLAND, C. I. 1938a. Experimental studies in rote-learning theory: I. Reminiscence following learning by massed and by distributed practice. *J. Exp. Psychol.*, **22**, 201–224.

HOVLAND, C. I. 1938b. Experimental studies i rote-learning theory: II. Reminiscence wit varying speeds of syllable presentation. *J Exp. Psychol.*, **22**, 338–353.

HUGUENIN, C. 1914. Reviviscence paradoxale *Arch. Psychol., Genève*, **14**, 379–383.

HULL, C. L. 1938. The goal-gradient hypothesis applied to some "field-force" problems i the behavior of young children. *Psychol. Rev.* **45**, 271–300.

HULL, C. L., and B. I. HULL. 1919. Parallel learning curves of an infant in vocabulary and in voluntary control of the bladder. *Ped Sem.*, **26**, 272–283.

HUMPSTONE, H. J. 1917. *Some aspects of the memory span: A study in associability.* Philadelphia: Psychological Clinic Press.

HUNTER, W. S. 1913. Delayed reaction in animals and children. *Behav. Monogr.*, **2**, No. 6 Pp. 86.

——. 1917. The delayed reaction in a child. *Psychol. Rev.*, **24**, 75–87.

HURLOCK, E. B. 1924. The value of praise and reproof as incentives for children. *Arch. Psychol., N. Y.*, **11**, No. 71.

——. 1931. The psychology of incentives. *J. Soc. Psychol.*, **2**, 261–290.

HURLOCK, E. B., and E. D. NEWMARK. 1931. The memory span of pre-school children. *J. Genet. Psychol.*, **39**, 157–173.

HURLOCK, E. B., and R. SCHWARTZ. 1932. Biographical records of memory in preschool children. *Child Develpm.*, **3**, 230–239.

IDE, G. G. 1920. The educability of five year old children. *Psychol. Clin.*, **13**, 146–172.

IVANOV-SMOLENSKY, A. G. 1927a. Neurotic behavior and the teaching of conditioned reflexes. *Amer. J. Psychiat.*, **84**, 483–488.

——. 1927b. On the methods of examining the conditioned food reflexes in children and in mental disorders. *Brain*, **50**, 138–141.

JACKSON, T. A. 1939. Studies in the transposition of learning by children: III. Transpositional response as a function of the number of transposed dimensions. *J. Exp. Psychol.*, **25**, 116–124.

JACKSON, T. A., and K. DOMINGUEZ. 1939. Studies in the transposition of learning by children: II. Relative vs. absolute choice with multidimensional stimuli. *J. Exp. Psychol.*, **24**, 630–639.

JACKSON, T. A., E. STONEX, E. LANE, and K. DOMINGUEZ. 1938. Studies in the transposition of learning by children: I. Relative vs. absolute response as a function of amount of training. *J. Exp. Psychol.*, **23**, 578–600.

JACOBS, J. 1887. Experiments in "prehension." *Mind*, **12**, 75–79.

JENSEN, M. B., and M. SCHRODT. 1936. Language difficulty in learning: The relative effectiveness of a series of study sheets of graded difficulty as teaching devices with children in the 6A grade. *J. Genet. Psychol.*, 49, 451–467.

JERSILD, A. T. 1932. Training and growth in the development of children: A study of the relative influence of learning and maturation. *Child Develpm. Monogr.*, 10, p. 73.

JONES, A. M. 1927. An analytical study of one hundred and twenty superior children. *Psychol. Clin.*, 16, 19–26.

JONES, H. E. 1930a. The galvanic skin reflex. *Child Develpm.*, 7, 106–110.

——. 1930b. The retention of conditioned emotional reactions in infancy. *J. Genet. Psychol.*, 37, 485–498.

——. 1931. The conditioning of overt emotional responses. *J. Educ. Psychol.*, 22, 127–130.

——. 1934. The laws of emphasis and effect in children's learning. *Psychol. Bull.*, 31, 597–598.

JONES, H. E., and D. DUNN. 1932. The configural factor in children's learning. *J. Genet. Psychol.*, 41, 3–15.

JONES, H. E., and J. G. YOSHIOKA. 1938. Differential errors in children's learning on a stylus maze. *J. Comp. Psychol.*, 25, 463–480.

JONES, M. C. 1924a. The elimination of children's fears. *J. Exp. Psychol.*, 7, 382–390.

——. 1924b. A laboratory study of fear: the case of Peter. *Ped. Sem.*, 31, 308–315.

JUDD, C. H. 1908. The relation of special training to general intelligence. *Educ. Rev.*, 36, 28–42.

KANTROW, R. W. 1937. An investigation of conditioned feeding responses and concomitant adaptive behavior in young infants. *Univ. Iowa Stud. Child Welfare*, 13, No. 3.

KASATKIN, N. I., and A. M. LEVIKOVA. 1935a. The formation of visual conditioned reflexes and their differentiation in infants. *J. Gen. Psychol.*, 12, 416–435.

——. 1935b. On the development of early conditioned reflexes and differentiations of auditory stimuli in infants. *J. Exp. Psychol.*, 18, 1–19.

KELLOGG, W. N., and L. A. KELLOGG. 1933. *The ape and the child: A study of environmental influence upon early behavior.* New York: McGraw-Hill.

KETTERLINUS, E. 1931. Learning of children in adaptation to mirror reversals. *Child Develpm.*, 2, 200–223.

KIRKENDALL, L. A. 1938. The influence of certain incentives in the motivation of children. *Elem. Sch. J.*, 38, 417–424.

KIRKPATRICK, E. A. 1894. An experimental study of memory. *Psychol. Rev.*, 1, 602–609.

——. 1899. Development of voluntary movement. *Psychol. Rev.*, 6, 275–281.

——. 1909. Studies in development and learning. *Arch. Psychol., N. Y.*, 2, No. 12.

——. 1914. Experiment in memorizing vs. incidental learning. *J. Educ. Psychol.*, 5, 405–414.

KIRKWOOD, J. A. 1926. The learning process in young children: an experimental study in association. *Univ. Iowa Stud. Child Welfare*, 3, No. 6.

KNOTTS, J. R., and W. R. MILES. 1929. The maze-learning ability of blind compared with sighted children. *J. Genet. Psychol.*, 36, 21–50.

KÖHLER, W. 1925. *The mentality of apes.* (Trans. by E. WINTER.) New York: Harcourt, Brace.

KOMATSU, H. 1931. A study on the reproduction of perceived forms by children. *Jap. J. Psychol.*, 6, 569–590.

KRASNOGORSKI, N. I. 1909. Ueber die Bedingungsreflexe im Kindesalter. *Jb. Kinderheilk.*, 19, 1–24.

——. 1925. The conditioned reflex and children's neuroses. *Amer. J. Dis. Child.*, 30, 753–768.

——. 1933. Physiology of cerebral activity in children as a new subject of pediatric investigation. *Amer. J. Dis. Child.*, 46, 473–494.

KRECHEVSKY, I. 1932. The genesis of "hypotheses" in rats. *Univ. Calif. Publ. Psychol.*, 6, 45–64.

KREEZER, G., and K. M. DALLENBACH. 1939. Learning the relation of opposition. *Amer. J. Psychol.*, 41, 432–441.

LACEY, J. T., and K. M. DALLENBACH. 1939. Acquisition by children of the cause-effect relationship. *Amer. J. Psychol.*, 52, 103–110.

LANGHORNE, M. C. 1933. Age and sex differences in the acquisition of one type of skilled movement. *J. Exp. Educ.*, 2, 101–108.

LEWIN, K. 1935. *A dynamic theory of personality.* New York: McGraw-Hill.

LINDLEY, E. H. 1897. A study of puzzles with special reference to the psychology of mental adaptation. *Amer. J. Psychol.*, 8, 431–493.

LODER, J. E. 1937. A study of oral learning with and without the speaker present. *J. Exp. Educ.*, 6, 46–60.

LONG, E. D. 1930. *The acquisition of skill by children as affected by distribution of practice.* Unpublished master's thesis, George Peabody College for Teachers.

LUH, C. W., and B. T. LIANG. 1933. Further studies in forgetting and reminiscence. *Yenching Stud. Psychol.*, No. 3, pp. 1–14. (Reviewed by MCGEOCH, 1935.)

LUMLEY, F. H., and S. W. CALHOUN. 1934. Memory span for words presented auditorially. *J. Appl. Psychol.*, 18, 773–784.

LUND, F. H. 1927. The role of practice in speed of association. *J. Exp. Psychol.*, 10, 424–433.

LYON, D. O. 1916. The relation of quickness of learning to retentiveness. *Arch. Psychol., N. Y.*, 5, No. 34.

MAIER, N. R. F. 1936. Reasoning in children. *J. Comp. Psychol.,* **21,** 357–366.

MALLAY, H. 1935. The latent memory span of the preschool child. *Child Develpm.,* **6,** 110–119.

MARINESCO, G., and A. KREINDLER. 1933. Des réflexes conditionnels: I. L'organisation des réflexes conditionnels chez l'enfant. *J. psychol., Genève,* **30,** 855–886.

MARINESCO, G., O. SAGER, and A. KREINDLER. 1931. Hystéria et réflexes conditionnels. *Rev. neurol.,* **38,** 721–731.

MARQUIS, D. P. 1931. Can conditioned reflexes be established in the newborn? *J. Genet. Psychol.,* **39,** 479–492.

MARTIN, J. R. 1940. Reminiscence and Gestalt theory. *Psychol. Monogr.,* **52,** No. 235.

MAST, E. T. 1937. Motivating factors in child learning. *Child Develpm.,* **8,** 273–278.

MATEER, F. 1918. *Child behavior.* Boston: Badger.

MATHESON, E. 1931. A study of problem solving behavior in preschool children. *Child Develpm.,* **2,** 242–262.

MATTSON, M. L. 1933. The relation between the complexity of the habit to be acquired and the form of the learning curve in young children. *Genet. Psychol. Monogr.,* **13,** 299–398.

McCAULLEY, S. 1928. A study of the relative values of the audito-vocal forward memory span and the reverse span as diagnostic tests. *Psychol. Clin.,* **16,** 277–291.

McELWEE, E. W. 1933. Further standardization of the Ellis memory for objects test. *J. Appl. Psychol.,* **17,** 69–70.

McGEOCH, G. O. 1931. The intelligence quotient as a factor in the whole-part problem. *J. Exp. Psychol.,* **14,** 333–358.

———. 1935*a*. The age factor in reminiscence: A comparative study of preschool children and college students. *J. Genet. Psychol.,* **47,** 98–120.

———. 1935*b*. The factor of degree of learning in reminiscence: A second comparative study of preschool children and college students. *J. Genet. Psychol.,* **46,** 455–462.

———. 1935*c*. The conditions of reminiscence. *Amer. J. Psychol.,* **47,** 65–89.

———. 1937. Reminiscence in maze learning by kindergarten children. *J. Genet. Psychol.,* **50,** 171–186.

McGEOCH, J. A. 1925. Fidelity of report of normal and subnormal children. *Amer. J. Psychol.,* **36,** 434–445.

———. 1928. The influence of sex and age upon the ability to report. *Amer. J. Psychol.,* **40,** 458–466.

McGINNIS, E. 1929. The acquisition and interference of motor-habits in young children. *Genet. Psychol. Monogr.,* **6,** 209–311.

McGINNIS, J. M. 1928. A child's stylus maze. *Amer. J. Psychol.,* **40,** 313.

McGRAW, M. B. 1935. *Growth: A study of Johnny and Jimmy.* New York: Appleton Century.

MEEK, L. H. 1925. A study of learning and retention in young children. *Teach. Coll Contr. Educ.,* No. 164.

MELCHER, R. T. 1934. Children's motor learning with and without vision. *Child Develpm.* **5,** 315–350.

MEUMANN, E. 1913. *The psychology of learning.* (Trans. by J. W. BAIRD.) New York: Appleton.

MILLER, N. E. 1934. The perception of children: A genetic study employing the critical choice delayed reaction. *J. Genet. Psychol.* **44,** 321–339.

MIRENVA, A. N. 1935. Psychomotor education and the general development of preschool children: Experiments with twin controls. *J. Genet. Psychol.,* **46,** 433–454.

MITRANO, A. J. 1939. Principles of conditioning in human goal behavior. *Psychol. Monogr.,* **51,** No. 230. Pp. 74.

MONROE, W. S. 1928. How pupils solve problems in arithmetic. *Univ. Ill. Bull.,* **26,** No. 23.

MORGAN, J. J. B. 1938. Treatment of enuresis by the conditioned reaction technique. *Psychol. Bull.,* **35,** 632–633.

MORGAN, J. J. B., and F. J. WITMER. 1939. The treatment of enuresis by the conditioned reaction technique. *J. Genet. Psychol.,* **55,** 59–65.

MORIYA, M. 1937*a*. An observation of problem-solving behavior in preschool children: I. Application of the principle of a lever. *Jap. J. Exp. Psychol.,* **4,** 63–81.

———. 1937*b*. An observation on problem-solving behavior in preschool children: II. Application of the principle of a lever (continued). *Jap. J. Exp. Psychol.,* **4,** 147–160.

MORSH, J. E. 1930. The development of right-handed skill in the left-handed child. *Child Develpm.,* **1,** 311–324.

MOSS, F. A. 1924. Note on building likes and dislikes in children. *J. Exp. Psychol.,* **7,** 475–478.

MOWRER, O. H., and W. M. MOWRER. 1938. Enuresis—a method for its study and treatment. *Amer. J. Orthopsychiat.,* **8,** 436–459.

MUNN, A. F. 1909. The curve of learning. *Arch. Psychol., N. Y.,* **2,** No. 12, pp. 36–52.

MUNN, N. L. 1933. *An introduction to animal psychology.* Boston: Houghton Mifflin.

———. 1938. *Psychological development.* Boston: Houghton Mifflin.

MUNN, N. L., and B. R. STEINING. 1931. The relative efficacy of form and background in a child's discrimination of visual patterns. *J. Genet. Psychol.,* **39,** 73–90.

MYERS, G. C. 1913. A study in incidental memory. *Arch. Psychol., N. Y.,* **26.**

NANKING EXPERIMENTAL ELEMENTARY SCHOOL. 1935. An experimental study of the trends of memory change. *Kiangsu Elem. Sch. Teach.*, 2, 936–971.

NELSON, V. L. 1936. An analytical study of child learning. *Child Develpm.*, 7, 95–114.

NEUMANN, G. 1907. Experimentelle Beiträge zur Lehre von der Oekonomie und Technik des Lernens. *Z. exp. Päd.*, 4, 63–101.

NICOLAI, F. 1922. Experimentelle Untersuchungen über das Haften von Gesichtseindrücken und dessen zeitlichen Verlauf. *Arch. ges. Psychol.*, 42, 132–149.

NORTHWAY, M. L. 1936. The influence of age and social group on children's remembering. *Brit. J. Psychol.*, 27, 11–29.

——. 1937. The nature of "difficulty"; with reference to a study of "whole-part" learning. *Brit. J. Psychol.*, 27, 399–402.

OSIPOVA, V. N. 1926. The speed of formation of association reflexes in children of school age. *Nov. Refl. Fiziol. Nerv. Sist.*, 2, 218–234. (*See* RAZRAN, 1933.)

PACHAURI, A. R. 1935a. A study of gestalt problems in completed and interrupted tasks: I. *Brit. J. Psychol.*, 25, 365–381.

——. 1935b. A study of gestalt problems in completed and interrupted tasks: II. *Brit. J. Psychol.*, 25, 447–457.

——. 1936. A study of gestalt problems in completed and interrupted tasks: III. *Brit. J. Psychol.*, 27, 170–180.

PAVLOV, I. P. 1889–1890. Innervation der Magendrüsen beim Hunde. *Centralbl. Physiol.*, 3, 113–114.

——. 1903. Psychologie et psychopathologie animale expérimentale. *C. R. Cong. int. Méd.*, Madrid.

PECHSTEIN, L. A. 1926. The whole vs. part methods in learning. *Yearb. Nat. Soc. Coll. Teach. Educ.*, 15, 181–186.

PENTSCHEW, C. 1903. Untersuchungen zur Oekonomie und Technik des Lernens. *Arch. ges. Psychol.*, 1, 417–526.

PERL, R. E. 1933. The effect of practice upon individual differences. *Arch. Psychol., N. Y.*, 24, No. 159.

PETERSON, G. M. 1932. An empirical study of the ability to generalize. *J. Gen. Psychol.*, 6, 90–114.

PETERSON, J. 1918. Experiments in rational learning. *Psychol. Rev.*, 25, 443–467.

——. 1920. The backward elimination of errors in mental maze learning. *J. Exp. Psychol.*, 3, 257–280.

——. 1926. Limits of learning by trial and error. *J. Exp. Psychol.*, 9, 45–55.

——. 1933. Learning in children, pp. 417–481. In C. MURCHISON (Ed.), *A handbook of child psychology.* (2d ed., rev.) Worcester: Clark University Press.

PETERSON, J., and P. V. HARRELSON. 1923. Comparative abilities of white and negro children: Part III. *Comp. Psychol. Monogr.*, 1, No. 5. Pp. 141.

PINTNER, R., and D. G. PATERSON. 1917. A comparison of deaf and hearing children in visual memory for digits. *J. Exp. Psychol.*, 2, 76–88.

PYLE, W. H. 1920. *A manual for the mental and physical examination of school children.* (Revised edition.) Columbia, Mo.: University of Missouri.

PYLES, M. K. 1932. Verbalization as a factor in learning. *Child Develpm.*, 3, 108–113.

RADOSSAWLJEWITSCH, P. 1907. Das Behalten und Vergessen bei Kindern und Erwachsenen nach experimentellen Untersuchungen. Leipzig: Nemnich.

RAY, J. J. 1936. The generalizing ability of dull, bright, and superior children. *Peabody Contr. Educ.*, No. 175.

RAY, W. S. 1932. A preliminary report on a study of fetal conditioning. *Child Develpm.*, 3, 175–177.

RAZRAN, G. H. S. 1933. Conditioned responses in children. *Arch. Psychol., N. Y.*, No. 148.

——. 1935. Conditioned responses: An experimental study and a theoretical analysis. *Arch. Psychol., N. Y.*, No. 191.

——. 1936. Attitudinal control of human conditioning. *J. Psychol.*, 2, 327–337.

RENSHAW, S. 1930. The errors of cutaneous localization and the effect of practice on the localizing movement in children and adults. *J. Genet. Psychol.*, 38, 223–238.

RENSHAW, S., R. J. WHERRY, and J. C. NEWLIN. 1930. Cutaneous localization in congenitally blind versus seeing children and adults. *J. Genet. Psychol.*, 38, 239–248.

RICHARDSON, H. M. 1932. The growth of adaptive behavior in infants: An experimental study of seven age levels. *Genet. Psychol. Monogr.*, 12, 195–359.

——. 1934. The adaptive behavior of infants in the utilization of the lever as a tool: A developmental and experimental study. *J. Genet. Psychol.*, 44, 352–377.

ROBERTS, K. E. 1932. The ability of preschool children to solve problems in which a simple principle of relationship is kept constant. *J. Genet. Psychol.*, 40, 118–135.

——. 1933. Learning in preschool and orphanage children: An experimental study of ability to solve different situations according to the same plan. *Univ. Iowa Stud. Child Welfare*, 7, No. 3.

ROSENZWEIG, S., and G. MASON. 1934. An experimental study of memory in relation to repression. *Brit. J. Psychol.*, 24, 247–265.

RUCH, F. L. 1934. The differentiative effects of age upon human learning. *J. Gen. Psychol.*, 11, 261–286.

RUCH, G. M. 1925. The influence of the factor of intelligence on the form of the learning curve. *Psychol. Monogr.*, 34, No. 160. Pp. 64.

RUGER, H. A. 1910. The psychology of efficiency. *Arch. Psychol., N. Y.,* 2, No. 15. Pp. 88.

SAWA, H. 1937. A simple detour problem in infants. *Trans. Inst. Child Stud.* (Japan), **17,** 139–160.

SAWDEN, E. W. 1927. Should children learn poems in wholes or in parts? *Forum Educ.,* **5,** 182–186.

SEHAM, M. 1932. The "conditioned reflex" in relation to functional disorders in children. *Amer. J. Dis. Child.,* **43,** 163–186.

SHAW, J. C. 1896. A test of memory in school children. *Ped. Sem.,* **4,** 61–78.

SHIMIDU, E. 1934. On the development of immediate memory and perception of children. *Trans. Inst. Child Stud.* (Japan), **16,** 723–740.

SKALET, M. 1931. The significance of delayed reactions in young children. *Comp. Psychol. Monogr.,* **7.** Pp. 82.

SLEIGHT, W. G. 1911. Memory and formal training. *Brit. J. Psychol.,* **4,** 386–457.

SMALL, W. S. 1899. Notes on the psychic development of the young white rat. *Amer. J. Psychol.,* **11,** 80–100.

——. 1900. An experimental study of the mental processes of the rat: I. *Amer. J. Psychol.,* **11,** 135–165.

SMEDLEY, F. 1902. *Rep. U. S. Comm. Educ.,* **1,** 1095–1115.

SOBEL, B. 1939. A study of the development of insight in pre-school children. *J. Genet. Psychol.,* **55,** 381–388.

SONTAG, L. W., and R. F. WALLACE. 1934. A study of fetal activity: Preliminary report of the Fels Fund. *Amer. J. Dis. Child.,* **48,** 1050–1057.

SPELT, D. K. 1938. Conditioned responses in the human fetus *in utero. Psychol. Bull.,* **35,** 712–713.

SQUIRE, C. 1912. Graded mental tests. *J. Educ. Psychol.,* **3,** 363–380.

STARR, A. S. 1923. The diagnostic value of the audito-vocal digit memory span. *Psychol. Clin.,* **15,** 61–84.

STEFFENS, L. 1900. Experimentelle Beiträge zur Lehre vom oekonomischen Lernen. *Z. Psychol.,* **22,** 321–382.

STERN, W. 1904. *Die Aussage als geistige Leistung und als Verhörsprodukt.* Leipzig: Barth.

STEVENSON, P. R. 1925. Difficulties in problem solving. *J. Educ. Res.,* **11,** 95–103.

STONE, C. P. 1929–1930. The age factor in animal learning. *Genet. Psychol. Monogr.,* **5,** 1–130; **6,** 125–202.

STRAYER, L. C. 1930. Language and growth: The relative efficacy of early and deferred vocabulary training, studied by the method of co-twin control. *Genet. Psychol. Monogr.,* **8,** 215–317.

STROUD, J. B. 1940. Experiments on learning in school situations. *Psychol. Bull.,* **37,** 777–807.

STROUD, J. B., and R. MAUL. 1933. The influence of age upon learning and retention of poetry and nonsense syllables. *J. Genet. Psychol.,* **42,** 242–250.

STUMP, N. F. 1927. A classroom experiment in logical learning. *J. Appl. Psychol.,* **11,** 117–125.

STUTSMAN, R. 1926. Performance tests for children of pre-school age. *Genet. Psychol. Monogr.,* **1,** 1–67.

SULLIVAN, E. B. 1924. *Attitude in relation to learning.* Unpublished thesis, Stanford University.

SWIFT, E. J. 1903. Studies in the psychology and physiology of learning. *Amer. J. Psychol.,* **14,** 201–251.

TAGAWA, S. 1937. The imitation of the detour problem solved with the stick. *Trans. Inst. Child Stud.* (Japan), **17,** 121–137.

TERMAN, L. M., and M. MERRILL. 1937. *Measuring intelligence.* Boston: Houghton Mifflin.

THORNDIKE, E. L. 1898. Animal intelligence. *Psychol. Rev., Monogr. Suppl.,* **2,** No. 8. Pp. 109.

——. 1924. Mental discipline in high school studies. *J. Educ. Psychol.,* **15,** 83–98.

TIERNAN, J. J. 1938. The principle of closure in terms of recall and recognition. *Amer. J. Psychol.,* **51,** 97–108.

TOLMAN, E. C. 1932. *Purposive behavior in animals and men.* New York: Appleton.

TOWN, C. H. 1921. Analytic study of a group of five and six year old children. *Univ. Iowa Stud. Child Welfare,* **1,** No. 4. Pp. 87.

VERTES, J. O. 1931. Behalten und Vergessen des Kindes. *Z. Psychol.,* **122,** 241–354.

WARD, L. B. 1937. Reminiscence and rote learning. *Psychol. Monogr.,* **49,** No. 220. Pp. 64.

WATSON, J. B., and R. RAYNER. 1920. Conditioned emotional reactions. *J. Exp. Psychol.,* **3,** 1–14.

WEES, W. R., and W. LINE. 1937. The influence of the form of a presentation upon reproduction: The principle of determination. *Brit. J. Psychol.,* **28,** 167–189.

WELCH, L. 1938. A preliminary study of the interaction of conflicting concepts of children between the ages of 3 and 5 years. *Psychol. Rec.,* **2,** 439–459.

——. 1939*a*. The development of the discrimination of form and area. *J. Psychol.,* **7,** 269–297.

——. 1939*b*. The development of size discrimination between the ages of 12 and 40 months. *J. Genet. Psychol.,* **55,** 243–268.

——. 1939*c*. The span of generalization below the two-year age level. *J. Genet. Psychol.,* **55,** 269–297.

——. 1940*a*. The genetic development of the associational structures of abstract thinking. *J. Genet. Psychol.,* **56,** 175–206.

——. 1940*b*. A preliminary investigation of

some aspects of the hierarchical development of concepts. *J. Gen. Psychol.*, **22**, 359–378.

WELCH, L., and L. LONG. 1940a. The higher structural phases of concept formation in children. *J. Psychol.*, **9**, 59–95.

——. 1940b. A further investigation of the higher structural phases of concept formation. *J. Psychol.*, **10**, 211–220.

WENGER, M. A. 1933. Path-selection behavior of young children in body-mazes. *J. Exp. Educ.*, **2**, 197–233.

——. 1936. An investigation of conditioned responses in human infants. *Univ. Iowa Stud. Child Welfare*, **12**, No. 1, pp. 7–90.

WENGER, M. A., and H. M. WILLIAMS. 1935. Experimental studies of learning in infants and preschool children. *Psychol. Bull.*, **32**, 276–305.

WHIPPLE, G. M. 1915. *Manual of mental and physical tests;* Vol. 2. Baltimore : Warwick and York.

WICKENS, D. D., and C. WICKENS. 1939. A study of conditioning in the neonate. *Psychol. Bull.*, **36**, 599.

WIEG, E. L. 1932. Bilateral transfer in the motor learning of young children and adults. *Child Develpm.*, **3**, 247–268.

WILLIAMS, O. 1926. A study of the phenomenon of reminiscence. *J. Exp. Psychol.*, **9**, 368–387.

WILSON, F. T. 1927. Learning of bright and dull children. *Teach. Coll. Contr. Educ.*, No. 292.

——. 1928. Learning curves of boys of IQ's 76–148. *J. Educ. Psychol.*, **19**, 50–57.

——. 1930a. A comparison of difficulty and accuracy in the learning of bright and dull children in a motor-memory task. *J. Educ. Psychol.*, **21**, 507–511.

——. 1930b. Factors of repetition and of directed and indirected attention in the learning of bright and dull children. *J. Genet. Psychol.*, **38**, 498–504.

——. 1931a. A comparison of difficulty and improvement in the learning of bright and dull children in reproducing a descriptive selection. *Genet. Psychol. Monogr.*, **9**, 395–435.

——. 1931b. Errors, difficulty, resourcefulness and the speed of learning of bright and dull children. *J. Educ. Psychol.*, **22**, 229–240.

——. 1931c. Difficulty in the learning of shorthand characters by bright and dull children. *J. Genet. Psychol.*, **39**, 113–122.

WILSON, F. T., and C. W. FLEMING. 1937. Correlations of perception with other abilities and traits in grade I. *Child Develpm.*, **8**, 223–240.

WINCH, W. H. 1904. Immediate memory in school children. *Brit. J. Psychol.*, **1**, 127–134.

——. 1908. The transfer of improvement in memory in school children. *Brit. J. Psychol.*, **2**, 284–293.

——. 1910. Transfer of improvement in memory in school children. *Brit. J. Psychol.*, **3**, 386–405.

——. 1911. Some relations between substance memory and productive imagination in school children. *Brit. J. Psychol.*, **4**, 95–125.

——. 1914. *Children's perceptions.* Baltimore : Warwick and York.

——. 1924. Should poems be learnt by schoolchildren as "wholes" or in "parts"? *Brit. J. Psychol.*, **15**, 64–79.

WINGFIELD, R. C. 1938. A study of alternation using children on a two-way maze. *J. Comp. Psychol.*, **25**, 439–443.

WOODROW, H. 1917. Practice and transference in normal and feeble-minded children. *J. Educ. Psychol.*, **8**, 85–96 ; 151–165.

WOODWORTH, R. S. 1938. *Experimental psychology.* New York : Holt.

WOODY, C. 1936. An analysis of differences in the learning of bright and dull children. *Univ. Mich. Sch. Educ. Bull.*, **8**, 37–39.

WOOLLEY, H. T. 1926. *An experimental study of children at work and in school between the ages of fourteen and eighteen years.* New York : Macmillan.

WUNDERLING, R. L. 1935. *Kind und Rätsel.* Frankfurt a. M. : Moritz, Diesterweg.

YERKES, R. M. 1921. A new method of studying the ideational behavior of mentally defective and deranged as compared with normal individuals. *J. Comp. Psychol.*, **1**, 369–394.

YOAKUM, G. A. 1921. The effect of a single reading. *Yearb. Nat. Soc. Stud. Educ.*, 20(II). Chap. 6.

YOUNG, H. H. 1922. A slot maze. *Psychol. Clin.*, **14**, 73–82.

YOUNG, M. 1928. A comparative study of audito-vocal digit spans. *Psychol. Clin.*, **17**, 170–182.

ZEIGARNIK, B. 1927. Über das Behalten von erledigten und unerledigten Handlungen. *Psychol. Forsch.*, **9**, 1–85.

CHAPTER 9

THE MEASUREMENT OF MENTAL GROWTH IN CHILDHOOD

FLORENCE L. GOODENOUGH

Historical Orientation

Until about thirty years ago, the topic of mental growth and its measurement occupied an almost negligible place in psychological literature. Just before the turn of the century, it is true, a number of attempts had been made to relate individual differences in the ability to perform simple motor and perceptual tasks to the differences in scholastic ability that have baffled educators since schools were first established. From the time of his student days in Wundt's laboratory, J. McK. Cattell's attention had been captured by the idea that the study of differences among individuals in their responses to the same stimuli might be of even greater psychological importance than the study of the typical effect upon people in general of a measured physical change in the stimulus itself. After his return to America, Cattell was one of the most energetic leaders in the development of these early tests. The first scientific use of the term *mental test* is to be found in an article by him that appeared in *Mind* in 1890, in which he described a number of tests of sensorimotor capacities which he was then using with his students at the University of Pennsylvania. The interest aroused by this article encouraged similar experimentation by a number of other leading psychologists, with the result that at the 1895 meeting of the American Psychological Association a committee, headed by Cattell, was ap-

pointed to consider the possibility of a cooperative effort to develop tests that would prove useful in gauging the probability of scholastic success among students entering college. A year later, Cattell and Farrand (1896) published a detailed account of the work of the committee in the form of a long series of tests which they planned to try out on Columbia freshmen.[1]

Although college students continued to make up the great body of subjects for these early experiments, tests for use with children were also devised. Of the investigations carried on during this period with children as subjects, by far the most important were Gilbert's (1894, 1897). His studies are of special importance because of his attempt to validate his tests by comparison of the results with teachers' judgments of the ability of their pupils. Inasmuch as the tests used were made up of such items as physical measurements—height, weight, and lung capacity—speed of simple reaction, tonal memory, estimation of distance, sensitivity to pain, rate of tapping, and the like, the modern student will not be surprised to learn that, in spite of a fairly regular improvement with advancing chronological age in most of these functions, their relation to teachers' judgments of the ability of their students was negligible.

[1] The results of the Columbia testing were later published by Wissler (1901). Correlations between college grades and standing on the various tests were consistently around zero.

The interest aroused by the early tests was short-lived. It soon became evident that the results obtained by their use were of little or no practical value for the understanding and guidance of children. Although, because of Cattell's example, these measurements were commonly known as mental tests, they were evidently not measuring *intelligence*, either in the sense that the word is used by the layman or as it is understood by the psychologist of today. This was a disappointing discovery, which led to a general loss of interest in the problem and a virtual cessation of experimental work in testing in this country for almost a decade.

Meanwhile Binet, in France, had also become interested in the measurement of individual differences in mental ability. From the outset, however, his approach to the problem was radically different from that of most others of his time. Most of his experimental articles were published in the journal that he himself established in 1895, *L'Année psychologique*. A critical reading of these studies in their chronological sequence shows the steady trend of his interest away from the artificially simplified tasks of the formalized laboratory to the more complex and realistic problems encountered in life as it is lived. Over and over again he notes that differences between individuals become increasingly evident as one progresses from the relatively "simple" performances to those that are more complex, and that it is the latter rather than the former type of difference with which we are mainly concerned in everyday life. He admits that the simple mental functions or processes are easier to measure objectively, but insists that this is a secondary consideration, inasmuch as measurement degenerates into mere busy-work unless the results are of some practical use. In this distinction between objectivity of measurement and the significance of the measures when made, Binet foreshadowed the discussions of *reliability* and *validity* that were to occupy so large a place in the literature on mental measurement a quarter of a century later.

Binet's first formalized scale for the measurement of intelligence was a direct outgrowth of his work as a member of the special commission appointed in 1904 by the Minister of Public Instruction in Paris for the purpose of devising means of selecting and segregating in special classes those children who were incapable of benefiting by the regular methods of instruction. This scale was published in collaboration with Simon in 1905. It consisted of thirty tests arranged roughly in order of difficulty. Age standards were not available at that time. As a matter of fact, although Binet, in his discussion of the scale, refers specifically to the desirability of comparing the performance of a child with that of others of his age, it seems improbable that the device of arranging tests in age groups for the purpose of ascertaining the mental age had as yet occurred to him. He does, however, indicate the levels of performance that divide the three classes of mental defectives—the idiots, the imbeciles, and the morons. Needless to say, the distinction as here used applies only to those who have attained their final level of development.

Crude as the 1905 scale was, it nevertheless proved to be sufficiently useful to encourage Binet and Simon in the feeling that they were on the right track. In 1908 they published a revision of the scale and in 1911 a second revision. The great feature of the two later scales lies in the fact that, instead of being arranged merely in order of difficulty, the items are grouped according to the age at which they are usually passed.[1] The selection of items was

---

[1] Binet was not the first to whom the general concept of mental age occurred, nor was he

also improved by the elimination of a number that had proved unsuitable and the addition of others that were more discriminative. The tests designed for idiots were also omitted as unnecessary in a scale designed for public school children. The 1911 scale, published just before Binet's death, included tests for the mental age range from three years to the adult level.

Both the 1908 and the 1911 Binet-Simon scales were translated into English by Goddard (1910, 1911a), with only such minor changes as were necessary to make them suitable for use with American children. After trying them out both with feeble-minded children in the institution at Vineland, New Jersey, and in the near-by public schools, Goddard became thoroughly

the first to adopt the device of arranging tests in age groups. It is not unlikely that crude comparisons between the behavior of backward adults and that of children have been made by laymen at all times, just as today we often hear such expressions as "No more sense than a baby" or "Has to be looked after like a little child" even from people who have never heard of such a term as *mental age*. Reference to early medico-legal papers discloses a number of instances in which the same idea has been made more or less explicit. It is said that, as early as 1848 at the trial of one William Freeman, who was charged with the murder of four persons without provocation, a psychiatrist called as witness in the case stated that "in point of knowledge the accused was like a child of three years." (Pintner, 1931.)

In 1887 Doctor S. E. Chaille published a series of simple tests for children under three years of age. These tests are arranged in groups according to the age at which normal infants may be expected to succeed with them, in order, so the author points out, that parents and others who have to do with children may know whether or not a given child is developing as he should. Although Chaille does not use the term "mental age," it is clear from his discussion that this type of comparison was intended. However, Chaille's scale, which appeared in a medical journal of limited circulation at a date when few people were interested in the question of mental measurement, attracted little or no attention and was soon forgotten. It is Binet, therefore, to whom we are indebted for the development of the mental age concept as a practicable means of expressing test results in a roughly quantitative form.

convinced of the superiority of the new tests over all other methods of assaying the intelligence of children that had been tried up to that date. His many books and papers dealing with this topic were read with great interest by psychologists and educators throughout the country.

The extraordinary rapidity with which Binet testing was taken up in America can be traced to a number of conditions. Most important is the fact that the tests appeared at an opportune moment. In many states the period of compulsory school attendance was being extended, and compulsory attendance laws were being more strictly enforced. The immediate result was that large numbers of backward children who would formerly have dropped quietly out of school and been forgotten were being herded into the primary grades at small profit to themselves and at the cost of much wasted energy on the part of teachers. Ayres's *Laggards in Our Schools*, which appeared in 1909, did a great deal to arouse public interest in the matter of school retardation, and to point the need for more adequate methods of dealing with the problems involved.

Scientific interest in questions of juvenile delinquency also became active at about this period. The first juvenile court was established in 1910. Inasmuch as the question of individual responsibility for delinquent behavior has been a predominating feature of the public attitude for generations, it was but natural that the idea of utilizing the new instrument as a means of securing more valid information on the mental level of delinquent children should have arisen almost as soon as the tests were introduced into this country. The fact (afterward learned) that the Binet tests as revised by Goddard were incorrectly standardized at the older ages, with the result that the mental ages obtained for adolescents who make up the great mass of juvenile delinquents were far too low, gave rise to astounding findings. Pintner (1931) has summarized the results of a number of the most striking of these early studies in which the proportion of "feeble-minded" among institutionalized delinquents is said to be as high as 50 to 90 per cent.[1] It was but natural to conclude that if the problems of mental deficiency could be solved the amount of juvenile delinquency would be greatly reduced.

Consideration of the cost of mental defect in terms of delinquency and of the special educational problems it presents led immediately to questions of causation and prevention. The rediscovery of the early work of Mendel by DeVries, in 1900, had by this time attracted the attention of a number of psychologists, among whom was Goddard. With characteristic energy, Goddard at once set about tracing the family histories of feeble-minded children in the Vineland institution in order to see if there might be evidence for the hypothesis that feeble-mindedness not only tends to "run in families" but is inherited according to strictly Mendelian principles as a "unit character." His three books, *The Kallikak Family* (1912), *Feeble-Mindedness; Its Causes and Consequences* (1914), and *The Criminal Imbecile* (1915), comprised what was then regarded by many people as a convincing body of evidence that a large proportion of all cases of mental defect is the direct result of biological inheritance of a defective nervous struc-

ture. Although Goddard's investigations, carried on as they were at a time when the technical aspects of the biological study of human beings were but little considered, have been severely and justly criticized,[2] their effect upon psychological thinking and upon social provisions for the care and training of delinquent and defective groups has been profound.

Another factor that gave impetus to the testing movement was the rapid increase of organized agencies for social welfare. Up to about 1910, family social work was largely in the hands of untrained volunteer workers from the various churches. With the appearance on the scene of the professionally trained worker, and the coordination of records from different organizations, the need for a better means of separating the cases for whom there was reasonable hope of rehabilitation from those who were unlikely ever to be able to "manage themselves and their own affairs with ordinary prudence,"[3] the importance of mental testing for improving the efficiency of social welfare work became increasingly apparent.

Two additional social changes that stimulated interest in testing should be mentioned. The first of these was World War I, when the possibility of testing large groups of individuals at one time was clearly demonstrated. The cost of administering individual tests has always proved to be a major stumbling block in the way of their application to the rank and file of individuals. With the advent of group testing, mental measurement as an aid to

[1] The fact that modern studies commonly show a far smaller percentage of low-testing individuals among institutionalized delinquents than do those made at this early date is in all probability attributable only in part to the standardization error in the tests. A part of the difference is presumably a true one, indicating the greater tendency of modern social agencies to recognize the special problems of the feeble-minded delinquent, and to transfer such cases to institutions for the feeble-minded rather than to reformatories.

[2] In *The Kallikak Family,* the entire case rests upon the unverifiable story of a casual intimacy alleged to have occurred at the time of the Revolutionary War between a Continental soldier of good family and a "feeble-minded" girl encountered in a tavern.

[3] This is Tredgold's criterion for separating the feeble-minded from the normal.

educational administration was at once put on a firm basis.

Finally, the cause of mental testing was materially advanced by the rise of the mental hygiene movement with its modern emphasis upon the establishment of behavior clinics for children. The determination of the mental level as a first step in diagnosis and as a partial guide to the kind of treatment most likely to be helpful rapidly became a part of the standard practice in organizations of this kind.

Looking backward along the path over which we have come, it is apparent that the development of mental testing, like many other scientific procedures of modern times, was by no means a result of the abstract curiosity of the "pure" scientist. First and primarily, mental tests as we know them today are practical instruments, devised to meet some specific and immediate social need. Their use as research implements has in practically all instances been secondary in time as well as in importance; it is only within comparatively recent years that new tests have been devised with the needs of the research worker rather than those of the clinician or educator primarily in mind. It is not unlikely that if the opposite condition had prevailed, if the demand for a practical working instrument had been less insistent, leaving the early workers more time to perfect their instrument before its pattern had crystallized into a tradition, the course of the testing movement might have been very different. In the white heat of early enthusiasm, many scientific blunders were made for which we are still paying the price in terms of mistaken concepts and conflicting practices. Nevertheless, these very blunders, with the spectacular conclusions to which they led, in many instances served to arouse public interest and support for the tests in a way that might never have been accomplished by an instrument designed for the service of pure science. Whether or not our present knowledge of the course of mental growth would have been greater had we postponed our studies until better techniques of investigation had been devised is at least an open question. We might have been better prepared to make such studies, but we might also have been less strongly urged to do so!

Be that as it may, it is of the utmost importance that students of mental growth continually bear in mind the fact that even the best of our present instruments for measuring mental growth are still fallible, although they have been shown to work surprisingly well in the practical situations for which they were designed. Even as tools for scientific research, they become extremely valuable in the hands of those who understand the basic principles by which they were constructed and their consequent possibilities and limitations, but they are by no means foolproof. That false as well as true conclusions have resulted from their use can hardly be attributed to the tests or to the test-makers, but rather, in great part, to the fact that their apparent simplicity has led many poorly qualified persons to apply them to the solution of problems that neither the tests nor their users were well equipped to handle.

The Present Status of Mental Testing in America

Within the short space of a quarter of a century, the literature on mental growth and its measurement has become so voluminous that a mere listing of titles requires an entire book. Hildreth's (1939) recent bibliography covers 251 pages and lists well over 4000 titles. Her "bibliography of bibliographies" alone covers six full pages. Nevertheless, even this extensive source book is selective rather than exhaustive. Buros (1936, 1937, 1938) finds the literature in the field to be increasing so rapidly as to justify the publication of an annual *Yearbook* in which the outstanding tests of recent date are reviewed by competent authorities.[1] It is obvious that nothing even approaching an adequate covering of the literature in this field can be compressed into the number of pages in this chapter. All that will be attempted, therefore, is to direct the reader to some useful sources for further reference and to devote the remaining space to a consideration of a few of the more crucial problems in the field of measurement.

The most competent account of the early history of testing is to be found in Peterson's *Early Conceptions and Tests of Intelligence* (1925). A more concise but very readable report of the early work in testing, with particular emphasis on the kind of contributions made by workers of different countries, has been given by Kimball Young (1924). Pintner's little book on intelligence testing (1931) is particularly well adapted for the use of beginning students because of its clear presentation of material and its orderly arrangement. The series of annual reviews on intelligence tests and methods of testing by the same author (see Part II of the bibliography at the end of this chapter) is well selected and reasonably complete for the period covered. A survey of testing methods by Schieffelin and Schwesinger (1930) includes much valuable information on specific tests that has not appeared elsewhere. Although the book is no longer new, a large proportion of the 186 tests listed are still in active use. For each of these tests they cite the author, the publisher, the date of

publication, the price, and the purpose of the test, together with a brief description of the materials and the testing procedure, the time required for giving and scoring the test, the number and age range of the cases used for standardization, and the kind of norms available. Such information as it was possible to obtain with respect to internal consistency and correlation with various criteria is also included. Hildreth's *Psychological Service for School Problems* (1930) is a good reference book for those primarily interested in the practical uses of tests in public schools. Other treatments of the same topic are to be found in Kelley's *Interpretation of Educational Measurements* (1927) and *Testing and the Use of Test Results* (1935) by Lincoln and Workman, as well as in most of the manuals of instruction for the administration of particular tests. More generalized treatments of the entire field of mental measurement have been given by Dearborn (1928) and by Freeman (1939). Further references may be found in Part II of the bibliography at the end of this chapter.

The Nature and Organization of Intelligence

Because the early use of intelligence tests was largely confined to the diagnosis of mental deficiency, little attention was at first paid to the question of what "intelligence" really is. Up to the middle of the second decade of the present century, attempts at definition were chiefly concerned with descriptions of individuals who were lacking in intelligence. As a result, we had many definitions of mental deficiency couched in terms of what the mentally defective person is like, but few attempts at defining or describing the trait in which he was alleged to be deficient. Although Spearman had formulated his "two-factor

---

[1] Although Buros's original plan was for an annual volume, financial limitations have made it impossible to carry out his arrangements. Only three volumes of the series have appeared to date. A fourth is now in preparation.

theory" of intelligence as early as 1904, it was not until much later, when, as a result of the extension of mental testing techniques to all levels of ability, the question of what the mental testers were actually trying to measure was brought clearly to the fore, that this theory became the matter of spirited controversy that it is today.

In 1921 a number of leading psychologists were asked to express their views on the nature of intelligence, and their replies were published (*Symposium*, 1921). Although at first reading the points of view seem rather diverse, a little consideration shows that in reality the differences are less important than they seem. Some emphasized the ability to profit by experience, others the ability to adjust to new situations. But since the crucial test of the extent to which an individual has profited by his experience is to be found in his ability to employ the knowledge thus gained in new situations, the two concepts reduce themselves to much the same thing in the end. Thorndike's practical suggestion that intelligence consists in the ability of the individual "to make good responses from the standpoint of truth or fact" is certainly in accordance with everyday practice, both in the judgment of intelligence from behavior and in the scoring of intelligence tests. However, it does not offer any clue to the types of behavior that make most demand upon intelligence. This, of course, is in line with his general point of view that intelligence is not a unitary trait. Terman, on the other hand, makes the distinction very explicitly. According to Terman, "an individual is intelligent in proportion as he is able to carry on abstract thinking." Although some have regarded this definition as too academic, giving too little weight to the more practical and concrete aspects of behavior, nevertheless, as was shown in the early sections of this chapter, most investigators have found so low a correlation between the ability to respond to simple, concrete situations and the ability to handle abstractions, symbols, relationships, as emphasized by Terman, that it seems doubtful whether anything but confusion can result from the attempt to embrace both within a single measure.

The above principle has been clearly recognized in selecting the material for inclusion in tests of intelligence designed for adults and older children. It is very probable that the low correlation universally found between the results of tests given at the early ages and those of tests of the same individuals at later ages is in large part due to the fact that the tests for infants and young children are so largely made up of simple motor and perceptual items that the type of ability measured by them may be very different from that measured later on by tests that conform more closely to Terman's definition. The latter tests, as, for example, following complicated directions, solving mathematical problems, or drawing analogies, show a fair amount of intercorrelation with each other. In contrast, even among young children the interrelationships of the abilities measured by such concrete motor performances as maze learning, ring tossing, completing form boards, and so on are not high. Apparently, motor performances such as these are at all ages relatively specific, which means in effect that a test sample that includes only a few of them can by no means be regarded as a reliable indication of "general" ability. If the correlation of one measure with another is sufficiently high, only one of these need be used, since performance on the second can then be predicted from the score on the first with considerable accuracy. It is because the more abstract types of tests do show this characteristic of interlinkage, one with another, over a wide area of differential content that it has been found practically feasible to secure a reasonably dependable estimate of the general ability [1] of any individual by the use of a relatively small number of tests that require not over an hour's time for their completion.

Modern students of the nature of intelligence and of the organization of mental traits tend to lean much more heavily upon mathematical analysis for the verification of theories than did their forerunners. We are moving rapidly from the descriptive to the quantitative level, not only with respect to our attempts to assay individual differences in general ability but also, through mathematical examination of the interrelationships between various types of ability, with respect to our attempts to gain a more precise knowledge of the nature of mental organization. Space does not permit me to do more than touch upon the large body of experimental work centering about this problem. For a more complete account of the investigations and the conclusions that have emerged therefrom the interested reader should consult the brilliant review of the entire field by Thomson (1939). Here it must suffice to say that four somewhat different hypotheses as to the nature of mental organization have emerged from these studies. At one extreme we have the view expressed by Thorndike, which, briefly stated, is that each mental act is a separate element, to some extent independent of all others but also having features in common with many others. Certain acts have so many of their

[1] Needless to say, the term *ability,* as here used, has reference only to the area covered by the tests. A measure of *abstract thinking* will not predict standing on a specific type of motor performance any more effectively than the latter will predict the former. The advantage of the *abstract* test is that the mental area for which it affords a useful means of prediction is wide, whereas motor tests, generally speaking, have little or no predictive value for any functions outside the narrow limits of each particular item.

elements in common that we find it convenient to classify them into separate groups to which class names are applied, such as arithmetical reasoning, completing omitted portions of sentences, and so on.

Provided certain basic conditions of measurement are fulfilled, intelligence, according to Thorndike, is a simple aggregate of all the abilities underlying each of these separate acts. Symbolically, it may be regarded as a surface of which the height or *altitude* represents the difficulty of the acts that the individual is able to perform within a certain one of these closely related areas, such as completing analogies, while the *breadth* represents the range or number of tasks that can be solved at any given level of difficulty. According to Thorndike, correlation between performance on different mental tasks is not to be explained in terms of any generalized quality of "mind" but is purely a function of the number of common elements involved in their solution. This leads of necessity to the rejection of the whole concept of *general intelligence* and the substitution therefor of *specific intelligences,* the number of which is purely an arbitrary matter, depending upon how fine a classification is needed in any particular instance. He suggests that for many crude purposes a three-way classification under the headings of *abstract intelligence,* or the ability to deal with words and other symbols, *mechanical intelligence,* or the ability to deal with concrete objects and materials, and *social intelligence,* or the ability to deal effectively with people, will be found sufficient. Most of our modern tests of intelligence are based almost entirely upon the first, neglecting the other two. Thorndike regards this as a good thing as far as it goes, which is to say that he feels that only confusion would arise from mixing them. Better tests for the other forms of intelligence, rather than a combination of all three, are needed. He also points out that each of these may be divided almost indefinitely. This is illustrated in the case of abstract intelligence by his famous CAVD test (1926) in which each letter stands for a particular kind of performance.[1] These four tests, needless to say, are not to be thought of as covering the whole area of abstract intelligence; they represent only certain segments of it. However, because of the fairly high intercorrelation of all measures within this area, the remaining portions can be estimated from scores on the measured portion with a degree of accuracy that is sufficient for many purposes.

The other two types of ability may be subdivided in a similar manner. Social ability unquestionably varies with the age, sex, social status, intelligence, and so on of the persons to be dealt with. Some people are very effective in handling children but are awkward and constrained in the company of adults; some get on well with their own sex but not with the opposite sex; some appear to be "born leaders," [2] others are happiest and most effective when someone else assumes the leading rôle. The limit of divisibility is reached only when the separate act can no longer be subdivided without losing its identity.

Moving upward in the organizational scale from Thorndike's view that the system of organization is external, inherent in the task rather than in the individual, we come to the theory of orthogonal traits proposed by Kelley (1928, 1935). By means of a statistical analysis of the inter-

correlations between performances on many different kinds of tests, Kelley arrived at the conclusion that all the varying abilities of an individual can be accounted for on the basis of a relatively small number of independent traits or separate abilities that are completely unrelated to each other. In everyday life, as in test performance, a given act usually calls for the simultaneous exercise of more than one of these abilities, and in varying degree. It is because of the almost infinitely great number of combinations and permutations thus made possible that mental abilities appear to be so diverse, inasmuch as it is only by mathematical analysis that a given ability can be "purified" and known for what it is. Nevertheless, the principle, if true, is not devoid of its practical applications, for, if we once knew what these abilities are and, furthermore, if we were able to ascertain the kind of measurable acts in which a given ability exercises the dominant rôle, we should be able to develop a series of tests that would be more nearly exact measures of these separate functions even though they might not be completely freed from intermixture.

Thurstone (1938), whose theories rank next in our organizational scheme, has attempted to do that very thing. Like Kelley, Thurstone developed his theory of mental organization by means of a factorial analysis of tables of intercorrelation. His mathematical approach is, however, somewhat different and although, like Kelley, he emerges with a theory of separate and independent mental traits, he differs from Kelley in that he considers these traits to be ranked in order of generality, and hence, we may say, in terms of their importance in individual mental life. Mathematically speaking, these traits, or *factors*, as the mathematicians prefer to call them, are indeterminate, by which is meant that there is nothing in the nature

---

[1] Sentence completion, arithmetic reasoning, vocabulary, following directions.

[2] This statement must, of course, not be taken literally. There is evidence that social abilities are at least in part the result of individual experience and training. The extent to which inborn characteristics may also be involved is unknown, though it is probable that they play some part in the matter. The expression is used here in the popular rather than the scientific sense.

of the analysis itself that tells what a given factor is like. They are simply Factor I (the most nearly general), Factor II, and so on. But it is possible to determine mathematically the part played by any single factor in determining the intercorrelations between tests. By comparing the subject matter of tests in which these *factor loadings* are markedly different, as, for example, tests that have a high loading for Factor I but a low loading for Factor II with those weighted in the opposite direction, hypotheses that are at least in accordance with common sense as to the probable nature of these factors may be drawn up [1] and the factors may then be named in everyday language.

In the attempt to develop tests that are more nearly "pure" measures of these factors, or *primary mental abilities*, as Thurstone has named them, the procedure followed is essentially a cut-and-try matter in which the guiding principle is finding tasks that differ as much as possible from all those in which the loading for the factor in question is low, and most of all from those in which it is lowest, and which at the same time resemble most strongly those for which this loading is high. By repeating this process a sufficiently large number of times it should be possible, at least on theoretical grounds, to come out eventually with a series of tests by which all the abilities of an individual may be measured with a minimum of wasted time and effort.

[1] The particular set of weights comprising the "factor pattern" for any given set of intercorrelations is not, however, arrived at by any simple or unequivocal method. In order to obtain such a pattern, axes must be rotated until the resulting set of weights appears to accord with good psychological judgment as to the similarities and differences of the various tests included in the table. It is not at all certain that uniform agreement would be found among psychologists as to the stage at which the most reasonable psychological meaning can be attached to the factor pattern then obtained. (See Stalnaker, 1940.)

Within a somewhat less ambitious range,[2] this is what Thurstone has attempted to do in his Primary Abilities Test (1938). By means of a procedure essentially similar to that just described he arrives at the conclusion that individual differences in human mental abilities can be measured and described in terms of only twelve basic abilities, each of which may be possessed in varying degrees. Seven of these are tentatively named as follows: S = spatial abilities, P = perceptual abilities, N = numerical abilities, V = verbal relations, M = memory, W = words (that is, single unrelated words), and I = induction. With less certainty two others are named as follows: R = reasoning and D = deduction. For the remaining three he is not yet ready to propose names. Thurstone has also developed a battery of tests by which each of the first seven abilities may be measured separately. These tests were originally designed for use with college students and students in senior high schools. More recently the procedure has been extended downward to the fourteen-year age level (Thurstone and Thurstone, 1941). By means of the new series it is possible to draw up a mental profile for each child which will show his comparative proficiency along the following lines: verbal comprehension, word fluency, spatial relations, numerical ability, memorizing, and reasoning. Thurstone states that of these the reasoning or induction factor is most closely associated with the other aspects of ability (that is, is the most nearly general), whereas memorizing is the most nearly independent of the six factors studied. Work

[2] Thurstone's primary abilities are not presumed to cover the complete range of human talent. They do not, for example, cover such specialized abilities as musical or artistic talent or motor skills. They involve only the abstract abilities needed for success in the conventional types of intelligence tests and in the academic pursuits of the classroom.

on a further extension of the tests for use with children in the lower primary grades is now in progress.

Spearman, in a series of brilliant books and essays dating from 1904, has expounded a theory that calls for an even higher degree of mental organization than that proposed by Thurstone. According to Spearman, all mental activity demands the exercise of a special attribute that he terms *mental energy* because in the realm of mind its place is analogous to that of physical energy in the world of physics. This attribute of mind he designates by the symbol *g*, or *general* factor, since it is possessed by all individuals, though in varying degree, and enters into all mental activity, though to a varying extent. Because all are to some extent dependent upon *g*, all measurable forms of truly intelligent behavior, as, for example, the ability to solve arithmetic problems, to complete analogies, to perceive relationships among geometrical forms, or to understand long and complicated sentences, show some degree of correlation with each other. However, individual differences in ability are not wholly traceable to differences in the amount of *g*. They are also dependent upon other factors, known as *s* factors, that are more or less specific to particular activities or situations, whereas *g* is common to all. Some activities involve the *g* factor to only a slight extent, being chiefly made up of *s* factors, and these will commonly show only low correlations with other mental acts. Others, in which the *g* factor is paramount, will intercorrelate highly with one another. Because this theory was the first to be proposed that was based upon mathematical demonstration (although in fairness it must be pointed out that there is not complete agreement among statisticians as to the interpretation of the results), it has attracted much attention and has stimulated a large number of important investigations. Indeed, it was largely the attempt to test Spearman's conclusions that led to the formulation of the three other hypotheses as to the organization of mind that have been described in the preceding pages.

In addition to the *g* factor, which is primarily intellectual in nature, since, according to Spearman, it involves mainly the "apprehension of one's own experience, the eduction of relations and the eduction of correlates," Spearman has obtained evidence of the existence of other general factors, some of which, as *w* (volition), appear to be related to what is commonly known as *personality*. Intermediate between these general factors that play a part in all mental activity and the decidedly specific *s* factors are others of less complete generality but nevertheless common to a rather wide range of mental acts. To these Spearman has given the name of *group factors*. He suggests that musical ability and mechanical ability are of this type.

Inasmuch as all these variant hypotheses as to the nature of mental organization have been arrived at by means of different statistical methods applied to the analysis of tables of intercorrelations, it becomes pertinent to ask whether any one of them is more than an artifact of the method employed. This point has been ably discussed in a monograph by Thomson (1939), with which all who are interested in factor theory should be familiar. Because Thomson's treatment of the subject cannot be condensed into a few lines without danger of distortion, no attempt will be made to summarize his conclusions in this chapter. The interested reader should consult the original source.[1]

[1] For an able discussion of the use of factor analysis in the construction of a scale designed to measure "general intelligence," together with the detailed results obtained from a factorial

The Quantification of Intellectual Performance

For some years after the appearance of Goddard's translations of Binet's 1908 and 1911 scales, the only way of expressing the amount of acceleration or retardation of an individual child was to state the difference between his actual or chronological age and his mental age. A child was said to "test" so many years "above age" or "below age." But, since the significance of a given number of years' acceleration or retardation varies with the age of the child, the use of the *intelligence quotient,* or IQ, first proposed by Stern and popularized by Terman in the Stanford Revision of the Binet tests (1916), gained rapidly in popularity. The intelligence quotient, which is the ratio between the mental age and the chronological age, was at first assumed to have a constant meaning regardless of the age of the child. For this reason it was often spoken of as an *absolute* measure of intelligence. More recent work, however, has shown that this is not always the case. Unless certain constant relationships are maintained between the dispersion of test scores at each age and the averages or *norms* for the successive ages, the IQ cannot remain constant either for individuals or for groups. This point has been discussed by a number of different persons, and especially by Freeman (1930). For example, if the curve of mental growth from age to age is assumed to be a straight line, as is done when the tests are arranged in the form of a *year scale* with an equal number of tasks at each age, then the dispersion of mental ages must increase from age to age in a ratio that is proportionate to age. If at the age of 6 the standard deviation of

analysis of the findings for the 1937 revision of the Stanford-Binet, the reader should consult Chapter 9 of McNemar's *Revision of the Stanford-Binet Scale* (1942).

mental ages is 12 months, then at the age of 9 it should be 18 months, at the age of 12 it should be 24 months, and so on. If this condition is not met, then an IQ of 120 earned at the age of 6 will not be comparable in meaning to one of the same apparent value earned at some other age.

If the tests are not arranged in year groups but in some other order, say in order of difficulty, and the number of items passed at each age is taken as the norm for that age, as was done in the so-called point score procedure, some definite relationship between the successive age increments and the dispersion of scores must still be maintained. What that relationship should be will depend upon the form of the growth curve for the test in question. If the curve follows the form of a logarithmic series, then the dispersion of test scores should be equal at all ages. If it follows some other form, the dispersion of test scores must change accordingly in such a way that the overlapping of scores from age to age will increase in proportion to age. In a few tests, notably the middle ranges of the 1916 Stanford-Binet, the necessary conditions appear to be fairly well fulfilled, but the uncritical use of the IQ technique for any and all tests for which age standards have been worked out is unwarranted. (Goodenough, 1942.)

A number of other methods for interpreting test scores, such as the *coefficient of intelligence* proposed by Yerkes, Bridges, and Hardwick and the *index of brightness* suggested by Otis, that were advocated during the early days of testing rapidly became obsolete as the superiority of the IQ method (when properly used) became increasingly evident. Rand (1925) has described and discussed a number of these early procedures in connection with a very able analysis of the underlying premises of *quotient methods* in general.

An early study by Kuhlmann (1921), based upon a large number of retests of feeble-minded persons by means of his revision of the Binet scale—in which it was shown that the IQ's obtained by this scale for feeble-minded children in institutions do not, as was then supposed, maintain a constant level either as regards the individual or the average of the (feeble-minded) group—has been much quoted. Instead, they tend to become lower with advancing age. This study was used by Heinis (1926) as a partial means for verifying a previous conclusion that this tendency of low IQ's to decrease with advancing age is a necessary characteristic of the IQ method of expressing test results, and that it is paralleled at the upper extreme by a corresponding tendency for high IQ's to increase with age. He therefore developed a new formula leading to a measure called the *personal coefficient* [1] (PC), which is defined as follows: "The personal coefficient of any given individual is equal to the result of the intelligence examination divided by the normal degree of intelligence corresponding to his age, both measures being given in absolute graduation." Because the method of reducing test scores to absolute values is somewhat complicated, Heinis adds a table by which mental ages can be transformed directly into PC values. This assumes that there is a single curve of mental growth independent of the scale used, and that Heinis's derivation of the formula for this curve, which was based upon data obtained by Descoudres and Vermeylen, and some unpublished material of his own, is correct. Heinis shows that when his formula is applied to Kuhlmann's data, the PC's thus obtained show no general tendency to change with age, a fact that he regards as sufficient evidence of the superiority of the PC over the IQ. This alleged superiority, however, has been in-

[1] Also known as the *personal constant*.

vestigated by several persons and they have come to no uniform conclusion. P. Cattell (1933) found it yielded a more constant result for backward children but not for bright ones. Kuhlmann, however, has expressed himself as being definitely in favor of it and has employed it in his new individual test (1939). An excellent discussion of the Heinis coefficient with special comments on Kuhlmann's reasons for favoring it has been given by McNemar (1942).

During the last few years the *percentile method* of interpreting test scores has become increasingly popular. The percentile score, or, as it is often called, the *percentile rank*, is expressed in terms of the percentage of a specified group, usually of the same age, whom the child in question surpasses. The fact that any group may be used for comparison gives the percentile method a degree both of flexibility and of specificity that the methods previously described lack. A mental age norm is always, supposedly, representative of children in general of the age in question. A little consideration, however, will show that it is rarely possible, in the actual standardization of a test, to secure the truly representative group that is implied by the term mental age. This difficulty has been recognized theoretically by practically all workers; nevertheless, the idea that the *mental age norms* which have been worked out in the course of the original standardization of a test have some kind of final or absolute value is implicit in most of the interpretations of results obtained for different groups by the use of various tests. Moreover, rarely are we actively concerned with a comparison between *individuals* in noncompeting groups. Ordinarily we compare college students with other college students, preferably of the same class. We are likely to be more interested in knowing how the eight-year-old daughter of a college professor compares with the eight-year-old offspring of other college professors or with the other children in her class at school than in knowing how she compares with the eight-year-olds in a backward mountain community or with the eight-year-old Negroes on a Louisiana plantation. Comparisons between contrasted *groups* of this kind are often interesting, but for this purpose other methods of quantifying test results are more suitable than the quotient methods so often used.

The percentile method has other very obvious advantages. It is easily understood even by the uninformed and is therefore particularly useful in explaining test results to parents, teachers, physicians, and others who may be interested. Since comparisons are made only between individuals of the same chronological age, the implications resulting from assigning equal basic scores to individuals of very different levels of physical maturity and life experience are avoided. An imbecile of fifteen with a mental age of three is a very different kind of human being from a normal child of three years even though he may happen to pass the same number of items on a certain mental test. Even his test score, although it may count up to the same number of items, will usually show decided qualitative differences in the particular items passed and the kind of responses that are made to them. Cunningham (1927) has shown that, even with so carefully standardized a test as the CAVD, differences between the performance of adult imbeciles and normal children between the ages of two and a half and six years on the separate items of the test are in some instances as great as ten times the standard error. Merrill (1924) found decided differences in the performance of gifted, average, and subnormal children of the same mental age on the different items of the Stanford-Binet. The groups also dif-

fered considerably in the amount of *scatter* on this test, that is, in the range which it was necessary to cover in order to meet the usual conditions of complete testing. Both the gifted and the subnormal groups "scattered" decidedly more than the group of average ability. Aldrich and Doll (1931) matched normal children of nineteen to thirty-eight months with idiot boys of corresponding mental ages and compared their performances on the Gesell developmental items and on the Merrill-Palmer series of performance tests. The idiots were markedly inferior to the normal children on all tests involving language but were superior in the tests involving experience and the use of concrete materials.

Although, when properly used and interpreted, the method of percentile ranks is a simple and valuable device for reducing test scores to meaningful quantitative terms, it must not be forgotten that, unless the distribution of test scores takes the form of a rectangle instead of the usual normal curve, the distances between successive percentiles cannot be equal. Instead, their values will increase steadily toward each extreme. This is easily understood if it is remembered that the percentiles are computed on the basis of the percentage of cases making each successive score, that is, in terms of the areas of successive segments above the base line of the curve. If the distribution of scores approximates the usual bell-shaped form, equal areas will subtend longer and longer segments of the base line as the extremes of the distribution are approached. The difference in score value between the ninety-seventh and the ninety-eighth percentile will be far greater than that between the fifty-seventh and the fifty-eighth. Percentile ranks, therefore, while they are useful methods for expressing individual standing within a specified group, should never be used as media for further computation. They cannot, justifiably, be added or subtracted or averaged. Neither do they lend themselves to the conventional forms of graphic expression such as bar diagrams or histograms. They are interpretative measures only.

Another method of expressing the test standing of an individual is in terms of the number of standard deviations by which he falls below or surpasses the mean standing of his group. As in the case of percentiles, the group may be defined in any way desired. If age is taken as a basis for the definition, however, the range of ages used for determining the standard deviation should equal those used in defining the age of an individual child. That is, if the ages of the children are taken to the nearest month, then the standard deviations used in computing the scores should be calculated within the limits of dispersion shown by children whose ages vary only within a month's range. The point is a rather obvious one, and is mentioned only because it has frequently been disregarded when this method of expressing scores has been used.

The direct expression of test results in terms of untransformed standard deviation units has two practical disadvantages. Such scores involve the use of a decimal point and they may be either negative or positive in sign. Both these factors make for errors in reading and recording. A device for overcoming this difficulty is rapidly gaining in popularity. It consists in setting the mean of every test or measure used at 50 and the standard deviation at 10. The score of each individual on any type of mental or physical measure thus becomes

$$\text{Converted score} = 50 + 10x$$

where x is the number of standard deviations (plus or minus) by which he deviates from the mean of his group.

Goodenough and Maurer (1942) have suggested a modification of this formula which is designed to make the numerical results correspond to the values which have already been made familiar through the use of the ordinary intelligence quotients. By a simple substitution of constants, the formula becomes

$$\text{Converted score} = 100 + 17.5x$$

This procedure has been used in the derivation of interpretative units for the Minnesota Preschool Scales. The values so obtained have been called IQ equivalents to distinguish them from IQ's obtained in the usual manner. It should be noted, however, that the significance of the two is the same, and the procedure itself is not subject to some of the criticisms often made of the intelligence quotient when calculated in the usual manner.

The use of either percentiles or standard deviation scores (the latter are often called "sigma" scores) is based upon the implicit assumption that the items making up the tests are equally spaced for difficulty. But in few, if any, of the group tests in common use has this requirement been fulfilled. Generally speaking, all that has been done is to arrange the items in an approximate order of difficulty, and then count the number passed by each child. This procedure commonly yields very unequal steps, particularly at the extremes. The irregular overlapping resulting from the unequal spacing made it impossible that interpretative measures such as intelligence quotients or sigma scores calculated from these tests should have equivalent meanings at different levels, even within the limits of the same test. When different tests were used the discrepancies were likely to be even more glaring. A number of scaling procedures designed to overcome these irregularities have been worked out and applied both to the older tests first standardized on the basis of a simple item count and to newly devised tests. Thus far, scaling methods have been more generally applied to the educational tests for the measurement of accomplishment in the different school subjects than to intelligence tests, but work on the latter is well under way, and it is to be expected that in the future the question of scaling will be given much more attention in the construction of tests of all kinds than has been done in the past.

Among the tests in present use for which norms are given in terms of scale values, the Arthur Performance Scale (1930) and the Minnesota Preschool Tests (Goodenough, Maurer, and Van Wagenen, 1940) may be mentioned. The procedure used in deriving the scale values for the Arthur tests is the so-called discriminative value method (D.V.) proposed by Arthur and Woodrow (1919). In scaling the Minnesota tests the C-score method used in a number of educational tests was used. Thorndike's work on the CAVD tests has already been mentioned. This is one of the most thoroughgoing pieces of methodological work that has appeared, and merits careful study. In the same volume, scaled values for a number of the leading intelligence tests originally standardized on an item count basis are also given.

Although the question of scaling is so fundamental a problem in all attempts at mental measurement, there is as yet no general agreement as to which of the various methods that have been employed will yield the most consistent results. Thurstone (1925, 1928a, 1928b), who has developed a method of scaling based on the overlapping of scores at successive age levels, is very critical of any method which takes account of variability only within a single age group. His method results in scale values which appear to yield an approximately linear relationship between age

and variability, a condition which, as was pointed out in an earlier paragraph, is necessary if quotients are to have the same relative significance from one age to another. Although the true linearity of this relationship has been called into question by Holzinger (1928), the error appears to be much smaller than that which would result if scores derived from a single age group were used as the basis for scaling, as Holzinger recommends.

Since the values derived from the so-called absolute scaling methods will vary according to the method employed and the extent to which the empirical data correspond to the assumptions under which these methods have been worked out, it is evident that at best the equality of spacing that these methods are presumed to yield is only approximate.[1] It is undoubtedly an improvement over the old item count method, but much further work needs to be done before we can be certain how and to what extent the results are affected by variations in the conditions of testing and in the sampling of subjects upon whom the test was standardized. All methods of scaling derive their units from the proportion of children at each age who pass each test item. Although the matter has not been adequately tested, it seems highly improbable that scale values can maintain their equality of spacing except for groups that are reasonably similar to the one on which the values were derived. This point has been recognized to some extent. Thurstone (1928a, p. 178), for example, specifically states that "the social and intellectual factors of selection must operate more or less uniformly for the several age-groups" if the conditions requisite for his method of scaling are to be observed.

Thorndike et al. (1926) have pointed out additional sources of error. The ordinary

[1] See the discussion of this point by McNemar (1942, Chapter XI).

criterion of test difficulty is the relative frequency with which an item is passed. A test that is passed by few children at a given age is regarded as more difficult than one which the majority can answer. The frequency of passing, however, is determined not only by intrinsic difficulty but also by the extent to which the fact in question has become a matter of general knowledge, that is, the likelihood that all or most of the children will have had opportunity to become acquainted with it. The word "broccoli" is not intrinsically more difficult than the word "spinach" or "cabbage," but until the last few years at least it would unquestionably have been classed much higher in a vocabulary test. Whether or not the concepts of elementary algebra are intrinsically more difficult than the concepts of long division is uncertain, but because most schools teach long division before elementary algebra more children will succeed with division problems than with algebra problems. Probably more city children than country children of the same age will be able to give a correct answer to the question. "What must you do if you are going some place and miss the streetcar?" but if the question were, "What must you do if the cows break into the wheatfield?" the opposite tendency might be shown. Sherman and Key (1932) report that many of the mountain children whom they studied were unable to give their family name, identifying themselves simply as " 'Lizy's Tom" or "Mose's Joe." Giving the family name is a test for three-year-olds in the 1916 Stanford Revision of the Binet, but if the three-year-olds upon whom this test was standardized had been asked to give their father's or their mother's first name, they might have been no more successful than the mountain children were in giving the family name. The difficulty of a task for any group is in part a matter of its familiarity or strangeness

for that group. It follows that *scale values,* though they may be equally spaced for a particular group, are likely to be quite unequally spaced for another group of similar intelligence but different experience.

No matter what method of quantifying test results is used, the standards obtained cannot safely be applied to other groups unless it has been shown that the latter are reasonably similar to the standardization group in all matters that may be expected to affect the relative value of the scores. In order that such comparisons may be made, it is essential that the main characteristics of the group used in standardization be defined as exactly as possible. This means that some information about the home background of each child needs to be obtained. Although elaborate social case histories are usually out of the question and would be difficult to handle in any case, a few simple facts such as paternal occupation and residence (city, town, or rural) are easy to ascertain. If these were uniformly classified and reported as a part of the routine information concerning every test that is worked out, many of the discrepancies that result from the use of differently standardized tests could be explained and the suitability of a particular test for use with a given group of children could be more safely judged. The relationship between socioeconomic status and mental test standing will be considered further in a later section.

Mental Growth Curves

A natural outgrowth of the attempts to calibrate mental tests in truly equal units is the plotting of the results thus obtained in the form of growth curves. Inasmuch as there is as yet no general agreement as to the method best suited for calibrating the items making up the tests, it is not surprising to find that even when the same procedure is used for plotting the growth curves, the "form of the mental growth curve" derived from one test may be radically different from that derived from another test. Dissimilarity of test content, not only from one test to another but at successive age levels within the same test, also confuses the picture. Dissimilarity of the sampling of subjects used, particularly when the selective factors resulting in a biased sampling have differed from one age level to another, is a further complicating factor.[1] And, finally, there is the fact that the statistical procedures used for plotting the growth curves have varied from one investigator to another.

Courtis (1930) believes there is no single type of growth curve that can adequately express the pattern of growth represented by a conglomeration of items varying irregularly both as to kind and level of difficulty, such as is included in the usual mental test. Such curves lack stability of form because they do not measure a uniform function in a uniform manner. Courtis insists that any adequate plan for the study of mental growth must take its origin from a consideration of the developmental progress in the performance of a single act. After plotting curves for many forms of biologic growth, ranging from the growth in weight of a pumpkin to the increase with age in the percentage of men who are married, he derives a unit called the *isochron*, which is defined as the percentage of the total period of maturation that has been attained by any individual at any time. Isochronic units, so Courtis thinks, have uniform significance for all forms of growth whether of structure or function. The idea is an interesting one but requires further confirmation.

Most present-day students of human de-

velopment accept the theory that mental growth proceeds most rapidly during infancy and early childhood. This is equivalent to saying that the curve of mental growth is negatively accelerated, even though its exact formula remains undetermined. Gesell (1928) has assumed a logarithmic form; Thorndike *et al.* (1926), utilizing the data and the scaling procedure of the CAVD test, arrive at the conclusion that the curve for CAVD altitude is parabolic in form, rising from zero at birth to a midvalue around the age of three years and attaining its final height at about the age of twenty-one. It is interesting to note that, although independently derived, this curve shows fairly close agreement with that for growth in brain weight. Although at first thought the idea that one-half of an individual's ultimate mental stature has been attained by the age of three years may seem a bit startling, the following exercise which the writer has repeatedly tried both with university students and with laymen may put the matter in a somewhat different light. The instructions given are:

First, try to forget all that you may have learned about mental tests.[2] Think only of children as you have known them.

Now try to get the clearest picture that you can of a newborn baby. Go over his abilities and inabilities in your mind in considerable detail. (A few moments time should be allowed for this.)

Now turn your mind to the adults whom you have known. Consider in detail the things that they are able to do, especially

---

[1] This point is discussed by Anderson in Chapter 1 of this book.

[2] This caution is necessary because of the strong tendency on the part of those who have been taught that mental maturity is attained at some specified age, as sixteen years, to assume that the midpoint of growth in ability would of necessity correspond with one-half the time span covered between birth and maturity. This, of course, is circular reasoning. The mere length of time required to accomplish something tells nothing whatever about the evenness or unevenness of the rate of accomplishment.

the things that we commonly think of as indicating "intelligence." (Pause.)

Now go back once more to the newborn baby. Holding in mind these two points of reference—the newborn and the adult—move slowly up the age scale, asking yourself at each point, "Is the typical child of this age more nearly like the adult or the newly born infant in respect to the things he is able to do? Continue this process until you reach an age at which, in your judgment, the resemblances and differences are so evenly balanced that you can no longer come to a decision. If your judgment is sound, that age will fix the halfway point in postnatal mental growth."

When this exercise has been tried with fair-sized groups who have thoroughly grasped the idea that what they are seeking is a point of balance, equally far removed from the two terminal points in the matter of resemblance, the mean estimate is, as a rule, not far from that set by Thorndike. The distribution of judgments tends to be skewed toward the lower ages, which is, of course, just what would be expected if the true form of the growth curve were parabolic in shape.

The Prediction of Later Status from Earlier Status

The idea that mental tests not only provide a measure of the present mental level of the individual but also yield some indication of his potentialities for further development has from the outset been implicit in the uses to which they have been put. Shortly after the IQ method of expressing test results had been popularized by Terman, the extent to which this measure tended to remain constant for the individual child became a popular subject of investigation. Until the late twenties, however, these studies dealt almost exclusively with children of school age. The few studies based upon younger children that

had appeared up to that time usually included only a small number of cases, with little or no attempt at experimental control either of the sampling of subjects or of age at initial and final testing. Sometimes even the results from different tests were thrown together in a single grouping. Only within comparatively recent years have sufficient data been accumulated to provide a tentative answer to this important question: With how great a degree of assurance may we predict the mental level likely to be attained by any child at maturity (or at any other specified age) on the basis of tests given at some stated earlier age?

Both the empirical evidence and the underlying theories on this topic have recently been summarized by Anderson (1939). His conclusion is essentially the same as that expressed by the writer in Murchison's *Handbook of Child Psychology* (1933, p. 322). Briefly stated, the conclusion is that *the younger the child at time of first testing or the longer the interval between tests, the less accurate will be the prediction of later status from earlier status.*

Recent findings for the Minnesota Preschool Scales by Goodenough and Maurer (1942), however, make it appear that the effect of interval between testings may be actually far smaller than that of the age at first test. The reason for this apparent exception to the results of other investigators is not clear. It may be a function of the particular scale used or of the unit of measurement employed. On the other hand, it is possible that certain functions of the human mind, although measured with very unequal accuracy at different ages, nevertheless remain relatively constant from early childhood to maturity. The latter hypothesis would be reassuring if true, but much further evidence is needed before we are warranted in accepting it at its face value.

Furfey and Muehlenbein (1932), Bayley (1933), Shirley (1933), Honzig (1938), and others who have followed the development of infants from early infancy up to the period at which mental tests show reasonable stability of results from one testing to another, all report an absence of relationship between mental test standing before the age of eighteen months and later test performance. After the appearance of speech, the tests begin to have predictive value, although the amount of confidence that can be placed in the results as indices to the child's ultimate level of development continues to be small up to the age of four or five years. Both Goodenough (1933) and Anderson (1939) have pointed out that the amount of overlap between earlier and later testings is a factor of major importance in determining the degree of relationship between the results of successive testings of the same individuals.

In an article of basic importance for all students of mental growth, Bayley (1940) has shown that when the same individuals are retested at regular intervals over a period of years, characteristic differences appear in the rate and pattern of their mental growth. Out of a total of 48 cases who were followed over a period of 9 years, 8 maintained fairly constant positions near the mean of the group as a whole throughout the entire period; 8 showed relatively slow rates of growth, with continued tendency to lose in standing when compared with the other members of the group; 8 showed the opposite tendency with continued gain in test standing as age advanced; 8 displayed a tendency to lose in standing during infancy and early childhood but later shifted to an accelerated rate whereby the early loss was regained; and in contrast to these, another group of 8 cases showed early rapid growth with subsequent loss. The growth curves of the

remaining 8 were not classified as to form, since the patterns appeared not to fall into any easily recognized class. These findings are in fairly close general agreement with those obtained by Goodenough and Maurer (1942) in a twelve-year study carried out at the Institute of Child Welfare at the University of Minnesota.

Relationship of Intelligence Test Standing to Other Factors

That more than chance relationship exists between the scores made by a given individual on standardized tests of intelligence and his scores on many instruments designed to measure other mental and physical traits is well known. In many instances, however, it is not wholly clear to what extent the relationships found may be ascribed to biological or social factors and to what extent the issue is in reality a matter of semantics. We know, for example, that practically all measures of language development, such as size of vocabulary, mean length of sentence used, complexity of sentence construction, and so on, show fairly high correlation with measures of intelligence. Whether this relationship between *scores* indicates a genuine tendency for two *different* aspects of mental development to vary together or is merely a necessary result of measuring the same thing twice by slightly different instruments and calling the results by different names, is a question about which opinions differ. When greater agreement with respect to factorial procedures has been reached, an answer may perhaps be reached. For the present we shall avoid the issue by specifying that, in the discussion to follow, we are dealing only with relationships between the results of tests *designed* to measure general intelligence and those of measurements *designed* for other purposes.

Although in many instances the correlations are too low to have practical utility, it is nevertheless true that standing on recognized tests of intelligence is positively related to standing on practically all other measurements of socially desirable traits. Even physical measurements such as height and weight have been found to conform to the general rule, although the relationships are not high and in many of the reported studies heterogeneity of race and the inclusion at the lower end of the intelligence scale of special clinical types such as Mongolian imbeciles have operated to make the apparent relation higher than would be the case had a truly representative selection of subjects been used. (See Paterson, 1930.)

That performance on intelligence tests varies according to the social class from which the subjects are drawn has been recognized since the days of Binet. That the relationship is not one of simple cause and effect is demonstrated by the fact that every level of intelligence can be found within each social level, though not in equal proportion. A greater percentage of the very bright come from families of superior socioeconomic status, whereas the frequency of backward children is proportionately greater among the lower social classes. The relationship is sufficiently marked to bring about a difference of 20 to 30 IQ points in the mean test standing of children of college professors and those of day laborers.

This relationship between socioeconomic status and intelligence must always be kept in mind when considering statistical findings on the correlation of intelligence test scores with other factors such as juvenile delinquency, social behavior, standing on the pencil-and-paper "tests" of emotional stability, and the like. Undoubtedly, children of the upper social classes have fewer incentives to delinquent behavior than those who live in the slums. Undoubtedly,

too, their offenses are more likely to be handled privately by cooperation between parents and police than are corresponding offenses by children from homes where little parental assistance can be expected. All this makes for a greater percentage of low-testing individuals among institutionalized delinquents than among children not classified as delinquent, but in all probability a large share of this difference is attributable to the socioeconomic factor rather than to intelligence *per se*. A study of the relationship between intelligence and delinquency by the method of analysis of variance might lead to very different conclusions on this point from those commonly drawn from the published literature.

Likewise, the finding that children of superior intelligence are on the average more popular with their mates than those of low intelligence might be considerably modified if the socioeconomic factor (which, particularly among older children, involves some degree of prestige, as well as the means for providing little treats or toys for group use) were made equal for all. In the paper-and-pencil tests designed to measure various nonintellectual traits, the almost uniformly positive correlations between scores on these tests and scores on intelligence tests may be interpreted in either of two ways. There may be a true relationship between intelligence and the social or emotional traits presumably measured by these tests, or, on the other hand, the obtained correlations may result wholly or in part from the greater ability of bright children to select the more socially acceptable responses.

The Modifiability of Intelligence

Few, if any, questions relating to mental growth crop up so persistently or have provoked more intensive study than those relating to its possible modification. The obvious practical importance of the problem and the occasional, though by no means universal, improvement in mental level that has been brought about through thyroid treatment in cases of cretinism or by other types of glandular therapy in analogous conditions of endocrine malfunctioning have served as constant examples of the mental gains that can be accomplished when the basis for the original deficiency is once understood. It is but natural, therefore, that theories on the etiology of mental differences should lead by the shortest possible route to theories as to the extent and manner by which these differences may be modified. Moreover, because the most obvious indications of mental superiority or inferiority have to do with the learning process, it is not strange that many should question whether differences in learning ability have any constitutional bases at all, or whether they might not better be ascribed to lack of opportunity or stimulation to learn, or to the failure to acquire proper techniques of learning.

Two of the annual *Yearbooks of the National Society for the Study of Education* (Whipple, 1928, 1940a and b), as well as a number of separate monographs and experimental articles, have been devoted entirely to this topic. As yet, however, no general agreement on the basic question involved has been reached, although the weight of evidence, when all the large number of investigations reported in the *Yearbooks* and elsewhere are taken into account, certainly does not support the view that the intellectual development of children is as readily modified as many wishful thinkers would like us to believe. Undoubtedly, a part of the disagreement has resulted from unclear thinking about the actual nature of the point at issue. In the scientific world it is idle to ask the *cause* of a present condition since causes lie in a past that cannot be reinstated.

Our knowledge of causal factors is always derived by inference; we check the accuracy of these inferences by instituting anew the conditions or factors that we hypothesize as the necessary antecedents of the present facts and wait to see whether or not similar consequences result. Because of the exceedingly complex nature of most biological phenomena, modern scientists are exceedingly wary of accepting at their face value any etiological theories that fail to meet the following generally accepted criteria:

(1) Have the experimental conditions necessary for testing the hypothesis been described with sufficient detail and accuracy to enable others to make the same tests? That is, is the hypothesis susceptible to experimental validation?

(2) When independent tests are made, are similar results obtained?

Whether or not it is theoretically possible *by any conceivable means* to modify the course of mental growth to any specified extent is an unanswerable question since no one knows what scientific discoveries the future may bring. Whether or not a method has now been found that can be described in such terms that others may profit by its use is a question that permits a straightforward answer. It is the second rather than the first question that the reader of the literature on this highly controversial issue must hold steadily in mind if he is to avoid becoming hopelessly entangled in a web of conflicting figures. The question involved is not, as many have been led to think, determining the factors that caused the present differences in mentality that we observe in children. That question cannot be answered because too many unknown variables are involved. The question is, has a practicable method been discovered by which the course of a child's mental development can be materially altered? And, if so, *in precisely what respects does this method differ from others that have proved ineffective?* To date, no useful description of such a method has been given us.

Concluding Discussion

In the treatment of this topic more emphasis has intentionally been placed upon the inadequacies and imperfections of our present methods of mental measurement than upon their positive values. The latter have been thoroughly demonstrated. In spite of minor inaccuracies, in spite of disagreement as to exactly what it is that we are trying to measure and uncertainty as to what units we shall employ for expressing the results of our measurement, the fact remains that for most purposes and in most cases the tests work amazingly well. In the schoolroom, the behavior clinic, the offices of the vocational counselor, the juvenile court, or the child-placing agency, their practical value has repeatedly been shown.

In one sense it may be said that in the success with which they have been used lies their greatest weakness, for too often this successful use has engendered a blind faith in all test results to which some kind of numerical score is attached. Figures are likely to have a hypnotic effect upon most of us. Although we may know that the significance of a test score varies with the test used, the conditions under which it is given, and the age of the child tested, even the well-informed are often far too prone to feel that, once it has been calculated, an IQ is an IQ with fixed and absolute meaning. This attitude has led to two unfortunate errors in thinking. On the one hand, we have those who, on the basis of a single test, even when given at a tender age, are ready to "diagnose" the child's present mental level, make predictions as to his future, perhaps even take

action with respect to matters of vital importance for his future. On the other hand, we have those who, with equally naïve confidence in the accuracy of the tests, regard every fluctuation in standing as indicating a "real" change in the child's mental level. Even a casual reading of the experimental literature on the extent and frequency of changes in IQ upon retesting children of different ages and after varying intervals of time should demonstrate the lack of scientific basis for either of these extreme views. Fortunately, the number who still adhere to them appears to be diminishing. A critical examination of the literature that has appeared during the thirty years since the publication of Goddard's translation of Binet's 1908 scale shows an encouraging shift from the wholesale production of new and half-tried testing devices to the critical examination of the significance and accuracy of those already in use. Improved statistical methods have been applied to problems of scale construction as well as to the investigation of sources of error in measurement. The day is past when a simple statement of the "reliability" and "validity" of a test was thought to provide sufficient information as to its effectiveness.

Bibliography

ALDRICH, C. G., and E. A. DOLL. 1931. Comparative intelligence of idiots and of normal infants. *J. Genet. Psychol.*, **39**, 227–257.

ANASTASI, A. 1936. The influence of specific experience upon mental organization. *Genet. Psychol. Monogr.*, **18**, 245–355.

ANDERSON, J. E. 1939. The limitations of infant and preschool tests in the measurement of intelligence. *J. Psychol.*, **8**, 351–379.

ARTHUR, G. 1930. *A point scale of performance tests:* Vol. I. *Clinical manual.* New York: Commonwealth Fund.

ARTHUR, G., and H. WOODROW. 1919. An absolute intelligence scale: A study in method. *J. Appl. Psychol.*, **3**, 118–137.

AYRES, L. P. 1909. *Laggards in our schools.* New York: Charities Publication Committee.

BAYLEY, N. 1933. Mental growth during the first three years: An experimental study of sixty-one children by repeated tests. *Genet. Psychol. Monogr.*, **14**, 1–92.

——. 1940. Mental growth in young children. *Yearb. Nat. Soc. Stud. Educ.*, **39**(II), 11–47.

BINET, A. 1911. Nouvelles recherches sur la mesure du niveau intellectuel chez les enfants d'école. *Année psychol.*, **17**, 145–201.

BINET, A., and T. SIMON. 1905a. Sur la nécessité d'établir un diagnostic scientifique des états inférieurs de l'intelligence. *Année psychol.*, **11**, 163–190.

——. 1905b. Méthodes nouvelles pour le diagnostic du niveau intellectuel des anormaux. *Année psychol.*, **11**, 191–244.

——. 1908. Le développement de l'intelligence chez les enfants. *Année psychol.*, **14**, 1–94.

CATTELL, J. McK. 1890. Mental tests and measurements. *Mind*, **15**, 373–381.

CATTELL, J. McK., and L. FARRAND. 1896. Physical and mental measurements of the students of Columbia University. *Psychol. Rev.*, **3**, 618–648.

CATTELL, P. 1933. The Heinis personal constant as a substitute for the IQ. *J. Educ. Psychol.*, **24**, 221–228.

CHAILLE, S. E. 1887. Infants, their chronological progress. *New Orleans Med. Surg. J.*, **14**, 893–912.

COURTIS, S. A. 1930. *The measurement of growth.* Detroit: Author.

CUNNINGHAM, K. S. 1927. The measurement of early levels of intelligence. *Teach. Coll. Contr. Educ.*, No. 259.

DEARBORN, W. F. 1928. *Intelligence tests: Their significance for school and society.* Boston: Houghton Mifflin.

FLANAGAN, J. C. 1935. *Factor analysis in the study of personality.* Stanford University. Calif.: Stanford University Press.

FREEMAN, F. N. 1930. Mental indices. In *Proceedings of the first conference on individual differences in the character and rate of psychological development.* Washington: National Research Council. Pp. 8.

——. 1939. *Mental tests: Their history, principles and applications.* (Rev. ed.) Boston: Houghton Mifflin.

FURFEY, P. H., and J. MUEHLENBEIN. 1932. The validity of infant intelligence tests. *J. Genet. Psychol.*, **40**, 219–223.

GESELL, A. 1928. *Infancy and human growth.* New York: Macmillan.

GILBERT, J. A. 1894. Researches on the mental and physical development of school children. *Stud. Yale Psychol. Lab.*, **2**, 40–100.

——. 1897. Researches upon school children and college students. *Univ. Iowa Stud. Psychol.*, **1**, 1–39.

GODDARD, H. H. 1910. A measuring scale for intelligence. *Train. Sch.*, **6**, 146–155.

——. 1911a. *The Binet measuring scale for intelligence.* (Rev. ed.) Vineland, N. J.: The Training School. (Manual and record forms.)

GODDARD, H. H. 1911b. A revision of the Binet scale. *Train. Sch.*, **8**, 56–62.

——. 1912. *The Kallikak family.* New York: Macmillan.

——. 1914. *Feeble-mindedness: Its causes and consequences.* New York: Macmillan.

——. 1915. *The criminal imbecile.* New York: Macmillan.

GOODENOUGH, F. L. 1942. Studies of the 1937 revision of the Stanford-Binet Scale: I. Variability of the IQ at successive age-levels. *J. Educ. Psychol.*, **33**, 241–251.

GOODENOUGH, F. L., and K. M. MAURER. 1942. *The mental growth of children from two to fourteen years: A study of the predictive value of the Minnesota preschool scales.* Minneapolis: University of Minnesota Press.

GOODENOUGH, F. L., K. M. MAURER, and M. J. VAN WAGENEN. 1940. *Minnesota preschool scale.* Minneapolis: Educational Test Bureau.

HEINIS, H. 1926. A personal constant. *J. Educ. Psychol.*, **17**, 163–186.

HILDRETH, G. 1930. *Psychological service for school problems.* Yonkers-on-Hudson: World Book.

HOLZINGER, K. J. 1928. Some comments on Professor Thurstone's method of determining the scale values of test items. *J. Educ. Psychol.*, **19**, 112–117. Comment by PROFESSOR THURSTONE, *ibid.*, 117–124. Reply to PROFESSOR THURSTONE, *ibid.*, 124–126.

HONZIK, M. P. 1938. The constancy of mental test performance during the preschool periods. *J. Genet. Psychol.*, **52**, 285–302.

HOTELLING, H. 1933. Analysis of a complex of statistical variables into principal components. *J. Educ. Psychol.*, **24**, 417–441; 498-520.

KELLEY, T. L. 1927. *Interpretation of educational measurements.* Yonkers-on-Hudson: World Book.

——. 1928. *Crossroads in the mind of man.* Stanford University, Calif.: Stanford University Press.

——. 1935. *Essential traits of mental life. The purposes and principles underlying the selection and measurement of independent mental factors, together with computational tables.* Cambridge: Harvard University Press.

KUHLMANN, F. 1921. The results of repeated mental re-examination of 639 feeble-minded over a period of ten years. *J. Appl. Psychol.*, **5**, 195–224.

——. 1939. *Tests of mental development: A complete scale for individual examination.* Minneapolis: Educational Test Bureau.

LINCOLN, E. A., and L. L. WORKMAN. 1935. *Testing and the use of test results.* New York: Macmillan.

McNEMAR, Q. 1942. *The revision of the Stanford-Binet Scale: An analysis of the standardization data.* Boston: Houghton Mifflin.

MERRILL, M. A. 1924. On the relation of intelligence to achievement in the case of mentally retarded children. *Comp. Psychol. Monogr.*, **2.** Pp. 100.

MURCHISON, C. (Ed.) 1933. *A handbook of child psychology.* (2d ed., rev.) Worcester: Clark University Press.

PATERSON, D. G. 1930. *Physique and intellect.* New York: Century.

PETERSON, J. 1925. *Early conceptions and tests of intelligence.* Yonkers-on-Hudson: World Book.

PINTNER, R. 1931. *Intelligence testing.* (2d ed.) New York: Holt.

RAND, G. 1925. A discussion of the quotient method of specifying test results. *J. Educ. Psychol.*, **16,** 599–618.

SHERMAN, M., and C. B. KEY. 1932. The intelligence of isolated mountain children. *Child Develpm.*, **3,** 279–290.

SHIRLEY, M. 1933. *The first two years: A study of twenty-five babies:* Vol. II. *Intellectual development.* (*Inst. Child Welfare Monogr. Ser.*, No. 7.) Minneapolis: University of Minnesota Press.

SPEARMAN, C. 1904. "General intelligence" objectively determined and measured. *Amer. J. Psychol.*, **15,** 201–292.

———. 1927. *The abilities of man.* New York: Macmillan.

STALNAKER, J. M. 1940. Results from factor analysis. *J. Educ. Res.*, **33,** 698–704.

SYMPOSIUM. 1921. Intelligence and its measurement. *J. Educ. Psychol.*, **12,** 123–147; 195–216.

TERMAN, L. M. 1916. *The measurement of intelligence.* Boston: Houghton Mifflin.

TERMAN, L. M., and M. A. MERRILL. 1937. *Measuring intelligence: A guide to the administration of the new revised Stanford-Binet tests of intelligence.* Boston: Houghton Mifflin.

THOMSON, G. H. 1939. *The factorial analysis of human ability.* London: University of London Press.

THORNDIKE, E. L., *et al.* 1926. *The measurement of intelligence.* New York: Teachers College, Columbia University.

THURSTONE, L. L. 1925. A method of scaling psychological and educational tests. *J. Educ. Psychol.*, **16,** 433–451.

———. 1928a. The absolute zero in intelligence measurement. *Psychol. Rev.*, **35,** 175–197.

———. 1928b. Scale construction with weighted observations. *J. Educ. Psychol.*, **19,** 441–453.

———. 1935. *The vectors of mind: Multiple-factor analysis for the isolation of primary traits.* Chicago: University of Chicago Press.

———. 1938. *Primary mental abilities.* Chicago: University of Chicago Press.

———. 1940. Current issues in factor analysis. *Psychol. Bull.*, **37,** 189–236.

THURSTONE, L. L., and L. ACKERSON. 1929.

The mental growth curve for the Binet tests. *J. Educ. Psychol.*, **20,** 569–583.

THURSTONE, L. L., and T. G. THURSTONE. 1941. Factorial studies of intelligence. *Psychometr. Monogr.*, No. 2. Pp. 94.

TREDGOLD, A. F. 1929. *Mental deficiency (amentia).* (5th ed., rev.) New York: Wood.

WHIPPLE, G. M. 1914–1915. *Manual of mental and physical tests: A book of directions compiled with special reference to the experimental study of school children in the laboratory or classroom.* (2 vols.) (2d ed., rev.) Baltimore: Warwick and York.

WHIPPLE, G. M. (Ed.) 1928. Nature and nurture: Their influence upon intelligence. *Yearb. Nat. Soc. Stud. Educ.*, 27(I).

———. 1940a. Intelligence: Its nature and nurture. (Comparative and critical exposition.) *Yearb. Nat. Soc. Stud. Educ.*, 39(I).

———. 1940b. Intelligence: Its nature and nurture. (Original studies and experiments.) *Yearb. Nat. Soc. Stud. Educ.*, 39(II).

WISSLER, C. L. 1901. The correlation of mental and physical tests. *Psychol. Rev. Monogr.*, Suppl., **3,** No. 6. Pp. 62.

YOUNG, K. 1924. The history of mental tests. *Ped. Sem.*, **31,** 1–48.

A CHRONOLOGICAL LIST OF GENERAL REVIEWS AND BIBLIOGRAPHIES ON MENTAL TESTS

FREEMAN, F. N. 1911. Tests. *Psychol. Bull.*, **8,** 21–24.

———. 1912. Tests. *Psychol. Bull.*, **9,** 215–222.

———. 1913. Tests. *Psychol. Bull.*, **10,** 271–274.

———. 1914. Tests. *Psychol. Bull.*, **11,** 253–256.

———. 1915. Tests. *Psychol. Bull.*, **12,** 187–188.

———. 1916. Tests. *Psychol. Bull.*, **13,** 268–271.

BOARDMAN, H. 1917. *Psychological tests: A bibliography.* New York: Bureau of Educational Experiments.

FREEMAN, F. N. 1917. Tests. *Psychol. Bull.*, **14,** 245–249.

———. 1919. Tests. *Psychol. Bull.*, **16,** 374–381.

———. 1920. Mental tests. *Psychol. Bull.*, **17,** 353–362.

PINTNER, R. 1926. Intelligence tests. *Psychol. Bull.*, **23,** 366–381.

———. 1927. Intelligence tests. *Psychol. Bull.*, **24,** 391–408.

BRONNER, A. F., W. HEALY, G. LOWE, and M. SHIMBERG. 1927. *A manual of individual mental tests and testing.* Boston: Little, Brown.

GAMBRILL, B. L. 1927. *An analytical list of kindergarten-primary tests.* New Haven: Whitlock's Book Store.

SANDIFORD, P. 1928. *A bibliography of intelligence and educational tests.* Toronto: University Toronto Press.

PINTNER, R. 1928. Intelligence tests. *Psychol. Bull.*, **25,** 389–405.

———. 1929. Intelligence tests. *Psychol. Bull.*, **26,** 381–396.

PINTNER, R. 1930. Intelligence tests. *Psychol. Bull.*, **27,** 431–457.

SCHIEFFELIN, B., and G. SCHWESINGER. 1930. *Mental tests and heredity: Including a survey of non-verbal tests.* New York: Galton Publishing Co.

ALLEN, C. N. 1931. Bibliographies in child study and developmental psychology. *Psychol. Bull.*, **28,** 277–296.

NEWELL, C. 1931. The uses of the form-board in the mental measurement of children. *Psychol. Bull.*, **28,** 309–318.

PINTNER, R. 1932. Intelligence tests. *Psychol. Bull.*, **29,** 93–119.

BAKER, H. J., *et al.* 1932. Tests of intelligence and aptitude. *Rev. Educ. Res.*, **2,** 271–342.

PINTNER, R. 1933. Intelligence tests. *Psychol. Bull.*, **30,** 488–504.

——. 1934. Intelligence tests. *Psychol. Bull.*, **31,** 453–475.

——. 1935. Intelligence tests. *Psychol. Bull.*, **32,** 453–472.

BUROS, O. K. 1936. Educational, psychological and personality tests of 1933, 1934 and 1935. *Stud. Educ., Rutgers Univ. Bull.*, **13,** No. 9.

——. 1937. Educational, psychological and personality tests of 1936. *Stud. Educ., Rutgers Univ. Bull.*, **14,** No. 11.

SOUTH, E. B. 1937. *An index of periodical literature on testing, 1921–1936.* New York: Psychological Corporation.

(See also very complete annotated bibliographies in the *Review of Educational Research* for years 1932, 1933, 1935, 1936, 1938, 1939, and 1941.)

BUROS, O. K. (Ed.) 1938. *The 1938 mental measurements yearbook.* New Brunswick, N. J.: Rutgers University Press.

HILDRETH, G. 1939. *A bibliography of mental tests and rating scales.* New York: Psychological Corporation.

WANG, C. K. A. 1940. *An annotated bibliography of tests and scales:* Vol. I. Peiping, China: Catholic University Press. (In English.)

CHAPTER 10

LANGUAGE DEVELOPMENT IN CHILDREN

DOROTHEA McCARTHY

Introduction

The amazingly rapid acquisition of an extremely complex system of symbolic habits by young children is a phenomenon which has increasingly attracted the attention of child psychologists as well as linguists in recent years. This area of child development is one of the most important for the child psychologist, not only because the possession of the ability to speak is one of the distinguishing characteristics which set man apart from the lower animals, but also because of the intimate relationship which exists between language and thought. The increased interest in language development in recent years appears to be due to the realization of the valuable insights which can be gained into the content of the child's mental life through the study of his linguistic expression, to the dependence on some form of verbal expression in introspective technique as well as in the adequate measurement of intelligence and other psychological traits, and to a recognition of the limitations of psychological observations which are restricted to the period of infancy, when language responses are not a part of the child's observable repertoire of behavior.

The word *language* has a very wide variety of meanings, but in the present review emphasis will be placed on the ontogenetic development of spoken language in normal children. Some attempt will be made to show the setting of this aspect of

language development in the broader relationships which are involved, and to show something of the relationships of normal speech development to the acquisition of the secondary forms of language development in reading and writing. Only brief mention will be made of the fields of speech pathology, the physiology of speech, phonetics, linguistics, and semantics, which are much too highly specialized areas for any detailed treatment in the present review.

Excellent discussions of the various definitions of language are to be found in DeLaguna (1927), Pillsbury and Meader (1928), Esper (1935), and McGranahan (1936). In general, the various theories that have been advanced place the emphasis on different aspects of this tremendously complex process, and some recognize its plurality of function. Wundt (1901, 1911–1912) emphasized the expression of mental content, including both ideas and feelings, through language and considered that communication was only a secondary function of language. Pillsbury and Meader (1928), however, stress the function of communication in language. In 1927 DeLaguna, after seriously criticizing Wundt's point of view, claimed that a fresh conception of speech as an essential activity of human life is needed. She thereupon advanced a social-behavioral view of the nature of language which has become rather popular with the increasing emphasis on the function of language in the total stimulating situation. J. Dewey (1926) also pointed out that "the heart of language is not 'expression' of something antecedent, much less expression of antecedent thought. It is communication; the establishment of cooperation in an activity in which there are partners, and in which the activity of each is modified and regulated by partnership" (p. 179). Esper (1935) states: "The exclusive preoccupation with 'ideas' which are held to be 'expressed' by speech leads to a neglect of the behavior and concrete environment to which the speech is related."

K. Bühler (1934) distinguishes three functions of spoken language: representation, expression, and appeal. McGranahan (1936) points out that a speech phenomenon may be considered (1) in relation to the person who produces it, (2) in relation to the person or persons who hear it, and (3) in relation to the objective fact represented by it. Whereas Bühler recognized these three aspects, he was more interested in the speech phenomenon itself than in the social-psychological situation. Gardiner (1932) emphasizes four factors: the speaker, the listener, the words said, and the things referred to or spoken about. Much theory has been concerned with the speaker and with the words, but little attention has been paid to the listener and the things spoken of.

Linguists, who in the past have been concerned chiefly with descriptive and historical accounts and comparative details of the grammar of various languages, have become increasingly interested in problems of semantics. When the linguist thus raises the question of meaning he is led directly into the field of psychology, for he finds that meaning must be explained in terms of the situation in which the word is used. Horn (1942) considers that significant trends which have emerged in theory involve a greater recognition of the importance of language in all human culture,

rejection of the view that language is the external reflection of psychical processes, as well as an acceptance of the fact that verbal symbols have a predominant function in thinking.

In order to realize the importance of language in the psychological development of the child, one needs only to consider the comparative mental vacuum in which the young deaf-mute lives before any means of communication has been established; and to compare his mental state with that of the normal child who not only can understand the language of others in order to acquire a wealth of information, but who also can use language to express his ideas, needs, and wants, as well as to influence the behavior of others. The intimate relationship which most writers claim exists between language and thought is further evidence of the importance of this aspect of the child's development. Language, although perhaps not essential for all thinking, is so frequently involved in thought, and especially in making abstractions and fine distinctions and shades of meaning, as well as in communicating to others the results of one's thought processes, that a certain basic level of attainment in linguistic skills is practically an essential prerequisite to the child's formal education. As will be shown in this review, a basic mastery of spoken language is normally acquired very rapidly during the preschool years, usually between the ages of one and five years, and the child whose language development is seriously delayed for any reason labors under an almost insurmountable handicap in his social and academic relationships. The earlier a child can acquire facility in linguistic expression, the sooner he is free to reap the benefits of the use of this valuable tool in all his social and intellectual pursuits.

Characteristics of the Literature

As in all aspects of child development, the study of language development began with the rather casual observation of isolated cases which were reported in the early biographical literature. Because linguistic development lends itself so readily to the method of direct observation without the use of instrumentation, it played a large part in the studies of the period of the child study movement in the eighteen-nineties. Many of them placed considerable emphasis on language development; still others were entirely restricted to this readily observed area of the child's development. Most of these early biographical studies were concerned chiefly with the acquisition of vocabulary from the time of the appearance of the first word up to the fourth or fifth year, when the extent of vocabulary was so great that the data tended to become unwieldy. A few of the more ambitious attempts deal with the prelinguistic utterances of early infancy, usually without benefit of phonetics; and others attempted analyses of all-day conversations extending into the fourth and fifth years of life. Although this wealth of observational material has proved stimulating and suggestive for later research workers, it has little scientific merit, for each of the studies has employed a different method, the observations have for the most part been conducted on single children who were usually either precocious or markedly retarded in their language development, the records have been made under varying conditions, and most of the studies are subject to the unreliability of parents' reports. More recently there seems to have been a revival of interest in the biographical method with the employment of more refined techniques and special safeguards of objectivity (Lewis, 1936; Low, 1936; Grégoire, 1937; Leopold, 1939).

Previous Reviews. The literature in the field has been brought together from time to time by various authors. In 1833 Feldmann reviewed the reports of the vocabularies of 33 children, and in 1883 Sikorski gave a brief review of studies in foreign languages. In 1899 Franke surveyed about two hundred titles for the German *Handbook on Education,* edited by Reins. Preyer (1889) compared his son's progress in speech with that reported by Sigismund (1856), Lindner (1882), and others. Tracy (1893) presented an excellent summary of the studies of children's language up to two years of age, and Meumann (1908) discussed the early anecdotal accounts in the foreign literature with emphasis on the work of Lindner (1882), Ament (1899), and Gheorgov (1905). In 1907 appeared the classic volume, *Die Kindersprache,* by Clara and William Stern, in which they presented detailed observations on their own three children and compared their studies with the previously reported studies in the literature. Between 1907 and 1920 tabular summaries of vocabulary studies were published by Doran (1907), Pelsma (1910), Grant (1915), Gerlach (1917), and Magni (1919). Doran (1907) compiled a summary table of the vocabularies of 98 children between 8 and 72 months of age, and Bateman (1917) summarized all the published reports on the first word.

The *Twenty-eighth Yearbook of the National Society for the Study of Education* (1929) includes abstracts of 123 published studies on language development in preschool children and 20 researches in progress at that time. The May, 1929, issue of the *Psychological Bulletin* was a "Special Language Number," but it placed little emphasis on linguistic development in the early years. In 1933 a special volume of the *Journal de Psychologie* consisted of a symposium by a number of well-known

French psychologists and linguists on "Psychologie du Langage." Most of these articles, however, deal with theoretical problems of the origin of language and of the relationship between thought and language, as well as with problems of imagery and phonetics. Only two, those by Grégoire and Cohen, deal with the acquisition of language in children. The former is concerned primarily with phonetics in the first two years and the latter with the effect of infantile speech on the history of a language. In 1929 the writer reviewed the reports on infants' vocalizations up to and including the appearance of the first word, and later published more extensive reviews in the *Handbooks of Child Psychology* edited by Murchison in 1931 and 1933. A rather comprehensive review of 162 titles by Decroly was published posthumously about 1934. E. Dewey (1935) devotes about forty pages of her survey of the literature on the period of infancy to a discussion of studies of language development which appeared between 1920 and 1934.

Whereas in 1930 scarcely more than an isolated paragraph or two on language was to be found in textbooks in psychology, nearly all of the textbooks in child psychology which have appeared in the last decade include a major chapter on this aspect of the child's development. Some of the best chapters on language appear in textbooks by Goodenough (1934), Stoddard and Wellman (1934), Brooks and Shaffer (1937), Munn (1938), and Jersild (1940).

Quantitative Studies. The past fifteen years have seen the appearance of a series of interesting major studies on large numbers of children which have employed scientific controls in the observation of more nearly representative groups. M. E. Smith (1926) standardized a vocabulary test for preschool children on 273 children ranging in age from 8 months to 6 years. She employed test words selected from the Thorndike (1921) word list which she elicited by the use of objects, pictures, and questions. In another part of this same study, she analyzed sentence structure in one-hour records of the conversations of 88 children taken in free play situations. Her vocabulary test has been revised more recently by Williams and McFarland (1937). Another vocabulary test by Van Alstyne (1929) measures only the understood vocabulary of three-year-olds, as the child is required only to point to the picture of the object named by the examiner, and is not required to speak the words. The test has a reliability of .87 and has the advantages of ease of giving, objectivity of scoring, and inherent interest value for the child.

In 1930 the writer published a study based on the recording of 50 consecutive verbal responses from each of 140 children ranging in age from 18 to 54 months. A representative sampling of the population was secured by using paternal occupation as a criterion of selection. The data were subjected to four major types of analysis according to (1) the length of response, (2) the complexity of sentence structure, (3) the function of the response, and (4) the proportions of the various parts of speech. Each of these analyses was carried on in relation to age, sex, paternal occupation, mental age, and age of associates.

The general plan and methods used by McCarthy (1930) have been followed with minor variations by Day (1932), who duplicated the study on 80 pairs of twins, and by E. A. Davis (1937a), who extended the work to higher age levels, and who compared single children with siblings, twins, and only children. Fisher's (1934) study of 72 children of superior mental ability uses larger samples of conversations, but her analyses have much in common with the approaches of the above-mentioned studies. Later studies by M. E. Smith

(1933*b*, 1935*a*, 1939) and Young (1941) also yield data which are fairly comparable with these investigations.

Piaget (1924), who attempted to study the child's thought processes through a study of his language, pointed out that the child's language was largely egocentric. His very stimulating approach served as a point of departure for the functional analyses employed in these major American studies. His claims have not been verified by most of these studies when his method is taken literally. Much interest in recent years has centered around the interpretation of, and the attempt to harmonize, these apparently conflicting findings.

Some of the most valuable material on the development of the language sequence has appeared in the longitudinal studies of infant development by Shirley (1933*a*, 1933*b*) and by Bayley (1933). The normative studies of Gesell (1925, 1928), Gesell, Thompson, and Amatruda (1934, 1938), Gesell, Halverson, Thompson, *et al.* (1940), and those of C. Bühler (1930), C. Bühler and Hetzer (1935), and Cattell (1940) have also yielded significant findings regarding linguistic development. These observations made under standardized conditions on larger numbers of cases have now come to supersede the earlier biographical reports in large part because of their greater scientific value.

The most elaborate attempt to study the development of articulation in young children was made by Wellman, Case, Mengert, and Bradbury (1931). Tests of language achievement were developed by Descoeudres (1921) in France, and more recently Williams (1937*a*) and his associates at Iowa (Little and Williams, 1937) have developed an interesting language achievement test and have attempted to discover something of the interrelationships of the various aspects of linguistic development which most other studies have treated separately. A study by Young (1941) presents the results of records of 360 minutes of conversation per child taken on 74 children in four different situations in a nursery school. Half of the subjects were from families on relief and half were from upper socioeconomic levels. Analyses are conducted on length of response, amount of talking, and the proportions of the various parts of speech. Very rigorous grammatical rules, formulated by Jespersen (1933), were employed in the parts-of-speech analysis, and the results are related to the findings of six other similar studies.

An excellent study of written composition has been contributed by LaBrant (1933). She used over a thousand subjects ranging from fourth-grade children to adult scientific writers. Although primarily interested in a comparison of deaf and hearing children, Heider and Heider (1940*b*) give data for a hearing group of 817 children, ranging in age from 8 to 14, which constitute one of the most valuable contributions on children's sentence structure in written language.

When appropriate allowances are made for selective factors as well as for differences in method and classification, a remarkable degree of uniformity emerges from these research projects regarding most of the important developmental sequences and group differences.

Developmental Stages

From the mass of data which has been collected on children's development during the past two decades in the various child development research laboratories, it seems as if it should now be possible to sketch an adequate picture of the child's linguistic development and to analyze it for the appearance of a developmental sequence. The various major longitudinal studies mentioned above were concerned with much broader aspects of child development and observed language as only one aspect of the development of the whole child. They yield data on language, however, which are of considerably more value than the materials on which it has been necessary to depend in the past. In the first place, they all involve fairly large numbers of cases (25 to over 100) per age level. There is some attempt to have moderately representative groups of children, the observations have all been made under identical conditions within each study, and the authors have in each case been consistent in the criteria which they have employed for the various items at different age levels. Furthermore, all these observations have been made by trained observers who were unrelated to the children examined and who could presumably be objective about the observations. In all the above respects, then, these data are far superior to the isolated biographical studies which have been available heretofore.

On the other hand, a careful analysis of the material on language development which emerges from such a group of comprehensive studies reveals a number of shortcomings. In the first place, since language development was only one aspect of development observed, it has not been observed at regular intervals throughout the developmental period except by Gesell, who includes language items at all levels. Many writers leave periods of several months, during which they evidently were more interested in motor, sensory, social, or emotional aspects of the children's development, and for which no language items appear in their scales. It is only by dovetailing the results of several studies, as the writer has done in compiling Table 1, that it is possible to fill in the developmental sequence for language during periods when this aspect of development is probably

being obscured by some other aspect which is developing in a more spectacular manner and thus attracts the attention of observers. On a few points many writers have reported data which are apparently in marked agreement. Many items were noted by only one author and hence cannot be compared with the results of other investigations. On other items there probably is considerable agreement, but, since most of these studies were carried on almost simultaneously, it was not possible for later writers to adopt the terminology of earlier ones and to make their data comparable. The reader is thus confronted with a confusion of terms which on the surface appear to be very similar but which do not guarantee that the various observers were actually noting the identical behavior in similar situations.

In this table the writer has assembled 126 items of linguistic development which have been reported in eight major infant studies covering the first two years. All items which involve vocalization on the part of the child have been included, as well as responses to the human voice, responses to verbal commands, and all responses which are indicative of the comprehension of spoken language. A few items listed by the authors as linguistic were omitted either because they were negative items, such as the report of absence of vocalization, or because they did not involve vocalization on the part of the child and could just as reasonably be classified in a social development sequence. The entries in the table have been retained in the terminology of the original authors and all ages have been converted into months to render them directly comparable. The items are arranged roughly in the order of their appearance. Tentative groupings, which seem reasonable to the writer on the basis of similarity of terminology and descriptions of the situations, have been made

TABLE 1

Composite Table Showing Age in Months at Which Selected Language Items Are Reported in Eight Major Studies of Infant Development

	Strictly Longitudinal		Principally Cross-Sectional					
	Bayley (1933)	Shirley (1933)	C. Bühler (1930)	C. Bühler and Hetzer (1935)	Gesell, Thompson, and Amatruda (1938)	Gesell and Thompson (1934)	Gesell (1925)	Cattell (1940)
1 Vocal grunt		0.25						
2 Differential cries for discomfort, pain, and hunger						1		
3 Vocalizes small throaty noises					1.3			
4 Vocalizations	1.5							
5 Makes several different vocalizations						2		
6 Makes several vocalizations							4	
7 One syllable		2						
8 Vocalizes *ah, uh, eh*					1.3			
See Items 26–33.								
9 Attends readily to speaking voice						2		
10 Reacts positively to human voice				2				
11 Responds to voice	1.3							
12 Turns head on sound of voice					4			
13 Voice, attends (supine)								2
14 Voice, turns to (sitting)								4
15 Cooing			2	3				
16 Coos					3		4	2
17 Babbles or coos								
18 Returning glance with smiling or cooing				3				
19 Coos to music							6	
See Item 22.								
20 Two syllables		3						
21 Gives vocal expression to feelings of pleasure						3		
22 Actively vocalizes pleasure with crowing or cooing						6		
23 Vocalizes pleasure	5.9							
See Items 15–19, 36–37, 43–44.								
24 Vocalizes to social stimulus	3.1							
25 Responds vocally when socially stimulated						4		
See Items 38, 60.								
26 Vocalizes in self-initiated sound play						4		
27 Articulates many syllables in spontaneous vocalizations							6	
28 Vocalizes several well-defined syllables						6		
29 Says several syllables	6.3							
30 Vocalizes *ma* or *mu*					6.5			
31 Vocalizes *da*					7			
32 Two syllables—2d repetition of 1st—*mama* or *dada*	8				7			
33 Says *da-da* or equivalent	8.5					9		
34 Gives vocal expression of eagerness						5		
35 Vocalizes eagerness	5.6							

TABLE 1 (*Continued*)

COMPOSITE TABLE SHOWING AGE IN MONTHS AT WHICH SELECTED LANGUAGE ITEMS ARE REPORTED IN EIGHT MAJOR STUDIES OF INFANT DEVELOPMENT

		Strictly Longitudinal		Principally Cross-Sectional					
		Bayley (1933)	Shirley (1933)	C. Bühler (1930)	C. Bühler and Hetzer (1935)	Gesell, Thompson, and Amatruda (1938)	Gesell and Thompson (1934)	Gesell (1925)	Cattell (1940)
36	Vocalizes displeasure on withdrawal of coveted object						5		
37	Vocalizes displeasure	5.9							
38	"Talks" to a person See Items 25, 60.		6						
39.	Distinguishes between friendly and angry talking			6					
40	Imitating sounds *re-re-re*—immediate or delayed response			6					
41	Imitates sounds								9
42	Incipient or rudimentary imitation of sounds See Items 65, 66, 68.						10		
43	Vocalizes satisfaction	6.5							
44	Vocalizes satisfaction in attaining an object See Items 21–23.						7		
45	Singing tones		7.3						
46	Vocalizes recognition	7.4							
47	Gives vocal expression to recognition						8		
48	Single consonants See Items 30, 31.		8						
49	Adjusts to words See Items 55, 62.					8			9
50	Vocalizes in interjectional manner						8		
51	Vocal interjection	8.1							
52	Listens to familiar words See Item 61.	8.5							
53	Listens with selective interest to familiar words See Item 62.						9		
54	Understands gestures			9					
55	Responds to *bye-bye*					9			
56	Can wave *bye-bye* and often can say it							12	
57	Expressive sounds		9						
58	Expressive jargon	13.5							
59	Uses expressive jargon						15		
60	Uses jargon conversationally						18		
61	Differentiates words See Item 52.	9.8							
62	Makes conditioned adjustment to certain words See Items 69–77.						10		
63	Vocalizes in cup-spoon situation					10			
64	Vocalizes in 2-cube situation					10			

TABLE 1 (*Continued*)

COMPOSITE TABLE SHOWING AGE IN MONTHS AT WHICH SELECTED LANGUAGE ITEMS ARE REPORTED IN EIGHT MAJOR STUDIES OF INFANT DEVELOPMENT

	Strictly Longitudinal		Principally Cross-Sectional					
	Bayley (1933)	Shirley (1933)	C. Bühler (1930)	C. Bühler and Hetzer (1935)	Gesell, Thompson, and Amatruda (1938)	Gesell and Thompson (1934)	Gesell (1925)	Cattell (1940)
65 Imitating syllables, *mama, papa, dada*	11.7		11					
66 Imitates words See Items 40–42, 68.								
67 One word		14						11
68 First imitative word (*bow-wow*, etc.) See Items 40–42, 65, 66.		15						
69 Adjusts to commands	11.5							
70 Inhibits on command					10			
71 Adjusts to simple commands						12		
72 Places cube in or over cup on command						12		
73 Comprehends simple verbal commissions							12	
74 Understanding simple commands				13–15				
75 Understanding a demand ("Give me that" with gesture)			15–17					
76 Understanding a command ("Sit down" or "lie down" or "stand up" with gesture)			21–23					
77 Putting watch to ear on command See Items 62, 95.			21–23					
78 Responds to inhibitory words					12			
79 Understanding a prohibition				16–18				
80 Understanding a forbidding			18–20					
81 Says 2 words	12.9					12		12
82 Says 2 words or more					12			
83 Says 2 words besides *mama* and *dada*							12	
84 Vocalizes when looking in mirror					12			
85 Says 3 words or more					13			13–14
86 Says 4 words or more					13	15		15–16
87 Words, 5						18	18	
88 Names 1 object (ball, pencil, cup, watch, scissors)	17.4							
89 Names picture in book (dog)		19						
90 Naming 1 object or more				19–24				
91 Names 1 picture	18.7					21		
92 Names picture in book (baby)		22.5						
93 Asks with words See Items 101–103.								17–18
94 Says "Hello," "Thank you," or equivalent							18	
95 Points to nose, eyes, or hair						18	18	
96 Comprehends simple questions See Items 69–77.							18	

TABLE 1 (*Continued*)

COMPOSITE TABLE SHOWING AGE IN MONTHS AT WHICH SELECTED LANGUAGE ITEMS ARE REPORTED IN EIGHT MAJOR STUDIES OF INFANT DEVELOPMENT

		Strictly Longitudinal		Principally Cross-Sectional					
		Bayley (1933)	Shirley (1933)	C. Bühler (1930)	C. Bühler and Hetzer (1935)	Gesell, Thompson, and Amatruda (1938)	Gesell and Thompson (1934)	Gesell (1925)	Cattell (1940)
97	Names Gesell watch on fifth picture See Item 113.	19.4							
98	Names 2 objects	19.6							
99	Repeats things said						21		
100	Repeats 4 syllables (2 words)				30				
101	Joins 2 words in speech						21		
102	Words, combines								21–22
103	Uses words in combination See Item 93.						24		
104	Names 3 pictures	21.2							
105	Picture vocabulary 3								23–24
106	Names 3 objects	21.5							23–24
107	Names 3 objects in picture							36	
108	Identifies 4 objects by name								23–24
109	Names 3 of 5 objects See Items 104–107.						24		
110	Names familiar objects like key, penny, watch							24	
111	Points to 5 objects on card						24		
112	Names 5 pictures	24.4					30		
113	Names Gesell watch end picture See Item 97.	24.5							
114	Points to 7 of 10 simple pictures							24	
115	Points to 7 pictures	25.1					30		28–30
116	Picture vocabulary 7 (1937 Stanford-Binet)								25–27
117	Names 7 pictures	32.9							25–27
118	Pictures, points to 6								25–27
119	First pronoun		23						
120	Uses pronouns past and plural							36	
121	First phrase See Items 124–126.		23						
122	First sentence		23						
123	Uses simple sentences and phrases							24	
124	Distinguishes *in* and *under*							24	
125	Understands 2 prepositions	25							
126	Understands 3 prepositions	28							

and are indicated by the horizontal lines which for the most part mark off groups of items which apparently are descriptions of almost identical behavior noted by different authors at about the same period. It will be seen that the range in months reported for the different items is rather narrow within the horizontal lines. Occasional items noted by only one author appear in isolation in their proper chronological place. The few exceptions, in which items which appear on logical grounds to belong together but where there is considerable divergence in the age at which the behavior is reported, have been cross-referenced. Such discrepancies can usually be understood if one examines the criteria employed by the various authors for crediting the particular items.

Although the writer holds no brief for the tentative groupings which have been indicated in this table summarizing data on the language sequence, nevertheless the table appears to have some interpretative value in suggesting possible groupings for future investigators who may be able to employ more uniform terminology and criteria in order to clarify this still obscure picture. Some additional items are available up to 60 months of age in this group of studies, but they consist largely of the familiar intelligence test items, such as naming parts of the body, naming objects, naming objects in pictures, picture vocabulary and action-agent tests, as well as repetitions of sentences of various lengths. The objects and pictures employed take on variety so that the increasing numbers of things named have little or no significance from one investigation to the other. These difficulties begin to appear in the latter part of the table, but, as the first few items named are probably more nearly comparable from study to study, and since several authors have data up to 24 months

of age, it was arbitrarily decided to terminate this analysis with the last group of items for which the earliest entries occurred in the twenty-fourth month.

At first inspection of the array of items in this table the reader may be impressed with the length of the list and the amount of detail. If, however, he will mentally cross out all the items which are apparently duplicates, and list on a single line many of the items between pairs of horizontal lines, the amount of available information on the language sequence from the major normative studies will shrink appreciably. The reader will probably be impressed also with the striking degree of uniformity which is noticeable for the age at which similar items are reported in many instances where more than one author has observed the same or similar behavior with the same or almost the same criteria. Items 1 to 8 are, in general, descriptive of the utterances and syllabic vocalizations observed by most of the authors in the first few months. From the second to the fourth month are clustered all the reports of the infant's response to the human voice; the group of observations of cooing appears during this same time. Observations of vocalizations expressive of pleasure are reported by Bayley [1] and Gesell from the third to the sixth and seventh months, and of recognition in the seventh and eighth months. Variety in syllabification is heard apparently from the fourth to the sixth months and some rudimentary imitation of sounds from the sixth to the tenth months. Interjectional vocalizations are reported at the eighth month and listening to familiar words from the eighth to the ninth months. Response to gestures and to "Bye-bye" occurs from the ninth to the twelfth months.

[1] For bibliography references in this section, see headings of Table 1.

The greatest discrepancies appear in the group of items from 57 to 60, in which the behavior is described in rather vague terminology and in which the various investigators may have employed different criteria for what constitutes "expressive sounds" and what constitutes "jargon." Differential responses to different words are reported by both Bayley and Gesell in the ninth and tenth months, and C. Bühler and Bayley agree in noting imitation of syllables and words in the eleventh month. Only two of these studies, those by Shirley and by Cattell, report data on the first word. Here, there is an apparent discrepancy, for Cattell notes a vocabulary of one word at 11 months, whereas Shirley notes it at 14 months. Shirley, however, recorded only words actually spoken in the presence of the examiner, although the mothers heard the first words considerably in advance of the time at which they were elicited during the examination. Cattell, however, accepted the mothers' reports of the occurrence of the first word. With the exception of C. Bühler,[1] all investigators report responses to commands of various sorts from the tenth to the twelfth months. Two words or more are reported quite uniformly at the twelfth month, with the third and fourth words apparently following very shortly. The naming of single objects and pictures appears quite consistently in the latter half of the second year, as do responses to questions. According to the data available from this group of studies, children begin to combine words in the last quarter of the second year, and, as the vocabulary increases and the child enters upon the naming stage, there is a steady increase in the number of items named and objects pointed to in pictures

on verbal request. Such items, numbered 104 to 126, are all clustered from the twenty-first to the thirty-sixth months with the majority of the reports occurring at about 24 months. The first phrases, sentences, pronouns, and prepositions, all of which occur in the twenty-third and twenty-fourth months for the most part, round out the most advanced accomplishments of the second year of life.

It is somewhat surprising that the same sequence of behavior should be described so variously by these authors, and even by the same author from time to time. It is also surprising that some items which are rather readily observable, and which one might expect to find reported on by all investigators as landmarks, are so often overlooked. Inspection of Table 1 for the lines on which there are single entries reveals an amazing number of items on which only one of the writers reports data. Inspection of vertical columns of this table also reveals that it is entirely possible for writers to conduct apparently very thorough studies of infant behavior of the inventory type, and yet to have serious gaps of several months without the notation of a single language item. For example, Bayley does not have any language items from the twelfth to the seventeenth months, Shirley has none between the ninth and fourteenth months, and C. Bühler has none from the sixth to the ninth months or from the eleventh to the fifteenth months.

Another limitation of this group of normative studies is that none of the observers was trained in phonetics or employed any kind of recording aids, and none gives data on the reliability of observation. For the phonetic studies on the appearance of the various speech sounds in infancy it is still necessary to depend to a large extent on biographical studies. Two of the most careful and detailed studies of this sort, that by Lewis (1936), and

---

[1] Bühler's group was definitely underprivileged and probably was a retarded group of infants.

that by Grégoire (1937), employ the International Phonetic Alphabet and thus overcome the earlier difficulties of spelling notation with diacritical marks to indicate the infant's incomprehensible babblings.

Recent reports by Irwin and Chen (1941) and Irwin and Curry (1941) do much to bridge this gap, for they have data on the vocalizations of 40 infants during the first 10 days of life in which they use the International Phonetic Alphabet and report 94 per cent agreement between two observers. Irwin (1941a) also has data on the responses of 15 infants during the second quarter of the first year.

As Gesell and Thompson (1934) have pointed out, "In spite of voluminous literature on the subject of children's speech, the ontogenesis of language in the first year of life has had relatively little systematic attention" (p. 234). They go on to point out the difficulties of restricting observations to language behavior in the infant by saying:

> Genetically it is impossible to confine any analysis of factors to the field of verbalization, for verbalization is preceded by syllabification, vocalization and respiration, to say nothing of the whole complex of autonomic systems, which determine the affective life, which in turn determines the earliest language phenomena. For example, it is impossible to exclude crying from consideration. Although crying is a very primitive function and one which is in a measure shared with lower animals, the human cry very early undergoes differentiations which bring the act within the category of language (p. 245).

In her review on the period of infancy, in which the section on language is based largely on Decroly's (c. 1934) survey, E. Dewey (1935) states:

> The literature is in general agreement that the first sounds of the newborn infant are the overt elements from which speech develops, that vocalizations are used as means of communication before words proper are used; that comprehension appears before the use of words; that the normal child has a repertoire of a very few words by one year of age, that development is slow in the first months of the second year, but that toward the end of that year a great increase in the speed of progress appears; that words are first used in a generalized sense, and that their use for specific meanings is a developmental process; that name words appear first, verbs and adjectives later, relational words still later, and pronouns are just beginning to be used by the most advanced children by the end of the second year; that the first words have the force of a phrase or sentence, and combinations of words do not begin for some time (p. 251).

The Birth Cry. The birth cry is of significance for the development of language only because it constitutes the first use of the delicate respiratory mechanisms which are to be involved in speech. Its function is entirely physiological, having to do with the establishment of normal respiration and the oxygenation of the blood. It is also the first time that the child hears the sound of his own voice and, as such, has significance for language development. The earlier interpretations of the child's first cry as having intellectual or emotional significance have largely been discarded and are now no longer held in the scientific literature. There is evidence to show, however, that the organs involved in speech are capable of producing sounds at birth and even, in fact, quite early in prenatal life. Carmichael (1933) states: "By operative technique Minkowski has found that crying occurs as early as the sixth month in the prematurely delivered fetus. In clinical practice many cases of *vagitus uterinus,* or fetal crying, have been reported" (p. 98). According to E. Dewey (1935), Minkowski reports that faint sounds were heard in a fetus of 280 mm. after exposure to the air, and Carmichael believes this fifth-month fetus to be the youngest for which the literature reports sounds. Weak cries and spontaneous movements, more feeble than those of an infant born at term, were reported in a fetus of 330 mm. by Bolaffio and Artom (E. Dewey, 1935, p. 50). Thus, although the mechanism for the production of vocal sounds is ready to function considerably before birth, it is necessary to have the auditory and environmental social stimulation for language itself to emerge.

Prelinguistic Utterances of Infancy. Students of child development have always recognized the tremendous importance of the period of infancy which is perhaps most often described as the period which precedes the assumption of the erect posture. Strictly speaking, however, the word *infancy* means the period *without speech,* since the word itself is derived from the Latin words *in* (meaning without) + *fari* (to speak). The derivation was pointed out in 1880 by Schultze, but this interpretation of the meaning of the period of infancy is rarely encountered in the modern child development literature, and one finds that the derivation of the word is overlooked and emphasis placed on the more dramatic and more readily observable change in motor behavior which happens to occur at about the same time as the onset of speech.

Research in this period when utterances are incomprehensible is fraught with many methodological difficulties, described by McCarthy (1929*b*). There is the problem of hearing correctly the fleeting meaningless sounds and of using phonetic notation correctly in order to record them accurately. The greatest refinement of technique in this area has been developed by Irwin and his associates at the University of Iowa. Using respiration units, Irwin and Chen (1941) have demonstrated that it is possible to secure accurate and reliable phonetic transcriptions of infants' vocalizations. They report that practice in recording for eighteen infants yields observer agreement scores of over 90 per cent. They also state that just as satisfactory observer reliability is obtained from the recording of a large number of sounds from a few infants as from a small number of sounds from a large number of children. Although much progress has been made in mechanical and electrical recording, little has been done to apply these techniques in the study of infant speech.

Most writers agree that the earliest vocalizations are largely reflex and that at first they are entirely devoid of meaning, no specific sounds being used in connection with one situation and not in any other situations. Between the second and fifth weeks, however, O'Shea (1907) reports that the primitive squall begins to be differentiated to denote special forms of discomfort and that from then on differentiation progresses rapidly, so that soon all the child's vital experiences may be revealed in specialized vocalizations. Many of the rather fantastic interpretations of children's vocalizations that have appeared in the literature in the past have been due largely to the fact that adults tend to read meaning into children's sounds long before the child is capable of using vocalization to convey meaning. Sherman (1927) showed that adults had little success in judging the emotional accompaniment of infants' cries when the stimuli were not known. Interpretations of the cries were most often based on what was known regarding the stimulating situation, and not on any peculiar characteristics of the cries themselves. Blanton (1917), who was the first to observe as many as twenty-five babies during the first month of life, states: "There were differences of vowels and consonants, of timbre and degree, but no one was used as response to one set of circumstances that was not at the same time used to others—the cry of colic was the one exception." She also states that the other cries of the infant in the first month of life in response to hunger, pain, and cold differ from each other only in intensity.

It is almost universally agreed that the first utterances of the child are vowels of some sort. Observations in support of this are presented by Taine (1876), Preyer (1893), Tracy (1893), O'Shea (1907), Blanton (1917), Gesell (1925), Bean (1932), Shirley (1933a, 1933b), Lewis (1936), and Irwin (1941a), but from this point on there are divergent reports as to the order of appearance of the various speech sounds. The cruder observational studies were almost unanimous in reporting m, p, and b as the first consonants to appear and to modify the early vowel sounds into syllables. In spite of the very general acceptance of the early appearance of labial sounds which have been said to be formed quite naturally when the child closes his lips while uttering a vowel sound, there is an accumulation of evidence from more recent studies which seems to indicate that the front consonants probably are not the most frequent early sounds. The very interesting study by Irwin and Curry (1941) shows that among more than 1000 vowel sounds recorded phonetically for 40 babies observed during the first ten days of life 92 per cent were front vowels, only 7 per cent were middle vowels, and back vowels amounted to only 1 per cent. With regard to the consonants they report that the aspirate h is the most frequently used consonant. Occasionally w and k are heard, but m, b, and p did not occur among these 40 babies in the first ten days of life. Irwin also reports data on 15 babies who were visited

twice a month in their own homes and of whose vocalizations during the second quarter of the first year phonetic transcriptions were made. He states that most of the vowels were used during the quarter, the exceptions being ɜ and o. About one third of the consonants did not appear during this period. Those which were not heard were p, r, ʒ, ð, s, and ʃ.

Individual differences among these infants were marked. The average number of vowels used was 8.4, with a range of 3 to 12 out of a total of 13 vowels, and the average number of consonants was 4.0, with a range of 1 to 9 out of a total of 22 consonants. No sex differences were revealed in these early utterances. When the consonants were classified according to the manner of articulation, fricatives were most frequent, followed by plosives, semivowels, and finally nasals. When the classification was made on the basis of place of articulation, glottals ranked first, followed in order by velars, postdentals, palatals, labials, and labiodentals. The sound h was found to be the most frequent consonant, comprising over half of all consonant sounds and about 20 per cent of the total. The use of vowels was found to be clearly predominant over consonants.

Schultze (1880) states that the evolution of *lallation* is subject to the law of least physiological effort and that infants' phonetic utterances evolve from labial phenomena to sounds requiring greater effort, namely, guttural sounds. Ombredane (1935), however, disagrees with this early observation and, in harmony with Irwin, points out that development proceeds from phenomena involving strong muscular tension (the glottic) to those having weak tension, but which are uttered by the lips, the most mobile speech organs. He considers that the pre-eminence of the labial phenomenon marks the beginning of cortical functioning and the approach of the period of imitation.

Since Irwin (1941*a*) finds middle and back vowels, which were not evident during the first ten days, have appeared by the beginning of the second quarter, he considers the first quarter-year of life to be the period of the emergence of middle and back vowels. He sets up tentative hypotheses for further checking that the direction of progress in the phonetic development of vowels is from those which are formed with the front part of the mouth to those which are formed in the back of the oral cavity; and that consonant formation progresses from the back part of the mouth to the front. These data, he concludes, do not bear out the view frequently expressed in the literature, largely on *a priori* grounds, that the labials are the earliest consonants. Irwin is supported in the finding of the *h* sound as among the earliest sounds by Blanton (1917), Fenton (1925), Bean (1932), and Shirley (1933*a*, 1933*b*), all of whom report it either as a final or initial sound or in combination with another consonant as among the earliest sounds. Lewis (1936) also gives an explanation of the early appearance of the *h* sound, which he says "is the sound heard if the voice is momentarily withheld in the act of uttering any vowel" (p. 30). Guttural sounds, particularly variations of *g* and *k,* as well as sounds described as "gurgles" and "sputters," are also reported as among the earliest sounds by Tracy (1893), Blanton (1917), Fenton (1925), Bean (1932), and Shirley (1933*a*, 1933*b*).

Irwin (1942) made transcriptions of the speech sounds made by ten low-grade feeble-minded children with an average age of about four years and with IQ's ranging from 48 to 7. Two samples of sounds made during thirty breaths were taken at an interval of about one year. Only one of the cases was using what might be called meaningful sounds. These feeble-minded children used back vowels more infrequently than front vowels, in which respect their speech resembled that of young infants rather than that of adults. Infants one month old, he found, had a vowel-consonant ratio of 4 to 1, the feeble-minded children of 2 to 1, whereas adults have a ratio of 1 to 1. This is suggestive of the fact that these measures may prove fruitful developmental indices in this hitherto uncharted area.

Lewis (1936), who presents one of the most detailed phonetic studies based on only one child, but carefully integrated with earlier reports of infant vocalizations, is also in substantial agreement with the findings of Irwin and his associates (1941). He makes the interesting distinction between sounds uttered in comfort and sounds uttered in states of discomfort. He groups all the back consonants of *g, x, g, k,* and *r* as the early consonants uttered in comfort and the front consonants, both nasal and oral, as later consonants which are usually uttered in comfort. With regard to the front consonants Lewis (1936) states:

> Many observers have noted the occurrence of the characteristic labial and dental consonants. In Stern's summary of the records we find that they appear after the back consonants and that the nasals (*m* and *n*) occur chiefly in states of discomfort (p. 26).

Lewis (1936) traces an interesting relationship between the child's movements which are characteristically made with the vocal apparatus in typical states of comfort, usually after feeding, and in states of discomfort, usually in anticipation of feeding. The back consonants, which appear early and are said to be typical of periods of comfort, are associated with the swallowing and belching movements which usually follow feeding, and in the prefeeding period the child typically makes mouthing movements with tongue and lips in anticipation of feeding which are most likely to result in the later *m, p,* and *b* sounds. It is obvious, however, that the infant needs some weeks of preliminary experience in the feeding situation in which to learn to make these anticipatory movements. It is probable that the earlier writers, who claimed that these labial and dental sounds appeared first, did not make their observations early enough in the neonatal period to get the first utterances. Hazlitt (1933) points out that no crying occurs in a state of comfort and that babbling occurs only in states of comfort. In general, the phonetic grouping of sounds for purposes of research in infant vocalizations appears to be quite promising. The reader who is interested in more detailed accounts of the phonetics of infant babblings should consult the works of Lewis (1936) and Grégoire (1937).

After the first acquisitions of sounds, there seems to be a rather rapid increase in the variety of sounds, so that by the third month most observers of infant behavior report cooing and babbling, which continue until about the end of the first year, when the first words are heard. K. C. Moore (1896) reports that her son had used all the sounds which occur in English by the fourth month. Lewis (1936) maintains that the child's first comfort sounds are really expressive and that they are subsequently transformed into mere playful babbling, that is, sounds uttered for the mere delight of uttering them. Most writers agree that children's speech sounds are much less precise and definite than those of adults, and that during this preliminary babbling period of infancy there occurs increasing definiteness of utterance of various syllables.

The often-reported facts that the very young infant at first uses only a few vowels and later adds more and more sounds to his verbal repertoire, and the frequent observation of the persistence of baby-talk which is gradually outgrown, have led many writers to assume that the speech sounds are acquired very gradually, and that the complex sounds are built up from the simple ones. A number of articles which have appeared recently tend to bring this theory of the learning of language into question. In the first place, many writers have indicated that they find a tremendous variety in the vocal repertoire of the infant and that they hear many sounds which defy spelling in our alphabet. Children whose mother tongue is to be English, and who are hearing only English, often use German umlaut sounds, French guttural *r*'s, and a wide variety of sounds which it is difficult or impossible to describe. These phenomena are usually attributed to the plasticity of the child's speech organs; and, since any child regardless of his parentage learns the language which he hears spoken by those in his environment, it is claimed that the sounds needed for any particular language which the child is to learn are selected from this extensive repertoire and are singled out for practice because they are heard so frequently. Latif (1934) states that out of this astonishingly rich and varied repertoire of sounds those which are used by the child's elders are reinforced and become habitual and others cease to be uttered. He goes on to state:

> Almost as soon as sounds begin to be produced at all they begin to be repeated rather slowly and monotonously. . . . This *repetition,* or *reduplication,* may well be considered the final step in that process by which the mere vocalizations become organized into language. It is here that explanation of the development of language must begin (p. 62).

This brings us to the point that children's babbling often consists of repetition of identical or similar syllables so that the first vocal utterances to acquire meaning are usually reduplicated monosyllables such as *mama, dada, nana, bye-bye, tick-tick, choo-choo,* and the like. Writers who hold to slow acquisition of sounds and building-up of the repertoire of speech sounds by imitation, and the gradual perfection of each, stress the difficulty of the sounds from the motor aspect, and claim that the sounds which are late in appearing are more difficult to execute. Others, who see extreme variety in the plasticity of the vocal organs, take the point of view that the child can make the various sounds necessary for the acquisition of any language at a very early age, but they stress the sensory and perceptual difficulties of the acquisition of speech. E. Dewey (1935), in summarizing the literature on this point, says:

> There are a number of theories as to the way in which speech develops from the early vocalizations. In general, two opposing points of view appear: one, that learning goes on by a very gradual process of building up the complex from the simple; the other, that the original phonetic equipment of the individual is very large, and that learning takes place by a process of adjusting and eliminating the sounds used, to the language learned. . . . Grégoire, on the other hand, believes that the sound repertoire of the young infant is phonetically great and that a particular language evolves by the elimination of some sounds. The first sounds the infant makes are uncoordinated, and precision is gained gradually. In the beginning, the infant tries hard to express himself without awareness of trying to use words. He usually ends by crying. Later, about the ninth month, the combination of syllables begins. This sounds in its rhythm like an imitation of adult speech, and in the tenth month he begins to imitate the rhythm of the language of his country. Before the question can be decided we must have more exact, complex, and phonetically correct records of all sounds made by infants, from the time of birth to the appearance of speech (p. 252).

Bean (1932), for example, holds that children's mispronunciations are due to crude perception rather than to any inability to pronounce the elemental sounds. If the latter theory of the beginnings of speech is substantiated by further investigation, it will be interesting to relate it to the known facts about the development of the gross motor skills in which there occurs individuation of specific movements from the random mass activity manifested by the newborn child. It is entirely possible that future research may demonstrate some such individuation occurring in the motor responses involved in the development of speech. Latif (1934) sets forth such an hypothesis in regard to the increase in specificity of meanings, for he says:

> An infant's awareness of some meaning does not imply any very precise appreciation. And, as a rule, the earlier meanings of an infant are exceedingly vague. Just as there are many grades of specificity between the random and the coordinated movements of a child, so also there are different degrees of precision in its meanings. . . . In short whenever there is a response on the part of the organism to a stimulus, there is always meaning. But not until the response becomes specific can there be precise meaning. The explanation of the absence of precise meaning for an infant is the same as the explanation of his lack of coordinated and specific movements.

McGranahan (1936) says that there are two main types of theories of the evolution of language. One which was popular in the nineteenth century conceived of the development of language as a building-up process involving the progressive combination and integration of a number of elementary units called *roots*. The other more recent theory championed by Jespersen (1922, 1923) considers the process of evolution to be one of progressive differentiation of a number of primitive mass units. McGranahan (1936) further points out:

> These two theories of linguistic development have interesting counterparts in modern physiological and psychological theories of development. The root theory, for example, corresponds to the reflex theory of behavioral development, according to which more mature and complex behavior results from the combination and integration of a number of elementary reflexes; and the mass theory to the modern psychological conception of behavioral development as the progressive differentiation of original mass activity.

The Rôle of Imitation. As has already been implied, imitation is a very important element in the child's linguistic development. The mere fact that the child learns the language of his environment is evidence of its importance. Children imitate the behavior of others in all aspects of their behavior, and it is especially apparent in motor and verbal areas. The fact that the congenitally deaf child does not learn to speak because he is deprived of the opportunity to imitate others also bears witness to the important rôle of this factor. Imitative behavior is reported most often after the ninth month and is especially prominent around the end of the first year and the beginning of the second year when language proper is just beginning to emerge. Champneys (1881) says, "From nine months the child distinctly imitated the intonation of the voice when any word or sentence was repeated several times." C. Bühler (1930) reports

some elemental imitation of sounds such as *re-re-re* observed as early as six months, whereas Cattell (1940) reports imitation of words as a test item at nine months, and Gesell (1928) at ten months. C. Bühler (1930) reports imitation of syllables such as *mama, papa,* and *dada* at the eleventh month and Bayley (1933) finds her group of infants imitating words at 11.7 months. Shirley (1933a, 1933b) reports the first imitative word heard in the presence of the examiners in the fourteenth month, although the mothers of the children in her group had reported such behavior considerably earlier. (See Table 1.)

The term *imitation* has been used in several different ways in the literature, and it is necessary to distinguish these types of behavior in order to appreciate the rôle of imitation in language development. Decroly (c. 1934) distinguishes the following forms of imitation (p. 88):

1. Imitation with and without intention to imitate which is sometimes designated as spontaneous or voluntary imitation.
2. Imitation with or without comprehension.
3. Immediate or deferred imitation.
4. Exact and inexact imitation.

It is over the last of these that so much controversy has centered. The most limited use of the term refers only to exact mimetic reproduction of the identical sounds said to the child as a model. Although this sort of reproduction undoubtedly does occur, it is much more rare than the second type, by which is meant the attempt to reproduce sounds heard, regardless of the accuracy of the accomplishment. Most present-day psychologists seem to agree with the opinion of Taine (1876) that new sounds are not learned by imitation of the speech of others, but rather that they emerge in the child's spontaneous vocal play more or less as a result of maturation, and that the child imitates only those sounds which have already occurred in its spontaneous babblings. This view holds that imitation of the speech of others serves only to call attention to new combinations of sounds already used. In speaking of his daughter, Taine (1876) says, "Example and education were only of use in calling her attention to the sounds that she had already found out for herself —but all initiative belongs to her."

Curti (1938) expresses the same point of view, for she states:

> By repeating to the child other sounds which he has already spontaneously practiced, adults may evoke the sounds again and again and thus lead to facility in their use. No sound, however, will be thus repeated which the child has not already used (p. 261).

Shirley (1933a, 1933b) calls attention to the fact that there is a marked tendency to imitate the intonations and inflections of the voice regardless of the specific sounds. The Hoyers (1924) also report that their son repeated easily the sounds which he was able to say spontaneously, but that he did not arrive at any new syllables in this way. An excellent discussion of the problem of imitation appears in Guillaume (1925), which is well summarized in French by Decroly (c. 1934) and in English by Lewis (1936).

It must also be pointed out that the child not only imitates the sounds made by others, but that he also imitates the sounds which he himself makes. This self-imitation is what contributes largely to the phenomenon of babbling and to the later echolalia. When the child accidentally, and later purposefully, reproduces sounds which he himself has made, the adults in the environment usually say a real word which the child's sounds appear to approximate.

This tends to give auditory reinforcement to the sounds the child has just made, at the same time making for more precise perception and rendition of the approved sound groups. Thus there occurs a progressive elimination of errors and a selection of movements which give the best approximation to the real word heard in the speech of adults. Continued practice thus results in the fixation of the sound groups, which come to be uttered habitually.

Basing his point of view largely on Guernsey's (1928) intensive study of 200 children between the ages of 2 and 21 months, Lewis (1936) outlines three stages of imitation. He cites the child's tendency in the first three or four months to respond to human utterance by making sounds as a rudimentary form of imitation. Most writers do not classify this early vocalization as imitation, but Lewis points out that it is really a question of the criterion of imitation to which one subscribes. He then notes a pause during which there is a "diminution, if not an entire cessation, of the vocal responses to speech typical of the first stage." The third stage which he recognizes is that which most writers report at about nine months of age. He says: "There can be no question that in the second and third months children normally respond vocally to speech as speech." He argues for the imitative nature of these early sounds which have been reported in the literature on the grounds that "first, they most readily occur when the child is attentive to the speaker; secondly, the child's utterance is specially evoked by hearing adult speech; and, thirdly, that this utterance consists of his own familiar sounds" (p. 73). He cites the Sterns (1907), the Hoyers (1924), Guillaume (1925), Valentine (1930), and C. Bühler (1931), as showing similarity of phonetic form between the vocalizations of the first two or three months and sounds spoken to the child by adults. He points out, however, that sometimes the child's responses do not resemble what he hears either in intonation or phonetic form and concludes:

> It would appear, then, . . . that the child's vocal response to adult speech in his earliest months consists of his own familiar sounds; when he hears a sound drawn from his own repertory, his response may occasionally resemble it in intonational and phonetic form.

Three different explanations of the phenomenon of imitation have been advanced in the literature and are well summarized by Lewis (1936) as follows: "First, that there is an innate tendency for the child to respond to speech by speech; secondly, that the child responds by expression to expression; and, thirdly, that vocal responses to speech arise from intervention of the adult into the child's activity of babbling" (p. 76). In discussing the third of these explanations, which has been accepted very widely by writers on children's imitation and language development, he points out that this is J. M. Baldwin's (1895) hypothesis of *circular reaction* which has been accepted by such writers as the Sterns (1907), Bekhterev (1913), F. H. Allport (1924), Koffka (1924), Guillaume (1925), and McDougall (1931), and Allport's description of the circular reflex has been followed by Markey (1928), Lorimer (1929), and many others.

The general principle is that "in the course of repetitive babbling, a pattern of alternating hearing and utterance is set up; if an adult repeatedly imitates one of a child's own sounds while he is babbling, the heard sound becomes a part of the pattern of alternation, so that ultimately it remains effective in evoking speech which may resemble the stimulus both in phonetic and in intonational form" (p. 79). Lewis

(1936) goes on to point out, however, that Baldwin's (1895) hypothesis which has been so widely accepted cannot by itself account for the child's learning of language through imitation, for the Sterns (1907), Koffka (1924), Guillaume (1925), and McDougall (1931) "have found it necessary to supplement Baldwin's principle by accepting at the same time the principle of a general tendency to respond to speech by speech."

Lewis (1936) believes he is the first, however, to point out that "the actually observed facts of early babbling and imitation demand that Baldwin's principle shall be modified and supplemented." He concludes then, that "our only alternative is to recognize that the hearing of the adult word can merely stimulate the child to the utterance of his *own* babbling sounds, and that from this the child may become trained to respond with a particular sound to a particular heard sound. Baldwin's [1895] hypothesis is certainly valuable, so long as we couple it with the fundamental assumption that the child tends to reply to speech by speech" (p. 80).

Training experiments in language presuppose imitation as a basic factor. One of the most conclusive experiments on this point is by Strayer (1930) in which one member of a pair of identical twins was given intensive training in naming objects, etc., for a period of five weeks, whereas the other twin was deprived of all opportunity to hear language during that period. After this initial experimental period, similar training was given to the other twin. The author concludes:

> A maturational difference of even five weeks has a definite influence on the relative effectiveness of training. . . . Not only was training which was begun with a maturational advantage of five weeks more effective than earlier training, but the pattern of response was more mature. Train-

ing cannot transcend maturational level as evidenced by the fact that intensive training failed to bring either retarded child up to average in the particular function though it is effective to some degree in improving vocabulary.

She adds that the typical stages in the learning process were strikingly alike for both children. Sommer (1932), who found a 28 per cent improvement in an untrained kindergarten group in articulation, also tends to show the influence of maturation, although her trained group showed a 57 per cent improvement due to the effects of both maturation and the training given in articulation.

Decroly (c. 1934) calls attention to an interesting controversy in the literature on the problem of the relationship between imitation and comprehension of language. He points out that Compayré (1896), Sully (1908), and Meumann (1908) consider that vocal imitation comes before true language, but that Preyer (1900) contends that imitation does not precede comprehension, since his son did not imitate the word *papa* until about the second year although he gave considerable evidence of understanding language in the period of 12 to 18 months. The Sterns (1907) are cited as pointing out in contradiction to Preyer (1900) that sound groups are imitated long before the appearance of comprehension, and that the imitation observed in their three children at about the ninth month was only imitation of gestures, inarticulate sounds, and intonations of the voice. Imitation of the combinations of articulate sounds did not appear until the end of the second year, at which time many words were understood and some pronounced correctly. As E. Dewey (1935) says:

Decroly [c. 1934] concludes that auditory differentiation must precede speech and is a necessary element in imitation, and that development of comprehension and auditory perception are inseparable. He says that words do not have a purely tonal or musical interest for the child, and that he distinguishes only those to which he gives a meaning. Therefore, imitation cannot precede understanding, for function must not only be within the capacity of the individual, it must also serve some individual need or interest (p. 260).

Language Comprehension. Most writers agree that the child understands the language of others considerably before he actually uses language himself. Abundant evidence for this appears in the anecdotal accounts in the early biographical studies indicating children's responses to commands and questions. Some of these incidents are rather subjective and are inadequately reported, that is, without complete description of the circumstances in which the utterances were made. From the normative studies included in Table 1 it would seem as if the child usually gives objective evidence in his overt behavior of his comprehension of the speech of others at about the end of the first year. There may, however, be a dawning comprehension at about the ninth month, when the child is reported as paying close attention to words and making differential responses to them

Bean (1932) states that long before his child could pronounce a word he knew the meanings of a great many words. As a training method, he attempted to converse with the child in single words or short phrases at this period and secured three repetitions per item as evidence that "association links" had been formed between 152 words and phrases and the objects or acts to which they belonged. The process of training in the comprehension of language is outlined by Lewis (1936) as follows:

The child responds affectively both to the intonational pattern of what he hears and to the situation in which he hears it. And at this very same time he hears a phonetic pattern, inextricably intertwined with the intonational pattern and—in many cases—linked expressively or onomatopoetically with the situation. Then his affective response fashions a new whole out of these experiences, this new whole including the intonational pattern, the situation, and the phonetic pattern. When at last the phonetic pattern acquires dominance so that irrespective of the intonational pattern it evokes the appropriate response from the child, we say that he has understood the conventional word. Finally, there comes a time when the child on hearing the particular word refers to a particular object (p. 122).

It is quite generally agreed that the child understands gestures before he understands words, and in fact that he uses gestures himself long before he uses language proper. He looks for objects he has dropped, he reaches for objects, etc., long before he can ask for them. These and other overt bodily movements which are used as means of early expression and communication are often accompanied by early vocalizations. It has often been claimed that words constitute substitutes for actual gross motor activity. The extreme point of view in this direction is represented by the behaviorists, who hold that the laryngeal movements involved in speech are actual substitutes for overt bodily movements.

An interesting analysis of gesture language is presented by Latif (1934), who says: "It is through the intervention of its elders that the general movements and postures of an infant gradually pass into symbolic gestures." He describes the hungry child seeking his bottle as manifesting *"whole-body* language, since the attitude and activity of its whole body convey meaning to an onlooker," but he goes on to point out:

This whole-body language of the infant soon comes to be abbreviated, through the solicitous participation of the mother. As soon as the infant shows a nascent attitude of food-adience, the mother brings the bottle and thus cuts short the adient efforts of the infant. Whenever it stretches out its hand toward an object, the attentive mother is there to put the object in its hand. Such cooperation on the part of the mother soon reduces the whole-body language of the infant to mere ("conventional") gesture, in which *only a part* and that the earliest part of an action is substituted for the entire action. The responses of the infant thus become merely symptomatic; i.e., symbolic (pp. 76–77).

The literature in many instances is very obscure on the comprehension of adult gesture and language by children, for so much of it involves notation of the child's responses to commands. Often it is not stated whether the commands are accompanied by gestures or not. As may be seen in Table 1, C. Bühler (1930) specifies in items 75 and 76 that the commands were accompanied by gestures. Other investigators, however, report responses to commands at much earlier ages than she does, and they do not specify that gestures accompanied the commands, although it is rather likely that some gestural cues were employed since that is the natural way for adults to give commands. Undoubtedly the authors would have specified any artificiality introduced into the situation by experimental controls. In all probability the discrepancy in ages is due to differences in the selection of cases in the Bühler group.

It is evident that just as the child's gesture may become reduced from the whole-body language to the merely conventional gesture, so those actions which are originally accompanied by vocalization may drop out entirely and the reduction of effort may limit the child's activity to only the vocalizations which come to have symbolic meaning. Latif (1934) also points out that "the child's understanding of the behavior of others does not begin with its appreciation of words; it begins with an appreciation of its elders' actions and gestures" (p. 79). The child's own use of gesture gradually recedes and its place is taken by real language. Cases of language retardation are often attributed to the fact that the child develops an elaborate system of gesture language which is so well understood by adults in the child's environment that his wants and needs are satisfied without his having to make the effort to learn to talk. If, in a particular case, it can be shown that such is the cause of linguistic retardation, a refusal on the part of the adults in the environment to understand and respond to the child's gesture language is usually effective in bringing about the emergence of true language. Latif (1934) points out, however: "As vocal language (tonal or verbal) develops, the gesture language recedes into the background. But not even at the highest levels of vocal communication do gestures ever entirely disappear" (p. 81).

Witte (1930) conducted some interesting experiments on gesture language in which he attempted to determine what are the limitations of gestures and to find out what concepts can and cannot be expressed in gestures. He finds that concrete ideas and things within the visual field can readily be expressed in gestures, as can commands, questions, and negations. Many verbs and adjectives he finds can be gesticulated, but equality and similarity, the pronoun *it*, and auxiliary verbs are difficult to express in this way. He states that a comparison between the language of gestures and the child's language had not been carried out in the German literature up to 1930, and the writer has not noted any such study in the American literature up to the present time.

In discussing gesture theories of the origin of language, McGranahan (1936) says that kinesthetic experience is often proposed as the basis of natural representation, and he cites Paget's (1930) extreme theory which claims that the origin and development of all language are based upon certain positions and movements of tongue, jaws, and mouth which instinctively imitate the events and objects of the outside world. The speech sound which comes from a particular imitative oral gesture is claimed to evoke the same gesture in the hearer and thereby to symbolize the referent of which the gesture is an imitation.

Lewis (1936) takes issue with the Sterns' (1907) view "that the early responses of the child to heard speech are fundamentally built up on natural gestures, whether of the speaker, or of the child himself," and he says that "the child responds first to a gesture, then to the gesture accompanied by words, finally to those words in themselves." Lewis (1936) considers that such a description leaves out of consideration the child's early responses to the human voice, for it is evident that the child is quieted by talking and that he distinguishes between friendly and angry talking, and in general is responsive to affective intonations of the voice long before he gives evidence of understanding gestures or of showing differential response to phonetic patterns of words. Usually language comprehension has been considered only at the later ages when the child gives evidence of responding differently to various sound patterns. Seldom is there any attempt to relate the very early responses to intonation to the sequence of development in the understanding of the speech of others.

After criticizing the Sterns' (1907) description as placing too much emphasis on training aspects and too little on the persistent tendencies already present, both in the acts that the child performs and in the words that he hears, Lewis (1936) says:

> The child's development cannot be fully understood unless we consider these tendencies in relation to whatever appears to be new in his comprehension. The persistent features are these: the child has at an earlier date already begun to perform specific acts, and to respond to sounds by expression. The new features are these: he now performs specific acts (or inhibits them) in response to specific phonetic patterns (p. 111).

Lewis describes the following three stages in the child's development of response to specific sound groups:

1. At an early stage, the child shows discrimination in a broad way, between different patterns of expression in intonation.
2. When the total pattern—the phonetic form together with intonational form —is made effective by training, at first the intonational rather than the phonetic form dominates the child's response.
3. Then the phonetic pattern becomes the dominant feature in evoking the specific response; but while the function of the intonational pattern may be considerably subordinated, it certainly does not vanish (pp. 115–116).

Whereas the Sterns and others have accepted the point of view that it is easier for the child to understand the gestures than the language of others, Lewis points to the findings of Bühler and Hetzer (1935), who report that before six months of age no child observed by them responded to coaxing or threatening gestures, and that an additional two months of maturity seemed necessary before such re-

sponse could be elicited, but specific responses to differences in the intonation of the voice were definitely established in these same children as early as the sixth month. Lewis concludes, therefore:

> What we cannot accept is Stern's suggestion that the response to gestures is prior to the response to the intonational patterns of speech. The child responds to both: each indeed may facilitate the effect of the other. Together they evoke an affective response from the child, initiating or inhibiting his acts (p. 121).

Decroly (c. 1934) also begins the discussion of the problem of language comprehension with a consideration of the child's earliest responses to sounds, especially to the sound of the human voice, and agrees that the first influence of heard words is affective in nature. He also discusses the problem of the length of the interval between the child's first comprehension of language and his actual use of linguistic expression. The Sterns (1907) are cited as maintaining that there is a relatively short interval between the time when the child first shows that he comprehends speech and his actual use of speech. Schäfer (1921), who took up this problem in detail, claims that most children show an interval of about three months between linguistic comprehension and expression.

The First Word. Although at first thought it might seem as if it would be very easy to determine the actual onset of speech by noting the child's first word, there are a number of difficulties surrounding the determination of the exact age at which the child uses his first word with meaning. The first use of sound with meaning is usually considered to constitute the child's first word. This event is so eagerly anticipated by parents that they often read meaning into the child's early babblings which happen to coincide with the presence of certain persons, objects, or events in the environment. If the child habitually uses *da-da* in his babbling, and sometimes uses it in the presence of his father, when can it be said that this is uttered with meaning to designate his father? If the criterion of using the word to mean only one person and not using it in any other situation is accepted, it is necessary to observe over a period of time, to note consistency of usage, and to see that the sounds are not used in other situations. This is rather a negative way of establishing the fact that the word is used with meaning, and it does not indicate positively the *first* time the word is *used with meaning*.

Other criteria are accompanying gestures which may make the interpretation of the child's usage more certain, and observation over a period of time for recurrences of the sound in similar situations. Some observers consider the child's first word to be his first spontaneous utterance of a word with meaning (meaningfulness being inferred by the adult with little or no objective evidence as to the correctness of the inference); others consider it to be the first word that he gives evidence of understanding; and still others consider it to be the speaking of a word in imitation of an adult's speech. With such varying criteria it is necessary to employ caution in interpreting data which have been reported on the appearance of the first word.

As Lewis (1936) puts the same problem:

> To discover how reference develops, we have to notice, by considering the child's behavior at times when he is speaking or responding to words, what is the function of a given sound-group both before and after he first appears to attach it to a given object. In other words, we have to judge of the meaning of a word by noticing its place in the child's activity.

Lorimer (1929) points out that "because of the variety of factors involved in the origin of words it is rather artificial to attempt ever to say exactly what is the child's 'first word.'"

Earlier sections on imitation and on language comprehension have already indicated the chief points of view which have been set forth as to how the child's utterances come to have meaning for him. There is a tremendous psychological gap which has to be bridged between the mere utterance of the phonetic form of a word and the symbolic or representational use of that word in an appropriate situation. As Sapir (1921) says in speaking of sound elements in speech: "What distinguishes each of these elements is that it is the outward sign of a specific idea," and again: "The mere phonetic framework of speech does not constitute the inner fact of language" (p. 43).

Sapir (1921, 1929) proposes a nativistic theory of phonetic symbolism which has given rise to considerable controversy and experimentation. He experimented with nonsense syllables and found that adults judged syllables containing the vowel *a* as "larger" than syllables containing the vowel *i* 80 per cent of the time. Newman (1933) conducted more elaborate experiments in which he showed a scale of relative symbolic magnitude corresponding to the vowel series and related to the various positions of articulation. McGranahan (1936), however, points out that such phenomena of phonetic symbolism in regard to size seem to work only when the factor of size is primary in attention and when the symbolic vowel in the word is also in the focus of attention. He thus tends to discredit the rôle of this phenomenon in the development of meaning. Wolfle (1932, 1934), who has shown that children are only slightly more prone to analogic change than adults, thinks that phonetic symbolism, word meaning, and the phenomenon of analogic change in language forms should all be explained psychologically as examples of the process of generalization. Heider and Heider (1940a) have demonstrated the phenomenon of phonetic symbolism among deaf children, and they consider that in many cases their subjective experience of their own speech is quite similar in its symbolism to that of hearing persons, although there are some differences which are traceable to the lack of the auditory factor.

As may be seen from inspection of Table 1, only two of the authors (Shirley and Cattell) included in this group attempt to assign an age level to the stage of linguistic development characterized by the use of a single word. Cattell (1940), who accepts the mothers' reports for this item, places it at 11 months, and Shirley (1933a, 1933b), who reports on the first comprehensible word spoken in the presence of the examiners, places it at the fourteenth month. She states, however, that most of the mothers reported that the babies had a vocabulary of two or three words at one year, but that speech did not occur so early during the tests as it did spontaneously in the presence of the mothers. Thus these two studies are probably in fairly close agreement that the first word actually does occur shortly before the end of the first year of life. C. Bühler (1930) reports the imitation of syllables such as *mama*, *dada*, and the like at 11 months, and Bayley (1933) also reports imitation of words at 11.7 months.

In Smith's (1926) study none of the 13 children studied at 8 months had begun to talk. The 17 children whom she observed at 10 months had an average vocabulary of one word (although Gesell, Halverson, Thompson, et al., 1940, estimate this group to have been somewhat highly

selected), and 52 children at one year of age had an average vocabulary of three words. Castner (in Gesell, Halverson, Thompson, et al., 1940), however, points out that Smith's group was probably somewhat precocious.

The scattered reports on the appearance of the first word in the biographical studies have been collated from time to time by various writers. Feldmann (1833) gave statistics on 33 cases in which the mode for the appearance of the first word was at 16 months. Bateman (1917) summarized 35 cases, 18 of whom were English-speaking, 12 German-speaking, and 5 Polish and Bulgarian. Since all these cases were children whose parents were sufficiently interested to write articles on their linguistic development for scientific journals, it is probable that they represent a very highly selected group. The age range in this group is 8 to 15 months, with 43 per cent of the cases using the first word between 10 and 11 months of age. The boys usually reached this stage somewhat later than the girls, and the English-speaking children somewhat in advance of those speaking other languages, with the Polish and Bulgarian children considerably later than other nationality groups. The Sterns (1907) also summarized 26 biographical reports, but most of these are included in Table 2, taken from C. Bühler (1931), who

TABLE 2

Tabulation of Age of Appearance of First Word

(After C. Bühler, 1931)

Age in months	8	9	10	11	12	13	14	15	16	17	18	19	20
Number of cases	3	7	13	6	5	5	4	1	1	1	0	0	3

presents data on 49 cases. The three cases reported as not using the first word until 20 months of age are reported by Bühler to be definitely pathological. Decroly

(c. 1934) reproduces this table of Bühler's with the addition of another case at 11 months. For these data for children drawn largely from superior socioeconomic backgrounds the mode for the use of the first word is at 10 months. The median for all cases is at 11 months of age. This agrees with the average age of talking reported by Terman *et al.* (1925) for his gifted group. His data were collected from the parents in retrospect after the children had been located as gifted children in school. Mead (1913), using rather crude techniques of parents' retrospective reports, gives the average age for beginning to talk as 15.3 months for normal children and 38.5 months for a group of feeble-minded children. The significance of these findings will be discussed in the section on the relationship between language development and intelligence (pp. 546 ff.).

In regard to the form of the first word there is rather striking agreement in the literature that it is usually a monosyllable or a reduplicated monosyllable such as *bye-bye, mama, dada, bebe, tick-tick,* and the like. Certainly the commonest words heard in the nursery of the child who is just beginning to talk are of the reduplicated monosyllable type. Perez (1889), the Sterns (1907), Kroeber (1916), and Shirley (1933a, 1933b) are among the many writers who call attention to this phenomenon. The frequently occurring syllables, which are heard again and again in the child's babble, readily become the familiar appellations of babyhood as soon as adults begin to note the child's consistent use of them in specific situations and begin to use them in talking to the child. The Sterns (1907) also point out how often these words are of an onomatopoeic character, having a natural connection between sound and meaning, such as *moo-moo* and *tick-tick.* Shirley (1933a, 1933b), who terms these "childish imitative words,"

states that they were apparently picked up from parents or older children in most cases rather than invented by the babies themselves.

Lewis (1936), after making a phonetic analysis of the first words of the 26 children reported on by the Sterns (1907), together with the observations on his own son, states:

> The great majority of the earliest words are of a definite phonetic form: they consist of single or duplicated syllables in which the consonants are either labials (*p, b, m, w*) or labio-dentals (*f, v,*) or tip-dentals (*t, d, n*): they are made with both lips or lip against teeth or tongue-tip against teeth (or gum ridge). . . . No less than 83 out of 110 (or 75 per cent) contain only front consonants, while 12 per cent contain one front consonant. Further, 85 per cent of the total are either monosyllabic or reduplicated (39 per cent of the former and 46 per cent of the latter) (p. 125).

It is interesting to note agreement between this report on first words and Irwin and Curry's (1941) findings of the preponderance of front vowel sounds.

It is difficult to say exactly what part of speech the first words usually are since they are used in isolation for lack of supporting vocabulary. They are usually used as whole sentences and function for a time as one-word sentences (Lukens, 1894; the Sterns, 1907; Pelsma, 1910; Koffka, 1924; Bean, 1932; and Brigance, 1934). However, if only the form of the words is considered in terms of the most frequent occurrence of the forms, the first words are characteristically nouns or interjections. Markey (1928) gives a detailed account calling attention to the verbal function of many of the early nouns. By the use of gestures and intonations of the voice the child often uses a single word to convey a variety of meanings in different situations

The single word "ball" may mean "There is the ball," if uttered in the presence of a ball accompanied by a pointing gesture, or it may mean "Where is the ball?" or "I want the ball," if uttered with a questioning or demanding inflection and accompanied by searching behavior. Meumann (1908) has stressed the point that first words are strongly affective and that they express wishes, feelings, and needs. He claims that if these early words do designate object names at the same time, such function is secondary to that of expressing the emotional relation between the child and the object. It is because of this wish or affective nature of the first words that they are sentence words, and Meumann (1908) claims that their word function develops only from the sentence function through a process of limitation.

The Growth of Vocabulary

After the appearance of the first few words which are used consistently with meaning in appropriate situations, there occurs a rapid increase in vocabulary as the child acquires the raw material of language which he is to use later in various combinations to express all degrees and shades of meaning. Many of the early biographical studies began with the appearance of the first word and proceeded to list cumulatively all new words as they were first heard in the child's speech. This method has proved moderately satisfactory for studies of the earliest stages of vocabulary growth, but soon the vocabulary becomes so extensive that the lists become unwieldy and adults find it increasingly difficult to detect the new words. Most such records have been kept on precocious children, and the various authors have not employed the same methods in counting plurals, inflections of verbs and adjectives, some counting the root word only once,

and others counting all derivatives as separate words, so that comparisons of the total vocabulary counts are almost impossible to interpret correctly. Other difficulties of interpretation arise, as Dale (1931) has ably pointed out, from the facts that various writers use different lengths of observation periods and employ different criteria for considering that a child "knows" a word. Some investigators recorded only words heard in spontaneous conversation, others recorded "words understood," some kept running cumulative accounts, others recorded all words heard within a week of the child's birthday, and some excluded words which had been in active use some months before, but which appeared to have dropped out of active use according to the latest sample.

The studies of vocabulary may be grouped into several types: (1) estimates of total vocabulary at specified ages (usually of single children); (2) analyses of total vocabularies according to parts of speech; (3) analyses of total vocabularies for subject matter content; (4) analyses of the occurrence of the various parts of speech in samples of conversation; (5) analyses of the occurrences of the various parts of speech in compositions; (6) estimates of total vocabularies of groups by the use of the free association technique; (7) estimates of total vocabularies by the use of vocabulary tests; and (8) word frequency counts. The vocabulary tests have all been devised by employing different methods of sampling, which raises serious methodological problems. Some of them involve the actual eliciting of the words, whereas others involve merely pointing to pictures and thus reveal only understood vocabulary.

Summaries of the vocabulary studies of preschool children have been attempted by Tracy (1893), Doran (1907), the Whipples (1909), Waddle (1913), M. D. Horn (1926–

1927*a*), and others. Outstanding among individual vocabularies recorded are those by Deville (1890), the Gales (1906), the Whipples (1909), Boyd (1914), Bateman (1914), Nice (1915, 1917), the Brandenburgs (1916), Haggerty (1930), and Brigance (1934). Attempts at complete enumeration of vocabulary have of necessity been confined to the preschool period, and at higher ages some form of sampling has been employed in the efforts to ascertain total vocabulary.

These studies indicate that there are marked individual differences in the size of vocabulary at any age. Shirley (1933*a*, 1933*b*) reports that on the average each baby in her group had spoken 36.9 different words in the presence of the examiners by the age of two years, the range being from 6 to 126 words. These figures are undoubtedly low estimates, for the sampling secured during the periodic visits of the examiners was probably much smaller than mothers would have reported for these same children had they kept complete records. Although tabular summaries of reported vocabularies have been compiled by some, they are not presented here because of the many reasons for lack of comparability of the data from one study to another. For estimates of the probable normal vocabulary at various preschool ages the reader is referred to Table 3 from Smith (1926) in the section on vocabulary tests (p. 510).

The vocabulary appears to increase rather slowly at first, then quite rapidly throughout the preschool period, and then more slowly at least until mental maturity. It probably never stops increasing, as the individual is constantly learning the meanings of new words and learning new usages of familiar words throughout life. The age at which the rapid increase in vocabulary occurs is probably related to the age of walking in individual children, for Shirley (1933*a*, 1933*b*), Brigance (1934), and others report that there seems to be a plateau in language development during the mastery of a new motor skill, especially that of walking. Although there is enormous variation in the age of onset of both developmental phenomena, most normal children begin to walk before they talk. In many cases, however, especially among girls and among children who are more precocious in their intellectual development, talking precedes walking. In such cases there is likely to be observed a slowing-up of rate of improvement in vocabulary while the child is devoting most of his attention to mastery of the skill of walking. After such a plateau, rapid progress in vocabulary is likely to be made. (See section on relation to motor development, p. 545.) Drever (1915–1916), Brigance (1934), and others report rapid vocabulary development associated with a vacation or trip to the seashore. With the broadening of the child's experience through travel there appears a marked increase in vocabulary. (See section on effect of environment, pp. 557 ff.)

Analyses of vocabularies for the content or for purposes of listing concepts known to children at various ages are of some value at early ages, but at later ages selective factors are probably operative to such an extent that generalizations based on such data are of little value. One of the most interesting recent studies of this type is by Shirley (1938), in which verbatim records were made for 336 cases 2 to 5 years old during a play period of 30 to 45 minutes. It was found that the four most common concepts related to the mother, home, father, and siblings. The eleven most frequently used word concepts all seemed to carry an emotional charge for the children. At least half the concepts seemed to arise out of common needs of children and another 20 per cent was largely expositional. These findings are of interest when the affective nature of infants' vocalizations is recalled as well as the high frequency of interjectional speech in the earliest words. It tends to emphasize the importance of the function of language to express feelings, wants, and desires.

The study of vocabulary is fraught with methodological problems. Three basic difficulties which have contributed much to the confused state of the literature on children's vocabularies may be pointed out. The first is the difficulty of deciding on the proper criterion for *knowing* a word. Dale (1931) points out in reference to this matter that *know* is a relative term, since there are accretions to the meanings of words throughout life. He argues, therefore, that the *knowing* of a word should be defined in terms of the specific reactions one is able to make to a word. For example, is the child able to understand the word when he hears it spoken, or is he able to use it in his spontaneous speech, or is he able to read it? How many different shades of meaning does he know for the word, and in what variety of situations can he use it? Is he able to define the word, and, if so, how well can he do it? Such questions about the degree of *knowing* a word, which are carefully brought out in the study of Bear and Odbert (1941), could be multiplied almost indefinitely, but they serve to show the psychological artificiality which enters into all vocabulary tabulations.

The second basic difficulty in vocabulary measurement which has been stressed by Seashore (1933), Seashore and Eckerson (1940), and M. K. Smith (1941) involves failure to define *the word* as a unit of measurement. Seashore cites particularly in earlier estimates such as those by Kirkpatrick (1891), Brandenburg (1918), and Holley (1919) the failure to distinguish

adequately between (1) spoken, written, and recognition vocabularies; (2) between root and derivative words, which he says occur in the proportion of 1 to 3.4 words; (3) between commonest and multiple usages of words; as well as (4) differences in policy regarding inclusion of special terms such as proper nouns, technical, foreign, obsolete, and provincial terms; and (5) differences associated with various criteria of knowledge of a word. Seashore states that methods of sampling word lists from dictionaries gave very stable proportions of each type of word. Seashore and Eckerson estimated by the use of a four-choice recognition vocabulary test, considering the commonest meaning as correct, that the average college undergraduate recognized 35 per cent of the common basic words in the sample, 1 per cent of the rare basic words, and 47 per cent of the derivative words in the test which was based on a numerical sampling of the items in the Funk and Wagnalls unabridged dictionary. The total vocabulary of college undergraduates, therefore, would be estimated at 155,736 words, the range being from 112,100 to 192,575 for the group studied. Comparisons of the various criteria employed to indicate different degrees of knowledge of a word showed high intercorrelations and yielded estimates of total vocabulary for a group within a range of 8 per cent.

In the third issue basic to the methods of vocabulary studies, Williams (1932) sounds a much-needed and wholesome note of warning to the makers of vocabulary tests regarding the methods of selecting words from the dictionary. Since all vocabulary estimates at higher ages are based on prediction from small samples, it is very important that great care be exercised in the selection of the words to be used in the test. Williams points out that all available vocabulary tests have selected the test words by the page method, that is, by taking the last word on alternate pages or according to some such plan. He determined the expected frequency of children's words in the International Kindergarten Union (1928) list of 2500 words and found that the actual number of words of high frequency selected by the page method greatly exceeded the expected proportion. He also found that the larger the dictionary used in the selection, the greater was the likelihood of the selection of these very common words for vocabulary tests. He attributes this phenomenon to differences in spatial allotment which favor the words in most common use and those which have the greatest richness of meaning. Naturally such words receive relatively more space in large than in small dictionaries. Williams recommends that the selection of test words in future vocabulary tests be based on the actual counting of ordinal position in the dictionary, taking every fifth or every tenth or every hundredth word. This appears to be a fundamental criticism of all previous vocabulary tests with the exception of the one just mentioned by Seashore· and Eckerson (1940). Their change in sampling method, as well as their use of an unabridged dictionary, undoubtedly accounts for the unusually high, but probably more nearly correct, estimates.

The Seashore-Eckerson vocabulary test published by the authors at Northwestern University is available for Grades 1 through 12. Norms have been established on 867 children by M. K. Smith (1941), who devised special adaptations of procedure for the lower grades. The odd-even reliability for this test was above .90 for Grades 5 to 9, inclusive, but was less satisfactory at higher and lower ranges. For Grade 1 the average number of words in the total vocabulary was 23,700 with a range of 6000 to 48,800 and for Grade 12 it was 80,300 with a range of 36,700 to 136,500.

Although the estimates of total vocabulary obtained by Seashore and Eckerson (1940) and by M. K. Smith (1941) are much larger than those previously noted in the literature, Hartmann (1941) in his critique of the common methods of estimating vocabulary size considers that even these may be gross underestimates by as much as 100,000 words. He used four lists of varying lengths from a single dictionary and found that all members of a group of normal school graduates had vocabularies in excess of 200,000 words.

Bear and Odbert (1941) studied the degree of insight which pupils have into their knowledge of words and found the often-used method of checking known or unknown words very unsatisfactory as pupils identified as unknown fewer than half the words they missed on a vocabulary test. Those having the poorest vocabularies had least insight into their own limitations.

Another vocabulary test for Grades 3 through 8 was devised by Gansl (1939). It consists of 100 items of the sentence type of multiple-choice questions. It has a reliability of .94 for 190 eleven-year-old boys, and norms are based on 3306 children. Items were carefully selected from among those of 22 current vocabulary tests; frequencies were determined on the basis of the Thorndike Word List (1931–32) and the order of difficulty was empirically determined. The author seriously questions "the naïve acceptance in many former tests of the frequency ratings as measures of difficulty," which she found to be wholly unwarranted. The test yields raw and derived, or "D scores," but no estimates of total vocabulary. The curve for vocabulary growth from age 8 to 13 was approximately a straight line with a tendency toward negative acceleration from 12 to 13 years.

Parts of Speech. In the analyses according to the various parts of speech three approaches have been used which yield quite different results. The first, which is suitable only for the vocabularies of very young children where there may be some reasonable expectation of approximating the total vocabulary, is to calculate the proportions of the total number of words in the entire vocabulary, however defined, which belong in each category of the various parts of speech. This method always yields a very large proportion of nouns merely because nouns are predominant in the language and hence are most numerous in any dictionary. The samples taken for very young children also yield an unusually high proportion of words usually classified as nouns, because during the early acquisition of vocabulary the child goes through the naming stage in which, after making the important discovery that everything has a name, he asks many "what questions" in order to learn the names of the various objects in his environment. As has been pointed out above, however, merely because a word used by a child has the form of a noun does not mean that it always functions as a noun in the child's usage, for he may use what appears to be a noun with a variety of meanings, and it may actually function as a verb, an adjective, an interjection, or even as a whole sentence in itself. Thus it is very difficult, if not impossible, to arrive at a satisfactory answer as to the relative proportions of the various parts of speech in a child's total vocabulary, first because of the difficulty of determining when a child *knows* a word, second because of the difficulty of determining the total vocabulary, third because of difficulty in classifying the word according to the part of speech it actually functions as in the child's usage, and fourth because of the difficulty of classifying the same word form according to different functions.

In the second type of study of the parts of speech no attempt is made to determine total vocabulary, but a fairly long sample of running conversation (or sometimes compositions or letters) is taken, and an attempt is made to determine the relative importance of the various parts of speech in the child's running language. After the child has passed beyond the naming stage and has ceased his early use of interjections, about the end of the second year, and when he has begun to combine words into sentences, the relative proportions of the various parts of speech are determined to a large extent by the limitations imposed upon the speaker by the conventional forms of sentence structure. Thus, whereas a child may have a high percentage of nouns in his "total vocabulary," roughly 60 per cent perhaps, at two years of age in the first type of analysis, in this second type of analysis he will probably have only about 20 per cent of the words in his running conversation consisting of nouns. This does not mean that he does not have the variety of nouns in his vocabulary, but merely that because he is speaking in sentences he does not need to draw heavily on his store of known nouns, since each simple sentence requires only one noun for the subject. In order to say anything about that noun, however, it is necessary for him to use a verb, and perhaps an adjective or an adverb; at least for every clause involving one noun he is forced by the rules of sentence structure (which he comes to know by the example of others) to use other parts of speech with it. It is also obvious that since such figures are relative and are expressed in percentages any change or trend in one part of speech will upset the balance of the parts of speech, and there may be an apparent trend in some part of speech which is really only an artifact and a reflection of the tendency already noted in another part of speech. Which trend is more significant psychologically is usually a matter for interpretation.

The third type of analysis according to parts of speech is that which is based, not on the total number of words in a given sample of running conversation or writing, but upon the total number of different words appearing in such a sample. A comparison of this method with that of the previous one immediately reveals the fact that the great bulk of language is made up of a small number of frequently recurring words, and that there is relatively infrequent use of the great majority of words in the total vocabulary. Zyve (1927), who recorded the conversations of third-grade children during a fifteen-minute story period for about three months, used both these methods of tabulation and obtained strikingly different results with the two procedures. Nouns constituted 51 per cent of the number of different words used and only 15 per cent of the total number of words used. Verbs represented 22 per cent of the number of different words used, and they amounted to 27 per cent of the total number of words used. Pronouns also show a striking difference when tabulated by the two methods, as they equaled only 1.5 per cent of the number of different words and 17.2 per cent of the total number of words used. Like the nouns, the adjectives showed a decrease, but the adverbs, prepositions, and conjunctions all showed relative increases when considered according to the total number of words used. The tabulations for the articles bring out very clearly the striking artificiality of these methods. There are only three different articles in the English language and all three of them are used by very young children, yet they represent only one-tenth of 1 per cent of the number of different words. These same three words recur so frequently in conversation, however, that

in Zyve's (1927) data they constituted 7 per cent of the total number of words used.

Uhrbrock (1936) reports interesting data on this point based on a sample of 24,000 words dictated into an Ediphone by a little girl during the six weeks immediately preceding her fifth birthday. He found that three-quarters of the dictated material involved the use of 141 different common words, each of which occurred 20 times or more in his sample. Forty per cent of the total number of different words (750) occurred only once. Separate samples of 1000 running words of dictation never contained fewer than 258 different words or more than 331, with the average number of different words at 290 per thousand words dictated. Some idea of the difficulty of determining total vocabulary for a five-year-old may be seen in Uhrbrock's report that 52 new words, not previously encountered in the data, appeared in the twenty-fourth thousand.

Vocabulary Tests for Preschool Children. The first serious attempt to devise a vocabulary test for young children was made by M. E. Smith in 1926. In this test 203 words were selected by a systematic sampling of the Thorndike (1921) 10,000-word list which had been checked against the vocabularies of a large number of children in order to eliminate words which these young children were almost certain not to know. Most of the words were elicited from the child by means of pictures although no standard pictures are available, the author merely providing verbal descriptions of the pictures which had been culled from magazine advertisements and similar sources. It is quite likely that the materials gathered by other investigators in attempting to elicit the words of the Smith battery differ widely from those used in the normative work. If the child failed to say the word in response to the appropriate pictures and questions, the examiner then used another type of question in which the test word was used in such a way that the child could not answer the question unless he understood the word involved. Credit for "knowledge" of the word was allowed if the child responded by using the word in the first type of test or if he answered the second type of question correctly. Thus the score on the test was made up of a composite of items, on some of which credit was allowed for recalling and speaking the word in the test situation, and on others of which credit was allowed for mere indirect evidence that he "understood" the word. On quite a large number of the test words no second form of the question is provided, however, and the word actually must be said by the child before credit is allowed. Smith reported a split-half reliability of .97 for a two-year range of talent with this test. On the basis of the fact that actual known total vocabularies were predicted fairly accurately by multiplying the total score by an appropriate multiplier, she argues that total vocabulary can be estimated with this test.

Williams and McFarland (1937) point out, however, that such estimates are really only fairly accurate predictions of the total number of known words in the Thorndike list of 10,000 words rather than accurate estimates of total vocabulary. M. E. Smith (1926) reports correlations of +.88 and +.84 with Descoeudres' (1921) tests of language and Cobb's (1922) rearrangement of the Stanford-Binet vocabulary test as evidence of validity of the test. The figures given by Smith as the total vocabularies of 278 preschool children ranging in age from 8 months to 6 years are widely quoted as the best available material on vocabulary estimates at these ages, although it must be remembered in interpreting them that they are subject to the above-mentioned limitations. (See Table 3.)

TABLE 3

INCREASE IN SIZE OF VOCABULARY IN RELATION TO AGE

(From M. E. Smith, 1926)

Age		N	Average IQ	Number of Words	Gain
Years	Months				
	8	13		0	
	10	17		1	1
1	0	52		3	2
1	3	19		19	16
1	6	14		22	3
1	9	14		118	96
2	0	25		272	154
2	6	14		446	174
3	0	20	109	896	450
3	6	26	106	1222	326
4	0	26	109	1540	318
4	6	32	109	1870	330
5	0	20	108	2072	202
5	6	27	110	2289	217
6	0	9	108	2562	273

Another approach to the measurement of vocabulary was made by Van Alstyne (1929). This test, which takes fifteen minutes to administer, is entirely a picture-vocabulary test involving a series of pen-and-ink drawings with four items to a card. It is limited to three-year-olds with regard to norms, and if children of other age levels are tested with it interpretations have to be made in terms of the three-year-old norm. The child is expected only to point to the one object out of four on each card which is named by the examiner and is not expected to speak the words being tested for. The test is thus limited to "understood" vocabulary. The reliability reported by the author is +.87 for split halves after using the Spearman-Brown prophecy formula.

Another attempt to develop a vocabulary test is the above-mentioned revision of the M. E. Smith test by Williams and McFarland (1937). These authors have overcome a number of defects in the earlier scale. The materials are now available in standard form; two equivalent forms of the test have been made consisting of only

42 words each. This considerably reduces the administration time, yet a satisfactory reliability of +.96 is reported by the authors between Forms I and II for 359 cases 2 to 6 years of age. The procedure has been modified to make for more rigid control of the recall method, and the test is given first as a recall test and later as a test of verbal recognition. This separates the administration of the two methods for the same word by the length of the test. Results are reported for 242 children who attended the Iowa preschool laboratories and for 64 orphanage children, but, since the authors emphasize that the original and also the revised tests are only relative measures and do not yield absolute figures on total vocabulary, no figures comparable with Smith's data are provided. The two groups tested could hardly be considered adequate normative samples since one group had a mean IQ of 124 and the other of 84. Grigsby (1932), using apparently a prepublication edition of Williams's revision of the M. E. Smith Vocabulary Test on 83 subjects between the ages of 2 years 8 months, and 6 years 4 months, reports the mean vocabulary at 3 years as 1507; at 4 years, 2148, at 5 years, 2527, and at 6 years, 3054. These estimates are somewhat higher than those reported by M. E. Smith (1926).

Jersild and Ritzman (1938), using extensive samples of the conversation of a group of very superior preschool children, report that there is a tendency for younger children to use a higher proportion of different words in relation to the total number of words spoken. Roughly every fourth word in their data was a "new" word, and one three-hour period yielded only about half as many different words as three periods of three hours each.

Word-Count Studies. Closely related to the general problem of vocabulary are the various word-count studies and frequency lists of words which have been published for various purposes. The most widely used is Thorndike's *Teacher's Word Book,* which as originally published in 1921 listed the 10,000 words most frequently encountered in extensive samplings of adult writing, including large samplings of children's literature. This list was revised and extended in 1931–1932 to include 20,000 words. The tables indicate in which thousand the words fall, and, in the first 5000 words, whether they fall in the first 500 or the second 500 of each 1000. It must be remembered in using this list for research purposes that these words were not actually used by children, that it does not include derivatives, and that no separate entries are made for homographs like *bear,* the animal, and *bear,* to carry. Word forms have been treated as units without any reference to differences in meaning.

Recently, however, there has appeared a very valuable list by Eaton (1940), the *Semantic Frequency List for English, French, German, and Spanish.* It is based on the first 6000 concepts, rather than word forms, in frequency lists which have been compiled for the four languages separately and then combined. It was issued by the Committee on Modern Languages of the American Council on Education.

Other word lists which have been devised especially as spelling lists include the lists of Ayres (1915), E. Horn (1925), and many others. Of greatest interest to the child psychologist, however, are the list of M. D. Horn (1926–1927a), sometimes spoken of as the International Kindergarten Union List, which is based on words actually used orally by children before entering the first grade, and Fitzgerald's (1934b) list, based on the letters written by elementary school children in life outside of school. Perhaps the most useful single source book on frequency word lists is Buckingham and Dolch's *A Combined*

Word List (1936), which presents data showing the degree of overlapping and disagreement on the frequencies of words in seven different word-count studies.

Zipf (1935) in his *Psycho-Biology of Language* points out that the words which occur most frequently are quite short and that longer words are much more rare. After elaborate word-count investigations he proposes a theory of linguistic change based on economy of time and effort. He has subsequently (1942) analyzed the records from Fisher's (1934) study as well as Uhrbrock's (1936) data and finds that his theory is substantiated in the oral language of young children. Thorndike (1937, 1938), while agreeing in general with the correctness of Zipf's (1935) observations, questions some of his interpretations. G. W. Allport (1936) in his review criticizes the saving of time and effort theory and feels that the more universal process of cue reduction in learning is more important. He considers hearer needs rather than ease for the speaker to be the more important factor. Although he is not satisfied with Zipf's interpretations, he admits that psychologists have nothing better to offer as interpretations of the mental counterparts of linguistic change.

Of the studies which employ the free association technique those by Dolch (1927) and by Prescott (1929) are typical. Elementary school children were asked to write all the words they could think of in 15 minutes. The former study showed an increase in the average number of words given from 35 at 7 years to 157 at 13 years, whereas the latter showed a steady increase from 73 words for the average second-grade child to 191 in the eighth grade. Shambaugh and Shambaugh (1928) used 400 stimulus words with 50 children in each grade from the fourth to the eighth inclusive. The stimulus words were chosen because of their close association with the daily lives of the children. The words were arranged in lists of 50, and no group of children responded to more than one list of words. In all, 1851 children participated and were asked to write in four or five words which they associated most closely with the stimulus word. The total number of words given ranged from 32,905 in Grade 4 to 46,505 in Grade 8, a total of 230,631 being given in all grades. The number of different words listed ranged from 2102 in Grade 4 to 3017 in Grade 7, there being a marked drop in the eighth grade probably due to selective factors. In all grades a total of 4515 different words was given, 1309 of which were common to all grades. Interesting comparisons are made with the Thorndike and Horn lists. For example, 51 per cent of these 1309 words common in the free associations of all grades from fourth to eighth were not found in Horn's first 3000 words. Shambaugh and Shambaugh (1928) also found 98 words which occurred in their data with a frequency of 500 or more, 61 of which did not appear in Thorndike's first 500 words, 15 of which were not in his first 1000, and it was necessary to go into the third 1000 of the words most frequently used in the Thorndike 10,000 word list to include all 98 words which occurred with a frequency of 500 or more in the free association data. This study is cited in detail to illustrate the elusive nature of frequency word lists and the difficulty of making valid comparisons among them. Tinker, Hackner, and Wesley (1940) found that those who have higher vocabularies also have more rapid word associations. There was a correlation of +.83 between the quality of the associative response and vocabulary score.

Comprehensibility of Speech

As is well known, adults usually have considerable difficulty in understanding the speech of young children. The degree of comprehensibility of the speech varies with a number of factors, especially with the child's accuracy of sound reproduction, his voice quality, the hearer's familiarity with children in general, and with the individual child in particular, as well as with the stage of the child's linguistic development, and with the amount of baby-talk used by adults in the child's environment, which often makes for perseveration of infantile speech habits. This means either that there are varying amounts of children's speech which go unrecorded in the studies which employ longhand or stenographic accounts of oral language, or that varying percentages of the flow of language are subject to separate treatment, owing to incomprehensibility. On the other hand, in spite of very poor pronunciation, there is much in children's speech that can be understood and interpreted correctly by adults who are familiar with children.

Since most of the major investigations of children's spoken language have been made by longhand recording, the degree of comprehensibility, as well as the speed and accuracy of the recorder, is a vital problem in methodology. Day (1932) obtained quite high coefficients of correlation for most indices among the records made by three examiners who noted children's speech simultaneously. These satisfactory degrees of agreement were obtained for indices based on samples of twenty-five responses even though the recorders did not always record the identical responses. Errors, which were chiefly those of omission, did not appear to be constant, and did not appreciably affect the measures used which were based on the total sample. Betts (1934), however, using the strict criterion of an electrical record of grade school children's oral compositions compared the relative completeness and accuracy of four types of recording: that of court reporters, longhand recorders, shorthand recorders, and phoneticians. Although the court reporters made the most complete records, they obtained only 80.4 per cent of the material. This was secured with an accuracy of 84.9 per cent. Shorthand reporters had the next most complete records with only 53.3 per cent of the material, and their accuracy was 82.9. Longhand recording yielded only 32 per cent of the flow of speech, but the accuracy remained high (83.9 per cent). Phoneticians had the most incomplete records, but the most accurate, as they noted only 14.9 per cent of the material with an accuracy of 87.6 per cent. The incompleteness of all these types of record is probably very significant from the standpoint of methodology. It is all the more surprising when it is remembered that the oral compositions were by fourth-, fifth-, and sixth-grade children whose speech undoubtedly was much more comprehensible than that of preschool children, and the compositions had common content, being based on a short motion picture which the children had seen in school. The greater length of the sentences found at this age level, however, probably operated to reduce the completeness and accuracy in comparison with records on younger children.

Some investigators of children's language development do not mention the incomprehensibility of children's speech, yet from the percentage of incomprehensible responses reported by other authors at the same ages it seems unlikely that any investigators could have understood 100 per cent of what the children said. Such studies should probably be interpreted as having recorded only comprehensible responses. Shirley (1933a, p. 293) states that "incomprehensible vocalization attained its highest frequency in the period between 12 and 18 months; after 82 weeks it reached a low level and thereafter (up to two years of age) varied around 10 per cent." McCarthy (1930) found 26 per cent of the responses of her 18-month-old children were comprehensible, two-thirds of the responses of the 2-year-olds, 89 per cent at 2½, 93 per cent at 3 years, and practically all responses from 3½ on. At most age levels the speech of the boys was much less readily understood than that of the girls. Day (1932) found about 35 per cent of the responses of the 2-year-old twins incomprehensible and only about 7 per cent of the responses of the 3-year-olds. Fisher (1934) reports that 8.1 per cent of the responses of her superior group ranging in age from 18 to 60 months consisted of "non-verbal speech." Young (1941) reports her data in terms of the mean number of comprehensible words spoken per 10-minute period. The results are in close agreement with Smith's (1926) figures, showing increases from about 20 words at 30 months to about 70 at 54 months. Sex differences here were strikingly in favor of girls.

Wellman, Case, Mengert, and Bradbury (1931) report a correlation of +.80 between age and the ability to give sounds correctly in their very detailed examination of 204 preschool children. They report that at 2 years approximately 32 per cent of the total number of sounds were given correctly, at 3 years 63 per cent, at 4 years 77 per cent, at 5 years 88 per cent, and at 6 years 89 per cent. The most marked increases in accuracy of articulation of all types of sounds appeared between 2 and 3 years of age. Davis (1937a) used a crude seven-point rating scale in conjunction with her very extensive investigation and reports that 75.7 per cent of the 5½-year-olds, 90.9

per cent of the 6½-year-olds, and 90.4 per cent of the 9½-year-olds had "perfect articulation" in a representative group of 173 singletons with siblings.

Studies of the incidence of speech defectives vary greatly in that they all employ different criteria of what constitutes a speech defect. Some are concerned only with articulatory difficulties exclusive of stuttering; others emphasize cases of stuttering to the exclusion of other problems. The methods of determining whether or not the child has a speech defect vary greatly, and much depends upon teachers' sensitiveness to such matters. Some teachers are much more aware of minor speech difficulties than others, and this results in percentages found varying from about 2 to 25 per cent. Many of the studies report only the total number of speech defectives located without giving the size of the population from which they were drawn.

The whole area of speech defects is such an important, extensive, and highly specialized field that no attempt can be made within the compass of this chapter to treat it adequately. However, one very important problem which arises from the point of view of the child psychologist is determining when a child is or is not a speech defective, and when the aid of a speech therapist is indicated. As has already been shown, the vast majority of children go through a period of baby-talk. For many children this is relatively brief and the articulatory imperfections are comparatively unimportant. Such children usually develop correct speech habits quite early. On the other hand, there are a fairly large number of children who have quite marked articulatory defects in their baby-talk which for various reasons persist for some time, even well into the elementary school period. It is an important practical problem for the clinician to be able to distinguish between the children who are likely to outgrow their infantile speech patterns at a reasonably normal age and those who need speech training from a specialist in order to overcome their articulatory defects. Too early introduction of formal speech training of young children who may outgrow their infantile speech normally without help, or whose speech infantilisms are only a symptom of general emotional immaturity, may result only in the child's becoming self-conscious and refusing to talk. With such children, practice in talking may be more essential than drill on correctness of articulation for a time. Gain in self-confidence, increased independence, and social contacts may often do much to improve the speech difficulties.

However, for the few children whose speech is so defective that they are not likely to overcome the difficulty without special training, it is desirable to have a measuring instrument to evaluate and diagnose the seriousness of the articulatory defect. A study by Sommer (1932) indicated that group training was quite effective with nursery school and kindergarten children. Her experimental group which received training improved 57 per cent, as compared with the control group which improved 28 per cent without training. This shows that, whereas in a group of children certain improvement occurs with maturation alone, speech training such as Sommer gave brings about twice as much improvement.

Springob (1930) selected as speech defectives children whose speech errors as detected with the Blanton-Stinchfield Articulation Test were 20 or more after the age of 4 years. A plot of the number of speech errors against age shows a distinct dropping-out of errors in his 5- and 6-year groups with a few exceptional cases persisting in a large number of errors at these ages, which apparently are the cases in need of therapy. Town (1921), after analyzing the speech of 42 children for speech defects, states:

It was found impossible on the basis of the examination results to divide the class into two groups, one of which contained children with perfect speech, and the other of which contained children with defective speech. In speech, as in other abilities, the transition is so gradual from normal performance to defective performance that it does not permit of an absolute dividing line.

However, 10 of her 42 cases were judged to have sufficiently defective speech to need corrective work.

Thus far no satisfactory test for the measurement of articulatory defects in young children has been devised and standardized. The most elaborate attempt to test for all the phonetic elements in all positions is by Wellman, Case, Mengert, and Bradbury (1931). This test, however, is extremely long, involving 583 sounds to be tested for by eliciting 352 test words with a variety of unstandardized pictures and questions. Only 75 per cent of the test words occur in the first 2000 words of the Thorndike Word List, and 7 per cent of them are not listed in Horn's 2500 words most commonly used by children of kindergarten age. Many of the sounds tested for are of rare occurrence in the language and hence are relatively unimportant as far as a child's articulation is concerned. Similar criticisms can be made of the West Test (1933), the Detroit Test by Stoddard and Languin (1934), the Voegelin-Adams Test (1934), and to a lesser extent the Blanton-Stinchfield Test (1926). In general they are all very long, test for rarely occurring sounds, and test for them with words which involve too much of a vocabulary burden for young children. The best one available so far seems to be the Blanton-Stinchfield, which tests for 100 sounds with 100 test words with standardized pictures, but it also places too much of a vocabulary burden upon the child of preschool or kindergarten age.

Poole (1934) reports having tested 140 preschool children for the ability to articulate 23 consonant sounds in words by evoking isolated words as responses to objects and pictures and questions, but she does not describe the test itself or supply the materials and questions. She reports that the sounds that the child uses most often in his everyday conversation are the ones in which he shows the greatest ability in articulation. Slightly over 64 per cent of the sounds that appear most often in the words of these children's conversations are articulated correctly before the age of 4½ years. About 35 per cent of the sounds used least often do not develop correctly in articulation until after 5½ years. The median child at 6½ years articulated all 23 consonant sounds correctly. Poole states that a normally developing child should be able to articulate all sounds at least by 8 years, and that failure to make notable progress in articulation at 6 years indicates that a speech therapist should be consulted. In another briefly reported study by Templin and Steer (1939) an apparently good articulation test was used, although the vocabulary load cannot be determined since the test words are not published. It tests for 84 sounds with one sound per word being tested. The test takes 7 to 40 minutes to administer and has been given to 93 children ranging in age from 1 year 11 months to 4 years 9 months.

As part of the development of their language achievement scale, Little and Williams (1937) modified the speech sounds test originally devised by Wellman and her collaborators (1931). They eliminated the testing for all sounds in medial positions and included only those sounds which occur in the first 1000 of the International Kindergarten Union List. The revised list of speech sounds was divided into seven steps according to level of difficulty as established by Wellman et al., and a child was given one point for any three sounds given correctly at each of the seven levels of difficulty, with seven the maximum score. They also devised a measure of intelligibility of children's speech by securing a sample of 50 syllables which Williams had previously found had a predicted reliability of +.94. The child is assigned a score of two points for each syllable pronounced correctly, one point for each syllable mispronounced but intelligible to an observer not familiar with the child's idiosyncrasies, and zero for syllables not intelligible to an observer who was not accustomed to the child's speech. Data are presented on 285 cases in which rapid improvement in speech sounds and intelligibility scores was found up to the forty-eighth month, at which time there occurred a leveling-off of the curve for both these functions when the children had attained almost maximum scores.

McCarthy (1935) made a preliminary report on the development of an articulation test for young children which is designed to overcome many of the difficulties of previously published tests. It is based on the frequency of English speech sounds as they occur in the count of 100,000 words by G. Dewey (1923) employing the Fonetic Key Alfabet approved by the Simplified Spelling Board. It is designed to elicit 46 test words which include 95 test sounds accounting for 94 per cent of the total number of sounds in the Dewey sample of adult language and for 90 per cent of the sounds occurring in the Horn list. All the test words are taken from the first 1000 words used by kindergarten children, and hence should not place a serious vocabulary burden on children of 3 and 4 years.

There is considerable difference of opinion among workers in this field as to whether articulation tests should employ the method of eliciting the words in the child's spontaneous manner by showing pictures or asking appropriate questions, or whether the examiner may pronounce the test words for the child in an effort to elicit them. Most writers have scrupulously avoided saying the word for the child, fearing that immediate imitation might occur which would fail to reveal habitual faulty sounds. Morrison (1914–1915) and others, however, have reported that when the children are asked to repeat sounds as best they can in imitation of the examiner, practically none of the sounds are pronounced correctly simply from hearing the correct form. It appears, then, that if the child habitually mispronounces a sound he will give only his own approximation to the sound in the test situation, even though he has just heard the correct form. Certain forms of careless speech might be eliminated in such a method, but if the child is actually unable to pronounce the correct forms or habitually fails to use them, the imitative method should reveal such defects just as readily as the eliciting of the child's natural way of saying the word independent of the immediate example of the examiner.

Quantitative Measures

There are two types of studies which undertake to determine only quantity and rate of speech output without reference to the quality of the expression or to any details of the complexities of sentence structure. These studies are limited in scope, but have the advantage of objectivity. Studies of the amount and rate of talking are involved here as well as studies presenting data on length of response. The latter, however, are usually more elaborate studies in which length of response is only one aspect of linguistic development measured.

Amount and Rate of Talking. Gesell (1925) reported on the results of a complete 24-hour record of the vocal activities of a 6-month-old child who spent 3 per cent of its waking time in vocal activity. He says: "There were 104 separate moments of vocalization during the day, varying in complexity from one-letter sounds to 32 repeated syllables; 75 sounds and combinations of sounds were used." The Brandenburgs (1919) reported on a child who at the age of 40 months used 11,623 words in a day or an average of 950 words per hour; by 52 months of age this same child used 14,930 words in a day. They compare these data with a study by Nice (1917) in which a child of 63 months used 10,500 words in a day and with one by Bell (1903) in which a child at 3½ years used 15,230 and another at 4 years used 14,996 words in one day. These are undoubtedly reports on children who were very precocious in linguistic development and who were undoubtedly encouraged to converse freely at home, but they serve to show the important rôle that conversation can play in the life of a young child.

There are very marked individual differences in loquacity, for McCarthy (1930) found that among 140 children observed under similar conditions the time required to record 50 consecutive responses varied from 7 to 50 minutes. Fisher (1934), who recorded the responses of a group of 72 children with a mean IQ of 132.6 for 9 hours of free play, found that the average number of remarks per hour ranged from 23 to 192, with a mean at 92. There was a correlation of +.56 between chronological age and the number of remarks per hour. M. E. Smith (1926) recorded children's responses for one hour during free play. This measure showed a steady increase from a mean of 78 words per hour for 2-year-olds to 400 words per hour at 4 years of age, with practically no change from 4 to 5 years. She states:

> The average total number of words used to the hour shows a regular increase with age; but the variability is too great from child to child, for it to be an adequate criterion. In fact, this number ranges from 0 to 1100 words for the entire group studied. The length of sentence, that is, the number of words to the sentence, seems to be a much better measure (p. 17).

A study by Olson and Koetzle (1936) presents an interesting technique for securing a quantitative statement of the amount and rate of talking. The groups they used were small and highly selected so the study is of value chiefly from the methodological standpoint. It involves the use of a mechanical hand tally and a time-out stop-watch in a modification of Olson's (1929) short sample technique of observation. Records were made for two 1-minute periods per day for 15 days. The examiner actuated the counter for each word heard and started and stopped the stop-watch as the child talked until a whole minute of continuous talking had elapsed. Measures of rate of talking were made in similar fashion, using 6 samples of 30 seconds each distributed over 6 weeks. Observers checked the reliability of the method against reading aloud and found a correlation of +.99 between the number of words recorded and the actual number of words in the passages read from a book. The mean error was 1.4 words in 12 samples of 144 words each and the errors were in the direction of omission. The reliability of the amount records as measured by comparison of odd and even observations was +.93 after application of the Spearman-Brown prophecy formula. Rate

samples were quite unreliable, but the authors believe that the reliability could be made satisfactory by increasing the number and length of the observation samples. It was found that the child who talked most talked seven times as much as the child who talked least, and that the most rapid talker spoke 1.4 times as fast as the slowest. Amount scores correlated +.40 in the nursery school and +.73 in the kindergarten with teachers' ratings of the quantity of the child's verbal output as measured on a five-point graphic rating scale. Amount scores showed a correlation of only +.14 and rate scores one of only +.02 with IQ on the Kuhlmann-Binet. The two types of scores correlate only +.13 with each other.

Jersild and Ritzman (1938) reanalyzed the same data used by Fisher (1934) with the addition of 16 more cases. They state that the increase in sheer quantity of speech is perhaps the most obvious indication of the rapid development of language in the early years of childhood. They also note a decelerating rate of increase around 4 to 5 years. The average half-yearly increase in amount of talking between 24 and 48 months for these bright children was 66 per cent.

One of the major types of analysis to which Young (1941) subjected her data was the number of comprehensible words spoken per 10-minute period. This measure showed a steady increase up to 60 months of age and reflected all the group differences, such as difference in sex, socioeconomic status, and setting, which were revealed in the other types of analysis in her study.

Length of Response. As noted earlier, the child uses his first words as whole sentences, but with the increase in vocabulary which soon follows he begins to combine the words in his vocabulary in varying degrees of complexity. One of the most objective and easily determined indices of the increase in complexity of sentence structure is the increase in length of response which has been reported by most serious investigators of children's language. A number of the studies on speech development in preschool children have employed similar methods and hence have yielded fairly comparable results, which are shown in Table 4. In general this table reveals quite striking agreement among a variety of workers, each employing a different group of subjects and slightly varying methods. Most of the discrepancies which appear can be accounted for in terms of known selective factors or by the methods of recording and analysis.

The data reported by McCarthy (1930) and those on Davis's (1937a) singletons are the most nearly representative and most nearly comparable groups, since they were selected so as to be representative of the population on the basis of paternal occupation. Fisher's (1934) group, being a gifted group intellectually, naturally yields much higher mean length of response at all ages. Day (1932) found that her twins who were selected by the same criteria as were used in the McCarthy study were seriously retarded in this aspect of language development, and Howard (1934) found a group of five-year-old triplets also seriously retarded in language development. In this connection it is interesting to note that the reports available on the language development of the quintuplets reveal that they are more seriously retarded in language development than twins and perhaps more so than triplets. It is indeed unfortunate that the data were not recorded and reported in such a manner as to make the results on the quintuplets directly comparable with this accumulated body of knowledge. (See section on age of associates, p. 560.)

The data from the McCarthy (1930),

Day (1932), Shirley (1933a), and E. A. Davis (1937a) studies, as well as the A (adult) data from the M. E. Smith studies (1935a, 1939), were taken when the child was alone with the examiner in most cases, except where a member of the family occasionally entered the room when data were being recorded in the home situation. The data from the Smith (1926) study, the Fisher (1934) study, the C (child) data from the M. E. Smith (1935a) study, and the Young (1941) study were all taken while the children were engaged in play with other children in free play situations in nursery schools. As may be seen by a comparison of the A and C situations (Smith, 1935a), children appeared to use somewhat longer sentences when alone with an adult than when engaged in conversation with other children, but since different numbers of cases were used in the two groups the comparison is obscured. The data reported by Shirley (1933a) are really longitudinal and represent the same measures taken on the same group of children at successive ages. All the other studies are of the cross-sectional type. In the E. A. Davis (1937a) twin group quite a number of the cases at 5½ and 6½ are the same cases used at an earlier age by Day (1932), although the exact amount of overlap is not specified. In some of M. E. Smith's studies the same children have contributed records at various ages, but it is difficult if not impossible to determine the number of overlapping cases from age to age. In Fisher's (1934) data 10 of her 72 records were obtained by having two records on the same cases about one year apart, the four-year-olds having also been measured as three-year-olds.

In M. E. Smith's (1926) study data were based on one-hour conversations in the free play situation. In Fisher's (1934) study the data represent 9 hours of recording of spontaneous conversation during free play

TABLE 4

MEAN LENGTH OF SENTENCE IN SPOKEN LANGUAGE AS SHOWN IN TEN INVESTIGATIONS

Author and Type of Study	Date	Group	N	1½	2	2½	3	3½	4	4½	5	5½	6	6½	9½
M. E. Smith * One-hour conversations in play situation. Miscellaneous cases. Not discrete age groups.	1926	Boys	64		1.3	2.2	3.3	4.4	4.1	4.8	4.7				
		Girls	60		2.2	2.4	3.5	3.8	4.4	4.7	4.6				
		All	124		1.8	2.2	3.4	4.3	4.2	4.7	4.6				
McCarthy Representative group. Fifty responses with adult.	1930	Boys	67	1.0	1.4	3.2	3.1	4.2	4.3	4.6					
		Girls	73	1.3	2.1	3.1	3.8	4.4	4.4	4.7					
		All	140	1.2	1.8	3.1	3.4	4.3	4.4	4.6					
Day Representative group of twins. Fifty responses with adult.	1932	Boys	79		1.3		2.5		3.0		2.9				
		Girls	81		1.7		2.5		3.0		3.5				
		All	160		1.5		2.5		3.0		3.2				
Shirley Fifty responses with adult. Longitudinal infant study.	1933	All	23		1.7	2.7	4.2	4.5							
Fisher Gifted group. Three 3-hour samples in play situation.	1934	Boys	35	3.4	4.7	3.4	5.0	8.4	6.9	10.1					
		Girls	37	3.9	4.8	5.3	6.3	5.6	7.6	8.3					
		All	72	3.7	4.8	4.7	5.6	6.9	7.2	9.5					
Howard † Triplets.	1934	All									3.0				

M. E. Smith ‡ — Miscellaneous cases. Overlapping in child-child and adult-child situations. (1935a)

E. A. Davis — Representative groups. Fifty responses with an adult. (1937a)

M. E. Smith — Bilingual groups in Hawaii. Fifty responses in adult situation. (1939)

Young — Regular nursery school and relief nursery school cases. Large samples. Four situations. (1941)

Study	Group	N	1	2	3	4	5	6	7	8	9	10	11
1935a	All	305	1.2	1.8	2.5	3.5	4.3	4.6	4.9	5.0	5.1	4.7	6.0
	Boys	153	1.2	1.5	2.4	3.3	4.3	4.4	5.0	4.9	5.4	5.4	7.0
	Girls	152	1.3	2.0	2.6	3.8	4.2	4.7	4.9	5.0	4.7	5.0	6.5
	All w. adult	198	1.3	2.1	2.8	3.6	4.8	5.1	5.6	6.1	5.7		
	All w. child	107	1.1	1.6	2.4	3.4	4.0	4.3	4.6	4.6	4.8		
1937a	Singletons Boys	86									4.4	4.7	6.3
	Singletons Girls	87									4.4	5.4	6.1
	Singletons All	173									4.4	5.0	6.2
	Twins Boys	83									4.5	5.5	7.4
	Twins Girls	83									4.4	5.3	7.2
	Twins All	166									4.4	5.4	7.3
	Only Boys	49									4.7	5.1	
	Only Girls	48									5.6	5.9	
	All	97									5.1	5.4	
1939	All	1000		1.9		3.0		3.4			3.6	3.7	
1941	Relief boys	20				2.8	3.0	3.9	4.2	4.3	4.5		
	Relief girls	17				3.1	3.7	4.3	4.4	4.6	5.0		
	Regular boys	20				3.3	3.6	4.4	4.9	5.0	5.2		
	Regular girls	17				3.4	4.1	4.8	5.1	5.4	5.9		
	All boys	37				3.1	3.3	4.2	4.6	4.7	4.9		
	All girls	37				3.3	3.9	4.6	4.8	5.0	5.5		

* Data from M. E. Smith's 1926 study have been recomputed from raw data presented in the appendix because of discrepancies between her Tables I and XII. Actually based on 124 records from only 88 children.

† As reported by E. A. Davis (1937a).

‡ Data from two situations have been grouped in the analysis according to sex.

taken in 3 periods of 3 hours each, and in Young's (1941) study they are based on 28 periods of 10 minutes each distributed over four different types of situations in the nursery school. These two studies may be thought of as the most intensive since they have the largest samples of conversation per child. The McCarthy (1930), Day (1932), Shirley (1933a), M. E. Smith (1935a, 1939), and E. A. Davis (1937a) studies employed 50 responses which have proved to be a sufficiently reliable sample for most purposes, provided the situation remains constant. Young's study was primarily concerned with a comparison of relief cases and privileged nursery school children, so her data are necessarily broken according to socioeconomic level. It should also be mentioned at this point that the Davis, Day, McCarthy, and Smith (1935a) studies found marked and consistent differences in length of sentence with change in socioeconomic level. This matter will be discussed in more detail in a later section. (See pp. 557 ff.)

In general, it may be seen that the child of 18 months is still essentially in the one-word-sentence stage and that he is just beginning to combine words. A year later sentences of two or three words are most typical, and by 3½ years he is using complete sentences averaging about four words each. By 6½ years the mean length of sentence is about five words, and by 9½ years it has increased to six or seven words. Note should be made at this point regarding sex differences in length of response in favor of girls which appear quite consistently in Table 4. More detailed discussion of this problem will be presented in the section on sex differences. (See pp. 551 ff.)

The measure of sentence length was first suggested by Nice (1925), who described four stages of sentence development. The complete sentence stage, she said, did not appear until after four years of age. Nice pointed out that the complete sentence usually consisted of six to eight words and was characterized by mastery of inflections. These conclusions, based on observations of only a few children and made before any of the quantitative studies had appeared, afforded a fairly accurate forecast of what was in store for later investigators.

This same measure can be and often has been applied to written language as well as to spoken language. The best available data on the length of sentence in written compositions are supplied by Heider and Heider (1940b), who present data for 817 normal cases aged 8 to 14 years who wrote compositions based on a short movie they had seen. It is interesting to compare these figures with those by Stormzand and O'Shea (1924) based on 10,000 sentences collected from children's compositions and letters in various grades as well as with length of sentence in adult writing as represented by the works of such writers as Macaulay, Stevenson and others. (See Table 5.)

J. E. Anderson (1937) also reports data on sentence length for 150-word samples from the compositions of college students; he obtained a mean length of written sentence at the college level of 20.4 words. He reports, however, that such short samples do not yield adequately reliable measures.

Apparently, then, sentence length is a measure which continues to show increase up until maturity. The use of the measure has been criticized by some writers and a few substitute measures have been suggested, but none seems to have superseded the mean length of sentence for a reliable, easily determined, objective, quantitative, and easily understood measure of linguistic maturity.

LaBrant (1933) used the mean length of clause in her study, for she argued that division into sentences may be rather arbi-

TABLE 5

MEAN NUMBER OF WORDS PER SENTENCE IN WRITTEN COMPOSITIONS BY AGE AND SCHOOL GRADE

Age Grade	8 3	9 4	10 5	11 6	12 7	13 8	14 9	10	11	12	College Fresh- men	College Upper Class- men	Adults
Heider and Heider	10.2	10.9	11.1	11.1	12.8	13.7	13.9						
Stormzand and O'Shea		11.1		12.0	13.5	15.2	17.3	17.8	18.0	19.8	19.9	21.5	20.9

trary, especially in the compositions of children who have not mastered punctuation and who may write several run-on clauses as a single sentence. LaBrant argues that the counting of predicates is easier, more objective, and psychologically more sound. It is interesting to note from this study, however, that length of clause remains fairly constant in Grades 4 to 12, although the subordination index, or ratio of subordinate to coordinate clauses, shows an increase. Apparently length of clause is somewhat controlled or restricted by the structure of the language, and whatever increase in sentence length occurs at higher age levels is brought about largely through the addition of more subordinate clauses. Anderson (1937) determined subordination indices for samples of 150 words each, taken from four different compositions written by college students, and found very low reliabilities averaging only +.07. Subordination indices based on two successive samples of this length taken from the same compositions correlated only +.23. The mean number of words to the sentence yielded reliabilities of only +.31 and +.35 when similarly treated. E. A. Davis (1941) found that the index of subordination was slightly higher in written than in oral products. Position of the clause within the sentence she found to be important as a developmental index, the older and brighter children more often placing clauses in the beginning of the sentence.

E. A. Davis (1937b) also compared the relative merits of the longest sentences with the mean length of all sentences. The measures of the longest sentences and that of the five longest sentences she found exaggerate developmental trends and group differences and tend to throw them into relief. Although they undoubtedly are a better indication of the child's maximum linguistic capacity at the time than the mean of all the sentences, they do not afford as reliable measures, especially at lower ages, as the mean length of all sentences. Although the longest sentence and the mean of the five longest sentences in a sample have the advantage of ease of computation, there is considerable sacrifice in reliability when either of these short-cut methods is employed, and the loss in reliability appears to be more serious at younger age levels. Davis advocates the use of the mean of the five longest sentences, but the writer is of the opinion that the use of this measure should be restricted to very rough group comparisons.

Sentence Structure and Grammatical Form

Most students of children's language development have been concerned not only with the quantitative approach in terms of length of responses, but they have also attempted some form of qualitative analysis to reveal the improvement in sentence structure which takes place as the child develops.

Emphasis has been placed on sentence structure because of the necessity of guiding children's writing and because of the rôle of grammar in the school curriculum. Symonds and Daringer (1930) state:

> Sentence structure in a language is a key to the logic and structure of thinking, inasmuch as the sentence is the smallest complete unit of thought. Growth in the power to form complete, concise, balanced, consistent sentences is an index of the growth in clear and accurate thinking.

The biographical studies usually give anecdotal accounts of the first sentence, but make little or no attempt to trace sentence formation further. According to a summary of these observations in the *Twenty-eighth Yearbook of the National Society for the Study of Education*, the time of the appearance of the first sentence is reported from the fifteenth to the twenty-sixth month by Moore (1896), Bateman (1914), Drummond (1916), Nice (1925), Guillaume (1927a), and Stern (1930). Nice (1925) reports the average age of the appearance of the first sentence for 20 children as 17.5 months. Shirley (1933a, 1933b) calls attention to the marked perseverative tendency which is apparent in the first sentences and suggests that possibly the variety of sentences would afford a better measure than the total number of sentences at the earliest stages. More detailed analyses of sentence structure are reported by Pollock (1878), Moore (1896), Boyd (1913), and Nice (1925). Nice outlines the various stages in sentence formation as follows: (1) the single word stage from 4 to 12 months; (2) the early sentence stage from 13 to 27 months, with an average at 17.5 months, lasting from 4 to 7 months and characterized by a preponderance of nouns, lack of articles, auxiliaries and copulative verbs, prepositions, and conjunctions; (3) the short sentence stage, which consists of sentences 3.5 to 4.5 words in length and having the same characteristics as the preceding stage, but to a lesser degree; inflections are not yet mastered, and only one or two sentences out of 50 are compound or complex; (4) the complete sentence stage, which appears at about 4 years and consists of sentences of 6 to 8 words, characterized by greater definiteness and complexity as shown by an increased use of relational words and a fairly good mastery of inflections.

The studies which have presented the most elaborate analyses according to sentence structure are those by McCarthy (1930), Day (1932), and E. A. Davis (1937a), which used comparable classifications. Day's figures are somewhat different from McCarthy's because of the general retardation which she found in the language development of twins. Davis used older children and does not have any overlapping age levels with the other two studies. However, since these three studies used the same methods of sampling, were done in the same community, and used the same categories in analyzing the data, they afford some interesting comparisons which may be seen in Table 6. This table is a modification of Davis's Table 40, in which Day's figures for 4-year-old twins, erroneously reported for 4½-year-old twins, are compared with McCarthy's 4½-year-old singletons. Day had no 4½-year-old subjects.

Other studies which have been concerned with construction analysis cannot be compared with this group of studies for various reasons. Fisher's (1934) data are presented only for her total group and are

TABLE 6

MEAN PERCENTAGES OF TOTAL RESPONSES IN EACH CONSTRUCTION CATEGORY AT VARIOUS AGE
LEVELS IN THREE COMPARABLE STUDIES

Age in Years	Investigator		Type of Sentence											
			Functionally Complete		Simple		Simple with Phrase		Compound and Complex		Elaborated		Incomplete	
	Singletons	Twins	Single-tons	Twins	Single-tons	Twins	Single-tons	Twins	Single-tons	Twins	Single-tons	Twins	Single-tons	Twins
1½	McCarthy		78.4		9.6		0.0		0.0		0.0		11.9	
2	McCarthy	Day *	53.8	70.0	17.3	7.5	1.4	2.0	.9	.2	.6	0.0	25.1	19.7
2½	McCarthy		35.3		38.7		5.3		1.5		1.2		18.1	
3	McCarthy	Day	27.2	48.0	45.1	23.0	8.7	4.0	1.5	.5	1.3	.3	16.2	24.6
3½	McCarthy		30.6		35.3		11.4		6.5		2.3		13.9	
4	McCarthy	Day	32.0	48.0	39.4	28.0	10.9	7.5	6.1	1.5	4.5	.9	6.8	13.3
4½	McCarthy		31.2		36.5		10.4		7.0		5.9		8.8	
5		Day		49.0		24.0		7.0		3.6		1.0		15.4
5½	E. A. Davis		39.4	38.0	29.4	31.4	7.8	7.8	4.6	4.6	3.6	2.8	15.0	15.4
6½	E. A. Davis		32.0	28.6	30.8	32.2	9.8	10.8	5.4	7.4	5.6	5.8	16.4	15.2
9½	E. A. Davis		33.6	34.8	18.8	22.2	11.4	10.8	6.8	5.4	10.0	10.2	19.4	16.6

* Figures from Day have been estimated from graphs.

not separated by age levels. In the series of studies by Smith (1926, 1935a, 1939) totally different classifications are employed, so that the figures are not comparable. In work of this sort change in one category affects the percentages in other categories if the authors have used classifications that account for 100 per cent of the responses. Smith reports on the percentage of complete sentences, simple sentences, and "yes" and "no" only; and the rest of her classification in all three studies is based on the functional classification of sentences into declarative, interrogative, imperative, and exclamatory sentences, which makes the data more comparable with the functional analyses of many of the other studies. She does not provide a classification for incomplete or fragmentary responses which often occur in records of conversation, so it is difficult or impossible to determine whether or not her classification covers 100 per cent of the data. If various types of sentences have merely been counted without necessarily accounting for all sentences, it is difficult to ascertain what was used as the base in determining percentages. Young's (1941) study, which in many respects is comparable with the group of studies in Table 6, does not attempt any analysis according to sentence structure.

Examination of Table 6 for developmental trends reveals that in general there is a decrease in the functionally complete but structurally incomplete sentences, although even at the 9½-year level they continue to constitute about one-third of the speech of the children studied by E. A. Davis (1937a). Simple sentences without phrases show an initial increase, followed by a decrease as the more elaborate forms of sentence structure begin to appear. Simple sentences without phrases constitute 9.6 per cent of the comprehensible sentences at 18 months and they practically double in number every half year up to 2½. They appear to reach a peak in the latter part of the preschool period and then decrease. The decrease is much later among twins in accordance with their general linguistic retardation, as this peak is not reached by twins until 6½ years of age. Phrases are first reported in small numbers—about 1 or 2 per cent—at 2 years and show a steady increase with age in both twins and singletons, although they never exceed about 10 or 11 per cent even by 9½ years of age. They are comparatively infrequent in the speech of the twins until after school age.

Compound and complex sentences also first appear in very small numbers at 2 years of age. Among singletons they quickly rise to 6 and 7 per cent of the total comprehensible sentences between 3½ and 4½ years and remain at about this level in the speech of the 9½-year-olds. The emergence of compound and complex sentences appears to be considerably slower in the preschool period for twins, but they appear to catch up in the use of the more complex forms after exposure to the school environment. The category of elaborated responses, first suggested by the writer, which consists of sentences containing two phrases, two clauses, or a phrase and a clause, proved to be an interesting developmental index for later linguistic development. Such sentences were very rare in the speech of the preschool children, and reached a maximum of about 6 per cent at 4½ years. However they increased to 10 per cent by 9½ years. The same trend appeared, although much more slowly, among the twins. Incomplete sentences, that is, sentences which were sufficiently complete to enable the scorer to detect omissions, decreased in McCarthy's data from 25 per cent at 2 years to about 8 per cent at 4½ years. For some unaccountable reason the percentage of incomplete sentences did not show similar decreases with age in the data of Day and Davis, as they continue to constitute 15 or 16 per cent of the responses even up to the 9½-year level.

Williams (1937a) has attempted to quantify the qualitative analysis of the complexities of sentence structure by assigning arbitrary scores to certain types of structure for his language achievement scale. He gives a score for completeness of the expression unit in which a response must have subject, verb, and object expressed if the verb requires an object. A score of 2 is given for a complete unit, 1 for an incomplete unit, and 0 for unintelligible responses. He also assigns weights for complexity of sentence as follows: unintelligible, 0; simple sentence, 1; compound, 2; complex, 3; and compound-complex, 4. In addition he has devised a score for word usage composed of the number of words given in conventional usage per 50 running words. These appear to be quite objective and easily applicable techniques which are deserving of further experimentation. They have the advantage of permitting correlational treatment of some dimensions of language development which have heretofore been restricted to treatment in terms of percentages of various types of response. In other words, they enable the investigator to assign a single quantitative score for several important dimensions of language development instead of depending on inspection of a series of categories.

The two studies by Stormzand and O'Shea (1924) and by Heider and Heider (1940b) yield valuable data on sentence structure in written composition, as may be seen in Table 7. In written language, sentences are much more likely to be complete, and hence there is not the necessity

TABLE 7

COMPARISON OF PERCENTAGES OF DIFFERENT TYPES OF SENTENCE STRUCTURE IN TWO STUDIES
OF WRITTEN LANGUAGE

Type of Sentence	Heider and Heider * / Stormzand and O'Shea †	Age	8	9	10	11	12	13	14				Freshmen	Upper Classmen	Adults
		Grade		4	5	6	7	8	9	10	11	12			
Simple	Heider and Heider		53	45	40	36	30	27	27						
	Stormzand and O'Shea			48		59	46	48	38	44	39	38	30	22	37
Compound	Heider and Heider		31	36	38	38	41	42	43						
	Stormzand and O'Shea			25		6	13	14	18	18	17	20	18	23	13
Complex	Heider and Heider		8	9	12	13	13	14	12						
	Stormzand and O'Shea			27		37	41	37	44	38	44	42	52	55	46
Compound-complex	Heider and Heider		8	10	10	12	15	17	18						

* N = 817 children who wrote short compositions on a movie they had seen in class.

† Based on 10,000 sentences selected from essays, newspaper articles and editorials, modern light fiction, adult letters, and compositions of university, high school, and fourth- to eighth-grade pupils.

of providing a category for fragmentary responses as in the records of oral responses of younger children. Stormzand and O'Shea report their data in terms of school grades, whereas the Heiders' material is in terms of ages. However, the results of the two studies have been aligned in Table 7 so as to compare the 9-year-olds with the fourth-graders, etc., which should be a fairly reasonable assumption if the children were normally placed in school for their ages. It is difficult to evaluate the developmental significance of such data, however, without any adult norm for the expected level at maturity. The nearest approach to such material is provided in a study by Thorndike, Evans, Kennon, and Newcomb (1926–1927), in which 45 samples of writing were analyzed for grammatical construction. There were 18,113 occurrences of the simple sentence in the sampling, and 438 other types of sentence construction were listed with their frequencies per 100,000 sentences. LaBrant's (1933) material is treated using the clause as the unit rather than the sentence, so again comparisons are impossible.

It is indeed unfortunate that more direct comparisons cannot legitimately be made among these various studies. The similarity of the labels of many of the categories is likely to mislead the naïve reader who has not handled data of this sort into thinking that many figures are comparable which actually are not because of differences in methodology, and the counterbalancing effect of the treatment in terms of percentages is likely to be confusing.

Various investigators have been concerned with the incidence of the different parts of speech as they occur in the running conversation of children. The most recent and most detailed study of this sort is by Young (1941), in which she presents, in addition to her own data on 74 cases, the results of six other investigations. The author is chiefly concerned with reconciling certain differences which appear in the literature which she interprets to be due to difference of definition of grammatical terms. She adheres strictly to the definitions in Jespersen's *Essentials of English Grammar* (1933). In the opinion of the writer, such analyses are of significance for child development only in the very early stages of sentence formation before all the various parts of speech have come into active use. As Young herself states, "The proportions of the parts of speech changed most rapidly before the age of three, and after that age the rate of change tended to be slower" (p. 87). As soon as the child begins to use full and complete sentences which are grammatically correct, the percentages of the various parts of speech become more or less set by the conventions of the language. The beginnings of the use of modifiers and of prepositions and connectives are probably quite significant and mark important milestones in the development of the child's speech, but as soon as they are employed characteristically their developmental significance becomes submerged in a number of other factors. In addition to being controlled by the demands of conventional usage, they are definitely related to the situation in which the language sample is taken, as Goodenough (1938) has shown in her excellent study of pronouns, in which she states:

> Proportions of the various parts of speech in the language of children are frequently quoted in a fashion that might lead the reader to think that these proportions depend almost wholly upon the child's level of development and vary but little with the conditions of observation. The unsoundness of this point of view will be apparent from an examination of the data here presented. As a matter of fact, while most of the pronouns here listed show a distinct difference in frequency of usage according to the immediate situation under which they are used, age differences are not always apparent, even when no allowances are made for the increasing length of the sentence (p. 338).

More promising leads are afforded by the recent search for additional indices of improvement in sentence structure as reflected in specific changes in various types of grammatical forms. Such approaches lead the investigator into more detailed treatment and classification, but this apparently is the direction in which the refinement of techniques will probably progress. Verb forms, especially the use of past and future tenses, have been studied by Lewis (1937), Adams (1938), and M. E. Smith (1939). The understanding of prepositions has been described by Grigsby (1932), and their use in written language has been treated by Heider and Heider (1940b). Connectives have received special treatment from E. A. Davis (1937a) and also from the Heiders. A very detailed study of determining and numerating adjectives has been presented by Carroll (1939), and pronouns have received detailed treatment from Goodenough (1938) and E. A. Davis (1938a). Infinitives have been studied by E. A. Davis (1937a), Young (1941), and Heider and Heider (1940b), and the various types of clauses which were brought to the fore by LaBrant (1933) have also been analyzed in greater detail by E. A. Davis (1937a) and by the Heiders.

Lewis (1937) brings out that at first the language of the child is concerned exclusively with the immediate situation in which it is spoken, and that gradually it begins to deal with things that are absent. This matter of reference to things absent has also been emphasized by both K. and C. Bühler (both 1930). Lewis relates the child's use of past and future tenses to the functions of his earlier undifferentiated speech. It is because of the child's use of speech as an instrument to draw others into his social circle that he begins to speak of absent things and events. Lewis points out that the child uses a word manipulatively in an effort to call attention to an object which he wishes brought into the present situation. In such instances he claims that the child's utterance is much more an expression of his needs within the present situation than a reference to an absent object. At this point the adult's conversation with the child becomes a potent factor in the emergence of the use of past and future tenses.

Adams (1938) approached the problem of verb forms by using the records of the speech of twelve 4-year-olds taken during nursery school activities. He tabulated the first 50 verbs in each child's record and compared them with those in 100 consecutive sentences of adult spoken language. He found that 59 per cent of the adult speech and 56 per cent of the children's speech were in the present tense. The adult speech was found to contain a larger percentage of sentences in the compound tense than the children's, and the children's speech contained a greater percentage of sentences in the present and present-progressive tenses. He found that at 4 years the future tense has come into common use and occurs 10 per cent of the time, and the preterite or simple past is found about as often as in adult speech. Interestingly enough, he points out, however, that whereas the verb takes on past and future forms, the times referred to are immediate rather than remote. Only 4 children made reference to any time earlier than the previous day. Children's use of future tense nearly always involved reference to the future of the day of speaking.

The data available on the use of various types of clauses and on the use of infinitives and auxiliary verbs are almost impossible to summarize. Much of this work has been done on written language, La-Brant (1933) using school compositions on different topics from Grade 4 to the adult level, and the Heiders (1940b) using compositions in response to a specific standardized situation. In the latter study emphasis is placed on the comparison of groups of deaf and hearing children rather than on the developmental trends in either the experimental or hearing group. E. A. Davis (1937a) attempted similar analyses on the oral language of her subjects recorded in a standardized situation on younger children. In most of these analyses she reports data only for the total group, although each age level is heavily weighted with twins and only children, both of which groups showed significant differences from the singletons in all other aspects of language development. Her samples are so short for each individual that these more complex and elaborate forms occurred so rarely as to make the means unreliable. J. E. Anderson (1937) pointed out in his study of indices of linguistic development that it is not possible to get an adequate sample for detailed analysis of written language in a passage of only 150 words. This is probably even more serious for oral language in which fragmentary remarks are likely to be more frequent, and hence samples of a given length are likely to yield fewer of the more complex forms in complete sentences for statistical treatment. Goodenough (1938) states, however, on the basis of her study of pronouns, that "a sample of 50 responses is not sufficient for the study of individual differences in the use of separate pronouns, but the consistency of the group trends . . . is evidence of their validity as group measures." A clue as to possible development of more detailed indices may be obtained from her finding that the percentage of pronouns in the total sample shows little consistent change with age or sex after three years, but that certain specific groups of pronouns showed very pronounced changes with age and with the conditions of observation. The chief trends noted in this analysis showed that there was an increase with age in the use of the first personal pronoun, and that it is used more frequently during play with other children than when conversing with an adult.

Gheorgov (1905) pointed out that the child has a fairly well-developed awareness of self long before he begins to express himself in language, but that it is only with the use of words that the higher types of concepts can be differentiated, such as the *I*, the *self*, and the *mine*. He also calls attention to the familiar phenomenon of the child's designation of himself by his own name which he hears others use when speaking or referring to him. This use of the own name often precedes the correct use of the first personal pronouns and is regarded by some as a sign of immaturity in speech. Goodenough (1938) also found that, contrary to popular opinion, the absolute number of pronouns shows no increase with age after the maximum has been reached at 3½ years, and in proportion to the total number of words used the number of pronouns actually declines. Young (1942b) also conducted a detailed study of the personal and possessive pronouns occurring in her major investigation. She found that they constituted 28 per cent of all the comprehensible words spoken by the nursery school children. The first person singular pronouns *I*, *me*, and *mine* constituted 36 to 39 per cent of the total, whereas the impersonal *it* accounted for 19 per cent. In face-to-face situations, *you* accounted for 15 per cent of the pronouns and the plural forms of *we* or *us* accounted for only 5 per cent.

Symonds and Daringer (1930) report that in written compositions the use of pronouns is high up to the ninth grade, but that thereafter it decreases as the writing takes on a more impersonal and more abstract nature. Goodenough (1938) concludes from her study that the use of an unusually large number of pronouns after the age of 3½ years may be interpreted as evidence of linguistic immaturity. As the vocabulary increases the use of the third person neuter pronoun declines, for proper and common nouns come to be substituted for it as the child is able to be more specific in his speech. In conclusion, Goodenough (1938) brings out a very important point for methodology in future research on language development, for she says:

> Many of the formal grammatical classifications of adult usage are inadequate to bring out significant developmental trends in the speech of children. The very marked changes that occur in the use of pronouns, for example, are almost wholly obscured when all pronouns are grouped into a single class. Developmental processes are qualitative as well as quantitative and in devising systems for classifying behavioral manifestations it is necessary to keep these qualitative changes in mind if the systems are to be useful. It is suggested that in the study of children's language, too much attention has been paid to the type of grammatical analysis used by adults and too little to the developmental changes in conceptual thinking and social drives that lie back of the verbal expression (p. 344).

Carroll (1939) made a special study of determining and enumerating adjectives in children's speech. The author recommends the study of adjectives as an easy approach to the minute details of syntax because, as he points out, they occur frequently and constitute a relatively large part of the total number of words (about 15 per cent). Numeratives are very infrequent at 2½ years and occur much more frequently at later ages. Both definite and indefinite adjectives excluding articles show increases with age, although the proportion of definite to indefinite adjectives is in the direction of relatively fewer definite adjectives and more indefinite adjectives as age increases. The growth curve for the use of *a* levels off between 3½ and 4½ years, but for *the* the curve shows a sharp rise throughout the age range studied, namely, 2½ to 4½ years. This appears to be in accordance with Young's (1941) finding of a steady increase in the use of articles from 30 to 60 months. This detail has been overlooked in most earlier work because articles have seemed like such insignificant words that most previous investigators have grouped them with adjectives and have not treated them separately. These results somewhat challenge research workers to comb the field of language development for other significant indices.

Another interesting measure which thus far has received very little attention is suggested by Busemann (1925), in which he uses a ratio of the activity words to the qualitative words. It really amounts to an activity quotient determined by dividing the total number of verbs by the total number of adjectives. Busemann claims that this index shows a rhythmical cycle of alternating action and qualitative periods throughout the life cycle. His data, however, do not appear adequate to support these claims, as the results he reports could be accounted for on the basis of sampling. He claims that high activity quotients are related to periods of emotional instability in the child's life. This index has been used by Boder (1940) on various types of adult writing, and he finds that it varies with the subject matter, scientific writing yielding the highest quotients, with fiction, legal writing, and plays following in the order named. He claims to find alternating activity quotients in the writings of Emerson.

The educational and English journals are replete with minor articles on the incidence of various types of grammatical errors in the oral and written language of school children. Most of them are poorly controlled with errors often being jotted down at the whim of the teacher at odd moments during the school day. In general they are extremely pessimistic and stress the fact that errors continue in the speech and writings of children throughout the school period in spite of the educational influences aimed to overcome them. One of the better studies on written language is by Symonds and Daringer (1930), in which the authors report that in the fourth grade there are on the average about two errors to every sentence, and that this ratio shows a gradual decrease until about the eighth or ninth grade, when there is about one error per sentence in children's writings.

One of the soundest and the most optimistic article on the study of errors is by E. A. Davis (1939). She points out that reports based on frequency of error alone are inaccurate and misleading, and that it is necessary to take into account the frequency of occurrence of a given construction in a given sample of language before it can be properly evaluated. Most teachers, she states, find it easier to note errors than correct usage. In an analysis of the most frequently occurring errors in her major study (1937a), she points out that when the inflection of pronouns is compared with the comparison of adjectives it appears that a pronoun is inflected correctly once for every 16 words and incorrectly once for every 873 words. Adjectives are compared correctly once for every 407 words and incorrectly once for every 16,211 words. The opportunity to inflect a pronoun occurred approximately 17 times for each child, while adjectives were compared less than once per child in the data analyzed. She tried a variety of measures of error approached from the positive rather than the negative angle and found that the mean occurrence per child, the number of occurrences per 1000 words, the ratio to the total words used, ratio of times correct to times incorrect, percentage of correct usage, and errors per 1000 chances to use the construction all revealed definite improvement with advancing age. In general, she found that the number of correct usages increased, and the number of incorrect usages decreased, with advancing age, both absolutely and when studied in relation to the total number of words used. For some constructions there was a marked difference in the children coming from the upper and lower socioeconomic levels, those from upper levels presumably having the better example and hence fewer errors. It is also interesting to note that the greatest improvement in the elimination of errors occurred in the less privileged group during the early school years.

The Functions of Language in the Child's Life

Of considerably more interest to the child psychologist than the use of various types of word forms are the analyses which attempt to answer the questions of why the child talks, what motivates him to use language in certain situations, what needs he satisfies by the use of language, and what functions language fulfills in the child's life. The early biographical studies approached this problem by classifying responses as declarative, interrogative, exclamatory, and imperative sentences in accordance with the formal classifications of conventional grammar. As has already been pointed out, however, this system does not lend itself well to the psychological analysis of the language of young children. These categories have been designed to fit written discourse, but prove unsatisfactory for the conversation of adults and especially unsuitable for the conversations of children.

Snyder (1914) was among the first to point out this inadequacy and modified the usual grammatical classifications in her study of a 2½-year-old boy. M. E. Smith followed Snyder's classification of sentences in her 1926 study in which several subdivisions and variations of the usual categories were provided. In that analysis she reported:

> There are more declarative sentences, at all ages, than any other type. Also the proportion of imperative sentences, including variations, is probably significantly greater than the proportion of questions at two, three, and four years.

With the appearance of Piaget's *Language and Thought of the Child*, an entirely new approach to the study of the functions of the child's language was suggested, which has stimulated much further research and controversy in the field. Piaget is chiefly interested in the child's language as a means of revealing his thought processes. He recognizes two major types of speech in the child's language: first, egocentric speech, and second, socialized speech. Piaget was the first to emphasize the rôle of egocentricity in the child's life. He claims to have discovered its importance through a functional approach to child language. In egocentric speech, as Piaget defines it, "the child does not bother to know to whom he is speaking nor whether he is being listened to. He talks either for himself or for the pleasure of associating anyone who happens to be there with the activity of the moment. . . . He does not attempt to place himself at the point of view of his hearer." Socialized speech, on the other hand, is speech "in which the child addresses his hearer, considers his point of view, tries to influence him or actually exchanges ideas with him." Piaget recognizes three types of egocentric speech, namely, echolalia, monologue, and dual or collective monologue. He subdivides socialized speech into: (1) adapted information, which occurs when "the child really exchanges his thoughts with others," (2) criticism, (3) commands, requests, and threats, (4) questions, and (5) answers. He reports on data consisting of about 1500 remarks recorded for each of two children 6½ years of age taken down during free play in La Maison des Petites in Geneva. He reports that about 38 per cent of the child's remarks fall in the egocentric categories and that only about 45 per cent are spontaneous socialized speech with an additional 17 per cent made up of answers, which are of course socialized remarks, making a total of 62 per cent socialized speech. Piaget reports a higher percentage of egocentric remarks at ages 3 to 5, and states that there occurs a definite socialization in the child's speech at 7 to 8 years of age. He implies that adult conversation is highly socialized and that this egocentrism is a symptom of psychological immaturity, which is outgrown with age.

McCarthy (1930), in seeking a more satisfactory method of treating children's language from the functional point of view, applied Piaget's categories to her data, consisting of 50 consecutive responses from each of 140 children ranging in age from 18 to 54 months, and selected so as to be representative of the population on the basis of paternal occupation. Although the method at first might appear to be quite subjective, she found that it possessed a fairly satisfactory degree of reliability, for when four scorers attempted to classify identical responses in the various categories of the functional analysis after studying Piaget's definitions, the average intercorrelation was +.78 and this value would have been +.88 if only three scorers were included, as one of the scorers who was obviously less interested in the task had consistently lower correlations with all the others. It appears then that really conscientious scorers can classify the re-

sponses of preschool children into these categories with a satisfactory degree of agreement. In the application of this classification scheme to her data McCarthy adhered as strictly as possible to a literal interpretation of Piaget's definitions of the terms for each category. Piaget's examples often do not fit his definitions, but where confusion occurred on this account the definition was used as the criterion rather than an isolated example. It was necessary to modify the classification slightly in order to make it include all the responses in McCarthy's data. She therefore added two classes, namely, social phrases and dramatic imitation. For convenience and in order to make it cover a few other responses not included in Piaget's group, his category of "commands, requests, and threats" was termed "emotionally toned responses" and made to include wishes and desires as well. The category of adapted information accounted for such a large percentage of the responses that it was broken into four subheads as follows: naming, remarks about the immediate situation, remarks associated with the situation, and irrelevant remarks.[1]

Egocentricity of Children's Speech. As a result of this analysis McCarthy (1930) found a much smaller percentage of egocentric responses than that reported by Piaget, as all egocentric categories together never exceeded 6.5 per cent at any age level; the average for all age levels was only 3.6 per cent. This seeming discrepancy, which is probably much more apparent than real, has aroused considerable interest and controversy. A number of other writers have since attempted to apply some sort of functional analysis suggested by the Piaget classification. None of the American writers has found his classification usable in its exact form, but unfortunately

[1] For more detailed description of these categories, see McCarthy (1930, pp. 37–42).

several investigators have made their own versions in modifying the classifications, so that direct comparisons are difficult if not impossible.

In general, the studies employing a functional approach are of two types from the standpoint of interpretation. The studies which attempt to classify on the basis of a literal interpretation of Piaget's definitions invariably emerge with a much smaller percentage of egocentric responses, as did McCarthy's. The second group of studies, particularly those by Rugg, Krueger, and Sondergaard (1929), Adams (1932), and Fisher (1934), who definitely set out to look for egocentrism as it is found in the speech of children, and devised their own definitions of egocentrism, usually in terms of the subject of the sentence, invariably find a high percentage of egocentrism which agrees rather closely with that reported by Piaget. The former group of studies have been summarized in Table 8, which represents the percentages found in each of the studies by McCarthy (1930), Day (1932), Smith (1935a), and E. A. Davis (1937a), for five of the major categories in the functional analysis.

As stated above, these figures must be interpreted with extreme caution because of the varying circumstances pointed out in the footnotes. Day used the identical method employed by McCarthy, but her subjects were twins and showed marked linguistic retardation and immaturity throughout. The data reported in this table from Davis's study are those given for singletons with siblings, since that group is most nearly comparable with McCarthy's and Smith's data. Davis unfortunately placed all criticism in the same class with adapted information, which would tend to raise the percentage in that category by 1 or 2 per cent. She also treated all expressions of liking and desire, which the other authors treat as emotionally toned responses under adapted information. Smith collected her data, which are shown in Table 8, in two different situations, one in which the child conversed with the experimenter as in the other three studies, and the other in which data were collected in the free play situation in a nursery school where the child was conversing with other children. Smith used a category called "monologue" and then grouped under "collective monologue" remarks about the immediate situation, remarks associated with the situation, and irrelevant remarks. These were all considered to be types of adapted information and were classed as socialized speech in McCarthy's investigation. Without defining her interpretation of egocentrism Smith computed coefficients of egocentrism which decreased from 40 at year 2 to 26 at year 5. Thus, Smith agreed with Piaget's findings but did not specify how she interpreted his categories or exactly how she classified her data. She also compared data on 84 cases whose remarks were recorded during conversation with an adult in a situation similar to McCarthy's study with data from 175 children who were playing in a free play situation in a nursery school and conversing with other children. She found no difference in the amount of egocentrism in the two situations, but the data have been grouped so as to mask any real trends which might appear, since age, sex, and occupational group differences were also operating to unknown degrees in the two sets of data being compared for situation.

One of the most crucial works on the effect of the situation on language responses, which will be treated in more detail in a later section, is an unpublished doctoral dissertation by McConnon (1935). Two records of twenty-five consecutive responses were taken in each of six situations both at home and at nursery school. The

TABLE 8

Percentages of Responses in Main Categories of the Functional Analyses in Four Major Studies

Age	Egocentric Speech				Emotionally Toned				Adapted Information				Questions				Answers			
	McCarthy (1930)	Day* (1932)	Davis† (1937a)	M. E. Smith‡|| (1935a)	McCarthy (1930)	Day* (1932)	Davis† (1937a)	M. E. Smith‡|| (1935a)	McCarthy (1930)	Day* (1932)	Davis†§ (1937a)	M. E. Smith‡|| (1935a)	McCarthy (1930)	Day* (1932)	Davis† (1937a)	M. E. Smith‡|| (1935a)	McCarthy (1930)	Day* (1932)	Davis† (1937a)	M. E. Smith‡|| (1935a)
1½	3.1				14.6				60.6				10.8				0.3			
2	6.5	16		40	18.3	30		32	40.8	37		17	13.9	2		5	16.6	13		3
2½	4.0				14.2				57.7				3.5				14.6			
3	3.6	1		33	9.4	18		30	50.9	52		20	13.2	7		8	19.1	19		6
3½	4.7				9.4				53.2				9.7				20.4			
4	1.3	1		26	6.5	15		28	45.2	51		23	12.1	8		12	31.0	22		9
4½	2.2				6.4				54.6				8.2				26.0			
5		2		26		14		22		50		25		9		16		21		7
5½			.4				3.8				59.7				10.6				25.5	
6½			.2				3.3				66.8				9.4				22.7	
9½			.7				1.4				60.7				3.8				37.1	

* Day's subjects were twins markedly retarded in all aspects of language development. Classification was identical with McCarthy's. Figures estimated from graph.

† Davis's data for singletons with siblings. She classed criticism and expressions of liking and desire with adapted information, whereas McCarthy and Day classed them as emotionally toned responses.

‡ M. E. Smith's figures given in this table are apparently based on a grouping of data from two types of situations. The adult-child situation which showed fewer egocentric and emotionally toned responses is comparable to the other studies. Smith did not use discrete age groups as was done in the other three studies.

§ Adapted information not given separately by Davis for different experimental groups. These figures probably include data from twins and only children as well as from singletons.

|| Figures from Smith under emotionally toned responses in this table were classed by her as "imperative sentences."

data were not reported in terms of mean percentage of occurrence of the various types of response, but in terms of inter-correlations and critical ratios for the various situations. In regard to the egocentrism controversy McConnon's data are of particular interest, however, for she found an average intercorrelation of only +.17 between various situations in the number of egocentric remarks recorded. She used McCarthy's classification and interpretation of Piaget's categories. The correlation between the home situation and the table-play situation, which probably were most comparable with the McCarthy and Piaget situations, respectively, is only −.135. In her critical ratio analysis the measure of egocentrism yielded the largest number of significant differences when the home situation was compared with the various nursery school situations.

In the study by Williams and Mattson (1942), in which children's language responses in different social groupings were studied, it was found that as the group becomes larger the language becomes more social and less egocentric. Only one of their six subjects indulged in speech while playing alone, and social speech was found to account for 60 to 78 per cent of the sentences, with the remainder being classified as parallel speech in their social usage analysis. When they used Piaget's analysis, however, the amount of egocentric speech ranged from 42 to 58 per cent in the various situations.

In another study McCarthy (1929a) compared two methods and found an appreciably higher percentage of egocentric responses in the free play situation (6.32 per cent) than in the adult situation (3.35 per cent). M. E. Smith's (1935a) findings on larger numbers of cases are also in the same direction. Unfortunately, however, for purposes of comparison, she grouped the data obtained by these two methods

by age levels separately, which are the figures necessarily reported in Table 8. When she compared the two methods of recording responses in the two different situations she put all age levels together and this rendered the material incomparable with other available data. The figures given in Table 8 for E. A. Davis's (1937a) data on adapted information were not given by her separately for singletons, twins, and only children, and hence the figures reported here probably include her total group, which is heavily weighted with twins and only children, both of which are deviate groups in linguistic development.

It thus appears that the data of Table 8 are very difficult if not impossible to interpret. In spite of similarity of purpose and methods of collecting data, the methods of presentation of the results have varied from study to study to such a degree that comparisons of data which should be comparable are rendered impossible.

Another study which is presented very briefly so that figures could not be added to the above table is that by Johnson and Josey (1931), who attempted to repeat some of Piaget's work on 55 children. They state that their results "substantiate few of Piaget's claims" and

instead of finding them egocentric we found them socially minded, willing and able to assume the position of another and even that of an hypothesis. They were quite able to make themselves understood. . . . Six-year-olds, he [Piaget] tells us, cannot reason because they are too egocentric. We found nothing in our investigation to support this view. On the contrary we found all of our children to be socially minded and in no manner dominated by an egocentric attitude.

The most significant American study which has apparently confirmed Piaget's findings with regard to egocentricity of language is that of Fisher (1934). Although she took the work of Piaget (1924) as her point of departure in the search for the degree of egocentricity in the child's language, she did not follow his classification in arriving at her coefficient of egocentrism. Instead she set up a much simpler and more objective method based on the proportion of the total remarks having the self as subject. Her coefficients of egocentrism obtained by this method were in striking agreement with those reported by Piaget, but, with the marked difference in method, the validity of a direct comparison of these indices bearing identical names is somewhat questionable. One of the chief difficulties is that the classification of the same set of remarks on the basis of Fisher's classification and on the basis of Piaget's would in all probability lead to quite different results, since many remarks can be about the self and yet be directed toward a hearer, require a response from the hearer, and in every other way qualify as a socialized response according to Piaget's definitions. Fisher found that 34 per cent of the remarks were about the self and she concluded that a high degree of concern with himself is characteristic of the preschool child. She does not, however, find any relationship between age and remarks about the self. Adams (1932), who also recorded language in a nursery school setting, defines egocentric remarks as remarks which contain self-references. He uses separate categories for monologue and social monologue which are subheads under egocentric remarks in Piaget's original classification. His egocentric remarks show a regular increase with age from 13 per cent at 2 years to 41 per cent at 4 years. It is not surprising that workers using such criteria should find results indicative of a relatively large percentage of egocentrism, for in the M. D. Horn (1926-1927a) list, of the words most frequently used by kindergarten children the word *I* is by far

the most frequent, with *my* occurring as the ninth and *me* as the twenty-fourth word in order of frequency.

Another investigation which apparently supports Piaget's conclusions, but arrives at the result by different methods, is that by Rugg, Krueger, and Sondergaard (1929). They found that 40.8 per cent of the remarks of kindergarten children were self-assertive. However, their definition of this category did not exclude socialized responses as was done in Piaget's classification, since self-assertive remarks could at the same time be highly socialized.

A recent article by Henle and Hubbell (1938) on egocentricity in adult conversations has occasioned some challenging re-evaluations of the significance of Piaget's work. Heretofore the implication had always been that as the child grows older his speech becomes more socialized, and that in the adult there is relatively little egocentric speech. The high degree of socialization of adult speech has always been implied, but never demonstrated. Henle and Hubbell undertook to determine the amount of egocentric speech in adult conversations. They also set up their own criteria of egocentricity. Criticizing the artificiality of Fisher's (1934) technique they proceeded to classify sentences from the point of view of their meaning as ego-related sentences. In this category they include statements of the activities of the speaker, of his feelings and emotions, his ambitions, desires, and interests as well as all opinions, attitudes, criticisms, and all evaluative and normative statements. The remarks classified were those of college students and other adults and were recorded by a variety of eavesdropping techniques in order to avoid artificiality and to assure spontaneity. They found 40.7 per cent of all the adult remarks fell in the ego-related category. Perhaps individuals of all ages are egocentric in about 40 per cent of their responses, if one uses a somewhat subjective classification scheme based on meaning rather than on the manner of utterance and attendant circumstances, as in Piaget's definitions. If this is true, it may be that the great concern of child psychologists regarding the developmental significance of the supposed outgrowing of the egocentrism of early childhood has been somewhat unnecessary.

Those who have disagreed with Piaget's findings when they employ his classifications are not all American investigators so the differences probably should not be explained on the basis of nationality. Ohwaki (1933), who studied her own two Japanese daughters, reports that at about the age of two years social expression is as frequent as monologue. She attempts to harmonize her findings with those of Piaget by pointing out that if all sentences not directed toward other people are considered as egocentric, talking with animals and the like would be considered egocentric. She thinks, however, that this kind of talking should be considered as very social since animals are often real companions to children. Huang and Chu (1936) recorded a total of 1500 sentences from 21 nursery school children 2½ to 5 years of age in the everyday environment and found 80 per cent of their speech socialized and 20 per cent egocentric. Language about other persons was 12.5 per cent of the total, language about the self classified as socialized was 11.6 per cent, and language about the group constituted only 3.3 per cent. Kuo (1937) recorded spontaneous language from 4 Chinese children 3 to 5 years of age and found egocentric speech occupies only 10 to 20 per cent of children's conversation and that it decreases with age.

In her third edition of *Kindheit und Jugend,* published in 1931, C. Bühler discusses this problem in some detail, referring to some unpublished German studies which have not yet found their way into American literature on the subject. She states that Piaget's very stimulating investigations were refuted by many different child psychologists, at least in regard to their main thesis (egocentricity). She says that W. Stern has always pointed out that the egocentric behavior of the children observed by Piaget was furthered by the special environmental conditions prevailing at La Maison des Petites, which she describes as a Montessori preschool in which each child is encouraged to work alone on an individual basis with relatively little social intercourse being developed within the group. She also states that, at the suggestion of Doctor Stern, M. Muchow tested the egocentricity coefficients in a preschool in Hamburg and found completely different ratios from those reported by Piaget. Another unpublished study by Elsa Köhler resulted in 82 per cent of the speech of preschool children being classified as socialized. This is of course much more in line with the American investigations which have employed Piaget's classifications. C. Bühler (1931) herself gives the interesting interpretation that the flow of speech which often accompanies a child's activity is really an expression of a need for social contact. She feels that much of the speech classed as monologue is merely expressing a desire to feel close to others, and that it is only in the second place to be considered as playful monologue. She considers that Piaget found reason to emphasize the egocentric aspects of children's language because of the rather peculiar characteristics of the play situation in which the children were observed, and because records were taken in only the one type of life situation. Although the drive for social contact may be interpreted as egoistic, the very striving for contact, she says, drives the child away from himself and toward others in social contact.

In summary, it appears that the controversy over egocentrism is more apparent than real, and that much of the discrepancy can be accounted for in terms of (1) differences in definition and interpretation of terms by various authors, (2) the situations in which responses are recorded, and (3) individual differences in the personality characteristics of the children observed. The writer is inclined to the belief that these three factors are of considerably more importance than the factor of nationality which has been stressed by some. It is evident that there is a high degree of egocentrism (about 40 per cent of all remarks) in the speech of young children if one sets out to look for its manifestations without artificial restraints imposed by a rigidly defined classification system (Rugg, Krueger, and Sondergaard, 1929; Adams, 1932; Fisher, 1934). It should be pointed out, however, that even the highest estimates of egocentrism rarely exceed 50 per cent and hence the enthusiastic statements one occasionally finds regarding the *predominance* of egocentrism in the speech of young children are quite unfounded. If, however, one accepts Piaget's definitions and adheres to them strictly, much smaller amounts of speech are classified as egocentric in any situation, although more egocentric responses are found in free play and in child-child situations than in adult-child situations. Whether or not such egocentrism as is found in studies reporting high incidence of it is characteristic of childhood, and whether it is outgrown with added maturity, is still an open question. The work of Henle and Hubbell (1938) points to the interpretation that perhaps the degree of egocentrism first called to attention in the speech of young children may be a characteristic of human nature which is merely somewhat more subtly manifested in adulthood.

Socialized Speech. Obviously, all the studies which have been cited above have been concerned with socialized speech as opposed to egocentric speech. The absolute percentages of socialized speech are the complements of the percentages of egocentric speech noted in the preceding section. Hence all the factors which influence the percentage of egocentrism also affect the percentages of socialized speech. As has already been pointed out, each author has made slight modifications of the classifications, and each of these changes upsets the balance of percentages in a closed system so that the actual figures available on the various categories of socialized speech are not readily comparable except in the few studies which have employed identical methods. In general those who have duplicated McCarthy's techniques have confirmed her main findings in regard to the general trends. The percentage of answers varies with the amount of participation of the adult to stimulate conversation and with the degree to which the observer waited for spontaneous remarks in the adult-child situations. As may be seen from Table 8, roughly one-fourth of the responses are answers in the data of McCarthy (1930), Day (1932), and E. A. Davis (1937a), whereas M. E. Smith (1935a) has only 9 per cent or less in this category at all ages.

The largest single category of socialized speech in most studies which have used this classification is adapted information which amounts to 40 to 60 per cent at the various age levels. It constitutes by far the bulk of the conversation, and as a total category shows no definite trend with age. M. E. Smith's (1935a) figures are lower than those of other investigators because she classed remarks about the immediate situation and remarks associated with the situation as collective monologue rather than as adapted information. The most interesting trend in adapted information is that the subgroup of naming is very prominent in the speech of young children, dropping from about 50 per cent of the comprehensible responses of McCarthy's (1930) 18-month-old children to about 10 per cent at the age of 4½, and E. A. Davis (1937a) reports only 6 to 8 per cent naming in the 5½- to 9½-year-old children studied by her. Corresponding to the decrease in the amount of naming there is an increase with age in the number of remarks associated with the situation. The child is able to recall information and bring his past experiences to bear on the present situation, and to look ahead into the future and to talk about related items as he grows older and gains in experience and in his ability to integrate his experiences and to verbalize about them.

Another striking trend which has emerged quite consistently from a number of investigations is that very young children usually begin to talk about things which have emotional content for them. The first word is often an interjection, and even words which are usually used as nouns are often uttered with exclamatory or interjectional inflection. Apparently young children are motivated to use language in the beginning to satisfy their needs, wants, and desires and to control their environment in accordance with their needs and wants; for the category of emotionally toned responses including commands, requests, threats, and desires constitutes a fairly large percentage of the responses of the youngest children and this category dwindles in importance with increase in age (Table 8).

In seeming conflict with these findings are those of Young (1942a), who reports children over 48 months using more exclamatory expressions than younger children. This apparently is due to the dif-ferent situations in which her data wer collected, as she also finds more command given to other children than to adults, an an increasing tendency to use verbal ex pressions instead of physical combat. Thi latter is undoubtedly due to nursery schoo training and to the fact that her data wer collected in the nursery school situation It is unfortunate that this study did no include a situational analysis in order to clarify this point.

The figures given by E. A. Davis (1937a) on emotionally toned responses are much lower than those of McCarthy (1930) and Day (1932) and are not comparable with them, because she classed expressions of liking and of desire under adapted information while retaining the category of emotionally toned responses only for exclamations and definite commands. The figures reported for Smith under the heading "emotionally toned" in Table 8 are actually classed by her as imperative sentences, but in all probability these are emotionally toned in the sense that the other investigators employed this term. It is interesting to note the decline in the percentage of such responses as the child gains in socialization and in facility of expression. There is also the possibility that the large amount of emotionality in early speech is an accompaniment of the early stage of learning to talk, for the child who understands the speech of others much better than he can express himself may go through a period of emotional stress comparable to the emotional accompaniment which has often been pointed out in the early stages of learning many motor and other skills.

The category of children's questions has received considerable attention from investigators in recent years, for it has been treated as a separate category in the major studies of language development and it has also received more detailed analysis in studies by Piaget (1926), E. A. Davis (1932), M. E. Smith (1933b), and Lewis (1938). This area has been reviewed by Fahey (1942). In most studies of preschool children, questions seem to make up 10 to 15 per cent of the conversation. There seems to be a slight, although irregular, tendency for the number of questions to increase with age, but by 9½ years Davis (1937a) reports a marked falling off. Smith (1933b) found a slightly larger percentage (16 per cent) of questions asked in the adult-child situation than in the child-child situation (12 per cent), although it must be remembered that the two records were not taken from the same group of children, and hence may be affected by sampling errors. McCarthy (1930) and Davis (1937a) found that children of the upper socioeconomic classes ask a much larger number of questions than children of the lower socioeconomic levels. This is undoubtedly due in part to the intellectual factor, but is probably also related to the satisfaction that such children are likely to get when they ask questions. A child from a superior home is somewhat more likely to get a satisfactory answer to his questions and hence will be encouraged to ask more. Davis (1937a) also found that only children tend to ask more questions than singletons or twins. This can probably be explained on the same grounds as the occupational group differences.

Piaget (1926) was interested in children's questions chiefly for the light they might shed on the development of child logic. He devotes an entire chapter in *The Language and Thought of the Child* to a treatment of 1125 questions asked of one adult by one child over a 10-month period between 6 and 7 years of age. He points out that early "why" questions appear at about 3 years, but, classifying the questions according to the type of answer he thinks is expected by the child, he claims

that these are not actually questions demanding causal explanations. He states that the earliest "whys" are affective rather than intellectual, and he postulates the hypothesis of precausality. He claims that children do not ask questions of causal relationship until 7 or 8 years of age.

Lewis (1938) is in essential agreement with this point of view although he tends to emphasize the social function of the child's questions. He attempts to show

that the growth of a child's questions is determined by social cooperation working upon two powerful tendencies in the child —namely, to use language as play and as a means of satisfying his vital needs. . . . Throughout, the growth of the various categories of questions depends very largely upon the replies that the child receives; that is, upon social cooperation.

This is very much in line with the hypothesis suggested above that the occupational group differences in the frequency of questions may depend upon the degree to which they are answered. Lewis stresses the fact that the child at first tends to use language as a form of play and in an attempt to satisfy his needs. The play is the game of question and answer in which the child calls another person in to help satisfy his needs. He points out that it gives the child pleasure to speak merely in order to be spoken to. Apparently children learn very early that they can gain the attention of adults and control others by the technique of asking questions. Lewis also points out that children often ask questions to which they already know the answers, often because they are learning to make formulations of events in words and seek social sanctions for these formulations. In building up his system of knowledge the child is said to begin by making tentative statements which, having an interrogative form, invite corroboration or rejection by others. He thinks that whereas there may be some rudimentary notion of causality in the early "why" questions, the child's real notion of causality develops only out of his constant experience with the causal answers that he receives from others.

E. A. Davis (1932) had mothers of 73 children record samples of 50 consecutive questions, totaling 3650 questions. These were classified and analyzed for form, length, and content. The questions are from children in the upper socioeconomic brackets, are subject to the unreliability of maternal report, and are not consecutive samples. Adequate tables on the frequency of the various types of question forms are not provided, although the author discusses this point at some length and presents a few critical ratios. When in her later study (1937a) she analyzed over 2000 questions many of the categories showed discrepancies with the earlier results.

M. E. Smith published (1933b) a separate article based on the 3095 questions recorded in running conversations of preschool children. Most of the analyses involve comparisons of responses recorded in the adult-child and child-child situations, but, as mentioned above, the two situations are not comparable, owing to the differences in selection of cases. She found, however, that "what" questions constituted 12 per cent of all questions and "where" questions 11 per cent, both of these categories showing increase with age. "Who," "whose," and "which" questions accounted for only 2 per cent and showed no relation to age. "How" questions were 6 per cent, "when" 1 per cent, and "why" questions amounted to 4 per cent. None of these groups showed significant change with age. Causal questions she found amounted to 8 per cent of all questions, questions of place 13 per cent, being most frequent at two years of age and showing a decrease with age. Questions of fact, time, and invention

showed an increase with age and accounted for 14 per cent. The category accounting for the largest percentage of the questions was that involving questions concerning human actions and intentions, which included 46 per cent of all. Of interest in connection with the recognition of the naming stage and the increase in nouns in the early vocabulary is the finding that questions asking for the name of an object or person constituted one-fifth of all the questions asked by two-year-olds and were third in frequency. She also reports that 94 per cent of all questions were concerned with some object, action, or person either in the immediate situation or desired to be there.

Interrelationships of Various Measures of Language Development

As is evident from the foregoing discussions, there is a wide variety of measures and indices of language development which have been employed and traced throughout childhood. Probably the two most widely used measures are those of vocabulary and of length of sentence, the latter having proved to be the most objective and reliable single index. However, comparatively little has been done in an attempt to determine the relative importance of the various aspects of linguistic development or to arrive at any single index of development in this tremendously complex function. One may still ask what is the relative importance of vocabulary, clearness of articulation, length of sentence, completeness and complexity of sentences, and the coefficient of egocentrism. So many of the analyses to which language development has been subjected, particularly the structural, functional, and parts-of-speech analyses, involve classification into percentages within a closed system that relationships can only be inferred from some of the shifts which occur in the percentages. One change or trend in such a system inevitably affects the other proportions, since all figures are relative. The result is that, upon completion of any one type of analysis, a set of values is obtained rather than a single index of the child's level of sentence structure or some other measure which can be correlated with other indices.

Only one study has appeared which has attempted to shed light on this vital question. This is a study by Williams (1937a) called "An Analytical Study of Language Achievement in Preschool Children." In Part IV of the same monograph by Little and Williams (1937) there appears a description of "An Analytical Scale of Language Achievement," with instructions in the appendix for the administration of the scale.

In Williams's (1937a) basic study, measures were obtained of ability to make speech sounds by the use of a modification and shortened form of the articulation test of Wellman, Case, Mengert, and Bradbury (1931), of the correctness of word usage, of the development of the sentence or expression unit, and of vocabulary. Word usage was measured by the number of words spoken correctly per fifty running words of conversation. Development of the expression unit was studied for length, completeness in terms of subject-predicate-object relationship, and in terms of complexity of grammatical construction. The scoring was entirely arbitrary and somewhat crude, yet it served to reveal individual differences in each of these measures in quantitative form with considerable reliability. Odd-even reliabilities for the several measures ranged from +.84 to +.91. Vocabulary was measured with the Van Alstyne Vocabulary Test (1929) and a modification of the M. E. Smith Vocabulary Test (1926), described above in the section on vocabulary tests. (See p. 510.)

The measures were obtained on 70 children, ranging in chronological age from 30 to 78 months, but considerably advanced in mental age. Unfortunately not all children had all the tests, so the complete tables of intercorrelations are based on only the 38 three- and four-year-olds for whom all measures were available. Although the probable errors of these correlations are large because of the small number of cases, the trends revealed are of interest. A condensed table of intercorrelations and the second order partial correlations reported by Williams (1937a) is given in Table 9. The reliabilities obtained by the odd-even method are shown in the diagonal cells. All the original intercorrelations are shown above and to the right of the diagonal and the partial correlations holding chronological and mental age constant are shown below and to the left of the diagonal. As may be seen, there is a rather strong positive relationship among the various language measures with the exception of vocabulary measures, which appear to be relatively independent of the others. These relationships are maintained at fairly high levels even when the influences of chronological and mental age are eliminated. Of particular interest is the strong degree of relationship which appears between the accuracy of speech sounds and the various measures of length, completeness, and complexity of the expression unit.

Such results are quite in accord with E. A. Davis's (1937a) conclusion that "at least during the kindergarten year, a child's mastery of articulation is closely related to other phases of language development. There are indications in the data that faulty articulation, if unduly prolonged, may become a major handicap preventing both adequate command of language and

TABLE 9

CORRELATIONS OF SEVERAL LANGUAGE INDICES WITH CA, MA, AND INTERCORRELATIONS AMONG THE LANGUAGE VARIABLES

(After Williams 1937a)

N = 38	MA	Speech sounds	Word usage	Length of unit	Complete-ness	Com-plexity	Van Alstyne vocabulary	Smith-Williams vocabulary
CA	.56	.31	.43	.54	.41	.45	.36	.16
MA		.12	.49	.78	.55	.59	.52	.47
Speech sounds		.91	.64	.60	.61	.62	.16	.01
Word usage		.60	.94	.62	.80	.57	.36	.27
Length of unit		.69	.42	.86	.65	.80	.56	.37
Completeness		.58	.66	.41	.89	.74	.41	.21
Complexity		.60	.38	.67	.61	.87	.56	.41
Van Alstyne vocabulary		.57	.13	.28	.16	.36	.84	.59
Smith-Williams vocabulary		.08	.09	.04	−.02	.22	.76	.87

Reliabilities are shown on the diagonal. Zero order r's above and to the right. Partial correlations holding CA and MA constant below and to the left.

wholesome development of the personality." This is based on a comparison of a group of 160 cases rated as having "perfect articulation" with a group of 88 cases rated as having "faulty articulation." Those with perfect articulation had a mean length of sentence of 4.85 as compared with 4.00 for those with faulty articulation, and they used 102.2 different words as compared with only 82.5 different words used by the group having faulty articulation.

The reasonableness of this finding is evident when it is pointed out that the child with faulty articulation usually has faulty sensory perception of speech sounds or faulty motor responses in attempting to make speech sounds, and the resultant model which he furnishes for himself to imitate is imperfect so that he continues to practice error. He is understood less well by others, and so gains less adequate social satisfaction and facilitation and probably practices his language less, simply because it is less satisfactory. The faulty articulation and the retardation in other aspects of language development may be due to a common cause in the last analysis, but it is entirely conceivable that in some cases the faulty articulation may exert a retarding effect on the other aspects of linguistic development. This area of the interrelationships among various measures of linguistic development is largely new and uncharted, and it is to be hoped that further researches along this line with improved techniques and adequate numbers of cases will follow in the near future.

Relation of Language Development to Other Aspects of Development

Unfortunately practically no research has been undertaken in an attempt to determine the degree of relationship between linguistic development and other aspects of the child's development. Most of the work has been confined to determining the relationship of various linguistic factors to measures of general intelligence, and a few suggestions of possible relationships to motor, emotional, and social development appear in isolation without supporting data. It is probable that the fact that no single general index of language development has been devised has prevented such studies from appearing heretofore.

Motor Development. Language is usually considered to be a substitute or short-cut type of behavior for overt bodily responses, as it is well known that gestures accompany language in the early stages. As has been pointed out earlier, gestures precede the appearance of language and constitute a more primitive form of communication. As language develops and becomes more precise, fewer gestures are needed, and it has often been pointed out that if a child develops an unusually effective gesture language his development of true language may be delayed for some time.

Shirley (1933a, 1933b), who made a careful analysis of the motor development of the same 25 children on whom language records were also kept, reported a cyclical relationship between linguistic development and the appearance of certain gross motor skills. Children's vocalizations decreased in frequency during periods when reaching for objects, sitting alone, and walking were being mastered. She found correlations between developmental scores on locomotion and vocalization which were all low or negative tending to "confirm the theory that speech development is held in abeyance at the time when motor progress is most rapid." She further states that, although the evidence is meager, "it points in the direction that early vocalization is held in check by rapid motor progress and that babbling is a type of behavior which a baby resorts to when there is nothing better to do, or when the novelty of a new type of motor activity has worn off." This phenomenon was pointed out as early as 1880 by the German observer, Schultze,

who said that children appear to learn only one thing thoroughly at a time, and that while the child learns to walk he pushes aside the development of speech almost entirely and resumes his linguistic task only after the locomotor one has been finished. It is possible that the slowing-up in rate of gain in vocabulary as shown in M. E. Smith's (1926) data (Table 3) at the age of 15 months, which was the age of learning to walk in Shirley's group, is another instance of this same phenomenon. Brigance (1934) also noted it in one child who showed a plateau in vocabulary development during the period of learning to walk. After walking became well established this child showed a rapid spurt in vocabulary development. It is relationships of this sort which are all too meager in the literature of child psychology because of the research worker's need to isolate functions for study. In all probability many interesting interrelationships such as these are being overlooked because of the methodology which characterizes so many current studies in child psychology.

Wellman, Case, Mengert, and Bradbury (1931), who give detailed tabulations on the ability of preschool children to articulate various sounds, report correlations of +.67 and +.65, respectively, between scores on a tracing path test and the total number of sounds and the number of consonant blends articulated. Bilto (1941) studied 90 speech-defective cases ranging in age from 9 to 18 years and found them to be definitely inferior as a group on three sets of motor ability tasks. Since articulation is so largely a motor function, this may be indicative of a general motor ability or both may be closely related to chronological age in the data presented. Shirley (1933b) found a moderate positive relationship between fine motor coordinations and language development after the age of 45 weeks. H. M. Johnson (1928) reports that nursery school children under three years of age frequently use rhythmic vocal accompaniments to their physical activity; Fisher (1934) reports a correlation of +.86 between the use of things by nursery school children and talking about things; and Goodenough (1930) reports a low positive correlation of +.17 with age constant between talkativeness and physical activity in nursery school children.

Although it is beyond the scope of this review to include the very extensive and specialized literature on pathological aspects of language, particularly on problems of aphasia and stuttering, a few interesting facts which may prove challenging to the investigator interested in developmental interrelationships might be pointed out. Neurological data seem to indicate that the speech area appears to be dominant on only one side of the brain and that it is on different sides in left-handed and in right-handed persons. Although the controversy as to the relationship between lack of, or disturbance of, lateral dominance and speech disturbances, particularly stuttering, still rages, and there are undoubtedly many cases of stuttering which do not appear to have any such explanation, there certainly are enough clinical cases on record to demonstrate rather clearly that at least in some cases there appears to be a relationship between lateral dominance and speech disturbance. From the developmental standpoint it is interesting to note that lateral dominance apparently becomes established toward the end of the first year of life and during the first months of the second year, which is just the period when speech begins to emerge from the infant's early babblings. It is interesting to speculate as to the possibility of a developmental relationship between these phenomena, but to date the writer has discovered no data on this very interesting point. Anticipating for the moment the

rather striking and consistent sex differences in favor of the girls which will be presented in detail in the section on individual differences, it is also interesting to point out that most studies report a higher incidence of left-handedness and a higher incidence of stuttering and also of reading disabilities among boys, who in comparison with girls are slightly more retarded in all measures of linguistic development. These facts also present a challenge to the research worker as to the possible relationships which may be involved between linguistic development and motor development, and more specifically between linguistic development and the establishment of lateral dominance. As Esper (1935) states, "The relationships between verbal and manual behavior offer a rich field for experimental investigation, the results of which might well be of great theoretical as well as practical (pedagogical) importance."

Intellectual Development. The age of onset of talking has often been regarded as symptomatic of the child's later intellectual development. One often hears favorable prognoses regarding the intellectual development of children who talk early, and mothers often become concerned over failure of their children to talk at least by the second birthday. From the scientific evidence available there appears to be some justification for these popular beliefs although the relationship is far from perfect, and the layman accepting such a generalization is quite likely to make serious errors in predicting a child's future mental development merely from a knowledge of the age at which he begins to talk. An idiot never learns to talk, and Terman et al. (1925) found that gifted children with IQ's above 140 talked on the average at about 11 months or approximately four months earlier than the average child. However, there were in this group of gifted children some who did not talk at all until 2, 2½, and even 3 years of age. So it is by no means certain that a child who is late in talking will be mentally retarded. However, in general, feeble-minded children usually talk much later than normal or superior children. The average age of talking of a group of feeble-minded subjects is reported by Mead (1913) as 38.5 months as compared with the normal age of 15.3 months. (See also Town, 1912–1913.) It thus appears that feeble-minded children are always late in beginning to talk, and a child who talks early is quite likely to be above average in intelligence. However, although delayed onset of speech is often due to general mental retardation, there are many other causes of delayed speech, and a diagnosis of mental retardation should never be made on the basis of delayed speech alone.

Irwin (1942) has thrown further light on this problem by showing that the speech sounds made by 10 low-grade feeble-minded children, none of whom was using real language (average age 4 years and average IQ 29), approximate those of normal children one year of age in such characteristics as vowel ratio, vowel-consonant ratio, and distribution of consonants. Sirkin and Lyons (1941) who examined 2500 institution mental defectives report that only one-third speak normally and that the lower the intelligence rating the lower is the incidence of normal speech. Speech correction with these cases was found to be unsuccessful below the moron level and they consider that a minimum mental age of five years six months combined with a cooperative attitude is essential to successful speech therapy.

In the studies of McCarthy (1930), Day (1932), and E. A. Davis (1937a) the same relationships which were traced with relation to chronological age also appeared when the data were analyzed according to mental age. The marked linguistic superiority of Fisher's (1934) subjects whose average IQ was 132 is also significant in considering the relationship between intellectual development and language development. It is also interesting to note that there are differences in intellectual status paralleling the differences in linguistic development, there being slight superiority of girls, of singletons as compared with twins, and of children from the upper as compared with the lower socioeconomic levels. This brings up a very interesting problem on which there are not sufficient data for a final answer: namely, whether the more precocious development of language among these groups is due to their greater intellectual endowment, or whether their higher scores on the intelligence tests, which are highly verbal in nature, are due to the more precocious linguistic development. Shirley (1933b) reports quite high correlations (five out of six between +.63 and +.76) between Minnesota Preschool Test scores and cumulative vocabulary, number of different words used per examination, and vocalization scores, all of them being higher at 2 years than at 18 months.

Only two studies have made any attempt to separate the factors involved in this relationship. Day (1932), in attempting to account for the differences which she found between twins and singletons in language development, matched her 4-year-old group of twins with singletons in regard to total test score, chronological age at time of testing, sex, and occupational class. The percentages of the total score which each group earned on verbal and nonverbal items of the test were then calculated and were found to match almost exactly. Day (1932) concludes therefore that "the language retardation of these 4-year-old twins does not seem to have been a factor in reducing the total test score and thus lowering the IQ." She also determined "language quotients" for her twins by obtaining ratios between the mean length of response of singletons and of twins of the same ages. The results indicate that "the language retardation is so significantly greater, that factors other than 'below average general intelligence' must be responsible for it. The language quotient decreases rapidly as age increases in spite of the fact that the intelligence quotient does not." It thus appears that differences in intelligence do not account entirely for the language retardation of twins, nor does the verbal element in intelligence tests appear to penalize the twin sufficiently to account for the differences in intelligence as measured.

The second study in which an attempt has been made to separate these two influences is that by Williams and McFarland (1937), in which a revision of the M. E. Smith (1926) vocabulary test was given to 242 Iowa City children and to 64 orphanage children. Here, again, the two groups showed marked contrast in both vocabulary and IQ. When orphanage and non-institutional children were matched on MA and IQ, there still remained a marked discrepancy between the vocabularies of the two groups, the vocabulary ratios of the orphanage children being only .48 to .68. The authors therefore state: "Thus the orphanage children have vocabularies which are inferior not only to those of children of the same chronological or mental age, but higher IQ, but also to those of children matched for IQ level as well." For the group living in the community the correlation between vocabulary and mental age, with chronological age held constant, was +.43, whereas for the orphanage group it was +.65.

Another interesting approach to this problem comes from learning studies in which subjects learn more readily when they have names for the learning materials.

It is well known that meaningful paired associates are learned more readily in the laboratory than nonsense syllables in the same type of learning situation. Pyles (1932) in an interesting study of the factor of verbalization in learning found that when young children were given names for nonsense molds which covered rewards, 44 per cent solved the problem in 25 trials or less, whereas only 14 per cent solved it when the molds remained unnamed. This brings us face to face with the very interesting problem of the relationship between thought and language. Carmichael, Hogan, and Walter (1932) demonstrated that in many cases merely saying a word before the presentation of a visual form definitely influences the manner in which the form is apprehended as well as the readiness with which it is recalled. It was also shown by Goodenough and Brian (1929) that verbal instructions were of considerable help to preschool children in acquiring a simple motor skill.

Space does not permit an adequate coverage of this controversial problem here. The various arguments as to whether or not thought occurs without language or whether subvocal speech is a necessary concomitant of thought are well presented in the symposium "Is Thinking Merely the Action of Language Mechanisms?" which appeared in the *British Journal of Psychology*, 1920. Other reviews on the subject are presented by McCarthy (1930), Mandell (1931), and Vigotsky (1939); and of course Piaget's (1926) approach to child thought through his language is a stimulating work on this topic. As Garrison and Garrison (1929) state, however:

> Language and mental development are mutually dependent. . . . With language man is able to acquire in a relatively short time a great share of the things discovered in the past. Since an individual grows only as he reacts to the things about him,

it is evident that language gives the individual a superior means of reacting and thus makes possible greater mental development.

Emotional Development. There is little or no information available on the relationship between linguistic development and emotional development, but evidence from isolated case studies indicates that there may be quite a marked relationship. Clinicians are familiar with cases of delayed or interrupted speech which cannot be accounted for on the basis of mental deficiency, deafness, or pathological condition of the organs of speech, and in which there seems to be evidence of severe emotional shock or psychic trauma which is responsible for the failure to speak. Blanchard (1933) gives one of the most helpful, although very brief, accounts of work with such cases in the Philadelphia Child Guidance Clinic in which she reports that they usually present a picture of general infantile and retrogressive behavior and that the most successful approach has been through the use of play therapy during which

> The whole course of the changes shown by the children . . . was one of growing out of infantile emotional patterns and behavior into those suitable for their age, and a turning from negative to positive modes of expression. The resumption of talking seemed to be an accompaniment of the emotional growth and the increasing ability to find satisfaction in positive rather than negative, or active rather than passive, ways.

At times overly critical attitudes of adults toward a child's early attempts to speak may result in a withdrawal type of behavior which involves the child's refusal to talk or a reduction of his conversational efforts to a minimum of single word responses. Relief from pressure and criticism often brings about an increased flow of language and increased practice in sentence structure, and a corresponding freedom in emotional expression. This often has a rather wholesome effect in spite of poor articulation, which may later need correction after the child has gained facility in the use of language as a means of expression.

A few writers, especially Low (1936), have suggested the possibility of tracing the developmental stages in reverse in retrogressive disturbances of speech in certain types of insanity. The suggestion is an interesting one, but it has not yet been put to the test scientifically so far as the writer has been able to determine.

Another line of evidence which is suggestive of a close relationship between emotional development and speech development is that which comes from the clinical experience with stutterers. Individuals who stutter only in the presence of certain persons and who respond favorably to situations of emotional calm bear witness to the existence of a rather intimate relationship of functions which have thus far been investigated only in individual cases or by very crude statistical surveys. The area of stuttering is much too specialized to be treated in detail here. Suffice it to say that there is apparently great need for basic psychological research to bring order out of the chaos which appears to exist in this controversial area. The reader who is interested in these problems is referred especially to the work of Travis (1931).

In the study by Busemann (1925) previously referred to, he claims that the action quotients, which he obtains roughly by determining the ratio of verbs to adjectives, reflect rhythmical changes throughout the child's life with alternating activity and quality phases. He also claims that these phases are related to periods of emotional instability. He thinks it is possible to determine from the action quotient analysis of a child's speech or composition whether a child is in a period of emotional stability or instability. When teachers marked personality check lists and the children were separated into vivacious as compared with quiet and reserved children, the children who were described as lively had higher action quotients in their language than those described as quiet. The data on cyclical changes with age are very dubious because of the manner of grouping and treating the data, but the hypothesis is interesting and might prove fruitful on further investigation. Portenier (1937) found that it took longer to elicit a specified number of responses from a group of children who were rated by their nursery school teachers as poorly adjusted than from a group rated as well adjusted.

In the discussion of functional analyses of children's speech it was pointed out that children first talk about things that have a strong emotional tone for them, and wishes, threats, requests, and commands bulk relatively large in the speech of the two-year-old. There appears to be a gradual waning in the relative amount of speech which is definitely emotional in character. This may be symptomatic of emotional maturation as may the decreasing frequency of the use of the first personal pronouns. McCarthy (1929a) found no very marked correlations between ratings of nursery school children on the Marston extroversion-introversion scale and various linguistic measures for 26 children observed in free play and in the controlled situation with an adult, except for a definite negative relationship between the percentage of emotionally toned responses and the ratings of extroversion. In general the correlations were slightly larger when the language was recorded in the free play situation.

Social Development. During the early preschool period when the child's language is not yet very useful as a means of social communication, he is still definitely an individualist, and it is probably significant that a marked degree of socialization of his behavior occurs during the later preschool period when language itself is becoming a more efficient means of intercommunication. Every nursery school teacher is familiar with the increased facility in controlling a child's behavior which comes as soon as his understanding of spoken language improves, and with the marked change in social behavior which comes about when a child learns to make verbal instead of physical contacts with his playmates. Children who talk very little are often solitary even in a group situation, and a spurt in a child's linguistic development sometimes appears to facilitate his social contacts so that a previously solitary child may develop friendships as soon as he begins to talk and make verbal approaches to other children. Schmidt (1941) has shown that speech therapy given to mental defectives facilitates their social adjustments and stimulates them to more gregarious behavior. A positive correlation between maturity of articulation and acceptable social behavior, as measured with the Haggerty-Olson-Wickman Behavior Rating Schedule B, was found in a study by I. P. Davis (1938). This she considers may indicate that the factors which retard a child's speech also retard his social development, or that the speech difficulty may in itself contribute to the retardation in social adjustment. The evidence is mainly indirect from studies of social behavior and from undirected observation in free play situations, but certainly careful research in this area is badly needed and should prove fruitful and yield results of considerable practical importance.

Language responses have been shown to differ from one play situation to another, as will be shown in more detail in the section on the effects of the environment. Further study should be made in order to determine whether the child's stage of linguistic development determines the types of companions he finds congenial and the sorts of play situations in which he will engage, or whether the situations themselves determine the linguistic pattern which is obtained.

Language Development and Individual Differences

Language is one area of the child's development in which more marked and more striking degrees of individual variation can be observed than in almost any other. From the idiot who grows to physical maturity without learning to talk, to the gifted child who begins to use words at eight months and sentences at the first year of life, there certainly is a wide span which is of considerable developmental significance. Suffice it to point out here that the individual differences in linguistic development closely parallel the differences which have been shown to exist in intellectual development, and certainly equal and perhaps even exceed them in magnitude. It is also quite certain that language development has contributed heavily to the variations in intellectual differences as they have thus far been measured. Whether or not this is an artifact due to the highly verbal nature of most of the more satisfactory intelligence tests, or whether there is a more basic fabric of intellectual development consisting largely of factors of linguistic maturation, is something which has not as yet been determined. The facts that thus far no satisfactory intelligence test has been developed for age levels before the emergence of language, and that all the intelligence tests which have proved to have a satisfactory degree of validity are heavily weighted with verbal factors, bear witness to the importance of language in mental development. The few studies that have attempted to separate the functions involved were treated under the section on the relationship of linguistic development to intellectual development. (See pp. 546 ff.)

Sex Differences. One of the most consistent findings to emerge from the mass of data accumulated to date on language development seems to be a slight difference in favor of girls in nearly all aspects of language that have been studied. Whenever groups of boys and girls are well matched in intelligence and socioeconomic background, and when the situation in which responses are recorded does not tend to favor the interests of one sex or the other, there appear slight differences in favor of girls. Whenever such sex differences fail to appear, or in rare instances are reversed, the result can nearly always be accounted for, when the data are available, in terms of selection on the basis of one of the aforementioned factors. The most clear-cut example appears in Table 4, where the mean length of response, which is the most objective single measure so far available, is shown for the sexes separately as obtained in 10 major studies. In this table there appear 55 comparisons of the two sexes for children of the same age groups. Of these, 39 favor the girls, 3 are identical for the two sexes, and only 13 favor the boys. Two of the figures where the sexes are equal come from Day's (1932) study of twins and one from E. A. Davis's (1937a) study, whereas four of the differences favoring boys come from the Davis study, which presented a situation that definitely favored boys' interests.

The toys used by Davis are described by the author as "a motley collection of little covered wagons with detachable oxen, lassoing cowboys, buffalo hunters, scouts,

Indians in attitudes of hostility, flight, or pursuit, and various animals and trees" (p. 20). It is difficult to understand the following justification for this choice of toys by a scientific investigator who is seriously interested in making valid comparisons with other available data on the matter of sex differences in language development. She states:

> Since no play object or situation was discovered which was of equal appeal to boys and girls of the ages studied, it was decided to choose objects known to be of especial interest to boys. This was done because (1) boys of five years are already "conditioned" against girls' toys, but girls if given the opportunity ordinarily enjoy boys' toys; (2) even if they are not interested in the toys, girls can easily be induced to cooperate in the experiment; and (3) since the language development of girls is slightly in advance of that of the boys, it is only fair that the advantage, if any, of a high degree of interest in the situation should be given to the boys. If the findings still show superiority on the part of girls, the significance becomes all the greater.

It should also be noted that in Davis's procedure picture books were shown "only when the toys had failed of their purpose," namely, to stimulate spontaneous language. Toys were considered to have "failed of their purpose" if the child volunteered no remarks after ten minutes and could not be induced to enter into conversation. Just how "happy" the choice of toys was for eliciting verbal responses from girls on an *equal* basis with boys, and how "easily" girls were "induced to cooperate in the experiment," can be gathered from the fact that Davis herself admits that "roughly about twice as many girls as boys were shown the books," and this following ten minutes of silence, and "at all ages boys show slightly more interest in the toys than do girls" (p. 21). "Boys are less likely to

be shy than girls. . . . Boys were slightly less negativistic than girls . . . [and] girls were somewhat more distractible than boys perhaps because they were less interested in the situation," and ratings on talkativeness revealed "a consistent tendency toward greater talkativeness in boys than in girls. . . . The mean time is slightly greater for girls than for boys" (pp. 25–26) (that is, to secure the same number of responses) and "greater spontaneity of speech is unquestionably characteristic of boys" (p. 67).

In view of these circumstances it does not appear that anyone should take seriously, as valid comparisons, the data on sex differences from Davis's investigation. The wonder is that, in spite of the very unequal conditions, the girls maintained their superiority in length of response in four of the nine comparisons and were equal to the boys in a fifth instance on length of response, and showed decided superiority on a number of other measures. The reversal of the usual trend seen in McCarthy's 2½-year-old subjects can be attributed to sampling errors, as the girls of that age group came in undue proportion from the lower socioeconomic levels. The reversals occurring in M. E. Smith's (1926) data can be accounted for on the basis of age differences as the boys are about a month and a half older than the girls at the ages at which they excel. In Young's (1941) study in which groups relatively homogeneous with respect to socioeconomic level were used, there was not a single exception to the general trend toward a slight superiority of girls in length of sentence.

Although length of sentence is the most objective and the most reliable single quantitative measure to use for comparison of the sexes, almost all other measures which show developmental trends with age also reveal a slightly more rapid linguistic maturity of girls. Mead (1913) found an earlier age of talking for feeble-minded girls, and Sirkin and Lyons (1941) report speech defects to be twice as frequent among mentally defective males as among defective females. I. P. Davis (1938) reports that girls reach maturity in articulation about a year earlier than boys, first grade girls having about the same articulatory patterns as second grade boys. Terman's (1925) gifted girls used short sentences at a slightly earlier age than the gifted boys. Doran (1907), after an extensive survey of the literature on vocabulary, reported that girls have larger vocabularies than boys of the same ages, but that the difference was smaller among older children, and M. E. Smith (1926) confirmed this in her vocabulary study.

Sex differences in favor of the girls appear in the comprehensibility of the speech at early levels. In McCarthy's (1930) study boys had only 14 and 49 per cent comprehensible responses at 18 and 24 months, as compared with 38 and 78 per cent for the same ages for the girls, and similar differences were found throughout the age range studied. Fisher (1934) also found a higher percentage of incomprehensible speech among the boys. They tended to repeat identical speech patterns more often. In the McCarthy (1930), Day (1932), M. E. Smith (1935a), E. A. Davis (1937a), and Young (1941) investigations, all other analyses, particularly functional and construction analyses, revealed that, when categories are studied for sex differences which reveal increasing or decreasing trends with age, the trend is evident at an earlier age among the girls. Davis summarizes the findings of her own study which revealed sex differences in favor of girls, in spite of a situation which was unfavorable to them, as well as that of other investigators as follows:

In nearly every phase of language studied, girls were found to retain up to the 9½-year level the superiority which has been previously demonstrated for the preschool period. This is true of articulation, word usage, and length, complexity, and grammatical correctness of sentences. Girls use more personal pronouns and conjunctions than boys, and less slang.

It is interesting to note that both Davis (1937a) and Young (1941) agree in finding the sex differences more marked among children of the lower socioeconomic levels than among those from superior homes. Fisher (1934), whose group was the most highly selected, found the smallest sex differences. This might seem to point to an early differential effect of the environment on the two sexes as revealed in linguistic development. In this connection it is interesting to note that in Davis's study twin boys who had twin sisters, rather than brothers, were less seriously retarded in language. One hypothesis which she suggests is that:

> The twin sister, developing a little faster than the boy, may act as a pacemaker for him; but it is equally possible that unlike-sex twins because of parental attitude or differing interests are less dependent on each other than twins of the same sex and more likely to seek out the wider contacts which stimulate and facilitate attempts at articulate speech (p. 126).

Wellman and others (1931) also found that girls articulate consonant elements better than boys.

The proverbial claim that the female is the more talkative is in general borne out by the results of scientific investigations and apparently is evident at a very early age. Jersild and Ritzman (1938) found that girls excel boys in the number of words spoken and in the number of different words used, but some might be surprised at the report by Olson and Koetzle

(1936) that, although boys tend to speak less than girls during given periods of time, when they do talk, it is at a slightly more rapid rate. Jersild and Ritzman state: "In summary, then, the present findings with regard to sex differences in verbosity and vocabulary indicate that girls tend quite consistently to surpass the boys, but not to a degree that is statistically significant."

The writer has previously pointed out that the magnitude of the sex differences usually found in young children's language is not large enough to yield statistically significant differences when the usual criterion is employed. Probably one reason why these differences have not proved significant is because of the small numbers of cases usually employed at a given age level, and also because of the fact that so many analyses are done in terms of percentages which are rather unreliable indicators. It should also be pointed out that there seem to be two methods employed by writers in the field for determining the significance of a difference although all claim to be using the critical ratio. Some use the number of children observed as the N in the formula, and others use the total number of sentences representative of the age level. Young (1941) obtains many very large critical ratios in various comparisons of subgroups by virtue of the fact that she employs the total number of cases in the study (74) when comparing data based on smaller subgroups. Obviously, a large number of sentences from a small number of children would yield more significant differences if the latter method is employed than if N is taken merely as the number of children observed. There is need for clarification of methodology on this point and for uniformity of procedure. It seems to the writer that the correct procedure is to use the number of children being studied in the particular subgroups as the N. When such a method is employed the sex differences seldom prove statistically significant.

The vast accumulation of evidence in the same direction from a variety of investigators working in different parts of the country, employing different situations and methods of observation, and employing different analyses and linguistic indices, certainly is convincing proof that a real sex difference in language development exists in favor of the girls. Critical ratios are employed and are interpreted to mean that if the ratio is sufficiently large we can be practically certain that if the experiment were repeated the difference would occur in the same direction again. In the array of data cited above we have presented experimental, rather than statistical, evidence of the reality of the differences, small though they may be, and when experimental trends check in study after study there appears to be little need for the reassurances of the statistical significance of critical ratios.

Apparently these small differences in the two sexes in linguistic development are related to later academic success in verbal skills. LaBrant (1933) found, for example, that girls used 148.3 words per theme, whereas the boys used only 124.7 words per theme. The boys in general wrote between 83 and 86 per cent as much as the girls. Bennett (1938) in reviewing the literature on reading disability presented a summary table showing 17 groups of cases requiring remedial reading work. The proportion of boys in all these reports is striking, ranging from 60 to 100 per cent of the total groups in the various studies. Is it not possible that exposure to the reading experience at the same chronological age, but at an earlier stage of linguistic maturity, may be partly responsible for the greater toll of reading disability cases among boys? Ley (1930) stated that all forms of difficulty in the development of language occur much more frequently in males than in females, and the higher incidence of stuttering and other speech defects among them is well known. Azoy (1935) found 202 boys to 119 girls in a group of speech defectives and 43 boys and only 22 girls in a group of 65 stammerers. He reported that the sex distribution is the same as that found in Germany. It is probable that this slight though apparently basic difference between the sexes is also partly responsible for the consistent reports of better scholarship among girls in high school and college.

With these data in mind it would be well to re-examine the data on sex differences in intelligence as reported in Terman (1916, 1925), Goodenough (1927, 1928), Monroe (1932), and others which show slight superiority of girls in intelligence as measured with the usual tests having a preponderance of verbal items likely to favor the girls. An unpublished study by Seidl (1937) showed that the Stanford-Binet scores of bilingual girls are apparently more depressed in comparison with their scores on the Arthur Point Scale of Performance Tests due to their bilingualism than are the scores of a similarly selected group of bilingual boys. It would seem then that bilingualism was a greater handicap to girls than to boys in the intelligence test as they characteristically tend to earn a greater proportion of their scores on verbal items.

Language Development in Handicapped Children. In certain groups of handicapped children, such as the deaf and the blind, sensory handicaps result in a definite restriction of the child's experiences which is often reflected in their language. Maxfield (1936) studied the language development of a group of eight totally blind preschool children, employing methods similar to those of McCarthy (1930),

Fisher (1934), and M. E. Smith (1935a) in a more or less exploratory investigation. Although conclusions were necessarily tentative on such a small number, Maxfield demonstrated that the method employed in these other studies of normal children is directly applicable to young blind children. There was an abundance of language among these children with about twice as high a percentage of their remarks being about things as occurred in Fisher's data. The blind children, as a group, asked many more questions, gave fewer commands, and had unusually high percentages of emotionally toned responses. They used fewer nonverbal responses, but more incomplete responses, and had an unusually high incidence of proper names. As Maxfield stated:

> It may be that the trends which have appeared in connection with some of the questions [raised in her study] will be found to group themselves around some fundamental need of the growing blind child. For instance, it seems reasonable to assume that the totally blind preschool child is satisfying his need for a feeling of security through talking a great deal, asking many questions, and using proper names frequently. . . . The trends disclosed . . . probably stand for the blind child's attempt to gain that assurance regarding his environment which seeing children obtain through visual observation (p. 85).

Thus, while the handicap of blindness does not appear to have a seriously retarding effect upon the child's linguistic development, and may on further investigation actually prove to have a stimulating effect, since the handicap itself forces dependence upon others and requires an abnormal amount of adult attention, the patterns of the functional analysis may be very different in a group of children having atypical needs.

The handicap of deafness of course has

a much more direct and more serious retarding effect upon language development, for the child who is totally deaf from birth does not acquire language in the normal way and has to be taught to speak by artificial techniques. Children with adventitious deafness, or hard-of-hearing children having various amounts of residual hearing, are much less seriously handicapped, the degree of linguistic retardation being a function of the age at onset of the acoustic handicap, and of the amount of residual hearing, as well as of the type of education and the age at which it was begun. Most of the literature in this field consists of reports of isolated cases, surveys of incidence and causes of hearing loss. There are reports of results obtained with specific educational techniques of interest to teachers of the deaf, and most of the studies of a psychological or educational nature are concerned with problems of the measurement of intelligence in the deaf and with the measurement of their academic achievement. The most interesting research work being carried on with deaf and hard-of-hearing subjects is that being conducted by Doctor and Mrs. Heider and their associates in the Psychological Division of the Clarence W. Barron Research Department at the Clarke School for the Deaf. One of their most interesting conclusions from this group of studies is that by Eberhardt (1940) which states:

> The experiments show that the world of the young deaf child is already organized beyond the perceptual level and that this organization closely follows that of speaking people. They show clearly that language is not essential for organized conceptual thought, at least during its first stages. They are interesting, from an educational point of view, in showing that much of the first language development of the young deaf child in school consists in the learning of words for ideas that he

already knows and uses in his everyday life. . . . Of course there are many instances in which a new word introduces a new conceptual relationship, but this is also true for hearing persons (pp. 4–5).

Heider and Heider (1940*b*) point out:

> The deaf child usually does not begin to learn language until he has reached an age at which the hearing child has already mastered most of the forms used in adult expression. The whole process by which he learns language is necessarily different from that of a hearing child. From the beginning it is based to a certain extent on the presentation of carefully selected examples from which rules can be derived, while the hearing child learns by free selection from a wealth of language forms.

They analyzed 1118 compositions consisting of accounts of a short motion picture written by 301 deaf and 817 hearing children of seven different age groups. The hearing children were 8 to 14 years and the deaf 11 to 17 years, the youngest children in each age group being the youngest children who were able to write the whole story. A very detailed analysis on complexity of sentence structure was conducted. Among the more significant findings were the facts that the sentences of the deaf were shorter both in number of words and number of clauses than those of the hearing, the deaf used relatively more simple and fewer compound and complex sentences, fewer verbs in coordinate and subordinate clauses, relatively more infinitives, and relatively more prepositional phrases. In all these, the authors report, except those of the infinitive and prepositional phrase, the performance of the deaf resembled that of the less mature hearing children. It appeared that the deaf used relatively simple language units, shorter sentences, and relatively few forms requiring precision of use. These differences were found even though the deaf children were approximately three years older than the hearing children with whose compositions their work was being compared.

Two very similar studies have appeared recently on the speech of deafened children. One by Hudgins and Numbers (1942) involved the analysis of phonographic records of the speech of 192 deaf pupils between the ages of 8 and 20 years who had been taught by the oral method. Teachers of deaf children served as auditors, and a reliability of +.90 was obtained for the method of analysis. Results were chiefly in terms of analysis of vowel and consonant errors and errors in rhythm. Approximately 21 per cent of all consonants and 12 per cent of all vowels were malarticulated by the deaf children. Correct rhythm was revealed to be an extremely important element contributing to the intelligibility of the speech of the deaf. The authors concluded:

> Speech is a dynamic process; it cannot be broken down into static positions and isolated movements. An *analytic* method of speech teaching of itself, therefore, violates basic physiological and phonetic principles. A synthetic method in which the basic phonetic unit is the syllable is in keeping with these physiological and phonetic principles; it is the natural method by which hearing children acquire speech.

They therefore advocate a basic revision of the methods which have heretofore been employed in the teaching of speech to the deaf.

The study by Hughson and others (1942) involved a detailed analysis of the voice and speech characteristics of 367 children resident in the Pennsylvania School for the Deaf, 249 of whom had never received auricular training and 118 of whom were enrolled in auricular classes, that is, classes using group hearing aids for children with residual hearing. Electrical transcriptions were employed. Children receiving auric-

ular training in speech were found distinctly superior to those taught by the traditional oral method. Their superiority was independent of the amount of residual hearing and age of onset of deafness. They estimate a two-year shortening in the education of the deaf child by the use of this method. The previously cited study by Hudgins and Numbers (1942) agrees that children having auricular training have more intelligible speech than those taught by the oral method.

The Effect of Various Environmental Factors

It has been pointed out above that investigators have not been very successful in their attempts to measure intelligence until the child is able to talk or at least to respond to verbal commands, in other words, to participate in verbal tests. We are faced with the dilemma of whether the differences in intellectual ability are responsible for the differences in linguistic development, or whether the differences in linguistic development account for the intellectual differences which are measurable with verbal intelligence tests. Before any attempt is made to resolve this problem, certain environmental factors should be considered. Socioeconomic status, of course, involves a combination of hereditary and environmental factors which cannot readily be separated. Perhaps a consideration of this and some of the more strictly environmental factors in their relation to linguistic development will serve to throw the picture into somewhat clearer relief.

Occupational Group Differences. There is considerable evidence in the literature to indicate that there exists a marked relationship between socioeconomic status of the family and the child's linguistic development. Chamberlain (1900) states that as early as 1847 Degerando reported that "the child of the rich understands more words and less actions, and the child of the poor less words and more actions." This early observation regarding the linguistic superiority of the privileged child has since been confirmed by a number of recent experimental studies.

Descoeudres (1921) studied 300 children of the upper and lower classes as they were distinguished by attendance at private or public schools and found that on practically all items of her extensive battery of tests, nearly all of which involved language, the children of the upper social classes were decidedly superior to those of the lower social classes. Stern (1930), who reworked these data, calculated that the difference between the educated class and the working class would be equivalent to about eight months in linguistic development.

Worbois (1942) compared the language of children from a one-room rural school and from a consolidated rural school. The groups were matched on IQ, age, home cultural index, and midparent education. Significant differences on the Stanford-Binet vocabulary test and on a verbal effectiveness test were found in favor of the group in the consolidated school. They also used almost twice as many words and half again as many different words in describing the pictures in the Stanford-Binet scale as the children from the one-room school. The principal environmental difference which seemed to be associated with these factors was the education of the teachers, for in the one-room school they had had on the average only 0.6 of a year beyond high school, whereas those in the consolidated school had had an average of 3.0 years of education beyond high school.

C. Bühler (1931) reported that children from a neglected milieu show retardation in all aspects of their development, but that the retardation is more evident in language development than in other aspects of development. She reported data of Hetzer and Reindorf, who compared a group of children from a "good" environ- ment with a group from an "underprivi- leged" environment. The children from the more favored environment used more words meaningfully at earlier ages, a larger percentage of them were using two- to three-word sentences at earlier ages, and the same differences were revealed when syntax, inflection, and sentence structure were analyzed.

Chamberlain (1900) reports a study by Lombroso in which 50 children of well-to-do and educated families were found to have much larger vocabularies than 100 children from poor families. In reviewing this study Markey (1928) states: "Both in the precocity with which they interpret the words and in the exactness reached, the children of the former families exceeded those of the poor in the proportion of two to one."

In the McCarthy (1930), Day (1932), and E. A. Davis (1937a) studies paternal occupation was used as a criterion of selection in efforts to secure representative samplings. In all these studies occupational group differences are consistent and strikingly in favor of the upper socioeconomic levels in all types of analysis. The children from the upper social levels not only use longer sentences, but also use more mature sentence forms at earlier ages. Functional categories, especially questions, which show trends with age, also reveal more rapid development of children from the more favored homes. In McCarthy's word analysis, children of the lower classes continued to use larger percentages of nouns up to higher age levels, which is probably indicative of linguistic immaturity. In Davis's study 73 per cent of the children from upper socioeconomic levels were rated as having "perfect articulation" at 5½ years, but only 58 per cent of the children of the lower levels received similar ratings on articulation at that age. It will be recalled that Fisher's (1934) cases which showed the greatest superiority in linguistic development came, nearly always, from the families of professional men. McCarthy (1930) and Day (1932) found a tendency for the differences between the occupational groups to increase with increase in chronological age, but this was not borne out by Davis's data on school age subjects.

The most recent and perhaps the most clear-cut study on this problem is that by Young (1941) in which six-hour language records were made on 74 cases, half of whom attended the nursery school at the University of Georgia during a period when tuition was charged and half of whom attended when the nursery school was run as a Federal Emergency Relief Project and served only families on relief. Comparisons are made between the "regular" and "relief" cases attending the same school in different years. It was found that the regular group surpassed the relief group in all aspects of language that were analyzed. Relief boys were by far the poorest in language development and regular girls the most advanced.

It is difficult or impossible to determine from available data the relative rôles of environmental factors and differences in native ability in bringing about these differences. It should be pointed out, however, that there are differences in intelligence as measured with verbal tests corresponding to the differences in linguistic development here reported. They were evident in the data of Yoakum and Yerkes (1920) on occupational status in the testing with the Army Alpha, and Haggerty and Nash (1924) and others have shown the presence of such differences among school children whose fathers are in the various occupational groups. Goodenough (1928), Kawin (1934), and others have shown that such differences in intellectual ability are present at a very early age, at least as early as two years.

Variety of Experiences. Several investigators have reported that travel and events which broaden the child's experiences are accompanied or followed by increases in vocabulary. Drever (1915–1916), after comparing the vocabularies of his own three children, who had had a broad environment with considerable travel, and those of slum children, concluded: "Expansion of a child's environment always tends to increase nouns relatively to other parts of speech. Conversely, with a constant or relatively constant environment, the other parts of speech will increase relatively to the nouns."

This is in agreement with Bean's (1932) observation that periods of rapid increase in vocabulary coincided with the widening of the child's experiences through travel, and that periods of sentence building paralleled uneventful interim periods. Most of these reports are on isolated cases, yet it is conceivable that the occupational group differences which have been found so consistently in the larger scale studies may be due in some measure to the more restricted environment commonly experienced by children of the lower socioeconomic classes. Parents of children in the lower classes are presumably less gifted linguistically than parents of children in the upper classes, and hence not only afford a poorer example of language for a model, but also probably provide less verbal stimulation. It would be interesting to conduct more extensive investigations which would be designed to reveal in greater detail the effects of specific environmental experiences. The effects of the amount and kind of language heard at home, of school field trips, etc., on vocabulary, sentence structure, oral and written composition would be interesting problems for further investigation.

Age of Associates. There have been a number of interesting facts revealed on the relationship between the age of the child's associates and his linguistic development. The Gales (1906), whose second and third children used twice as many words as the first child at the same age, claimed that "the later children have an advantage in learning much from contact with the older child." Others hold, however, that children understand each other much better than they do adults who are too far above their level. G. S. Hall (1891a), in speaking of children of approximately the same age, said: "Their noises are too well understood by each other, the younger holding the older back."

McCarthy (1930) found that the median percentile rank on length of response of the children in her experimental group who associated chiefly with adults was 70. For those who associated with older children it was 42.5. This latter group was drawn chiefly from large families who usually came from lower socioeconomic levels. The children who associated chiefly with younger children had a mean length of response very close to the median for their ages, namely, 52.5. It appears, then, that association with adults is likely to be associated with linguistic acceleration. Further evidence along this line comes from M. E. Smith's (1935a) study in which children were shown to use longer sentences and to use more advanced patterns of language development during the situation in which they conversed with an adult than in the situation involving conversation with other children. If association with adults is frequent in the child's experience, and he follows the pattern found by M. E. Smith, he will get more and more practice in using more mature language in situations which are conducive to better language usage.

Another striking fact which fits into the picture on age of associates is the marked superiority of only children. Of all the groups studied, only children, especially only girls, seem to be the most precocious in all aspects of language development. It is true that only children most frequently come from homes of the upper socioeconomic levels and are somewhat higher in intelligence, but their linguistic superiority appears to be out of all proportion to what would be expected on the basis of their age, sex, and socioeconomic status alone. Because of the nature of the family pattern, only children usually have more adult contacts than other children. Although these children are undoubtedly of superior native endowment, it must be remembered that their environments differ from that of other children chiefly in affording greater association with adults and greater opportunities for practice in the use of language under optimum conditions.

At the opposite extreme, children in orphanage and institution environments can be cited as the most seriously retarded group in language development. Little and Williams (1937), Skeels, Updegraff, Wellman, and Williams (1938), and Flemming (1942) have found marked retardation in vocabulary development among institution children. Although the children of this group undoubtedly come from lower socioeconomic levels, are somewhat below the average in native ability, and probably have had very restricted environmental experiences, their retardation appears so marked that it is necessary to look for other factors to account for the magnitude of the differences found. Even when Little and Williams (1937) match cases on mental age, the institution children are much more retarded in vocabulary than are noninstitution children of the same mental age. If these data are fitted into the picture on age of associates it appears that children living in an orphanage have the maximum amount of association with other children, and a minimum of association with, and attention from, adults. If, therefore, association with adults is a facilitating factor in language development, it is understandable why this group of orphanage children should show such marked retardation in linguistic development.

Environmental Effect of Multiple Births. Another line of evidence on the effect of environment comes from studies of children whose environment differs from the normal by reason of multiple birth. Day (1932), who duplicated McCarthy's (1930) techniques with 80 pairs of twins, using the same criteria of selection, found that the twins were markedly retarded in all aspects of language development when compared with McCarthy's singletons. She reported that "the mean length of response for five-year-old twins is slightly below that of three-year-old singletons," and a comparison of the yearly gains indicated that the rate of increase in length of response among singletons was about double that found among twins. She attributes the differences found to the peculiar social situation of the twin, stating, "One surely could not learn as much or as rapidly, from companionship with an individual so nearly on his own plane, as from one in advance. Satisfactions from this companionship may be adequate to the twin . . . whereas the single child . . . may be motivated to gain his satisfactions from a wider field."

Following up these results, E. A. Davis (1937a) set out to compare twins, singletons, and only children at higher age levels. She found the twins retarded in language as compared with the other groups, but the discrepancy between their linguistic status and that of singletons was not nearly so great after the age of school en-

trance as Day found at the preschool period. It seems that the home situation of the twins during the preschool period is not likely to promote normal linguistic growth, but that after school experience comes in with its opportunities for wider social contacts much of the initial handicap appears to be overcome. The twins of the upper socioeconomic groups made most of the linguistic gains after school entrance, whereas those in the lower economic brackets made comparatively little progress. An unpublished study by Howard (1934) on a large number of triplets revealed even more serious linguistic retardation than Day found among twins, for her 5-year-old triplets had a mean length of sentence of only 2.98 words, which is about equal to Day's 4-year-old twins, and McCarthy's 2½- to 3-year-old groups.

Interestingly enough, the Dionne quintuplets have been found to show even more marked linguistic retardation. Blatz, Fletcher, and Mason (1937) reported that Annette, who was the most advanced of the five in language, began to use words by the nineteenth month and that all children were using a few words by the twenty-second month. They compare the total vocabularies spoken by the quintuplets with McCarthy's (1930) and Day's (1932) data showing the mean number of words used in a sample of 50 consecutive responses by singletons and twins, and state that the quintuplets are about 16 to 18 months retarded as compared with the normal children. The real comparison which should be made would indicate even more serious retardation, since the figures for the quintuplets represent the total cumulative vocabulary ever heard before that age. Obviously, if a short sample of 50 responses recorded in 15 or 20 minutes yielded 66 words for McCarthy's singletons and 55 for Day's twins and the quintuplets did not have as many words in their entire known vocabularies until 32 or 33 months, their retardation in language was indeed serious at that age. It must be remembered also that they were living in a bilingual environment, but up to the time of the report cited above they had used only French and were just about to begin to learn English. It is difficult to explain this retardation entirely in terms of the social situation, since the quintuplets had so much individual attention from adults during their preschool years that it should compare favorably with the amount of adult time and attention which children in smaller families normally receive, unless, perhaps, their environment was psychologically more nearly comparable to that of institution children.

Effect of the Situation. Considerable interest has been shown in recent studies in the effect of the immediate situation in which language responses are recorded on the general pattern of results. Attention was called to this factor by McCarthy (1929a), who in an effort to reconcile the results of her major study with those of Piaget (1926) recorded the language of the same children in a situation in which the child was conversing with an adult and also in a nursery school free play situation. Although the odd-even reliability of length of response samples of 50 responses taken in the adult-child situation was +.91, the correlation found between mean lengths of response for samples taken in the two different situations was only +.54. Some children who were somewhat shy and restrained in the adult situation talked more freely on the playground, and others who were talkative with adults talked relatively little in this group, thus tending to lower the correlation.

McConnon (1935) conducted a study of 28 nursery school children in which two samples of conversation were recorded in each of six different situations; lunch, morning outdoor play period, indoor free play situation, table-play, afternoon outdoor play, and an outdoor play situation at home. Twenty-five responses were recorded in each situation for the same group of children. McCarthy's (1930) methods of recording and analysis were followed quite closely although no construction analysis was conducted. Surprisingly low coefficients of agreement between the two observations in each situation were found, the quantitative analyses yielding the highest mean coefficient of only +.431, the functional analysis yielding a mean correlation coefficient of only +.289 between various situations, and the parts of speech analysis one of only +.072. The two reasons which obviously account for the differences found here are, first, that the quantitative measures such as length of response and total number of words and the like are more objective and do not involve judgment and classification by the experimenter, and, second, that they are based on the total sample while the functional and parts-of-speech analyses are based on only parts of the sample, in some instances certain categories being represented by a relatively small number of responses. On the whole, McConnon reports, the home situation yielded the greatest consistency from one occasion to the next. The category of emotionally toned responses yielded the highest consistency coefficient from one situation to another. Of the various nursery school situations, the lunch period apparently offered more controlled conditions than the other school situations. The two outdoor situations both showed low consistency, as did also the indoor play situations.

A recent inquiry on the relationship between children's language and their play by Janus (1943) is so inadequately controlled that the conclusions should be disregarded. Space does not permit detailed criticism here, but the article has been severely criticized in print by Dennis (1943).

Williams and Mattson (1942) studied the effect of different social groupings on the language of six nursery school children. A Fonda recorder enabled them to secure responses for several children at one time. Records were taken when the child was alone, with the experimenter, with the experimenter and one, two, and three other children. Most talking and the most social speech occurred when in the largest social group, but the mean length of sentence remained fairly constant for the various social situations. The data were also analyzed for parts of speech and according to Piaget's analysis.

Comparing the various situations with one another, all the intercorrelations were low, being more than three times their standard errors in only nine instances. For the quantitative indices they averaged +.31 to +.40, and for the functional indices −.05 to +.20, and for the parts of speech −.07 to +.23. The same children used longer responses and more words in samples of conversation taken in an outdoor home situation than in any of the nursery school situations studied.

In a very interesting study by Van Alstyne (1932) it was found that over half the time preschool children tended not to talk to other children while working with play materials. Certain materials appeared to have considerably more "conversation value" than others. Doll play, blocks, crayons, and clay ranked high for percentage of time that their use was accompanied by conversation, whereas painting, scissors, and books were low in conversation value. It is interesting in view of the sex differences previously shown that the doll-corner activities and dishes, which are typical girl activities, were among the highest in conversation value. It is rather easy to conclude that certain differences in language may be due to the effect of the situation, but perhaps the situations may attract children whose language development is at different levels. It would be interesting, however, to attempt experimentally to stimulate the linguistic development of children who were not naturally very talkative by deliberate efforts to interest them in play materials which appear to be conducive to conversation.

It appears from McConnon's investigation that the results of language analyses are dependent upon the situation in which the data are gathered and on the type of index of language development employed. It is extremely important, therefore, in comparing language studies and in setting up experimental situations for future investigations, to control the situation with great care, to make comparisons only of situations which have been shown to be comparable, and to generalize regarding language development only for the specific situation in which the data have been collected. Apparently there are sufficient differences in the same children's use of language from one situation to another to make it extremely hazardous to infer that a given sample is representative of a child's language development in general. M. E. Smith (1935a) also attacked this problem by comparing children's language recorded in a nursery school free play situation and in the adult-child situation, but since the personnel of her groups differed it is difficult to interpret her findings. She claims, however, superior language usage by children in the adult-child situation. However, as McConnon concludes, "If a typical picture of the child's behavior is to be obtained, a number of situations must be sampled. Observational studies cannot continue to ignore the situational factor in response if the results are to have significance for child development." She further points out, "In order to obtain a stable index of the child's language responses it is necessary to take a number of samples in a number of situations."

In the recent study by Young (1941) samples of language in four different nursery school situations were obtained. Each child was observed for 6 hours in periods of 10 minutes each during about 15 days. The situations studied were outdoor play, indoor play, dinner, and a period in which the children were looking at picture books. It was found that the setting in which the responses are collected has a marked relation to the amount of language obtained in a given time, that is, to talkativeness. Young states:

> The amount of comprehensible verbal behavior varies significantly from setting to setting. The Outdoor and Picture situations were the scenes of the largest amounts of speech. The results indicate that in order to secure truly representative samples of the language of preschool subjects it is important to procure records in several relatively distinct types of environmental situations. If this is impossible the setting which is used should be carefully described and the limitations recognized (p. 127).

In length of response, however, twelve correlations between compared situations ranged from +.90 to +.94. These and all other intersituation correlations reported by Young are unbelievably high considering the degree of reliability which is usually found for data of this type. They are all the more surprising when one considers the small homogeneous groups upon which they are based. Barring computational errors, the only possible explanation of them seems to be in the relatively longer samples employed, which may have yielded more reliable data. These correlations seem to indicate that sentence length in any one setting tends to be markedly similar to that used by the subjects in the other situations studied. However, Young states:

> Apparently the four groups were not identically affected by the four different settings in which they were placed. Judging from the results of the combined groups of "All Subjects," studies of sentence length made in the Picture setting, a situation somewhat similar to that used by McCarthy, may be expected to yield findings representative of those which would be secured in any of the other three settings, if the subjects are of both sexes and come from widely differing socioeconomic levels, as in the present investigation. If, however, a relatively homogeneous group is being studied it seems advisable to secure responses in several different types of situation. This appears to be especially important if the subjects are of low socioeconomic status (pp. 43–44).

The analysis for parts of speech showed rather marked differences from setting to setting corresponding to the changes found in amount of comprehensible verbal behavior. It seems as if this contribution to methodology is very timely and should be a helpful guide to future investigators in this rapidly expanding field.

Results such as those cited above raise some interesting questions regarding the effects of nursery school experience on children's language. Undoubtedly there are some instances in which the social stimulation of association with other children brings about increased use of language, and the usual findings of tendency to increase in intelligence quotient during nursery school attendance would argue in favor of a probable facilitating effect. However, for most children of the upper socioeconomic levels nursery school experience results in more child contacts and fewer adult contacts, and in the light of the evidence presented earlier it would not be surprising if in some cases there were revealed a retarding effect of nursery school experience, especially for only children of upper socioeconomic levels. This possibility, even if later demonstrated, however, should not be interpreted as an indictment of nursery school experience, because such factors need to be evaluated in the light of the child's total development. Social facilitation from contacts with other children might counterbalance any linguistic retardation which might be present owing to less adult contact, and, even if the net result should show a slight retarding effect, there would undoubtedly be other advantageous factors which would more than offset it, should later investigation confirm this possibility. This is an area of evaluation which needs to be explored further.

Bilingualism. Another environmental factor which is of prime importance in the acquisition of language by the preschool child is bilingualism. In adulthood the ability to use a second language is thought to be a decided cultural advantage, and considerable time and effort are spent in secondary school and college to acquire even a rudimentary knowledge of another language; yet a young child can acquire two languages during the preschool years with apparently little difficulty. However, there are many examples of confusion which children who hear two languages are likely to experience. The usual situation for bilingual children in this country is to hear a foreign language in the home and English at school, and in such instances educational experience reveals that the bilingualism is a handicap to the child's school adjustment and academic achievement. Parents who can speak two languages often ask whether it is advantageous or detrimental to permit the child to hear and speak two languages during the preschool years, when language development normally is progressing so rapidly, and whether a certain mastery of one language should be attained before the second one is introduced. Scientific evidence on these very practical and important problems has been seriously lacking. Most of the studies on bilingualism have been concerned with the effect of this factor on intelligence as measured with verbal tests. Seidl (1937) found that bilingual Italian children usually test on the average 5 or 6 points below average in verbal intelligence and that their scores on performance tests generally run 10 or 12 points higher than on verbal tests. Few studies have been concerned with the effect of bilingualism on the development of the child's language.

Leopold (1939), a linguist, has conducted one of the most careful and detailed studies based on diary records, phonetic transcriptions, and vocabulary counts of his own two daughters who were brought up to hear both English and German. M. E. Smith (1935b) studied the language development of eight children in the same family who had varied experiences with English and Chinese. On the basis of this study she concluded that it is probably better for young bilingual children to receive their two languages from quite separate sources, each adult in the home using one language consistently, and that change from a monolingual to a bilingual environment has a more serious effect on the child's language than change from bilingual to monolingual environment. Such changes she thinks are more difficult for infants 12 to 18 months of age than for children who have acquired greater facility in the use of speech. It does not appear to delay the first use of words, but does seem to have a handicapping effect at later ages.

In 1939 Smith published the most comprehensive investigation that has ever been reported on the effect of bilingualism on language development. She studied 1000 children of varying racial backgrounds and varying amounts of bilingualism in Hawaii.

The major findings were that in general these children preferred to use English. The Japanese children who heard the least English used 50 per cent English words, but the total group used about 88 per cent English words. In comparison with *haole* [1] children and those studied on the mainland, the Island children were seriously retarded in the use of the English language, a retardation which is not compensated for by greater advancement in other languages used. The more bilingual groups use more nonverbal sentences and shorter sentences than do children in a less polylingual environment. They are found to use more exclamatory and fewer interrogative sentences, and to use compound and complex sentences much less frequently. The bilingual groups were also retarded in the use of connectives and pronouns and in the use of the copula and inflected forms, as well as in the expected decrease in the use of interjections. When a language is disappearing in competition with a new language, nouns and interjections (which, it will be recalled, are the first to be acquired) persist for the longest time. Those words that pertain to intimate aspects of family life and to eating are the last to be abandoned. In general, it was found that the children of Hawaii from non-*haole* homes are retarded in language development to a degree so marked that, on most criteria, they are at about the level of three-year-old children from a less polyglot environment at the time of school entrance. Smith considers that this retardation is due to the bilingualism of many homes and the prevalent use of pidgin English in the Hawaiian Islands.

There is need for further study of bilingualism in the United States with other languages as the foreign language, and uncomplicated by the presence of a mutilated

[1] *Haole* is an Hawaiian word used to apply to almost all Caucasians except the Portuguese.

form of English. Most of the studies are seriously obscured by the factor of socioeconomic status, for most bilingual children either come from highly cultured homes of the upper social levels where the language is being deliberately preserved for cultural reasons, or they come from the lower socioeconomic levels where the parents have not been sufficiently intellectual to acquire the second language. On the other hand, there are a number of children whose parents remain in lower socioeconomic brackets than those in which they would be found in their native countries because the very fact of a language handicap has necessitated their remaining at manual occupations rather than undertaking more verbal or more intellectual tasks. In McCarthy's (1930) study 10 per cent of the cases were bilingual. These children were more advanced than would be expected on the basis of their age, sex, and paternal occupation as measured by mean length of response. It may be that the handicap is more readily detectable in articulation and in quality of speech than in quantitative measures like length of response. Numerous reports seem to indicate that as far as pronunciation is concerned there is a definite advantage to learning the second language at an early age. Yoshioka (1929), however, states on the basis of meager data that older children can handle two languages better than younger ones and that bilingualism seems to require a certain degree of mental maturation for its successful mastery.

Conclusion

Recent experimental and observational studies of language development that have been reviewed here have indicated that there is increasing interest in the social function of language in the child's life and in the effect of the situation in which speech is used. This emphasis in the literature was perhaps anticipated by Weiss, who in 1925 described language as a "form of *behavior* through which the individual adjusts himself to a social environment." This trend toward more emphasis on the psychological and behavioral study of language is an interesting realization of the early statement of Max Müller (1862) that "researches into the origin of language transcend the domain of the physiologist as well as of the philologist, and require for their solution a complete mastery of the problems of psychology."

Since the writer last reviewed the literature in this field in 1933 a number of interesting tendencies have become evident indicating rather significant changes in areas of research interest. These changes seem to be symptomatic of the coming of age of the science of child psychology, for, since the first exploratory and descriptive researches have blocked in the major outlines, investigators have become more concerned with refinement of methods in an effort to fill in the details of the picture.

As has been indicated, there appears to have been a trend away from the emphasis on language as a form of thought and a means of expressing ideas, and toward an approach which treats language as a form of social behavior, and as a major area in the behavior of the integrated organism. In the methods of analysis which have been employed there is evident an abandonment of the more formal grammatical analyses of sentence structure which has been balanced by an intense interest in the functional approach, which has centered largely around the controversy regarding egocentrism.

Investigators have been increasingly concerned with a search for more promising measures which would be better indices of linguistic development. This has led to an interesting series of detailed studies of separate types of speech units. Some of these include studies of the use of questions, pronouns, adjectives, the use of past and future tenses, as well as the use of connectives and subordinate clauses. Except for Young's (1941) investigation, interest in parts of speech seems to have drawn almost completely away from the study of the proportions of the various parts of speech in the child's total vocabulary and to have shifted to interest in the psychological and developmental significance and function of the various parts of speech and of the various types of inflection in the child's sentence structure.

Recent studies have tended to employ larger numbers of subjects and to carry the investigation of oral language up to higher age levels. Although the biographical method has continued to appear in the literature, the modern studies are much more comprehensive, employ refined techniques such as phonetic recording of infant responses, and are much more detailed in their reports of, and analyses of, the situations in which the responses are recorded (Lewis, 1936; Grégoire, 1937; Leopold, 1939). In addition, these authors relate their work in detail to the earlier biographical studies. Reports of this type afford valuable checks by the longitudinal method on the results of cross-section studies on larger numbers of cases.

There have also been an increasing interest in and refinement of methods of recording. Betts (1934) was concerned with the reliability of electric recording, records of court reporters, shorthand reporters, longhand reporters, and phoneticians. McConnon (1935) and Young (1941) were concerned with the effect of the situation in which the child was speaking upon the reliability of speech records. Along with the interest in language as a form of social behavior, numerous studies have appeared which treat the problem of the effect of environment on the child's language development, including the influence of the age of associates. Although most of them have been concerned primarily with qualitative analyses of children's language, a few have appeared which employ a quantitative approach and which are concerned more with talkativeness and the amount and rate of talking than with the quality of the expression (Olson and Koetzle, 1936; Jersild and Ritzman, 1938). Following the studies which have described the development of language in normal children, some studies have appeared dealing with the development of language in handicapped groups, particularly in the blind (Maxfield, 1936) and in the deaf (Heider and Heider, 1940b).

In spite of the tremendous volume of research in this area there are a number of important questions which have scarcely been touched, or upon which only very tentative exploratory studies have appeared. As has been indicated, there is need for further investigations of the prelinguistic utterances of infancy, especially in relation to the total stimulating situation and to the condition of the infant at the time of utterance. The work of Irwin (1941a) and his associates in this area seems to indicate that analysis of these sounds from the point of view of place of phonation may prove promising. Language is so tremendously complex that no one has as yet worked out any single index of linguistic development which takes account of several aspects. One reason why this has not been realized is that the interrelationships of the various aspects of language development are not as yet known and understood. There is need also to carry over into the elementary school age levels some of the wealth of information which has accumulated regarding the preschool period and to attempt to relate the development of spoken language to the acquisition of the secondary forms of language; namely, reading and writing. The very important problem of determining the relationship of linguistic development to other aspects of the child's total development and its rôle in the development of an integrated personality also remains unsolved, and probably will have to wait upon the appearance of better linguistic measures.

Bibliography

ADAMS, S. 1932. A study of the growth of language between two and four years. *J. Juv. Res.*, **16**, 269–277.

——. 1938. Analysis of verb forms in the speech of young children, and their relation to the language learning process. *J. Exp. Educ.*, **7**, 141–144.

ADAMS, S., and F. F. POWERS. 1929. The psychology of language. *Psychol. Bull.*, **26**, 241–260.

ALLPORT, F. H. 1924. *Social psychology.* Boston: Houghton Mifflin.

ALLPORT, G. W. 1936. Book review of G. K. ZIPF. *The Psycho-biology of language.* (Boston: Houghton Mifflin, 1935.) *Psychol. Bull.*, **33**, 218–221.

AMENT, W. 1899. *Die Entwicklung von Sprechen und Denken beim Kinde.* Leipzig: Wunderlich.

ANDERSON, I. H., and G. FAIRBANKS. 1937. Common and differential factors in reading vocabulary and hearing vocabulary. *J. Educ. Res.*, **30**, 317–324.

ANDERSON, J. E. 1937. An evaluation of various indices of linguistic development. *Child Develpm.*, **8**, 62–68.

——. 1939. The development of spoken language. *Yearb. Nat. Soc. Stud. Educ.*, 38(I), 211–224.

ANON. n.d. Speech retardation: A case study. *Child Res. Clin. Ser.*, **1**, No. 1.

ANON. n.d. Language development in a nursery school child: A case study. *Child Res. Clin. Ser.*, **2**, No. 4.

ARLITT, A. H. 1930. *Psychology of infancy and early childhood* (2d ed.), Ch. XIII, pp. 276–293. New York: McGraw-Hill.

AYRES, L. P. 1915. *A measuring scale for ability in spelling.* New York: Russell Sage Foundation.

AZOY, A. 1935. [Results of the investigation of speech defects among the school children of Barcelona.] *Rev. Psicol. Pedag.*, **3**, 265–266.

BAIN, R. 1936. The self-and-other words of a child. *Amer. J. Sociol.*, **41**, 767–775.

BALDWIN, B. T., and L. I. STECHER. 1924. *The*

psychology of the preschool child. New York: Appleton.

BALDWIN, J. M. 1895. *Mental development in the child and the race: Methods and processes.* (3d ed., 1906.) New York: Macmillan.

BALLENGER, H. L. 1931. The validation of the Iowa Elementary Language Tests. *Univ. Iowa Stud. Educ.,* 6, No. 3.

BARNES, W. 1930, 1931. Language as behavior. *Elem. Engl. Rev.,* 7, 241–245; 8, 14–17, 24, 44–46, and 48.

———. 1937. Language as social behavior. *Educ. Meth.,* 16, 275–288.

BATEMAN, W. G. 1914. A child's progress in speech. *J. Educ. Psychol.,* 5, 307–320.

———. 1915. Two children's progress in speech. *J. Educ. Psychol.,* 6, 475–493.

———. 1916. The language status of three children at the same ages. *Ped. Sem.,* 23, 211–240.

———. 1917. Papers on language development: I. The first word. *Ped. Sem.,* 24, 391–398.

BAYLEY, N. 1933. Mental growth during the first three years. *Genet. Psychol. Monogr.,* 14, No. 1. Pp. 92.

BEAN, C. H. 1932. An unusual opportunity to investigate the psychology of language. *J. Genet. Psychol.,* 40, 181–202.

BEAR, R., and H. ODBERT. 1941. Insight of older pupils into their knowledge of word meanings. *Sch. Rev.,* 49, 754–760.

BECK, R. L. 1933. A natural test of English usage. *J. Exp. Educ.,* 1, 280–286.

BEKHTEREV, W. M. 1913. *La psychologie objective.* (Trans. from the Russian by N. KOSTYLEFF.) Paris: Alcan.

BELL, S. 1903. The significance of activity in child life. *Independent,* 55, 911–914.

BENNETT, C. C. 1938. An inquiry into the genesis of poor reading. *Teach. Coll. Contr. Educ.,* No. 755.

BENTLEY, M., and E. J. VARON. 1933. An accessory study of "Phonetic Symbolism." *Amer. J. Psychol.,* 45, 76–86.

BETTS, E. A. 1934. An evaluation of certain techniques for the study of oral composition. *Res. Stud. Elem. Sch. Lang.,* No. 1, *Univ. Iowa Stud. Educ.,* 9, No. 2. Pp. 7–35.

BETZNER, J. 1930. Content and form of original compositions dictated by children from five to eight years of age. *Teach. Coll. Contr. Educ.,* No. 442.

BEYER, T. P. 1915. The vocabulary of two years. *Educ. Rev.,* 49, 191–203.

———. 1916. The vocabulary of three years. *Educ. Rev.,* 52, 478–489.

BILTO, E. W. 1941. A comparative study of certain physical abilities of children with speech defects and children with normal speech. *J. Sp. Disord.,* 6, 187–203.

BLACHLY, M. E. O. 1922. Further notes on eighteen months vocabularies. *Proc. Okla.*

Acad. Sci., 2 (*Univ. Okla. Bull.,* N.S., No. 247), 106–108.

BLACHLY, M. E. O. 1923. A comparison of the sizes of vocabularies of fifty children of the same age. *Proc. Okla. Acad. Sci.,* 3 (*Univ. Okla. Bull.,* N.S., No. 271), 151–155.

BLANCHARD, P. 1933. The child with difficulties of adjustment. In C. MURCHISON (Ed.), *A handbook of child psychology.* (2d ed., rev.), Ch. XXII, pp. 858–881. Worcester: Clark University Press.

BLANTON, M. G. 1917. Behavior of the human infant during the first thirty days of life. *Psychol. Rev.,* 24, 456–483.

BLANTON, M. G., and S. M. STINCHFIELD. 1926. *Articulation Test A.* Chicago: Stoelting.

BLANTON, S., and M. G. BLANTON. 1927. *Child guidance.* New York: Century.

BLATZ, W. E., M. I. FLETCHER, and M. MASON. 1937. Early development in spoken language of the Dionne quintuplets. In W. E. BLATZ *et al., Collected studies on the Dionne quintuplets. Univ. Toronto Stud. Child Develpm. Ser.,* No. 16.

BLOCH, O. 1921. Les premiers stades du langage de l'enfant. *J. psychol.,* 18, 693–712.

———, 1924. La phrase dans le langage de l'enfant. *J. psychol.,* 21, 18–43.

BLOOMFIELD, L. 1933. *Language.* New York: Holt.

BODER, D. P. 1940. The adjective-verb-quotient: A contribution to the psychology of language. *Psychol. Rec.,* 3, 310–343.

BOHN, W. E. 1914. First steps in verbal expression. *Ped. Sem.,* 21, 578–595.

BOYD, W. 1913. The beginnings of syntactical speech: A study in child linguistics. *Child Study,* 6, 21–24, 47–51.

———. 1914. The development of a child's vocabulary. *Ped. Sem.,* 21, 95–124.

———. 1927. The development of sentence structure in childhood. *Brit. J. Psychol.,* 17, 181–191.

BRANDENBURG, G. C. 1915. The language of a three-year-old child. *Ped. Sem.,* 22, 89–120.

———. 1918. Psychological aspects of language. *J. Educ. Psychol.,* 9, 313–332.

BRANDENBURG, G. C., and J. BRANDENBURG. 1916. Language development during the fourth year. *Ped. Sem.,* 23, 14–29.

———. 1919. Language development during the fourth year: The conversation. *Ped. Sem.,* 26, 27–40.

BRIGANCE, W. N. 1934. The language learning of a child. *J. Appl. Psychol.,* 18, 143–154.

BROOKS, F. D., and L. F. SHAFFER. 1937. *Child psychology* (Chap. 7, pp. 173–206). Boston: Houghton Mifflin.

BROWN, M. S. 1935. Study of the vocabulary used in oral expression by a group of fourth grade children. *Educ. Meth.,* 15, 39–44.

BUCKINGHAM, B. R., and E. W. DOLCH. 1936. *A combined word list.* Boston: Ginn.

BÜHLER, C. 1930. The first year of life. [Trans. by P. GREENBERG and R. RIPIN from the following three German publications: C. BÜHLER and H. HETZER, Inventar der Verhaltungsweisen des ersten Lebensjahres (*Quell. u. Stud. z. Jugendk.*, No. 5), Jena: Fischer, 1927, pp. 125–250; H. HETZER and K. WOLF, Babytests, *Zsch. f. Psychol.*, 1928, **107**, 62–204; H. HETZER and L. KOLLER, Vier Testreihen für das zweite Lebensjahr, *Zsch. f. Psychol.*, 1930, **117**, 257–306.] New York: Day.

——. 1931. *Kindheit und Jugend*. (3d ed.) Leipzig: Hirzel.

BÜHLER, C., and H. HETZER. 1935. *Testing children's development from birth to school age*. New York: Farrar and Rinehart.

BÜHLER, K. 1930. *Die geistige Entwicklung des Kindes*. (6th ed.) Jena: Fischer. (1st ed., 1918.) (*The mental development of the child.*) New York: Harcourt, Brace; London, Kegan Paul.

——. 1934. *Sprachtheorie*. Jena: Fischer.

BURTT, H. E. 1932. An experimental study of early childhood memory. *J. Genet. Psychol.*, **40**, 287–295.

——. 1937. A further study of early childhood memory. *J. Genet. Psychol.*, **50**, 187–192.

BUSEMANN, A. 1925. Die Sprache der Jugend als Ausdruck der Entwicklungsrhythmik: Sprachstatistische Untersuchungen. (*Quel. Stud. Jugendk.*) Jena, Verlag von Gustav Fischer.

BUSH, A. D. 1914. The vocabulary of a three-year-old girl. *Ped. Sem.*, **21**, 125–142.

CAMPBELL, C. V. 1901. Two recent studies of children's vocabularies. *Child Stud. Mo.*, **6**, 277–280.

CARD, M. S., and F. L. WELLS. 1936. Vocal symbol formation as a function of reading ability. *J. Genet. Psychol.*, **48**, 149–176.

CARMICHAEL, L. 1933. Origin and prenatal growth of behavior. In C. MURCHISON (Ed.), *A handbook of child psychology* (2d ed., rev.), pp. 31–159. Worcester: Clark University Press.

CARMICHAEL, L., H. P. HOGAN, and A. WALTER. 1932. An experimental study of the effect of language on the reproduction of visually perceived forms. *J. Exp. Psychol.*, **15**, 73–86.

CARROLL, J. B. 1939. Determining and numerating adjectives in children's speech. *Child. Develpm.*, **10**, 215–229.

CATTELL, P. 1940. *The measurement of intelligence of infants and young children*. New York: The Psychological Corporation; Lancaster, Pa.: Science Press.

CHAMBERLAIN, A. F. 1900. *The child: A study in the evolution of man*. London: Scott; New York: Scribner's.

CHAMPNEYS, F. H. 1881. Notes on an infant. *Mind*, **6**, 104–107.

CHIPMAN, C. E. 1935. The vocabulary of mental defectives. *Proc. Amer. Ass. Stud. Ment. Def.*, **40**, 485–503.

CHRISTIAN, A. M., and D. G. PATERSON. 1936. Growth of vocabulary in later maturity. *J. Psychol.*, **1**, 167–169.

CIAMPI, L. 1933. La patología del lenguaje en la edad evolutiva. *Bol. Inst. Psiquiat.*, **5**, 147–163.

COBB, M. V. 1922. Tentative order of difficulty of the Terman vocabulary with very young children. *J. Educ. Psychol.*, **13**, 357–362.

COHEN, M. 1933. Observations sur les dernières persistances du langage enfantine. *J. psychol.*, **30**, 390–399.

COMAS, J. 1931. Contribución al estudio de la génesis psicobiológica del lenguaje hablado. *Rev. de ped.*, **10**, 484–490.

COMPAYRÉ, G. 1896. *The intellectual and moral development of the child:* Pt. 1. (Trans. by M. E. WILSON.) New York: Appleton.

CONRADI, E. 1904. The psychology and pathology of speech development. *Ped. Sem.*, **11**, 328–380.

——. 1912. Speech development and intellectual progress. *J. Educ. Psychol.*, **3**, 35–38.

COOLEY, C. H. 1908. A study of the early use of self-words by a child. *Psychol. Rev.*, **15**, 339–357.

CORNIOLEY, H. 1935. *Die sprachliche Entwicklung eines Kindes von ihren Anfängen bis zum dritten Lebensjahr*. Bern: Lang.

COURT, S. R. A. 1910–1920. Linguistic creativeness of a child. *Proc. Okla. Acad. Sci.*, **1** (*Univ. Okla. Bull.*, N.S., No. 220), 70.

——. 1926. Some sentences of a boy three years eight months. *Proc. Okla. Acad. Sci.*, **6**, Pt. II (*Univ. Okla. Bull.*, N.S., No. 348), 334–343.

——. 1927. The growth of a small boy's linguistic interest. *Proc. Okla. Acad. Sci.*, **7** (*Univ. Okla. Bull.*, N.S., No. 409), 224–234.

COUSINET, R. 1936. Le monologue enfantin. *J. psychol.*, **33**, 28–39.

CUFF, N. B. 1930. Vocabulary tests. *J. Educ. Psychol.*, **21**, 212–220.

——. 1935. Social status and vocabulary. *J. Genet. Psychol.*, **46**, 226–229.

——. 1937. *Child psychology*, Ch. IX, pp. 160–180. Louisville: Standard Printing Co.

CURTI, M. W. 1938. *Child psychology*. (2d ed.) New York: Longmans, Green.

DALE, E. 1931. Difficulties in vocabulary research. *Educ. Res. Bull.*, **10**, 119–122.

DARWIN, C. 1877. Biographical sketch of an infant. *Mind*, **2**, 285–294.

DAVID, D. 1925. The development of language habits. *J. Educ. Meth.*, **5**, 155–160.

DAVIS, D. M. 1939. The relation of repetitions in the speech of young children to certain measures of language maturity and situational factors: Pt. I. *J. Speech Disorders*, **4**, 303–318.

DAVIS, E. A. 1932. The form and function of children's questions. *Child Develpm.*, **3**, 57–74.

——. 1937a. *The development of linguistic skill in twins, singletons with siblings, and only children from age five to ten years.* (*Inst. Child Welfare Monogr. Ser.*, No. 14.) Minneapolis: University of Minnesota Press. Pp. ix + 165.

——. 1937b. Mean sentence length compared with long and short sentences as a reliable measure of language development. *Child Develpm.*, **8**, 69–79.

——. 1937c. Development in the use of proper names. *Child Develpm.*, **8**, 270–272.

——. 1937d. The mental and linguistic superiority of only girls. *Child Develpm.*, **8**, 139–143.

——. 1938a. Developmental changes in the distribution of parts of speech. *Child Develpm.*, **9**, 309–317.

——. 1938b. Basic English in the speech of American children. *Sch. and Soc.*, **48**, 665–668.

——. 1939. Accuracy versus error as a criterion in children's speech. *J. Educ. Psychol.*, **30**, 365–371.

——. 1941. The location of the subordinate clause in oral and written language. *Child Develpm.*, **12**, 333–338.

DAVIS, I. P. 1938. The speech aspects of reading readiness. *Newer Practices in Reading in the Elementary School.* [In] *Seventeenth Yearb. Dept. Elem. Sch. Prins.* Washington, D. C.

DAY, E. J. 1932. The development of language in twins: I. A comparison of twins and single children. *Child Develpm.*, **3**, 179–199.

DEARBORN, G. V. N. 1910. *Moto-sensory development: Observations on the first three years of childhood.* Baltimore: Warwick and York.

DECROLY, O. 1930. *Le développement du langage parlé chez l'enfant.* Liège: Edition Biblio.

——. c. 1934. *Comment l'enfant arrive à parler.* Vols. I and II. Cahiers de la Centrale. (Revu et complété par J. DECROLY et J. E. SEGERS.) *Cent. du. P.E.S. de Belgique*, Vol. 8.

DELACROIX, H. 1930. *Le langage et la pensée.* (2d ed.) Paris: Alcan.

DELAGUNA, G. A. 1927. *Speech: Its function and development.* New Haven: Yale University Press.

DELLA VALLE, G. 1931. Le prime fasi dello sviluppo del linguaggio infantile. *Riv. ped.*, **24**, 1–35.

DENNIS, W. 1943. Mr. Janus on children's language. *J. Genet. Psychol.*, **63**, 183–185.

DESCOEUDRES, A. 1921. Le développement de l'enfant de deux à sept ans. Neuchâtel et Paris: Delachaux et Niestlé.

——. 1924. La mesure du langage de l'enfant. *J. psychol.*, **21**, 43–47.

DEVILLE, G. 1890. Notes sur le développement du langue. *Rev. linguistique et philol. comp.*, **23**, 330–343.

DEWEY, E. 1935. *Infant behavior.* New York: Columbia University Press.

DEWEY, G. 1923. *Relative frequency of English speech sounds.* (*Harv. Monogr. Educ., IV.*) Cambridge: Harvard University Press. Pp. xii + 148.

DEWEY, J. 1894. The psychology of infant language. *Psychol. Rev.*, **1**, 63–66.

——. 1926. *Experience and nature.* New York: Norton.

DOLCH, E. W. 1925. *Reading and word meanings.* Boston: Ginn.

——. 1927. Grade vocabularies. *J. Educ. Res.*, **16**, 16–26.

DORAN, E. W. 1907. A study of vocabularies. *Ped. Sem.*, **14**, 401–438.

DREVER, J. 1915–1916. A study of children's vocabularies: I, II, and III. *J. Exp. Ped.*, **3**, 34–43; 96–103; 182–188.

——. 1919. The vocabulary of a free kindergarten child. *J. Exp. Ped.*, **5**, 28–37.

DRIGGS, H. W. 1934. The vocabulary of letters of boys and girls 12 to 15 years of age inclusive. *J. Exp. Educ.*, **2**, 339–354.

DRUMMOND, M. 1916. Notes on speech development: I. *Child Study*, **9**, 83–86.

——. 1925. *Five years old or thereabouts.* London: Arnold.

EATON, H. S. 1940. *Semantic frequency list for English, French, German, and Spanish: A correlation of the first six thousand words in four single-language frequency lists.* Chicago: University of Chicago Press.

EBERHARDT, M. 1940. A summary of some preliminary investigations of the deaf. *Psychol. Monogr.*, **52**, No. 1, 1–5.

EGGER, M. E. 1879. *Observations et reflexions sur le développement de l'intelligence et du langage chez les enfants.* Paris: Picard.

ELLESOR, M. V. 1934. The relation between situation and response in vocalization of a three-year-old child. *Child Develpm.*, **5**, 158–164.

ESPER, E. A. 1921. The psychology of language. *Psychol. Bull.*, **18**, 490–496.

——. 1925. A technique for the experimental investigation of associative interference in artificial linguistic material. *Lang. Monogr.*, No. 1. Pp. 46.

——. 1933. Studies in linguistic behavior organization: I. Characteristics of unstable verbal reactions. *J. Gen. Psychol.*, **8**, 346–381.

——. 1935. Language. In C. MURCHISON (Ed.), *A handbook of social psychology*, pp. 417–460. Worcester: Clark University Press.

FAHEY, G. L. 1942. The questioning activity of children. *J. Genet. Psychol.*, **60**, 337–357.

FELDMANN, H. 1833. *De statu normali functionum corporis humani.* Dissertation, Bonn.

FENTON, J. C. 1925. *A practical psychology of babyhood.* Boston : Houghton Mifflin.

FIRTH, J. R. 1930. *Speech.* London : Benn.

FISHER, M. S. 1932. Language patterns of preschool children. *J. Exp. Educ.*, **1**, 70–74.

———. 1934. Language patterns of preschool children. *Child Develpm. Monogr.*, No. 15. Pp. xvi + 88.

FITCHEN, M. 1931. Speech and music development of a one-year-old child. *Child Develpm.*, **2**, 324–326.

FITZGERALD, J. A. 1934a. Letters written outside the school by children of the 4th, 5th, and 6th grades : A study of vocabulary, spelling errors and situations. *Univ. Iowa Stud.*, **9**, No. 1, 9–50.

———. 1934b. The vocabulary of children's letters written in life outside the school. *Elem. Sch. J.*, **34**, 358–370.

———. 1936. The overlap of child and adult vocabularies. *J. Exp. Educ.*, **4**, 364–367.

———. 1938. The vocabulary and spelling errors of third grade children's life-letters. *Elem. Sch. J.*, **38**, 518–527.

FLEMMING, V. V. 1942. A study of Stanford-Binet vocabulary attainment and growth in children in the city of childhood, Mooseheart, Ill., as compared with children living in their own homes. *J. Genet. Psychol.*, **60**, 359–373.

FOULKE, K., and S. M. STINCHFIELD. 1929. The speech development of four infants under two years of age. *J. Genet. Psychol.*, **36**, 140–171.

FRANKE, C. 1899. Sprachentwickelung der Kinder und der Menschheit. In REINS (Ed.), *Encyklopädischem Handbuch der Pädagogik.* Langensalza : Beyer.

FRIEDRICH, G. 1906. Psychologische Beobachtungen an zwei Knaben : Beiträge zur Kinderforschung und Heilerziehung. *Beih. z. Kinderforsch.*, No. 17.

FRIES, C. C., and A. A. TRAVER. 1940. *English word lists: A study of their adaptability for instruction.* Washington, D. C. : American Council on Education.

GALE, H. 1902. The vocabularies of three children in one family at two and three years of age. *Ped. Sem.*, **9**, 422–433.

GALE, M. C., and H. GALE. 1901. Children's vocabularies. *Pop. Sci. Mo.*, **61**, 45–51.

———. 1906. Vocabularies of three children in one family to two and one-half years of age. *Psychol. Stud., Univ. Minn.*, No. 1, pp. 70–117.

GANSL, I. 1939. Vocabulary : Its measurement and growth. *Arch. Psychol., N. Y.*, No. 236.

GARDINER, A. H. 1922. The definition of the word and the sentence. *Brit. J. Psychol.*, **12**, 352–361.

———. 1932. *The theory of speech and language.* New York : Oxford University Press.

GARRISON, K. C. 1930. The relationship between three different vocabulary abilities. *J. Educ. Res.*, **21**, 43–45.

GARRISON, K. C., and M. THOMAS. 1930. A study of some literature appreciation abilities as they relate to certain vocabulary abilities. *J. Educ. Res.*, **22**, 396–399.

GARRISON, S. C., and K. C. GARRISON. 1929. *The psychology of elementary school subjects*, pp. 207–266. New York : Johnson.

GATES, A. I. 1935. A reading vocabulary for the primary grades. (Rev. ed.) New York : Teachers College, Columbia University.

GERLACH, F. M. 1917. *Vocabulary studies.* (*Stud. Educ. Psychol.*, No. 1.) Colorado Springs : Colorado College.

GESELL, A. 1925. *The mental growth of the preschool child: A psychological outline of normal development from birth to the sixth year, including a system of developmental diagnosis.* New York : Macmillan.

———. 1928. *Infancy and human growth.* New York : Macmillan.

———. 1940, 1941. *Wolf child and human child: Being a narrative interpretation of the life history of Kamala, the wolf girl.* New York : Harper.

GESELL, A., H. M. HALVERSON, H. THOMPSON, F. L. ILG, B. M. CASTNER, L. B. AMES, and C. S. AMATRUDA. 1940. *The first five years of life, a guide to the study of the preschool child.* Ch. VIII, by B. M. CASTNER. New York : Harper.

GESELL, A., and E. LORD. 1927. A psychological comparison of nursery-school children from homes of low and high economic status. *J. Genet. Psychol.*, **34**, 339–356.

GESELL, A., and H. THOMPSON, assisted by C. S. AMATRUDA. 1934. *Infant behavior: Its genesis and growth*, pp. 243–257, 286–291. New York : McGraw-Hill.

GESELL, A., H. THOMPSON, and C. S. AMATRUDA. 1938. *The psychology of early growth.* New York : Macmillan.

GHEORGOV, I. A. 1905. Die ersten Anfänge des sprachlichen Ausdrucks für das Selbstbewusstsein bei Kindern. *Arch. ges. Psychol.*, **5**, 329–404.

GOODENOUGH, F. L. 1927. Consistency of sex differences in mental traits at various ages. *Psychol. Rev.*, **34**, 440–462.

———. 1928. *The Kuhlmann-Binet tests for children of preschool age: A critical study and evaluation.* (*Inst. Child Welfare Monogr. Ser.*, No. 2.) Minneapolis : University of Minnesota Press. Pp. viii + 146.

———. 1930. Interrelationships in the behavior of young children. *Child Develpm.*, **1**, 29–47.

———. 1934. *Developmental psychology*, pp. 248–259. New York : Appleton-Century.

———. 1938. The use of pronouns by young children : A note on the development of self-awareness. *J. Genet. Psychol.*, **52**, 333–346.

GOODENOUGH, F. L., and C. R. BRIAN. 1929.

Certain factors underlying the acquisition of motor skill by preschool children. *J. Exp. Psychol.,* **12,** 127–155.

GOODENOUGH, F. L., K. M. MAURER, and M. J. VAN WAGENEN. 1935, 1940. *Minnesota preschool scale manual,* Forms A and B. Minneapolis: Educational Test Bureau.

GOODMAN, M. 1936. Language development in a nursery school child. *Child Res. Clin. Ser.,* **2,** No. 4.

GRABO, R. P. 1930. *A study of comparative vocabularies of junior high school pupils in English and Italian speaking homes.* Schenectady, N. Y.: Public Schools.

GRAFF, W. L. 1932. *Language and languages.* New York: Appleton.

GRANT, J. R. 1915. A child's vocabulary and its growth. *Ped. Sem.,* **22,** 183–203.

GRAY, L. H. 1939. *Foundations of language.* New York: Macmillan.

GRÉGOIRE, A. 1933. L'apprentissage de la parole pendant les deux premières années de l'enfance. *J. psychol.,* **30,** 375–389.

———. 1937. *L'apprentissage du langage: Les deux premières années.* Paris: Droz.

GRIGSBY, O. J. 1932. An experimental study of the development of concepts of relationship in preschool children as evidenced by their expressive ability. *J. Exp. Educ.,* **1,** 144–162.

GUERNSEY, M. 1928. Eine genetische Studie über Nachahmung. *Z. f. Psychol.,* **107,** 105–178.

GUILER, W. S. 1926. Analysis of children's writings as a basis for instruction in English. *J. Educ. Meth.,* **5,** 258–264.

GUILLAUME, P. 1925. *L'imitation chez l'enfant.* Paris: Alcan.

———. 1927a. Les débuts de la phrase dans le langage de l'enfant. *J. psychol.,* **24,** 26–77.

———. 1927b. Le développement du langage chez l'enfant. *J. psychol.,* **24,** 203–229.

HAGGERTY, L. C. G. 1930. What a two-and-one-half-year-old child said in one day. *J. Genet. Psychol.,* **38,** 75–100.

HAGGERTY, M. E., and H. B. NASH. 1924. Mental capacity of children and paternal occupation. *J. Educ. Psychol.,* **15,** 559–572.

HALL, G. S. 1891a. Notes on the study of infants. *Ped. Sem.,* **1,** 127–138.

———. 1891b. The contents of children's minds on entering school. *Ped. Sem.,* **1,** 139–173.

HALL, MRS. W. S. 1896–1897. The first 500 days of a child's life: V. *Child Study,* No. 2, pp. 586–608.

HARTMANN, G. W. 1941. A critique of the common method of estimating vocabulary size, together with some data on the absolute word knowledge of educated adults. *J. Educ. Psychol.,* **32,** 351–364.

HAWK, S. S. 1938. Does the intelligence quotient change with speech training? *West. Speech,* **2,** 1, 4.

HAWTHORNE, J. W. 1934. An attempt to measure certain phases of speech. *J. Gen. Psychol.,* **10,** 399–414.

HAZLITT, V. 1933. *The psychology of infancy,* Ch. V, pp. 49–63. New York: Dutton.

HEIDBREDER, E. 1936. Language and concepts. *Psychol. Bull.,* **33,** 724.

HEIDER, F. 1935. The rôle of language in the psychological situation of the child: A comparative study of free play among deaf and among hearing children of preschool ages. *Psychol. Bull.,* **32,** 728–729.

HEIDER, F. K., and G. M. HEIDER. 1940a. A study of phonetic symbolism of deaf children. *Psychol. Monogr.,* **52,** No. 1, pp. 23–41.

———. 1940b. A comparison of sentence structure of deaf and hearing children. *Psychol. Monogr.,* **52,** No. 1, pp. 42–103.

HEILIG, M. 1913. A child's vocabulary. *Ped. Sem.,* **20,** 1–16.

HENLE, M., and M. B. HUBBELL. 1938. "Egocentricity" in adult conversation. *J. Soc. Psychol.,* **9,** 227–234.

HETZER, H., and B. REINDORF. 1928. Sprachentwicklung und soziales Milieu. *Z. angew. Psychol.,* **29,** 449–462.

HILLS, E. C. 1914. The speech of a child two years of age. *Dialect Notes,* **4,** 84–100.

HINCKLEY, A. C. 1915. A case of retarded speech development. *Ped. Sem.,* **22,** 121–146.

HOLDEN, E. S. 1877. On the vocabularies of children under two years. *Trans. Amer. Philol. Ass.,* **8,** 58–68.

HOLLEY, C. E. 1919. Holley sentence vocabulary scale. Bloomington, Ill.: Public School Publishing Co.

HOLLINGWORTH, H. L. 1927. *Mental growth and decline.* New York: Appleton.

———. 1938. Verbal Gestalt experiments with children. *J. Exp. Psychol.,* **23,** 90–95.

HOLMES, U. T. 1926–1927. The phonology of an English child. *Amer. Speech,* **2,** 219–225.

HOPPES, W. C. 1934. Considerations in the development of children's language. *Elem. Engl. Rev.,* **11,** 66–70.

HORN, E. 1925. The commonest words in the spoken vocabulary of children up to and including six years of age. *Yearb. Nat. Soc. Stud. Educ.,* 24(I), 186–198.

HORN, E. 1942. Language and meaning. *Yearb. Nat. Soc. Stud. Educ.,* 41(II), 377–413.

HORN, M. D. 1926–1927a. The thousand and three words most frequently used by kindergarten children. *Child. Educ.,* **3,** 118–122.

———. 1926–1927b. Sectional differences in the vocabulary of kindergarten children. *Child. Educ.,* **3,** 180–182.

HOWARD, R. 1934. *A developmental study of triplets.* Unpublished Ph.D. Dissertation, University of Minnesota.

HOYER, A., and G. HOYER. 1924. Über die Lallsprache eines Kindes. *Z. angew. Psychol.,* **24,** 363–384.

HUANG, I., and Y. J. CHU. 1936. The social

function of children's language. *Chung Hua Educ. Rev.*, **23**, No. 7, pp. 69–94.

HUDGINS, C. V. 1934. A comparative study of the speech coordination of deaf and normal subjects. *J. Genet. Psychol.*, **44**, 3–48.

——. 1939. Report of the Clarence W. Barron Research Department: Experimental phonetics. *A. R. Clarke Sch. for the Deaf*, **72**, 31–39.

HUDGINS, C. V., and F. C. NUMBERS. 1942. An investigation of the intelligibility of the speech of the deaf. *Genet. Psychol. Monogr.*, **25**, 289–392.

HUGHSON, W., A. CIOCCO, E. G. WITTING, and P. S. LAWRENCE. 1942. Studies of pupils of the Pennsylvania School for the Deaf: III. An analysis of speech characteristics in deafened children with observations on training methods. *Child Develpm.*, **13**, 131–158.

HULL, C. L., and B. I. HULL. 1919. Parallel learning curves of an infant in vocabulary and in voluntary control of the bladder. *Ped. Sem.*, **26**, 272–283.

HUMPHREYS, W. 1880. A contribution to infantile linguistics. *Trans. Amer. Philol. Ass.*, **9**, 5–17.

INTERNATIONAL KINDERGARTEN UNION. 1928. *A study of the vocabulary of children before entering the first grade.* Baltimore: Williams and Wilkins.

IRWIN, O. C. 1941*a*. Research on speech sounds for the first six months of life. *Psychol. Bull.*, **38**, 277–285.

——. 1941*b*. The profile as a visual device for indicating central tendencies in speech data. *Child Develpm.*, **12**, 111–120.

——. 1942. The developmental status of speech sounds of ten feeble-minded children. *Child Develpm.*, **13**, 29–39.

IRWIN, O. C., and H. P. CHEN. 1941. A reliability study of speech sounds observed in the crying of newborn infants. *Child Develpm.*, **12**, 351–368.

IRWIN, O. C., and T. CURRY. 1941. Vowel elements in the crying vocalization of infants under ten days of age. *Child Develpm.*, **12**, 99–109.

JANUS, S. Q. 1943. An investigation of the relationship between children's language and their play. *J. Genet. Psychol.*, **62**, 3–61.

JEGI, J. I. 1901. The vocabulary of the two-year-old child. *Child Stud. Mo.*, **6**, 241–261.

JENKINS, F. 1915. A test of the ability of children to use language forms. *J. Educ. Psychol.*, **6**, 335–344.

JERSILD, A. T. 1940. *Child psychology*, Ch. V, pp. 112–155. (Rev. and enlarged.) New York: Prentice-Hall.

JERSILD, A. T., and R. RITZMAN. 1938. Aspects of language development: The growth of loquacity and vocabulary. *Child Develpm.*, **9**, 243–259.

JESPERSEN, O. 1922, 1923. *Language: Its nature, development and origin.* London: Allen and Winous; New York: Holt.

JESPERSEN, O. 1933. *Essentials of English grammar.* New York: Holt.

JOHNSON, E. C., and C. C. JOSEY. 1931. A note on the development of the thought forms of children as described by Piaget. *J. Abnorm. Soc. Psychol.*, **26**, 338–339.

JOHNSON, H. M. 1928. *Children in the nursery school.* New York: Day.

JOHNSON, W. 1939. Language and speech hygiene: An application of general semantics. *Monogr. Inst. Gen. Semantics*, No. 1. Pp. 54.

KANTOR, J. R. 1928. Can psychology contribute to the study of linguistics? *Monist*, **38**, 630–648.

KATZ, D., and R. KATZ. 1927. *Gespräche mit Kindern* (*Untersuchungen zur Socialpsychologie und Pädagogik*). Berlin: Springer.

KAULFERS, W. 1928. The prognostic value of general language. *Sch. and Soc.*, **28**, 662–664.

KAWIN, E. 1934. *Children of preschool age.* Chicago: University of Chicago Press.

KEILHACKER, M. 1933. Beobachtungsbagen über sprachliche Entwicklung im Schulalter. *Z. Pädag. Psychol.*, **34**, 286–289.

KELLER, H. 1904. *The story of my life.* Garden City: Doubleday Page. (New ed., 1922.)

KENEYERS, E. 1927. Les premiers mots de l'enfant et l'apparition des espèces de mots dans son langage. *Arch. psychol.*, **20**, 191–218.

KERN, A. 1929. Vom innern Sprechen. Eine experimentelle Studie. *Z. Kinderforsch.*, **35**, 420–447.

KERN, E. 1933. Die Sprechmotorik des beschulten Taubstummen. Eine experimentelle Untersuchung. *Z. Kinderforsch.*, **41**, 503.

KIRKPATRICK, E. A. 1891. The number of words in ordinary vocabularies. *Science*, **18**, 107–108.

——. 1903. *Fundamentals of child study.* New York: Macmillan.

KOFFKA, K. 1924. *The growth of the mind: An introduction to child psychology.* (Trans. by R. M. OGDEN.) New York: Harcourt, Brace; London: Kegan Paul.

——. 1935. Psychology of learning, with reference to the acquisition of language. *Engl. J.* (Coll. ed.), **24**, 388–396.

KROEBER, A. L. 1916. The speech of a Zuni child. *Amer. Anthrop.*, **18**, 529–534.

KUHLMANN, F. 1939. *Tests of mental development.* Minneapolis: Educational Test Bureau.

KUO, H. H. 1937. [A study of the language development of Chinese children.] *Chin. J. Psychol.*, **1**, 334–364.

LABRANT, L. L. 1933. A study of certain language developments of children in grades four to twelve inclusive. *Genet. Psychol. Monogr.*, **14**, 387–491.

——. 1934. Changing sentence structure of children. *Elem. Engl. Rev.*, **11**, 59–65; 85–86.

LANGE, G., and W. NEUHAUS. 1934. Der Strukturwandel der Kindersprache während der Zeit vom 6. bis 9. Lebensjahr. *Arch. Ges. Psychol., 91*, 200–228.

LANGENBECK, M. 1915. A study of a five-year-old child. *Ped. Sem., 22*, 65–88.

LATIF, I. 1934. The physiological basis of linguistic development and of the ontogeny of meaning: I, II. *Psychol. Rev., 41*, 55–85; 153–176.

LEMAITRE, A. 1902. Le langage intérieur chez les enfants. Recherches Pedologiques extrait de l'Educateur, 3S. Pp. 22.

LEOPOLD, W. F. 1939. Speech development of a bilingual child: A linguist's record: Vol. I. Vocabulary growth in the first two years. *Northw. Univ. Stud. Human., 6.*

LEWIS, M. M. 1936. *Infant speech; A study of the beginnings of language.* New York: Harcourt, Brace.

——. 1937. The beginning of reference to past and future in a child's speech. *Brit. J. Educ. Psychol., 7*, 39–56.

——. 1938. The beginning and early functions of questions in a child's speech. *Brit. J. Educ. Psychol., 8*, 150–171.

LEY, J. 1930. Les troubles de développement du langage. *J. Neurol. Psychiat., 30*, 415–457.

LINDNER, G. 1882. Beobachtungen und Bemerkungen über die Entwicklung der Sprache des Kindes. *Kosmos, 9*, 321–430.

——. 1898. *Aus dem Naturgarten der Kindersprache. Ein Beitrag zur Kindlichen Sprach- und Geistesentwickelung in den ersten vier Lebensjahren.* Leipzig: Grieben.

LINFERT, H. E., and H. M. HIERHOLZER. 1928. A scale for measuring the mental development of infants during the first year of life. *Stud. Psychol. Psychiat. Cathol. Univ. Amer., 1*, No. 4.

LITTLE, M. F., and H. M. WILLIAMS. 1937. An analytical scale of language achievement. *Univ. Iowa Stud. Child Welfare, 13*, No. 2, pp. 49–94.

LOOMIS, C. P., and A. M. MORAN. 1931. Relation between use of different parts of speech in written composition and mental ability. *J. Educ. Psychol., 22*, 465–475.

LORIMER, F. 1929. *The growth of reason: A study of the rôle of verbal activity in the growth of the structure of the human mind,* pp. 32–77. New York: Harcourt, Brace.

LOW, A. A. 1936. *Studies in infant speech and thought.* (*Ill. Med. Dent. Monogr., 1*, No. 2.) Urbana: University of Illinois Press. Pp. 71.

LUKENS, H. 1894. Preliminary report on the learning of language. *Ped. Sem., 3*, 424–460.

LULL, H. G. 1929. The speaking and writing abilities of intermediate grade pupils. *J. Educ. Res., 20*, 73–77.

LURIA, A. R. 1930. *Language and intelligence in the city child, the country child and the child without a home.* Moscow: Gosizdat.

LURIA, A. R. 1932. *The nature of human conflicts.* (Trans. by W. GANNT.) New York: Liveright.

LYMAN, R. L. 1929. *Summary of investigations relating to grammar, language and composition.* (*Suppl. Educ. Monogr.*, No. 36. Pp. viii + 302. Chapter III.) Chicago: University of Chicago Press.

MABIE, E. 1931. A study of the conversation of first grade pupils during free play hours. *J. Educ. Res., 24*, 135–138.

——. 1933. Language ability and personality adjustment. *Elem. Engl. Rev., 10*, 165–168.

MACDOUGALL, R. 1912, 1913. The child's speech. *J. Educ. Psychol., 3*, 423–429, 507–513; *4*, 29–38.

MAGNI, J. A. 1919. Vocabularies. *Ped. Sem., 26*, 209–233.

MAJOR, D. R. 1906. *First steps in mental growth: A series of studies in the psychology of infancy.* New York: Macmillan.

MALINOWSKI, B. K. 1923. The problem of meaning in primitive languages. In C. K. OGDEN and I. A. RICHARDS, *The meaning of meaning,* pp. 451–510. London: Kegan Paul.

MANDELL, S. 1931. Relation of language to thought. *Quart. J. Speech, 17*, 522–531.

MANDELL, S., and B. SONNECK. 1935. Phonographische Aufnahme und Analyse der ersten Sprachäusserungen von Kindern. *Arch. Ges. Psychol., 94*, 478–500.

MARKEY, J. F. 1928. *The symbolic process and its integration in children.* New York: Harcourt, Brace.

MATEER, F. 1908. The vocabulary of a four-year-old boy. *Ped. Sem., 15*, 63–74.

MAXFIELD, K. E. 1936. The spoken language of the blind preschool child: A study of method. *Arch. Psychol.*, No. 201.

MCCARTHY, D. 1929a. A comparison of children's language in different situations and its relation to personality traits. *J. Genet. Psychol., 36*, 583–591.

——. 1929b. The vocalizations of infants. *Psychol. Bull., 26*, 625–651.

——. 1930. *The language development of the preschool child.* (*Inst. Child Welfare Monogr. Ser.*, No. 4.) Minneapolis: University of Minnesota Press.

——. 1933. Language development. In C. MURCHISON (Ed.), *A handbook of child psychology* (2d ed., rev.), pp. 329–373. Worcester: Clark University Press.

——. 1935. A preliminary report on a new articulation test for young children. *Psychol. Bull., 32*, 699.

MCCONNON, K. 1935. *The situation factor in the language responses of nursery school children.* Unpublished Ph.D. Dissertation, University of Minnesota.

MCDOUGALL, W. 1931. An outline of psychology. (5th ed.) London: Methuen.

McGranahan, D. V. 1936. The psychology of language. *Psychol. Bull.*, **33**, 178–216.

McGraw, M. B. 1935. *Growth: A Study of Johnny and Jimmy.* New York: Appleton-Century.

McKee, P. 1937. Vocabulary development. *Yearb. Nat. Soc. Stud. Educ.*, 36(I), 277–302.

Mead, C. D. 1913. The age of walking and talking in relation to general intelligence. *Ped. Sem.*, **20**, 460–484.

———. 1916. The relation of general intelligence to certain mental and physical traits. *Teach. Coll. Contr. Educ.*, No. 76.

Meumann, E. 1908. *Die entstehung der ersten Wortbedeutungen beim Kinde.* (2d ed.) Leipzig: Engelmann.

Miller, G. F., F. D. Miller, and M. M. Nice. 1923. A boy's vocabulary at 18 months. *Proc. Okla. Acad. Sci.*, **3** (*Univ. Okla. Bull.*, N.S., No. 271), 140–144.

Monroe, M. 1932. *Children who cannot read; the analysis of reading disabilities and the use of diagnostic tests in the instruction of retarded readers.* Chicago: University of Chicago Press.

Moore, C. E. A. 1938. Preliminary study of the emotional effects of letter sounds. *Quart. J. Speech*, **24**, 134–149.

Moore, K. C. 1896. The mental development of a child. *Psychol. Rev. Monogr.*, **1**, No. 3. Pp. 150.

Morgan, J. J. B. 1934. *Child psychology,* Chapter IX, pp. 270–308. New York: Farrar and Rinehart.

Morrison, C. E. 1914–1915. Speech defects in young children. *Psychol. Clin.*, **8**, 138–142.

Müller, M. 1862, 1865. *Lectures on the science of language.* (2 vols.) New York: Scribner's.

Munn, N. L. 1938. *Psychological development,* Ch. XII, pp. 372–398. Boston: Houghton Mifflin.

Murchison, C., and S. Langer. 1927. Tiedemann's observations on the development of the mental faculties of children. *J. Genet. Psychol.*, **34**, 205–230.

National Society for the Study of Education. 1929. Preschool and parental education. *Yearb. Nat. Soc. Stud. Educ.*, **28**, 495–568.

Nausester, W. 1904. Das Kind und die Form der Sprache. *Geb. Pädag. Psychol. Physiol.*, **7**, No. 7.

Newman, S. S. 1933. Further experiments in phonetic symbolism. *Amer. J. Psychol.*, **45**, 53–75.

Nice, M. M. 1915. The development of a child's vocabulary in relation to environment. *Ped. Sem.*, **22**, 35–64.

———. 1915–1916. Speech of a left-handed child. *Psychol. Clin.*, **9**, 115–117.

———. 1917. Speech development of a child from eighteen months to six years. *Ped. Sem.*, **24**, 204–243.

Nice, M. M. 1918. Ambidexterity and delayed speech development. *Ped. Sem.*, **25**, 141–162.

———. 1920. Concerning all-day conversations. *Ped. Sem.*, **27**, 166–177.

———. 1922. A child that would not talk. *Proc. Okla. Acad. Sci.*, **2** (*Univ. Okla. Bull.*, N.S., No. 247), 108–111.

———. 1924. The speech development of a little girl. *Proc. Okla. Acad. Sci.*, **4** (*Univ. Okla. Bull.*, N.S., No. 322), 147–168.

———. 1925. Length of sentences as a criterion of a child's progress in speech. *J. Educ. Psychol.*, **16**, 370–379.

———. 1926. A child's vocabularies from fifteen months to three years. *Proc. Okla. Acad. Sci.*, **6**, Pt. II (*Univ. Okla. Bull.*, N.S., No. 348), 317–333.

———. 1926–1927. On the size of vocabularies. *Amer. Speech*, **2**, 1–7.

———. 1932. An analysis of the conversation of children and adults. *Child Develpm.*, **3**, 240–246.

———. 1933. A child's attainment of the sentence. *J. Genet. Psychol.*, **42**, 216–224.

Noiré, L. 1917. *The origin and philosophy of language.* Chicago: Open Court.

Norsworthy, N., and M. T. Whitley. 1933. *The psychology of childhood.* (Rev. ed.) (Chapter XII, pp. 243–264.) New York: Macmillan.

Ogden, C. K., and I. R. Richards. 1923, 1929. *The meaning of meaning.* London: Kegan Paul; New York: Harcourt, Brace.

Ohwaki, Y. 1933. Die ersten zwei Jahre der Sprachentwicklung des japanischen Kindes. Ein Beitrag zur Psychologie der Kindersprache. *Tohoku Psychol.*, **1**, 71–110.

Olson, W. C. 1929. *The measurement of nervous habits in normal children.* (*Inst. of Child Welfare, Monogr. Ser.*, No. 3.) Minneapolis: University of Minnesota Press. Pp. 97.

Olson, W. C., and V. S. Koetzle. 1936. Amount and rate of talking of young children. *J. Exp. Educ.*, **5**, 175–179.

Oltuszewski, W. 1897. *Die geistige und sprachliche Entwickelung des Kindes.* Berlin: Fischer's Medic. Buchhandlung, H. Kornfeld.

Ombredane, A. 1935. Études sur le langage. Sur les premières manifestations du langage enfantine et sur la prétendue loi de Fritz Schultze. *Hyg. Ment.*, **30**, No. 4, 69–89.

Orton, S. T. 1937. *Reading, writing and speech problems in children.* New York: Norton.

O'Shea, M. V. 1907. *Linguistic development and education.* New York: Macmillan.

Paget, R. 1930. *Human speech.* New York: Harcourt, Brace.

Paterson, D. G., and T. A. Langlie. 1926. The influence of sex on scholarship ratings. *Educ. Adm. and Supervis.*, **12**, 458–468.

PAYNE, C. S. 1930. The mispronunciation of words. *J. Genet. Psychol.*, **38**, 427–444.

PELSMA, J. R. 1910. A child's vocabulary and its development. *Ped. Sem.*, **7**, 328–369.

PEREZ, B. 1878, 1885, 1889, 1894. *La psychologie de l'enfant: Les trois premières années.* Paris: Alcan. (5th ed., 1894.) *The first three years of childhood.* (Ed. and trans. by A. M. CHRISTIE.) London (1885); Chicago: Marquis (1885); Syracuse, N. Y.: Bardeen (1889). (1889 Ed. used in preparing this chapter.)

PIAGET, J. 1924. *Le langage et la pensée chez l'enfant.* Neuchâtel et Paris: Delachaux & Niestlé. *The language and thought of the child.* (Trans. by M. WARDEN.) New York: Harcourt, Brace; London: Kegan Paul (1926).

——. 1928. *Judgment and reasoning of the child.* New York: Harcourt, Brace.

PICHON, E. 1932. Aperçu sur le développement moteur et psychique de l'enfant. *Paris Méd.*, **22**, 38–44.

PILLSBURY, W. B., and C. L. MEADER. 1928. *The psychology of language.* New York: Appleton.

POLLOCK, F. 1878. An infant's progress in language. *Mind*, **3**, 392–401.

POOLE, I. 1934. Genetic development of articulation of consonant sounds in speech. *Elem. Engl. Rev.*, **11**, 159–161.

PORTENIER, L. G. 1937. Factors influencing the social adjustment of children of preschool age. *J. Genet. Psychol.*, **51**, 127–139.

POS, H. J. 1934. Het affect enzijn uitdrukking in de taal. *Ned. Tijdschr. Psychol.*, **5/6**, 209–238.

POWERS, F. F. 1929. Psychology of language learning. *Psychol. Bull.*, **26**, 261–274.

PRESCOTT, D. A. 1929. Le vocabulaire des enfants des écoles primaires de Genève. *Arch. Psychol., Genève*, **21**, 225–261.

PRESSEY, S. L. 1925. A statistical study of children's errors in sentence structure. *Engl. J.*, **14**, 529–535.

PREYER, W. 1882, 1889, 1900. *Die Seele des Kindes.* Leipzig: Fernau. (5th ed., 1900.) *The mind of the child: Pt. 2. The development of the intellect.* (Trans. by H. W. BROWN.) New York: Appleton (1889). (Only 1900 ed. consulted.)

——. 1889. *The soul of the child.* (Trans. by E. MARWEDEL.) Pt. 2 of E. MARWEDEL, *Conscious motherhood.* Boston: Heath.

——. 1893. *Die geistige Entwicklung in der ersten Kindheit.* Stuttgart: Union. *Mental development in the child.* (Trans. by H. W. BROWN.) New York: Appleton.

PROBST, C. A. 1931. A general information test for kindergarten children. *Child Develpm.*, **2**, 81–95.

PUTCHKOWSKY, M. A. 1931. ["Lalling" and its role in the development of children's speech.] *Sovietskaya Psikhonevrol*, No. 2–3, 103–106.

PYLES, M. K. 1932. Verbalization as a factor in learning. *Child Develpm.*, **3**, 108–113.

RAND, W., M. E. SWEENEY, and L. VINCENT. 1930. *Growth and development of the young child.* Philadelphia: Saunders.

RASMUSSEN, V. 1920, 1921, 1923. *Child psychology: Vol. I. Development in the first four years.* (Trans. by G. C. BERRY.) London: Gyldendal (1920); New York: Knopf (1923). Vol. II. *The kindergarten child; its conception of life and its mental powers.* Vol. III. *Thought, imagination and feeling: Will and morale.* (Trans. by D. PRITCHARD.) London: Gyldenddl (1921); New York: Knopf (1923).

REMER, L. L. 1932. Handicaps of school entrants. *Univ. Iowa Stud. Child Welfare*, **6**, 195–207.

RICHTER, F. 1927. *Die Entwicklung des psychologischen Kindersprachforschung bis zum Beginn des 20 Jahrhunderts. Ein Beitrag zur Geschichte der Kinderseelenkunde.* Münster: Münsterverlag.

RICKARD, G. E. 1935. The recognition vocabulary of primary pupils. *J. Educ. Res.*, **29**, 281–291.

RIGG, M. G. 1938a. A superior child who would not talk. *Child Develpm.*, **9**, 361–362.

——. 1938b. The international Kindergarten Union Word List compared with eight spoken vocabularies. *Child Develpm.*, **9**, 363–364.

ROBINSON, E. W., and H. S. CONRAD. 1933–1934. The reliability of observations of talkativeness and social contact among nursery children by the short time sample technique. *J. Exp. Educ.*, **2**, 161–165.

ROWE, E. C., and H. N. ROWE. 1913. The vocabulary of a child at four and six years of age. *Ped. Sem.*, **20**, 187–208.

ROWLAND, E. H. 1907. The psychological experiences connected with different parts of speech. *Psychol. Rev. Monogr. Suppl.*, **8**, No. 32, 36–37.

RUGG, H., L. KRUEGER, and A. SONDERGAARD. 1929. Studies in child personality: I. A study of the language of kindergarten children. *J. Educ. Psychol.*, **20**, 1–18.

SALISBURY, A. 1894. A child's vocabulary. *Educ. Rev.*, **7**, 289–290.

SANFORD, E. C. 1891. Notes on studies of the language of children. *Ped. Sem.*, **1**, 257–260.

SAPIR, E. 1921. *Language, an introduction to the study of speech.* New York: Harcourt, Brace.

——. 1927. Language as a form of human behavior. *Engl. J.*, **16**, 421–433.

——. 1929. A study in phonetic symbolism. *J. Exp. Psychol.*, **12**, 225–239.

——. 1933. Language. In H. R. A. SELIGMAN (Ed.), *Encyclopedia of the social sciences.* (Vol. IX, pp. 155–169.) New York: Macmillan.

SCHÄFER, P. 1921. Die kindliche Entwicklungsperiode der reinen Sprachverständnisses nach ihrer Abgrenzung. *Z. pädag. Psychol.*, **22,** 317–325.

SCHÄFER, P. 1922. Beobachtungen und Versuche an einem Kinde in der Entwicklungsperiode des reinen Sprachverständnisses. *Z. pädag. Psychol.*, **23,** 269–289.

SCHMIDT, B. G. 1941. Language development as an aid to the social adjustment of mental defectives. *Ment. Hyg.*, **25,** 402–413.

SCHULTZE, F. 1880. *Die Sprache des Kindes: Eine Anregnung zur Erfarschung des Gegenstandes.* Leipzig: Ernst Gunther's Verlag.

SEAGO, D. W. 1925. An analysis of language factors in intelligence tests. *Ment. Meas. Monogr.*, **1,** No. 1. Pp. 125.

SEARS, I., and A. DIEBEL. 1917. A study of the common mistakes in pupils' oral English. *Elem. Sch. J.*, **17,** 44–54.

SEASHORE, R. H. 1933. The measurement and analysis of extent of vocabulary. *Psychol. Bull.*, **30,** 709–710.

SEASHORE, R. H., and L. D. ECKERSON. 1940. The measurement of individual differences in general English vocabularies. *J. Educ. Psychol.*, **31,** 14–38.

SECHEHAYE, A. 1917. Les problèmes de la langue. *Rev. Phil.*, **84,** 1–30.

SEGALLA, F. L. 1934. Writing vocabularies of negro and white children. *Sch. Rev.*, **42,** 772–779.

SEIDL, J. C. G. 1937. *The effect of bilingualism on the measurement of intelligence.* Unpublished Ph.D. Dissertation, Fordham University.

SETH, G., and D. GUTHRIE. 1935. *Speech in childhood; its development and disorders.* London: Oxford University Press.

SHAMBAUGH, C. G., and O. L. SHAMBAUGH. 1928. An association study of vocabularies of grade children. *J. Educ. Res.*, **18,** 40–47.

——. 1929. A core vocabulary for elementary school pupils. *J. Educ. Res.*, **19,** 39–46.

SHERMAN, I. 1935. *Articulation test with reading disability feature.* Winona, Minn.: Winona Public Schools. (Mimeographed.)

SHERMAN, I., and B. KENEVAN. 1935. *Kindergarten-primary articulation test.* Winona, Minn.: Winona Public Schools.

SHERMAN, M. 1927. The differentiation of emotional responses in infants: II. *J. Comp. Psychol.*, **7,** 335–351.

SHINN, M. W. 1893. Notes on the development of a child: I. *Univ. Calif. Publ. Educ.*, **1,** 1–178.

——. 1900. *The biography of a baby.* Boston: Houghton Mifflin.

SHIRLEY, M. M. 1933a. *The first two years: A study of twenty-five babies:* Vol. II. *Intellectual development. (Inst. Child Welf. Monogr. Ser.,* No. 7.) Minneapolis: University of Minnesota Press. Pp. xvi + 513.

——. 1933b. *The first two years: A study of twenty-five babies:* Vol. III. *Personality manifestations. (Inst. Child Welf. Monogr. Ser.,*

No. 8.) Minneapolis: University of Minnesota Press. Pp. xi + 228.

SHIRLEY, M. M. 1938. Common content in the speech of preschool children. *Child Develpm.*, **9,** 333–346.

SIGISMUND, B. 1856. *Kind und Welt. Vätern, Müttern, und Kinderfreunden gewidmet: I. Die fünf ersten Perioden des Kindesalters.* Braunschweig: Vieweg.

SIKORSKI, M. 1883. Du développement du langage chez les enfants. *Arch. de Neurol.*, **6,** 319–336.

SIMS, V. M. 1929. The reliability and validity of four types of vocabulary test. *J. Educ. Res.*, **20,** 91–96.

SIRKIN, J., and W. F. LYONS. 1941. A study of speech defects in mental deficiency. *Amer. J. Ment. Def.*, **46,** 74–80.

SKEELS, H. M., R. UPDEGRAFF, B. L. WELLMAN, and H. M. WILLIAMS. 1938. A study of environmental stimulation: An orphanage preschool project. *Univ. Iowa Stud. Child Welfare*, **15,** No. 4. (Chapter V, pp. 75–121.)

SMITH, L. Z. 1930. An experimental investigation of young children's interest and expressive behavior, responses to single statement, verbal repetition and ideational repetition of content in animal stories. *Child Develpm.*, **1,** 232–247.

SMITH, M. E. 1926. An investigation of the development of the sentence and the extent of vocabulary in young children. *Univ. Iowa Stud. Child Welfare*, **3,** No. 5.

——. 1931. A study of five bilingual children from the same family. *Child Develpm.*, **2,** 184–187.

——. 1932. The preschool child's use of criticism. *Child Develpm.*, **3,** 137–145.

——. 1933a. A study of language development in bilingual children in Hawaii. *Psychol. Bull.*, **30,** 692–693.

——. 1933b. The influence of age, sex, and situation on the frequency, form, and function of questions asked by preschool children. *Child Develpm.*, **4,** 201–213.

——. 1933c. Grammatical errors in the speech of preschool children. *Child Develpm.*, **4,** 182–190.

——. 1935a. A study of some factors influencing the development of the sentence in preschool children. *J. Genet. Psychol.*, **46,** 182–212.

——. 1935b. A study of the speech of eight bilingual children of the same family. *Child Develpm.*, **6,** 19–25.

——. 1939. Some light on the problem of bilingualism as found from a study of the progress in mastery of English among preschool children of non-American ancestry in Hawaii. *Genet. Psychol. Monogr.*, **21,** 121–284.

——. 1940. A comparison of the English vocabulary used by children of non-American ancestry in Hawaii before they reach the age of seven years with that of kindergarten children in Continental United States. *J. Exp. Educ.*, **9**, 121–132.

SMITH, M. K. 1941. Measurement of the size of general English vocabulary through the elementary grades and high school. *Genet. Psychol. Monogr.*, **24**, 311–345.

SNYDER, A. D. 1914. Notes on the talk of a two-and-one-half-year-old boy. *Ped. Sem.*, **21**, 412–424.

SOMMER, A. T. 1932. The effect of group training upon the correction of articulatory defects in preschool children. *Child Develpm.*, **3**, 91–107.

SPRINGOB, J. R. 1930. *Factors influencing the incidence of articulatory speech defects in preschool children.* Unpublished Master's Thesis, University of Minnesota.

STALNAKER, E. 1933. The language of preschool children. *Child Develpm.*, **4**, 229–236.

STERN, C., and W. STERN. 1907. *Die Kindersprache: Eine psychologische und sprachtheoretische Untersuchung.* (*Monogr. seel. Entwick. d. Kindes,* Vol. I.) Leipzig : Barth. (3d ed., rev., 1922.) Pp. xii + 434.

STERN, W. 1930. *Psychologie der frühen Kindheit, bis zum sechsten Lebensjahre.* (6th ed., rev.) Leipzig : Quelle and Meyer. (1st ed., 1914.) *Psychology of early childhood: Up to the sixth year of age.* (Trans. from the 3d German ed. by A. BARWELL.) New York : Holt; London : Allen (1924). (2d ed., rev., 1930.)

STEVENSON, A. 1893. The speech of children. *Science,* **21**, 118–120.

STINCHFIELD, S. M. 1924. The formulation and standardization of a series of graded speech tests. *Psychol. Rev. Monogr.*, **33**, No. 149. Pp. 54.

——. 1928. *The psychology of speech.* Boston : Expression Co.

STINCHFIELD, S. M., and E. H. YOUNG. 1938. *Children with delayed or defective speech: Motor-kinesthetic factors in their training.* Stanford University, Calif.: Stanford University Press.

STODDARD, C. B., and H. K. LANGUIN. 1934. *Articulation Test I. Speech improvement.* Detroit : Board of Education, City of Detroit.

STODDARD, G. D., and B. WELLMAN. 1934. *Child psychology.* New York : Macmillan.

STORMZAND, M. J., and M. V. O'SHEA. 1924. *How much English grammar?* Baltimore : Warwick and York.

STOUTEMYER, J. H. 1930. Some psychological aspects of language. *Kadelpian Rev.*, **9**, 331–337.

STRANG, R. 1938. *An introduction to child study.* New York : Macmillan.

STRAYER, L. C. 1930. Language and growth : The relative efficacy of early and deferred vocabulary training studied by the method of

co-twin control. *Genet. Psychol. Monogr.*, **8**, 209–319.

STUMPF, C. 1900. Eigenartige sprachliche Entwicklung eines Kind. *Z. pädag. Psychol.*, **2**, 1–29.

STUTSMAN, R. 1931. *Mental measurement of preschool children.* Yonkers-on-Hudson : World Book.

SUKHOV, G. D. 1939. [The acquisition of speech by the child in the play process.] In *Psikhologitchni doslidzennia. Naookovi zapiski.* Kharkov : Derj. Ped. Inst.

SULLY, J. 1896, 1908. *Studies of childhood.* London and New York : Appleton. (New ed., 1908.) (The 1908 ed. consulted.)

SUNNE, D. 1933. The effect of locality on language errors. *J. Educ. Res.*, **8**, 239–251.

SYKES, J. 1940. A study of the spontaneous vocalizations of young deaf children. *Psychol. Monogr.*, **52**, No. 1, 104–123.

SYMONDS, P. M., and H. F. DARINGER. 1930. Studies in the learning of English expression. IV. Sentence structure. *Teach. Coll. Rec.*, **32**, 50–64.

SYMONDS, P. M., and B. LEE. 1929. Studies in the learning of English expression. III. Vocabulary. *Teach. Coll. Rec.*, **31**, 50–58.

SYMPOSIUM. 1920. Is thinking merely the action of language mechanisms? *Brit. J. Psychol.*, **11**, 55–104.

TAINE, H. 1876. Note sur l'acquisition du langage chez les enfants et dans l'espèce humaine. *Rev. Phil.*, **1**, 3–23. (Trans. in *Mind,* 1877, **2**, 252–257.)

TANNER, A. E. 1904. *The child, his thinking, feeling and doing.* Chicago ; New York ; London : Rand, McNally.

TEMPLIN, M., and M. D. STEER. 1939. Studies of growth of speech in preschool children. *J. Speech Disorders,* **4**, 71–77.

TERMAN, L. M. 1916. *The measurement of intelligence: An explanation of and a complete guide for the use of the Stanford revision and extension of the Binet-Simon intelligence scale.* Boston : Houghton Mifflin.

TERMAN, L. M., *et al.* 1925. *Genetic studies of genius:* Vol. I. *Mental and physical traits of a thousand gifted children.* Stanford University, Calif. : Stanford University Press.

THORNDIKE, E. L. 1921. *The teacher's word book.* New York : Teachers College, Columbia University.

——. 1931–1932. *A teacher's word book of the twenty thousand words found most frequently and widely in general reading for children and young people.* New York : Teachers College, Columbia University.

——. 1937. On the number of words of any given frequency of use. *Psychol. Rec.*, **1**, 399–406.

——. 1938. Studies in the psychology of language. *Arch. Psychol.*, No. 231.

THORNDIKE, E. L., A. L. EVANS, L. H. V. KEN-

NON, and E. I. NEWCOMB. 1926–1927. An inventory of English constructions with measures of their importance. *Teach. Coll. Rec.*, 28, 580–610.

TINKER, M. A., F. HACKNER, and M. W. WESLEY. 1940. Speed and quality of association as a measure of vocabulary knowledge. *J. Educ. Psychol.*, 31, 575–582.

TÖGEL, H. 1905. 16 Monate Kindersprache. *Beih. z. Kinderforsch.*, No. 3.

TOWN, C. H. 1912–1913. Language development in 285 idiots and imbeciles. *Psychol. Clin.*, 6, 229–235.

——. 1921. An analytic study of a group of five- to six-year-old children. *Univ. Iowa Stud. Child Welfare*, 1, No. 4.

TRACY, F. 1893. The language of childhood. *Amer. J. Psychol.*, 6, 107–138.

TRAVIS, L. E. 1931. *Speech pathology.* New York: Appleton.

TRETTIEN, A. W. 1904. Psychology of language interest in children. *Ped. Sem.*, 2, 113–177.

UHRBROCK, R. S. 1936. Words most frequently used by a five-year-old girl. *J. Educ. Psychol.*, 27, 155–158.

UNDERWOOD, A. 1931. Investigations in the study of language. *J. Educ. Res.*, 23, 162–164.

VALENTINE, C. W. 1930. The psychology of imitation. *Brit. J. Psychol.*, 21, 105–132.

VAN ALSTYNE, D. 1929. The environment of three-year-old children: Factors related to intelligence and vocabulary tests. *Teach. Coll. Contr. Educ.*, No. 366.

——. 1932. *Play behavior and choice of play materials of preschool children.* Chicago: University of Chicago Press.

VASEY, F. T. 1919. Vocabularies of grammar school children. *J. Educ. Psychol.*, 10, 104–107.

VENDRYES, J. 1921. *Le langage: Introduction linguistic à l'histoire.* Paris: Renaissance du Livre.

VIGOTSKY, L. S. 1939. Thought and speech. *Psychiatry*, 2, 29–54.

VIGOTSKY, L. S., and A. R. LURIA. 1929. The function and fate of egocentric speech. *Proc. and Pap. 9th Int. Cong. Psychol.*, 464–465.

VOEGELIN, C. F., and S. ADAMS. 1934. A phonetic study of young children's speech. *J. Exp. Educ.*, 3, 107–116.

WADDLE, C. W. 1913. *An introduction to child psychology.* Boston: Houghton Mifflin.

WAGONER, L. C. 1933. *The development of learning in young children.* (Chapter XII, pp. 181–197.) New York: McGraw-Hill.

WARING, E. B. 1927. The relation between early language habits and early habits of conduct control. *Teach. Coll. Contr. Educ.*, No. 260.

WEISS, A. P. 1925. Linguistics and psychology. *Language*, 1, 52–57.

WELLMAN, B. L., I. M. CASE, I. G. MENGERT, and D. E. BRADBURY. 1931. Speech sounds of young children. *Univ. Iowa Stud. Child Welfare*, 5, No. 2.

WEST, R. M. 1933. *Disorders of speech and voice.* (2d ed.) Mimeographed by College Typing Co., Madison, Wis. Pp. 141.

WHIPPLE, G. M., and Mrs. G. M. WHIPPLE. 1909. The vocabulary of a three-year-old boy with some interpretive comments. *Ped. Sem.*, 15, 1–22.

WILKE, W. H. 1938. Development and application of a scale for measuring diction. *Quart. J. Speech*, 24, 268–281.

WILLIAMS, H. M. 1932. Some problems of sampling in vocabulary tests. *J. Exp. Educ.*, 1, 131–133.

——. 1937a. An analytical study of language achievement in preschool children. Part I of Development of language and vocabulary in young children. *Univ. Iowa Stud. Child Welfare*, 13, No. 2, 9–18.

——. 1937b. A qualitative analysis of the erroneous speech sound substitutions of preschool children. Part II of Development of language and vocabulary in young children. *Univ. Iowa Stud. Child Welfare*, 13, No. 2, 21–32.

WILLIAMS, H. M., and M. L. McFARLAND. 1937. A revision of the Smith vocabulary test for preschool children. Part III of Development of language and vocabulary in young children. *Univ. Iowa Stud. Child Welfare*, 13, No. 2, 35–46.

WILLIAMS, R. M., and M. L. MATTSON. 1942. The effect of social groupings upon the language of preschool children. *Child Develpm.*, 13, 233–245.

WILLOUGHBY, R. R. 1932. The functions of conversation. *J. Soc. Psychol.*, 3, 146–160.

WILSON, F. T. 1937. Correlations of vocabulary knowledge with other abilities and traits in Grade I. *Elem. Sch. J.*, 37, 451–457.

WILSON, G. M. 1922. Language error tests. *J. Educ. Psychol.*, 13, 341–349.

WITTE, O. 1930. Untersuchungen über die Gebärdensprache. Beiträge zur Psychologie der Sprache. *Z. Psychol.*, 116, 225–308.

WITTY, P. A., and M. FRY. 1929. The vocabulary content of compositions written by college students. *J. Educ. Res.*, 19, 135–138.

WITTY, P. A., and L. L. LABRANT. 1930. Vocabulary and reading. *Sch. and Soc.*, 31, 268–272.

WOLFE, H. K. 1917. On the color vocabulary of children. *Nebraska Univ. Stud.*, 1, No. 3, 205–234.

WÖLFFLIN, E. 1901. Reduplikation in der Kindersprache. *Z. dents. Wortforsch.*, 1, 263.

WOLFLE, D. L. 1932. The relation between linguistic structure and associative interference in artificial linguistic material. *Lang. Monogr.*, No. 11. Pp. 54.

WOLFLE, D. L. 1934. The role of generalization in language. *Brit. J. Psychol.,* **24,** 434–444.

WORBOIS, G. M. 1942. Language development in two different rural environments. *Child Develpm.,* **13,** 175–180.

WUNDT, W. 1901. *Sprachgeschichte und Sprachpsychologie.* Leipzig: Engelmann.

——. 1911–1912. *Völkerpsychologie:* Vol. I. *Die Sprache.* (3d ed., two parts.) Leipzig: Engelmann (Kroener).

YOAKUM, C., and R. M. YERKES. 1920. *Army mental tests.* New York: Holt.

YOSHIOKA, J. 1929. A study of bilingualism. *J. Genet. Psychol.,* **36,** 473–479.

YOUNG, F. M. 1941. An analysis of certain variables in a developmental study of language. *Genet. Psychol. Monogr.,* **23,** 3–141.

——. 1942a. Certain social indices in the language of preschool subjects. *J. Genet. Psychol.,* **61,** 109–123.

YOUNG, F. M. 1942b. Development as indicated by a study of pronouns. *J. Genet. Psychol.,* **61,** 125–134.

ZAGOROVSKII, P. L. 1928. [Clinical methods of investigating the speech reaction of children.] *Z. Psikhol. Ped. Psikhotekh.,* **1,** 96–106.

ZAPOROSHETZ, A. V. 1939. [The role of elements of practice and speech in the development of thinking in children.] In *Psikhologitchni doslidzennia. Naookovi zapiski.* Kharkov: Derj. Ped. Inst.

ZEROV, V. 1930. [The evolution of written language in primary school children.] *Pedologiya* (Russian), 683–697.

ZIPF, G. K. 1935. *The psycho-biology of language.* Boston: Houghton Mifflin.

——. 1942. Children's speech. *Science,* **96,** 344–345.

ZYVE, C. I. 1927. Conversation among children. *Teach. Coll. Rec.,* **29,** 46–61.

CHAPTER 11

ENVIRONMENTAL INFLUENCES ON MENTAL DEVELOPMENT [1]

HAROLD E. JONES

The Nature of Mental Ability

The studies reported in this chapter are based primarily upon results from the use of standard intelligence tests. The influence of environment on mental ability will therefore, in the first instance, be observed only through its effect upon mental test scores. The validity or general significance of such scores rests upon the extent to which they serve as indicators of a wider range of adaptive behavior (that is, of mental capacities or potentialities). No test is as valid as we would like to have it, but the significance of scores is particularly open to question in the case of subjects who have had special practice, or who are outside the cultural or educational range of the sample on which the test was standardized. If these or other conditions have

disturbed the appropriateness of the test in question for the individuals in question, the effect of the environment can, of course, be interpreted only with reference to a narrow range of test functions, and not with regard to a broader concept of intelligence.

Individual differences in mental ability have been discussed by E. L. Thorndike (1927) as involving three principal aspects, *level, range,* and *speed.* The level of ability which a person reaches is defined by the difficulty of mental tasks which he can perform; the range or breadth of ability is defined by the number of different tasks which he can perform at various levels. If the items of an intelligence test are classified from "easy" to "hard," two individuals may be able to solve problems at the same level of difficulty, but one may achieve a higher total score than the other because he solves a greater variety of problems at that or at preceding levels. Speed, or rate of work, is also a factor in mental efficiency, although regarded as of less direct importance than the other aspects of ability.

A useful line of inquiry would be the study of the effects of environment upon specific aspects of intelligence, as represented for example in level, range, or speed scores, or even more specifically in test items, groups of items, or component scores derived from factor analysis. In this field, however, few attempts have been made to deal analytically with constituent factors; the principal studies are limited

[1] The subject of this chapter has been covered in comprehensive reviews in two *Yearbooks of the National Society for the Study of Education,* prepared respectively by Terman *et al.* (1928) and Stoddard *et al.* (1940) ; in three issues of the *Review of Educational Research,* edited by Stoddard (1933, 1936) and Jones (1939) ; in *Heredity and Environment* by Schwesinger (1933) and *The Dynamics of Population* by Lorimer and Osborn (1934) ; and also in numerous textbook treatments. With our knowledge still inconclusive at many points, the rapid growth of research in this field testifies to its continuing vitality and also to the continued need for critical summaries and appraisals. The present treatment deals with research through the year 1941.

Acknowledgments are due to Miss Jane Loevinger for assistance in connection with this chapter, and also to Doctor Herbert S. Conrad for reading the manuscript and for numerous suggestions.

chiefly to general measures of mental function. These general measures, concerned with the capacity to utilize symbols and to acquire *intellective* adaptations, are ordinarily expressed in terms of a composite score, such as the IQ.

It is readily seen that, in our present state of theory, intelligent behavior can be designated more readily by illustration than by abstract definition. This implies, of course, an empirical and functional point of view concerning the nature of intelligence. The reader who wishes a fuller statement as to current emphases in the theory of intelligence is referred to a discussion of this problem by Freeman (1940).

The Nature of Environmental Influences

The individual organism comes into being and develops in a maternal environment which supplies nourishment and other biological needs and also provides both protective shielding and some opportunity for functional stimulation. These environmental supports are essential if the organism is to grow, or even to survive. In this connection, no one asks the question, "Which is more important, nature or nurture?" for both are obviously indispensable. Structural and, ultimately, functional development is an outcome of (1) the interaction of genes with their intracellular environment, (2) the interaction of cells in the intraorganic environment, and (3) the interaction of the organism with its extraorganic surroundings. The hereditary "determiners" or genes cannot function unless the various aspects of the environment play their necessary rôles. On the other hand, the influence of environmental factors is subject to very definite limitations, for (to cite one example) no normal environmental force can change an individual with

chromosomes of one species into an individual with the characteristics of a different species. Developmental differences large enough to distinguish species are thus hereditary effects which extrinsic factors cannot (in any given individual) wholly simulate or counteract.

The problem of environmental influences becomes less a matter of general principles, and more a matter for specific analysis, when we turn our attention from the growth of the single individual to the consideration of factors which affect individual differences. In this area we may with reason ask, "Which is more important, nature or nurture?" If, however, we attempt to reply to the question (as applied to mental abilities) with an over-all generalization, we shall immediately find ourselves in logical difficulties. Suppose that we address ourselves to the task of determining the causes of illiteracy. Haldane (1938) has pointed out that, among adults in England under forty years of age, illiteracy is probably most often due either to mental deficiency or to blindness. But among adults in Elizabethan England, or in India today, illiteracy may be attributed primarily to the lack of educational opportunity.

Thus we are led to say that hereditary and environmental influences on intelligence do not constitute a single problem for which a single quantitative answer can be found, but a family of problems, each with its own relatively complicated answer.

Quantitative Approaches

Hogben (1933), in a book rich with illuminating examples of the interaction of heredity and environment, points out that statistical methods are useful in detecting the *presence* of either sort of influence, but he questions the meaningfulness of attempts to *quantify* the relative influence of genetic and nongenetic causes of variations.

"No statement about a genetic difference has any scientific meaning unless it includes or implies a specification of the environment in which it manifests itself in a particular manner" (p. 14). Haldane (1938) has similarly made the point: "The question of the relative importance of nature and nurture has no general answer, but . . . a very large number of particular answers" (p. 36). The analysis by Whipple (1928) and by Schwesinger (1933) of the heredity-environment problem is also relevant to the present discussion. In a cogent statement as to the relation of specific conditions to the effects of training, Whipple has urged that results should be formulated in detailed terms of the approximate percentages of a given group which can be expected to show improvements of various amounts.

One of the earliest and most widely criticized quantitative statements was Burt's (1921) regression equation for predicting Binet mental age from schooling, "reasoning ability," and chronological age. Both Holzinger and Freeman (1925) and Burks (1928a) have demonstrated the error in direct inference from regression coefficients to proportional contributions.

Fisher (1918) has developed methods by means of which, granted the applicability of certain assumptions, "it is possible to calculate the numerical influence not only of dominance, but of the total genetic and nongenetic causes of variability" (p. 433). These methods have been used by Conrad and Jones (1940) to test hypotheses concerning the nature of hereditary transmission of intelligence but not for the purpose of calculating the numerical influence of nature and nurture.

Methods for determining the proportional influence of causal factors have been applied to studies of foster children by Burks (1928b), Wright (1931), Leahy (1935), and Wallis (1936), and to studies

of twins by Newman, Freeman, and Holzinger (1937). Leahy's computations gave the home environment the very meager credit of determining not more than 4 per cent of the variation in mental ability (stated in terms of variance, or the square of the standard deviation). A more liberal estimate by Burks was 17 per cent. Wright (1931) and Shuttleworth (1935) have reworked the data of these investigators, applying statistical corrections which give results differing somewhat from each other and from the original studies.

We need not at this point be greatly concerned about reconciling these statements or interpreting the highly mathematical criticisms which various members of the quantitative school of thought have leveled at each other's techniques. For all these statements, it is important to understand that: (1) The proportional contribution of heredity and environment does not refer to the make-up of individual IQ's nor to the general level of intelligence, but either to average effects upon *individual differences* or to differences between groups. (2) Existing studies are based on fallible and incomplete measures both of intelligence and of the environment; this fact should be remembered when the data are being manipulated to yield an apparently highly exact result. (3) Even if it is logically feasible to seek a single value for the effect of environment, this particular value may not apply in samples involving (*a*) a different environmental level, (*b*) a different hereditary selection, (*c*) a change in variability of either of the above factors, or (*d*) a change in any special conditions which may affect the interaction of these factors.

The remainder of this discussion will be concerned with results from several different types of approach. Each of these contributes in its own way to our understanding of what environment can and cannot do; each provides some clue as to the relative importance of environmental factors under specified circumstances. For the time being, however, we must think of these results as rough approximations rather than as precise and final statements.

Mental Growth Curves

One approach to the analysis of environmental influences is based on the study of mental growth curves. If the intelligence of children (relative to age) were generally found to be constant throughout childhood, few questions would be raised about the rôle of differential environmental factors, except perhaps as these may be assumed to operate in the prenatal period or in early infancy.

If, on the other hand, mental development of individuals is marked by variable or systematic changes (that is, by fluctuations or age trends, relative to the group), the nature and extent of possible environmental influence become an issue of some interest. Such changes, if they occur, are not necessarily due to the environment or subject to educational controls. They may be attributable to errors of measurement; to normative defects of the test; or to changes in the composition of the test, or of intelligence, at different levels. They may be due to variations in the temporary state of the subject, dependent upon physical condition, rapport, and motivation. Or they may express a neurophysiological growth pattern differing in rate of evolution for different children; such maturational changes are well established in the patterns of physical growth for various organs, and for the body as a whole. Any of these factors, in any combination, may conceivably operate to alter the apparent or actual course of mental development. One of our first problems, therefore, is to ascertain the facts as to the regularity of

growth, and then to attempt an assessment of the various agencies which may be responsible for irregular or unpredicted variations.

Growth in Terms of Averages. An implicit belief in the lawfulness and uniformity of mental development has at times accompanied the acceptance of IQ and mental age as indices of intelligence most convenient for general use. For any group of children with an average IQ of 100 at age 10, the average will remain substantially the same at 11 and at 12 years if we allow for slight practice effects which tend to increase the IQ, and slight standardization errors which in our present instruments usually tend to decrease it. This constancy, however, is the necessary outcome of a scale conceived in terms of mental age.[1] In such a scale, a gain of one year in mental age is that increment which occurs (on the average) in one chronological year, and the average rate of development during childhood must appear to be constant since it is expressed in terms of constant and equal increments of mental age. It is, of course, now generally understood that such a picture of growth is merely a convenient artifact— convenient largely because of its adaptability for use in connection with an educational grade system based on chronological age.

A theory of environmental influence should be able to deal with the fact that in terms of units other than mental age the growth of intelligence may not be

1 Heinis (1926) has derived a logarithmic formula for mental growth and proposed the use of a "Personal Constant," based on the logarithmic equation, to avoid alleged arbitrary features of the mental age scale. This proposal has been analyzed in a definitive discussion by Bradway and Hoffeditz (1937). Gesell (1928), in plotting developmental age, has also used a logarithmic method to express the relative rate of what is "arithmetically implicit" in an age scale.

linear, but with increasing age may show a decreasing rate of change. This is illustrated in Table 1, adapted from Freeman

TABLE 1

MEANS AND STANDARD DEVIATIONS, BY AGE, FOR THE *VACO* GROUP INTELLIGENCE TEST

Age	Mean Score	SD	Annual Gain	Gain / SD
8	82.3	....	....	....
9	106.1	24.4	23.8	0.98
10	127.7	28.8	21.6	0.75
11	150.0	31.5	22.3	0.71
12	172.2	34.6	22.2	0.64

and Flory (1937). The intelligence scale used in this study consisted of vocabulary items, analogies, a completion test, and an opposites test. In terms of point scores, it can be seen that the annual gains are quite constant or linear within this age range. Annual gains, however, decrease sharply when expressed as a fraction of the SD; this is a more rational way of indicating age changes than merely in terms of raw scores or of mental age.

Rate changes in mental growth can also be estimated in terms of the overlapping of distributions of scores at successive ages. In a somewhat selected group, Bayley (1933) has shown that in early childhood overlapping is very small even when retests are given at short intervals. Thus, at 5 months no cases in her sample equal or exceed the average mental score attained at 6 months. At 5 years, on the other hand, evidence of age changes can hardly be seen within a period so short as a month. The distributions for tests given at month intervals overlap to such an extent that they are almost identical.[1]

[1] Individual development involves a multiplication of environmental contacts, and also an increasing scope of response to the environment. This might reasonably be expected to produce an orderly *increase* in the rate of mental growth during early childhood and adolescence, if envi-

IQ Constancy. Another source of evidence concerning variability in growth is based on the study of changes in individual scores. Although average IQ's maintain approximate constancy by force of standardization, individual IQ's are under no such requirement. The common finding that the probable error of an IQ (Stanford-Binet) is approximately 5 points appears reassuring from the point of view of those who wish to classify children on the basis of a single test, but, when we consider this statement, we should also bear in mind the fact that with a probable error of 5 points (if differences are normally distributed) one child in five may deviate as much as 10 points in a retest.[2] Such a difference is of sufficient practical importance to justify an inquiry into its possible causes.

Predictive Correlations. IQ differences on retests may be influenced not merely by changes within the group but also by upward or downward trends of the group as a whole; such trends could be due to practice effects, to errors in standardization, or to other factors which will be discussed in a later section. If our interest is primarily in the constancy with which individuals maintain their relative rate of mental growth, the most straightforward index is the coefficient of correlation between mental status on two different occasions.

ronment is of predominant importance in mental growth. Current research, however, has shown that basic mental test abilities decrease in their rate of growth, that they reach a peak in the late teens or early twenties, and that they decline in later maturity; these facts suggest the presence of innate or organic limitations in the individual's response to his environment.

[2] The reader may consult Hildreth (1926) for empirical evidence on this point. However, the probable error of the IQ is not a fixed value, but may vary according to the age, intelligence level, and test experience of the subject. In the Terman and Merrill (1937) standardization, the average difference between IQ's on Form M and L was 5.9 for cases with IQ of 130 or above, decreasing to 2.5 for cases with IQ below 70.

Various reviews [1] have shown that retest correlations are rarely as high as .95, and most commonly fall between .80 and .90. Reports on this subject, however, are often difficult to interpret, since they have usually included cases at many different age levels and with different test intervals. R. L. Thorndike (1933) has shown that on an immediate retest the most probable correlation is .89. This value falls to .87 at 10 months; .81 at 30 months; .70 at 60 months. It is recognized, however, that age as well as test interval may influence the results. If the first test is given as late as at 10 years of age, prediction may be better than Thorndike's estimate; thus, in a study by Byrns and Henmon (1935), 250 college students were located who had been tested 8 to 10 years previously. For this selected group the initial IQ (National Intelligence Test) correlated .81 with a group test score obtained in college. On the other hand, if the initial test is given in infancy, correlations with later status may fall close to zero.

During the first year of life, adequately reliable measurements can be obtained of mental functions on the basis of various types of items involving problem solving, imitation, memory, and other forms of adaptive reaction. Such measurements are of possible importance in adapting a régime to a child's developmental level at any given time. Moreover, individual differences in these mental functions are reasonably consistent over periods of several months. Bayley (1940a) has obtained mental scores with a reliability of .94 by averaging scores obtained at 7, 8, and 9 months. These correlate .81 with scores

3 months later, but only .39 with scores at around 21 months; .22 with scores at around 30 months, and practically zero with all later measurements, to 6 years and beyond. Although other studies have not covered this age range, similar results have in general been reported between mental tests given at 1 year and 3 to 4 years later.[2]

From such results, it might be expected that in the case of mental scores obtained still earlier in infancy, the correlations with later status would also vary around zero. It is interesting to note, however, that Furfey and Muehlenbein (1932), L. D. Anderson (1939), and Bayley (1940a) all report negative correlations between test scores obtained at 6 months or earlier and test scores obtained at 4 years or later. Although the prediction indices found in these studies are not statistically significant, they are sufficiently consistent to suggest that early status and later growth rates may be negatively related. Speculation on this point may well be re-

1 The best of these are by R. L. Thorndike (1933, 1940). Earlier reviews have been published by Foran (1926, 1929) and by Nemzek (1933). Useful summaries are also given by Pintner (1931) and by Hirsch (1930a), the latter adding further evidence from a cumulative study of a large sample.

2 For 91 cases, L. D. Anderson (1939) reported a correlation of .06 between Gesell scores at 1 year and the Stanford-Binet at 5 years. Furfey and Muehlenbein (1932) found a correlation of −.20 between mental scores at 12 months, on the Linfert-Hierholzer scale, and Stanford-Binet IQ's given at an average age of 4.8 years.

With the feeble-minded and in cases involving a definite pathology, such as mongolian idiocy and some birth injury cases, it would be expected that a fairly consistent picture of retardation would be observable from infancy. Case records reported by Gesell, Castner, Thompson, and Amatruda (1939) give convincing evidence on this point. In a representative sampling, however, such cases are either absent or too few to produce much effect upon the retest coefficients.

A number of writers have been optimistic as to the possibility of obtaining improved prediction through the selection and differential weighting of items in the infant tests. The practical possibilities of this procedure remain to be demonstrated, although current studies by Nelson and Richards (1938, 1939) and Richards and Nelson (1939) have yielded promising preliminary results.

served until the findings are confirmed by other studies. Of possible relevance is the investigation by Dubnoff (1938), who tested 489 infants in Kazan, U.S.S.R., by the California First Year Mental Scale. Approximately one-third of the group was of Tatar extraction; one-half was tested in homes, and one-half (factory workers' children) in crèches or factory nurseries. Scale scores during the first year favor the Kazan group; in terms of the variability of the Kazan group, the difference is about 2 SD at one month. From the fourth to the eighth month the difference drops to about 1 SD and by the tenth month the averages become approximately equal in the two groups. It could be contended that the relative gain of the California group from 1 to 10 months is due in part to a more favorable environment with regard to medical care, diet, sunlight, and to a more intelligent régime of care by the mother. Dubnoff comments:

> Due to the cold winters, the Kazan child is heavily clothed, and often wrapped in blankets which prevent freedom of movement. Except for about two months of the year he is never exposed to sunlight. Rickets is prevalent. . . . The level of education of the parents is very markedly lower than that of the California sample (p. 70).

Environmental factors, however, cannot be adduced to explain the initial superiority of the Kazan infants. Dubnoff's work, together with other related studies, may lead to the speculative suggestion that between natio-racial groups, as within a given group, a slight tendency exists for early precocity to be associated with a slower mental growth at later ages, and perhaps with a lower average intelligence level at maturity. A parallel situation may be noted when we compare different animal species; among the primates, for example, the maturity of performance at a given age in infancy can be used *inversely* to predict the general level of adaptive ability that will be attained at adolescence.

To summarize the foregoing, we have noted an apparent slight tendency for mental scores in early infancy to be negatively correlated with mental scores at 4 years or later. At 12 months of age the correlation is close to zero. Beyond that point, however, a positive relationship emerges. Figure 1 shows the correlations of scores at 10 years with scores at each preceding year for the sample of cases previously reported on by Bayley (1933, 1940a) and by Bayley and Jones (1937). The index of forecasting efficiency $(1 - \sqrt{1 - r^2})$ is also shown. It is apparent that as early as 2 years of age individual differences are beginning to appear which carry forward to some extent into later childhood.[1] The increase in predictive power is somewhat more rapid in the preschool period than later.

The Age Ratio. J. E. Anderson (1940) has pointed out that as we go up the age scale the prediction of later from earlier status involves an increasing proportion of similar elements. The 10-year tests are in content more similar to the 9- than to the 8-year tests. Moreover, the cumulative composites of performance which are represented in test scores are more similar between adjacent than between separated age levels. They become increasingly similar for adjacent levels as we approach maturity, since the increment from one year to another will have a proportionately smaller effect upon total scores.

Figure 1 represents correlations based upon actual scores (point scores or mental ages). The scores for each individual change each year as a result of successive increments of growth. What would happen if we were to set up an artificial

[1] See also reports by Honzik (1938) and L. D Anderson (1939).

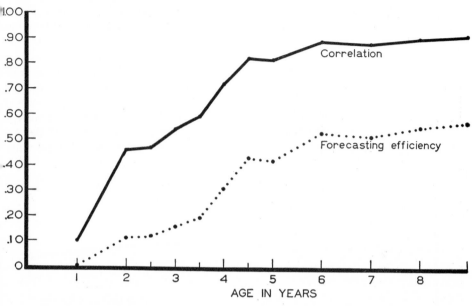

FIGURE 1. Mental scores at 10 years as related to scores in each preceding year.

series in which the increments for each year were cumulated at random? Thus, at 3 years individual A would be given an arbitrary score consisting of his own score at 2 years plus B's increment from 2 to 3 years. The resulting 3-year score could then be added to C's actual increment from 3 to 4 years, in order to obtain an arbitrary 4-year score for A. Such a series (as Anderson has shown by cumulating random numbers) would necessarily result in a correlation curve very similar to that actually obtained in Figure 1. Several factors might operate to produce differences in the two curves. For example, if actual mental growth involves greater annual increments for those who already have higher status, then the correlation curve for actual scores, other things being equal, will be higher than that based on arbitrary cumulations. But in any event we must expect that the predictive power of our tests will be proportionate to the age of testing. It will also be inversely propor-

tionate to the length of the interval over which prediction is attempted. Honzik (1938) has proposed the concept of the Age Ratio $\left(\dfrac{CA \text{ at Test } 1}{CA \text{ at Test } 2}\right)$ to express both these factors. The Age Ratio shows a high positive correlation with retest coefficients during the first ten years.

Two consequences of this may now be pointed out. If hereditary components in mental ability are more fully manifested at maturity than at earlier ages, children whose eventual status is to be either high or low will tend to fall nearer the mean in earlier tests, and in later tests will gradually approximate their final position.[1]

[1] This appears to be illustrated in a study by P. Cattell (1937), who made ability classifications of children on the basis of an average of initial tests and retests (thus eliminating changes within extreme groups due to regression). Children of superior average ability tended to increase in IQ on the retest. Among mental defectives, Roberts, Norman, and Griffiths (1938) have reported an average downward shift of about 2 IQ points per year in the age range

The foregoing argument should also be considered in relation to statements about the "plasticity" of early childhood (susceptibility to environmental influences). Figure 2 illustrates an individual growth curve of a fairly typical or normal form. The curve is based on sigma or standard scores and is smoothed, the actual points being also shown. It may be noted that this is a relative, not an absolute, growth curve.

years. Such a growth pattern has been variously interpreted as due to the changing nature of early tests, to a fundamental instability in early growth (related to physiological instability), and to a sensitive response to environmental changes. Although these factors cannot be wholly excluded, it may be pointed out that, in terms of the previous analysis of the Age Ratio, curves of this general type would

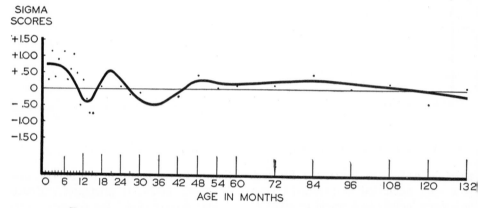

FIGURE 2. An individual mental growth curve, based on sigma scores.

A horizontal line indicates that the child is maintaining his position in the group; an ascending or descending line indicates that he is growing faster or slower than the group average. The mental growth[1] of the individual represented in Figure 2 is marked by some irregularities during the first four years. At 4, however, he achieves a fairly even, stable position which is maintained with only very minor changes to 10

be expected to be fairly common even in a constant environment, or in a function insensitive to differential environmental factors. We should be cautious in attributing greater retest changes in early childhood to some inherent factor of modifiability if it is possible that they are chiefly due to a statistical factor, namely, to a relatively small proportion of similar elements in successive tests.

from 10 to 14 years. It is, of course, possible that this latter finding is associated with an earlier limit of growth in the feeble-minded.

[1] Sigma score curves indicate changes in status, relative to the group, from one measurement to another. They do not provide a direct measure of growth, and, since they are usually based on unanalyzed composite scores, they do not permit inferences as to the composition or dynamics of growth. From this point of view, it may be sounder to regard them as "status curves" than as growth curves.

A Classification of Factors Influencing Changes in Test Scores

In order to assess the importance of environmental influences on mental growth, we should attempt to gain some conception of the range and magnitude of other influences which affect test scores. These were briefly indicated on page 585 and are here discussed in greater detail.

Changes in Test Composition. Changes due to the measurement of different abilities cannot be attributed to "chance" factors and yet are not true variations in the growth rate of any one function. For example, consider two children, one possessing unusual motor aptitudes but poor at verbal tasks, the other showing an opposite pattern of abilities. Prior to two years of age, the first child is likely to stand relatively high, but these positions will be reversed at later ages when intelligence tests become more verbal in content. Marked shifts in status due to such factors are probably not very common, since, in general, mental test abilities are intercorrelated positively.

Administrative Factors. "Error" factors other than a shift in the ability stressed are of many sorts, including differences in the test situation, errors in administering or scoring tests, and differences in the "personal equation" of different examiners. This latter was apparently a negligible factor in studies by Goodenough (1928b) and Kawin (1934), but has been emphasized by P. Cattell (1937) in connection with the interpretation of mental test data from the Harvard Growth Study.

Negativism. An important aspect of the relation between subject and examiner, especially in preschool years, arises from the tendency of young children toward negativistic responses, which reduce test scores.[1] Of several studies on this subject, Mayer's (1935) report on negativism encountered in the normative group of the Revised

Stanford-Binet is probably most comparable with the ordinary test situation, since the effort was primarily toward getting the best possible response, with the study of negativistic responses only a secondary aim. Under good testing conditions and with highly trained examiners, the average number of negativistic responses per child ranged between 4 and 7, at ages 2½ to 4½ years. About 75 per cent of the cases in that age range gave at least one negativistic response in one of the two testing periods. At 2 years of age less than 25 per cent of the total negativism could be overcome by adroit management, but at 5½ years 90 per cent was overcome. This latter would be true, however, only with skilled examiners, and it is possible that at these ages slight differences in examining technique may be of critical importance to test scores.

Practice Effects. Practice and special training on the part of the subject may introduce spurious changes in mental test scores. According to Terman and Merrill (1937), the *average* gain from a first to a second test is, at different age levels, 2 to 4 IQ points. Successive additional tests may produce smaller gains, but in a longitudinal study the cumulative effect may be so great that results cannot be appropriately stated in terms of IQ, but must be transformed into percentile or scale scores based on cases receiving equivalent amounts of practice. Analyzing results from several group tests, Adkins (1937), following Thorndike, has suggested that the improvement of scores on retest with the same examination may be largely a matter of increased speed on tasks previously solved. The implication is that work-limit tests are of greater value than time-limit tests for longitudinal studies. The reader interested in recent work on practice effects and other conditions of testing will find a list of such

[1] Whereas error factors are frequently susceptible to environmental changes, and thus operate to reduce constancy coefficients, it may be noted that retest correlations may be spuriously raised if an error factor occurs systematically; for example, if children negativistic on one occasion tend also to be negativistic on succeeding tests, with similar effects upon scores.

studies in a review by R. L. Thorndike (1940).

Coaching. One special case of practice effect which deserves separate mention is the effect of coaching or specialized training.[1] Although our present studies in this field point to no very clear-cut conclusion, they suggest, as might be expected, that training is most effective when devoted to material similar to that in the test, and that the effects of training are, characteristically, to produce a temporary but not permanent rise in IQ. The application of these findings is greatest at the preschool level, since the test materials at those levels are more like everyday playthings than at later ages. Although it has not been demonstrated that children of preschool age are particularly susceptible to the effects of special coaching, it is highly probable that nursery schools differ more than grade schools with respect to the similarity of school "curricula" to the testing situation. Earlier reports on the effects of coaching have been reviewed by Burks (1928c).

Intrinsic and Extrinsic Factors. All the factors discussed above may be regarded as involving errors in measurement. In addition to these error factors, mental growth may be conceived as involving actual changes, which have an origin in either intrinsic or extrinsic factors. Intrinsic alterations may arise from specific or general changes in the rate of growth. Relevant factors are the form of the growth curve, with reference to possible cyclical changes, and the age of completion of growth; a neurophysiological basis is implied.

Extrinsic influences on mental growth are roughly of two sorts, social and personal. The social factors include general environ-

mental conditions, such as socioeconomic factors in the home and neighborhood and specific educational régimes. What are here called personal factors are those nonability aspects of a person's make-up which actually affect the course of growth in ability rather than merely modify the score at a particular test period. The personal factors, if traumatic, such as physical diseases or extreme emotional episodes, may affect mental growth fairly directly. The more permanent aspects of physical and mental constitution may influence mental development by virtue of the fact that they comprise part of the equipment through which the individual assimilates the environment.

The main problem of this chapter is the evaluation of the extent and nature of *extrinsic influences* on mental development. We are concerned with *error factors* mainly to discount them in considering irregularities in obtained growth curves. The maturational factor leading to intrinsic differences in growth rates can only be mentioned; as yet there is no evidence to separate its effects from those of other factors. Among the extrinsic influences, the reviewer's emphasis will reflect the status of the present literature and will not attempt a systematic evaluation of the relative importance of these factors.

One of the first facts with which we are confronted is that in the preschool period the prediction of later intelligence can be improved by taking into account a measure of the home environment. The varying interpretations of this finding will be discussed in the ensuing section.

Relationships to Cultural-Economic Factors

Education of the Parents. Figure 3, from Bayley's data, shows, at successive ages, the correlation between mental scores of children and the education of their par-

[1] The studies of Greene (1928) and Casey, Davidson, and Harter (1928), reported in the *Twenty-seventh Yearbook of the National Society for the Study of Education,* are particularly relevant to this problem.

nts (in terms of the average years of chooling of father and mother). This is n admittedly imperfect index of the cultural status of the parents and an even less perfect index of the extent to which cultural factors actually enter into the child's nvironment. Nevertheless, if we compare

For such findings the most obvious interpretation is that better-educated parents provide environments more stimulating to mental growth and that in general children tend to acquire the intellectual status characteristic of the environment to which they are exposed. Equally logical,

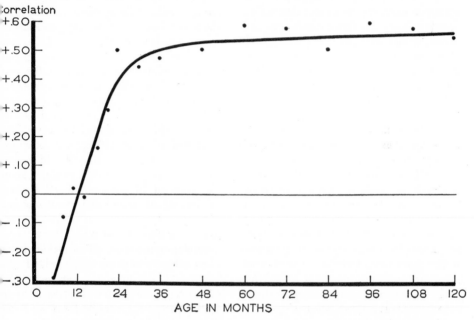

FIGURE 3. Children's mental scores at successive ages as related to parents' education.

Figures 3 and 1, we can see that the parents' education (obtained prior to the birth of the child) yields a better prediction of the child's intelligence at 10 years than does the child's own test score at ages prior to 2 years.

The relation of parents' education to the child's test score is negative in infancy (a fact consonant with the discussion on page 587). It increases sharply during the period of one to two years, and thereafter shows only minor changes. Somewhat similar correlation curves have been reported by Bayley and Jones (1937) for other measures of social and economic factors.[1]

however, is an interpretation based on the maturing of hereditary potentialities. As a corollary to the discussion of the Age Ratio, the argument has been advanced

[1] Correlations with social status are usually lower than with measures of parent education. Stroud (1928) reported an *r* of .25 between IQ and tax assessments; Chapman and Wiggins (1925), an *r* of .32 between IQ and the Chapman-Sims Scale of Socio-economic Status. These studies were based on large samples. When cultural items are included in a home rating or an environmental scale, Burks (1928b) found a correlation of .42 and Leahy (1935) one of .53 with intelligence measures. In interpreting correlational data in this field, attention must be given to the characteristics of the socio-economic measures, particularly with regard to skewness of the distributions.

that, as children approach their eventual intelligence level, they manifest the degree of relationship to parents' intelligence (or to other factors correlated with parents' intelligence) that would be expected on the basis of the inheritance of abilities. The correlation curve as given in Figure 3 presents us with hypotheses rather than with definitive evidence of causal relationship. Each of these hypotheses may serve as a partial explanation of the facts as obtained, but their relative cogency cannot be estimated unless we turn to evidence involving some form of experimental design. Such evidence will be presented in connection with a discussion of studies of foster children.

Perhaps the most elaborate study employing correlational methods is by Van Alstyne (1929), who examined the relationship between children's intelligence (Kuhlmann-Binet) and various factors in the home environment. The sample, consisting of seventy-five 3-year-old children, was drawn from very diverse environments in New York City, and the obtained correlations are probably somewhat higher than would be found in a more representative group. Table 2 presents illustrative results from this study. Van Alstyne pointed out

TABLE 2

The Mental Age of Children As Related to Environmental Factors

(From Van Alstyne [1929].)

Child's MA by:	r
Mother's education	.60 ± .05
Father's education	.51 ± .06
"Opportunity for use of constructive play materials"	.50 ± .06
"Number of hours adults spend daily with child"	.32 ± .07
"Number of playmates in home"	.16 ± .08
"Number of hours father reads to child"	.06 ± .08
Nutrition index	− .03 ± .08

that these correlations do not permit any conclusion as to causal factors. It is of interest that several positive correlation emerged in the case of variables which could have little conceivable direct effect upon intelligence: thus, a biserial r of .54 ± .08 was found between the child MA and whether or not he slept alone in his own bed. This is merely one aspect of the general relation between socioeconomic status and intelligence.

Occupation and "Social Class." The principal sources of material on the relationship of intelligence to socioeconomic factors include a volume by Schwesinger (1933) and one by Lorimer and Osborn (1934). Subsequent reviews have been published by Neff (1938) and Loevinger (1940). Neff pointed out that in various studies of school children a range of about 20 points in IQ has been found between children of the highest and lowest socioeconomic groups. This is also found for preschool children, as shown in Table 3.

Similar occupational differences are found when other criteria are employed. If, for example, we examine the percentage distribution of the parents of gifted children or the parents of persons listed in *Who's Who in America*, we find a very disproportionate number in the higher occupational brackets. On the other hand, parents of children admitted to feeble-minded institutions tend to cluster in the lower brackets. The assertion has been made by Neff that the occupational hierarchy in IQ can be accounted for entirely in environmental terms. This would also seem to be implied in Pieter's (1939) suggestion of a "coefficient of innate intelligence," to be obtained through dividing the IQ by an environmental index. Conceding that a difference in IQ may have a somewhat different significance when children are compared within the same occupational class and in sharply separated classes, it still appears

TABLE 3

Mean IQ's of Preschool Children, Classified by Father's Occupation *

Father's Occupation	Goodenough (1928b)	Terman and Merrill (1937)
I. Professional	116	116
II. Semiprofessional and managerial	112	112
III. Clerical and skilled trades	108	108
IV. Semiskilled and minor clerical	105	104
V. Slightly skilled	104	95
VI. Unskilled	96	94

* Goodenough's sample consisted of 380 Minneapolis children between the ages of 18 and 54 months the Kuhlmann-Binet was given twice to each child, the means reported in Table 3 being based on the initial test only. The Terman and Merrill sample consisted of 831 children, ages 2 and 5½ years, in the standardization groups for Forms L and M of the revised Stanford-Binet. In this latter sample, an additional classification of "rural owner' was included, with a mean IQ of 99.

unwarranted to explain group differences wholly in terms of extrinsic factors.

The hypothesis that the intelligence differential between the social classes is to some extent an hereditary sampling difference follows from two assumptions: (1) individual variations in intelligence are, in part, genetic in origin; and (2) differences in the selection of occupations and in occupational success are, in part, determined by intelligence. At the present time probably the majority of psychologists regard these assumptions as plausible. Current efforts are directed not toward proof or disproof, but rather toward assessing the approximate importance of different factors under specified conditions.

Special interest attaches to the fact that the social differential in intelligence is well established as early as 2 or 3 years of age, and relatively constant in later childhood. If due chiefly to environmental effects acting directly, one would expect it to be small at 2 years but to increase gradually with age. Another line of evidence, contrary to the environmental hypothesis, has been supplied by Lawrence (1931), who showed a relationship between children's IQ and the occupational status of their parents, even where environmental differentials were ruled out (in the case of children removed from their homes in infancy and brought up in an institution). D. C. Jones and Carr-Saunders (1927) have added a further relevant finding in comparing the intelligence of children of different social origins who have lived in an orphanage for varying lengths of time. Continued residence in this less differential environment apparently had little or no effect in reducing or "leveling" the original social differential in intelligence.

A study by Outhit (1933) provides an interesting comparison between the intelligence of children and their parents. Fifty-one families were represented, with four or more children in each family. The Army Alpha was used with adults and with children above 12, scores being transformed into IQ's for comparison with the Stanford-Binet IQ's of the younger children. Figure 4 indicates a tendency toward greater occupational differences among parents than among children or, in other words, a tendency for children of either superior or inferior parents to regress toward the mean of the total group. This result would be predicted on the basis of genetic factors, but, so far as home environments are concerned, it is not entirely clear that environmental theory would lead to the same expectation.

Asher (1935) and others have with some justice argued that tests standardized on one social group may give misleading re-

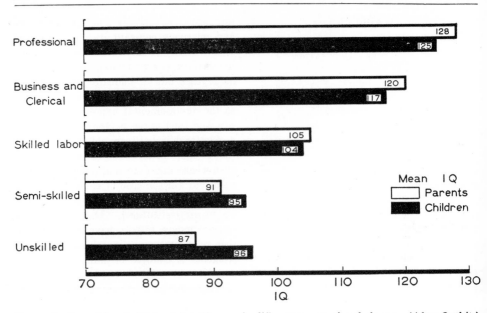

Figure 4. Parents' and children's intelligence, in different occupational classes. (After Outhit.)

sults when applied to other groups. This is a special case of the general principle that the validity of items varies according to the experience or cultural background of subjects taking the tests. Another example can be found in the case of experience dependent upon age, as in the study by Jones (1931) of juveniles and adults who had the same mental ages but who performed very differently on different types of test items. Although such studies are illuminating with regard to the specific composition of group differences, little attention has been given to comparative item analyses in connection with occupational groups. The technique has, however, been employed in several studies of rural and urban children.

Rural-Urban Studies. That rural children in the United States attain lower average IQ's than urban children has been confirmed in a number of investigations summarized by Shimberg (1929) and Pintner (1931). It has sometimes been suggested that this is an artifact of the tests used. Tests are usually devised by city dwellers and validated on city children; it is reasonable to expect that their content and perhaps also their time limitations will tend to handicap rural children. Peterson (1928) has emphasized the rôle of test experience and of competitive exercises in school in producing a "set" for efficient performance. Relevant attitudes and incentives may be stimulated in varying degrees by different school systems, and rural children in general probably receive less practice than urban children in working at high pressure under speed and accuracy requirements.

The ever-present problem of test content has been considered by Shimberg (1929), who demonstrated that the urban superiority on an information test could be reversed if the test were originally scaled from items supplied by rural teachers and standardized on a rural group. A similar experiment has not been attempted with ther types of material; it is probable that distinctive "urban" and "rural" content is more apparent in an information test than in other tests. Several investigations have reported not merely a low IQ for rural children, but also an IQ diminishing with age: (1) the well-known study by Gordon (1923) of English gypsies and canal boat children, showing marked negative correlations between age and IQ; (2) Asher's (1935) study of children in the east Kentucky mountains (in this group the median IQ dropped steadily from 84 at 7 years to 60 at 15 years); (3) a report by Edwards and Jones (1938) on school children in the mountains of north Georgia (IQ's dropped from around 100 at ages 7 to 9 years to 76 at age 14, and 70 for those older); (4) Jordan's (1933) study of the children of mill workers in a North Carolina town (IQ's decreased from 100 at the age of 6 to 85 at 13 years); (5) studies of Iowa children by Baldwin, Fillmore, and Hadley (1930) and by Skeels and Fillmore (1937). In the last report, children from underprivileged homes (either rural or urban) were examined at the time of entrance to an orphanage; the mean IQ diminished from 93 at age 4 to 80 at age 14.[1]

These findings have been variously interpreted as due to (1) "the retarding effect of poor homes on mental development" (Skeels and Fillmore, p. 438); (2) the ef-

[1] Speer (1940a, 1940b) and a number of other investigators have utilized similar material from children referred to institutions because of conditions in their own homes. Older children, who have lived longer in homes characterized by poverty and frequently by other undesirable factors, have lower average IQ's than younger children from similar environments. It must be noted, however, that these test scores are not based on cumulative records or on sibling comparisons, but on different samples which may have been subjected to different selective factors. Thus it seems likely that among the older children in very inferior environments some of the brighter ones have already been removed by relatives or other agencies.

fect on the Stanford-Binet of "continued existence at a critically low level of social and cultural status" (Neff, 1938, p. 739); or (3) the effect of using tests which at higher age levels become increasingly inappropriate for the groups to which they are applied (Asher).

The first of these interpretations, in line with other Iowa studies, proposes an actual psychological handicap resulting from a poor environment. The second and third interpretations are more purely psychometric, although the second seems to imply some actual cumulative handicap in mental test abilities, whereas the third is concerned primarily with an age differential in the tests which lowers their validity.

It would be permissible to hold all these interpretations simultaneously, but they would still fail to give an adequate picture of the complex situation involved in the comparison of different cultural groups. Terman and Merrill (1937) have called attention to the fact that in their standardization sample the mean IQ for rural children was 99.2, for urban children 105.7. The urban group was defined as including all subjects from areas having a population density of 1000 or more per square mile, and the rural group as all others. A slight tendency was noted for the rural group to show a decreasing IQ at the beginning of the school period, whereas children of slightly skilled and unskilled laborers show an increase at this period. The authors comment:

These trends are too small to be very reliable and should be regarded merely as suggestive. Even if the trend were reliable it would require an extensive research, carefully planned for that purpose, to determine whether the lowered IQ of rural children can be ascribed to the relatively poorer educational facilities in rural communities, and whether the gain for children from the lower economic strata can be attributed to an assumed enrichment of intellectual environment that school attendance bestows (p. 49).

In the attempt to study the possibility of differential environmental handicap on different test items, Jones, Conrad, and Blanchard (1932) made an item analysis of test results for 351 New England rural children, aged 4 to 14, as compared with 905 cases in the 1916 Stanford-Binet standardization, and also with 212 cases from a relatively homogeneous urban sampling, highly superior in socioeconomic status. The three groups had mean IQ's of 92, 101, and 117, respectively. When the individual items were scaled, marked differences were found in the relative difficulty of the items in the three samples, leading to the conclusion that even when an attempt is made to attain "equal units" on a psychological scale these are strictly relative to the sample. A test scaled on one group may show marked inequalities when applied to other groups. Several tests were identified as showing a sharp differentiation between the three groups, with a tendency for the differences to increase with age. These were all verbal items. In a common environment, the acquisition of verbal skill may, by and large, be regarded as a good index of intelligence; but in widely differing environments it may become predominantly a good index of the environment, and the resulting intelligence quotients will then require reinterpretation.

In this particular study, the authors estimated that social and educational factors could on the average account for about half the mean difference of 10 points in IQ between the rural and the normal urban group. These environmental handicaps, however, appeared to be specific to certain test items, rather than general. As would be expected if the rural-urban difference is in part due to a difference in

hereditary capacities, certain types of test were found with a marked difference which could not readily be explained in terms of differential opportunities for special training, or differential interest or motivation. On the basis of this item-and-age analysis the conclusion was offered that the rural group (although representative for the communities studied) presented an inherently poorer selection than the urban comparison groups.

The study of selective rural migration (selective drainage into urban centers and urban occupations) may in the future result in a fuller understanding of rural-urban differences. It is interesting that both in the study discussed above and in an English study by Thomson (1921) fewer high IQ's were found in rural communities accessible to city districts than in comparable communities more remotely located. Areas supplied by good transportation and near a growing urban center are probably in some regions more subject to selective drainage. Similar interpretations may apply to results obtained by Bickersteth (1919) in the Yorkshire dales and by Macmeeken (1939) in isolated rural and coastal sections of northern and western Scotland. It is hard to see how the children in these remote localities could have acquired relatively high average IQ's on the basis of superior cultural opportunities. Economic factors are important in determining the nature of selective migration. Lorimer and Osborn (1934) have cited a number of surveys indicating that in relatively prosperous rural areas the cities attract from both the upper and lower extremes of social status. In depressed rural areas, on the

[1] These included the ball-and-field test, memory for designs, digit memory, picture description, and comprehension.

Results which are in general similar to those of this study have been obtained by Bruce (1940) in a Virginia survey of rural white and Negro children.

her hand, a survey by Gee and Corson
(1929) indicated that the less intelligent
are more frequently "bound to the land,"
whereas those of higher social, educational,
and intellectual status tend, in greater proportions, to migrate to urban centers. This
is supported by Mauldin (1940) and Sanford (1940), on the basis of data from
small southern communities.[1]

In concluding this section, the interpretation of rural handicap as due to lack of
cultural privilege is seen to provide only a
partial explanation. Commenting on the
lack of schooling of southern mountain
children,[2] Goodenough (1940a) points out
that our pioneering New England ancestors
did not find schools ready made in the
wilderness.

They made schools, and it did not require two centuries of residence for them
to do so. Accordingly, I find it hard to
accept the idea that the low IQ's of the
mountain children are to be explained
solely on the basis of educational deprivation. One is forced to ask: Why were they
so deprived? (p. 329).

The principal outcome of the socioeconomic and rural-urban studies is to emphasize the fact that, among groups as
among individuals, differences cannot be
explained in terms of a fixed structure of
relationship. With changes in any of the
related factors (test composition, hereditary selection, or environment) group or
individual differences will represent chang-

ing degrees of hereditary or environmental
influence.

Racio-Cultural Comparisons. According
to the bias or special interest of different
investigators, comparative studies of Negroes and whites have been quoted as providing evidence of (1) hereditary racial
differences or (2) environmental effects.[3]
It is well established that in the same communities white children tend to show higher
average IQ's than Negro children, with an
increasing difference manifested during the
school period. Several studies have also
indicated, among mixed bloods, a relationship between intelligence and the degree of
white admixture; this has not always been
confirmed in studies controlling the factor
of social status. Until further more crucial evidence is supplied, we must remain
in some doubt as to the bearing of Negro-
white investigations upon the nature-nurture problem.

In the case of other natio-racial differences, such as have been reported in
studies of migrant groups in the United
States, the problem is even more complicated by questions of intragroup selection
(selective migration) as well as questions
bearing on environmental handicaps and
the appropriateness of tests. On the basis
of tests ordinarily accepted for measuring
intelligence, the weight of evidence points
to the probability of a difference, in terms
of averages, between United States native
whites and Negroes, and between American
citizens of North European and South European descent. It is possible, but not certain, that this difference would wholly disappear if a correction were made for social
status and educational differences. The effect of such a correction can hardly be predicted at the present time, for no one as
yet has conducted an experiment in which

[1] For other studies of rural groups, see Clark
and Gist (1938), who reported the occurrence of
selective migration in Kansas, and Klineberg
(1938), who reported its occurrence in a study
of southern Germany, but found no evidence for
it in a parallel investigation in New Jersey.
Conflicting evidence in this field is not an indication of inadequacy in the studies involved, but
rather of the varying balance of the complex
factors influencing selection.
[2] See Sherman and Key (1932) and Sherman
and Henry (1933).

[3] For research summaries with contrasting interpretations, see Pintner (1931) and Anastasi
(1937).

controlled selections of children varying as to racial background have been reared under similar environmental conditions. This would be entirely feasible either in an appropriately planned institution or in foster homes where precautions are taken to insure comparable physical and social environments.

Another approach which has given suggestive results is represented in the work of Klineberg (1935), who studied the intelligence of Negro migrants from the South in relation to their length of residence in New York City. Children newly arrived had an average IQ of 81.4 (Stanford-Binet), as compared with 84.5 for those who had been in New York two to three years, and 87.4 for those in residence longer than four years. It is reasonable to interpret this as an environmental effect, provided that similar selections of migrants arrived in successive years, and provided also that no selective factors have operated with regard to continued residence in New York. Could an educationally improved environment, exerting its effects early enough and long enough, bring the average IQ of these children not merely to 87 but to the norm of 100 or even higher? Such a conclusion has sometimes been offered, but would seem to involve a premature "extrapolation" from the facts now available.

Mental and Physical Relationships

A slight positive relation has frequently been reported between intelligence and various measures of physique and physical condition. The best-known treatise in the field is Paterson's *Physique and Intellect* (1930). Jones (1933b, 1936, 1939), in a series of reviews, has summarized approximately three hundred studies, and reviews by Shock (1939a, 1939b), Carmichael (1940), and Shock and Jones (1941) cover recent research on physiological relationships.

Physical Measures. It is well known that in certain types of dwarfism (cretins the arrest of physical growth is accompanied by mental retardation. A similar relationship also holds, in some degree within normal samples. One of the most competent studies in this field is by Abernethy (1936), who found positive correlations between intelligence and various physical measures at all ages from 8 to 1 years; in the case of height the average was .26 for boys and .16 for girls. These results are supplemented at the lower ages by Bayley (1940b), who reported an average age correlation (between intelligence an height) of .20 for boys and .22 for girls in the age range of 2 to 8 years.[1]

The relevance of this topic to the present problem is in part indicated by B. S Sanders' (1934) discussion of differential physical growth:

Evidence of differential growth, or i end result—differential size—shows tha everywhere children with a superior socio economic environment are on the averag heavier and taller than their age-mates ex posed to a less favorable environment. . . The study does not dispute the fact tha in all probability there are inherent di ferences between the various socio-economi classes. Its one and only contention that the role of environment cannot b overlooked. . . . And, if environmental di ferences are important enough to affec physical growth, it is most probable tha they affect psycho-social adaptations an behavior as well (p. 299).

[1] More recently, Katz (1940) has reported co relations approaching .40 between median IQ five tests and height at successive ages from to 5 years. Such atypically high coefficients ar less surprising than the fact that for boys th corresponding r's are close to zero. Over on hundred cases are included for each sex. Thes results have not been confirmed by other inve tigators.

The hypothesis implied in the foregoing was subjected to a test by Honzik and Jones (1937), who examined the relationship of height to intelligence in a group of approximately 200 children representative of Berkeley, California. Correlations close to zero were found at each age from 21 months to 7 years, but the uniformly positive coefficients for both boys and girls suggested the presence of a genuine, even if meager, relationship; there was, moreover, a slight tendency for growth rates in height or weight to be correlated with increments in mental scores. As in other samples, mental test scores showed an increasing relation to social status [1] (.04 at 21 months, rising to .42 at 7 years). Height also showed a positive but not an increasing relation to social status (.20 at 21 months, and also at 7 years).

In the study of this problem, correlational procedures, dealing with average relationships in a total group, may be less effective than the comparative study of individual growth curves. Honzik and Jones have presented such curves for height, weight, and intelligence, with raw measurements transformed into sigma scores to permit direct comparison as to changes in status in the group. Although some cases showed independent or even diverging curves, a number exhibited a striking concomitance in trend. The suggestion has been made that mental-physical relationships are due to a common influence of the social environment, acting upon intelligence through social example and education, and upon physical factors through nutrition and hygiene. In this study, however, the relationship between height and intelligence was found to be independent, or nearly so, of the measured factors in the environment, since the partialing out of social status (as measured) had little ap-

1 A socioeconomic index based on parent education, occupation, income, and social ratings.

preciable effect upon the correlations. For the sample in question it seems probable that genetic factors, and the association of traits in assortative mating, are more important than cultural-economic factors in determining the fact that brighter children tend to be taller and heavier than children of below-average intelligence.

Health and Physical Defects. If physical condition exerts a direct effect upon mental functioning, it may perhaps be expected that intelligence will show a closer relation to measures of health than to measures of physical growth. Our concern here is with studies of general health, nutritional status, or minor physical defects, and not with neurological or endocrine disorders, or psychopathologies. In one of the earliest studies in this field, Ayres (1909) computed the incidence of physical defects in three groups of children classified as dull, normal, and bright on the basis of progress in school. Three thousand three hundred and four cases were included. The percentage of each type of defect is given in Table 4.

TABLE 4

PERCENTAGE INCIDENCE OF PHYSICAL DEFECTS IN THREE GROUPS

	Bright	Normal	Dull
Defective teeth	34	40	42
Adenoids	6	10	15
Enlarged tonsils	12	19	26
Enlarged glands	6	13	20
Defective breathing	9	11	15
Defective vision	29	25	24
Other defects	11	11	21
Average number of defects per child	1.07	1.30	1.65

Similar findings have been reported by Sandwick (1920) and Kempf and Collins (1929). Where correlations have been computed, these are approximately of the same order as for other physical traits such as height or weight. Among the highest *r*'s reported are those found by Dayton (1928–1929) for approximately 14,000 retarded school children in Massachusetts (−.29 ± .01 for boys, −.25 ± .01 for girls, IQ by physical defects). These correlations, similar to those found for other physical-mental relationships, serve merely to describe the fact that physical and mental handicaps are associated in the same samples. We cannot conclude that one type of handicap has caused the other, although to a very small degree such causal relationships may be present.[1]

In such defects as infected tonsils, a quasi-experimental approach is possible through studying the mental test performance of children before and after surgical removal of the infection. It has not been possible to show that such focal infections progressively impair mental ability, or that their removal has a beneficial effect upon intelligence (see reports by Rogers, 1922; Lowe, 1923; and Richey, 1934). In a few studies, evidence is available concerning the effect of an improved physical régime upon mental functions. Westenberger (1927) selected the poorest 10 per cent, with regard to physical defects, from a sample of approximately four hundred school children in Wisconsin. Medical and surgical treatment was provided over a nine-month pe-riod, but without observable effects upon mental development. The investigator concluded: "The influence of defects upon academic performance and intelligence has been somewhat exaggerated in the past." Similar negative results were obtained by Kohnky (1913) in connection with a program of dental treatment and instruction in dental hygiene, and by Hoefer and Hardy (1928) in a carefully planned three-year study of the effect of health education.

Effects of changes in physical condition are more likely to be noted in school achievement than in measures of intelligence. Thus, in later reports Hardy (1936) and Hardy and Hoefer (1936) have shown that children participating in a health instruction program improved in their school work to a greater degree than members of a control group. Even these gains, however, are not entirely attributable to changes in health régime, since the special attention given to the experimental cases may have had not merely indirect psychological effects, but also more direct effects, through changes in motivation.

Nutrition. Fritz (1935) and Jones (1939) have summarized a number of studies dealing with the effects of nutritional factors upon mental abilities. It is of course to be expected that small positive coefficients will be obtained when measures of nutritional status are correlated with IQ. These correlations arise from the same causes that determine a positive relationship between socioeconomic status and IQ (see pp. 592 ff.) and tend to disappear if nutritional variations are examined within a single social group. An exception to the latter statement may be found in cases close to a subsistence margin. Thus, among 293 children from slum areas, O'Hanlon (1940) found a significant correlation (.18 ± .04) between nutritional condition and IQ.

A more satisfactory approach to this

[1] In a study of fifth-grade children in New York City schools, Maller (1933) determined the correlation between the average IQ for each school and the percentage in each school having a given defect. The coefficients were −.50 for defective teeth, −.40 for visual defect, −.28 for malnutrition. These relatively high correlations are due to the use of averages, and can be used for predictions about neighborhoods rather than about individuals. It is clear that districts with better health records tend to have higher average IQ's; these districts also have superior socioeconomic status, as shown by a correlation of .50 between average IQ and average rentals. Although Maller's results are of unusual interest in describing important aspects of urban social structure, they of course give no indication as to the source of the relationships.

problem is through an experimental procedure, as illustrated in the following two examples. Twenty-five children selected by Smith and Field (1926) as markedly underweight were given school lunches over a 6-month period, together with health lessons and various motivational devices designed to bring about physical improvement. As compared with normal controls, striking gains were shown in weight, but mental development appeared to be unaffected. A similar experiment was conducted by Seymour and Whitaker (1938) in a group of 25 underprivileged children (6½ years old) matched with a control from a similar social selection. The experimental group was given daily breakfasts in school, adequate as to variety and amount, whereas the control group received their usual inadequate breakfast of bread and tea at home. Differences between the two groups began to appear on standardized tests (such as cancellation) by the tenth day, but the superiority of the experimental group diminished after the breakfasts were discontinued. Neither of these two experiments points to any actual change in mental growth as a result of nutritional gains.

Among mental defectives Poull (1938) has reported that when malnourished children receive an improved régime IQ gains are greater than in a control group. This was particularly true of children below 5 years of age, leading to the question as to whether persistent malnutrition, beyond 5 years, might do "irreparable" harm in mental development. The cases, however, are too few for definite conclusions. It has frequently been noted that the relationship of mental and physical traits is more readily demonstrated among the feeble-minded than among normals. This may be due in part at least to a larger proportion of the feeble-minded who suffer, in various degrees, from the effects of organic handicaps

expressed both in physical structures and in mental function. Stout (1937) has summarized a study of 10-year-old children by the statement: "The fact that a child is normal in intelligence gives little or no clue as to what his health or physical condition may be." On the other hand, among the 2 per cent at the lowest extreme in intelligence it is clear that we have a disproportionate incidence of many different types of physical defects.

More specific aspects of nutrition (such as the effects of vitamin B_1 or vitamin C administration) have been considered in a number of studies of young children, but in regard to psychological relationships the work in this field is still very preliminary.

Seasonal Factors. An interesting subsidiary problem has been raised by a number of investigations showing a relationship between IQ and month of birth. These studies, principally by Pintner and his associates (Pintner and Forlano, 1934, 1939; Pintner and Maller, 1937; Mills, 1941), but supported by other investigators, purport to show that both in the northern and southern hemispheres children born in the late spring, summer, or fall have slightly higher average IQ's than children born in the winter months. These differences are related to health statistics for the warmer as compared with the colder months. In the case of children of exceptionally high intelligence the most favorable month of birth appears to be slightly different than for the total population. For children with IQ's above 130, and also for individuals of distinction listed in the *Dictionary of American Biography,* Huntington (1938) has reported a high rate of births in the late winter or early spring months. In conformity with his theories of climatic influence, he has argued that children born from February to April have a maximum developmental advantage due to the fact that the early months of the pregnancy fall in the preceding late spring and summer. It is these months, he believes, that provide the most favorable extrinsic conditions for promoting physical vigor and general development. Huntington has been criticized to the effect that he has failed to account for the complex operation of cultural factors influencing conceptions and abortions. "The various seasonal trends in births cannot be denied, but their explanation in terms of meteorological and resulting physical factors must be subject to doubt until more direct evidence is obtainable" (Jones, 1939, p. 99).

More recently, Goodenough (1940c) has shown for a sample of over three thousand cases that seasonal differences in the *frequency* of births occur in the higher but not in the lower occupational groups. Since children at the higher socioeconomic levels also average higher in IQ (see p. 595), the birth month factor in intelligence can apparently be fully accounted for on the basis of selective planning or other conditions related to cultural status. This argument is supported by the fact that in samples presenting a restricted socioeconomic range, as in studies of college students (E. L. Clark, 1939; Held, 1940; Forlano and Ehrlich, 1941), intelligence differences related to birth month are either reduced or eliminated.

A different aspect of seasonal variation is considered in studies which have dealt with IQ changes in young children in relation to the month of testing. Wellman (1934) has reported that children in the University of Iowa Nursery School tend to show higher IQ's in the spring than in the fall. She attributed this to the effect of nursery school attendance. Lodge (1938), however, and Jones (1941) obtained similar results among children not in nursery school. In the latter study, data for 1798 tests, given to children between the ages of 2 and 5 years, were examined with reference to the month of testing. The cases were balanced in such a way as to eliminate the influence of age and of test practice. The highest average IQ's were found in November, December, and January; the lowest in May, June, and July. Several alternative interpretations were offered for these results, in terms of (1) the influence of climatic factors (such as periodic storms) upon mental performance, (2) the influence of climatic factors upon basic rates of mental growth, and (3) seasonal variations in play activities which have a positive transfer in mental test performance. Further studies are needed in different geographic areas in order to confirm these findings and, if they are confirmed, to provide an adequate explanation of the results.

Physiological Maturing. Chronological age is not always a good index of the *physiological time* through which a child has lived. In a group of the same age, wide individual differences will occur in the level of maturity assessed by physiological methods. These developmental indications include dentition, pubescence, the age of menarche, skeletal age assessed from X-rays, and anatomical age assessed from physical growth patterns. It has been suggested that a child's IQ at any given time should be computed by referring mental age to physiological rather than chrono-

logical age $\left(IQ = \dfrac{MA}{PA} \text{ rather than } \dfrac{MA}{CA} \right)$.

This is illustrated in Figure 5. Case 9M presents a mental growth curve, in terms of raw scores, consistently superior to the average of the total group. He is, however, somewhat retarded in physiological maturing, and if allowance is made for this we find that his growth curve (plotted against skeletal age) is even further above the group average. Case 25M has a men-al growth curve which agrees very closely with the average, but in skeletal development he is markedly accelerated. In terms of the number of *physiological years* he has lived, we note that his mental development lags considerably behind expectation. When data are treated in this way, (at a given level of chronological age) are usually too low to command special interest.[1] In one of the most comprehensive studies yet reported, Gates (1924) obtained a measure of skeletal age as well as height and some other physical measurements; the multiple r of these with men-

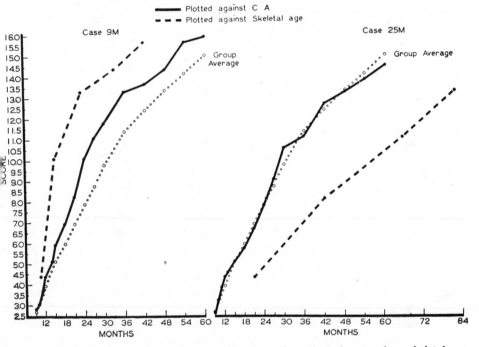

FIGURE 5.   Individual mental growth curves, based on chronological age and on skeletal age. (After Bayley.)

it is possible that clues will sometimes be uncovered which will be useful in interpreting deviate mental growth curves or even in improving the prediction as to subsequent growth.

Unfortunately, however, the concept of physiological age is still somewhat vague. The various measures of physiological maturity agree with each other very imperfectly, and a satisfactory composite measure has not yet been achieved. When we correlate a single index, such as skeletal maturity, with mental age, the coefficients tal age was only .21.   In the same sample, mental age predicted educational achievement to the extent of a correlation of .60; when the physical measures were added, this correlation was increased only to .63.

Zuck (1936) and Todd (1938) have sponsored the belief that environmental influences acting through illness or nutri-

1 Abernethy (1936) and Bayley (1940b) have reported correlations which at most ages are positive but close to zero.   Higher correlations were obtained by Severson (1920–1921) and by West (1936), although in the latter case the coefficients dropped with increasing age.

tional disturbance have a direct effect upon mental development, and also that a prior effect is frequently manifested in the X-rays of the skeleton. Individual cases can no doubt be found to support this view, but the general importance of such relationships remains to be demonstrated.

Several studies have investigated mental test performance in relation to the age at puberty. In general, these have led to the tentative finding that IQ's are on the average lower in late-maturing individuals and higher in the early-maturing.[1] If these indications are confirmed, they can be interpreted as due either to a stimulating effect of sexual maturing upon mental growth or to a tendency of early-maturing individuals to represent a superior selection. The first interpretation would lead us to look for a spurt in the rate of mental growth accompanying the increased physical growth in adolescence; this has never been clearly demonstrated.[2] The second and more probable interpretation might rest upon one or several selective factors. It is possible, for example, that (for quite different reasons) the lower socioeconomic groups are more heavily weighted with late-maturing individuals as well as with those of lower intelligence (see p. 595).

A readily measured aspect of physical condition is basal metabolism. At the pathological extremes, with which we are not here directly concerned, striking evidence of correlated physical and mental effects can be found in such conditions as cretinism and myxedema, with equally striking evidence as to the mental improvement following thyroid treatment in certain cases. It is reasonable to inquire as to whether thyroid function, measured through basal metabolic rate, is related to intelligence in a normal range of cases. This is important for our present topic, since within this normal range thyroid functioning may be disturbed by illness and other extrinsic factors and may also be controlled to some extent by appropriate régime and treatment. Shock and Jones (1940), however, for a school sample of approximately 90 children at an average age of 12 and 14 years, have at each of these ages and for each sex found no demonstrable relationship between highly reliable measures of intelligence and of basal metabolism.[3] This is another instance in which correlations which are quite clear in pathological cases vanish or become obscured when sought in a normal representative group. The authors suggest that "slight variations in functional activity of the thyroid gland are not reflected in changes in mental capacity because in most individuals other adaptive mechanisms are present which may compensate for this thyroid deficiency" (p. 374). To carry over this conception to the general problem of environmental influence, it is a reasonable hypothesis that intelligence itself involves an adaptive mechanism which can to some degree compensate for variations in the environment, at least within an ordinary range of social and physical conditions.

[1] A review by Shock (1939a) has summarized a number of investigations (Baldwin, Terman, Lutz, Stone and Barker, Freeman and Flory, Abernethy) in which positive results were obtained. Negative results (as by Reymert, 1940) have occasionally been reported. It is of course well known that at the pathological extreme exceptionally early maturity (pubertas praecox) occurs without corresponding precocity in mental functions (Keene and Stone, 1937).

[2] The Harvard Growth Study, summarized by Dearborn and Rothney (1941), contains a large body of material pertinent to this hypothesis. No relation was found between the physical growth cycle and performance on intelligence or achievement tests.

[3] Similar results have been obtained in other investigations reviewed by these writers, with the exception of two reports by Hinton (1936, 1939), asserting correlations ranging from .80 at age 6 to .53 at age 15 between IQ and basal metabolic rate. The study is difficult to evaluate because complete data are not furnished.

Environmental Factors in the Family Constellation

Birth Order. The hypothesis has been advanced that children who are the first-born in their families suffer, on the average, a handicap in mental development due to both physical and social disadvantages. The fact of physical disadvantage is well established. Many studies have shown that the first-born are on the average smaller and lighter at birth than later-born in the same families. They include more prematures, and more cases of abnormal confinement. Jones and Hsiao (1933), in a study of 310 pairs of pregnancies, found among the first-born a greater proportion of instrumental delivery and of cases marked by poor physical condition after birth. A smaller proportion of the first-born receive normal breast-feeding (Schlesinger, 1923). Studies of later health and physical development [1] have not yielded consistent results; there is, however, a tendency to report a higher incidence of tuberculosis among the first-born.

The educational and social handicaps of the first-born are a matter of speculation rather than of direct proof. It is argued that first-born have the disadvantage of less experienced nurture by the parents, of less social stimulation (from older sibs), and frequently also of a less well-established economic security. However great or little these environmental differences may be, it is apparent that even in combination with a certain degree of physical handicap the average effects upon mental development are negligible.

It is unfortunate that investigators of this problem have been deceived by a number of errors of interpretation, the most important of which arises from the relation between birth rate and social status. Since families of higher social status

[1] Summarized by Hsiao (1931).

tend to have fewer but, on the average, more intelligent children, in a mixed population the first- or second-born, for example, will have higher average IQ's than third or fourth children. This, of course, is not actually a consequence of order of birth but is due merely to the fact that the earlier birth orders are weighted with children from small families, who constitute a superior selection. If we attempt to remedy this difficulty by limiting our comparisons to children of the same family, a new difficulty arises from the fact that many intelligence tests are so standardized that the IQ tends to drop slightly with age. This artifact produces a lower average IQ among children of the earlier birth orders (since they are, on the average, older when tested). Another factor to be considered is the unfavorable weighting of late birth orders due to maternal age. It has been clearly shown that the offspring of mothers near the end of the childbearing period are marked by a slightly greater incidence of certain types of mental defect, including mongolism.

In an earlier critique (Jones, 1933a) of research in this field evidence has been given that when these and other methodological difficulties are properly controlled no birth order differences in intelligence occur in normal samples. So far as this problem is concerned, we must then dismiss the environmental arguments as having little net weight. Atypical results, however, have been encountered in certain highly selected samples. Studies of gifted children by Terman (1925) and of eminent men by Ellis (1926), Cattell (1927), and Huntington (1938) have shown a distribution of birth orders differing from chance expectation, and strongly favoring the first-born (see Figure 6). No satisfactory explanation of this finding has been given. It is possible that the first-born more often become eminent because of greater incentive, but one would hesitate to apply this interpretation to the Terman material. An explanation in terms of differential educational opportunity would have even greater difficulty in including Terman's results with children. At least for this latter study, which is the only one dealing directly with intelligence test data, it is

sampling or of tests deficient in reliability or validity.[1]

In one of the earliest studies in this field Pearson (1903) found that family resemblances in mental traits were of the same degree as those in physical traits such as height, eye color, span, and head measurements. From this he concluded,

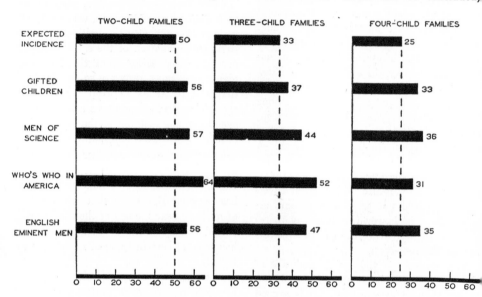

FIGURE 6. Percentage incidence of first-born, according to size of family.

likely (as suggested by Terman) that the true explanation will involve some selective factor, such as the greater tendency to locate older than younger members of incomplete families in a restricted age range.

Sibling Resemblance. The significance of a correlation of .50 is sometimes described as "that degree of resemblance which is ordinarily found among brothers and sisters living in the same family." This order of relationship is now so well established that a study reporting a markedly lower sibling correlation in intelligence would be immediately suspected of an inadequate

"We are forced . . . to the conclusion that the physical and psychical characters in man are inherited within broad lines in the same manner and with the same intensity" (p. 204). Two considerations, however, must lead us to a more cautious interpretation of the evidence. First, our present knowledge of genetic mechanisms suggests that if intelligence has an hereditary basis it is genetically more complex than a trait such as eye color; differences in genetic composition might well be expected to produce differences in family resemblance coefficients. Second, a given degree of re-

1 See Schwesinger (1933) for a summary of earlier investigations.

semblance may (theoretically) be attained not only through the influence of a common heredity but also through the effects of living in a common environment.

Still another consideration involves the degree of selective mating in the population. Pearson, in his theoretical calculations, assumed that the correlation between husband and wife in intelligence was close to zero, but more recent studies show that the husband-wife coefficient tends to be as high as, if not higher than, the sibling coefficient.[1] Differences in selective mating with respect to different traits would be expected to have important effects upon family resemblances in these traits. We must conclude, then, that from a given degree of sibling resemblance no *immediate* inferences can be drawn as to causal factors. The pattern of sibling correlations, however, may prove significant when considered in relation to certain hypotheses of environmental influence. These hypotheses are:

I. Siblings of the same sex share, on the average, a more common social environment than siblings of opposite sex. Hence on an environmental basis higher correlations could be predicted for brothers or for sisters than for brothers-and-sisters.

II. Siblings close together in chronological age share a more similar environment than children widely separated as to age. Changes in social and economic status of the family, in home and neighborhood, and in the age and personal characteristics of the parents, as well as differences in schools and teachers, might be expected to have some average effect in lowering correlations for siblings with a wide natal interval, that is, separated by several years in age.

III. Older siblings have lived together longer than younger siblings, and hence share a greater accumulation of environmental influences. It may also be assumed that as

children grow older they become responsive to a wider range of environmental factors; in these factors families are more diverse than in factors to which younger children are sensitive. The effect of a greater variability in family environments should (on an environmental hypothesis) be to increase sibling correlations.

Each of these hypotheses may, at certain points, be questioned on theoretical grounds, but they have a sufficient common sense basis to justify an empirical test. Table 5 gives data relevant to the

TABLE 5

SIBLING CORRELATIONS

	Like-Sex Siblings		Opposite-Sex Siblings	
	Pairs	r	Pairs	r
Group A	159	.47	153	.55
Group B	178	.40	144	.55
Group C	158	.44	169	.46

first of these hypotheses, from a study by Conrad and Jones (1940). A representative sample of 777 pairs of children in New England rural communities was divided into three groups, on the basis of the tests used (Stanford-Binet, Army Alpha, or Stanford-Binet and Alpha).

The correlations tend to vary around .50, with no tendency for like-sex siblings to show higher r's. As a matter of fact (although the differences are not reliable), the higher r's are attained by the opposite-sex pairs.[2] The authors comment:

[2] Studies by Willoughby (1927) and S. K. Richardson (1936) also report no reliable differences in the coefficients for like-sex and opposite-sex siblings.

[1] Reviewed by Jones (1929) and H. M. Richardson (1939).

It is possible that the family constellation involved factors of interstimulation, rivalry or identification, that are somewhat different for same-sex than for opposite-sex siblings, and these may be reflected in the correlations.

Such factors, if they are conceived as influencing the development of basic mental abilities, may tend to balance out other factors associated with the more common environment of children of the same sex. On the present evidence, however, it is apparent that a defense of Hypothesis I will require ambitious ventures into speculation.

Data relevant to Hypothesis II have been supplied by Conrad (1931) for a sample of 778 pairs of siblings. Correlations were calculated for three different age groups and for siblings who were (1) less than three years apart in age and (2) more than three years apart. The coefficients varied around .50, and no comparisons yielded significant differences. The natal interval problem may be approached also by correlating the score difference (IQ, or sigma score) of each sib pair with the age difference (natal interval) of the pair. A positive correlation would be expected if a greater age separation of siblings is accompanied by a greater difference in IQ. For large samples, Conrad in the above-mentioned study and Finch (1933) found all correlations unreliably different from zero. The temporal factor has been examined by S. K. Richardson (1936) in a different way by determining correlations for siblings tested at similar ages (on the average, six months apart in age) and at separated ages (on the average, three and a half years apart). For 101 cases in each group, identical coefficients (.49) were obtained. It is evident that the environmental influences associated with age differences of siblings

are (on the average) without perceptible effect.

With regard to Hypothesis III, Figure 7 presents evidence as to increase of sibling correlation with age. This material, from unpublished data of Jones and Conrad, is based on a sample of 225 pairs of rural children tested with the Stanford-Binet, and 210 pairs tested with the Army Alpha. For each subgroup, the maximum age interval between each pair of siblings is five years. In each test, the correlations show a definite tendency to increase with age. Although this is consonant with the hypothesis of increasing or cumulative environmental influence, it is unfortunately impossible to eliminate other factors which may also contribute to the age trend.

One might inquire why the correlation drops so sharply when we shift, at around ten years, from the Stanford-Binet to the Army Alpha. The Stanford-Binet is not more reliable than the Alpha at this age, but it is probably more valid. The difference between these two tests at the same age may be due to much the same validity factors that operate to produce a difference within a given test at different ages. In other words, although the results indicated in Figure 7 can be plausibly attributed to environmental factors, it is equally plausible to account for them in terms of an increasingly valid measurement of basic abilities involving, with increasing age, the more complete expression of hereditary potentialities. It is interesting to note that in the case of the Alpha the highest sibling r (.54) is obtained in an age range extending into maturity, with many of the sibling pairs no longer living in the same homes. Environmental separation has apparently not tended to reduce measures of resemblance. Comparable results have been reported by Hildreth (1925), who found a correlation of .49 for 78 pairs of siblings

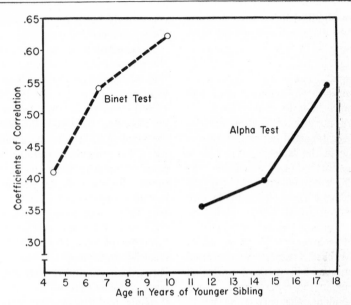

FIGURE 7.   Sibling correlations, according to age of the younger sibling.

separated, on the average, from four to five years.[1]

Before leaving this topic, reference should be made to one other type of sibling study which is of considerable interest for the present problem. This involves the measurement of resemblance among siblings reared in an institutional environment. If the similarity of brothers and sisters is due

[1] In the well-known Chicago study by Freeman, Holzinger, and Mitchell (1928) incidental data were reported for 130 pairs of siblings who had been separated for at least four years in different foster homes. The sibling correlation was .25, a diminished resemblance which may have been due to the reduced similarity in their environments. Burks (1928b, p. 321), however, has shown that this correlation rises toward the customary value if cases are omitted below 5 and above 14 years of age, eliminating individuals who are less adequately measured by the Stanford-Binet scale. In future studies, it will be desirable to know the sibling correlation before as well as after separation. If adoptive children are for any reason selected members of their families, and if the families themselves are a selected group, initial as well as the final correlations may be low because of reduced variability.

in part to the fact that they are reared in the same homes, the correlations would be expected to drop not merely when they are separated in different homes, but also when they are brought together into the relatively homogeneous physical and social conditions of an orphanage. The best-known evidence on this topic is from a study of 216 pairs of siblings in California orphanages; the reported correlation (.53) shows no evidence of an effect of institutional life.[2] For siblings in a Hebrew orphan asylum in New York, Hildreth (1925) obtained a lower correlation, but, on the other hand, found no evidence of a reduced variability such as would be expected if a common environment is influential. Similar results as to variability

[2] Originally reported by K. Gordon (1918–1920, 1919), the data were reanalyzed by Pearson (1918–1919) and Elderton (1923) in order to control age factors and also to render the correlation tables symmetrical. In correlations of siblings and of twins, the recommended procedure is to plot each pair of cases twice, transposing the axes (Fisher, 1930, pp. 178 ff.).

changes were obtained in an English study by Lawrence (1931), who compared institution children with a control group of children living in their own homes. The evidence suggests that when children move to a more uniform environment their IQ's do not become similarly standardized.

In a small number of studies, correlations have been reported between *unrelated* siblings living in the same homes. This is a promising method for examining the effect of the environment provided the original placement has not been made with reference to any social factor related to intelligence. Perhaps the best evidence on this problem is given by Freeman, Holzinger, and Mitchell (1928), who measured the intelligence of 112 pairs of unrelated children living in the same homes. On a genetic basis alone, the correlation would be expected to be zero, whereas the coefficient actually obtained was .25. Although significantly lower than for true siblings, it suggests that a common environment tends to produce some degree of resemblance among individuals living together. However, a part of this relationship must be assigned to a selective rather than to an environmental factor, since the evidence concerning foster child studies (see p. 621) indicates that placement agencies tend to locate children with some regard to the social and educational status of their true parents.

Twins. Studies of twins offer unusual advantages in the assessment of environmental influence, but up to the present few "crucial" results can be reported from investigations in this field. The following types of comparisons have been employed:

1. *Fraternal twins versus ordinary siblings.* On a genetic basis, fraternal twin correlations should be of the same order as coefficients for sibling resemblance (approximately .50). In fact, however, they tend to range slightly above this figure,

occasionally being reported as high as .70. This difference in correlation, if genuine,[1] may be attributable to the more common environment shared by twins. In line with this interpretation are the results from an ingenious study by S. K. Richardson (1936), who artificially "twinned" siblings by recording their IQ's for tests given at the same ages. Under these conditions (as noted in a previous section), the sibling correlations were the same as when computed with the ordinary age intervals (.49 in each computation). On the other hand, true twin correlations tended to diminish when control measurements were employed for different ages (for example, one twin recorded at 8 years and the other at 10). Richardson concluded that "the environment of twins from birth is so similar that it tends to increase their natural resemblance" (p. 197). The twin correlation in this case was .73 for 92 pairs; the correlation for twins as of different ages was .57 for 45 pairs. This difference is not fully significant, and would, moreover, be considerably diminished if Richardson had corrected for variability differences. The procedure is nevertheless a promising one and should be applied in further study with a larger number of cases.

2. *Younger versus older twins.* In the earliest twin study using mental test data, E. L. Thorndike (1905) found that in various traits twins 12 to 14 years of age exhibited correlations no higher than those of twins 9 to 11 years of age. He argued that, if twin resemblance is due to environment, correlations ought to increase with age. We have here a possibility of a more sensitive test of the hypothesis discussed on page 610, but still with difficulties in

---

[1] Twin correlations are subject to spurious inflation because of defects in test standardization, producing slightly lower average IQ's at higher ages. Some investigators have not understood the necessity of partialing out CA in order to control this factor.

interpretation. Thorndike's negative results (supported, in general, by later studies) have suggested to some writers that small environmental factors may be acting in opposite directions. The effect of longer residence in the same home may make for greater resemblance; but, on the other hand, with increasing age twins may become more independent in their choice of activities.[1]

3. *Fraternal versus identical twins.* More definitive results have been expected in this than in the preceding types of analysis, since we have a comparison in which environmental factors have been assumed to operate in a similar manner while genetic factors vary. The genetic difference consists in the fact that identical twins share the same gene determinants, whereas fraternal twins share a similar heredity only to the extent of ordinary brothers and sisters. Investigations have agreed that identical twins are on the average much more similar in intelligence than fraternal twins. Table 6 shows the twin correlations obtained in two representative studies.

Newman, Freeman, and Holzinger found a mean IQ difference of 9.8 for pairs of siblings, of 9.9 for pairs of fraternal twins, and of 5.9 for pairs of identical twins. This latter difference, it will be noted, is similar to that reported on page 586 in connection with studies of the constancy of the IQ.[2]

Such results would be expected if twin

<hr>

[1] This can also be expressed by saying that interfamilial variations (differences among families) may tend to produce correlated changes in twins, with an increasing degree of resemblance, whereas intrafamilial variations may lead to uncorrelated or even negatively correlated changes.

[2] Assuming that in representative samples identical twins correlate .90 in intelligence, ordinary siblings .50, and random pairs .00, Page (1941) has applied a formula predicting that the average intrapair IQ difference will be approximately 6 points for identical twins, 13 for siblings, and 19 for unrelated pairs, in terms of the 1916 Stanford-Binet.

TABLE 6

RESEMBLANCE OF IDENTICAL AND FRATERNAL TWINS IN INTELLIGENCE

(Stanford-Binet IQ, corrected for age.)

Investigator	Fraternal Twins		Identical Twins	
	N	r	N	r
Stocks and Karn (1933)	119	.65	68	.84
Newman, Freeman, and Holzinger (1937)	52	.63	50	.88

similarities were primarily genetic, but we must also take into account the fact of a greater degree of environmental similarity. Several studies have shown that identical twins spend more time together, enjoy more similar reputations, are more likely to be in the same classrooms, have more similar health records, and in many other respects share a more common physical and social environment than that ordinarily experienced by fraternal twins (Stocks, 1930–1931; Jones and Wilson, 1932–1933; Wilson, 1934; Lehtovaara, 1938).

Comparisons of twin populations are sometimes made not in terms of resemblance coefficients but more coarsely in terms of intrapair "concordance" or "discordance" as to specified traits. Thus Rosanoff, Hardy, and Plesset (1937) found that among identical twins in whom one member of the pair had been identified as mentally deficient 91 per cent of the co-twins were also classed as deficients. Among fraternal twins this measure of concordance dropped to 47 per cent.

4. *Twin resemblance in contrasted abilities.* Here we are concerned with the comparison of (a) abilities subject to training and (b) traits usually thought to be relatively independent of training. In E. L. Thorndike's (1905) study it was found that the degree of twin resemblance in various traits bore little or no relationship to the susceptibility of traits to training. Hence it could be argued that for both kinds of traits twin resemblance is primarily an expression of genetic factors. Lauterbach (1925) and Wingfield (1928) have also used this method in demonstrating, to their own satisfaction, the relatively minor importance of environmental factors. For identical and fraternal twins combined, Wingfield found twin correlations of .75 for IQ, .76 for educational quotient, .78 for arithmetic scores, and .85 for spelling scores, with no fully reliable differences. The problem is, however, one of great complexity, and many factors affecting (a) the incidence of training and (b) the genetic constitution of the trait in question may operate to produce results which make direct comparisons difficult between different traits.

5. *The method of co-twin control.* Technically superior to the preceding method is a procedure limited to identical twins, in which one member of a twin pair receives specific training while the other is reserved as a control. During the experimental period both twins undergo mental growth owing to intrinsic maturation and to general functioning, and any residual difference between the twins must be attributed to the experimental factor in the environment. First introduced by Gesell in the study of motor traits, the application of this method by Strayer (1930) in studying language development, and by Hilgard (1933) in connection with memory tests, has led to conclusions emphasizing the importance of intrinsic factors. A co-twin study covering a limited age period can, however, yield no general statement as to the comparative rôle of training and maturation. Its results will apply *only* to that particular age level and to the *specific functions* which are experimentally trained.

During the past decade a number of investigators in the U.S.S.R. have employed the co-twin method, with reference to various traits including intelligence (reviewed by Levit, 1935). Although we must regard this as a potentially powerful tool in the study of factors influencing development, in this country at any rate we have not yet been able to apply it to a sufficient number of cases (usually, only to a single pair of twins) or over a sufficiently long period of time to throw much light on our present problem.

6. *The comparison of identical twins reared apart.* In the absence of opportunities for the experimental separation of twins, the next best thing is to make use of separations which have occurred as a result of adoption in different homes. Here also reports have usually dealt with a single pair of twins, but in the well-known volume by Newman, Freeman, and Holzinger (1937) results have been assembled for a total of 19 pairs. The sample is, of course, a heterogeneous one, consisting of twins separated at ages ranging from 2 weeks to 6 years; at the time they were studied, their ages ranged from 12 to 60 years.

Ratings of the differences in the educational environments of the twins were made by five judges, three of whom knew only the case histories and two of whom also knew the twins. For all except six pairs of twins, the differences in ability were of about the same size as are found among identical twins reared together. Twelve pairs had small or negligible differences both in ability and in educational environment; for one pair there was no marked difference in ability even though a large difference in formal schooling had occurred. One pair with similar formal schooling showed a marked difference in ability corresponding to other differences in cultural opportunity; the remaining five pairs had experienced large or fairly large differences in education and showed corresponding differences in ability. Correlations for the nineteen pairs were below the usual coefficient for identical twins, but higher than the usual coefficients for siblings reared together (.67 for the Stanford-Binet IQ; .73 for the Otis IQ). Conclusions from this research, emphasizing environmental factors more strongly than in most twin studies, have been challenged in a number of reviews.[1] The method remains, however, a most important one, and, following the lead of Newman, Freeman, and Holzinger, we may expect significant results from a gradual accumulation of further cases of twins reared apart.

7. *Longitudinal studies of twins.* Psychological case studies of twins have been exemplified not only in the work of Freeman and his associates, but also in an interesting report by Koch (1927) on a pair of Siamese twins, and in several studies by Carter (1934) on mature identical twins. These have been based on cross-section and retrospective records rather than on cumulative data. Detailed studies are greatly needed in which the year-to-year development of twins is examined with reference to the relationship of developmental and environmental changes, the consistency of small differences, and the interrelationship of differences. With cumulative observations it is possible to examine the rôle of factors which are usually inaccessible to experimental techniques (illness, accidents, and various "crises" of development).

More complete reviews of twin research have been made by several investigators.[2] Although frequently exploited in journalistic treatments, it is clear that twin studies are not merely a scientific "stunt," but deserve continued serious attention as a basic approach to nature-nurture problems. Certain safeguards, however, must be maintained with regard to the following difficulties in twin research:

1. *Number of cases.* Plural births occur only in the proportion of about 11 per 1000.[3] A large population must be covered in order to establish an adequate sample. Thus, in locating approximately 500 pairs of twins, Wilson and Jones (1931) found it necessary to survey a school enrollment of over 75,000 pupils.

2. *Sampling methods.* The best method of locating twins is through birth records, or by a questionnaire placed in the hands of all members of the group that is to be sampled. If reliance is placed on a census of twins by teachers, this method may lead to reporting all fraternal twins who are

[1] Burks (1938a), McNemar (1938), Woodworth (1941). Woodworth has emphasized the fact that when twins of identical heredity are subjected to environments differing about as much as those of the children in an ordinary community, the twins nevertheless remain much more similar than random pairs of children in such a community. This would suggest that interfamilial and general educational differences are not of primary importance in determining variations in IQ in the general population.

[2] Some of the best-known treatments are by Dahlberg (1926), Hirsch (1930b), Gesell (1931), Levit (1935), Newman, Freeman, and Holzinger (1937), Carter (1940), and Newman (1940). Especially valuable is an analysis of twin and foster-child studies by Woodworth (1941).

[3] Triplet births occur in the proportion of approximately 1 per 8000, and other forms of plural birth are so rare as not to provide dependable scientific material. Considerable interest, however, is commanded by the recent volume by Blatz, Chant, Charles, *et al.* (1937) on the quintuplets, and by several publications dealing with small samples of triplets. The best known of these is by Anderson and Scheidemann (1933).

sufficiently similar to be in the same classrooms, but may fail to place on record the fraternal twins who, being less similar, are located in different grades or different schools. Such a factor would spuriously increase coefficients of twin resemblance among fraternals, and may be responsible for unexpectedly high correlations reported by some investigators. A representative sample of twins may ordinarily be expected to include about one-quarter identicals and three-quarters fraternals.

3. *The classification of twins.* In classifying twins as fraternals or identicals, various methods have been used, including reference to obstetric data on fetal membranes; physical measurements; skeletal X-rays; finger prints and palm prints; hair color, form, and distribution; eye color and the pattern of iris pigmentation; microscopic capillary examination; blood agglutination grouping; and also more subjective methods based on the impression of similarity in general appearance. No one of these methods provides an infallible means of diagnosing identical twins, but with the application of a variety of methods a very high degree of agreement can be obtained in independent assessments by different investigators. In studying a given trait, such as intelligence, it is unsafe to use this trait as a part of the basis for diagnosis. Thus Hirsch (1930b) selected identicals in terms of criteria which included mental similarity, a procedure which may have had the effect of exaggerating differences in correlations between the two types of twins. In general, however, errors in diagnosis will spuriously *reduce* the difference between identical and fraternal twin correlations. It is sometimes a wise policy to exclude a small percentage of cases as "undetermined," if these cases show a conflict in the objective criteria employed for classification.

4. *General selective factors.* Twins are subject to a heavier infant mortality than are the single-born. The effect of this upon the selection of surviving twins is not fully known. One would expect it to improve the selection slightly; but, if this is so, then the prenatal or circumnatal factors affecting the development of twins must impose a decided handicap, for those surviving into school age are on the average slightly inferior to single-born in terms of a number of physical and mental criteria. This factor may also operate to eliminate divergent members of twin pairs, with the effect of increasing our measures of resemblance for those that survive.

An additional factor to be considered in interpreting research findings is that twins live in a very special social environment. Except in the case of twins reared apart, general conclusions from twin studies may not be immediately applicable to other selections of cases or other types of environment.

Parent-Child Resemblance. Chiefly because of the difficulty of obtaining intelligence test data for adults, relatively few studies of parent-child resemblance have been reported. In an early investigation, Pearson (1910) obtained a correlation of .49 between father and son, using ratings of mental ability. Subsequent studies employing intelligence tests have in general supported his finding that the resemblance of parents and children is of the same order as that of brothers and sisters.[1] This is not unexpected on the basis of hypotheses of genetic causation, but on an environmental hypothesis one would expect

[1] Somewhat lower coefficients have been reported by Willoughby (1927) and Freeman, Holzinger, and Mitchell (1928), but Pearson's results agree closely with those of Burks (1928b), Jones (1928), Banker (1928), Outhit (1933), Leahy (1935), and Conrad and Jones (1940). A review of earlier studies may be found in Carter (1932).

the sibling correlation to be higher, since the conditions under which brothers and sisters are reared, in a given family, are more similar than the conditions under which the members of two different generations are reared. It is a matter of unusual interest that these markedly differential factors in childhood environments seem unable to exert any distinguishable effect upon the family coefficients.

The suggestion has sometimes been made that, since the mother spends more time with her children during early childhood and has more direct supervision over their activities, a greater resemblance might be expected between mother and child than between father and child. So far as mental abilities are concerned, this does not appear to be the case. With the largest sample reported to date, Conrad and Jones (1940) found no differences in parent correlations. In this study the parents and children over 14 years of age were tested with the Army Alpha; between 10 and 14 either the Alpha or Stanford-Binet was used; and below 10 the Stanford-Binet was used exclusively. Table 7 summarizes the results.

TABLE 7

PARENT-CHILD CORRELATIONS

	Stanford-Tested Offspring		Alpha-Tested Offspring	
	N	r	N	r
Father	232	.49	196	.49
Mother	269	.49	245	.48

The striking uniformity in these results would of course be predicted on a genetic basis, since on the average the two parents play an equal rôle in transmission of hereditary characters. The greater rôle of the mother in the intimate determination of the child's early environment appears to have no differentiating effect with regard to intelligence. An alternative interpretation, however, might be that such an effect, if present, is balanced out by some other environmental factor.

As in the case of the sibling coefficients, a tendency exists for parent-child correlations to increase with age, especially if we compare results for preschool children and for adolescents. But again, as in the case of the sibling coefficients, the results are difficult to interpret, since an age change could be expected on the basis of both environmental and hereditary hypotheses, and also as a result of any increase in validity of the tests.

We have seen that studies of family resemblance have frequently led to ambiguous results as to the relative importance of environmental factors in mental development. In general, however, they have emphasized interfamilial differences in heredity as equally or more potent than differences in family environments, for a normal range of subjects. These studies not only have their own implications, but they are also of value in providing a normative background for the interpretation of results from a quasi-experimental type of investigation, in which "true" family resemblance is compared with the degree of resemblance achieved in foster relationships (see the section on children in foster homes, p. 621).

The Effects of Schooling

The theory of intelligence or capacity measurement implies a curvilinear relationship between education and test scores (for children of a given age). Children of school age with no education will make low scores, regardless of their natural talents or "educability." But it is assumed that, beyond a certain level of educational advance, and within a normal range of school opportunities, increments in training will not be accompanied by corresponding increments in mental test score. To assume otherwise would be to regard intelligence tests merely as tests of schooling. We know, however, that in groups relatively homogeneous as to education wide differences occur in test performance and that these differences persist even after extended exposure to a similar educational environment.

If it is maintained that mental growth can be controlled within narrow limits by educational factors, the burden of proof rests with those making this claim. It would appear to be a simple matter to set up an experiment in which an adequately large group is given experimental training of a type regarded as basically stimulating to mental development, and to compare the subsequent mental test records of this group with records obtained from a carefully matched control. In such an experiment, however, numerous precautions need to be taken. It is unfortunately true that in previous work these precautions have rarely been observed in their entirety:

1. The experimental and the control group should consist of matched pairs from the same population, one member of each pair being assigned at random to the experimental or the control procedure. It usually happens that the experimental group is already "given" to the experimenter, in the membership of a specific school sample. He must then make a search for suitable controls. Unless he is fully conversant with the factors which have determined the selection of the experimental sample, it is unlikely that he will succeed in matching this selection completely. Thus, if exceptional intelligence of the parents is a factor determining the placement of children in nursery schools, a matching on the basis of children's IQ will be unsatisfactory, since the children in the experimental group will show differential gains merely as a result of increasing approximation to the level of ability characteristic of their families.

2. In the selection of cases, homogeneous groups are needed. In the nursery school, for example, it is possible that educational experiences provided in the school exert differing effects according to the age and cultural background of the children concerned. The mixture of cases of various ages and various social groups (as usually occurs) may yield results extremely difficult to interpret. An additional factor to consider in selection is the much-discussed phenomenon of statistical *regression to the mean*. If, for example, a group of children of below-average ability is selected for special educational attention, retests will probably show a movement toward the mean not necessarily because of true changes but because of compensation for errors of measurement which influenced the original selection. These difficulties, as well as other ambiguities, can be reduced by increasing the reliability of our measurements, as, for example, by the procedure of basing all scores on the average of two tests on successive days.

3. The criteria for matching the experimental and control pairs should include chronological age, initial IQ, and physical status of the children, intelligence (or, at any rate, education) of the parents, and a socioeconomic index for the home. It is important to obtain the initial IQ's under comparable conditions. Thus, if the nursery school children are tested in the stress of their first attendance at school and the control children are tested under familiar conditions at home, the experimental group may show larger gains on a second test, owing chiefly to gains in rapport. With

young children, attention should be given to assessments of effort, cooperation, freedom from inhibition, response to success or failure, and other motivational factors considered with reference to possible effects upon test performance. It would, of course, be desirable to establish controls on the basis not merely of a single period, but of a series of tests representing a segment of the growth curve prior to the beginning of the experiment. Children are sometimes given superior educational opportunities because their mental growth appears to be temporarily restricted. This apparent restriction, however, may be due to any of the intrinsic or extrinsic factors discussed on page 592. Later gains, giving the impression of an improved rate of growth, may represent changes in these factors rather than the effects of the nursery school experience.

4. The experimental situation should be analyzed and described in detail. Investigations which give a vague report of positive effects from undefined "school experience" can neither be interpreted nor repeated unless the specific basis of these effects is made known. Such information is also necessary in order to determine whether the effects are (*a*) merely specific transfers to certain kinds of test items, (*b*) the result of attitude changes or increased incentive, or (*c*) a more generalized change in mental efficiency.

5. Subsequent test comparisons of the experimental control pairs must involve equal amounts of test practice, comparable tests, and comparable conditions in testing. If retests are made by persons who are strangers to the control group, but (as teachers or staff members) are well known to the children in the school, differential apparent gains may occur as a result of this factor.[1] These considerations lead to

a further requirement; namely that, when a test is given, the examiner should not be familiar with the results of previous tests and should not know whether the child is in the experimental or in the control group. Subjective factors in the administration and scoring of such a test as the Stanford-Binet may lead to a conscious or unconscious biasing of the results by examiners who think they know how the results "ought" to turn out. Krugman (1939) and Goodenough (1940*b*) have discussed the possible rôle of these subjective factors in determining basal and final ages and in reaching decisions as to the scoring of marginal successes or failures.

6. The test program should be continued for several years, in order to determine whether possible effects are temporary (and specific to certain test items at certain ages) or whether they are expressed in more lasting effects upon mental development.

7. Finally, since any obtained effects are likely to be small in magnitude, a substantial number of cases is needed in order to reach a well-founded decision as to the significance of differences.

The reports on the effects of nursery school training should be examined in the light of the foregoing experimental criteria.

gains were also those regarded by the teacher as showing the greatest improvement in personality traits. Krugman (1939), in difficult clinical cases, attributed the largest changes in test performance to changes in rapport or cooperation. The following comment by Black (1939) is also illuminating:

"In our experience at the Harriet Johnson Nursery School we have found resistance and shyness to be far less characteristic of the nursery school than of the non-nursery school child, regardless of age. The school situation itself tends to produce rapport between examiner and child before the examination begins. Freedom, a feeling of security in the school situation, and increasing sense of the friendliness and trustworthiness of adults recognized as belonging to the school make the test situation relatively easy for the child and the examiner" (p. 164).

[1] In the report by Barrett and Koch (1930) the nursery school cases making the greatest IQ

An early study by Woolley (1925), with inadequate controls, reported an apparent effect of preschool education upon mental development. Similar results were obtained a few years later by Barrett and Koch (1930) in an orphan asylum group. Because of the small number of cases and the lack of adequately defined experimental conditions, and also because of negative evidence in two other studies (Hildreth, 1928; Goodenough, 1928a), the majority of workers in this field turned from the problem as presenting little hope of further reward. It is to the credit of the Iowa group of investigators that they maintained a persistent interest in the possible effects of nursery school education and formulated an extensive and versatile program of research. In general, this research has been interpreted by Wellman and her associates as indicating potency of the preschool environment in generating marked and persistent changes in mental growth. The *Thirty-ninth Yearbook of the National Society for the Study of Education* (Stoddard *et al.*, 1940) contains a summary of the Iowa studies, together with reports on nine other preschool investigations, the majority of which were stimulated (in 1938 and 1939) by the strikingly positive findings reported from Iowa.

It may be noted that for the most part the various studies show a negligible relation between IQ change and length of attendance in nursery school. With a few exceptions they agree in showing a slight difference in favor of nursery school groups when these are compared with control groups. Although in nearly every case the difference is statistically unreliable, the findings are sufficiently consistent to be of interest.[1] At the present time disagree-

ment exists as to the extent to which errors of measurement, of experimental procedure, and of statistical treatment may be responsible for results which have been so enthusiastically advocated as evidence that mental growth responds promptly and permanently to educational influences in the nursery school. In our discussion of IQ constancy and the mental growth curve it was shown that with many children the preschool period is marked by a considerable degree of irregularity or variation in mental growth. It is tempting to the educator to believe that these variations are readily subject to his management and control, but as yet we cannot regard the evidence in this field as satisfactory. No one doubts, however, that the nursery school presents opportunities for promoting development in traits more directly amenable to environmental influence, and perhaps more essential for adjustment at this age level. In commenting on the Iowa studies, Burks (1939) has stressed the importance of such factors:

> The preschool ages constitute the period *par excellence* not only for developing constructive attitudes toward tasks, but for integrating these with a sense of personal value and with feelings of security in social relationships. To accomplish this integration, however, would not necessarily mean that maximal mental growth during the preschool years was necessary or even desirable for all children. Rather, it would seem that the growth of adaptive behavior should be stimulated and guided—often in special instead of in all areas—so as to achieve an harmonious balance with the

---

[1] Of the nine studies referred to above, one (Starkweather and Roberts, 1940) tends to support the Iowa conclusions, but unfortunately does not include a control group. The remaining eight investigations, all published in 1940 (L. D. Anderson, Bird, Frandsen and Barlow, Goodenough and Maurer, Jones and Jorgensen, Lamson, Olson and Hughes, and Voas), point to essentially negative conclusions.

The highly controversial literature on this topic includes discussions by McNemar (1940), Goodenough (1940a), R. L. Thorndike (1940), Stoddard and Wellman (1940), and Wellman, Skeels, and Skodak (1940).

expanding personality needs of each particular child (p. 555).

It seems probable that such gains in IQ as have been reported are not too large to be accounted for in terms of the effect of personality improvement upon mental functioning.

The effect of environmental factors in later schooling will not be considered here in detail. The evidence in this area is even less satisfactory than in the nursery school studies, chiefly because of the lack of data from comparison groups in definitely contrasting educational situations. Goodenough (1940a) has summarized relevant studies in this field through the year 1939, concluding that "the attempts to demonstrate the differential effects of different kinds of school practice upon child achievement have been disappointingly meager when suitable controls have been employed," and that differential effects upon intelligence are even harder to demonstrate by methods used up to this time (p. 330). This should not be taken to imply that the problem has already been answered in the negative, but rather that our present need is for more definitive research.

Children in Foster Homes

Only a limited view of the possible effects of environmental influence can be given through the experimental control of the school environment. Unfortunately, no studies have been made of a representative sample of children observed under conditions involving an experimental, and parallel, modification of factors both in the home and in the school. Such a study would require the random separation of pairs of siblings (or, preferably, identical twins) and their rearing in homes and schools possessing certain specified differences. We do, however, have a number of investigations of children placed in foster homes. These, though limited in a number of respects, provide us with some of our most penetrating evidence concerning the nature-nurture problem.

Studies of foster children have been discussed in reviews by Goodenough (1940a) and Loevinger (1940), and need not be presented here in detail. The two researches which are most comparable as to procedure are by Burks (1928b) in California and by Leahy (1935) in Minnesota. Each investigated approximately 200 children placed in foster homes before 12 months of age. Each obtained intelligence tests of the foster parents, a cultural-economic assessment of the home environment, and a record of the foster child's IQ after he had reached school age (between 5 and 14 years). Moreover, in each investigation a "true child" control group was set up which would permit comparisons of parent-child relationship with and without the presence of a systematic hereditary factor.

It is often found that the selection of children available for adoption in official placement agencies is slightly superior in average intelligence; for Burks's 204 cases the mean IQ was 107.4, and for Leahy's 194 cases (all of whom were illegitimate) the mean IQ was 110.5. Figure 8 presents some of the more important results from these studies. The degree of resemblance to measures of the home environment, or to parents' intelligence, is clearly greater for true children than for foster children. From this an inference can be drawn that the correlations with home environment which have been found in the case of true children are due primarily to the common factor of the parents' intelligence rather than to the environment acting as a causative agent. That is to say, the intelligence of the parents finds expression both in the culture of their home and in the IQ's of their children. What, now, will happen when the hereditary factor is eliminated from parent-child correlations (through drop to low values, ranging from .07 to .21. That they remain higher than zero can perhaps be ascribed in part to the

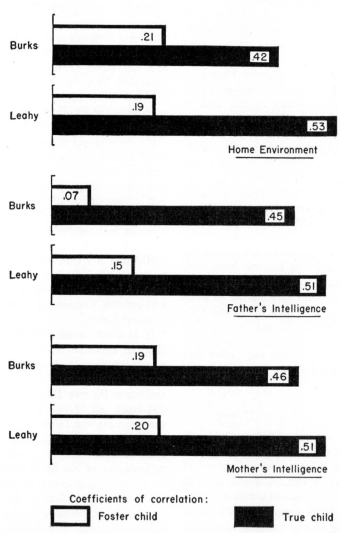

Coefficients of correlation:

☐ Foster child   ■ True child

FIGURE 8. A comparison of foster child and true child correlations.

the use of foster children)? Should we not expect that this elimination will also directly affect the correlation of the child's IQ with measures of the (foster) home environment? These correlations do actually tendency for adopted children to shift toward the level of the homes in which they are placed. However, an additional factor is present in that the placement of children is rarely experimentally random. In other words, when placement officers have knowledge of the cultural circumstances of the true parents, this is likely to influence their choice of foster homes. Even with elaborate precautions against selective placement, a positive relation has been shown to exist between the occupations of true and foster parents.

When children are placed at ages later than infancy, the aim of "fitting the child to the home" will result in an increased likelihood of selective placement. This appears to have been a factor in the study of Freeman, Holzinger, and Mitchell (1928) of 401 children in Illinois who were placed at an average age of 4 years, 2 months. When tested at around 11 years, the correlation with a measure of the foster home [1] was .48. This value, as high as would be expected in a "true child" sample, was apparently influenced somewhat by a choice of foster homes appropriate to the intelligence or to the family origins of the children. If this choice were made without including intelligence tests of the true parents, the subsequent correlation of children's IQ with foster parents' intelligence would be expected to be lower than for true parent-child relationships. This proved to be the case; for 255 mothers and 180 fathers who were tested when the children were 11 years of age, on the average, the correlation with the foster child's IQ was .28 for the mothers and .37 for the fathers. For a subgroup of 74 children another and more direct type of analysis is possible since tests were available both before and after the children had been in a foster home. The average age of the children at placement was 8 years; at the time of the retest, approximately 12 years. A significant average gain in IQ

[1] Based on ratings of the material environment, evidences of culture, education of the parents, occupation of the father, and social activity of the parents.

was shown for children placed in superior homes, and a less significant gain for those placed in poorer homes.

Similar results have been reported in a number of studies in which children were removed from bad home situations and placed in an orphanage or a boarding home (Lithauer and Klineberg, 1933; Wells and Arthur, 1939; Skeels, 1940; Speer, 1940a, 1940b). In such cases, apparent gains are suspect because of difficulties in obtaining a valid test at a time when a child's home is broken, or when emotional factors may be present from previous home conditions. Poverty, drunkenness, sex delinquency, inadequate food and housing, and many other disturbing factors are frequently cited as characteristic of the true homes and as giving rise to the need for placement elsewhere. It is difficult or impossible to appraise IQ gains in foster homes unless the initial tests are given under conditions in which test performance can genuinely register the child's ability. A further, and perhaps the chief, explanation of differences between the results of this study and those of Burks and Leahy can be sought in terms of random sampling differences.

An incidental outcome of the Freeman, Holzinger, and Mitchell study has been pointed out by Lorimer and Osborn (1934). For 156 children classified as members of good, average, and poor foster homes, mean IQ's were obtained of 111, 103, and 91. These differences could be attributed both to environmental influence and to selective placement. However, when the group was subdivided into legitimate and illegitimate children, the former were found to have a mean IQ of 95 and the latter of 106, with similar differences present in each grade of homes. The illegitimate children apparently represent a superior hereditary selection, and this superiority has by no means been obliterated by removal from their true parents.

Similar inferences can be drawn from a recent preliminary report by Stippich (1940) involving a comparison between 48 children whose mothers were feeble-minded, and 29 children of normal mothers; all had been placed in boarding homes before 12 months of age. On the basis of tests given after they were 3 years old, marked differences were noted between the two groups, although they were developing in apparently comparable environments. Twenty-one per cent of the experimental group (children of mentally deficient mothers) and none of the control group fell below 75 IQ. Here again, the ubiquitous problem of selective placement must be considered. Comparability of the two groups of foster homes appears to be more a matter of assertion than of proof; if there was any tendency to place the children of feeble-minded mothers in less adequate homes this might to some extent account for the results obtained.

Somewhat different results have been reported by Skeels (1941) for a sample of 87 children of mothers who were mentally retarded. After placement in adoptive homes the children attained a mental level "equaling or exceeding that of the population as a whole." For the present purpose, comparisons of small samples of children of feeble-minded and normal mothers are unsatisfactory unless there is adequate information about (1) the diagnosis of the mothers, (2) the conditions of placement, and (3) the mental status of the fathers. Cases should be ruled out in which the mothers' mental deficiency is of clearly secondary origin, as from injury or disease, and in which there is no other record of mental defect in the family. It is also important to know whether the children who have become available for adoption repre-

sent a genuinely unselected sample for the families considered. Results would be extremely difficult to interpret if the more retarded children of a defective mother are kept at home or sent to an institution, whereas the more normal offspring are accepted by foster homes. Finally, the mental status and family origins of the fathers cannot be neglected. In the case of illegitimate children of feeble-minded mothers, the ordinary principles of assortative mating may not be operative. It is obvious that "crucial" findings cannot be expected if a substantial proportion of the true fathers are of normal intelligence or derive from families of normal intelligence.[1]

The remaining principal study in this field, by Skodak (1939), dealt with 154 children who were placed before the age of six months in average or superior foster homes. Since selective placement was involved, the most effective comparison to be made is between children coming from true homes within a given occupational classification and those placed out in homes of varying classification. The conclusion is offered that the effect of superior home environments is clearly shown in the results, and also that in general the children exhibit higher test scores than would be ex-

[1] Foster child studies have not as yet utilized intelligence scores for true fathers. The first study making use of test scores for true mothers was carried out by Skeels (1936). His group, including 39 mothers, was a preliminary subgroup of that later used by Skodak. More recently, results have been reported from Stanford-Binet IQ's of 312 true mothers and adopted children, in a Toronto study by Snygg (1938). Parent-child correlations in these two investigations were .09 and .13, respectively; mean IQ's of the mothers were, respectively, 84 and 78, and of the children, 115 (?) and 95. These results are not in line with those based on our most carefully controlled and most fully reported foster child studies. Unfortunately, a further interpretation is difficult because sufficiently complete data have not been presented concerning methods of sampling and conditions of testing.

pected on the basis of their true homes.[1] In view of the fact that further reports are expected from these Iowa studies, with additional cases, it may be desirable to delay an evaluation until more evidence is in. One striking finding, however, somewhat contrary to what would be looked for on the basis of Skodak's main conclusions, is that after an average of several years in the foster home the children show correlations of .16 to .19 with education of the foster parents. These are comparable to coefficients reported by Leahy and Burks and are in part due to selective placement. With the education of the true parents, however, a more marked correlation was shown of .33 to .38,[2] in spite of the fact that there had been little or no contact with the true parents since earliest infancy.

One of the most important types of research to be conducted in the future will involve the placement of foster children on the basis of a planned experimental design, rather than the study of children whose location has been previously determined by uncontrolled and incompletely known factors. To appraise the results of such an investigation, it would be necessary to have intelligence tests of all the true and foster parents, a goal that has never yet been reached. The intelligence of the children should be observed cumulatively rather than stated, as at present, on the basis of one or two tests, and a cumulative inventory should also be maintained of relevant environmental factors in and outside the home. Previous studies, which are neces-

sarily inconclusive at many points, may be regarded as preparing the ground for more thorough and better-controlled investigations which still remain to be conducted.

So much has been written on the topic of environmental influence that it has not been possible within a single chapter to review all the significant reports and discussions, or even to refer to all the principal methods of approach. Little mention has been made, for example, of studies of feeble-minded or gifted children, of the mental growth of institutionalized children, or of mental growth or achievement gauged in other ways than by intelligence tests. Reference has been given, however, to numerous other sources in which further materials can be found. A topic as yet very incompletely studied involves the relationship between intelligence and personality and the effect of variations in emotional adjustment and personal integration upon the nature and the efficiency of mental functioning.[3]

Burks (1939) has pointed out that in this general field

> ... there is, in fact, less of a cleavage between pure research and application than is true of many scientific fields, since the most crucial data for the nature-nurture problem are obtained not through laboratory experiments, but through experiments which society itself has undertaken for social goals. This circumstance seems to lower the emotional thresholds of research workers, but paradoxically it places upon them an added responsibility to disengage themselves from emotional biases. If the results of scientific research are of the kind that find immediate application, errors are costly to society. On the other hand, sound data have immeasurable social value (p. 548).

In its social import the nature-nurture problem extends not merely into every

---

[1] A number of the assumptions and procedures in this study have been vigorously criticized by Burks (1939), McNemar (1940), and Goodenough (1940a), with replies from Skeels (1940), Stoddard and Wellman (1940), and Wellman, Skeels, and Skodak (1940).

[2] These coefficients represent a correction from original coefficients of .28 to .33. The correction was suggested by Goodenough (1940a), to take account of a difference in variability of the two groups of parents.

[3] Cf. discussions by L. S. Hollingworth (1940), Lorge (1940), and Lund (1940).

branch of education but also (because of the differential birth rate) into the field of population and social planning. It is evident that the approach to this problem has, during the past two decades, led to striking improvements in research method and to a clearer awareness of the complexity of the issues with which we must deal. When we seek a better understanding of human potentialities in intelligence, we are at the same time appraising the rôles which environmental factors can play in the functional development of our capacities for adaptation. It must be emphasized that this is an extremely varied task. Future research must address itself not to a single ultimate solution of the problem, but to an examination of its many aspects, in many specific situations.

Bibliography

ABERNETHY, E. M. 1936. Relationships between mental and physical growth. *Monogr. Soc. Res. Child Develpm.*, **1**, No. 7. Pp. 80.

ADKINS, D. C. 1937. The effects of practice on intelligence test scores. *J. Educ. Psychol.*, **28**, 222–231.

ANASTASI, A. 1937. *Differential psychology.* New York: Macmillan.

ANDERSON, F. N., and N. V. SCHEIDEMANN. 1933. A study of triplets. *Genet. Psychol. Monogr.*, **14**, 93–176.

ANDERSON, J. E. 1940. The prediction of terminal intelligence from infant and preschool tests. *Yearb. Nat. Soc. Stud. Educ.*, **39**(I), 385–403.

ANDERSON, L. D. 1939. The predictive value of infancy tests in relation to intelligence at five years. *Child Develpm.*, **10**, 203–212.

——. 1940. A longitudinal study of the effects of nursery-school training on successive intelgence-test ratings. *Yearb. Nat. Soc. Stud. Educ.*, **39**(II), 3–10.

ASHER, E. J. 1935. The inadequacy of current intelligence tests for testing Kentucky mountain children. *J. Genet. Psychol.*, **46**, 480–486.

AYRES, L. P. 1909. The effect of physical defects on school progress. *Psychol. Clin.*, **3**, 71–77.

BALDWIN, B. T., E. A. FILLMORE, and L. HADLEY. 1930. *Farm children: An investigation of rural child life in selected areas of Iowa.* New York: Appleton.

BANKER, H. J. 1928. Genealogical correlation of student ability. *J. Hered.*, **19**, 503–508.

BARRETT, H. E., and H. L. KOCH. 1930. The effect of nursery-school training upon the mental test performance of a group of orphanage children. *J. Genet. Psychol.*, **37**, 102–122.

BAYLEY, N. 1933. Mental growth during the first three years. A developmental study of 61 children by repeated tests. *Genet. Psychol. Monogr.*, **14**, 1–92.

——. 1940a. Mental growth in young children. *Yearb. Nat. Soc. Stud. Educ.*, **39**(II), 11–47.

——. 1940b. Factors influencing the growth of intelligence in young children. *Yearb. Nat. Soc. Stud. Educ.*, **39**(II), 49–79.

BAYLEY, N., and H. E. JONES. 1937. Environmental correlates of mental and motor development: A cumulative study from infancy to six years. *Child Develpm.*, **8**, 329–341.

BICKERSTETH, M. E. 1919. The application of mental tests to children of various ages. *Brit. J. Psychol.*, **9**, 23–73.

BIRD, G. E. 1940. The effect of nursery-school attendance upon mental growth of children. *Yearb. Nat. Soc. Stud. Educ.*, **39**(II), 81–84.

BLACK, I. S. 1939. The use of the Stanford-Binet (1937 revision) in a group of nursery school children. *Child Develpm.*, **10**, 157–171.

BLATZ, W. E., N. CHANT, M. W. CHARLES *et al.* 1937. *Collected studies on the Dionne quintuplets.* Toronto: University of Toronto Press.

BRADWAY, K. P., and E. L. HOFFEDITZ. 1937. The basis for the personal constant. *J. Educ. Psychol.*, **28**, 501–513.

BRUCE, M. 1940. Factors affecting intelligence test performance of whites and Negroes in the rural south. *Arch. Psychol., N. Y.*, No. 252. Pp. 100.

BURKS, B. S. 1928a. Statistical hazards in nature-nurture investigations. *Yearb. Nat. Soc. Stud. Educ.*, **27**(I), 9–33.

——. 1928b. The relative influence of nature and nurture upon mental development: A comparative study of foster parent-foster child resemblance and true parent-true child resemblance. *Yearb. Nat. Soc. Stud. Educ.*, **27**(I), 219–316.

——. 1928c. A summary of literature on the determiners of the intelligence quotient and the educational quotient. *Yearb. Nat. Soc. Stud. Educ.*, **27**(II), 248–353.

——. 1938a. Review of twins: A study of heredity and environment. *J. Abnorm. Soc. Psychol.*, **33**, 128–133.

——. 1938b. On the relative contributions of nature and nurture to average group differences in intelligence. *Proc. Nat. Acad. Sci. Wash.*, **24**, 276–282.

——. 1939. Review of "Children in foster homes: A study of mental development," by

MARIE SKODAK. *J. Educ. Psychol.*, 30, 548–555.

BURT, C. 1921. *Mental and scholastic tests.* London : King.

BYRNS, R., and V. A. C. HENMON. 1935. Long range prediction of college achievement. *Sch. and Soc.*, 41, 877–880.

CARMICHAEL, L. 1940. The physiological correlates of intelligence. *Yearb. Nat. Soc. Stud. Educ.*, 39(I), 93–155.

CARTER, H. D. 1932. Family resemblances in verbal and numerical abilities. *Genet. Psychol. Monogr.*, 12, No. 1. Pp. 104.

——. 1934. Case studies of mature identical twins. *J. Genet. Psychol.*, 44, 154–174.

——. 1940. Ten years of research of twins : contributions to the nature-nurture problem. *Yearb. Nat. Soc. Stud. Educ.*, 39(I), 235–255.

CASEY, M. L., H. P. DAVIDSON, and D. I. HARTER. 1928. Three studies on the effect of training in similar and identical material upon Stanford-Binet test scores. *Yearb. Nat. Soc. Stud. Educ.*, 27(I), 431–439.

CATTELL, J. McK. 1927. *American men of science.* (4th ed.) Garrison, N. Y. : Science Press.

CATTELL, P. 1937. Stanford-Binet IQ variations. *Sch. and Soc.*, 45, 615–618.

CHAPMAN, J. C., and D. M. WIGGINS. 1925. Relation of family size to intelligence of offspring and socio-economic status of family. *Ped. Sem.*, 32, 414–421.

CLARK, C. D., and N. P. GIST. 1938. Intelligence as a factor in occupational choice. *Amer. Sociol. Rev.*, 3, 683–694.

CLARK, E. L. 1939. Significance of month of birth as judged by test scores and grades. *Psychol. Bull.*, 36, 629 (abstr.).

CONRAD, H. S. 1931. *Sibling resemblance and the inheritance of intelligence.* Ph.D. Dissertation, University of California.

CONRAD, H. S., and H. E. JONES. 1940. A second study of familial resemblance in intelligence : Environmental and genetic implications of parent-child and sibling correlations in the total sample. *Yearb. Nat. Soc. Stud. Educ.*, 39(II), 97–141.

DAHLBERG, G. 1926. *Twin births and twins from a hereditary point of view.* Stockholm : Bokförlags-A.-B. Tidens Tryckeri.

DAYTON, N. A. 1928–1929. The relationship between physical defects and intelligence. *J. Psycho-Asthenics*, 34, 112–139.

DEARBORN, W. F., and J. W. M. ROTHNEY. 1941. Predicting the child's development. Cambridge, Mass. : Sci-Art Publishers.

DUBNOFF, B. 1938. A comparative study of mental development in infancy. *J. Genet. Psychol.*, 53, 67–73.

EDWARDS, A. S., and L. JONES. 1938. An experimental and field study of north Georgia mountaineers. *J. Soc. Psychol.*, 9, 317–333.

ELDERTON, E. M. 1923. A summary of the present position with regard to the inheritance of intelligence. *Biometrika*, 14, 378–408.

ELLIS, H. 1926. *A study of British genius.* (New ed., rev.) Boston : Houghton Mifflin.

ENGLAND, N. J. 1936. The relation between health and intelligence in school children. *J. Hyg.*, 36, 74–94.

FINCH, F. H. 1933. A study of the relation of age interval to degree of resemblance of siblings in intelligence. *J. Genet. Psychol.*, 43, 389–404.

FISHER, R. A. 1918. The correlation between relatives on the supposition of Mendelian inheritance. *Trans. Roy. Soc. Edinburgh*, 52, 399–433.

——. 1930. *Statistical methods for research workers.* (3d ed.) London : Oliver and Boyd.

FORAN, T. G. 1926. The constancy of the intelligence quotient : A review. *Cath. Univ. Amer. Educ. Res. Bull.*, 1, No. 10. Pp. 40.

——. 1929. A supplementary review of the constancy of the intelligence quotient. *Cath. Univ. Amer. Educ. Res. Bull.*, 4, No. 9. Pp. 29.

FORLANO, G., and V. Z. EHRLICH. 1941. Month and season of birth in relation to intelligence, introversion-extroversion and inferiority feelings. *J. Educ. Psychol.*, 32, 1–12.

FRANDSEN, A., and F. P. BARLOW. 1940. Influence of the nursery school on mental growth. *Yearb. Nat. Soc. Stud. Educ.*, 39(II), 143–148.

FREEMAN, F. N. 1940. The meaning of intelligence. *Yearb. Nat. Soc. Stud. Educ.*, 39(I), 11–20.

FREEMAN, F. N., and C. D. FLORY. 1937. Growth in intellectual ability as measured by repeated tests. *Monogr. Soc. Res. Child Develpm.*, 2, No. 2. Pp. xi + 116.

FREEMAN, F. N., K. J. HOLZINGER, and B. C. MITCHELL. 1928. The influence of environment on the intelligence, school achievement, and conduct of foster children. *Yearb. Nat. Soc. Stud. Educ.*, 27(I), 103–217.

FRITZ, M. F. 1935. The effect of diet on intelligence and learning. *Psychol. Bull.*, 32, 355–363.

FURFEY, P. H., and J. MUEHLENBEIN. 1932. The validity of infant intelligence tests. *J. Genet. Psychol.*, 40, 219–223.

GATES, A. I. 1924. The nature and educational significance of physical status and of mental, physiological, social, and emotional maturity. *J. Educ. Psychol.*, 15, 329–358.

GEE, W., and J. J. CORSON. 1929. Rural depopulation in certain Tidewater and Piedmont areas of Virginia. *Univ. Va. Inst. Res. Soc. Sci. Monogr.*, No. 3.

GESELL, A. 1928. *Infancy and human growth.* New York : Macmillan.

——. 1931. The developmental psychology of twins. In C. Murchison (Ed.), *A handbook of child psychology,* pp. 158–203. Worcester: Clark University Press.

GESELL, A., B. M. CASTNER, H. THOMPSON, and C. S. AMATRUDA. 1939. *Biographies of child development. The mental growth careers of eighty-four infants and children.* New York: Hoeber.

GOODENOUGH, F. L. 1928a. A preliminary report on the effect of nursery school training upon the intelligence test scores of young children. *Yearb. Nat. Soc. Stud. Educ.,* 27(I), 361–369.

——. 1928b. *The Kuhlmann-Binet tests for children of preschool age: A critical study and evaluation.* (*Inst. Child Welfare Monogr. Ser.,* No. 2.) Minneapolis: University of Minnesota Press. Pp. 146.

——. 1940a. New evidence on environmental influence on intelligence. *Yearb. Nat. Soc. Stud. Educ.,* 39(I), 307–365.

——. 1940b. Some special problems of nature-nurture research. *Yearb. Nat. Soc. Stud. Educ.,* 39(I), 367–384.

——. 1940c. Intelligence and month of birth. *Psychol. Bull.,* 37, 442 (abstr.).

GOODENOUGH, F. L., and K. M. MAURER. 1940. The mental development of nursery-school children compared with that of non-nursery-school children. *Yearb. Nat. Soc. Stud. Educ.,* 39(II), 161–178.

GORDON, H. 1923. Mental and scholastic tests among retarded children: An enquiry into the effects of schooling on the various tests. *Educ. Pamphlets, Bd. Educ., London,* No. 44.

GORDON, K. 1918–1920. The influence of heredity on mental ability. *Rep. Children's Dept., State Bd. Control, Calif.*

——. 1919. Report on psychological tests of orphan children. *J. Delinq.,* 4, 46–55.

GREENE, K. B. 1928. The influence of specialized training on tests of general intelligence. *Yearb. Nat. Soc. Stud. Educ.,* 27(I), 421–428.

HALDANE, J. B. S. 1938. *Heredity and politics.* New York: Norton.

HARDY, M. C. 1936. Improvement in educational achievement accompanying a health education program. *J. Educ. Res.,* 30, 110–123.

HARDY, M. C., and C. H. HOEFER. 1936. *Healthy growth: A study of the influence of health education on growth and development of school children.* Chicago: University of Chicago Press.

HEINIS, H. 1926. A personal constant. *J. Educ. Psychol.,* 17, 163–186.

HELD, O. C. 1940. The influence of month of birth on the intelligence of college freshmen. *J. Genet. Psychol.,* 57, 211–217.

HILDRETH, G. H. 1925. The resemblance of siblings in intelligence and achievement. *Teach. Coll. Contr. Educ.,* No. 186.

——. 1926. Stanford-Binet retests of 441 school children. *Ped. Sem.,* 33, 356–386.

HILDRETH, G. H. 1928. The effect of school environment upon Stanford-Binet tests of young children. *Yearb. Nat. Soc. Stud. Educ.,* 27(I) 355–359.

HILGARD, J. R. 1933. The effect of early and delayed practice on memory and motor performances studied by the method of co-twin control. *Genet. Psychol. Monogr.,* 14, 493–567.

HINTON, R. T. 1936. The rôle of the basal metabolic rate in the intelligence of ninety grade school students. *J. Educ. Psychol.,* 27, 546–550.

——. 1939. A further study of the basal metabolic rate in the intelligence of children. *J. Educ. Psychol.,* 30, 309–314.

HIRSCH, N. D. M. 1930a. An experimental study upon three hundred school children over a six-year period. *Genet. Psychol. Monogr.,* 7, No. 6, 487–549.

——. 1930b. *Twins; heredity and environment.* Cambridge: Harvard University Press.

HOEFER, C., and M. C. HARDY. 1928. The influence of improvement in physical condition on intelligence and educational achievement. *Yearb. Nat. Soc. Stud. Educ.,* 27(I), 371–387.

HOGBEN, L. 1933. *Nature and nurture.* London: Allen and Unwin.

HOLLINGWORTH, L. S. 1940. Intelligence as an element in personality. *Yearb. Nat. Soc. Stud. Educ.,* 39(I), 271–275.

HOLLINGWORTH, L. S., and P. WITTY. 1940. Intelligence as related to race. *Yearb. Nat. Soc. Stud. Educ.,* 39(I), 257–269.

HOLZINGER, K. J., and F. N. FREEMAN. 1925. The interpretation of Burt's regression equation. *J. Educ. Psychol.,* 16, 577–582.

HONZIK, M. P. 1938. The constancy of mental test performance during the preschool period. *J. Genet. Psychol.,* 52, 285–302.

HONZIK, M. P., and H. E. JONES. 1937. Mental-physical relationships during the preschool period. *J. Exp. Educ.,* 6, 139–146.

HSIAO, H. H. 1931. The status of the first-born with special reference to intelligence. *Genet. Psychol. Monogr.,* 9, 1–118.

HUNTINGTON, E. 1938. *Season of birth; its relation to human abilities.* New York: Wiley.

JONES, D. C., and A. M. CARR-SAUNDERS. 1927. The relation between intelligence and social status among orphan children. *Brit. J. Psychol.,* 17, 343–364.

JONES, H. E. 1928. A first study of parent-child resemblance in intelligence. *Yearb. Nat. Soc. Stud. Educ.,* 27(I), 61–72.

——. 1929. Homogamy in intellectual abilities. *Amer. J. Sociol.,* 35, 369–382.

——. 1931. The pattern of abilities in juvenile and adult defectives. *Univ. Calif. Publ. Psychol.,* 5, 47–61.

——. 1933a. Order of birth, pp. 551–589. In C. MURCHISON (Ed.), *A handbook of child psy-*

chology. (2d ed., rev.) Worcester: Clark University Press.

JONES, H. E. 1933b. Relationships in physical and mental development. *Rev. Educ. Res., 3,* 150–162; 177–181.

——. 1936. Relationships in physical and mental development. *Rev. Educ. Res., 6,* 102–123; 146–152.

——. 1939. Relationships in physical and mental development. *Rev. Educ. Res., 9,* 91–103; 134–137.

——. 1941. Seasonal variations in IQ. *J. Exp. Educ., 10,* 91–99.

JONES, H. E., *et al.* 1939. Mental and physical development. *Rev. Educ. Res., 9,* 1–141.

JONES, H. E., H. S. CONRAD, and M. B. BLANCHARD. 1932. Environmental handicap in mental-test performance. *Univ. Calif. Publ. Psychol., 5,* No. 3, 63–99.

JONES, H. E., and H. H. HSIAO. 1933. Pregnancy order and early development. *Child Develpm., 4,* 140–147.

JONES, H. E., and A. P. JORGENSEN. 1940. Mental growth as related to nursery-school attendance. *Yearb. Nat. Soc. Stud. Educ., 39* (II), 207–222.

JONES, H. E., and P. T. WILSON. 1932–1933. Reputation differences in like-sex twins. *J. Exp. Educ., 1,* 86–91.

JORDAN, A. M. 1933. Parental occupations and children's intelligence scores. *J. Appl. Psychol., 17,* 103–119.

KATZ, E. 1940. The relationship of IQ to height and weight from three to five years. *J. Genet. Psychol., 57,* 65–82.

KAWIN, E. 1934. *Children of preschool age.* Chicago: University of Chicago Press.

KEENE, C. M., and C. P. STONE. 1937. Mental status as related to puberty praecox. *Psychol. Bull., 34,* 123–133.

KEMPF, G. A., and S. D. COLLINS. 1929. A study of the relation between mental and physical status of children in two counties of Illinois. *U. S. Publ. Health Rep., Wash., 44,* No. 29, 1743–1784.

KLINEBERG, O. 1935. *Negro intelligence and selective migration.* New York: Columbia University Press.

——. 1938. The intelligence of migrants. *Amer. Sociol. Rev., 3,* 218–224.

KOCH, H. L. 1927. Some measurements of a pair of Siamese twins. *J. Comp. Psychol., 7,* 313–333.

KOHNKY, E. 1913. Preliminary study of the effect of dental treatment upon the physical and mental efficiency of school children. *J. Educ. Psychol., 4,* 571–578.

KRUGMAN, M. 1939. Some impressions of the Revised Stanford-Binet Scale. *J. Educ. Psychol., 30,* 594–603.

LAMSON, E. E. 1940. A follow-up study of a group of nursery-school children. *Yearb. Nat. Soc. Stud. Educ., 39* (II), 231–236.

LAUTERBACH, C. E. 1925. Studies in twin resemblance. *Genetics, 10,* 525–568.

LAWRENCE, E. M. 1931. An investigation into the relation between intelligence and inheritance. *Brit. J. Psychol. Monogr. Suppl., 16,* 1–80.

LEAHY, A. M. 1935. Nature-nurture and intelligence. *Genet. Psychol. Monogr., 17,* 236–308.

LEHTOVAARA, A. 1938. *Psychologische Zwillingsuntersuchungen.* Helsinki: Academiae Scientiarum Fennicae.

LEVIT, S. G. 1935. Twin investigations in the U.S.S.R. *Character and Pers., 3,* 188–193.

LITHAUER, D. B., and O. KLINEBERG. 1933. A study of the variation in IQ of a group of dependent children in institution and foster home. *J. Genet. Psychol., 42,* 236–242.

LODGE, T. 1938. Variation in Stanford-Binet IQ's of preschool children according to the months in which the examinations were given. *J. Psychol., 6,* 385–395.

LOEVINGER, J. 1940. Intelligence as related to socioeconomic factors. *Yearb. Nat. Soc. Stud. Educ.,* 39(I), 159–210.

LORGE, I. 1940. Intelligence and personality as revealed in questionnaires and inventories. *Yearb. Nat. Soc. Stud. Educ.,* 39(I), 275–281.

LORIMER, F., and F. OSBORN. 1934. *Dynamics of population.* New York: Macmillan.

LOWE, G. M. 1923. Mental changes after removing tonsils and adenoids. *Psychol. Clin., 15,* 92–100.

LUND, F. H. 1940. Intelligence and emotionality. *Yearb. Nat. Soc. Stud. Educ.,* 39(I), 282–285.

MACMEEKEN, A. M. 1939. *The intelligence of a representative group of Scottish children.* London: University of London Press.

MALLER, J. B. 1933. Vital indices and their relation to psychological and social factors: A study of 310 health areas in New York City with reference to birth rate, death rate, juvenile delinquency, school progress, and intelligence. *Human Biol., 5,* 94–121.

MAULDIN, W. P. 1940. Selective migration from small towns. *Amer. Sociol. Rev., 5,* 748–758.

MAYER, B. A. 1935. Negativistic reactions of preschool children on the new revision of the Stanford-Binet. *J. Genet. Psychol., 46,* 311–334.

MCNEMAR, Q. 1938. Special review: Newman, Freeman and Holzinger's *Twins: A study of heredity and environment. Psychol. Bull., 35,* 237–249.

——. 1940. A critical examination of the University of Iowa studies of environmental influences upon the IQ. *Psychol. Bull., 37,* 63–92.

MILLS, C. A. 1941. Mental and physical development as influenced by season of conception. *Human Biol., 13,* 378–389.

NEFF, W. S. 1938. Socioeconomic status and intelligence: A critical survey. *Psychol. Bull.,* **35,** 727–757.

NELSON, V. L., and T. W. RICHARDS. 1938. Studies in mental development: I. Performance on Gesell items at six months and its predictive value for performance on mental tests at two and three years. *J. Genet. Psychol.,* **52,** 303–325.

——. 1939. Studies in mental development: III. Performance of twelve-months-old children on the Gesell Schedule, and its predictive value for mental status at two and three years. *J. Genet. Psychol.,* **54,** 181–191.

NEMZEK, C. L. 1933. The constancy of the I.Q. *Psychol. Bull.,* **30,** 143–168.

NEWMAN, H. H. 1940. *Multiple human births.* (*Publ. Amer. Ass. Adv. Sci.*) New York: Doubleday-Doran.

NEWMAN, H. H., F. N. FREEMAN, and K. J. HOLZINGER. 1937. *Twins: A study of heredity and environment.* Chicago: University of Chicago Press.

O'HANLON, G. S. A. 1940. An investigation into the relationship between fertility and intelligence. *Brit. J. Educ. Psychol.,* **10,** 196–211.

OLSON, W. C., and B. O. HUGHES. 1940. Subsequent growth of children with and without nursery school experience. *Yearb. Nat. Soc. Stud. Educ.,* 39(II), 237–244.

OUTHIT, M. C. 1933. A study of the resemblance of parents and children in general intelligence. *Arch. Psychol., N. Y.,* No. 149. Pp. 60.

PAGE, J. D. 1941. Twin, sibling, and chance IQ differences. *J. Educ. Psychol.,* **32,** 73–76.

PATERSON, D. G. 1930. *Physique and intellect.* New York: Century.

PEARSON, K. 1903. On the inheritance of the mental and moral characters in man, and its comparison with the inheritance of physical characters. *J. Anthrop. Inst.,* **33,** 179–237.

——. 1910. *Nature and nurture.* (*Eugen. Lab. Lect. Series,* 1910, **6.**) London: Dulau.

——. 1918–1919. The inheritance of psychical characters. *Biometrika,* **12,** 367–372.

PETERSON, J. 1928. Methods of investigating comparative abilities in races. *Ann. Amer. Acad. Sci.,* **140,** 178–185.

PIETER, J. 1939. Intelligence quotient and environment. *Kwart. Psychol.,* **11,** 265–322.

PINTNER, R. 1931. *Intelligence testing: Methods and results.* (2d ed.) New York: Holt.

PINTNER, R., and G. FORLANO. 1933. The influence of month of birth on intelligence quotients. *J. Educ. Psychol.,* **24,** 561–584.

——. 1939. Season of birth and intelligence. *J. Genet. Psychol.,* **54,** 353–358.

PINTNER, R., and J. B. MALLER. 1937. Month of birth and average intelligence among different ethnic groups. *J. Genet. Psychol.,* **50,** 91–107.

POULL, L. E. 1938. The effect of improvemen in nutrition on the mental capacity of youn children. *Child Develpm.,* **9,** 123–126.

REYMERT, M. L. 1940. Relationships betwee menarcheal age, behavior disorders, and intel ligence. *Character and Pers.,* **8,** 292–300.

RICHARDS, T. W., and V. L. NELSON. 1939 Abilities of infants during the first eightee months. *J. Genet. Psychol.,* **55,** 299–318.

RICHARDSON, H. M. 1939. Studies of menta resemblance between husbands and wives an between friends. *Psychol. Bull.,* **36,** 104–12C

RICHARDSON, S. K. 1936. The correlation o intelligence quotients of siblings of the sam chronological age levels. *J. Juv. Res.,* **20** 186–198.

RICHEY, A. 1934. The effects of diseased ton sils and adenoids on intelligence quotients o 204 children. *J. Juv. Res.,* **18,** 1–4.

ROBERTS, J. A. F., R. M. NORMAN, and R. GRIF FITHS. 1938. Studies on a child population IV. The form of the lower end of the fre quency distribution and the fall of low intel ligence quotients with advancing age. *Ann Eugen., Cambridge,* **8,** 319–336.

ROGERS, M. C. 1922. Adenoids and disease tonsils; their effect on general intelligence *Arch. Psychol., N. Y.,* No. 50.

ROSANOFF, A. J., L. M. HARDY, and I. R PLESSET. 1937. The etiology of mental defi ciency with special reference to its occurrenc in twins. *Psychol. Monogr.,* 48, No. 4. Pp 137.

SANDERS, B. S. 1934. *Environment an growth.* Baltimore: Warwick & York.

SANDERS, M. 1932. Similarities in triplets. *J Hered.,* **23,** 225–234.

SANDWICK, R. L. 1920. Correlation of physica health and mental efficiency. *J. Educ. Res. ,* **1,** 199–203.

SANFORD, G. A. 1940. Selective migration ir a rural Alabama community. *Amer. Sociol Rev.,* **5,** 759–766.

SCHLESINGER, E. 1923. Die Kinder des kin dereichen Familien. *Arch. f. Kinderheilk,* **73** 50–68.

SCHWESINGER, G. C. 1933. *Heredity and envi ronment.* New York: Macmillan.

SEVERSON, S. O. 1920–1921. The relation of the anatomical age to the chronological, peda gogical, and mental ages with special refer ence to sex differences. *J. Psycho-Asthenics* **25,** 150–170.

SEYMOUR, A. H., and J. E. F. WHITAKER. 1938 An experiment on nutrition. *Occup. Psychol.* **12,** 215–223.

SHERMAN, M., and T. R. HENRY. 1933. *Hollou folk.* New York: Crowell.

SHERMAN, M., and C. B. KEY. 1932. The intel ligence of isolated mountain children. *Child Develpm.,* **3,** 279–290.

SHIMBERG, M. E. 1929. An investigation into the validity of norms with special reference to urban and rural groups. *Arch. Psychol., N. Y.,* No. 104. Pp. 84.

SHOCK, N. W. 1939*a.* Physiological factors in mental development. *Rev. Educ. Res.,* **9,** 103–110 ; 137–139.

——. 1939*b.* Some psychophysiological relations. *Psychol. Bull.,* **36,** 447–476.

SHOCK, N. W., and H. E. JONES. 1940. The relationship between basal physiological functions and intelligence in adolescents. *J. Educ. Psychol.,* **31,** 369–375.

——. 1941. Mental development and performance as related to physical and physiological factors. *Rev. Educ. Res.,* **11,** 531–552.

SHUTTLEWORTH, F. K. 1935. The nature *versus* nurture problem : II. The contributions of nature and nurture to individual differences in intelligence. *J. Educ. Psychol.,* **26,** 655–681.

SKEELS, H. M. 1936. Mental development of children in foster homes. *J. Genet. Psychol.,* **49,** 91–106.

——. 1940. Some Iowa studies of the mental growth of children in relation to differentials of the environment: A summary. *Yearb. Nat. Soc. Stud. Educ.,* **39**(II), 281–308.

——. 1941. Children with inferior social histories : Their mental development in foster homes. *Psychol. Bull.,* **38,** 594 (abstr.).

SKEELS, H. M., and E. A. FILLMORE. 1937. Mental development of children from underprivileged homes. *J. Genet. Psychol.,* **50,** 427–439.

SKODAK, M. 1939. Children in foster homes : A study of mental development. *Univ. Iowa Stud. Child Welfare,* **16,** No. 1.

SMITH, A. J., and A. M. FIELD. 1926. A study of the effect of nutrition on mental growth. *J. Home Econ.,* **18,** 686–690.

SNYGG, D. 1938. The relation between the intelligence of mothers and of their children living in foster homes. *J. Genet. Psychol.,* **52,** 401–406.

SPEER, G. S. 1940*a.* The mental development of children of feeble-minded and normal mothers. *Yearb. Nat. Soc. Stud. Educ.,* **39**(II), 309–314.

——. 1940*b.* The intelligence of foster children. *J. Genet. Psychol.,* **57,** 49–56.

STARKWEATHER, E. K., and K. E. ROBERTS. 1940. IQ changes occurring during nursery-school attendance at the Merrill-Palmer school. *Yearb. Nat. Soc. Stud. Educ.,* **39**(II), 315–335.

STIPPICH, M. E. 1940. The mental development of children of feeble-minded mothers : A preliminary report. *Yearb. Nat. Soc. Stud. Educ.,* **39**(II), 337–350.

STOCKS, P. 1930–1931. A biometric investigation of twins and their brothers and sisters. *Ann. Eugen., Cambridge,* **4,** 49–108.

STOCKS, P., and M. N. KARN. 1933. A biometric investigation of twins and their broth-

ers and sisters. *Ann. Eugen., Cambridge,* **5,** 1–55.

STODDARD, G. D., *et al.* 1933, 1936. Mental and physical development. *Rev. Educ. Res.,* **3,** 81–181 ; **6,** 1–152.

——. 1940. Intelligence : Its nature and nurture. Part I. Comparative and critical exposition. Part II. Original studies and experiments. *Yearb. Nat. Soc. Stud. Educ.,* **39**(I), 39(II).

STODDARD, G. D., and B. L. WELLMAN. 1940. Environment and the IQ. *Yearb. Nat. Soc. Stud. Educ.,* **39**(I), 405–442.

STOUT, H. G. 1937. Variations of normal children. *J. Exp. Educ.,* **6,** 84–100.

STRAYER, L. C. 1930. Language and growth : The relative efficacy of early and deferred vocabulary training, studied by the method of co-twin control. *Genet. Psychol. Monogr.,* **8,** 209–319.

STROUD, J. B. 1928. A study of the relation of intelligence-test score of public-school children to the economic status of their parents. *J. Genet. Psychol.,* **35,** 105–110.

TERMAN, L. M., *et al.* 1925. *Genetic studies of genius:* Vol. 1. *The mental and physical traits of a thousand gifted children.* Stanford University, Calif. : Stanford University Press.

——. 1928. Nature and nurture : Part I. Their influence upon intelligence : Part II. Their influence upon achievement. *Yearb. Nat. Soc. Stud. Educ.,* 27(I), 27(II).

TERMAN, L. M., and M. A. MERRILL. 1937. *Measuring intelligence.* Boston : Houghton Mifflin.

THOMSON, G. H. 1921. The Northumberland mental tests. *Brit. J. Psychol.,* **12,** 201–222.

THORNDIKE, E. L. 1905. *Measurement of twins.* New York : Science Press. (Also in *J. Phil., Psychol. and Sci. Meth.,* **2,** 547–553.

THORNDIKE, E. L., *et al.* 1927. *The measurement of intelligence.* New York : Teachers College Press, Columbia University.

THORNDIKE, R. L. 1933. The effect of the interval between test and retest on the constancy of the IQ. *J. Educ. Psychol.,* **24,** 543–549.

——. 1940. "Constancy" of the IQ. *Psychol. Bull.,* **37,** 167–186.

TODD, T. W. 1938. Objective ratings of the constitution of the growing child : Based on examination of physical development and mental expansion. *Amer. J. Dis. Child.,* **55,** 149–159.

VAN ALSTYNE, D. 1929. The environment of three-year-old children. Factors related to intelligence and vocabulary tests. *Teach. Coll. Contr. Educ.,* No. 366.

VOAS, W. H. 1940. Does attendance at the Winnetka nursery school tend to raise the IQ? *Yearb. Nat. Soc. Stud. Educ.,* **39**(II), 363–376.

WALLIS, W. D. 1936. Observations on Leahy's *Nature-Nurture and Intelligence*. *J. Genet. Psychol.*, **49**, 315–324.

WELLMAN, B. L. 1934. Growth in intelligence under differing school environments. *J. Exp. Educ.*, **3**, 59–83.

WELLMAN, B. L., H. M. SKEELS, and M. SKODAK. 1940. Review of McNemar's critical examination of Iowa studies. *Psychol. Bull.*, **37**, 93–111.

WELLS, J., and G. ARTHUR. 1939. Effect of foster-home placement on the intelligence ratings of children of feeble-minded parents. *Ment. Hyg., N. Y.*, **23**, 277–285.

WEST, E. D. 1936. Stage of ossification as a measure of growth and its relation to intelligence-test score. *Harv. Teach. Rec.*, **6**, 162–168.

WESTENBERGER, E. J. 1927. A study of the influence of physical defects upon intelligence. *Cath. Univ. Amer. Educ. Res. Bull.*, **2**, No. 9.

WHEELER, L. R. 1932. The intelligence of east Tennessee mountain children. *J. Educ. Psychol.*, **23**, 351–370.

WHIPPLE, G. M. 1928. Nature and nurture: Their influence upon intelligence and upon achievement. (Selected papers read at the Boston meeting of the Nat. Soc. Stud. Educ.) *J. Educ. Psychol.*, **19**, 361–409.

WILLOUGHBY, R. R. 1927. Family similarities in mental-test abilities. *Genet. Psychol. Monogr.* **2**, 235–277.

WILLOUGHBY, R. R. 1928. Family similarities in mental-test abilities. *Yearb. Nat. Soc. Stud Educ.*, **27**(I), 55–59.

WILSON, P. T. 1934. A study of twins with special reference to heredity as a factor determining differences in environment. *Human Biol.*, **6**, 324–354.

WILSON, P. T., and H. E. JONES. 1931. A study of like-sexed twins. I. The vital statistics and familial data of the sample. *Human Biol.*, **3**, 107–132.

WINGFIELD, A. H. 1928. *Twins and orphans. The inheritance of intelligence.* London and Toronto : Dent.

WOODWORTH, R. S. 1941. *Heredity and environment: A critical survey of recently published material on twins and foster children.* New York : Social Science Research Council.

WOOLLEY, H. T. 1925. The validity of standards of mental measurement in young childhood. *Sch. and Soc.*, **21**, 476–482.

WRIGHT, S. 1921. Correlation and causation. *J. Agric. Res.*, **20**, 557–585.

———. 1931. Statistical methods in biology. *J. Amer. Statist. Ass.*, **26**, 155–163.

ZUCK, T. T. 1936. The relation of physical development to mental expansion. *Proc. 3 Inst. Except. Child, Child Res. Clin. Wood Schs*, 6–15.

CHAPTER 12

THE ADOLESCENT [1]

WAYNE DENNIS

Historical Introduction

The earliest recorded scientific views in many fields were those of Aristotle, and this master of observation and compilation did not fail to mention puberty. He gave a description of the pubertal changes and recorded an approximate date for puberty in Greek youth. The following is from *Historia Animalium* (as cited in bibliography):

> When twice seven years old, in most cases, the male begins to engender seed; and at the same time hair appears on the pubes, in like manner so Alcmaeon of Croton remarks, as plants first blossom and then seed. About the same time the voice begins to alter, getting harsher and more uneven, neither shrill as formerly nor deep as afterward, nor yet as any even tone, but like an instrument whose strings are frayed and out of tune; and it is called, by way of by-word, the bleat of the billy-goat (p. 581a).

Aristotle knew that these changes depended upon some activity of the testes, for he noted that if a boy is castrated the pubertal hair does not appear and the voice remains high-pitched (*Historia Animalium*, p. 631b).

Concerning puberty in women, Aristotle wrote:

> At the same age in the female,[2] the breasts swell and the so-called catamenia commence to flow; and this fluid resembles fresh blood. . . . In the majority of cases the catamenia are noticed by the time the breasts have grown to the height of two fingers' breadth. In girls, too, about this time the voice changes to a deeper note.

Of the psychological changes accompanying the physiological phenomena which he described, Aristotle had nothing to say except that girls at this age are in need of constant surveillance because of their developing sexual impulses. It is true that in his *Rhetoric* Aristotle described many traits which he held to be characteristic of youths as contrasted to persons in their prime or in old age. He did not indicate, however, that he believed these attributes to be associated with puberty. In regard to several traits, he stated explicitly that it is the youths' immaturity of experience rather than their physical constitution which explains their propensities. Thus young men are not desirous of gain because they have never experienced want; they do not view things in a bad light by reason of their never having witnessed much depravity; they are credulous because they have not been often deceived; they are

[1] We wish to acknowledge our indebtedness to Dr. R. T. Sollenberger of Mount Holyoke College for many excellent suggestions, particularly in regard to the delimitation of the field. We wish also to express our gratitude to the Institute for Research in the Social Sciences at the University of Virginia for providing clerical assistance and for defraying expenses incurred in consulting the literature.

[2] Prior to this, Hippocrates also named the fourteenth year as the year in which the menarche is most frequently reached.

high-minded because they have not as yet been humbled by the course of life. Some characteristics, on the other hand, although not specifically pubertal, belong to the young by virtue of their biological make-up rather than because of their naïveté. Among such traits are their tendencies to be ardent, passionate, irritable, and sanguine, which are due to the warmer nature of youth.

Aristotle's method was that of generalized observation. We find no instance of the application of a different method to the phenomena of puberty until near the beginning of the nineteenth century, nor do we find before that time any general descriptions of adolescence which are much better than that written by Aristotle. According to Mills (1937), Osiander in 1795 compiled a distribution table for the onset of the menarche, which must be placed as the first detailed investigation of puberty. Buffon (1812) wrote an excellent general account, first published in 1749.

Since 1800 considerable attention has been given to puberty, especially by physicians. In the *Catalog of the Surgeon General's Library* are listed many monographs on puberty which appeared between 1800 and 1850. These consist chiefly of French medical dissertations and, in the main, they are concerned with puberty in women. Typical of these is the volume by Raciborski (1844). Medical, anatomical, and physiological topics are the primary concern, psychological observations remaining secondary and casual. All observations are of the generalized sort.

The lack of reliable facts about puberty which existed one hundred years ago is shown by the statement of Roberton (1832):

> Even the illustrious Boerhave has assured us that there are whole nations whose women are destitute of the catamenia; and that Scythian women approach

nearly to the nature of the male! Haller's opinion is that in the warm regions of Asia the menses appear from the eighth to the tenth year; in Switzerland, Britain, and other equally temperate regions, at the age of twelve or thirteen, and later the further we ascend toward the north.

Roberton in 1831 tabulated the age at menarche of a series of British women. His data had to do with 326 patients in a lying-in hospital, who were questioned concerning the onset of the first mensis. The range of these cases was from the eleventh to the twentieth years, with a median of 13.75 years. This pioneer investigation furnished the basis for a series of comparative studies by the same author.

Roberton was interested in the theory that puberty in tropical countries is extremely early. As noted above, he cited Haller as favoring this view, but Roberton also found this theory espoused by Montesquieu. Roberton attacked the theory in a group of papers (1842, 1843, 1844, 1845b, 1848) in which he showed that the average age at menarche was greater among some groups of tropical and semitropical women than among the women of England. A fuller discussion of this topic must be deferred to a later section. Roberton, by comparing several tabulations, established a research pattern which has yielded a multitude of data relative to the age of female puberty.

These statistical studies, however, did not serve to establish a psychology of adolescence. For the establishment of adolescence as a topic in modern psychology, the chief credit must be given to G. Stanley Hall. As early as 1882 he called attention to what he considered the psychological characteristics of the adolescent and stressed the importance of the study of the period of adolescence. He was the first (1882) to hold that adolescence is an age of special religious impressionability.

As was typical of Hall, he readily succeeded in interesting others in what was of interest to himself, and we find several of his students making early contributions to the subject (Burnham, 1891; Daniels, 1893; Lancaster, 1897; and Starbuck, 1899).

Burnham made use of questionnaire returns and of accounts of personal experiences of "storm and stress" obtained from correspondents. That he was really studying puberty is doubtful in view of the fact that the episodes with which he was concerned occurred in the main when his informants were in college or in theological seminary and seem to have been occasioned by a very narrow religious background in childhood rather than by puberty. He also cited the autobiographical accounts of the youth of several well-known men and thus became one of the first to use autobiographical and diary material in connection with adolescence. Daniel's article described some puberty ceremonies of primitive peoples and portrayed the alleged psychological accompaniments of adolescence. Lancaster continued the questionnaire approach and, in addition, studied numerous biographies in his search for a psychological picture of adolescence.

Starbuck's work is better known than that of any other of Hall's students. His earlier publications in journal form were followed by a book entitled *The Psychology of Religion*. This volume, whose main thesis is that religious conversion is closely related to adolescence, will be reviewed in a later section.

In the later part of the nineteenth century the work of Marro (1897) appeared. Following the earlier tradition, this work was chiefly physiological and anatomical in its emphasis.

The history of the development of a psychology of adolescence now brings us to the publication of Hall's two-volume work, *Adolescence,* which appeared in 1904, although it had been preceded by many years of interest in this subject on Hall's part. Hall's guiding idea, in this as in other fields of genetic psychology, was that of a psychical evolution in the individual which in some way paralleled and, finally, complemented the evolution of the race. Hall's conceptions, and likewise his vocabulary and style, are well illustrated by the following paragraph:

> The individual in a general way repeats the history of its species, passing slowly from the protozoan to the metazoan stage, so that we have all traversed in our own bodies ameboid, piscian, amphibian, anthropoid, ethnoid, and we know not how many intercalary stages of ascent. How these lines of heredity and growth along which the many thousand species, extant and extinct, these viatica of the holy spirit of life, the consummate products of millennia of the slow travail of evolution, have been unfolded, we know scarcely more than we do what has been the impelling force, or will to live, which seems so inexhaustible and insistent (1904, Vol. I, p. 2).

The idea of unraveling the course of evolution by studying the development of the individual proved wonderfully stimulating to Hall and led him to indulge in profuse theorizing. In Hall's evolutionary scheme, the adolescent had his appropriate place. Whereas the child harks back to a remote past of the race,

> . . . the adolescent is neo-atavistic, and in him the later acquisitions of the race slowly become prepotent. Development [in adolescence] is less gradual and more saltatory, suggestive of some ancient period of storm and stress when old moorings were broken and a higher level attained.

We need not present here the reasons why the theory of recapitulation has been, to a large extent, abandoned. But the relinquishment of this approach by no means reduced Hall's work to nothing. The recapitulatory viewpoint served as a thread on which to string a multitude of data. When the thread is removed, the facts remain, although, to be sure, their arrangement becomes amorphous. Hall's assemblage of data on the period of youth was monumental, and, although many data have accumulated since 1904, no later writer has equaled Hall in the marshaling of material on the adolescent period. Hall dealt with the growth of many parts of the body, with adolescent diseases, with juvenile delinquency, with sexual development, with periodicity, with pubertal changes in the voice and in the senses, with the instincts of adolescence, with religious conversion, with the adolescent feelings toward nature, with primitive public initiations, and with what he called the adolescent races. He also had a chapter on education during adolescence, with a special chapter on the education of the adolescent girl. Nor was his exposition of these topics perfunctory; it was detailed and involved. Yet Hall's completeness was somewhat like the completeness of an inventory. It served the purpose of taking stock of our knowledge; it did not serve to establish any causal connections between so-called adolescent behavior and any biological phenomena. It did not pose clear-cut experimental problems nor did it stimulate well-directed research.

Hall's volumes, however, set the pattern for later books on the psychology of adolescence. Nearly all the books since 1904, many of which were written by Hall's students, have dealt with the same list of topics with which Hall was concerned, but in a less vigorous, less inspired, and less lofty manner.

The data which have been gathered since the publication of Hall's treatment we shall review in subsequent sections. To present the material here in chronological order would entail excessive duplication, but in the separate sections we shall pay some attention to the sequence in which these studies have appeared. We turn first, however, to a consideration of the various meanings attached to the term *the psychology of adolescence*.

Definition of the Field

The psychology of adolescence is often treated as the psychology of the teen age, or at least as the psychology of a certain age period. When adolescence is defined in the literature as an age period, its definition is vague and without general agreement. Burnham's questionnaire study (1891) asked specifically about phenomena appearing between the ages of 12 and 17. Hall (1882), however, referred to adolescence as lasting until the twenty-fourth or twenty-fifth year.

The classification of psychological facts may, of course, proceed in a variety of ways, and we cannot deny to another the privilege of dealing with a certain decade of life if he chooses. However, we see no more reasonableness in treating separately the psychology of the teen age than we do in considering separately the psychology of the twenties, the psychology of the forties, etc. All such treatments might have essentially the same table of contents since all, or nearly all, human responses can occur in any decade after the period of early childhood. Books on the psychology of adolescence frequently deal with leadership, yet it is clear that leadership can be studied at any age. So with religion, with intelligence, with emotional stability, with neuroticism, and a variety of topics which are often treated in books on the second decade of life.

Another tendency of recent years is to assert that adolescence is a social phenomenon (Reuter, Foster, Mead, *et al.*, 1936; Reuter, 1937). If this means that biological changes have nothing to do with adolescent behavior, the statement is a radical one which goes far beyond the current evidence. If, on the other hand, it means that behavior is determined not only by biological status but also by the society in which the organism is found, the view is, of course, incontrovertible. Neither the organism nor its environment can be ignored. When social influences are adequately recognized, the organism still constitutes an important variable. This conception has recently been stated in excellent form by Sollenberger (1939a). To those who are chiefly interested in the adjustment of young people to the rôles imposed upon them by society and scarcely concerned with the bearing of physiological status upon this adjustment, we suggest that for their subject matter the term social psychology of youth be employed. The present use of the term *adolescence* to cover these phenomena is not in accord with the older use of the term, and the double usage leads to confusion. The statement that adolescence is a social phenomenon is a paradox which could have arisen only by a process of redefinition.

In contrast to the age distinctions and social distinctions mentioned above, some "studies" of adolescence prove to be concerned solely with high school pupils. When such is the case, the subjects with which the psychologist is dealing form neither an age group, a social group, nor a physiological group. They constitute a section of the student population of a particular nation, a population segment heterogeneous in age, pubertal status, and in almost every respect except academic classification. On various grounds, a separate treatment of high school students is advantageous. However, to call a study of high school pupils, whose pubertal status the investigator does not mention, an investigation of adolescence is to misrepre-

sent greatly the nature of the research. A similar situation exists in many textbooks entitled "the psychology of adolescence." These are primarily treatises on the psychology of secondary education, or on the handling of youth, whose titles have a physiological and sexual connotation which is not appropriate to their contents.

Adolescence originally had a meaning which was biological, not temporal, social, or educational. We believe that it is desirable to maintain certain distinctions between the psychology of age periods, the social psychology of youth, the educational psychology of the high school pupil, and the psychology of adolescence. The central interest of the psychology of adolescence, as we conceive it, is to portray the effects of biological adolescence upon the behavior of the individual. Its aim is to examine a certain set of mental-physical correlations, not to treat those aspects of behavior which, although present in adolescents, are also present to the same degree in all other biologically defined classes of subjects.

Using the definition of the psychology of the adolescent which we have indicated above, we shall, in the remainder of this chapter, deal first with the biological changes of adolescence, which must be known before psychological phenomena can be related to them. Later we shall examine the behavioral accompaniments of these biological phenomena in so far as we know these accompaniments at the present time.

The Biological Changes of Adolescence

Chief Landmarks. The changes which lead to maturity are far from being ascertained with completeness. It seems probable that the sequence of these changes is roughly the same in all individuals, but it is not invariable. As a landmark in the study of adolescence, the menarche of the girl is of course the most outstanding, and all other changes are usually located with reference to this event, those coming before the menarche being called prepubertal or premenarcheal and those subsequent to it being referred to as postpubertal or postmenarcheal.

In boys no such distinct event occurs, but criteria employed by Crampton (1908a, 1908b) have gained wide acceptance, and will be employed here. They refer to the maturity of the pubic hair. Boys who have no pigmented pubic hair are classified as prepubertal, those with pigmented but straight pubic hair as pubescent, and those whose pubic hair is not only pigmented but in addition has attained the typical twist or kink are called postpubertal.

The use of a single line of demarcation in describing the maturity of girls and of two dividing lines in estimating the maturity of boys is far from an ideal method. Undoubtedly many other changes occur during adolescence. The menarche of the girl and the appearance of pubic hair in the boy may be found eventually to be relatively unimportant events in the developmental process. Nevertheless, nearly all studies of behavior which have related behavior to some stage of adolescence have chosen to make use of the criteria which have been described above. We shall not be misunderstood, then, if we use the terms prepubertal and postpubertal, prepubescent and postpubescent in this review in the limited sense in which they have been defined, acknowledging that future efforts should be directed toward attaining finer distinctions. Puberty, as defined here, is equivalent to the menarche in the girl and to the appearance of the first pigmented pubic hair in the boy. In using these terms, there is no assumption that these steps, as defined, mark equivalent stages in male and female development.

Prepubertal Acceleration in Growth.
Numerous investigators have shown that puberty is preceded by a period of rapid growth. We are unable to name the first investigator to record evidence on this point; it has, of course, been a matter of common observation. Buffon showed a clear recognition of the relation of puberty to growth in the following passages (*Natural History of Man*, 1812):

> The growth of the body, in length, generally terminates at the age of puberty. Before this period, young people commonly shoot up several inches in a short time. . . . At the age of puberty, or a few years after it, the human body attains its full stature. The growth of some persons stops at the fourteenth or fifteenth year; in others, it continues until they arrive at twenty-two or twenty-three years (pp. 151, 172).

Among the early anthropometric studies which yielded evidence of an acceleration in growth in height and weight just before puberty was that of Bowditch (1891). He found that this acceleration comes at an earlier period in large children than it does in small children. Crampton (1908a) recorded differences in weight and height between prepubertal and postpubertal boys of the same age. For instance, in the age group from 15½ to 16 years he found postpubertal boys to be 34 per cent heavier than prepubertal boys. He reported that he found no postpubertal boys who weighed less than 30 kilos and no boys who weighed above 55 kilos who were still prepubertal. Similar data for height were obtained. There are differences in height and weight between prepubertal and pubescent boys and between pubescent and postpubertal boys as well as between the first and third stages. Girls show differences comparable to those described for boys. Carey (1935), Dimock (1937), Stone and Barker (1937a), Shuttleworth (1937, 1938b, 1939), as well as others, have fully verified the earlier findings.

Baldwin (1916) corroborated the findings of Bowditch, showing that children who mature early are heavier and taller than children who mature late, even in the age period of 8 to 10 years, before other signs of puberty have appeared. Richey (1931) extended this type of study downward to the age of 6 years, and showed that even at that period boys and girls who will mature early on the average are heavier and taller than those who will mature at a late age. This difference exists between groups at all ages from 6 years until both of the groups which are being compared approximate adult stature. In making these comparisons, Richey divided his subjects into three groups, namely, those reaching puberty before the fourteenth year, those reaching puberty in the fourteenth and fifteenth years, and those reaching puberty after the fifteenth year. Shuttleworth (1939) also found consistent differences between early-maturing and late-maturing children from 6 years of age onward. No one has, as yet, obtained data with reference to whether or not these differences appear before 6 years of age. It is worthy of note that postpubescent individuals do not suddenly become superior in bodily measurements to their later-maturing associates at puberty but have, as a rule, been superior for several years.

Boas (1932), by repeated measurements upon the same individuals, found that the moment of most rapid growth somewhat preceded the menarche, the most rapid increase in height occurring usually about one year before the establishment of menstruation. Shuttleworth (1939) also reported that the most rapid growth took place before the onset of the menses. He discovered a substantial correlation between the period of most rapid increase in height and the age at menarche, the r being .754 in one group of 174 cases and .702 in another group of 246 cases.

At this point we may raise the question as to whether the early-maturing individuals merely attain adult dimensions at an earlier age or whether they reach adult dimensions differing from those of late-maturing persons. The answer to this question is still somewhat uncertain, since but few subjects have been followed sufficiently long to assure that maximum height has been reached. Barker and Stone (1936) studied college girls of ages 17 to 21. In this period they found early-maturing girls to be somewhat shorter than late-maturing girls. At the college level, girls who reached the menarche at or before 11 years averaged one inch shorter than girls who reached puberty at 15 years. These investigators found that early-maturing girls tended toward the pyknic type, the late-maturing girls tended toward the leptosome body build. However, Viteles (1929) in examining 236 first-year normal school girls found no correlation between height and weight and the age at menarche. Richey (1931) likewise found no significant differences between the average heights of groups of different menarcheal ages, and no significant differences in boys of different pubertal ages. Boas (1930) observed that, although persons differ greatly in the age at which maximum growth is achieved, the time of maximum growth appears to have little or no effect upon adult stature.

The investigations of Flory (1935) and of Shuttleworth (1937, 1939) have to do with the relation of various anatomical measurements, other than height, to the menarche. Flory reported correlations between various measures taken on 80 girls at 9, 10, 11, and 12 years and the age at the onset of menses. Every characteristic with which he deals is correlated with the age at which the menarche was reached. Most of the correlations are between .20

and .50, but some are higher. Age at menarche correlated to the extent of .57 with iliac width at 12 years, .58 with trochanteric width at 12 years, and .64 with the skeletal age at 11 years. The highest correlation, .76, was with age at the appearance of the sesamoid on the distal end of the first metacarpal. All cases reached puberty within the 24 months following the appearance of the sesamoid.

Secondary Sex Characteristics. We may inquire next concerning the position in the adolescent sequence of changes in pubic and axillary hair in both sexes, of facial hair in the male, and of breast development in the female. Although many general statements have been made, carefully recorded data are few. Marro's data (1897) on boys, concerning the percentage of cases at each age which show various characteristics, tend to indicate that in general pubic hair appears before the axillary and the axillary before the labial. However, different degrees of hirsutal development are not distinguished. H. B. Pryor (1936) in a serial study of 74 girls reported upon the status of various secondary sex characteristics at the time of the menarche. The traits which were observed were the presence of axillary hair and of pubic hair and enlargement of the breasts and of the thyroid gland. Considerable variation was noted in the status of each of these characteristics at the time the first menses took place. However, the most frequent conditions at puberty were as follows: the pubic hair in 64 per cent of the cases was fully pigmented and wavy but the terminals were sparse; the axillary hair was only 5–10 mm. in length in the majority of cases (54 per cent); the breasts in 72 per cent of the cases exhibited adipose tissue and protrusion of the areola. Although many general statements concerning the order of development of the female secondary sexual characteristics are

to be found in the literature, to our knowledge Pryor's study is the only observational report to date. Her study, as we have seen, does not reveal the sequence of changes, since it deals only with those conditions which are concomitants of the menarche.

Endocrine Changes and Physiological Changes. It has long been recognized that pubertal phenomena are somehow related to the gonads, since persons who are castrated before maturity do not undergo puberty. Furthermore, it has been surmised that the influence of the gonads is exerted by means of secretions which are carried throughout the body, and hence are able to influence the entire organism. The identification of the specific sex hormones, their extraction, their assay, and their synthesis, on the other hand, are events which have occurred only in recent years. Despite the recency of this work, its volume is tremendous, and the investigation of sex hormones is going on apace at the present time. The survey by Allen, Danforth, and Doisy (1939) runs into thirteen hundred pages, and every new issue of physiological and endocrinological journals sees the publication of further facts.

As yet the preponderant part of such investigations is concerned with animal subjects, whose comparability to man requires testing. When researches dealing with man are reported, they prove, thus far, to be concerned in almost all cases with adult subjects. It is natural that investigators should first study sex hormones where they are most certain to be found—in the mature individual. The developmental process, much as it interests us, will be investigated only after the sex hormones of the adult are well understood. The index of the comprehensive survey of Allen, Danforth, and Doisy shows only one reference to puberty. A few brief reports on the hormone status of children have appeared since the publication of the review mentioned above.

Dorfman, Greulich, and Solomon (1937) performed sex hormone assays by the method of Dorfman and Greulich (1937) on the urine of 18 boys and 5 girls and found that the hormone status, in this limited number of cases, appeared to be closely related to the physical maturity of the subjects. Immature boys of 13 years evidenced little hormone activity, whereas several mature boys of the same age possessed a hormone activity nearly as great as that of normal men. Nathanson, Towne, and Aub (1939) also found androgenic substances to be present in very small quantities in immature boys. Rush, Bilderback, Slocum, and Rogers (1937) assayed the sex hormones of two cases of precocious puberty in boys, one 4 and the other 8 years of age. These boys, in contrast to normal children, exhibited a considerable amount of hormone activity.

These preliminary studies are not adequate to show whether the hormone content increases slowly or suddenly at puberty, nor do they indicate the relation between the onset of androgens and estrogens and the time of appearance of the skeletal, vocal, hirsutal, and other features of puberty. Knowledge of puberty will be greatly extended by the application of already available endocrinological techniques of investigation to the problems of pubertal development.

A number of investigators (Topper and Mulier, 1932; Bruen, 1933; Molitch and Cousins, 1934) have found irregularities in the basal metabolic rate at roughly the period of puberty. The basal metabolic rate decreases from childhood to maturity, but this decrease is arrested during adolescence. Topper and Mulier (1932) find that this relative increase in basal metabolic rate is, for girls, most pronounced from 1 to 8 months before the menarche.

The metabolic irregularity is not always associated with an increase in the size of the thyroid, although it has been shown that the thyroid gland commonly enlarges at about the time of the menarche.

Burlage (1923) found that postpubescent girls have a higher average systolic blood pressure than do prepubescent girls of the same age. This difference, however, was discovered to be associated with weight rather than with puberty *per se*, for when postpubescent and prepubescent girls were matched for weight the difference no longer appeared.

Age at Menarche. Having now examined some of the biological changes of adolescence and their relation to puberty, we may now ask at what time in the life of the individual puberty is likely to occur. We shall review the data on girls first, turning later to the age of puberty in boys.

Every study, without exception, reveals very great variation in the age at which individual women reach puberty. The limits of the variation are extraordinarily great. There are some cases of extremely precocious puberty in which menstruation occurs regularly from birth. On the other hand, one finds instances in which the menses do not appear until the third or fourth decade. Both sorts of cases, however, are often caused by some pathological condition, and do not represent merely the extremes of a normal distribution. Women of excellent health may reach puberty as early as the ninth year and as late as the twentieth. This fact renders utterly unsound the division of the decade from the tenth to the twentieth years into early, middle, and late adolescence on a purely chronological basis. Some girls are in late adolescence at 10 years of age; some are in early adolescence at 20 years. This fact again reminds us that investigations whose subjects are described only in terms of chronological age cannot be classified as studies of adolescence.

An immense body of data is extant on the average age at menarche of women of different races, climates, occupational classes, etc. These observations establish the fact that groups often differ in central tendency but the causes of the differences for the most part are unknown. We cannot, in the present connection, discuss causes, but shall be content merely to display some of the differences.

To begin with the United States, we should call attention to the collection of data from various sources assembled by Engelmann (1901). He found the average menarcheal age of 1360 American college women to be 13.50 years. The average figure for 5552 American women of all classes was 14.20. Most American averages lie between the two just cited. Gould and Gould (1932) found the average menarcheal age of 680 students of Louisiana State University and of Sophie Newcomb College to be 13.61 years. Lintz and Markow (1923), taking 800 consecutive cases from private practice, arrived at the figure of 13.50 years. Boas (1932) reported an average of 13.1 years for students of Horace Mann School.

Different racial groups in America appear not to differ appreciably. Mills and Ogle (1936) reported an average of 13.6 years for the Negroes of Cincinnati and Richmond. Engelmann, writing in 1901, presented an average of 14.05 for 2339 Negroes living farther south. Boas (1932) found Jewish and non-Jewish students of the Horace Mann School to have the same average menarcheal age, 13.1 years.

American women attain puberty at as early a period as do any other social or national groups which have been studied. Women of tropical and subtropical countries mature no earlier than American women. Mills (1937), summarizing recent data, reports the following averages: for white Brazilians, 14.47 years; for white Cubans, 13.87 years; for Hindu women of Calcutta, 14.12 years. Curjel (1920) found for both Moslem and Hindu women of India an average of 13.6 years. We have noted that Roberton (1845b) showed that the view that puberty is unusually precocious in the tropics is false.

The evidence for northern European countries shows that in these regions the menarche occurs somewhat later than in America, southern Europe, and the tropics. Again taking our data from Mills's recent summary (1937), we cite the following means: for Edinburgh women, 15.04 years; for Norwegian women, 14.5 years; for Finnish women, 15.95 years; for Russian women, 15.85 years. The two latter groups are retarded approximately two years in relation to American standards.

Many Chinese groups are late in reaching puberty. Mondière (1880) found the average menarcheal age of all his groups to be beyond 16 years. Mills (1937) reported 16.65 years as the average for Formosa Chinese. Westbrook, Lai, and Hsiao (1934) reported, however, for *college students* in Shanghai and Wuchang an average of 13.56 years, a result which suggests that the menarche may be greatly influenced by environmental (probably nutritional) factors.

Because of their far northern location, interest has been directed to the menarcheal age of Eskimo women. Roberton (1845a) reported an average of 15.94 years for 16 Labrador Eskimos; Engelmann (1901) published an average of 16.0 for 100 Greenland Eskimos.

Some evidence indicates that within the past century the average menarcheal age has decreased in several countries. Mills (1937) has called attention to the fact that Husemann in 1868 found an average menarcheal age of 16.1 for Norwegian women, whereas Skerlj in 1935 obtained a mean of 14.5 years. Schlichting at Munich in 1864, according to Mills (1937), recorded an average of 16.3 years, whereas in 1880, only sixteen years later, the same investigator obtained 15.4 years as an average for the same city. Again, Mills has shown that Osiander (1795) obtained for South Germany a record of 16.6 years, whereas Dieterich in 1920 (reported by Mills, 1937) recorded a result of 14.5 years from the same region. It will be seen that the difference is 2.1 years. Bolk (1923) found for Dutch women born before 1880 a menarcheal age approximately one year greater than that reported by their daughters.

Within the United States also the average age of menarche may be decreasing. Gould and Gould (1932) found that, whereas the records of 680 Louisiana college women yielded a mean of 13.61 years, their mothers' average was 13.99 years. Mills (1937) in 1935 determined menarcheal ages for women then in different decades of life, from age 20 to age 90. The average menarcheal age of women over 60 years of age was one year greater than that of women who were in their twenties. (The number of cases is such that all the differences to which we have referred in the preceding paragraphs are highly significant.) Such differences may, of course, be explained otherwise than as a result of a change in the age at maturity. One interpretation which suggests itself is that older women may yield higher menarcheal ages through some constant error of memory. Another possibility of interpretation is a differential mortality rate for early-maturing and late-maturing women. If late-maturing women should live longer, this fact would account for the relatively great menarcheal ages of the women who were questioned between the sixtieth and the ninetieth years. Mills (1937) has

taken no cognizance of these alternative explanations of his results.

However, the possibility that a change in the onset of puberty has occurred or will occur deserves serious attention, since a decrease in the age of puberty would seem to require some readjustment of social standards for adolescents, or else demand of them a longer period of sexual deprivation than was required in former times. The differences in menarcheal ages between countries, and between social classes, may also be important from the point of view of what the sexual taboos demand of the individual.

Although we cannot discuss in full the factors which may influence the onset of puberty, we wish to mention the very interesting study of Dworzak (1936), which shows that girls who have had rickets reach the menarche on the average two years later than do those who have been free of rickets. The great decrease in rickets in the past century, due to advances in medical knowledge, is of course well known, and may have led to a change in the average menarcheal age.

Age of Puberty in Boys. Information concerning the onset of any phase of adolescence in boys is extremely scanty in comparison with reports on the menarche of girls. No doubt this situation arises because no aspect of the boy's adolescence is so precipitous or so memorable as is the beginning of menstruation for the girl. Whereas most of the studies of the menarche in girls have been questionnaire studies, few of the investigations of puberty in boys have made use of this method. An exception is the work of Starbuck (1899), who asked 96 men to date their puberty. One wonders to what phenomenon the results refer; nevertheless, Starbuck reported an average of 15.6 years, whereas the same question presented by Starbuck to 119 women resulted in an average of 13.8 years.

Westbrook, Lai, and Hsiao (1934) were more specific in their questionnaire study of adolescence in 1000 Chinese college students. We reproduce the author's averages: for change of voice, 15.2 years; for the appearance of pubic hair, 15.24 years; for the first emission, 15.48 years; for the appearance of axillary hair, 16.01 years. It is obvious that such data must be subject to serious memory errors.

We have noted that it is customary to divide boys into three classes by means of an examination of the pubic hair. Those having no pubic hair or colorless hair are classified as prepubescent, those with pigmented straight hair as pubescent, and those with pigmented kinky hair as postpubescent. Crampton (1908b) believed that the pubescent condition lasts only about six months. One way in which the data of the examinations have been treated has been to determine the average age of those individuals who were found to be pubescent. Crampton (1908b) found the average age of his pubescent subjects (New York City) to be 13.4 years; Baldwin (1916) arrived at an average of 14.4 for his urban subjects and 13.9 for his rural subjects; Dimock (1937) obtained a mean of 13.08. The last two averages cited above were based on more than 1000 cases; the first two were derived from more than 3000 cases each. Considering the subjective factors in the diagnosis of pubescence, the agreement among the studies seems good. Dimock (1937) noted that his average is the lowest yet obtained, and called attention to the fact that this agrees with the trend toward earlier puberty in girls, but he was not willing to conclude that the difference between his study and those of Crampton and Baldwin represented anything other than a difference in the subjective standards of the examiners.

These investigations, like the studies of the age at menarche, reveal a wide variation in the onset of puberty. Crampton's range for pubescence was from 12 to 17.5 years; Dimock's was from 10 to 15 years. Further perusal of Dimock's data shows even more striking contrasts. One of his subjects was postpubescent at 10 years, two were prepubescent at 15 years.

If the pigmentation of the pubic hair in boys is really equivalent to the menarche in girls, it would appear that the two sexes reach comparable stages of adolescence at approximately the same age. This would be contrary to the usual view that boys, in a general way, mature later than girls. There is, however, no reason for claiming that the two conventional signs of puberty are really homologous. The popular impression of the relative maturity of boys and girls probably derives from their height and weight. Girls attain the adult standards of height and weight earlier than boys. Furthermore, Shuttleworth (1939) has found that boys, on the average, reach the period of most rapid growth about two years later than do girls. This difference also upholds the general belief in the earlier maturity of girls.

Adolescent Sterility. Much interest attaches to the question of the age of nubility; that is, the age at which reproduction becomes possible. Concerning boys, little evidence is at hand. Crampton (1908b) stated in a footnote that microscopical examination of secretion (presumably of emissions, but he does not so state) shows that well-formed and motile spermatozoa make their appearance in the months of transition to postpubescence. It is not clear that this brief statement was based upon sufficient evidence. Baldwin (1928) described a preliminary attempt to find the relation between various adolescent features and the appearance of sperm in urine collected upon arising in the morning, but the study was not carried far enough to determine the relationships which it was desired to examine. It is interesting to note, especially in view of the recent literature on adolescent sterility, that Aristotle (*Historia Animalium*, p. 582a) made the flat statement that in boys the seminal discharge is infertile until the individual is twenty-one years of age. Although a statement which allows so little individual variation is clearly erroneous, Aristotle's belief that a period of infertility follows puberty may be correct. Evidence on the fertility of boys is, however, difficult to obtain, whereas pregnancy in the girl renders evidence of feminine fertility more readily obtainable.

As noted above, considerable attention has been attracted recently to the view that girls do not become fertile immediately following the menarche. The period between the menarche and the onset of fertility has been called the period of adolescent sterility (Hartman, 1931). Ashley-Montagu (1939) has summarized a convincing array of evidence for the existence of adolescent sterility in man as well as in animals. This author is in error, however, in crediting the first evidence for adolescent sterility in women to Waddy (1846). Roberton, who has been previously mentioned, in 1845 reported data on the age at menarche of 71 Hindu women of Bangalore, India. Hindu girls are almost always married before puberty, and usually go to live with their husbands as soon as the menarche occurs, although there are some exceptions. Roberton reported for each woman the time at which the marriage was consummated as well as the age at menarche. In 64 of the 71 cases the interval between these two events was no greater than a year, and in the majority of the instances the period was negligible. Nevertheless, the average time elapsing between the menarche and the age at which the first conception occurred for the 68 who had borne children before the time of the

report was two years and seven months. In 1846 Roberton published similar records for Bombay women. The evidence reviewed by Ashley-Montagu is of the same character. For instance, Mondière (1880) [1] showed that among Chinese women, who also begin to live with their husbands at puberty, the average period elapsing between the menarche and the first pregnancy was about three years. These observations are borne out by the testimony of anthropologists, including Malinowski (1929), who reported that in a primitive society in which adolescent promiscuity is common pregnancy is rare until several years after the menarche.

Behavioral Phenomena Associated with Normal Puberty

Sex Behavior. It is not an uncommon notion that erotic feelings and sexual behavior begin suddenly at about the time of puberty. Although scientific data on human sexual development are notably scanty,[2] still they are sufficient to show that sexual behavior is not absent in childhood. As Willoughby (1937) has said in an excellent review of sexuality in the second decade of life, "There is abundant evidence that adolescence does not initiate, but only intensifies, specifically sexual behavior." Some of the best material on human sexual development is contained in

[1] Ashley-Montagu (1939) credits Mondière (1880) with the first study of the reproductive life of non-European women. We should like to call attention to the fact that Roberton nearly forty years earlier reported on various aspects of the reproductive life of the Hindus (1845b), of the Negroes (1842), and the Eskimos (1845a).

[2] The literature on sex drive has been reviewed recently by Stone (1939). The review shows how little information we possess concerning human sex drive as compared with a vast array of observational and experimental data on animals. Stone is strongly in favor of attempting to devise ways of supplementing the usual questionnaire method in the study of human sexual attitudes, feelings, etc.

the collection of case histories presented by Ellis (1936, Vol. 1, pp. 278–341, Vol. 2, Pt. I, 223–259, Vol. 2, Pt. II, 92–200). Unfortunately, case histories do not lend themselves readily to review. These documents, which are in the nature of sexual autobiographies, show that sexual interests and other sexual manifestations in many cases do appear before puberty. Bell (1902) and Moll (1912) also provided material to support this view.

It is in the earliest and least self-conscious period that direct observation can be applied most easily. Evidence exists that sexual behavior may occur within the first year of life. Townsend (1896) has described five cases of masturbation, some with apparent orgasm, beginning within the first year. In these instances, there were no physical precocity and no abnormalities of the genitals. Townsend recorded a further case, cited by Ellis (1936, Vol. 1), as follows:

> An infant, eight months old, would cross her right thigh over the left, close her eyes and clench her fists; after a minute or two there would be complete relaxation, with sweating and redness of face; this would occur about once a week or oftener; the child was quite healthy, with no abnormal condition of the genital organs.

The existence of such cases indicates the need of study directed at finding the rôle which maturity plays in sexual development.

Bender and Blau (1937) have presented a report of 16 children admitted consecutively to the children's ward of a hospital after sexual relations with adults. There were 11 girls and 5 boys, all between 5 and 12 years of age and all prepubescent. In several instances the children were active partners in a continuing sexual relationship. Their emotional reactions were in general free of guilt and fear; the subjects as a whole were children of charming personality. These facts, like many other previously reviewed, raise seriously the question of the exact relationship of puberty to the development of sexual responses. They also throw very grave doubts upon the Freudian theory (see E. Jones, 1922–1923) that the period from 5 to 10 years of age is a latent period in sexual development, since we have seen evidence for the presence of sexual behavior within that period.

Willoughby (1937), in summarizing the data on masturbation, has stated that it is not clear what influence puberty exercises over autoerotic practices, but it is certain that these practices frequently begin before puberty. Of 320 children between 1 and 14 years of age who were brought to a general pediatric clinic, Huschka (1938) reported that 142 were known to have masturbated. Of these, 54 per cent began to masturbate before 5 years of age. Davis (1929), in a questionnaire study of college women, received returns which showed that, of those who reported the practice of masturbation at some time, 40 per cent stated that it was indulged in before 10 years of age. This age must have been prepubertal in nearly all instances. Harvey (1932) has treated the data of numerous investigators so as to exhibit the percentage of male and female respondents to questionnaires who had practiced masturbation prior to 12, 15, 18, 21, and 24 years of age. Among boys and girls alike, 15 per cent of those to whom the data refer (the subjects were chiefly of superior intelligence and of the higher economic classes) reported autoerotic behavior before 12 years. Some of these must have been prepubescent at the time the practices began; how many were so, the data do not show. After 12 years, there is a marked increase in frequency of masturbation, which is much greater for boys than for girls. Between the ages of 12 and 18, the frequency for boys increases from 15 per cent to 75 per cent. However, we do not know whether those who matured earliest were those who began masturbation first.

Few data exist regarding the percentage of cases of prepubertal masturbation in which the orgasm is experienced or the frequency with which the orgasm is reached. From Davis' (1929) study of college women it is found that, of those who practiced masturbation at some period, a few experienced the orgasm before 10 years of age, whereas many first experienced it in the twenties. Again, the relation of sexual manifestations to puberty is far from clear.

Ellis (1936, Vol. 1, p. 215) presented a report on the first appearance of sexual feeling in 12 women about whom he felt that his information was precise. In 2 of the women, sexual feeling occurred spontaneously at about 7 or 8 years, but complete orgasm was experienced only some years after puberty. In 5 of them, sexual feeling appeared spontaneously soon after puberty. In another case, sexual feeling also was felt soon after puberty; however, this was not a spontaneous experience but a result of her suitor's advances. In contrast to the 8 who had experienced sexual feelings by the time of early postpubescence, the remaining 4 women did not have this experience until they were past the twenty-fifth year. Twelve cases are, of course, a very small sample, but they do indicate that sexual feelings are not an invariable accompaniment of puberty. In G. V. N. Hamilton's study (1929) of 100 women, he asked whether or not they recalled any change in sex feeling in connection with the first menstruation. Ninety-three per cent of the subjects answered in the negative.

One of the most objective phenomena which might be related to other adolescent changes is nocturnal emissions. Yet even here an attempt to correlate sexual phenomena with physiological development is lacking. Willoughby (1937) has reviewed data which show the proportion of boys of various ages who have experienced nocturnal emissions, but no observer has determined the degree to which the nocturnal emissions tend to be associated with age of maximum growth, with change of voice, with the appearance of pubic hair, or any other pubertal phenomenon. Gualino (1907), with 100 Italian professional men subjects, obtained reminiscent accounts of the erotic dreams which sometimes accompany nocturnal emissions. All his subjects had had erotic dreams by the age of 17. For 37 of them, erotic dreams were the first erotic experiences; that is, neither masturbation nor intercourse had preceded the spontaneous sex experience. Of Hamilton's 100 male subjects, 51 had erotic dreams before 15 years, 81 before 20 years. Here again there are no data which make it possible to find the place of erotic dreams in the adolescent sequence. In reference to erotic dreams with orgasm in women, Ellis (1936, Vol. 1, p. 198) has made the statement that they rarely occur in women who have not experienced coitus. The survey made by G. V. N. Hamilton (1929) revealed that only 4 women in 100 had orgastic dreams before the age of 20 years. This feature of female sexual life would seem, therefore, to be decidedly postpubertal in its appearance.

Heterosexual relations occasionally occur before puberty. In lower-class American Negroes, Childers (1936) has noted the frequent occurrence of sex activities among prepubescent children. In this ethnic group, children may speak freely of their sex experiences without objection from their parents. In various primitive societies, also, sexual relations before puberty are common. Malinowski (1929), who described copulatory behavior among the Trobriand Island children, was inclined to think that it was in the nature of play, without strong emotional significance to the individual. He wrote:

As the boy or girl enters upon adolescence the nature of his or her sexual life becomes more serious. It ceases to be mere child's play and assumes a prominent place among life's interests. What was before an unstable relationship culminating in an exchange of erotic manipulation or an immature sexual act becomes an absorbing passion, and a matter for serious endeavor (p. 54).

Malinowski did not make clear the meaning with which he used "adolescence" in the preceding quotation. Mead (1928), however, dealing with Samoan girls, related heterosexual experience definitely to the menarche. Of the girls known to her, only one in the group had sexual intercourse prior to the first menstruation, and hers was clearly a case of delayed menstruation, several other signs of adolescence being present. Moreover, sex experience for the Samoan girl does not immediately follow puberty; a period of one, two, or three years often elapses between the menarche and the first affair with a boy. Similar results for American female sex delinquents have been reported by Glueck and Glueck (1934). This delay, however, seems to be due to the social attitudes of the males concerning the proper age of a partner rather than to physiological maturity per se.

Ellis (1936) has indicated that male homosexuality often has its roots in the prepubertal years. Of 72 cases from whom he obtained fairly complete sexual histories, 54 per cent exhibited an abnormal attachment to men or boys before the eleventh year, and 37 per cent evidenced homosexual trends at about the age of puberty. These early manifestations were not overt homosexual acts, however, but were "purely psychic." Ellis has presented the case histories in full.

Strength and Skill. Crampton (1908b) was the first to show that pubescence is accompanied by an increase in strength. Comparing prepubescent, pubescent, and postpubescent boys at each of several age levels from 13 to 16 years, he found the average strength of grip of the right hand to be greater among the more mature boys than among the less mature subjects. At any age level, the grip of the postpubescent boys exceeded that of the prepubescent boys by about one-third. This difference was greater than that induced by two years of chronological age among those whose pubertal status was unchanged during a two-year period. No attempt was made by Crampton to determine whether the superiority of the pubescents was due solely to the greater weight and height which his data showed to be characteristic of mature boys.

Crampton's study proved that premenarcheal and postmenarcheal girls of equivalent ages also differed in regard to strength of grip. In this case, however, the superiority of the mature group amounted to only 10 per cent.

To the reviewer's knowledge, Crampton's researches upon the strength of girls have not been repeated. His findings relative to boys, however, have been corroborated by Carey (1935) and Dimock (1937). Both these recent investigators find that postpubescents are stronger than pubescents and that pubescents exceed prepubescents in strength at each age level at which the numbers in each group enabled the investigators to make a significant comparison. Dimock's researches not only involved strength of grip but also included measures of strength of back extension, leg extension, arm and shoulder extension, and arm and shoulder flexion. These indices of strength showed the same trends as the manual grip tests.[1]

A popular impression exists to the effect that at puberty a loss in skill is to be noted. Adolescence, indeed, is often called the "awkward age." Mead (1928) has referred to the awkward gait of the adolescent Samoan girl, indicating that the impression of awkwardness is not limited to our society. Awkwardness at this period would not be surprising in view of the rapid growth of the extremities and of the relatively sudden changes in bodily proportions. Nevertheless, pubertal changes take place over a period of time, and it is possible that the young boy or girl can adjust his coordinations to his new bodily dimensions as rapidly as they are achieved.

In apparent contradiction to the popular view, age norms for skilled performances, which have been summarized by others (Whipple, 1915; Miles, 1935) reveal a consistent increase in speed and dexterity with increasing age and show no halt at the ages at which puberty is commonly reached.

The only direct comparison of mature and immature individuals, equated with respect to age, is that of Dimock (1937), who utilized a motor skills test which had been standardized by Brace. His subjects were boys. Making comparisons at each of several age levels, he found no consistent differences among the three commonly accepted levels of maturity. He discovered that improvement in skill took place even during periods of most rapid increase in

height and weight, as revealed by his longitudinal data. His investigation therefore supports the negative evidence for adolescent awkwardness which has been derived from examination of age trends. Espenschade's (1940) recent study also corroborates these facts, although she dealt with an insufficient number of prepubertal cases.

The general impression of awkwardness given by the adolescent may be due to the fact that he often performs under conditions of "razzing" or under knowledge that he is being closely scrutinized, as when he first begins to wear adult clothing, begins to dance, etc. Under these circumstances he may show a deficiency which is not apparent in routinely administered tests of manual dexterity. If he exhibits malcoordination in social situations, his awkwardness should not be attributed to adolescence unless further data indicate that the awkwardness is not due to the situation in which the performance has occurred.

Another factor which may contribute to the impression of awkwardness in the adolescent is the familiar size-age illusion which enters into many judgments concerning children. The larger child is perceived as older and is expected to behave accordingly. Attention has repeatedly been called to the fact that the sexually mature boy in most cases is large for his age. This fact arouses expectations of agility and skill above average for his age. Dimock's study, however, shows that his skill is not greater than that of his age-mates who are prepubescent. This discrepancy between expected skill and actual skill may be one of the most important bases for the belief that the adolescent is awkward.

Developmental Age. By means of a test devised by Furfey (1931) the maturity of the interests of a boy may be determined by noting his selection of paired alternatives, which have been shown, em-

[1] It is noteworthy that whereas the increase in strength, size, and weight at puberty is well known, we have been unable to find any statements as to whether or not high school athletes are recruited largely from among the sexually mature. It seems unlikely that many prepubescent boys could successfully compete in athletics with their more mature companions, but no evidence on this point is available.

pirically, to differentiate between age groups. Developmental age (DA) and developmental quotient (DQ) are derived from the data by methods comparable to those already familiar in the field of intelligence testing. In a normative survey of 982 grammar school and high school pupils, Furfey found that the increase in DA between 8 and 12 years of age is followed by a much sharper increase from the twelfth to the sixteenth years. There is no increase whatsoever in the average DA after age 16. The facts naturally suggest that DA is related to physiological maturity. In accordance with this view is Furfey's further finding that until age 12 there is no correlation between DA and height (within one-year age groups), whereas after 12 years there is a slight correlation (from .12 to .27). These correlations, he felt, might be due to the contribution of sexual maturity to variation in both height and DA after 12 years of age.

In 1933 Rauth and Furfey reported a more direct attack upon this problem. DA was correlated with a number of anatomical measurements in a group of 70 prepubescents and in a group of 43 postpubescents. In the former group the correlations had a central tendency of approximately zero, whereas in the second group all coefficients were between .22 and .60. In several instances the latter correlations were significantly higher than those observed in the former group.

Carey (1935) compared the DQ's of boys of the same age but of different degrees of sexual maturity and found that the physically more mature scored higher on Furfey's test. In another treatment of the same data, Carey found a significant difference between 64 boys who were decidedly accelerated physically and 64 who were markedly retarded. Although the difference was statistically reliable, in ab-

solute units it amounted to only 4 DQ points.

In the only study in which behavioral measures have been related to the male hormone content of the urine, rather than to anatomical criteria, Sollenberger (1940), using 23 reform school subjects between the ages of 12.75 and 16.84 years, found the hormone index to correlate with DA to the extent of .51. The correlation between CA and DA was only .14. A second group of 10 cases yielded an r between hormone index and DA of .65.

A DA test for girls has been devised by Sullivan (1934), who, in a study similar to those of Furfey and of Rauth and Furfey cited above, correlated DA with height and with weight. One-year age groups were employed. The r's were unreliable and were irregular as to sign. However, a direct comparison by Stone and Barker (1937b) of the DA's of premenarcheal and postmenarcheal girls of matched ages revealed a highly reliable difference between the two groups, the mature group exceeding the average of the immature group by 11 DA months.

Other Personality Studies. Only in recent years has it been possible to make use of objective instruments in attempts to measure the psychological effects of puberty. In consequence, the investigations are few and we have an incomplete picture. Studies now in progress, particularly the Adolescent Growth Study at the Institute of Child Welfare of the University of California, should soon add greatly to our knowledge of this subject.

Stone and Barker have published several comparisons of premenarcheal and postmenarcheal subjects, matched as to age and approximately equal in respect to socioeconomic status. In their 1937 study, they not only found the postmenarcheal girls more advanced in developmental age, as we reported in an earlier section, but also found that their postmenarcheal subjects yielded a reliably more mature average score on the Pressey Interest Attitude Test (Pressey and Pressey, 1933). The Bernreuter Test revealed no group differences. In a later study Stone and Barker (1939) utilized a personality test made up largely by selecting from earlier scales those items which they thought might differentiate between postmenarcheal and premenarcheal girls of matched ages. Their test did succeed in showing that the postmenarcheal subjects were *more* interested than the premenarcheal subjects in heterosexual social activities, adornment, display of person, and in daydreaming, whereas postmenarcheal girls were *less* interested in games and sports requiring vigorous activity. There were no differences between the groups in regard to the amount of friction within the family or in respect to the degree of revolt against parental discipline.

In an earlier study (1934) these authors correlated age at menarche with various Bernreuter scores which were obtained from one to ten years after puberty. Zero correlations were found. However, Stone and Barker (1937b) later found, as noted previously, that the Bernreuter scoring did not serve to differentiate between pubescent and prepubescent girls tested in the early teens. As yet we have no information as to whether or not the pubescent-prepubescent differences obtained by Stone and Barker at 12-, 13-, and 14-year levels are traceable at later ages. However, we do have the report of Terman and Miles (1936) upon the result of the application of the Masculinity-Femininity Test to a small number of early-maturing and late-maturing boys and girls, tested at the average age of 16.5 years. Although the number of cases is inadequate, the results show the early-maturing boys to be more masculine and the early-maturing girls to be more feminine than their respective comparison groups.

Dimock (1937) applied the Lehman-Witty Play Quiz to 200 boys on several occasions during a two-year period. Comparing prepubescent and postpubescent boys of matched ages, he found a reliable difference in play interests in regard to only one activity—driving an automobile. As Dimock remarked, this difference may have been due solely to the fact that parents, because of the greater size of the sexually mature boy, were more willing to permit him to drive. This investigation supersedes that of Furfey (1929), who found that the age incidence of choices of several types of boys' games followed Crampton's curves for the incidence of the postpubescent condition and concluded that puberty might be the causal factor. Dimock (1937) found that, whereas several activities exhibited age trends similar to the onset of physiological changes, nevertheless these really bore no relationship to puberty; this was revealed by the fact that at each age pubescent and prepubescent subjects participated in these activities with equal frequency. Another case in point is Lehman's (1927) report that, on the Play Quiz, the decline in girls' interests in dolls is similar to the decline in the number of girls who are prepubescent. It remains to be demonstrated that girls who mature early give up doll play sooner than do late-maturing girls. We shall see in a later section that girls who undergo precocious puberty do not cease to occupy themselves with dolls. We cannot overemphasize the fact that phenomena having average ages of cessation which are roughly equivalent to pubertal phenomena are not thereby demonstrated to be a result of physiological maturity.

Of interest is the case reported by Dicks and Childers (1934) of a boy who was reared as a girl during the first 14 years of life and who readily transferred to a masculine rôle at puberty.

Religious Interests and Activities. Starbuck's well-known book, *The Psychology of Religion* (1899), succeeded in publicizing widely his claim of an association between religious manifestations, particularly conversion, and adolescence. The chief evidence for this association consisted of the age incidence of conversions, which paralleled roughly the age incidence of puberty. These facts, of course, merely showed that the two phenomena had similar central tendencies, so far as the age at which they occurred was concerned. They did not show that early puberty tended to be accompanied by early conversion, nor did Starbuck's data give any evidence for a causal connection between the two sets of observations with which he was concerned.[1]

It needs scarcely be called to the reader's attention that, since Starbuck's time, social change has been sufficient to demonstrate that religious life need not be marked by conversion (see Clark, 1929) and that puberty, when it is associated with religious awakening, possesses this association by virtue of social, not physiological, forces. In fact, data which proved these points were available in the first decade of this century when the notion of a connection between puberty and religion was being promulgated. Although Starbuck often receives credit for the theory of the religious character of adolescence, G. Stanley Hall (1904, Vol. 2) rightly claimed that he had published on this topic (Hall, 1882)

before Starbuck became his student. Certainly no one more staunchly believed that adolescence was characterized by religious sentiments than did Hall, who brought together from various sources the age of conversion of some four thousand persons. In keeping with the folkways of the times, conversions then commonly occurred in that indefinite period called adolescence. Hall, with scientific impartiality, printed all the data which came to his attention. It is important to note that in connection with his tabular summary of conversions there were two columns of figures of which Hall (1904) wrote as follows:

> The last two columns are compiled from the covenant book of Rev. E. P. Hammond, whose specialty is revival work with children, which he has kindly loaned me for the purpose [*sic*]. They represent the converts in two series of meetings in two small cities (Vol. 2, p. 290).

These two sentences, which are not typical of Hall's style, are his only comment on data which could have served to reverse his views. The data are plentiful; they represent 1142 conversions. The Reverend Hammond's cases form a continuous distribution from 6 to 28 years of age. In contrast to other groups, the median age at conversion for the Reverend Hammond's cases was approximately 11 years. In other words, when revival services were prepared especially for children, children were converted. What then should have become of the argument for a "nascent" religious period peculiar to adolescence?

Among recent studies of puberty, we have noted only one which has investigated the relation between maturity and religious experience. Hillery (1937), employing the controlled-diary method, secured a one-year record of religious experiences from 96 girls, 47 of whom reached the menarche during the year. Although Hillery found

[1] Starbuck's table (1899, p. 44), which shows the number of years by which conversions preceded or followed puberty, is no exception to the above statement, because he did not show that the proximity of conversion to puberty was any greater than would arise from chance, given the two distributions with which he was dealing. Of course, since he was writing in 1899, Starbuck cannot be taken to task for lack of statistical refinements.

hat certain changes in religious experience occurred with age, she could discover no difference between the religious experiences of premenarcheal and postmenarcheal subjects whose ages were equated.

Leadership. We wish now to call attention to a field in which it seems likely that an effect of puberty may be observed, but in respect to which only very indirect evidence is at hand. This field is that of leadership of several sorts among high school pupils.

There are reasons to believe that height is an aid in establishing dominance and prestige in face-to-face situations. Depth of voice may also be effective. Since we know that differences in pubertal status are among the important determinants of height and depth of voice at the secondary school level, an effect of puberty upon leadership, dominance, and prestige seems therefore not unlikely.

Nutting (1923), in an investigation of girls who were chosen by their teammates as captains of gymnasium squads, found them noticeably above average in strength and in physical abilities, but also in age. Caldwell and Wellman (1926) found junior high school athletic leaders of both sexes to be above average in physical achievement and in height. Class presidents were also superior in height but not in regard to physical achievement. Bellingrath (1930), who investigated high school seniors, found elective officers of both sexes to average higher than their classmates in both height and weight. Cabot (1938) discovered that his tallest subjects were more marked social leaders, more extraverted, and more influential than short subjects of the same age. Although these studies suggest that certain types of leaders may often be selected from among the postpubescent rather than from among the prepubescent, no investigation of high school leadership has ever reported upon the pubertal status of its subjects, although these researches are often labeled as studies of adolescence. This subject recommends itself for future examination.

Intelligence. Since the growth of intelligence is treated with fullness in another chapter, it will suffice at this point to comment very briefly on the relation between puberty and intelligence. Because sexual maturity and intellectual maturity are reached at about the same chronological age, it has seemed reasonable to suppose that there is some causal relationship between these two forms of development. The near equality of the two average ages —for puberty and for adult intelligence— has led to the claim that *in the individual* the two may be associated; that is, early maturity implies early mental development and mental growth ceases at puberty. All the evidence, however, is opposed to this view. Abernethy (1925) correlated menarcheal age with mental age in 359 high school girls, holding chronological age constant, and obtained an unreliable coefficient. She found no difference in IQ between 19 girls who reached puberty before 11.5 years and 19 who matured after 15.5 years. Dimock (1937), dealing with boys, obtained an unreliable difference between his early-pubescent and late-pubescent subjects. The difference found was in favor of those reaching maturity at an early age. The early-maturing group, however, were significantly superior in socioeconomic status. In view of the well-known relationship between socioeconomic status and intelligence, any correlation between age at puberty and intelligence should be examined to determine whether it is merely a secondary result of occupational level. Stone and Barker (1937b) compared the intelligence of 175 premenarcheal girls and 175 postmenarcheal girls of approximately equal socioeconomic status and of equal age. The average score on the Otis group test was 2.25 points higher for the post-menarcheal subjects, but this difference did not quite meet the usual criterion for significance.

Of interest in this connection are cases of precocious puberty, in which physiological growth is greatly accelerated. The reviews of Doe-Kulmann and Stone (1927) and of Keene and Stone (1937) and of Singer show that no accompanying acceleration of mental growth occurs, nor does mental growth stop when premature puberty is reached. Some of the best data on this topic have been derived by longitudinal studies of a few cases. Outstanding in this connection is the report, covering a fifteen-year period, of Gesell, Thoms, Hartmen, and Thompson (1939).

Delinquency. Delinquency is often said to be an "adolescent phenomenon," meaning, we suppose, that delinquency commonly occurs between the ages of 10 and 20 years. To state that most delinquency takes place within this period does not show that it has a physiological basis, since before puberty children are commonly under adult supervision at all hours and after this period there can be, by definition, no delinquency, but only crime.

In view of the claim that delinquency is an adolescent phenomenon it is surprising that for boys there are no facts whatsoever concerning the proportion of delinquents who are pubescent and postpubescent. It may be that physical maturity plays some rôle in delinquency, perhaps as a determinant of its onset, but no facts relative to the problem are available in the extensive literature on juvenile delinquency. In the entire literature, so far as the reviewer knows, the only observation concerning puberty is the clinical judgment of Burt (1925) that adolescent instability was the principal cause of delinquency in 2 per cent of the cases examined by him.

The association between boys' gangs and delinquency has been noted, and the term "the gang age" has also been used in conjunction with adolescence. Although Thrasher (1927) reported the ages of the members of the gangs which he investigated, here, as in so many other fields, there are no reports which indicate the stage of sexual maturity of the boys who were studied.

Because delinquency in girls so often consists of sexual delinquency, a slight amount of attention has been given to the physiological development of female offenders. We have previously referred to the finding of Glueck and Glueck (1934) that the sexual offenses of delinquent girls seldom occur until after the menarche. Burt (1925) recorded early or excessive sexual development in 10 per cent of the delinquent girls examined by him, whereas the same conditions were found in less than 1 per cent of his control group. Healy (1925) found that puberty was premature in 10 per cent of his female subjects. Healy did not define his criteria for prematurity; in Burt's study, prematurity was defined as puberty occurring two or more years before the average age of menarche. Seventy per cent of the female delinquents included in Healy's investigations were above the weight norms for their age. Healy noted that this is in line with the common-sense observation that physical overdevelopment in girls has a tendency to be related to delinquency, particularly with sex delinquency.

Miscellaneous Behavior Observations. In this section we shall call attention to negative evidence, or to lack of evidence, for a relationship between puberty and each of several forms of behavior. The list of alleged but unproved concomitants of puberty could be extended greatly; we shall limit it, however, to those topics which ave received the most attention in the literature on adolescence.

At one time, it was believed that sexual maturity ushered in a susceptibility to mental disease. In opposition to this point of view are the results of many statistical studies, such as those of Pollock and Malzberg (1929) and Malzberg (1931), which showed that in New York state the incidence of all forms of mental disease is negligible below the age of 15 years. A very large proportion of boys and girls have reached puberty before that date. The incidence for all forms of mental disease is higher after the age of 20 years than it is in any earlier year. This is true of schizophrenia, which was first called dementia praecox because of its relatively early onset. As yet there are no data on the pubertal condition of persons incurring mental disease at early ages, nor are there any facts concerning a possible correlation between the age at puberty and the age at the onset of mental disease.

Although adolescent suicides often receive attention, this is apparently due to their rarity. Cavan (1928), summarizing the data of others, showed the suicide rate to be very much less at ages before 20 years than thereafter. Whatever storm and stress, whatever emotional instability, whatever depression and moodiness may accompany any phase of adolescence, these mental conditions are seldom sufficient to cause the individual to take his own life.

"Crushes" commonly occur at the high school and college levels. Ellis (1936, Vol. 2, Pt. 2, pp. 368–384) has summarized the literature on crushes among adolescent girls in Italy, England, the United States, and South America. Recently, Hurlock and Klein (1934) have contributed to the literature. Whatever else these studies may have proved, they have failed to show whether or not the persons who experienced the crush were prepubescent or postpubescent.

Although the reviewer does not know of a direct statement concerning the matter in the anthropological literature, it is his impression that in many societies, such as those studied by Mead (1928, 1930a), no such crushes are experienced. If crushes are culturally transmitted forms of behavior, that, of course, does not obviate their having a relationship to physiological drives. The phenomenon is in need of a more analytical treatment than it has received in the past.

Hetzer (1926) has called attention to a "negative phase" which she holds to be characteristic of adolescence in girls. Hetzer's description (1927), as translated by Hurlock and Sender (1930), is:

> This phase is characterized by passivity and restlessness; loss of interest; desire for isolation; neglect of productive activity; instability; restlessness; loss of skill of performance; withdrawal from friends, parents and teachers.

Hetzer discovered the negative phase during the course of a year which she spent as manager of a retreat for children. Of 28 children who were in the institution, 2 were in the negative phase when they first came under Hetzer's observation and 5 entered upon this phase in the course of the year. In other words, Hetzer observed only seven cases of the negative phase. The negative phase was ended before the menarche was reached in three cases. In three other cases, the menarche occurred during the phase and in one case the relationship was undetermined because the negative phase was not ended nor the menarche reached during the period of observation.

In evaluating Hetzer's conclusions concerning an adolescent negative phase, it must be remembered that variations in mood and in other psychological traits occur in many persons at times other than at puberty. The fact that 7 girls exhibited certain behavior at or near the time of puberty does not constitute evidence that this behavior was in any way associated with puberty. We do not know that the negative phase takes place more frequently at puberty than at any other period. In connection with a later work of Hetzer (1927), in which she identified the negative phase through a study of diary records, it must be borne in mind that scarcely ever do diaries permit one to determine the time at which physiological maturity took place,[1] so that it is impossible to relate diary events to puberty. This criticism also holds for Bühler's (1926) claim that the negative period is followed by a more joyous, light-hearted, exuberant period indicated by the German word *Schwärmerei*, since the discovery of this period by Bühler was derived from diaries of girls whose age at menarche was unknown. Furthermore, the identification of the condition of negative phase and of *Schwärmerei* is subjective to an unknown degree. To what extent two investigators examining the same material would agree in their demarcation of these periods we do not know.

Behavioral Phenomena in Precocious Puberty

That puberty, in rare instances, may be attained at a very early age, even shortly after birth, has been known for centuries. With the great increase in medical publication in modern times, the number of such cases which have been described has become large and at the present time it probably exceeds five hundred. The literature on the topic has been reviewed by

[1] The recent psychological interest in the analysis of adolescent diaries is not novel. Hall (1904) made extensive use of diary and autobiographical material.

Neurath (1909), Lenz (1913), Reuben and Manning (1922–1923), Doe-Kulmann and Stone (1927), Keene and Stone (1937) and Singer (unpublished study).

The reviews show a general agreement as to the physical characteristics of uncomplicated cases of hypergonadal prematurity. This form is usually distinguishable from pituitary and adrenal-cortex types of precocity, and it alone will be discussed here. Dawkes' report (1747) presents a fairly typical case, should the reader care to consult one. The individual whether male or female, who undergoes precocious puberty shows a pubertal acceleration in growth. In consequence, the sexually precocious child is for a while greatly in excess of the physical norms for his age. However, growth practically ceases at or near the date that puberty is attained, so that as an adult the individual is small and short and may even approach dwarfism. The secondary sex characteristics are present. A child a few months old who is undergoing precocious sexual development possesses a deep voice and pigmented pubic hair. In the girl, the breasts enlarge and the body form becomes more feminine; in the boy, the beard may begin to appear. Ossification of the bones is far in advance of the normal. We have mentioned earlier that recently devised methods of endocrine assay show the presence of considerable amounts of sex hormones in these individuals. Other recent reports (J. B. Hamilton 1937a, 1937b; Kunstadter, 1938) show that the administration of androgens in the treatment of cryptorchidism will induce premature puberty.

On the behavior side, one of the most apparent characteristics is the greatly superior strength of the sexually precocious child. This is particularly noticeable in the boy. So-called infant Herculeses are almost always instances of precocious pu rty. The excessive size and strength of e premature male make it easy for him dominate his age-mates.

A considerable amount of attention has een paid to mental development in precious puberty. The reviews of Doe-Kulann and Stone (1927) and of Keene and tone (1937) show that children who have own precocious sexual development are ot advanced mentally beyond the expections of their chronological age. The ngitudinal study reported by Gesell 1926, 1928) and by Gesell, Thoms, Harten, and Thompson (1939) reveals no efct of physical precocity upon mental evelopment.

Of great interest is the question of the fect of sexual precocity upon social beavior. The investigation of this problem beset with difficulties. The data must e sought in the case reports; in most of ne case studies the reporting physician is aterested only in the physical and medical spects. When behavioral data are present ney are scanty and of doubtful interpreation.

Singer has completed the most extensive eview of the literature with respect to onintellectual aspects of behavior. He ound some behavioral data in the reports or 50 males and 59 females, all of whom nderwent precocious puberty of the hypergonadal type before the age of nine years, nd most of them at much earlier ages. The data collected by Singer show coniderable evidence for sexual behavior in he precociously mature boys. Of the 50 nale cases, 25 were stated to have had rections, 16 were reported to have masurbated and most of these had experienced rgasm, 15 exhibited some form of heterosexual interest, and for 8 nocturnal emisions were reported. It should not be asumed that these phenomena were absent n the remainder of the cases, since many f the reports which contain some refer-

ence to behavior omit any mention of sexual responses.

In some instances the sexuality of the child is marked. Le Marquand (1932) wrote of his subject, who attained puberty shortly after the first birthday and who was 2½ years of age at the time of the report, that the child could not be left alone with an adult woman because of the obvious sexual advances which he made. In contrast, he was not attracted by immature girls. These statements which were made by the parents were corroborated by observation in the hospital. Harris' case (1870–1871) reached puberty at 9 years. When he was 12 years old he was reported to have had the sexual passions of a man, which he indulged to a marked degree. Devon's case (1905) was arrested at 11 years for attempted rape; he had attained maturity at 8 years. These cases suggest that pubertal endocrine changes greatly increase the strength of the sexual drive, since the sex activities of immature children, referred to in a previous section, are not known to rise to the intensity of those of the three cases of precocity just mentioned. It is true, however, that in some cases of precocity, in contrast to those described above, no sex behavior occurs. In this connection, it should be borne in mind, first, that the sex drive differs greatly in its strength in different individuals, and, second, that sexual impulses may be repressed. Undoubtedly most parents would employ strong repressive measures in the case of the precocious child.

The positive evidence for sexual behavior in girls who are precociously mature is small. In only 5 of the 59 case reports reviewed by Singer was there evidence of heterosexual interests and in only 3 reports was genital manipulation mentioned. However, it may be that parents were loath to report such behavior, and perhaps physicians also were unwilling to do so, since the fact that the physical precocity of the child is apparent to all makes anonymity of report an impossibility. Of the 5-year-old girl reported by Craven (1932), it was reported that she was affectionate to the point of being highly sexual. Stein's subject (1907), who reached the menarche at 14 months, at 3½ years had begun to masturbate, to exhibit her genitals to other children, and to show inclination toward the opposite sex. The child described by Wallentin (1885), mature at 15 months, and 6 years of age at the time of the report, was sexually excitable and had to be kept away from boys. Kennard (1858) made the statement that the sexual passions were strong in the 4½-year-old described by him. Certainly one could not obtain such extensive evidence of sexuality in 59 girls of comparable age picked at random. However, one cannot ignore the fact that the child of precocious maturity no doubt attracts more sexual interest and is more likely to receive advances than is the case with the normal child.

Beyond the topic of sexuality, evidence concerning the behavior of young children who are physically mature is more meager still. Some of them are described as serious and as preferring the company of adults rather than the company of children; however, the majority are described as being childlike in behavior and as playing the usual juvenile games. These are general impressions, and they usually refer to a short period of observation. Longitudinal studies with measures such as Furfey's and Sullivan's developmental age scales would be highly desirable.

Behavioral Phenomena in Delayed Puberty

Eidelsberg and Ornstein (1940) have presented four very interesting cases of young men with retarded sexual development, whose physique and behavior have been markedly affected by the administration of the recently identified male sex hormone, testosterone proprionate. These cases seem worth reviewing in some detail. The first case is that of a young man of 26 who developed normally until he was about 13 years of age. He then began to realize that he was lagging behind others in physical development. At 26 years he was obese, possessed a high-pitched voice, had little pubic hair and no axillary or facial hair. His genitals were infantile. His movements, carriage, and mannerisms were somewhat feminine. He was extremely shy and suffered so much from constant teasing that he entertained thoughts of suicide. The medical diagnosis was pluriglandular dysfunction with hypogonadism and eunuchoidism. Testosterone proprionate was administered after the physician had employed other drugs which proved ineffective. Within two weeks of the beginning of the administration of the sex hormone, the primary and secondary sexual characteristics changed markedly. The genitals grew rapidly, erections became frequent, and orgasms were occasioned by friction with clothing. Facial, axillary, and pubic hair underwent rapid development and the voice deepened. Accompanying these physiological changes was a noticeable increase in self assurance.

The second case was that of a young man of 22 whose testes had been destroyed before he had attained puberty. He presented a picture of physical immaturity with psychological concomitants. He was keenly aware of his sexual shortcomings and despaired of ever possessing love, sex life, and marriage. He was depressed and frequently wept. One month of medication by means of testosterone proprionate induced dramatic changes. Hirsutal development took place; the voice became deeper

He experienced marked libido with erections, masturbation with orgasm, and, later, satisfactory coitus. In mental outlook, he became happy and hopeful and contemplated early marriage.

The two remaining cases reported by Eidelsberg and Ornstein were essentially similar to those which have just been described. They were cases of young men who had never attained full sex development and who suffered keenly from a knowledge of the difference between themselves and normal men. In each case it would seem that their physiological status was due solely to organic causes, but that their feelings of inferiority, inadequacy, and depression were due largely to their appreciation of the fact that they could not meet the social norms. With administration of the sex hormone by repeated small doses, all the physiological changes of puberty took place in the course of a few weeks, showing that pubertal changes can occur much more rapidly than they ordinarily do. Accompanying these developments came the attainment of libido and of sexual potency, and there were also an observed increase in aggressiveness, masculinity, and in general social adjustment.

The cases reported by Miller, Hubert, and Hamilton (1938) present similar features, although some of the men had undergone castration after the age of puberty. The cases, both of prepubertal and postpubertal emasculation, were subject to uncontrollable shifts in mood, severe depression, tears, irritability, sullen anger, apathy, and fatigability. Endocrine therapy which restored the sexual urge and sexual capacity led to greater euphoria, more stability and control, and to more energy and stamina.

Stolz, Jones, and Chaffey (1937), in a report upon the 10 boys among the 100 studied by them whose puberty was most retarded, found that 8 of the 10 gave evidence of emotional insecurity, probably because of "feelings of difference." They also reported that every one of 7 boys whose structural characteristics were feminine were significantly disturbed by it.

Levy (1936) has published a psychological study of 33 boys characterized by the Fröhlich syndrome; that is, obesity of the mons-mammary-girdle type. Twenty-eight of these were definitely hypogenital; 7 had feminine mannerisms. Levy found that 79 per cent of them were submissive, whereas of 1000 other cases chosen at random from the files of the same clinic only 31 per cent were classified as submissive. Although Levy made no general statement concerning the sexuality of these hypogenital cases, it would appear from the brief case histories which he included that sex behavior was almost nonexistent among them.

Concerning delayed puberty and hypogonadism in girls, very few data are available. We know only the study of Abernethy (1925), who paid special attention, in a group of 487 girls, to the 19 whose menarche occurred at ages beyond 15.5 years. Sixteen of them were markedly below the norms in height and weight; 11 had histories of poor health. Nine of the 19 were rated deficient in social qualities, particularly in cooperation, leadership, and responsibility.

Summary

We first attempted, in this chapter, to demonstrate that adolescence should not be defined in chronological terms or in terms of educational level. To be sure, if one wishes to treat either the second decade of life or the high school years as an arbitrarily defined period, the right to do so cannot be denied. The growth of intelligence from age 10 to age 20, racial attitudes in the teens, reading comprehension in high school students—these and hundreds of topics like them are valuable, and they may be called studies of adolescence if one wishes to do so. But this usage does violence to the common significance of the word *adolescence*. Such studies avoid what was originally the fundamental problem of the psychology of adolescence, namely, that of investigating the relationship between physiological maturation and psychological functioning. In accordance with this conviction that adolescence should retain a physiological definition, we have limited our survey to studies of mental-physical relationships at or near puberty.

A contrasting emphasis which is familiar at the present time is that which holds that adolescence is a social phenomenon. This view proposes that the cultural demands which are placed upon the adolescent are the chief factors controlling his behavior. We have no wish to deny the importance of culture as a determinant of behavior, but studies of the effects of social situations ordinarily belong to social psychology. They become a part of the psychology of adolescence only when they seek to discover the relation between pubertal stage and the effectiveness of various social situations. A denial that such a relationship exists should be based upon more evidence than is available at the present time.

In reviewing the relationships between puberty and behavior, we have found that investigators have made use of but few physiological distinctions in the adolescent period. In girls, scarcely any pubertal categories have been employed except those of premenarche and postmenarche. In boys, the traditional practice, following Crampton (1908b), has been to classify subjects into three groups on the basis of the status of the pubic hair. Obviously these characteristics are but the more superficial pubertal changes, and attention should be directed to other aspects of sexual maturation as well.

The sequence of bodily changes at puberty is still imperfectly known. It is certain, however, that a rapid increase in size and weight ordinarily precedes the attainment of puberty, as commonly defined Ossification also is accelerated during this period of rapid growth. Recent progress in the assay and in the synthesis of sex hormones should lead soon to valuable studies of the pubertal endocrine changes It is already apparent that the endocrine aspects of puberty, like the anatomical changes, may occur years earlier in some persons than in others, making it impossible to treat age groups as if they possessed clear-cut physiological differences.

The chief method which has been employed in determining the psychological accompaniments of puberty is that of comparing groups of different pubertal status which have been equated in several other respects. The equating of pubertal groups has been carried out with particular reference to age, intelligence, and socioeconomic status. However, the number of researches which have presented behavioral comparisons by this method is quite limited.

Among the behavioral manifestations which appear at puberty are undoubtedly certain increases in sexual sensitivity and interest. However, the psychology of sex has been concerned almost exclusively with adult subjects, leaving the sexual phenomena of puberty relatively unknown and unanalyzed. Such data as exist, although not adequate, indicate that probably sexual drive increases markedly at about the time of puberty but does not reach the adult level until some time after puberty.

Postpubescents, in comparison with prepubescents of the same age, are much heavier and taller, and can exert considerably more muscular force. This difference in strength is more marked in boys than in girls. How postpubescents and prepubescents, matched in height and weight, would compare in strength has not been determined, but it seems likely that they too would differ, as endocrine factors in themselves probably are capable of affecting the degree of muscular force. These differences in size and strength, together with the differences in voice and in hirsutal development, create an impression upon others and upon the subject himself, and this may be the chief cause of whatever changes in social behavior are found to accompany puberty.

The evidence does not indicate that there is any loss in skill at puberty, as is commonly held. This belief may be derived from the size-age illusion, since the adolescent's skillfulness does not improve at the same rate as do his height and weight. Because of their greater strength postpubescents are probably superior to prepubescents of the same age in many athletic abilities, although this also has not yet been demonstrated by research.

Postpubescents are superior to matched prepubescents in respect to scores made on certain tests of social maturity. Specifically the tests which have revealed this difference are Furfey's and Sullivan's Developmental Age Tests, the Pressey Interest-Attitude Test, and a test devised by Stone and Barker. Very few personality measures have been employed in connection with this problem, so it is likely that in the future many more personality differences will be discovered.

Studies of high school leaders show that some forms of leadership are associated with superior height and weight. It seems reasonable that the size, the deeper voice, and the greater social maturity of postpubescents in comparison with prepubescents of the same age give the former an advantage in situations which provide opportunities for dominance, prestige, and leadership. As yet, no test of this hypothesis has been made. The possibility that early maturity may give the boy or girl habits of social domination which persist into later years is also an untested theory. In fact, the persistence of the effects of early or late maturity into the adult years has been almost totally unexplored.

Many of the early views concerning the psychological consequences of puberty seem to have arisen from the fact that phenomena which occur at about the same ages as puberty were thought of as consequences of puberty. At one time religious conversion frequently occurred at puberty. We now know, however, that a religious emphasis may take place at almost any time in the life cycle. There is no evidence to indicate that adolescence differs in this respect from other periods.

The fact that intellectual maturity is achieved at about the same time as sexual maturity has been proved to be an instance of concomitance rather than of causal relation. Sexual maturity has no effect upon the mental growth of the individual, as is shown by studies of puberty praecox and by comparisons of prepubescent and postpubescent individuals of the same age.

In regard to delinquency, the conclusion seems justified that its only relationship to puberty lies in the fact that sex delinquency is infrequent until after puberty has been reached. Postpubescent boys may exhibit an increased aggressiveness but this may or may not incline them toward delinquency, according to the social situation in which they find themselves. Gang formation has not been shown to be intimately related to physiological maturation. In regard to other alleged adolescent phenomena, such as the negative phase and the *Schwärmerei*, it has not been adequately shown that they are peculiar to adolescence or that they are unusually frequent at any pubertal stage.

Although some behavioral differences have been demonstrated to exist between postpubescents and prepubescents of the same age, we still lack analytical researches which will show the extent to which these differences are direct physiological effects of adolescence and the extent to which they result from the subject's perception of his relationship to the social norms or result from the effect of the subject's maturity upon the social attitudes of other individuals. Studies of cases of exceptionally precocious puberty and of delayed puberty suggest that the individual's treatment by others, as it is conditioned by his bodily development, is highly important. That is not to deny, however, that some pubertal conditions, especially endocrine secretions, may have fairly direct psychological effects.

Only within recent years have techniques become available for the measurement of pubertal indices other than skeletal dimensions and total weight. Likewise, it has only been within the last decade that there have come into existence instruments which are capable of measuring the attitude and personality manifestations which may result, either directly or indirectly, from sexual maturation. In view of these facts, the studies here reviewed must be regarded as pioneer researches which will soon be supplemented by more extensive, more systematic, and more analytical investigations. The psychology of adolescence, the psychology of sex, the social psychology of youth, and the psychology of secondary and higher education are related and overlapping fields, each one of which is more active today than it has ever been before in contributing to an understanding of the adolescent individual.

Bibliography

ABERNETHY, E. M. 1925. Correlations in physical and mental growth. *J. Educ. Psychol.*, 16, 458–466; 539–546.

ALLEN, E., C. H. DANFORTH, and E. A. DOISY (Eds.). 1939. *Sex and internal secretions.* Baltimore: Williams and Wilkins.

ARISTOTLE. 1908–1931. *The works of Aristotle.* (Translated into English under the editorship of W. D. ROSS.) Vol. IX: *Historia animalium;* Vol. XI. *Rhetorica.* Oxford: Clarendon Press.

ASHLEY-MONTAGU, M. F. 1939. Adolescent sterility. *Quart. Rev. Biol.*, 34, 192–219.

BALDWIN, B. T. 1916. A measuring scale for physical growth and physiological age. *Yearb. Nat. Soc. Stud. Educ.*, 15(I), 11–23.

——. 1921. The physical growth of children from birth to maturity. *Univ. Iowa Stud. Child Welfare*, 1, No. 1.

——. 1928. The determination of sex maturation in boys by a laboratory method. *J. Comp. Psychol.*, 8, 39–43.

BARKER, R. G., and C. P. STONE. 1936. Physical development in relation to menarcheal age in university women. *Human Biol.*, 8, 198–222.

BELL, S. 1902. The emotion of love between the sexes. *Amer. J. Psychol.*, 13, 325–354.

BELLINGRATH, G. C. 1930. Qualities associated with leadership in the extra-curricular activities of the high school. *Teach. Coll., Contr. Educ.*, No. 399.

BENDER, L., and A. BLAU. 1937. The reaction of children to sexual relations of adults. *Amer. J. Orthopsychiat.*, 7, 500–518.

BOAS, F. 1930. Observations on the growth of children. *Science*, 72, 44–48.

——. 1932. Studies in growth. *Human Biol.*, 4, 307–350.

BOLK, L. 1923. The menarche in Dutch women and its precipitated appearance in the youngest generation. *Konin. Akad. van Wetenschappen te Amsterdam*, 26, 650–663.

BOWDITCH, H. P. 1891. The growth of children studied by Galton's percentile grades. *Ann. Rep. Mass. Board of Health, Boston*, 22, 479–525.

BRUEN, C. 1933. Variations of basal metabolic rate per unit surface area with age: II. The pubertal acceleration. *J. Nutrit.*, 6, 383–395.

BÜHLER, C. 1926. *Die Schwärmerei als Phase der Feifezeit.* Z. Psychol., 100, 1–17.

BUFFON, COUNT DE. 1812. *Natural history, general and particular:* Vol. III. *The history of man and quadrupeds.* (Trans. by H. SMELLIE.) London. (1st ed., 1749.)

BURLAGE, S. R. 1923. The blood pressure and heart rate in girls during adolescence. *Amer. J. Physiol.*, 64, 252–284.

BURNHAM, W. H. 1891. The study of adolescence. *Ped. Sem.*, 1, 174–195.

BURT, C. 1925. *The young delinquent.* New York: Appleton.

CABOT, P. S. DE Q. 1938. The relationship between characteristics of personality and physique in adolescents. *Genet. Psychol. Monogr.*, 20, 3–120.

CALDWELL, O. W., and B. WELLMAN. 1926.

Characteristics of school leaders. *J. Educ. Res.*, **14**, 1–15.

AREY, T. F. 1935. *The relation of physical growth to developmental age in boys.* Washington, D. C.: Catholic University of America.

AVAN, R. S. 1928. *Suicide.* Chicago: University of Chicago Press.

CHILDERS, A. T. 1936. Some notes on sex mores among Negro children. *Amer. J. Orthopsychiat.*, **6**, 442–448.

CLARK, E. T. 1929. *The psychology of religious awakening.* New York: Macmillan.

CRAMPTON, C. W. 1908a. Anatomical or physiological age versus chronological age. *Ped. Sem.*, **15**, 230–237.

——. 1908b. Physiological age. *Amer. Phys. Educ. Rev.*, **13**, 144–154; 214–227; 268–283; 345–358.

CRAVEN, J. D. 1932. Precocious menstruation. *Amer. J. Dis. Child.*, **43**, 936–941.

CURJEL, D. F. 1920. The reproductive life of Indian women. *Indian J. Med. Res. (Calcutta)*, **8**, 366–371.

DANIELS, A. D. 1893. The new life; a study of regeneration. *Amer. J. Psychol.*, **6**, 61–106.

DAVIS, K. B. 1929. *Sex factors in the lives of twenty-two hundred women.* New York: Harper.

DAWKES, T. 1747. *Prodigium Willinghamense, or authentic memoirs of the more remarkable passages in the life of a boy, born at Willingham, near Cambridge, October 31, 1741, who before he was three years old was three feet eight inches high and had the marks of puberty, with some reflections on his understanding, strength, temper, memory, genius and knowledge.* London: C. Davis.

DEARBORN, W. F., J. W. M. ROTHNEY, and F. K. SHUTTLEWORTH. 1938. Data on the growth of public school children. *Monogr. Soc. Res. Child Develpm.*, **3**, No. 1. Pp. 136.

DEVON, J. 1905. Case of precocious development. *Glasgow Med. J.*, **64**, 339–343.

DICKS, G. H., and A. T. CHILDERS. 1934. The social transformation of a boy who had lived his first fourteen years as a girl: A case history. *Amer. J. Orthopsychiat.*, **4**, 508–517.

DIMOCK, H. S. 1937. *Rediscovering the adolescent.* New York: Association Press.

DOE-KULMANN, L., and C. P. STONE. 1927. Notes on the mental development of children exhibiting the somatic signs of puberty praecox. *J. Abnorm. Soc. Psychol.*, **22**, 291–324.

DORFMAN, R. I., and W. W. GREULICH. 1937. The response of the chick's comb to naturally occurring endrogens and estrogens. *Yale J. Biol. Med.*, **10**, 79–88.

DORFMAN, R. I., W. W. GREULICH, and C. I. SOLOMON. 1937. The excretion of androgenic and estrogenic substances in the urine of children. *Endocrinology*, **21**, 741–743.

DWORZAK, H. 1936. Rachitis und Menarche. *Med. Klin., Berlin*, **32**, 17–19.

EIDELSBERG, J., and E. A. ORNSTEIN. 1940. Observations on the continued use of male sex hormone over long periods of time. *Endocrinology*, **26**, 46–53.

ELLIS, H. 1936. *Studies in the psychology of sex.* (4 vols.) New York: Random House.

ENGELMANN, G. J. 1901. Age of first menstruation on the North American continent. *Trans. Amer. Gynecol. Soc.*, **26**, 77–110.

ENGLE, R., and M. C. SHELESNYAK. 1934. First menstruation and subsequent menstrual cycles of pubertal girls. *Human Biol.*, **6**, 431–453.

ESPENSCHADE, A. 1940. Motor performance in adolescence, including the study of relationships with measures of physical growth and maturity. *Monogr. Soc. Res. Child Develpm.*, **5**, No. 24. Pp. 126.

FLORY, C. D. 1935. Predicting puberty. *Child Develpm.*, **6**, 1–6.

FURFEY, P. H. 1929. Pubescence and play behavior. *Amer. J. Psychol.*, **41**, 109–111.

——. 1930. *The growing boy.* New York: Macmillan.

——. 1931. A revised scale for measuring developmental age in boys. *Child Develpm.*, **2**, 102–114.

GESELL, A. 1926. The influence of puberty praecox upon mental growth. *Genet. Psychol. Monogr.*, **1**, 507–588.

——. 1928. Precocious puberty and mental maturation. *Yearb. Nat. Soc. Stud. Educ.*, 27(I), 398–409.

GESELL, A., H. THOMS, F. B. HARTMEN, and H. THOMPSON. 1939. Mental and physical growth in pubertas praecox; report of 15 years study of case. *Arch. Neurol. Psychiat., Chicago*, **41**, 755–772.

GLUECK, S., and E. GLUECK. 1934. *Five hundred delinquent women.* New York: Knopf.

GOLDSMITH, M. 1846. Precocious children. *Boston Med. Surg. J.*, **34**, 481.

GOULD, H. N., and M. R. GOULD. 1932. Age of first menstruation in mothers and daughters. *J. Amer. Med. Ass.*, **98**, 1349–1352.

GREULICH, W. W., H. G. DAY, S. E. LACHMAN, J. B. WOLFE, and F. K. SHUTTLEWORTH. 1938. A handbook of methods for the study of adolescent children. *Monogr. Soc. Res. Child Develpm.*, **3**, No. 2. Pp. xvii + 406.

GUALINO, L. 1907. Il sogno erotico nell' uomo normale. *Riv. Psicol.*, January–February. (Abstracted by ELLIS, *Auto-erotism*, p. 191.)

HALL, G. S. 1882. The moral and religious training of children. *Princeton Rev.*, **10**, 26–48.

——. 1904. *Adolescence; its psychology and its relations to physiology, anthropology, sociology, sex, crime, religion, and education.* (2 vols.) New York: Appleton.

HAMILTON, G. V. N. 1929. *A research in marriage.* New York: Boni.

HAMILTON, J. B. 1937a. Treatment of sexual

underdevelopment with synthetic male hormone substance. *Endocrinology*, 21, 649–654.

HAMILTON, J. B. 1937b. Induction of penile erection by male hormone substances. *Endocrinology*, 21, 744–749.

HARRIS, R. P. 1870–1871. Early puberty. *Amer. J. Obstetr.*, 3, 611–622.

HARTMAN, C. G. 1931. On the relative sterility of the adolescent organism. *Science*, 74, 226–227.

HARVEY, O. L. 1932. Some statistics derived from recent questionnaire studies relative to human sexual behavior. *J. Soc. Psychol.*, 3, 97–100.

HEALY, W. 1925. A review of some studies of delinquents and delinquency. *Arch. Neurol. Psychiat.*, *Chicago*, 14, 25–30.

HETZER, H. 1926. *Der Einfluss der negativen Phase auf soziales Verhalten und literarische Production pubertierender Mädchen.* Jena: Fischer.

——. 1927. Systematische Dauerbeobachtungen am Jurgendlichen über den Verlauf der negativen Phase. *Zsch. pädag. Psychol.*, 28, 80–96.

HILLERY, M. P. 1937. *The religious life of adolescent girls.* Washington, D. C.: Catholic University of America.

HOSKINS, R. G. 1933. *The tides of life.* New York: Norton.

HURLOCK, E. B., and E. R. KLEIN. 1934. Adolescent "crushes." *Child Develpm.*, 5, 63–80.

HURLOCK, E. B., and S. SENDER. 1930. The "negative phase" in relation to the behavior of pubescent girls. *Child Develpm.*, 1, 325–340.

HUSCHKA, M. 1938. The incidence and character of masturbation threats in a group of problem children. *Psychoanal. Quart.*, 7, 338–356.

HUSEMANN, T. 1868. Normales Verhalten der Menstruation in Norwegen. *Monatsbl. med. Statist. öff. Gesundheitspflg.*, *Berlin*, 20, 24–28.

JONES, E. 1922–1923. Some problems of adolescence. *Brit. J. Psychol.*, 13, 31–47.

JONES, H. E. 1938. The California adolescent growth study. *J. Educ. Res.*, 31, 561–567.

KEENE, C. M., and C. P. STONE. 1937. Mental status as related to puberty praecox. *Psychol. Bull.*, 34, 123–133.

KENNARD, T. 1858. Remarkable precocity in the female. *St. Louis Med. Surg. J.*, 16, 201–202.

KUNSTADTER, R. H. 1938. The induction of premature puberty with androgenic substance. *Endocrinology*, 23, 661–665.

LANCASTER, E. G. 1897. The psychology and pedagogy of adolescence. *Ped. Sem.*, 5, 61–128.

LEHMAN, H. C. 1927. A study of doll play in relation to the onset of pubescence. *J. Genet. Psychol.*, 34, 72–76.

LE MARQUAND, H. S. 1932. Suprarenal virilism. *Proc. Roy. Soc. Med.*, 25, 804–806.

LENZ, J. 1913. Vorzeitige Menstruation, Geschlechtsreife und Entwicklung. *Arch. Gynäk. Berlin*, 99, 67–144.

LEVY, D. M. 1936. Aggressive-submissive behavior and the Fröhlich syndrome. *Arch. Neurol. Psychiat.*, *Chicago*, 36, 991–1020.

LINTZ, W., and H. MARKOW. 1923. Relation of onset of menstruation to environment. *Endocrinology*, 7, 57–60.

MALINOWSKI, B. 1927. *Sex and repression in savage society.* New York: Harcourt, Brace.

——. 1929. *The sexual life of savages in north-western Melanesia.* London: Routledge.

MALZBERG, B. 1931. A statistical study of the prevalence and types of mental disease among children and adolescents. *Psychiat. Quart.*, 5, 511–537.

MARRO, A. 1897. *La puberta studiata nell' uomo e nella donna in rapporto all' antropologia, alla psichiatria, alla pedagogia ed alla sociologia.* Torino: Bocca. (French trans. by J. P. MEDICI, Paris: Schleicher, 1902.)

MEAD, M. 1928. *Coming of age in Samoa.* New York: Morrow.

——. 1930a. *Growing up in New Guinea.* New York: Morrow.

——. 1930b. Adolescence in primitive and modern society, pp. 169–188. In V. F. CALVERTON and S. D. SCHMALHAUSEN (Eds.), *The New Generation.* New York: Macaulay.

MILES, W. R. 1935. Age in human society, pp. 596–682. In C. MURCHISON (Ed.), *A handbook of social psychology.* Worcester: Clark University Press.

MILLER, N. W., G. HUBERT, and J. B. HAMILTON. 1938. Mental and behavioral changes following male hormone treatment of adult castration, hypo-gonadism, and psychic impotence. *Proc. Soc. Exp. Biol.*, *N. Y.*, 38, 538–540.

MILLS, C. A. 1937. Geographic and time variations in body growth and age at menarche. *Human Biol.*, 9, 43–56.

MILLS, C. A., and C. OGLE. 1936. Physiological sterility of adolescence. *Human Biol.*, 8, 607–615.

MOLITCH, M., and R. F. COUSINS. 1934. Variations of basal metabolic rate per unit surface area with age. *J. Nutrit.*, 8, 247–251.

MOLL, A. 1912. *Sexual life of the child.* New York: Macmillan.

MONDIÈRE, A. T. 1880. Sur la monographie de la femme de la Cochinchine. *Bull. Soc. Anthrop.*, 3, 250–261.

NATHANSON, J. T., L. E. TOWNE, and J. C. AUB. 1939. The daily excretion of urinary androgens in normal children. *Endocrinology*, 24, 335–338.

NEURATH, R. 1909. Die vorzeitige Geschlechtsentwicklung. *Ergeb. inn. Med. Kinderheilk.*, 4, 46–81.

NUTTING, L. R. 1923. Some characteristics of leadership. *Sch. and Soc.*, **18**, 389–390.

OSIANDER, F. B. 1795. Resultate von Beobachtungen und Nachrichten über die erste Erscheinung des Monatlichen. *Denkwrdgkth. Keilk. Geburtsh., Göttingen*, **2**, 380–388.

POLLOCK, R., and B. MALZBERG. 1929. Expectation of mental disease. *Ment. Hyg., N. Y.*, **18**, 132–163.

PRESSEY, S. L., and L. C. PRESSEY. 1933. Development of the interest-attitude test. *J. Appl. Psychol.*, **17**, 1–16.

PRYOR, H. B. 1936. Certain physical and physiologic aspects of adolescent development. *J. Pediat.*, **8**, 52–62.

PRYOR, W. R. 1887. A case of precocious development. *Amer. J. Obstetr.*, **20**, 245–251.

RACIBORSKI, M. A. 1844. *De la puberté et de l'âge crétique chez la femme.* Paris : Balliere.

RAUTH, J. E., and P. H. FURFEY. 1933. The maturational factor in adolescent conduct. *Child Develpm.*, **4**, 90–93.

REUBEN, M. S., and G. R. MANNING. 1922–1923. Precocious puberty. *Arch. Pediat.*, **39**, 769–785 ; **40**, 27–44.

REUTER, E. B. 1937. The sociology of adolescence. *Amer. J. Sociol.*, **43**, 414–427.

REUTER, E. B., R. G. FOSTER, M. MEAD, *et al.* 1936. Sociological research in adolescence. *Amer. J. Sociol.*, **42**, 81–94.

RICHEY, H. G. 1931. The blood pressure in boys and girls before and after puberty. *Amer. J. Dis. Child.*, **42**, 1281–1330.

——. 1937. The relation of accelerated, normal and retarded puberty to the height and weight of school children. *Monogr. Soc. Res. Child Develpm.*, **2**, No. 1. Pp. vi + 67.

ROBERTON, J. 1831. Period of puberty in women. *N. Eng. Med. Surg. J.* (Abstracted in *Amer. J. Med. Sci.*, p. 513.)

——. 1832. An inquiry into the natural history of the menstrual function. *Edinb. Med. Surg. J.*, **38**, 227–254.

——. 1842. On the period of puberty in Negro women. *Edinb. Med. Surg. J.*, **58**, 112–120.

——. 1843. Early marriages so common in oriental countries no proof of early puberty. *Edinb. Med. Surg. J.*, **60**, 1–18.

——. 1844. On the alleged influence of climate on female puberty in Greece. *Edinb. Med. Surg. J.*, **62**, 1–11.

——. 1845a. On the period of puberty in Esquimaux women. *Edinb. Med. Surg. J.*, **63**, 57–65.

——. 1845b, 1846. On the period of puberty in Hindu women. *Edinb. Med. Surg. J.*, **64**, 423–429 ; **66**, 56–64.

——. 1848. On the period of puberty in the Negro. *Edinb. Med. Surg. J.*, **69**, 69–77.

RUSH, H. P., J. B. BILDERBACK, D. SLOCUM, and A. ROGERS. 1937. Pubertas praecox (macrogenitsomia). *Endocrinology*, **21**, 404–411.

SCHLICHTING, F. E. 1880. Statistisches über den Eintritt der ersten Menstruation und über Schwangerschaftsdauer. *Arch. Gynäk.*, **16**, 203–232.

SHUTTLEWORTH, F. K. 1937. Sexual maturation and the physical growth of girls age six to nineteen. *Monogr. Soc. Res. Child Develpm.*, **2**, No. 5. Pp. xx + 253.

——. 1938a. The adolescent period : A graphic and pictorial atlas. *Monogr. Soc. Res. Child Develpm.*, **3**, No. 3. Pp. 246.

——. 1938b. Sexual maturation and skeletal growth of girls age six to nineteen. *Monogr. Soc. Res. Child Develpm.*, **3**, No. 5. Pp. 56.

——. 1939. The physical and mental growth of girls and boys age six to nineteen in relation to age at maximum growth. *Monogr. Soc. Res. Child Develpm.*, **4**, No. 3. Pp. vi + 291.

SINGER, M. R. D. 1941. *Precocious puberty and behavior.* Unpublished manuscript.

SKERLJ, B. 1935. Die Menarche in Norwegen und ihre Beziehungen zum Klima. *Arch. Gynäk.*, **159**, 12–21.

SOLLENBERGER, R. T. 1939a. The concept of adolescence. *Psychol. Bull.*, **36**, 601.

——. 1939b. Adolescence, pp. 91–109. In J. DOLLARD, *et al.*, *Frustration and aggression.* New Haven : Yale University Press.

——. 1940. Some relationships between the urinary excretion of male hormone by maturing boys and their expressed interests. *J. Psychol.*, **9**, 179–189.

STARBUCK, E. D. 1899. *Psychology of religion.* New York : Scribner's.

STEIN, A. 1907. Eine dreijahrige Virgo. *Dtsch. med. Wschr.*, **33**, 224.

STOLZ, H. R., M. C. JONES, and J. CHAFFEY. 1937. The junior high school age. *Univ. High Sch. J. (Calif.)*, **15**, 63–72.

STONE, C. P. 1939. Sex drive. In E. ALLEN, C. H. DANFORTH, and E. A. DOISY (Eds.), *On sex and internal secretions.* Baltimore : Williams and Wilkins.

STONE, C. P., and R. G. BARKER. 1934. On the relationships between menarcheal age and certain aspects of personality, intelligence and physique in college women. *J. Genet. Psychol.*, **45**, 121–135.

——. 1937a. On the relationship between menarcheal age and certain measurements of physique in girls of the ages nine to sixteen years. *Human Biol.*, **9**, 1–28.

——. 1937b. Aspects of personality and intelligence in postmenarcheal and premenarcheal girls of the same chronological age. *J. Comp. Psychol.*, **23**, 439–455.

——. 1939. The attitudes and interests of premenarcheal and postmenarcheal girls. *J. Genet. Psychol.*, **54**, 27–71.

SULLIVAN, SISTER CELESTINE. 1934. A scale for measuring development age in girls. *Stud. Psychol. and Psychiat., Cathol. Univ. Amer.*, **4**.

TERMAN, L. M., and C. C. MILES. 1936. *Sex and personality.* New York: McGraw-Hill.

THRASHER, F. M. 1927. *The gang.* Chicago: University of Chicago Press.

TOPPER, A., and H. MULIER. 1932. Basal metabolism of normal children. The puberty reaction. *Amer. J. Dis. Child., 43,* 327–336.

TOWNSEND, C. W. 1896. Thigh-friction in children under one year. *Trans. Amer. Ped. Soc., 8,* 187–189.

VITELES, M. S. 1929. The influence of age of pubescence upon physical and mental status of normal school students. *J. Educ. Psychol., 20,* 360–368.

WADDY, J. M. 1846. Birmingham Lying-In Hospital, medical and statistical report. *Lancet, 1,* 673–675.

WALLENTIN, G. 1885. *Menstruatio praecox.* Breslau.

WESTBROOK, C. H., S. G. LAI, and S. D. HSIAO. 1934. Some physical aspects of adolescence in Chinese students. *Chin. Med. J., 48,* 37–46.

WHIPPLE, G. M. 1915. *Manual of mental and physical tests:* Pt. II. Baltimore: Warwick & York.

WILLOUGHBY, R. R. 1937. Sexuality in the second decade. *Monogr. Soc. Res. Child Develpm., 2,* No. 3. Pp. 54.

CHAPTER 13

RESEARCH ON PRIMITIVE CHILDREN

MARGARET MEAD

Introduction

The value of research upon primitive children to students of psychology is part of the whole larger problem of the relationship of researches made among primitive people to the hypotheses and theories of psychology. Therefore, the history of the uses to which psychology has put data about primitive children and data about primitive peoples when constructing theories of developmental psychology is a history of the changing relationship between anthropology and psychology.

The first use to which psychologists put ethnological data was in constructing biogenetic theories in which the postnatal behavior of the child was regarded as recapitulating the past history of the race. In a thorough examination of this position Hallowell (1939) has shown that any such theory involves these untenable positions: (1) an acceptance of the doctrine of acquired characters, (2) a direct equation between the type of culture found among our primitive contemporaries and previous stages in the history of more advanced cultures, and (3) a demonstrable correspondence between the behavior of civilized children and primitive adults. In its crudest form this old biogenetic theory continues to crop up in the literature, and psychologists continue to make investigations to disprove it (Schubert, 1930; Anastasi and Foley, 1936, 1938). More seriously, it lies, as Hallowell has shown, behind much current psychoanalytic thinking and therefore compromises investigations made among primitive people within the psychoanalytic frame of reference.

All the evidence which we have at the present time goes to suggest that the only cases in which the savage adult can be compared with the child within our society are those in which primitive societies have failed to pattern some aspect of behavior which we have patterned extensively. In those cases, the thinking of the primitive adult, not trained, for example, in scientific logic, may resemble to a certain extent the thinking of civilized children *not yet* trained in the methods of scientific thinking. This resemblance, however, will be negative in terms of slightness of exposure to some cultural patterning and may not be attributed to a greater degree of "primitiveness" in the thinking of the savage adult than of the civilized adult in the sense that primitive means a simpler, a more rudimentary, or an earlier form. Similarly, the drawing of primitive adults who have *never drawn before* often resembles the drawing of civilized children who have *never drawn before,* but when the art of a primitive or non-European society has some positive characteristic—for example, the technique of phenomenal regression instead of perspective—this must be attributed either to the circumstance that the societies have developed and institutionalized different approaches to the problem of representation or to differences in the cultural conditioning of perception (Thouless, 1933). There is the further possibility that, since types of thinking or ways of solving problems may tend to appear in a given order in the development of the child, different cultures may select an earlier ontogenetic tendency than others for elaboration. When this occurs we can find elaborations in given primitive cultures of types of behavior manifested for a brief period and within a restricting and limiting frame in our own culture. In such cases there are available to the psychologist data upon ways in which potentialities of human thought which we leave unexploited or definitely overlay or distort may develop.

This generalization holds in many fields. We can find cultures which develop the potentiality for animistic thought, as we can also find primitive societies which give their children a training which discourages animistic thought even more rigorously than does our own (Mead, 1932), and cultures which fail either to give encouragement and elaborate channeled forms, or to discourage, but leave man's capacity to begin thinking animistically, in childhood, so unpatterned that it will survive merely as an idiosyncrasy in some adults confronted with a new situation (Mead, 1928a).

Roheim (1934b), working within the psychoanalytic frame of reference in the study of primitive children, continues to refer those aspects of primitive culture which are common to all primitive societies to a phylogenetic Oedipus situation, although allowing (Roheim, 1939) more and more for the specific elements in given cultural family situations which account for the particular form which the Oedipus complex takes in the character of members of a given primitive tribe. The most promising attempt to state the relationship between developmental phases in the emerging personality and the institutional-

ized cultural forms of contrasting societies is to be found in Erikson's (1939) theory of the social implications of *epigenesis*. By handling the assumed developmental stages formally (Figure 1) in terms of *zones* predominantly involved at any given stage of development and *modes* of behavior appropriate to each zone, Erikson has constructed a theoretical scheme within which different cultures can be classified according to the extent to which they abbreviate or lengthen these stages, emphasize or deprecate the various modes of behavior associated with given zones, and so produce, as the standard cultural personality, a *monstrum in excessu* or *monstrum in defectu*, stated in terms of developmental possibilities. This approach permits, as did the discredited biogenetic theory, a stimulating cross-comparison between the behavior of children in any given culture, at any given stage, and the behavior of adults in other cultures.

The biogenetic theory and much of the thinking that has replaced it all worked with the concept of *the primitive*, a synthetic personality, built up partly deductively from a hybrid of sociological, pseudo-biological theory, and partly through a miscellaneous mass of detail collected and systematized by such comparative writers as Lévy-Bruhl and Frazer. Such material was further systematized by psychologists like Wundt, Freud, and Stanley Hall, and "the primitive" as an analogue of "the child" or "the neurotic" or "the psychotic" became a theoretical counter in later psychological research (Piaget, 1924; Storch, 1924). Despite the enormous amount of ethnological research that has been done to demonstrate the great complexity and diversity of preliterate cultures (Evans-Prichard, 1934; Beaglehole, 1940) and the untenability of any such concept as "the primitive," this concept still recurs with monotonous frequency in psychological writing today. Meanwhile, there arose a counter tendency to document the extent to which primitive man must be regarded as an acculturated adult, subject to the patterning of his culture, and in no sense more archaic, or simple, in his methods of thinking than are we (Boas, 1938). The very great differences between cultures of the world appear then as comparable to the smallest local variations which obtain at home. This approach, in the hands of members of other disciplines, again tended to crystallize into a series of synthetic primitives, as unreal as their single predecessor, members of a given tribe who were just like us except for a few conspicuous details; the Zuni had a distaste for violence, and the Kwakiutl a freer exaltation of himself. These stereotypes have proved to be almost as mischievous an idea as the primitive who thought prelogically and represented the childhood of the race.

Current sophisticated treatments of the data from primitive society tend to use, in one part of their argument, the data showing that primitive man is just like us in all the respects in which he has been accused of being most different, and in another part of the discussion discrete items of difference as recorded for particular tribes, who become unreal counters for "nonviolence," "jealousy," "lack of knowledge of paternity," etc. This is the result of combining the generalized rebuttals of the older position, based upon a large number of miscellaneous instances, with a certain amount of data on conspicuous differences.

Neither stereotype is of any genuine use to psychologists; one leads to untenable theory, the other to mere dull disbelief, for the average student who is taught that a given kind of native is just like himself except for a few conspicuous and striking differences of behavior of which he knows he would be absolutely incapable, very

properly rejects the whole argument. To convert these stereotypes it will be necessary for psychology gradually to assimilate and reduce to useful form the more recent findings of ethnologists which stress that a fully acculturated member of a living culture differs in *every* respect, and *systematically*, from members of any other culture (Mead, 1934a; Bateson, 1936; Erikson, 1940; see also Köhler, 1937). Lee (1940) shows, for instance, that the Trobriand lack of recognition of paternity is not merely a prop for matriliny or an isolated piece of illogicality among a people who are just like us, but that this nonrecognition stands in a systematic relationship to many other Trobriand ways of thought, a system of thought different from our own.

It is necessary to recognize that the growing child is systematically patterned in every detail, in posture as well as in gesture, in tempo as well as in speech, in his way of thinking as well as in the content of his thinking, in his capacity to feel as well as in the forms which his feeling takes, and that only by an understanding of the extent and internal interrelationships of any of these systems of socialization can the psychologist operate usefully with "the Zuni child" or "the Arapesh child." The use of isolated instances of cultural differences, in the most abstract form possible, so that for the statement "The Mundugumor native feels shame in the outside of his upper arm" the psychologist will substitute "The localization of specific emotions may be introspectively referred to different parts of the body, and parts so identified in one culture may be ignored in another," will enable the psychologist to keep his thinking from becoming culturally limited, but the effect will be negative. Such an abstraction keeps him from making obvious errors of the order of "All children are more animistic than adults," but it does

CHART I : MALE

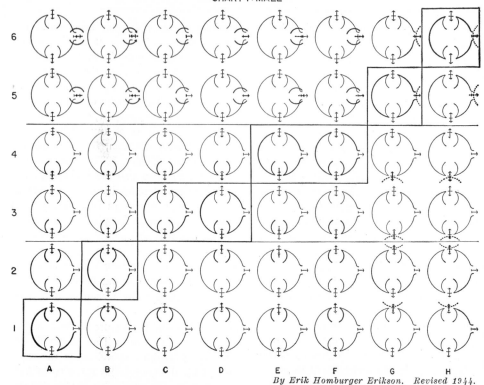

By Erik Homburger Erikson.   Revised 1944.

FIGURE 1. CHART OF MODES AND ZONES.
The chart was first designed as a means for
reducing to a nonverbal common denominator,
namely, that of organ-mode, certain infantile
habits, play acts, and symptoms and their resi-
dues in adult psychopathology. Such seemingly
unrelated acts as the wilful closure of a body
orifice, the retention of objects in containers,
the hiding of feelings in oneself and of oneself
in some claustrum are not only "similar" in
configuration, but also genetically and psychologically related. They have in common the
retentive mode. The chart offers signs for such
modes and arranges them to signify their initial
relation within the successive libidinisation and
training of the body orifices and of the peripheral zones during the "pregenital" phases (Freud)
of infancy and early childhood.

Each large circle is a (topologically and
anatomically naïve) sign for one mode emphasis
in one zone of the organism; nothing more. In
1A and 2B the modes of incorporation (A) as
if sucking a fluid, (B) as if biting off a solid,
are placed in their model zone, the oral zone
(top of circles). The outlining of the larger
circle indicates that the mode is generalized to
include a peripheral system; sense organs and
body surface, also, express and develop by incor-
porative receptivity. In 3CD and 4EF the mode
of closing of a body orifice (C and E) for the
purpose of retention and that of opening it (D
and F) for emission or expulsion are emphasized
in connection with the zone in which they come
to full differentiation, namely, in the anal-
urethral zone (bottom of circles). They are peripherally associated (outlined circle) with the

discriminative function of muscular development
(i.e., holding on, pushing away). The four
modes mentioned so far belong to both sexes
although their basic relatedness to the different
location and mode of the procreative zones (on
the male chart reproduced here: right side of
circles) is potential throughout. The mode of
intrusion (G and H), i.e., the use of a protruding body part for entering another body, is
located in the male genito-urethral zone and,
peripherally, in aggressive locomotion (5G, 6H).
(On the female chart, which is not reproduced
here, the corresponding genito-urethral zone is
the modal orifice for the inceptive mode and its
concomitants in tactual receptivity.)

The mode-zone combinations outlined represent the time-space organization of infantile
body experience during three overlapping phases:
1, 2: oral-respiratory-sensory-tactual; 3, 4: anal-
urethral-muscular; 5, 6: infantile genital-ure-
thral-locomotor. Broken arrows signify that the
mode has been developed and "trained"; the
zone has become society's ward. All modes, however, are partial tendencies in all zones. Horizontally, all the modes appear connected with
one zone, i.e., the oral zone rejects, retains,
eliminates, and intrudes. Vertically, one and the
same mode appears connected with all zones, i.e.,
genitals as well as anus and mouth can become
zones for a generalized closing up.

By varying the assumed duration for each
phase, by outlining different modes, zones, and
peripheral systems one may chart variations in
infantile experience. For example, infants may
be pictured to move from 1A to 1B and further
horizontally in an attempt to "clutch" an uncer-

not permit him to say anything new, to advance any more fruitful hypothesis.

Looking at the development of psychology's use of primitive data from another point of view, we find that in the first stage, that of *analogy*, there was an efflorescence of unprofitable and unsound parallels between primitive man and civilized children which led to a dead end in psychological thinking. This period was followed by the period of disproving the assumptions made in the previous period and using primitive material *negatively*, to call in question psychological assumptions which had contained a Western European premise (Malinowski, 1927a; Mead, 1928b, 1932; Benedict, 1934b). During this period it was further the function of the ethnologist who oriented his work to psychological preoccupations to phrase his material as "Yes, but among the . . . such and such is the case, and so your hypothesis will not hold."

The effect of this type of criticism is to drive the theorist toward higher degrees of abstraction. The Yale frustration-aggression hypothesis (Dollard, Doob, Miller, *et al.*, 1939) is a case in point. The hypothesis states that if a series of acts which would have led to a final satisfying act is interrupted, the subject will either turn toward some other analogous goal (substitution), or he will exhibit aggressive behavior. The critic replies, "Yes, but the Balinese do not see their own behavior in this way. They see their own behavior either as an infinite continuum leading nowhere, or else as separate atomic pieces;

they do not see life as we do, as composed of a series of acts punctuated with satisfactions." This criticism calls attention to the whole problem of "time gestalt" and "purpose," and it is now possible to look at the goal-seeking and at the aggressive behavior in terms of this new abstraction and to see that both are alike in their punctuation, in that both end in climax. This leads us to this generalization: "If an individual has been conditioned to a certain time gestalt and if a sequence of his acts is interrupted, he will turn toward some other sequence in which a similar gestalt is implicit."

Our criticism has led to a higher degree of abstraction and so to a reduction in the number of entities invoked. In place of the alternative entities, "substitution" or "aggression," we now have only one entity, the "time gestalt" (Bateson, 1941). However, a correction of this order, introduced into an hypothesis which had been carefully framed with an attempt to allow for and rule out the cultural factor, can be introduced only on the basis of an exceedingly detailed study of character formation in other cultures. It is therefore to be expected, in terms of the continual cross-fertilization between psychology and anthropology, that, as the field worker takes more cross-culturally useful frames of reference into his field, he will return with material which will be relevant at a higher level of theoretical abstraction in psychology.

This most recent stage in the application of primitive material to psychological theory has a positive aspect, in which the eth-

---

tain source of food or to resist an undesirable one before mode *B* is integrated in 2*B;* or they may persist on the relatively more passive expectancy of mode *A* and continue to 2*A* before proceeding to 2*B*. Wherever on the chart such (vertical) mode or (horizontal) zone fixations occur, meaningful systematic correlates are found in individual life patterns or within the institutions of groups. Some mode-zone combinations correspond only to rare phantasies, perversions, and "strange" customs.

During early childhood the battle of the modes can be observed in wilful or playful, outgoing or regressive habits. Then (beyond this chart) an integration takes place which provides mastery over the basic modalities of existence as learned by the particular organism in the particular society. In such integration the modes become a firm foundation for the infinite variability and specialization of human existence. Isolated, they remain potential stereotypes for rigid and magic defenses against danger and anxiety.

The chart is intended to serve the study of configurational relations as a first step in analysis.

nologist attempts upon the basis of primitive data to develop concepts which could not be arrived at on the basis of any data which we possess. The contribution of the ethnologist here may be likened to the contribution which a chemist might have made in discovering a new element *before* the periodic table was constructed. Because our theories of human nature must always be constructed on the basis of subjects who have been socialized, our progress is exceedingly slow in constructing any theoretical picture of the range of human potentialities and the systematic interrelationship of different parts of this range. Until we have enough data to fill in the analogue of the periodic table for human development, it will be necessary to have more and better-detailed studies of the process of character formation and the resulting personality structure in different cultures. Erikson's (Homburger, 1937) chart makes it possible to make an intelligible statement about certain aspects of character formation in about half the primitive societies upon which we have relevant data about the way in which the zonal behavior is patterned. By developing the method further it would be possible to include not only the trunk, as he does in his groundplan, but also the arms and legs and skin and eyes, etc.; but mere theoretical extension will not tell us the systematic way in which cultural emphasis on other organs is related to the zones which he does treat. The extension will, however, raise problems both for the psychologist and the field worker.

So the psychologist will continue to demand from material gathered by the ethnologist data for correcting his hypotheses —*negative* material—and data for amplifying his hypotheses—*positive* material. Upon the formulation of significant cross-cultural hypotheses which the ethnologist can take into the field will depend the amount of significant materials of this sort

which the ethnologist can bring back; and, if the science of human behavior is to proceed at maximum speed, the field ethnologist concerned with psychological problems must be working with hypotheses even before they reach the point of publication, and not with the formal psychological statements of some years back.

The Psychologist among Primitive Peoples

We can now turn to the history of the attempts of the psychologist to work in the field or to set specific problems or provide tests for the use of the field worker. His first contacts with primitive peoples, like his first use of primitive material, were cast in a biological mold. He wanted to study racial differences. Klineberg (1935) and Goodenough (1936) summarize the state of research here. Goodenough says:

> In view of the relatively small amount of information concerning the mental characteristics of various cultural and racial groups that is based upon direct measurement of simple functions, it is greatly to be regretted that up to the present time psychological interest has been so closely centered about the problem of classification on the basis of general broad assumptions the validity of which is uncertain.

The first research was done on the sense organs and, as Goodenough (1936, p. 6) points out, psychologists were satisfied with the disproof of the extravagant claims of racial differences which had been made and ignored the differences which were found. There was then a very infertile period of applying intelligence tests to primitive children, usually in culture contact environments, which necessitated an equally infertile effort to refute these findings. New efforts are now being made (Porteus, 1937; Cattell, 1940; Stewart, ms. *c*) to develop tests which can be standardized on the members of preliterate cultures and which will yield positive data on how the individuals think, not merely on how we may classify them. To date, no data have been advanced which actually call into question the basic ethnological assumption of the nonexistence of innate psychological differences between races. The principal importance of this type of research lies in its background relationship to other problems, for if there were significant and constant differences between all the members of one primitive group and those of another group, then any study of the socialized individual would have to take them into account.

A second attempt on the part of psychologists to collect primitive data has been prompted by problems which they themselves formulated and for which they collected supporting data. Porteus (1937) set out to test the theory that environment was responsible for the poor showing of natives in a culture contact setting. He made a study of primitive people in two differentially difficult *physical* environments, to find that, if anything, the individuals in the harder environment were superior, but that, on the whole, the differences were unsystematic. Greater reliance upon ethnological data would have suggested that this problem, as it was phrased, was not worth attempting. Dennis (1940a) posed the problem of whether the cradle board affected the age of walking and tested it out in two Hopi communities—one in which the cradle board was still used and one in which its use had been abandoned. Setting aside the reliability of Indian mothers' reports on a problem that involved accuracy in months, the question, like Porteus's, was phrased in a way that tremendously oversimplified the problem. It is to be expected that infants subjected to a type of environmental pressure of which the cradle board is one expression will differ from infants differently reared, but not on such

simple items as "age of walking." Rather will they differ in manner of walking, occasions when they walk, significance of walking for the personality, type of balance disturbance to which the individual is subject, etc. It is even probable that most of these effects would remain even if the cradle board itself disappeared, as long as the whole complex of cultural behavior of which the cradle board had been a part survived (Erikson, 1939).

On the other hand, Dennis (1940c) has developed a concept which has important cross-cultural uses, the concept of autogenous behavior:

> I believe a useful sub-classification of the learned aspects of behaviour can be attained by distinguishing between those things which the individual learns by himself without being aided or directed by others, and those things, like language, which are socially transmitted. The former I have called autogenous, the latter sociogenous behaviour.

However, he does not give this concept its maximum usefulness, as he tends to limit it to behavior during the first year. It might more usefully be rephrased to read that all through life some autogenic behavior will develop, making its appearance in forms determined by the culture, but always present—for example, giggling and awkwardness at puberty, forgetfulness in old age—in at least a great proportion of the individuals of a given culture, etc., without drawing any sharp line between the very early behavior and the later, although granting that, with the introduction of language, the impact of cultural patterning becomes quantitatively greater.

It may also be useful to bear in mind two possible uses for the word *autogenous*. We might apply the word, as Dennis does, to behavior patterns, leaving open the possibility that cultural factors may determine what stimuli will evoke them; or again we might apply the word autogenous to sensitivities (for example, cold, hunger, fatigue, sex, etc.) which are biologically determined, though the behavior patterns exhibited in response to the appropriate stimuli may be culturally determined.

When the emphasis was upon the contribution of research in primitive society as a negative corrective to culturally limited hypotheses, taking a problem into the field, such as the incidence of conflict at adolescence (Mead, 1928b) or the effect of a harsh environment on the intelligence quotient (Porteus, 1937), seemed to be an effective use of primitive material. From such oversimplified studies, however, we could not expect anything except negative, corrective, precautionary conclusions, and such an approach is now definitely out of date.

New Approaches

The new approaches take as a focusing point, not a simple presence or absence, concomitance or nonconcomitance problem, but instead the investigation of the developing individual within the cultural matrix, emphasizing the new knowledge of complex interrelationships between cultural forms and the developing personality. The older approaches relied upon primitive societies to provide laboratories within which different sorts of children could be found whose behavior could be used to disprove or call in question some hypothesis. The value of primitive societies was regarded as lying principally in the fact that the culture was a different one and that special sets of conditions, such as cradle boards, prolonged suckling, nonrecognition of paternity, absence of formal schooling, and no knowledge of graphic techniques, could be found and their "effects" upon the developing personality studied.

We now know that more is to be gained by asking another kind of question, and by utilizing two aspects of primitive cultures: (1) that they have developed historically along different lines from our own and therefore present social forms which we can neither produce experimentally nor derive by extrapolation from known forms, and (2) the circumstance that in small groups of preliterate peoples sharing a common culture it is possible to deal with the individual within the whole society, in relation to his total culture, in a way that is not possible in large groups, in a stratified society, characterized by great heterogeneity of culture. The new questions that the psychologist or the ethnologist working in terms of psychology must ask are positive questions: What is the mechanism of character formation within the new society? What sorts of learning are emphasized and what are the results? How is a personality type which places no value on aggression developed and how do individuals of this sort function within society? Emphasis is laid first upon collecting data upon the total socialization process, and then focal points within that process may be studied.

This approach has grown out of increased emphasis upon personality and culture (Malinowski, 1927a; Frank, 1931, 1938, 1939a; Fromm, 1933; Benedict, 1934a; Mead, 1934a, 1937; Lasswell, 1935; Bateson, 1936; Dubois, 1937a, 1937b; Horney, 1937; Maslow, 1937; Gorer, 1938) and upon an increasing rapprochement between psychoanalytic findings and cultural studies (Mead, 1930c; Glover, 1932; Roheim, 1932, 1934a, 1934b; Dollard, 1935a, 1935b; Horney, 1935; Mekeel, 1935; Opler, 1935; Erikson, 1939; Kroeber, 1939; Lasswell, 1939; Levy, 1939; Schilder, 1940). It has expressed itself in a type of field work most of which is still unpublished (see pp. 704–706). From this type of investigation we may expect data upon the whole socialization process within a given society which are sufficiently precise to give a greater understanding of specific aspects of socialization, such as types of learning (by conditioned reflexes, by "empathy," by different sorts of identification, by dependence upon verbal or nonverbal cues); patterning of interpersonal relationships in preponderantly symmetrical or asymmetrical terms; utilization of biologically given differences, such as sex differences, in building character; interaction between autogenic behavior and cultural forms; minimization or maximization of hereditary defects or special abilities; psychosomatic problems of the relationship of disease pictures to culturally determined forms of character structure; development and utilization of symbolic forms; orders of congruence between sorts of character structure and politicoeconomic forms, etc. Even further illumination is to be expected from using a series of such detailed findings in cross-cultural comparisons which will bring out general tendencies, on the basis of which hypotheses, later to be tested in other ways, can be formed.

A first attempt at such a study was made in *Cooperation and Competition among Primitive Peoples* (Mead, 1937). Kardiner, moreover (1939), using suggestive data upon the formal aspects of the culture, has recently attempted to indicate the lines along which such investigations might proceed. To be more than suggestive, such cross-comparisons must be made of a series of cultures upon which we have data derived from the study of children and individual adults. When such material is available, it will then be possible to develop a number of ways of handling it. But to be significant a cross-cultural survey must compare *systems* of charac-

ter organization, not aggregations of items of behavior, each one of which may be a focal point of learning or cultural discipline, which are merely aligned by the investigator (Ford, 1939).

The most successful survey of primitive education based upon a mass of indifferent sources, but made valuable because it was confined to the North American Indian area, and informed by unusually acute analysis, is that of Pettitt (1940), who has organized his data to show various fundamental aspects of North American Indian educational procedure such as the tendency to delegate disciplinary powers to someone —a relative, or a supernatural outside the immediate family; the use of praise as an incentive to learning and the accompanying inflation of the ego, resulting in sensitivity to the widespread American sanction of shame; and the conscious invocation of imitation in training. The only area upon which we have even the beginning of the necessary material for an intensive local study of socialization is the Southwest, in the studies of Bunzel (Zuni), Dennis, the Beagleholes, and Asch (Hopi), Harper (Jemez), the Whitmans (San Ildefonso), Hawley (Zia), Opler (Apache), and Kluckhohn and Dyk (Navaho). Even here, however, the material is very uneven and has been collected within very different frames of reference. This, however, is the area where there is the largest amount of cultural background material against which psychologists can profitably make detailed studies (Asch, 1936; Dennis, 1940b). Cultures which have been described with sufficient data on socialization to make detailed cross-comparisons possible are the Manus (Mead, 1930a, 1932, 1934b, 1937; Fortune, 1935), the Arapesh (Mead, 1935, 1937, 1940b), the Lepchas (Gorer, 1938), with a far larger amount of material which was collected in 1936–

1939 on the Iatmul and the Balinese (Bateson, E [1]; Mead, E).[2]

A differently oriented set of studies of socialization in which the emphasis is upon the place of the growing individual within a social group, with the data collected and organized to show the way in which status, class, and kin facets of the personality are developed, is to be found in the field studies of Malinowski (1929), and of Hogbin (1931), Firth (1936), and Wedgwood (1938). Fortes (1938) combines this approach with data on more definite psychological problems, such as the rôle of imitation in education.

The new emphasis upon the study of the total socialization process and the investigation of the development of the personality within the whole culture does not obviate the need for precise psychological studies within the primitive societies which will use more controlled methods for the study of small, delimited problems. Without these basic studies, however, the precise investigations are meaningless. The psychologist who used anthropological data in the past had been inclined to pick at random illustrative details torn from the context (Miller, 1928) or recorded in the absence of context, or to content himself with insisting that more precise methods should be used, without formulating the interrelationships between the problems which the precise methods were to solve and the delineation of the total socialization process (Bartlett, 1937).

[1] E = Expedition, that is, field work upon which there are no publications indicating that work has been done on children. (See prefatory note to Bibliography, p. 700.)

[2] On the basis of preliminary reports and published statements of aim or brief summaries, material upon the socialization process may be expected to appear on Alor (Dubois, E), Navaho (Kluckhohn, E), Pilaga (Henry, E), Quiche (Bunzel, E), Zuni (Bunzel, E), Pukapuka (Beagleholes, E), S. Bougainville (Olivers, E), and Kwoma (Whiting, E).

Once this connection is recognized, it will be possible to take more precise psychological methods into the field. For example, in Bali, it may be observed that the incidence of fatigue seems to be much lighter than in other societies. In the absence of other data, for the psychologist to make a precise determination of the degree of fatigue under different sorts of tasks, among the Balinese, would get us absolutely no further than the original observational statement. It would back up the original observation but would not add any further understanding. However, a study of the total picture in Bali shows: the way in which learning takes place, by direct manipulation of the learner's body or by participation by the carried infant in the rhythm of the mother's acts, by observing what others do, but with a minimum of verbal teaching of any sort; the way in which the child's behavior is controlled by the effectively toned exclamation accompanied by the invocation of one of an assortment of fear symbols—wildcat, witch, scorpion; the way in which gradual detachment from other persons and a decrease in and finally the disappearance of bids for personal attention takes place in the Balinese child whose responsiveness is continually played upon by adults and older children; the absence of any manifestation of guilt or remorse; the high degree of hypochondria, coupled with a great preoccupation in playing upon one's own body; the way in which a craftsman uses only the particular muscles absolutely essential to a given task, so that there is no spread to total involvement; the premium that the Balinese put upon orientation in space, and their objection to drunkenness; their interruptibility and apparent lack of perseveration; the absence of goal-oriented behavior.

When these and a great number of comparable motifs have been identified and documented, the psychologist skilled in the measurement of fatigue could go in and make significant, precise studies of the amount of fatigue shown by the Balinese in various relevant contexts—in the presence of strangers, in a strange environment, under exhortation to make an effort, in dangerous occupations involving a threat of personal injury, when given verbal instruction as over against a demonstration of the task, etc.—and from such an investigation as this a real addition to our knowledge of fatigue might be made.

This general principle holds true of all precise measurements of individuals in primitive society; differences in visual acuity are of merely academic interest and lack any theoretical significance unless they can be correlated with a total behavior picture in which they may be shown to play a systematic rôle. Ability to solve a maze, endurance, perseveration, discontinuity of learning, etc., are important to measure if it is possible to show that these identified mental habits have an organized relationship to the type of character standardized in that particular culture. (For example, K. Stewart [ms. *b*] found that Ainu women showed a definite inability to tackle new problems which could be correlated with the special circumstances of older women's social rôle.)

If the field worker is trained in both psychological and ethnological techniques, a great deal of this work can go hand in hand, the areas in which precise measurement, or control groups, would be useful can be identified in the field, and the necessary tests given. Alternatively, ethnologists in the field can carry out various suggestions given them in consultation with psychologists, either before they set out or, more fruitfully, after they have identified the foci of their problem. Examples of such cooperation are Nadel working with Bartlett's suggestions (Nadel, 1937*a*,

1937*b*); Mead working with the Abel Free Design Test (Abel, 1938); Henry and Mirsky working in cooperation with D. Levy (Levy, 1939; Henry, 1940*a*); and conversely Stewart, as a testing psychologist, using techniques of hypnotism, dream analysis, maze-testing, Goodenough test, etc., and working with a knowledge of the cultural background provided by Noone (Stewart, E, ms. *e*); Erikson making his observations among the Sioux with cultural orientation provided by Mekeel (Erikson, 1939) and among the Yurok with cultural orientation provided by Kroeber (Erikson, 1943); and Dennis's extensive use of the manifold published Hopi cultural material (1940*b*).

With the recent elaboration of techniques of recording and observing single-handed, field work is becoming steadily less rewarding, and expeditions in which scientists trained in different disciplines cooperate on the spot will have to take the place of the single worker.

Methods of Research

In discussing methods of field research, certain absolute requirements will be taken for granted and not discussed in detail.[1] In the primitive culture studied, the investigator must have a specially detailed knowledge of the data most immediately relevant to childhood: prenatal care, care of children, family structure, children's play patterns, both formal and informal (Mead, 1931; Flannery, 1936), age grades, initiation system, rituals associated with *rite de passage* (Van Gennep, 1909), etc. He must furthermore have a systematic understanding of the whole culture—the sociopolitical system, the economic arrangements, etc.—so as to be able to place this detailed material in its context. Such an understanding can, of course, be gained

[1] For practical consideration, see Mead (1931).

in several ways: by direct ethnological research, by the use of existing ethnological sources, by cooperation with an ethnologist in the field, or by working with the cooperation and advice of an ethnologist who has been in the field. Work must be done either in the native language or in a contact language in which the children and the investigator have facility (Mead, 1939a). The direct use of an interpreter is not adequate, but educated natives may be used to give tests, record results, etc. The subjects should be known as individuals, so that at no time will an individual's behavior on a test, in a social situation, as recorded in a photograph, have to be interpreted without reference to that individual's known personality and status within the family, the age group, and the community. As most research on primitive children is highly qualitative and utilizes a very limited number of subjects, this condition is not difficult to meet. The research should be done with a closed group, a village, a clan, a locality, a horde, as the case may be, so that the total social situation within which the individuals studied live can be accurately stated (Moreno, 1934). Observations of "forty Indian children gathered from twelve different tribes at a government school," etc., are relatively valueless until an enormous amount of work has been done on the twelve tribes involved, and then it would be more rewarding to study forty children within one of the twelve tribes.

We may now consider the more specific methods by which children's behavior can be studied and by which the implications of the cultural setting as expressed in the behavior of the growing child can be evaluated.

The Natural History Approach. This method is based upon careful observation of primitive children within ordinary life situations: infants in their mothers' arms; siblings struggling over the mother's breasts; children's behavior at the death of a parent or during a quarrel between their parents; behavior of individuals during initiation; etc. In such an approach the investigator is minimally present, effaces himself or his camera as much as possible, and records the surrounding context of behavior as well as the actual behavior. So a struggle witnessed between an old woman and a child, in which the old woman is putting (culturally) excessive energy into attempting to drag the child with her, is given retrospective illumination by the circumstance of the old woman's death three hours later (Bali). A child's display of fear in the arms of a young-girl nurse which is not paralleled by similar behavior in the arms of a different nurse may be placed against the knowledge that the nurse has just quarreled with her guardian and been expelled from the temple society of unmarried girls (Bali). A child who has never been observed refusing food before may suddenly refuse food from his mother with an accompanying temper tantrum (Iatmul). This behavior becomes relevant if the investigator knows that the child was adopted a short time before, had been taught that his mother was not his mother, and that the adoption arrangement had been abruptly terminated the preceding night as a result of a quarrel among the adults.

There are various stages of refinement with which these methods can be used. The records kept may be taken at random whenever significant behavior is observed (Mead, 1928b, 1930b; Hogbin, 1931; Firth, 1936; Gorer, 1938); a large enough sample of different types of observation— for example, "daughters with fathers in mothers' absence," "mimetic play immediately following a cultural spectacle," etc.— may be taken to make quantitative statements possible; or they may be taken at definite intervals (Bateson, E, and Mead,

FIGURE 2. Expression of fear of foreigners by Balinese children. Bajoeng Gede, Bali. G. Bateson. (Reading from left to right and from top to bottom.)

Doemoen, aged ca. 18 months, in her mother's brother's wife's arms. (Dec. 12, 1936. Leica, 3V-34.)

Patera, ca. one year, in his father's arms. (Dec. 8, 1936. Leica, 3T-9.)

Karbo, 310 days old, in his mother's arms. (Dec. 11, 1936. Leica, 3T-34.)

Badera, girl ca. one year, in arms of a neighbor child. (Oct. 10, 1936. Leica, 3A-21.)

E, for Bali and Iatmul; Brown, E; Kluck-hohn, E, for definite periods, once a year). The records themselves may be *retrospective,* that is, written down after the observations have been completed, or *simultaneous.* Simultaneous records may be of many types: running verbal records of behavior (varying in value as to whether the recorder has to look at the medium of recording, so that writing without looking, touch-typing, and stenotyping are superior to methods of recording which require visual attention, such as stenography); records made by one observer or by several observers who concentrate on different aspects of the situation and synchronize against a time scale (available only for Bali); records made with a parallel still photographic record, varying from illustrative photographs (Figures 3, 4, 5, 6) giving a general setting to a short series of photographs in a sequence (Figure 7); a sequence of photographs taken with a miniature camera permitting more lavish expenditure of film and automatically giving a permanent sequence record (Figure 8); a sequence taken with a rapid winder, presenting a far more detailed record (Figure 9); or a set of stills taken simultaneously with a cinematograph record. Cinematograph records represent the most complete behavioral record (exclusive of sound), and vary in refinement from short Ciné sequences interspersed with verbal records and short Ciné sequences interspersed with verbal and still records through the final refinement of two 16-mm. Ciné cameras, staggered so as to give a complete record.[1]

There are two further possibilities of obtaining photographic records which have not yet been tried out. The first is the use of a motor-driven camera and the inclusion of a sound-recording apparatus. Such a method would be very costly and would require three persons, one for the Ciné camera, one for the sound apparatus, and one to keep a verbal situational record, which the sound record would not replace. If it were desired to expand in the direction of equipment rather than in the number of investigators, it is probable that a 35-mm. Ciné camera, equipped with a foot release, a device for taking single frames, and an automatic clock device, might permit a single investigator to approximate but not to equal the record kept by two investigators, in which one makes the photographic record, the other the verbal.[2]

The most significant cleavage among these methods lies between the *retrospective* and *simultaneous* types of records. As this difference applies both to completely "natural," that is, nonexperimental situations, and behavior within experimental set-ups, it will be discussed in detail here. Examples of retrospective records are the following:

> (Dennis, 1939.) (Observation within a contrived set-up among the Hopi.) (1940*b,* p. 145.) Joe seems sleepy and cross. He cries easily. He was sitting on Etta's lap and protested when she tried to get him to sit alone. When he cried, she hugged him

[1] Bateson, Mead, and Belo have experimented with all the various methods described above. Costs of still photographs are enormously reduced by using bulk film and loading it into cassettes in the field, and by supplementing the use of Ciné film by much less expensive series of stills. The use of two Ciné cameras and two miniature cameras makes it possible to record simple behavioral sequences without any break, if it is possible to have an operator for each

Ciné miniature pair. This method, however, necessitates *three* observers, for it has been found that even Ciné records are of very limited value without a complete simultaneous verbal record.

[2] All records made by more than one observer must be made against a time scale, and all records, even by a single observer, are enormously improved by the use of a time scale, not only for behavioral sequences, but also for single bits of behavior observed out of any known context, as the context may later be filled in, or the interval before another observed bit of behavior may become significant.

FIGURE 3. Contrasting ways of handling children. (Reading from left to right and from top to bottom.)

Arapesh, New Guinea. Bischu's ca. week-old baby, carried in a net bag, in which the infant's body gets all-round support as *in utero*. (1932. M. Mead.)

Iatmul, New Guinea. Kalugwaimali's 11-day-old infant on mother's outstretched arm. (May 31, 1938. Leica, 23P. G. Bateson.)

Lepchas, Sikkim. Tafoor's two middle daughters. The Lepcha child spends nearly all waking hours securely fastened to the back, in which position it has to yield passively to every move of the carrier. (1937. G. Gorer. [Gorer, 38 Pl. 23.])

Manus, Admiralty Islands. Ngamel's wife with ca. 8-month-old baby on her back. (1929. M. Mead.)

Pilaga, Argentina. Carrying child in sling. (1936–1937. J. Henry.)

Bajoeng Gede, Bali. Lenjad, carrying her 42-day-old infant girl. Balinese babies are suckled in the sling. (May 6, 1937. Leica, 8E-4. G. Bateson.)

FIGURE 4.   Contrasting ways of carrying older children.   Mandated Territory of New Guinea.
(Reading from left to right and from top to bottom.)

   Mundugumor, Sepik-Aitape District.   Kwenda, carrying adopted twin girl, ca. 2 years.   Child is
given no support by woman whose hands hang idle.   (1932.   M. Mead.)
   Tchambuli, Sepik-Aitape District.   Woman of Wompun hamlet carrying child in ceremonial dress.
No support given by hands of woman.   (1933.   M. Mead.)
   Arapesh, Sepik-Aitape District.   Kamawon, ca. 2-year-old girl, on the back of a young girl,
Wadjubel.   Both of child's legs supported.   (1932.   R. F. Fortune.)
   Manus, Admiralty Islands.   Piwen, aged ca. 2½ years, on the back of her father, Luwil, holding
on herself.   (1929.   M. Mead.)

FIGURE 5. Sleep postures. Iatmul, Balinese, Pilaga, Pitjentara. (Reading from left to right and from top to bottom.)

Bajoeng Gede, Bali. Kenjoen, 266-day-old baby girl, in arms of elder sister, Gati, aged ca. 5 years. (Dec. 24, 1936. Leica, 3Wa-35. G. Bateson.)

Iatmul, New Guinea. Pulembelua, seated on a log, with her ca. 3-month-old baby girl on her lap. (Oct. 5, 1938. Leica, 32A. G. Bateson.)

Pilaga, Argentina. Child asleep at breast. (1936–1937. J. Henry.)

Pitjentara, Central Australia. Tuma, wife of Kanakana, demonstrating how mothers sleep over their children. (1929. G. Roheim.)

FIGURE 6. Children's symbolic play. (Reading from left to right and from top to bottom.)

Siwai, Bougainville, Solomon Islands. Girls dancing in imitation of women. (1938–1939. D. Oliver.)

Iatmul, New Guinea. Kowi and Wanggi, boys ca. 12 years old, making play pots by pouring water into mounds of sand. (Aug. 26, 1938. Leica, 29C-45. G. Bateson.)

Pilaga, Argentina. Naicho and Tapeni, girls making themselves clay breasts. (Henry, 1940b.) (1936–1937. J. Henry.)

Bajoeng Gede, Bali. Karni, ca. 10 years, preadolescent girl, with hair still cropped short, wearing false hair made of grass. (April 14, 1937. Leica, 6V-21. G. Bateson.)

and rocked him back and forth. Then she reached to the window and brought along a half-consumed sucker which apparently had been brought along with such a use in

kept pushing the pig off with his pole and slithering the canoe around for about five minutes. No one came to his aid. Finally the pig gave up and he, still wail-

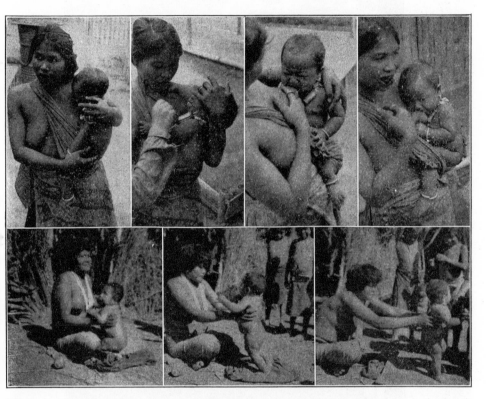

FIGURE 7. Child behavior sequences. (Reading from left to right and from top to bottom.)

Bajoeng Gede, Bali. Raoeh, 312-day-old boy, in mother's arms, while ethnologist medicates his skin. Mother brings child in typical limp fear state; covers his eyes during medication; offers breast to crying child; finally child actively sucks. (Oct. 24, 1936. Leica, 3A-2-5. G. Bateson.)

Pilaga, Argentina. Mother teaching child to walk. Before standing the child up, the mother raises and lowers the baby, never lifting it from the ground, just flexing and unflexing its legs. (1936–1937. J. Henry.)

view. This quieted him but he remained on her lap.

(Mead, 1929. Field notes.) (Observation in natural set-up on a Manus child, aged 2½ to 3 years.) Ponkob, 43–4. Ponkob was in a canoe alone, a fairly shallow one, punting. A great pig started to attack the canoe. He screamed with fright but nevertheless didn't lose his head, and

ing, made for his house. This happened right behind his own house.

We may compare such records with simultaneous running records of behavior:

(Fortes, 1938, p. 31.) (Observation of three Tallensi children who had been building a play cattle kraal which had collapsed in the course of their play.) Suddenly,

FIGURE 8. Characteristic teasing situation. Bali. Selection from a sequence of 23 frames (Leica, 5A-3-28), covering about 10 minutes of scenes among wedding guests in Bajoeng Gede. March 1, 1937. G. Bateson. (Reading from left to right and from top to bottom.)

Karsa, unweaned boy ca. 3 years, crouches laughing behind his mother, Men Singin, who holds her sister's crying baby girl, Meres.

Karsa begins to show anger when his mother gives her breast to the baby.

Mother has returned the baby to her child nurse but is unresponsive to Karsa's continued temper tantrum.

Mother covers her mouth; Karsa still in a temper.

Mother finally picks up Karsa, who pushes her face away.

with a shout, Gomma began to scramble off the baobab branch, followed by Zoo, calling out, "Let's swing." For a minute or two they rocked back and forth on the branch and then descended. Now Gomma remembered his cows. Vehemently he ac-

(Beagleholes, 1941.) (Account of weaning of a Pukapuka child.) Mata, a childless married woman, is minding her sister's baby, William (aged 8 months), for the day, while his mother works in the taro gardens. The child is soon to be weaned

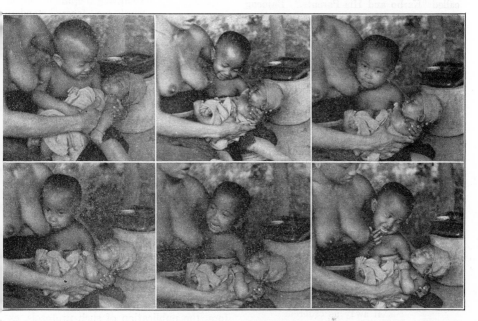

FIGURE 9. Sibling behavior sequence. (Bajoeng Gede, Bali. April 30, 1937. Leica, 7V-34-39. G. Bateson.) (Reading from left to right and from top to bottom.)

Njawa, girl ca. 3 years, infant brother, aged 30 days, in mother's arms, at a birthday feast for another child. End of a 14-frame sequence. At the beginning of the incident, the mother puts the baby in Njawa's lap, a standard way of making children show off. In the frames shown, the mother's attention wanders and the weaned older child absently steals to the breast, then grins back at the baby.

cused his sister of having taken them, and when she denied this, challenged her to "swear." "All right," she said placidly. Gomma took a pinch of sand in his left hand and put his right thumb on it. Zoo licked her thumb and pressed down with it on Gomma's thumbnail. He stood still a moment, then suddenly withdrew his thumb. (This is a children's play ordeal.) Gomma examined his sister's thumb and found sand adhering. "There you are," he said, rapping her on the head with a crooked finger.

and has already started to eat taro and nuts. Mata's keeping the child for the whole day is part of the weaning process. The child gets restless and fretful, so Mata picks it up in her arms and rocks it violently, cuddling it fiercely, bumping it about and patting it with no gentle hand. To soothe the child further she gives it her dry breast to suck. The baby sucks hard and then, when he can get no milk, he stands up and suddenly bites Mata's neck. Then he returns to the breast and ends by giving her nipple a severe nip with his teeth. Mata slaps the child on the head. The child cries hard, throws itself about in her lap. It is given some coconut flesh to eat but continues to whimper for some time.

(Mead. Notes.) (Excerpt from record called "Karbo and His Parents." Bajoeng Gede, Bali, October 11, 1937. Karbo is 19 months old; natives speaking Balinese.)

11.32 A.M. K comes to step, sits and wiggles on his bottom.

N. Oera (father of Karbo) rattles some money on the cement.

K turns and looks at him.

K drops a piece of banana skin.

K takes an enormous mouthful (of banana).

N. Oera exclaims in alarm then, "There, chew it."

K pounds with bracelets on the cement.

K takes banana and pounds with it.

N. Oera, "Eh! Eh!" (mild exclamation of pain) "Throw it away!"

K pounds again and throws it away as ordered.

K pounds another piece.

N. Oera, "Throw it away!"

11.35 A.M. K. "Away," and throws it away also. (Repeating the last syllable of the Balinese *koetang*, "throw away." This form of syllable clipping is culturally standardized for baby talk, and between intimates.)

A record of this sort can be compared in detail with the following excerpt from "Scaring Children," November 10, 1937, in which Karbo, aged 20 months, is carried by Moespa, a girl of about 11, onto my veranda. (Natives speaking Balinese.)

9.50 A.M. K reaches toward my papers, out of Moespa's arms.

Moespa, holding him, says, "*Aroh*" (an exclamation of fright or pain), "*aroh*, contains worms."

K puts a marble into his mouth.

Moespa, "Spit it out. Contains faeces, contains faeces" (omitting the initial *t* in the word *tae*, faeces, standard baby talk).

K spits it out.

K puts marble in his mouth again.

I say "*Aroh!*" as closely imitating Moespa's tone as possible.

K takes marble out and *then* spits.

We may now consider the advantages of the two types of records. The retrospective type of recording is only as valuable as the questions which were already formulated in the investigator's mind. He selects for later recording certain aspects of the behavior, and later he makes generalizations based upon these illustrations. They may suggest new problems, but they will rarely yield answers to problems which the investigator has not formulated. Therefore, the publication of such protocols, except illustratively, to show the type of data used, is hardly justified, in terms of publication costs, because they will already have been squeezed almost dry of theoretical implications. Simultaneous records, on the other hand, although inevitably somewhat affected by the frame of reference also, contain a great deal more spontaneous observation and may yield to analysis and reanalysis, not only by the investigator, but also by other investigators. Records of this type permit detailed comparisons between many aspects of the behavior of children of the same age, of the same child at different ages, and between children from different cultures. Retrospective recording is an efficient method for solving the negative type of problem which has now been outdated. For the new approach, what we need is a mass of very detailed material about the way in which the individual child develops within his culture; simultaneous records which are ultimately to be made available in full are an absolute requirement.[1]

A further advance in the natural history approach is made when the same situations are recorded for a number of children, for the same child over time, and in different cultures. Advances in this respect have been due to practical considerations which rather limit the number of comparable situations as between cultures, for example, bathing a baby; and theoretical considerations, mainly contributed by various psychoanalytic frames of reference, which have suggested that some situations (suckling, weaning, cleansing after excretion, handling of genitals, sibling rivalry, etc.) were specially significant in the process of character formation and therefore important to observe in detail. Although materials for cross-comparison become immediately much more usable if such standard observations have been made, it is possible to overemphasize the importance of these crucial situations. Erikson's more abstract statement suggests the need for recording tendencies which find many different expressions during the socialization process. Because the simplest way to demonstrate a type of child training is to give a vivid illustration, as Roheim's illustration of the way in which a Normanby Island mother sings a song as she suckles her child, which is accompanied by pulling the nipple out of the child's mouth at the end of each phrase (Roheim, 1932), there is a tendency to oversimplify the problem and say that

such an experience as this in itself produces the type of character formation observed in the adult.

A more discriminating and accurate way of stating the matter would be to say that in the illustrative incident there are a number of details—for example, the rhythm, the deprivation, the returning of the nipple, etc.—and that of these some one or more are specially significant inasmuch as they are backed up by innumerable other small habitual details of daily life. An identical sort of behavior where, however, it was the rhythm and not the deprivation which was the more typical element, might be found elsewhere, associated with quite different character structure. Similarly, in Iatmul, the nipple is frequently pulled out of the child's mouth in order to transfer the child to the other breast, hoped to contain more milk. Such a deprivation will have a very different effect from that produced by interrupting a child's sucking before it has finished because the mother dislikes suckling, as Mundugumor mothers do (Mead, 1935). Similarly, in the Iatmul custom by which the mother subjects the child to a mock weaning, wreathing her nipples with human hair for fifteen hours or so, and then going on nursing the child again, until, a month or so later, she finally weans it with a hair wreath, the significant element is the false alarm, which ties up with many other aspects of Iatmul behavior, while the use of human hair as a weaning mechanism, although found in many societies, has no very important tie-up in Iatmul.

If we emphasize too heavily a formal set of data, on suckling, weaning, sphincter control, etc., some of these most important nuances are likely to be lost. So, while continuing to collect as much material on these standard situations as possible, in order to assure comparable masses of data, the next task is to make simultaneous, de-

---

1 Such records need not necessarily be printed. They may be mimeographed and given a small library circulation, or they may be put on microfilm. This latter technique, however, is not very fully adapted to methods of detailed cross-comparison between sets of data.

tailed, and, if possible, multiple-observer and multiple-technique records of large sequences of behavior in normal situations. Such sequences will be valuable in direct proportion to their length, continuity, and the amount of detail recorded. From long records of the interactions of about three human beings in a culturally natural context we may be able to answer great numbers of problems not yet formulated; we can attack such points as cadence and tempo of behavior, proportion of symbolic to nonsymbolic activity at different age levels, the sequence in which one type of activity is substituted for another, etc.

Recording of Verbal Behavior. The various American schools of anthropology and the Malinowski school have all insisted upon the value of collecting ethnological materials in text, that is, literally recorded in the native language. Text collection has usually been regarded as a corrective for overenthusiastic interpretation, and very little emphasis has been given, except by Malinowski (1935, Vol. II), to the extent to which a record of words spoken in sequence is a record of behavior. Even without a photographic record of the posture of the individual, and with no formal system for recording tone of voice, large masses of spoken or written (where writing has been introduced) comment from native children is a specially usable form of data.

(Mead. Notes.) (Monologue [directed toward the investigator] of a Manus child, Kawa, aged 4-5 years, February 19, 1929.)
I am called [i.e., someone is calling me].
My tobacco is in the box of Kopal.
There is no paper but someone will get some in the house of mourning.
Give me some paper to smoke.
Pwailep is at the house of Katu.
Pwailep is the niece [*kaka,* literally, sister's daughter].

Ponap and Posuman have gone to work for the white man.
Topal [her brother] wants to take my tobacco to the Usiai [members of another tribe with whom the Manus trade].
Someone calls.
We have no food, it is all in the bush [i.e., not yet traded for].
The ghosts are about. [There has been a death in the village and the presence of inimical ghosts makes going about, and trading, dangerous.]
We haven't a big canoe.
Ngawa wants to go to make a ceremonial exchange in Dropal.
Do you want to buy it?
I. What?
K. Some paper. My tobacco is in the box of Kandra in our [exclusive possessive pronoun] house.

It is also possible to get children from about nine years to adolescence to dictate material, sometimes quite lengthy texts.

(Mead, 1928b.) (Portraits of themselves dictated in Samoan by two Samoan adolescent girls. 1926.)

I

I am a girl. I am short. I have long hair. I love my sisters and all the people I know how to weave baskets and fishing baskets and how to prepare paper mulberry bark. I live in the house of the pastor (p. 255).

II

I am clever at weaving mats and fine mats and baskets and blinds and floor mats. I go and carry water for all of my household to drink and for others also. I go and gather bananas and breadfruit and leaves and make the oven with my sisters. Then we [herself and her sisters] go fishing together, and then it is night (p. 256).

(Bateson, 1938. Notes.) (Informant Kowi, boy, aged 12. October 22, 1938. In the presence of Mbetna, aged 14.) In the

Agamora Reach [of the river] there she went to *undumbu* [Land of the Dead], they took her. They brought [her] to the village. Having put [her] in the house, they wept. Then "turn pancakes" when he had said and looked [and there were none], he hit [her with] adze. Here [holding his own wrist] the spirits put her heart he hit her. She went to *undumbu*. They wept for her. What [shall I say now]? In the morning, going in the top of a malay apple tree he went and hung himself. He—first having tied it badly he fell. Having fallen with a good rattan having tied it he fell. He hanged. Djaneimbuangga [and] Ambwanembindo undid him. They buried him.

Text records of conversations between children and parents, or between children, are also much more valuable than translations, but the problem of getting down more than brief exchanges is very great, whereas in dictated texts or slow, dreamy monologues, the recorder has a chance to keep up with the child.

(Mead. Notes.) (Conversation between Kawa, girl, aged 4, and Tjokal, boy, aged 11–12, immediately following the monologue recorded above. February 19, 1929.)

Tj. Kawa, your father is calling you.
K. I have no canoe.
Tj. The child-of-Ngandiliu has one, go on.
Tj. (To me.) Her father is calling her. He says: "This evening all the ghosts will emerge."
Kawa comes back.
K. We haven't any food in our house. They didn't go to the bush. To-morrow we'll go.

The Cross-section Method. The investigator of primitive children is usually limited to a brief period, seldom exceeding a year, and if he wishes to describe the way in which children develop within that culture he must perforce use the cross-section method, that is, construct a picture of the total socialization process by reference to the observed behavior of groups of children at each age level. Many criticisms of the limitations of the cross-section method as it applies specifically to the study of the individual, culturally seen, have been made (Mead, 1928b, pp. 261–262; Dollard, 1935b, p. 4; Beagleholes, 1941). Supplemented by the *retrospective* and the *simultaneous* (see below) life history, however, cross-sectional methods are likely to remain one of the principal standbys of the study of children in other cultures. Two methodological devices can increase their usefulness. The first of these is maximum and detailed attention given to the behavior of individuals in periods of maturation, *defined as transitional* for purposes of the investigation. So, if the adolescent girls have been classified by the usages of the culture or by the investigator into groups of preadolescent, adolescent, and postadolescent, there will be certain individuals who stand conspicuously, in physique or behavior or status, whatever the criteria are, at transitional points. The task of the investigator will then be to define the central tendency in the group which the transition individuals are on the point of leaving and the central tendency in the group toward which the transition individual is moving. These individuals will then be observed in the greatest detail, and every alteration or variance of behavior relevant to the defined behavior of the two groups will be recorded, analyzed, and subjected to immediate scrutiny in terms of situational or constitutional or social structural factors which might make it atypical.

This transitional behavior will furthermore be utilized to get introspective comments from preadolescents and adolescents about the behavior, and to get the adults to make retrospective and valuational comments of the order of "I remember when

I reached menarche, my mother said . . . ," and "She is just about to reach menarche, she should stop dancing," or "Yes, he refused to carry her even though she had a sore foot because he is not *sapta*" (brave enough to raise a momentarily nubile girl above his shoulder). A year usually provides enough time to study a significant number of transitional cases, whether it be a suckled child through weaning to post-weaning, a child with an unpregnant mother through the mother's recognition that she is pregnant, a child with all milk teeth through loss of several milk teeth, a child who is still too young to go anywhere alone through the period when he is entrusted with his first older-boy tasks, etc.

The second method is one invented by Lasswell (1937), and requires a greater refinement of data and knowledge of age level than are usually available in a small primitive group. It might, however, be available for work in an alien culture with a large population, if the observer had a limited amount of time but almost unlimited resources for observation. By this method the observer keeps under simultaneous observation, in terms of a detailed schedule of behavior items, a series of overlapping age or status groups, so that the transition from *a* to *b* to *c* is recorded for two different groups, when the group in stage *a* was entering *b*, and when the group in stage *b* was entering stage *c*. The detailed utilization of this method is dependent upon knowledge of age of subjects or the substitution of some physiological criteria which are systematically related to behavior, that is, classification according to change of voice in one culture and height in another. It would be difficult to handle cross-culturally but would not interfere with the adequacy of the method within a given culture. In a general way it may be utilized in any cross-section study of individuals in a living culture and provides the technique for correcting any error which may come from observing individuals, for instance, from one point of view, so that the group in period *b* is thought of more in terms of having left period *a* than as approaching period *c*, etc.

Other Methods Which Can Be Combined with Cross-section Studies. The field worker is always under far greater pressure than the psychological investigator working within our society. He usually has a definite and very inadequate time allowance, he is working in the medium of a foreign language with subjects unaccustomed to any sort of routine or discipline, and even if the main outlines of the culture are known he has to pay constant attention to the unraveling of the cultural implications of the simplest acts. Furthermore, a great deal of time has to go to subsistence and supporting activities, buying food, medical care of the natives, maintaining rapport, etc. Any techniques which can short-cut this problem are doubly useful.

I shall discuss these three in detail: Fortune's handling of *events*, my own method of utilizing the *deviant case*, and an adaptation of Levy's method of *pure cases*. In the use of *events*, extensively developed by Fortune (1935), events of a certain type, illness, misfortunes, quarrels, etc., are taken as focusing points for the study of the behavior of all individuals involved in that particular situation. This method, applied to the study of children, means that at the end of a field trip one would have a systematic account of the behavior of children of given age and sex when confronted with comparable situations within their households, such as birth, death, quarrels, major *rite de passage* ceremonials, etc. If this method is to be used systematically, a type of event must be chosen which is likely to occur often enough o provide a real sample; for example, quarrels would be a suitable selection for a six-month investigation among the Iatmul, but no large sample of quarrels could be obtained in a two-year study of Bali.

In my method of the *deviant case*, cases which vary from the observed norm, either environmentally or in personality, are selected for study. These cases are analyzed in terms of generalizations already made about the group behavior and the factors molding it. For example, individuals from biological families are analyzed to show whether hypotheses made about the influences of large households can be supported (Mead, 1928b, pp. 141–143), or single cases of early weaning are examined to see what light they throw on the rôle of late weaning (Mead, 1935, p. 38); the behavior of little boys whose fathers are dead is examined in cultures where the father plays an important part in education (Mead, 1930b, pp. 112–116). Then, as a related method, deviations in behavior, such as the individual child who has temper tantrums beyond the customary age limit (Mead, 1935, p. 51) or the girl who bursts out with a suicidal wish at a funeral ceremony in a society where all such outbursts of emotion are disallowed (Mead, E) or the child who steals in a society where stealing is most unusual (Mead, 1928b, pp. 178–180), are analyzed to discover what elements in the social background or experience of the individual may explain the behavior. The fullest published material on cases of this latter sort is that of Henry (1940b), in which three cases of Pilaga children who refused to speak were analyzed to show the emotional deprivation which the children had undergone. A final use of deviant cases is the study of the behavior of individuals whose personality approximates least accurately the type of behavior for that age and sex approved by the group, as a device for illuminating the functioning of the more successfully acculturated individuals (Mead, 1935).

Levy (1938–1939), in his method of *pure cases*, selects from a large set of full case records a series of cases, all having several hypothetically significant criteria in common, and then analyzes these cases in detail to show a pattern of interaction between the developing personality and the social environment. This method can be applied in the field by making the criteria of "purity" a series of items of conformance to the cultural ideal, for instance, or conformance to the statistical norm. So a series of cases which were "pure" because they were ideal, or "pure" because they were statistically usual, could be analyzed to show what sort of personality developed under the circumstances which the culture postulated, and those which actually obtained in the culture. For the Mountain Arapesh, for instance, this would mean studying a series of children from families where the father and mother had been betrothed in childhood, the mother had grown up in the father's parents' home, and there had been no other wife and both father and mother were mild personalities; these would be the pure cases of the cultural ideal. Such a series could be set against children in homes where there were two wives, at least one of whom had not been "grown" by the husband during a child betrothal, which is the statistically usual condition.

The Life History. The significance of the life history in the study of the development of personality within a cultural setting has been most fully stated by Dollard (1935b), and the most satisfactorily annotated published life history of a member of a living native culture is Gorer's life of Kurma (1938). Radin's *Crashing Thunder* (1926) is still a classic in this field, and Dyk's *Son of Old Man Hat*, published in 1938, falls far behind it in usefulness, because it lacks cultural annotation. Perham's (1936) set of life histories of ten Africans affords interesting data on available types of material, and Barton's (1938) *Philippine Pagans* throws considerable light on adolescence. Collected and unpublished life history materials are listed below (summary table in bibliography).

It is usual to characterize the life history approach as dynamic and involving time as an active dimension, and the cross-section approach as static, but actually the use of transitional cases in cross-sectional studies shows the individual acting in time, whereas time is merely an implied dimension when the individual relates past events as they appear to him in the present. Life histories may be distinguished in respect to what point in the individual's life is taken as the focus. In the *retrospective* life history, or autobiography, adults relate the story of their lives as they now appear to them; in the *simultaneous* life history, a section of the life of an individual capable of introspective comment is recorded, both in terms of actual events and of the individual's comment upon those events. Parallel with this utilization of introspection are *longitudinal* methods, designed especially for the study of young children or the application of tests, in which the behavior of individuals is observed over a period of time, or at stated intervals with wide gaps, throughout a period of development.

The Retrospective Life History. Much has been claimed for this technique as restoring the organic locus to the study of personality. It is undeniable that an adult's account of his early memories and childhood experiences furnishes valuable data on the way in which adults see childhood experience, their own and other peoples'. However, they are essentially data upon how the narrator feels, what significance those experiences have for him in the present, not data upon his actual development in the present. This distinction has been lost sight of because for therapeutic purposes a false memory is as good as a real one. When our object is the study of the impact of culture upon the growing personality, however, data derived from these introspective accounts must be taken with the greatest caution. This is particularly so when the material is gleaned from the memories of survivors of an earlier cultural era and there are no living children against whose experiences these memories can be checked (Eastman, 1902; Michelson, 1918–1919, 1932, 1933; Radin, 1926; Linderman, 1930, 1932; Stewart ms. *d*; Devereux, 1937; Landes, 1938).

The survivors of an earlier period may well give a record of their childhood training which jibes perfectly with the data they give on their attitudes as young men and women, on their accounts of cultural values and emphases, and on their present attitudes toward life. There is, however, no guarantee that this internal consistency has not been imposed by the narrator upon the actual facts of their experience and, whereas consistency among a large number of unrelated observations on individuals of different ages within a living society can be regarded as strengthening the presumption of accuracy for any one observation (if the observations are of such an order that the coherence which might be introduced by the investigator can be ruled out, for example, myths, formal rituals, literal texts, photographic records, as well as observations on behavior), such consistency in retrospective life histories is not of any such value.

The only circumstances under which life histories from members of broken cultures unsupported by any observational data can be of value is when there are several of them, with systematic differences among them, and sufficient data about the person lities of the narrators so that some day these personalities may be placed in a theoretical frame of reference and we may be able to say, "The formal culture, as seen through the eyes of three individuals of type x, two of type y, three of type z, etc., appears to be of type x, and the differences in the versions given by the various narrators confirm this hypothesis." It is probable that by the time that we know enough to make any such systematic statement we shall not need to reconstruct the childhood experience of members of cultures on which we have only this very limited kind of data. Because there is a possibility that we might need it, however, investigators are urged to get as many data as possible on the present personality of their informants (including moving pictures showing posture and gesture, or at least long continuous portrait sequences, literal records of responses to situations which can be standardized for all informants, disease pictures, if any, performance on projective methods such as the Rorschach, etc.).

In the meantime, retrospective life histories are useful mainly in the study of the parents of children who are also being studied and may throw valuable light upon the way in which the child's behavior is being interpreted and reacted to by the parent. They are especially valuable if the informants combine memories of their own past with a running comment upon their children's present behavior and if such records can then be put beside observational records of the children's behavior. Children's own accounts of their pasts are even more valuable.

However, such records as these become, in effect, what I propose to call *simultaneous* life histories, in which the emphasis is upon the individual's comment, whether it includes retrospective material or not, upon current events, the substance of which is known to the investigator. When such records stretch over several months and are carefully correlated with events in the real life situation, very valuable data can be obtained on the behavior of parents when got from adults, and also on their own behavior when the material is gathered from adolescents and children. This method was extensively pursued among the Iatmul. Such simultaneous life histories can be continually checked against the events which have stimulated the memories,[1] and the memories themselves can be compared with other individuals' memories of the same event and with the way in which similar situations are being handled in the lives of contemporary children. So an adult's comment on his own adoption, made at a time when he is giving back, in a fit of petulance, a name owned by his adoptive father, may be placed against the actual circumstances under which a child of three is at the moment being adopted.[2]

Longitudinal Studies. It is generally recognized that all the above methods, cross-sectional studies and various types of life-history techniques, are imperfect compro-

[1] This method was used by Gorer (1938, p. 403) in checking up on Kurma's belief, not shared by the rest of the group, that his brother had been murdered. The excerpt from Kowi's account of his father's suicide (see p. 691) is taken from a check series of eighteen accounts of a suicide in Iatmul, in which the fourteen lengthy and detailed versions fail to agree upon any point except the fact that the man killed his wife and hanged himself, after the rope broke once.

[2] A still more relevant procedure is obtaining personal comments from children themselves on current events in their own lives. No records of this sort have been published. I collected, among the Iatmul, a fair number of verbatim monologues from preadolescent and just-adolescent boys, with one series of material from a boy just passing through change of voice, which practically amounts to a life history, in which present reverie, memories of the past, daydreams about the future, and comment on immediate events, such as a threat of sorcery or the destruction of his gardens by a careless fire, are all woven together.

mises and substitutes for the on-going life history in which the course of individual lives would be recorded, within the full social setting, from infancy to maturity. The Beagleholes are committed to the absolute necessity of such a measure, and on the basis of a seven-and-a-half-month study of Pukapuka children (E. Beaglehole, 1941) assert that, no matter how great the mass of data accumulated in a short-time study, these data cannot be interpreted without a study of selected children over a longer period. I have just completed a study in which I followed a series of Balinese mountain children for a period of a year, with some interruptions over a second nine months, and during a check-up visit a year later, so that there are records of their behavior over a period of thirty-three months. Placing the data of this study against intensive cross-sectional studies made in four other cultures, I do not find that the advantages of a longitudinal study are anything like those which the Beagleholes predicted. There is obviously a richer body of material collected over thirty-three months than over periods of seven to nine months (the periods of the other studies), and for purposes of exposition it is useful to be able to show a film of a thirty-three-month spread in the same child's life. This material has not yet been analyzed in detail, and it is possible that as yet unguessed values will come out of the longitudinal aspects of the study. To date, however, I do not see them. If the proper checks are used in the cross-sectional method, as outlined above, and the field worker has a theoretical framework within which individual behavior can be translated into an understanding of the dynamics of socialization, the increased understanding to be derived from work in two cultures, rather than the time spent on a longitudinal study of one, would in my opinion be more rewarding.

Kluckhohn, working on the same assumption as the Beagleholes, but with less insistence upon continuous observation over a period of time, is undertaking a fifteen-year study of Navaho children, with periodic observations at yearly intervals. Only a very general statement of his plan is as yet available (Kluckhohn, 1939). For the success of such a plan, consistency and objectivity of records, holding the rôle of the observer constant, and not too great cultural change are all desirable, and difficult to attain.

Projective Methods. Projective methods are particularly suited to the study of primitive children, and the results are excellent expository devices. The general discussions of projective methods (Homburger, Erikson, 1937; Lerner, 1937; Frank 1939b) have to be supplemented by a few further remarks when the methods are to be used not primarily to study children as individuals but to throw light upon cultural processes. The projective techniques should be as free from culturally limiting elements as possible. For example, Stewart's metal maze tests (Stewart, ms. e) are less culturally limited than is the Porteus maze test; and the Goodenough drawing test, used freely, is more useful than forcing children to draw a white man so as to make it possible to score it. Methods which do not require isolation of the subject are preferable to those that do, for any method, such as Levy's sibling rivalry test, which requires privacy will be definitely ruled out for some cultures. Surprise and bizarre elements are undesirable because the news of the tests will be spread too rapidly through the group and standards of behavior will be imaginatively elaborated outside. Tests which require complicated but recordable responses will be valuable in proportion to the amount of response they elicit; tests to which motor responses are important should be avoided unless they can be given in front of a cinema, as our vocabulary for describing motor responses is not capable of any sort of cross-cultural accuracy.

At the same time, the simpler the situation to which the children are asked to respond, the more probability there is that the responses will reveal a high proportion of cultural patterning. For example, in the use of toys a small series permits a great number of repeats as every child is likely to use all three or four of the toys presented; a large assortment permits each child to make an idiosyncratic choice and the underlying pattern is less apparent. As the number of cases will always be few, any test which encourages range is more difficult to deal with. It is also desirable to eliminate tests in which the prompting given by the experimenter is stereotyped (for our own culture, of course) and tests in which expected responses in terms of our culture have been incorporated in the test.[1] Some projective methods, like the Rorschach, depend for their interpretation upon the compiling of cultural norms for age and sex groups.[2]

Useful projective methods may be classified into experimental situations which permit a variety of responses, varying from the presentation of a simple situation in which responses are recorded (for example,

Japanese paper flowers which open in water, Mead, 1932) through stylized situations, of which the Levy sibling rivalry test is the best example (Levy, 1939; Henry, 1940a), to free play with a series of toys.[3]

Children's drawings are perhaps one of the most generally usable projective methods (Figure 10). They are the simplest to collect. It is necessary to keep a record of the composition of each drawing group, the date, the sequence of sheets if a child does more than one, and interpretations, either spontaneously given or systematically elicited. However, the bulk of the data is provided by the children's work, which can be analyzed at leisure out of the field. The material, if white paper and a black pencil or crayon are used, is easily reproduced and very comparable from culture to culture. To make any use of such material, further than to say that each set of drawings betrays a definite style (which shows up sharply in Stewart's, ms. a, enormous collection of Goodenough drawing tests from different tribes), it is necessary to have a proper record of the adult art style and particular knowledge of the children's own art styles as portrayed in sand drawings, mud sculpture, scratching on walls, etc. With such data, a variety of problems can be attacked in terms of drawing material, more positive than the old biogenetic theory. (Relationship of children's drawings to this theory is summarized in Hallowell [1939]. Compare also Anastasi and Foley [1936] and Schubert [1930].)

Examples of such problems are the ex-

1 In giving the Weigl test to Balinese boys, Jane Belo followed the prescribed procedure and stopped the test when they had sorted for form and content, these being the two usual responses for individuals in our society. A later analysis of test results showed that many Balinese used other categories, such as position, and place in a color pattern, as categories of equal importance with form and color, so that, in stopping the test when form and color had been sorted for, a culturally limited "right answer" had been forced upon the subject.

2 Doctor Dubois tells me that the analysis of her series of thirty Rorschachs, all on adults, shows this number to be insufficient, and the collection of Rorschachs on children, when the adult standards are not known, would not in the opinion of her consultants be rewarding.

3 In visual terms, these types of specificity are represented by picture interpretation (Mead, 1928a), to the setting of a problem (Draw something you are afraid of [Stewart, E]; draw a man killing a man [Mead, E]) or by cutting the drawing paper to specified shapes (Mead, 1940b) or by permitting the children to draw whatever they like.

FIGURE 10. Children's drawings showing stylistic differences. (Reading from left to right and from top to bottom.)

Iatmul tribe, Sepik-Aitape District, New Guinea. Man, woman, and animal figures. Gambu-kundiavwan, boy, ca. 12 years. (July 28, 1938. Collected by M. Mead.)

Arapesh tribe, Sepik-Aitape District, New Guinea. Human beings, lizards, trees, houses, moon and stars. Nigimarib, boy, ca. 7 years. (April 4, 1932. Collected by M. Mead.)

Manus, Admiralty Islands, New Guinea. Fishing for turtle from a European schooner. Loponiu. (February 24, 1929. Collected by M. Mead.)

Sajan village, Bali. Two figures from shadow play. I Gandir, boy, ca. 6 years. (1934. Collected by J. Belo.) (Belo, 1937.)

tent to which personalization is character-istic of the children's thought (Mead, 1932); the formation of style (Mead, E; Belo, 1937); emotional attitudes (Stewart, E, drawings of dreams; Mead, E, "draw a man and woman"); and the problem of identifying basic patterns of symbolism. The contrast between drawings of Balinese and Iatmul children is extremely interest-ing in this connection. The Balinese way of life is exceedingly formal, stereotyped, and static, interpersonal relations are con-ducted with a minimum of emotional ex-pression, the minutiae of etiquette govern every act; Balinese children's drawings are full of activity, with free-flowing lines and the depiction of vigorous movement.

The Iatmul way of life is in the strongest contrast to the Balinese. Interpersonal relations of greatest vigor and assertiveness are the rule, quarrels and reconciliations a continual feature of village life. The Iatmul child's drawings, however, are static and scattered aimlessly over the page; there is no movement and no relationship between one design element and another; when told to draw two men fighting they would draw a figure of a man and say, "He is dead." When it is realized that Balinese children are persistently discouraged when they attempt to bring human relations to a climax, whereas Iatmul children are taught to exert maximum personal pressure in order to induce others to satisfy their needs, the importance of these materials becomes evident.[1]

Extensive use of play technique among primitive peoples was first made by Roheim among the Central Australians and on Normanby Island, where he found the Australian children dominantly interested in genital play, the Normanby Islanders in mother-child play in which the same characters become alternately mother and child and husband and wife. Roheim, however, controlled the plot of his play situations by interjecting such remarks as "What does the husband do to the wife?" I have used toys among the Iatmul, and the Henrys (Henry, J. and Z., 1944) have extensive records for the Pilaga.

All attempts to use projective techniques will be fruitful to the extent that the attention of the investigator is focused upon the rôle of the culture. He should not merely look for isolated types of behavior similar or different from our own in situations which are experimentally controlled,

but should try to see the behavior as produced by the cultural setting.

Future Research

The general trends in research among primitive children have already been indicated above as being (1) increased emphasis upon the study of the developing child within the culture seen as a whole; (2) possibilities for detailed psychological exploration of aspects of development which a preliminary study of the total situation have shown to be relevant; and (3) accumulation of masses of simultaneous records, verbatim accounts of behavior, photographic records, multiple-observer records, performance on tests of the projective type, etc., which will be amenable to subsequent analysis as our hypotheses become more refined. If problems are to be taken into the field, they should be problems of the constellative type, hypotheses which involve a fair number of factors assumed to be interrelated, rather than problems which seek to isolate the effects of one factor. The large amount of existing unpublished material on primitive children, some of which is summarized in the table below, provides another source for research. Psychologists may phrase their problems in such a way that field workers may be able to provide relevant material from their existing notes.[2] Nothing, however, is so pressing as more intensive detailed studies of the development of children in living primitive societies. These data are invaluable in extending our knowledge of the possible range of human behavior. Only with this sort of material can we lay the foundations of a psychology free from the limitations of our own cultural bias; and, once the few surviving primitive societies

[1] Iatmul children's use of toys in free play is congruent. They construct tableaux and state, for example, that "The snake has killed the child [a female]. The 'possum [who represents the male child] has killed the snake, and the 'possum now mourns [a female activity] over the dead child."

[2] See *Introduction to Cooperation and Competition among Primitive Peoples* (Mead, 1937) for discussion of this point.

have yielded to culture contact, we shall have no possible way of replacing them.

Bibliography

PREFATORY NOTE

Publications in anthropology differ from publications in psychology, where short, formal summaries of masses of concrete observations are the acceptable form in which detailed studies are presented to the student. In anthropological research, a full account of the background against which the individual is studied cannot be omitted in a final statement of the material, and the publication is delayed until facilities for complete monograph publication are available. As a result, a large part of the work on primitive children which has been done in the last ten years is still unpublished. I have therefore adopted a procedure rather different from that which will be employed by the authors of other chapters. I placed notices in anthropological journals asking for unpublished results, in manuscript or summary, to be sent to me, and I circularized such field workers as were known to have done some work on children, asking specific questions about methods employed and types of results obtained. Where the information which I have received is merely that a given worker has used such and such a method in such and such a tribe, but no manuscript or supporting evidence has been forwarded to me, I can only publish this statement without taking any responsibility for the extent and fullness of the results.

As an appendix to the bibliography, I have presented a summary table of the information which has been supplied to me in response to these requests. Manuscripts to which I have had access are listed in the regular bibliography. Field work upon which there are no publications indicating that work has been done on children has been listed as Expeditions (E), under the name of the field worker. By including this list of unpublished materials and completed but unorganized field work, I hope to encourage the use of these materials by workers interested in collecting as much comparative material as possible.

ABEL, T. M. 1938. Free designs of a limited scope as a personality index. *Character and Pers.,* **7,** 50–62.

AGINSKY, B. W. (E) Skokomish, Pomo. New York University.

ANASTASI, A., and J. P. FOLEY, Jr. 1936. An analysis of spontaneous drawings by children of different cultures. *J. Appl. Psychol.,* **20,** 689–727.

——. 1938. A study of animal drawings by Indian children of the North Pacific Coast. *J. Soc. Psychol.,* **9,** 363–374.

ARKIN, E. A. 1935. *The child and its toy in primitive culture.* (In Russian.) Moscow: Zentralny Institut Ochrany Zdorovya Detyei i Podrostkov.

ASCH, S. E. 1936. *The social life of the Hopi child.* (Unpublished manuscript.)

BARTLETT, F. C. 1937. Psychological methods in anthropological problems. *Africa* (London), **10,** 400–420.

BARTON, R. F. 1938. *Philippine pagans: The autobiographies of three Ifugaos.* New York: Routledge.

BATAILLE, G. 1930. L'art primitif. *Documents,* **7,** 389–397.

BATESON, G. 1936. *Naven.* Cambridge: University Press.

——. 1941. *The frustration-aggression hypothesis and culture.* (Contribution to the symposium on the effects of frustration. Eleventh Annual Meeting, Eastern Psychological Association, April 5, 1940.) *Psychol. Rev.,* **48,** 350–355.

BATESON, G., and M. MEAD. 1942. *Balinese character: A photographic analysis.* New York: New York Academy of Sciences (Special Publications, Vol. II).

——. (E) Iatmul, New Guinea, Bali.

BEAGLEHOLE, E. 1940. Psychic stress in a Tongan village. *Proceedings, Sixth Pacific Science Congress,* **4,** 43–52.

——. 1941. Interpersonal theory and social psychology, *Psychiatry,* **4,** 61–77.

BEAGLEHOLE, E., and P. BEAGLEHOLE. 1941. *Personality development in Pukapukan children.* In *Language, culture, and personality,* pp. 282–298. L. SPIER, A. I. HALLOWELL, S. S. NEWMAN, Editors. Menasha, Wis.: Sapir Memorial Publication Fund.

BEAGLEHOLE, P. 1935. Notes on personal development in two Hopi villages. *Mem. Amer. Anthrop. Ass.,* **44,** 25–65.

BELO, J. 1937. Balinese children's drawing. *Djawa,* 5 and 6.

BENEDICT, R. 1934a. *Patterns of culture.* Boston: Houghton Mifflin.

——. 1934b. Anthropology and the abnormal. *J. Gen. Psychol.,* **10,** 59–82.

——. 1938. Continuities and discontinuities in cultural conditioning. *Psychiatry,* **1,** 161–167.

BERNDT, R. M. (E) Boldea, Jaraldi tribe. Sydney University.

BLACKWOOD, B. 1927. A study of mental testing in relation to anthropology. *Ment. Meas. Monogr.,* No. 4. Pp. 117.

BOAS, F. 1938. *The mind of primitive man.* New York: Macmillan.

BROWN, G. (E) Hehe, Tanganyika. Temple University.

BUNZEL, R. (E) Guiché, Guatemala; Chamula, Mexico; Zuni, New Mexico. Columbia University.

CAMBOUÉ, P. P. 1907. Notes sur quelques coutûmes malagaches. *Anthropos*, **2**, 981–989.

CATTELL, R. B. 1940. A culture-free intelligence test. *J. Educ. Psychol.*, **31**, 161–179.

CHÉMALI, B. 1910. Naissance et premier age au Liban. *Anthropos*, **5**, 734.

COOPER, J. M. 1928. Child training among primitive peoples. *Primitive Man*, **1**, No. 1. 10–16.

DELORIA, E. (E) Dakota. Columbia University.

DENNIS, W. 1940a. The effect of cradling practices upon the onset of walking in Hopi children. *J. Genet. Psychol.*, **56**, 77–86.

——. 1940b. *The Hopi child.* New York: Appleton-Century.

——. 1940c. Infant reaction to restraint: An evaluation of Watson's theory. *Trans. N. Y. Acad. Sci.*

——. 1940d. Does culture appreciably affect patterns of infant behavior? *J. Soc. Psychol.*, **12**, 305–317.

——. 1941. *The socialization of the Hopi child.* In *Language, culture, and personality*, 259–271. Menasha, Wis.: Sapir Memorial Publication Fund.

——. (E) Cochiti, Zuni, New Mexico. University of Virginia.

DENNIS, W., and M. G. DENNIS. 1940. Cradles and cradling customs of the Pueblo Indians. *Amer. Anthrop.*, **42**, 107–115.

DEVEREUX, G. 1937. Institutionalized homosexuality of the Mohave Indians. *Hum. Biol.*, **9**, 498–527.

DOLLARD, J. 1935a. Mental hygiene and a scientific culture. *Int. J. Ethics*, **45**, 431–435.

——. 1935b. *Criteria for the life history.* New Haven: Yale University Press.

DOLLARD, J., L. W. DOOB, N. E. MILLER, O. H. MOWRER, R. R. SEARS, *et al.* 1939. *Frustration and aggression.* New Haven: Yale University Press.

DOLS, P. J. 1908. L'enfance chez les Chinois de la province Kan-sou. *Anthropos*, **3**, 761.

DOOLEY, C. T. 1934–1936. Child training among the Wangaru. *Primitive Man*, **8**, 22–31; **8**, 73–81; **9**, 1–12.

DUBOIS, C. 1937a. Some anthropological perspectives on psychoanalysis. *Psychoanal. Rev.*, **24**, 246–273.

——. 1937b. Some psychological objectives and techniques in ethnography. *J. Soc. Psychol.*, **8**, 285–300.

——. 1944. *The people of Alor; A sociopsychological study of an East Indian island.* University of Minnesota Press. (In Press.)

DYK, W. 1938. *Son of Old Man Hat.* New York: Harcourt, Brace.

EASTMAN, C. A. 1902. *Indian boyhood.* New York: McClure.

EDEL, M. M. (E) Batciga, East Africa. Brooklyn College.

ERIKSON, E. HOMBURGER. 1939. *See also* HOMBURGER, E. Observations on Sioux education. *J. Psychol.*, **7**, 101–156.

——. 1940. Problems of infancy and early childhood. In *Cyclopedia of Medicine, Surgery, and Specialties.* Philadelphia: Davis.

——. 1943. Observations on the Yurok: Childhood and world image. *Univ. Calif. Publ. in Amer. Archaeol. Ethnol.*, **35**, 257–302.

EVANS-PRICHARD, E. E. 1934. Lévy-Bruhl's theory of primitive mentality. *Bull., Faculty of Arts, Univ. Egypt, Cairo*, **2**, Pt. 1.

FIRTH, R. 1936. *We the Tikopia.* London: Allen and Unwin.

FLANNERY, R. 1936. Some aspects of James Bay recreative culture. *Primitive Man*, **9**, 49–56.

——. 1937. Child behavior from the standpoint of the cultural anthropologist. *J. Educ. Sociol.*, **10**, 470–478.

FORD, C. S. 1939. Society, culture, and the human organism. *J. Gen. Psychol.*, **20**, 135–179.

FORTES, M. 1938. Social and psychological aspects of education in Taleland. Supplement to *Africa*, **11**, 4. Or *Internat. Inst. of African Languages and Cultures*, Memorandum 17.

FORTUNE, R. F. 1935. Manus religion. *Mem. Amer. Phil. Soc.*, **3** (Oct.).

——. 1939. Arapesh warfare. *Amer. Anthrop.*, **41**, 22–41.

——. 1942. Arapesh texts and grammar. *Publ. Amer. Ethnol. Soc.*, **19**, 237.

FRANK, L. K. 1931. The concept of inviolability in culture. *Amer. J. Sociol.*, **36**, 607–615.

——. 1938. Cultural control and physiological autonomy. *Amer. J. Orthopsychiat.*, **8**, 622–626.

——. 1939a. Cultural coercion and individual distortion. *Psychiatry*, **2**, 11–27.

——. 1939b. Projective methods for the study of personality. *J. Psychol.*, **8**, 389–413.

FROMM, E. 1933. Die psychoanalytische Charakterologie und ihre Bedeutung für die Sozialpsychologie. *Z. Sozialforsch.*, **1**, 253–277.

GILHODES, P. C. 1911. Naissance et enfance chez les Katchins (Birmanie). *Anthropos*, **6**, 868–884.

GLOVER, E. 1932. Common problems in psychoanalysis and anthropology. *Brit. J. Med. Psychol.*, **12**, 109–131.

GOODENOUGH, F. 1936. The measurements of mental functions in primitive groups. *Amer. Anthrop.*, **38**, 1–11.

GORER, G. 1938. *Himalayan village.* London: Michael Joseph.

GRIMBLE, A. 1921. From birth to death in the Gilbert Islands. *J. Roy. Anthrop. Inst.*, **51**, 5–54.

GRINNELL, G. B. 1923. *The Cheyenne Indians.* New Haven: Yale University Press.

HALLOWELL, A. I. 1939. The child, the savage,

and human experience. *Proc. 6th Inst. Except. Child., Child Res. Clin.*, 8–34.

HAMBLY, W. D. 1926. *Origins of education among primitive peoples: A comparative study in racial development.* London : Macmillan.

HARPER, B. W. ms. *Infancy; childhood; adolescence; pregnancy and birth, Pueblo of Jemez, 1926–1935.*

HARRIS, J. S. (E) S. E. Nigeria. Columbia University.

HAWLEY, F. (E) Zia Pueblo. University of Chicago.

HENRY, J. 1936. The personality of the Kaingang Indians. *Character and Pers.*, 5, 113–123.

——. 1940a. Some cultural determinants of hostility in Pilaga Indian children. *Amer. J. Orthopsychiat.*, 10, 111–112.

——. 1940b. Speech disturbances in Pilaga Indians. *Amer. J. Orthopsychiat.*, 10, 362–365.

HENRY, J., and Z. HENRY. 1944. *The doll play of Pilaga Indian children. Amer. J. Orthopsychiat.*, Research Monograph, No. 4. 160 pp.

HOGBIN, H. I. 1931. Education at Ontong Jaya, Solomon Islands. *Amer. Anthrop.*, 33, 601–614.

——. 1943. A New Guinea infancy : From conception to weaning in Wogeo. *Oceania*, 13, 285–309.

——. (E) Malaita, Solomon Islands. Sydney University.

HOMBURGER, E. 1937. (*See also* ERIKSON, E. HOMBURGER.) Configurations in play-clinical notes. *Psychoanal. Quart.*, 6, 139–214.

HORNEY, K. 1935. The problem of feminine masochism. *Psychoanal. Rev.*, 22, 241–257.

——. 1937. *The neurotic personality of our time.* New York : Norton.

HOVEY, E. O. 1918. Child-life among the Smith Sound Eskimo. *Nat. Hist.*, 18, 361–371.

KARDINER, A. 1939. *The individual and his society.* New York : Columbia University Press.

KIDD, D. 1906. *Savage childhood: A study of Kafir children.* London : Black.

KLER, J. 1938. Birth, infancy, and childhood among the Ordos Mongold. *Primitive Man*, 11, 58–67.

KLINEBERG, O. 1928. An experimental study of speed and other factors in "racial" differences. *Arch. Psychol.*, No. 93.

——. 1935. *Race differences.* New York : Harper.

KLUCKHOHN, C. 1939. Theoretical bases for an empirical method of studying the acquisition of culture by individuals. *Man*, 39, 98–103.

——. (E) Navajo ; Hopi (Moencopi). Harvard University.

KÖHLER, W. 1937. Psychological remarks on some questions of anthropology. *Amer. J. Psychol.*, 59, 271–288.

KROEBER, A. L. 1939. Totem and taboo in retrospect. *Amer. J. Sociol.*, 45, 446–451.

LANDES, R. 1938. *The Ojibwa woman.* New York : Columbia University Press.

LASSWELL, H. D. 1935. Collective autism as a consequence of culture contact. *Z. Sozialforsch.*, 4, 232–247.

——. 1937. The method of interlapping observation in the study of personality and culture. *J. Abnorm. Soc. Psychol.*, 32, 240–243.

——. 1939. Person, personality, group, culture. *Psychiatry*, 2, 533–561.

LAYARD, J. (E) Atchin (Malekula) ; New Hebrides. 17 Parkhill Road, London, N.W. 3.

LEE, D. 1940. A primitive system of values. *Phil. of Sci.*, 7, 355–378.

LERNER, E. 1937. New techniques for tracing cultural factors in children's personality organization. *J. Educ. Sociol.*, 10, 479–486.

LEVY, D. 1938–1939. Maternal overprotection : I, II, III. *Psychiatry*, 1, 561–562 ; 2, 99–109 ; 3, 563–597.

——. 1939. Sibling rivalry studies in children of primitive groups. *Amer. J. Orthopsychiat.*, 9, 205–214.

LINDERMAN, F. B. 1930. *American.* New York : Day.

——. 1932. *Red mother.* New York : Day.

LINDGREN, E. J. 1935. Field work in social psychology. *Brit. J. Psychol.*, 26, 177–182.

LIPKIND, W. (E) Karajá of Brazil. Columbia University.

MALINOWSKI, B. 1927a. *Sex and repression in savage society.* New York : Harcourt, Brace ; London, Kegan Paul.

——. 1927b. *The father in primitive psychology.* New York : Norton.

——. 1929. *The sexual life of savages in North-Western Melanesia: An ethnographic account of courtship, marriage, and family life among the natives of Trobriand Islands in British New Guinea.* New York : Liveright ; London, Routledge.

——. 1935. *Coral gardens and their magic.* (2 vols.) London : Allen and Unwin.

MANDELBAUM, D. (E) Kota, India. University of Minnesota.

MASLOW, A. H. 1937. Personality and patterns of culture. In R. STAGNER, *Psychology of personality*, pp. 408–428. New York : McGraw-Hill.

McPHEE, C. 1938. Children and music in Bali. *Djawa*, 6, 1–15.

MEAD, M. 1928a. A lapse of animism among a primitive people. *Psyche*, 9, 72–79.

——. 1928b. *Coming of age in Samoa.* New York : Morrow.

——. 1928c. The role of the individual in Samoan culture. *J. Roy. Anthrop. Inst., London*, 58, 481–495. Reprinted in A. L. KROEBER and T. T. WATERMAN, *Source book in anthropology,* pp. 545–561. New York: Harcourt, Brace, 1931.

MEAD, M. 1930a. Adolescence in primitive and modern society. In F. V. CALVERTON and S. D. SCHMALHAUSEN (Eds.), *The new generation: Symposium.* New York: Macaulay.

——. 1930b. *Growing up in New Guinea.* New York: Morrow.

——. 1930c. An ethnologist's footnote to "Totem and Taboo." *Psychoanal. Rev.,* **17,** 297–304.

——. 1931. The primitive child. In C. MURCHISON (Ed.), *A handbook of child psychology.* Worcester: Clark University Press.

——. 1932. Investigation of thought of primitive children with special reference to animism. *J. Roy. Anthrop. Inst.,* **62,** 173–190.

——. 1933. More comprehensive field methods. *Amer. Anthrop.,* **35,** 1–15.

——. 1934a. The use of primitive material in the study of personality. *Character and Pers.,* **3,** 1–16.

——. 1934b. Kinship in the Admiralties. *Anthrop. Pap. Amer. Mus. Nat. Hist., N. Y.,* **34,** Pt. II.

——. 1935. *Sex and temperament in three primitive societies.* New York: Morrow; London: Routledge.

——. 1937. *Cooperation and competition among primitive peoples.* New York: McGraw-Hill.

——. 1939a. Native languages as field work tools. *Amer. Anthrop.,* **41,** 189–205.

——. 1939b. Researches in Bali and New Guinea. *Trans. N. Y. Acad. Sci.,* **2,** 1–8.

——. 1940a. Character formation in two South Sea societies. *Proc. Amer. Neurol. Ass.,* **66,** 99–103.

——. 1940b. The mountain Arapesh: II. Supernaturalism; III. The socio-economic life; IV. Record of Unabelin. *Anthrop. Pap. Amer. Mus. Nat. Hist., N. Y.,* **37,** No. 3, 319–451; ms. *b.*

——. (E) Bali; Iatmul, New Guinea.

MEKEEL, S. 1935. Clinic and culture. *J. Abnorm. Soc. Psychol.,* **30,** 292–300.

——. 1936. An anthropologist's observations on American Indian education. *Progr. Educ.,* **13,** 151–159.

MICHELSON, T. 1918–1919. Autobiography of a Fox woman. *Ann. Rep. Bur. Amer. Ethnol.,* **40,** 291–337.

——. 1932. Narrative of a Southern Cheyenne woman. *Smiths Misc. Coll.,* **87,** 1–13.

——. 1933. Narrative of an Arapaho woman. *Amer. Anthrop.,* **35,** 595–611.

MILLER, N. 1928. *The child in primitive society.* New York: Brentano.

MIRSKY, J. (E) Comanche; Coban, Guatemala. Columbia University.

MORENO, F. 1934. Who shall survive? *Nerv. Ment. Dis. Monogr. Ser.,* No. 58.

NADEL, S. F. 1937a. The typological approach to culture. *Character and Pers.,* **5,** 267–284.

——. 1937b. Experiments on cultural psychology. *Africa* (London), **10,** 421–435.

NISSEN, H. W., S. MACHOVER, and E. F. KINDER. 1935. A study of performance tests given to a group of native African Negro children. *Brit. J. Psychol.,* **25,** 308–355.

OLIVER, D., and E. OLIVER. (E) Siwai, Bougainville. Peabody Museum, Cambridge, Mass.

OPLER, M. E. 1935. The psychoanalytic treatment of culture. *Psychoanal. Rev.,* **22,** 138–157.

——. 1941. An Apache life-way. The economical, social, and religious institutions of the Chiricahua Indians. *Univ. of Chicago Publ. in Anthropol.*

——. (E) Jicarilla Apache, Lipan Apache, Mescalero Apache. Claremont College.

PERHAM, M. 1936. *Ten Africans.* London: Faber and Faber.

PETTITT, G. A. 1940. *Primitive education in North America: Its processes and effects.* Unpublished Dissertation, University of California.

PIAGET, J. 1924. *Le jugement et le raisonnement chez l'enfant.* Neufchâtel et Paris: Delachauz et Nièstlé.

——. 1928. *Judgment and reasoning in the child.* (Trans. by M. WARDEN.) New York: Harcourt, Brace; London: Kegan Paul.

PORTEUS, S. D. 1937. *Primitive intelligence and environment.* New York: Macmillan.

——. 1939. Racial group differences in mentality. *Tabulae biologicae,* **18,** 66–75.

PROBST, M. 1906. Les dessins des enfants Kabyles. *Arch. Psychol., genève,* **6,** 131–140.

RADIN, P. (Ed.). 1926. *Crashing Thunder; the autobiography of a Winnebago Indian.* New York: Appleton.

RADIN, P. 1936. Ojibway and Ottawa puberty dreams. In R. H. LOWIE (Ed.), *Essays in anthropology,* presented to A. L. KROEBER. Berkeley.

READ, M. H. 1937. Songs of the Ngoni people: Lullabies and initiation songs. *Bantu Studies,* **11,** 1–35.

——. (E) Chewa, N. Rhodesia. London School of Economics.

ROHEIM, G. 1932. Psychoanalysis of primitive cultural types. *Int. J. Psycho-anal.,* **13,** 2–221.

——. 1934a. *The riddle of the Sphinx.* London: Hogarth Press and Institute of Psycho-Analysis.

——. 1934b. The study of character development and the ontogenetic theory of culture. In E. E. EVANS-PRICHARD, R. FIRTH, B. MALINOWSKI, and I. SCHAPERA (Eds.), Essays presented to C. G. SELIGMAN. London: Kegan Paul. Pp. 281–292.

——. 1939. Racial differences in the neuroses and psychoses. *Psychiatry,* **2,** 386.

ROHEIM, G. 1941. Play analysis with Normanby Island children. *Amer. J. Orthopsychiatry*, 11, 524–529.

——. 1943. Children's games and rhymes in Duau. *Amer. Anthropologist*, 45, 99–119.

SAPIR, E. 1934. Emergence of the concept of personality in the study of culture. *J. Soc. Psychol.*, 5, 408–415.

SCHILDER, P. 1940. Cultural patterns and constructive psychology. *Psychoanal. Rev.*, 27, 159–170.

SCHUBERT, A. 1930. Drawings of Orotchen children and young people. *J. Genet. Psychol.*, 37, 232–244.

SLEGTENHORST, H. J. 1930. Karakterologisch Onderzoek van de Rijpere Jeugd in Nederlandsch-Indie. *De Indische Gids*, 970–978.

SMITH, E. W. 1934. Indigenous education in Africa. In E. E. EVANS-PRICHARD, R. FIRTH, B. MALINOWSKI, and I. SCHAPERA (Eds.), *Essays presented to C. G. Seligman*, pp. 319–334. London: Kegan Paul.

SPITZ, R. A. 1935. Frükindliches Erleben und Erwachsenenkultur bei den Primitiven. Bemerkungen zu Margaret Mead, *Growing up in New Guinea*. Imago, vol. 21.

STERN, B. 1934. The Lummi Indians of Northwest Washington. (*Columbia Univ. Contr. Anthrop.*, 17.) New York: Columbia University Press. (For sale in U. S. by J. J. Augustin.)

STEWARD, J. H. 1934. Two Paiute autobiographies. *Univ. Calif. Publ. Amer. Archaeol. Ethnol.*, 33, 423–438.

STEWART, K. R. ms. a. The Goodenough "draw-a-man" test.

——. ms. b. Psychometric studies among the Ainu.

——. ms. c. A report on the results of Porteus maze tests among some of the racial groups of South-Eastern Asia and the Peripheral Islands.

——. ms. d. A study of dreams in Temiar culture (*Malaya*). (In collaboration with S. D. NOONE, Perak Museum.)

——. ms. e. Stewart ring puzzle test.

——. (E) Negritos, Luzon; Ainu, Japan; Yami, Botto Tobago; Senoi, Malaya. 176–11 East Street, Salt Lake City.

STORCH, A. 1924. The primitive archaic forms of inner experience and thought in schizophrenia: A genetic and clinical study of schizophrenia. *Nerv. Ment. Dis. Monogr. Ser.*, No. 36.

STRONG, D. (E) Naskapi. Columbia University.

TAX, S. (E) Fox, Guatemalan Indians. University of Chicago.

THOMPSON, L. (E) Fiji (Lau Island); Guam. Bishop Museum, Honolulu.

THOULESS, R. H. 1933. A racial difference in perception. *J. Soc. Psychol.*, 4, 330–339.

TURNER, S. 1938. Infant life in Yuanling. *Primitive Man*, 11, 1–25.

UNDERHILL, R. 1936. The autobiography of a Papago woman. *Mem. Amer. Anthrop. Ass.*, 46, No. 3, Pt. 2.

VAN GENNEP, A. 1909. Les rites de passage. Étude systematique de rites. Paris: Librairie Critique.

WAGLEY, C. (E) Guatemala, Taperape, C. Brazil. Columbia University.

WARD, E. 1936. The parent-child relationship among the Yoruba. *Primitive Man*, 9, 56–63.

WEDGWOOD, C. 1938. The life of children in Manam. *Oceania*, 9, 1–29.

WHITING, J. W. M. (E) Temino of Oregon; Kwoma, New Guinea; Painte (Harvey Valley). Yale University.

WHITING, J. W. M., and S. REED. Kwoma culture. *Oceania*, 9, 197–199.

——. 1941. Becoming a Kwoma. Yale University Press.

WHITMAN, W., and M. WHITMAN. ms. Education at San Ildefonso.

Unpublished Research [1]

[1] This table was compiled in the spring of 1940 on the basis of a questionnaire sent to all workers in the field. Owing to conditions caused by the war, it has not been possible to do a second follow-up of the small amount of work which has been done since. One considerable study, instituted in 1941, must, however, be mentioned. The Committee on Indian Education, jointly sponsored by the Committee on Human Development and the U. S. Bureau of Indian Affairs, has undertaken the study of six modern Indian tribes in the United States: the Hopi, Zuni, Zia, Navaho, Papago, and Sioux. The Committee on Indian Education is composed of W. Lloyd Warner, Chairman, Dr. Robert J. Havighurst, and Dr. Ralph Tyler, all of the University of Chicago. The Coordinator of Research is Dr. Laura Thompson. The goal of the research is to synthesize and integrate the various approaches to a single study for each tribe, and then, through the comparative method, to discover the social factors that are most important in the development of personality and the factors that seem to be more individually and psychically determined. Perhaps of equal importance is an interest in refining and developing present techniques for the analysis of personality development and for the study of social behavior among groups of people. The methods used include those from anthropology, sociology, and psychology. The social organization of each tribe has been studied and psychological tests, including intelligence tests (Arthur performance), projective techniques (Rorschach tests and Murray's thematic apperception tests), psy-

TABLE SUMMARIZING THE UNPUBLISHED RESEARCH METHODS AND MATERIALS REPORTED BY 24 INVESTIGATORS
(The investigators are listed in the bibliography with addresses in case they have not published.)

	Legend
General	1. Observations of children in ordinary life situations.
	2. Detailed material on the standardized treatment of and training of children.
	3. Time samples of child behavior.
	4. Studies of group behavior.
	5. Tests of any sort.
	6. Experimental methods of any sort.
	7. Childhood material obtained from adults by life history method.
	8. Life history materials obtained from children or adolescents.
Projective Methods	9. Children's drawings, modeling, or carving.
	10. Rorschach records.
	11. Tests of the Levy Sibling Rivalry Type.
	12. Tests involving cognitive processes of the Nadel (1937) type.
	13. Intelligence tests used as projective methods, for example, Porteus Maze or Goodenough.
	14. Use of free play techniques.
Miscellaneous	15. Collection of children's games and songs.
	16. Intelligence tests.
	17. Tests of sense perception.
	18. Collections of children's dreams.
Photographed	19. Typical treatment of children, for example, suckling position.
	20. Standard activities of children's games, etc.
	21. Studies of parent-child behavior.
	22. Studies of individual children.
	23. Studies of series of children in any standard set-up.
	24. Body-build pictures.
Language Development	25. Baby talk or special children's language.
	26. Records of the way in which children learn a language.
	27. Material on the formation of concepts by children.

AGINSKY, B.   1, 2, 4, 7, 8.
BATESON, G.   7, 8, 19, 20, 21, 22, 23.   (Leicas, Ciné.)
BUNZEL, R.   1, 2, 7, 11, 14.
DENNIS, W.   1, 2, 3, 4, 5 (Dennis and Russel Animism Tests), 9, 15, 25, 27.
DUBOIS, C.   1, 2, 4, 5, 7, 9, 11 (modified Levy Sibling Rivalry), 13 (Goodenough Drawing Tests), 14.
FLANNERY, R.   1, 2, 7, 15.
FORTES, M.   1, 2, 3, 4, 5, 7, 8, 9, 13, 14, 15, 16, 19, 20, 21, 22.   (Perceptual tests based on Spearman: Lowenfeld's colored shapes.   Sex life and moral development, economic activities of children.)
HARPER, B. W.   1, 2, 4, 7, 15.   (Material on sex play.)
HARRIS, J. S.   1, 2, 15, 27.   (Concepts of property.)
HAWLEY, F.   1, 2, 3, 4, 7, 8.
HENRY, J., and Z.   1, 2, 4, 5 (toys used to test logical approach to a problem), 6 (Piaget type

chological investigations of moral and psychic development (Eugene Lerner's, Jean Piaget's, and Bavelas' methods and techniques) have been given.   A number of well-known social anthropologists and psychologists are involved in this study.   The work on the Navaho is being done by Dr. Dorothea Leighton, Dr. Clyde Kluckhohn, and Mrs. Malcolm Collier; the work on the Hopi by Dr. Laura Thompson, Dr. Alice Joseph, and Ray Birdwhistell; the research on the Papago by Rosamund Spicer and Jane Chesky; on the Sioux by Dr. Gordon McGregor and Dr. Royal Hasserick; on the Zia by Florence Hawley.   There will be four types of publication: (1) monographs on personality development in each of the six tribes; (2) critiques of methods and techniques; (3) a general book presenting the conclusions for the entire study; and (4) publications on the application of this scientific knowledge to the problems of administration.

of question), 9, 10, 11 (modified Levy SR), 14, 15, 19, 20, 21, 22, 23 (stills), 25.

KLINEBERG, O. 5 (speed and accuracy), 6 (photographs of emotions expression of adults, submitted to Chinese children), 16.

KLUCKHOHN, C. 1, 2, 3, 4, 7, 9, 11 (Levy toys), 14, 18, 19, 20, 21, 22 (stills and Ciné), 26 (reaction of child to cradle; development of attitudes of modesty and of attitudes and practices with relation to excreta).

LAYARD, J. 15. (Attitudes of adults towards children, particularly in regard to the concept of the soul; attitudes of novices and initiators in initiation ceremonies.)

LIPKIND, W. 1, 7, 9, 19, 20, 24. (Stills.)

MANDELBAUM, D. 1, 2, 7 (material on sex play, drawing test), 14, 15, 19, 20 (stills), 25, 26, 27.

MEAD, M. 1, 2, 3, 4, 5 (animism tests, ink blots. Bender tests), 7, 8, 9, 10, 11 (toys), 12, 13 (Goodenough).

MEKEEL, S. 1, 2.

OLIVER, D., and E. 1, 2, 3, 4, 5 (animism tests used by M. Mead), 7, 8, 9, 15, 19, 20 21, 22 (stills), 25, 26, 27 (concepts of kinship, totemism, status, supernaturalism).

OPLER, M. E. 1, 2, 4, 7, 8, 15, 19, 20, 21, 22 (stills), 27.

READ, M. H. 1, 2, 4, 7, 8, 9, 15, 19, 20 (stills). (Special studies in relation to nutrition.)

ROHEIM, G. 1, 7, 8, 14, 15, 19, 20, 22 (stills and Ciné). (Daydreams.)

Chapter 14

CHARACTER DEVELOPMENT IN CHILDREN—AN OBJECTIVE APPROACH

Vernon Jones

Definition and Distinctions

Any attempt at the objective study of character development is beset with many difficulties, such as the varying concepts as to what is meant by character, the extreme complexity of the phenomenon, and the subtle manner in which nature and nurture exert their influences upon it. Recognizing this, let us attempt at the outset to eliminate as many unnecessary difficulties as we can by delimiting and defining the area of study. The concept of character is related to, and sometimes confused with, such concepts as moral or ethical behavior, temperament, and personality. Impossible as it may be to draw hard and fast boundary lines between these conceptual areas, working distinctions can be made which may help to avoid confusion.

In any strict interpretation of character it is clear that it is not coextensive with ethical or moral behavior. Morality concerns itself with conformity to existing standards of a given time or place. Character does not necessarily imply such conformity. Often in history the individuals who have been rated greatest in point of character have been nonconformists from the point of view of certain existing standards of their day. Moreover, conformity to existing standards sometimes demonstrates not so much character as behavior along lines of least resistance. This does not mean, of course, that character is not related to morality. It means that character is a more dynamic and more inclusive concept. In character development much more attention is given to volitional factors and to individual creativeness in the realm of goals to be achieved than is true in moral or ethical growth. If we add to morality the ability to reconstruct one's values and the volitional powers sufficient to direct conduct progressively toward such evolving values, then we have character as we shall think of it in this chapter.

The area of temperament is perhaps less often confused with character than is morality, but illustrations of such confusion are not hard to find. Morton Prince (1914), for example, said: "Hence the character of one is said to be 'good-tempered,' and the other 'bad-tempered.'" Whether a person is good-tempered, sanguine, phlegmatic, melancholic, or choleric is certainly of interest to anyone rating him for practical purposes of living or working with him, and no claim can be made that such characteristics have no relation to character. Strictly speaking, however, the readiness and capacity of an individual for such relatively prevailing affective experiences are not central to the problem of his character. Roback (1928) thinks that the influence of a man's character has a farther reach than his temperament. The value of a man's character, he says, does not fluctuate with our nearness

707

to him in time or space, but his temperament is a matter of only "passing interest." "That Carlyle was bilious, choleric, or grouchy," he says, "is certainly deplorable, but Carlyle's temperament, which counted so much with those he came in contact with, does not determine our estimate of the man from the point of view of character." Whether or not we agree fully with Roback that temperament is of only passing interest, we can readily agree that character concerns itself more with the volitional powers of the individual and the directions or goals of his striving.

Finally we come to the confusion of character with personality. Personality, of course, is a very broad concept, being defined by Allport (1937) as the "organization within the individual of those psychophysical systems which determine his unique adjustments to his environment." It will be granted that there is little that psychologists wish to study about human behavior that could not be subsumed under so broad a definition. If we may judge by actual research emphasis in personality, however, there is relatively little interest manifested in the problems of moral behavior coupled with the allied problems of values and there is not very intense interest in the problems of volition as they relate themselves to the values or goals of achievement. These are the very problems in which the student of character development is most interested. Normally the student of personality is interested in the adjustments or maladjustments which individuals make to frustrations and conflicts, and the goal of his therapy is adjustment. The student of character is not interested so much in the mechanisms of adjustment adopted or the types of personality developed by the individual who feels inferior, or deludes himself, becomes introverted, or develops various stereotypes; he is much more interested in what values accepted by the individual underlie his feelings of inferiority or stimulate him to attempt to maintain his self-esteem by such mechanisms as the students of personality have uncovered.

In the area of character, adjustment is not the end of therapy. Aspiration, striving, and all the volitional factors related thereto are considered to be aspects of character which are never outgrown. Instead of adjustment being an end in the character development of an individual, the kind of adjustment which he makes (whether, for example, by honesty and cooperation, or by deceit, cajolery, and self-deception) is a measure of his character.

In attempting to make a distinction between character and personality, we do not wish to give the impression that they can be divided off into compartments. Personality as defined by some may include all that has been emphasized under character. From the practical point of view, however, research in personality has usually neglected, or touched only very lightly, the central problems here raised under the term *character*.

In a study of character development where the aim is to include the maximum of concrete data and the minimum of abstract speculation, as is the aim in this chapter, it is necessary to confine oneself as closely as possible to measurable behavior. If one is interested in building theories or in interpreting facts in terms of some theory already accepted, there is ample opportunity for such in the interpretation of the responses of children in situations involving persistence, feelings of guilt, values, and the like. There are, for example, the very difficult but important problems of the source of values and the genesis of volition. With these particular problems little scientific progress has been made, and too often they have been neglected in the testing of theories. However, it is easy to point to many areas in character development which have been attacked by experimental methods. Tests and rating scales have been used to study the behavior of children in situations involving cooperation, generosity, honesty, persistence, self-control, truthfulness, levels of aspiration, and the like. There has also been a large amount of statistical and experimental work done in comparing the responses of delinquent and nondelinquent children. The contributions of various native and environmental factors to character development have been studied. It will be the aim of this chapter to bring together the most significant facts from these and similar studies and to interpret them in the light of modern psychological principles.

Individual Differences in Character

One of the first facts which one notes in the inspection of the character responses of children in controlled situations is that the individuals do not fall into two groups: the strong and the weak, or the persistent and the nonpersistent, or the honest and the dishonest. There are individual differences in character just as truly as there are individual differences in general intelligence or in the knowledge of history. In tests of persistence, for example, Ryans (1938b) finds that persistence scores made by a group of subjects spread from very low to very high with no gaps in the distribution. Similarly in tests of honesty, where dishonest responses are easily accessible and where motivation for such responses is strong, children have been found to distribute themselves all along the scale. Figures 1 and 2 illustrate this point.

Figure 1 is based on the results of Hartshorne, May, and Shuttleworth (1930) on twenty-one tests of honesty-dishonesty of children in school and play situations.

Figure 2 is based on the original data of Jones (1936) on one test of cheating in school. Both figures represent results for children ranging in age, for the most part, from 12 to 15. It is important to emphasize that the results in both these studies are based not on what children's attitudes toward honesty seemed to be, or on what

DISTRIBUTION OF HONESTY SCORES FOR 265 CHILDREN, EACH SCORE BEING MEAN OF 21 TESTS

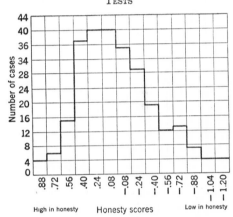

FIGURE 1. Based on data from *Studies in the Organization of Character*, by H. Hartshorne, M. A. May, and F. K. Shuttleworth. New York: Macmillan, 1930, 480, 486.

they said they would do in different situations, but on tests of what they actually did under rather well-controlled conditions. In both figures the distributions are seen to be continuous.

At first glance one might be inclined to say that the individual differences which are spoken of here apply only to the degrees of dishonesty among the dishonest, and that the honest students are still in a class by themselves. This view, although seemingly logical enough in the case of a given set of data, runs into difficulty when it is found that an individual may be completely honest in one situation, or under one degree of motivation, while he may show a considerable number of lapses from perfect honesty in another situation, or under a higher degree of motivation.

To appreciate the fact that honest-dishonest behavior varies with the nature of situations and the motivation involved, at

DISTRIBUTION OF SCORES ON MALLER SELF-MARKING (CHEATING) TEST FOR 191 BOYS AND GIRLS IN SEVENTH AND 133 IN EIGHTH GRADE

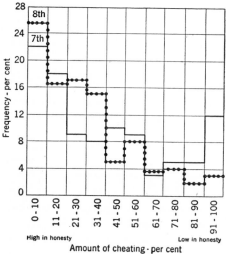

High in honesty   Low in honesty
Amount of cheating - per cent

Scores given in percentages, that is, the percentage that the number of cheatings bears to the number of chances to cheat.

FIGURE 2. From original unpublished data of Jones, 1936.

least among children, one has only to think how different so-called character traits get in one another's way. Truthfulness at times conflicts with loyalty to one's group; truthfulness to one's host or benefactor may run counter to courtesy or gratitude; truthfulness to the sick may come into collision with tact and helpfulness. Thus, if a child deviates in a given situation from "the truth, the whole truth, and nothing but the truth," shall we think of him and treat him as belonging in a separate category from the honest? It seems more con-

sistent with the experimental facts—and also sounder from the point of view of education and therapy—to say in a case like this that the child's inhibitions against dishonesty and deceit have weakened under the particular motivation or particular conditions of conflict with other "traits," and that in spite of a certain amount of dishonesty some degree of the organization of behavior which we call honesty remains intact. It is in this sense that we may think of a given individual in different situations or different individuals in the same situation as differing in degrees of honesty. From the point of view of genetic develop-

DISTRIBUTION OF TOTAL HELPFULNESS SCORES

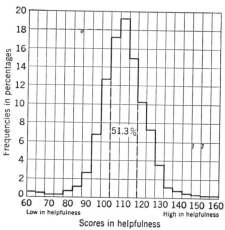

Low in helpfulness   High in helpfulness
Scores in helpfulness

Frequencies given in percentages. Number of cases = 800.

FIGURE 3. Adapted from *Studies in Service and Self-control,* by H. Hartshorne and M. A. May. New York: Macmillan, 1929, 109. By permission of the publisher.

ment of honest behavior in a child, there seems to be much merit in this concept of degrees of honesty because it is consistent with the basic hypothesis of the gradual organization of behavior and assumes neither a sudden springing into perfection of patterns of behavior, or "traits," on the one hand, nor the sudden and complete collapse of such patterns on the other.

What has been said about individual differences in honesty seems to apply to all other traits which have been measured. Space, however, will permit the giving of only one more distribution. Figure 3 represents a distribution of scores in helpfulness.

From a study of Figures 1, 2, and 3 it is not possible to generalize about the shape of the different distributions further than to say that they are continuous from the low to the high end of the scale and that the dispersion in all cases is wide. Figures 1 and 3 show a tendency toward normality of distribution, but this is not borne out by Figure 2, where the units of measurement are the simplest. In addition to the statistical fact that the shape of distributions may be affected by the units of measurement employed,[1] it is known that it will vary with different degrees of motivation. It is also quite possible that the shape will differ in groups of different ages and different amounts of training.

Methods of Character Measurement

Before going further in the discussion of the results obtained in the objective study of character, perhaps brief mention should be made of the measurement techniques which have been employed in these studies. These techniques can be grouped under four headings: (1) rating scales, (2) measurement of actual behavior, (3) measurement of knowledge and attitudes, and (4) intensive interviews and clinical case studies employing certain psychoanalytical and projective methods.

Rating Method. The oldest and one of the best methods available for measure-

[1] This is especially true if standard scores, or some other derivative of the standard deviation, are used as the unit of measurement, as frequently happens in character measurements.

ment in character traits is some form of rating. In the measurement of character these ratings are usually obtained from teachers, parents, or friends. The reliability and validity of ratings will, of course, vary with the traits rated and with the training and care of the raters. Ratings, however, if carefully made and based on averages of two judges, will ordinarily have reliabilities ranging from .60 to .80 for such traits as dependability, persistence, and determination.

The reader who is interested in an extended review of the methodology and results of the rating method is referred to the very adequate treatment by Symonds (1931). Suffice it to say here that the best results have ordinarily been obtained with ratings under the following conditions: (1) when ratings were made only after careful observation of the trait or traits in question; (2) when definite manifestations of the trait or traits were rated and these ratings combined to yield a measure of the trait *in toto;* (3) when raters who were abnormally biased were avoided, or their ratings weighted very lightly; (4) when ratings were based on the composite of several competent judges; (5) when rating devices were employed to encourage raters to distribute their ratings over the scale range and thus avoid undue bunching of scores.

Test of Actual Conduct. Among the most interesting and convincing measures of character have been the tests of actual performance. In such tests the subject does not know that he is being measured in character. Voelker (1921), a pioneer worker in this field, devised several tests which measured the trustworthiness of children. He measured such behavior as the following: whether or not children would return borrowed property and overchange, the degree to which they would cheat in marking their own test papers, the extent to which they would make overstatements about knowledge possessed and books read, and whether or not they would receive a tip for small favors.

Cady (1923) and Raubenheimer (1925) built upon the work of Voelker and used these tests rather extensively in attempts to devise measures which would predict incorrigibility and juvenile delinquency. The most extensive work in the devising and using of concealed tests of performance has been done by Hartshorne and May, who worked with hundreds of school children. They employed the best of available tests and devised many new ones for the measurement of honesty, self-control, cooperativeness, and allied traits. Extensive statistical data were obtained concerning the validity and reliability of such tests, regarding the intercorrelations among different measures of behavior in these fields, and on the relation of various factors, such as intelligence and home background, to such behavior. For detailed discussions of tests of this variety, the reader is referred to Hartshorne and May (1928, 1929), Hartshorne, May, and Shuttleworth (1930), and Symonds (1931).

Another trait in which performance tests have been employed is persistence. An extensive review of the methods and results of testing in this field has been made by Ryans (1939a). He (1938a, 1938b) has experimented rather intensively with a test battery consisting of these three subtests: amount of consecutive effort at a task in learning, standing on a functional schedule, and endurance in the face of physical discomfort.

Physiological Methods. In attempts to measure certain character responses, notably truthfulness and deceit, several physiological measures have been tried. Changes in blood pressure, pulse, respiration, and galvanic skin reactions have been the responses most frequently studied in their relation to deception. Lombroso, as early as 1912, refers to his use of the hydrosphygmograph in proving a suspect guilty of stealing. Since that time there has been a gradual development of instruments designed to detect deception by the measurement of several physiological reactions simultaneously. Probably the most successful instruments of this type to date are those devised by Keeler, Lee, and Ohio State University. The Keeler (1934) "polygraph" (or, more exactly, pneumo-cardio-sphygmo-galvanograph) is somewhat more widely known than the others. Results from this instrument were permitted as evidence in a jury trial in Wisconsin in 1935. This is the first time that such physiological measures have been accepted as evidence before a jury in the United States, although a few earlier cases are on record where such results had been presented directly to judges in nonjury trials. The Lee polygraph has been used rather extensively with juvenile delinquents. A good report on such work is given by Lyons (1936).

The key problem in the use of such physiological measures for research or for practical purposes of detection of deception or guilt is one of validity. One question that is particularly significant concerns the probabilities that an honest or innocent person may, in the face of the excitement involved in taking such tests, react as if dishonest or guilty. The measurement of several physiological reactions simultaneously is designed to reduce the probabilities of such errors; but the attitude of the more careful experimenters concerning the validity of present instruments is illustrated by Keeler, who said in the Wisconsin case that he recommended his findings as only one element in the evidence and that he would not convict upon such results alone.[1]

Intensive Interview and Projective Methods. Signs have been accumulating for several years now that one of the most fruitful approaches to the measurement and thoroughgoing analysis of character development is the intensive interview. Healy has for a long time used the "child's own story" in his study of individual delinquents. He carefully avoids any claim that these intensive interviews are psychoanalytical in nature, although he uses informally some of the same techniques as those used by psychoanalysts for diagnosis. Künkel (1938) gives a good demonstration of the possibilities of this method for studying the relation of the character development of a child to the total integration of his mental and emotional life. From this treatment of Künkel, and that of Freud on the superego and ego-ideal, we get challenging suggestions as to the possibilities of the use of intensive interview in evaluating character responses at a depth where such responses are viewed not in isolation but in relation to fundamental patterns of accepted authority and of aspiration.

Other Methods. The most promising of the projective methods for application to the study of character development are the thematic apperception method (see Murray *et al.*, 1938), the "world test" method of Bühler and Kelly (1941), and the Rorschach method (see Klopfer and Kelley, 1942).

No mention has been made of tests of moral knowledge and attitudes as measures of character. Numerous tests of this kind have been employed, involving such devices as ranking of offenses, marking suggested responses in complex situations as right or wrong, giving cause-and-effect relations, predicting probable consequences of acts, and the like.[2] The obvious weakness of such tests is that measures of knowledge and verbally expressed attitudes do not accurately reveal to what extent such knowledge and attitudes will be translated into action. Of course, it might be maintained that such tests are of value because knowledge of, and proper attitude toward, desirable conduct is a prerequisite for such conduct, even though they are not guarantors of it. There is much cogency in this argument, especially as it applies to the use of such tests for revealing points at which education in knowledge and attitudes might be profitably applied. However, for purposes of measurement and analysis of overt character development, tests of knowledge and verbally expressed attitudes seem to be of relatively little value. In saying this, there is no intention of indicating that the effectual knowledge and attitudes of a child are of little value in his character development, but rather that present surface tests of these are not very dependable measures of this development. It is quite possible that research in the future may reveal ways of measuring attitudes and aspirations at depths which are nearer the mainsprings of action than present methods which lean so heavily on the verbalized and censored reports of subjects. This may be a part of the contribution which the intensive interview and projective methods mentioned above may make to the measurement of character.

Finally, mention should be made of serious violations of social standards as measures of character. In such social institutions as law enforcement agencies, the church, the school, and the home, certain

---

[1] See Imbau (1935a, 1935b). For good historical treatments on the use of physiological methods for detection of deception and guilt, the reader is referred to Larson (1932), Jordan (1938), and Trovillo (1939).

[2] For descriptions of such tests and for rather complete bibliographies, see Hartshorne and May (1926), Symonds (1931), and Jones (1933).

minimum standards are set up, and any individual who falls below them is looked upon as a social offender by those interested in maintaining these standards. The standards set up by civil law particularly are quite generally accepted, and consequently any serious violation of these is usually considered as indisputable evidence of inferior character development. All studies of juvenile delinquents have proceeded on the assumption that these young people have been measured and found deficient by one of society's most widely accepted tests. The fact that this measure places an individual in one of two classes, the nondelinquent or delinquent, does not alter the fact that it is a widely accepted —although none too critically analyzed— yardstick. We mention it particularly because its verdict is taken so seriously and uncritically by society, when as a matter of fact it is but a crude measure of character and is in need of all the supplementary measures which research with more exact and penetrating methods can reveal.

The Contribution of Nature to Character Development

Having considered briefly the question of individual differences in character development and their measurement, we come now to the problem of the factors contributing to such differences. Does a child of a given age show up poorly in character because he was born short in those factors which make for character development, or because the conditioning and education which his environment afforded were faulty? This raises the age-old controversy of nature and nurture, and it raises it in a most complex field of behavior.

If one were starting out, at the present stage of knowledge, to arrive at any percentage contribution of nature and nurture in accounting for individual differences in character development, he would be doomed to failure. There is such a multitude of unmeasurable variables subsumed under each of these concepts, and they interact in such intricate ways, that the crucial experiment to determine the exact relative influence of each is at present out of the question. However, sufficient data are available to indicate that at least intelligence, age, sex, and certain emotional and volitional factors are sufficiently related to differences in character to justify their discussion, if we can accomplish that difficult task of treating one of these factors at a time without losing sight of the fact that none of them operates singly or in isolation from environmental forces. One fundamental thesis of this chapter is that character development of an individual at any given time is an integration based upon certain native and biological factors, upon certain conditionings and learnings, and upon the ever-present impacts of the environment. It is hoped, therefore, that the following discussion of some of the native factors which influence character development will never become so involved in particulars that it seems to lose sight of this larger framework of relationships.

Influence of Intelligence. The relation of intelligence to character development is probably most readily seen in the rôle which intellect plays in orienting the individual in his environment. The dull and the bright intellectually are not alike in their ability to foresee the consequences of their acts; neither are they alike in their capacity to sense when greater advantages inhere in remote goals than in immediate gratifications. The more able the individual, the better can he select his environment and mold it in accordance with the ends he would achieve. Moreover, the same environment does not produce the same total organization of learned behavior and values in the bright and in the dull.

ndeed, differences in intellect make of identical physical environments different psychological environments. Of course, his does not mean that superior intellect can so alter inferior environments as to guarantee good character under any circumstances. Good intelligence, however, should enable one to achieve the skills, knowledge, and orientation that will help him to make the most of a superior environment, on the one hand, or to resist most efficiently the restricting effects of a poor environment, on the other.

With these preliminary remarks concerning the meaning of any possible relation found between intelligence and character development, let us turn now to a consideration of the objective studies. The statistical facts which are available on the relation between intelligence and character can be summarized under three headings: 1) the comparison between intellectually gifted children and unselected children on certain tests of character; (2) the correlation between general intelligence and scores on certain tests of character; and (3) the intelligence of serious offenders or delinquents.

Terman et al. (1925) compared a group of 532 children having IQ's over 130 with an equal number of unselected children by means of a battery of seven tests of moral ability. They found that 85 per cent of the gifted group equaled or exceeded the mean of the unselected, or control, group. The results for each age group are given graphically in Figure 4. It is seen that the gifted boys and girls exceeded the unselected by a significant amount at each age level. Terman also had teachers rate the children of the gifted and the control groups on 25 traits. If we select out of this list those traits most closely related to the problem of character development and compare the ratings assigned to the two groups, we find that 73 per cent of the

gifted boys and 74 per cent of the gifted girls exceeded the respective means of the control groups. The five traits upon which the above figures are based are conscientiousness, truthfulness, sympathy and tenderness, will and perseverance, and prudence and forethought.

From the results on the tests and the total ratings, Terman concludes that intel-

MEAN TOTAL SCORES OF GIFTED AND CONTROL CHILDREN, BY AGE, ON SEVEN CHARACTER TESTS

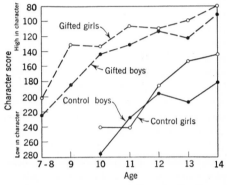

FIGURE 4. Adapted from *Genetic Studies of Genius,* by L. M. Terman, *et al.* Vol. 1. Stanford University, Calif.: Stanford University Press, 1925, 515. By permission of the publisher.

lectually gifted children surpass unselected children in tests and ratings of honesty, truthfulness, and similar moral traits. As he points out, the gifted are not free from faults in character development; indeed, he says that one out of five of the gifted has more faults than the average of the general population. However, the average difference between the two groups on the basis of total scores is certainly striking.

There is, however, one significant point growing out of the detailed analysis of Terman's data which the above composite results do not reveal. It is with regard to whether the gifted surpassed the average more in traits directed to self-success than in those directed to social responsibilities and to consideration of others. The gifted children exceeded the average in every trait, but they exceeded the average most in "will and perseverance" and least in "sympathy and tenderness." In the volitional, aggressive traits, 85 per cent of the gifted exceeded the mean of the unselected; in the sympathy-service traits only 59 per cent of the gifted exceeded the mean of the unselected. When one considers the much greater capacity on the part of the gifted to achieve power over others, this difference between their standing on ego-directed and on alter-directed traits takes on much social significance. This result of Terman's is based on only one investigation and, of course, needs verification in other studies before too much stress is placed upon it. However, the writer knows of no evidence to contradict this conclusion, and some of the results of Spaulding (1938) and of Wilson (1938), working in the field of education, may be interpreted as at least complementary evidence. Spaulding made an extensive study of the social-civic knowledge and attitudes of high school students and found that, whereas the abler students had mastered factual material much better than the average, their insight into and concern about the social problems of their community or nation were far from commensurate with their mental abilities or general scholastic achievements. Wilson, in a study along similar lines, found that young people with high intelligence quotients consistently surpassed the average in comprehension of social terms, knowledge of history, and the like, but that these same students differed from the average very little indeed in knowledge of or attitude toward such community affairs as relief, health, and recreation.

So much for the relation of intelligence to character development as revealed by studies which contrast the bright and the average. These results can be summarized by saying that the gifted exceed the average on all composite tests and ratings reported, but that there are some definite signs that gifted children in our present culture are developing their superiority more in those character traits making for individual success than in those making for social responsibility.

The second line of evidence concerning the influence of intelligence on character development involves results from correlational studies. Hartshorne and May (1928, 1929), using an extensive battery of tests with elementary school children, found correlations which average about $+.50$ between intelligence and honesty in school situations. They attempted to measure the home background of their subjects and to partial out this factor by using the partial correlation technique. The partial r between intelligence and honesty, with home background constant, was found to be $+.40$. Jones (1936), working with honesty tests similar to those of Hartshorne and May, found correlations ranging from $+.32$ to $+.43$ with seventh- and eighth-grade pupils who were rather homogeneous in home background. The correlation between intelligence and helpfulness was found by Hartshorne and May to be $+.16$ and that between intelligence and cooperative behavior was found by Jones to be $+.09$.[1] These are samples of the correlations found between intelligence and tests of actual performance in situations where the subjects do not know that they are being tested in moral behavior.

If we may judge from the rather wide range of correlations extending from $+.09$ for cooperation to $+.40$ for honesty, it seems that intelligence is related in differ-

[1] The correlation ratio between the cooperation test and intelligence was found to be .37. When this is compared with the Pearson r of .09, it is clear that the regression is curvilinear.

ent ways to different aspects of character. If we examine all the correlations in the literature we never find the relation to be really close. On the other hand, we almost never find it to be zero or negative.

The correlations between tests of moral knowledge and intelligence are appreciably higher than those mentioned above involving performance tests. This is to be expected because intelligence effectively serves to assist the individual to make fine distinctions between what society approves of and what it condemns. These correlations, however, are of little worth in predicting character as judged in terms of actual conduct.

The third source of evidence on the relation of intelligence to character development is the studies of juvenile delinquency. Healy and Bronner (1926) in their classic study reported that 13 per cent of the 4000 delinquents examined by them in Boston and Chicago were feeble-minded, that is, below 70 IQ. This should be compared with 1.5 to 2 per cent, which is the percentage of feeble-mindedness in the general population. More recent studies tend to substantiate these findings of Healy and Bronner. Indeed Glueck and Glueck (1934, 1940), working with 1000 delinquents, found exactly the same percentage. These results on the incidence of feeble-mindedness among delinquents are interesting and relevant as far as they go, but it is clear from these figures that feeble-mindedness cannot be considered a factor in the large majority of cases. It is the dull and the dull-normal groups, not the feeble-minded, that are the chief sources of juvenile delinquency. Lane and Witty (1935) reported that 80 per cent of their group of 700 delinquent boys were below the average of unselected children in intelligence. Glueck (1935) found 58 per cent of her group of 1000 delinquents to be below 91 IQ as compared with 21 per cent of unselected school children. Owen's (1937)

summary of twenty-one studies of delinquents showed a mean IQ of 82.4. These are but a few of the many studies of the intellectual status of delinquents, but they give results which are typical.[1] There is no need to multiply the evidence. It shows clearly that feeble-mindedness and dullness are much more frequent in delinquent than in normal populations.[2]

In presenting these three lines of evidence to the effect that intelligence is somehow related to character, care has been exercised to avoid any intimation that any single-line causal relation exists between intelligence and character development. It is clear that all the evidence can be interpreted as meaning only that those factors which ordinarily go with good intelligence also go with good character development. However, the results are interesting and significant if we are not too much bent on arguing back to single lines of causation. Our first conclusion is that dull and dull-normal children will, on the average, be more likely to be brought before juvenile courts for serious antisocial

[1] For a review of this and other correlates of delinquency, see Metfessel and Lovell (1942). The position taken by these writers is essentially the same as that taken in this chapter, namely, that neither feeble-mindedness nor dullness in and of itself produces juvenile delinquency. There are always mediating factors. It is probable, for example, that low mental ability leading to difficulties and frustrations at school is one important mediating factor. It is possible that abilities to foresee consequences of one's acts are dimmed and the capacities to visualize possible punishment ahead are weak as a result of dullness. This may be a second factor. Moreover, when dullness is combined with the inferior home background that ordinarily accompanies it, the training is likely to be defective, the prestige of the family as a restraining force is likely to be negligible, and the individual aspiration level is likely to be low.

[2] It is interesting to note that with the rise in juvenile delinquency in England after the outbreak of hostilities, the increase was greatest among the dull normals. It appears that the war conditions served to afford more opportunities for crime and tended to intensify almost all the causal factors.

conduct than average or bright children, if everything else, including the environment, is left alone to work itself out as it will. The second is that, although good intelligence does not guarantee normal or superior character development, good intelligence, plus all the other advantages and opportunities which usually go with it in a given culture, does give one a better chance to avoid or counteract the stimuli leading to inferior character, on the one hand, and to select more worthy stimuli and more challenging goals, on the other.

Influence of Chronological Age. The influence of maturation upon character development, like the influence of intelligence, cannot be studied in complete isolation from certain other variables. In a strict sense, therefore, it may be maintained that maturation as such cannot be investigated here at all, for it cannot be divorced from improved ability to learn and increased experience. However, the influence of age, coupled with all the attending advantages in ability and learning opportunities, can be studied. At least tentative answers can be given to such practical questions as whether older children exceed younger in those aspects of character which have been measured, or whether increased age and experience in our culture influence some areas more than others. Let us take up first the evidence for the age range from about seven to fourteen, the range upon which most of the objective studies have concentrated.

Slaght (1928) compared younger and older boys on their ideas as to whether it was wrong "to cheat if you can," "to lie to keep a secret," and "to lie to get even with someone," and found that a significantly greater percentage of the younger children condemned each of these as wrong. Tudor-Hart (1926), working in collaboration with Bühler, found that lying from a social motive was considered wrong more often by younger children than by older ones. These experimenters also reported that, although selfishness may change in its manifestations, its amount did not seem to decrease with age or advancement in school. In the study of gifted and unselected children, mentioned earlier in this chapter, Terman *et al.* (1925) reported a clearly defined tendency for total character scores, as determined by an average of seven tests, to increase with age (see Figure 4). A study of the separate distributions for the various tests, however, revealed the interesting fact that the older children obtained their advantage very largely from verbal tests in which knowledge of the most acceptable answer counted most, such as tests of reading preferences and social standards and attitudes. On the tests of overstatement with respect to books read or knowledge possessed, there was no perceptible increase in honesty with age. Also on the "peeping," or cheating, test there was no consistent tendency for the older children to be more trustworthy than the younger. Jones (1936), in a study of the influence of age on improvement in moral behavior during a nine-month period of special training in character and citizenship, found an average r of $+.03$ between age and improvement scores on three tests of honesty.

All these negative results make a rather discouraging picture when it is considered that the older children in the above investigation had the advantage of increased mental age over the younger and the benefit of several years of training in home and school. In comparing these results obtained under objective test conditions with uncontrolled observations it is, of course, important to recognize that with changes in age there are frequently definite changes in the manifestations of conduct. The types of untruthfulness and dishonesty, for example, which are practiced at different age evels will vary with the amount of experience and foresight possessed and with the values at stake. However, it seems safe to conclude from the above experiments that the process of growing older (at least between 7 and 14) will not, on the average, decrease the amount and the seriousness of the dishonesty and deceit of children who at a younger age displayed genuine dishonest behavior.

The results on tests of moral knowledge and of persistence are more favorable to the older children than are those on tests of honesty and truthfulness. All studies are in agreement that children as they grow older learn better what the accepted standards of society are, both those which are practiced and those which are preached. It also seems definitely established that children, on the average, increase somewhat in persistence as they grow older. Hartshorne and May (1929), for example, found a correlation of +.33 between test scores on persistence and age. This result is in marked contrast to the finding of these same experimenters on cooperation and service. Here no consistent increase with age was found. The children improved in persistence in working for individual goals, but not when working for other persons or for group goals.

This summarizes the main results on the relation of age to character development of children ranging in age from about 7 to 14. It is unfortunate that there are so few studies above age 14 with which to compare the above results. Probably the most extensive investigation made over a fairly wide range at the upper ages is that of Vakellariou (1938), who studied truthfulness and falsehood among 2000 boys and girls in Greece ranging in age from 12 to 20. He found that, with one or two exceptions, lying was somewhat less frequent in the higher ages than in the lower. He reported, however, that older adolescents become less sincere with teachers, relatives, and strangers than they were at an earlier age, while they become more sincere and truthful with their friends. In discussing his results, he made the interesting observation that the main "causes" of lying at these higher ages are fear, egoism, and social habit.

Moore (1934), Parr (1936), Howells (1938), and others have made studies of the amount of dishonesty among college students when they are permitted to mark their own papers. The percentage of students who cheated in these different investigations ranged from 33 to well above 50.[1] MacKinnon[2] had college students solve problems under an experimental set-up where they had opportunities to cheat and where their behavior could be observed through a one-way screen. Forty-six per cent of his subjects cheated.[3] Strictly comparable results are not available for students of high school age, but, from some unpublished data of the writer's on several hundred high school students, it seems safe to say that there has been little or no improvement in honesty in this type of situation between freshmen and senior years in high school, especially when the selective factors in the senior group are taken into account. Ryans (1939b) studied the rela-

[1] Two interesting sidelights in Howells's study were: first, that on a very hard test in history there was a larger percentage of students who were dishonest (about 10 per cent more) than on an easier test in that subject; and, second, that there were 25 per cent more who cheated on that form of the test which seemed less suspicious and unusual.

[2] See Murray et al. (1938), pp. 491–495.

[3] An interesting comparison was made by MacKinnon between the cheaters and noncheaters in their reactions to difficult problems. Thirty-one per cent of the cheaters who expressed themselves verbally vented their anger upon the problem, whereas none of the noncheaters did this. The reaction of blaming oneself for failures with hard problems did not appear among the cheaters, but 10 per cent of the noncheaters showed definite signs of such intropunitive responses.

tion of age to persistence among subjects ranging in age from 14 to 22. He found no consistent change in persistence with age at this level.

So much for the sketchy results on the influence of age on character development. They do not tell us what part maturation alone plays. They make no pretense of revealing how much of the difference (or sameness) from age level to age level is due to increased learning ability and experience and how much is due to conscious training by parents, teachers, and others who try to encourage their children to exceed the prevailing practices in their cultural milieu. The results, although unanalyzable along these lines, do indicate conclusively that increase in age, plus all that ordinarily accompanies it, does not produce large changes in any of the aspects of character which have been investigated, except in moral knowledge. They support the conclusion that children do not "naturally outgrow" their earlier faults as they become older. They lead one to believe that there is no age level which can be properly referred to as the "age of discretion," before which children's actions may be considered unimportant or insignificant for future development, and after which conduct greatly improves as a result of natural maturation.

Influence of Sex. Appreciable differences are found here and there in experimental studies between boys and girls in character development. In referring to these results we must recognize, of course, that any unanalyzed differences noted between the sexes are not necessarily native. Our culture does not expect the same social patterns of girls that it expects of boys, and the training which it gives them is different. Having granted this, however, we wish first to call attention to at least one line of evidence which argues for a biological or native contribution. The glandular systems of boys and girls are obviously different, and there is much evidence to indicate that differences in glandular balance and functioning are related to difference in character and personality. It would take us far afield to attempt to review here the extensive evidence on this, but one very relevant study might be mentioned in passing. Bize and Moricard (1937) gave injections of testosterone to young boys and found a definite increase in aggressiveness in all social relations. This and many other studies lead one to the conclusion that one example of a character difference between the sexes which may result in part from native differences is the greater aggressiveness of the male, other things being equal.

Most of the gross differences which have been found in the comparison of the character development of boys and girls are probably the resultant of a very intricate interaction of a few native differences, such as greater aggressiveness on the part of boys, and a host of environmental differences.

Tudor-Hart (1926) asked a large number of young boys and girls in Austria and in America to name any cases which they could think of where lies were necessary. She found, in comparing the answers of boys and girls, that the girls gave a much larger number of conventional lies, such as "Mother is not at home," "Glad to see you," or "I've had a fine time at your party." An appreciable difference was found in all lies which might be grouped under the heading of social, including lies to keep secrets, to conceal surprises, to protect others, to keep from offending, and the like. Thirty-two per cent of all the lies named by the girls, as compared with 18 per cent of those by the boys, were of this type. Hartshorne and May (1928) found that on the basis of averages on several tests there was no significant difference etween the sexes in honesty in school, but he girls cheated more than the boys on a party test" where cheating consisted of eeping in order to make a good showing 1 a social situation. Terman *et al.* (1925) lso found, on the basis of a peeping test, hat gifted girls were a little more dishon-st than gifted boys, although on all hon-sty tests combined the girls were slightly 1ore honest than the boys. Jones (1936), mploying several tests of honesty in chool, found no appreciable sex difference t the initial testing, but the girls tended o show somewhat more improvement dur-ng nine months of instruction in charac-er and citizenship than the boys.

With regard to possible sex differences in olitional behavior, the evidence is rather 1eager and not conclusive, it being par-icularly difficult here to control for dif-erences in motivation and early condition-ng. In a study of approximately 800 boys nd girls, ranging in age from 9 to 16, heehy (1938) found that boys are more ggressive, dominant, fearless, and boastful han girls, whereas girls are more suspi-ious, more fanciful, and more amenable to ocial controls than boys. Ryans (1939*b*) ound no sex difference in his test of per-istence.

On cooperative and "helpful" behavior, Iartshorne and May (1929) reported that oys and girls differ very little on the aver-ge, but, wherever small differences do oc-ur, the advantage is usually on the side of he girls. On the average, the girls were ound to be consistently more generous han boys in voting money for charitable auses, although in any given social group-ng it is not unusual to find that it is a oy who shows the greatest aggressiveness n leadership and action.

In studying the incidence of serious chool conduct and delinquent behavior mong boys and girls, we find the evidence o be conclusive. More boys than girls are found guilty of serious behavior. Olson (1930) found by means of a behavior rat-ing scale that boys have more tendencies toward serious conduct disorders than girls. Rundquist (1938), working with large sam-ples of boys and girls in the first and sec-ond grades in school, came to the same conclusion as Olson. It is a well-known fact, of course, that many more boys than girls fall so far below the minimum stand-ards of moral conduct that they run afoul of the law. The Children's Bureau, U. S. Department of Labor (1937), reported, on the basis of returns from 30 states, that the ratio of boys to girls among juvenile delin-quents was 6 to 1. In New York Maller (1937) found the ratio to be 7 to 1.

When a study is made of the types of offenses for which boys and girls are ar-raigned before the courts, significant dif-ferences are found. An investigation by the U. S. Department of Labor (1942) showed the usual results, namely, that girls were referred to the courts most frequently for sex offenses, for running away, and for being ungovernable, whereas boys were ar-raigned most often for stealing and other crimes against property. (See Table 1.) Dollard *et al.* (1939) interpreted such sex differences in crime largely in terms of the greater aggressiveness of boys, their whole theory of delinquency being that it is a form of aggression to frustration.

Of course, the facts concerning sex dif-ferences obtained from the study of juve-nile court cases cannot be interpreted apart from the differences in moral standards set by society for boys and girls. One might say, for example, that the greater percent-age of sex offenses charged against the girls does not represent so much a difference in moral behavior as it does a "double stand-ard" of judging the "morality" of boys and girls. These facts, however, are very rele-vant to the question of sex differences if we think of them as differences in ade-

TABLE 1

Offenses and Frequencies of Occurrence among 83,389 Delinquents of 473 Cour from 28 States for the Year 1939

(Taken from U. S. Department of Labor, Children's Bureau, 1942.)

Reason for Reference to Court	Number			Per Cent		
	Boys	Girls	Total	Boys	Girls	Tota
Stealing	34,767	1,484	36,251	49	12	44
Mischief and traffic violation	21,144	1,279	22,423	30	10	27
Truancy	3,677	1,471	5,148	5	12	6
Running away	3,337	1,895	5,232	5	15	6
Being ungovernable	3,233	3,267	6,500	4	26	8
Sex offense	1,827	2,355	4,182	3	19	5
Injury to person	1,642	325	1,967	2	3	2
Other reasons	1,341	345	1,686	2	3	2
Totals	70,968	12,421	83,389	100	100	100

quacy of response to situations where the adequacy of response is judged in terms of existing standards and practices in our present culture.

It is hazardous to attempt to draw any broad generalizations from the above results, but for the purpose of bringing some of the lines of evidence together we submit the following two tentative conclusions.

In the first place, it seems from the results of Hartshorne and May, Terman, Tudor-Hart, Jones, and others that girls may be more influenced than boys by what they think is expected of them by adult society. Second, the fact that there are more boys than girls who fail to meet the minimum standards of moral conduct, coupled with the finding of equality of the sexes in honesty, cooperativeness, etc., among random samplings of school children, may indicate either that there is greater variability among boys than among girls, or that the boys are more aggressive, or both. If either or both of these prove to be true, w should expect to find not only a greate number of boys than girls at the lower en of the scale, committing crimes, as has bee found, but also a larger number at the u per end, exercising leadership for superio conduct.

Influence of Accidents and Diseases A fecting Brain Functioning. Among th unlearned factors which are known to in fluence character development at least neg atively are injuries and disease which in terfere with the normal function of th higher cortical centers. Probably the mos interesting point to be emphasized in thes studies is that in not a few cases the injur, or the disease seems to operate directly [1] t upset the organized patterns of characte

[1] Of course not all the total result is neces sarily attributable directly to the injury or di ease, for important character results may com from an individual's emotional reactions to th injury or disease. The point is, however, tha the injury or the disease was basic at some poin or points.

sponses. Many individual case histories e on record to show that after a cerebral jury the individual has been left not only th reduced intellectual ability but also th greatly altered patterns of inhibition d control. Newell (1937) made a study 20 children who had had brain injuries d reported that the most frequent effect the injury was an increase in irritability th "a general decrease of inhibitory func- ns." Ten of these cases showed neurotic mptoms after the injury and 5 were found ilty of delinquent behavior. Rylander 937) studied 32 patients after brain op- ations had been performed. Changes in tellectual ability appeared in 21 of these ses, whereas in 25 cases diminished inhi- tions of affective responses occurred, and 22 notable changes in volitional powers. In the case of severe mental diseases it is ell known that changes in the character of e victims occur. The disease which has tracted most attention recently in its re- tion to character changes is encephalitis. any writers, including Levi (1930), ertz (1931), and Ciampi (1937), have ted cases showing notable changes in aracter following this disease. Sometimes e change in the behavior occurs soon 'ter the onset of the disease; sometimes it ppears in a serious form much later. The ief offenses noted are disobedience, ly- g, stealing, sex irregularities, cruelty, and olence. These occur in individuals who ere, presumably, well adjusted previous the contraction of the disease. Heer- na (1940) stresses the point that the ef- cts of the disease, and any attending in- ctions, are more pronounced in children, hose personality and character are still ndergoing rapid development.

Such changes in moral behavior attend- g disease present an interesting theoreti- l problem. If we knew the mechanisms y which satisfactory moral behavior was ther suddenly replaced by a definitely

unsatisfactory behavior in such cases, then perhaps we should have a better idea as to just what happens in the organism in the development of character. Unfortunately, however, the studies shed little light on this. The most promising hint which we get is that the disease may so affect neuro- logical functioning as to throw out of equi- librium, so to speak, the integrations which the individual has achieved. Some evi- dence for this is presented by Bond and Appel (1931), who state that they find in the postencephalitic condition not only ly- ing and stealing but also heightened feel- ings of insecurity, stronger regressive tend- encies, and more intense introversion or extroversion. We should expect that, at- tending these signs of increased inner con- flict following this disease, the integration in behavior which had been previously achieved would be unsatisfactory and that changes would appear. We should also ex- pect that remnants of old integrations might remain and that the victim might alternate, as he usually does, between the new patterns of conduct and remorse for having forsaken the old.

Volitional and Other Possible Nonintel- lectual Factors Running in Families. Nu- merous studies, including the much-debated family histories of the Kallikak, Jukes, and Edwards families, could be cited to indi- cate that superior and inferior conduct, es- pecially the latter, tends to run in families. To quote evidence on this, however, is un- necessary, for few if any readers will ques- tion the statement that family, including all the hereditary and environmental fac- tors that are subsumed under that term, is a powerful determiner of character. The only question which the reader is likely to ask is whether there is any evidence that there is anything more in the influence of family upon the character development of children than training and environment, on the one hand, and the possible inheritance of intelligence, on the other. The influence of mental abilities has already been discussed, and the influence of environmental factors connected with the home will be treated at length in a later section. What, if anything, else is left?

Perhaps the problem can be illustrated best by the results from the study of twins. From the point of view of social conditioning there is no reason why monozygotic twins should be more alike than dizygotic, whereas genetically the monozygotic are much more closely related than the dizygotic. If, therefore, the monozygotic are found to be more alike in character than the dizygotic, it would seem safe to attribute this to nonlearned factors.

One of the most striking of the twin studies bearing on this problem is that by Lange (1930). In investigating kinship among criminals he found in institutions 30 individuals who had twin brothers. Thirteen of these pairs were monozygotic and 17 were dizygotic. In the case of the 17 dizygotic pairs, both members of the pair had been sentenced in 2 cases, whereas among the monozygotic both members had been sentenced in 10 out of the 13 pairs. Rosanoff, Handy, and Rosanoff (1934) found 65 adults with prison records each of whom had a like-sexed twin. Of the 37 pairs which were probably monozygotic, both twins had a criminal record in 68 per cent of the cases; of the dizygotic pairs both members had criminal records in only 18 per cent of the cases. Stumpfl (1939) reported that identical twins who are guilty of crime or delinquency show similarities even in the types of offenses committed—much greater similarity than fraternal twins. Eckle and Ostermeyer (1939) compared 18 pairs of monozygotic with 12 pairs of dizygotic twins. They found much greater similarity in various character and personality traits between the monozygotic twins. The greatest variation within pairs

occurred in the area of emotional beha ior, but the variation was definitely less the monozygotic pairs. On the Bernreut Personality Inventory, Carter (1933) four the coefficient of correlation to be +.32 f dizygotic twins and +.63 for monozygoti Holzinger (1929) obtained correlations +.37 and +.56, respectively, for dizygot and monozygotic twins on neurotic ten encies as measured on the Woodwort Matthews test. Woltring (1938) fou that monozygotic twins were striking similar in selfishness, stubbornness, ascen ance, and ambition.

These and other similar results lead us the conclusion that the force of the fami in determining the character developme is perhaps greater even than is common supposed by either the environmentalists hereditarians. The average environmenta ist stresses the great power of the fami and all the social milieu which is dete mined by where and how the family live The average hereditarian in psycholog stresses the contribution of the family inheritance, usually singling out intelligen for major emphasis. In the study of cha acter development we seem to be forced grant the strength of both sets of factor and we are led to postulate that inheri ance operates not only in such abilities general intelligence and special aptitude but also in such nonintellectual areas volition and possibly even the area of d rectional tendencies and impulses.

The Problem of the Inheritance of Moral Sense. In any discussion of th nonlearned factors connected with chara ter development, the old question arises to whether or not a moral sense can inherited. The intuitionists of the seve teenth and eighteenth centuries postulate an intuitive faculty which could perceiv without training what was moral and wha was not. The special application of th notion to the study and treatment of youn elinquents was made by Maudsley (1883). is belief was that probably most young criminals were deficient in the common power of forming moral intuitions. The concept of the moral imbecile which is found in the literature from time to time, even today, harks back to a view akin to that of the intuitionist. Among relatively recent writers this view is represented best perhaps by Tredgold (1937), who maintains that a certain proportion of delinquents and criminals are fundamentally lacking in moral sense. The term *moral deficiency* is used frequently in a recent report of the Mental Deficiency Committee in England.

This we believe is an outmoded concept, and it is mentioned here primarily for the purpose of sharpening up the distinction which should be made between saying that inherited nature affects the substructures upon which character is built and maintaining that inheritance affects character directly. The view represented in this chapter, and the only one which seems consistent with the data presented, is that children do not inherit their moral values and their character. They inherit capacities for responding to stimuli and for experiencing satisfactions and annoyances; probably they inherit or biologically develop certain glandular and volitional strengths and weaknesses; and possibly they inherit some propensities toward overdevelopment or underdevelopment of certain impulses. They gradually acquire their character, within the broad limits set by their native make-up, by responding in certain ways in the situations which the environment affords.

The Influence of Nurture

The environmental factors which relate themselves to the character development of a child are legion. Indeed, it would be difficult to name a factor in the environment calling forth a psychological reaction which might not have some relation to character development. All that can be done here is to group under a few headings what seem to be the most potent factors for the majority of children and treat each of these groupings rather generally. Those which will be discussed briefly are: home influences, associates, church schools, day schools, recreational activities, motion picture attendance, and reading.

Influence of the Home. The first and most important place in a list of environmental factors influencing character development must be assigned to the home. As Groves (1940) says, the home, itself enmeshed in a cultural milieu, is the most powerful transmitter of the culture of the group. It complements such institutions as government, education, sex status, and religion, but it begins its work long before the child is conscious of these other institutions. In the early ages it is in almost complete control of his joys and sorrows. When the home smiles upon the young child, all the world is bright; when it frowns, all is dark. Parental harmony and discord cast their spell upon him before he understands scarcely any of the words spoken around him. Parental precepts and example get in their conditioning long before conscious teaching of other institutions of society can reach the child, and they are continually reinforced as long as the child is in the home.

Paynter and Blanchard (1928), in their analysis of the factors underlying the conduct disorders of the 330 children brought before their clinics, place the factor of poor training and discipline first, and assign this as an important factor in 90 per cent of the cases. The third place in their list is given to broken homes, and this is assigned as a contributing factor in 40 per cent of the cases. Wallenstein (1937) studied 3000 school children with a battery of character and personality tests to determine the influence of broken homes on measurable conduct. Seventeen per cent of his group was from broken homes. A comparison of the children from such homes with those from normal homes leads this investigator to conclude that inferior development in several aspects of character could be attributed directly to broken homes. Hartshorne, May, and Shuttleworth (1930) correlated children's ideas of right and wrong with the ideas of each of the following: parents, friends, club leaders, day school teachers, and Sunday school teachers. They found the correlation between child and parent to be the highest, with r equaling .55, and that between child and Sunday school teacher to be the least, r equaling .002. Within the home it was found that there is a closer relation between the ideas of child and mother than between those of child and father. The influence of the size of family on the moral behavior of children has received some attention from experimenters, but no general conclusions can be drawn. If a child gets the impression that he is not wanted by his parents, or if the presence of a younger brother or sister is interpreted as detracting from the affection and attention which he was receiving, he has greater difficulties in making satisfactory personality adjustments. Whether the adjustments finally made, however, will lead to stronger or weaker character development remains an open question. Probably it will depend both upon the individual child and upon the degree to which he feels that he is rejected. Symonds (1939), after an extensive study of parent-child relationships, came to the conclusion that if one or both parents strongly reject a child he tends to become overaggressive, or hostile, and may resort to truancy, lying, and stealing. If, on the other hand, one or both parents exercise overprotection with

a child, he tends to become infantile in his demands upon others, overdependent, and relatively noncooperative in situations requiring give and take.

The economic situation in the home is an important factor in the moral development of children when all the other variables correlated with it are considered. If, however, one may judge from the trends in delinquency during the depression years, it seems that the effect of economic status is small when such factors as parental supervision and the level of a child's associates are held constant.[1] Jones (1932) and Dawson (1938) have shown that in the State of Massachusetts juvenile delinquency did not rise during the economic depression of 1929 to 1937. Adult theft increased, but crime on the part of children and youth below 17 decreased slightly. The Federal Children's Bureau showed a decrease of 16 per cent in the number of juvenile cases handled in a sampling of the courts of the United States from 1929 to 1937. Rundquist (1938) found no greater incidence of behavior problems among children whose parents were on relief during the depression than among comparable children of more normal economic status.

Influence of Associates. The influence of home and of associates cannot, of course, be separated because the place where a child's home is located often sets limits to

[1] Carr-Saunders, Mannheim, and Rhodes (1944), working in England, equated delinquent and nondelinquent children for neighborhood and school district, and Healy and Bronner (1936) working in the United States, paired delinquent and nondelinquent children of the same family. In both studies the attempted equating of home background decreased the apparent importance of formal sociological factors as contributing causes of juvenile delinquency but such equating did not eliminate the psychological factors. Even in the same home Healy and Bronner found that the delinquent child felt more often discriminated against and thwarted, more often disliked by one or both parents, and more subject to general emotional stress than did the nondelinquent child.

e neighborhood and the range of cultural background from which he will select is friends. Granting these interrelations, however, it seems justifiable to treat the influence of associates separately. Some of the clearest evidence of the influence of associates on character growth or decline comes from the studies of juvenile delinquency. Burt (1925) and Healy and Bronner (1936) stress the fact that there are few other factors comparing in strength with that of intimate companions in determining whether or not an individual will commit a crime, and, if he commits one, what the crime will be.

It is interesting to note in these and in other recent studies that there has been a shift in the direction of greater emphasis upon intimate friendships as contrasted with larger groups such as boys' gangs. Thrasher (1927) stressed the great power of the gang to mold the conduct of its members, and there is no gainsaying that such effects are very real. There are, however, intimate loyalties and counterloyalties even within the most solidified gang, and many students of delinquency today are stressing particularly the power for good or ill of the relationships among intimate pals—the twos and threes. There is no intention, in stressing this point, of implying that the influence exerted upon a boy by one or two intimate companions detracts from the power of the gang upon him. On the contrary, one may supplement the other. However, some of the influence which was formerly attributed to the gang in molding conduct may really belong to smaller groupings of intimate companions. Hartshorne and May (1928) have made some interesting, although not surprising, finding that the influence of one's associates upon his conduct is greatest when they are actually with him. They found that the correlation between children's standing on tests of deception and that of

their best friends not in the same classroom was .23, whereas the correlation between best friends in the same classroom was .66. These results justify the conclusion that the effect exerted upon one by his companions is greatest when they are present and in a position to influence his behavior through immediate example, suggestion, and the passing of judgment.

This leads to the mention of the influence of group morale. In small intimate groups, the standard of behavior accepted in the group molds the behavior of all its members at least while they are together. This phenomenon is frequently noted in schools and especially in individual classes. If a class group remains fairly well intact for a year or two, certain habits and attitudes toward neatness, cheating, courtesy to teachers, etc., may gradually be developed. These habits and attitudes are usually rather specific, however. A case is known, for example, where a whole school developed a sort of taboo against cheating, but extreme snobbishness was condoned if not actually encouraged by the group. In a given class in school a good group spirit may develop under one teacher and manifest itself in a high degree of honesty and cooperation in her room and in her presence, but under another teacher the conduct of the group may be very different.

Jones (1936) has found that improvement in measurable character made under the conditions of good group morale is largely dependent for its permanence upon the maintenance of the group intact. He used eight classes of seventh- and eighth-grade students in his experiment and gave instruction in character and citizenship over a period of one school year. The class with the best group morale made the greatest gain. But a few months after promotion time, when the previous class groupings had been dissolved, the students of each class were brought together again for testing. It was found that the original gains were maintained most poorly by the students of the class which had developed the best group morale, and they were maintained best by those students who improved in spite of the weakest group morale. The experimenter refers to these gains made under the very favorable conditions of good group morale as *group-linked gains*. They were, in other words, largely dependent for their operation upon the total group and the spirit which welded it together. This concept implies that, if a child rather suddenly shows improved character responses in a social setting where the group morale favors superior conduct, it does not necessarily follow that such conduct has become firmly interiorized at this level. Similarly, if an individual suddenly displays an abrupt drop from his customary level of conduct when in the company of companions where the group morale favors such retrogression, it does not necessarily follow that his individual habits and standards have crystallized at this lower level.

It seems that group-linked gains and losses become interiorized gradually. On the side of remedial treatment this would seem to mean that a child who rather suddenly deteriorates under bad influences may be saved from much of his loss by speedy removal from these surroundings. In the case of a child whose conduct has improved under the impetus of superior surroundings, it means that provision should be made for rather protracted exposure to such conditions to allow the gains to become integrated into individual standards and habits.

Influence of Church Instruction. Historically, the problem of character has always been intimately associated with religion, and no discussion of children's character development would be complete without at least a recognition of the question of this relationship. There is, however, a notable scarcity of objective data on certain crucial questions.

Ligon (1939) has effectively raised many of these questions and has given a plausible account of the influence which well-directed religious education should have upon the character and personality development of children and youth. Theoretically, the opportunities for religious instruction gradually to internalize the controls of conduct of the individual and to provide emotional toning for such controls would seem very challenging.

A few studies have been conducted in which comparisons have been made between church school attendance and character, as measured by tests of honesty and cooperativeness, and between knowledge of the Bible and character ratings. Hartshorne and May (1928), working with large numbers of children in public schools compared the amount of cheating done in a group attending Sunday school and in a group not attending. In their first sampling the percentage of cheating in the former group was 31 as against 40 in the latter group. In their second sampling the percentages were respectively 38 and 43. The same experimenters (1929), working with another group of 84 children, found that those who attended church schools obtained somewhat higher scores on tests of helpfulness than those who did not, and those who were regular in attendance did better than those who were irregular. Maller (1930) found on the basis of objective tests that the honesty of a group of Jewish children increased appreciably during attendance at religious schools.

All these differences are rather small, but they are consistent in their direction. Of course, it may be argued that the differences noted in favor of the church school group are due not so much to church school attendance as to factors in the hredity and homes of children whose parents are sufficiently concerned about their welfare to send them to such schools. Unfortunately, the accuracy of such an argument cannot be proved or disproved because of the impossibility of measuring and controlling all relevant variables. The fact remains, however, that the children who attended church schools, and who had all the other advantages that might have gone with church school attendance, did better on the tests than those who did not attend.

With regard to the influence of Biblical knowledge on the moral conduct of children, it is impossible to draw any definite conclusions at present. Taylor and Powers (1928), working with school children, correlated the results on the Laycock Bible Test with character ratings based on the combined judgments of two teachers and found a correlation of $.50 \pm .06$, whereas the correlation between the character ratings and intelligence was only $.24 \pm .08$. On the surface of it, this seems to mean that children who knew many Biblical facts impressed their teachers more favorably than those who knew few, and that this difference could not be fully accounted for by the influence of intelligence. Hightower (1930), however, made a study of the same problem and found little or no relationship between Biblical knowledge and the different phases of moral behavior tested. He compared Biblical knowledge scores with teachers' ratings of character and with test results in cheating, lying, unselfishness, etc. The differences in the results of these two studies serve to stress the difficulty of controlling all relevant variables and getting to the bottom of the matter. Until the interrelationships among intelligence, Biblical knowledge, home influence, and various aspects of moral conduct are known, we cannot hope to draw any conclusions about the relation of Biblical knowledge to character.

Influence of Day Schools. Several investigations have been made of the influence of day schools upon the character development of pupils as they progress through the grades. Jones (1936) found no significant difference in character development in the seventh and eighth grades with which he worked. During a program of rather intensive character training, however, extending over a school year, he found that a majority of the students in most of his experimental classes improved. In one class under a superior teacher the improvement was very noticeable, whereas in another class, where the discipline gradually deteriorated during the year, the losses outweighed the gains. Hartshorne and May (1928) found that one section of a fifth grade under one teacher cheated only half as much at the end of a year as it did at the beginning, whereas another section of the same grade under another teacher cheated more at the end than at the beginning.

The improvement of a child in school, therefore, seems to be contingent not primarily upon mere attendance but on specific experiences in his relation with his teacher and with his class or school group. The mere fact of being in a class where the group spirit supports a certain mode of conduct is certainly one important factor in the behavior of a child. It is impossible to say how much contribution is made by teacher-pupil relations and how much by class-pupil relations, but if we consider these two together we have the two factors in the school situation which are most clearly related to character development. Level of advancement in school in itself does not seem to be a significant determiner of character, at least not in the grade range of five to eight, which has been most extensively studied.

Influence of Recreational Activities. The main objective studies in this field have been made on club activities, motion picture attendance, and reading. Consequently, the discussion here will be confined to these three.

(1) *Club membership.* The pioneer investigation of character development employing controlled test situations was made in the field of club activities. This study was conducted by Voelker (1921) for the purpose of determining the influence of Boy Scout work on trustworthiness. He worked with 57 boys, ranging in age from 10 to 14. At the beginning of the experiment he gave a series of performance tests. Then, during an experimental period of seven weeks, two groups of boys were given intensive work on trustworthiness, which consisted of the learning of codes, discussions, exhortations, and actual practice of honesty wherever possible. Thus a very definite attempt was made to build up the ideal of honesty. In two other groups of boys, having about the same scores on the initial test, regular Scout training was given with the usual emphasis on honesty. Finally, there were two control groups which received no Scout training and no special training in trustworthiness. At the end of the experimental period all six groups were retested with a test battery similar to the initial one. It was found that most progress had been made by the two Boy Scout groups receiving the intensive training, and that the least progress was made by the two groups which received no Scout training. Though these results alone are based on too few cases to justify any unqualified conclusions, they agree with the findings of other experimenters in indicating that training in the development of trustworthiness must be rather specifically and intensively directed to that end to lead to measurable improvement over short periods of time such as are involved in the usual experiments.

Hartshorne and May (1928, 1929), working with their extensive test data, made a comparison of the scores obtained by children who were members of clubs and those who were not. They found that club members, no matter what the organization, were more cooperative than nonmembers; but club members did not consistently exceed nonmembers in resisting temptation to cheat in school tasks.

Numerous results, based on studies of delinquency in urban areas after club activities have been organized or expanded, have appeared to show that clubs providing good recreational programs and capable leadership have accomplished striking results. In such studies, however, the factor or factors accounting for the improvement have not usually been rigorously isolated. Frequently increased club activities in a community are accompanied by better leadership, better housing, etc. It is easy to believe that any opportunities that are provided for children to engage in desirable club activities under supervision and to derive proper meanings and generalizations should help, but proof of just what contribution is made by each of the interlocking variables would require many more controls than are involved in these studies.

(2) *Motion picture attendance.* The effect of motion picture attendance on character development of children and youth has been the subject of a considerable number of research investigations. One topic of study has been the frequency of attendance. In urban areas it has been found that, on the average, attendance is slightly over once per week per child. There are, of course, wide variations in different areas of the country and in different sections of a given community. It is interesting to note that in some crowded areas of cities a substantial percentage of children begin rather regular attendance at the movies by or before age 8, and in such sections it is not uncommon to find children attending

s frequently as four or five times a week. Dale (1935) reported that in a large congested area in New York, 17 per cent of the movie audience was under 7 years of age and 53 per cent was under 20. During the war period this attendance of younger children increased in many communities with the improved economic situation and the increase in the number of working mothers.

In Dale's study an analysis was made of what children see at the movies. The outstanding result of this analysis from the point of view of character development was the great frequency of crimes, deaths, and overdrawn love scenes. The lack of reality in the films was also emphasized. Dale found, for example, that most of the characters in the films do not show any signs of working and yet 75 per cent of them wear evening clothes at one time or another.

Success is depicted in the movies as coming fast and often easily. In the interest of making the story compelling, there are few normal and average people depicted in average homes. Extremes are the rule. The rich are lavishly rich; the poor are desperately so. Luck and physical strength, beauty and prowess, are out of proportion to their true place in reality. For adults who have experienced life widely, and can easily distinguish between the unreality of a good story and the reality of life, this is not serious. But for children who start their motion picture attendance at young ages and see life depicted in this manner year in and year out, it may be serious, especially if the home, school, church, or some other institution of society does not correct these warped impressions.

The influence of motion pictures upon emotional responses and upon restlessness during sleep has been studied by Renshaw, Miller, and Marquis (1933). It was found that the restlessness after seeing motion pictures increased 26 per cent on the average with boys and 14 per cent with girls. Using measures of change in pulse rate as a measure of emotional response, Dysinger and Ruckmick (1933) found that while seeing a picture children 6 to 11 years of age displayed responses which averaged three times those of adults.[1]

Many studies have been made to determine the influence of motion picture attendance on delinquency and crime. The results are conflicting. In general, the investigations which have employed interviewing and questionnaire methods with delinquents have reported that motion pictures were direct causal factors in 10 to 20 per cent of the cases. Blumer and Hauser (1934), for example, have concluded that the movies were important factors in directing 10 per cent of the boys studied and 25 per cent of the girls into delinquent and criminal careers. Cressey and Thrasher (1934) interviewed 139 delinquent boys, age 15 and below, and concluded that 17 per cent of them "were clearly influenced by the movies toward delinquency."

On the other hand, such specialists in the study of delinquents as Healy and Bronner (1926, 1936) in America and Burt (1925) in England find much smaller percentages. They are inclined to discount much that delinquent boys and girls say in interviews and questionnaires about the "cause" of their delinquency and seek for objective evidence beyond the delinquent's self-analysis. Healy and Bronner conclude that only about 1 per cent of their cases were clearly motivated in their acts of delinquency by motion pictures. Burt does not give any percentage figure but says that the influence is very small.

With such conflicting results before us it

---

[1] Of course a given change in pulse rate is not so serious with children as with adults, but such wide changes are certainly worthy of note.

is impossible to generalize concerning the exact percentage of delinquents who were stimulated toward their misconduct by motion pictures. All investigations agree, however, that some motion pictures have deleterious effects on delinquents and near-delinquents. It seems probable that the greatest effects of movies do not appear suddenly and in such ways that they can be accurately measured by existing methods. Probably any detrimental effects are most likely to manifest themselves through a gradual influencing of attitudes over a long period of time, and through supplying to individuals and small groups just enough added stimulation to serve as "trigger action" when they already have rather strong antisocial inclinations or pent-up resentments.

The potentialities of motion pictures for improving standards and conduct have received less attention than their potentialities for harm. However, positive values have not been entirely overlooked. As examples of studies showing positive gains in moral attitudes and standards, we may mention the studies of Thurstone (1931) and Jones (1936). The former showed that attitudes toward gambling were changed in a desirable direction as a result of seeing a film. The latter found that ethical standards of children could be raised or lowered as a result of seeing specially selected films. The films which were most effective in raising standards were those which unqualifyingly condemned specific types of undesirable conduct. A large factor in determining whether undesirable conduct was really being condemned in a given picture was the attitude taken toward that conduct by the actor with whom the spectator identified himself.

(3) *Reading of books, magazines, and newspapers.* Reading is believed by many writers to be one of the foremost methods which can be employed for character development. The great stress on Bible reading in church schools and the confidence which many writers have expressed in the values of reading biography and great fiction are illustrations of this belief. Moreover, it is well known that some of the greatest characters of the past have been ardent readers of biography and of superior literature of all types. The difficulties, however, of demonstrating in an objective manner the value of such reading, divorced from all other desirable factors that may surround it, are very great. Jones (1931b) prepared a group of biographical episodes and tried these out as reading and discussion material in the seventh and eighth grades. In comparing results in trained groups with control groups, he did not find a statistically significant difference on a test of moral knowledge, although subjective judgments seemed to indicate that there were probably some positive gains. More controlled investigations of this matter with children and youth are definitely needed.

With regard to the deleterious effects of inferior reading matter, there is more evidence. Healy (1915) and Healy and Bronner (1936), who base their conclusions on wide experience with delinquents, are very emphatic in their claim that cheap novels and magazines dealing with bandit and underworld life act as a pernicious influence upon the character development of young people. Their conclusion is based on the verified confessions of boys and on the fact that many delinquents were found to have among their possessions a well-fingered book or magazine article which described crimes bearing marked resemblances to the ones committed. In condemning such reading, Healy (1915) says: "A definite habit and craving for this type of reading is developed just as the individual develops a habit for alcoholic stimulants. The fires of the spirit of adventure are not only kindled, but are kept going by this fuel"

. 305). The excessive reading of over-
rawn, erotic stories by young people af-
rds undue stimulation toward sexual beavior, which often results in dangerous
ractices. Novels and magazine articles
re ordinarily sufficiently long and read
nder such conditions of relaxation as to
ermit suggestion effects to be at a high
oint. Such stories are considered failures
y the reader unless they arouse his emo-
ons and encourage him to identify him-
lf with the hero. Particular parts of
ne written story, as contrasted with the
rama, can be turned back to by the
eader and reread for more stimulation
r specific details. These are doubtless
ome of the features of the bandit, under-
vorld, and amatory types of stories which
ontribute to the effects which Healy and
thers emphasize. Carr (1941) points to
he relatively wide use of outright salacious
vritings and pictures in certain sections of
he population, and stresses the evil re-
ults from such material upon adolescents.

Comic books have come in for some ex-
verimental study, but the results are too
onflicting to justify any general conclusion. One of the most interesting of the
studies is that by Bender and Lourie
(1941), who come to the conclusion that
comic book material often fits the needs of
a child in his striving to solve problems of
aggression of others toward him and of
his own impulses of aggression toward others. Future research, however, must reveal what kinds of solutions to these strivings result from the reading of the comics.

A few studies have been made to determine the influence of the reading of newspaper accounts of crime upon delinquency
and crime. From the examination of such
evidence one is led to doubt that the average newspaper account of crime influences
unfavorably the character development of
young readers. Sometimes a particular
paper or a particular reporter tends to

make of the criminal something of a hero
or daring adventurer. But usually the
newspaper reports are brief and factual,
and they record the losses to the victims
of the crime and the arrests of the perpe-
trators as well as the daring get-aways.

Motivation in Moral Behavior

Up to this point the discussion has been
confined largely to phenomena upon which
objective data are available, and it is not
our intention in this chapter to venture
far from such objective material. However, when we come to the question of motivation in character we are confronted
with the choice of ignoring the problem altogether or of attempting to discover what
the general theories of motivation in psychology have to offer which will apply here.
In the face of this dilemma it seems best
to adopt the latter course, even though the
limitation of space will necessitate a sketchy
treatment.

The points of view found in the literature concerning the dynamics of conduct
are varied. There are writers who believe
that all behavior springs from many instincts; there are those who believe in one
or two instinctive roots from which all specific motives can be derived; and there are
those who deny the theory of instinctive
drives and stress learned wants and the
motivating power of the ongoing organism
in preparatory and consummatory activity.

The clearest and boldest treatment of
motivation from the standpoint of instincts
has been given by McDougall (1908).
"The human mind," he says, "has certain
innate or inherited tendencies which are
the essential springs or motive powers of
all thought and action . . . and are the
bases from which the character and will of
individuals and nations are gradually developed under the guidance of intellectual
faculties" (p. 20). He lists among in-

stincts: curiosity, pugnacity, self-assertion, self-abasement, reproduction, gregariousness, acquisition, etc. The chief difficulties which have been faced by those who hold this view are: first, the inability to demonstrate what the unitary instincts are, and, second, the failure to show the degree to which the manifestation of an instinct which is noted at any given time is native and the degree to which it is acquired. With the advance of the researches on the processes and results of conditioning, on the one hand, and the growing interest in the integrative behavior of the organism, on the other, the belief in an hereditary equipment consisting of rather independent, broad, unitary tendencies to action was appreciably undermined.

In the fields of psychoanalysis and of individual psychology there has been a tendency to look for the dynamics of behavior in two or three instinctive roots. Freud (1924) regarded the sex tendency and the self-preservation tendency to be the main elements in human motivation, at least on the side of the life instincts as he later called them. The sex tendency encompassed all the direct and indirect derivatives of the sex motive whether conscious or "repressed in the unconscious." The self-preservation tendency included among other things the protection of all of one's moral and social standards. Adler (1927) postulated two universal tendencies: first, a desire for personal power and superiority; and, second, a "social feeling which binds man to man." "With these two points of view," he said, "we can understand how the relation between human beings is conditioned by the relative degree of their social feelings, as contrasted to their strivings for personal aggrandisement, two tendencies which are always in opposition to each other. It is a dynamic game, a parallelogram of forces whose external manifestations are what we call character (p. 190).

Murphy, Murphy, and Newcomb (1937) suggest for descriptive purposes the following four groups of "human motives" visceral drives, activity drives, aesthetic drives, and emotions. They do not think of these as instinctive, however. They stress the point that there is no separation of the fundamental drives from the means which serve them. The process of motivation they think of as going on unremittingly and they believe that the patterns of habitual responses are as fully motivated as unlearned responses.

Numerous other views have been held, such as Dunlap's theory of "fundamental desires," Woodworth's theory of preparatory and consummatory activity as the essential feature in drives, Stern's concept of pheno-motives and geno-motives, and Troland's theory of retroflexes. Space will not permit a discussion of these here, but the reader may find a rather extensive treatment of most of them given by Troland (1928) and Allport (1937).

These conflicting theories serve to illustrate the difficulty of arriving at a comprehensive and integrated concept of motivation in character. However, a few suggestions will be given as proposed guides in the search for such a concept. The first suggestion is that the attempts to reduce the motivation for conduct to two or three pervading tendencies have probably oversimplified the native equipment of man. Such attempts have derived, in what often seems a forced manner, too much from a very few tendencies and have not given sufficient consideration to the possibility that there may be a multitude of unlearned patterns of response, rather than just two or three, which may form the cores for broad tendencies. We know that the child can without training make the responses of sneezing, coughing, and crying to appropriate stimuli. It seems no less certain that the human organism after a certain degree of maturation has an unlearned capacity to experience a tension-expulsion impulse on genital stimulation. This may be the core of the structure which, when elaborated, has been called the sex instinct. Thus it seems quite possible that there is a multitude of fine patterns of actions in the innate structure of individuals and that around these patterns motivations are built up. It is possible also that these patterns differ in strength from individual to individual and that they are integrated in different ways. Thus two children raised under the same environmental circumstances might not be similarly motivated in the same situation.

A second suggestion to be offered is that the instincts given by McDougall and others, and the "fundamental desires" given by Dunlap, and all the supposedly unitary factors in lists like these, are probably products of an intricate combination, elaboration, and integration of a multitude of simpler urges. The mainsprings of moral behavior are probably not few and simple, but many and complicated; and genetic psychology may in the future show us how these tendencies develop and from what biological nuclei. The recent work on conditioning leads us to believe that the influence of training begins much earlier and has much more to do with the manifestation and relative potency of "wants" than the classical treatment of instincts has indicated.

Third, motivation for superior and inferior character responses is probably not static, but is evolving. This is, of course, in one sense simply a corollary of the conclusion that the motivation of behavior at any given time is dependent partly on conditioning and training. But, besides this, it seems probable that some of the innate patterns, such as the sex impulse, change

with age because of the process of maturation in the nervous system. Such a study as Gesell and Thompson's (1929), which indicated that growth in climbing ability among young children is partly a process of maturation in neural patterns, suggests that such a possibility is well within reason. The change in motivation with age is well illustrated by the work of Piaget (1932), who studied the nature of the rules made and followed by children in their own games and the reasons why they followed them. He distinguished what he calls two moralities among children. One he found in all very young children: an egocentric type of behavior characterized by a tendency to follow rules because they are handed down by elders. He found no tendency for the child, regardless of amount of training, to think of revising rules in games for mutual advantage, and he found nothing upon which he can build a desire on the part of the child to do this or that because of any "mutual respect of child for child." The second type of morality he found to have its beginning later in the life of the child than the first, but not suddenly to replace it—indeed it is not infrequently crowded out or prevented from appearing by the first. It is a morality motivated by a desire to change the rule in a game if in its working some child is not being treated as he himself would like to be. It is the beginning of the desire for creativeness, as opposed to conformity, in character.

No one probably would contend that Piaget's "two moralities," which we have used to illustrate our point of the changing nature of "wants," are due purely to differences in maturation. But Piaget's observation that the second one never precedes the first, coupled with the common observations concerning growth in cooperative play among children and the change in interests of youth with the maturation of the sex functions, leads one to believe that the "wants" of children change not only through training but also through maturation in neural patterns.

A fourth point which should be made is that motivation for character responses is not some potential power existing somewhere, unrelated to what the organism is doing at the moment, and waiting to be turned on like a starter in an automobile. Woodworth (1934) has particularly emphasized this and has pointed to the fact that any activity in progress may be a motive for the time being. As an illustration of this in the area of character, one would say that a child's motivation for truthfulness or honesty, lying or cheating, at any given time is a part of a chain of on-going activities; that is, his motivation is not unrelated to what he is doing and where he is.

Fifth, emotional conditioning may pronouncedly affect motivation. Bekhterev (1928) has found in working with children afflicted with kleptomania, "in which the emotion of satisfaction is associated with theft," that reconditioning can take place in just a few sittings so that the feeling of extreme annoyance instead of satisfaction is associated with theft. Watson (1926) has found that the emotion of fear may be connected by a conditioning process with situations to which it was not previously connected, and that it may, by the same process, he disconnected from situations to which it was connected. It is interesting that so little attention has been given to this problem in studies of character development, especially in view of the fact that the church has made use of it to such an important extent, as have also primitive tribes, particularly in connection with adolescent initiation ceremonies. It seems probable that one of the chief effects which literature, drama, oratory, and other arts may have upon character development is along this line of linking strong emotionally

toned reactions to certain motivating forces of the individual.

Our sixth suggestion concerns conscious and unconscious motivation. It is a matter of common observation that very small children misrepresent facts oftentimes not as a result of any conscious desire to deceive but rather as a regular part of their wishful thinking and imagining. Among older children and adults a very large part of their honest behavior is a matter of habit, where it would be impossible to say that they are consciously motivated to refrain from lying or stealing. Moreover, the psychoanalysts have emphasized what they call unconscious motivation in cases where thwartings in certain lines of activity have led to "repressions," which in turn have led to undesirable acts which do not seem to fit in logically with any conscious motivation of the subject. Cases have been cited, for example, where a youth who has been thwarted in certain desires derived from the sex impulse may turn to stealing. From a practical point of view there seems to be no doubt that the genesis of stealing in particular, and other forms of immoral behavior to some extent, may often be traced back to some important conflict or thwarting. It is possible, however, to lay so much emphasis on this type of explanation as to make it seem that almost all character responses are motivated by what "escapes from the unconscious." It would seem a more inclusive and less mysterious explanation to say that conflicts play their part, as do all experiences, in affecting the on-going activity of the individual, but that it is the on-going activity at any given time, including conscious processes, reactions to frustration, and habit mechanisms, rather than some entity in the "unconscious," which provides the motivation for action.

The final suggestion which we wish to make is that verbalized concepts may motivate character responses. This point is implied in much that has been said about activity motivating further activity. Those who subscribe to the view that no behavior, regardless of how much it may benefit society, can be described as moral unless the motive of the agent is consciously moral, will say that all motivation in moral behavior *must* depend on verbalized and conscious concepts. This problem has led to an age-old controversy in philosophy which cannot be reviewed here. Suffice it for our purposes to emphasize the contention that verbalized concepts do motivate moral behavior at times. As will be shown later, generalized principles and ideals are gradually built up in accordance with the laws of learning out of experiences which are verbalized. Once these verbalized principles are acquired, they become tools not only for considering the present but also for reconstructing the past and planning the future. Through them, the distant and the past are made a part of the here and now. With them, we build the goals we would achieve. By them, individual characters of the past and present, both great and small, may exert motivating influences upon us.

Such a verbalized concept, for example, as cheating-is-a-form-of-stealing may, under some circumstances, act as one motivating factor for honesty in an examination. In the presence of conflicting motivations the ideal of acting-toward-others-as-we-would-have-them-act-toward-us may become for the individual the prepotent "drive" in the situation. It would be a mistake, of course, to assume that the major part of the motivation in the character of children is dependent upon the prepotency of such a highly complex concept or principle as the last one named. The goal of character development, however, is in that direction. The striking gap which so frequently exists between verbally expressed principles and actions has so impressed some observers that they seem to doubt or belittle the motivating power of ideals. The frequency of the gap must, of course, be granted. However, any account of character development which underestimates the potential motivating power of ideals and other verbalized principles, because they seldom if ever produce action completely consistent with them, would be short-sighted indeed. It would be guilty of discerning nothing in a direction of striving except the goals achieved and of minimizing worthy intentions that do not eventuate in accomplishment.

Knowledge, Will, and Conduct

Knowledge. In popular analyses of ethical conduct it is often assumed that knowledge of "right" and "wrong" and the will to follow the right when it is known are the *sine qua non* of moral responsibility. This assumption is shown most interestingly in attempts made in courts and homes to decide upon punishment for misconduct. Roscoe Pound (1930) says, "Our traditional criminal law thinks of the offender as a free moral agent who, having before him the choice whether to do right or do wrong, intentionally chooses to do wrong." This clearly assumes, in the first place, that the individual knew which act was right and which wrong, and, in the second place, that the individual "willed" to do the wrong. Before the courts, an individual, whether child or adult, is considered to be either responsible for his acts or irresponsible. There are no in-betweens. If it can be established that an individual's powers have not developed sufficiently for him to know the difference between right and wrong or for him to have adequate "will power" to control his acts, then he is pronounced irresponsible for his acts. In many states, children under six or seven years of age are considered irresponsible if they commit serious offenses, but children slightly older are considered responsible and are punished accordingly. In the home, too, it is sometimes assumed that young children should not be held very strictly accountable for their acts because they have not reached an "age of discretion."

One purpose of this section is to point to the oversimplification in the above concepts. In the first place, there is no point in the development of a child at which he suddenly passes from the age of irresponsibility to that of responsibility. Study after study has shown that children develop gradually in their moral knowledge as well as in conduct. Two or three such studies which deal primarily with moral knowledge may be cited by way of illustration. Written descriptions of 64 childhood situations were presented by Jones (1929a) to 177 children of Grades 7 and 8. The instructions were that the proposed action in each situation should be marked as "right," "excusable," or "wrong." There were only 9 situations out of the 64 where as many as 90 per cent of these children agreed as to the rightness or wrongness or excusability of the proposed action. The same situations were presented to several hundred school teachers and prospective teachers, and among these there were only 12 situations where as many as 90 per cent agreed. These findings were subsequently corroborated by Maller (1932).

Even at the college level the question of cheating on quizzes and examinations seems to be a moot issue with many. An intensive study by Katz and Allport (1930), at Syracuse University, revealed that 26 per cent of the college students examined considered "cribbing" to be as bad as lying or stealing, but that 22.5 per cent definitely condoned it. The remainder took stands in between these two positions. From these results it seems certain that persons cannot

be divided into two categories, those who know the difference between right and wrong and those who do not. There is no time in life when one is suddenly endowed with ability to discern right from wrong. Strictly, there is no age that can be called "the age of discretion." Throughout life one is continually learning and modifying his views of the right and wrong as he faces new situations.

This leads to a second point of oversimplification in popular comments upon knowledge and action in character. There seems to be a rather widespread assumption that there is something automatic about knowledge of desirable conduct even in novel situations, and that the only task of the individual is to make his conduct harmonize with his intuitive knowledge of what he ought to do. If, however, one questions the concept of intuitive knowledge, as is done here, he is faced with the problem of proposing another explanation of how an individual arrives at his notions as to what is right in *novel* situations. This is very important because character development cannot be conceived of as mere repetition of isolated learned responses. There must be a place for creativeness. New issues must be faced by every developing individual, and with increasing maturity he must make his responses more and more independently of parents, teachers, or other counselors. In real life, virtues not infrequently run counter to each other and one has to choose among them. How does the individual arrive at his conception of what is the "right" course of action in a novel situation? The view subscribed to here is that moral knowledge is derived by a process of generalization from past experience and that the more the child is taught to generalize from his knowledge and conduct in those stages of development when he has guidance from parents and teachers, the more will he be able to use the process of ethical problem solving in novel situations. A young child who is properly taught learns that it is wrong to steal jam at home, a pencil at school, and candy in a store, but he may gradually generalize that stealing in any situation is wrong. Thus a hierarchy of values is built up. Any line of activity in a novel situation which in his judgment involves stealing will be considered wrong.

As an illustration, take the case of a boy who for the first time faces the situation of not having his fare collected on a train, owing to the oversight of the conductor. He is faced with the choice of keeping quiet and retaining his fare or of paying for the service which he is obtaining. In deciding what is right and what is wrong in this new situation, the boy may consider the paying of the fare as linked up with honesty, and the retaining of the money or ticket as associated with dishonesty. If this happens, he is no longer faced solely by the specific choice between paying and not paying, but he is faced by the choice as it has allied itself with the "honesty constellation" or the "dishonesty constellation." If, as a result of development and of training, the honesty constellation is greatly preferred to the dishonesty one, the choice between paying and not paying is largely made. Following this same reasoning there may be further interlinkages. The boy may look upon honest behavior as a sort of subhierarchy in the higher hierarchy of respect for rights of others and dishonesty as a violation of these rights for selfish interest. The simplest choice may be made, therefore, by an individual in the light of his most fundamental values. We call this choosing on "principle." But the principle is not some mysterious and suddenly acquired power for knowing right from wrong; it is an acquired generalization based on specific experiences.

It is an oft-repeated fact that knowledge of the right does not insure right conduct. This is so strongly emphasized by some writers, however, that one sometimes wonders if they have not overlooked the fact that, whereas one may not choose the right course after he discerns it, one cannot choose the right in a situation except by utter chance if he does not have knowledge or proper habit patterns. In cases of conscious choice knowledge is a prerequisite of character, even though, as everyone knows, it is not a guarantor of it.

Conscience. At this point we come to the crux of the age-old problem of conscience. We cannot hope to do justice to this very complex problem here, but we do wish to recognize it as a problem worthy of psychological study. Most psychologists today are very circumspect about the use of the term *conscience,* but they recognize that tensions accompanying the consciousness of an individual of a serious gap between what he thinks he ought to do and what he does are among the chief sources of personality conflicts.

Freud freely uses the word conscience, and we are indebted to him for what is probably the most systematic attack on tensions growing out of moral values that has been made from the instinct point of view. To Freud feelings of guilt and sense of inferiority are manifestations of the tensions between the ego and the ego ideal. But how is this ego ideal or conscience built up? Freud (1930) thinks that the ego ideal develops by the child's gradual "internalizing" certain controls upon himself, motivated by his early helplessness and dependence upon others. Thus, according to Freud, conscience grows out of child-parent relationships which go back fundamentally to instinctive bases. The child identifies himself with the parent and gradually the ego ideal develops, taking **over** certain controls and **exercising the** same aggressiveness toward the ego that the father would have exercised toward the child. Out of concepts such as these, Freud builds a systematic structure of urges, controls, and tensions.

In some of the more recent work in anthropology and psychoanalysis less stress is being placed on instincts than characterized Freud's writings. More emphasis is being placed on early conditioning and societal influences. Kardiner (1939), for example, maintains that Freud's explanation falls short in that it does not give sufficient recognition to the dependencies, affections, and values which are built up from the earliest age by direct conditioning and learning from the social environment. He says:

> In his orientation on instinct, Freud left little room for the operation of societal influences. . . . If we see the super-ego as a mental function, we tend to lose sight of the fact that it represents an habitual and automatic method of reacting to other individuals to the end of being loved and escaping punishment. . . . Fully recognizing the important rôle of helplessness of the child, Freud does not follow its influence on the acceptance of disciplines, but continues to view the relationship of the child and parent from the point of view of sexual object and aim.

Horney (1937) also stresses the cultural basis of many of the wants, values, and aspirations of individuals, and contrasts this approach with the more purely instinctive and biological approach of Freud. This author particularly emphasizes the important rôle played in anxiety and other neuroses by the conflict between what the individual does and what he feels is expected of him.

There is much to be said for extending the sources of moral standards, values, and ideals along the lines suggested by Kardiner, Horney, and others. That one has the power to acquire conscience is a gift of nature. The limits to which one's conscience can be made to function in making intricate and subtle distinctions are probably dependent at least in some measure on native endowment. There may even be certain prepotent impulses which influence the kind of conscience which an individual develops. But, within certain very broad limits, children and adults acquire their consciences by reacting to the stimulation which such environmental factors as home and friends, church and school, afford.

Level of Aspiration. The nearest approach which has been made by laboratory experimentation to the problem above is the work which has been done on *aspiration level.* Hoppe (1930), who did pioneer research on this problem, defined level of aspiration as the goals, the expectations of a person, or the claims on his future achievement. In his experiments he was not concerned with aspiration in any ethical sense. Some of his results and conclusions, however, like those of others who have worked on this problem under well-controlled laboratory conditions, are suggestive in the present discussion. He found, for example, that success on the part of a subject in reaching his aspiration level encouraged him to try harder tasks, whereas failure had the opposite effect. Individual differences in reaction to success and failure in meeting the aspiration level seemed to him to be related to self-confidence, fear of inferiority, caution, ambition, and the like. Frank (1935) concludes in his study that the difference between the average level of aspiration and median level of past performance is related to the ego level of the individual in the task, to tenacity of purpose, to ability to withstand failure, and to ability to look objectively at one's past performance. Gould (1939) concludes that different subjects react differently to the gap between level of aspiration and erformance. Some subjects react to feelings of failure by trying to do better; others by becoming discouraged and losing the desire to go on; others by overcoming the consciousness of the gap by dreaming of success, making excuses, etc.; and still others by various combinations of these.

Will. In many treatments of character the gap between knowledge of desirable conduct and action consistent with such knowledge is attributed to weaknesses in volitional factors or will. Indeed, not a few writers consider will to be the central problem of character and maintain that strong characters are strong primarily in will and weak characters are weak in will. Stephenson (1935), for example, says that it is "in the sphere of volition and conation that we hope to find the secrets of character."

In psychological literature, notably that of Germany and England, there are many treatises upon the will. Typical of the best of these is the analysis of Ach (1935) and the stimulating but equally subjective discussion of Stern (1938). The chief difficulty with all such analyses of the will is the absence of supporting experimental evidence.

Attempts to study objectively the phenomenon of willing in some of its manifestations have usually fallen under one of three headings. First, there are the studies of a statistical nature which have sought to determine whether or not there was a general factor in the realm of volitional behavior. Notable in this line of attack has been the work of Webb (1915), Spearman (1927), and others. By use of the factor analysis technique applied to tests and ratings of character, Spearman and his students have obtained results which lead them to conclude that a general factor, w, can be identified. Moreover, they believe that this general factor of will is quite basic to character.

The chief criticism of this line of attack is that it is difficult to see what the next step psychologically is to be after the factor of w has been identified. To the genetic psychologist, the operation of willing seems to be contributed to by at least the following: motivation for the specific activity in question; strength of the tendency to self-assertiveness, or the determination not to be outdone; habits of completing what has been undertaken; strength and persistence of reacting. To subsume all these under the general factor of w is well enough in contrasting volitional factors with, say, intellectual factors; but in the study of the development of character this seems too general and too much like a faculty to stimulate much research.

A second area of research on volitional factors is that dealing with perseveration. One of the most interesting contributions to the study of character development coming out of the work on perseveration has been the finding of Pinard (1932) and Cattell (1933) that those persons at or near the extremes in perseveration, either very low or very high, are likely to be low in character development. In commenting upon this, the latter experimenter has argued as follows: When neural stimulation toward a certain goal lasts only a very short time, we have an individual who is changeable, lacking in ability to stick to a task, and undependable; whereas when the neural stimulation towards a goal lasts too long we have an individual who cannot put aside one task when he needs to do another, who is almost obsessed by unfinished tasks, and who cannot give vigorous attention to any one task because of the residual stimulation from previous tasks.

From the above results it seems that perseveration bears some relation to character, but it is also clear that much more research upon perseveration and other measures of willing will be required before basic relationships and meanings become at all well understood. Kendig (1937) and Shevach (1937) have particularly stressed this latter point. Shevach does not find in his experiments that the perseverative tendency is very consistent from situation to situation and doubts that any general factor of perseveration, such as has been suggested by some writers, could have any very real psychological meaning. Kendig shares this same view and attempts to explain perseveration in terms of residual tensions growing out of disequilibrium in the organism.

A third set of studies on volitional factors has concentrated on persistence. Ryans (1938a, 1939b) and Thornton (1939), for example, have conducted valuable studies. They reach very different conclusions, however, regarding the generality of a trait of persistence in factor analysis studies. The former obtained results which led him to postulate a general factor of persistence; the latter failed to find this. There is rather general agreement in the literature, however, that persistence correlates positively with other measures of willing, that it increases with age, at least between 9 and 15, and that it is related to self-control. It seems to be contributed to by hereditary factors and is probably related, as Ryans (1939a) suggests, to organic drives.

So much for a very brief review of some of the objective results on volitional factors and their relation to character development. That the ground has scarcely been scratched in this complex area is very apparent. The results, however, have served at least to show that will cannot be thought of as any single power which an individual possesses. It seems safe to say that will exists psychologically only in the operation of willing. Experiments indicate that the native make-up and the physiological conditions of an individual affect the strength and duration of his reactions at all times, but there are equally good rea-

sons for believing that acquired interests, goals, motivations, and habits are also potent factors in any character responses which would be popularly referred to as showing will or will power.

Specificity versus Generality of Traits. One of the most interesting theoretical problems in the study of character is the problem of the consistency or inconsistency in the behavior of an individual in different situations involving honesty, cooperativeness, persistence, or the like. There is a considerable body of evidence on this problem, most of it consisting of correlational studies in which children's scores on one measure of a *trait* are correlated with their scores on another measure of the trait. As will be seen from the few typical results given below, there is relatively good agreement among the statistical results obtained by the different experimenters. Jones (1936), working with 185 seventh-grade pupils, found an average inter-*r* of .35 among three tests of honesty in school situations. Hartshorne and May (1928, 1929), using elementary and junior high school children as subjects, found an average inter-*r* of .39 among four tests of honesty. Crutcher (1934) reports a median inter-*r* of .47 among six persistence tests on children ranging in age from 7 to 16. Cushing (1929) obtained an average inter-*r* of .42 among five tests of persistence among preschool children.[1] These, we believe, are fair samples of the results which have been obtained, and we need not multiply the evidence.

What does it mean so far as specificity or generality of traits is concerned? On the

[1] It is interesting in passing to compare these inter-*r*'s among different tests within the same "trait" with inter-*r*'s among different "traits." Jones found an average inter-*r* of .15 between each of his honesty tests and a test of cooperation. Hartshorne and May found an average inter-*r* of .21 among tests of honesty, helpful ness, self-control, and persistence.

face of it, it means that an observer cannot predict very accurately what a child's unanalyzed behavior will be in one situation, involving a supposed trait, from his behavior in another situation presumably involving the same trait. For example, a child may be honest on a test where he has a good chance to cheat, and yet he may dishonestly get an advantage over other pupils in a prize contest by peeping when he has promised to compete with his eyes closed. Moreover, a child may cheat under one teacher but not under another. From such observations and statistical facts as the above, an advocate of specificity, such as Symonds (1928), argues against the concept of generality of traits. "It has been found," he says, "that no one acts perfectly consistently with regard to a trait as would be the case if conduct was an expression of inner traits" (p. 320). He believes that the central element in character development is more or less specific habit. He admits that conduct may be generalized in accordance with the principles of habit formation by responding to the likenesses and differences in situations; but, he says, "this generalization of conduct does not extend as far as most people suppose, with the result that conduct for the large masses of people remains unorganized, a rather loose bundle of unrelated and disassociated habits" (p. 325).

Allport (1937), starting with the same statistical results as Symonds, comes out with a very different interpretation. He calls attention to a correlation of .13, found by Hartshorne and May, between stealing pennies and the telling of lies about cheating, and he admits that the "dishonest habit aroused by one of these situations is quite independent of the dishonest habit in the other." He maintains, however, that under this surface specificity there are generalized traits. He admits that a given child who is tested may not steal pennies and yet may cheat in school and lie about the cheating. But he interprets this as showing not so much the lack of a general trait of honesty as the presence of a general trait of timidity. "Each of these children," he says, "behaved as he did toward these tests, not because of specific habits but because he had some deep-lying and characteristic trait" (p. 251).

These are illustrations of the different interpretations based on the very same facts. It seems possible that a beginning of rapprochement between these two views may be achieved by making a distinction between the behavior of an individual as seen by an observer and the behavior of the individual from his own point of view. Certainly no one who has experimented with children can avoid the conclusion that many children are not very consistent in honesty as judged by their overt behavior alone. This is not to say that specificity is the rule, for the correlations are no more zero than they are 1.00. Some children, even as judged by observers who see nothing but their outward behavior, are quite consistent; and all who stand high in one aspect of a trait are more likely than not to stand high in another. This is what the positive correlations reported above really mean.

Furthermore, if we could see the child's total behavior in these situations from his own point of view, there seems little doubt that we should see much more consistency than his unanalyzed behavior reveals. This would be true not so much because we could, if we fail to find a general trait of honesty, postulate, as Allport does, some underlying personality trait such as timidity; it would be true because a situation which is designed from the point of view of the examiner to test honesty may not test honesty—and nothing but honesty—from the point of view of the subject. A child, for example, who refrains from cheating with one teacher, but cheats freely with another, may not think of the two situations as comparable at all. He may not cheat in the one case because he feels that he is on his honor not to try to "put anything over" on someone who treats him fairly and whom he likes; he may cheat in the other because he considers it an opportunity to "steal a march on," or to get even with, someone whom he dislikes or distrusts. As observers of only the honest-dishonest aspects of these situations, we might well conclude that honesty for this child is rather specific. If, however, we view the total situations from the child's position we may see much to account for what may seem inconsistency in behavior from situation to situation besides specificity in the trait of honesty.

Another point which should be considered is that generality or specificity of traits probably varies with the age and training of the individual. There is no clear-cut statistical or experimental evidence which can be given here to demonstrate this, but all that we know of early conditioning as well as later learning of children leads us to believe that there should be greater specificity of conduct at the lower levels of learning and greater generality at the higher level.

One of the main theses of this chapter is that development in character should be away from specificity and in the direction of generality. When a child at a very young age makes a response which is judged to be undesirable or wrong in a situation, there come along simultaneously from the parent disapproving gestures, facial expressions, vocal tones, or such words as "no-no," "that's bad," "that's wrong," "that's not yours," "that's being a tattle-tale," "that's dishonest," and the like. By repeatedly experiencing annoyance in connection with a response or class of responses the child is conditioned against it.

On the other hand, if the child makes a response which is judged to be the proper one, his action is rewarded by a smiling countenance, approving gestures, and such words as "that's a good boy," "that's right," "that's being honest," et cetera. He has similar experiences on every side, and, just as he learns gradually the names and uses of objects, he learns that certain acts are looked upon with approval and others with disapproval. This is the beginning of the process of generalizing, but his generalizations are based on only a very few acts which he has learned are not approved of and which he pronounces in a parrotlike fashion to be bad. At this stage of development a child's conduct seems to be highly specific.

But as time goes on, the child finds that there are approved-of or not-approved-of aspects in a large number of situations; he learns that such words as "right," "wrong," "ought," "mustn't," "truthful," "untruthful," "honest," "dishonest," "loyal," "disloyal," refer to certain common factors in many situations. No other behavior of his is so violently responded to by adults as that where questions of right and wrong are raised, and consequently no other becomes so quickly and so thoroughly emotionally toned. With the increasing ability of the child to use verbalized concepts goes increasing use of and understanding of the generalizations of right and wrong, good and bad, honesty and deceit, loyalty and disloyalty. He experiences what is referred to by various trait names in a great variety of situations. Gradually there develops whatever consistency of behavior occurs under trait names for him. These trait names assist him to generalize further, and emotional accompaniments become increasingly attached not only to specific acts but also to classes of acts. This process continues on into adulthood.

However, even when an individual reaches

his highest stage of maturity we cannot say that his traits are completely generalized in the sense that we can predict with anything like absolute certainty how he will behave in a relatively new situation involving a "trait" in which we rate him highly. When we describe a youth or man as honest, for example, we do not mean that we have observed any unitary or generalized trait of honesty on his part. We mean only that we have observed honest behavior in his case in a variety of situations and that we predict that in further sampling of situations he will respond similarly. This prediction is made partly on the assumption that in new situations involving honesty which he will face he will have systems of detailed habits that will make highly probable such and such conduct, and partly also on the assumption that he has a certain orientation, a certain hierarchy of values which will tend to insure behavior consistent with it.

Unfortunately, experimental facts are not available by which to test the above hypothesis that generality increases with growth in character. Taking all things into account, however, it seems that neither thoroughgoing specificity nor generality is likely to be adequate in any universal sense. The degree of specificity or generality characterizing an individual's conduct will depend, we believe, on his maturity and character development. Thus, looked at genetically, specificity and generality seem to be not so much opposing explanatory concepts as descriptive terms depending in their relative applicability upon the stage of development of the individual.

Some Practical Principles in Character Development

In concluding this chapter a few practical suggestions concerning character development in home, church, and school may be in order.

The Importance of Early and Continuous Training in Character Development. In some of the older doctrines, before the advent of modern research on child development, great faith was placed in sudden changes in the character development of children and youth. The old notion that a child rather abruptly reached an age of moral responsibility after which time he could be "reasoned with" is one illustration of the belief in sudden changes. It is not our purpose here to maintain that rather sudden changes in the values and moral outlook of individuals never occur. Sufficient psychological data are not available on the dramatic cases that are usually cited in support of sudden changes to enable us to judge, but such cases are at least rare in comparison with the multitude of individuals who develop gradually from day to day.

The parent or the teacher who waits for the sudden dawning of an age of discretion seems, in light of research results on mental growth, to be doomed to disappointment. While parents wait for their small child to be "old enough to understand," certain preliminary orientation on the part of the child is achieved about the relative importance of truthfulness and of not getting caught. Young children have often learned a great deal before their parents stop recounting with amusement their "cute" escapades and "white lies."

Teachers, also, often delay too long or overlook good opportunities in giving early training. Such a simple lesson, for example, as the distinction between mutual helpfulness among classmates and cheating is frequently put off or taught only sporadically until serious confusion develops. The result is that many children in our elementary and secondary schools do not consider cheating as an ethical question at all. It is rather a question of what one can "put over on" the teacher and what one can "get by with" in general. What an older child subsumes under the concepts of honor, cheating, tattling, or being a goody-goody or a thief, and what his emotionally toned attitudes toward these are, at any given age, are dependent in no small degree upon his conditioning and learning which began very early. Moral concepts and behavior are in continuous process of formation and revision throughout life, of course, but the earlier a child is oriented toward desirable conduct and generalizations, the earlier does he begin to internalize the controls upon him and to evolve his own sense of relative values.

Motivating Character Development: Rewards and Punishments. A child learns desirable character responses by experiencing satisfaction in connection with those responses which are ethically and socially acceptable and annoyance with those which are undesirable. Thus rewards and punishments are basic in character development as in all learning. In no other form of learning, however, is it quite so important that they be adjusted accurately to the stage of development of the child. In the early period of development, especially, it seems that intensity of rewards and punishments are less important than promptness and consistency. Much evidence is accumulating to indicate that reward is often more effective than punishment, and that punishment should be recognized mainly as a deterrent to undesirable behavior since it lacks the constructive qualities required to motivate desirable conduct.

Tangible awards for desirable responses are sometimes valuable means for making such responses satisfying, but they are valuable only in so far as they become less and less necessary as the child grows older. If at any age tangible awards tend to establish and perpetuate desirable conduct

only on the basis of the artificial stimulant, they are to that extent undesirable, as Dimock and Hendry (1929) have interestingly demonstrated.

The types of rewards which seem to be most universal and permanent are those involving social approval and self-approval. Manifestations of genuine approval in the form of compliments, personal acceptance, and added responsibilities are among the strongest satisfactions for a child when they come from an adult or an associate whom he admires. As an individual becomes older, he never becomes insensitive to social approval, but a more and more important place may gradually be taken by the satisfaction accompanying the consciousness of self-approval or inner harmony. As Dewey says, "The community without gradually becomes a forum and tribunal within." Thus, in the most advanced stages of character development, the most important function which the teacher can perform in associating satisfaction or annoyance with a specific act is to show the learner new light on the relation of that act to his existing patterns of generalized responses which already have strong satisfactions or annoyances connected with them. Once an act is viewed as being in harmony with one's ideals and values, it becomes satisfying; once it is viewed as out of harmony, it becomes annoying. Perhaps most of the choices of life are made at lower levels of ethical consciousness than this, but the choices with the greatest significance to character it seems are made in this manner. All teaching of youth should make provision for the development of such inner satisfactions and annoyances. Without such internalized motivation character would always depend upon the short-range stimulation of more or less exteriorly derived rewards and punishments and would lack the sustained pull of ideals and values.

Transfer of Training. In character development, as in all other aspects of development where learning plays an important rôle, one of the major practical problems is the degree to which training received in one situation will function outside the narrow confines of that situation. Space will not permit a detailed discussion of even the most directly relevant studies in this field. However, two or three of the main generalizations from four such studies— those of Voelker (1921), Hartshorne and May (1928, 1929), Zyve (1931), and Jones (1936)—will be given.

One conclusion which seems justified from these experiments is that the learner in developing the responses which are called by any trait name should be led to practice such responses in a variety of situations if much transfer is to be expected. In school, for example, trustworthiness cannot be effectively taught if the only situations involving this trait which are called to the attention of the children are cheating and noncheating on tests.

A second suggestion growing out of the experiments is that, in the interest of greatest transfer, learners should be stimulated and assisted to respond to the *relations* among the various manifestations of a trait in different situations. The potential power of children to generalize has been repeatedly emphasized in this chapter. The development and use of this power to see relations among different situations and to generalize are among the main objectives of any education designed for character development. Without the attempt on the part of parents and teachers to help the child, in learning honest behavior, for example, to cull out the honesty "element" in a variety of situations and to respond to this generalized concept, the learner would be left without the most promising bridge between one honesty situation and another, and his concept of honesty would be an unorganized, unintegrated collection of "do's" and "don't's."

The synthetic process of gradually building up trait concepts and other generalizations, and the analytical process of seeing "elements" in new situations to which these generalizations apply, should go hand in hand. The most advanced education in character which is supplied by home, school, church, drama, literature, and philosophy functions largely in this area of stimulating young and old, on the one hand, to generalize, and, on the other, to analyze out of the ever new and increasingly complex problems which they meet those familiar virtues which earlier training revealed and toned with emotional attachments.

Résumé

The aim of this chapter has been to raise the main psychological problems involved in character development and to present evidence wherever possible toward their solution. Character has been considered as the sum total of an individual's ways of behaving which are judged in terms of ethical rightness or wrongness and which typically involve for him volitional factors and feelings of personal adequacy (or guilt) and social responsibility.

Both native and environmental factors have been stressed, the view being taken that character development in an individual is a resultant of both sets of factors. A central thesis of the chapter has been that every individual acquires his character in conformity with the usual laws of conditioning and learning, but that the possibilities for such acquisition and the broad limits thereto are provided by nature. One's character is deeply integrated with his social and personality adjustments and therefore environmental factors influence character only as they are converted from outer stimuli and presses into inner habits and motives.

In accordance with the laws of conditioning and learning one acquires not only the habits and motives which control his conduct, but also the goals or ideals he would achieve. The *gaps* between such aspirations of an individual and his achievements afford important sources of personality and character maladjustments which psychological research is only beginning to reveal.

Bibliography

ACH, N. 1935. *Analyse des Willens.* Berlin: Urban and Schwarzenberg.

ADLER, A. 1927. *Understanding human nature.* (Trans. by W. B. WOLFE.) New York: Greenberg.

ALLPORT, G. W. 1937. *Personality.* New York: Holt.

BEKHTEREV, V. M. 1928. Emotions as somato-mimetic reflexes. In M. L. REYMERT (Ed.), *Feelings and emotions: The Wittenberg Symposium,* pp. 270–283. Worcester, Mass.: Clark University Press.

BENDER, L., and R. S. LOURIE. 1941. The effect of comic books on the ideology of children. *Amer. J. Orthopsychiat.,* 11, 540–551.

BIZE, P. R., and R. MORICARD. 1937. Psychic changes following injection of testosterone in young boys. *Bull. soc. pédiat., Paris,* 35, 38.

BLUMER, H., and P. M. HAUSER. 1934. *Movies, delinquency and crime.* New York: Macmillan.

BOND, E. S., and K. E. APPEL. 1931. The treatment of post-encephalitic children in a hospital school. *Amer. J. Psychiat.,* 10, 815–828.

BÜHLER, C., and G. KELLY (Eds.). 1941. *The world test.* New York: Psychological Corporation.

BURT, C. 1925. *The young delinquent.* London: University of London Press; New York: Appleton.

CADY, V. M. 1923. The estimation of juvenile incorrigibility. *J. Delinq. Monogr.,* No. 2.

CARR, L. J. 1941. *Delinquency control.* New York: Harper.

CARR-SAUNDERS, A. M., H. MANNHEIM, and E. C. RHODES. 1944. *Young offenders.* London: Cambridge University Press; New York: Macmillan.

CARTER, H. D. 1933. Twin-similarities in personality traits. *Ped. Sem. and J. Genet. Psychol.,* 43, 312–321.

CATTELL, R. B. 1933–1934. Temperament tests: II. Tests. *Brit. J. Psychol.,* 24, 20–29.

CIAMPI, L. 1937. Postencephalitic ethical defect in children. *Ann. Soc. Argent. Criminol.,* 3, 69–88.

CRESSEY, P. G., and F. M. THRASHER. 1934. *Boys, movies, and city streets.* New York: Macmillan.

CRUTCHER, R. 1934. An experimental study of persistence. *J. Appl. Psychol.,* 18, 409–417.

CUSHING, H. M. 1929. A perseverative tendency in preschool children: A study of personality differences. *Arch. Psychol., N. Y.,* 17, No. 108.

DALE, E. 1935. *Attendance at motion pictures and the contents of motion pictures.* New York: Macmillan.

DAWSON, L. L. 1938. *The relation of unemployment to certain types of crime in Massachusetts.* Unpublished M.A. Thesis. Clark University.

DIMOCK, H. S., and C. E. HENDRY. 1929. *Camping and character.* New York: Association Press.

DOLLARD, J., L. W. DOOB, N. MILLER, O. MOWRER, and R. SEARS. 1939. *Frustration and aggression.* New Haven: Yale University Press.

DYSINGER, W. S., and C. A. RUCKMICK. 1933. *The emotional responses of children to the motion picture situation.* New York: Macmillan.

ECKLE, C., and G. OSTERMEYER. 1939. Erb-charackterologische Zwillingsuntersuchungen. *Beih. Z. angew. Psychol.,* No. 82.

FORD, R. 1939. *Children in the cinema.* London: Allen and Unwin.

FRANK, J. D. 1935. Some psychological determinants of level of aspiration. *Amer. J. Psychol.,* 47, 285–293.

FREUD, S. 1924. *Collected papers:* Vol. 1. London: Hogarth Press and Institute for Psycho-Analysis.

——. 1930. *Civilization and its discontents.* (Trans. by J. RIVIÈRE.) New York: Cape and Smith.

GARNETT, M. 1939. *Knowledge and character.* London: Cambridge University Press.

GESELL, A., and H. THOMPSON. 1929. Learning and growth in identical infant twins: An experimental study by the method of co-twin control. *Genet. Psychol. Monogr.,* 6. Pp. 124.

GLUECK, E. T. 1935. Mental retardation and juvenile delinquency. *Ment. Hyg., N. Y.,* 19, 549–572.

GLUECK, S., and E. T. GLUECK. 1934. *One thousand juvenile delinquents.* Cambridge: Harvard University Press.

——. 1940. *Juvenile delinquents grown up.* New York: Commonwealth Fund.

GOULD, R. 1939. An experimental analysis of "level of aspiration." *Genet. Psychol. Monogr.,* 21. Pp. 115.

GROVES, E. R. 1940. *The family and its social functions.* Philadelphia: Lippincott.

HARTSHORNE, H., and M. A. MAY. 1926. Testing knowledge of right and wrong. *Relig. Educ.*, **26**, 539–554.

——. 1928. *Studies in deceit:* Book I. *General methods and results;* Book II. *Statistical methods and results.* New York: Macmillan.

——. 1929. *Studies in service and self-control.* New York: Macmillan.

HARTSHORNE, H., M. A. MAY, and F. K. SHUTTLEWORTH. 1930. *Studies in the organization of character.* New York: Macmillan.

HEALY, W. 1915. *The individual delinquent: A text-book of diagnosis and prognosis for all concerned in understanding offenders.* Boston: Little, Brown; London: Heinemann.

HEALY, W., and A. F. BRONNER. 1926. *Delinquents and criminals: Their making and unmaking.* New York: Macmillan.

——. 1936. *New light on delinquency and its treatment.* New Haven: Yale University Press.

HEALY, W., A. F. BRONNER, E. M. H. BAYLOR, and J. P. MURPHY. 1929. *Reconstructing behavior in youth.* New York: Knopf.

HEALY, W., A. F. BRONNER, and A. M. BOWERS. 1930. *The structure and meaning of psychoanalysis.* New York: Knopf.

HEERSENA, P. H. 1940. Prognosis in postencephalitic behavior disorders. *Med. Clin. N. Amer.*, **24**, 1179–1190.

HIGHTOWER, P. R. 1930. Biblical information in relation to character conduct. *Univ. Iowa Stud. Char.*, **3**, No. 2.

HOLZINGER, K. J. 1929. The relative effect of nature and nurture on twin differences. *J. Educ. Psychol.*, **20**, 241–248.

HOPPE, F. 1930. Erfolg und Misserfolg. *Psychol. Forsch.*, **14**, 1–62.

HORNEY, K. 1937. *The neurotic personality of our time.* New York: Norton.

HOWELLS, T. H. 1938. Factors influencing honesty. *J. Soc. Psychol.*, **9**, 97–102.

IMBAU, F. E. 1935a. Detection of deception technique admitted as evidence. *J. Crim. Law Criminol.*, **26**, 262–270.

——. 1935b. The lie-detector. *Sci. Mon.*, **40**, 81–87.

JONES, V. 1929a. Ideas on right and wrong among teachers and children. *Teach. Coll. Rec.*, **30**, 529–541.

——. 1929b. Disagreement among teachers as to right and wrong. *Teach. Coll. Rec.*, **31**, 24–36.

——. 1931a. *What would you have done?* Boston: Ginn.

——. 1931b. *Character education through cases from biography.* Boston: Ginn.

——. 1932. Relation of economic depression to delinquency, crime, and drunkenness in Massachusetts. *J. Soc. Psychol.*, **3**, 259–282.

——. 1933. Children's morals. In C. MURCHISON (Ed.), *A handbook of child psychology* (2d ed., rev.), pp. 482–533. Worcester: Clark University Press.

JONES, V. 1936. *Character and citizenship training in the public school.* Chicago: University of Chicago Press.

JORDAN, H. W. 1938. Admissibility of deception (lie-detector) tests. *J. Crim. Law Criminol.*, **29**, 287–291.

KARDINER, A. 1939. *The individual and his society.* New York: Columbia University Press.

KATZ, D., and F. H. ALLPORT. 1930. *Students' attitudes.* Syracuse, N. Y.: Craftsman Press.

KEELER, L. 1934. Debunking the lie-detector. *J. Crim. Law Criminol.*, **25**, 153–159.

KENDIG, I. 1937. Studies in perseveration: II, III, IV, and V. *J. Psychol.*, **3**, 231–264.

KENDIG, I., and B. J. SHEVACH. 1937. Studies in perseveration: I. A survey of researches in perseveration. *J. Psychol.*, **3**, 223–230.

KLOPFER, B., and D. M. KELLEY. 1942. *The Rorschach technique.* Yonkers: World Book.

KÜNKEL, F. 1938. *Character, growth, education.* (Trans. by B. KEPPEL-COMPTON and B. DRUITT.) Philadelphia: Lippincott.

LANE, H. A., and P. A. WITTY. 1935. The mental ability of delinquent boys. *J. Juv. Res.*, **19**, 1–12.

LANGE, J. 1930. *Crime and destiny.* (Trans. by C. HALDANE.) New York: Boni.

LANKES, W. 1915. Perseveration. *Brit. J. Psychol.*, **7**, 387–419.

LARSON, J. A. 1932. *Lying and its detection.* Chicago: University of Chicago Press.

LEVI, L. 1930. Sul decorso e la prognosi dell'encefalite epidemica nei ragazzi. *Quad. di Psichiat.*, **17**, 89–102.

LIGON, E. M. 1939. *Their future is now.* New York: Macmillan.

LYONS, V. W. 1936. Deception tests with juvenile delinquents. *J. Genet. Psychol.*, **48**, 494–497.

MALLER, J. B. 1930. Character growth and Jewish education. *Relig. Educ.*, **25**, 627–630.

——. 1932. Conflicting ideals and their bearing upon character education. *J. Educ. Res.*, **25**, 161–167.

——. 1937. Juvenile delinquency in New York: A summary of a comprehensive report. *J. Psychol.*, **3**, 1–25.

MARSTON, W. M. 1938. *The lie detector test.* New York: R. R. Smith.

MAUDSLEY, H. 1883. *Responsibility in mental disease.* New York: Appleton.

MAY, M. A., and F. K. SHUTTLEWORTH. 1935. The relationship of moving pictures to the character and attitudes of children. (Bound with R. C. PETERSON and L. L. THURSTONE. *Motion pictures and social attitudes of children.* New York: Macmillan.)

McDOUGALL, W. 1908. *An introduction to social psychology.* London: Methuen; Boston: Luce.

METFESSEL, M., and C. LOVELL. 1942. Recent literature on individual correlates of crime. *Psychol. Bull.*, 39, 133–164.

MOORE, E. H. 1934. A technique for scoring honesty in classroom performance. *J. Educ. Sociol.*, 8, 34–43.

MURPHY, G., L. B. MURPHY, and T. M. NEWCOMB. 1937. *Experimental social psychology.* Rev. ed. New York: Harper.

MURRAY, H. A., *et al.* 1938. *Explorations in personality.* New York: Oxford University Press.

NEWELL, H. W. 1937. Effect of head injury on the behavior and personality of children: A study of twenty cases. *Med. Clin. N. Amer.*, 21, 1335.

OLSON, W. C. 1930. *Problem tendencies in children: A method for their measurement and description.* Minneapolis: University of Minnesota Press.

OWEN, M. B. 1937. The intelligence of the institutionalized juvenile delinquent. *J. Juv. Res.*, 21, 199–206.

PARR, F. W. 1936. The problem of student honesty. *J. Higher Educ.*, 7, 318–326.

PAYNTER, R. H., and P. BLANCHARD. 1928. *Educational achievement of children with personality and behavior difficulties.* New York: Commonwealth Fund.

PIAGET, J. 1932. *The moral judgment of the child.* (Trans. by M. GABAIN.) New York: Harcourt, Brace; London: Kegan Paul.

PINARD, J. W. 1932–1933. Tests of perseveration: Their relation to character. *Brit. J. Psychol.*, 23, 5–19.

POUND, R. 1930. *Criminal justice in Cleveland.* New York: Holt.

PRINCE, M. 1914. *The unconscious; the fundamentals of human personality, normal and abnormal.* New York: Macmillan.

RAUBENHEIMER, A. S. 1925. An experimental study of some behavior traits of the potentially delinquent boy. *Psychol. Monogr.*, 34, No. 159. Pp. 107.

RENSHAW, S., V. L. MILLER, and D. MARQUIS. 1933. *Children's sleep.* New York: Macmillan.

ROBACK, A. A. 1928. *The psychology of character.* New York: Harcourt, Brace.

ROSANOFF, A. J., L. M. HANDY, and I. A. ROSANOFF. 1934. Criminality and delinquency in twins. *J. Crim. Law Criminol.*, 24, 923–934.

RUNDQUIST, E. A. 1938. Behavior problems and the depression. *J. Abnorm. Soc. Psychol.*, 33, 237–260.

RYANS, D. G. 1938a. An experimental attempt to analyze persistent behavior: I. Measuring traits presumed to involve persistence. *J. Gen. Psychol.*, 19, 333–353.

——. 1938b. An experimental attempt to analyze persistent behavior: II. A persistence test. *J. Gen. Psychol.*, 19, 353–371.

RYANS, D. G. 1938c. A study of the observed relationship between persistence test results, intelligence indices, and academic success. *J. Educ. Psychol.*, 29, 573–580.

——. 1939a. The measurement of persistence: An historical review. *Psychol. Bull.*, 36, 715–739.

——. 1939b. A note on variations in persistence test score with sex, age, and academic level. *J. Soc. Psychol.*, 10, 259–264.

RYLANDER, G. 1937. Personality changes after operations on frontal lobes. *Acta Psychiat. Kbh.*, Suppl. 20.

SAKELLARIOU, G. T. 1938. A study of lies told by Greek adolescents. *Ereunai Psuchol. Ergasteriou*, Thessalonike, No. 3.

SHEEHY, L. M. 1938. *A study of preadolescents by means of a personality inventory.* Washington, D. C.: Catholic University Press.

SHEVACH, B. J. 1937. Studies in perseveration: VI and VII. *J. Psychol.*, 3, 381–427.

SLAGHT, W. E. 1928. Untruthfulness in children: Its conditioning factors and its setting in child nature. *Univ. Iowa Stud. in Charact.*, 1, No. 4.

SPAULDING, F. T. 1938. *High school and life.* New York: McGraw-Hill.

SPEARMAN, C. 1927. *The abilities of man: Their nature and measurement.* New York: Macmillan.

STEPHENSON, W. 1935. Perseveration and character. *Character & Pers.*, 4, 44–52.

STERN, W. 1938. *General psychology.* New York: Macmillan.

STERTZ, G. 1931. Encephalitische Wesensveränderungen und Mord: Gutachten über dei Zurechnungsfähigkeit. *Mschr. Krimpsychol. Strafrechtsref.*, 22, 320–332.

STUMPFL, F. 1939. Kriminalität und Vererbung. *Handb. Erbbiol.*, 5, Pt. 2, 1223–1274.

SYMONDS, P. M. 1928. *The nature of conduct.* New York: Macmillan.

——. 1931. *Diagnosing personality and conduct.* New York: Century.

——. 1939. *The psychology of parent-child relationships.* New York: Appleton-Century.

TAYLOR, H. R., and F. F. POWERS. 1928. Bible study and character. *J. Genet. Psychol.*, 35, 294–302.

TERMAN, L. M. 1916. *The measurement of intelligence: An explanation of and a complete guide for the use of the Stanford Revision and Extension of the Binet-Simon Intelligence Scale.* Boston: Houghton Mifflin.

TERMAN, L. M., *et al.* 1925. *Genetic studies of genius:* Vol. 1. *Mental and physical traits of a thousand gifted children.* Stanford University, Calif.: Stanford University Press.

THORNDIKE, E. L. 1940. *Human nature and the social order.* New York: Macmillan.

THORNTON, G. R. 1939. A factor analysis of tests designed to measure persistence. *Psychol. Monogr.*, 51, No. 229. Pp. 42.

THRASHER, F. M. 1927. *The gang; a study of 1313 gangs in Chicago.* Chicago: University of Chicago Press.

THURSTONE, L. L. 1931. Influence of motion pictures on children's attitudes. *J. Soc. Psychol.,* **2,** 291–305.

TREDGOLD, A. F. 1937. *Mental deficiency (amentia).* (6th ed.) Baltimore: Wood.

TROLAND, L. T. 1928. *The fundamentals of human motivation.* New York: Van Nostrand.

TROVILLO, P. V. 1939. A history of lie detection. *J. Crim. Law Criminol.,* **29,** 848–881; **30,** 104–119.

TUDOR-HART, B. E. 1926. Are there cases in which lies are necessary? *Ped. Sem.,* **33,** 586–641.

UNITED STATES DEPARTMENT OF LABOR. 1937. Juvenile court statistics (1934). *Child. Bur. Publ.* 235.

——. 1942. Children in the courts, 1938 and 1939. *Child. Bur. Publ.* 280.

VOELKER, P. F. 1921. The function of ideals and attitudes in social education: An experimental study. *Teach. Coll. Contr. Educ.,* No. 112.

WALLENSTEIN, N. 1937. Character and personality of children from broken homes. *Teach. Coll. Contr. Educ.,* No. 721.

WATSON, J. B. 1926. Experimental studies in the growth of the emotions. In C. MURCHISON (Ed.), *Psychologies of 1925,* pp. 37–58. Worcester: Clark University Press.

WEBB, E. 1915. Character and intelligence. *Brit. J. Psychol. Monogr. Suppl.,* **1,** No. 3. Pp. 99.

WILSON, H. E. 1938. *Education for citizenship.* New York: McGraw-Hill.

WOLTRING, B. 1938. *Gelijkenis von Tweelingen. Een psychologisch Onderzock.* Amsterdam: University of Nijmegen.

WOODWORTH, R. S. 1934. *Psychology.* (3d ed.) New York: Holt.

ZYVE, C. 1931. Experiments in the teaching of integrity. *Teach. Coll. Rec.,* **32,** 359–374.

CHAPTER 15

EMOTIONAL DEVELOPMENT

ARTHUR T. JERSILD

This chapter is based primarily upon studies that have dealt with emotional behavior from a developmental point of view. During recent years the rôle of emotion in the conduct of children has received increasing emphasis. Many theories have been proposed, and many empirical studies have been undertaken to throw light upon the almost limitless mixtures and gradations of feeling, impulse, physiological reaction, and overt expression that constitute emotional behavior. Such studies have been prompted in part by a desire to understand the behavior of children at various stages of growth and, in part, by the hope that a study of children might help to explain the oftentimes baffling complexity of the emotional behavior of adults.

The Beginnings of Emotional Behavior

Some Earlier Psychological Interpretations. Ribot (1903) gives an account of "primitive" emotions that cannot be reduced to previous manifestations. The first of these emotions to appear, according to Ribot, is fear or the "defensive" emotion. Somewhat later appears the "offensive" emotion of anger. Then comes affection (from which later are derived the "social and moral" emotions). In addition, there are the more "purely human" emotions: self-feeling or egoistic emotion, which may appear in negative or positive forms, and the sexual emotion. McDougall's (1909) well-known formulation lists a number of instincts with each of which is

associated emotional excitement of a given quality.[1]

Much research has been precipitated by John B. Watson's (1919; Watson and Morgan, 1917) description of the original emotional reactions of infants. These reactions were designated as fear, rage, and love. Fear was described as a startle reaction to loud sound or sudden loss of support, characterized by responses such as catching of the breath, trembling, sudden closing of the eyes, clutching with the hands, puckering of the lips, whimpering, and crying. Rage was described as a stiffening reaction to hampered movements, involving responses such as slashing movements with hands and feet, holding of the breath, crying, or screaming. Love was described as an expansive reaction to gentle patting, warmth, and stroking of sensitive zones, characterized by responses such as stretching, spreading of fingers and toes, cooing, and extension of the arms. Hollingworth (1928) suggests that these reactions, as distinguished from the more highly differentiated emotions of later life, might be designated *startle, resistance,* and *content,* and recommends that a fourth form of response, *gloom,* be added.

Psychoanalytic Interpretations. In some accounts based upon psychoanalytic interpretations it is stated quite confidently that the child at birth is capable of profound

[1] Included in the bibliography are references to other writings of an earlier date, including Bain (1875), Darwin (1877, 1913), Preyer (1888), and Moore (1896).

and intense feeling. One writer, for example (Isaacs, 1936), says that "knowledge is lacking, understanding has not yet begun; but wants and wishes, fears and angers, love and hate are there from the beginning." Another writer (Rank, 1932) states that the child brings anxiety with him into the world. This anxiety is then attached to the parents and often extends far beyond the time of the child's helplessness. Freud (1936) also emphasizes the view that the "biological factor of helplessness . . . brings into being the first situations of danger and creates the need to be loved which the human being is destined never to renounce" (p. 130). He takes issue, however, with Rank's formulation of anxiety as related to the vicissitudes of birth. He states that the infant indubitably has a disposition to anxiety, but this is not at its maximum immediately after birth since it is "not credible that the child has preserved any other than tactile and general sensations from the act of birth" (p. 97).

Klein (1932) emphasizes, among other things, that the satisfactions associated with nursing reside not simply in the alleviation of hunger but in the pleasure which the baby experiences through contact with the mother's breast. Klein says that "this gratification is an essential part of a child's sexuality and is indeed its initial expression" (p. 31). The feelings associated with bodily contact with the mother in the feeding situation are similarly emphasized by Sharpe (1938), and Isaacs (1933) speaks also of the "intensely personal" feelings associated at the very beginning of the infant's life with unsatisfied longings for food and love. In the present state of knowledge, pronouncements such as the foregoing cannot be taken as statements of fact based upon tested scientific data.

Evidences of Lack of Differentiation. In a well-known study by Sherman (1927a) it was found that no clear-cut emotional patterns could be detected in the responses of infants to stimuli such as delay of feeding, sudden loss of support, restraint of head movements, or being pricked with a needle. When adult observers saw motion pictures of the behavior of the children, without knowledge of the stimuli that had been applied, they failed to identify the provocations or to agree among themselves as to what emotion was being expressed. Adults similarly showed little agreement in identifying the cries of children from behind a screen (1927b). Sherman's observations revealed that there was much uncoordinated, unspecialized, and diversified response.

In an earlier study by the Shermans (1925) restraint of movement was imposed through pressure upon the chins of infants by means of the experimenter's forefinger. No coordinated defense movements appeared during the first twenty-four hours but defensive movements did appear by the fifth day. Pratt, Nelson, and Sun (1930) observed infants when their nostrils were compressed in such a way as to prevent breathing (for periods ranging from five to fifteen seconds), or when their arms were pinned to their sides. The investigators report that the findings did not substantiate Watson's earlier statements regarding defense reactions in the newborn child. In the nose-holding experiment, movements of the hands that might be described as defense movements constituted only about 1 per cent of the reactions. The authors emphasize the extent to which generalized reactions predominate over specific reactions in early childhood and the fact that distinctive patterns are difficult to detect. Dennis (1940) in a study of a pair of non-identical infant twins reports that restraint of movement as such does not produce negative reactions in the newborn but any form of intense and prolonged stimulation, including rough restraint of movement, can elicit crying and restlessness. In due time stimuli calculated to restrain activity may elicit negative reactions if such stimuli interfere with customary sequences of behavior. What constitutes thwarting depends upon postnatal developments.

In observations by Irwin (1932), 24 infants under the age of one month were observed in a situation that presumably might produce fear. They were held above the experimenter's head and were dropped and caught again after they had fallen a distance of two feet. In only 2 instances out of 85 did the infants exhibit crying in response to sudden loss of support as described by Watson, and in 12 per cent of the trials no overt responses could be detected. Lack of differentiation in early emotional reactions has been emphasized also by Taylor (1934), in a study of 40 children aged 1 to 12 days.

Reformulated Theories Concerning Emotional Behavior at Birth. On the basis of his own observations, Sherman (1928) offers the theory that in the beginning emotion is not differentiated beyond rather generalized positive and negative reactions, but with the passage of time the child's behavior becomes increasingly differentiated and adaptive. On the basis of somewhat less carefully controlled observations, Bridges (1932) likewise maintains that in early infancy: "The most common response to highly stimulating situations seems to be one of general agitation or excitement. . . . This vague emotional response to a large variety of circumstances must surely be one of the original emotions, if not the only one" (p. 326).

The Startle Pattern. M. C. Jones's (1933) conjecture that finer methods of recording might possibly reveal features or patterns that cannot be detected by ordinary observation is reinforced by findings reported by Landis and Hunt (1939) concerning the *startle pattern* in studies of infants and older persons by means of high-speed motion picture records. The startle pattern is described as "a complex, almost invariable, involuntary, innate reflex response," elicited by sudden or intense stimuli from any sense modality, and notably by sudden, sharp noises. It includes elements such as blinking, closing of the eyes, a thrusting-forward of the head and neck, and flexion of the bodily musculature that resembles "protective contraction or 'shrinking,'" and involves forward movements of the trunk, contraction of the abdomen, and pronation of the lower arms. It is described as a pre-emotional reaction rather than as an emotional state. It is more simple in its organization than the so-called emotions, and it may or may not be followed by emotion proper. Landis and Hunt point out that more study is necessary to establish the relationship between this response and the Moro Umklammerungsreflex.

Differentiation of Emotional Behavior during Infancy

Answers concerning the nature of the newborn child's emotional experiences and concerning what are the primary emotions must be regarded as tentative and theoretical. It is clear, however, that as a child matures emotional responses emerge that roughly can be labeled with such terms as anger, fear, and delight. Gesell (1928) reports, for example, that at the age of one month a child will give different cries for hunger, pain, and discomfort and that the beginnings of what perhaps might be regarded as delight or pleasure appear in smiles and vocal expressions of apparent feelings of pleasure at the age of three months. Blatz and Millichamp (1935) note the progressively expanding repertoire of emotional behavior which becomes progressively more adaptive with age.

Accounts of the differentiation of emotional behavior during the first months of life have been offered by Bühler (1930) and Bridges (1932). A graphic representation of Bridges's formulation is shown in Figure 1.

and successful achievement in procuring desired objects is noted at 7 and 8 months. At 8 months appear what Bridges regards as the earliest demonstrations of affection, which are differentiated from the emotion of delight and appear in the form of

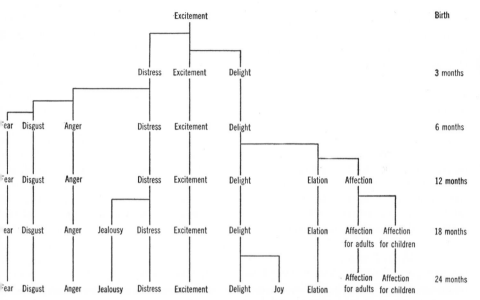

FIGURE 1. Approximate ages of differentiation of the various emotions during the first two years of life. (Adapted from "Emotional Development in Early Infancy," by K. M. B. Bridges. *Child Development,* 1932, **3**, 340. By permission of the publisher.)

Bridges (1932) recognizes only a general state of excitement or agitation at birth. First to be differentiated from the original state of general excitement is distress, which, according to Bridges's account, is distinguishable from excitement at 3 weeks. The beginnings of delight are described as perhaps starting at 2 months, with fleeting smiles in response to being nursed, patted, or cared for, but this emotion is more clearly differentiated at 3 months. More active signs of delight, such as loud laughter, are noted at 4 months; signs of pleasure in self-initiated movements and sounds are described at 6 months, and elation in connection with personal accomplishment

waving, patting, cooing, drawing in long breaths, watching attentively, and smiling.

Need for Further Study Concerning Early Differentiation. There are points of similarity as well as disagreement in the accounts given by Bühler (not here reproduced) and Bridges. Neither account can be regarded as definitive, but each represents a developmental approach that is much needed in the study of early emotional behavior.

In the study of the differentiation of emotion there is need for longitudinal study of representative samplings of infants and young children, with due regard for individual differences, with safeguards to insure reliable observations, and with carefully defined criteria for classification and interpretation. Thorough study would require attention also to phenomena that cannot be ascertained by direct observation. Instructive in this connection are studies of galvanic skin reflexes by H. E. Jones (1930b, 1935), which show that it is practicable to use the galvanometer in work with infants at an early age. Wechsler, Crabbs, and Freeman (1930) likewise have found that "the psychogalvanic experiment [is] an available and reliable method for the investigation of the affective responses of preschool children to various types of stimuli." They add, however, that "what is not yet clear is the significance of these [galvanic] responses as measures of the child's emotional make-up or [their] precise correlation with autonomic excitability." M. C. Jones (1933) also points out that the galvanometer is directly concerned with only a limited segment of autonomic reaction. H. E. Jones (1930b) found that the galvanic skin reflex was exhibited by infants as young as three months (notably in response to mild pain stimuli and loud sounds). Although the reflex in infants was smaller and less easily aroused than in older children, the results "unquestionably demonstrate the functional completeness of the arcs involved in the galvanic skin reflex, at least as early as three months of age." Jones noted furthermore that there may be discrepancies between the overt response to a stimulus and the internal response, in so far as the galvanometer may be regarded as indicating visceral changes.

Factors in the Development of Emotional Processes

The Rôle of Learning. That emotional behavior is modified through learning and that emotional responses become associated with new situations through the process of conditioning are obvious from everyday observation. These facts have been emphasized also in experimental studies. The classic study in this field is Watson's (Watson and Rayner, 1920) work with a little boy called Albert. When first presented with a white rat, Albert showed interest and curiosity, but as his hand touched the animal a loud noise was made which caused Albert to be startled and to withdraw. After several repetitions, Albert no longer reached for the rat but shrank and showed evidences of fear at the sight of the animal. Conditioned emotional responses have also been described by H. E. Jones (1930a, 1931). Conditioning techniques have also been used in studies of reactions to pain stimulation (Aldrich, 1928), to stimuli associated with disagreeable tastes (Moss, 1924; Gauger, 1929; Herring, 1930), and in a study by M. C. Jones (1924a) of the elimination of fears. The manner in which the associations occurring during dreams may reinforce waking fears has been described by Anderson (1927).

The concept of the conditioned response is useful in describing certain modifications of emotional behavior that can be observed in the laboratory and in everyday life. The concept *per se* does not, however, provide an adequate basis for predicting under what circumstances an emotional response will occur or under what circumstances conditioning is likely to "take" in a laboratory setting or in everyday situations (English, 1929; Valentine, 1930; Bregman, 1934; Jersild and Holmes, 1935a). Neither does the concept of conditioning *per se* fully account for changes in susceptibility and in modes of expression that are due not simply to the additive or cumulative effects of external stimuli but are determined also by developments that take place within the child himself in the process of growth.

The Stimulus Situation and Individual Differences in Response. The problem of identifying emotional responses and of tracing the manner in which emotional behavior is modified through learning involves, among other things, the problem as to what constitutes an adequate stimulus. There is quite general agreement that certain stimuli sooner or later become especially potent, such as interference with activity in producing anger, and noise, sudden jars, and sudden or unexpected visual stimuli or cutaneous contacts in producing fear. The appearance of an emotional reaction is determined, however, not simply by the occurrence of a stimulus of a given class but also by the intensity, duration, and novelty of the stimulus, factors in the context in which the stimulus occurs (Sherman, 1927b; English, 1929; M. C. Jones, 1933; Jersild and Holmes, 1935a), and variable factors within the individual himself.

At a given age, mild restraint of movement may, for example, produce little response; more forcible restraint may produce signs of anger; more violent restraint, suddenly imposed, may elicit signs of fear. Moreover, the effectiveness of a stimulus cannot, of course, be gauged by its external characteristics alone. In a study of a five-month-old baby, Sears and Sears, as reported by Dollard, Doob, Miller, *et al.* (1939), found, for example, that the amount of time that elapsed before the onset of crying when the infant's bottle was withdrawn varied in proportion to the amount of milk that had already been consumed. Again, a given stimulus, such as a banging door, may have little effect, as when a young child is seated in his mother's lap, but a marked effect if he is alone in an unfamiliar place. The potency of a present stimulus will also be determined by stimuli that have gone before, such as cumulative thwartings, setbacks, or other disturbing circumstances.

Practically all studies of young children likewise emphasize the fact that children differ in emotional susceptibility and responsiveness. Shirley (1933b), for example, describes differences in timorousness and irritability that appear early in infancy and persist throughout ensuing months. Gesell and Thompson (1941) describe how seemingly minor differences in the early responsiveness of two monozygotic twins may have a bearing on later behavior.

Changes Associated with Growth. Many studies have emphasized the fact that a child's susceptibilities change as he matures and that the concept of conditioning alone does not explain these changes in the child's susceptibilities, or the emergence of new or changed emotional responses as a child grows older. Bühler (1930) describes, for example, the manner in which new occasions for delight occur as the child becomes able to undertake new performances. Similarly, the development of a child's ability to discriminate and perceive will render him responsive to stimuli to which he was impervious at an earlier time. Shirley (1933a) notes the appearance in some children of timidity or fear in response to strangers at about half a year. Jersild and Holmes (1935a) similarly report the appearance of fears of events that earlier attracted little notice but now seem to strike the child as unfamiliar and challenging. Although the possibility of a conditioning factor cannot be eliminated, it appears that such responses are associated with an increased capacity to discriminate rather than being the result primarily of a conditioning frightening event.

Gesell (1929) describes the manner in which fear "waxes and alters with growth. . . . This pattern is as much the product of organic growth as the various stages in the elaboration and perfection of prehension" (pp. 656–657), and illustrates with a description of reactions shown at different age levels by an infant when confined in a small pen. In an earlier study, Jones and Jones (1928) noted changes with age in response to a large, harmless snake. They point out:

> The arousal of fear depends not only upon situational changes, but also upon the individual's general level of development. . . . As a child develops . . . new things startle him because of his new perception of the fact that they are new and unusual. . . . Fear arises when we know enough to recognize the potential danger in a situation but have not advanced to the point of complete comprehension and control of the changing situation (pp. 142–143).

Further indications of the changes in fear in relation to maturity appear in findings by Jersild and Holmes (1935a) to the effect that responses that may be described as fear of failure, or of humiliation in the eyes of others, begin to be reported at the age range when children are becoming increasingly aware of competitive standards and are acquiring an increasing capacity for self-criticism.

The varying effects of a given external event as children grow older can also be noted in occasional shifts in emotional response. At about five to eight months, for example, a hungry but hitherto relatively calm infant may show signs of anger if there is a momentary delay in his feeding after he has caught sight of the bottle, but at about eight or nine months in the same circumstances a child may show signs of pleasant anticipation rather than anger (Bühler, 1930) if the delay is brief. Similarly, as a child's abilities increase with age, an event that previously frightened him may provoke anger, and at a still later time the event may provoke amusement. As the child grows up, there not only are changes in his susceptibility but he also, of course, acquires many immunities.

Obviously, learning may have a considerable effect on changing reactions such as those described above. The point remains however, that the reaction to a situation will depend not simply upon the cumulative or spreading effect of specific emotional stimuli that have gone before but also upon the changes in capacity and changes in scope of behavior that are associated with growth.

Differentiation of Early Expressions as Related to Growth. A study by Goodenough (1931a) of judgments of facial expression of emotion offers an interesting supplement to the observations by Sherman and others of newborn children. Judges were shown photographs of a ten month-old child. These photographs were taken under conditions designed to elicit various emotional states. Although the photographs represented only single brief phases of the child's reactions to relatively mild forms of stimulation, the judges correctly identified the situation or emotion depicted by various photographs in 47.4 per cent of the instances. The chance expectancy was only 8.3 per cent of correctness. Moreover, errors were in the main confined to descriptions that corresponded quite closely to the emotions imputed to the child by the original investigator. Goodenough points out that, since the subject of the photographs was an infant of ten months, it seems improbable that the form of behavior displayed by him had been appreciably modified by social tradition or by camera consciousness. According to Goodenough:

> The findings suggest that however greatly the overt expression of emotional states may be inhibited, modified or intentionally assumed in the social relationships of adult life, the language of expression is nevertheless built upon a core of native reaction

patterns which appear at so early an age that they can hardly be ascribed to training (p. 101).

Findings in keeping with this conclusion are also reported by Goodenough (1932) in a study of a ten-year-old child who had been blind and deaf from the time of birth. Photographs snapped at opportune moments were utilized by Thompson (1941) in an investigation of the facial expressions of emotion exhibited by 26 blind and 29 seeing children aged 7 weeks to 13 years. Patterns of emotional response identical with those designated as anger, sulkiness, annoyance, and sadness in seeing children were also exhibited by blind and deafblind children, but such responses did not occur as uniformly among the blind as among the seeing. No typical expressions of fear were observed in the blind but this, Thompson explains, may be due to the fact that no very frightening situation occurred. The older blind children showed decrease in facial activity in connection with smiling. Thompson concludes that the facial expressions exhibited by the blind "seem to be maturational since there is no other obvious way in which they could have been brought about." On the other hand, the effects of mimicry, as distinguished from maturation, appear in certain stylized expressions exhibited by older seeing children. Darwin (1913) earlier reported that the expressions of the blind resemble those of persons who can see. That facial expressions of emotions in adults show much variability is indicated in a study by Landis (1929).

Some Developmental Trends

Widened Scope of Effective Stimuli. The younger the child, the more his emotions tend to be aroused by tangible events that impinge directly upon him. As he grows older he becomes increasingly responsive to signs and symbols that betoken furtherance or hindrance of his welfare and his wishes, and more and more of his emotional reactions concern anticipated events. Also, of course, as a child grows older, emotions become associated with an enlarging repertoire of activities, plans, and interests, and he becomes increasingly able to entertain lingering or recurrent fears, joys, and resentments.

When the child is on the threshold of new experiences or achievements he may for a time react emotionally to situations that subsequently are "laid by." Roughly speaking, each new hurdle in the child's development, or in his impact with new environmental conditions, may involve a thrill or a hazard. As the child continues his stride, these occasions recede into the realm of the familiar and come increasingly to be taken for granted. Children, however, sometimes fail to "lay by" fears or resentments that are precipitated at a given period of their growth, and such reactions may persist as infantile or childish forms of behavior at later stages of growth.

Changes in Expression. The differentiation of overt expressions of emotion is especially noteworthy during the first year of life, but there are further elaborations after the first year in nuances of facial, vocal, and postural expression. There is a trend away from gross and explosive overt responses toward more subtle and indirect expressions, and from momentary outbursts to more prolonged emotional states.

In the display of anger, for example, Goodenough (1931b) notes:

> With advancing age behavior during anger becomes more overtly directed toward a given end. At the same time the primitive bodily responses of the infant and young child gradually become replaced by substitute reactions of a somewhat less violent and more symbolic character. [Also, with advancing age,] There are more evi-

dences of persisting generalized reactions toward a single person and more attempts to retaliate by means of indirect attacks designed to hurt the feelings rather than to injure the body of the offender.

There is also an increase in observable after-reactions, particularly resentfulness and sulkiness.

The length to which the substitution of other forms of expression has gone by the time of maturity is indicated in a study by Richardson (1918), who found that, in about six hundred instances of anger reported by twelve adults, no blows were struck "except with those persons who have the correction of children." In a study of college women by Gates (1926), the subjects described impulses to do physical injury in forty instances, but in only three did physical violence occur.

A shift from overt expression to more subtle reactions and preoccupations is noteworthy also in the case of fear (Jersild and Holmes, 1935a). As a result of this, observations of the child's overt behavior fail increasingly as he grows older to reveal apprehensions that a child might habitually conceal or might confide in an interview with a trusted adult.

A decrease in the frequency of overt emotional manifestations with increase in mental age at the school-age level was noted in a study by Blatz, Chant, and Salter (1937). They noted also that manifestations became better directed toward the problem situation as well as more socially acceptable. The substitution of language for physical expressions of anger is quite pronounced during the preschool years (Jersild and Markey, 1935), and this trend continues during later years (Blatz, Chant, and Salter, 1937).

The manner in which fears and resentments may be expressed through make-believe situations is shown in studies of preschool children by Markey (1935) and Griffiths (1935). One child in Markey's study, for example, went through the motions of burning a baby (doll). The child was jealous of a younger sister and the make-believe behavior seemed to be an expression of hostility against the sister. The fact that a child sometimes will reveal his feelings through a make-believe setting or a play situation has been taken into account in the use of projective methods and play technique in the study of children (Horowitz and Murphy, 1938; Frank 1939).

The decline with age in frequency of emotional outbursts does not, of course, depend solely upon the development of the inhibitions, gradations, and the substitution of less overt responses. It arises also in part by reason of changes in the nature of the emotion. Persisting apprehensions resentments, and pleasant anticipations cannot be expressed so appropriately by outbursts such as may occur in an episodic response to a concrete happening.

The expectation that a child will show more calm and fortitude in the face of passing provocations is implicit in the practice of characterizing a child as "emotionally immature" if he continues, as he grows older, to display fear, anger, or grief in response to events that presumably should not arouse normal children of his age. Mitrano (1939) has pointed out that the concept of emotional maturity is important for the understanding of what constitutes *emotional stability*. He found that the forms of emotional behavior conspicuously shown by children who were judged to be unstable included many items that might be described as immature forms of behavior (such as temper tantrums, crying spells display of anger in response to teasing etc.). The data now available from direct observation or experimental study do not provide the basis for a systematic account of *normal* and *immature* emotional behavior at various age levels.

Decline in Crying as an Expression of Emotion. Crying at first usually occurs in connection with bodily movement, but by the age of six months crying may occur without the accompaniment of such movements (Bühler, 1930). In a study of sixty-one children during mental and physical examinations throughout the first year of life, Bayley (1932) found that children cried an average of 15 per cent of the total examination time. In the early months crying resulted mainly from internal causes, but in later months factors in the external environment, such as strangeness of place or persons and continued handling, became increasingly potent.

A sharp decline with age in crying in connection with preschool children's social contacts and in their conflicts with one another has been noted in several studies (Arrington, 1932; Ding and Jersild, 1932; Brackett, 1934; Jersild and Markey, 1935). It has also been noted that at the preschool level crying occurs less in response to the child's own falls and bruises than as an expression of anger when a child is hurt or thwarted by someone else (Ding and Jersild, 1932). Ricketts (1934) found that crying occurred relatively more often in connection with anger episodes exhibited at home by preschool children than in connection with displays of anger in a preschool situation.

The decline in crying is, of course, expedited by social pressures. Blatz, Chant, and Salter (1937) found a relatively high incidence of crying in an institution for the feeble-minded, where there was less disapproval of crying in public than usually prevails in other situations.

In a study by Bell (1940), in which about a hundred children three to eight years old were observed during dental treatment, crying was displayed by only 25 per cent of the children, whereas 51 per cent of them smiled or laughed. The average frequency of crying was 0.9 per ten minutes of treatment; the average of smiling was 1.1. The children who cried showed somewhat more rebellious forms of behavior than did the non-criers. Incidentally, it was found that there were no significant differences between boys and girls in their tendency to cry during dental treatment. At the adult level, however, Landis (1924b) found that women cried more often than did men in trying experimental situations.

Among older children, as among adults, there is a relative increase in crying in private by reason of grief as distinguished from momentary pains or annoyances.

Studies of Various Emotional Reactions

The ensuing sections will give a résumé of studies that have dealt with such topics as anger, fear, affection, and other reactions. Systematic investigations have been organized mainly in terms of these topics, but this does not imply that emotional reactions can be segregated into distinct bundles of anger, fear, joy, and the like. As emphasized earlier, the mixtures and gradations of emotional response are limitless in variety. In the child's everyday life there may arise various forms of excitement of mild or severe degree that cannot be described by any single label. When a child, for example, participates in an exciting game, or follows a stirring motion picture or radio program, his behavior may appear to involve varying reactions of joy, anger, fear, pleasant anticipation, disappointment, and grief, all of which are related features of the larger experience. Similarly, in his everyday life he may be subject to varying degrees of depression, boredom, restlessness, uneasiness, anxiety, irritability, or elation that are not adequately portrayed in such terms as "anger," "joy," or "grief." Again, there may be a high degree of interaction between various impulses, as when a child shows hostility when he is denied affection or fears the consequences of his anger.[1]

FEAR

Situations Feared at Various Age Levels.[2] Startle or apparent fright in early infancy may be precipitated by sudden or intense stimulation through any sense modality, although the responses of individual children are likely to be varied and unpredictable. During later infancy and early preschool years a large proportion of children's fears are exhibited in response to noise and agents of noise; situations, persons, or objects previously associated with pain; strange objects, situations, and persons; falling and insecure support; sudden and unexpected movements (Jersild and Holmes, 1935a). In a series of experiments, M. C. Jones (1924b, 1925) found that the factor of unexpectedness was especially potent in producing fear. From two years to the end of the preschool period these stimuli continue to elicit fear. There is also an irregular increase with age in the everyday display of fear of animals; being abandoned or left alone; dangers associated with imaginary creatures and the dark; and possible bodily injury through drowning, fire, traffic accidents, physical accidents, and so forth. Near the end of

[1] This chapter does not deal extensively with physical correlates of emotion that have been made mainly with adults as subjects. It also omits extensive mention of emotional maladjustments, since these are considered in other sections of this book.

[2] Among the earlier studies dealing with fear and listed in the bibliography are investigations by Calkins (1894–1896), Binet (1895), Mosso (1896), and Hall (1897). Certain studies by Watson and others have been referred to in an earlier section.

the preschool period and into the elementary school years children increasingly exhibit apprehensions concerning failure and humiliation. At the adolescent period, fears and anxieties relating to the sexual functions, physical inadequacies or asymmetries, social, vocational, and academic inadequacies may arise (Bonar, 1942; Marsh, 1942).

Figure 2 shows the trends in the frequency of various fear situations that were noted in a study (Jersild and Holmes, 1935a) in which parents recorded fears manifested by their children during a period of 21 days.

An irregular decline with age in the percentage of children who showed fear in response to seven of eight situations was noted in an experimental study by Holmes (1935) of over one hundred children aged 2 to 6 years. In this study the presence of fear was determined in terms of various overt and vocal manifestations concerning which independent observers showed a high degree of agreement. Stimuli such as being left alone, a strange person, a high place, and a loud sound elicited signs of fear in 12 to 36 per cent of children aged 24 to 35 months and in none of the children aged 60 to 70 months. In response to a snake the respective percentages of children exhibiting fear at 2 to 5 years were 35, 56, 43, and 31.

As the child acquires increasing ability to discriminate, to act in terms of past impressions, to imagine and anticipate the future, his fears are formulated increasingly in terms of remote or imaginary dangers or misfortunes that might befall at a future time. By the time children reach the school age level, there is a good deal of discrepancy between children's most acute fears and "worst happenings" as reported by themselves (Jersild, Markey, and Jersild, 1933). For example, 73 per cent of "worst happenings" reported by children aged 5 to 12 years fell in the category that included such events as bodily injury, falling, illness, accidents, and operations, but ing their fears. Similarly, a child's preoccupation with the possibility of misfortune may be quite disproportionate to the like-

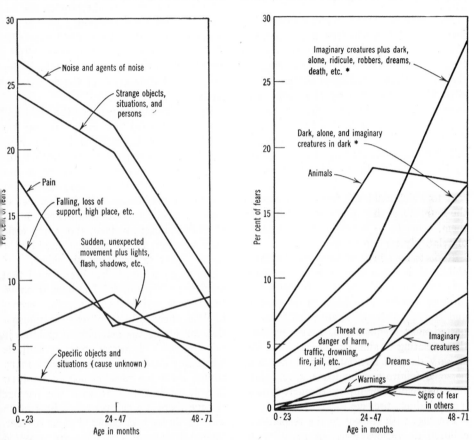

FIGURE 2. Relative frequency of various fear situations as described by parents and teachers, including 146 records of observation of children for periods of 21 days (31, 91, and 24 at the respective age levels), combined with occasional records of 117 additional children (27, 67, and 23 at the respective age levels). (Adapted from "Children's Fears," by A. T. Jersild and F. B. Holmes. *Child Development Monographs*, 1935, No. 20, 54. By permission of the publisher.)

Starred items represent the cumulative tally of two or more categories that also are depicted separately.

only 13 per cent of the fears were described in these terms. Only about 2 per cent of the children reported that they actually had been attacked by animals, but 14 per cent of them mentioned animals in describ- lihood that misfortune actually will strike. In one study it was found, for example, that 53 per cent of 1124 children responded on a check list that they sometimes or often "worried" about "being left back in school" (non-promoted), whereas, according to the promotion policies in effect, only about 1 per cent would be "left back."

An analysis of the factors underlying fears described by children would perhaps disclose that there is less discrepancy between such fears and actual happenings in their lives than is indicated in the figures cited above, since the apprehensions may have their roots in past misfortunes or deprivations, or may be due to threats, reminders of failure, or conditions leading to self-disparagement that are not recognized by the child when he describes his fear. It still is of interest to note, however, the extent to which children's fears, regardless of the happenings that may have precipitated them, come to be conceptualized in terms of relatively remote dangers.

Reports by adults of fears recalled from childhood indicate that a relatively large proportion of childhood fears persist in one form or another into adult years (Jersild and Holmes, 1935a). Among the fears reported most frequently as persisting were those relating to animals, the dark and imaginary dangers associated with the dark, personal failure and inadequacy, and dangers of accident or injury through drowning, collisions, fire, etc.

Findings with respect to the response of children at various levels of maturity to acute dangers such as prevail during air raids are as yet too meager for anything but tentative generalizations (see, for example, Bodman, 1941; John, 1941; Vernon, 1941; Gillespie, 1942). Although there have been many emotional casualties, children at all ages have shown less manifest fear or panic and more ability to "take it" than generally had been anticipated before bombings began. Predictions or pronouncements to the effect that bombing and evacuation would make "nervous wrecks" of a large proportion of children have not been borne out by the children themselves. It is too early to verify other occasional predictions to the effect that children's wartime experiences might provide the basis for neurotic symptoms in later life. It is possible that the response will vary with changes in the severity of other vicissitudes associated with war, such as malnutrition and general dislocation of the habits and facilities of everyday life.

By and large, the younger the child and the more limited his understanding the more his reactions will be influenced by wartime happenings that fall within the range of his immediate experience as distinguished from apprehensions concerning the larger ramifications of the fortunes of war. While failing to comprehend many of the meanings involved, the young child may, however, still be much affected by the signs of fear exhibited by his elders.

For many adults it has been found that anxious anticipation of bombing is sometimes more trying than the actual event; to date, there is little systematic information concerning the reactions of children in this respect. Informal reports indicate that many children, in common with many adults, show the phenomenon of habituation or acclimatization: with the passage of time there is a conspicuous falling off in fear, or at least in outward signs of fear, when warnings or bombings are repeated from day to day. (The ensuing sections include other occasional items dealing with children's fear reactions in a war situation.)

Contributing Factors. In many cases the cause-and-effect relationships in children's fears are relatively clear: a child is frightened by a given event and subsequently fears that situation or events associated with it. Examples of such fears have been cited in an earlier section. Sometimes, also, it is possible to trace fears through rather devious channels. For example, a child who was frightened when hurt by an automobile on the street later showed fear of crossing streets and also had nightmares involving traffic accidents, following which, for the first time, he showed fear of being alone in a dark room (Jersild and Holmes, 1935b). In has been observed that after an especially harrowing event, such as bombing by airplanes, some children (but far from all) may, for a period of several months, exhibit a higher than usual incidence of fear not only in response to stimuli that presumably are associated with the event, such as noise and darkness, but also in response to other stimuli (John, 1941). There are outstanding individual differences in the responses children show to a frightening situation and the manner in which fears thereafter become generalized. John (1941) reports that the after-effects of an air raid are likely to correspond more to the intensity of the emotional excitement exhibited at the time than to the severity of the raid as such. Other things being equal, the after-effects of a harrowing or trying experience are likely to be more severe for a child who has a past history of many fears or other emotional disturbances than for a child who hitherto has been quite stable.

Fears of a young child may be influenced to a considerable degree by the example of his parents, whose display of fear not only suggests to the child that there is danger but also may have the effect of weakening the child's confidence in the protection which his parent can afford. Hagman (1932), in a study by means of the interview method, found numerous similarities between the fears of mothers and children of preschool age and found also a correlation of .67 between the gross number of fears reported by mothers and the number of fears reported for children. A young child's fears and the persistence of after-effects following an especially alarming event, such as an air raid, are likely to be influenced to a marked degree by the extent to which his elders display calm or terror (John, 1941).

When adults report fears recalled from their childhood they attribute many such fears to lurid threats used by older children and adults as a means of discipline or intimidation. Frequently it appears that such intimidation represents a form of rejection of the child and leaves him distressed, not only by reason of the specific threat but also by reason of a vague impression that he is an outcast.

In many instances of such intimidation it also appears that feelings of guilt and apprehensions concerning future punishment are engendered. Apprehensions that seem to involve a certain amount of self-derogation also appear quite frequently when children themselves describe their worries. In a study of fifth- and sixth-grade children by Pintner and Lev (1940), in which the subjects reported their worries by checking the items of an inventory, a substantial number of children checked items concerning punishment, "making your parents sad," being scolded, telling lies, doing wrong, etc. That overtly expressed fears may be associated with underlying conflicts or guilt feelings is stressed also in psychoanalytic writings. Klein (1932), for example, maintains that one four-year-old child's fear of being left alone or abandoned by her mother arose as a result of the child's desire to rob and kill her mother (by reason of the fact that her mother was pregnant). She also maintains that the unruly behavior of children while being bathed or having their hair washed represents a hidden fear of being castrated or having their own bodies destroyed. Freud (1936) gives an account of a person who expressed fear of a horse. According to Freud's analysis, this fear represented attitudes associated with the person's father. In the clinical literature there are frequent references to anxieties associated with impulses and conflicts related to sex. Levy (1940) reports that his data confirm "the psychoanalysts' finding" that the "typical response of the child in our culture, when he becomes aware of the primary differences in sex anatomy" is that "castration anxiety is aroused in boys, and a feeling of envy with destructive impulse toward the penis in girls." Conn (1940), on the other hand, in a study by means of a play interview technique with 200 children ranging in age from 4 to 12 years, reports that, whereas some children are disturbed, a large majority of boys and girls respond to the first sight of genital differences without upset or disturbance. He concludes that "healthy children are not as easily upset" by these matters as "some theorists would lead us to believe."

In a study by Stratton (1929) it appeared from reports of college students that persons who have a history of many illnesses during childhood are likely to exhibit more fear reactions than do persons who have been free from serious disease. Deaf children of school age in a study by Pintner and Brunschwig (1937) reported more fears than did children whose hearing was normal.

In many instances fears are precipitated through vicarious stimulation by way of stories, radio programs (Jersild, 1937), motion pictures (Dysinger and Ruckmick, 1933), and the like. Such stimulation sometimes may evoke apprehensions that otherwise would not have arisen, but it also frequently appears that the story or picture does not operate as a primary cause but serves rather to supply an image or a focus for vague apprehensions that already prevail. Of incidental interest in this connection is the fact that, although children of today are in some respects perhaps exposed to more sources of vicarious excitement than children of earlier generations, it appears that the fears of present-day children, as described by themselves correspond quite closely to the fears of the preceding generation who recall as best they can their childhood fears (Jersild and Holmes, 1935a).

Occasionally the fears exhibited by children appear to represent a desire for attention or for exemption from uninteresting duties. Sometimes, also, fears are precipitated by pressures involved in the child's everyday work. In the study by Pintner and Lev (1940) it was found, for example, that about 90 per cent of the children reported that they sometimes or often worried about "failing a test." Among other items were worries concerning everyday mishaps, such as not having nice clothes or losing property.

Fear often occurs in connection with children's dreams and especially in nightmares.[1] In the study by Foster and Anderson (1936), records were obtained, through the cooperation of mothers, of unpleasant dreams exhibited over a period of several days by children in the age range of 1 to 12 years. One or more unpleasant dreams during the course of a week were reported for 43 per cent of the children aged 1 to 4 years, and 39 and 22 per cent, respectively, at the age ranges of 5 to 8 and 9 to 12 years.

Most difficult to trace is the process by which fears come to be formulated in terms of imaginary or remote dangers and the cumulative effect of setbacks and uncertainties in a child's life that underlie the development of persisting fears. Sometimes children, like adults of the "worrying kind," will fix now upon this, now upon that, as the subject of their apprehensions. In such cases, the underlying disposition is more significant than the specific expres-

[1] See, for example, G. H. Green (1927); Jersild, Markey, and Jersild (1933); Foster and Anderson (1936); Pintner and Lev (1940).

sions of fear at a given moment. In case studies of children, underlying causal factors can sometimes be noted. For example, Holmes (1936) describes a child who was making progress in overcoming fear and then suffered a relapse when he seemed to be especially disturbed by circumstances in his home situation, notably the fact that his nurse left the household and his mother went to the hospital to have a baby.

To probe the development of lingering apprehensions and forebodings, persisting habits of shyness, and similar conditions that seem to involve elements of fear obviously would require inquiries into the life history of the individual. In a study of forty timid children, for example, Nicholson (1931) found that most of the children who were above ten years of age had always had difficulty in making social contacts and that complex emotional factors in the home seemed to be linked with the children's shyness.

Factors in Overcoming Fear. In the normal course of development, many fears appear and then wane, without special treatment, as the child himself gains in experience and competence. Many fears that first arose through association with a frightening event weaken with time if they are not reinforced by further misfortunes. Likewise, fear of the unfamiliar recedes as the child becomes acquainted with his environment. When adults describe childhood fears that no longer prevail, they frequently report that they simply "outgrew" them as they became abler and wiser (Jersild and Holmes, 1935a). The process of habituation to a new situation frequently is quite rapid, as shown in a study by Slater, Beckwith, and Behnke (1939) which notes the decline from day to day in signs of fear and uneasiness exhibited by children who attended nursery school for the first time.

In dealing with fear, as in dealing with other emotional disturbances, it is, of course, important to give attention to factors in the general background that may contribute to the child's disposition to be afraid—his state of health, his situation at home, his relations with members of his family and people outside the home, and various conditions that might produce strain or uneasiness. There also are many concrete steps that may be taken. Many of these occur in connection with the everyday care of children. Gesell and Ilg (1937) speak, for example, of the importance of feedings that are regularized according to the child's own requirements as one safeguard against anxiety and distress.

With older children, forewarning as a safeguard against sudden surprise sometimes may forestall fears that otherwise might arise, although occasionally a forewarning may simply suggest to the child that there is something to fear (Jersild and Holmes, 1935a). Most useful, wherever feasible as a preventive measure, is the procedure of introducing the child to a new situation by degrees under friendly auspices.

In an experimental study of methods of eliminating fear, M. C. Jones (1924b) used a number of procedures described as the methods of disuse, verbal appeal, negative adaptation, repression, distraction, direct conditioning, and social imitation. Only the methods of direct conditioning and social imitation proved to be very successful. Hagman (1932) found that among the methods which mothers reported they had used were explanation, explanation combined with efforts to confront the child with the feared situation, and explanation combined with gradual exposure to the feared situation. Explanation alone was unfruitful in a large number of cases, but was superior to no treatment at all. Explanation was more effective when combined with exposure to the situation. Conn (1941) has described the use of a play interview technique for helping children to understand and to cope with their fears.

Findings in an investigation by Jersild and Holmes (1935c) by means of interviews with parents and reports by other observers, and results in a later experimental study by Holmes (1935), confirm some of the general findings mentioned above and emphasize supplementary procedures. Parents most frequently reported that they tried to talk the child out of his fears by means of explanations and reassurances. This method sometimes helped but it was not very effective when used alone. Somewhat more effective was verbal reassurance combined with a demonstration that there was nothing to fear. Effective also in some instances was an example of fearlessness. Efforts to effect reconditioning or uncon- ditioning through association of the feared situation with a pleasant event or experi- ence resulted in a few reported successes, and in just as many failures. The investi- gators point out that this method might have been more successful if it had been used more skillfully, but they also empha- size that a technique aimed merely at ef- fecting a more or less passive association between an acceptable situation and a feared event has little practical value.

In several instances, the procedure of providing opportunities for the child to be- come acquainted with the feared situation on his own accord and in his own way, or of providing a graded presentation of the feared stimulus, was successful. Relatively little success was achieved with methods such as ignoring the fear, temporarily re- moving the cause, or introducing pallia- tives, or using methods of compulsion by means of physical force, verbal pressure, or ridicule.

The highest percentage of success was reported for procedures that helped the child to gain increased competence and skill, aided him in finding practical meth- ods of his own for dealing with the feared situation, and helped him by degrees to have active experience with, or successful direct participation in, the feared situation.

In an experimental study in which efforts were made to foster active experience with feared situations and skill in handling them, Holmes (1936) worked with thirteen chil- dren who were afraid to enter a dark room (as manifested by refusal to retrieve a ball with which the child and experimenter had been playing in an adjacent room, after urging, reassurances, and an offer by the experimenter to accompany the child into the room). After three to seven exposures each child in the experiment entered the room alone, without hesitation or requests for company, felt his way through the darkness, turned on the light, and retrieved the ball. Although, as Holmes points out, the results do not indicate whether the gains made by the children would transfer to other situations, the findings, as far as they go, have significant practical impli- cations.

In another experiment, Holmes worked with two children who showed fear of walking across a plank at a height of 4 feet. After eight exposures, during which the board was adjusted to various heights of one foot upward, one of the children (aged 39 months) walked the length of the board alone at a height of 6 feet. She also walked happily at the same altitude after one exposure to a modified apparatus that was set up in a different situation. The other child also made progress at first, but then reverted to earlier forms of behavior and showed "babyish" responses that were conspicuous also in his general behavior on the playground. After eleven exposures the experiment was discontinued. Inquiry revealed that his early motor development had been retarded by reason of illness and that he exhibited other maladjustments that seemed to be linked to his relations with his parents. It also appeared that he displayed fear of the high board in part as a means of gaining attention.

This case emphasizes, as is known from everyday experience, that direct dealings with fears that represent primarily a symptom of complex maladjustments may fail to have much effect. This does not, however, detract from the value of such procedures in dealing with many fears that will yield to specific treatment. A point that may be emphasized in this connection is that children themselves often are eager to come to grips with fears that impede their everyday activities and they will sometimes devise quite ingenious ways of their own to gain mastery over a feared situation (Jersild and Holmes, 1935a, 1935c).

Occasionally, a change in the child's general environment will give him an opportunity to overcome behavior in which there are elements of fear. In a study by Lowenstein and Svendsen (1938) thirteen six-to-ten-year-old children, who showed notable symptoms of shyness among other evidences of personal difficulty, were placed in a small summer camp in which they were free to make their own way as they pleased. In this situation, the children, after a time, proceeded to make contacts with one another and to assert themselves; evidences of shyness waned and most of the children continued to show improved behavior after they left the camp. In a study by Jack (1934), which does not deal specifically with the subject of fear but with nonascendant behavior, it was noted that five children who were conspicuously nonascendant at the start showed considerably more poise and self-assertiveness in their social contacts with others in connection with projects in which the children had gained competence through a period of training.

Emphasis on improved competence in dealing with situations that are feared does not, of course, rule out the use of other indirect approaches that are employed in the general practice of mental hygiene.

ANGER, HOSTILITY, AND AGGRESSIVENESS

Provocations to Anger. In characterizing situations that elicit anger,[1] as distinguished from fear, Bridges (1931) points out that "anger is prompted by a situation which instead of being a sudden call to action is a more or less sudden stoppage or interference with action." Bridges also states that the call for a quick readjustment appears in the arousal both of anger and of fear but the factor of suddenness is not as essential in anger as in fear. Blatz and Millichamp (1935) neatly describe anger as due to "thwarted approach," whereas fear arises from "thwarted withdrawal."

The most systematic evidence concerning anger in young children is provided in a study by Goodenough (1931b) in which parents cooperated in observing and recording anger episodes. Goodenough describes changes with advancing age in the nature of the immediate provocations leading to anger. In the case of two infants less than one year old, one-fourth of all outbursts arose in connection with routine care such as dressing, bathing, and the like. About one-fourth of the outbursts arose in connection with social relationships, chiefly those described as involving a desire for attention. Minor physical discomforts were reported as responsible for about one-fourth of the outbursts. Direct restriction of bodily movements accounted for slightly over 6 per cent of the outbursts.

At two years, a large percentage of anger outbursts arose in connection with the establishment of routine physical habits, and second in frequency were conflicts with authority over matters not directly concerned

[1] Questionnaire studies of anger by Hall (1899) and Malapert (1902) are listed in the bibliography.

with habit training. Problems of social relationship represented a third important source of difficulty. Provocations arising in connection with matters of self-help or minor physical discomfort or restriction of bodily movement were less prominent.

At the two-to-three-year level, the three outstanding sources of provocation were conflicts with authority, difficulties connected with the establishment of routine physical habits, and social difficulties with playmates. Between the ages of three and four years, provocations arising in connection with social difficulties and disagreements with playmates reached their maximum, and conflicts with authority accounted for about one-third of the outbursts that were noted. At four years and upward, difficulties arising in connection with social relations continued to represent the most frequent sources of provocation. Next in order came difficulties arising over physical habits and conflicts with authority over matters not connected with physical habits or self-help.

As a child grows older, occasions for interferences that lead to anger occur increasingly, of course, in connection with the thwarting of plans, interests, and anticipated satisfactions, as distinguished from direct physical interference.

Varying Expressions. An inventory of manifestations of anger at the school age and adolescent level would embody not only violent outbursts of temper but also the numberless less volcanic expressions of anger such as are found in surliness, resistance, refractory conduct, prejudice, teasing, bullying, hostile criticism, as well as many forms of so-called antisocial behavior which frequently represent a form of aggression, such as stealing, lying, vandalism, truancy, and cruelty. Dollard, Doob, Miller, *et al.* (1939) have described numerous forms of aggressive behavior that occur as a consequence of frustration. They note that

these may sometimes include deliberate self-injury. The following anger reactions at the adult level, as described by Richardson (1918) and Gates (1926), include many forms of behavior that also are exhibited by children: impulses to make angry, sarcastic, or sullen retorts; crying, screaming, swearing; impulses to tell others or to appeal to authority; visual and motor images and imaginary invectives and cutting remarks; irascible words and actions that are intended to cause discomfort but are disguised as playful; the use of witticism and irony, insinuations, etc.; imaginary exaltation of self and preoccupation with behavior that might be displayed in response to future provocation.

Contributing Factors. Apart from conditions that lead to direct thwarting of activity, there are, of course, many factors both within the individual and in the environment that cumulatively influence a child's irascibility. From an early age the child is subject to many inevitable thwartings. Many of these occur as he goes about his own affairs and meets with obstacles, such as a stubborn knot. Many, as already noted, occur in connection with the discipline and training imposed by his elders and his contemporaries. One result is that a large proportion of children may show outcroppings of hostility when, for example, their behavior is observed in a play situation with dolls representing members of their families (Baruch, 1941). As noted elsewhere in this chapter, hostile feelings associated with various aspects of sex development and behavior have been emphasized in psychoanalytical writings. It is possible to make an imposing list of frustrations that may lead a child to become angry and aggressive (see, for example, Dollard, Doob, Miller, *et al.*, 1939). Fortunately, as Horney (1939) has pointed out, any healthy person, whether child or adult, can endure a considerable amount of rustration without becoming chronically hostile.

Anger in situations in which the individual is called upon to perform an impossible task has been studied by Dembo (1931). Keister and Updegraff (1937) observed displays of anger, among other "immature" reactions, in situations in which children were asked to perform difficult tasks (such as fitting objects of various shapes into a tray). Needless to say, interferences that lead to anger do not depend simply upon the exactions of the external environment, for a child's susceptibilities are influenced in complex ways by factors within himself, such as his lack of competence in handling problems that other children take in their stride, the persistence of infantile habits of resistance and of attitudes of resentment, and discrepancies between aspiration and ability to achieve. Anger as related to jealousy is discussed later in this chapter.

Among the factors in the external environment that seemed to contribute to a greater frequency of anger outbursts among Goodenough's subjects were the number of adult members in the household and the number of older brothers and sisters in the family group; the presence of adult or child visitors; a disposition on the part of the child's elders to be critical and overanxious, to exhibit worries and feelings of uncertainty, to nag over minor issues, and to show concern about the goodness or badness of the child's behavior rather than to regard it from a practical point of view. Anger outbursts appeared also to be positively related to inconsistency in methods of discipline. The frequency of anger outbursts is also likely to be correlated with the degree to which the child succeeds in solving pressing difficulties or gaining desired ends by means of such outbursts.

Among the organic factors noted by Goodenough (1931b) as contributing to increased irascibility were the child's state of health as indicated by colds, bed-wetting, constipation, etc.; delays in feeding; the presence of fatigue and previous sleeplessness. The influence of factors such as fatigue and hunger on irascibility has been noted also by Gates (1926) and Young (1937) in studies of college students. Stratton (1929) found that adults who had a history of illness during childhood tended to be somewhat more subject to anger than persons who had no history of serious illnesses.

In a study by Meltzer (1937), based upon diaries kept by ninety-nine college students, it was found that there was practically a zero relationship between frequency of anger episodes and intelligence and achievement. In an earlier study, Morrison (1924) found a positive relationship between anger outbursts and intelligence in feeble-minded persons.

Relative Frequency of Overt Manifestations of Anger and Fear. At the three-to-five-year level, Felder (1932) found that anger outbursts were about eight times as frequent as displays of fear. It appears that in a well-protected environment it is easier to shield a child from specific events that are likely to frighten him than to eliminate thwartings of the kind that lead to anger. Moreover, many occasions for anger arise in connection with the child's own enterprises, as noted above. In some instances, however, the higher incidence of anger than of fear may be more apparent than real, since there are children who may express their anger quite overtly but may conceal their fears or find means of avoiding direct contact with the situations which they dread.

Although passing displays of temper may be more frequent than manifestations of fear, the latter are regarded as quite often constituting a "problem" in the behavior of young children. In a classification by Foster and Anderson (1930) of the problems exhibited by children of two to six years, fears were reported in a larger percentage of cases than were temper tantrums. Among children who have been labeled as maladjusted or neurotic there are likely to be many who exhibit symptoms of withdrawal or anxiety (Burt, 1940; Isaacs et al., 1941).

Some Factors in Dealing with Anger. A consideration of factors that provoke anger suggests some policies that an adult might bear in mind in trying to cope with anger in children. Avoidance of needless restraint, confinement, overexacting requirements, impossible tasks, peremptory or arbitrary practices is indicated. On the basis of findings from her study of anger in young children, Goodenough (1931b) concludes:

> The control of anger in children is best achieved when the child's behavior is viewed with serenity and tolerance, when the standards set are within the child's ability to achieve, and when these standards are adhered to with sufficient consistency to permit the child to learn through uniformity of experience, without such mechanical adherence to routine that the child's emotional or physical well-being is sacrificed to the demands of an inflexible schedule. However, when departures from the established schedule are made, they should be determined by a recognition of the needs of the child and not simply by the convenience or mood of the adult in charge. Self-control in the parents is, after all, likely to be the best guarantee of self-control in the child.

From everyday observation it is possible to note many occasions in which a child's disposition to show anger in response to a given event recedes as he gains skill in handling it. In the study by Keister and Updegraff (1937) cited above, it was found that immature reactions, including displays of anger, declined after the children had received an opportunity to achieve more skill in the performance of a difficult task

One difficulty in dealing with anger is that it frequently involves the disposition to assign blame to somebody or something other than oneself, and that a show of anger is likely to arouse a response in kind. Sometimes it is possible to break this by reducing the area of friction through yielding points except those directly at issue, by seeking ways in which the angry person's feelings may be assuaged through praise, successful achievement, and friendly attentions in matters not directly concerned with the issue that is under dispute. A study by Tucker (1937) of pupil "troublemakers" offers many illustrations of the manner in which such friendly attentions and recognition of merit may have a salutary effect upon children who have grown resentful or rebellious by reason of difficulty in meeting the school's demands. Such remedies are, of course, likely to be more effective in dealing with anger that is provoked by restricted and readily ascertainable circumstances than in dealing with pervasive and long-continued resentments that are interwoven in complex ways with other factors in the child's personality.

Aggressive Behavior in Extrafamilial Social Relationships. Expressions of anger in connection with the fights, quarrels, and other forms of aggressive behavior in children's contacts with one another have been noted in several investigations (Goodenough, 1931b; Isaacs, 1933; E. H. Green, 1933; Dawe, 1934; Jersild and Markey, 1935; Jersild and Fite, 1939; Fite, 1940). Such aggressive behavior frequently is mild in nature and arises as an incidental feature of the child's general activity as he moves about, explores his environment, interferes with others, or seeks to obtain their material or to protect his own possessions. Occasionally a child's anger is aroused when he is rebuffed by other children whose play he tries to join. It has been noted, also, that children will sometimes, apparently by reason of previous irritations, go out of their way to attack; and sometimes a youngster will expose himself to attack seemingly in order that he may find justification for retaliation.

Fighting and bickering, usually of a relatively mild sort, are likely to occur most frequently in the relations of children who associate with each other a good deal and whose relationship with one another is predominantly of a friendly sort (E. H. Green, 1933). Again the child who is most active socially and who is most versatile in his social contacts is also likely to get into a larger number of situations in which controversy may arise than is a child who is less enterprising. In two studies (Jersild and Markey, 1935; Murphy, 1937) it has been noted that children who tend to show aggressive behavior most often also tend to show sympathy most often, although there are notable exceptions.

In one study there was some evidence, although not conclusive, to the effect that children are more likely to enter into many conflicts if they occupy small play space (Jersild and Markey, 1935). Lippitt (1940) and Lewin, Lippitt, and White (1939) have described the manner in which rigid "autocratic" techniques used by an adult who presides over a group of children may precipitate aggressive behavior in the relations between the children.

A study by Fite (1940) indicates that the extent to which a child exhibits aggressive behavior in his relations with other children may bear little relationship to the child's own professed attitude concerning the rightness and wrongness of hitting, or to pressures against fighting that have been brought to bear by his parents. In some instances, parental admonitions against fighting appeared to lead to evidences of feelings of guilt when the child did commit an aggressive act. In one study it was found that one group of children whose combative behavior was curtailed by the teachers during one year showed a sharp increase in the frequency of their combative behavior the following year when they moved into a situation where there was less teacher interference (Jersild and Markey, 1935); another group of children who were subjected to less interference showed a slight decline in their combativeness from one year to the next. The evidence on this point, however, is not entirely conclusive.

Relative Incidence of Hostile and Friendly Forms of Behavior in Children's Social Relationships. Although aggressive behavior often is quite conspicuous, studies of young children indicate that neutral or relatively friendly contacts outnumber overtly hostile advances in the case of the normal child. In observations of two-year-old children who were paired with each other in an experimental situation, Mengert (1931) found that overtly friendly contacts far outnumbered overtly unfriendly contacts. Preliminary findings in observations by McKinnon (1940) of children in a relatively free school situation indicate that apparently friendly comments and contacts outnumbered hostile criticisms and unfriendly contacts in the ratio of about three to one. A relatively high incidence of friendly responses likewise was found by McFarland (1938) in the behavior of sisters observed in their homes.

JEALOUSY

Feelings and Impulses Associated with Jealousy. Jealousy has not usually been described as a primary emotion but has been treated as a hybrid. Ribot (1903) notes that the gradations of jealousy range from "mild cases up to madness and homicide" and cites Descartes' definition of jealousy as "a kind of fear related to the desire we have for keeping some possession." Components of jealousy, as described by Ribot, include a pleasurable element related to something desired or possessed, an element of depressing vexation arising through the idea of dispossession or privation, and destructive tendencies, such as hatred and anger, directed toward the real or imagined cause of this dispossession or privation. Among the feelings mentioned as components of jealousy by adult subjects in an investigation by Gesell (1906) were anger (which was most frequent, and was sometimes combined with feelings of hatred and with vengeful thoughts), self-pity, grief, sadness and dejection, mortification, fear and anxiety. The most frequent combinations were anger, self-pity, and grief. These descriptions by adults seem to conform to symptoms exhibited by jealous children, but just what are the feelings of a jealous child would be difficult to appraise, since children are not very articulate about such matters.

Overt Expressions of Jealousy. Prominent among the overt symptoms of jealousy as described by S. Foster (1927) and others are expressions of anger, ranging from open hostility to substitute forms of attack. These may be directed toward the person whom the child looks upon as a rival for affection and attentions which he desires for himself, or they may be directed against the person whose affection is desired. The latter may also be subjected to reproaches and appeals designed to arouse sympathy. The child who is jealous of a younger sibling may revert to infantile habits, such as demands to be fed and dressed when actually he is able to take care of himself (Sewall, 1930). As a bid for attention he may also exhibit fears that previously did not exist, show relapses in bladder and bowel control and idiosyncra-

sies with regard to food. Various expressions of hostility have been described by Levy (1937) in a study which utilized dolls to represent a mother, a baby, and an older brother or sister.

Among other expressions may appear an unwonted display of affection or helpfulness, or a tendency to lie and tattle, and varying forms of competitiveness. The child may also be very subdued in his behavior, as though he were grieving, or he may resort to vindictive make-believe and fantasies of self-glorification. Children who are afflicted sometimes will show quite contrasting behavior at different times and in different situations, and their reactions to the same person at different times may range from attack to attempts to curry favor. The repertoire of the jealous child is likely to be that of a troubled person who tries many different techniques in meeting a problem.

The label "jealous child" commonly refers to children who exhibit marked symptoms, or whose elders are unusually alert to any symptoms that may appear. A systematic study of normal children would no doubt show that all of them exhibit symptoms of jealousy to a greater or lesser degree.

It should be noted that many of the forms of behavior described above may also be exhibited by a child who is not directly competing with a sibling but who seems to be uncertain or "insecure" in his relations with his parents or teachers or other associates.

Causal Factors. Studies of children who are conspicuously jealous (S. Foster, 1927; Sewall, 1930; Smalley, 1930; Ross, 1931) and of children who show rivalry (McFarland, 1938) do not reveal any other single, outstanding factor that distinguishes such children from others. Differences in intelligence and age between two siblings may have an influence in individual cases. More important are the complex factors involved in the relationships between parents and their children, between the father and the mother, and disturbing influences such as friction in the home, favoritism, and rejection of one child. Minor expedients, such as the mere academic step of informing a child that a new baby is coming, or the policy of providing "two of everything" to eliminate friction over possessions, seem to be of little avail (Sewall, 1930; McFarland, 1938). One line of study, among others, that is much needed is an investigation of jealousies exhibited by normal children, the varying rôles played by different children in everyday situations, and the manner in which varying affinities are established within the family by reason of distinctive qualities possessed by one child and not by the others.

AFFECTION

Generalizations concerning early signs of affection and the course of its development depend to a large extent upon what one chooses to label as affectionate behavior. Interpretations range from those that ascribe to the newborn child a powerful drive to love and be loved to those that reserve the term affection for forms of behavior that do not appear until some time after birth, such as smiling, patting, and fondling. In any event, during the first year of life, and even more noticeably thereafter, children exhibit both the desire to receive evidences of fondness and the impulse to display fondness for other persons and things.

The ways in which a child's attachments to objects and persons are influenced by learning are too apparent to need elaboration. It is possible, however, that some of the forms of behavior that seem to denote the beginnings of affection, or at least what appears to be a friendly disposition toward others, emerge naturally in the child's normal growth. Bühler (1930), for example, in discussing the smiling of the infant at about the age of six weeks in response to the human voice and glance, states:

> Possibly this smiling is a conditioned reflex transferred from the situation of satiety to the human being present at that moment. Yet, considering that this is only one of the many situations, painful as well as comforting, in which people surround the child, it is even more likely that the smiling is an original and primary reaction to the human voice and look.

Objects of Affection. In a study by Simpson (1935), of children aged five to twelve years, it was found that a majority both of boys and of girls (69.6 and 61 per cent, respectively) expressed greater fondness for their mothers than for their fathers. These findings are not in keeping with the popular view that children are likely to be most fond of the parent of the opposite sex. Simpson discusses factors that might have influenced the replies, but her reservations do not lead to the conclusion that the results would have been different if other approaches had been used. Investigations with older subjects (for example, Hamilton, 1929; Stagner and Drought, 1935; Terman, 1938) reveal that at later age levels there is a more nearly equal balance of reported fondness for both parents. Investigations in this area, utilizing various techniques, indicate that children do not at all eventually show a universal tendency to become attached to the parent of the opposite as distinguished from the parent of the same sex, or to show more antagonism toward the like-sexed than toward the opposite-sexed parent, such as is presumed in Freud's (1920) account of the Oedipus situation. In a review of research dealing with this and other features of sexual development as formulated by Freud, Sears (1943) points out that culture patterns for familial inter-relationships vary, as do the specific learn-ing conditions in one home as compared with another, and that object choices are far more variable than Freud has supposed.

A study by McFarland (1938) of chil-dren aged two to five years describes the interplay of various forms of emotional be-havior in the interrelations between sib-lings, including frequent instances of un-friendly responses intermingled with a high frequency of helping, protecting, sympa-thizing, and conventional expressions of affection (patting, kissing, and verbal ex-pressions of endearment). Affectionate re-sponses often occurred when the sisters were in close proximity and seemed stimu-lated by the physical closeness, but in some instances such responses "seemed to arise out of a general feeling of delight and well-being. . . ."

The extension of affection beyond the family circle to other persons, and to groups and institutions in the form of loy-alties of various kinds, overlaps with the general field of social psychology. An ex-ample of the way in which the normal child acquires more or less sentimental re-gard for characters outside the home circle appears in studies of children's heroes and ideals. Hill (1930) found that, when chil-dren aged six to eight years named ideal persons, 58 per cent were characters from the immediate environment, and that by the age of 13 years the percentage had fallen below 30. Macaulay (1925) reports an even greater increase from 7 to 13 years in the mention of names of characters out-side the immediate environment. The up-swing in sentimental regard for the oppo-site sex at the time of puberty has been noted in a study by E. H. Campbell (1939) of age trends in the reactions of boys and girls to one another. In a study by But-terfield (1939) of the love problems of ado-lescents it was noted that many questions

raised by the young people concerned the social conventions and the physical aspects of sex relationships, but there also were many questions concerning the sentimental aspects (such as "What is the meaning of true love?").

Affection and Adjustment. Numerous writings, including clinical studies, empha-size the importance of affection for the child's normal development and the rôle played by parental affection or rejection in behavior disorders.[1] Evidences of parental affection are valuable not only for the an-chorage and security which they afford, but also as an aid toward the development of the child's own affections for others and the learning of means whereby affection may effectively be expressed. The impor-tance of emotional ties between a child and his parents and his home has been empha-sized especially by observations of reactions to bombing, evacuation, or the idea of evac-uation, and other stresses connected with war (see, for example, Isaacs, Brown, and Thouless, 1941; Burt, 1941; and Bender and Frosch, 1942). In the remainder of this paragraph are some generalizations that have emerged from observations of children's (and parents') response to evac-uation. For a great many children, the prospect or actuality of evacuation from parents and home, be it ever so humble, is more sinister than the prospect of bombing or actual nonfatal exposure to air raids at home. As against this, it also has been found that most children who have stayed for a reasonable length of time in a foster home make an apparently good adjustment. By and large, children who are most "se-cure" in parental affection at home are likely to be the least disturbed, as time passes, in a temporary new home. Tokens of affection, such as visits from parents

1 This topic is not elaborated here since it over-laps with the topics treated in Chapters 11 and 12.

(even if followed temporarily by new out-croppings of homesickness), letters, and gifts from home, may have a helpful effect. If the children are older, parental appeals to the children's sympathies, or any suggestion that their enjoyment of the foster home is tantamount to disloyalty toward their own parents, may have a disturbing effect. In many instances, evacuation of children has brought more grief and bereavement to the parents who remain at home than to the comfortably evacuated child; the parent's need for the child frequently has been greater than the child's expressed need for the parent.

Affection and Hostility. The fact that a child at different times or almost simultaneously may exhibit affection as well as hostility toward the same person has been noted in many studies. The term *ambivalence* was applied by Bleuler (1924) to manifestations of "double" feelings. The concept of ambivalence has also been elaborated by Freud and by other writers. Isaacs (1933) states that even the child's loved mother is not only loved, but is feared and hated as well, by reason of the inescapable denials and thwartings he receives at her hands. Peller (1939) maintains that such ambivalence is sharper with children than with adults and that neurotic behavior may ensue through failure to reconcile these two contradictory feelings.

Whether varying manifestations of friendliness and hostility that are displayed by the normal child represent a basic emotional conflict is open to question. In McFarland's study, cited above, as well as in several studies of aggressive behavior, cited earlier, it has been noted that many children show all manner of positive and negative reactions toward their peers and their elders. These reactions do not seem uniformly to represent a form of emotional conflict grounded in uncertainty and vacillation between incompatible feelings of love and hate. Instead, it appears that the normal child responds now with one form of behavior, now with another, as the occasion demands or as provocations arise. Bleuler states that ambivalent feeling tones are the exception with the normal person. He apparently is speaking of adults, but the same statement seems also to describe the behavior of normal children.

Emotional "Insecurity"

In recent years the designations *security, insecurity,* and *desire for security* have attained wide usage in discussions of the emotional behavior of children. The label insecurity has been used quite loosely to cover a variety of conditions with varying emotional reactions, such as the condition of the jealous child; the child who is "rejected" by his parents and whose condition may or may not be complicated by jealousy of a sibling; the child who is insecure in his relationships with his peers and who may exhibit symptoms of fear or aggressiveness or now one reaction and now the other; the child who is insecure by virtue of inability to understand or to cope with his own impulses and temptations; and so forth.

A step in the direction of clarification of some of the meanings denoted by insecurity in its popular usage has been taken in a study by Prichard and Ojemann (1941). Records were kept of the behavior of preschool children who had been labeled as secure or insecure by their teachers. The results indicated that the insecure children exhibited conspicuously more withdrawal (solitary play, few attempts to join the group), "nonacceptance" (unsuccessful efforts to join group), "bidding for attention" (from adults), crying, and evidences of apprehensiveness than did the secure children. A similar approach, coupled with inquiry into underlying motives, to the study of insecurity in other situations and contexts would be helpful.

PLEASURE

Active signs of pleasure, as distinguished from quiescence, appear later than active signs of distress. As noted earlier, Bühler (1930) reports signs of pleasure at one month and describes the appearance of pleasure in movement or activity at two months. Bridges, as noted earlier, states that the emotion of delight perhaps begins at about two months, as manifested by fleeting smiles in response to being cared for, and that more positive signs of delight in the form of laughter and smiling in response to another's smile appear at about four months. She places pleasure in self-initiated activities somewhat later than does Bühler (at about six months) and describes elation in connection with successful achievement at seven or eight months.

Available data do not provide the basis for a precise classification of behavior that might be described as joy or pleasure. Even more tenuous are the nuances of feeling, mood, and expression involved in later forms of behavior that are described by such terms as positive self-feeling, pleasant anticipation, interest, contentment, and happiness. Laughter frequently seems to denote delight but it cannot be regarded as synonymous with joy since, at least in older persons, it may occur without pleasant accompaniments, and frequently there is pleasure without laughter. The topic of laughter will be treated separately below. Certain overt reactions that accompany pleasant emotional states have been described by Dearborn (1898) and Goodenough and Brian (1929).

A consideration of the ramifications of the feeling of satisfaction or joy would carry us into the field of children's inter-

ests, play activities, and also into the larger field of personality development. In a study based upon compositions written by children in the elementary school grades, Stryker (1898) found that outstanding specific occasions for joy named by the children included gifts, expeditions and excursions, parties and games, and experiences with new places and things.

Throughout life it can be noted that satisfactions may arise from unimpeded activity, successful achievement, and ventures into new activities. Children will themselves often seek hurdles, including mild forms of danger, for the satisfaction of overcoming them (Valentine, 1930; T. D. Jones, 1939; Gutteridge, 1939).

Everyday observation likewise testifies to the value of being active or gainfully occupied as an antidote to boredom, discontent, and self-reproach. Even if a person is not particularly aware of pleasure when he has something to do, he may become acutely aware of discontentment if he has nothing to do or if what he does seems not worth while. Gillespie (1942) in an account of some reactions of English adult civilians and children to the stresses of war, emphasizes the morale-preserving values of work and activity. Moreover, to have something to do, especially if it involves some degree of responsibility, may fortify the individual against stimuli that might otherwise elicit anger or fear. Vernon (1941), among others who have reported on the behavior of British adults and children during air raids, notes that activity is valuable in helping people to bear up in times of stress; those on active defense service, for example, have managed better, on the whole, than those who have no assignment.

Prominent among the gratifications of everyday life are, of course, the numerous pleasures derived from ministering to bodily needs and the satisfying of physical appetites—pleasures associated with food and drink, fragrant odors, relief from itches, the comforts of rest and relaxation, of coolness or warmth as the occasion demands, and numerous other forms of gratification or relief from cravings of various kinds. The development of liking or distaste for various foods is especially significant in relation to the establishment of good feeding habits, but there is space in this writing to mention only two observations in connection with this complicated topic. Among the factors that influence a child's likes and dislikes for various articles of food is the example set by his elders (McCarthy, 1935). Davis (1928) in a study of newly weaned infants, under conditions that perhaps would be difficult to duplicate in the usual home, found that children made wholesome choices of food when presented from day to day with a variety of articles of food and were free to make their own selections and to eat as much or as little of any available item as they pleased.

Relative Rôle of Pleasant and Unpleasant Events in Everyday Experience and in Recollections of the Past. Needless to say, it is difficult to appraise the "feeling level" of children from their overt behavior, especially at the school age and beyond. As pointed out earlier, smiling and laughter are displayed considerably more frequently in normal children at the preschool age than is crying as a symptom of anger or grief. To the extent that such overt signs may be trusted, it would appear that pleasant, or at least neutral tones, predominate greatly over unpleasant states in normal children, as seems also to be true of normal adults (see, for example, Flügel, 1925; G. Watson, 1930; Hersey, 1931; Jersild, 1931; Hartmann, 1934–1935; Johnson, 1937). Wolgemuth (1922–1923) found that children of school age reported a greater number of pleasant than unpleasant events when asked to record their experiences during an immediately preceding vacation period.

In a study by Lee (1932) of eighteen two- and three-year-old nursery school children, records which proved to show a high degree of reliability were made of shifts in mood as judged by observed facial and vocal expressions, ranging from "audible expression of rage or grief" (rated as −3) to "audible expression of pleasure" (rated as +3). The average mood level was found to vary under different circumstances: it was higher, for example, on bright, sunny days, and during outside free play, than during routine activities under the direction of adults.

A classification of the events reported by adolescents when called upon to describe their earliest memories (Dudycha and Dudycha, 1933) revealed a somewhat larger proportion of apparently unpleasant than pleasant earliest recollections. However, the phenomenon of more complete recall of pleasant than unpleasant everyday experiences, which has been noted in several studies of adults, has also been noted in work with children (Wolgemuth, 1922–1923). The tendency of children to avoid words with unpleasant connotations is shown impressively in a study by Davis (1937), who found, in an analysis of the remarks of children aged five to nine years, that the ratio of words with pleasant connotations to words with unpleasant connotations was 1057 to 80. A classification of dreams reported by 400 five-to-twelve-year-old children during private interviews (Jersild, Markey, and Jersild, 1933) revealed a larger proportion of apparently unpleasant than pleasant dreams, but, when directly questioned as to the relative frequency of various types of dreams, more of the children reported a predominance of "good" over "bad" dreams. About 50 per cent of the subjects said that they preferred to continue having dreams, whereas the rest gave negative or equivocal replies.

SEX BEHAVIOR

Much research has been devoted to behavior that might throw light upon the development of sex impulses and feelings in children. That there is sensitivity in the genital areas in early infancy, and that many children before the age of three engage in manipulation or other forms of self-stimulation has been reported by several investigators. Halverson (1940), in systematic observations of 9 male infants aged 3 to 20 weeks, found that tumescence was exhibited at least once daily by 7 of the 9 children and on 8 and 9 days, respectively, by the other two. The incidence of tumescence per day varied in the case of different children. The feelings that may be associated with the phenomenon of tumescence and detumescence cannot be ascertained by observation, but the indications were that tumescence had a disquieting effect (it was accompanied, in a large percentage of instances, by manifestations such as restlessness, fretting, crying, stretching or flexing the limbs stiffly), whereas the behavior following detumescence was distinctly more in the nature of playful activity or relaxation. In commenting on this finding, Sears (1943) points out that it should not be surprising that children would themselves learn to perform an act that might reduce restlessness and crying such as were noted in connection with tumescence. By the age of three years, direct manual stimulation, such as holding, stroking, or pressing the genital organ, was reported in the case of 26 of 49 boys whose mothers were interviewed by Levy (1928). Manual stimulation was reported also in the case of 4 of 26 girls, but this, as Levy points out, does not take account of the possible occurrence of other forms of stimulation that are dif-

ficult to detect, such as thigh-rubbing. Koch (1935), in systematic observations of children of nursery school age, also found a higher incidence of masturbatory activities in boys than in girls. Isaacs (1933), on the basis of direct observation, has presented an impressive collection of anecdotes showing ways in which children of preschool age express an interest in genital functions.

The advantage of systematic, direct observation, such as was employed in some of the studies mentioned above, cannot be so readily exploited with older children. The findings at later levels are subject, accordingly, to such limitations as arise by reason of the reticence of children in raising questions or supplying answers, errors of recall when adults try to reconstruct childhood experiences, bias that the investigator may show in pressing his inquiry or in recording or interpreting his data, and the temptation (which seems to be strong) to generalize from select clinical cases to the child population at large. In any event, the findings indicate [1] that there is a wide, and perhaps almost universal, prevalence of varying degrees of interest and curiosity concerning sex in the prepubertal years roughly corresponding to the elementary school period. Many children during this period engage in experimentation, manipulation, and sex play, but no definitive answer can be given to the question as to the incidence of such activities in the normal population. As one would expect, there is an accentuation of such interests and activities at puberty. By the time adulthood is reached, findings in various studies indicate that upward to 90 per cent of males and upward to 50 per cent of females have engaged in masturbation at one time or another with varying duration.

[1] For reviews, or reports of original findings, see Willoughby (1937), Sears (1943), C. Landis, A. Landis, Bolles, et al. (1940).

Likewise, varying but quite substantial percentages report other forms of sex experimentation, ranging from mild petting to intercourse, crushes, love affairs, exposure to mild or major forms of sex aggression, and the like. Such endeavors are accompanied by varying degrees of placidity and enjoyment. As would be expected, by reason of the cultural counter-pressures that are brought to bear, they are also accompanied by varying degrees of fear and guilt.

The evidence from various systematic studies indicates that many children are perplexed by questions relating to sex, that curiosity and interest are more prevalent than provision for informing children or opportunities for frank discussion with adults. As noted elsewhere in this chapter, however, the weight of evidence does not indicate that in addition to these distresses the typical child is also burdened with feelings of anxiety, guilt, or hostility that have been described in accounts of the Oedipus complex or in some accounts of children's attitudes toward their own sexual organs and those of the opposite sex. It is interesting to note that, whereas the literature properly emphasizes the distresses that are involved in sexual development, there is relatively little emphasis on the positive side of the ledger. On this side may be listed such matters as the pleasure a child may experience when his curiosity is satisfied in ways that do not conflict with his scruples; the pleasures incident to activities that happen to be acceptable to his elders, such as dating, mixed parties, dances, and the like; the exhilaration he may feel when he engages in petting and other forms of play that in his case happen to be congenial to his conscience.

LAUGHTER AND HUMOR

Although laughter does not represent any distinct emotion, it deserves consid-eration as an outstanding expressive reaction. References have been made in an earlier section to the accounts by Bühler (1930) and Bridges (1932) of the appearance of laughter during the early months of life. Washburn (1929) noted laughter at twelve weeks in response to a "chirruping" sound as the experimenter bent over the child. The most effective laughter stimulus (at sixteen weeks) was the "threatening head."

Several studies at the preschool age have shown that laughter is most likely to appear in association with bodily activity, especially in connection with social play (M. C. Jones, 1926; Enders, 1927; Kenderdine, 1931; Ding and Jersild, 1932; Brackett, 1934). Jones found that the following circumstances were most effective in producing laughter at the preschool level: those relating to a feeling of well-being (running, romping, chasing); exciting physical contacts, such as tickling; and situations which provide an opportunity for self-assertion (teasing, overcoming difficulties, making noises or musical sounds). Kenderdine found that at two years laughter in response to motions made by the child himself or others was highest in frequency, and next in order came laughter in response to socially unacceptable situations. At three years the latter situations led the former. She also noted laughter in response to circumstances such as grimaces, pleasure in accomplishment, and word play. In a study of preschool children, Ding and Jersild found little evidence for the theory that laughter commonly denotes feelings of derision or superiority. Kenderdine, however, noted some instances of laughter in response to inferiority in others. Blatz, Allin, and Millichamp (1936), from a study of preschool children, conclude: "Laughter and probably smiling may be considered as socially acceptable tics or compensatory motor mechanisms accompanying the resolution of conflicts that have, for a shorter or longer period, kept the individual on the horns of a dilemma."

Justin (1932), in a study of children aged three to six years, used a number of situations to represent the following conditions: (1) surprise or defeated expectation; (2) superiority and degradation; (3) incongruity and contrast situations; (4) social smile as a stimulus; (5) relief from strain; (6) play situation. Some children at all age levels laughed or smiled in response to all the experimental situations. Incongruity and superiority, and the play situations, became somewhat more laughter-provoking as age increased, but the main change noted in relation to age was an increased tendency to laugh at more of the specific situations that were used to represent each of the large classes of laughter-provoking stimuli.

Children of high intelligence in the group studied by Kenderdine tended to laugh more than children of average or somewhat above average IQ. Justin also found a positive correlation between IQ and tendency to laugh, especially in response to incongruity. It seems plausible that bright children might be more responsive than less intelligent children to laughter-provoking subtleties; in a study of older children, Brumbaugh (1939) found, for example, that brighter children were better able to recognize absurdities. Other factors in a child's social and emotional adjustment, however, are likely to have a more important bearing upon his disposition to laugh than the factor of intelligence alone.

In a study of children aged 7 to 18 years, Laing (1939) concluded from data obtained through questioning, essays, and reports by the subjects concerning their best jokes that the development of a sense of humor parallels the child's intellectual and emotional development. At 7 to 10 years, the major sources of humor are described as deviation from the normal; and at 11 to 13 years, important sources were the discomfiture of others and deviation from the normal. In the range from 7 to 13 years, situations regarded as humorous were mostly visual, but at 14 to 18 there was an increased appreciation of verbal humor. Herzfeld and Prager (1930) likewise describe changes in children's understanding of the comic as related to intellectual development. They note, for example, that when the child has acquired a grasp of size relationships he finds amusement in inanimate objects that show gross disproportions in size or colors, and at later ages other forms of distortion and incongruity, including human frailties, become effective. Brumbaugh (1939), in a study of children in Grades 3 to 6, found that incongruity was the most frequent stimulus to laughter and that the children liked comedy of the sort that was disapproved by many of their elders.

SYMPATHY

Sympathy by definition denotes suffering with another, and therefore an account of sympathetic behavior should emphasize feelings that are involved. In the case of young children such feelings can only be inferred from the child's language and actions. Ribot (1903) maintains that sympathy in its primitive manifestations represents merely a passive phenomenon, the active aspect of which is imitation.

In a study by Boeck (1909) based upon parental reminiscences and questionnaire returns, the largest number of reported sympathetic responses was directed toward people (358, of which 285 were directed toward the father, mother, sisters, or brothers); 207 responses were directed toward animals; and 65 responses were directed toward other objects.[1] Berne (1930), in a study that utilized rating scales, found evidence of a slight increase in sympathy at the four-year level as compared with the three-year level.

In a study by Murphy (1937) of preschool children, sympathetic responses were classified under headings such as helping, comforting, punishing, or removing the causes of distress, protecting, defending, warning, suggesting a solution, anxious or disorganized responses (such as showing an anxious expression, evidences of worry, and crying). Murphy utilized a number of semiexperimental situations that provided an opportunity for the display of sympathy, and also observed children during their free play.

Murphy noted that children two and three years old did not generally respond sympathetically to black-and-blue wounds, swellings, and other minor distortions of flesh which to an adult would suggest discomfort or illness, or to Red Riding Hood's being eaten up by the Wolf, pictures of accidents, funerals, being crippled, and the like. Three-year-olds responded generally, although not universally, to such evidences of distress as bandages, blindness, injuries colored with iodine, red swellings, and the like; also to crying, accidental falls, attacks by another person, deprivation of toys, food, or of mother; interferences such as being caught in a pen or having to stay in bed; incompetence to do a job undertaken.

Records obtained during 188 hours of observation of the behavior of one group of children disclosed 318 sympathetic responses and 195 responses that were classified as unsympathetic. In another nursery school group, 398 sympathetic and 60 unsympathetic responses were observed during 234 hours of observation. These

1 These statements concerning Boeck's findings are taken from a review by Murphy (1937).

frequencies of sympathetic behavior are considerably lower than the frequencies of resistant or combative behavior exhibited by children of this age. Such frequencies are not directly comparable, however, since the number of times sympathy occurs will depend, among other things, upon the occasions that arise for a display of sympathy.

The older children showed sympathy more frequently than the younger ones; the older children also responded to a wider range of distress situations, and they exhibited more active responses of comfort and defense as distinguished from passive staring or inquiries concerning another's misfortunes. Factors in the personality of the individual children were, however, more important than the factor of age. Murphy describes many such factors. For example, a child who is sympathetic when he himself is disturbed or uncertain of his status in the group may become less sympathetic as he gains in confidence, whereas another child may show the reverse tendency. Again, a child may shift from sympathetic to unsympathetic behavior if his own self-interest is involved. McFarland (1938) likewise found that a child was less likely to sympathize with another's distress if the child himself was the cause of the distress.

Needed Research

Practically all sections of the foregoing account bespeak the need for further study. There is much unanimity in a number of objective studies dealing with the emotional reactions of the newborn, but refinements of method may bring new light and different interpretations. At the infancy level there is especially a need for longitudinal study of changes in emotional behavior that appear from week to week and from month to month. Such studies would be especially fruitful if supplemented by more complete information concerning the development of the neural mechanisms involved in emotional behavior and concerning physical and physiological factors.

The studies that have been made of emerging emotional reactions have revealed much, but the evidence notably lacks the precision of observation and of definition of terms that characterizes some studies of other aspects of early development, such as motor behavior and language. The use of safeguards that have been developed in the application of the method of direct observation should be helpful. Quite as necessary would be the application of safeguards that have been devised for checking the interpretation of behavior through the aid of independent observers, and for making definitions and classifications of behavior so explicit that other workers can understand and use them.

Many of the studies of developmental trends stop quite abruptly at the school-age level. It would be especially helpful to have further systematic studies concerning the ways in which emotional expressions become modified and subject to various gradations, are intertwined with other aspects of the child's personality, and are modified through the child's impact with a changing environment and by virtue of internal changes associated with his own growth. Judging by discrepancies that have been noted in studies of younger children between facts ascertained by direct observation and information reported by the subjects themselves, it appears that the solution to many problems can be found only through a combination of direct observation of overt behavior, procedures designed to help the child to reveal subjective aspects of his emotions, and laboratory instruments.

Further longitudinal studies of representative samplings of children would be very helpful in indicating normal manifestations of emotion at various age levels and in clearing up some of the confusion tha' now seems to prevail concerning what con stitutes a "problem" as distinguished from behavior that lies within the normal range

Bibliography

ALDRICH, C. A. 1928. A new test for hearin, in the newborn. The conditioned reflex *Amer. J. Dis. Child.*, **35**, 36–37.

ANDERSON, J. E. 1927. The dream as a re conditioning process. *J. Abnorm. Soc. Psy chol.*, **22**, 21–25.

ARRINGTON, R. E. 1932. Interrelations in th behavior of young children. *Child Developm Monogr.*, No. 8. Pp. 156.

BAIN, A. 1875. *The emotions and the will* (3d ed.) London : Longmans, Green.

BARD, P. 1939. Central nervous mechanism for emotional behavior patterns in animals *Res. Publ. Ass. Nerv. Ment. Dis.*, **19**, 190–218

BARKER, R., T. DEMBO, and K. LEWIN. 1937 Experiments on frustration and regression i children. *Psychol. Bull.*, **34**, 754–755.

BARRETT, W. G. 1937. A childhood anxiety *Psychoanal. Quart.*, **6**, 530–535.

BARUCH, D. W. 1941. Aggression during dol play in a preschool. *Amer. J. Orthopsychiat* **11**, 252–260.

BAYLEY, N. 1932. A study of the crying o infants during mental and physical tests *J. Gen. Psychol.*, **40**, 306–329.

BELL, J. 1940. *Psychological aspects of denta treatment of children.* Unpublished Ph.D. Dis sertation, Teachers College, Columbia Univer sity.

BENDER, L., and J. FROSCH. 1942. Children' reactions to the war. *Amer. J. Orthopsychiat* **12**, 571–586.

BENDER, L., and P. SCHILDER. 1936. Aggres siveness in children. *Genet. Psychol. Monogr* **18**, 410–525.

BERNE, E. V. C. 1930. An experimental inves tigation of social behavior patterns in youn children. *Univ. Iowa Stud. Child Welfare,* **4** No. 3.

BINET, A. 1895. La peur chez les enfants *Année psychol.*, **2**, 223–254.

BLATZ, W. E., K. D. ALLIN, and D. A. MILL CHAMP. 1936. A study of laughter in th nursery school child. *Univ. Toronto Stud Child Develpm. Ser.*, No. 7.

BLATZ, W. E., S. N. F. CHANT, and M. D SALTER. 1937. Emotional episodes in th child of school age. *Univ. Toronto Stud Child Develpm. Ser.*, No. 9.

BLATZ, W. E., and D. A. MILLICHAMP. 1935 The development of emotion in the infant *Univ. Toronto Stud. Child Develpm. Ser* No. 4.

BLEULER, E. 1924. *Textbook of psychiatry.* (Trans. of author's 4th German ed., by A. A. BRILL.) New York : Macmillan.

BODMAN, F. H. 1941. War conditions and the mental health of the child. *Brit. Med. J.,* **II,** 486–488.

BOECK, W. 1909. *Das Mitleid bei Kindern.* Giessen : v. Münchow.

BONAR, H. S. 1942. High-school pupils list their anxieties. *School Rev.,* **50,** 512–515.

BORGQUIST, A. 1906. Crying. *Amer. J. Psychol.,* **17,** 149–205.

BOSTON, M. V. 1939. Some factors related to the expression of fear in a group of average and superior children. *Smith Coll. Stud. Soc. Work,* **10,** 106–107.

BOYD, W. A. 1919. A child's fears. *J. Exp. Ped.,* **5,** 128–139.

BOYNTON, P. L., H. DUGGER, and M. TURNER. 1934. The emotional stability of teachers and pupils. *J. Juv. Res.,* **18,** 223–232.

BRACKETT, C. W. 1934. Laughing and crying of preschool children. *Child Develpm. Monogr.,* No. 14. Pp. 91.

BREGMAN, E. O. 1934. An attempt to modify the emotional attitudes of infants by the conditioned response technique. *J. Genet. Psychol.,* **45,** 169–198.

BRIDGES, K. M. B. 1931. *Social and emotional development of the preschool child.* London : Kegan Paul.

——. 1932. Emotional development in early infancy. *Child Develpm.,* **3,** 324–334.

BRUMBAUGH, F. N. 1939. *Stimuli which cause laughter in children.* Ph.D. Dissertation, New York University.

BÜHLER, C. 1930. *The first year of life.* New York : Day.

——. 1933. The social behavior of children. In C. MURCHISON (Ed.), *A handbook of child psychology* (2d ed., rev.), pp. 374–416. Worcester : Clark University Press.

BURT, C. 1940. The incidence of neurotic symptoms among evacuated school children. *Brit. J. Educ. Psychol.,* **10,** 8–15.

——. 1941. The billeting of evacuated children. *Brit. J. Educ. Psychol.,* **11,** 85–98.

BUTTERFIELD, O. M. 1939. Love problems of adolescence. *Teach. Coll. Contr. Educ.,* No. 768. Pp. 212.

CALKINS, M. W. 1894–1896. The emotional life of children. *Ped. Sem.,* **3,** 319–330.

CAMPBELL, E. H. 1939. The social-sex development of children. *Genet. Psychol. Monogr.,* **21,** 461–552.

CAMPBELL, H. F. 1938. Types of fear. *Brit. J. Educ. Psychol.,* **8,** 314.

CANTRIL, H., and W. A. HUNT. 1932. Emotional effects produced by the injection of adrenalin. *Amer. J. Psychol.,* **44,** 300–307.

CHAMBERS, O. R. 1925. A method for measuring the emotional maturity of children. *J. Genet. Psychol.,* **32,** 637–647.

COLLMAN, R. D. 1931. The psychogalvanic reactions of exceptional and normal school children. *Teach. Coll. Contr. Educ.,* No. 469.

CONN, J. H. 1940. Children's reactions to the discovery of genital differences. *Amer. J. Orthopsychiat.,* **10,** 747–755.

——. 1941. The treatment of fearful children. *Amer. J. Orthopsychiat.,* **11,** 744–752.

DARWIN, C. 1877. Biographical sketch of an infant. *Mind,* **2,** 285–294.

——. 1913. *The expression of the emotions in man and animals.* New York : Appleton.

DAVIS, C. M. 1928. Self-selection of diet by newly weaned infants. *Amer. J. Dis. Child.,* **36,** 651–679.

DAVIS, E. A. 1937. The tendency among children to avoid words with unpleasant connotation. *Amer. J. Psychol.,* **49,** 315–316.

DAWE, H. C. 1934. An analysis of 200 quarrels of preschool children. *Child Develpm.,* **5,** 139–157.

DEARBORN, G. V. N. 1898. The emotion of joy. *Psychol. Rev. Monogr.,* **2.** Pp. 70.

DEMBO, T. 1931. Der Ärger als dynamisches Problem. *Psychol. Forsch.,* **15,** 1–144.

DENNIS, W. 1938. Infant development under conditions of restricted practice and of minimum social stimulation : A preliminary report. *J. Gen. Psychol.,* **53,** 149–157.

——. 1940. Infant reaction to restraint: An evaluation of Watson's theory, *Trans. N. Y. Acad. Sci.,* **2,** 202–218.

DING, G. F., and A. T. JERSILD. 1932. A study of the laughing and smiling of preschool children. *J. Gen. Psychol.,* **40,** 452–472.

DOLLARD, J., L. W. DOOB, N. E. MILLER, O. H. MOWRER, R. R. SEARS, *et al.* 1939. *Frustration and aggression.* New Haven : Yale University Press.

DUDYCHA, G. J., and M. M. DUDYCHA. 1933. Adolescents' memories of preschool experiences. *J. Genet. Psychol.,* **42,** 468–480.

DUFFY, E. 1930. Tensions and emotional factors in reaction. *Genet. Psychol. Monogr.,* **7.** Pp. 79.

——. 1932. The measurement of muscular tensions as a technique for the study of emotional tendencies. *Amer. J. Psychol.,* **44,** 146–162.

DUNBAR, H. F. 1938. *Emotions and bodily changes: A survey of literature on psychosomatic interrelationships.* (2d ed.) New York : Columbia University Press.

DUREA, M. A. 1937. The emotional maturity of juvenile delinquents. *J. Abnorm. Soc. Psychol.,* **31,** 472–481.

DYSINGER, W. S., and C. A. RUCKMICK. 1933. *Emotional responses of children to the motion picture situation.* (Payne Fund Studies.) New York : Macmillan.

ELLESOR, M. V. 1933. Children's reactions to novel visual stimuli. *Child Develpm.,* **4,** 95–105.

ENDERS, A. C. 1927. A study of the laughter of the preschool child in the Merrill-Palmer nursery school. *Pap. Mich. Acad. Sci., Arts, Letters,* **8,** 341–356. (Cited in *Yearb. Nat. Soc. Stud. Educ.,* 1929, **28,** 603–604.)

ENGLISH, H. B. 1929. Three cases of the "conditioned fear response." *J. Abnorm. Soc. Psychol.,* **24,** 221–225.

FELDER, J. G. 1932. Some factors determining the nature and frequency of anger and fear outbreaks in preschool children. *J. Juv. Res.,* **16,** 278–290.

FISHER, V. E., and A. J. MARROW. 1934. Experimental study of moods. *Character and Pers.,* **2,** 201–208.

FITE, M. D. 1940. Aggressive behavior in young children and children's attitudes toward aggression. *Genet. Psychol. Monogr.,* **22,** 151–319.

FLÜGEL, J. C. 1925. A quantitative study of feeling and emotion in everyday life. *Brit. J. Psychol.,* **15,** 318–355.

FOSTER, J. C., and J. E. ANDERSON. 1930. *The young child and his parents.* (*Inst. Child Welfare Monogr. Ser.,* No. 1.) Minneapolis: University of Minnesota Press.

——. 1936. Unpleasant dreams in childhood. *Child Develpm.,* **7,** 77–84.

FOSTER, S. 1927. A study of the personality make-up and social setting of fifty jealous children. *Ment. Hyg., N. Y.,* **11,** 53–77.

FRANK, L. K. 1939. Projective methods for the study of personality. *J. Psychol.,* **8,** 389–413.

FREUD, S. 1920. *General introduction to psychoanalysis.* New York: Boni and Liveright.

——. 1930. Three contributions to the theory of sex. (4th ed., trans. by A. A. BRILL.) *Nerv. Ment. Dis. Monogr. Ser.,* No. 7. Pp. xiv + 104.

——. 1936. *The problem of anxiety.* New York: Norton.

GATES, G. S. 1926. An observational study of anger. *J. Exp. Psychol.,* **9,** 325–336.

GAUGER, M. E. 1929. The modifiability of response to taste stimuli in the preschool child. *Teach. Coll. Contr. Educ.,* No. 348.

GESELL, A. 1906. Jealousy. *Amer. J. Psychol.,* **17,** 437–496.

——. 1928. *Infancy and human growth.* New York: Macmillan.

——. 1929. The individual in infancy. In C. MURCHISON (Ed.), *The foundations of experimental psychology* (1st ed.), pp. 628–660. Worcester: Clark University Press.

GESELL, A., and F. L. ILG. 1937. *Feeding behavior of infants.* Philadelphia: Lippincott.

GESELL, A., and H. THOMPSON. 1941. Twins T and C from infancy to adolescence. *Genet. Psychol. Monogr.,* **24,** first half.

GHOSH, R. 1939. An experimental study of humour. *Brit. J. Educ. Psychol.,* **9,** 98–99.

GILLESPIE, R. D. 1942. *Psychological effects of war on citizen and soldier.* New York: Norton.

GOODENOUGH, F. L. 1931a. The expression of the emotions in infancy. *Child Develpm.,* **2,** 96–101.

——. 1931b. Anger in young children. (*Inst. Child Welfare Monogr. Ser.,* No. 9.) Minneapolis: University of Minnesota Press.

——. 1932. Expression of the emotions in a blind-deaf child. *J. Abnorm. Soc. Psychol.,* **27,** 328–333.

GOODENOUGH, F. L., and C. R. BRIAN. 1929. Certain factors underlying the acquisition of motor skill by preschool children. *J. Exp. Psychol.,* **12,** 127–155.

GREEN, E. H. 1933. Friendships and quarrels among preschool children. *Child Develpm.,* **4,** 237–252.

GREEN, G. H. 1927. *The terror dream.* London: Kegan Paul.

GRIFFITHS, R. 1935. *The study of imagination in early childhood.* London: Kegan Paul.

GUTTERIDGE, M. V. 1939. A study of motor achievements of young children. *Arch. Psychol., N. Y.,* No. 244.

HAGMAN, R. R. 1932. A study of fears of children of preschool age. *J. Exp. Educ.,* **1,** 110–130.

HALL, G. S. 1897. A study of fears. *Amer. J. Psychol.,* **8,** 147–249.

——. 1899. A study of anger. *Amer. J. Psychol.,* **10,** 516–591.

HALVERSON, H. M. 1940. Genital and sphincter behavior of the male infant. *J. Genet. Psychol.,* **56,** 95–136.

HAMILTON, G. V. 1929. *A research in marriage.* New York: Boni.

HARTMANN, G. W. 1934–1935. Personality traits associated with variations in happiness. *J. Abnorm. Soc. Psychol.,* **29,** 202–212.

HERRING, J. P. 1930. The measurement of liking and disliking. *J. Educ. Psychol.,* **21,** 159–196.

HERSEY, R. B. 1931. Emotional cycles in man. *J. Ment. Sci.,* **77,** 151–169.

HERZFELD, E., and F. PRAGER. 1930. Verständnis für Scherz und Komik beim Kinde. *Z. angew. Psychol.,* **34,** 353–417.

HILL, D. S. 1930. Personification of ideals by urban children. *J. Soc. Psychol.,* **1,** 379–392.

HOLLINGWORTH, H. L. 1910. Obliviscence of the disagreeable. *J. Phil. Psychol. Sci. Meth.,* **7,** 709–714.

——. 1928. *Psychology: Its facts and principles.* New York: Appleton.

HOLMES, F. B. 1935. An experimental study of the fears of young children. In A. T. JERSILD and F. B. HOLMES (1935a), pp. 167–296.

——. 1936. An experimental investigation of a method of overcoming children's fears. *Child Develpm.,* **7,** 6–30.

RNEY, K. 1939. *New ways in psychoanalysis.* New York: Norton.

ROWITZ, R., and L. B. MURPHY. 1938. Projective methods in the psychological study of children. *J. Exp. Educ.,* **7,** 133–140.

RLOCK, E. B., and E. R. KLEIN. 1934. Adolescent "crushes." *Child Develpm.,* **5,** 63–80.

VIN, O. C. 1932. Infant responses to vertical movements. *Child Develpm.,* **3,** 167–169.

ACS, S. 1933. *Social development in young children: A study of beginnings.* New York: Harcourt, Brace.

—. 1936. *The nursery years.* New York: Vanguard Press.

—. 1938. The nursery as a community. In J. RICKMAN (1938), pp. 167–232.

ACS, S., S. C. BROWN, and R. H. THOULESS (Eds.). 1941. *The Cambridge evacuation survey.* London: Methuen.

CK, L. M. 1934. An experimental study of ascendant behavior in preschool children. In L. M. JACK, E. M. MANWELL, I. G. MENGERT, *et al.* (1934), pp. 7–65.

CK, L. M., E. M. MANWELL, I. G. MENGERT *et al.* 1934. Behavior of the preschool child. *Univ. Iowa Stud. Child Welfare,* **9,** No. 3.

MES, W. 1890. *The principles of psychology.* Vol. II. New York: Holt.

SILD, A. T. 1931. A note on pleasures and unpleasures of college men and women. *J. Abnorm. Soc. Psychol.,* **26,** 91–93.

—. 1935. The nature and prevention of childhood fears. In A. T. JERSILD and F. B. HOLMES (1935a), Pt. 4, pp. 297–350.

—. 1937. *A study of children's reactions to radio programs.* Unpublished.

—. 1940. *Child psychology.* (Rev. Ed.) New York: Prentice-Hall.

SILD, A. T., and M. D. FITE. 1939. The influence of nursery school experience on children's social adjustments. *Child Develpm. Monogr.,* No. 25. Pp. 112.

SILD, A. T., B. GOLDMAN, and J. J. LOFTUS. 1941. A comparative study of the worries of children in two school situations. *J. Exp. Educ.,* **4,** 323–326.

SILD, A. T., and F. B. HOLMES. 1935a. Children's fears. *Child Develpm. Monogr.,* No. 20. Pp. 356.

—. 1935b. Some factors in the development of children's fears. *J. Exp. Educ.,* **4,** 133–141.

—. 1935c. Methods of overcoming children's fears. *J. Psychol.,* **1,** 75–104.

SILD, A. T., and F. V. MARKEY. 1935. Conflicts between preschool children. *Child Develpm. Monogr.,* No. 21. Pp. xi + 181.

SILD, A. T., F. V. MARKEY, and C. L. JERSILD. 1933. Children's fears, dreams, wishes, daydreams, likes, dislikes, pleasant and unpleasant memories. *Child Develpm. Monogr.,* No. 12. Pp. 172.

SILD, A. T., and W. S. THOMAS. 1931. Influence of adrenal extract on behavior and mental efficiency. *Amer. J. Psychol.,* **43,** 447–456.

JOHN, E. 1941. A study of the effects of evacuation and air-raids on children of preschool age. *Brit. J. Educ. Psychol.,* **11,** 173–182.

JOHNSON, W. B. 1937. Euphoric and depressed moods in normal subjects. *Character and Pers.,* **6,** 79–98.

JONES, H. E. 1930a. The retention of conditioned emotional reactions in infancy. *J. Genet. Psychol.,* **37,** 485–498.

—. 1930b. The galvanic skin reflex in infancy *Child Develpm.,* **1,** 106–110.

—. 1931. The conditioning of overt emotional responses. *J. Educ. Psychol.,* **22,** 127–130.

—. 1935. The galvanic skin reflex as related to overt emotional expression. *Amer. J. Psychol.,* **47,** 241–251.

JONES, H. E., and M. C. JONES. 1928. Fear. *Childhood Educ.,* **5,** 136–143.

JONES, M. C. 1924a. A laboratory study of fear: The case of Peter. *Ped. Sem.,* **31,** 308–316.

—. 1924b. Elimination of children's fears. *J. Exp. Psychol.,* **7,** 382–390.

—. 1925. A study of the emotions of preschool children. *Sch. and Soc.,* **21,** 755–758.

—. 1926. The development of early behavior patterns in young children. *Ped. Sem.,* **33,** 537–585.

—. 1933. Emotional development. In C. MURCHISON (Ed.), *A handbook of child psychology* (2d ed., rev.), pp. 271–302. Worcester: Clark University Press.

JONES, T. D. 1939. The development of certain motor skills and play activities in young children. *Child Develpm. Monogr.,* No. 26. Pp. 180.

JUSTIN, F. 1932. A genetic study of laughter-provoking stimuli. *Child Develpm.,* **3,** 114–136.

KEISTER, M. E. 1938. The behavior of young children in failure: An experimental attempt to discover and to modify undesirable responses of preschool children to failure. *Univ. Iowa Stud. Child Welfare,* **14,** 27–82.

KEISTER, M. E., and R. UPDEGRAFF. 1937. A study of children's reactions to failure and an experimental attempt to modify them. *Child Develpm.,* **8,** 241–248.

KELCHNER, M. 1929. Kummer und Trost jugendlicher Arbeiterinnen. *Forsch. Völkerpsychol. Soziol.,* **6,** 1–90.

KENDERDINE, M. 1931. Laughter in the preschool child. *Child Develpm.,* **2,** 228–230.

KLEIN, M. 1932. *The psycho-analysis of children.* New York: Norton.

—. 1938. Weaning. In J. RICKMAN (1938), pp. 31–56.

KOCH, H. L. 1935. An analysis of certain forms of so-called "nervous habits" in young children. *J. Genet. Psychol.,* **46,** 139–170.

LAING, A. 1939. The sense of humour in childhood and adolescence. *Brit. J. Educ. Psychol.,* **9,** 201.

LANDIS, C. 1924a. Studies of emotional reactions: I. A preliminary study of facial expression. *J. Exp. Psychol.,* **7,** 325–341.

——. 1924b. Studies of emotional reactions: II. General behavior and facial expression. *J. Comp. Psychol.,* **4,** 447–509.

——. 1929. The interpretation of facial expression in emotion. *J. Gen. Psychol.,* **2,** 59–72.

LANDIS, C., and W. HUNT. 1939. *The startle pattern.* New York: Farrar & Rinehart.

LANDIS, C., A. LANDIS, M. BOLLES *et al.* 1940. *Sex in development.* New York: Hoeber.

LEE, M. A. M. 1932. A study of emotional instability in nursery school children. *Child Develpm.,* **3,** 142–145.

LEVY, D. M. 1928. Fingersucking and accessory movements in early infancy. *Amer. J. Psychiat.,* **7,** 881–918.

——. 1937. Studies in sibling rivalry. *Res. Monogr. Amer. Orthopsychiat. Ass.,* No. 2. Pp. 96.

——. 1940. "Control-situation" studies of children's responses to the difference in genitalia. *Amer. J. Orthopsychiat.,* **10,** 755–763.

LEVY, D. M., and S. H. TULCHIN. 1923. The resistance of infants and children during mental tests. *J. Exp. Psychol.,* **6,** 304–322.

LEWIN, K., R. LIPPITT, and R. K. WHITE. 1939. Patterns of aggressive behavior in experimentally created "social climates." *J. Soc. Psychol.,* **10,** 271–299.

LIPPITT, R. 1940. An experimental study of the effect of democratic and authoritarian group atmospheres. *Univ. Iowa Stud. Child Welfare,* **16,** 43–195.

LOWENSTEIN, P., and M. SVENDSEN. 1938. Experimental modification of the behavior of a selected group of shy and withdrawn children. *Amer. J. Orthopsychiat.,* **8,** 639–653.

LUND, F. H. 1939. *Emotions: Their psychological, physiological and educative implications.* New York: Ronald.

MACAULAY, E. 1925. Some social, age and sex differences shown in children's choice of ideals. *Forum Educ.,* **3,** 105–114.

MACFARLAND, J. W. 1938. Studies in child guidance: I. Methodology of data collection and organization. *Monogr. Soc. Res. Child Develpm.,* **3,** No. 6, Ser. 19. Pp. vii + 254.

MACFARLANE, J. W. 1938. Relationships between young sisters as revealed in their overt responses. *Child Develpm. Monogr.,* No. 23. Pp. 230.

MALAPERT, P. 1902. Enquête sur le sentiment de la colère chez les enfants. *Année psychol.,* **9.** 1–40.

MARKEY, F. V. 1935. Imaginative behavior in preschool children. *Child Develpm. Monogr.,* No. 18. Pp. 138.

MARSH, C. J. 1942. The worries of the college woman. *J. Soc. Psychol.,* **15,** 335–339.

MATHEWS, E. 1923. A study of emotional stability in children by means of a questionnaire. *J. Delinq.,* **8,** 1–40.

MCCARTHY, D. 1935. Children's feeding problems in relation to the food aversions in the family. *Child Develpm.,* **6,** 277–284.

MCDOUGALL, W. 1909. *An introduction to social psychology.* Boston: Luce.

MCGRAW, M. B. 1935. *Growth: A study of Johnny and Jimmy.* New York: Appleton Century.

MCKINNON, K. 1940. *Consistency and change in personality and behavior manifestations—as observed in a group of 16 children during a five year period.* Unpublished, Teachers College, Columbia University.

MELTZER, H. 1933. Students' adjustments in anger. *J. Soc. Psychol.,* **4,** 285–309.

——. 1937. Anger adjustments in relation to intelligence and achievement. *J. Genet. Psychol.,* **50,** 63–82.

MENGERT, I. G. 1931. A preliminary study of the reactions of two-year-old children to each other when paired in a semi-controlled situation. *J. Genet. Psychol.,* **39,** 393–398.

MIRK, M. 1930. The difference of emotional stability in girls of different ages. *Aust. J. Psychol. Phil.,* **8,** 229–232.

MITRANO, A. J. 1939. Preliminary construction of a schedule of emotional stability for children. *Amer. J. Orthopsychiat.,* **9,** 360–367.

MOORE, K. C. 1896. The mental development of a child. *Psychol. Monogr.,* No. 3. Pp. 150.

MORRISON, B. M. 1924. A study of the major emotions in persons of defective intelligence. *Univ. Calif. Publ. Psychol.,* **3,** 73–145.

MOSS, F. A. 1924. Note on building likes and dislikes in children. *J. Exp. Psychol.,* **7,** 475–478.

MOSSO, A. 1896. *Fear.* (Trans. by E. LOUGH and F. KEISOW.) New York: Longmans Green.

MURPHY, L. B. 1937. *Social behavior and child personality.* New York: Columbia University Press.

NICHOLSON, J. 1931. A study of 40 shy and timid children. *Smith Coll. Stud. Soc. Work,* **1,** 310.

PELLER, L. E. 1939. The child's approach to reality. *Amer. J. Orthopsychiat.,* **9,** 503–513.

PINTNER, R., and L. BRUNSCHWIG. 1937. A study of certain fears and wishes among deaf and hearing children. *J. Educ. Psychol.,* **28,** 259–270.

PINTNER, R., and J. LEV. 1940. Worries of school children. *J. Genet. Psychol.,* **56,** 67–76.

PRATT, K. C., A. K. NELSON, and K. H. SUN. 1930. The behavior of the newborn infant. *Ohio State Univ. Stud., Contr. Psychol.,* No. 10.

PREYER, W. 1888, 1889. *The mind of the child:* Pt. 1. *The senses and the will;* Pt. 2. *The development of the intellect.* (Trans. by H. W. BROWN.) New York: Appleton.

PRICHARD, E., and R. H. OJEMANN. 1941. An approach to the measurement of insecurity. *J. Exp. Educ.,* **10,** 114–118.

RANK, O. 1932. *Modern education: A critique of its fundamental ideas.* New York: Knopf.

RAY, W. S. 1932. A study of the emotions of children with particular reference to circulatory and respiratory changes. *J. Genet. Psychol.,* **40,** 100–117.

REYNOLDS, M. M. 1928. Negativism of preschool children. *Teach. Coll. Contr. Educ.,* No. 288.

RIBOT, T. 1903. *The psychology of the emotions.* New York: Scribner's.

RICHARDSON, R. F. 1918. *The psychology and pedagogy of anger.* (*Educ. Psychol. Monogr.,* No. 19.) Baltimore: Warwick & York. Pp. 100.

RICKETTS, A. F. 1934. A study of the behavior of young children in anger. In L. M. JACK et al. (1934), pp. 159–171.

RICKMAN, J. (Ed.). 1938. *On the bringing up of children, by five psychoanalysts.* (S. Isaacs, M. Klein, M. P. Middlemore, N. Searl, E. F. Sharpe.) London: Kegan Paul.

ROSS, B. M. 1931. Some traits associated with sibling jealousy in problem children. *Smith Coll. Stud. Soc. Work,* **1,** 364–376.

RUCKMICK, C. A. 1936. *The psychology of feeling and emotion.* New York: McGraw-Hill.

SEARS, R. R. 1943. *Survey of objective studies of psychoanalytic concepts,* Bulletin 51. New York: Social Science Research Council.

SEWALL, M. 1930. Two studies in sibling rivalry: I. Some causes of jealousy in young children. *Smith Coll. Stud. Soc. Work,* **1,** 6–22.

SHARPE, E. F. 1938. Planning for stability. In J. RICKMAN (1938), pp. 1–30.

SHERMAN, M. 1927a. The differentiation of emotional responses in infants: I. Judgments of emotional responses from motion picture views and from actual observation. *J. Comp. Psychol.,* **7,** 265–284.

——. 1927b. The differentiation of emotional responses in infants: II. The ability of observers to judge the emotional characteristics of the crying of infants, and of the voice of an adult. *J. Comp. Psychol.,* **7,** 335–351.

——. 1928. The differentiation of emotional responses in infants: III. A proposed theory of the development of emotional responses in infants. *J. Comp. Psychol.,* **8,** 385–394.

SHERMAN, M., and I. C. SHERMAN. 1925. Sensori-motor responses in infants. *J. Comp. Psychol.,* **5,** 53–68.

SHIRLEY, M. M. 1933a. *The first two years, a study of twenty-five babies:* Vol. II. *Intellectual development.* (*Inst. Child Welfare Monogr. Ser.,* No. 7.) Minneapolis: University Minnesota Press. Pp. xvi + 513.

SHIRLEY, M. M. 1933b. *The first two years, a study of twenty-five babies:* Vol. III. *Personality manifestations.* (*Inst. Child Welfare Monogr. Ser.,* No. 8.) Minneapolis: University of Minnesota Press. Pp. xi + 228.

SIMPSON, M. 1935. Parent preferences of young children. *Teach. Coll. Contr. Educ.,* No. 652.

SLATER, E., R. BECKWITH, and L. BEHNKE. 1939. Studies from the Center for Research in Child Health and Development, School of Public Health, Harvard University: II. Types, levels, and irregularities of response to a nursery school situation of forty children observed with special reference to the home environment. *Monogr. Soc. Res. Child Develpm.,* No. 4. Pp. 148.

SMALLEY, R. E. 1930. Two studies in sibling rivalry: II. The influence of differences in age, sex and intelligence in determining the attitudes of siblings toward each other. *Smith Coll. Stud. Soc. Work,* **1,** 23–40.

STAGNER, R., and N. DROUGHT. 1935. Measuring children's attitudes toward their parents. *J. Educ. Psychol.,* **26,** 169–176.

STRATTON, G. M. 1927. Anger and fear: Their probable relation to each other, to intellectual work and to primogeniture. *Amer. J. Psychol.,* **39,** 125–140.

——. 1929. Emotion and the incidence of disease: The influence of the number of diseases, and of the age at which they occur. *Psychol. Rev.,* **36,** 242–253.

STRYKER, M. F. 1898. Children's joys and sorrows. *Child Stud. Mon.,* **4,** 217–225.

STUMP, N. F. 1939. Sense of humor and its relation to personality, scholastic aptitude, emotional maturity, height, and weight. *J. Gen. Psychol.,* **20,** 25–32.

SULLIVAN, E. T. 1922. Mood in relation to performance. *Arch. Psychol.,* No. 53.

SWAN, C. 1938. Individual differences in the facial expressive behavior of preschool children: A study by the time-sampling method. *Genet. Psychol. Monogr.,* **20,** 557–650.

SYMONDS, P. M. 1938. A study of parental acceptance and rejection. *Amer. J. Orthopsychiat.,* **8,** 679–688.

TAYLOR, J. H. 1934. Innate emotional responses in infants. *Ohio Univ. Stud. Contr. Psychol.,* **12,** 69–81.

TERMAN, L. M. 1938. *Psychological factors in marital happiness.* New York: McGraw-Hill.

THOMPSON, J. 1941. Development of facial expression of emotion in blind and seeing children. *Arch. Psychol. N. Y.,* No. 264.

THORNDIKE, E. L. 1913. *Educational psychology: Vol. I. The original nature of man.* New York: Teachers College, Columbia University.

TUCKER, L. E. 1937. A study of problem pupils. *Teach. Coll. Contr. Educ.*, No. 720.

VALENTINE, C. W. 1930. The innate bases of fear. *J. Genet. Psychol.*, **37**, 394–420.

VERNON, P. E. 1941. Psychological effects of air-raids. *J. Abnorm. Soc. Psychol.*, **36**, 457–476.

WASHBURN, R. W. 1929. A study of the smiling and laughing of infants in the first year of life. *Genet. Psychol. Monogr.*, **6**, 397–539.

WASHBURNE, J. N. 1932. The impulsions of adolescents as revealed by their written wishes. *J. Juv. Res.*, **16**, 193–212.

WATSON, G. 1930. Happiness among adult students of education. *J. Educ. Psychol.*, **21**, 79–109.

WATSON, J. B. 1919. *Psychology from the standpoint of a behaviorist.* Philadelphia: Lippincott.

WATSON, J. B., and J. J. B. MORGAN. 1917. Emotional reactions and psychological experimentation. *Amer. J. Psychol.*, **28**, 163–174.

WATSON, J. B., and R. RAYNER. 1920. Conditioned emotional reactions. *J. Exp. Psychol.*, **3**, 1–14.

WEBER, C. O. 1930. The concept of "emotional age" and its measurement. *J. Abnorm. Soc. Psychol.*, **24**, 466–471.

WECHSLER, D., L. M. CRABBS, and R. G. FREEMAN, JR. 1930. Galvanic responses of preschool children. *J. Genet. Psychol.*, **38**, 203–222.

WENGER, M. A. 1938. Some relationships between muscular processes and personality and their factorial analysis. *Child Develpm.*, **9** 261–276.

WHITE, M. A., and H. M. WILLIAMS. 1939. The approach-withdrawal pattern in the social behavior of young children. *J. Genet. Psychol.*, **54**, 73–84.

WILLOUGHBY, R. R. 1937. Sexuality in the second decade. *Monogr. Soc. Res. Child Develpm.*, **2**, No. 10.

WOLGEMUTH, A. 1922–1923. The influence of feeling on memory. *Brit. J. Psychol.*, **13**, 405–416.

YOUNG, P. T. 1937. Laughing and weeping, cheerfulness and depression: A study of moods among college students. *J. Soc. Psychol.*, **8** 311–334.

ZILLIG, M. 1928. Über das Verständnis des Kindes für den Erwachsenen. *Arch. ges. Psychol.*, **62**, 135–179.

CHAPTER 16

BEHAVIOR AND DEVELOPMENT AS A FUNCTION
OF THE TOTAL SITUATION

KURT LEWIN

If one wishes to use the facts concerning development, personality, social relations, cognition, and motivation which are discussed in the various chapters of this book for the purpose of understanding, guiding, or predicting the behavior of the child, these data will have to be linked in such a way that they become applicable to a particular child at a particular time. This chapter discusses procedures and concepts which have been found to be instrumental for this purpose. Some of the relevant methodological questions are considered and certain problems of cognition, motivation, and development are treated as examples. Frequently, reference is made to data which are discussed in more detail in other chapters; but no attempt to achieve completeness could be made within the limitations of this chapter.

ANALYSIS, CONCEPTS, AND THEORY IN CHILD PSYCHOLOGY

The Psychological Field

STIMULUS AND SITUATION: THE BASIC FORMULA FOR BEHAVIOR

Scientific procedure is analytical in that it tries to determine or to "isolate" the effect of the various factors. It studies, for instance, the effect on the child of different intensities of light, of different degrees of hunger (Irwin, 1930; Pratt, 1933), of failure or praise. It is widely agreed, however, that the effect of a given stimulus depends upon the stimulus constellation and upon the state of the particular person at that time. The perceived form, size, and color of a visual object corresponding to the same retinal stimulus vary widely according to the visual background and the nature of the rest of the visual field (Gelb, 1938). The toys and other objects in a room may lead to very different reactions of the year-old child when the mother is present and when she is not (MacDonald, 1940). In general terms, behavior (B) is a function (F) of the person (P) and of his environment (E), $B = F(P, E)$. This statement is correct for emotional outbreaks as well as for "purposive" directed activities; for dreaming, wishing, and thinking, as well as for talking and acting.

PERSON AND PSYCHOLOGICAL ENVIRONMENT

In this formula for behavior, the state of the person (P) and that of his environment (E) are not independent of each other. How a child sees a given physical setting—for instance, whether the frozen pond looks dangerous to him or not—depends upon the developmental state and the character of that child (Murray, 1938) and upon his ideology (Mead, 1928). The worlds in which the newborn, the one-year-old child, and the ten-year-old child live are different even in identical physical or social surroundings. This holds also for the same child when it is hungry or satiated, full of energy or fatigued. In other words, $E = F(P)$. The reverse is also true: The state of the person depends upon his environment, $P = F(E)$. The state of the person after encouragement is different from that after discouragement (Fajans, 1933), that in an area of sympathy or security from that in an area of tension (Murphy, 1937), that in a democratic group atmosphere from that in an autocratic atmosphere (Lewin, Lippitt, and White, 1939). The momentary intellectual ability of a child as measured by an intelligence test (MA) is different in an atmosphere of good rapport with the examiner from what it is in one of poor rapport. In regard to the effect of the environment upon development there is a consensus that environment may change intelligence, although opinion differs in regard to how much intelligence can be changed by environment (Terman, 1919; Wellman, 1932–1933; Stoddard and Wellman, 1934; Burks, 1940; Goodenough, 1940). Certainly the ideology, values, and attitudes of the growing individual depend greatly upon the culture in which he is reared (Mead, 1937; L. K. Frank, 1938) and upon his belonging to a privileged or underprivileged group (Dollard, 1937; Lewin, 1940b).

In summary, one can say that behavior and development[1] depend upon the state of the person and his environment, $B = F(P, E)$. In this equation the person P and his environment E have to be viewed as variables which are mutually dependent upon each other. In other words, to understand or to predict behavior, the person and his environment have to be considered as *one* constellation of interdependent fac-

[1] The possibility of treating the factors determining development formally in the same way as the factors determining behavior simplifies psychological theory considerably. I owe this idea to Donald K. Adams.

tors. We call the totality of these factor the life space (LSp) of that individual, and write $B = F(P, E) = F(LSp)$. The life space, therefore, includes both the person and his psychological environment. The task of explaining behavior then become identical with (1) finding a scientific representation of the life space (LSp) and (2 determining the function (F) which link the behavior to the life space. This function F is what one usually calls a *law*.

GENERAL CHARACTERISTICS OF A PSYCHO LOGICAL FIELD

The novelist who tells the story behind the behavior and development of an individual gives us detailed data about his parents, his siblings, his character, his intelligence, his occupation, his friends, his status. He gives us these data in their specific interrelation, that is, as part of total situation. Psychology has to fulfil the same task with scientific instead of poetic means. The method should be analytical in that the different factors which influence behavior have to be specifically distinguished. In science, these data have also to be represented in their particular setting within the specific situation. A totality of coexisting facts which are conceived of as mutually interdependent is called a *field* (Einstein, 1933). Psycholog has to view the life space, including the person and his environment, as one field

What means are most appropriate for analyzing and representing scientifically psychological field have to be judged on the basis of their fruitfulness for explaining behavior. In this respect, the following general points should be remembered:

(1) A prerequisite for properly guiding a child or for the theoretical understanding of his behavior is the distinction between that situation which the teacher, the parents, or the experimenter sees and that situation which exists for the child as his life

pace. *Objectivity* in psychology demands representing the field correctly as it exists for the individual in question at that particular time. For this field the child's friendships, conscious and "unconscious" goals, dreams, ideals, and fears are at least as essential as any physical setting. Since this field is different for every age and for every individual, the situation as characterized by physics or sociology, which is the same for everybody, cannot be substituted for it. It is important, however, to know the physical and social conditions because they limit the variety of possible life spaces—probably as *boundary conditions* (Lewin, 1936a) of the psychological field.

(2) The social aspect of the psychological situation is at least as important as the physical. This holds even for the very young child.

(3) To characterize properly the psychological field, one has to take into account such *specific* items as particular goals, stimuli, needs, social relations, as well as such more *general* characteristics of the field as the *atmosphere* (for instance, the friendly, tense, or hostile atmosphere) or the amount of freedom. These characteristics of the *field as a whole* are as important in psychology as, for instance, the field of gravity for the explanation of events in classical physics. Psychological atmospheres are empirical realities and are scientifically describable facts (Lewin, Lippitt, and White, 1939).

(4) The concept of the psychological field as a determinant of behavior implies that everything which affects behavior at a given time should be represented in the field existing at that time, and that only those facts can affect behavior which are part of the present field (Lewin, 1936a).

(5) To avoid unnecessary assumptions, one can represent the psychological field scientifically by the interrelation of its parts in mathematical terms without asking what the "essence behind" this field is.[1] Such a mathematical representation of the psychological field and the equations expressing the psychological laws are all that have to be known for predicting behavior.

Theories and Constructs: Law and the Individual Case

THEORIES ARE UNAVOIDABLE

Without theories it is impossible in psychology, as in any other science, to proceed beyond the mere collection and description of facts which have no predictive value. It is impossible to handle problems of conditions or effects without characterizing the *dynamic* properties behind the surface of the directly observable *phenotypical* properties.

The terms *need, association, conditioned reflex, excitatory tendency, gestalt, libido,* and *super-ego* are examples of theoretical constructs with which various psychological schools have attempted to characterize certain underlying dynamical or genotypical facts. It is important to distinguish those facts which are essential for prediction and explanation from their various symptoms. For instance, an emotional state such as anger can lead to a variety of very different symptoms (noisiness, as well as extreme politeness [Dembo, 1931]); tension can lead to aggressiveness as well as apathy (Lewin, Lippitt, and White, 1939). The same personality may manifest itself in practically opposite actions. In other words, a given state of a person corresponds to a variety of behavior and can, therefore, be inferred only from a combined determination of overt behavior and the situation. This is only another way of saying that behavior (B) is deter-

[1] What here is called *life space* is more or less identical with or closely related to the concept of brain field (Köhler, 1920) or regnancy (Murray, 1938).

mined by the person and the environment $[B = F(P, E)]$ and not by the person or the environment alone.

Psychology has never avoided, nor can it avoid, theory (Reichenbach, 1928; Hull, 1930; Tolman, 1935; J. F. Brown, 1936; Lewin, 1938), but it can try to eliminate those speculative theories which are frequently introduced without clear intent or in a hidden way, and try instead to make use of openly stated empirical theories. The main desiderata for an efficient empirical theory are: (1) constructs which (a) are linked to observable facts (symptoms) by a so-called operational definition or by a number of operational definitions corresponding to the possibilities of observation under different circumstances; and constructs which (b) have clearly defined conceptual properties. These properties are coordinated to certain mathematical (logical) concepts. Such a coordination is a prerequisite for logically strict derivations (Hull, 1930; J. F. Brown, 1936; Lewin, 1938). (2) The laws (that is, the relation between behavior, on the one hand, and the field characterized by certain constructs, on the other, or between various factors determining the field) should be verified by experiment. A law should be accepted as valid only if it is not contradicted by data in any branch of psychology. In this sense, a law should always be general.

GENERAL LAWS AND INDIVIDUAL DIFFERENCES

The problems of general laws and of individual differences frequently appear to be unrelated questions which follow somewhat opposite lines. Any prediction, however, presupposes a consideration of both types of questions.

To give just one example of the linkage between the study of general laws and of individual differences: The velocity with which an activity is satiated increases, according to Karsten (1928) (see p. 825) with the degree to which the activity is psychologically central (as against peripheral). This proposition has the nature of a general law. If correct, it would explain why both agreeable and disagreeable activities are more quickly satiated than relatively neutral ones, and why fashions in women's clothes change faster than in men's clothes. By means of this law one can account for variations in the speed of satiation exhibited by the same person in different states. Certain activities, for example, are more central during menstruum than during intermenstruum and, in accordance with the general law, these activities are satiated more quickly during menstruum. When applied to age differences the law would explain why the velocity of satiation of certain activities is slower in older than in younger children. Finally, it would explain why certain types of problem children who are oversensitive reach the satiation point more quickly than the average child of that age.

This example may show that problems of individual differences, of age levels, of personality, of specific situations, and of general laws are closely interwoven. A law is expressed in an equation which relates certain variables. Individual differences have to be conceived of as various specific values which these variables have in a particular case. In other words, general laws and individual differences are merely two aspects of one problem; they are mutually dependent on each other and the study of the one cannot proceed without the study of the other. This implies that the data about the various age levels provided by child psychology have practical value for the understanding and guiding of individual children only if these data are linked with the concrete situation which is dominating the behavior of a given child at a given time.

This example concerning psychological atiation illustrates also that laws should, nd usually can, be applied to all parts of psychology. One of the main functions of heories and constructs is to bind together ll the various fields of psychology which otherwise would tend to fall apart into a number of unconnected disciplines. Child psychology, which necessarily has to deal with such apparently divergent questions is nutrition, growth, emotions, perceptions, culture, personalities, social relations, actions, and thought (L. K. Frank, 1938), demands the synthetic ties offered by theories and constructs probably more than any other branch of psychology and is a particularly good testing ground for their validity.

Microscopic and Macroscopic Units in Psychology

A problem where prejudices have greatly hampered progress of research is the treatment of units of different sizes. In child psychology we want to know the development of, and conditions for, the movement of the various fingers in the action of grasping (Halverson, 1931) or the movement of the tongue (Gesell *et al.*, 1940), as well as the effect of the home background upon the school work of a child, or the effect of his childhood relations with his parents on his behavior as an adult. Child psychology is concerned with questions regarding time units of a fraction of a second ("reaction of the eyelid, eye movements in the act of reading") and with time units of many years (problems of life history, Dollard, 1935; Allport, 1937; Bühler, 1939).

For instance, the investigation of stuttering involves the study of the position of a sound or syllable in a word (S. F. Brown,

1938*a*), of a word in a sentence (S. F. Brown, 1936–1937; 1938*b*); it involves the study of the importance of the sentence in the text of the paragraph (Johnson and Knott, 1937); the relation of this verbal expression to the immediate social situation—speaking alone or to a small or large audience (Porter, 1939; Barber, 1939); the effect of the family's classification of the child as a stutterer (Gray, 1940); the individual's position in his family—for instance, his position in the rank order of siblings (Rotter, 1939); his position within the population at large (Travis, Johnson, and Shover, 1937); and the general atmosphere of his life space. In other words, it is necessary to investigate units of action of widely different sizes and situations of widely different scope, such as the "immediate situation" and the "situation at large."

Dealing with units of different sizes is common in every science. Physics, for instance, deals with the ion, the atom, the molecule, and the so-called macroscopic physical objects up to units of the size of the stars. Each size of unit has to be approached technically in a somewhat different way and has some characteristics of its own. However, there is no logical reason to call one type of unit—for instance, the smaller one—more real than the other.

In psychology, too, it is possible to obtain objective and reliable observations in regard to units of any size if one uses methods fitted to the various types (Ronald Lippitt, 1940; Barker, Dembo, and Lewin, 1941). The attempt to determine reliably large macroscopic units by observing microscopic units, however, is bound to fail (Thomas, 1932) in psychology as in other sciences. It is technically impossible to describe the movement of the sun by describing the movement of every ion contained in it.

Laws usually are concerned with the relations between various parts of a situation and are independent of the absolute size to a high degree. Without this dependence of laws upon structure rather than upon size, experimentation would be infinitely more difficult.

Constructs Basic for Representing the Psychological Field

It seems to be possible to represent the essential properties of the life space with the help of relatively few (perhaps a dozen) related constructs. To some degree it is a matter of convenience which of a group of interrelated constructs are to be considered the basic ones (Reichenbach, 1928). For the purpose of this representation we shall use mainly the following constructs: psychological force, psychological position, and potency of a situation.

(1) The concept of force in psychology refers to phenomena which have been called *drive, excitatory tendency,* or by any other name expressing "tendency to act in a certain direction." The term *force* intends to express this directed element, attributing to it, in addition, a magnitude (strength of force) and a point of application, without assuming any additional implications (Lewin, 1938).

(2) The position of the person within the total psychological field and the position of the other parts of the field in relation to one another are of prime importance. This holds for the relative position of various areas of activities the child might enter, the relative position of social groups to which the child belongs, or would like to belong, and of areas of security and insecurity. Although it is not possible today to measure psychological distance or direction quantitatively, it is possible to treat some problems of position by means of the qualitative geometry called topology.

(3) Potency refers to the weight which a certain area of the life space has for a child relative to other areas. This concept is particularly valuable in case of "overlapping situations," that is, when the belongingness to two groups or the involvement in two or more activities at the same time is pertinent.

THE BEHAVIOR IN A GIVEN PSYCHOLOGICAL FIELD

Cognitive Structure of the Life Space

THE LIFE SPACE AS A WHOLE DURING DEVELOPMENT

Differentiation of the Various Dimensions of the Life Space. An outstanding characteristic of the change of the life space during development is an increasing differentiation. The importance of this factor has been shown in regard to the development of language (Gesell and Thompson, 1934), knowledge (Tolman, 1932), social interrelations (Murphy, 1937), emotions (Jersild, 1936), and actions (Fajans, 1933).

The life space of the newborn child may be described as a field which has relatively few and only vaguely distinguishable areas (Koffka, 1928). The situation probably corresponds to a general state of greater or less comfort. No definite objects or persons seem to be distinguished. No area called "my own body" exists. Future events or expectations do not exist; the child is ruled by the situation immediately at hand.

Some of the first areas which get a definite character seem to be connected with food and elimination. As early as three to six days the child reacts to being prepared for nursing (Marquis, 1931). A similar increase in size and differentiation of the life space occurs in other respects. The child studies his own body (Bühler, 1939) nd his immediate physical surroundings. Within the first few months, certain social relations develop.

The increase of the life space in regard to the psychological time dimension continues into adulthood. Plans extend farther into the future, and activities of increasingly longer duration are organized as one unit. For instance, between two and six years of age the duration of play units increases (Barker, Dembo, and Lewin, 1941).

The differentiation of the life space also increases in the dimension of reality-irreality. The different degrees of irreality correspond to different degrees of fantasy. They include both the positive wishes and the fears. Dynamically, the level of irreality corresponds to a more fluid medium (J. F. Brown, 1933; Erikson, 1940) and is more closely related to the central layers of the person. This fact is particularly important for the psychology of dreams (Freud, 1916; T. French, 1939). Play can be understood as an action on the level of reality closely related to the irreal level (Sliosberg, 1934). The play technique (Homburger, 1937), in the study of personality, makes use of the fact that the irreal level is closely related to the central layers of the person.

The level of irreality in the psychological future corresponds to the wishes or fears for the future; the level of reality, to what is expected. The discrepancy between the structure of the life space on the levels of irreality and of reality is important for planning and for the productivity of the child (Barker, Dembo, and Lewin, 1941). Hope corresponds to a sufficient similarity between reality and irreality somewhere in the psychological future; guilt to a certain discrepancy between reality and irreality in the psychological past. In the young child, truth and lying, perception and im-

agination are less clearly distinguished than in an older child (Piaget, 1932; Sliosberg, 1934; L. K. Frank, 1935). This is partly due to the fact that the younger child has not yet developed that degree of differentiation of the life space into levels of reality and irreality which is characteristic of the adult.

The speed with which the life space increases in scope and degree of differentiation during development varies greatly. A close relation seems to exist between intelligence or, more specifically, between mental age and the degree of differentiation of the person and the psychological environment (Lewin, 1935; Kounin, 1939). If this is correct, differences in IQ should be considered as different rates of increasing differentiation of the life space. Similar considerations apply to motor development (McGraw, 1935) and to social development.

The growth of the life space has a different rate at different times. Such differences are particularly important for the so-called developmental crises, as in adolescence (Dimock, 1937; Lewin, 1939).

Figure 1a and b represents schematically the scope and degree of differentiation of the life space as a whole at two developmental stages. The differentiation concerns the psychological environment as well as the person. The increasing differentiation of needs, for instance, can be represented as an increase in the differentiation of certain intrapersonal regions. The main differences between these developmental stages are: (1) an increase in the *scope* of the life space in regard to (a) what is part of the psychological present; (b) the time perspective in the direction of the psychological past and the psychological future; (c) the reality-irreality dimension; (2) an increasing *differentiation* of every level of the life space into a multitude of social relations and areas of activities; (3) an increasing *organization;* (4) a change in the general *fluidity* or *rigidity* of the life space.

Not all the areas of this life space are accessible to the child. He sees older chil-

tance for behavior and development of the normal and abnormal child (Lewin, 1936a).

Regression. A change of the life space as a whole in the direction opposite to that characteristic of development may be called *regression.* Regression may include

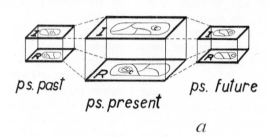

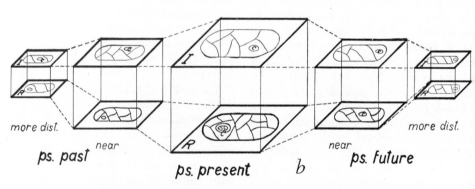

FIGURE 1. The life space at two developmental stages.

Figure 1a represents the life space of a younger child. Figure 1b represents the higher degree of differentiation of the life space of the older child in regard to the present situation, the reality-irreality dimension, and the time perspective. *C,* child; *R,* level of reality; *I,* level of irreality; *Ps Past,* psychological past; *Ps Present,* psychological present; *Ps Future,* psychological future.

dren engaged in certain activities, which he would like to do himself, but into which he finds he cannot enter because he is not strong or clever enough. Additional limitations of his space of free movements are established by the prohibitions of the adult or by other social taboos.

The relation between accessible and inaccessible regions in the life space, the size of the space of free movement, and the precision of boundary between accessible and inaccessible areas are of great impor-

a decrease in time perspective, dedifferentiation or disorganization, leading to behavior more or less typical for children on a younger age level.

Regression may be either permanent or temporary. It is a common phenomenon and may be due, for instance, to sickness (Jersild, 1936), frustration (Barker, Dembo, and Lewin, 1941), insecurity (Murphy, 1937), or emotional tension (Dembo, 1931; Jersild, 1936). Regression, in the sense of a narrowing-down of the psychologically resent area, may result from emotional ension, for instance, if the child is too ager to overcome an obstacle (Köhler, 925).

Regression may occur not only as a result of such frustration in the immediate tuation but also as the result of a back-

THE POSITION OF THE PERSON. BEING INSIDE AND OUTSIDE A REGION

Position, Neighboringness, and Locomotion. The determination of the position of the person within the life space is the first prerequisite for understanding behavior. His social position within or outside of

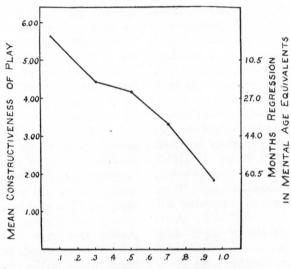

FIGURE 2. Decrease in constructiveness with a background of various degrees of frustration. (From "Studies in Topological and Vector Psychology: II. Frustration and Regression," by R. Barker, T. Dembo, and K. Lewin. *University of Iowa Studies in Child Welfare*, 1941, **18**, 166. By permission of the publisher.)

ground of frustration. Barker, Dembo, and Lewin (1941) have shown that the constructiveness of play of a five-and-one-half-year-old child may regress to the level of a three-and-one-half-year-old child as a result of a background of frustration. This is due to the fact that constructiveness of play is closely related to time perspective, the degree of differentiation within an organized unit of play, and the functional relation between irreality and reality. The amount of regression increases with the potency of the background of frustration (Figure 2).

various groups should be known; his position in regard to various activities, in regard to his goal regions, and in regard to physical areas should be determined. This is fundamental because the region in which the person is located determines (1) the quality of his immediate surroundings, (2) what kinds of regions are adjacent to the present region—that is, what possibilities the individual has for his next step—and (3) what step has the meaning of an action toward his goal and what step corresponds to an action away from his goal.

Most behavior can be conceived of as a

change of position—in other words, as a locomotion of the person. (The other cases of behavior are changes of structure.) In turn, every behavior changes the situation. We shall mention only a few examples of the effect of the region in which the person is located.

"Adaptation" to a Situation. A common phenomenon is what is usually called adaptation in the sense of "getting tuned to the present atmosphere." H. Anderson (1939) found that children of preschool age reacted to an aggressive approach with aggression, to a friendly approach in a friendly manner. Ronald Lippitt's (1940) study on democratic and autocratic atmospheres found similar adaptation of the children to the cultural atmosphere produced by the leader. J. R. P. French, Jr. (1944) found adaptation to group atmospheres in experiments with college freshmen. There are many indications from case studies that the tenseness of the mother easily affects the emotional state of the young child. There are indications that this occurs even during the first few months of life. It is a common observation that children who are learning bladder control may resume bed-wetting if exposed to the sound of running water.

The adaptation to the present region is frequently employed to make a child do something "against his will." A child of a few weeks may be induced to drink at the breast when he does not like to by keeping his head pressed to the breast in the position of feeding. Waring, Dwyer, and Junkin (1939) describe how the child and the adult both commonly use this technique for their own purposes when they differ about the desirability of eating a certain food. The child tries to avoid the pressure of the adult by leaving the eating-situation (for instance, by going to the toilet) or by making the adult leave the eating-situation psychologically (for instance, by starting conversations about noneating topics). On the other hand, the adult frequently uses one of two methods of coercion. He may lower the potency of the eating-situation (see later), and thus the resistance of the child, by "distracting his attention" from the eating (that is, by making the child enter a psychologically different region) and then slip in the food. Or he may heighten the potency of the eating-situation and of his own pressure and in this way induce the child to eat. In the latter case he frequently uses the "step-by-step method": having the child sit at the table, then putting the food on the spoon, and so on.

J. D. Frank (1944) has found, in an experiment with college students, that the step-by-step method is more efficient in coercing the person to eat than the attempt to make him go the whole way at one step. The effectiveness of the step-by-step method seems to be based on the gradual acceptance of the situation in which the person finds himself so that he resists less the making of the next step. A similar method is frequently used in domestic and international politics. People who are ready to fight against being pushed into a situation may accept the *fait accompli.*

Group Belongingness. Most social goals can be characterized as a wish to belong or not to belong to a certain group. This group may be a group of friends, an athletic organization, or a favorite subgroup within a larger group. It may be a group of only two persons, as with the friendship between mother and child. Belonging or not belonging to the group is equivalent to having a position inside or outside this group. This position determines the rights and duties of the individual and is decisive for the ideology of the individual.

The feeling of belonging to certain groups is a crucial factor for the feeling of security in children of minorities (Dollard, 1937; Lewin, 1940b). MacDonald (1940) found that the security of the child is greatly increased by the presence of the mother. The tendency to enter a certain group and to keep certain children in and feeling of group belongingness (as expressed, for instance, by the use of the term "we" instead of "I") is stronger in democratic than in autocratic clubs. In the autocratic atmosphere the larger group is actually composed of a number of sub-

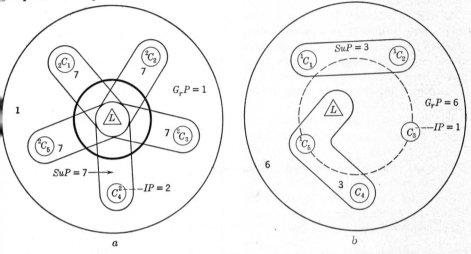

FIGURE 3. Subgrouping and potency of the group as a whole in (a) an autocratic and (b) a democratic setting. (Derived from "Studies in Topological and Vector Psychology: I. An Experimental Study of the Effect of Democratic and Authoritarian Group Atmospheres," by Ronald Lippitt. *University of Iowa Studies in Child Welfare*, 1940, **16**, 133–135. By permission of the publisher.)

In the autocratic situation two distinct social strata exist, a higher one containing the leader (L) and a lower containing the children (C). (The social distance between these strata is indicated by the heavy black circle.) In democracy the status differences are less marked (dotted line). In the autocratic setting distinct subgroups of two exist containing one child and the leader. Therefore, if the leader is taken away, no strong bond between the members remains. In democracy the subgrouping is varying and less rigid. The potency of the group as a whole (GrP) is higher there than in the autocratic setting where the potency of the individual goal (IP) and of the subgroup (SuP) is relatively higher.

other children out of that group plays a great rôle in the behavior of the nursery school child (Murphy, 1937; Rosemary Lippitt, 1940). This tendency is important for the children's gang (Shaw, 1933). Juveniles in the reformatory who have not fully accepted their belonging to the criminals have a tendency to name as their best friends persons outside the reformatory (Kephart, 1937).

Ronald Lippitt (1940) found that the groups containing the leader and one child each, whereas in the democratic group the group as a whole has a greater potency (Figure 3a and b). This is one of the reasons why children in these autocracies are more likely to be aggressive against their fellows although submissive to the leader. M. E. Wright (1940) found that friendship between two children increases in certain situations of frustration partly because these situations favor a group structure in which the children see themselves opposed to the adult.

Bavelas (1942a) found that the degree of cooperation between children in a day camp increased after their adult leaders were retrained from autocratic to democratic leadership techniques.

Moreno (1934) has developed a technique which permits an easy determination of group structure and group belongingness under certain circumstances. Other techniques have been developed, for instance, by Bogardus (1933) and by Ronald Lippitt (1940).

The difference between being inside and outside a region is basic not only for social groups but for all goal-seeking activities, and for the problem of frustration. Seeking a certain goal is equivalent to a tendency to enter a region outside of which one is located. We shall take up this question when discussing psychological forces.

CHANGE IN COGNITIVE STRUCTURE

The structure of the life space is the positional relations of its parts. Structure may be expressed by the topology of the life space. Locomotion of the person, that is, the change of his position from one region to another region, can be viewed as one type of change in structure. Other examples are those changes which occur during "insight" or learning. The infinite variety of changes in structure may be classified roughly into (1) an increase in differentiation of a region, that is, an increase in the number of subregions; (2) a combination of separated regions into one differentiated region; (3) a decrease in differentiation, that is, a decrease in the number of subregions within a region; (4) a breaking-up of a whole, that is, previously connected subparts of a region are separated into relatively independent regions; and (5) a restructuring, that is, a change

in pattern without increase or decrease of differentiation.

Detour. Insight. Restructuring of certain areas of the life space can be readily

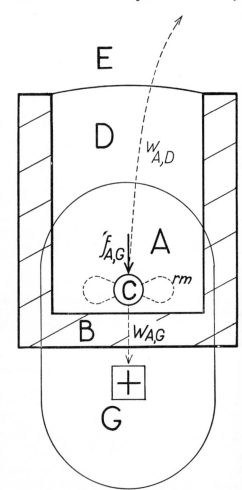

FIGURE 4. A simple detour problem as seen by the young child.

observed in the solution of detour problems. The basic questions can be illustrated by a simple example: A goal *G* (Figure 4) lies behind a U-shaped physical barrier *B*. The child *C*, of a mental age of one year (this may be a chronologically young child, or an older feeble-minded child) is likely to try to reach the goal by an action toward the barrier along the path $w_{A, G}$.[1] A child of five years, under the same circumstances, will have no difficulty. It will

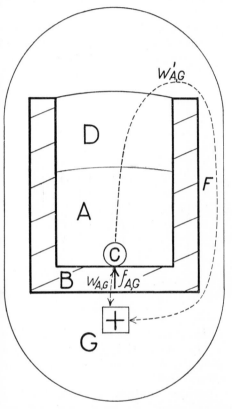

FIGURE 5. The detour problem represented in Figure 4 as seen by the older child.

reach the goal by way of a roundabout route along the path $w'_{A, G}$ (Figure 5). What are the difficulties of the younger child? Both children have the tendency to locomote from their present situation A toward the goal G. (As we shall see later, we can say there exists a psychological

[1] A fuller discussion of the problems of direction and path in psychology may be found in Lewin (1938).

force $f_{A, G}$ acting on the child in the direction from A toward G.)

We can understand the difference in difficulties if we consider what "direction toward G" means for both children. For the young child the direction from A to G, $d_{A, G}$, is equal to the direction toward the barrier B, $(d_{A, G} = d_{A, B})$. A movement from A to D along the path $w_{A, D}$ would have, for this child, the meaning of going away from G. In other words, the direction toward D, $d_{A, D}$, is opposite to the direction toward G, $d_{A, G}$ $(d_{A, D} = d_{\overline{A, G}})$. For the older child (Figure 5) the direction toward D, $d_{A, D}$, has not the character of being opposite to the direction but of being equal to the direction to G $(d_{A, D} = d_{A, G})$, because the step from A to D is seen by this child as a part of the roundabout route $w'_{A, G}$ toward G. The difference in the meaning of the direction $d_{A, G}$ toward G is due mainly to two facts: (1) For the younger child the immediate situation is less extended than for the older one (this is but one result of the fact that the life space of the younger child is smaller in many aspects than that of the older child). It includes only the regions A, B, and G (Figure 4). For the older child, a wider area is psychologically present, including, for instance, the areas D and F. As an effect of this difference in scope of the present situation the younger child sees the areas A and G separated by the impassable barrier B. For the older child, regions A and G are connected by way of passable regions D and F.

Directions in the psychological life space are defined by certain paths as a whole. The older child sees the step from A to D as a part of the path A, D, F, G toward G. The young child sees the step A, D as a part of the path A, E, that is, away from G. The difference in the cognitive structure of the situation for the young and older child leads, therefore, to a different meaning of the direction toward G and, accordingly, to a different locomotion resulting from the same tendencies of both children to reach G.

(2) For the young child, the path $w'_{A, G}$ simply does not exist psychologically. For the older child two paths toward G exist psychologically, namely, the roundabout route $w'_{A, G}$ and the blocked "direct" path $w_{A, G}$. The "direct" direction toward G can be interpreted, in this case, as the direction of looking toward G; the less "direct" direction as that of walking toward G. For the young child, "direction toward G" has not yet been differentiated into these two directions. (This is an example of the lesser degree of differentiation of the life space of the younger child.)

A two-year-old child placed in the same situation may at first have a cognitive structure corresponding to that of the younger child (Figure 4). After a few attempts the structure of the situation may change to that of the older child (Figure 5). These changes frequently occur as a sudden shift. They are an example of what has been called *insight* (Köhler, 1925).

Insight can always be viewed as a change in the cognitive structure of the situation. It frequently includes differentiation and restructuring in the sense of separating certain regions which have been connected and connecting regions which have been separated. For instance, to use a branch of a tree as a stick (Köhler, 1925) for reaching a goal behind a fence (Figure 6) it is necessary to see the branch br as a relatively separate unit instead of a part within the larger unit of the tree Tr. In addition, it is necessary to connect this branch br with the goal G behind the fence.

From the theory of insight in detour problems certain conclusions in regard to factors facilitating insight can be derived. Becoming emotional leads frequently to a narrowing-down of the psychologically existing area. A state of strong emotionality should, therefore, be detrimental to finding intellectual solutions (see p. 815). A distance sufficient to permit a survey of the larger situation helps in the solution of intellectual problems. Katona (1940) discusses the effect of various settings upon the change of the cognitive structure and the ability to find new solutions.

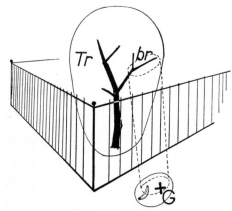

FIGURE 6. Problem solving. A case of change in cognitive structure.

The principles of change in cognitive structure discussed here are as applicable to social and mathematical problems as to physical problems.

Learning. Orientation. Learning is a popular term referring to such different processes as learning to like spinach, learning to walk, and learning French vocabularies, that is, problems of changes of goals or needs, changes of posture and muscular coordination, and changes in knowledge. Therefore, no one theory of learning is possible. Problems of change in goals will be discussed later. Insight is an example of learning in the sense of change of cognitive structure. Learning, in this sense, usually involves several of those types of structural changes which we have mentioned previously, combined with a change in the degree of organization.

A change in the direction of greater differentiation takes place, for instance, when a child gets oriented in a new surrounding. Being in an unknown surrounding is equivalent to being in a region which is unstructured in the double sense that neither the quality nor the subparts of the present region, nor the immediately neighboring regions, are determined. Orientation means the structurization of the unstructured region. In this way, direction within the life space becomes determined (Lewin, 1938). Orientation is a process which, on a smaller scale, shows significant parallels to the development of the life space of the young child.

An unstructured region usually has the same effect as an impassable obstacle. Being in unstructured surroundings leads to uncertainty of behavior because it is not clear whether a certain action will lead to or away from the goal. It is undetermined whether the neighboring regions are dangerous or friendly. Waring, Dwyer, and Junkin (1939) found that children during the meals of the first nursery school day were more ready to acquiesce to the advice of the adult than later on when they felt themselves to be on better-known ground for resisting.

The problem of learning is treated in detail in another chapter (Chapter 8). We shall add, therefore, but one remark about the relation between repetition and learning. Repetition of a certain activity may lead to differentiation of a previously undifferentiated region of the life space, and to unification of previously separated activities. This is frequently the case in motor learning. However, if continued long enough, repetition may have the opposite effect, namely, a breaking-up of the larger units of actions, a dedifferentiation, unlearning, and disorganization similar to that of primitivation or degeneration. These processes are typical of psychological satiation and oversatiation.

Force and Force Field

FORCE AND VALENCE

Resultant Force, Locomotion, and Force Field. The structure of the life space determines what locomotions are possible at a given time. What change actually occurs depends on the constellation of psychological forces. The construct *force* characterizes, for a given point of the life space, the direction and strength of the tendency to change. This construct does not imply any additional assumptions as to the "cause" of this tendency. The combination of a number of forces acting at the same point at a given time is called the *resultant force.* The relation between force and behavior can then be summed up in the following way: Whenever a resultant force (different from zero) exists, there is either a locomotion in the direction of that force or a change in cognitive structure equivalent to this locomotion. The reverse also holds; namely, whenever a locomotion or change of structure exists, resultant forces exist in that direction.[1]

Psychological forces correspond to a relation between at least two regions of the life space. A simple example is the force $f_{A, G}$ acting on a child C in the direction toward a goal G (Figure 7). This force depends upon the state of the child C, particularly upon the state of his needs, and upon the nature of the region G. If the region G (which may represent an activity, a social position, an object, or any other possible goal) is attractive to the person,

[1] We are not discussing here the complicated problems of the alien factors, that is, those physical and social factors which may be viewed as the boundary conditions of the life space (Lewin, 1936a; 1943; 1944). We keep within the realm of psychology.

it is said to have a positive valence $(Va(G) > 0)$.

Such a valence corresponds to a field of forces which has the structure of a positive central field (Figure 7). If no other valences existed, the person located in any region A, B, D, E ... would always try to move in the direction toward G. In other words, the valence G corresponds to a force $f_{A, G}, f_{B, G}, f_{D, G}$, etc. The observation of behavior permits not only the

bend his head toward the goal. The older, more differentiated child is likely to react in a more "controlled" way with only a part of the body.

Strength of Force and Distance of Valence. We shall discuss later what factors determine a change of valence. First, let us ask what effect a given valence, or distribution of valences, has on behavior. The strength of the force toward or away from a valence depends upon the strength of

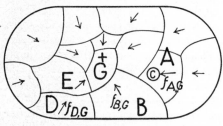

FIGURE 7. A positive central field of forces corresponding to a positive valence.

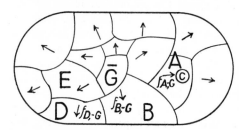

FIGURE 8. A negative central field of forces corresponding to a negative valence.

determination of conscious goals but also of "unconscious goals," as Freud uses the term.

If the person is repulsed, we speak of a negative valence of G ($Va(G) > 0$), corresponding to a negative central field (Figure 8), which is composed of forces $f_{A, -G}$, $f_{B, -G}, f_{D, -G}$, etc., away from G.

The effect of forces may be observed from earliest infancy: Movements toward or away from the breast during feeding are noted in the first weeks of life. Looking toward an object (fixation) is another example of directed action. Later on, there is grasping. More elaborate directed actions presuppose a correspondingly higher differentiation of the life space. In a young child a force is more likely to affect directly every part of the child than it is at a later age. For instance, the child of six months reaching out for a toy may move both arms and legs in this direction (Figure 9). He may open his mouth and

that valence and the psychological distance $(e_{A, G})$ between the person and the valence $[f_{A, G} = F(Va(G), e_{A, G})]$.

Fajans (1933) found that the persistence of children (ages 1 to 6 years) trying to reach a goal from various physical distances (8 to 100 cm.) increases with decreasing distance. This may mean that, with increasing distance, either the force decreases or the child sees more quickly that the barrier is insurmountable. If the first factor is dominant, emotional tension should decrease with distance (see p. 815). Fajans found this to be true only for the infants. For the older children, the second factor seems to be dominant, probably because these children view the obstacle as dependent upon the will of the experimenter rather than as physical distance.

In some experiments with rats, the velocity of running toward a goal was found to increase with decreasing distance (Hull, 1932). H. F. Wright (1937) found no consistent indication of such a speed gradient in experiments where nursery school children pulled the goal (a marble) toward themselves. This indicates that the relation between strength of force and bodily locomotion is rather complicated in psychology and that physical and psychological distance may be related quite differently under different circumstances.

FIGURE 9. Action in the direction of a positive valence. (From *Dynamic Theory of Personality*, by K. Lewin. New York: McGraw-Hill, 1935, 82. By permission of the publisher.)

As a particular example, the situation may be mentioned where the person "nearly" reaches a goal. In animals (Hull, 1932), as in children (H. F. Wright, 1937), a marked slowing-down has been observed at the last section before the goal is reached. If the force were related simply to the physical distance, there should be no sudden drop in velocity at this point. Obviously, after the individual is inside the goal region, the force $f_{A, G}$ can no longer have the direction "toward" the goal region but changes to a force $f_{G, G}$, which properly has to be interpreted as a tendency to resist being forced out of the goal region (for details see Lewin, 1938). Being in the goal region is frequently not equivalent to consumption of, or to bodily contact with, the goal, but it is equivalent to having the goal in one's power, to being sure of it. This is probably the reason for the slowing-down in the last section before the goal. This also explains the frequent "decrease of interest" after possession, illustrated by the following example. A nine-month-old child reaches out for two rattles lying before him. When he gets one he does not begin to play but is interested only in the rattle he does not have.

An example of a decrease of the strength of a force with the distance from the negative valence can be found in certain eating-situations (Lewin, 1938, p. 117). For a child who dislikes his spinach, the act of eating might consist of a series of relatively separate steps, such as putting the hand on the table, taking the spoon, putting food on the spoon, etc. (Figure 10a). The strength of the force away from eating the disagreeable food and, therefore, the resistance against making the next step increases with the nearness of the step to the actual eating (Re). After the child starts chewing, the structure of the situation in regard to this bite usually is fundamentally changed, as shown in Figure 10b. Instead of resisting, the child tries to finish the bite. This is an example of how the direction and strength of the forces acting on the person depend upon the region in which the person is located.

The change of the strength of the force with the distance to the valence is different for positive and for negative valences. The latter usually diminishes much faster (see later, Figure 15). The amount of decrease depends also upon the nature of the region which has a positive or negative valence. It is different, for example, in case of a dangerous animal which can move about, from the amount in case of an immovable unpleasant object.

The effect of temporal distance on the strength of the force seems to parallel that of physical distance in some respects. E Katz (1938), in experiments with nursery school children, found that the frequency of resumption of interrupted tasks increases with the nearness of the interruption to the completion of the task, but that it drops for interruptions very close to the end. Institutionalized adolescents,

The restraining forces, just as the driving forces, are due to a relation between two regions of the life space, namely, the nature of the barrier region and the "ability" of the individual. The same social or physical obstacle corresponds, therefore, to different restraining forces for different individuals.

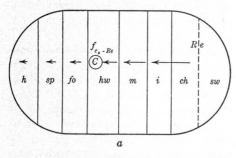
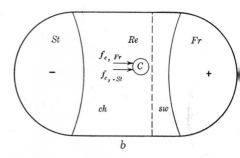

$$a \qquad\qquad\qquad b$$

FIGURE 10. (a) Eating situation in case of disliked food. (b) Change of direction of forces after the child started real eating. (From "The Conceptual Representation and Measurement of Psychological Forces," by K. Lewin. *Contributions to Psychological Theory*, 1938, **1**, 117. By permission of the Duke University Press, publisher.)

(a) C, child; Re, real eating; h, putting hand on table; sp, taking spoon; fo, putting food on spoon; hw, bring spoon halfway to mouth; m, bringing spoon to mouth; i, taking food into mouth; ch, chewing; sw, swallowing. Eating has a negative valence; the force away from eating $f_{C,-Re}$ increases stepwise with the decrease of distance between C and Re.

(b) C, child; Re, real eating; St, struggle with adults; Fr, freedom; $f_{C,Fr}$ force in the direction of freedom; $f_{C,-St}$ force away from struggle.

like other prisoners, may attempt to escape shortly before they are eligible for release. Frequently they become rebellious (Farber, 1944). Their emotional tension is heightened by the temporal nearness of the goal.

TYPE OF FORCES

Driving and Restraining Forces. The forces toward a positive, or away from a negative, valence can be called *driving forces.* They lead to locomotion. These locomotions might be hindered by physical or social obstacles. Such barriers correspond to *restraining forces* (Lewin, 1938). Restraining forces, as such, do not lead to locomotion, but they do influence the effect of driving forces.

Induced Forces, Forces Corresponding to Own Needs and Impersonal Forces. Forces may correspond to a person's own needs. For instance, the child may wish to go to the movie or to eat certain food. Many psychological forces acting on a child do not, however, correspond to his own wishes but to the wish of another person, for instance, of the mother. These forces in the life space of the child can be called *induced forces,* and the corresponding positive or negative valence "induced valence." (A force acting on the child in the direction to the goal G induced by the mother M may be written $i^M f_{C,G}.$)

There are forces which psychologically correspond neither to the own wish of the child nor the wish of another person, but have, for the child, the character of something "impersonal," a matter-of-fact demand. We call them *impersonal forces*. It is of great importance for the reaction of the child and for the atmosphere of the situation whether an impersonal request or the personal will of another individual is dominant.

Point of Application. Forces may act on any part of the life space. Frequently, the point of application is that region of the life space which corresponds to the own person. The child may, however, experience that the "doll wants to go to bed," or that "another child wants a certain toy." In these cases the points of application of the forces are regions in the life space of a child other than his own person. Such cases are most common and play an important part, for instance, in the problems of altruism.

CONFLICT SITUATIONS

Definition of Conflict. A conflict situation can be defined as a situation where forces acting on the person are opposite in direction and about equal in strength. In regard to driving forces three cases are possible: The person may be located between two positive valences, between two negative valences, or a positive and negative valence may lie in the same direction. There may be, also, conflicts between driving and restraining forces. Finally, there may be conflicts between own forces and various combinations of induced and impersonal forces. The effect and the development of conflicts vary with these different constellations, although all conflicts have certain properties in common.

Conflicts between Driving Forces. What is usually called a *choice* means that a person is located between two positive or negative valences which are mutually exclusive. The child has to choose, for example, between going on a picnic (G^1, Figure 11a) and playing (G^2) with his comrades. (Figure 11 and some of the later figures represent situations where the physical directions and distances are sufficiently important psychologically to be used as frames of reference for the life space. One can speak in these cases of quasi-physical fields.) An example of a child standing between two negative valences is a situation in which punishment (G^1) is threatened if he does not do a certain disagreeable task (G^2, Figure 11b). Figure 11a and b represents the corresponding force fields. If the child is located at A and the strength of the valences are equal, he will be exposed to forces which are equal in strength but opposite in direction. In the first example, the opposing forces f_{A, G^1} and f_{A, G^2} are directed toward the picnic and play. In the second example, the opposing forces $f_{A, -G^1}$ and $f_{A, -G^2}$ are directed away from the task and the punishment.

From these force fields certain differences of behavior can be derived. In the case of two negative valences, there is a resultant force in the direction of "leaving the field" altogether. If the two negative valences are very great, the child may run away from home, or try to avoid the issue. To be effective, the threat of punishment has to include the creation of a set-up which prohibits this avoidance (Lewin, 1935), that is, the creation of a prisonlike situation, where barriers B prohibit leaving the situation in any other way than by facing the task T or the punishment P (Figure 12). If there is a choice between two positive valences, no force in the direction of leaving the field exists. Instead, the child will try to reach both goals if possible.

An example of a conflict due to the presence of a negative and a positive valence is the promise of reward for doing a disagreeable task (Figure 13). Here a conflict is brought about by the opposition of the force $f_{A,\,R}$ toward the reward R and the force $f_{A,\,-T}$ away from the disagreeable activity T. The structure of the situation is similar to that characteristic of a

The necessity for setting up a barrier around the reward indicates one of the differences between this method of making the child perform a disagreeable activity T and the methods which try to change the negative valence of T itself into a posi-

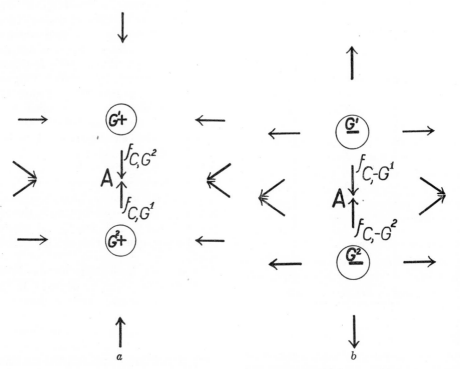

FIGURE 11. (a) Force field corresponding to two positive valences. (b) Force field corresponding to two negative valences.

detour problem. Indeed, the child frequently tries to reach the reward R along a roundabout route $w_{A,\,C,\,R}$ without passing through the disagreeable activity. The reward will be effective only if all other paths to R are blocked by an impassable barrier B which permits entrance to R only by way of T. The barriers in this case, as in the case of the threat of punishment (Figure 12), are usually social in nature: The child knows that the adult will prevent certain actions by social force.

tive one. A "change of interest" in T may be brought about by imbedding the activity T (for instance, the disliked figuring) into a different setting (for instance, into playing store), so that the meaning, and consequently the valence, of T is changed for the child. Such a method makes the creation of a barrier unnecessary and secures spontaneous actions of the child toward the previously disliked activity as a result of the newly created positive central field.

Another example of a conflict between a positive and a negative valence can be observed in a setting where a child of three years is trying to seize a toy swan S from the waves W on the seashore (Figure 14). Following the forces $f_{C, S}$, the child will

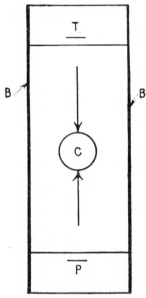

FIGURE 12. Threat of punishment. (From *Dynamic Theory of Personality*, by K. Lewin. New York: McGraw-Hill, 1935, 91. By permission of the publisher.)

T, disagreeable task; *P*, threat of punishment; *C*, child; *B*, barrier preventing the child from leaving the situation through other regions than *T* or *P*.

approach the swan. If, however, he comes too close to the waves W, the force away from the waves $f_{C, -W}$ may be greater than those toward the swan. In this case the child will retreat. The force corresponding to the negative valence of the waves decreases rather rapidly with the increasing distance because of the limited range of the effect of the waves (Figure 15). The forces corresponding to the positive valence of the swan diminish much

more slowly with the distance. There exists, therefore, an equilibrium between the opposing forces at point E where their strengths are equal ($f_{E, S} = f_{E, -W}$). The children may be observed wavering around this point of equilibrium until one of these forces becomes dominant as a result of changes of circumstances or of a decision. In this example the force field corresponding to the swan is a positive cen-

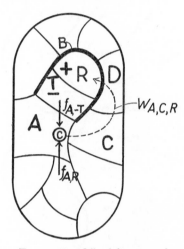

FIGURE 13. Offer of a reward.

tral field; the forces corresponding to the waves have a direction perpendicular to the shore.

Conflicts between Driving and Restraining Forces. A most common type of conflict arises when a child is prevented from reaching a goal G by a barrier B. Two basic cases may be distinguished: (1) the child is surrounded by a barrier with the goal outside (Figure 12); (2) the goal is surrounded by a barrier with the child outside (Figure 16). The first case is a prison-like situation which gives the child little space of free movement. In the second case, the child is free except in regard to the region G. Each of these cases leads to specific reactions (Lewin, 1935). We shall now discuss in greater detail a sequence of behavior typical of the second case.

At first, a certain amount of change in structure usually occurs: The child tries to investigate the nature of the obstacle with the purpose of finding a sector s within the barrier which will permit passage. Such a

barrier at first as a physical obstacle (as too great a physical distance). For the children above two years, after some time the social aspect of the situation became clear and led to social approaches toward the goal (the children asked the adult for help).

The barrier acquires a negative valence

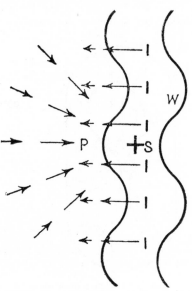

FIGURE 14. Force field in a conflict resulting from a positive and negative valence. (From *Dynamic Theory of Personality*, by K. Lewin. New York: McGraw-Hill, 1935, 92. By permission of the publisher.)

S, attractive toy; *W,* waves perceived as dangerous; *P,* point of equilibrium.

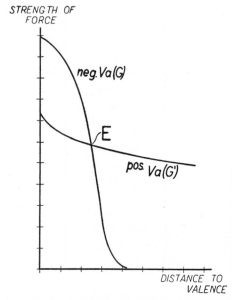

FIGURE 15. Schematic representation of the change of the strength of a force with the distance to a positive and a negative valence.

change in cognitive structure is similar to that observed in detour problems. It is very common for a child to be in situations where an obstacle could be overcome with the help of an adult. In these situations the barrier is composed of at least two sectors, one corresponding to the physical obstacle (*ph,* Figure 16), the other to the social obstacle (*sl*). In the experiment of Fajans, mentioned above, practically all children conceived of the

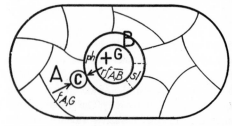

FIGURE 16. Conflict between driving and restraining forces in the case of a physical and social obstacle to a goal.

$f_{A,G'}$ driving force; $rf_{\overline{A,B'}}$ restraining force; *ph,* physical sector of the barrier (*B*); *sl,* social sector of the barrier.

for the child after a number of unsuccessful attempts to cross it. This change is equivalent to a change in the force field from the structure represented in Figure 17 to that of Figure 18. If the barrier is an obstacle but has no negative valence, the corresponding force field does not reach much beyond the barrier (Figure 17). The

Fajans (1933) has given a detailed report about the form and sequence of events in such a situation. Usually the child leaves the field at first only temporarily. After some time, the forces toward the goal again become greater than the forces away from the barrier, and the child returns. If the new attempts are still unsuccessful,

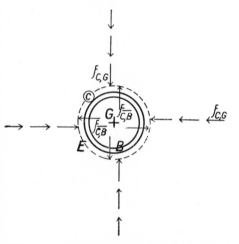

FIGURE 17. Line of equilibrium between driving and restraining forces in case of a circular barrier.

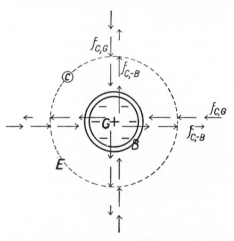

FIGURE 18. Line of equilibrium after the barrier has acquired a negative valence.

restraining forces $rf_{c,B}$ merely hinder a locomotion in the direction of the force $f_{c,B}$ without driving the person away from B. The line of equilibrium E between driving and restraining forces lies, therefore, close to the barrier region. If, after failure, the barrier acquires a negative valence, the corresponding negative central force field will reach out farther (Figure 18) so that the line of equilibrium E between the force $f_{c,G}$ toward the goal and the force $f_{c,-B}$ away from the barrier is located at a greater distance.

With increasing failure, the negative valence tends to increase. This enlarges the distance between the line of equilibrium and the barrier until the child leaves the field altogether.

the negative valence increases again until the child leaves. On the average, these later attempts show less duration. Finally, the child leaves the field permanently; he gives up. Barker, Dembo, and Lewin (1941) report similar sequences of behavior in children between two and six years in a slightly different setting of frustration.

Active children, on the average, are more persistent than passive ones (Fajans, 1933). Some active children, however, are particularly quick to leave the situation, probably because they decide soon that the barrier is impassable. A state of equilibrium in such a conflict can lead to passive, gesturelike action toward the goal: The child stays below the goal with his arm erect but he makes no actual attempts to reach it. Children frequently leave the field psychologically without leaving the room bodily. They may try to enter a different activity, may daydream, or start self-manipulation with their clothes or their body (Fajans, 1933; Sliosberg, 1934; Mac-Donald, 1940).

A conflict between driving and restraining forces may also occur if the child is prevented by an obstacle from leaving the field of a negative valence. Such a situation exists, for instance, if a child is oversatiated with an activity but prevented from leaving it, or in any other prison-like situation. The sequence of behavior is, in many respects, similar to that discussed above. Attempts to leave are followed by the giving-up of such attempts as the result of the relation between the strength of the force $f_{A, -A}$ away from the region A and the increasing negative valence of the barrier. Frequently a state of high emotional tension results.

Conflicts between Own and Induced Forces. Every one of the conflict situations discussed above might be due to the opposition of two forces corresponding to the child's own needs, to the opposition of two induced forces, or to the opposition between an own and an induced force. Many effects of conflict situations are independent of these differences. Certain effects, however, are typical of conflicts between own and induced forces.

A force induced by a person P on a child C can be viewed as the result of the power field of that person over the child (Figure 19). The person having power over the child is able to induce positive and negative valences by giving orders. By a restraining command, he can change the character of a region which would be passable according to the child's own ability into an impassable barrier. In other words, "the power of P over C" means that P is able to create induced driving or restraining forces $^{iP}f_{C, G}$ which correspond to P's will.

A conflict between own and induced forces always permits at least one other solution in addition to those discussed above: The child may attempt to undermine the power of the other person, at least in the area of conflict. The tendency of a conflict between own and induced

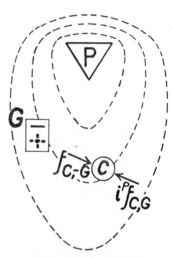

FIGURE 19. Power field.

P, stranger; C, child; G, activity having positive valence for the child and an induced negative valence; f_{C-G}, own force away from G; $^{iP}f_{C,G}$, force induced by P in the direction of G. ———, lines corresponding to equal strength of power field.

forces to lead to fights has been observed by Waring, Dwyer, and Junkin (1939) in nursery school children in an eating-situation. Dembo (1931) and J. D. Frank (1944) have observed similar tendencies in students. M. E. Wright (1940) found an increasing aggression against the experimenter in pairs of nursery school children in a setting of frustration induced by the experimenter. The children showed greater cooperation among themselves. This might be interpreted as due partly to the tendency to increase their own power relative to the power of the experimenter. Lewin, Lippitt, and White (1939) found a strong endency toward aggression in autocratic atmospheres which are dominated much more by induced forces than by forces coresponding to the own needs of the children. This aggressiveness, however, was usually not directed against the supreme powers of the leader but diverted toward their fellows or toward material objects. If the suppressive power of the leader is too great, even this aggression ceases.

EMOTIONAL TENSION AND RESTLESSNESS

Emotional Tension and Strength of Conflict. If two opposing forces, $f_{A, G}$ and $f_{A, D}$ (Figure 20a and b), are equal in strength the resultant force will be zero, independent of the absolute strength of the forces. As far as changes in position are concerned, therefore, no difference should exist in the effect of conflicts between weak and between strong forces. Actually, the state of the person is quite different in a weak and in a strong conflict. One of the main differences is the intensity of emotional tension (*et*), which seems to be a function of the strength of the opposing forces $[et = F(|f_{A, G}|)]$ (Sears and Sears, 1940). As mentioned above, greater emotionality is found in infants if the distance to an inaccessible goal is small than if it is larger. This is one of the reasons why increasing incentives favor the solution of detour and other intellectual problems only up to a certain intensity level. Above this level, however, increasing the forces to the goal makes the necessary restructurization more difficult, partly because the person has to move against stronger forces, partly because the resultant emotionality leads to primitivation (regression). Barker, Dembo, and Lewin (1941) found that the frequency of negative emotional behavior increased with the intensity of frustration. The same holds for the amount of regression as measured by the constructiveness of play (Figure 2).

The Form of Restless Movement. One of the simplest expressions of emotionality is restless movements, movements which are not directed to a certain goal but are merely an expression of tension. (Actually, all combinations of undirected expression, such as restlessness and purposeless behavior, occur [Dembo, 1931].) Irwin (1932) found that general activity as meas-

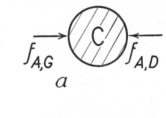

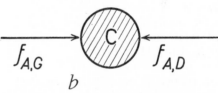

FIGURE 20. Emotional tension in case of (*a*) weak conflict and (*b*) strong conflict.

ured by the stabilimeter increases in infants with the time after the last feeding. This indicates that the amount of undirected activity is a good measurement for the state of tension accompanying hunger at that age level.

Restless movements are usually perpendicular to the direction of the force to the goal, or, more generally, they proceed as much as possible along the line of equilibrium. In the case of the six-month-old child reaching to the goal (Figure 9), restless movements of his arms and legs occur perpendicular to the direction of the goal. Behind a U-shaped barrier (Figure 4), the restless movements are parallel to the barrier along the line *rm*. In a constellation corresponding to Figure 17 or 18 the restless movements will follow the line *E*. This is verified in a situation where a one-and-one-half-year-old child tries to reach a toy *G* behind a circular physical barrier *B*. The restless movements of the child take the form of circling around that barrier. (For details see Lewin, 1938.)

The restless movement can be understood as a tendency to move away from the present situation, that is, as a movement corresponding to a force $f_{A, -A}$.

Overlapping Situations

OVERLAPPING SITUATIONS DEFINED. RELATIVE POTENCY

Frequently the person finds himself at the same time in more than one situation. The simplest example is that of divided attention: A child in the classroom listens to the teacher but also thinks about the ball game after school. The amount to which the child is involved in either of these two situations, S^1 and S^2, is called their relative potency, $Po(S^1)$ and $Po(S^2)$.

The effect a situation has on behavior depends upon the potency of that situation. In particular, the effect a force has on behavior is proportional to the potency of the related situation.

OVERLAPPING ACTIVITIES

Barker, Dembo, and Lewin (1941) speak of secondary play, as distinguished from primary play, when the child does not give his full attention to play. The constructiveness of secondary play is decisively below that of primary play. In experiments about psychological satiation (Karsten, 1928; Kounin, 1939), a person who is supposed to do an activity over and over again tends to perform the repetition as a secondary activity on a peripheral level. Activities such as writing may be considered as an overlapping of two activities, namely, (1) conveying a certain meaning, (2) writing symbols. The first has

the nature of a steadily progressing action, the second that of a repetition. The velocity of becoming satiated depends upon the relative potency of the repetitive aspect of the activity. Writing a letter, therefore, may lead more quickly to satiation in a child for whom writing is more difficult. Similarly, walking or other activities which usually have very low potency for the adult may soon lead to satiation in the child (see p. 825).

DECISION

A situation of choice can be viewed as an overlapping situation. The person be-

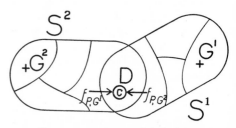

FIGURE 21. State of indecision.

S^1 and S^2, the two possibilities with the corresponding goals G^1 and G^2; *D*, a region of making a decision.

ing in the process of making a decision *D* (Figure 21) usually alternates between seeing himself in a future situation corresponding to the one and to the other possibility (S^1 and S^2). In other words, the potency of the various possibilities fluctuates. When a decision is reached, one of these situations acquires the dominant potency permanently. In a choice between activities of different degrees of difficulty, the decision is influenced by the probability of success or failure on each task. Escalona (1940) has shown that this probability is equivalent to the potency of the corresponding future situation.

The decision time increases also, the more the opposing forces are equal in strength (Barker, 1942). B. A. Wright (1942a, 1942b) found, in a study of altruistic and egoistic choices, that eight-year-old children whose choices were all either altruistic or egoistic arrived at a decision more quickly than those who made sometimes the one type of choice and sometimes the other (Figure 22). Cartwright (1941), in experiments on discrimination of figures or of meaning, found the decision time to be longest if the forces in opposite directions were equal. Recently the theory has been elaborated and quantified by Cartwright and Festinger (1943).

Decision time also increases with the importance of the decision (the valence of the goals). Jucknat (1937), in a study of the level of aspiration with children, and Barker (1942), in a study of choices between more or less agreeable or disagreeable foods, found that the choice time increases with the intensity of the conflict.

The decision time is longer in choices between two negative than between two positive valences (Barker, 1942). This latter fact derives from the different equilibria existing in the different constellations of forces (Lewin, 1938). Decision time shows great individual variations. Extreme decision-retardation is typical of certain types of depression (Escalona, 1940; Deri, 1943).

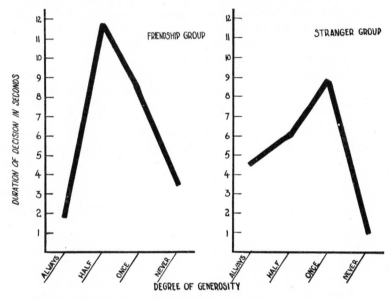

FIGURE 22. Time of decision in various degrees of conflict. (Derived from "Altruism in Children and the Perceived Conduct of Others," by B. A. Wright. *Journal of Abnormal and Social Psychology*, 1942, **37**, 218–233.)

IMMEDIATE SITUATION AND BACKGROUND

The influence which the background of a situation has on behavior can be understood as an overlapping of an immediate situation and of the situation at large (Barker, Dembo, Lewin, 1941). A background of frustration decreases constructiveness of play even if the play itself is not hampered from the outside. The amount of regression increases with increasing potency of the background of frustration (Figure 2).

Sheffield (1937) and others report cases where school work was greatly changed by a change of the home background.

THE EFFECT OF THE GROUP ON THE INDIVIDUAL. THE MARGINAL CHILD

The effect of group belongingness on the behavior of an individual can be viewed as the result of an overlapping situation: One situation corresponds to the child's own needs and goals; the other, to the goals, rules, and values which exist for him as a group member. Adaptation of an individual to the group depends upon the avoidance of too great a conflict between the two sets of forces (Lewin, 1938).

A child usually belongs to a great number of groups, such as his family, the school, the church, friends. Within the family he may belong to a subgroup containing him and his closest sibling. The effect of the various groups, particularly whether or not the child is ruled by the ideology and values of the one or the other, depends on the relative potency of these groups at that time. Schanck (1932) has found that the influence of public or private morale is different at home and in the church. In school children, the tendency to cheat changes with the social setting (Hartshorne and May, 1929).

Many conflicts in childhood are due to forces corresponding to the various groups to which the child belongs. Such conflicts are particularly important for children in marginal positions, that is, for children who are standing on the boundary between two groups. One example is the adolescent who no longer wants to belong to the children's group but who is not yet fully accepted by the adults. Uncertainty of the ground on which the child stands leads to an alternation between the values of the one and of the other group, to a state of emotional tension, and to a frequent fluctuation between overaggressiveness and over-timidity (Lewin, 1939). The degree to which such adolescent behavior is shown depends upon the degree to which children and adolescents are treated as separate groups in that culture (Benedict, 1934; Reuter, 1937).

A similar effect of marginality can be observed in regard to other types of groups. Emotional tension is high in inmates of reformatory schools as a result of the marginal position of these children between the criminal and the "honest citizen" (Kephart, 1937). Emotional tension diminishes when the child accepts his belongingness to a definite group. A decrease in emotionality was observed in those inmates who accepted their belonging to the criminal class. Marginality is an important problem for the crippled or the otherwise handicapped child (Bartõs, 1932; Dresdner, 1933). Shaw et al. (1929) have shown the influence of residing in marginal sections of a city on criminality of children. Marginality raises important problems for children belonging to minority groups, such as Negroes or Jews (Lewin, 1940b; Frazier 1940). The effect, in many respects, is similar to that typical of the adolescent.

FACTORS DETERMINING THE FIELD AND ITS CHANGE

In the preceding section we have discussed the results of the cognitive structure and of certain constellations of forces on behavior. We shall now discuss factors which determine the constellation of forces. This second problem is equivalent to the question of how one part or aspect of the life space depends upon other parts or aspects. Of course, both problems are interrelated since any behavior resulting from a certain situation alters the situation to some degree. We shall here limit our discussion to problems related to needs. They refer to the relation between the state of

hat region in the life space which repre-
ents the person and the psychological
nvironment.

Need, Force Fields, and Cognitive Structure

NEED AND VALENCE

During the development of the child,
1eeds are constantly changing in intensity
1nd degree of differentiation. The so-called
rises of development are periods of par-
icularly important or particularly quick
hanges in needs (Dimock, 1937; Bühler,
1939). In addition, there is a change of
1eeds in briefer periods corresponding to
he states of hunger, satiation, and over-
atiation.

Needs have the character of "organizing"
)ehavior. One can distinguish a hierarchy
)f needs (Allport, 1937; Murray, 1938;
3arker, Dembo, Lewin, 1941). One need
)r a combination of several needs may set
1p derived needs (quasi-needs) equivalent
'o specific intentions.

Needs are closely related to valences.
Vhat valence a certain object or activity
$[Va(G)]$ has depends partly upon the na-
ure of that activity (G), and partly upon
he state of the needs $[t(G)]$ of the per-
on at that time $[Va(G) = F(G, t(G))]$.
An increase in the intensity of need (for
nstance, the need for recreation) leads
o an increase of the positive valence of
:ertain activities (such as going to the
novies or reading a book) and to an in-
:rease in the negative valence of certain
)ther activities (such as doing hard work).
Any statement regarding change of needs
:an be expressed by a statement about cer-
:ain positive and negative valences.

As a result of the increase in positive
valence which accompanies the state of
1unger of a particular need, areas of activ-
ties which are negative or on a zero level

when the need is satiated acquire a positive
valence. The hungrier person is usually
satisfied with poorer food (D. Katz, 1937).

The valence of an activity is related to
its consummatory value for satisfying the
need. Not all activities, however, which
have positive valence also have satisfaction
value in case of consumption; on the other
hand, activities with no or even negative
valence may have satisfaction value. Valence and satisfaction value should, therefore, be clearly distinguished. It is surprising how frequently valence and value
actually go hand in hand. D. Katz (1937)
reported an increase in the valence of foods
which contain minerals for which deficiencies had been established in chickens.
When the deficiency was removed the
valence again decreased. Similar results
have been claimed for children. Experience may change the valence as well as
the meaning which an activity has for the
child. The child has to make many important decisions (for instance, in regard
to occupation) on the basis of the valence
of an activity rather than on the basis of
clear knowledge of its satisfaction value.

NEED AND COGNITIVE STRUCTURE

The cognitive structure of the life space
is influenced by the state of the needs.
Murray (1938) found that faces of other
people appear more malicious to children
in a state of fear than normally. Stern
and MacDonald (1937) found that pictures
without definite meanings will be seen according to the mood of the child.

The effect which a need has on the structure of the life space depends upon the
intensity of the need and upon the fluidity
of the related areas of the life space.
Dembo (1931) found hallucination-like wish
fulfillments in highly emotional situations.
If the visual field is sufficiently fluid, its

structure may be considerably changed by intention (quasi-need) (Gottschaldt, 1926; Lewin, 1935). Levels of irreality, being more fluid than the level of reality, are, consequently, more easily influenced by both wishes and fears. This is the reason why dreams and daydreams mirror the needs of the child. This also explains why, in fantasy and dreams, needs may come into the open which are kept from "public life" by social taboos.

Sliosberg (1934) has shown that the meaning of objects and events is more fluid in *play* than in nonplay situations. The so-called play technique (Homburger, 1937; Erikson, 1940) and other projective methods (Murray, 1938) make use of this greater flexibility of play to study the deeper desires and suppressed wishes of children. (It should be mentioned, however, that play frequently mirrors the actual home situation rather than the wishes and fears of the child.)

Needs affect the cognitive structure not only of the psychological present but, even more, of the psychological future and past. This is particularly important for the level of aspiration (see p. 830). If the effect of the needs on the psychological future is particularly great, one speaks of an unrealistic person. One form of the influence of needs on the structure of the psychological past is called *rationalization;* other forms are *repression* and *lying.* The lying of the child in the first years of life seems frequently to have the nature of an actual change of the psychological past in line with the child's needs.

There are great individual differences (Davidson and Klopfer, 1938) in the way in which a child sees ink blots (Rorschach test). Unstable problem children are more likely to be carried away by wishes and fears than the average child as a result of their greater fluidity.

Satisfying a Need

A need may be satisfied either by reaching the desired goal or by reaching a substitute goal.

THE EFFECT OF SATISFIED AND UNSATISFIED NEEDS. SATISFACTION THROUGH REACHING THE ORIGINAL GOAL

The intention to carry out a certain action is equivalent to the creation of a quasi-need (Lewin, 1935). As long as that need is not satisfied, a force corresponding to the valence of the goal region should exist and lead to an action in the direction of that goal (Lewin, 1940a).

Ovsiankina (1928) studied the resumption of interrupted activities. She found a high tendency to resume the task (about 80 per cent) if the inner goal of the person was not reached. In some cases, after resumption, the person stopped as soon as a substitute satisfaction was reached. The frequency of resumption depends upon the nature of the task (it is high for tasks with a definite end as against continuous tasks) and upon the attitude (need) of the subject. Children between nine and eleven showed a percentage of resumption (86 per cent) similar to that of adults. Children who had the attitude of being examined and of strict obedience showed little resumption owing to the lack of involvement; they were governed mainly by induced forces (see p. 808). E. Katz (1938), in a study of resumption of interrupted activities on nursery school children, found practically the same frequency of resumption as Ovsiankina (88 per cent). Differences of intelligence, within the normal range, did not affect the resumption significantly.

The tendency to resume is not diminished if the unfinished work is out of sight (Ovsiankina, 1928). On the other hand, the presence of uncompleted work of anther person does not lead (or extremely seldom leads) to spontaneous completion in adults (Ovsiankina, 1928) or in children (Adler and Kounin, 1939). Both results indicate that the state of the need of the child is decisive for resumption. Such a need might be instigated if the child becomes sufficiently involved through watching another person doing the work. (The results of Rosenzweig [1933] with children of various ages differ somewhat from those of E. Katz and Adler and Kounin. These differences are probably due to factors peculiar to his situation.)

The forces in the direction of the goal which correspond to a need can be observed in thinking as well as in action. Zeigarnik (1927) studied the effect of quasi-needs on the tendency to recall. She found the quotient of the recollection of uncompleted to completed tasks to be 1.9 for adults and 2.5 for children between five and ten years old. This quotient, like the frequency of resumption, depends on the degree of involvement of the subject. The difference between children and adults is probably due to a greater involvement of the children in the particular type of activity and to a more immediate dependence of thinking upon the valences. Zeigarnik found that certain types of unintelligent children are particularly persistent in their tendency to come back to the unfinished tasks, whereas easily distractable children show a low quotient.

Marrow (1938) investigated the effect of praise and condemnation in a competitive situation on the Zeigarnik quotient. He found that in both cases it rises. This indicates that the strength of the force in the direction of spontaneous recollection is a function of the intensity of the need. When the subject was told that he would be interrupted as soon as the experimenter saw that he could complete the activity successfully, the quotient was slightly be-

low one. The findings of Marrow and Zeigarnik show that the decisive factor for the release of the need tension is the reaching of the individual's goal rather than the finishing of the work as such. Experiments by Schlote (1930), Sandvoss (1933), and Pachauri (1935) generally substantiate Zeigarnik's findings.

Rosenzweig (1933) studied the Zeigarnik quotient under conditions where the interruption created a feeling of failure. Some children recollected more unfinished, others more finished, tasks. The latter children had a higher average rating on pride. In Rosenzweig's setting, the force in the direction of recalling a task, which is due to the need tension, is counteracted by a force away from this task, which is due to the negative valence of failure. For the children who show a high rating in pride, this negative valence should be higher, thus producing Rosenzweig's results.

SUBSTITUTE SATISFACTION

The term *substitution* has been introduced into psychology by Freud (1916). Frequently one activity is called a substitute for another if they show similarity. However, as any two types of behavior show some kind of similarity, this terminology is misleading. Functionally, substitution can be linked either to the valence of an activity or to its satisfaction value.

Substitute Value, Similarity, and Degree of Difficulty. Lissner (1933) studied the value which one activity has for satisfying a need originally directed toward another activity by a technique of resumption. The substitute value is measured by the amount of decrease in resumption of the interrupted original activity after a substitute activity has been completed. The substitute value increases (1) with the degree of similarity between the original and the substitute activity and (2) with the degree of difficulty of the substitute activity. The latter factor seemed to be related to the higher level of aspiration corresponding to a more difficult task.

Substitution on Fantasy Level. If reaching the original goal (for instance, that of attacking another person) is hindered, frequently a substitute action on the level of fantasy or talk can be observed (Doob and Sears, 1939). Freud views the dream in part as such a substitute activity. Have these substitute activities substitute value?

Mahler (1933), using as her subjects children six to ten years old, has studied the substitute value of finishing an interrupted activity by talking or thinking instead of acting. She, too, measured substitute value by the decrease of the frequency of resumption. On the average, the substitute value (2.3) for finishing by action was considerably higher than for finishing by talking (1.2). (Little difference was found between children and adults.) For some activities, such as figuring, however, finishing by talking had a high substitute value. According to Mahler, the same factor which determines the substitute value of actions is decisive for the substitute value of talking, namely, whether or not the individual's goal is reached. For *problem tasks* the intellectual solution is decisive; therefore, talking can have a very high substitute value. For *realization tasks* the building of a material object (such as making a box) is the goal; therefore, talking has practically no substitute value. Thinking through an activity had no measurable substitute value for realization or problem tasks. This finding indicates that frequently a condition for satisfaction value is the creation of a social fact (letting another person know). "Magic" solutions performed in a "make-believe" manner seemed to have a certain amount of substitute value, but only if the subject had accepted the magical nature of the situa-

tion. This was accepted more readily by children than by adults.

Substitute Value and Cognition. Adler (1939) studied the relation between certain cognitive processes and substitute value at three age levels (seven to ten years chronological age). After interruption of the original task, the child had to finish a second task which was physically identical to the interrupted one. For the younger children, building a house for Mary had no substitute value for building a like house for Johnny, although these children were able to see the similarity of the two activities. For older children, too, the substitute value was low in a situation which favored the "concrete attitude" (that is, viewing each house as specifically related to Mary or Johnny). If, however, a *categorical attitude* (that is, if house-building as such) was stressed, the two activities showed considerable substitute value in the older children. For the younger children the substitute value was low even in the "categorical" situation.

Theoretically, the substitute value of one activity for another depends upon a communication between the two underlying need systems in such a way that satisfying the one also satisfies the other. The results of Lissner, Mahler, and Adler indicate that this communication depends partly on the cognitive similarity of the activities, and this in turn on the nature of the situation and the developmental state of the person. These results are in line with the finding that the more primitive person is more *concrete-minded* (Gelb and Goldstein's [1924] work on patients with brain lesions; Werner's [1940a, 1940b] findings concerning the increase of "objectivation and abstraction" during development; Weigl's [1941] experiments on children; common observations of feeble-minded). They support Vigotsky's (1934) theory that "situational" thinking precedes the "abstract" conceptual" thinking in the development of the child. The relatively high age (ten years) at which the "categorical situation" became effective in Adler's experiment indicates, in addition, that the mere ability to see abstract similarities does not necessarily have sufficient weight to establish substitute value for needs.

SUBSTITUTE VALENCE IN PLAY AND NON-PLAY SITUATION

If reaching a goal, that is, satisfying a need in a particular way, is hindered, spontaneous substitute goals may arise. Students who were unsuccessful in their attempts to throw rings over a bottle were found to throw them over near-by hooks (Dembo, 1931). Such spontaneous substitute actions, according to Dembo, have frequently no permanent substitute value. Instead of satisfying, they seem only to heighten the emotional state. This indicates that activities which appeal as substitutes, that is, which have substitute valence, do not need to have satisfaction value. We have mentioned a similar discrepancy between valence and value in ordinary consumption.

Sliosberg (1934) studied substitute valence with children between three and six years in play and in a serious situation. In a serious situation, children would not accept make-believe candy (cardboard) for a piece of chocolate if the make-believe candy was offered after they had started to use real chocolate. If the make-believe candy was offered from the beginning, 17 per cent of three- and four-year-old children accepted it and treated it in a gesture-like way as real candy. Also, make-believe scissors were accepted (in 15 per cent of the cases) for real ones only if they were offered before the real ones.

In a play situation, the children accepted the make-believe chocolate or scissors in almost 100 per cent of the cases (some of them even started to chew the chocolate cardboard). If the make-believe object was introduced without relation to the particular play at hand, the percentage of acceptance decreased slightly to 75. The child was less ready to accept the substitute object if the related need was in a state of greater hunger.

Important for the acceptance or refusal of a substitute is the plasticity of the meaning of the object and of the situation. A toy animal has a more fixed meaning than a pebble or a piece of plasticene and is, therefore, less likely to be accepted as a substitute for something else. The acceptability of substitutes depends more on the plasticity of meaning of the substitute object than on that of the original object. That substitutes are more readily accepted in play is due to greater plasticity of play in respect to social rôles, to the child's own position and goals, and to the meaning of objects.

Changes of Needs and Goals

The emergence of a substitute valence can be viewed as one example of a change of needs or valences. How needs arise in the long-range history of a person and in momentary situations is one of the basic problems of child psychology. New needs, or, more correctly, a change in needs, may result from a great variety of circumstances (Murray, 1938). A child may find out that his friend thinks highly of certain actions and he then comes to value them himself. A change in a social setting, such as attending a children's party, may significantly change the needs of the child in regard to his table manners. Reaching a goal, as well as not reaching it, may change the valences in a momentary or permanent way. During development, new needs may arise by way of differentiation from the previous ones. Behavior in a specific situation usually results from a combination of several needs; in this way, a "derived need" for this behavior may arise. Such a derived need may be kept dependent upon the *source needs* or may become functionally autonomous (Allport, 1937). Some needs seem to die gradually in various periods of the life history of the individual.

Generally speaking, needs may be changed by changes in any part of the psychological environment, by changes of the inner-personal regions, by changes on the reality level as well as on the irreality level (for instance, by a change in hope), and by changes in the cognitive structure of the psychological future and of the psychological past (Lewin, 1942). This is well in line with the fact that the total life space of a person has to be considered as one connected field. The problem of emergence of needs lies at the crossroad of cultural anthropology, developmental psychology, and the psychology of motivation. Its investigation has been hampered by premature speculative attempts to systematize needs into a few categories. In the following pages we shall discuss a few of the related questions.

RESTRAINING FORCES AFFECTING NEEDS

Giving Up. Persistence. We have seen (p. 813) that a failure to reach a certain goal may increase the negative valence of the obstacle until the constellation of forces is changed in such a way that a person will withdraw temporarily or finally. This withdrawal is frequently accompanied by an open or concealed conflict which may show itself in aggressiveness. The withdrawal can, however, go hand in hand with a full acceptance of the inaccessibility of the goal. This is equivalent to an actual giving-up: The inaccessible region ceases to be an effective part of the life space. If the child reaches a state where the in-

accessibility becomes a "matter of fact," he is no longer in a state of frustration or conflict.

What is usually called persistence is an expression of how quickly goals change when the individual encounters obstacles.

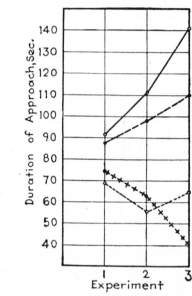

FIGURE 23. The effect of success, encouragement, substitution, and failure upon persistency. ———, success with concomitant encouragement; — — —, success; ― ― ―, substitute success; +++, failure. (From *Dynamic Theory of Personality*, by K. Lewin New York: McGraw-Hill, 1935, 253. By permission of the publisher.)

Fajans (1933) found previous failure to decrease persistence in one- to six-year-old children when they were again confronted with the same type of difficulty. Success led to a relative increase in persistence (Figure 23). When the same task was repeated, a combination of success and praise increased persistence 48 per cent, a success alone 25 per cent; a substitute success led to a decrease of 6 per cent, failure to a decrease of 48 per cent. Similar effects o.

praise and failure were found by Wolf (1938). We have seen that such a change in goals depends on the change in the cognitive structure and on individual differences (Wolf, 1938) which can be observed even in the infant (Fajans, 1933). These experiments indicate that the velocity with which these goals change depends, in addition, upon the psychological past and the social atmosphere. Jack (1934) and Keister (1936) found that it is possible to change the reaction of nursery school children to failure through proper training. The increase of persistence and the decrease of rationalization and of emotional and destructive reactions showed a certain amount of transfer to different areas of activity.

Difficulties Intensifying Needs. H. F. Wright (1937) has shown in experiments with adults and children that a difficulty may increase the need for an object behind a barrier. Children, like adults, will prefer a goal which is more difficult to reach, provided that the barrier is not too strong and that both goal objects are not fully identical. This preference is observed if the object itself has the nature of a goal, but not if it is merely a means. For instance, the child will prefer (everything else being equal) a toy which is slightly more difficult to reach. If, however, he has to choose between two tools with which to get the same object, he will prefer that tool which is easier to reach. Wright's investigations indicate that the so-called law of parsimony (using the easiest way) holds only for psychological means, but not for ends. This latter fact is closely related to the problem of the level of aspiration (see p. 830).

PSYCHOLOGICAL SATIATION

One can distinguish in regard to all or most needs a state of hunger, of satiation, and of oversatiation. These states correspond to a positive, a neutral, and a negative valence of the activity regions which are related to a particular need. Karsten (1928), in experiments with college students, has studied the effect of repeating over and over again such activities as reading a poem, writing letters, drawing, and turning a wheel. She found the main symptoms of satiation to be (1) small variations; (2) large variations; (3) the breaking-up of larger units of actions into smaller parts, loss of meaning; (4) mistakes, unlearning; (5) fatigue and similar "bodily" symptoms.

These results provide one more reason for revising the older theories which explain the genesis of larger units of actions in terms of associations between smaller units established through repetition. Repetition may lead to the combining of smaller units of action into larger ones, but sufficient repetition will break up larger units. This involves, in case of meaningful material such as poems or sentences, a destruction of the meaning. A similar disintegration may also occur for the situation as a whole.

Satiation occurs only if the activity has, psychologically, the character of an actual repetition, of marking time as opposed to making progress. If the character of making progress can be maintained, the usual symptoms of satiation will not appear.

Psychological satiation frequently leads to muscular fatigue or such bodily symptoms as hoarseness. It is frequently the main cause of "fatigue" in children. Like hysterical symptoms, these bodily symptoms cannot be eliminated by voluntary effort, although they are caused by psychological factors and may disappear with the transition to other activities even though the new activity makes use of the same muscles in practically the same way. Imbedding an activity in a different psychological whole so that its meaning is changed has practically the same effect in satiation as shifting to a different activity. The superiority of the method of learning to read and write whole sentences or words rather than single letters is based partly on the fact that the former method is less likely to lead to satiation. The good primer is careful to repeat the same words in such a way that they are imbedded in somewhat different wholes, and that a "progress of meaning" rather than actual repetition occurs.

Repetition not only changes the needs related to the activity which is carried out, but usually also affects the needs related to psychologically similar activities, by way of cosatiation.

The velocity of satiation (that is, how quickly repetition leads to a change in needs) depends, according to Karsten, mainly upon (1) the nature of the activity (particularly the size of its units of action), (2) the degree of centrality, and (3) the individual character and state of the person. Pleasant as well as unpleasant activities are more quickly satiated than neutral activities which in other respects are equivalent. Giving more attention to an activity (without changing its meaning) seems merely to quicken satiation. Freund (1930) found that the velocity of satiation of minute tasks is greater during menstruum. All three results can be interpreted as indicating that the velocity of satiation increases with the centrality of the activity. Frequently a person tries to avoid satiation by doing the activity in a peripheral manner. Automatic activities such as breathing or walking do not become satiated if they are not carried out consciously as mere repetition. The effect of primary and secondary aspects of an activity can be handled with the concept of relative potency (see p. 816).

Children, in line with their lesser degree of differentiation, are likely to be involved in an activity with their whole person. The velocity of satiation should, therefore, vary inversely with mental age. Experimental results seem to confirm this expectation, although they are not univocal (Lewin, 1935; Wolf, 1938). The apparent divergence of findings is probably due to the fact that child psychology treats the problems of satiation under the title of persisting or perseverant behavior and that the term *persistence* is used to refer to dynamically rather different situations (for instance, persistence in overcoming an obstacle and persistence in carrying on an activity without an obstacle). Shacter (1933) found satiation time to be longer for a complex task than for a simpler one, without much age difference between three-, four-, and five-year-old children.

Wolf (1938) studied satiation in situations of praise, competition, and of no incentive with children of four and six years, making a careful analysis of the individual cases. She found the individual goal of the child to be of primary importance and this goal to depend upon the level of aspiration (see p. 830).

Kounin (1939) compared the satiation and cosatiation of normal 7-year-old children with 12- and 30- to 40-year-old feeble-minded persons of the same mental age. He found (Figure 24) that the velocity of satiation (drawings of different patterns) decreased with increasing age. The younger child shows greater cosatiation in spite of the small number of repetitions required for satiating an activity. In other words, the velocity of satiation and the degree of cosatiation decrease with chronological age even if mental age is kept constant. Kounin (1939) and Seashore and Bavelas (1942) found about the same symptoms of satiation in children which Karsten has described with adults.

The phenomena of satiation indicate (1) that there is a close relation between activities and needs, and (2) that an activity can be viewed as a consumption which changes the underlying need and, therefore, the positive valence of the activity into a negative one. As a result of this consumption the valence of "similar activities" also becomes negative, whereas certain different types of activities acquire an increasingly positive valence.

A satiated or oversatiated need, after a

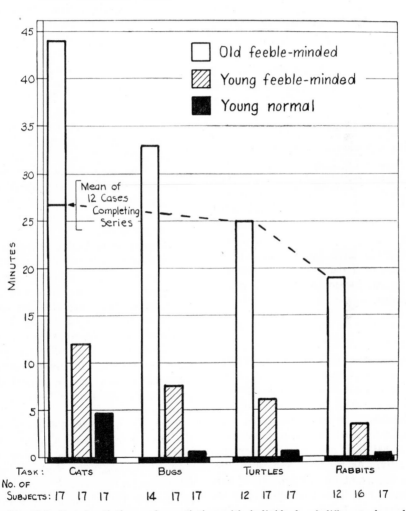

FIGURE 24. Velocity of satiation and cosatiation with individuals of different chronological age and the same mental age. (From *Experimental Studies of Rigidity as a Function of Age and Feeblemindedness,* by J. S. Kounin. Unpublished Ph.D. Dissertation, University of Iowa, 1939.)

lapse of time, frequently changes back into a state of hunger. The conditions of these changes need investigation.

INTENTION

The effect of an intention can be viewed as the setting-up of a quasi-need (Lewin, 1935). A quasi-need is dynamically equivalent to other needs in that it tends to create actions in the direction of satisfying the need with or without the presence of a corresponding goal object. Intentions are made, as a result of a given time perspective, to secure a certain behavior in the future which is expected to bring nearer the fulfillment of one or of several needs. The newly established quasi-need usually remains dependent on these source needs.

Experiments of Birenbaum (1930) show that the tension level of such a quasi-need depends upon the tension level of the more inclusive set of needs of which this quasi-need is a part. An intention will be "forgotten," that is, not carried out, if these source needs have been satisfied in the meantime, or if the state of the person as a whole has become one of high general satisfaction.

NEEDS AS PART OF MORE INCLUSIVE NEEDS. GOAL STRUCTURE

It has been stated that goals or other valences are closely related to needs. Changes of goals depend largely upon the interdependence of needs. Needs may be interdependent in different ways. (a) Two or more needs can be in communication so that their need tensions vary concomitantly. As we have seen, such relation is important for the problem of substitution. (b) The interdependence between needs can be one of ruling and being ruled. For instance, quasi-needs which correspond to intentions are induced by ruling needs. In both cases of interde-

pendence, the need becomes a part of a more inclusive need system.

We have discussed the effect of completion and noncompletion in regard to satisfying or not satisfying the need behind an action. We shall discuss now the effect of those actions on the setting-up of new goals.

Maturity of Aspiration. To a child of six months, lying on his stomach and trying to reach a rattle, it seems to make no difference whether he finally reaches the rattle as the result of his own effort or whether the rattle is brought within his reach by someone else. The child will be satisfied both ways. A child of three, trying to jump down from the third step, may refuse help. He will not be content unless he has reached certain results by his own effort. The very young child seems to know only satisfaction and dissatisfaction but not success and failure. In other words, he has needs and goals but not yet a level of aspiration.

We speak of *aspiration* in regard to an action if the result of this action is seen as an achievement reflecting one's own ability; if, in addition, different degrees of difficulty can be distinguished, we speak of a *level of aspiration.* The level of aspiration is of basic importance for the conduct of human beings and influences most of their goal-seeking. In this connection we have the paradox that the individual may prefer something more difficult to something more easy.

Fales (C. Anderson, 1940) has studied the development, over a period of six months, of aspiration in two- to three-year-old children. She observed such activities as putting on and removing snow suits. Refusing help is probably the best behavioral symptom for the existence of an aspiration in regard to an activity. Such insistence on independence indicates that one's own action has become a part of the goal. Observing manipulations of various degrees of difficulty (such as opening the zipper, getting an arm out of the coat, hanging the cap on the hook), she found that children at this age have an aspiration only in regard to particular activities.

grees of "maturity of aspiration," corresponding to different types of goals and procedures in attaining them at various age levels. C. Anderson (1940) developed a scale of maturity of aspiration for children between two and eight years, using

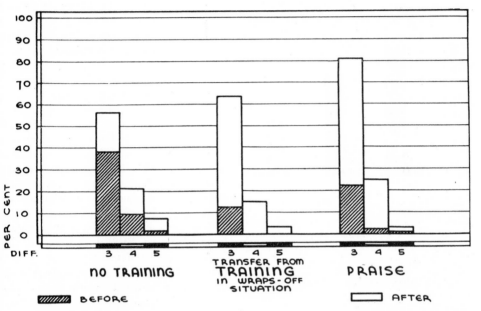

FIGURE 25. Development of aspiration as a function of difficulty of task, training, and praise. (From an incomplete study by Fales, quoted in *The Development of a Level of Aspiration in Young Children,* by C. Anderson. Unpublished Ph.D. Dissertation, University of Iowa, 1940.)

Ordinate refers to per cent of refusal of help.   Numbers on abscissa refer to degrees of difficulty of task.

tivities. One of the determining factors is the ability of the child; he will not refuse help for activities definitely beyond his reach. As he becomes older or is better trained (Figure 25) an aspiration develops in regard to the more difficult actions. Fales also found that social situations or praise (Figure 25) facilitate the rise of an aspiration. This indicates that a social component is important for aspiration from its earliest development.

It is possible to distinguish different de-

activities such as throwing a series of rings over a stick and knocking down tenpins with a ball. A child of eight will consider the series of five throws as one unit and will not, therefore, rethrow single rings which miss the stick before counting his score. Children of the youngest group (three years old) always pick up the single rings after missing the stick and rethrow them or place them directly on the stick (Figure 26). The youngest children do not hold to the rule of standing behind a given place. These and other symptoms indicate that the development of a level of aspiration, the choosing of a goal of a particular degree of difficulty, presupposes (1) that a number of goals are seen as subgoals within a larger goal structure, (2) that the action itself is conceived as a part of the goal, and (3) that the child under-

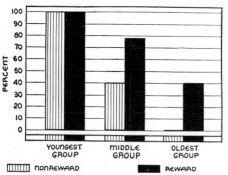

FIGURE 26. Maturity of aspiration at three age levels and amount of regression in case of social pressure (reward situation). (From *The Development of a Level of Aspiration in Young Children*, by C. Anderson. Unpublished Ph.D. Dissertation, University of Iowa, 1940.)

The frequency with which the child places the missed ring on a stick or rethrows the single ring instead of finishing the series of rings is indicated.

stands the meaning of rules and is ready to keep them.

If pressure is brought to bear on a child by offering a reward, the level of aspiration (that is, the degree of difficulty chosen) will decrease. If a lowering of the level of aspiration is made impossible, the maturity of aspiration may regress (Figure 26); that is, a procedure is used which is characteristic of a younger age level. Regression of the maturity of aspiration can be observed in adults in emotional situations.

Level of Aspiration. Level of aspiration has been defined (Hoppe, 1930) as the de-

gree of difficulty of that task chosen as a goal for the next action. One may distinguish two main problems: (1) under what condition the individual experiences success or failure and (2) what factors influence the level of aspiration.

Conditions for the experience of success or failure. The experience of success or failure depends on the level of performance within a frame of reference (Lewin, Dembo, Festinger, and Sears, 1944). This frame of reference can be the level of aspiration (that is, the goal which has been set for that action), the past performance, or the standards of a group. A feeling of success will prevail if a certain level, related to the dominant frame of reference, is reached. What frame of reference will be dominant depends upon a number of factors, one of which is the tendency to avoid the feeling of failure.

It has been shown (Gould, 1939; P. Sears, 1940; Festinger, 1942) that to avoid the feeling of failure after a poor performance the frame of reference is frequently shifted. Other ways to avoid failure are various forms of rationalization (Hoppe, 1930; Gould, 1939), such as blaming a poor instrument for the shortcomings of the performance. In this way the link between performance and one's own ability is cut, which is, as we have seen, one of the conditions for the phenomenon of aspiration.

Jucknat (1937) distinguishes different intensities of the feeling of success and failure. They are to be related to the amount of discrepancy between goal and performance. This holds, however, only within the range of difficulties which is close to the boundary level of ability. "Too easy" and "too difficult" tasks do not lead to feelings of success and failure. This may be the reason why rivalry among siblings is less frequent when there are relatively great differences of age among them (Sewall, 1930).

The relation between the feeling of success and failure, on the one hand, and the boundary of ability, on the other, is operative only if other frames of reference, such as certain group standards, do not become dominant. The mentally retarded child might have permanently the feeling of failure in a group of children of high ability even though the tasks were actually far beyond the limit of his own ability.

Case studies (Kanner, 1935) and experimental data (Fajans, 1933) show that change in group status (for instance, gaining recognition or love or being rejected by an individual or a larger group) is, in many respects, equivalent to success or failure.

Factors determining the level of aspiration. After the experience of success or failure the person may either quit or continue with a higher, equal, or lower level of aspiration. The difference between the level of aspiration for the new action and the level of past performance is called the "discrepancy" between level of aspiration and performance. (For details see Lewin, Dembo, Festinger, and Sears, 1944.)

The factors determining a change in the level of aspiration are manifold. Jucknat (1937) found that with children from nine to fifteen and with adults the direction and the amount of the change in the level of aspiration depend upon the degree of success and failure (Figure 27). In addition, within a given series of tasks, the discrepancy is smaller for the same amount of success and greater for the same amount of failure the closer the previous level of performance comes to the extreme of the series of difficulties.

The level of aspiration is much influenced by social factors. In a situation of competition it might be increased (J. D. Frank, 1935). The knowledge of group standards may affect the level of aspiration (Festinger, 1942). For instance, the discrepancy between aspiration and performance increases toward a higher level of aspiration if the person learns that his performance is below the standard of his

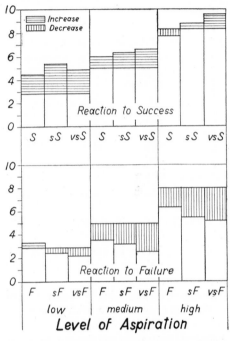

FIGURE 27. Change in the level of aspiration as a function of (*a*) strength of the feeling of success and failure; (*b*) the relative difficulty of the previous level of performance. (From "Performance, Level of Aspiration and Self-consciousness," by M. Jucknat. *Psychologische Forschung,* 1937, **22,** 102. By permission of the publisher.)

S, success; *sS,* strong success; *vsS,* very strong success; *F,* failure; *sF,* strong failure; *vsF,* very strong failure. Ordinate refers to degrees of difficulty of task.

own group or of a group which he considers to be lower. The discrepancy decreases if the opposite conditions obtain. The level of aspiration is affected also by the degree of realistic judgment about one's own ability (J. D. Frank, 1935). P. Sears (1940) found the average positive discrepancy (that is, the amount by which the level of aspiration exceeds past performance) to be greater in children after failure than after success, indicating a greater degree of realism after success than after failure.

For the same individual, the direction and amount of discrepancy seem to be constant to a certain degree for a number of activities (J. D. Frank, 1935; P. Sears, 1940; Gardner, 1939). P. Sears (1940) and Jucknat (1937) found the discrepancy to be greater in children of poor standing than in children of good standing in school. The degree to which the level of aspiration in one activity affects the level of aspiration in another activity depends upon their similarity and upon how well previous experience has stabilized the level of aspiration in these activities (Jucknat, 1937). The influence of success in one activity on the level of aspiration in another is slight if the child has clearly found out his ability in the latter.

The level of aspiration is closely related to the time perspective with respect to both the psychological past and the psychological future. According to Escalona (1940), the level of aspiration at a given time depends upon the strength of the valence of success and failure and upon the probability of success at that time. By representing this probability as the potency of the future success or failure situation, the basic facts concerning the level of aspiration can be understood (see Lewin, Dembo, Festinger, and Sears, 1944).

INDUCED NEEDS. GROUP GOALS AND INDI-
    VIDUAL GOALS

The needs of the individual are, to a very high degree, determined by social factors. The needs of the growing child are changed and new needs induced as a result of the many small and large social groups to which he belongs. His needs are much affected, also, by the ideology and conduct of those groups to which he would like to belong or from which he would like to be set apart. The effects of the advice of the mother, of the demand of a fellow child, or of what the psychoanalyst calls *super-ego*, all are closely interwoven with socially induced needs. We have seen that the level of aspiration is related to social facts. We may state more generally that the culture in which a child grows affects practically every need and all his behavior and that the problem of acculturation is one of the foremost in child psychology.

One can distinguish three types of cases where needs pertain to social relations: (1) the action of the individual may be performed for the benefit of someone else (in the manner of an altruistic act); (2) needs may be induced by the power field of another person or group (as a weaker person's obedience of a more powerful one); (3) needs may be created by belonging to a group and adhering to its goals. Actually, these three types are closely interwoven.

Sources of Ideology. The frequency with which children named the teacher as a source for praise or scolding of behavior in school remained relatively constant from the fourth to the eighth grade in certain schools (Bavelas, 1942b). An individual classmate (as distinguished from the concept "children") was frequently named as source for evaluation of behavior at the fourth grade (Figure 28); this frequency declined to zero at the eighth grade. The school superintendent was practically never named as source at the fourth grade (Figure 28); he was named with increasing frequency later on, mainly as a source for scolding.

Kalhorn (1944) compared positive and negative values (Figure 29a) and sources of values (Figure 29b) in Mennonite and non-Mennonite children in rural areas. She found differences in the emphasis on such values as individual achievement and religion. In both groups the parents are indicated by the children to have the most dominant influence as a source of values.

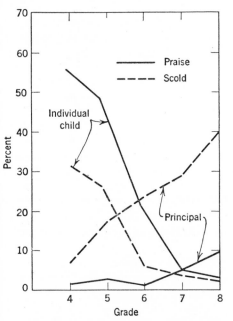

Fig. 28. Frequency with which an individual child and the school principal are given as source for praise or scolding of school conduct at different grades. (From "A Method for Investigating Individual and Group Ideology," by A. Bavelas. *Sociometry*, 1942, **5**, 376. By permission of the publisher.)

The same conduct may have different psychological meaning in different cultures. For instance, going to church is linked with God as the source of approval by the Mennonite children, with everyone by the non-Mennonite children. This indicates that church-going is primarily a religious affair with the former, a social affair with the latter.

Egoism and Altruism. In an experiment by Moore (1931), children between the ages of two and three were asked to share orange juice with a companion who was seated beside the subject. Her results show wide individual differences and no correlation with the degree to which the child respects the rights of others as determined by other methods. Hartshorne and May (1929) studied test situations in which service (altruism, cooperation) of the children could be observed. They claim that the tendency to serve is "specific" rather than "general" in children between ten and fourteen years (for a discussion of the problem of generality of traits see Allport, 1937). McGrath (1923), using a questionnaire technique, reports that an altruistic response to a hypothetical situation increases with age. Piaget (1932) orders his findings on the moral development of children in terms of two psychologically different moralities which are an outgrowth of two types of social relations: up to seven or eight years, there exists a social relation of unilateral respect in which the child is subjected to adult authority. Gradually a relationship of mutual respect is set up in which each member has a more equal part of the control.

B. Wright (1941, 1942a, 1942b) studied children in a situation where they had a choice of keeping a preferred toy or giving it to someone else. The other child (who was not present) was either someone unknown or a best friend. The five-year-old child was practically always egoistic; the eight-year-old child showed considerable altruism, and more so toward the stranger (58 per cent generous choices) than to the friend (23 per cent generous choices). When acting as an umpire between a friend and a strange child in distributing the toys, the five-year-old child favored the friend more frequently than the stranger. The eight-year-old favored the stranger more frequently than the friend.

Praised Conduct

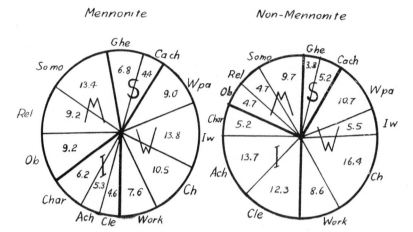

Source for Praise

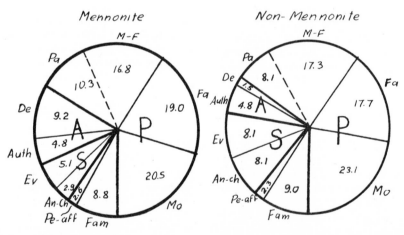

FIGURE 29. (a) Praised conduct. (b) Source for praise. (From "Studies in Topological and Vector Psychology: III. Values and Sources of Authority among Rural Children," by J. Kalhorn. *University of Iowa Studies in Child Welfare*, 1945, **20**. By permission of the publisher.)

(a) *W*, work area (work; *Ch*, chore; *Iw*, intensive work; *Wpa*, work for parents); *S*, social area (*Ca ch*, care of other children; *Ghe*, generalized help); *M*, morality area (*So mo*, social morality; *Rel*, religion and virtues; *Ob*, obedience); *I*, individual area (*Char*, character; *Ach*, individual achievement; *Cle*, cleanliness).

(b) *P*, parents (*Mo*, mother; *Fa*, father; *M-F*, mother and father; *Pa*, parents); *A*, authority (*De*, deity; *Auth*, authority); *S*, society (*Ev*, everybody; *An-ch*, another child; *Pe-aff*, person affected; *Fam*, family).

Theoretically, the altruistic or the egoistic choice can be viewed as the result of the relative strength of forces acting on different regions of the life space and of the potency of various situations. In the life space of child C (Figure 30), a force $f_{C, G}$ acts on his own person in the direction to a goal G. In addition, a force $f^C_{Ot, G}$ exists in his life space, acting on the other child, Ot, in the direction of the same goal. (The situation permits only one person to obtain the goal.) This second force, $f^C_{Ot, G}$, corresponds to the need of the other child as perceived by the child whose life space is represented and the readiness of the child C to back the goal of the child Ot. Formalistically speaking, the altruistic or egoistic choice depends on the relative strength of these two forces. According to Wright, the need of the other child is not perceived by the very young child. This may be the reason for the absence of cooperative play in the young child. With increasing age, the potency of the perceived need of the other child increases. Similarly, the potency of the outgroup increases relative to the potency of the ingroup (friend).

The greater altruism toward the stranger than toward the friend seems to be due partly to the fact that the child sees himself in the position of a host toward the stranger, but not toward the friend, and that his ideology requires that he be hospitable. The children judged other people to be altruistic or egoistic to the same degree as they themselves were. A preliminary study seems to indicate that adults in a similar setting are more egoistic than the eight-year-old child.

Obedience and Social Pressure. In discussing problems of conflicts we have seen that the force acting on a person in the direction of a goal might be counteracted by induced forces corresponding to the will of another person. In view of the relation between psychological forces and psychological needs we can also speak of *induced needs.* The relation between two persons might be that of friends or that of enemies; the need of each would depend greatly on the power field of the other.

Wiehe (Lewin, 1935) observed children between two and four years of age when a stranger entered the child's room. He found the strength of the power field of

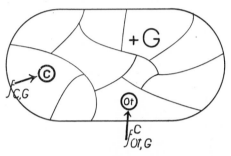

FIGURE 30. The situation of altruism. (Derived from *The Development of the Ideology of Altruism and Fairness in Children*, by B. A. Wright. Unpublished Ph.D. Dissertation, University of Iowa, 1942.)

the stranger at a given moment to be influenced by the physical position of both persons. The effect of the power field on the child increases with decreasing distance (see Figure 19). It is very high if the child is placed on the adult's lap. The power field is weaker back of the stranger, or where the child cannot be seen, than in front of the stranger. In other words, the strength of the power field of one person on another differs for different areas. J. D. Frank (1944), in experiments with students, and Waring, Dwyer, and Junkin (1939) in experiments with nursery school children at the dinner table, also found the effectiveness of the power field for creating induced forces to be greater if the distance between the persons is smaller.

Lippitt and White (1943), in experiments with ten-year-old children, tested the effect of induced needs during the presence and the absence of the inducing power field. They found that the amount of work output in an autocratic group atmosphere dropped very decisively within a few minutes when the leader left the room. This was in contrast to a democratic group

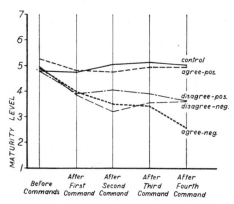

FIGURE 31. The effect of conflicting authorities on constructiveness. (From "Studies in Topological and Vector Psychology: III. The Effect of Conflicting Authority on the Child," by C. E. Meyers. *University of Iowa Studies in Child Welfare,* 1944. By permission of the publisher.)

atmosphere, where the work had been chosen and planned by the group itself, and where the work output was unchanged when the leader left. C. E. Meyers (1944) studied the effect of conflicting adult authority on children of nursery school age. He found that the opposing orders lower the children's constructiveness of play very considerably (from 4½ to 2½ on his constructiveness scale) (Figure 31). The child may stop action altogether (aside from self-manipulation similar to that described by MacDonald, 1940) if he does not find a way to follow the orders of both authorities. Even if the orders of both adults agree, too frequent interference with the child's play lowers his constructiveness

somewhat. Negative commands were more damaging than positive commands, and vague commands more damaging than specific ones.

Induced needs which are opposite to own needs may lead to a permanent state of conflict which is more or less concealed. If such a conflict cannot be resolved by breaking the dominant power field (see p. 814), the child may become aggressive toward less powerful persons. Lewin, Lippitt, and White (1939) found that, on several occasions, one of the children was attacked as a scapegoat in the autocratic group (Figure 32).

Taking Over Foreign Goals. An induced need may slowly change its character in the direction of an own need. In other words, the person not only will follow orders but also "accept" them (in the meaning of taking them over). Waring, Dwyer, and Junkin (1939) have observed changes in this direction with nursery school children.

Duncker (1938) studied changes in food preferences of children from two to five years of age, as affected by a story in which the hero abhorred one and enthusiastically relished the other of two kinds of food. After the story, the children preferred the hero's favorite food, although previously it had been unattractive to them. This effect decreased with time, but could still be detected after six days. Thompson (1940) studied the effect of prejudicial leadership on ten-year-old children. The leader set up an underprivileged minority within a group of children who originally had equal status. After a number of club meetings the children of the privileged majority continued to treat the rest of the children as underprivileged even when the leader left the room. This discrimination, however, was not so strong as in the presence of the leader. This shows both that the presence of the power field of the leader has some influence and that the induced goals have been taken over in some measure.

Lippitt and White (1943), in a study of autocratic, democratic, and laissez-faire values." Children who follow boy values are more sociable among themselves but less obedient at school.

Horowitz (1936) found no prejudices against Negroes in white children under

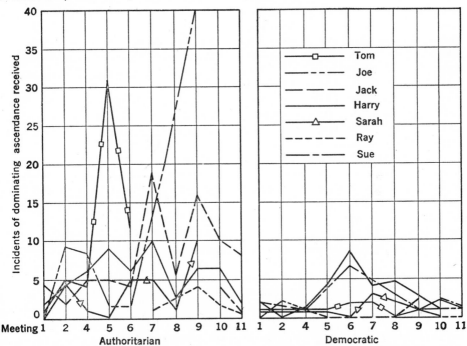

FIGURE 32. The emergence of scapegoats. (From "Studies in Topological and Vector Psychology: I. An Experimental Study of the Effect of Democratic and Authoritarian Group Atmospheres," by Ronald Lippitt. *University of Iowa Studies in Child Welfare*, 1940, **16**, 165. By permission of the publisher.)

The curves indicate that the amount of dominating behavior directed against the various individuals was much greater in autocracy than in democracy. In autocracy two individuals (Tom and Joe) were treated as scapegoats (at the fifth and ninth meetings, respectively).

groups, have found that the readiness of an individual to accept autocracy in the club depends partly upon the home background. A combination of a firm and warm home atmosphere seems to be most favorable to that end; that is, an atmosphere of relative autocracy which, nevertheless, by its warmness, prohibits the child from becoming independent of the family. These children are likely to adhere to "adult values" rather than "boy three years. The prejudices increased between four and six years. This increase was as great in New York as in the South. It was independent of the degree of acquaintance of the children with Negro children, and of the actual status of the Negro child in the class which the white child attended. The prejudices are, however, related to the attitude of the parents of the white child. This indicates that the prejudices against the Negroes are due to an induction and gradual taking-over of the culture of the parents by the child.

A phenomenon which is probably partly due to the acceptance of originally induced needs and partly to the problems of group belongingness (see p. 800) is the hatred against one's own group in persons belonging to an underprivileged group. This hatred against the own group is frequent among the bodily handicapped and among socially underprivileged groups (Davis and Dollard, 1940; Lewin, 1940b). It means that the values and prejudices of the privileged group have been taken over by the members of the socially lower group even if they are directed against their own group. This hatred of one's own group may lead to self-hatred. It is augmented by the need of the individual to raise his status and, therefore, to separate himself from the underprivileged group.

Whether or not an induced need has changed its character and has become an own need is frequently difficult to decide. Lippitt and White (1943) distinguished two types of reaction to an autocratic atmosphere: one called *aggressive autocracy,* and the other *apathetic autocracy.* In the latter case the children seem to work willingly. Signs of discontent or obstruction may be entirely absent. Particularly strict obedience may have the appearance of a voluntary action. This holds also for the behavior of children in institutions. Nevertheless, the effect of the removal of the leader in the experiment shows how great the actual difference in both situations is for the child.

Needs of a Child as a Group Member. As mentioned above, the children in the democratic group studied by Lippitt and White did not decrease the intensity of their work if the leader left. The plan for this work had been decided upon by majority vote after consideration. This shows that under these conditions a need

corresponding to a group goal is more like an own need than an induced need. This problem is closely related to the difference between "we"-feeling and "I"-feeling. Lewin, Lippitt, and White (1939) found "we"-feeling, as measured by the verbal expression and the attitude toward the work, to be greater in the democratic group than in the autocratic group where an egocentric attitude prevailed.

One can consider two factors to be basic for the kind and degree of influence which group goals have for the goals of the individual: (1) the degree of dependence of the person on the group; (2) the character of enmity or friendship of this dependence. According to Ronald Lippitt (1940), the power fields of enemies weaken each other in areas where they overlap, whereas the power fields of friends strengthen each other. In addition, friendship as distinguished from enmity includes the readiness to accept and to back up the intention of the other person. According to M. E. Wright (1940), both characteristics can be expressed by the degree of accessibility of one's own power field to the power field of the other person.

Individual Differences

We have seen that it is not possible to determine the specific characteristics of individuals by classifying them according to their overt behavior. Instead, one has to look for factors which can be inserted as constant values into the variables of the equations which represent psychological laws. In this way also the variability of behavior, that is, the difference in behavior of the same individual in different situations, becomes susceptible to treatment. This variability does not mean merely that the absolute frequency or intensity of a certain type of behavior depends upon the situation. Actually, the rank-order of individuals in regard to a certain trait may also be different in different situations. For instance, Lewin, Lippitt, and White (1939) found in clubs of ten-year-old boys that, in regard to some "traits," such as "demanding attention from other club members" and "out-of-field conversation," the rank-order of the individual in different atmospheres remains rather constant ($r = .85$ and $r = .78$). In other traits, such as "dependence upon leader," there is scarcely any consistency of rank-order ($r = .02$). There are more extreme changes in the rank-order in "work-mindedness" than in "aggressiveness." The changes seem to be linked to the differences of meaning of the particular atmospheres to the particular children.

The attempts to link positively problems of individual differences and of general laws are relatively new in psychology. We shall mention but one example, which is related to differences in age, intelligence, and rigidity of the person. Lewin (1935) has outlined a theory according to which differences in mental age are closely related to the degree of differentiation of the person. The variety of states which an organism can assume, and the corresponding variety of patterns of behavior, must logically be conceived of (Barker, Dembo, and Lewin, 1941) as a function of the degree of the differentiation of that organism. Therefore, with increasing mental age, the individual should show an increasing flexibility, in the sense of richness, of behavior. This is in line with empirical observations of individuals of different mental age and with the peculiar pedantry and stubbornness of the young child.

The increase of flexibility with increasing mental age is somewhat counteracted by a decrease in plasticity which seems to go hand in hand with chronological age and which seems to be important for senility. A certain type of feeble-minded-

ness is characterized by the fact that these individuals show at the same level of differentiation (the same mental age) less plasticity (Lewin, 1935). If this theory is correct, one should expect less cosatiation in feeble-minded persons than in normal persons of the same mental age. Kounin (1939) demonstrated this with individuals whose chronological ages were 7, 12, or 30, all having a mental age of 7 (see p. 826). One can derive from the same set of premises that feeble-minded individuals should be less able to tolerate overlapping situations. One should expect, therefore, that the feeble-minded person would make fewer mistakes in case of change of habits under certain conditions, that he would show greater difference in speed of performance between overlapping and nonoverlapping situations, and that he would be less able to change the cognitive structure in a test requiring several classifications of the same group of objects. Kounin's experiments substantiate all these derivations. The results of Koepke (Lewin, 1935) and of Gottschaldt (1926) indicate that the readiness of the feeble-minded person to accept or to refuse a substitute is either very small or very great, according to the specific situation. This is in line with what should be expected from a relatively rigid individual.

The coordination of certain individual differences with differences in the degree of differentiation and rigidity of the person makes it possible to link behavior in quite a variety of fields, such as cognition, stubbornness, substitution, and satiation, and to understand apparent contradictions of behavior. A greater rigidity of the feeble-minded person also explains why his development is slower than that of the normal child (that is, the relative constancy of the IQ) and why he reaches his peak of development earlier.

It can be expected that all problems of

individual differences will be linked more and more with the general psychological laws of behavior and development and that in this way a deeper understanding of both the individual differences and the general laws will be possible.

Bibliography

ADLER, D. L. 1939. *Types of similarity and the substitute value of activities at different age levels.* Unpublished Ph.D. Dissertation, State University of Iowa.

ADLER, D. L., and J. KOUNIN. 1939. Some factors operating at the moment of resumption of interrupted tasks. *J. Psychol., 7,* 355–367.

ALLPORT, G. W. 1937. *Personality: A psychological interpretation.* New York: Holt.

ANDERSON, C. 1940. *The development of a level of aspiration in young children.* Unpublished Ph.D. Dissertation, University of Iowa.

ANDERSON, H. H. 1939. Domination and social integration in the behavior of kindergarten children and teachers. *Genet. Psychol. Monogr., 21,* 287–385.

BARBER, V. 1939. Studies in the psychology of stuttering: XV. Chorus reading as a distraction in stuttering. *J. Speech Disorders, 4,* 371–383.

BARKER, R. 1942. An experimental study of the resolution of conflict by children. In Q. McNEMAR and M. A. MERRILL (Eds.), *Studies in personality.* New York and London: McGraw-Hill.

BARKER, R., T. DEMBO, and K. LEWIN. 1941. Studies in topological and vector psychology: II. Frustration and regression. *Univ. Iowa Stud. Child Welfare, 18,* No. 1.

BARTOS, A. 1932. Die psychologischen Grundlagen der seelischen Erziehung bei Verkrüppelten. *4. Vers. f. Kinderforsch.,* 244–253.

BAVELAS, A. 1942a. Morale and the training of leaders. In G. WATSON (Ed.), *Civilian morale,* second yearbook of the SPSSI. Boston: Published for Reynal and Hitchcock by Houghton Mifflin.

——. 1942b. A method for investigating individual and group ideology. *Sociometry, 5,* 371–377.

BENEDICT, R. 1934. *Patterns of culture.* Boston: Houghton Mifflin.

BIRENBAUM, G. 1930. Das Vergessen einer Vornahme. Isolierte seelische Systeme und dynamische Gesamtbereiche. *Psychol. Forsch., 13,* 218–285.

BOGARDUS, E. S. 1933. A social distance scale. *Sociol. and Soc. Res., 17,* 265–271.

BROWN, J. F. 1933. Über die dynamischen Eigenschaften der Realitäts- und Irrealitätsschichten. *Psychol. Forsch., 18,* 1–26.

BROWN, J. F. 1936. *Psychology and the social order.* New York: McGraw-Hill.

BROWN, S. F. 1936–1937. Influence of grammatical function on the incidence of stuttering. *J. Speech Disorders, 2,* 207–215.

——. 1938a. A further study of stuttering in relation to various speech sounds. *Quart. J. Speech, 24,* 390–397.

——. 1938b. Stuttering with relation to word accent and word position. *J. Abnorm. Soc. Psychol., 33,* 112–120.

BÜHLER, C. 1939. *The child and his family.* New York: Harper.

BURKS, B. S. 1940. Mental and physical developmental pattern of identical twins in relation to organismic growth theory. *Yearb. Nat. Soc. Stud. Educ., 39(II),* 85–96.

CARTWRIGHT, D. 1941. Decision-time in relation to the differentiation of the phenomenal field. *Psychol. Rev., 48,* 425–442.

CARTWRIGHT, D., and L. FESTINGER. 1943. A quantitative theory of decision. *Psychol. Rev., 50,* 595–621.

DAVIDSON, H. H., and B. KLOPFER. 1938. Rorschach statistics: II. Normal children. *Rorschach Res. Exch., 3,* 37–42.

DAVIS, A., and J. DOLLARD. 1940. *Children of bondage.* Washington, D. C.: American Youth Commission.

DEMBO, T. 1931. Der Ärger als dynamisches Problem. *Psychol. Forsch., 15,* 1–144.

DERI, S. 1943. *The psychological effect of the electric shock treatment.* M.A. thesis. State University of Iowa.

DIMOCK, H. S. 1937. *Rediscovering the adolescent.* New York: Association Press.

DOLLARD, J. 1935. *Criteria for the life history.* New Haven: Yale University Press.

——. 1937. *Caste and class in a southern town.* New Haven: Yale University Press.

DOOB, L. W., and R. R. SEARS. 1939. Factors determining substitute behavior and the overt expression of aggression. *J. Abnorm. Soc. Psychol., 34,* 293–313.

DRESDNER, I. 1933. Ueber Körperbehinderung und seelische Entwicklung. *Z. angew. Psychol., 44,* 399–437.

DUNCKER, K. 1938. Experimental modification of children's food preferences through social suggestion. *J. Abnorm. Soc. Psychol., 33,* 489–507.

EINSTEIN, A. 1933. *On the method of theoretical physics.* New York: Oxford University Press.

ERIKSON, E. H. 1940. Studies in the interpretation of play: I. Clinical observation of play disruption in young children. *Genet. Psychol. Monogr., 22,* 556–671.

ESCALONA, S. K. 1940. The effect of success and failure upon the level of aspiration and behavior in manic-depressive psychoses. *Univ. Iowa Stud. Child Welfare, 16,* No. 3.

FAJANS, S. 1933. Erfolg, Ausdauer, und Activität beim Saügling und Kleinkind. *Psychol. Forsch.*, **17**, 268–305.

FARBER, M. L. 1945. Studies in topological and vector psychology: III. Imprisonment as a psychological situation. *Univ. Iowa Stud. Child Welfare*, **20**.

FESTINGER, L. 1942. Wish, expectation, and group performance as factors influencing level of aspiration. *J. Abnorm. Soc. Psychol.*, **37**, 184–200.

FRANK, J. D. 1935. Some psychological determinants of the "level of aspiration." *Amer. J. Psychol.*, **47**, 285–293.

——. 1944. Experimental studies of personal pressure and resistance: II. Methods of overcoming resistance. *J. Gen. Psychol.*, **30**, 43–56.

FRANK, L. K. 1938. Cultural control and physiological autonomy. Reprinted from *Amer. J. Orthopsychiat.*, **8**, No. 4, 622–626.

——. 1939. Cultural coercion and individual distortion. *Psychiatry*, **2**, 11–27.

FRAZIER, E. F. 1940. *Negro youth at the crossways*. Washington, D. C.: American Council on Education.

FRENCH, J. R. P., JR. 1945. Studies in topological and vector psychology: III. Organized and unorganized groups under fear and frustration. *Univ. Iowa Stud. Child Welfare*, **20**.

FRENCH, T. 1939. Insight and distortion in dreams. *Int. J. Psycho-Anal.*, **20**, 287–298.

FREUD, S. 1916. *The interpretation of dreams*. (Trans. by A. A. BRILL.) (rev. ed.) New York: Macmillan.

FREUND, A. 1930. Psychische Sättigung im Menstruum und Intermenstruum. *Psychol. Forsch.*, **13**, 198–217.

GARDNER, J. W. 1940. The relation of certain personality variables to level of aspiration. *J. Psychol.*, **9**, 191–206.

GELB, A. 1938. Colour constancy, pp. 196–209. Article in W. D. ELLIS (Ed.), *Source book of gestalt psychology*. London: Kegan Paul.

GELB, A., and K. GOLDSTEIN. 1924. Über Farbennamenamnesie nebst Bemerkungen über das Wesen der amnestischen Aphasie überhaupt und die Beziehung zwischen Sprache und dem Verhalten zur Umwelt. *Psychol. Forsch.*, **6**, 127–186.

GESELL, A., H. M. HALVERSON, H. THOMPSON, F. L. ILG, B. M. CASTNER, L. B. AMES, and C. S. AMATRUDA. 1940. *The first five years of life: A guide to the study of the preschool child*. New York: Harper.

GESELL, A., and H. THOMPSON, assisted by C. S. AMATRUDA. 1934. *Infant behavior: Its genesis and growth*. New York: McGraw-Hill.

GOODENOUGH, F. L. 1940. New evidence on environmental influence on intelligence. *Yearb. Nat. Soc. Stud. Educ.*, 39(I), 307–365.

GOTTSCHALDT, K. 1926. Über dem Einfluss der Erfahrung auf die Wahrnehmung von Figuren: I. Über den Einfluss gehäufter Einprägung von Figuren auf ihre Sichtbarkeit in umfassenden Konfigurationen. *Psychol. Forsch.*, **8**, 261–318.

GOULD, R. 1939. An experimental analysis of "level of aspiration." *Genet. Psychol. Monogr.*, **21**, 3–115.

GRAY, M. 1940. The X family: A clinical study and a laboratory study of a "stuttering" family. *J. Speech Disorders*, **5**, 343–348.

HALVERSON, H. M. 1931. An experimental study of prehension in infants by means of systematic cinema records. *Genet. Psychol. Monogr.*, **10**, 107–286.

HARTSHORNE, H., and M. A. MAY. 1929. *Studies in service and self-control*. New York: Macmillan.

HOMBURGER, E. 1937. Configurations in play: Clinical notes. *Psychoanal. Quart.*, **6**, 139–214.

HOPPE, F. 1930. Erfolg und Misserfolg. *Psychol. Forsch.*, **14**, 1–62.

HOROWITZ, E. L. 1936. The development of attitude toward the Negro. *Arch. Psychol., N. Y.*, No. 194.

HULL, C. L. 1930. Simple trial-and-error learning: A study in psychological theory. *Psychol. Rev.*, **37**, 241–256.

——. 1932. The goal gradient hypothesis and maze learning. *Psychol. Rev.*, **39**, 25–43.

IRWIN, O. C. 1930. The amount and nature of activities of newborn infants under constant external stimulating conditions during the first ten days of life. *Genet. Psychol. Monogr.*, **8**, 1–92.

——. 1932. The distribution of the amount of motility in young infants between two nursing periods. *J. Comp. Psychol.*, **14**, 429–445.

JACK, L. M. 1934. An experimental study of ascendant behavior in preschool children. *Univ. Iowa Stud. Child Welfare*, **9**, No. 3, 7–65.

JERSILD, A. T. 1936. The development of the emotions. In C. E. SKINNER (Ed.), *Educational psychology*. New York: Prentice-Hall.

JOHNSON, W., and J. R. KNOTT. 1937. Studies in the psychology of stuttering: I. The distribution of moments of stuttering in successive readings of the same material. *J. Speech Disorders*, **2**, 17–19.

JUCKNAT, M. 1937. Performance, level of aspiration and self-consciousness. *Psychol. Forsch.*, **22**, 89–179.

KALHORN, J. 1945. Studies in topological and vector psychology: III. Values and sources of authority among rural children. *Univ. Iowa Stud. Child Welfare*, **20**.

KANNER, L. 1935. *Child psychiatry*. Springfield, Ill.: Thomas.

KARSTEN, A. 1928. Psychische Sättigung. *Psychol. Forsch.*, **10**, 142–154.

KATONA, G. 1940. *Organizing and memorizing: Studies in the psychology of learning and teaching.* New York: Columbia University Press.

KATZ, D. 1937. *Animals and men.* New York and London: Longmans, Green.

KATZ, E. 1938. *Some factors affecting resumption of interrupted activities by pre-school children.* (Inst. Child Welfare Monogr. Ser., No. 16.) Minneapolis: University of Minnesota Press. Pp. 52.

KEISTER, M. E. 1936. *The behavior of young children in failure.* In BARKER, KOUNIN, and WRIGHT, *Child Behavior and Development.* New York: McGraw-Hill.

KEPHART, N. C. 1937. Studies in emotional adjustment: II. An experimental study of the "disorganization" of mental functions in the delinquent. *Univ. Iowa Stud. Child Welfare,* **15,** No. 1.

KOFFKA, K. 1928. *The growth of the mind: An introduction to child psychology.* (Trans. by R. M. OGDEN.) (2d ed.) New York: Harcourt, Brace.

KÖHLER, W. 1920. *Die physischen Gestalten in Ruhe und im stationären Zustand.* Braunschweig: Germany: Friedr. Vieweg & Sohn.

——. 1925. *The mentality of apes.* (Trans. by E. WINTER.) New York: Harcourt, Brace.

KOUNIN, J. S. 1939. *Experimental studies of rigidity as a function of age and feeblemindedness.* Ph.D. Dissertation, University of Iowa.

LEWIN, K. 1935. *Dynamic theory of personality.* New York: McGraw-Hill.

——. 1936a. *Principles of topological psychology.* New York: McGraw-Hill.

——. 1936b. Psychology of success and failure. *Occupations,* **14,** 926–930.

——. 1938. The conceptual representation and measurement of psychological forces. *Contr. Psychol. Theor.,* **1,** No. 4.

——. 1939. Field theory and experiment in social psychology: Concepts and methods. *Amer. J. Sociol.,* **44,** 868–896.

——. 1940a. Studies in topological and vector psychology: I. Formalization and progress in psychology. *Univ. Iowa Stud. Child Welfare,* **16,** No. 3, 7–42.

——. 1940b. Bringing up the child. *Menorah J.,* **28,** 29–45.

——. 1942. Time perspective and morale. In G. WATSON (Ed.), *Civilian morale,* second yearbook of the SPSSI. Boston: Published for Reynal and Hitchcock by Houghton Mifflin.

——. 1943. Defining the "field at a given time." *Psychol. Rev.,* **50,** No. 3, 292–310.

——. 1945. Studies in topological and vector psychology: III. Constructs in psychology and psychological ecology. *Univ. Iowa Stud. Child Welfare,* **20.**

LEWIN, K., T. DEMBO, L. FESTINGER, and P. SEARS. 1944. Level of aspiration. In J. McV. HUNT (Ed.), *Handbook of personality*

and the behavior disorders. New York: Ronald.

LEWIN, K., R. LIPPITT, and R. WHITE. 1939. Patterns of aggressive behavior in experimentally created "social climates." *J. Soc. Psychol.,* **10,** 271–299.

LIPPITT, RONALD. 1939. Field theory and experiment in social psychology: Autocratic and democratic group atmospheres. *Amer. J. Sociol.,* **45,** 26–49.

——. 1940. Studies in topological and vector psychology: I. An experimental study of the effect of democratic and authoritarian group atmospheres. *Univ. Iowa Stud. Child Welfare,* **16,** No. 3, 45–195.

LIPPITT, R., and R. WHITE. 1943. The "social climate" of children's groups. In BARKER, KOUNIN, and WRIGHT, *Child behavior and development.* New York: McGraw-Hill.

LIPPITT, ROSEMARY. 1940. *Popularity among preschool children.* Unpublished Ph.D. Dissertation, University of Iowa.

LISSNER, K. 1933. Die Entspannung von Bedürfnissen durch Ersatzhandlungen. *Psychol. Forsch.,* **18,** 218–250.

MACDONALD, J. M. 1940. *The behavior of the young child under conditions of insecurity.* Unpublished Ph.D. Dissertation, Harvard University.

MAHLER, V. 1933. Ersatzhandlungen verschiedenen Realitätsgrades. *Psychol. Forsch.,* **18,** 26–89.

MARQUIS, D. P. 1931. Can conditioned responses be established in the newborn infant? *J. Genet. Psychol.,* **39,** 479–492.

MARROW, A. J. 1938. Goal tension and recall. *J. Gen. Psychol.,* **19,** 3–35; 37–64.

McGRATH, M. C. 1923. A study of the moral development of children. *Psychol. Monogr.,* **32,** No. 2, 1–190.

McGRAW, M. B. 1935. *Growth: A study of Johnny and Jimmy.* New York: Appleton-Century.

MEAD, M. 1928. *Coming of age in Samoa.* New York: Morrow.

——. 1937. *Cooperation and competition among primitive peoples.* New York: McGraw-Hill.

MEYERS, C. E. 1945. Studies in topological and vector psychology: III. The effect of conflicting authority on the child. *Univ. Iowa Stud. Child Welfare,* **20.**

MOORE, E. S. 1931. The development of mental health in a group of young children: An analysis of factors in purposeful activity. *Univ. Iowa Stud. Child Welfare,* **4,** No. 6.

MORENO, J. L. 1934. *Who shall survive? A new approach to the problem of human interrelations.* Washington, D. C.: Nervous and Mental Disease Publishing Co.

MURPHY, G., L. B. MURPHY, and T. M. NEWCOMB. 1937. *Experimental social psychology* (rev. ed.). New York: Harper.

MURPHY, L. B. 1937. *Social behavior and child*

personality: An explorative study in some roots of sympathy. New York: Columbia University Press.

MURRAY, H. 1938. *Explorations in personality.* London: Oxford University Press.

OVSIANKINA, M. 1928. Die Wiederaufnahme von unterbrochener Handlungen. *Psychol. Forsch.,* **11,** 302–379.

PACHAURI, A. R. 1935. A study of Gestalt problems in completed and interrupted tasks: I. *Brit. J. Psychol.,* **25,** 447–457.

PIAGET, J. 1932. *The moral judgment of the child.* (Trans. by M. GABAIN.) New York: Harcourt, Brace; London: Kegan Paul.

PORTER, H. VON K. 1939. Studies in the psychology of stuttering: XIV. Stuttering phenomena in relation to size and personnel of audience. *J. Speech Disorders,* **4,** 323–333.

PRATT, K. C. 1933. The neonate. In C. MURCHISON (Ed.), *A handbook of psychology,* pp. 163–208. (2d ed., rev.) Worcester: Clark University Press.

REICHENBACH, H. 1928. *Philosophie der Raum-Zeitlehre.* Leipzig: De Gruyter.

REUTER, E. B. 1937. The sociology of adolescence. *Amer. J. Sociol.,* **43,** 414–427.

ROSENZWEIG, S. 1933. The recall of finished and unfinished tasks as affected by the purpose with which they were performed. *Psychol. Bull.,* **30,** 698 (abstract).

ROTTER, J. B. 1939. Studies in the psychology of stuttering: XI. Stuttering in relation to position in the family. *J. Speech Disorders,* **4,** 143–148.

SANDVOSS, H. 1933. Über die Beziehungen von Determination und Bewusstsein bei der Realisierung unerledigter Tätigkeiten. *Arch. ges. Psychol.,* **89,** 139–192.

SCHANCK, R. L. 1932. A study of a community and its groups and institutions conceived of as behaviors of individuals. *Psychol. Monogr.,* **43,** No. 2, 1–133.

SCHLOTE, W. 1930. Über die Bevorzugung unvollendeter Handlungen. *Z. Psychol.,* **117,** 1–72.

SEARS, P. S. 1940. Levels of aspiration in academically successful and unsuccessful children. *J. Abnorm. Soc. Psychol.,* **35,** 498–536.

SEARS, R. R., and P. S. SEARS. 1940. Minor studies in aggression: V. Strength of frustration-reaction as a function of strength of drive. *J. Psychol.,* **9,** 297–300.

SEASHORE, H. E., and A. BAVELAS. 1942. A study of frustration in children. *J. Genet. Psychol.,* **61,** 279–314.

SEWALL, M. 1930. Some causes of jealousy in young children. *Smith Coll. Stud. Soc. Work,* **1,** 6–22.

SHACTER, H. S. 1933. A method for measuring the sustained attention of preschool children. *J. Genet. Psychol.,* **42,** 339–371.

SHAW, C. R. 1933. Juvenile delinquency—a group tradition. (*Child Welfare Pamphlets,*

No. 23.) *Bull. State Univ. Iowa, New Ser.,* No. 700.

SHAW, C. R., *et al.* 1929. *Delinquency areas: A study of the geographic distribution of school truants, juvenile delinquents, and adult offenders in Chicago.* (*Behav. Res. Monogr.*) Chicago: University of Chicago Press. Pp. xxi + 214.

SHEFFIELD, A. 1937. *Social insight in case situations.* New York: Appleton-Century.

SLIOSBERG, S. 1934. A contribution to the dynamics of substitution in serious and play situations. *Psychol. Forsch.,* **19,** 122–181.

STERN, W., and J. MACDONALD. 1937. Cloud pictures: A new method of testing imagination. *Character and Pers.,* **6,** 132–147.

STODDARD, G. D., and B. L. WELLMAN. 1934. *Child psychology.* New York: Macmillan.

TERMAN, L. M. 1919. *The intelligence of school children.* Boston: Houghton Mifflin.

THOMAS, D. S. 1932. An attempt to develop precise measurements in the social behavior field. *Sociologus,* **8,** 436–456.

THOMPSON, M. M. 1940. *The effect of discriminatory leadership on the relations between the more and less privileged subgroups.* Unpublished Ph.D. Dissertation, University of Iowa.

TOLMAN, E. C. 1932. *Purposive behavior in animals and men.* New York: Century.

——. 1935. Psychology versus immediate experience. *Phil. Sci.,* **2,** 356–380.

TRAVIS, L. E., W. JOHNSON, and J. SHOVER. 1937. The relation of bilingualism to stuttering. *J. Speech Disorders,* **3,** 185–189.

VIGOTSKY, L. S. 1934. Thought in schizophrenia. *Arch. Neurol. Psychiat., Chicago,* **31,** 1063–1077.

WARING, E. B., F. M. DWYER, and E. JUNKIN. 1939. Guidance: The case of Ronald. *Cornell Bull. for Homemakers,* No. 418, 1–112.

WEIGL, E. 1941. On the psychology of so-called processes of abstraction. *J. Abnorm. Soc. Psychol.,* **36,** 3–33.

WELLMAN, B. L. 1932–1933. The effect of preschool attendance upon the IQ. *J. Exp. Educ.,* **1,** 48–69.

WERNER, H. 1940a. *Comparative psychology of mental development.* New York: Harper.

——. 1940b. Perception of spatial relationships in mentally deficient children. *J. Genet. Psychol.,* **57,** 93–100.

WHITE, R. K. 1940. An analysis of conversation in autocratic and democratic atmospheres. *Psychol. Bull.,* **37,** 476.

WIEHE, F. 1935. *Die Grenzen des Ichs.* Quoted in LEWIN (1935.)

WOLF, T. H. 1938. *The effect of praise and competition on the persistent behavior of kindergarten children.* (*Inst. Child Welfare Monogr. Ser.,* No. 15.) Minneapolis: University of Minnesota Press.

WRIGHT, B. A. 1941. An experimentally created conflict expressed in a projective technique. *Psychol. Bull.*, **38**, 718 (abstract).

——. 1942a. Altruism in children and the perceived conduct of others. *J. Abnorm. Soc. Psychol.*, **37**, 218–233.

——. 1942b. The development of the ideology of altruism and fairness in children. Ph.D. thesis, State Univ. Iowa. (Also, *Psychol. Bull.*, **39**, 485–486 [abstract].)

WRIGHT, H. F. 1937. The influence of barriers upon the strength of motivation. *Contr. Psychol. Theor.*, **1**, No. 3.

WRIGHT, M. E. 1940. The influence of frustration upon the social relationships of young children. Ph.D. thesis, State Univ. Iowa. (Also, *Psychol. Bull.*, **38**, 710 [abstract].)

ZEIGARNIK, B. 1927. Über das Behalten von erledigten und unerledigten Handlungen. *Psychol. Forsch.*, **9**, 1–85.

CHAPTER 17

THE FEEBLE-MINDED CHILD [1]

EDGAR A. DOLL

The Concept

In all societies there are some individuals who do not make a successful "go" of life. They fail to manage their affairs with ordinary discretion. They are incapable of economic independence at more than a marginal standard of living. They get into various social difficulties, perhaps adding delinquency to dependency. They are the socially incompetent who live their lives at ineffectual levels of social, occupational, and educational activity (Jastrow, 1938).

[1] *Author's note:* This formulation extends the excellent treatment of this topic in *A Handbook of Child Psychology*, edited by C. Murchison (Pintner, 1933). The accompanying bibliography supplements that of Pintner in accordance with the difference in emphasis. The material has been organized to emphasize standpoints rather than to survey the detailed literature. The illustrations are designed to portray the feeble-minded as living people rather than as morbid specimens. The emphasis is on mental deficiency as a clinical symptom-complex or syndrome rather than as simple subnormality of intelligence. The terms *feeble-mindedness* and *mental deficiency* are used synonymously but with some exposition of current variation from this practice. Also, the term *child* is used somewhat loosely to include mentally deficient adults, as in general institutional practice. The rather common medical practice of referring to the feeble-minded as *patients* is avoided so far as practicable on the ground that mental deficiency in general represents a condition rather than a disease. While the subject matter of this chapter is related to the scientific and popular literature, the emphasis naturally reflects the author's point of view, which may here and there be at variance with those of individual authorities. In lieu of direct quotation, liberal bibliographic references are provided in the running text as well as in indented passages of elaborative comment.

Such a person may be a burden to his family or a liability to his community. Or he may "get along" in a fairly good state of social adjustment at a low degree of personal, family, and group attainment. Among these socially dubious individuals there are many types of associated conditions (Goddard, 1912; Kostir, 1916; Rogers and Merrill, 1919; Estabrook and McDougle, 1926; Wembridge, 1926; Sherman and Henry, 1933; G. M. Whipple, 1940).

Consider, for example, the socially marginal whose level of adjustment has been handicapped by limited environmental opportunities, poor financial circumstances, unfavorable homes and associates, ill health, crushing personal misfortunes, with consequent loss of pride or ambition.[2] These are the socially impoverished, the "submerged tenth," whose personal qualities operate somewhat obscurely to prevent their rising to positions of social self-sufficiency. They may have a fair amount of native capacity and aptitude which has not been stimulated or exercised to the point of personal social independence. We may designate them as the socially subcultural or borderline (Wood, 1929; Penrose, 1933) without specific handicap except generally low *élan vital*.

Others among the socially incompetent are handicapped by various physical infirmities such as crippling, defects of sight

[2] Compare sociological fiction (for example, *The Grapes of Wrath, Tobacco Road, Of Mice and Men*). Classical literary examples have been assembled by MacMurchy (1920).

or hearing, or chronic diseases (Berry, 1931; Scheidemann, 1931; Ellis, 1933; Heck, 1940). In the otherwise normal person, and under favorable environmental conditions, these handicaps do not of themselves produce social incompetence. They may, however, serve to depress the socially

successful. These mental abnormalities, such as insanity and epilepsy, frequently lead to serious mental deterioration.

A fourth group, distributed throughout all socioeconomic levels but predominating at the lower margin, is composed of those with generalized developmental deficiencies.

FIGURE 1. Familial mental deficiency. (From *Clinical Studies in Feeble-mindedness,* by E. A. Doll. Boston: Badger, 1917, 26, 54. By permission of the publisher.)

Left. Mag and two of her boys at the county almshouse. She was able to tell the number of her children (by various fathers) so long as she had only ten. The arrival of the eleventh child overtaxed her limited ability to count. She was committed to a state institution shortly after this picture was taken; LA (life age) 35, Binet MA (mental age) 6. The boy at her right was committed to a training school at the same time; LA about 7, Binet MA 3.5, IQ (intelligence quotient) about 50. This family had extensive ramifications in a rural district where their borderline mentality and subcultural habits constituted a serious moral and economic burden to the community.

Right. Poverty, domestic incompetence, and child neglect in a subcultural home and family. The mother has "run off" on another sexual escapade leaving her potentially feeble-minded children in the dubious care of her putative father (right). The IQ's of the children are within borderline limits, but family history and personal characteristics suggest ultimate borderline mental deficiency. The domestic interior of this rural shack reveals extreme slovenliness and submarginal home life. Later investigation showed some of these children clearly feeble-minded, others dubiously within low normal limits.

marginal person to submarginal levels, especially when coupled with reinforcing deficiencies of weak personality or low stimulation.

Another group has its origins in general and specific mental disorders which produce aberrations of such manner or extent as to interfere with the full exercise of native aptitudes (Hillyer, 1926; Morgan, 1928; H. L. Hollingworth, 1930; "Inmate Ward 8," 1932). These disorders may develop early in life, but most of them become critical in the later years among persons who have previously been socially

They owe their social subnormality to incomplete mental maturation, apparent from birth or from a relatively early age, as a result of limited native endowment or various influences which arrest normal mental growth (Tredgold, 1937). *These are the feeble-minded.* Their condition reflects early and relatively permanent inhibition of ontogenetic evolution of the organism as a whole, which is made manifest at maturity by a constitutional incapacity for adequate self-direction and self-support (Doll, 1941).

For a clear concept, correct diagnosis,

and sound classification the feeble-minded must be separated from the merely impoverished, the unadjusted, the antisocial, the physically handicapped, the feeble personalities, and the mentally disordered. These conditions may be associated with or may be consequences of feeble-mindedness, but as such are only suggestive symptoms which may be due to causes other than or in addition to feeble-mindedness.

A satisfactory criterion of feeble-mindedness involves four essential attributes, namely, social (including occupational and educational) inferiority, intellectual retardation, developmental arrest, and constitutional deficiency or defect. No one of these criteria may be omitted without weakening the concept. Thus, mental deficiency in the limited sense of low mental test performance which is not accompanied by social incompetence is not synonymous with feeble-mindedness in its traditional and legal definition (Wood, 1929; Doll, 1936a, 1940c). Similarly, developmental deficiencies which are not primarily mental in nature and do not result in social inaptitude cannot be considered as the genuine feeble-mindedness with which the term *mental deficiency* has long been associated (Humphreys, 1936; Wechsler, 1939).

Since this condition is essentially one of developmental incompleteness, its criteria may not always be fully satisfied prior to maturity except in extreme cases where the presumptive maturity level can be safely predicted from other characteristics. Moreover, the condition is considered as essentially incurable because of its organic basis (Kuhlmann, 1915). These constitutional limitations to normal function may in some cases be ameliorated by treatment and training, and to this extent the condition is improvable. Through environmental stimulation and favorable situations the social incompetence which is the essential earmark of the condition may be alleviated sufficiently to enable the borderline individual to pass temporarily from high-grade deficiency to dull normality in social adaptation. Correspondingly, unfavorable environmental opportunity may depress the borderline dull-normal to apparent high-grade deficiency, especially when coupled with marginal constitutional aptitudes (Skeels and Dye, 1939; Strauss and Kephart, 1939). Thus, favorable personality, social habits, attitudes, and achievements may *pro tem* change marginal failure to marginal success and *vice versa*. Care must be exercised, however, not to confuse this temporary amelioration of the behavioral *symptoms* with the relatively permanent nature of the constitutional symptom-complex.

Hence the complete concept of the feeble-minded child must include lack of ultimate maturation to normal adult levels of attainment. Consequently, the diagnosis of feeble-mindedness in children is tentative or prognostic (Doll, 1917; Bisch, 1925; Gesell, 1928; Louttit, 1936; Gesell, Castner, Thompson, and Amatruda, 1939). In certain grades and types this diagnostic prognosis can safely be made prior to maturity, but in the less severe degrees and especially in the familial types can be only presumptive during the genetic period (Huey, 1912; Blackfan, 1932; Baller, 1936).

The childlikeness which results from incomplete ontogenesis is reflected in current terminology. The term *feeble-mindedness* is traditionally synonymous with mental deficiency, mental defect, mental defectiveness, or more technically amentia, oligophrenia, hypophrenia.[1] This is reflected in the generic German term *Schwachsinnigkeit*, the French *faiblesse mentale*, the Italian *frenastenia*, and so on (Bösbauer,

[1] The student should be on guard for the careless and often indiscriminate use of these terms in other meanings.

Miklas, and Schiner, 1909; De Sanctis, 1912).

In the American literature *mental deficiency* is generically synonymous with feeble-mindedness, but in British usage the latter term is specifically employed for the highest grade of mental deficiency, corresponding to the American term *moron*. More recently the term mental deficiency has been loosely used for various degrees of intellectual attainment as measured by specific mental tests without reference to the diagnostic syndrome. This tendency is regrettable because of (*a*) the earlier authoritative identification of mental deficiency with feeble-mindedness, (*b*) the serious social implications, (*c*) the uncertainty of the standards employed in specifying varying degrees of mental retardation, and (*d*) the discrepancies of differentiation as among the specific tests employed. Until the relation of mental retardation to social retardation is specified, and until the results from different tests are harmonized, scientific consistency and sound social practice cannot be attained. Since the personal characteristics and the recognized methods of treatment established for the mentally deficient who are feeble-minded do not apply to the so-called mentally deficient who are only intellectually retarded (Ellis, 1933), grave errors of scientific classification and public policy may result. Social welfare and educational programs for the mentally subnormal who are not feeble-minded differ radically from the programs for those who are feeble-minded (Davies, 1930).

Since the early work with the feeble-minded was conducted principally under medical auspices, the medical term *patient* came into use and the concept of mental deficiency as a disease acquired authoritative standing. But in the majority of cases feeble-mindedness is a condition rather than a disease (Wolfe, 1935) and, since those so affected are not ill or sick, the term patient may be thought of as more conventional than literal. For this reason and because of the essential resemblance of the feeble-minded at all ages to the developmental stages of childhood, the term *feeble-minded child* has come to be used rather widely, especially among institutional workers, for any feeble-minded person regardless of his age. In careful usage the word *child* is employed without quotation marks for juveniles (say under 16 to 20 years of age), and with quotation marks for those who are beyond the developmental age period in years but not in maturity. Much of the literature applies to both children and adults, and the differentiation of characteristics and treatment according to life age has not usually been very clearly specified. In this chapter an effort will be made to reserve the term feeble-minded child for those individuals who are under approximately 20 years of age, although much of the material applies to the feeble-minded in general, regardless of age.

The history of this topic has been so well covered in Murchison's *Handbook* (Pintner, 1933) that it is unnecessary to repeat that material here. Briefly, prior to the beginning of the nineteenth century and the work of the French physician, Itard, the feeble-minded were not systematically cared for except as other social dependents. They were thought of as social outcasts, or public fools, and left to perish or survive as best they might. Legal recognition of mental deficiency is evident in English law in the sixteenth century, and by the nineteenth century various forms of asylum care had been established (Barr, 1904). Following the work of Itard (1932) with the Wild Boy of Aveyron,[1] about 1800, and the work of his pupil, Seguin (1907; original in 1866), public institutions for the treatment and sympathetic custodial care of the feeble-minded were established. In the United States such care began about 1840 and de-

[1] A summary of earlier observations and experiments on "wild children" is offered by Briffault (1927).

eloped rather rapidly toward the end of he nineteenth century (Fernald, 1917). ince the first decade of the twentieth entury, state care has been widely extended so that by 1935 there were approximately 130 public and private residential institutions in 47 states caring for 4,000 individuals (Zubin, 1938). Coincidentally, programs of special education ave been developed for the feeble-minded n the public schools in 43 states, whereby 43 city systems reporting special schools r classes serve 99,621 children (Foster nd Martens, 1938). These developments n the United States have been paralleled y similar developments in Europe and lsewhere throughout the world, especially n England. As yet, however, institutional rovision for the feeble-minded is available for less than 5 per cent of the generally estimated total number of the feebleminded (about one person per hundred in he general population) and hardly anywhere exceeds 10 per cent of that total Doll, 1929, 1933b).

Definition and Classification

As already noted, the feeble-minded are hose children and adults who are socially ncompetent because of serious degrees of ntellectual subnormality resulting from ubnormal psychosomatic development.

There is some uncertainty as to what constitutes mental subnormality and arrested development since these, like social inferiority, vary with time, place, and circumstances. There has been ample measurement of intelligence (Pintner, 1931), but such measurement has been only crudely correlated with total social success.

Differential standards of arrested development have been vague because so little is known regarding the comparative course of progressive maturation in normal and defective children. Work in the field of mental tests has led many to conclude that mental development proceeds at a rate which is constant throughout the genetic period. This is true for averages, but does not necessarily apply to individuals or to some specific groups. Some authorities assume that arrested mental development occurs suddenly, and others assume that it occurs gradually. The evidence suggests both possibilities and further indicates that this may vary in individual cases and for different degrees and types of deficiency (L. S. Hollingworth, 1920; Doll, 1921; Blackfan, 1932; Wechsler, 1939).

The hereditary feeble-minded usually show degrees of brightness which are close to the normal average during the period of infancy and early childhood; progressive developmental retardation may then occur any time prior to the preadolescent period, but usually not later than about six to ten years of age. In the more severe and pathological types mental arrest may be evident at birth or in early infancy. Arrest may also occur suddenly at any age prior to maturity when adventitious circumstances, such as accident or disease, interrupt development in a person of normal endowment. Other children may show delayed maturation or delayed retardation for reasons not yet well understood. Hence some initially retarded children may later attain average status, whereas other children may show early average attainment with later serious retardation (Burt, 1921; Jewell, 1929; Baller, 1936; Gesell, Castner, Thompson, and Amatruda, 1939; Doll, 1940c; cf. Fig. 10, this Chapter, p. 870.

It should be noted that, although all the feeble-minded have some characteristics in common, this condition is not a clinical entity in the sense that all cases show the same attributes, the same course of development, the same onset, the same cause, or respond to the same methods of care, treatment, and training. On the contrary, mental deficiency is revealed in a succession of "grades," types, and etiologies, and the failure to distinguish these has led to ambiguity in the interpretation of research data.

It is customary to classify the feeble-minded according to (1) form, (2) grade, and (3) type (Tredgold, 1937). *Form* refers to the presumptive etiology grouped as primary, secondary, and mixed. *Grade* refers to the degree of severity of the mental deficiency. *Type* refers to the clinical varieties of amentia. These may be combined with accessory influences such as health, age, and behavior in a supplementary administrative classification for purposes of social disposition and control (Doll, 1929).

Primary (hereditary, endogenous) mental deficiency includes those cases where the cause is simple familial transmission. Some authorities include congenital cases in which abnormalities occurring at the time of fertilization or during the period of gestation produce conditions which are recognizable at birth or are directly related to the prenatal and birth histories. Intra-uterine anomalies of development, and birth abnormalities, are more generally considered as producing secondary amentia because they are postconceptional or because the true causes are not clearly understood. Some authorities class these as complications or special cases of primary amentia rather than as separate conditions.

Secondary (acquired, exogenous) amentia includes those cases which are attributable to developmental anomalies, accidents, or diseases which adversely affect the healthy fruition of normal genetic endowment. These causes are sometimes referred to as adventitious or accidental and may occur at any time between conception and adult maturity.

The terms *endogenous* and *exogenous* are sometimes used etiologically and sometimes symptomatically, the descriptions serving as presumptive indications of etiology.

The endogenous group includes the organically sound individuals of hereditary origin where deficiency rather than defect is the outstanding feature. This is generally referred to as uncomplicated (simple) feeble-mindedness. The exogenous group includes persons with marked neurological, glandular, and other organic defects which are superimposed upon, or are the major cause of, the ultimate feeble-mindedness without familial heredity (Strauss, 1939).

Extrahereditary influences may be added to the handicap of genetically poor endowment, thus producing the *mixed* form. The temporal onset and severity of these adventitious influences are specially relevant to the type and degree of ensuing mental deficiency.

Classification by form is of special importance in the interpretation of research data, since the various characteristics of the feeble-minded, the course of maturation, the practicability of treatment and care are intimately related to the etiology.

Classification by *grade* of deficiency includes the subdegrees of idiot, imbecile, and moron. In careful clinical practice these grades of feeble-mindedness are viewed as fairly distinct symptom-complexes without appreciable overlapping (Doll, 1936a). More commonly this classification is made in terms of Binet-Simon mental age (Rogers, 1910) or IQ (Fernald, 1921) as convenient points on a continuum, without reference to other characteristics. The latter practice has the disadvantage of not allowing for variations in the course of mental development, and, since there is

[1] The MA and IQ standards for feeble-mindedness are derived from Binet-Simon (most commonly 1916 Stanford revision) tests. Results from other tests may not be so used without specific validation as to their statistical and diagnostic equivalence. As noted elsewhere, test data alone, and *a fortiori* data from single test systems, do not constitute a proper basis for clinical designations. Classification by MA grade is determined *after* the feeble-mindedness has been determined by other (additional) evidence.

tendency for the mental ages (and con-sequently the IQ's) of the feeble-minded to become progressively retarded with ad-vancing life age, such a mental test grada-tion leads to recurrent shifts of classifica-tion. Each of the three grades of defi-ciency is further subdivided into low, middle, and high.

Idiocy, the most severe degree of mental deficiency, includes those who at maturity are unable to care for their personal needs, protect themselves from ordinary danger, develop useful command of speech, or mas-ter even the simplest occupational tasks. As children, idiots give little promise of such social attainments. The physical and physiological signs of idiocy are more se-vere than in the higher grades, with a greater prevalence of retarded growth, physical stigmata, physiological anomalies, specific diseases, motor handicaps, and other constitutional symptoms. Learning, emotionality, and initiative are at the in-fant level (Aldrich and Doll, 1931c). The ultimate Binet mental age of idiots is be-low 3 years, and final arrest in develop-ment is common by 6 or 8 years of age. Their social maturity is practically com-plete at 10 years of age with "social ages" below 4 years. Idiots are predominantly of the secondary form and include a high percentage of the clinical anomalies of men-tal development (Bradway, 1935). Al-though among these attributes the social and the mental are the most distinguishing traits, the total clinical combination rein-forces these distinctions, especially among young children where early prediction of ultimate status is desired. This symptom-complex determination of idiocy is useful as an effective basis for early disposition, treatment, care, and training.

Imbeciles are those who can be taught to care for their personal needs, to pro-tect themselves from ordinary dangers, and to master simple routine tasks under supervision, but are incapable of benefiting appreciably from scholastic instruction or of acquiring more than the most rudimen-tary occupational skills. Imbeciles stand midway between idiots and morons in most respects. They have a fair command of speech but marked poverty of ideas. They are more than vegetative and are even so-cially helpful under sympathetic direction. Such initiative as they have is feebly exer-cised. In personality they are bland or inane rather than aggressive or antago-nistic. Mental maturity is usually com-plete at about 10 or 12 years of age with Binet mental age ranging from 3 to 7 years, inclusive. Social maturity is ordi-narily complete at 15 years of age with social ages between 4 and 9 years. Both forms of amentia are found about equally in this grade, the secondary form being relatively more prevalent at the lower levels and the primary form at the higher levels (Penrose, 1938).

Morons represent the highest grade of feeble-mindedness, and care should be taken not to confuse them with the lower degrees of dull normality. Morons under favorable conditions are capable of looking after themselves in routine matters, may acquire apprentice levels of skill in the simpler occupations, and may master the rudiments of scholastic education below the fifth school grade but without much successful use for practical purposes. Mo-rons are lacking in social judgment and do not usually develop sufficient discretion for economic independence or for more than marginal social success except under the most favorable conditions. Many morons "get on" after a fashion, but their social success is generally precarious and in the long run falls short of the normal standard of personal independence (Wood, 1929). Morons may, however, be happy, useful, and well adjusted so long as the demands of their environment do not overtax their

FIGURE 2. Grades of mental deficiency. The reader is urged to estimate the degree of feeble
mindedness represented in each case and then compare the accompanying descriptive data
(Photographs courtesy Dr. E. R. Johnstone, Director, The Training School at Vineland, N. J
and Dr. H. Robert Otness.)

Left to right, beginning top row: [MA's are from the 1916 Stanford-Binet Scale; SA's (socia
ages) are from the Vineland Social Maturity Scale. IQ's are based on 14-year adult divisor; SQ"
(social quotients) are based on 25-year adult divisor. Res. (length of residence) indicates period o
continuous years of institutional care at The Training School to present LA.]

Henry B. Potential moron. LA 12.7, MA 7.2, IQ 57, SA 7.0, SQ 55, Res. 2.4. Familial typ
(mother feeble-minded, sister at State School). Binet annual growth rate .74 (initial IQ 53) fo
past 2.4 years (testing period), with rising IQ.

Karl H. High-grade imbecile. LA 40.8, MA 6.0, IQ 43, SA 8.0, SQ 32, Res. 27.8. **Right-side**
hemiplegia. Etiology birth lesion. Mental age static since first test at LA 13.

Nora H. Low-grade moron. LA 14.8, MA 8.3, IQ 59, SA 10.0, SQ 68, Res. 4.5. Familial typ
(father unknown, mother feeble-minded, five defective siblings). Binet annual growth rate .1
(initial IQ 77) for past 4.5 years (testing period), with falling IQ.

George Q. Middle-grade imbecile. LA 43.5, MA 4.3 (at LA 36.8), IQ 31, SA 7.6, SQ 30, Res. 32.6

imited capacities, or so long as the condi-ions in the community or the supervision hey receive protect them from the more erious readjustments required by chang-ng conditions. Morons are principally of he familial type and primary form; the ther types and secondary form are rela-ively infrequent. Although abnormalities f physique are common among the insti-utional cases, morons generally are of ;ood physical constitution (Kaplun, 1935). They have a fair degree of initiative, espe-ially prior to the adult years, but this is ssociated with naïve judgment which often produces unfavorable conduct. Intellectual naturity is usually complete by 15 years of ge (compare, however, Raymond, 1927; Voodall, 1931), with Binet mental age anging from 8 to 12 years. Individual ases reveal a somewhat longer period of levelopment and a somewhat higher men-al age limit, but this is unusual and not rdinarily functionally significant. Social naturity is complete by about 20 years of ge, with social ages between 10 and 18 ears.

Classification by *clinical type* includes, n addition to familial (primary) feeble-nindedness, such distinctive pathological onditions as mongolism, birth lesion, micro-ephaly, hydrocephalus, and a number of ess common syndromes associated with

feeble-mindedness (Bisch, 1925; Tredgold, 1937; Penrose, 1944). The nonfamilial types are not always classifiable as primary or secondary because of uncertainties of knowledge regarding their etiology. It should be noted, however, that the feeble-mindedness itself may have a variable rela-tionship to different clinical types. For example, while mental deficiency is as-sumed always to accompany mongolism or microcephaly, it only sometimes results from or is accompanied by birth lesion or hydrocephalus. These clinical types may be thought of as more or less definite syn-dromes in the sense that they severally represent similarities of etiology, attributes, course, and treatment.

Familial mental deficiency is the most common type. Such individuals show sim-ple developmental retardation as a result of low genetic potential for development. This group includes at least one-third of all the mentally deficient, and by many authorities is thought to include two-thirds or more of all cases. However, it must be understood that what is known scien-tifically about mental deficiency today is limited to those individuals who have re-ceived specific attention. Since, as noted previously, less than 10 per cent of all the feeble-minded are identified 'for clinical study, and since familial feeble-mindedness

---

ncertain etiology (family history negative, birth lesion, congenital hypothyroidism, malnutrition). farked cretinism at LA 7; conspicuous improvement following thyroid medication. Macrocephalic.)eaf. Mental age static since first test at LA 13.

Evelyn N. Low-grade imbecile, mongolian type. LA 12.0, MA 3.3, IQ 27, SA 3.8, SQ 32, Res. 3.0. Binet annual growth rate .10 (initial IQ 33) for past 3.0 years (testing period), with falling IQ.

Irvin T. Low-grade moron. LA 15.4, MA 9.0, IQ 64, SA 8.9, SQ 58, Res. 8.6. Macrocephalic. tiology cerebral birth hemorrhage with congenital hydrocephalus; family history negative. IQ 52 t LA 7.1 (first test), with Binet annual growth rate .86 for following 5.7 years, with rising IQ o LA 12.8, followed by annual rate .15 to present LA.

Frances D. High-grade moron. LA 21.4, MA 10.7 (at LA 19.4), IQ 76, SA 14.1, SQ 66, Res. 8.3. 'amilial type. Socially unstable. Fourth-grade literacy. Competent cook. Mental age static ince LA 14.

Samuel S. Excitable middle-grade idiot. LA 13.0, Kuhlmann-Binet MA 1.7, IQ 13, SA 2.6, SQ 20, Res. 5.1. Etiology undetermined; presumption of exogenous form. Mental age static since first est at LA 9.

Daniel B. Low-grade moron. LA 60.4, MA 7.3, IQ 52, SA 10.3, SQ 41, Res. 49.3. Familial type. Iental age static since first test at LA 30.

easily escapes attention as a low degree of pseudonormal development, the vast majority of the hereditary feeble-minded have not yet been clinically observed. The majority of the unrecognized feeble-minded are probably of the hereditary type, which, if true, would greatly increase their pro-

versely fissured lips, deeply furrowe tongue, rough edematous skin, and so o Other characteristics include relatively lo stature, infantile body form, stubby hand poor circulation, and hoarse voice (Brous seau, 1928; Kuenzel, 1929; Penrose, 1933 Tredgold, 1937).

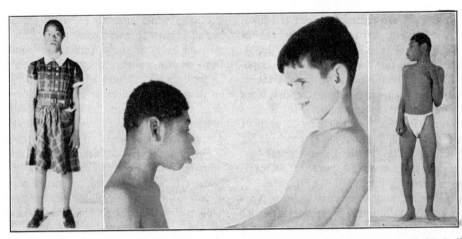

FIGURE 3. Clinical types of mental deficiency. (Photographs and data courtesy: (left) G. I Thorn, Superintendent, Vineland State School, Vineland, N. J.; (center and right) E. I Johnstone, Superintendent, State Colony, Woodbine, N. J., and H. von Bulow.)

Left. Negro mongolian low-grade imbecile. (Note that mongolism is comparatively infreque among Negroes.) LA 16.6, Binet MA 3.7, IQ 27, SA 3.7, SQ 22. (Cf. Fig. 2, Evelyn N., and Fig. 6 *Center.* Negro microcephalic low-grade idiot compared with white macrocephalic high-grade idio *Microcephalic*—LA 10.8, Kuhlmann-Binet MA 0.7, IQ 6, SA 0.8, SQ 7. Etiology undetermine (brother-sister incest parenthood). Height 123 cm. (average for 8 years), weight 25.4 kg. Cep alometric measurements: circumference 420 mm., length 138 mm., breadth 114 mm., height 107 mm cubic capacity (Lee-Porteus) 830 cc. (below average for age 0–1). *Macrocephalic*—LA 12.7, Kul mann-Binet MA 3.0, IQ 24, SA 3.5, SQ 28. Etiology undetermined (three sisters at State School Height 139 cm. (average for 11 years), weight 31.4 kg. Cephalometric measurements: circumfe ence 545 mm., length 193 mm., breadth 146 mm., height 139 mm., cubic capacity 1465 cc. (averag for 18–19 years).
Right. Full-length view of Negro microcephalic at center left.

portion of all the feeble-minded (Goddard, 1914; Wildenskov, 1934; Myerson, 1936; Penrose, 1938).

The *mongolian type* of mental deficiency derives its name from a minor resemblance to the Mongol race, namely, the almond-shaped ocular orifice. The most obvious physical signs are almond-shaped slanting eyes, epicanthus, small brachycephalic head, flat occiput, adenoid facies, trans-

The condition occurs within the Mong race and among Negroes, as well as in t white race (Thompson, 1939). In spite the ease with which this type is recognize from its appearance, the characteristi enumerated by different authorities as cli ically significant are not in close agre ment. One study of the statistical inc dence of these traits comparing mongolia feeble-minded subjects with paired no ongolian feeble-minded has developed a st of sixteen differential traits, a mini-um of eight of which are present among ongolians and a maximum of six of which re present in nonmongolian feeble-minded f the same age, mental age, and sex.[1]

This is a conspicuous type of mental de-ciency which includes about 10 per cent f the population of most institutions. hese patients look and act remarkably ike, and this suggests a unique genetic athology, but the basic etiology is not yet early understood (Jenkins, 1933).

Mongolism occurs sporadically in fami-es of good social status and is obscurely lated to advanced maternal age. It has een attributed to various anomalies of nception and early embryonic evolution. Iorphologically, it is related to multiple docrine dysmetabolism, especially of the yroid gland, the pituitary body, and robably the gonads. Because of thyroid volvement there is some physical resem-ance of mongolism to cretinism. In some ses endocrine medication has yielded atifying mental and physical improve-ent, but seldom if ever has it brought ch patients to normal limits of social d educational proficiency (Jervis, 1942).

Mongolism is predominantly of idiot and becile grade, seldom exceeding a Binet ental age of six or eight years. Indeed, e condition is commonly referred to as ongolian idiocy because of the usually w level of intelligence. Their social com-tence is generally less than that antici-ted from the associated mental level. hey ordinarily are short-lived; many esumably unidentified cases die early in fancy and relatively few live much be-nd thirty or forty years. They are rticularly subject to respiratory, circula-

tory, and gastrointestinal disorders as well as disorders of metabolism.

Intracranial birth lesion as associated with mental deficiency is about equal to mongolism in numerical incidence. The evi-dence is comparatively recent and it may well be that further study will indicate a higher proportion of cases than is at pres-ent recognized (Doll, 1933c; McIntire, 1938). The condition arises from damage to the intracranial portion of the central nervous system incidental to untoward cir-cumstances of intrauterine growth, par-turition, and early postnatal development. These mishaps include anomalies of devel-opment, infectious disease, birth trauma, neonatal asphyxia, early postnatal trauma, prematurity, rapid delivery, improper han-dling of the infant following birth, and other accidents which may attend the com-plete process of reproduction, birth, and early life experience. The essential symp-tom is brain damage, especially in the cerebral cortex and the basal ganglia (Doll, Phelps, and Melcher, 1932; Doll, 1933a; Schreiber, 1939).

Motor disturbances and an unfavorable birth history are common among these pa-tients. However, in a larger number than is now generally suspected, mental defi-ciency without marked motor symptoms is produced by brain damage resulting from birth difficulties. Recent surveys suggest that perhaps one-third of recognized con-genital cerebral palsy is accompanied by mental deficiency, the remaining two-thirds being mentally normal. Such surveys also suggest that, among mental defectives as a group, birth injuries account roughly for 10 per cent of the cases.

Patients with mental deficiency resulting from birth damage are chiefly character-ized by such motor symptoms as spasticity or athetosis. The less obvious handicaps include generalized or localized motor inco-ordination, synkinesia and ataxia, with per-

[1] Kuenzel (1929) gives a brief preliminary re-rt of this study, but subsequent (unpublished) alysis has modified the list of traits in some rticulars.

haps specific involvement of vision, hearing, speech, breathing, digestion and elimination. Among those without evident motor symptoms there may be significant disturbances of personality, unstable behavior, and irregularities of mental development. Delayed development is an outstanding characteristic of the motor group which, taken

plete idiocy to the upper limits of menta deficiency. Motor handicaps due to birt conditions without resulting mental def ciency are also observed among the men tally normal, even including the mentall superior (Hoopes, 1939; Hoskins, 1939 Carlson, 1941). The consequences depen on the amount and location of the intra

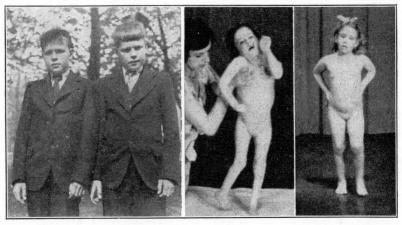

FIGURE 4. Cerebral birth lesions in identical twins. (From "Birth Lesions in Identica Twins," by K. P. Bradway. *American Journal of Orthopsychiatry*, 1937, 7, 198, 195. Illus trations courtesy Vineland Training School and *American Journal of Orthopsychiatry*.)

Left pair. Mental deficiency without noticeable motor impairment in one (right) of identica twins. Other twin is mentally and physically normal.

Right pair. Extreme athetosis and spasticity without mental deficiency in one (left) of identica twins. Other twin is mentally and physically normal.

in combination with the expressive limitations due to the physical handicaps, frequently leads to mistaken diagnosis.

This condition has been specifically recognized for nearly a century, but has received comparatively little emphasis as a special category of feeble-mindedness until the past decade. Muscle training alleviates the motor handicaps, whereas regimen and education ameliorate the other symptoms. The mental grade of the birth-injured [1] feeble-minded extends from com-

cranial damage, which only can be inferre *ante mortem* from the behavioral an physical symptoms.

The other clinical types of mental def ciency are relatively infrequent. Like mor golism and birth lesion, they are of scier tific importance because of their etiologic: and organic bases. These secondary forn offer some ultimate hope of medical pr phylaxis and therapy. They also reve: some of the constitutional mechanisn which determine the course of human d

[1] Patients with intracranial birth lesions are commonly referred to as *birth-injured*. In careful usage this term is avoided because of certain unwarranted implications. *Paranatal intracra-*

nial lesions (Schreiber, 1939) is a more sat factory expression. Other terms (for examp *infantile cerebral palsy*) emphasize the mot features.

elopment and the limits of behavioral modifiability.

Microcephaly derives its name from the extremely small brain which is character-

for two years.[1] Others emphasize cranial form as well as size, noting markedly receding forehead and "sugar-loaf" form of head. Such a cranium can usually be en-

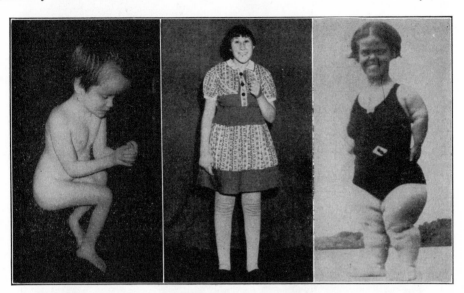

FIGURE 5. Clinical types of mental deficiency. (Illustrations and data courtesy Vineland State School. Photographs left and center by R. W. Taylor.)

Left. Severe progressive hydrocephalus, with associated spasticity. LA 8.4, Kuhlmann-Binet MA 0.3, IQ 4, SA 0.1, SQ 1. Vegetative idiot (bed case). Presumptive etiology birth lesion. Standing height 119 cm. (average for 7 years), weight 26.2 kg. Cephalometric measurements: circumference 745 mm., length 250 mm. (greatest diameter 270 mm.), breadth 192 mm., height 205 mm., cubic capacity (Lee-Porteus) 3226 cc. (far above adult average).

Center. Microcephalic low-grade imbecile. LA 12.8, Binet MA 4.1, IQ 32, SA 4.0, SQ 31. Etiology undetermined (premature 7 months). Standing height 140 cm. (average for 11 years), weight 33.3 kg. Cephalometric measurements: circumference 420 mm., length 135 mm., breadth 108 mm., height 80 mm., cubic capacity (Lee-Porteus) 686 cc. (below average for age 0–1).

Right. Achondroplasia, with borderline mentality (not to be confused with cretinism). LA about 30, Binet MA (at LA 23) 11.1, IQ (14-year basis) 79, SA (at LA 32) 17.3, SQ (25-year basis) 69. MA increase of 3 years after LA 13. Note micromelia and relative macrocephaly. Height average for 6 years (115 cm.); cranial capacity (1646 cc.) above adult average. Etiology undetermined (eighth in line of birth; no similar cases recorded in this family history). (Cf. Landauer, 1940; Mörch, 1940.)

istic of this clinical type of mental deficiency. Persons in this category are easily recognized from mere observation of head size (Barr, 1904; Tredgold, 1937). More precisely, some authorities define the condition in terms of a cranial circumference of less than about 440 mm., or a cranial content of less than about 1000 cc., or cephalic measurements below the norm

compassed within the adult hand. Cranial height is relatively less subnormal than

[1] Literally microcephaly means "small brain." In practice the term is used for those instances of mental deficiency in which the intracranial volume is very small. However, the precise limits of size are not clearly established and are usually expressed in terms of cranial circumference rather than brain volume. Moreover, the shape of the head and the relation of head size to body size must be taken into account. Clini-

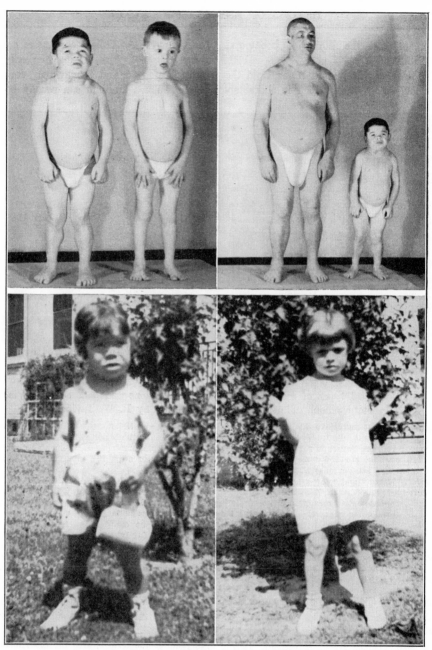

FIGURE 6. Clinical types of mental deficiency. (Photographs and data courtesy: (upper) Woodbine State Colony; (lower) Vineland State School, assistance Margaret E. Shirlock, M.D., and Dorothy M. Bassett, M.A.) (Cf. Engelbach, 1932; Brown, Bronstein, and Kraines, 1939.)

ngth or breadth. The fontanelles have usually closed prematurely owing to lack : brain growth. The head is small in re-.tion to stature, but body growth as a hole is also subnormal.

"True" microcephaly should not be con-ised with merely small head size, which is .latively frequent among other mentally eficient persons and even among the men-.lly normal. In the mongolian type, for xample, the cranial capacity is usually

lly, therefore, diagnosis is determined by symp-m-complex rather than by head size alone. he decision as to head size is embarrassed by .adequate standards, and the exact amount of eviation in relation to age has not been authori-.tively specified. In general the absolute meas-rements for microcephaly may be considered as .ose below the norms for one or two years of ɾe age when the subject under examination is, y, at least five years of age. Broadly speak-g, this criterion is equivalent to minus three gma deviation, but this is inferred from mul-ple considerations rather than from exact an-ropometric data. In extreme cases micro-phaly may be evident at birth or early in the eriod of infancy without reference to precise ead measurements.

below the ten-percentile for age, with the average at the five-percentile. Head size must also be related to other body pro-portions (Porteus, 1923; R. J. A. Berry, 1933).

These patients show generally good mo-tor development except for skilled activi-ties. They resemble the highest anthro-poids in physical alertness, and "little monkey" is a term as appropriate as it may be affectionate. Their general level of behavior is that of high-grade idiocy or low-grade imbecility with Binet MA about two to four years coupled with marked imi-tativeness, euphoric disposition, and habit-conditioned learning. Language develop-ment is meager and stereotyped, often with echolalia.

Marked microcephaly is observed in about one case per two or three hundred of mental defectives. It occurs occasion-ally among siblings (Bernstein, 1922), but this is apparently due to reproductive anomalies rather than to ancestral trans-mission. The specific causes are not clearly

---

Upper left. Cretin idiot (left) compared with mongolian idiot (right). Physical resemblances ɾe apparent in low stature, body form, skin condition, hands, feet. Differences include facies, ranial size and form, weight, personality, aptitudes. *Cretin*—LA 15.3, Kuhlmann-Binet MA 3.2, Q 23, SA 2.5, SQ 16. (Compare with sister in illustrations below.) "Glandular therapy" from A 4 months to 9 years, during which he "appeared to be more alert." Height 107 cm. (average ɔr 5 years), weight 25.9 kg., cranial capacity 1410 cc. (average for 16 years). *Mongolian*—LA 7.1, Kuhlmann-Binet MA 1.3, IQ 18, SA 2.3, SQ 32. History meager. Height 112 cm. (average for 6 ears), weight 18.9 kg., cranial capacity 1074 cc. (average for 1 year). Cretins tend toward macro-ephaly, mongolians toward microcephaly. Note hallux varus in both cases.

Upper right. Cretin acromegalic "giant" compared with cretin dwarf. *Acromegalic*—LA 37.7, Kuhlmann-Binet MA 2.7, IQ 19, SA 3.4, SQ 14. Sporadic cretin idiot in good family; three bright ɔrmal siblings. Continuous thyroid therapy from LA 5 to 17. MA "about 3" at LA 13. Relative allness not noted prior to LA 22. Presumptive pituitary involvement, undated. Present height 70 cm. (average for 17 years), weight 95.0 kg., cranial capacity 1785 cc. (above adult average). At LA 15 height was average for 12 years (144 cm.), cranial capacity (1522 cc.) above adult verage, with MA 2.6. *Dwarf*—same case as in illustration at left.

Lower left. Cretin idiot (congenital myxedema, congenital hypothyroidism) before effective reatment. LA 9.8, Kuhlmann-Binet MA 1.3, IQ 13. Etiology congenital (familial?) thyroid de-iciency. Brother (cretin dwarf in upper illustrations) and sister also cretins. Father hypothyroid; eputed to resemble his three children when a child but not cretinoid in appearance as adult. Aother reported mentally borderline. "Glandular treatment" from LA 2 to LA 6, but apparently vithout marked improvement. No measurements made.

Lower right. Same child as at left, 13 months later following thyroid medication. LA 10.8, Kuhlmann-Binet MA 1.7, IQ 16, SA (at LA 12.2) 2.0, SQ 16. Improvement noted in height (gain ɔf 30 cm.), weight, hair texture, hair color, skin, face, lips. Reduction in edema and umbilical aernia. Poor gait, enlarged tongue, and protruding abdomen still present. Height (at LA 12.2) 120 cm. (average for 8 years), weight 28.2 kg., cranial capacity 1215 cc. (average for 10 years).

understood. Maternal pelvic irradiation is one cause which can definitely be avoided by medical precautions (Doll and Murphy, 1930; Murphy, Shirlock, and Doll, 1942).

Treatment is limited to regimen and training. The earlier practice of craniotomy has proved of little value since the condition is one of cerebral hypoplasia rather than of premature cranial resistance to brain expansion.

Hydrocephalus is an intracranial condition due to excess of spinal fluid in the ventricles (internal) or in the subarachnoid space (external), which usually produces cerebral aplasia or atrophy with consequent mental deficiency (Tredgold, 1937), but is sometimes associated with mental normality. Some microcephalics are also hydrocephalic, and macrocephaly [1] (large-headedness) may occur without hydrocephalus. In some instances the condition is not evident until autopsy. In other cases it may be plausibly inferred from cranial form (extreme frontal, occipital, parietal, or altitudinal dimensions), extreme volume, cerebrospinal pressure, or encephalogram.

The incidence of hydrocephalus is somewhat uncertain because of the difficulty of diagnosis from either cranial size or behavioral symptoms. Extreme cases occur

[1] Literally macrocephaly is the antithesis of microcephaly and refers to excessive cranial volume without reference to abnormal significance. Similarly, the precise limits for macrocephaly have not been specified as to cranial measurements or their normative deviations, but might be considered as representing plus three sigma deviation from relevant age norms. But whereas in clinical practice microcephaly commonly refers to a category of mental deficiency, macrocephaly is used without reference to degree of intelligence except for its abnormal manifestations. Macrocephaly may be associated with hypertrophic amentia (macroglia or gliosis), hydrocephalus, subdural hematoma, intracranial neoplasm, rickets, and other conditions. Therefore, one should not too readily assume hydrocephalus from macrocephaly, whether or not mental deficiency is at issue.

perhaps once in about two or three hundred cases of mental deficiency, but this is a rather random estimate. Although an infrequent cause of feeble-mindedness, must be regarded as a specific etiology with widely variable degree but perhaps similar type of behavioral attributes. The pathology of the condition itself need not be considered here.

The behavioral characteristics have not been very clearly set forth as distinguishing features. The mental level ranges from helpless idiocy to normal degrees of intelligence, and this range of general talent obscures the traits said by some to be common to this type. In extreme cases the patients may be bedridden because of inability to balance the extraordinary cranial weight. Motor handicaps may be one of the sequelae. Language development is generally favorable in relation to degree of intelligence.

The *cretin type* of clinical amentia is product of extreme deficiency in thyroid metabolism. The physical signs are short stature, infantile body proportions, obesity, pallid edematous skin, and peculiar facies. These somatic features somewhat resemble those of mongolism. The mental symptoms include a fatuous type of personality, usually idiot level of intelligence, sluggish activity, and extremely limited response to training (Tredgold, 1937).

Marked cretinism occurs rather less often than microcephaly or hydrocephalus, perhaps about once per four or five hundred of institutional cases of mental deficiency. Less marked cretinoid symptoms are observed more frequently as severe degrees of thyroid deficiency. Endemic cretinism appears to be not always associated with a genuine mental deficiency but with a tendency toward subnormal type of development. Cretinism may show particularly striking response to treatment, with occasional instances of extraordinary facilitaon of mental and physical development om thyroid medication. This condition therefore of special theoretical interest s revealing one of the endocrine precon- itions of mental development. The causes f the insufficient thyroid metabolism pro- ucing cretinism are not clearly understood. odine supply appears to be one environ- ental factor, but this in turn may be in- uenced by physiologic utilization.

Other clinical types of mental deficiency re still less frequent than those mentioned bove. The cranial anomalies include such onditions as oxycephaly, anencephaly, and orencephalus. Comparatively rare syn- romes are found in tuberous sclerosis epiloia), hypertelorism, phenylketonuria, maurotic family idiocy, Schilder's disease, he Lawrence-Moon-Biedl syndrome, and o on. These and other conditions result- ng from trauma, infection, endocrinopathy, vitaminoses, disorders of metabolism, de- eneration, or deprivation are relatively oo infrequent to warrant treatment here.[1] ome of these and similar conditions or iseases may be considered merely as com- lications added to mental deficiency with- ut necessarily producing it. Thus epi- epsy or syphilis may either cause or, like chondroplasia, only accompany feeble- nindedness. Similarly, mental defectives re subject to the same illnesses or dis- bling defects as may affect normal per- ons.

[1] References to these comparatively rare al- though medically and scientifically significant conditions are omitted from this chapter as repre- senting material of limited interest here. They are of special import in those aspects of child development included under the general field of auxology. The specialized student will find such material in standard works on neurology, physi- ology (especially endocrinology), and neuropsy- chiatry, in such compendia as Engelbach's *Endo- crine Medicine,* such digests as *The Yearbook of Neurology, Psychiatry and Endocrinology,* such transactions as the *Journal of Mental Science* and the *American Journal of Mental De- ficiency.*

These scientific groupings of the feeble- minded may be supplemented by the fol- lowing administrative classification which is useful for purposes of social disposition, treatment, care, and training. This group- ing was adopted by the White House Con- ference on Child Health and Protection (Ellis, 1933) to emphasize the combina- tions of factors which underlie a compre- hensive program of social control.

(1) *Helpless Low-Grades.* These are the most severely handicapped feeble- minded from the point of view of total ability. They require constant assistance in the simplest matters of everyday living. They are burdens in their families and an embarrassment to the neighborhood. Un- der favorable family circumstances they may be continuously cared for at home, but as a rule this imposes physical, finan- cial, and social embarrassments which are difficult to meet. These patients are gen- erally best cared for in public or private institutions.

(2) *Maladjusted High-Grades.* These in- clude the higher degrees of mental defi- ciency at the adolescent and early adult years where problems of conduct and morality require some special safeguard. These individuals disrupt public school classes and are unstable in gainful occupa- tions. Without close supervision, they drift into prisons, reformatories, and institutions for juvenile delinquents. Their own best interests, as well as those of the family and community, are best served by institutional custody.

(3) *Physically Handicapped High- Grades.* These are the brighter feeble- minded who could get along fairly well if it were not for some physical handicap. These defects aggravate the social depend- ence resulting from low intelligence and make occupational employment or home care impracticable. This group therefore

also is best provided for under institutional conditions unless favorable family circumstances make this unnecessary.

(4) *Well-Adjusted Young High-Grades.* These are the potential morons who get along fairly well at home and in the community but who embarrass the regular

(5) *Well-Adjusted Older High-Grade* This group is much the same as the preceding, except for their more advance age. These individuals get along fairly well in the community, especially if supervised by some welfare agency, and if assisted during the period between school

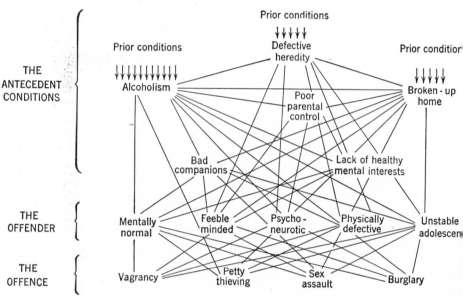

FIGURE 7. Schematic indication of sequential and multiple factors in crime and delinquency (From *The Individual Delinquent*, by W. Healy. Boston: Little, Brown, 1915, 165. By permission of the publisher.)

classes of the public schools by their inaptitude for learning and the consequent social friction. Under favorable conditions they can be cared for at home or in the community if special classes in the public schools are provided for their educational needs. If the family situation is unfavorable, many of this group will be greatly benefited by temporary institutional care, especially during the period of later schooling and during the adolescent years. Well-directed home visiting and special parent-education assistance are of great benefit to these children and their families.

attendance and stable employment. Their principal menace is from the point of view of family reproduction. It is particularly in this group that selective sterilization is helpful.

(6) *Aged and Infirm High-Grades.* This is a group whose marginal dependence is increased by loss of vigor with age or the onset of physical infirmity. In many of these cases initially favorable family supervision may have been discontinued because of the loss of the parents and the embarrassment and burden of continuing home care at the expense of other relatives.

Many of these individuals are adequately cared for in almshouses or homes for the aged and infirm if the feeble-mindedness self has no serious complications.

(7) *Clinical Anomalies.* In this group are found the more or less remediable clinical varieties of mental deficiency who are susceptible to medical treatment. Many of them can be adequately cared for in their own homes, but as a rule the medical problems and related difficulties are so specialized as to fall outside the skill of the ordinary family physician and the resources of the parents. These individuals are best cared for under a program of hospitalization designed to provide systematic medical treatment and training which might either overcome or ameliorate their special disabilities. The mongols and the birth-injured constitute the largest portion of this group.

(8) *Psychiatric Cases.* These include the luetic, epileptic, psychopathic, and otherwise disordered or deteriorated feeble-minded where psychopathology added to feeble-mindedness makes home and community care impracticable. These individuals are best cared for in special institutional units such as a feeble-minded unit at a mental hospital or a psychiatric unit at an institution for the feeble-minded.

Incidence

The prevalence of feeble-mindedness in the general population is of greater extent than is commonly appreciated. The information on frequency of occurrence, although still inadequate, has become much more satisfactory in the last two decades as a result of numerous local, state, and national surveys. The data on incidence are limited by the definition of mental deficiency and the methods of examinations employed, as well as by the extent and specificity of the inquiries. The results are further influenced by age and sex, as well as by geographic and cultural areas.

At the beginning of the current century the number of the feeble-minded in the general population was found to be about five persons per thousand (Pintner, 1933). This was prior to the use of mental tests and the criterion was essentially one of social inadequacy resulting from arrested mental development. These as well as later figures are only minimum estimates since they are based on only known instances encountered in incomplete surveys. Occasionally, however, the estimates have risen to unwarrantedly high figures because of applying to the total population the proportions found in local areas, or employing only a mental test method of determination.

In the second decade of the current century Goddard startled this country by finding 3 per cent of an elementary school population feeble-minded (Goddard, 1911). This result was derived from the application of the 1908 Binet-Simon scale without employing a comprehensive standard of clinical diagnosis. Subsequent local, county, and state surveys during that decade in this country revealed the minimum number as approximating at least 10 per 1000.

These inquiries were conducted under different auspices and employed different standards of detection. They indicated marked differences according to geographic and cultural areas. They also indicated a much higher incidence among children as compared with adults. This latter result was influenced partly by the greater accessibility to examination of children of school age, and partly by the use of mental tests in the public schools. In the case of adults the life test of social competence was more generally relied upon.

Numerous investigations have reported results ranging from 4 to 10 per cent of school children "testing" within the Binet IQ limits of mental deficiency. Obviously, these could not all be considered feeble-minded without supporting evidence from other criteria and other mental tests. Evidence regarding the relatively low life expectancy (Kaplan, 1940) of the feeble-minded (about twenty-five years for institutionalized cases) lends support to the presumption of higher incidence in populations of school age as compared with adult groups. Studies of specially handicapped groups and of less-favored environments yield a wide range of incidence.

These data have always been difficult to evaluate because of the variations in standards and methods employed and especially because of the failure to specify the selective factors involved. It is still difficult to appraise the true incidence of mental deficiency at different levels of social organization and with respect to different types of social adjustment with dependable clarity.

Key (1915) demonstrated the extreme differences in incidence according to type of community studied. In this inquiry more than half the individuals in one small isolated area and more than a quarter in another were considered feeble-minded. In a surrounding area of larger scope this proportion dropped to 17 per 1000. For the entire area (about 700 square miles and 16,000 inhabitants) the proportion was 32 per 1000.

Similarly, the estimates of mental deficiency found in correctional groups such as institutions for juvenile delinquents, reformatories, and prisons have varied from 5 per cent to 95 per cent (Zeleny, 1933). In New Jersey, where a standard method of detection was employed in all correctional institutions, the percentages of mental deficiency were found to be (1) about 30 in state schools for juvenile delinquents, (2) roughly 15 in reformatories, and (3) approximately 8 in prison. This *decrease* in correctional incidence with increase in

age and severity of offense is particularl[y] significant but has not been confirmed else where, partly because of wide variation i[n] selection and particularly because of varia tion in methods of standards of detectior Indeed, even in New Jersey these result[s] have been modified by more recent meth ods of examination.

Other results on the relation of menta[l] deficiency to crime and delinquency ar[e] still unsettled because of the difficulty o[f] controlling selective influences and of em ploying comparable standards of concep[t] and detection (Crafts and Doll, 1917; Dol[l] 1930). Mental test surveys in some insti tutions have indicated no marked differ ences between the intelligence of prisoner[s] and comparable adults in the general popu lation except for the selection of prisoner[s] in the direction of the less-favored socia[l] strata, which in turn show a lower level o[f] intelligence as compared with higher strat[a] (Doll, 1920; Murchison, 1926).

The use of mental tests in the Unitec[d] States Army in the year 1918 afforded a[n] unusual opportunity to evaluate the varia bility of intelligence in a selected group o[f] male adults. These results in terms o[f] Stanford-Binet mental ages indicated a[n] average adult level of intelligence at 13.5 years, with as many as 10 per cent of al[l] army recruits falling below the standard of 10 years. Such data suggested that the av erage mental age of adults is lower than previously supposed. They also for the first time indicated the lower limits of mental age for normal adults (Doll, 1919; Yerkes, 1921). This, in turn, exposed the previous logical error of assuming that the upper mental age limit for feeble-mindedness was also the lower limit of normality. Hence mental age alone could not be a sufficient criterion of mental deficiency.

The fallacy of distribution (error of the converse) has troubled workers in this field and may haunt the readers of this chapter. If we say that "all morons have mental ages above 8 years," the converse inference that "all persons with mental ages bove 8 years are morons" is seen to be in rror. But the proposition that "the eeble-minded have mental ages below 12 ears" (or some other limit) has been con- erted to "those with mental ages below 2 years (or some other limit) are feeble- inded," and this error has persisted for any years. Similarly, if we say that "the eeble-minded have IQ's below 70" (which s itself a debatable proposition), we may ot *therefore* infer that "persons with IQ elow 70 are feeble-minded." Yet this fal- cy pervades most of the work in this eld since 1910. To give the MA or IQ mits of feeble-mindedness (mental defi- iency), then, does *not* mean that *all*, but nly *some*, persons within those limits are nentally deficient. We must caution the eader not to misinterpret these pages by llogical conversion or obversion of state- nents herein.

The 1920 report of the Surgeon-General f the Army (Ireland, 1920) indicated the umber of men drafted under the 1917 elective Service Act who were rejected by amp and local boards as unfit for mili- ary duty because of mental deficiency. These results were based on the use of a gen- ral standard which probably gave a more eliable index of mental deficiency in the Army than did the army mental test exami- ations. When one considers how many eeble-minded remained in the Army after hese rejections by camp and local boards, ne is further inclined to believe that the tandard employed must have been con- ervative. These results indicated that 12 er 1000 of all men drafted for military luty during World War I were rejected ecause of mental deficiency.[1] The dis- ribution by states varied from one-quarter

[1] Other reports raise this estimate to as high s 5 per cent. The data vary with locale, color, ationality, standard of diagnosis, and other ariables. About one-third of all neuropsychi- tric disabilities were classed as mental deficiency Ireland, 1929).

of 1 per cent in Arizona to 3 per cent in Vermont. These percentages show some correlation with other aspects of socio- economic selection.

One of the most informing surveys of the incidence of mental deficiency is that published by the Wood Committee in Eng- land (Wood, 1929). This investigation was carefully planned to insure a uniform standard of detection. Representative sam- ples of the population according to age, sex, and social and geographic distribution were carefully studied by various means under the direction of E. O. Lewis (Wood, 1929, Part IV). The total results present one of the most dependable revelations of this problem yet available. The Wood Committee found at least 8 mentally defi- cient persons per 1000 for the total popu- lation of England and Wales. The per- centages varied significantly with age, lo- cale, sex, and degree of deficiency, being higher for young than for old, for males as compared with females, for urban communi- ties in contrast with rural areas, for high- grades *versus* low-grades.

The difficulties of identifying the feeble- minded in terms of symptom-complex cri- teria have led some authorities to substi- tute a statistical definition of mental de- ficiency as the lowest 1 per cent (in intel- ligence) of the total population. That this point of view, usually based on results from Binet-Simon mental testing, continues to receive serious attention in fact and im- plication is astonishing in view of the vari- ations in incidence with time, place, age, mental test employed, and other circum- stances. How this lowest percentage of the total population is to be determined inde- pendently of social, multiple intellectual, developmental, and etiological standards is not clear. The lack of correlation between any of these standards and the percentage concept of mental deficiency makes this plan an all too simple solution of the diffi- culty. It can readily be demonstrated that

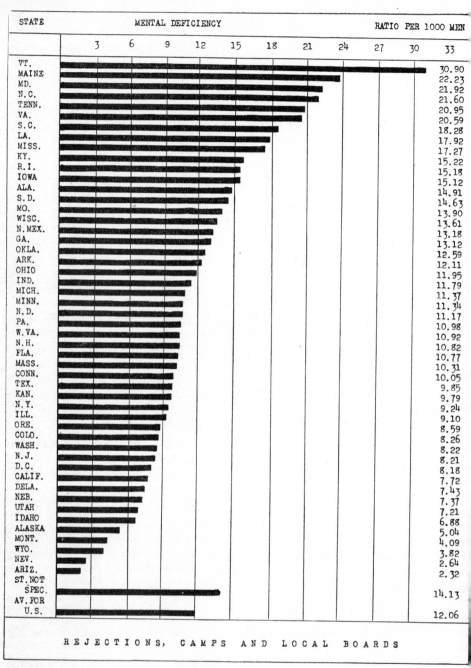

FIGURE 8. Incidence of mental deficiency among men drafted for military service. Note geographic variability. (From *Defects Found in Drafted Men,* by M. W. Ireland (Director). Washington, D. C.: Government Printing Office, 1920, 176. By permission of the Surgeon-General, United States Army.)

many individuals who occupy the 1 percentile of a random distribution on the Binet-Simon scale may occupy some higher rank on some other criterion, or on some other mental test, or in some larger sample (Doll, 1925, 1927). Moreover, by such a standard the concept of mental deficiency will definitely vary from place to place unless the percentage definition is itself validated against other criteria and in terms of some total standard of population distribution.

The question of incidence may also be considered in relation to types and degrees of deficiency (Roberts, Norman, and Griffiths, 1936, 1937, 1938a, 1938b). Some suggestions have already been made in the section on grades and types. The data, however, are restricted to cases which have thus far come to attention. For example, intracranial birth lesions, once assumed to be of negligible incidence, are now known to constitute the second, if not the first, most frequent nonhereditary cause of mental deficiency.

The data on the institutionalized feeble-minded indicate that perhaps 10 per cent of institutional cases are idiots, 30 per cent imbeciles, and 60 per cent morons (Frankel, 1940). Outside institutions, the proportions are less well known. The Wood Committee found four times as many imbeciles as idiots and four or five times as many morons as imbeciles (Wood, 1929). These proportions depend, however, on the other variables already noted. Such data reveal the greater proportion of institutionalization among low-grades *versus* high-grades. Public school surveys confirm these results, with approximately 70 per cent of the cases above IQ 50 during the developmental age period (Dayton, 1938). However, in view of the uncertainties of the IQ diagnosis of mental deficiency, and in view of the fact that during the developmental period many familial cases of mental defi-

ciency score above IQ 70, the interpretation of the data regarding the moron type is distinctly hazardous. In this connection it may be noted that the moron degree of mental deficiency completely overlaps the lower range of dull normality for the adult mental ages of 8 to approximately 12 years.

Characteristics

Social. The social insufficiency of the feeble-minded is manifest in subnormal personal dependence, self-direction, social responsibility, and self-support. If a person is able to get along at more than a marginal level of self-sustenance without need of more than ordinary aid or supervision from others, he can hardly be considered feeble-minded (Wood, 1929). Society's interest in the feeble-minded is one of social control and social assistance.

The social criterion of mental deficiency is principally applicable to youth and adults, since children in general are considered socially dependent and subject to parental care and guidance. Normal standards of social competence at all life ages have only recently been clearly formulated. Social success for adults has always implied personal and economic independence, sound practical judgment, discreet behavior, and occupational adequacy. The degree of success is reflected in socioeconomic status and the cultural standard of living. For children, these social standards must be conceived in relation to developmental maturation at successive age levels as progressive stages of self-reliance, acceptable conduct, response to instruction, and "getting along" with others.

Such concepts of social competence have been reduced to systematic definition and measurement in the Vineland Social Maturity Scale (Doll, 1936b, 1940a). In this scale social maturation has been formulated

Figure 9. Genetic maturation in social performance. (From *Your Child Grows Up*, by E. A.
Doll. Boston: John Hancock Mutual Life Insurance Company, 1939. Illustrations courtesy
John Hancock Life Insurance Company.)

Sequences from the Vineland Social Maturity Scale for measuring social competence. On this
scale the SA (social age) limits for successive grades of mature mental defectives are, approximately, idiocy 0 to 3.5 years, imbecility 3.5 to 9.5 years, moronity 9.5 to 19.0 years, and for mature
normality 19.0 to 30+ years (adult average 25 years). SQ's (social quotients) are comparable to
IQ's and may be used clinically during the period of genetic maturation for early prediction of
presumptive ultimate deficiency.

Reading left to right, beginning top row, the sketches illustrate: Moves about on floor
(Year 0-I, Scale item 12). Eats with spoon (Year I-II, Scale item 28). Relates experiences
(II-III, 44). Helps at little household tasks (III-IV, 48). Washes face unassisted (IV-V, 52).
Is trusted with money (V-VI, 60). Uses tools or utensils (VIII-IX, 71). Writes occasional short
letters (X-XI, 78). Buys own clothing accessories (XII-XV, 87). Goes to distant points alone
(XVIII-XX, 96). Assumes responsibilities beyond own needs (XX-XXV, 103). (Cf. Doll, 1936*b*,
1940*a*.)

categorical aspects of behavior as pro-essive degrees of personal initiative and cial responsibility. This indicates the egree of differential social attainment in elation to age and affords a reliable means distinguishing between the feeble-minded and the normal. Such an instrument ob-ectifies and quantifies the social criterion a relation to which the other character-tics of the feeble-minded may be vali-ated. It also affords a means of classify-ig the idiot, imbecile, moron, dull-normal, and superior levels of social attainment.

Mental. The mental characteristics of he feeble-minded are most evident in level f intelligence, degree of brightness, rela-ive energy, initiative, judgment, emotional rganization, motor facility, and linguistic xpression. The feeble-minded at any age re essentially childlike in these respects. n standard intelligence tests the feeble-ninded are consistently subnormal, but the degree of subnormality varies with the test mployed, being relatively more obvious in bstract verbal (oral and literate) tests as ompared with nonverbal (manipulative nd nonliterate) tests (Goddard, 1919; Baker, 1927; Doll, 1927).

The sound use of such tests requires not only that they be normatively standard-ized but also differentially validated against the social criterion of mental deficiency, or against some reliable diagnostic symptom-complex from which the intelligence test is itself excluded. The most widely used test for this purpose is the Stanford-Binet. Ac-cording to this scale, idiocy is incompletely conceived as permanent mental arrest at a mental age below 3 years, imbecility at a mental age between 3 and 7 years inclu-sive, and moronity at a mental age from 8 to some uncertain upper age limit which may approximate the average normal level.

It is important for careful work that these mental ages represent in fact or by reliable prediction the ultimate attainment of the persons tested, the interpretation of

mental ages during the developmental pe-riod being subject to many uncertainties in the present state of knowledge regard-ing intellectual maturation. That this course of development is not constant for the feeble-minded is evident from many studies, and that the maturity level may be reached at an earlier age among the feeble-minded as compared with the normal is also indicated by the trend of evidence (Doll, 1921; Kuhlmann, 1921).

The principle of the constancy of the IQ has proved invalid in the case of the fee-ble-minded generally (Doll, 1940c). Since the ultimate level of development among the different degrees of feeble-mindedness is reached at life ages which are correlated with these degrees of attainment, there is a tendency for the IQ of the feeble-minded to decrease progressively with increase of age (since the denominator of the IQ frac-tion increases while the numerator remains relatively stationary or increases at a pro-gressively decreasing rate). Thus, if the maximum MA of the idiot is taken at 3.0 years, and the average life age of normal maturation is taken at 14.0, the maximum IQ of the idiot becomes approximately 20. Similarly, the different degrees of imbecil-ity range from IQ 20 to 50, and moronity from 50 to some as yet uncertain upper limit. Moreover, the IQ standard for de-ficiency itself varies with life age (Roberts, Norman, and Griffiths, 1936, 1937, 1938a, 1938b; Wechsler, 1939).

In considering these and other mental aspects of feeble-mindedness, one encoun-ters a wealth of psychological investigation which is extremely difficult to evaluate be-cause of confusing contradictions. In many of these studies there is little or no regard for the basic diagnoses of the subjects and the differential groupings by form, grade, and type. The interpretations are further often embarrassed by lack of evidence re-garding age, sex, and other relevant selec-tive variables.

It is obvious from observation, as well

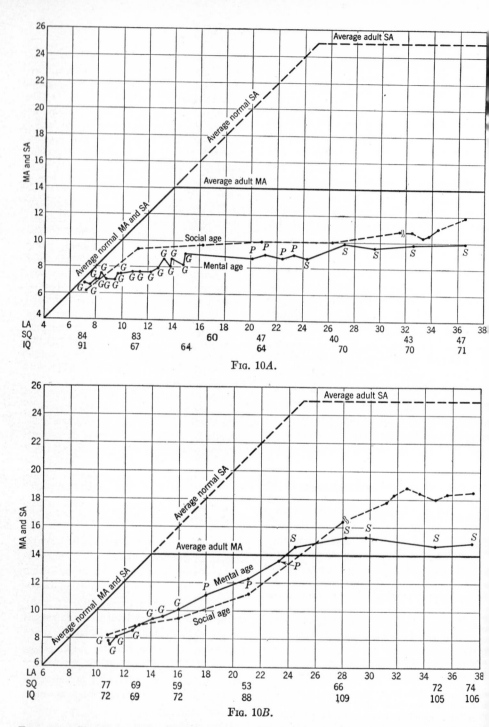

Fig. 10A.

Fig. 10B.

FIGURE 10. Developmental social age and mental age curves for clinically borderline subjects. (Data from Vineland Laboratory.)

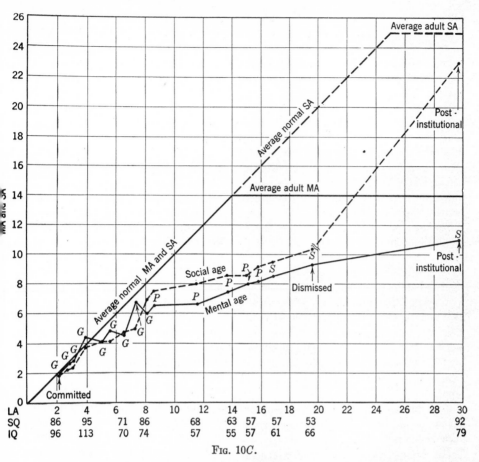

FIG. 10C.

Social ages in these graphs are derived from the Vineland Social Maturity Scale (determined retrospectively on history data for scores at left of breaks). Mental ages are from Binet-Simon tests (G = Goddard 1911 form; P = Porteus form; S = 1916 Stanford form). IQ's are based on 14-year adult average, SQ's on 25-year adult average. Note MA and SA similarities in these three subjects at about LA 10 with subsequent differentiation in type and degree of development. Careful evaluation of symptoms, history, environmental conditions, and certain artifacts of the data yields no satisfactory explanation of these diverse courses of development.

Fig. 10A. Delayed retardation with slight adult acceleration in a middle-grade moron girl, potentially feeble-minded at first test. Familial type, socially marginal stock; no known pathology. Period covers institutional residence. Note (a) relative lack of practice effect in relation to interval between tests; (b) final MA and SA within feeble-minded limits; (c) SA consistently above MA.

Fig. 10B. Delayed development continued through early adult years in a high-grade borderline girl of debatable diagnosis. Subcultural stock; mother of borderline intelligence and sexually promiscuous; putative father low-grade moron; numerous feeble-minded siblings; no known pathology. Period covers institutional residence. Subsequently transferred to employee status. Social performance, although above MA, falls below MA expectation (cf. Doll, 1937). Note (a) MA annual growth rate continued at .50 from LA 11 to 24 years; (b) final SA at borderline, and final MA at average normal levels; (c) SA below MA up to LA 21.

Fig. 10C. Variable status in an ultimately dull-normal male. Subcultural stock; paternity doubtful; mother low-grade moron; putative father low-grade moron; presumptive father dull-normal; no known pathology. Institutionalized because of parental neglect and assumption of ultimate hereditary mental deficiency. Note favorable early development, followed by period of apparent mental deficiency, with postinstitutional social normality in spite of relatively low MA. Note (a) MA annual growth rate continued at .25 from LA 8 to 30 years; (b) final SA at normal adult lower quartile and final MA within borderline limits; (c) SA above MA after LA 8.

as from numerous studies, that the feeble-minded react through established habits, that they learn by drill rather than by precept. In personality, they are generally naïve, with marked tendency toward self-reference, extreme weakness in generalization, and low power of deduction and induction. They generally have low energy, show marked limitations in initiative, originality, and resourcefulness, are emotionally immature, reveal generally dull perception, limited alertness, and so on.

The general psychology of the feeble-minded still awaits comprehensive development. A systematic review of previous work requires a more critical appraisal than is herein practicable. The numerous writings of Binet and Simon (1916a, 1916b) offer rich material in brief and lucid treatment for the beginner. The more advanced student will find the *Proceedings of the American Association on Mental Deficiency* a major source of experimental reports.

If to the strictly mental aspects of behavior we add those motor functions which have been the object of recent psychological inquiry, we observe again a general tendency toward deficiency and defect (Kreezer, 1935; Glanville and Kreezer, 1937; Heath, 1944). Likewise, the psychological study of the neurological and physiological correlates of mental deficiency as recently developed in studies of chronaxy, action currents, and the electroencephalogram offer spheres of research of great theoretical and practical value (Kreezer, 1933, 1935, 1936, 1937, 1938, 1939; Kreezer and Bradway, 1935). That such investigations may open new vistas regarding the organic and functional conditions which subserve normal behavior as well as mental deficiency seems amply justified by the significant work of recent years in these directions.

Developmental. Feeble-mindedness reveals correlated deficiencies of development which are represented in practically all details of the growth of the organism and the maturational exercise of its consequent functions (Doll, 1917; Bisch, 1925; Humphreys, 1936). The condition reflects a general tendency toward infantility, and this is correlated with the degree of deficiency. The mental age aspect of development has served usefully as a basic criterion for correlating the diverse results from different fields of study of mental deficiency (L. S. Hollingworth, 1920) which may in the future be supplemented or even superseded by the social age concept of maturation. In either case, the study of feeble-mindedness is essentially a problem of genetic psychology against a background of incomplete or abnormal organic morphology. To this over-all characteristic of genetic retardation we may add a few of its more specific manifestations.

Somatic. The general tendency toward incomplete behavioral maturation is only somewhat less obvious in terms of developmental somatic evolution. This is the major field of medical interest in mental deficiency, the fundamental importance of which has been emphasized during fourteen decades of scientific study of its biological preconditions. From this point of view, feeble-mindedness is a state of incomplete or pathological development of the organism which is significantly reflected in subnormal or abnormal structure and function of the central and autonomic nervous systems. This, in turn, limits the growth of intelligence which is manifested in educational, behavioral, and social incompetence.

This organic hypoplasia is grossly evident in skeleton and musculature. There is also retardation in general psychophysical attributes, such as sensorium, general health, body tone, or total physique. And this tendency toward physical hypoplasia, like the behavioral traits, is related to degree and type of deficiency.

In the pathological cases somatic subnormality is accompanied by various physical stigmata as well as by structural and functional abnormalities as noted in the section on clinical types. Among the familial cases deficiencies of physical development are less obvious. In both primary and secondary forms there are general and specific deficiencies and defects in the circulatory, respiratory, glandular, and other systems as well as those already noted.

As in the fields of social and psychological interest, these deficiencies cannot be clearly comprehended without normative standards. Much of the work on the physical and physiological characteristics of the mentally deficient is difficult to evaluate because of the lack of objective definition and statistical norms. Further work will undoubtedly furnish an indispensable basis for the evaluation of the other attributes of mental deficiency which, theoretically at least, must be reduced to their physical preconditions for a psychobiological theory of functional immaturity.[1]

Educational. Other symptoms and consequences of mental deficiency are evident in the direction of spontaneous learning and response to teaching. Since learning depends principally on organic maturity, it is obvious that the educational attainments of the feeble-minded cannot rise appreciably beyond their native incapacity to profit from experience and instruction. This is evident in all forms of learning in which the feeble-minded have been observed, whether simple habit conditioning, environmental imitation, original adaptation, or response to training (Seguin, 1907;

[1] It is impracticable to review here the extensive literature on the medical and morphological aspects of the problem, but this deficiency should not be permitted to obscure the essential importance of the constitutional basis of feeble-mindedness.

Aldrich and Doll, 1931a, 1931b; Aldrich, 1932; Itard, 1932). Indeed, feeble-mindedness, especially among children, has been defined in terms of incapacity for learning and as lack of profit from instruction. The degree of learning may even be inferred from the degree and type of deficiency. The idiot is grossly retarded in mastering the rudiments of self-care, the beginnings of linguistic expression, and the simplest forms of occupational activity. The imbecile masters these but makes no progress in scholastic subjects. The moron may learn the scholastic rudiments (up to about fourth grade) but rarely makes appreciable use of such accomplishments (De Sanctis, 1912; Anderson, 1921; Wallin, 1924; Baker, 1927; H. D. Whipple, 1927; C. S. Berry, 1931; Scheidemann, 1931; Ingram, 1935).

The expression "vegetative idiot" is to a degree redundant, as are the corresponding expressions of "stupid imbecile," or "indiscreet moron." These very adjectives indicate the incapacity for the acquisition of certain types of experience which are common to mankind in all times and places. This incapacity for behavioral acquisitions is most evident in those forms of learning which are essential to the higher stages of phylogenetic and societal evolution.

The incapacity of the feeble-minded for profiting from abstract instruction in the public schools is a major earmark of mental deficiency and one of the principal symptoms employed in recognizing the feeble-minded at an early age. As in mental test situations, the feeble-minded are less apt in mastering scholastic learning than in mastering handwork. Even with relatively good language development, there is poverty of thought, expression, reasoning, and inference. The deficiency of the feeble-minded is so generalized that even their relative proficiency in occupational and recreational pursuits is still below that of the normal individual. This is in contrast with the verbally handicapped dull-normal child in the public schools who masters manual and trade instruction at normal levels while handicapped in those directions which put a premium on language facility. It is chiefly in linguistic learning that the moron is most readily confused with the dull-normal. Retarda-

nature and even then only under relatively constant supervision except for those tasks which have been reduced to a simple habit routine. The imbecile acquires but little command of machinery and does not possess the degree of judgment necessary for

FIGURE 11. Institutional training of feeble-minded children. (Photographs courtesy Vineland Training School: (left) Royce Studio, and (right) Larry Keighley.)

The education of feeble-minded children in an institution includes, in addition to academic classroom instruction, other forms of training such as those illustrated above. Such instruction is based on homogeneous grouping according to age, mental age, and special aptitudes. This is materially facilitated by scientific appraisal of individual development.

tion in academic work alone is only a suggestive indication of the possibility of mental deficiency and should not be taken as an all-sufficient criterion even when supported by mental test subnormality.

Occupational. The educational consequences of mental deficiency are further evident in limited occupational attainment. The idiot masters no occupational skills of any moment. The imbecile succeeds at only simple occupational tasks of a routine

successful use of tools. The moron, under persistent instruction and continued supervision, may succeed at the apprentice levels of the simpler occupations not requiring independent judgment or much motor skill. At the upper levels of moronity there is observed some simple use of machinery but very little resourcefulness in the adjustment or repair of tools. Yet the moron may become occupationally well adjusted through habituation, and under favorable circumstances may acquire certain industrial virtues, such as persistence and patience in monotonous activities, which make him desirable for simple kinds of work. Indeed, the very faithfulness of the moron is something of an asset in situations not requiring ready adaptation or (Porteus, 1923; Raymond, 1926; Unger and Burr, 1931; Kaplun, 1935).

Causes

As noted previously, the most common cause of mental deficiency is heredity.

FIGURE 12. Occupational training of high-grade mental defectives. (Photographs courtesy: (upper and lower left) Vineland Training School, (upper right) Vineland Training School and Larry Keighley, (lower right) Vineland State School and R. W. Taylor.)

"The proper education for feeble-minded boys and girls is to teach them what they can learn and will make use of when they become men and women in years."—S. Olin Garrison.

the expression of personal judgment. It may broadly be said that the feeble-minded at best are limited to routine occupational activity not requiring more than simple judgment or ready adaptation. Moreover, the conditions of their employment have much to do with their occupational success It has long been known that mental deficiency "runs in families." Indeed, one of the first considerations in establishing the etiology of mental deficiency is to search for familial transmission (Goddard, 1912, 1914; Kostir, 1916; Wildenskov, 1934; Humphreys, Watts, and Boldt, 1937; Tred-

gold, 1937; Penrose, 1938; Town, 1939).
Where both parents are feeble-minded, *and
are themselves of the familial type,* it is
extraordinary for any of the children not
to be feeble-minded. Indeed, such few

principally limited to institutionalized cases.
Bearing in mind the comparative rarity of
all the nonfamilial types other than those
recognized as mongolians or birth-palsied,
and considering the nature of the clinical

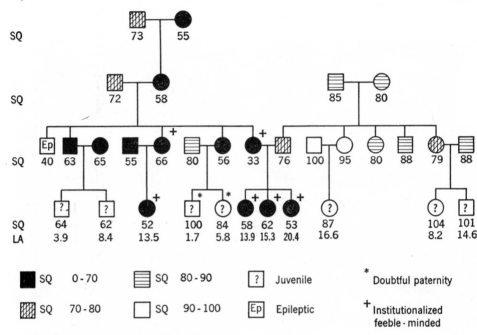

FIGURE 13. Familial mental deficiency. (From "The Inheritance of Social Competence," by
E. A. Doll. *Journal of Heredity,* 1937, **28** (May), 153–166. Courtesy *The Journal of Heredity.*
Adapted from Figure 3 and Table 1, above reference.)

In this chart Vineland Social Maturity Scale SQ's (unless affected by special handicaps) have
been segregated in categories which suggest: below 70, presumptive mental deficiency; from 70–80,
doubtful mental deficiency; from 80–90, dull-normality; from 90–100, average normality. Immature
subjects (under LA 25) classed as "?" unless already institutionalized.

exceptions as have been noted immediately
raise the question of maternal fidelity or
putative fatherhood. Few authorities in
the field of etiology question the likelihood
that at least one-third of all cases are due
to familial transmission, and few modern
authorities doubt that less than one-third
are nonhereditary (Myerson, 1936). The
argument usually centers about the middle
one-third of all cases. It must be recalled
that the information regarding etiology is

symptoms which are associated with the
nonhereditary types, it is likely that the
problem of etiology will ultimately be clarified by a definite correlation between etiology and characteristics.

   In judging a case as familial, definite
evidence should also be provided that the
case is *not* nonfamilial, and *vice versa.* It
is unfortunate that in many studies the
presumption of either hereditary or nonhereditary etiology is not reinforced with

confirming negative evidence regarding both the affected and the relevant ancestral propositi.

As to the causes of the secondary form and detailed clinical varieties, these considerations are better reserved for more specific treatment. As previously noted, mongolism is now generally attributed to imperfections in the ovum, or to circumstances obtaining in close temporal relation to conception such as imperfect fertilization or imperfect implantation of the

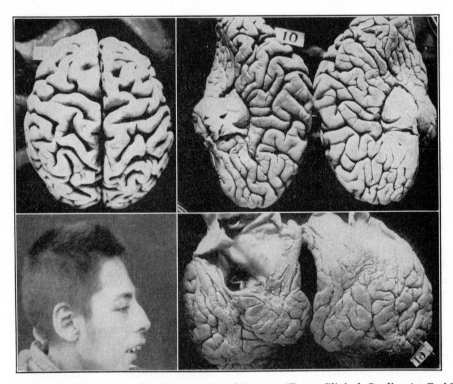

FIGURE 14.   Cerebral anomalies in mental deficiency.   (From *Clinical Studies in Feeble-mindedness,* by E. A. Doll.   Boston: Badger, 1917.   Illustrations courtesy Vineland Training School and R. G. Badger.)

The brain structures in endogenous feeble-mindedness typically show deficiencies rather than defects of neuronic organization. Conspicuous cerebral abnormalities are more commonly associated with exogenous feeble-mindedness or the special conditions which sometimes accompany the mixed forms of mental deficiency. (Cf. Canavan and Taft, 1939.)

Upper left. Asymmetry and hypoplasia in a low-grade imbecile. Age at death 44. Weight of cerebrum 906.5 g.; left hemisphere 455.5 g., right hemisphere 451.0 g.; cerebellum 122.0 g.; stem 25.6 g.; total weight 1054.1 g. Etiology uncertain; presumptive cause early meningitis. (See Goddard (1914), Case 285.)

Upper right. Absence of corpus callosum in a middle-grade imbecile. Age at death 32. Etiology uncertain; family history negative; difficult birth. No brain measurements.

Lower left. Hydrocephalic microcephalic helpless spastic idiot.

Lower right. Severe aplasia with degeneration in brain of patient at left. Age at death 21. Etiology: "Congenital, no reasons known by parents." Total weight 348.8 g.; cerebrum 264.3 g.; cerebellum 72.0 g.; stem 12.6 g. For view of mesial surface of this brain, see Doll (1917), illustration in lower right of cut facing p. 30.

ovum. The particular causes producing cerebral birth lesions are manifold, and the reader is referred to the technical literature for these as well as for the specific etiology of the more exceptional clinical types. Likewise mental deficiency following toxic or infectious diseases such as severe cerebral meningitis, whooping cough, scarlet fever, diphtheria, encephalitis, and the like, while infrequent, must not be disregarded as arresting or deteriorating agencies in cerebral structure and function.

Social Control, Disposition, and Treatment

The great majority of the feeble-minded grow up in their own families, and most of them throughout their lives receive but little other attention except such as may be obtained through special classes in the public schools, attention at the hands of the family physician or consulting specialist, and the assistance of relatives. A systematic program for disposition and treatment outside the feeble-minded child's own family is best considered in terms of incidence, characteristics, grade, and type (Davies, 1930; Doll, 1933b; Stevenson, 1940).

Idiocy is a burden rather than a menace, and the number of cases is relatively small. These children are best cared for, at least after the period of early childhood, in public or private institutions where they can receive specialized care, safe custody, and skilled training.

Imbeciles, similarly, are a social embarrassment rather than a social menace except as high-grade imbecile women of child-bearing age may present special hazards from the point of view of parenthood. Imbeciles are likewise not easily or well cared for except custodially and profit little from ordinary instruction in the special classes of the public schools. While more important in point of numbers than idiots, they still do not constitute a very large part of the total population or even of the mentally deficient population. Imbeciles likewise are usually socially well adjusted and are not as a rule a serious menace from the point of view of sexual reproduction.

The major problem of social welfare in relation to mental deficiency is the care and training of morons. The majority of morons continue to live in the community in their own families at marginal levels of social success. They are frequently unrecognized and are held socially accountable for a higher degree of social performance than is consistent with their constitutional aptitudes. The social policy for morons depends on plus factors (Doll, 1929), such as physical handicaps, family circumstances, unfavorable conduct, and especially the likelihood of sexual promiscuity and familial reproduction. The principal danger with the moron is the frustrated maladjustment ensuing from social expectation greater than he can accomplish.

Special class instruction in the public schools for feeble-minded children who live at home affords an exceptionally good means of assisting moron children to make a favorable social adjustment.

Public institutional care and training are necessary or advisable in many cases, especially for morons during whose adolescent periods family situations are unfavorable (Johnstone, 1923; Byers, 1934). One of the most practicable means of providing for morons, especially those of adult years, is some form of community supervision supplemented by boarding-home family care (Pollock, 1936). Another means is colony and hostel care for morons under institutional or public welfare supervision (Bernstein, 1920; Doll, 1940b).

The word *treatment* is somewhat loosely employed for all forms of custody, care, training, placement, and other forms of social and educational disposition, as well as in the more specific sense of medical therapy. Medical treatment as such has not yet proved notably effective except in

problems have proved custodial, social, and educational rather than medical in the narrow sense. Their designations have accordingly been changed in most cases from hospitals to training schools.

FIGURE 15.   Recreational activities of institutionalized feeble-minded. (Photographs courtesy Vineland Training School: (left) Larry Keighley, and (right) Royce Studio.)

Upper left.   Playhouse constructed by these moron boys under leadership of boy in doorway.
Upper right.   Leisure-time activities among moron girls.
Lower left.   Moron members of winning team playing in community league. Other sports include swimming, field events, football, tennis.
Lower right.   Boy Scouts of America, Troop 39, Cumberland County, N. J. (Cf. Heath, 1940.)

the case of a limited number of clinical types. As already noted, cretinism sometimes yields to thyroid medication, and the motor handicaps of the birth-palsied feeble-minded respond favorably to muscle training.

Most public institutions for the care and training of the feeble-minded were founded by physicians, and most of them are still medically superintended. But the major

It is a common error to assume that because a person is feeble-minded he should *therefore* be committed to an institution for permanent custody. Many feeble-minded are well cared for in their own homes or under community supervision. The need for and the kind of institutional care vary with the individual mental defective in relation to his social circumstances. However, the proper education of the feeble-minded child in his own home continues to be a major family problem (Gesell, 1925) which often puts a heavy burden on the family and results in serious handicaps to the child.

method of control. There is general agreement that sterilization is one useful means of restricting the increase in the number of the feeble-minded under some conditions, and that this surgical procedure does

FIGURE 16. The Vineland Laboratory. (Photograph by Helen F. Hill.)

Founded in 1906 by E. R. Johnstone, Director of The Training School at Vineland, N. J., as the first formal department of research for the scientific study of mental deficiency. Under the initial direction of H. H. Goddard (1906–1918) and later of S. D. Porteus (1919–1925), the pioneering investigations of this Laboratory have continuously promoted scientific and welfare interests in the diagnosis, prevention, treatment, and control of feeble-mindedness. While engaged primarily in psychological research, this Laboratory has made important contributions in such related fields as eugenics, education, medical and social science, and public welfare administration. It has also served as a center for graduate internships and professional collaboration, as well as for promoting numerous standard scientific procedures. (Cf. Doll, Ed., 1932.)

Selective sterilization as a method of control applies primarily to the familial cases (Popenoe and Johnson, 1918; Laughlin, 1922; Landman, 1932; Myerson, 1936). The evidence on familial reproduction in submarginal families lends weight to the advisability of this means of social prevention. Many practical difficulties as well as scientific reservations have restricted this

not result in the unhappy consequences so frequently predicted for it (Popenoe, 1927, 1930). Sterilization has also been favored with reference to undesirable *social* parenthood.

Research Significance

It is fitting to close this chapter with some brief comment on the significance of mental deficiency as affording a field of theoretical and experimental value for related sciences. Public and private institutions for the feeble-minded afford exceptionally favorable centers for research on the problems of mental deficiency and associated problems of biological, psychological, educational, physical, and social development (Doll, Ed., 1932). The feeble-minded, by the very nature of their condition, constitute a favorable field for studying the numerous influences involved in personal maturation and self-expression (Doll, 1940*d*). Certain it is that the study of mental deficiency has already greatly stimulated important research in many specific fields of human development and adjustment.

Bibliography

This bibliography is only briefly representative of the extensive literature on this subject. It may be amplified by use of the further citations contained in many of the references and by consulting journals in this and related fields, notably the *Proceedings of the American Association on Mental Deficiency* (previously the *Journal of Psycho-Asthenics* and now published as the *American Journal of Mental Deficiency*). References other than English have been kept to a minimum because of their relative difficulty of access to all but specialized students. For a more careful interpretative review of the recent literature in this field than is herein practicable or desirable, see Penrose (1944). Supplementary references in the broad field of child psychology (of which only a few are listed here) will be found elsewhere in this *Handbook*.

ALDRICH, C. G. 1932. Lessons in child training gleaned from idiots. *Child Develpm.*, **3**, 75–80.

ALDRICH, C. G., and E. A. DOLL. 1931*a*. Problem-solving among idiots. *J. Comp. Psychol.*, **12**, 137–169.

——. 1931*b*. Problem-solving among idiots: The use of implements. *J. Soc. Psychol.*, **2**, 306–336.

——. 1931*c*. Comparative intelligence of idiots and normal infants. *J. Genet. Psychol.*, **39**, 227–257.

ANDERSON, M. L. 1921. *Education of defectives in the public schools.* Yonkers-on-Hudson: World Book.

BAKER, H. J. 1927. *Characteristic differences in bright and dull pupils.* Bloomington, Ill.: Public School Publishing Co.

BALLER, W. R. 1936. A study of the present social status of a group of adults, who, when they were in elementary schools, were classified as mentally deficient. *Genet. Psychol. Monogr.*, **18**, 165–244.

BARR, M. W. 1904. *Mental defectives: Their history, treatment and training.* Philadelphia: Blakiston's.

BERNSTEIN, C. 1920. Colony and extra-institutional care for the feeble-minded. *Ment. Hyg., N. Y.*, **4**, 1–28.

——. 1922. Microcephalic people sometimes called "pin heads." *J. Hered.*, **13**, 30–39.

BERRY, C. S. (Chmn.) 1931. *Special education: The handicapped and the gifted.* (Report of the Committee on Special Classes, White House Conference on Child Health and Protection.) New York: Century.

BERRY, R. J. A. 1933. *Stoke Park monographs on mental deficiency and other problems of the human brain and mind: I. The Burden Memorial Volume.* London: Macmillan.

BERRY, R. J. A., and R. G. GORDON. 1931. *The mental defective: A problem in social inefficiency.* London: Kegan Paul.

BINET, A., and T. SIMON. 1916*a*. *The development of intelligence in children.* (Trans. by E. S. KITE.) (*Publ. Train. Sch., Vineland, N. J.,* No. 11.) Baltimore: Williams and Wilkins.

——. 1916*b*. *The intelligence of the feeble-minded.* (Trans. by E. S. KITE.) (*Publ. Train. Sch., Vineland, N. J.,* No. 12.) Baltimore: Williams and Wilkins.

BISCH, L. E. 1925. *Clinical psychology.* Baltimore: Williams and Wilkins.

BLACKFAN, K. D. (Chmn.) 1932. *Growth and development of the child: IV. Appraisement of the child.* (Report of the Committee on Growth and Development, White House Conference on Child Health and Protection.) New York: Century.

BÖSBAUER, H., L. MIKLAS, and H. SCHINER. 1909. *Handbuch der Schwachsinnigenfürsorge.* (2d ed.) Vienna: Graeser.

BRADWAY, K. P. 1935. Paternal occupational intelligence and mental deficiency. *J. Appl. Psychol.*, **19**, 527–542.

——. 1937. Birth lesions in identical twins. *Amer. J. Orthopsychiat.*, **7**, 194–203.

BRIFFAULT, R. 1927. *The mothers: A study of the origins of sentiments and institutions.* Vol. I. New York: Macmillan.

BROUSSEAU, K. 1928. *Mongolism: A study of the physical and mental characteristics of mongolian imbeciles.* (Rev. by H. G. BRAINERD.) Baltimore: Williams and Wilkins.

BROWN, A. W., I. P. BRONSTEIN, and R. KRAINES. 1939. Hypothyroidism and cretinism in childhood. *Amer. J. Dis. Child.*, **57**, 517–523.

BURT, C. 1921. *Mental and scholastic tests.* (Rep. London County Council.) London: King.

BYERS, J. P. 1934. *The Village of Happiness: The story of The Training School.* Vineland, N. J.: Smith Printing House.

CANAVAN, M. M., and A. E. TAFT. 1939. *Waverley researches in the pathology of the feebleminded.* (Research Series, Cases XXXI to XL.) Boston: Mass. Dept. of Mental Health.

CARLSON, E. R. 1941. *Born that way.* New York: John Day.

CRAFTS, L. W., and E. A. DOLL. 1917. The proportion of mental defectives among juvenile delinquents. *J. Delinq.,* 2, 119–143; 191–208.

DAVIES, S. P. 1930. *Social control of the mentally deficient.* New York: Crowell.

DAYTON, N. A. 1938. Report of the Division of Mental Deficiency. *Ann. Rep. Comm. Ment. Health, Mass.*

DE SANCTIS, S. 1912. *Les enfants anormaux.* (Reprinted from *Premier Congrès International de Pédologie.*) Brussels: Ledeberg-Gand.

DOLL, E. A. 1917. *Clinical studies in feeblemindedness.* Boston: Badger.

——. 1919. The average mental age of adults. *J. Appl. Psychol.,* 3, 317–328.

——. 1920. The comparative intelligence of prisoners. *J. Crim. Law Criminol.,* 11, 191–197.

——. 1921. The growth of intelligence. *Psychol. Monogr.,* 29, No. 2. Pp. vi + 130.

——. 1925. Further note on the intelligence quotient. *Educ. Res. Bull.,* 4, 148–150.

——. 1927. Borderline diagnosis. *Proc. Amer. Ass. Stud. Feeble-mind.,* 32, 45–59.

——. 1929. Community control of the feebleminded. *Proc. Amer. Ass. Stud. Feeble-mind.,* 34, 161–175.

——. 1930. The relation of intelligence to criminality. *J. Soc. Psychol.,* 1, 527–531.

——. 1933a. Birth lesion as a category of mental deficiency. *Amer. J. Orthopsychiat.,* 3, 1–13.

——. 1933b. Community control of mental deficiency in the United States. *J. Ment. Sci.,* 79, 578–589.

——. 1933c. Psychological significance of cerebral birth lesions. *Amer. J. Psychol.,* 45, 444–452.

——. 1935. The clinical significance of social maturity. *J. Ment. Sci.,* 81, 766–782.

——. 1936a. Idiot, imbecile, and moron. *J. Appl. Psychol.,* 20, 427–437.

——. 1936b. *The Vineland Social Maturity Scale: Revised condensed manual of directions.* (*Publ. Train. Sch., Vineland, N. J.,* Series 1936, No. 3.) Vineland, N. J.: Smith Printing House.

——. 1937. The inheritance of social competence. *J. Hered.,* 28 (May), 153–166.

DOLL, E. A. 1939. *Your child grows up.* Boston: John Hancock Mutual Life Insurance Co.

——. 1940a. Annotated bibliography on the Vineland Social Maturity Scale. *J. Consult. Psychol.,* 4, 123–132.

——. 1940b. Foster care for mental defectives. *Train. Sch. Bull.,* 36, 193–205.

——. 1940c. IQ and mental deficiency. *J. Consult. Psychol.,* 4, 53–61.

——. 1940d. The nature of mental deficiency. *Psychol. Rev.,* 47, 395–415.

——. 1941. The essentials of an inclusive concept of mental deficiency. *Am. J. Ment. Def.,* 46, 214–219.

DOLL, E. A. (Ed.) 1932. *Twenty-five years: A memorial volume in commemoration of the twenty-fifth anniversary of the Vineland Laboratory.* (*Publ. Train. Sch., Vineland, N. J.,* Series 1932, No. 2.) Vineland, N. J.: Smith Printing House.

DOLL, E. A., and C. G. ALDRICH. 1932. Simple conditioning as a method of studying sensory discrimination among idiots. *J. Gen. Psychol.,* 7, 104–143.

DOLL, E. A., and D. P. MURPHY. 1930. A case of microcephaly following embryonic Roentgen irradiation. *Amer. J. Psychiat.,* 9, 871–878.

DOLL, E. A., W. M. PHELPS, and R. T. MELCHER. 1932. *Mental deficiency due to birth injuries.* New York: Macmillan.

ELLIS, W. J. (Chmn.) 1933. *The handicapped child.* (Report of the Committee on Physically and Mentally Handicapped, White House Conference on Child Health and Protection.) New York: Century.

ENGELBACH, W. 1932. *Endocrine medicine.* (3 vols.) Springfield, Ill.: Thomas.

ESTABROOK, A. H., and I. E. McDOUGLE. 1926. *Mongrel Virginians: The Win Tribe.* Baltimore: Williams and Wilkins.

FERNALD, W. E. 1917. The growth of provision for the feeble-minded in the United States. *Ment. Hyg., N. Y.,* 1, 34–59.

FERNALD, W. E. (Chmn.) 1921. *Statistical manual for the use of institutions for the feeble-minded.* New York: National Committee for Mental Hygiene.

FOSTER, E. M., and E. H. MARTENS. 1938. Statistics of special schools and classes for exceptional children. (*Biennial Survey of Education in the United States: 1934–1936,* Vol. II, Chap. VI.) [*Bull. U. S. Dept. Interior, 1937,* No. 2 (advance pages).] Washington, D. C.: Government Printing Office.

FRANKEL, E. 1940. The development of the program for the mentally deficient in New Jersey—a statistical review. *Amer. J. Ment. Def.,* 45, 110–118.

GESELL, A. 1925. *The retarded child: How to help him.* Bloomington, Ill.: Public School Publishing Co.

GESELL, A. 1928. The diagnosis of mental defect in early infancy. *Proc. Amer. Ass. Stud. Feeblemind.*, 33, 211–218.

GESELL, A., B. M. CASTNER, H. THOMPSON, and C. S. AMATRUDA. 1939. *Biographies of child development: The mental growth careers of eighty-four infants and children.* New York: Hoeber.

GLANVILLE, A. D., and G. KREEZER. 1937. Deficiencies in amplitude of joint movement associated with mental deficiency. *Child Develpm.*, 8, 129–138.

GODDARD, H. H. 1911. Two thousand normal children measured by the Binet measuring scale of intelligence. *Ped. Sem.*, 18, 231–258.

——. 1912. *The Kallikak family: A study in the heredity of feeble-mindedness.* New York: Macmillan.

——. 1914. *Feeble-mindedness: Its causes and consequences.* New York: Macmillan.

——. 1919. *Psychology of the normal and subnormal.* New York: Dodd, Mead.

HEALY, W. 1915. *The individual delinquent.* Boston: Little, Brown and Co.

HEATH, S. R. 1940. Scouting in an institution for the mentally deficient. *Train. Sch. Bull.*, 37, 28–32.

——. 1944. Clinical significance of motor defect, with military implications. *Amer. J. Psychol.*, 57, 482–499.

HECK, A. O. 1940. *The education of exceptional children.* New York: McGraw-Hill.

HILLYER, J. 1926. *Reluctantly told.* New York: Macmillan.

HOAKLEY, Z. P. 1932. The variability of intelligence quotients. *Proc. Amer. Ass. Stud. Feeble-mind.*, 37, 119–148.

HOLLINGWORTH, H. L. 1930. *Abnormal psychology: Its concepts and theories.* New York: Ronald.

HOLLINGWORTH, L. S. 1920. *The psychology of subnormal children.* New York: Macmillan.

HOOPES, G. G. 1939. *Out of the running.* Springfield, Ill.: Thomas.

HOSKINS, F. H. 1939. The broken string: An autobiography. *Train. Sch. Bull.*, 36, 41–51; 67–75; 119–123.

HUEY, E. B. 1912. *Backward and feeble-minded children.* Baltimore: Warwick and York.

HUMPHREYS, E. J. 1936. Development deficiencies as the essential problem of mental deficiency. *Proc. Amer. Ass. Ment. Def.*, 41, 215–224.

HUMPHREYS, E. J., G. W. T. WATTS, and W. H. BOLDT. 1937. An investigation into the case records of one thousand high-grade mentally or developmentally defective children. *Proc. Amer. Ass. Ment. Def.*, 42, 9–46.

INGRAM, C. P. 1935. *Education of the slow-learning child.* Yonkers-on-Hudson: World Book.

"INMATE WARD 8." (M. M. WOODSON.) 1932. *Behind the door of delusion.* New York: Macmillan.

IRELAND, M. W. (Director.) 1920. *Defects found in drafted men.* Washington, D. C.: Government Printing Office.

——. 1929. *Neuropsychiatry.* (The Medical Department of the United States Army in the World War, Vol. X.) Washington, D. C.: Government Printing Office.

ITARD, J.-M.-G. 1932. *The wild boy of Aveyron.* (Trans. by G. and M. HUMPHREY. Original in 1894.) New York: Century.

JASTROW, J. 1938. Wise man's burden. *Curr. Hist.*, 48, 25–30.

JENKINS, R. L. 1933. Etiology of mongolism. *Amer. J. Dis. Child.*, 45, 506–519.

JERVIS, G. A. 1942. Recent progress in the study of mental deficiency: Mongolism. *Amer. J. Ment. Def.*, 46, 467–481.

JEWELL, E. J. 1929. Research in progress: The mental growth of borderline feeble-minded. *Train. Sch. Bull.*, 26, 38–42.

JOHNSTONE, E. R. 1923. *Dear Robinson: Some letters on getting along with folks.* Vineland, N. J.: Smith Printing House.

KAPLAN, O. 1940. Life expectancy of low-grade mental defectives. *Psychol. Rec.*, 3, 295–306.

KAPLUN, D. 1935. The high-grade moron—a study of institutional admissions over a ten-year period. *Proc. Amer. Ass. Ment. Def.*, 40, 69–91.

KEY, W. E. 1915. *Feeble-minded citizens in Pennsylvania.* (Publ. Pub. Charities Ass. Pa., No. 16.) Philadelphia: Public Charities Association of Pennsylvania.

KOSTIR, M. S. 1916. *The family of Sam Sixty.* (Publ. Ohio Bd. Adm., No. 8.) Columbus: Ohio Board of Administration.

KREEZER, G. 1933. Neuromuscular excitability in the mentally deficient. *Proc. Amer. Ass. Ment. Def.*, 38, 193–201.

——. 1935. Motor studies of the mentally deficient: Quantitative methods at various levels of integration. *Train. Sch. Bull.*, 32, 125–135.

——. 1936. Electric potentials of the brain in certain types of mental deficiency. *Arch. Neurol. Psychiat., Chicago*, 36, 1206–1213.

——. 1937. Electrical phenomena of the brain among the feeble-minded. *Proc. Amer. Ass. Ment. Def.*, 42, No. 2, 130–141.

——. 1938. The electroencephalogram and its use in psychology. *Amer. J. Psychol.*, 51, 737–759.

——. 1939. Intelligence level and occipital alpha rhythm in the mongolian type of mental deficiency. *Amer. J. Psychol.*, 52, 503–532.

KREEZER, G., and K. P. BRADWAY. 1935. Relation between Binet mental age and motor chronaxia. *Arch. Neurol. Psychiat., Chicago*, 34, 1149–1171.

KUENZEL, M. W. 1929. Research in progress:

A survey of mongolian traits. *Train. Sch. Bull.*, **26**, 49–59.

KUHLMANN, F. 1915. What constitutes feeble-mindedness? *J. Psycho-Asthenics*, **19**, 214–236.

——. 1916. Part played by the state institutions in the care of the feeble-minded. *J. Psycho-Asthenics (Proc. Amer. Ass. Stud. Feeble-mind.)*, **21**, 3–24.

——. 1921. The results of repeated mental re-examinations of 639 feeble-minded over a period of ten years. *J. Appl. Psychol.*, **5**, 195–224.

LANDAUER, W. 1940. The nature of disproportionate dwarfism, with special reference to fowl. *Sigma Xi Quart.*, **28**, 171–180.

LANDMAN, J. H. 1932. *Human sterilization: The history of the sexual sterilization movement.* New York: Macmillan.

LAUGHLIN, H. H. 1922. *Eugenical sterilization in the United States.* Chicago: Psychopathic Laboratory of the Municipal Court.

LOUTTIT, C. M. 1936. *Clinical psychology: A handbook of children's behavior problems.* New York: Harper.

MACMURCHY, H. 1920. *The almosts: A study of the feeble-minded.* Boston: Houghton Mifflin.

McINTIRE, J. T. 1938. The incidence of feeble-mindedness in the cerebral palsied. *Proc. Amer. Ass. Ment. Def.*, **43**, No. 2, 44–50.

MINER, J. B. 1918. *Deficiency and delinquency: An interpretation of mental testing.* Baltimore: Warwick and York.

MÖRCH, E. T. 1940. Achondroplasia is always hereditary and is inherited dominantly. *J. Hered.*, **31**, 439–444.

MORGAN, J. J. B. 1928. *The psychology of abnormal people.* New York: Longmans, Green.

MURCHISON, C. 1926. *Criminal intelligence.* Worcester: Clark University.

MURPHY, D. P., M. E. SHIRLOCK, and E. A. DOLL. 1942. Microcephaly following maternal pelvic irradiation for the interruption of pregnancy. *Amer. J. Roentgenology and Radium Therapy*, **48**, 356–359.

MYERSON, A. (Chmn.) 1936. *Eugenical sterilization: A reorientation of the problem.* (By the Committee of the American Neurological Association for the Investigation of Eugenical Sterilization.) New York: Macmillan.

PENROSE, L. S. 1933. *Mental defect.* London: Sidgwick and Jackson.

——. 1938. *A clinical and genetic study of 1280 cases of mental defect.* (Privy Coun., Med. Res. Coun., Special Rep. Ser., No. 229.) London: His Majesty's Stationery Office.

——. 1944. Mental defect. *J. Ment. Sci.*, **90**, 399–409.

PINTNER, R. 1931. *Intelligence testing: Methods and results.* (2d ed.) New York: Holt.

——. 1933. The feeble-minded child. In C.

MURCHISON (Ed.), *A handbook of child psychology.* (2d ed., rev.), pp. 802–841. Worcester: Clark University Press.

PINTNER, R., and D. G. PATERSON. 1916. A psychological basis for the diagnosis of feeble-mindedness. *J. Crim. Law Criminol.*, **7**, 32–55.

POLLOCK, H. M. (Ed.) 1936. *Family care of mental patients: A review of systems of family care in America and Europe.* Utica, N. Y.: State Hospitals Press.

POPENOE, P. 1927. Success on parole after sterilization. *Proc. Amer. Ass. Stud. Feeble-mind.*, **32**, 86–103.

——. 1930. Feeble-mindedness today. *J. Hered.*, **21**, 421–431.

POPENOE, P., and R. H. JOHNSON. 1918. *Applied eugenics.* New York: Macmillan.

PORTEUS, S. D. 1923. *Studies in mental deviations.* (Publ. Train. Sch., No. 24.) Vineland, N. J.: Smith Printing House.

PRESSEY, S. L., and L. C. PRESSEY. 1926. *Mental abnormality and deficiency: An introduction to the study of problems of mental health.* New York: Macmillan.

RAYMOND, C. S. 1926. Industrial possibilities of the feeble-minded within an institution. *Proc. Amer. Ass. Stud. Feeble-mind.*, **31**, 28–39.

——. 1927. Intellectual development in morons beyond the chronological age of sixteen years. *Proc. Amer. Ass. Stud. Feeble-mind.*, **32**, 243–248.

ROBERTS, J. A. F., R. M. NORMAN, and R. GRIFFITHS. 1936. Studies on a child population: I. Definition of the sample, method of ascertainment, and analysis of the results of a group intelligence test. *Ann. Eugen., Camb.*, **6**, 319–338.

——. 1937. Studies on a child population: II. Retests on the advanced Otis and Stanford-Binet scales, with notes on the use of a shortened Binet scale. *Ann. Eugen., Camb.*, **8**, 15–45.

——. 1938a. Studies on a child population: III. Intelligence and family size. *Ann. Eugen., Camb.*, **8**, 178–215.

——. 1938b. Studies on a child population: IV. The form of the lower end of the frequency distribution of Stanford-Binet intelligence quotients and the fall of low intelligence quotients with advancing age. *Ann. Eugen., Camb.*, **8**, 319–336.

ROGERS, A. C. (Secy.) 1910. Report of Committee on Classification of Feeble-minded. *J. Psycho-Asthenics*, **15**, 61–67.

ROGERS, A. C., and M. A. MERRILL. 1919. *Dwellers in the Vale of Siddem: A true story of the social aspect of feeble-mindedness.* Boston: Badger.

SCHEIDEMANN, N. V. 1931. *The psychology of exceptional children.* Boston: Houghton Mifflin.

SCHREIBER, F. 1939. Mental deficiency from

paranatal asphyxia. *Proc. Amer. Ass. Ment. Def.*, **44**, No. 1, 95–106.

SEGUIN, E. 1907. *Idiocy: And its treatment by the physiological method.* (Reprint of 1866 ed. by Committee on Publication, Teachers College, Columbia University.) Albany: Brandow Printing Co.

SHERMAN, M. A., and T. R. HENRY. 1933. *Hollow folk.* New York: Crowell.

SKEELS, H. M., and H. B. DYE. 1939. A study of the effects of differential stimulation on mentally retarded children. *Proc. Amer. Ass. Ment. Def.*, **44**, No. 1, 114–136.

STEVENSON, G. S. (Chmn.) 1940. Practical state program for care of the mentally deficient. (Report of Committee on Public Relations of the American Association on Mental Deficiency.) *Amer. J. Ment. Def.*, **45**, 325–328.

STRAUSS, A. A. 1939. Typology in mental deficiency: Its clinical, psychological and educational implications. *Proc. Amer. Ass. Ment. Def.*, **44**, No. 1, 85–90.

STRAUSS, A. A., and N. C. KEPHART. 1939. Rate of mental growth in a constant environment among higher-grade moron and borderline children. *Proc. Amer. Ass. Ment. Def.*, **44**, No. 1, 137–142.

THOMPSON, W. H. 1939. A study of the frequency of mongolianism in Negro children in the United States. *Proc. Amer. Ass. Ment. Def.*, **44**, No. 1, 91–94.

TOWN, C. H. 1939. *Familial feeble-mindedness: A study of one hundred and forty-one families.* Buffalo: Foster and Stewart.

TREDGOLD, A. F. 1937. A text-book of mental deficiency (amentia). (6th ed.) Baltimore: William Wood and Co.

UNGER, E. W., and E. T. BURR. 1931. *Minimum mental age levels of accomplishment: A study of employed girls of low-grade intelligence.* Albany: University of the State of New York.

WALLIN, J. E. W. 1917. *Problems of subnormality.* Yonkers-on-Hudson: World Book.

——. 1924. *The education of handicapped children.* Boston: Houghton Mifflin.

WECHSLER, D. 1939. *The measurement of adult intelligence.* Baltimore: Williams and Wilkins.

WEMBRIDGE, E. R. 1926. *Other people's daughters.* Boston: Houghton Mifflin.

——. 1931. *Life among the lowbrows.* Boston: Houghton Mifflin.

WHIPPLE, G. M. (Ed.) **1928.** Nature and nurture: Their influence upon intelligence. *Yearb. Nat. Soc. Stud. Educ.*, 27(I).

——. 1940. Intelligence: Its nature and nurture: Comparative and critical exposition. *Yearb. Nat. Soc. Stud. Educ.*, 39(I). (See also supplement, *Addresses and discussions presenting the Thirty-ninth Yearbook.* Salem, Mass.: Newcomb and Gauss.)

WHIPPLE, H. D. 1927. *Making citizens of the mentally limited: A curriculum for the special class.* Bloomington, Ill.: Public School Publishing Co.

WILDENSKOV, H. O. 1934. *Investigations into the causes of mental deficiency.* (Trans. by H. ANDERSEN.) London: Oxford University Press.

WOLFE, M. M. 1935. President's address. *Proc. Amer. Ass. Ment. Def.*, **40**, 348–356.

WOOD, A. H. (Chmn.) 1929. *Report of the Mental Deficiency Committee: Pt. I. General; Pt. II. The mentally defective child; Pt. III. The adult defective; Pt. IV.* (By E. O. LEWIS.) *Report on an investigation into the incidence of mental deficiency in six areas, 1925–1927.* London: His Majesty's Stationery Office.

WOODALL, C. S. 1931. Analysis of IQ variability. *Proc. Amer. Ass. Stud. Feeble-mind.*, **36**, 247–266.

YERKES, R. M. (Ed.) 1921. *Psychological examining in the United States Army.* (*Mem. Nat. Acad. Sci.*, **15**.) Washington, D. C.: Government Printing Office.

ZELENY, L. D. 1933. Feeble-mindedness and criminal conduct. *Amer. J. Sociol.*, **38**, 564–578.

ZUBIN, J. 1938. Regional differences in the care of mental defect and epilepsy. *Proc. Amer. Ass. Ment. Def.*, **43**, No. 2, 167–178.

Chapter 18

GIFTED CHILDREN

Catharine Cox Miles

"Gifted" as a Term of Distinction

Children who acquire the traditional culture of their group with extreme ease and rapidity have always been especially prized. Those who show an unusual interest in and facility with its more difficult intellectual branches or its higher creative expressions have seemed to merit the special group name of *gifted*. We hardly need consult the dictionary to know that gifted means talented, endowed with superior natural abilities which clearly distinguish their possessor from the average of those of the same age or experience. Children gifted in the higher mental processes—in thinking, reasoning, and making judgments—comprise one of two generally differentiated groups of the gifted. The other is made up of the children who are highly endowed with special talents for creative or inventive production. Terms including *supernormal, highly endowed, intellectually talented, bright, apt,* and *competent* have been supplanted by the simpler term *gifted* in referring to the first of the two groups, and since about 1910 the term has gradually assumed a specific technical meaning. Still applied to children with special capacity or skill in the arts, the term in psychology is now more often used to designate those of very high general intelligence.

The gifted in both categories may be differentiated from children popularly labeled *precocious*. The former are those who have been shown by objective test to possess to a certain high degree the trait of intelligence, or some special, highly valued skill. Precocious children, on the other hand, are those who at an earlier age than others show behavior not necessarily of specific merit in terms of intellectual or creative development, but popularly supposed to be characteristic of older children or adults. It is clear that the gifted may be precocious and that the precocious may be gifted, but the two terms are not necessarily synonymous. Precocious children are overtly expressive in ways that are directly recognized by their day-to-day associates. A child may thus be precocious in simple surroundings who would seem no better than average and perhaps even retarded in a superior setting. Gifted children, on the other hand, are those objectively certified on the basis of a generalized norm system which recognizes absolute values in terms of standard tests. Early specific precocity may be merged even under favorable conditions in later general mediocrity. The gifted are presumed to possess abilities that tend to continue at a high level of competence.

In the past gifted children have been described in qualitative and quantitative terms. The earlier qualitative definitions were influenced by recognition of the presence of creative geniuses in the population, and the term when so used implied the presence of something different in the personality from the traits of the average human being. Child prodigies—children with unusual gifts in art, music, or literaure, or children with some phenomenal gift in rapid calculation or in memory; in fact, the precocious and the special talent groups—were thought of as having this quality of subjective giftedness. The quanitative definitions are of more recent development. They ascribe to gifted children a greater amount of the same kind of ability possessed by average individuals. The fairly recent discovery that feebleminded children generally have not a special disease, but are simply less well endowed than others with the same kinds of power that the average person has, supported the view, now generally held in scientific psychology, that gifted individuals are differentiated from the majority of mankind by a superior endowment in the measurable human abilities characteristic of all. Both types of definitions are an expression of an endeavor to identify in childhood the individuals likely to become the ablest adult leaders, the most productive mature contributors to human culture.

When intelligence tests of the Binet type were first applied to the general population the purpose of measurement was the differentiation of the dull from the average. But the earliest surveys showed quite another possibility, for these tests, found to be singularly effective as indicators of mental power, at once set off a small group of superior individuals whose test scores were as far above the generality as those of the feeble-minded were below it. The rarity of individuals scoring 130 or 140 IQ and higher, and their extraordinary facility in performance, naturally aroused a feeling of wonder and surprise. In the first 1000 children tested, only 1 per cent rated as high as 130, and the 4 or 5 whose IQ's passed the 140 mark seemed indeed phenomenal. It was natural to think of these unusually brilliant test performers as the probable leaders of the future, those among

whom the most distinguished personalities, including geniuses of all kinds, were most likely to appear. Furthermore, by assuming an appropriate critical point they could be arbitrarily defined as geniuses or near-geniuses in Galton's special sense of possessing unusually superior mental ability, if this were defined as mental test ability. What the significance of their high competence might be for future attainment could only be surmised.

The limitation of the term gifted to those scoring within a specified part of the IQ scale is necessarily arbitrary. Statistical habit and popular custom suggested restricting the term to the highest 1 per cent of the population, specifically, those rating IQ's 130 and upward. In the larger researches limitation to the highest ½ per cent has been practiced, and this usage has been suggested for general adoption. It has not been said, nor does serious consideration of the complexity of intellect, motivation, and other personality factors lead investigators to suppose, that the measure of intelligence alone can serve fully to predict later social or intellectual accomplishment or creative achievement. Yet the view is now generally accepted that intelligence measurement, more satisfactorily than any other one available criterion, sets limits within which the several levels of potential competence will essentially be found.

Consideration of the numbers of gifted children in the community indicates their absolute frequency as well as their relative rarity (Table 1). There are usually, as in the first reported sample, some 4 or 5 children scoring at or above 140 IQ in an average thousand, and the top 1 per cent rate generally beyond 130 IQ. In the public school population of the United States, numbering some 28,000,000, there are probably not less than 110,000 to 140,000 of the very highly gifted children, and somewhere

TABLE 1

PERCENTAGE OF GIFTED CHILDREN IN SCHOOL POPULATIONS AS REPORTED BY VARIOUS INVESTIGATORS

(IQ 140 Plus and Upper Centile)

Stanford-Binet Intelligence Test

Population	Revised 2904	Old Form 874	905	112	149	100
Investigator	Merrill	Macmeeken	Terman	Terman	Terman	Malherbe
Date	1938	1939	1916	1919	1919	1921
School status	Grades 1–8	Single age	Grades 1–8	Kindergarten	Grade 1	Grades 1–8
Percentage of group rating 140+	1.33	1.03	.55	2.7	1.30	13.0
Percentage of group rating 136+						
Upper 1 per cent	143 IQ+		130 IQ+			
Median IQ of group	100	100	100	106	88	124

Group Intelligence Tests

Population	4925	13,220	27,642	53,751	1295	3522	4075	10,982
Investigator	Pintner	Duff and Thomson	Witty	Cohen and Coryell	Dearborn and Cattell	Rogers	Educ. Rec. Bureau	
Date	1931	1923	1934	1935	1930	1928	1940	
School status	Grades 1–8	Grades 11–12	H. S.	Senior H. S.	Grades 1–8	Grades 1–8	Grades 1–8	Grades 7–8
Percentage of group rating 140+	1.20	.12	.34	3.34	6.3	6.4	3.9	7.4
Percentage of group rating 136+							6.5	11.2
Median IQ of group	96	100	104		119	115	116	117

near twice this number who rate as high as 130 IQ. An average American town of 10,000 with a school population of roughly 2000 may be expected to have 20 children with IQ's of 130 or higher, of whom 10 or so rate as high as 140. Certain regions of the United States have relatively more, others relatively less, than the average approximations. Communities and cities vary within themselves in the density of the gifted population. Schools also differ, high schools generally attracting more of the superior intellects than elementary schools, and colleges more than either. Private schools also differ among themselves, some of them having as high populations of gifted children as the average or even the superior college. The frequency statistics for specific studies of the gifted are based on the use of the Stanford-Binet Intelligence Test. Results from group tests may be used as a method of approximation in groups, but their results are only roughly comparable and quite inadequate for individual evaluation.

The children rating as more or less gifted have many traits in common with each other. It may be difficult to distinguish the performance of many 130 IQ's from the 140's, but the group as a whole, whether more or less rigorously defined, differs unmistakably from average lower school children with IQ's between 85 and 115, and its educational needs are quite divergent from the generality. Exceptions prove the rule by their infrequency and by the evidence they offer of factors other than the intellectual which form part of the total personality picture.

The gifted child defined in intelligence test terms may not be the adult genius. The latter clearly combines with high mental ability traits of personality, and in many cases also special talents, not necessarily closely correlated with intelligence. An objective test index of the combined traits essential for eminent success in maturity might be more useful than our present index of giftedness in IQ terms. But the more ideal measure is not available, and estimates of later accomplishment can at present be arrived at only partially and in approximate terms by the careful use of tests and observations found relatively effective for the purpose.

Terman has not defined the term gifted psychologically; neither has Hollingworth. They and others have been content to study children with high intelligence test scores in the hope that the results would eventually throw light on the characteristics of superior human personalities. In using the term *genius* with reference to children of high IQ, Terman has directly allied himself with the historic effort to discover in childhood the characteristics of the exceptional adult. In his early studies of leadership, of precocity, and of bright contrasted with dull boys, he long ago began the search for measurable traits or qualities which may ultimately be found to represent the more persistent elements or trends toward superiority of endowment in personality. This search he and others have pursued with fruitful results, although the final summing-up to date shows that the complex problem of prediction is still far from solved.

Study of the most superior specimens of a species is of importance for pure and applied science. It is essential for pure science to determine the upper limits of superiority, the nature of the characteristics of the upper deviates, the ways in which they differ from the average, the individual differences among them, and their similarities. It is not to be expected in any biological series that they will prove to be a type, yet there will be certain traits in which they tend to resemble one another more than they resemble the average of their species.

It is of importance to applied science to know under what circumstances these superior deviates appear. If it should be found that the function of intelligence can be measurably increased through training methods, through environmental influences, and the like, then the hope would be justified that the effective number of the gifted may be considerably enlarged. If, on the other hand, biological elements are chiefly involved, it is not likely, under existing conditions, that the present percentage can be appreciably augmented. The attention of psychologists, which has been directed toward the study of background as well as foreground, is now being turned especially to a consideration of the environmental conditions favorable for the development of gifted children, that is, toward the discovery of opportunities and influences which can stimulate their talents to strong, healthy, optimal growth.

History

Philosophers and other teachers who have tried to work out systematic methods of producing a good human society have given thought to the selection and education of superior children. Plato spoke of the importance of discovering and suitably educating the most able youths for leadership in the state. He suggested that tests of native ability should be the basis of the selection. From his day until the introduction of modern universal school systems, education was, however, generally the prerogative of the children of the well-born and the able, plus a few outstanding minds from the lower economic or social groups. State administrators, teachers, and priests tried to recruit pupils of superior natural gifts who might be trained to carry on community institutions and maintain or extend the group culture. Under the apprentice system skilled specialists tried to attract gifted youngsters apt in learning and capable of superior accomplishment. Practical rather than scientific methods of finding and training gifted children are still in general use today. Ostwald in 1909 formulated his scheme for the selection of gifted university students for advanced research. Present-day personnel methods involve essentially similar problems and procedures. With or without the use of special technical aids, education and industry seek the gifted and train those who are expected to qualify for later leadership (E. L. Thorndike, 1939).

Prescientific Observation of Gifted Children. Parents in all times have been alert to recognize superior competence in their offspring, and it has often been they who discovered and brought to wider attention children with special mental ability. When the parents were themselves teachers they not infrequently attributed the unusual competence of the children to their own superior methods of instruction. Superior children have frequently been reported singly and in interesting collections. One of the more famous prodigies was Christian Heinrich Heineken, who showed remarkable powers of observation and speech at the age of 10 months. Before the age of one year he could recite stories and verses. Under a tutor's instruction he soon learned arithmetic fundamentals, anatomical systems, and world history. At the age of 4 years he could read printed and written German, relate stories in French, and recite 1400 sentences from good Latin authors; he knew all the important places on the map. His knowledge was said to be more than mere memory, for he could discuss what he knew with intelligence. His fame spread through Europe and he was invited to visit the Danish king, who was delighted and amazed by his conversation. Unfortunately, his health failed and he died at the age of 4 years and 4 months. Like Christian Heinrich, some others cited down to our own time (Braun, 1920; Bridgman, 1938) died at an early age and before their unusual promise could show complete fulfillment.

In happy contrast, the life story of Karl Witte gives the sequel to a gifted childhood in terms of superior, highly esteemed adult achievement. Considered to be quite unprepossessing as an infant, he was so carefully trained that at 6 his thinking was logical and his information accurate. He learned foreign languages readily and by the age of 9 was proficient in several. Science, art, and history he acquired by a natural project method devised by his father. Entering the university at 9 he completed a distinguished course in all his subjects and at 14 received the Ph.D. degree. When, at 16, he was appointed university instructor his youthful appearance caused objection and it was suggested by a royal patron that he devote some years to travel. During a residence abroad he was led to the literary study in which he became distinguished while continuing his chosen career in jurisprudence. At 21 he became a university teacher, at 23 a full professor. His long and active life was happy in domestic as well as in wider social relationships. He was devoted to community, professional, and scholarly activities in which, before his death at the age of 83, he had won high honor and distinction.

From many accounts we may conclude that, as in Witte's case, rapid mental development in superior healthy children can further unfold at a high level of adult distinction. On the other hand, precocity due to overtraining may regress to a mean of mediocrity. The one-sided advancement of the emotionally unstable may later deteriorate or end in mental illness. A typical early collection of case studies of historical precocious children is that of Buckley (1853). A more recent report of seven American prodigies illustrates the late pretest point of view (Dolbear, 1912).

Beginning of Scientific Psychological Observation. Early scientific method was injected into the study of the gifted and a new phase of interest aroused in their investigation by the genetic and statistical researches of Galton (1869) and his contemporaries. These constituted the first quantitative psychological studies of human endowment. DeCandolle (1885) and, subsequently, Ward (1906) introduced scientific method into the classification of the social influences favorable to the appearance of the gifted, contending that these are at least as important as the constitutional endowment in determining achievement. J. McK. Cattell (1915, 1917) combined the two points of view and methods in his studies of *American Men of Science.*

Yoder (1894) included childhood traits in his statistical study of the natural history of fifty eminent men, and Ellis (1904) devoted special attention to interrelationships of precocity and health in the childhood of eminent Britons.

Three studies already referred to, by Terman, belong to the intermediate period in which the methods of psychology as of all natural science were gradually evolving. A study of leadership, suggestibility, and other traits in school children (Terman, 1904) was followed by a summary of contemporary opinion regarding precocity, prematuration, and the new concepts of mental hygiene (Terman, 1905). By laboratory study employing a large variety of early intelligence test items, the abilities of bright and dull boys were compared (Terman, 1906). In the title of this study, "Genius and Stupidity," Galton's concept of genius as superior mental ability was introduced.

In 1905 Binet's mental test scale was published, Goddard's translation appeared in 1911, and Terman's revision in 1916.

Case studies of gifted children soon showed the possibilities of the new methods to discover superior mentality. The first of these utilized mental ratings based on early versions of Binet's scale preceding the Stanford standardization. The author of the earliest report was incredulous (Bush, 1914); the second (Langenbeck, 1915) found in the Binet data gratifying proof of obvious precocity.

Modern Period of Quantitative Study. The small group of children with exceptionally high IQ's revealed by the revised Binet method proved to be neither peculiar nor one-sidedly intellectual as had been suggested in some earlier studies of precocious children. They were found rather to be essentially normal, well-adjusted children (Terman, 1915). Brief reports of four whose IQ's reached 140 or above were included as the highest in a series covering the IQ range and illustrating the measurement of intelligence (Terman, 1916). The definition of 130 IQ as the scoring point exceeded by the highest centile of mental ability was enunciated in the same volume.

The following year Garrison, Burke, and Hollingworth (1917) published the first account of an IQ in the 180's. Rusk (1917) described the test performance of an English child whose repeated Binet scores gave IQ's near 200, and Terman (1917), from biographical data, appraised Galton's childhood IQ as near 200. Other cases described in the first decade of measurement included an IQ of 167 (Coy, 1918); a phenomenally precocious reader (Terman, 1918), later found to have an IQ of 140 (Terman and Chase, 1920); and some 35 individuals in the IQ range from 140 to 184 (Terman, 1919). Besides affording case reports, these 35 gifted children with 14 other top centile individuals were the subjects of the first group study of the intellectual, educational, and social characteristics of gifted public school children.

Gillingham (1920) reported seven IQ's of 140 and higher in a study of superior private school children with personality handicaps. Whipple (1919) outlined and illustrated methods of selection and instruction for superior, including technically gifted, children, reporting experimental results and norms and appending a bibliography. Clearly the new method of measurement had provided a means for differentiating intellectually able individuals in childhood, and psychologists soon became aware of the possibilities for the further study of individuals and groups thus differentiated.

The period from Henry's "Classroom Problems in the Education of Gifted Children," in the 1920 *Yearbook of the National Society for the Study of Education,* to Whipple's "Education of Gifted Children," in the 1924 *Yearbook* (Part I) of the Society, shows gradually developing systematization in method and presentation. The two volumes mentioned give cross-sections of contemporary interest and knowledge. Their bibliographies are extensive and valuable. Detailed studies of the educational status and progress of superior children in special classes published in this period include Coy (1923), in which the use of the term gifted was first specifically limited to the top centile; Cobb and Taylor (1924); and Stedman (1924). Goddard's monograph in this succession appeared in 1928. Root's (1921) descriptive study of superior children gave an experimental-psychological analysis of the mental processes of 53 cases, 23 of them of IQ 140+. A. M. Jones (1925) reported a detailed classification from clinical and educational data of material confirming for 120 children in Pennsylvania conclusions drawn by Terman for his first group of 59 upper centile Californians. Investigators at this time characteristically grouped their results and summarized the trends indicated by ranges and central tendencies. Their studies of superior children included school or clinic children variously restricted, in terms of IQ level, some extending consideration to include children within the average intelligence range. The researches dealing chiefly with groups of IQ 130+ or 140+ or presenting individual case studies at this level form the material basis for the present review. Other supportive works concerning above-average groups are occasionally referred to briefly.

Yates's account, in 1922, of 25 superior high school students marked the first use of group tests for the selection of notably high intelligence. The assumption that the reported scores corresponded to individual IQ's of 140 or higher is open to question. The upper centile criterion may, however, have been approximately fulfilled in this early work.

Whipple's *Yearbook* in 1924 contained the first statistically developed results from studies of the traits and achievements of large populations of the gifted. In this volume Terman outlined the Stanford study of more than 1000 gifted children with IQ's of 140 or higher. The methods of sifting the population by group and individual tests were described, and results obtained in the first cross-sectional research were briefly enumerated (Terman, 1924b). Terman and DeVoss (1924) also presented a preliminary summary of the educational test achievements later reported in detail. Waddle's (1924) case studies included a number of exceptionally high IQ's and reported remarkable achievements. The *Yearbook* researches describing upper centile intelligences and reporting many cases with IQ's 140 and higher include the studies by Hollingworth and Taylor (1924) of physical size and strength, Cobb and Taylor (1924) of achievement test scores, and Patrick (1924) of school achievement and personality traits. Standard educa-

tional tests with the devices of educational ages and quotients had added considerably to the effectiveness of statistical techniques for gifted child study.

In the next six years, 1925 to 1930 inclusive, the essential descriptive and statistical picture of the gifted child as we recognize it today was drawn. The researches of Terman and his associates, frequently referred to in this article as the California or Stanford studies, and Hollingworth's monograph were primarily responsible. Other investigators made valuable additions, generally by way of supporting evidence. Terman's researches were published in 1925 and 1930 as Volumes I and III of his *Genetic Studies of Genius*. These compendia afford the most complete available store of factual data about large groups of gifted boys and girls in childhood and adolescence. The first volume devoted 19 chapters to the history, methods, and results of the Stanford study of 1000 gifted preschool and elementary school children and 300 gifted high school pupils. A brief report of a follow-up study after 2 years and an important review of conclusions and problems completed the work (Terman *et al.*, 1925). In Volume III were reported methods and results in a cross-section follow-up after 7 years, 13 chapters; 86 cases illustrating individual differences and personality problems, 9 chapters; personal histories and achievements of seven gifted juvenile writers, 5 chapters; and a summary of retrospect and prospect in a critical, evaluative presentation, 1 chapter (Burks, Jensen, and Terman, 1930). The work presented in these two volumes is invaluable (1) because of the large number of subjects, representing about nine-tenths of the highest IQ's in a population of 250,000 public school children of their age, (2) because of the combination of longitudinal and cross-sectional study, (3) because statistical treatment is supported by case illustrations, and (4) because the basic data are made available for direct study and comparison.

Hollingworth, in 1926, published her monograph, *Gifted Children*, a general summary presentation of the background and foreground of the field of study. A series of researches by the same author and her associates on special problems concerning gifted children included further, before 1931, a study of the regression of the IQ's of the siblings of the gifted (Cobb and Hollingworth, 1925), measurements of motor functions (Hollingworth and Monahan, 1926), measurements of special musical abilities (Hollingworth, 1926a), a follow-up account 10 years after the first study of an unusually gifted boy, IQ 187 (Hollingworth, 1927), the important evidence of the superiority in school achievement of the more gifted over the less gifted (Hollingworth and Cobb, 1928), and a study of the growth in stature of the gifted (Hollingworth, 1930a).

In the same period Lamson (1930) reported on gifted children studied in the senior high school 7 years after their identification in the lower grades; Gray (1930) contributed a study of young college students; Lehman and Witty (1927) examined the play behavior of gifted school children; and Witty (1930) reported his first research on 100 gifted children with a follow-up after 6 years. The Witty studies covered many of the points studied also by Terman, and their similar findings gave direct support to the larger researches. Baumgarten in 1930 reviewed the studies of precocious children and described, psychologically, children with special artistic gifts.

In the year following the publication of Volume I of the *Genetic Studies of Genius*, Volume II of the series appeared: a study of the early mental traits of historical geniuses (Cox, 1926). This work belongs in the succession, from Galton through Yoder, Ellis, and Cattell, of quantitative evaluations of historically recorded biographical data concerning persons of eminent achievement. It differs from the older studies in the introduction of the new concept of intelligence measurement. The appraisal of the IQ's of historical persons in childhood as proposed and illustrated by Terman (1917) was here applied to a large number of the most eminent men of the past, including many of the world's greatest geniuses. Previsaged by Terman, this work reported by Cox, from data gathered by her and her associates, approached the problem of the gifted by making available for comparison the IQ ratings, personality trait evaluations, and environmental appraisals from available childhood data for 300 of the most distinguished figures in the history of American and European progress.

In the 1930's and the early 1940's individual and group studies of gifted children contributed many additional details to form the gradually emerging outline picture as it appears in later sections of this chapter. Three reviews and summaries gave the findings and conclusions to date (Terman, 1931; Terman and Burks, 1933; Hollingworth, 1940). Hollingworth's (1942) final volume directed attention to the rare individuals whose childhood IQ's reached 180 or higher. Case studies of 12 such unusual children were here prefaced by a detailed historical section with résumés of the previously published accounts of 19 other children with similarly high IQ's. The book contains also a summary (five chapters), with critical comments and amplifications, of the author's findings and conclusions hitherto available only in scattered periodical form.

The most significant contributions of recent research include (1) the increasing evidence of the persistence in the gifted as they grow older of high intellectual ability and achievement as demonstrated by test performances and academic standing (Hollingworth and Kaunitz, 1934; Lorge and Hollingworth, 1936; Hildreth, 1939; Hollingworth, 1940; Terman and Oden, 1940a; Witty, 1940a; Hollingworth, 1942; Witty and Theman, 1943) and (2) the beginnings of differential study of subgroups of the gifted as in Lewis's (1941) comparison of the traits of gifted children of superior and inferior educational achievement and in Terman and Oden's (1940b) comparison of the most and the least successful of the California gifted group who had reached adulthood.

The more extensive bibliographies for the twenty-five-year period of research include those of Terman and Chase (1920), Henry (1920), Coy (1923), Whipple (1924), Hollingworth (1926b), Terman and Burks (1933), Blair (1938), Hollingworth, Terman, and Oden (1940), and Hollingworth (1942). Bibliographies on the education of the gifted in the 1940's were prepared by Newland (1941) and Hildreth and Ingram (1942).

Emerging Search for Further Defining Traits. A series of essentially duplicate studies tends to follow the elaboration of a new scientific technique. This occurred when the Binet method appeared. Many psychologists sought to discover or verify the presence of high IQ children in populations available for testing. To this primarily scientific interest a practical educational one was joined. Recognition of the desirability of segregating gifted children for educational economy and effectiveness made demands for adequate methods of selection. The mental tests provided a practical and objective basis that was found to be increasingly useful, especially when applied in conjunction with other methods of appraisal.

When the high IQ groups had been segregated, further progress depended on accurate measurement of behavior capacities and personalities. Again two interests converged. The need for scientific knowledge about the accomplishments, abilities, and traits other than the intellectual of the high IQ's was a compelling incentive to research; and the needs of teachers faced with the problems of instructing children 40 to 100 per cent accelerated intellectually gave the problem immediate practical urgency. The results have exceeded early anticipations in their extent and concurrence, and they have raised many new problems demanding further investigation.

With the preliminary publication of the 16-year follow-up of Terman's gifted thousand (Terman and Oden, 1940a, 1940b), research concerning gifted children entered a new phase. Personal characteristics, hereditary factors, school progress, and achievement were here for the first time compared for gifted children, apparently intellectually indistinguishable in childhood, who later became (1) successes or (2) failures in terms of professional, occupational, and economic achievement. The ground was thus cleared for the next step: the identification of those within the gifted groups who are likely to become in terms of total personality the most competent adults. A basis for a more restricted definition of the term gifted may result, or a new classificatory term may be found for the high IQ children of greatest potentiality, the gifted in childhood who in exceptional accomplishment in their maturity realize the rare promise of their youth.

Children who have not only the superior intellects to which the term gifted now attaches, but also the other traits and characteristics in which later superior achievement is rooted, are intrinsically gifted in a broad psychosocial meaning of the word. Whether there are others not so highly gifted in intelligence as the 130 or 140+ IQ's discovered in childhood, nor so precocious in the unfolding of their mental powers, who later display equal or superior success in their mature work, only further research can prove. The indications now available seem to show that it is the integrated totality of personality, with its varying physical, emotional, intellectual, and social components forming more rather than less effective patterns, in which success in contrast to failure is conditioned under appropriate environmental stimulations. Tracing forward the life progress of large groups of gifted children and upper centile children and tracing backward the developmental course of equally successful adult individuals who were not labeled as gifted in childhood must eventually solve the puzzle.

Characteristics of Gifted Children

The understanding, care, and training of gifted children and the theory of their origin and psychological constitution depend on knowledge of their background, their emotional and social traits, and their physical characteristics and on adequate measures of their intellectual endowment. Detailed observation and extensive quantification must precede analysis, and hypotheses are not to be accepted as conclusions. Parents, teachers, even psychologists, may cling to certain prejudices regarding the problems of the gifted which only many facts can ultimately dispel. Some of these are now available and from them parts of the picture of the gifted children can be distinctly discerned; others are still fragmentary and unclear, with contradictory elements. In the following pages the present knowledge is briefly reviewed.

Racial Origin. Gifted children in the United States have been more frequently found in the racial groups in which in the past century economic, social, educational, and professional leadership has been generally centered. Yet exceptions have also appeared, indicating that superiority may occur in any of the races or ethnic groups that have contributed to the American population. In Terman's main group 51 per cent are of British descent; 17 per cent, German and Austrian; 6 per cent, French; 4 per cent, Scandinavian; and 10.5 per cent, of combined Jewish stock. Old American families from New England and the Middle West have contributed substantially more than their quota to the California group, whereas foreign-born parents are numerically less well represented. Whatever groups are in the general population are also represented in the gifted group; Negroes, Mexicans, and Orientals are included in the California studies. In the Middle West (Witty, 1930, 1940a), in Ohio (Cleveland, 1921), and in Pennsylvania (A. M. Jones, 1925), the gifted groups have drawn heavily on the hereditary stocks constituting the more favored and enterprising elements of the population. In New York City, Jewish children are especially in excess in the public school gifted groups (Hollingworth, 1926b).

The racial contributions to the gifted populations in the various studies correspond roughly to the rank order of IQ means of the same stocks in the public schools. They are also in general agreement with the draft army results of 1918. Yet conclusions as to the superiority of parent stocks or future groups of gifted children should not be drawn from results limited geographically, economically, and in terms of migration. Certain elements have never been adequately surveyed, as, for example, children of Irish descent in parochial schools. Indians and Negroes have been insufficiently represented in the public school groups surveyed. When looked for in city Negro communities many high IQ Negro children can be found (Jenkins, 1943; Witty and Theman, 1943), and the degree of giftedness is uncorrelated with the extent of white ancestry (Jenkins, 1936). A Negro girl of 200 IQ has been reported (Witty and Jenkins, 1936). Studies of IQ distributions in England and Scotland show that roughly the same IQ level marks the upper centile in those countries as in the United States (Duff and Thomson, 1923; Macmeeken, 1939). We may say in summary that, although it is true that under existing social conditions certain racial or ethnic groups produce relatively more gifted children than others, no final conclusions about the relation of giftedness and race should be drawn until wider regions are sampled and conditions for the study of social inheritance are more fully understood (Hollingworth, 1940).

Sex Ratio. An excess of boys over girls has been found in the higher IQ brackets in the majority of groups of gifted children so far described. Among elementary school children Terman *et al.* (1925) found a ratio of 121 boys to 100 girls in 643 preschool and elementary school children; A. M. Jones (1925), 135 boys to 100 girls in 120 cases. In contrast, Witty's (1930) 100 numbered 51 boys and 49 girls, and Jenkins's (1936) Negroes showed excess in favor of the girls. In none of these researches, however, was the sex ratio a primary problem, and representative selection had not been attempted. The method of nomination used by Terman and the admission of volunteered subjects are both known to increase the numbers of higher scoring boys, as has been shown, among others, in the Scottish study of 1000 "representative" single age 11-year-olds (Scottish Council, 1933). In proof, the only completely objective sample, a rigid single age group in which all the Scottish children born on certain days were tested, was found to contain 4 boys and 5 girls of IQ 140+ (Macmeeken, 1939). Lewis's (1940) study also shows more girls than boys in the higher IQ categories. His ratio is 46 to 40 for IQ 140+.

Terman's high school group (Terman *et al.*, 1925) of 200 gifted boys and 109 gifted girls selected by nomination and group intelligence test offered an even larger numerical sex contrast than his younger populations, and other comparisons of the sexes with respect to numbers at the highest group test score levels seemed at one time to confirm a disproportion largely increasing with age (Terman and Burks, 1933). However, many of the reported results were drawn from groups unequally selected or were based on tests of unequal difficulty for boys and girls. Recent results for large high school and college populations derived from fairly homogeneous distributions with equal mean scores for the sexes show generally smaller contrasts than the earlier studies. In illustration (Table 2), Witty's (1934) group test results for IQ's 140+ in high school populations are compared with high school seniors' scores reported by Henmon and Holt (1931) and the Thurstones' (1937, 1938) statistics for college freshmen. The ratios show the boys generally but not always outnumbering the girls at the highest levels, but no regular age-sex trend appears consistently.

Causes for lack of agreement in the present results probably include lack of homogeneity in the population samples compared and inadequacy of the tests as measures equally fair to both sexes at the upper extremes even when the means are satisfactorily equated. Essential for fair comparison of superior deviates are sufficiently high "ceilings" in different sections of the tests, equality in population samples, and statistical adequacy of sample size at the gifted level. Appropriate consideration should also be given to the pos-

TABLE 2

Sex Ratio in Top Range of Group-Test Distributions in High Schools and Colleges

Investigator and Tests Used	Population Tested	Numbers Tested			Ratio *
		Boys	Girls	Total	Boys to Girls
Witty (1934) Terman Group Test	Pupils in high schools: Indiana, Kansas, Oklahoma, Illinois Top 0.34 per cent (140 IQ+)	14,149 47	13,493 48	27,642 95	94 to 100
Henmon and Holt (1931) National Intelligence Test, etc. Ohio State Univ. Psychological Test	Seniors in high schools: Wisconsin Top 0.46 per cent	6,458 39	8,636 31	15,094 70	168 to 100
Henmon and Holt (1931) American Council on Education Test (1929)	Seniors in high schools: Wisconsin Top 1.18 per cent (97th college percentile)	7,503 111	9,451 90	16,954 201	156 to 100
Thurstone and Thurstone (1937) American Council on Education Test (1936)	College students Top 2.71 per cent † (97.3 percentile)	28,185 802	25,179 643	53,364 1,445	112 to 100
Thurstone and Thurstone (1938) American Council on Education Test (1937)	Students in 323 colleges Above 97th percentile ‡	32,500 1,207	26,450 771	68,899 1,978	123 to 100
	Students in private men's and women's colleges Above 97th percentile ‡	6,787 417	6,590 262	13,377 679	161 to 100
	Students in private coeducational colleges Above 97th percentile ‡	8,951 379	6,914 253	15,865 632	116 to 100
	Students in public coeducational colleges Above 97th percentile ‡	11,355 283	5,651 138	17,006 421	101 to 100

* Relative to numbers tested. Calculations made for this table from data reported by investigators as cited.
† Wrenn (1935) gives ave. IQ 140 = 97th percentile A.C.E. ‡ Approximate.

sible involvement of differences beside the intellectual, such as social motivation, physical endurance, and fatigability in learning situations and examinations, and amount of practice and experience with different kinds of subject matter. Such factors may complicate the measurement of intelligence more at the extremes than at the means. The existence of a sex difference or its amount can be indicated certainly only when the secondary factors are eliminated and the comparisons are made with group or individual test techniques equally fair to both sexes at the part of the scoring range involved.

Heredity and Home Background. Gifted children may come from humble or from superior homes. In Terman's group 31 per cent of the fathers were professional; 50 per cent, semi-professional or in business; 12 per cent, skilled laborers; and less than 7 per cent, semi-skilled or unskilled. In Witty's group 64 per cent were in business, 34 per cent were professional. In terms of proportional representation in the general population the professional class has ten times its quota of gifted children; the commercial and public service groups exceed their quota by 50 per cent, whereas the industrial group contributes less than half its share. Even so, the large non-professional general population is so great that its numerical contribution to the gifted group is more than twice that of the professions. Groups of superior, but not gifted, children show relatively similar distributions in occupational and professional homes (Blair, 1938). Rated on the Barr Occupational Scale, the fathers of Terman's children show a much higher average index than the theoretical norm for the general population. And the fathers of two gifted children rate higher than the fathers of one. Witty has pointed out that the average Barr rating for the fathers of high school children, average IQ

111, is approximately halfway between the index of the fathers of gifted children and the estimated theoretical index for the general population.

The good stock producing the gifted is further indicated by the statistics for education and various measures of social value in the parents. The education of the fathers and mothers in the California study averages 12 years; the grandparents had less schooling than this, but more than the average in their day. Witty's Kansas and Missouri mothers also average 12 years of education; his fathers, 13 years. Among the parents of Jones's group, which seems to have been drawn from a university clinic, 55 per cent of the fathers and 24 per cent of the mothers were college graduates. These figures are higher than are generally found for the parents of typical gifted pupils in public schools. In the California group one or both parents of a fourth of all the children held a college degree. In Witty's group 50 per cent of the parents had 2 years or more of college training.

It is characteristic for gifted children to be born in families where positions of honor, trust, and responsibility are the rule rather than the exception. Terman found among the members of 528 families of gifted children more than twice that number of political, religious or fraternal, professional, financial, or executive positions. Witty reports similar results. Eminent relatives are also numerous in the families of the gifted in Terman's group, including 14 members of the Hall of Fame, 25 men and women listed in *Who's Who*, and 57 relatives in the *American Encyclopedia of Biography*, or an equivalent source. The fathers and mothers of the gifted children report a large and varied interest in hobbies (Witty, 1930). Teachers regard gifted homes as probably favorable in 85 per cent of Terman's cases, unfavorable in 9 per cent; in a control group the corresponding figures are 62 and 24 per cent. Further statistics indicate energy and stability in the families of the gifted. The average family containing a gifted child has 3.35 children when completed, showing a relatively small decline from the 3.67 children in the completed families of the parents. The correlation coefficient between the schooling of the parents and the size of the family is $-.21 \pm .07$; between IQ and size of family, $-.27 \pm .06$. Seven per cent of the parents of the gifted have been divorced or separated as compared with an estimated rate in the general population of 8 to 9 per cent. Infant mortality and morbidity rates are low in the families of the gifted; only 8 per cent of the fathers and 12 per cent of the mothers report as much as one or more, often minor, chronic illnesses. In agreement with Cattell's findings for men of science, where there are two or more children in the family, the gifted is likely to be the first-born.

Physical Traits and Health History. Baldwin's study of the California gifted group finds them superior to the age norms in thirty-four anthropometric measurements, including height, weight, general physical development, and muscular energy (Burks, Jensen, and Terman, 1930). Age for age, they exceed the developmental norms for average children. In height and weight they resemble private school children and other select groups drawn from superior population samples and enjoying more adequate physical care than average children (Table 3). At each reported age the gifted boys considerably exceed Shuttleworth's (1939) superior socioeconomic group; they are slightly taller and heavier than Baldwin and Wood's (1923) norms; and they almost equal Gray and Jacomb's (1921) norms derived from exclusively healthy, private school children. Witty's

(1930) results also show better than average bodily development.

Hollingworth and Taylor's (1924) data for 45 gifted Jewish children in New York City are in agreement with the other results with respect to height, and show, in a comparison of their results with norms for average and feeble-minded children, that a positive intelligence-height relationship is present. These children were also especially well nourished, as indicated by height-weight coefficients, and their strength, measured by dynamometer test, was supe-

TABLE 3

HEIGHT AND WEIGHT OF GIFTED AND OTHER GROUPS OF BOYS

Age *	Gifted		Shuttle- worth ‡ (1939)	Gray and Jacomb† § (1921)	Baldwin and Wood ‡ (1923)	Faber ‡ California Terman *et al.* (1925)
	Baldwin † (1923) Terman *et al* (1925)					
Height (in Inches)						
7	48.5		46.2	48.1	48	47.1
8	50.6		48.7	52.1	50	49.2
9	52.3		50.8	55.8	52	51.2
10	53.7		52.8	56.0	54	53.3
11	56.2		54.8	56.8	56	54.7
12	57.9		56.6	59.7	58	56.8
13	59.9		58.6	60.1	60	58.8
14	62.6		61.1	62.8	63	61.4
15	64.7		64.6	66.2	65	62.8
Weight (in Pounds)						
7	55.8		47.8	45	53	51.3
8	57.8		53.8	59	58	57.5
9	68.6		59.5	71	64	62.9
10	71.4		65.5	72	71	71.1
11	82.2		71.8	77	78	75.3
12	87.5		79.0	85	85	83.2
13	95.4		86.4	86	94	91.1
14	109.3		97.6	104	111	103.3
15	118.8		114.8	120	123	111.1

* Age to nearest birthday.
† Net weight.
‡ Weight with clothing.
§ Weights read from height-weight table.

rior to that of average and vastly superior to that of dull children of the same age. The height of these children measured year by year for a 6-year period continued on the average about 5 per cent above the norms (Hollingworth, 1926b). Monahan and Hollingworth (1927) found gifted children appreciably superior in neuromuscular capacity as measured in strength of grip, in jumping, and in tapping speed. The early studies of Cleveland (1921), Yates (1922), and A. M. Jones (1925) are in agreement with the more recent and more detailed results in indicating superior physical development and energy with infrequent physical defects. Hildreth's (1939) 50 upper centile elementary school children of Jewish race were superior to a matched control group in energy, physique, activity, and resistance to fatigue. In this connection the exploratory psychogalvanic research of Collmann (1931) is of interest. He found that superior children (average IQ 138) are less disturbed emotionally by an experimentally stimulating situation than average children.

Health histories were secured in Terman's and Witty's studies. The general conclusion from both researches is that gifted children are generally above the average in physical health and strength. The parents of the gifted are in the prime of life when the children are born, the fathers in the early thirties, the mothers in the late twenties, in agreement with Cattell's figures for the parents of 865 men of science. In the California group only 4.4 per cent of the children were born prematurely. The mother's health during pregnancy was rated as poor or very poor in but 7.8 per cent of the cases. The mean birth weight for both the California and Middle Western infants was approximately 12 ounces above the norm as given by Faber and Holt. Of the California gifted children, 57 per cent were breast-fed 8 months or longer as compared with 39 per cent reported by Woodbury in a norm group. In three successive health reports of Witty's gifted, superiority was maintained by upwards of 84 per cent; 90 per cent were reported to have good or excellent health during the first year. Sixty-eight per cent reached or exceeded a control group in health index in Witty's first study. Witty's children cut the first tooth at 6.8 months, Terman's at 7 months, in comparison with the norm range from 6 to 9 months. Terman's group talked at 11.3 months; the boys at 11.74 and the girls at 11.01. The average age for taking the first step was 13.05 months; for the boys, 13.10 and for the girls, 12.87. These results were compared by Terman et al. (1925) with Mead's norms: walking, 13.88; talking, 15.3 months. Talking appears in Witty's and Terman's gifted children to be slightly more precocious than the other activities reported from this early age. Comparison of the California elementary school gifted children with a control school group shows relatively fewer gifted children with defective hearing, mouth breathing, stuttering, headaches, or other symptoms of nervousness. The hours of sleep for the gifted are, age for age, more than those for the control group. Increasing from year 7 the difference amounts to about three-quarters of an hour at 12 and 13 years.

Pubescence was reached somewhat earlier by the gifted than by control children. Thus 100 per cent of Terman's 14-year-old boys were postpubescent as compared to 53 per cent of the control boys; and 48 per cent of 13-year-old girls had reached menarche in contrast to 25 per cent of control girls.

In the California study detailed medical examinations were given by two pediatricians to 783 gifted children. The careful individual appraisals by the physicians led to an expressed impression that major and minor defects are much less common among the gifted than among unselected children, and that "other things being equal there is a direct correlation between physical health and mentality in children when studied in groups." The home care, cleanliness, and health habits of the majority of the children indicated by their diet, hours of sleep, etc., were evidence of the superior intelligence of the parents. The conclusion was reached that, physically, the gifted child ranks above the average child of the community.

School Progress. Early attendance, relatively rapid grade advancement, and more than average interest in the more theoretical subjects characterize gifted children in school. Of the California gifted group in the early 1920's, 3 out of 5 attended kindergarten before entering the elementary grades at the average age of 6 years, 3 months. One out of 5 skipped half the first grade, and 1 out of 10 was immediately entered in the second grade on beginning school. Acceleration tended gradually to increase so that by the time the elementary school course was completed one entire grade had commonly been skipped. Of Terman's children 85 per cent skipped one or more half grades. After skipping, and so missing a segment of the curriculum content, the gifted children were, in the teacher's opinion, entitled to still further advancement, 8 out of 10 deserving additional promotion. Although 4 per cent had actually repeated a half grade, no elementary school child in the California group was retarded in terms of age-grade standards. In terms of mental age and of tested educational accomplishment, however, the group was far below the appropriate placement, a characteristic condition of gifted children in school. The mean progress quotient (grade age divided by chronological age) was 114 for the Cali-

fornia group, 116 for Witty's group. If the average gifted child were promoted in terms of mental age, he would be at least 2.8 years advanced at age 7, and at age 11 he would be entitled theoretically to placement in the tenth grade or higher by reason of his 5 or more years of acceleration. It is not, however, suggested that promotion in the regular school should be made in these terms, although the frequently serious misplacement of the gifted is clearly indicated by these figures.

The school work of the gifted is rated subjectively by their teachers as superior to that of their classmates in debating, history, composition, literature, grammar, general science, geography, civics, reading, and arithmetic. The contrast in the quality of the work is most conspicuous in subjects requiring verbal comprehension, usage, and formulation; least so in activity subjects little correlated with intelligence, such as physical training, sewing, drawing, clay modeling, penmanship, manual training, painting, and shopwork. In five elements of musical sensitivity measured by the Seashore tests, Hollingworth (1926a) found 49 gifted children (IQ 135+) undistinguished from a control group of the same age. In speed and quality of penmanship Hollingworth and Cobb (1928) found the performance of the gifted children very close to the norms for their age. Because of their more frequent superiority, the average excellence of the gifted in 29 subjects combined is one step higher on a 7-point scale than that of control children (Terman *et al.*, 1925). Witty's results are in agreement in showing excellence, whether qualitatively or quantitatively measured (Witty, 1940a).

The weaknesses of the gifted appear most often in subjects requiring manual coordination or dexterity; those of the control children, in work requiring abstract thought. For the gifted, 68 per cent of the weaknesses are in writing, art, and handwork, as against 16 per cent for the control. Conversely, 17 per cent of the gifted are reported weak in such subjects as arithmetic, English, and history, whereas 61 per cent of the control children are weak in these subjects (Terman *et al.*, 1925).

Gifted children's school subject preferences correlate with the teachers' estimates of the quality of their work in the different subjects to the extent of .41 (Terman *et al.*, 1925). Witty found the same trends of preference, especially toward the verbal subjects (Witty, 1930). The boys are more alike in their preferences than the girls, and the gifted girls resemble the gifted boys in their choices more than they do the control girls. Subjects rated as easy by the gifted more often than by the control are again the more abstract and verbal: literature, debating, history, and grammar; and the preference and ease ratings correlate to the extent of .59. The normality of the gifted is indicated by their resemblance to control children in giving a high preference rating to games and sports as a school subject (Terman *et al.*, 1925).

Gifted children are regular in school attendance, very infrequently dislike school, and in more than half the cases—54 per cent for the boys and 70 per cent for the girls—have a "very strong liking for school." In the grades they devote on the average two hours of homework per week to school lessons (Terman *et al.*, 1925).

School Achievement. Educational achievement quotients from the Stanford Achievement Tests of gifted groups indicate without exception performance notably above the average, yet these scores age for age are little correlated in gifted children with years of grade school attendance. Intelligence, not formal schooling, largely determines their level (Terman *et*

al., 1925). For the brightest children in regular public school classes they are generally relatively lower than for the moderately superior children (Cohler, 1941; Johnson, 1942). The highest quotients so far reported are those from two New York City groups: (1) two opportunity classes where half the regular school time was devoted to the prescribed grade school curriculum, the other half to an enrichment program; (2) a mixed group of individual pupils in regular classes where no special enrichment had been attempted (Gray and Hollingworth, 1931). The unusually high scores in both groups suggest that exceptional motivation had been elicited through some technique of test administration. Relative to their IQ's, the two groups are closely equated in achievement, thus demonstrating neither advantage nor disadvantage in regular school accomplishment from (1) segregation, (2) shortened time for prescribed subjects, or (3) enrichment in the addition of special subjects. However, the fact that the opportunity class children achieved thus well after spending only half as much time on the subjects should not be lost sight of. Terman's large groups reported in 1925, Witty's 1930 group, and Terman's 11-year-olds from the 1925 group reported in 1930 also show high standing in terms of achievement quotients. But children, especially girls, selected in California for their high IQ's in 1922 and tested in achievement as 11-year-olds 5 to 7 years later show considerable regression in score from the means of those whose achievement was measured near the time of their qualification for the gifted group. Other score series may be compared with these (see Table 4): Patrick's (1924) upper centile opportunity group, Cobb and Taylor's (1924) gifted opportunity groups, Hildreth's (1938*b*) three IQ levels from regular classes in the Lincoln School, and

TABLE 4
EDUCATIONAL ACHIEVEMENT QUOTIENTS OF GIFTED AND OTHER SCHOOL CHILDREN

Investigator	Terman et al. (Boys)	Terman et al. (Girls)	Witty	Gray and Hollingworth (P.S.)	Gray and Hollingworth (O.C.)	Burks, Jensen, and Terman (Boys)	Burks, Jensen, and Terman (Girls)	Burks, Jensen, and Terman (Boys)	Burks, Jensen, and Terman (Girls)	Hildreth	Hildreth	Hildreth	Cobb and Taylor	Cobb and Taylor	Patrick	Jenkins (Boys)	Jenkins (Girls)	Wood: Educ. Records Bureau	Wood: Educ. Records Bureau
Date	1925†	1925†	1930†	1931†	1931†	1930†	1930†	1930†	1930†	1938b*	1938b*	1938b*	1924*	1924*	1924*	1936†	1936†	1929*	1929*
Number of cases	307	259	100	36 P.S.	56 O.C.	68	52	24	29	36	51	50	29	16	25	29	64	72 to 183	55 to 81
Sex	Boys	Girls	Both	Both	Both	Boys	Girls	Boys	Girls	Both	Both	Both	Both	Both	Both	Boys	Girls	Both	Both
Age (years or years and mos.)	6 to 14	6 to 14	Gr. 3 to 7	11-1	11-6								9	10	11-3	6 to 14	6 to 14	11-9	9-10
IQ average	151	151	152	151	157	153	155	146	136	147	134	104	152	146	142	135	134	124‡	112‡
Composite EQ			136	150	153	153	148	136	139						133	130	126	121 (90)	118 (55)
Reading	145	145	143	152	152	149	145	143	129	140	139	113	151	145	143	136	135	134 (163)	118 (65)
Arithmetic	138	136	134	153	156	139	137	129	127	140	131	102	142	141	139	124	121	114 (183)	118 (81)
Spelling	140	138	131	149	154	139	140	129	120	129	119	102	150	153	124	126	129	113 (62)	116 (56)
Nature study			137	145	144			134	125						129			115 (72)	114 (34)
Hist. and lit.	146	148	132	152	156	141	147	134	125				147	144	139	133	134	127 (91)	118 (57)
Lang. usage	151	142				151	145	141	128						141			132 (117)	128 (80)
Sci. inform.	157	152				159	156	139	142							132	120		
Lang. and lit.	148	138				158	140												
Hist. and civ.	154	153				157	158												
The arts																			

* Medians reported.   † Means reported.   ‡ Approximate based on group tests.

Woods's (1929) private school children with superior group IQ scores.

The differences in the various series of data raise many questions. To the extent that they are in agreement they show marked superiority in the average scores for the gifted; persistent excellence as compared with superior, but not exclusively gifted, private school pupils. In general, differing IQ levels are seen to maintain their relative status in achievement test scores. Differences in teaching emphasis may be involved in the contrasts and perhaps, as mentioned above, test motivation also. These factors, together with regression, here produce diverse score patterns under varying conditions of age, grade, and school curriculum.

Hollingworth and Cobb (1928), comparing a series of achievement test scores of two gifted groups of 20 children each as they progressed in a special public school opportunity class during a two-year period, found a brighter group, clustering around 165 IQ, maintaining its superior status over a less bright group (145 IQ), although educational opportunity had been the same for both. Results showed the excess for the higher IQ group to be most marked in tests measuring the more complex abilities. The higher IQ group was more than a year in advance of the lower group in all the reading comprehension tests, in spelling, in nature study and science information, and in difficult mathematical processes including fractions and long division. Later Hildreth (1938b), comparing three IQ levels from grade to grade in the same private school classes, also found no tendency for IQ differences to become ineffective under conditions of similar class instruction plus special coaching for the lower IQ's.

Studies of achievement scores have been reviewed by Gray and Hollingworth (1931) and by Terman and Burks (1933). The reported researches are in agreement with hose cited here in showing (1) superior school achievement scores of the gifted as compared to their age norms, (2) relative inferiority in most groups of educational age scores as compared to mental age scores, (3) equivocal evidence with respect to the advantages and disadvantages, as measured in available test scores, of special opportunities and programs.

DeVoss (Terman, 1925) made a careful study of the specialization of ability in achievement test terms, which he illustrated with case studies. He concluded that the achievement profiles of the gifted are like those of average children in pattern, but they rate at a much higher level. The score disparities in the various school subjects are similar and the gifted are no more one-sided than average children. Typical good readers tend to be relatively deficient in arithmetical computation, good calculators excel in science information, but are somewhat less capable in the language functions. Good spellers are relatively more successful with exact scientific work, including arithmetic, and less successful in verbal interpretation. In both gifted and control profiles the range from the best to the poorest single performance level is relatively narrow. The unevenness of scores, in younger children especially, can hardly be accounted for by differences in training and is believed to show the influence of innate factors. When measured in terms of standard scores with the intelligence level at 100 per cent, the high achievement level of the gifted is only 62 per cent above the chronological age norm. Measured in terms of educational quotient, the corresponding percentage is 80. Abilities in the various school subjects correlate more closely with general intelligence ratings than with any special ability for which measures were available in the gifted study.

As a corollary to the study of the evenness of achievement, the evenness of mental ability was rated by the teachers for the gifted and a control group with results favorable to the gifted. The question, as stated to the teacher, "Is child's mental ability very even, ordinarily even, rather uneven or very uneven?" may be interpreted in terms of day-to-day stability of performance or in terms of capacity for various types of work.

Extracurricular Pursuits and Interests. Somewhat more than half Terman's gifted group study music, drawing, painting, dancing, language, etc., outside the regular school curriculum. An average of 6½ hours a week is devoted to these studies by those who pursue them. The parents report noting superior ability in special subjects and in general intelligence as indicated in Table 5. It is of interest that 8 per cent of the parents report that they have never observed indications of superior intelligence in their children; 6 per cent more give no response to this item. Those who report recognition of intellectual superiority state that it was first noted just before 3½ years of age in the girls and a little later in the boys. Musical ability is noted on the average at 5 and the other special abilities at 6. The parents enumerate quick understanding, great curiosity, retentive memory, early speech, unusual vocabulary, and extensive information as the most frequent early indicators of superior intelligence.

Approximately 70 per cent of the parents state that they allowed the child to go his own pace in school, 19 per cent encouraged rapid progress, and 9 per cent held the child back. Most of the parents attempted to encourage progress by answering questions and by taking interest in the child's interests; few parents carried out systematic plans of home training.

Approximately half the California gifted children learned to read before starting to school. In Witty's group 38 per cent

TABLE 5

Percentages of Gifted Children Reported by Their Parents as Showing Various Kinds of Superior Ability *

	General Intelligence	Music	Arith. or Math.	Science or Nat. Study	Dramatics	Drawing or Painting	Dexterity, Handwork	Mechanical Ingenuity
Boys	84%	31%	52%	29%	18%	27%	21%	31%
Girls	85%	42%	45%	29%	42%	31%	31%	7%

* From Table 103, p. 278, L. M. Terman *et al.*, *Genetic Studies of Genius*, Vol. I. *Mental and Physical Traits of a Thousand Gifted Children*, Stanford University Press, 1925. By permission of the publishers.

learned to read before the age of 5; and of Terman's children 20 per cent learned at this age, 6 per cent before 4, and nearly 2 per cent before 3. This precocious activity among gifted children is stated to have occurred generally with little or no formal instruction. Learning to read at an unusually early age appears to be a correlate of high IQ in childhood.

Reading is the favorite pastime of the gifted children as well as their best-liked and easiest school subject. Teachers report that 9 out of 10 in a group of 400 read more than the average, and that nearly 60 per cent read very much, in contrast with about 12 per cent of a control group who do so. Parents estimate that their gifted children devote each week 6 hours at age 7 up to 12 hours at age 13 to their favorite pursuit.

A record of two months' reading shows that the gifted read more than twice as many books as control children of the same age. From the age of 9 the gifted exceed the average children of all ages up to 14 in number of books read (Terman *et al.*, 1925). That superiority in this respect is not necessarily a favorable sign of later achievement is shown by the comparison of the reading records of Terman's adult success and failure groups. The members of the failure group had reported in childhood a greater number of books read than had the success group (Terman and Oden, 1940b). Excess in this respect may admit of two interpretations beside the appar-

ently favorable one: overstatement may be characteristic of some gifted children, and social withdrawal or flight from reality may be present in some children who read excessively.

Gifted, like control, children prefer, if they are boys, first of all stories of adventure or mystery; if girls, stories of home and school life; but gifted children name also many more works of genuine literary excellence, including two to ten times as many books of poetry and drama, science, history, biography and travel, and definitely less popular, emotional fiction. Another investigation concurs with these results of Terman's in reporting superior quality in a larger proportion (49 per cent) of high IQ than of control (9 per cent) children (Cleveland, 1921). The Californians' best-liked book was a favorite for both gifted and control children; but boys and girls had only 5 of 20 favorites in common.

Gifted children express slightly stronger interest than do unselected children in the various activities that occupy their out-of-school hours. Sex differences rather than intellectual differences largely determine the trend of activity choices, yet a real contrast is shown between the gifted and unselected children in the number of collections made at all ages from 6 to 13. The gifted make about twice as many collections as the control, and the number of these having scientific interest and value is twice as large (Terman *et al.*, 1925).

The vocational ambitions of the gifted as compared to those of control children rate one and a half to two and a half points higher on the Barr Scale, a significant difference for the group as a whole. In the gifted group the preferred occupation rates nearer to the occupational status of the fathers than in the control group. The ambitions of the unselected tend, in terms of their abilities, to be more wishful than realistic, whereas the gifted may in most cases fortunately combine these two trends. Among the gifted, a small fraction chooses in childhood, and subsequently enters, occupations generally followed by people of average intellect and opportunity. Culture and custom limit the choices and the careers of the girls, as in some cases temperament or the lack of social or educational advantages does those of the boys (Terman et al., 1925).

Results from Wyman's (Terman et al., 1925) association test of (1) intellectual, (2) social, and (3) activity interests show characteristic contrasts between gifted and control groups in these interests, at each of four ages from 10 to 13. The largest differences are in the intellectual interests, but the social interest contrasts are also significant statistically. The differences in the activity interests are significant only at ages 10 and 11 for the boys and at 10 for the girls. Measurement by correlation of the relative effect of intelligence and intellectual interests upon school achievement shows that when the factor of intellectual interests is rendered constant intelligence and achievement correlate .76; with intelligence constant, intellectual interests and achievement correlate .49. Intellectual interest, although not so potent as intelligence, is thus found to be a possibly significant factor in school accomplishment. It is significant for all the school subjects except spelling and is greatest in the case of arithmetical reasoning. By a similar method, social interest and activity interest prove to be uncorrelated with school achievement scores.

Play Activities. The play interests, knowledge, and practice of 554 gifted children have been compared with those of 474 control children from the same elementary school grades (Terman et al., 1925). In play knowledge the quotient of the gifted is found to be 136; that is, a 10-year-old intellectually superior child has as much play information as an average 13-year-old child. The boys of both groups somewhat exceed the girls in play information. The gifted express as much liking for games and fondness for playing with others as average boys and girls. The gifted are inclined to prefer playmates who are older than themselves and they show less sex preference in the choice of playmates than do average children of the same age. The average amount of play with other children, 2¾ hours a day for the boys and 2¼ hours a day for the girls, is somewhat less than the time so spent by the average child. Yet the normality of the gifted is indicated by their devotion of more time to play than to reading and study combined (Terman et al., 1925; Coy, 1930). The play interests of gifted and average children are generally similar rather than contrasting. The slight differences appear to be associated with the somewhat greater mental maturity of the gifted. They tend to prefer games played typically by older children, and interest in the childish games wanes with them at an earlier age than in the average. These results derive from ratings on a play maturity scale (Terman et al., 1925).

Lehman and Witty (1927) report 50 gifted and 50 matched control children interested in the same diversity of plays and games. The gifted girls engage in a somewhat larger number of play activities than the average girls; the gifted boys in a slightly smaller number of play activities. The averages of the sexes combined prove to be identical. The gifted less frequently take part in certain kinds of vigorous physical play exercises and more often in games and pursuits in which reading is an element. Aside from reading itself, the best-liked activities are similar for the gifted and the control groups. The like sex intercorrelations of the preference ratings for 90 plays, games, and amusements, based on the children's own expression of attitude and participation, are above .80. This demonstrates that the games enjoyed most and played oftenest by gifted and average children are generally the same active social games, although gifted children prefer thinking games and those that are mildly social and quiet. Boys, whether gifted or average, prefer boys' games, and similarly girls, whatever their mental endowment, generally prefer typical girls' activities.

Personal and Social Character Traits. The traits of gifted children have been appraised by means of various tests and by ratings on elements of behavior defined for the purpose. The results, although lacking the statistical reliability and objectivity of the intellectual and educational measurements, seem to indicate through cumulative agreement that gifted children as a group tend to differ characteristically and favorably from unselected children. A wide range of tests and ratings has been reported by Terman and his associates (1925) for more than 500 gifted children and an equally large unselected control group. Witty's (1930) results for 100 gifted children are corroborative. In a number of other studies top centile or other superior children have been reported whose traits tend to resemble the strictly gifted groups.

When compared with control children in scores on tests of personal and social standards and ideals (Raubenheimer-Cady Series), the gifted children show far more favorable social preferences and social attitudes, more desirable preferences, less boastful exaggeration, less cheating, and considerably greater trustworthiness under stress. Sixty to 80 per cent of the gifted exceed the median scores on the separate tests of the battery (Terman, 1925).

On a total score, combining results for the entire series of tests, the average excess for the gifted children was 85 per cent, and the typical gifted nine-year-olds equaled or exceeded control children through age 14. Although both groups showed wide individual differences with interesting age-sex trends, the characteristic contrasts were maintained between gifted and control children. Witty's 100 gifted children were also superior on three of the same tests.

Freedom from psychopathic trends, as measured by Cady's version for children of the Woodworth Personality Inventory, showed a further superiority of the gifted children, with 67 per cent of the boys and 75 per cent of the girls equaling or exceeding the control median. Emotional stability measured by this test rates for the gifted more than 0.5 SD above the control children's average, a position maintained or slightly increased after four or five years, as demonstrated by retest (Burks, Jensen, and Terman, 1930). The individual consistency in earlier and later test scores (.42) is sufficient to indicate at least some degree of predictability of the characteristics thus measured.

The developmental-maturity quotients of some 50 top centile opportunity class pupils aged 9 to 12 were found by R. L. Thorndike (1940b) to indicate an acceleration approximately equal to that of their school progress. On the Furfey Developmental Scale the boys rated an average quotient of 114; on its adaptation by Sullivan the girls' quotient was 118. Wide item variation was characteristic, with high maturity shown in the choice of books to read, things to think about, and future vocations. Interest and attitude scores on the Pressey Test were reported for a similar group (R. L. Thorndike, 1939). The total test scores of interests and attitudes corresponded more closely to the mental than to the chronological ages of these children. The boys rated as definitely more mature than the girls. Both sexes scored highest in the traits which they admire in others and in their freedom from fears and worries. Judgments of wrong and interests rated as less mature, although above average for both sexes. Individuals showed wide variability in item and subtest scores.

Character trait ratings made by teachers and parents on more than 1000 gifted and control children indicate that the gifted as a group appear normal or better in the estimation of the adults most closely associated with them (Terman et al., 1925). Compared to a control group, their ratings are equal or higher on 25 traits including intellectual, volitional, emotional, moral, physical, social, and special ability traits. Parents and teachers are agreed ($r = +.70$) in ranking the order of superiority from marked excess in the case of the intellectual and volitional traits (difference more than 1 SD) to approximate equality in the physical and social traits. The ratings are found to be discriminative, and the "certainty of judgment" is fairly high. Single traits showing the largest excess for the gifted include common sense, originality, desire to know and to excel, self-confidence, sense of humor, truthfulness, prudence and forethought, conscientiousness, and leadership. In each of these traits 70 per cent or more of the gifted exceed the rated mean of the control children. In fondness for large groups, in freedom from vanity, and in cheerfulness the gifted differ least from average boys and girls. Although distinguished for leadership, in popularity they are close to the general mean. In ratings made five years later, the gifted still showed excess in the same traits when compared to a control group (Table 6), although the contrast was now not quite so sharply drawn. The rank orders of the trait differences were similar. Parents were inclined to see improvement with respect to conscientiousness and freedom from vanity, whereas teachers reported little change in these respects (Burks, Jensen, and Terman, 1930).

Teachers of New York City gifted children reported their pupils average or superior in a series of desirable traits (Specht, 1919). Reports by 31 teachers of superior children in St. Paul, Minnesota, are in agreement in finding the gifted children above the average in many traits, including courtesy, cooperation, imaginativeness, inquisitiveness, and willingness to take suggestions. These children have a keen sense of humor and are not inclined to become discouraged. Contrary to an older popular opinion, they are not considered especially forward, domineering, egotistical, or self-willed (Johnson, 1923; Laycock, 1933). Hildreth (1939) found 50 upper centile children, including 20 with IQ's in the 140's or higher, superior in personality traits to matched children of average IQ in the same school. Recorded notations for intellectual, personality, and character traits included nearly five times as many favorable entries for the superior as for the control children, whereas the latter showed excess in the unfavorable traits. The superior children excelled in activity and vivacity, independence, and self-assurance, they had more experiences to relate, their sense of humor was more often noted, as was also their willingness to face difficulties.

Simmons (1939) studied the suggestibility of 47 top centile, special opportunity class

TABLE 6

PERSONALITY TRAIT RATINGS OF GIFTED AND CONTROL CHILDREN
(MEANS AND SD's) *

Trait Names		Teachers' Ratings						Parents' Ratings			
		1927–28 Gifted		1921–22 Gifted		1921–22 Control		1927–28 Gifted		1921–22 Gifted	
		Boys	Girls	Boys	Girls	Boys	Girls	Boys	Girls	Boys	Girls
Traits in which gifted children differ little from control children											
Fondness for groups	M	6.4	5.9	6.2	5.6	6.1	5.9	6.2	5.0	5.5	4.7
	SD	2.2	2.1	2.1	2.2	2.1	2.0	2.7	1.8	2.6	2.2
Freedom from vanity	M	5.9	5.7	5.9	5.4	6.1	5.6	5.1	5.1	5.7	5.9
	SD	2.6	2.5	2.7	2.3	1.9	2.0	2.4	2.4	2.2	2.3
Sympathy	M	5.9	5.6	5.8	5.2	6.3	5.7	4.9	4.3	3.9	3.7
	SD	2.2	2.1	2.1	2.1	1.8	1.8	2.4	2.2	2.3	2.2
Popularity	M	6.5	6.4	6.4	5.7	6.5	6.2	5.6	5.2	5.5	5.2
	SD	2.1	2.2	2.0	2.0	1.8	1.9	2.1	1.5	2.0	2.1
Traits in which gifted children differ significantly from control children											
Leadership	M	6.6	6.3	6.3	5.8	7.2	7.0	5.2	5.0	5.3	4.9
	SD	2.0	2.2	1.9	2.0	2.1	2.2	2.0	2.0	2.2	2.1
Desire to excel	M	5.0	4.2	4.2	3.6	6.1	5.6	4.5	3.6	3.7	3.3
	SD	2.5	2.4	2.2	1.9	2.4	2.0	2.1	1.9	1.9	1.9
Conscientiousness	M	5.0	4.5	4.8	4.0	6.2	5.4	4.2	3.7	4.4	4.3
	SD	2.6	2.4	2.5	2.2	2.3	2.2	2.4	2.2	2.1	2.2
Common sense	M	4.9	4.9	4.2	4.1	6.2	5.9	4.3	4.0	4.4	4.3
	SD	2.0	2.0	1.9	1.9	1.8	1.8	2.1	1.9	2.0	1.9
Perseverance	M	5.1	4.4	4.4	4.1	6.4	6.1	5.2	4.2	4.9	4.1
	SD	2.4	2.3	2.1	1.9	2.2	2.0	2.0	2.2	2.3	2.0
Traits in which gifted children differ largely and significantly from control children											
Desire to know	M	4.6	4.4	3.5	3.9	6.3	6.2	3.5	3.4	2.7	2.8
	SD	2.3	2.4	1.9	2.1	2.0	2.1	2.2	2.0	1.9	1.8
Originality	M	5.0	4.9	4.4	4.5	6.8	6.9	4.1	4.0	4.0	3.9
	SD	2.2	2.2	2.1	2.1	1.9	1.9	2.2	2.1	2.2	2.1
General intelligence	M	4.0	3.8	3.1	3.1	6.4	6.2	3.3	3.3	3.1	3.1
	SD	1.9	1.7	1.6	1.8	1.9	1.8	1.3	1.4	1.6	1.6

* Data rearranged from B. S. Burks, D. W. Jensen, L. M. Terman, *Genetic Studies of Genius,* Vol. III, *The Promise of Youth* (Table 77, p. 190), Stanford University Press, Stanford University, California, 1930. By permission of the publishers.

children, aged 8 to 11, matched for age and sex, with a below-average group. In each of the experimental test situations employed, the group of higher intelligence yielded to fewer suggestions than the lower intelligence group, the differences being statistically reliable. Subjective ratings on independence from others in thinking also showed a reliable difference in favor of the gifted.

Classroom attitudes of high IQ children are found satisfactory and in general superior to the average. The children take active part in class discussions (Johnson, 1923), they respect authority (Woods, 1929), and are responsive to school discipline (Terman, 1925; Witty, 1930). In Root's (1921) study, conformity and traditional orthodox behavior were reported as characteristic of superior as of average children. The favorable conditioning of behavior by home influences is suggested in the conclusions of McGehee and Lewis (1940) from a study of teachers' estimates of the attitudes of their parents toward 45,000 children in 36 different states. Superiority of the parents' attitude was highly correlated with the intelligence of the children. The gifted boys and girls had the advantage of parental attitudes rated as superior in 66 and 61 per cent of the cases as compared with the attitudes toward the normative groups in which 20 and 23 per cent were so rated.

Summary of the Traits of the Gifted. Studies of young gifted children, beginning with Terman's report in 1919 and including the work of Root, Jones, Goddard, and Whipple, are in agreement with the larger, more recent, more strictly defined (IQ 140+), statistically more fully treated results of Terman, Hollingworth, Witty, and their associates, Hildreth, and other contemporary investigators. The various aspects of the background, development, interests, and achievements of gifted chil-

dren are found to be clearly marked by superiority, characteristically greater the more the trait in question is correlated with intellect. Gifted children are superior specimens physically as well as psychologically, and they tend to express a superior energy in their activities. They come from better homes and in many cases have had better educational backgrounds and opportunities. Yet, as we shall see in the consideration of individual cases, superior environments and educational advantages do not insure the production of crops of gifted children, and in capacity and accomplishment individual gifted children generally appear as unique and isolated individuals even against their superior backgrounds. We must, therefore, believe that inheritance of gifted traits is individual and complex and that training can only develop, never create, gifted capacity.

That there is no one-to-one correlation between intelligence and character traits is no surprise in view of the vast complexity of human personality. However, cumulative evidence seems clearly to demonstrate the better endowment of the gifted and their better training and development in social terms, as compared with average children. Techniques for precise measurement of causal relationships in this realm are not available to present-day research.

Progress of the Gifted from Childhood to Maturity

The relatively large populations of gifted children who have been intensively studied by psychologists no doubt include many all-round, highly superior individuals of whom it is reasonable to expect persistent growth at a level demonstrably above average and sustained continuity with respect to behavior and achievement. Because tests are fallible and the range of tested traits is narrow, some individuals who would rate below more broadly defined gifted standards are by current practice necessarily included in the groups selected for study. Moreover, test errors and changes in developmental rate, whether constitutionally or environmentally conditioned, lead to score and rating regressions. However, the subsequent histories of children selected as gifted in childhood indicate that the errors and changes are not sufficient to invalidate the selection technique as a basis for group prediction, and the accumulated results point to the ultimate possibility of individual clinical predictions of fair reliability.

Gifted children were first reported at the elementary school level, where their presence was revealed in the earliest individual test surveys and where the problems of their education appeared most urgent. Studies of older gifted children have included (1) follow-up surveys, after a period of years, of groups investigated in childhood and (2) surveys of various young groups not previously studied, adolescents, and college students, usually selected in terms of group test scores, or of youth in relation to academic status. Duff (1929) and Witty (1940a) have reported the progress of gifted school children in the grades. Terman and Hollingworth and their associates have contributed the majority of studies of gifted adolescents and college students, and the only studies so far reported of gifted young adults. The data from all these researches are in agreement in indicating relative persistence in the characteristic trait patterns of the gifted as they grow older and continued contrast between them and average children in intellectual achievements and superiority of interests. A summary of illustrative results is presented.

In a preliminary follow-up of more than 1000 gifted children made two years after his first study, Terman et al. (1925) found that the typical educational acceleration was continued and the indications of superior ability appeared consistently in the school and home reports. Gains far outweighed losses in deportment, in group activities, in breadth of interests, and in the social adaptability of the group as a whole Children who had skipped grades were reported to have gained in application and to be more often eligible for further rapid advancement.

In a more detailed follow-up carried out seven years after the first study, data for 900 children were gathered and analyzed (Burks, Jensen, and Terman, 1930). As far as possible the traits and characteristics measured in the first study were again evaluated. Intelligence was rechecked by two individual and two group tests in four population samples. The Stanford-Binet IQ results for children within the appropriate age range disclosed for the boys a small average decrease of 3 points, from 147 to 143; for the girls a sizable loss of 14 points, 149 to 135. The changes were apparently not correlated with age. In the groups of age 13 and under 20 who were given the Terman group test, the boys were significantly superior to the girls in score. The median Terman group test IQ for the retested children was judged equivalent to a Stanford-Binet IQ above 130, thus indicating maintenance of top centile status by 50 per cent of the group The ninetieth centile was exceeded by 73 per cent. The retest Terman group scores were very little lower than those taken age by age in the high school group tested seven years before. Analysis of factors of environment, personality, health, race, and Stanford-Binet test structure failed to reveal causes of the score decrement. The slight drop in scores for the boys was attributed, in the absence of any other explanation, to a difference in the tests used or to simple regression; for the girls the larger decrement was attributed to these factors or to a change in developmental rate and age of intellectual maturation. A sex difference in social motivation might also have been involved. Roughly paralleling the IQ scores, the Stanford Achievement Test quotients proved to be a little lower than they were in the first survey. For the boys the drop amounted to 6 points, for the girls, 10 points. Here again test standardization and regression factors were probably involved. Yet the scores were still far in excess of those of average children of like age.

Elementary School. The acceleration of the group in school grade status had continued and the projected Ayres-Strayer standards of educational progress showed no case of retardation. In comparison to the earlier acceleration of 67 per cent of the group, a slight gain had resulted in acceleration for 74 per cent of the boys and 84 per cent of the girls. Grade status continued typically above the chronological norm but far below the mental age status. School attendance continued to be regular, although liking for school had become slightly less strong. Attitude toward school was rated by the teachers as favorable for more than 80 per cent of the children. The amount of time devoted to homework had increased steadily with age. The gifted boys graduated from the eighth grade at the early age of 13 years, 1 month; the girls at 12 years, 10 months (Burks, Jensen, and Terman, 1930).

High School. Lamson (1930) studied the high school careers of 56 gifted children who had been identified as of top centile IQ status before the age of 9 years and placed on the basis of their high intelligence in special opportunity classes. They had entered high school from the special classes on the average before the age of 12 and they were about to graduate at age 16. Compared with a control group of 106 students in the same high school grades, the gifted were significantly superior in scholastic achievement and had a smaller percentage of failures, although in age they were two years younger. The gifted had participated in extracurricular activities to an extent exceeding the control group by 25 per cent. Lack of time and participation in other activities, including the reading of modern current fiction, study of music, and social dancing, prevented greater participation. The gifted impressed their teachers by their intelligence, the general quality of their work, and their sustained effort to an extent significantly in excess of the impression made by the control children. In self-control, general deportment, and appearance, they were rated as somewhat superior to the average pupils; in popularity and in conceit there was little difference between the two groups. In the teachers' estimations general deportment and quality of work improved for the gifted during a 2½-year period. Generally good health was reported for the high school years, and 6 out of 10 of the gifted expressed no regret at having entered high school at an exceptionally early age. Age 13 they considered the most favorable for high school entrance. Four out of five were glad to have had the advantages of the opportunity classes. Reasons for failures, activities participated in, offices held, honors, books read, and attitudes toward scholastic work were reported in detail.

Terman's gifted children (Burks, Jensen, and Terman, 1930) had consistently superior high school reports; a sample of 77 cases won "A" grades in their separate studies about four to eight times as frequently as the unselected high school pupils in the same classes. In every course, including science and mathematics, the gifted girls were given higher average marks than the boys. For the girls the "A" grades amounted to approximately three-quarters of their school work; for the boys, to something approaching half. In the estimation of the teachers about one-third of the group showed remarkable ability in some special subject or subjects, whereas only 15 per cent were rated as weak. Excellence and weakness generally appeared in the same subjects as before. Parents reported specialized ability in something over 60 per cent of all the cases, including for the boys mathematics, science, debating, public speaking, or mechanical ingenuity; for the girls, art, dramatics, dancing, writing, household art, and music.

Tests of high school achievement showed marked superiority of upwards of 150 gifted children reported above the high school norms (Burks, Jensen, and Terman, 1930). In comprehension of literature (Burch Test) the two-years-younger gifted group rated more than 1 SD above the control mean; in algebra problems (Hotz Test) the average difference is .5 SD. In the Iowa Content Examination, including tests of achievement in English, mathematics, science, and history, the girls exceeded the norm by 1 to 1.5 SD; the boys by 1.5 to 2 SD. The high school senior norms for the separate parts of this test were exceeded by 10 per cent or more of the gifted group. In total score 97 per cent of the gifted boys and 100 per cent of the gifted girls exceeded the control mean.

Characteristic sex differences in preference for school subjects were shown by the gifted group, 241 boys tending to prefer the sciences and to show distaste for ancient languages, 196 girls liking art, English, and modern languages and disliking mathematics and civics (Burks, Jensen, and Terman, 1930). The amount of time spent on general reading outside school studies was slightly greater for the girls, with an average of 7.6 hours per week for them in contrast to 7.2 hours for the boys. After 14 the boys spent more time on home study than on general reading whereas before this age the opposite was true. For the girls this change occurred at 13. Sex and age differences in reading interests continued, and reading was still preferred to all other occupations by both gifted boys and gifted girls. Active games were preferred to those that required little exercise, and games and exercise were next in preference to reading. About a third of the boys and nearly half the girls stated that they had been greatly influenced by a single "person, book, philosophy, or religion." The strongest influence was most often that of one or both parents. Interest in collecting tended to decline after 14, the boys having continued to make on the average more collections, including a larger number with scientific interest.

Acceleration was characteristic, as before. The boys graduated from high school at 16 years, 10 months; the girls two months younger. In high school and also in college the group as a whole was generally about two years younger than the age norm of their class. More than 80 per cent of the gifted group in high school expressed the intention of going on to college.

Characteristics and Aptitudes of Gifted High School and College Students. Social and personality traits (Raubenheimer-Cady series), when remeasured after a lapse of 4 or 5 years, showed little change in mean scores in similar age ranges (Burks, Jensen and Terman, 1930). The correlation coefficient was .42 for 150 gifted children twice tested. The Wyman test of intellectual, social, and activity interests showed very small changes in average scores for the children retested 5 years after the original study. However, the correlations between the tests of individuals were not very high, ranging from .15 in activities to .37 in social interests and showing only mild degree of permanence in interest type as measured by this test.

Personality ratings on 12 traits selected from the 25 used in the earlier investigation in general supported the previous findings in indicating marked divergence of the gifted group from unselected children in intellectual traits, moderate divergence in volitional and moral traits, and similarity tending toward equality in social traits (Table 6). Teachers and parents agreed fairly closely in the rank order of ratings and their estimates showed little change from those made 7 years before. Field visitors' appraisals placed the gifted at or above the hypothetical norms as follows: in achievement, boys 98 per cent, girls 99 per cent; in social adjustment, boys 81 per cent, girls 80 per cent; in environmental conditions, boys 95 per cent, girls 91 per cent (Burks, Jensen, and Terman, 1930).

The good looks of gifted children of high school age may contribute to their favorable social adjustment. Hollingworth (1935) reported that 10 judges rating from photographs agreed in finding the faces of 40 gifted children more attractive than those of a control group.

Tests given for the first time in the California study in 1927–1928 were the Watson Test of Fair-Mindedness, the Terman-Miles Masculinity-Femininity Test, and the George Washington University Social Intelligence Test. For each of these, results have been reported in detail for groups ranging in size from 75 to 175 individuals (Burks, Jensen, and Terman, 1930). In fair-mindedness the gifted differ little from other, generally older, groups of similar education. In mental masculinity adolescent gifted boys and girls resemble college men and women more than they do the youth of their own age. The boys differ from college men in more masculine ratings in the two sections of the Terman-Miles test where intelligence is associated with high masculinity of score; in items where culture, domestic sentiment, and literary taste have a feminizing influence on response, the ratings are less masculine than those of the college students. The gifted girls' profile resembles that of college women in showing a masculine score trend where this is generally correlated with high intelligence. In parts of the test where intelligence and intellectual interests exert little influence (Terman and Miles, 1936) gifted girls respond and score like average groups of their sex. On the Social Intelligence Test the median scores for the gifted are high above the age norms and even exceed the college norms. The high correlation known to exist between the scores on this test and intelligence test scores may largely account for these excessive ratings.

The Bernreuter personality profiles of 36 boys and 19 girls, mainly Jewish, of average age 18 years, 6 months, reported by Hollingworth and Rust (1937) are in general agreement with Terman's personality appraisals of the gifted in showing excess for both sexes in the traits of self-sufficiency and dominance and a lower neurotic tendency as compared to college students and adult norm groups. The differences tend to be significant for the boys, although for the girls they are so only in self-sufficiency.

Of 169 boys past 14 who took the Strong Occupational Interest Test (Burks, Jensen, and Terman, 1930) 23 per cent received "A" ratings in their chosen vocation (indicating interests like those of men in the three highest scoring quartiles in the vocation in question), 50 per cent received "B" ratings (resembling the interests of the men in the given vocation who rate within the lower quartile), and 27 per cent received "C" ratings (resembling the lowest 2 per cent of the men in the occupation in question). These results compare favorably with the scores for Stanford University seniors, who rate 32 per cent "A," 50 per cent "B," and 18 per cent "C" in their chosen vocations. Chance ratings give only 5 or 6 per cent "A," 25 per cent "B," and 70 per cent "C." The gifted boys, although considerably younger than the Stanford seniors, have, as revealed by this test, already developed almost to an equal extent the interests characteristic of their probable future vocations. Although this is in part due to the fact that young boys of potential college ability resemble one another in showing the characteristic likes and dislikes of chemists and engineers, yet the presence of fair-sized groups of "A" raters in other "most likely" occupations indicates that there are here probably true occupational interests exhibited by gifted boys at a fairly early age.

Scientific aptitude scores of 41 gifted boys measured by the Zyve Test equal as a group the mean for nonscientific faculty members, rating above the mean for unselected freshmen and very close to halfway between the latter and the high average of graduate students in scientific departments (Burks, Jensen, and Terman, 1930).

That the gifted are by no means characterized by studious reclusiveness is shown in their social and leadership ratings and in their community activities. Both boys and girls report social interests, enjoyment in leadership and in managing other people (Burks, Jensen, and Terman, 1930). Eighty-seven per cent of the boys and 96 per cent of the girls report having held one or more offices or honors in a wide variety of extracurricular activities. It proves to be as likely for them to have won notice in any one of several kinds of extracurricular activities as in scholarship. The girls more often participate in dramatics, the boys in student organization and scout troop activities. Yates's (1922) group numbered more than twice as many gifted (28 per cent) as control (12 per cent) leaders in high school activities. Finch and Carroll's

(1932) gifted high school seniors had held twice as many elective offices as the average high school pupil.

Studies of school and college leaders and leadership support these results by indicating the extent to which intelligence is a factor in social recognition and administrative distinction. High school honor students have been found to be younger, to rate higher in intelligence, and to graduate in less time than the average, although they carry more extracurricular activities (Zeigel, 1927).

In the reported studies there is no conflicting opinion regarding the value of superior intellect for leadership. Emphasis is sometimes laid on the need for due recognition of other desirable traits (Witty, 1930), but these, too, especially wisdom (prudence and forethought), motivation (will and perseverance), truthfulness, cheerfulness, stability of mood, generosity and unselfishness, conscientiousness, and sympathy, are more often found in conjunction with superior intellect than otherwise (Terman *et al.*, 1925).

Good health has persisted in 77 to 90 per cent of the gifted during the six-year period since the first survey. No more than 1 to 5 per cent report "poor health." Colds, headaches, and worry are relatively infrequent, and no more prevalent in the older gifted children than in the control group measured in 1921 and 1922. As compared with themselves in early childhood, fewer gifted boys but somewhat more gifted girls are reported to show signs of nervousness in the adolescent period. Organic disease is infrequent, occurring in only 4 per cent of the boys and 5 per cent of the girls. Serious eye trouble is present in less than 2 per cent of the gifted, and subnormal hearing shows decrease with age to less than 2 per cent of the group. The gifted children sleep less than they did at a younger age, but they continue to sleep more at each age than unselected children; their parents report that 98 per cent of the boys and 95 per cent of the girls sleep soundly. Five deaths, or less than 1 per cent, occurred in the 643 members of the regular group in the seven-year period between the first study and the second (Burks, Jensen, and Terman, 1930).

The Gifted Children in College and After. In their college years the gifted children as a group have maintained their status intellectually, academically, and in social adjustments. Their later occupational and economic careers have also developed on the whole favorably. Six reports give psychological test scores of gifted groups in college. The academic and social adjustments are presented in two confirmatory studies. The college progress of Terman's gifted children was briefly reported in 1930 and again in 1940 for the larger population who had progressed so far (Terman and Oden, 1940a). Gray (1930) studied the scholastic aptitude ratings, scholastic records, physical measurements, and the extracurricular and social activities of 126 boys and 28 girls who entered Columbia and Barnard colleges at 15 years of age or younger. Although these youngsters had not been identified by high IQ's in childhood, we may tentatively group them with the gifted because their Thorndike Scholastic Aptitude Test scores average as high at college entrance as the means reported by Terman for gifted children in California (Burks, Jensen, and Terman, 1930). Special investigations of the intelligence scores at college entrance or later of groups of gifted children have been supplied by Hollingworth and Kaunitz (1934), Lorge and Hollingworth (1936), and Hildreth (1939).

The data from the follow-up reports concerning late adolescent or young adult mental status are in agreement regarding the extent to which the gifted maintain after 6 to 16 years from their first selection their early demonstrated capacity to reach the highest levels of tested intelligence. Eighty-two per cent of Army Alpha scores of 116 top centile children rated 10 years after first identification by Stanford-Binet test reached the adult top centile norm. Of the remainder all were in high centiles, none regressed to the mean. Gifted boys 18 years of age or older all scored above the ninety-seventh centile. Fifty-seven cases with IQ's 150 or above rated without exception in the top centile. About one-third of the 140's scored somewhat lower (Hollingworth and Kaunitz, 1934). In their CAVD scores, cooperative general culture and general science tests, and Army Alpha scores, and in academic accomplishment, 21 individuals identified as gifted in childhood attained as a group the high standing predictable from their early Stanford-Binet and school achievement test scores (Lorge and Hollingworth, 1936). Data for a selection of these appear in Table 7. The scores reported for the science and culture tests fall for the most part within the upper quartile on the college norms. In the CAVD test 18 out of the entire group of 21 score above the seventy-fifth centile for law school freshmen and A.M. candidates in Teachers College, Columbia University.

Hildreth (1939) reports the American Council Psychological Test scores in senior high school of 70 children identified as to Stanford-Binet IQ before the age of 13. On this test, in which children of average eleventh and twelfth grade ability rate near the fiftieth centile, the mean rating for 12 gifted children with early IQ's of 140+ reaches the 97.5 centile for college students the country over. This result is in agreement with a statement by Wrenn (1935), based on results for 39 of Terman's gifted children, that the gifted of 140 IQ status rate at college entrance at the ninety-

TABLE 7

Test Scores of Highly Intelligent Children in Childhood and in Early Maturity *

Child	IQ First Stanford Binet †	Stanford Achievement Tests								Form 8 Army Alpha ‡	CAVD	General Science Centile	General Culture Centile	Age	Educational Status: College Degrees, Advanced Study, Major Subject, and Scholastic Honors
		Reading Par. Mng. EQ	Arithmetic Computation EQ	Arithmetic Reasoning EQ	Nature Study and Science EQ	History and Literature EQ	Language Usage EQ	Spelling Dictation EQ	Composite EQ						
1	190+	163+	168	180	170	164	159	182	171	210	454	93	100	21-0	B.A. + 1 yr. med. sch.; Phi Beta Kappa; major, premedical.
2	188+	183	165	197	173	179	175	203	184+	198	439	93	98	19-6	H.S. gr. + part of a semester in college.
E	187+										445	84	100	26-4	B.A., M.A., Ph.D., major hist.; ordained clergyman; Phi Beta Kappa.
3	187+	158	152	185	162	172	151	163	168	204	435	93	93	20-9	B.A., in 1st yr. grad. wk., major, statistics and economics.
D	183+										444	98	98	24-6	B.A. + 3 yrs. grad. wk. in physics; Phi Beta Kappa; research physicist.
E.B.	175										438	80	98	21-1	B.A. + 1st yr. grad. wk.; major, social science.
7	174	155+	161	149	152	146	146	166	154	192 §	435	98	98	21-6	B.A., major English.
8	173 or 177	180	171	161	167	177	182	171	175	181 §	435	75	98	20-5	B.A.
9	172	149	173	183	158	190	132	177	193	188	429	98	84	20-2	B.A., M.A.; chem. and premed. + 1 yr. medical school.
14	168	162	171	163	176	176	173	187	171	191	425	98	84	19-7	B.A., major premed.; + nearly 2 yrs. med. sch.; Phi Beta Kappa.
15	168	162	155	158	138	152	151	156	154	193	431	50	93	21-8	3 yrs. college; major economics.
16	167	164	151	170	154	163	160	181	164	197	423	80	98	21-0	B.A., major philosophy.
68	145	152	162	130	114	136	129	144	139	159	421	10	84	21-6	B.A. + 1st yr. grad. wk. in political science.
67	145	161	156	153	152	156	159	173	159	193	425	98	93	21-1	B.A., major chemistry.
95	138	144	162	142	123	140	137	162	144	166	412	60	75	22-3	B.A.
115	133									183 §	431	75	93	20-8	B.A., Phi Beta Kappa.

* Reprinted from ... "Status of Highly Intelligent Children." J. Gen. Psychol., 1936, 48, 215-226. Table 1. By permission of the editor, C. Murchison.

eventh centile on the A.C.P. examination. ifty-seven of Terman's gifted girls rated a ean score of 84, and 69 of his boys a mean f 87 on the Thorndike College Entrance xamination as reported in 1930 (Burks, ensen, and Terman). These scores were pproximately 1 SD above the Stanford niversity average for the corresponding ears. In 1940 Terman reported the cores of some 400 gifted as rating 1 SD bove the "highly selected Stanford popu- tion and only a few points below the ean of graduate candidates for the Ph.D. egree in psychology." Gray's young Co- mbia entrants averaged 92, his young arnard students 84 on this test, the for- er rating 1 SD above the Columbia Col- ge mean, the latter approximately .3 SD oove the Barnard mean.

These various scores at college entrance re in approximate agreement.[1] They in-

dicate (1) that gifted children tend to pre- serve at late adolescence or early adult- hood their high centile test competence; (2) that children with IQ's of 140+ in childhood tend to rate within the top 5 to 10 per cent on the national college entrance psychological test norms and to average scores about 1 SD above the mean of highly selected student distributions; and (3) that a tendency to regression toward the college mean occurs in many cases, more often among the girls than among the boys. Hollingworth's conclusion that the gifted are those at and above the seventy-fifth percentile of college graduates for the country at large perhaps underesti- mates the Columbia norms and the gifted ability in view of Hildreth's results and Wrenn's conclusion. Further adult scores from larger groups are needed to define more precisely the college and adult test score level of the gifted and to determine the extent, if present, of a regressive tend- ency in scores from childhood to maturity.

The first large-scale study in adulthood of children identified in childhood as gifted was made by Terman in 1936, sixteen years after his initial cross-sectional survey (Terman and Oden, 1940a). Of 1500 gifted subjects on record 93 per cent were located; and of these 755 males and 555 females cooperated with information deemed un- usually adequate and reliable, a high record

[1] *Group Test IQ and Prediction.* Keys (1940), a study of the college achievement of Uni- rsity of California students who had been ven a Terman Group Test during their high hool years, found an average IQ of 111 for e entering college group who failed to obtain e qualifying certificate for the third college ar, an IQ of 115 for those who obtained the rtificate but did not graduate, an IQ of 117 r those who graduated, and an IQ of 125 for nor graduates. A student whose IQ was 140 higher on the group test proved to have 0 times as many chances of graduating with nors as the student with an average IQ ore. Yet there were 6 of 19 honor students om the IQ range 105–119, and 8 from the nge 120–139. Traxler (1940) has reported the edian group test IQ of 68,899 college students 323 colleges as 109, Q₃ 117, Q₁ 101, in terms Otis equivalents of American Council Test res. These and other similar results raise several estions as yet unanswered by experimental idence: (1) Were the early group test IQ's of e students scoring at relatively low levels, t later achieving university success, inade- te measures of their ability at the time the ts were given? (2) Had a change occurred them in the rate of development between the ne of the test and the time of graduating from llege? (3) Can students adequately measured IQ's no higher than these achieve college duation and even distinction by reason of the

excellence of nonintellectual personality traits? Terman's 1940 study of the later achievement of gifted children shows that for the top half of 1 per cent in IQ score other factors than the high IQ are involved in young adult success. What then of 130 IQ's, 120 IQ's, and so on? It has been definitely demonstrated by studies such as that of Keys that there are relatively few individuals from the lower levels achieving the more distinguished successes. The formula for the diminishing returns is, however, as yet not determined. Further investigation is needed paralleling Keys' work, also systematic studies for comparison with the gifted and upper centile groups of the personality traits and careers of 130 and 120 IQ's.

in questionnaire response. Parents and teachers added their observations with similar completeness. Two age groups are included in the survey: the elementary school children of 1922 now in their twenties, median age 26; and the high school group of 1922 in the late twenties and early thirties, median age 32. The preliminary report of 1940 combines these in a single group. The reported loss by death, 3 per cent, is probably less than the expectation for a group of this age.

The girls' history is, as would be expected, shorter and less obviously significant than the boys', with only a few exceptional careers to mark the limits of high attainment. Eighty-five per cent of the girls attend college, and of these 90 per cent graduate. Class and student honors are frequent. Of the graduates, one-fifth are elected to Phi Beta Kappa, 3.5 per cent to Sigma Xi; half continue in graduate work, but few go beyond the M.A. degree. A fifth earn part of their college expenses as undergraduates, a third are self-supporting as graduate students. The occupational distribution of the 244 women who have completed their education and are gainfully employed shows 38 per cent in office work or business, 27 per cent in teaching, 9 per cent in music, art, or drama, 5 per cent in library work, 2 per cent in nursing, and 1.6 per cent in medicine. Of those who are not married or gainfully employed a number are engaged in volunteer social work. The average earnings (in 1936) of the high school graduate women are $90 per month; of those who attended college without graduating, $95; of the college graduates, $120. At each level the salaries amount to about half the corresponding income of the gifted boys. Fifty-one per cent of the girls were married at the time of the survey, and of these some 8 per cent had been divorced. The mean age at marriage was just under 23 years. Half the girls married college graduates; and the remaining half, men of more than average education. Four gifted intermarriages have occurred. Inclusion in the gifted groups has not, in their estimation, affected 65 per cent of the girls; 19 per cent record a favorable effect, 11 per cent an unfavorable one, and 5 per cent a mixed influence. The moral record has been good for the group as a whole. Sex delinquencies have been specifically reported for less than 1 per cent; alcoholic excess has been known in a few cases. Marriage and social life rather than intellectual pursuits have, as for girls generally, furnished the goals of the majority of the gifted. A few have achieved the Ph.D. or the M.D. degree or graduate distinction in law or engineering. A small number is carrying on superior administrative, business, or professional work.

Gray's (1930) study of 28 college women of unreported childhood IQ who averaged Thorndike college entrance scores equal to the Stanford gifted girls at the same or a younger age traces a similar picture for the college years. The 28 as a group had fewer college entrance deficiencies than the average student in the same college; three had state scholarship awards as freshmen; 79 per cent graduated, a relatively high percentage; but only 1 girl entered a graduate professional school. General honors were won by 3.6 per cent, special subject honors by 10.7 per cent, and Phi Beta Kappa election by over 21 per cent. One graduate fellowship and one scholarship were granted to members of the group. The health histories were favorable, and physical fitness test scores rated above the college average. In anthropometric tests the 28 were below the college average by reason of being younger; in motor ability, however, they exceeded the norms. They engaged in more athletic and other extracurricular activities than average college women.

Their responses to an emotionality questionnaire indicated more favorable adjustments than those of the comparable norm group. The later history of these students is not available.

Terman's 755 males surveyed sixteen years after their childhood IQ identification contribute a sketch outline of early adult gifted achievement in present-day educational, domestic, occupational, and economic life (Terman and Oden, 1940a). Nine out of ten enter college, and of these 95 per cent graduate. The gifted college student is three times as likely as the average to win graduation honors. About 16 per cent of the boys are elected to Phi Beta Kappa, 12 per cent to Sigma Xi, and some of the others win departmental distinction. Two-thirds continue in graduate work and of these 25 per cent receive a Ph.D. or M.D. degree, 25 per cent a degree in law, and 30 per cent the M.A. or some other predoctoral degree. Forty per cent are partially self-supporting as undergraduates, 14 per cent earn their entire expenses. The group as a whole earned more than half a million dollars in the undergraduate years. As graduates one-third are wholly self-supporting. A fourth of the entire group has won scholarships, fellowships, and assistantships to the extent of $200,000. The total record in class and student body honors is above average, and the course grade records are superior. Exceptions are attributed to poor work habits, lack of interest, maladjustment, or deliberate neglect of studies in the interest of special projects or social activities.

Forty-six per cent of the group are married, and of these 8 per cent are divorced. The mean marriage age is 24. The education of the spouse is above average with four of every ten of the wives college graduates. Forty per cent of all the married gifted of both sexes have offspring, numbering for the entire group 350. Seventy-three per cent of the gifted boys report no effects from inclusion in the gifted group; 13 per cent state that the effect has been favorable; 5 per cent regard it as unfavorable. The moral record has been above average. Exceptions include for the boys three criminal records and some cases of chronic alcoholic excess.

The occupational accomplishment of the group seems reasonably appropriate. Of the professions in which 50 per cent of the gifted engage, law recruits 13 per cent; engineering and geology, 10 per cent; medicine, 7 per cent; college teaching, 8 per cent; laboratory research, 5.5 per cent; religious or social work, 6 per cent. About 25 per cent enter semiprofessional or higher business pursuits and the remainder are engaged in office work, skilled trades, retail business, and a variety of other occupations. Less than 1 per cent of the employable members of the group were unemployed in 1936, and none was reported on relief. The salaries (in 1936) of the young adult gifted ranged from an average of $122 at 21 or 22 to $250 at 30. Ph.D. and M.A. graduates earned on the average $200 a month, physicians $217. High earnings include those of a lawyer, $12,000; a radio advertising executive, $10,000; an investment expert, $7000; a college professor, $8000; two musicians, $6000 or more. Some of these individuals may be on their way to the top salary class of adults (E. L. Thorndike, 1939). Half the entire group are launched upon careers worthy of their abilities. The arts have claimed several successful devotees, scientific research a number of others now already known for their publications. Bearing in mind that the financial and industrial depression of the 1930's coincided with the entrance of these youths on their mature careers, we find that the record as a whole is favorable.

Gray's (1930) 126 boys are younger

(under 16) at college entrance than Terman's gifted children (age **17**). Their Thorndike entrance examination scores rate higher (92) than the mean (87) reported by Burks, Jensen, and Terman in 1930. Thirty-nine of the 126 had state scholarship awards constituting approximately one-quarter of the total number granted to 25,000 Columbia freshmen in the same period. The total group had fewer deficiencies at entrance than the average student. Eighty-four per cent graduated from college, 79 per cent in four years as compared to 72 per cent for Columbia students generally. Sixteen per cent won Phi Beta Kappa honors, 10.3 general honors, as compared to 8 to 10 per cent and 3.1 per cent, respectively, of their classmates thus distinguished. In correlation with their younger age, Gray's boys were shorter, lighter, and inferior in strength as compared to the average college freshmen; however, they exceeded their own age norms in both height and weight. In interclass athletics and in nonathletic extracurricular activities they participated to a larger extent than their classmates and they were more successful in winning recognition. In emotional adjustment scores they rated more favorably than reported norm groups, and they were, according to their own statements, capable of profiting by early college entrance in spite of the difficulties of such a course. About one-fifth of the group expressed the belief that guidance in establishing habits of thought and work was essential for younger college students, and an equal number stated that in their opinion the superior student is neglected by his parents and college.

As a whole the results of the several researches show the level of attainment reached by the gifted under existing social, economic, and educational conditions. The contrast between the careers of the girls and the boys shows a lower level of economic and professional competence in the former and illustrates a well-known sex difference in social expectation and occupational opportunity. Nor can it be denied that a deeper, psychophysiological contrast may also be involved (Miles, 1935; Johnson and Terman, 1940).

Successful and Unsuccessful Adult Achievement of Gifted Children. In a short survey Terman and Oden (1940b) present a fascinating preview of a comparison between the most and the least successful of 600 gifted boys, selected in childhood, and at the time of this survey 23 years of age or older. Success was rated by three judges in terms of the extent to which native intellect had been utilized in life accomplishment. The upper and lower quarters of the resulting distribution were compared with respect to educational and occupational status, intelligence scores, achievement scores and school marks, extracurricular activities, books read, family background, racial differences, marital statistics and offspring, home environment, social adjustment and traits of personality, occupational preferences, masculinity-femininity scores, and pubertal changes. The results are summarized in Table 8. The statistical significance of the enumerated contrasts is not stated in the brief report, but many of the differences seem large enough to be clearly meaningful and the trends revealed by series of small differences may prove cumulatively important.

The successful group had generally the more satisfactory family background in terms of occupational status, marriage permanence, parental education, quality of the home, home instruction, and mental stock as indicated by higher sibling IQ and by fewer cases of abnormality in the relatives. Racially, a relatively small but noteworthy contrast appeared in the greater number of Jews in the success group. In child-

TABLE 8

Characteristics in Childhood and as Young Adults of Most and Least Successful Members of the California Gifted Groups *

	A Most Successful	C Least Successful		A Most Successful	C Least Successful
	N = 167	*N* = 146		*N* = 167	*N* = 146
Age (1939)	27.6	27.4	A marks in high school	62.5%	28.0%
Binet IQ (1922)	153.6	150.5	Iowa High School Con-		
T.G.T. IQ (1922)	148.5	147.5	tent Examination		
			Score:		
Home instruction	70.4%	52.0%	Above 99th percentile	45.2%	26.5%
Learned to read before			At or below 95th per-		
age 5	45.0%	45.0%	centile	3.2%	20.7%
Read 10 or more books					
in 2 mos. (1922)	56.0%	69.1%	Entered college	98%	70%
AQ (1922)	142.5	138.8	Of these, graduated		
Information Q (1922)	156.8	154.4	from college	90%	50%
Personality in childhood:			Thorndike Score in col-		
All traits, teachers'			lege	91.4 (57)	90.9 (25)
ratings	4.77	5.16	Postgraduate study	72.5%	19.4%
Adjustment difficulties	23.5%	33.1%	Phi Beta Kappa	32.5%	1.3%
Teased or thought			Sigma Xi	21.8%	2.8%
queer	7.0%	12.0%	Both	9.9%	0
Nervous symptoms	35.0%	43.0%			
			Self-supporting, half or		
Reported age of puberty	14.3	15.2	more	36.7%	45.8%
Masculinity score	+73	+64			
Paid jobs to age 16	63.0%	75.0%	Scholarships, fellow-		
			ships, etc.	50.0%	10.0%
Occupational preference			Total stipends from		
expressed	82.8%	68.5%	above	$116,000	$5,600
Social adjustment rat-					
ings normal or supe-			Mean earned income:		
rior (1928)	87.1%	74.6%	Age 23–24	$210	$96
			Age 28	$336 }	
Education of parents:			Age 35	$500 }	Less than $162
Post-graduate college	Fa. Mo.	Fa. Mo.			
work	25.3% 5.3%	14.0% 3.8%	Married (1938)	64.5%	48.6%
College graduate	41.0 18.5	22.6 12.0	Have offspring	46.0%	46.0%
8th grade only	11.6 5.3	19.5 16.3	Wives gainfully em-		
			ployed	10.7%	29.5%
Divorce or separation of			Divorced	4.6%	14.1%
parents	11.9%	19.8%			
Mental abnormality in			Occupational classifica-		
relatives	33.5%	41.0%	tion:		
			I. Professional	70.0%	17.1%
Home environment supe-			II. Semiprofessional		
rior (1928)	90.3%	79.0%	or higher busi-		
			ness	25.6%	11.1%
Occupational classifica-			III. Clerical, retail,		
tion of father:			skilled trades	3.8%	33.6%
I. Professional	36.7%	21.1%	IV to VI. Others	.6%	34.3%
II. Semiprofessional			Unemployed	0.0	3.6%
or higher business	23.9%	20.2%			
III to VI. Others	39.4%	58.7%			

* Data from L. M. Terman and M. Oden, "Correlates of Adult Achievement in the California Gifted Group," *Yearb. Nat. Soc. Stud. Educ.*, 1940, 39(I), 74–84, ed. by G. M. Whipple. Quoted by permission of the Society.

hood the less successful groups learned to read as early as the more successful, reported more books read, and performed approximately as well on school achievement, information, and intelligence tests. Parents and teachers had been able to discern in the successful gifted at a fairly young age slightly more favorable intellectual, social, moral, emotional, and especially volitional traits (Table 9). The successful cent graduated. The disproportion in the graduate schools is even greater. Somewhat more C's than A's had to earn their expenses in college, but five times as many A's as C's received honor appointments with stipends. The contrast in the amount of financial support thus won and in upper class and senior honors is more than 20 to 1 in favor of the A's. The slump in academic grades may too often be traced

TABLE 9

MEANS OF PARENTS' AND TEACHERS' RATINGS OF (1) THE TRAITS OF 300+ GIFTED BOYS AND 250+ GIFTED GIRLS, COMPARED WITH (2) SIMILAR MEANS OF 167 GIFTED BOYS RATED SUCCESSFUL IN YOUNG ADULT LIFE AND 146 GIFTED BOYS RATED UNSUCCESSFUL, AND (3) THE MEANS OF TEACHERS' RATINGS OF THE TRAITS OF 267 CONTROL BOYS AND 256 CONTROL GIRLS *

Traits	Gifted [1] Boys *	Control Boys †	Girls †	Gifted [1] Girls *	Gifted [2] A Group	C Group
Intellectual	3.66	6.4	6.3	3.70	3.5	3.8
Volitional	4.66	6.4	6.2	4.32	4.4	4.9
Emotional	4.83	5.9	5.8	4.80	4.3	4.7
Moral	4.82	6.2	5.6	4.50	4.4	4.7
Physical	5.53	6.4	6.1	5.42	5.3	5.3
Social	5.79	6.5	6.1	5.38	5.7	6.0
All Traits	4.88	6.3	6.0	4.82	4.77	5.16

* Teachers' and parents' ratings combined.   † Teachers' ratings.

Data derived or computed from [1] L. M. Terman et al., Genetic Studies of Genius, Vol. I, Mental and Physical Traits of a Thousand Gifted Children, Stanford University Press, 1925 (Table 192, p. 542), and [2] L. M. Terman and M. Oden, "Correlates of Adult Achievement in the California Gifted Group," Yearb. Nat. Soc. Stud. Educ., 1940, 39(I), p. 82, (Ed., G. M. Whipple), Public School Publishing Co.

or A group was slightly more accelerated in school than the unsuccessful C's; they reached puberty somewhat younger and during the high school period they showed superiority in school work, school performance tests, and extent of extracurricular activity. The differences in extracurricular activity are large, and they are probably significant in school marks, in Iowa Content Examination scores, and in leadership expressed in terms of the number of activities engaged in. Of the A's 98 per cent entered college, and 90 per cent graduated; of the C's 70 per cent entered and 50 per to an unsuitable educational régime which retarded the child or youth until he lost interest or forgot how to study.

After college, or in some cases after high school, occupational or professional activity was rewarded by salaries showing a greater than 2-to-1 contrast in the early years and reaching a 3-to-1 difference by age 35. The occupational classification reveals the typical adult contrast of the two groups, with 95.6 per cent of the A's and only 28 per cent of the C's in the two higher brackets. Earning power and general success may be causal in the larger number of marriages among the A's, but so also may be psychophysiological stability and balance. These factors may be involved in the 1-to-3 contrast in divorce frequency. The authors conclude: "The data reviewed indicate that *above the IQ level of 140, adult success is largely determined by such factors as social adjustment, emotional stability, and drive to accomplish.* To what extent these qualities are the product of environmental influences and to what extent they have a genetic basis, no one can say" (Terman and Oden, 1940*b*, p. 84, *Yearb. Nat. Soc. Stud. Educ.*, 1940, 39 (I). Quoted by permission of the Society.)

Individual Differences among Gifted Children

The large statistical studies of the gifted have necessarily stressed group trends, measured by averages, comparing these when possible with norms for unselected groups. Thus the typical traits and behavior patterns of highly intelligent children have been outlined against the background of the generality. However, as Terman, Hollingworth, and Witty have been at pains to emphasize, gifted children as individuals are not adequately represented by this method alone. The gifted, superior deviates as they are, are farthest perhaps from constituting a stereotype. Each individual is unique in the patterns of behavior that express character and in the traits whose vastly complex integration forms the personality. Essential statistical measurements of central tendencies in the intellectual, emotional, and social aspects of individual behavior result in oversimplified generalizations. These are qualified theoretically, it is true, by mathematical measures of dispersion indicating the wideness of contrasts in each separate trait of the gifted. Only acquaintance with

individual gifted children can create the appropriate lively sense of unduplicated human personalities, differing even in the patterns and expressions of their exceptional intellects and in other traits covering the whole wide range of constitutional and functional potentialities.

Well-drawn case studies afford individual illustrations that diversify the interesting individualities whose performance and characteristics furnish the basis for the important statistical studies. Hollingworth, Terman, and others have provided long series of case descriptions indicating some of the possible trait combinations within the gifted group.

Superior mental endowment itself, the qualifying basis for the rating of gifted, may show contrasting characteristics in its expression. Thus the scientific, analytically ingenious, inventive child differs from the literary, generalizing, verbally expressive and retentive, interpretative child. In adulthood the former becomes characteristically the experimental scientist, the latter the writer or lecturer. Hollingworth's D and E illustrate this contrast (Hollingworth, 1926*b*; Burks, Jensen, and Terman, 1930).

Sustained intellectual capacity proved by repeatedly high intelligence test ratings is a characteristic of gifted children. Yet wide individual differences from test to test and large IQ changes are not infrequent with regressive score losses somewhat outweighing gains, especially in the girls. Thus Bertha, in a comfortable superior home and with an IQ of 139, deteriorated in scored IQ to 107 in six years. Clara, a clairvoyant's daughter, showed after six years a drop from IQ 148 to a T.G.T. score far below the gifted mean. In contrast, Terman's Madeline (IQ's 192 and 190) and David (IQ 184, Thorndike score 106) in childhood, and Hollingworth's cases 1 (IQ 190+, CAVD 454) and 20 (IQ 162 and

CAVD 429) in childhood and early adulthood, illustrate persistence in high scoring capacity. Madeline and David, described in detail, are able personalities with varied active interests and achievements (Burks, Jensen, and Terman, 1930).

In school achievement the gifted are superior as a group by whatever measure is applied. Test scores of accomplishment as a whole rate far above the general age norms (Terman and DeVoss, 1924). Yet here also wide individual differences are present in separate subject scores and in the total composite rating. Gray and Hollingworth (1931) have reported subject-quotient ranges for the gifted extending from 100 (average) to the upper test limit (210) and composite-quotient ranges from 119 to 187. The highest and the lowest of these quotients represent vastly divergent performance and competence. Achievement ratios (educational quotient divided by IQ) giving approximate measures of educational capability show extremely wide contrasts in the extent to which gifted children utilize their potential capacity. Lorge and Hollingworth (1936) report 105 and 106 as their highest childhood achievement ratios for 19 gifted children now college graduates, and yet these two scores belong to individuals with IQ's as diverse as 145 and 172. The two lowest achievement ratios, 83 and 85, in the same series, belong to children with IQ's of 162 and 174. Motivation and special influences may make high as well as low intellects more or less effective in the tests and also in the school work they are designed to measure (Tiebout, 1943). Two cases of gifted children with inferior scholarship records illustrate this deviation from the gifted mean. Edwin, IQ 141, failed eight subjects, rated C in sixteen units of work, and was finally asked to withdraw from high school because of his poor standing. His explanation was that he didn't like to work. Glandular

disfunction was suspected by medical examiners. Thomas, IQ 142, had a mediocre school record as a result of devoting his time and effort to music, in which he excelled. In contrast with these rare cases whose performance is distinctly poor are the more characteristic gifted who do well in school, find the work in the lower grades relatively easy, score in the superior range on educational tests, lead the class in high school, and win distinguishing honors. Hollingworth's (1942) C, G, and L and Verda, one of Jensen's gifted juvenile writers, are among these (Burks, Jensen, and Terman, 1930).

In nonintellectual traits the gifted range from high to low in test scores and in behavior. Physical, mental, emotional, and social traits show wide deviations from the typical, superior averages of the group as a whole. Statistical expression generally shows about as great divergences from the highest to the lowest trait measures of the gifted as occur in unselected groups. Case studies again give concrete form to the statistics (see especially Burks, Jensen, and Terman, 1930). Beside the characteristically healthy, strong, well-developed gifted from superior stock and excellent homes there are also a few like Terman's Marshall. Hampered in childhood by physical frailty, lameness, poverty, bad heredity, and sordid environment, he became by 1940 a member of the young adult success group. Although coming generally from superior economic and social backgrounds, the gifted group includes the daughter of a Negro Pullman porter and the sons of an inflexible, Austrian-born laborer. Above the average in emotional stability, they number their share of behavior and adjustment problems, of hampering shyness, self-consciousness and inferiority complexes, of overbearing aggressiveness and conceit, of disobedience, dishonesty, laziness, and even a case or two of "queerness" and psycho-athy. Lack of motivation may appear or excessive driving ambition; neurotic avoidance of responsibility, and zealous, single track pursuit of personal objectives.

Hollingworth (1931) outlined special sources of personality disability to which the highest IQ's are liable and illustrated the consequences of these under varying conditions (Hollingworth, 1942). Gillingham (1920) described unstable and neurotic children at various high IQ levels. Terman enumerated the emotional adjustment hazards of the most superior deviates (Burks, Jensen, and Terman, 1930). Regensburg (1926) described clinically cases of instability and maladjustment and outlined methods of treatment. Nevill (1937) recently reported a statistical study of maladjusted gifted children referred for clinical diagnosis and guidance. Zorbaugh (1936) has enumerated the specific problems for which gifted children were referred to the New York University Clinic for the social adjustment of the gifted, and which cover the whole range of psychophysiological maladjustment indicators (enuresis, masturbation, stuttering, compulsions and mild obsessions, excessive daydreaming and fantasy, seclusiveness, temper tantrums, quarreling, defiance of discipline, truancy, lying, stealing, sex delinquency, and the like).

Terman described an unstable neurotic girl, IQ 152, a persistently delinquent boy, IQ 143, and a constitutional psychopath, IQ 165, who was finally a suicide. The statistics for high IQ's among neuropsychiatric cases are of interest in this connection. Schott (1931) found 18 patients able to rate a top score on the 1916 Stanford-Binet scale in a tested hospital sampling of 450 cases. The 4 per cent of highly intelligent individuals in this representative psychopathic group roughly equals the expectation as defined by Terman (1916) for the general population.

It is important to recognize that differences and contrasts are present in the superior intellectual trait profiles of the gifted and that these children, like unselected boys and girls, show unfavorable as well as favorable deviations from the group averages in measures of performance and personality. But a well-balanced picture of the gifted as a group shows more successful than unsuccessful members, more who maintain than who lose the superior quality of their intellectual interests and achievements, more who are stable, effective, and well-motivated than unstable, irresponsible, or deficient in ambition and drive. Favorable deviations are more frequent than unfavorable in the scores on tests of accomplishment and ability, whether scientific, literary, or artistic, in scholastic and extracurricular interests, in vocational choices, in indications of mental masculinity-femininity, of fair-mindedness and of social intelligence, of mental independence from suggestibility, of leadership, and of moral responsibility. Case studies of favorable rather than unfavorable deviates among the gifted illustrate the predominating membership of the group as a whole. Many such single cross-sectional pictures are available in which high IQ's are accompanied and supported by superior physical and social traits, excellence in studies and in extracurricular activities, and the favorable opinions of their companions. A few cases studied and described at intervals from childhood to adulthood afford the most striking proof of the persistence of gifted personality. Hollingworth's E, four times described (Lorge and Hollingworth, 1936, and Hollingworth, 1942), and Terman's David, Francis, and Henry Cowell are among the best examples (Burks, Jensen, and Terman, 1930). Adequately representative, in IQ terms, of the group as a whole, they exemplify in personality traits the effective, goal-seeking, eagerly, patiently, and persistently ambitious whose ability is equal to the demands of their objectives and whose objectives are adequate for the realization of their potential talents.

Adjustment Problems of Gifted Children

The special problems of adjustment of the gifted are not, as was at one time supposed, primarily due to an essential emotional instability. Terman's results showed that children of high IQ's are not as a group less stable emotionally than a control population. On the Woodworth-Cady emotional stability questionnaire they rated as more stable than the control children at every age from 7 to 14. The critical ratios for the group differences were 6.11 for the boys (284 gifted, 258 control) and 7.61 for the girls (248 gifted, 275 control). Ratings of emotional traits by parents and teachers showed a statistically significant advantage of the gifted, and this was further indicated by an excess for them (68 per cent) above the control median. In social traits involving emotional elements a further series of ratings showed approximate equality of the group, 58.5 per cent of the gifted scoring as high as or higher than the average control child (Terman et al., 1925).

Comparing superior with inferior school children, Laycock (1933) found that the superior individuals made superior adjustments. Conklin (1940), investigating the infrequent school failures of top centile children, came to the conclusion that in these relatively rare cases personality factors, as yet unanalyzed, were involved. Witty (1940a), following the careers of his 100 gifted children identified ten years earlier, found his group generally superior in poise and stability. Yet exceptions were present, and, although no child was

rated as "queer" by his associates, 10 per cent were maladjusted. Of these there were two types: the anxious, withdrawn, insecure, and the indifferent, bored, socially inadequate. The failure of the environment to stimulate maximally and to develop habits of industry was mentioned.

Nevill's (1937) study of behavior problems in gifted children suggests no correlation between IQ and type of emotional difficulty or adjustment, although it does indicate that a high IQ is generally an advantage in accomplishing good adjustment. This research supports the conclusions of Gillingham's (1920) early report in indicating that gifted children, although as a group above average in stability, are not all as individuals free from emotional and social adjustment difficulties. No conclusion as to relative prevalence of problems can be made from either of these reports, as control group data are not available. That Nevill's gifted cases constitute 12 per cent of her clinical practice indicates the social and intellectual status of the clientele in the private clinic where the study was made rather than the incidence of instability among superior children.

Beside the typical constitutional-emotional problems coincident to nervousness, overanxiousness, sensitivity, and other typical personality disorders, and infrequent social problems such as lying and stealing, conditions now known to be less rather than more frequent among gifted than unselected children, there appear in certain of Nevill's gifted patients handicaps perhaps in part specifically related to their high intelligence. These include excessive quickness, resulting in inaccuracy, awkwardness, and clumsiness in writing and handwork when correlated with the younger life age, and impracticality, associated with lack of experience. Complaint is made in several cases of too much time spent in reading, of being self-centered

nd bossy, and in a few instances of mix-
ig poorly, being teased easily, solitary,
esistant, or bumptious. These problems,
nore or less closely interassociated in in-
ividual children with high IQ's, are sim-
ar to those summarized by Hollingworth
fter years of close personal study of the
ifted. Hollingworth's (1936b) classifica-
on includes: (1) problems of physique
being weaker and smaller than their class-
aates); (2) problems of adjustment to
ccupation (preferring self-direction to di-
ection by others); (3) problems involved
1 "suffering fools gladly" (difficulty in ac-
epting the dogmatism of lesser intellects);
nd (4) the tendency to be isolated in in-
erests and goals. When a gifted child is
lso a sensitive or nervous child his adjust-
tent difficulties naturally tend to increase
Hollingworth, 1942).

Nevill and Hollingworth agree that the
ifficulties inherent in brilliance do not
reate maladjustment, although they may
redispose to unsatisfactory behavior not
frequently based on a sense of inferiority
ue to relative backwardness in social and
hysical development. The gifted become
ltracritical, self-sufficient, or mentally lazy
s a result of their semi-awareness of
tental superiority, insufficient social expe-
tence, and incomplete independence in
he development of personal responsibility.
uccessful treatment comes through early
ecognition of the problems and through
ooperation of home and school in (1)
reating a relatively normal milieu with
ppropriate social contacts and without
verstimulation and (2) in building the
ntellectual understanding and the social
abits of the child to meet the contrast
ifficulties that cannot be avoided.

Nevill reports that good adjustment oc-
urs when parents and teachers (1) with-
ut expecting too much at first and with-
ut exaggerating the child's superiority
ave built in him a healthy natural pride

in his powers, (2) have treated him as
older intellectually while recognizing his
emotional immaturity, (3) have encouraged
his all-round development, and (4) have
taxed his mental powers sufficiently at
school. Hollingworth concludes that "intellectually gifted children between 130 and
150 IQ seem to find the world well suited to
their development." They are superior in
size, strength, health, and beauty, well balanced emotionally, and of good character;
they tend to win confidence and to be
granted leadership. Above 150 IQ the conditions may be less favorable.

Both Hollingworth and Terman have
given attention to the highest IQ level
where they find the need of special opportunity classes and special social adjustment
most essential in order to avoid a sense of
alienation and resulting negativism. The
very exceptional children have few congenial playmates in childhood and little
opportunity for normal social contacts with
their peers. That 10 cases out of 35 IQ's
170+ are reported by Terman as lacking
youthful social intercourse or even being
seriously maladjusted is not surprising, in
view of these considerations. It is perhaps
more surprising that the average for this
very high scoring group is only half a step
below the mean on a five-step scale of
social adjustment and that 64 per cent of
the group rate as average or better on the
same scale (Burks, Jensen, and Terman,
1930). Case studies of the highest IQ children show that their adjustments and satisfactions are mainly achieved in strictly
intellectual fields and that these tend generally to be solitary. Their absorption in
their interests and their individual emotional stability equations no doubt condition the extent of their comfort in their
almost necessarily restricted social relationships. That their experiences have been
sufficiently satisfactory and that they hold
their own emotionally under the prevailing

conditions seem to be indicated by the presence of six of them in Terman's (Terman and Oden, 1940b) adult success group as contrasted with but two in his failure group.

Potentiality and Realization

The report of gifted accomplishment in young adults confirms the view that equality of IQ in childhood does not insure, although it predisposes to, equality of achievement in maturity. Intelligence is an important factor in accomplishment, but it proves to be only one factor among others, perhaps many others. Interrelationships among the factors may be as important for accomplishment as the presence of the factors themselves. The follow-up studies so far made suggest that more effective personalities emerge when heredity and environment are both favorable. No single unfavorable element in the picture has been found to block accomplishment in the gifted if a sufficient number of others are favorable. Similarly, no single favorable element has proved sufficient to insure the realization of potential ability along the many possible lines of gifted accomplishment or even along a single line. The highest IQ's (170 or 180 and above), although more often predisposing to success than to failure, do not necessarily insure the highest achievement. Nor do they, although sometimes associated with serious problems in childhood development, produce a condition of social maladjustment essentially thwarting (Terman and Oden, 1940b; Hollingworth, 1942).

Gifted groups include individuals of many possibilities. Intercorrelations between intelligence and special skills and abilities are generally positive, and the scores of the gifted have been demonstrated as above the average, sometimes far above, in tests and childhood achieve-ments prognostic, under favorable conditions, of later distinguished accomplishment. Both boys and girls are capable of superior literary and artistic work and produce examples of superior merit at an early age, often in the preschool years. However, the social influences of our athletic, industrial, mechanized age are opposed to the cultivation of these gifts in childhood, especially in boys.

History and biography show few examples of high achievement in adulthood along lines requiring special skills of manual or verbal expression where practice has not developed native ability from youth. The economic pressures of our time direct the emphasis of school instruction toward the primary aim of individual self-support. Mechanical invention may be included as an objective in practical education, but the development of literary, artistic, and musical creation is usually secondary and generally occurs only occasionally in individual extracurricular experience. Literary juvenilia of merit in Terman's gifted group were all the work of girls, although boys are known to produce superior literary work in childhood and youth under appropriately stimulating circumstances. Writing has at present little prestige value among boys except occasionally in the homes of successful literary or artistic parents or in schools, generally private schools, where literature is cultivated as a highly valued expression of superior personalities. Lang (1897) believed that youthful literary achievement is a poor indicator of later work of merit, but in the arts the child is father of the man and we are therefore not surprised that Terman's adult gifted include fewer writers than scientists, business administrators, or professional men. It is natural to believe that any sizable group of gifted children probably contains many more who could become successful creative workers than who do, but the means of developing these latent talents are not available and a valuable potential asset is thus usually wasted.

Scientific aptitude is another example of a talent present in the gifted group to a far greater extent than its probable realization in adult achievement. Social influences are opposed to superior scientific education and development in girls, and few of the potential scientists among them will reach a higher goal than high school teaching. Of the boys with this aptitude, the majority become industrial workers and engineers rather than contributors to the advancement of essential scientific progress.

Talents of superior grade in all the fields of human activity are no doubt present in any large group of gifted children. They are suggested or demonstrated by high scores on appropriate tests wherever these have been applied. No single individual, however, can in our complex society carry to a high level of achievement more than one or two human talents even under the most favorable circumstances. Mathematicians are seldom also superior artists or facile linguists, nor are engineers generally able to achieve high rank as poets or musicians even if talent for the necessary skills had been present in childhood. In science a man can today scarcely master more than a single branch, and literature, music, or art require complete devotion. A practical education, a brief apprenticeship, a few years of ill-paid junior business or professional service, the founding of a home, and the rearing of a family give little opportunity for the development of secondary or even primary talents in superior individuals even under favorable conditions. And conditions are frequently not favorable. Poverty, ill health, excessive responsibilities, social limitations, emotional handicaps increase the burdens of the personal, social, and economic life and prevent the realization in many gifted personalities of their potential capacity. For the feeble-minded, society undertakes to lift some of the burdens and cast off the restrictions as far as this may be. The gifted, the potential leaders, discoverers, and creators, however, are usually left to develop their own skills in their own way and in terms of personal initiative alone. Fortunately many of them have the energy, the ability, and the plasticity to make the necessary adjustments, overcome the environmental obstacles, and win the necessary economic support (Bridgeman, 1930). Others, as Terman's (1940) young adult study shows, are more or less exhausted by the struggle and fall by the way. Discovering means of preventing failure and of increasing the effectiveness of the possible life contribution of the gifted is a challenging task. Identifying talent and cultivating it maximally is an essential in the development of the natural resources of a progressive society (Terman, 1939b).

The Education of Gifted Children

Systematic attempts to segregate and specially train gifted children have developed in some of the more progressive localities as a practical consequence of the selection and study of the gifted by mental test methods. Many schools emphasize enrichment and individualized instruction within their regular groups. Before these methods were systematically formulated a few far-seeing educators had tried to meet the needs of the brighter pupils by various administrative plans. These included flexibility in promotion, double or multiple track curricula with varying rates of speed, constant and shifting group systems, promotion on the basis of separate subject mastery, and self-reliant programs with or without preparatory training centers for the rapid advancement of the more successful pupils at certain crucial points in the curriculum. In these procedures and their variations two aspects of individual and group differences in learning may be recognized: (1) diverse rates of advancement are appropriate for children of varying abilities, and the pupils at widely different levels on the intelligence scale can best be accommodated by some form of segregation or system of diversified progress; (2) wide differences in the amount and complexity of content that can be readily acquired by children of differing degrees of competence can be met by some flexible form of curriculum enrichment.

These principles were recognized and methods based upon them were developed by individual teachers of brilliant pupils long before they became the concern of administrative educators. Parents and tutors of able and precocious children developed their own systems of acceleration and enrichment. Karl Witte, Macaulay, and John Stuart Mill were instructed individually at rates of speed far beyond those of even the most superior private schools or opportunity classes, and the curricula devised for them were designed to cover by the age of 10 or 12 the elements and many of the higher aspects of liberal education, including the languages, literature, history, mathematics, theoretical science, and philosophy. Many other children besides, including Lord Kelvin, physicist, his brother James Thomson, engineer, Grotius, founder of international law, and the philosophers Bentham and Schleiermacher, were prepared by tutors or under flexible school plans which permitted college or university matriculation at the age of 11 or 12, followed by long careers of brilliant and active accomplishment. Men who achieve the distinction of inclusion in *Who's Who* and the notable group of starred American men of science have as a rule passed more rapidly through the elemen-

tary and college preparatory school years than the average boy. Enrichment of educational content came to them in part through superior private school instruction, in part through the personal interest of public school teachers, tutors, or friends, and in part as a result of personal initiative (Hollingworth, 1926b and 1942; Gray, 1930).

Private schools in the United States and elsewhere are actually carrying on the segregated education of superior pupils. Reports of the Educational Records Bureau (1940, 1943) and other sources indicate that approximately 90 per cent of the children in these schools are average or above in tested intelligence and educational competence, and that 5 to 25 per cent of them are gifted in the technical sense, having IQ ratings of 130+ or 140+. The average rate of learning in private schools is 15 to 20 per cent faster than that in the average public elementary school, an advantage that has generally been utilized in thoroughness and enrichment rather than by accelerated promotion.

Exceptional pupils are not adequately taken care of by the usual routine of the public schools. Often their very presence is not recognized. Thus Terman, among others, found that the more able public school children are discovered more readily in terms of birth date than by teachers' subjective nominations.

Public schools that have adopted multiple track or xyz class systems have partially met the need by their segregation of the average (y) from the dull (z), and the high average and superior (x) from the middle group. The x classes in many public schools enroll pupils approximately equal in ability to private school children. But just as the dull classification fails to meet the needs of the feeble-minded, so the above average group cannot sufficiently adapt its needs to its most gifted members. Children with IQ's of 140 or even 130 and above have quite different learning needs from the group averaging below 120.

Special classes explicitly for gifted children are a development of the mental test period. Race (1918) reported one of the first where selection was based on IQ tests. The pupils, IQ 120+, were described as healthy, stable, and capable of more and better work than the average. Without excessive effort they covered the prescribed course content in half the regular time. Specht (1919) described in similar terms work of children of the same level of superiority in a segregated New York class. Whipple (1919), Coy (1923), and others have also reported success with above average children. Cleveland (1920) stated that the scholastic records of the segregated gifted children and their extracurricular pursuits exceeded, sometimes considerably, the typical student performance of their class group.

From 1920 onward until 1930 there was a gradual increase in the number of special classes. The children were generally chosen early in the elementary school course. Usually, due regard was given to health and personality factors. The teachers were as carefully selected as the pupils and they were given much freedom in the planning and conduct of the work. The cost per pupil was somewhat greater than in the regular classes, and for this reason small school systems with few high IQ children infrequently attempted segregation.

From 1918 to 1923 educational psychologists in Germany as well as in the United States were experimenting successfully with the segregation of superior children for school instruction. Selection by test, supplemented by teachers' appraisals of health, motivation, and personality, gradually took the place of reliance on either test or teachers' judgments alone. Alert, competent, well-adjusted teachers were given charge of the instruction of the gifted (Lämmermann, 1931). In other European countries mental tests have been used as a basis for the granting of scholarships in special schools rather than for segregation within the regular schools.

In the period from 1923 onward attention was directed in the United States chiefly to the curriculum and problems of enrichment. Early considerations were summarized and discussed by Whipple (1919), Freeman (1924), Stedman (1924), Henry and others, in the *Yearbook of the National Society for the Study of Education* (1924), Hollingworth (1926b), Jensen (1927), and Goddard (1928). Later methodology and objectives have been formulated by Adams and Brown (1930), Osburn and Rohan (1931), Dransfield (1933), Cohen and Coryell (1935), and in terms of basic principles by Hollingworth (1942). Bentley (1937), Carroll (1940), Heck (1940), and Garrison (1940) have summarized present school attitudes and practices in the teaching of gifted children. Bibliographies have been prepared by Newland (1941), Gray (1942), and Hildreth and Ingram (1942).

Intraclass segregation of small groups and individualized project programs are developing where class segregation has proved nonfeasible. Hollingworth (1936c), from experience in special opportunity classes for the gifted, advises enrichment in the regular elementary school curriculum, including (1) courses in the development of civilized culture, using the project method; (2) biography of world leaders; (3) the tools of learning, including foreign languages; and (4) special work in art and music, including an introduction to appreciation. In the high school course Cohen, Coryell, and their associates (1935) emphasize the value and importance of teacher leadership and stimulation. Gifted pupils need to be associated with teachers who are themselves enthusiastic devotees of the subjects they teach and of the culture to which these are essential.

The most usual method of dealing with the rapid progress possibilities of the gifted in the public schools is by the simple expedient of grade skipping. The average gifted child in Terman's group skipped at least one grade, and those who skipped more were reported by their teachers as doing better work than those who skipped less. An unpublished study of Hoskinson is reported by Henry (1924) in which high school and college students who had skipped one or more half grades were found to be characteristically rapid readers, quick learners, industrious, and able to concentrate. They had learned to study independently and they brought from home a good attitude toward school and school work. Eighty-seven per cent believed that the skipping had been advantageous to them. The more recent study of McElwee (1932) in which the personality traits of accelerated children were compared with average and retarded groups finds the traits of the advanced pupils consistently superior. Their attitudes toward school work and their school habits are reported to be especially good.

Results reported by Wilkins (1936) on the high school achievement and social adjustment of accelerated pupils are in harmony with these findings and seem "to give further evidence that the dangers attributed to acceleration (unless of course practiced unwisely) have been largely overestimated."

The United States Office of Education reported, for 1935–1936, 3009 gifted children enrolled in special classes of public school systems in fourteen cities at a cost of $176,672. The enrollment had decreased 25 per cent during the period of financial curtailment beginning in 1930. "The education of gifted children," the report explains, "has always constituted a subject for debate with a rather definite difference of opinion as to the effect of membership in a special class upon their social adjustment. Many fine things are being done for this group without separate organizations for their instruction" (Foster and Martens, 1938, p. 1). In many large cities the xyz systems are now expected to take care of intelligence grouping sufficiently to meet the needs of the gifted at the elementary school level. Enthusiasts for segregation repeatedly emphasize the values of the method in making possible the maximal mental stimulation and better social adjustment of the abler pupils (Orleans, 1940). Enrichment within class groups is said to offer a successful solution without the organizational and administrative complexities of specific segregation. Recently Witty (1940b) has re-emphasized the undemocratic trend of gifted segregation in the public schools. He also contends that homogeneous grouping on a mental test basis is impossible. The evidence from the New York and other opportunity classes seems at variance with this view. Myers (1935) believes that the best all-round development of the gifted child results when he works at school at his own rate but in a regular class of normal children.

Research since 1930 has added little more than general confirmation to the earlier findings regarding the benefit of segregation (Heck, 1940). Lamson's (1930) segregated children excelled in high school above the average of their older classmates. Gray and Hollingworth's (1931) segregated gifted children, devoting only half their time to the prescribed curriculum, rated as high on educational achievement tests as nonsegregated children of equal intelligence who were spending full time on the prescribed work. A study of segregated and unselected first-grade children by Dvorak and Rae (1929) led to the conclusion that both segregation and enrichment had positive value. Studies by Danielson and Herschberger (reported by Terman and Burks, 1933) record comparisons of special class gifted children with gifted pupils from the regular grades. The subject marks for the former were higher and their participation in art activities, athletics, dramatics, committee work, and office holding was greater. Teachers' ratings of the two groups were approximately equal on accuracy, dependability, and leadership. The former special class group received the higher ratings in cooperation, initiative, and industry. In answering the question "In which grades have you been the happiest?" the segregated twice as often as the nonsegregated mentioned those grades in which the special class experience occurred. A study by Herr (1937) showed that superior children (average IQ 125) completed the work of the seventh and eighth grades in one year without loss in school marks, achievement scores, or extent of participation in extracurricular activities as compared with groups of equal ability who performed the work in a two-year period. Health and attendance were satisfactory in the accelerated group. Personality ratings showed possibly significant differences which are not necessarily indicators of unfavorable effects from the acceleration.

The experimental work with gifted children in which segregated are compared with nonsegregated groups seems to point to the more favorable progress of the former as compared with the latter. The studies are too few to be completely convincing. Enrichment and intragroup instruction may be almost equally effective. The important finding with reference to the education of the gifted relates to the development of attitude and motivation. Gifted children, like others, require ade-

quate opportunity and stimulation, and this can be more or less successfully given with due planfulness under various systems, so long as diverse rates of advancement are permitted and an adequately enriched curriculum is maintained. If segregation is used, selection in terms of total personality assets and needs is certainly desirable.

The Childhood of Genius

Biographical accounts of the early development of distinguished contemporaries or historic geniuses furnish psychological material of special interest for comparison with the observed and tested behavior of gifted children. Rate of mental development, frequency and type of precocious achievement, personality traits, especially the volitional, family background, educational opportunity, and social environment can be traced in biography and measured by the statistical methods of historiometry. It is true that tradition has not infrequently invested geniuses of the past with phenomenal characteristics and has popularly given them personalities unparalleled in contemporary cross-sectional studies. The factual material of reliable biography, however, can be viewed and weighed apart from exaggeration and excessive eulogy. When so examined the data, although often unfortunately too few, are comparable with current records. Gifted children of today undoubtedly include many of the leaders of tomorrow, and the childhood traits of the leaders of the past objectively evaluated can enlighten us about the most superior contemporary personalities.

Inquiry and controversy in this field have centered in the problems of the mental growth, the heredity, the special interests, the cultural opportunities and development, and the early physical and mental health of world leaders. Popular conclusions about these matters drawn from biased selections of illustrative data have gained a hold on popular opinion that gives way only slowly in the face of careful, objective, statistical studies of large representative populations. The view that ability finds a way to distinction, whatever the social handicaps, probably takes insufficient account of the demonstrable advantages in the environment of successful leaders. On the other hand, the opposite opinion that training and opportunity make the man must finally fall before rigorous comparisons of achievements of the equally schooled but unequally gifted. Fallacious evidence of the presence in geniuses generally of instability, psychopathy, delay in development, and degenerative precocity has been brought forward by the fascinating, subjective method of descriptive anecdote (Lombroso, 1891). Conclusions based on selected data of this kind have no place in a scientific natural history of genius, although they may serve the desirable end of stimulating research for proof or disproof.

The first studies of large samples of objective data were made by Galton, who elaborated a statistical psychobiographical method. The superior hereditary background of eminent men of science, letters, art, and public life was demonstrated in every such study (for example, Galton, 1869; DeCandolle, 1885; and Ellis, 1904). Correlation was demonstrated between the appearance of genius and such factors as social and economic security, educational opportunity, and favorable cultural influences. The importance of environmental stimulation for the emergence of ability and the possible veto power of poverty or educational restrictions were emphasized (Ward, 1906). Reviewing his own results and those of others, Ellis advised caution in the interpretation of cause and effect in the nature-nurture composite of genius.

Sully (1886) and Ellis (1904) found healthy, persistent precocity characteristic of leaders and geniuses. Precocity in the field of special interest was demonstrated by 80 per cent in a group of 287 geniuses representing the principal fields of human endeavor. Mental acceleration was noted by the biographers of one-third of Ellis's cases, and only 4 per cent were said to have been "not precocious." Those who failed to show early mental superiority or strong intellectual interest were not among the more distinguished for original intellectual achievement in maturity. "In order to go far," Ellis concluded, "it is evidently desirable to start early."

The first general statistical survey of the boyhood development of great men was Yoder's (1894) study of fifty geniuses and leaders. The tabulated results minimized the importance of poor health stressed by Lombroso, although they showed how in individual instances, as in the case of Dickens, delicate physique could be of advantage in intellectual pursuits. Yoder's great men were above average in size, born of parents in the period of mature energy, and were normal in childhood development and pursuits, including sports. At an early age they had already displayed strong memories, active imaginations, and many of them had shown a scientific spirit of investigation. "Like ordinary men, they were influenced by their environment."

Characteristic advantages in background and education were enjoyed by 1036 noted American men of science selected by their scientific associates at the instigation of Cattell (1915, 1917), who planned, organized, and interpreted the statistics. The national and racial heredity of the scientists showed trends similar to those of the gifted, with the northern European and British stocks preponderant. Professional men contributed a disproportionate share of members to the group. The sex difference in numbers is commented upon. Contrast in the production of various geographical regions is statistically expressed and interpreted with respect to the influence of universities and great teachers. Thus Massachusetts and Connecticut were, for example, fifty times as likely to rear a distinguished scientist in the period studied as the Southeastern States. Centers of learning where eminent investigators attracted the best students produced many times their share of younger scientific leaders. Thus from Agassiz at Harvard came thirteen first-rank naturalists; from Brünnow at Michigan, a quarter of the leading astronomers of their day. Teaching and inspiration directed the line of study and interest, and the effective expression of native ability was augmented through personal contacts.

The studies from Galton to Cattell showed the importance for achievement of superior innate ability, good heredity, and adequate education. As yet superior ability had been defined in such terms as school achievement, literary or scientific accomplishment, or creative artistic production. These were not interchangeably meaningful. An index of general mental measurement became available in the Binet tests and these, as revised at Stanford, Terman proposed to apply to biographical material for the evaluation of the childhood development of great men. The IQ of Francis Galton thus appraised on the basis of early records proved to be near 200 (Terman, 1917).

To Terman's plan for IQ evaluation the Stanford investigator of the childhood of geniuses added appraisals of heredity, environmental factors, and ratings of personality traits (Cox, 1926). The results may with due caution be compared to the test results and ratings that make up the picture of the gifted children. The subjects of the genius study were 301 persons

objectively rated among the 500 most eminent leaders of history and selected as adequately representing adult human distinction. The data from several thousand biographical works pertaining to the youth of these men, gathered into individual case studies, served as the basis for mental and personality trait ratings and evaluations of background and environment. Résumés of these materials are presented in the published study. Three experienced psychologists rated the items concerning mental behavior on an IQ scale, adding also in each case an appraisal of the adequacy of the data for this purpose. The agreement of the series of ratings is indicated by correlation coefficients of the order of .70. Two psychologists rated the environmental factors. One psychologist and one experienced teacher rated a series of personality traits for a representative third of the group. Tabulations of longevity and of fields of activity and a collection of early literary productions were also included in the published report.

The evidence of superior mental capacity in the subjects of this study is unequivocal. No individual, however meagerly reported by his biographers, was rated below average on the sum total of available childhood information. The three psychologists, advised to rate conservatively on the data alone, and as if the identity of the child were not known, found sufficient indication of superior intelligence to justify the conclusion that the group average IQ lies well within the gifted range. Ratings below 140 IQ resulted from regression of estimate when the data were too few for self-corroboration, or when they were of a sort as yet not adequately indexed in IQ terms (Table 10). Data evaluated as equal in reliability to an abbreviated Stanford-Binet test consisting of as many as two items per year-group gave an average IQ of 152. When the data reached the reliability of a Stanford-

TABLE 10

Scale of IQ Ratings of Geniuses in Childhood and Youth Indicating Increase of Rating as a Function of Completeness of the Data *

	Average IQ	Relative Coefficient
134 case studies with data equal to ⅟₁₂ to ½ test item per year group	124	.29
32 case studies with data equal to ¾ test item per year group	139	.53
54 case studies with data equal to 1 test item per year group	142	.60
41 case studies with data equal to 2 test items per year group	152	.75
13 case studies with data equal to 3 test items per year group	171	.82

* Based on data in Table 8, p. 53, and Table 18, p. 76, C. M. Cox, *Genetic Studies of Genius*, Vol. II, *The Early Mental Traits of Three Hundred Geniuses*, Stanford University Press, 1926. By permission of the publisher.

Binet test of three items per year-group, the average IQ was 171. Psychological and statistical considerations indicated that if all the facts were available for the genius group the average rating would well exceed 160.

Wide individual differences were present in the mental scores of the members of the group as a whole and even in the smaller numbers of the more completely recorded cases. It was not possible to conclude that a high, narrow IQ range accounted for all. Men eminent as soldiers showed least conclusively the childhood behavior associated with high mental test ratings; yet a fairly satisfactory appraisal of their probable average IQ registered above 140. Adequately reported artists and musicians averaged 160; statesmen and imaginative writers, 165; religious leaders and prose writers, 170; scientists, 175; and philosophers, 180. The lowest uncorrected, individual appraisals based on material sufficient for a single, relatively dependable IQ estimate (reliability coefficient .75) were at 135, the highest reached 200. Among the estimates based on more complete and, hence, for this purpose more reliable material were those for John Quincy Adams, 165; Pope and Chatterton, 170; Coleridge, 175; Voltaire and Macaulay, 180; Grotius, J. S. Mill, and Leibnitz, 190; and Goethe, 200. IQ values statistically corrected to offset the error due to brevity in the records gave Darwin, Scott, and Mozart IQ's of 165; Longfellow, Luther, and Faraday, 170; Agassiz and Kant, 175; Dickens and Hume, 180; Davy and Galileo, 185; Berkeley and William Pitt, 190. The correlation between IQ and the rank order of eminence in the group as a whole was low. Eminence in terms of illustrious achievement qualifying for this particular group, although associated with superior intelligence, was therefore not demonstrably a function of the high IQ as estimated. Other traits or circumstances generally rather obviously accounted for the presence of the intellectually lower-scoring members of the group, for the occasional low scores of some who probably deserve much higher ratings, and for the low eminence ratings of a few whose IQ's were found equal to the highest ever reported. The author was of the opinion that even the statistically corrected values were in many cases too low to serve as fully satisfactory measures of these rare intellects. Yet the purpose of the study had been served in bringing to light the levels of intelligence which had been exceeded by the illustrious, as indicated even in the often scanty reports of their early achievement.

Ratings of the fathers' occupations showed the trends of superior heredity and the advantages of background available to the geniuses; 80 per cent of the fathers belonged to Taussig's two upper economic classes. Ratings of home training and discipline of a representative third of the group averaged two steps higher than the assumed norm on a seven-step scale. Breadth, intensity, and kind of interests also proved superior to the assumed mean for children of equal mental age. Intellectual interests, intensity of a single interest, and breadth of interrelated interests rated especially high. Social and activity interests showed a slight negative correlation with the intelligence rating.

Sixty-seven character traits defined by Webb (1915) were made the basis of a personality profile of 100 of the more fully reported geniuses. Ratings considerably above average for the group as a whole were found (1) in four emotional traits: cheerfulness, imaginativeness, esthetic feeling, and excitability; (2) in three emotional-social traits: family affection, friendship, and loyalty; (3) in eleven social traits: fondness for a small circle of intimate friends, impulsive kindness, kindness on principle, trustworthiness, conscientiousness, desire to be liked, sense of corporate responsibility, sense of justice, religious interest, pure-mindedness, wideness and intensity of influence; (4) in two physical activity traits: energy or restlessness and physical bravery; (5) in all of the five positive self-traits: desire to excel, desire to be a leader, adequate self-confidence, self-esteem, and esteem of his own special talents; (6) in eleven intellectual traits: absence of suggestibility, degree to which action and thought are dependent on reason, keenness of observation, attention to detail, extent of mental work bestowed on studies and on special interests, soundness of common sense, originality and creativeness, strength of memory, quickness and profoundness of apprehension; (7) in four traits of persistence: degree to which he works with distant objects in view, degree of will and perseverance, tendency not to abandon tasks in the face of obstacles, or from mere changeability; (8) in balance; and (9) in strength or force of character as a whole. In Table 11 the personality traits are listed in which the geniuses are as distinguished or more so than they are in terms of their superior mental ability. In these traits they rate as a group at or above +1.5 on a seven-point scale in which 0 represents the mean and +3 the upper limit.

The conclusions from the data for geniuses support the view that good heredity and good home training are valuable assets for mature achievement and that superior interests are a basis of desirable stimulation. The youths in the genius group were probably without exception endowed with high, many of them with the highest, intellectual capacity of which human beings are capable. All of them had the capacity and the opportunity to develop motivation of a rarely superior order. The composite in their personalities of intellectual and emotional traits was so integrated and functioned so dynamically as to produce original, creative achievement in science, art, literature, philosophy, religion, or statesmanship. If leaders like these appear from among our gifted children they will probably also be found to possess not only high, often the highest, intellectual capacity, but also superior traits of personality, especially motivating power. Moreover, like these geniuses, they will no doubt benefit optimally from whatever favorable circumstances may enhance the effectiveness of their developing capacities.

The mental and physical health in childhood of fifty representative and well-reported members of this same group of geniuses and illustrious persons was rated and reported on by Miles and Wolfe in 1936. The mean physical health ratings showed 12 per cent of the group above average, 58 per cent average, 28 per cent somewhat below average, and 2 per cent with definitely frail health. In mental health 14 per cent were rated above average, 64 per cent at the average, 14 per

TABLE 11

HIGH PERSONALITY TRAIT RATINGS OF ONE
HUNDRED GENIUSES IN CHILDHOOD*

(Ratings are averages of two raters on a
seven-point scale, +3 to −3, when 0 is the
assumed average of the general child population.)

Intellectual Traits:

Mental work devoted to routine studies	1.7
Independence of thought	1.8
Keenness of observation	1.9
Strength of memory	2.0
Quickness of apprehension	2.0
Originality, creativeness	2.1
Profoundness of apprehension	2.3
Mental work devoted to special pursuits	2.4

Social Traits:

Trustworthiness	1.7
Conscientiousness	1.7
Wideness of influence	1.7
Intensity of influence on intimates	2.0

Self-traits and Motivation:

Desire to be a leader, to impose his will	1.7
Correctness of his own self-appraisal	1.7
Correctness of self-appraised special talents	2.0
Belief in his own powers	2.0
Force of character as a whole	2.0
Devotion of effort toward distant goals	2.0
Strength of will in perseverance	2.3
Persistence in the face of obstacles	2.3
Steadfastness of effort	2.5
Desire to excel in efforts	2.6

* Data from Table 49, C. M. Cox, *Genetic
Studies of Genius*, Vol. II, *The Early Mental
Traits of Three Hundred Geniuses*, Stanford
University Press, 1930. By permission of the
publishers.

cent as showing mental or emotional weakness, and 8 per cent with considerable or
serious mental or emotional weakness. In a
single case, that of Chatterton, definite emotional disorganization was clearly present,
leading at a young age to suicide. Equated
with Olson's Schedule B of mental health
for children, the ratings of the fifty geniuses
show a similar distribution of percentages
reaching or exceeding a certain point on
the scale (Table 12). In spite of the differences in method of arriving at the results compared in the table, there is a fair
agreement between them, and it may be
concluded therefore that the mental health
of this representative group of the illustrious was on the average no less satisfactory than that of unselected school children today. A relationship subtle or otherwise between genius and insanity is not
indicated by this particular comparison.

The apparent contradiction between
these results and the conclusions of Lombroso, Lange-Eichbaum, and others who
have found mental peculiarity or psychopathy a characteristic of their geniuses is
discussed by Miles and Wolfe. The conclusion is reached that the disagreement
among investigators regarding the relationship of genius and psychopathy or insanity is largely due to the definition of
the term. Many imaginative geniuses have
been unstable emotionally. Men of action,
on the other hand, have less often shown
psychopathic traits. White (1930) had arrived at a similar conclusion from a study
of the adult careers of the entire group of
Cox's geniuses.

Gifted Children and Genius

Human beings differ with respect to
traits and trait constellations. Both capacities and accomplishments are subject
to quantitative and to qualitative measurement, and superiority may therefore be of
either kind. Economic necessity generally
calls for quantity, cultural progress for
quality. Objective psychological measurement has differentiated primarily capacities. Evaluation of products is an interpretative function. The correlation be-

TABLE 12

MENTAL HEALTH RATINGS BY C. C. MILES AND L. S. WOLFE OF 50 GENIUSES IN CHILDHOOD COMPARED WITH THE RATINGS REPORTED BY W. C. OLSON OF 798 PRIMARY SCHOOL BOYS

	Below Average				Average				Above Average	
Subjective mental health scale	2	2.5	3	3.5	4	4.5	5	5.5	6	6.5	7
Rating on Olson's Schedule B	116	99		82		73	69	66		48	
Percentage of Olson's cases at or above a given percentage	98	91		72		59	52	45		5	
Percentage of 50 geniuses at or above a given scale point	100	98		82		62	56	40		16	

tween capacity and accomplishment has been assumed to be high. Measures or indices of one have often been accepted as satisfactory substitutes for the other. Recent psychological study attempts the difficult task of comparing capacity with accomplishment. The multiple measurable factors are analyzed in each by the method of intercorrelation.

Gifted children selected on the basis of early test performance represent a capacity group. Geniuses selected on the basis of past careers constitute an accomplishment group. Both are superior human specimens deviating exceptionally from the average. The problem of correlation between the factors contributing to the superiority of these two groups and between the traits of the personalities qualifying for membership in each can be approached only indirectly through descriptive comparisons. Such comparisons can give no final answers. They may, however, clear up certain misconceptions, define the problems more precisely, and throw some light on the larger relationships. Perhaps we may better understand what gifted children are and what is meant by genius if we attempt some consideration of their similarities and differences.

The term *genius* is popularly applied to a human being when he has accomplished altogether original creative work of the highest quality, such as is recognized as extraordinary in some valued field of human enterprise. The genius has been most often identified in the arts and in scientific discovery, because here individual origination and independent creation were most obvious. Political leadership has sometimes been recognized as possessing the individual quality essential to genius. Originally restricted to a few fields, the term has been used more and more to designate the individuals endowed with the power for whatever extraordinary feats the culture of the period chose to value as most significant.

In the early development of the genius concept the extraordinary accomplishment was attributed not to human capacity but to divine inspiration. This was the mystical or supernatural theory of genius. Its significance is idealistic and religious; its basis is emotional. It persists even at the present day, though its objects are generally historically remote. It has, unfortunately for the scientific use, tinged the word *genius* emotionally and subjectively, while popularly and poetically emphasizing in a desirable way the high value of original creative activity. The repudiation by some psychologists of the use of the term *genius* or *near-genius* as applied to gifted children may originate in the experience of contrast when elementary school boys and girls, even the brightest of them, are compared with the idealized characters whom we identify as the great men of history (Lange-Eichbaum, 1928, 1931).

While poets and popular philosophers perpetuated the subjective interpretation of genius, scientists attempted to objectify the picture. The rationalists said genius can be developed through training, but it will be recognized as genius only if it is expressed in production at the right time and place. The sociologists further developed this view, emphasizing environmental influences in the development of the product of genius and in the readiness of the world to accept it (Ward, 1906). Social conditions, they said, not individual accomplishments, are responsible for works of genius. Men of ordinary gifts may, according to this hypothesis, become leaders and be acclaimed as great. This view valuably emphasized the importance of social influences for the development of superior achievements, and in this it is amply supported by results from the studies of gifted children. However, the further conclusion that great leaders are men of mediocre capacity has not been substantiated by scientific evidence at least with respect to intelligence, although it does appear to be true that a rather wide range of superior ability is represented in the world's leadership group (Cox, 1926).

The contributions of clinical psychiatry include the various explanations of genius as abnormal personality function. The attempts to relate genius to insanity have classical roots and show also the influence of the subjective, unique quality interpretation. Pathological material especially available in the biographies of literary geniuses has given support to these efforts. The psychoanalysts belong to the clinical group in their identification of genius as a neurosis or as a compensatory reaction. A valuable contribution from the psychiatric point of view is in the emphasis on the total dynamic function of the personality with its complex factors and deeply conditioned impulses (Reid, 1911–1912; Witty and Lehman, 1930; Schott, 1931).

The relatively small number of insane geniuses in representative groups of the illustrious suggests that the relationship between genius and mental abnormality has been exaggerated (White, 1930). Also the fact that among gifted children, who, however, may not especially include those with subjective and creative gifts, mental as well as physical health has generally rated above the average seems to point in the same direction (Burks, Jensen, and Terman, 1930). It is not known whether this is simply the result of a sound mental hygiene in superior families or a consequence of the repression of subjective factors by the more intelligent children, or a consequence of unintentional exclusion from the studies of psychopathic gifted children.

That many geniuses have shown eccentric traits has been mentioned by Ellis, Galton, and others. How much more eccentric they were than average men has never been stated exactly. The eccentricities of the great have always been of interest to people of lesser accomplishment, and they may be more often reported or weighted with more serious consideration than those of the generality. The evidence from the childhood of eminent men fails to support the view of frequent idiosyncrasy except in the subjective, sensitive individuals already mentioned. Among the gifted children queerness and peculiarity are infrequent. Deviation from the typical, mentally healthy average is not regarded with favor by parents and teachers today. Capable self-control is the popular ideal, and children are encouraged not to be "different." The children who have shown unfavorable emotional developments have not been those among whom later distinction seemed probable (Witty, 1940b).

Genius as Most Superior Native Ability

The position of genius at the top level on a scale of ability was first suggested by Galton. His theoretical ability scale, constructed according to the requirements of the normal probability curve, differentiated levels of competence from the lowest (idiocy) to the highest (the genius level) in terms of frequency of occurrence and the correlated statistical measures of deviation from the mean. Although superiority in scale terms was expressed as degree of achievement, Galton emphasized the native capacity factors which made the achievement possible. He devoted much careful research to the definition of scale points as indicators of the statistical frequency of mediocrity, superiority, and eminence, including the high level of distinction of the genius. The lowest level of eminence defined from historical and contemporary statistics of achievement he placed at a point on the scale beyond which not more than one individual in 4000 of the general adult population could rate. Position at this level Galton illustrated in the careers of successful English judges and bishops. Higher levels specifically defined included, first, men of great national reputation, each being as one in 79,000; and, second, the rare illustrious characters of history, who rank as one in a million or more, and include only men of the greatest, internationally recognized distinction. From the life histories of his highest ability groups Galton deduced the basic psychological traits of genius: superior ability, persistent and intense motivation, and great physical power for work. These traits he found in all, but he discovered that they differed in relative weight according to the field of eminent accomplishment.

Galton's ingenious scale is arbitrary and fallible, as are all methods of measuring achievement and capacity. Its merit lies in the application of statistical psychological techniques to the rating and equating of human ability and superiority and in its objectification of the native traits of men of genius as measurable quantities.

The traits of adult genius discovered by Galton have in a relatively recent study been found to characterize illustrious historical personalities in childhood (Cox, 1926). A high general level of accomplishment and versatility which suggested that achievement might have resulted for many in any one of several fields was mentioned by Galton and demonstrated by White (1931) from Cox's data.

Intelligence and ability tests have proved for many specific lines of mental capacity and accomplishment that Galton's theory of the normal distribution of human ability meets the criterion of present-day objective measurement. Terman's results in the study of gifted children show close agreement between the statistics for the distribution of intelligence at the highest levels and Galton's upper segments on the normal curve constructed in terms of the threefold native ability that constitutes "genius." Among Terman's gifted are not a few who possess besides high test intelligence also high motivation and great power for accomplishment. These are especially well represented in the 1940 success group. Had Galton's threefold criterion been applied in the original selection of the California gifted children, there would be statistical grounds for the expectation that somewhere near 4 per cent (about thirty individuals) of those chosen might qualify for classification at Galton's lowest eminence level, a small fraction of 1 per cent (one or two persons) at his second eminence level, but by reason of the relatively small numbers perhaps none at the level of the "illustrious."

In statistical terms the majority of Terman's group may be as far below the level of Galton's "eminence" as the average 100 IQ child is below the child rating at 120 IQ. We may recall that 4 or 5 per cent, but not generally more, 100 IQ children do sometimes later reach the 120 IQ level in test terms (Merrill, 1938), and this analogy may illustrate the possibility of a similar gain in status from a lower to a higher level on a general achievement or eminence scale. The 1940 report of Terman's success group gives reason to suppose that somewhere near the appropriate proportion of gifted boys, who are highly superior in motivation and energy as well as in intellect, are on their way to the levels of eminence corresponding to Galton's statistical prediction.

Contemporary psychology views personality at every level as vastly complex. Each individual is recognized to be the product of numerous constitutional elements mutually interacting, and at every stage in the course of their development variously stimulated by many combinations of environmental influences. Individual differences occur in every dimension involving every possible combination of the multiple external and internal factors and their relationships. Rare genius offers no exception, nor does the superior segment of intellectual capacity represented by the gifted children (Carmichael, 1934).

Measurement of the traits of superior human specimens offers as many problems today as in the past. The proof, accumulated through many series of studies, of the importance of hereditary factors in the production of superior individuals is generally accepted today. The evidence of environmental influences and of the acquisition or modification of traits through external pressure or stimulation is also profoundly convincing.

Recent study in all the biological sciences including psychology has emphasized the importance in growth and experience of changes of developmental rates and the consequent need for very complete analyses and appraisals of total personality units and total social backgrounds before even conservative predictions of probable later achievement can safely or wisely be made. The rate changes themselves offer important foci for experimental research. Another line of investigation has indicated that the traits, factors, and skills combined in the effective individual personality are not all of equal present strength or potential vitality. Various divergent weightings of the usual factors, rather than an undifferentiated level of traits, are not uncommon. Multiple analysis gives relatively exact expression to the higher interrelationships of certain factors, such as the intellectual, and the lower intercorrelations of these with artistic or manual skills essential in many kinds of creative work. Traits and series of abilities may vary in strength within the individual gifted child or the genius as in the average person, and so the personality patterns of gifted children or of geniuses may offer contrasts even when some total unitary psychological or social measure or score suggests equality. Group studies have proved the group superiority of gifted children. Individual clinical developmental studies of gifted individuals when accumulated in sufficient numbers may indicate the best points of attack for further group studies of those subgroups of the gifted and other superior children who are most likely to become adult leaders. They may also indicate in greater detail and with increasing reliability the environmental influences which hinder or help the realization of potential human ability.

Bibliography

ADAMS, F., and W. BROWN. 1930. *Teaching the bright pupil.* New York : Holt.

ADAMS, F. J. 1940. College degrees and elementary school intelligence quotients. *J. Educ. Psychol.,* **31,** 360–368.

ALLTUCKER, M. M. 1924. Is the pedagogically accelerated student a misfit in the senior high school? *Sch. Rev.,* **32,** 193–202.

ALPERN, H. 1939. Educating the superior student in the high schools of New York City. *J. Educ. Psychol.,* **13,** 112–119.

ATKINS, H. A. 1929. The gifted child and his teachers. *Ment. Hyg., N. Y.,* **13,** 719–739.

AUSTIN, M. 1925. *Everyman's genius.* Indianapolis : Bobbs Merrill.

BAER, M. V. 1939. How St. Louis schools serve their bright pupils. *Nat. Educ. Ass. J.,* **28,** 121.

BAISCH, H. 1939. Wahrsinn oder Wahnsinn der Genius? *Beih. Z. angew. Psychol.,* No. 85.

BAKER, H. J. 1927. *Characteristic differences in bright and dull pupils.* Bloomington, Ill. : Public School Publishing Co.

BALDWIN, B. T. 1924. Methods of selecting superior or gifted children. *Yearb. Nat. Soc. Stud. Educ.,* 23(I), 25–47.

BALDWIN, B. T., and T. D. WOOD. 1923. *Weight-height-age tables.* (Tables for boys and girls of school age.) Washington, D. C., American Child Health Association.

BAUMGARTEN, F. 1930. *Wunderkinder. Psychologische Untersuchungen: VIII.* Leipzig : Barth.

BECKHAM, A. S. 1942. A study of social background and music ability of superior Negro children. *J. Appl. Psychol.,* **26,** 210–217.

———. 1942. A study of social background and art aptitude of superior Negro children. *J. Appl. Psychol.,* **26,** 777–784.

BENTLEY, J. E. 1937. *Superior children.* New York : Norton.

BERKHAN, O. 1910a. Otto Pöhler, das frühlesende Braunschweiger Kind. *Z. Kinderforsch.,* **15,** 166–171.

———. 1910b. Das Wunderkind Christian Heinrich Heineken. *Z. Kinderforsch.,* **15,** 225–229.

BERMAN, A. B., and A. KLEIN. 1942. A personality study of maladjusted pupils of superior mentality. *High Points,* **24,** 57–63.

BESSEN, M. 1934. *Suggestibility of normal and abnormal school children.* Unpublished Master's Thesis, Columbia University.

BINET, A. 1909. La psychologie artistique de Tade Styka. *Année psychol.,* **15,** 316–356.

BLAIR, G. M. 1938. Mentally superior and inferior children in the junior and senior high school ; a comparative study of their backgrounds, interests and ambitions. *Teach. Coll. Contr. Educ.,* No. 766.

BOODSTEIN, O. 1909. Frühreife Kinder. *Psychologische Studie.* (*Beitr. Kinderforsch. u. Heilerziehung,* **61.**) Langansalza, Beyer.

BRAUN, O. 1920. *Aus den nachgelassenen Schriften eines Frühvollendeten.* (Ed. by J. VOGELSTEIN.) Berlin : Cassirer.

BRIDGEMAN, D. S. 1930. Success in college and business. *Person. J.,* **9,** 1–19.

BRIDGMAN, A. S. 1938. *My valuable time.* Brattleboro, Vt. : Stephen Daye Press.

BROWN, A. W. 1926. The unevenness of the abilities of dull and bright children. *Teach. Coll. Contr. Educ.,* No. 220.

BRUCE, J. A. 1911. New ideas in child training. *Amer. Mag.,* **72,** 286–294.

———. 1912. Lightning calculators. *McClure's Mag.,* **39,** 586–596.

BRUNER, H. B. (Ed.) 1941. Some issues and problems raised by the Conference on Education for the Gifted. *Teach. Coll. Rec.,* **42,** 432–460.

BUCKLEY, T. A. 1853. *The dawnings of genius.* London : Routledge.

BURKS, B. S. 1925. A scale of promise and its application to 71 nine-year-old gifted children. *Ped. Sem.,* **32,** 389–413.

BURKS, B. S., D. W. JENSEN, and L. M. TERMAN. 1930. *Genetic studies of genius:* Vol. III. *The promise of youth; follow-up studies of a thousand gifted children.* Stanford University, Calif. : Stanford University Press.

BURNSIDE, L. H. 1942. Psychological guidance of gifted children. *J. Consult. Psychol.,* **6,** 223–228.

———. 1942. An experimental program in the education of the intellectually gifted adolescent. *School Rev.,* **50,** 274–285.

BUSH, A. D. 1914. Binet-Simon tests of a thirty-nine-month-old child. *Psychol. Clinic,* **7,** 250–257.

CARMICHAEL, L. 1934. The psychology of genius. *Phi Kappa Phi J.,* 149–164.

CARROLL, H. A. 1930. Generalization of bright and dull children : A comparative study with special reference to spelling. *Teach. Coll. Contr. Educ.,* No. 439.

———. 1940. *Genius in the making.* New York : McGraw-Hill.

———. 1940–1941. Intellectually gifted children. *Teach. Coll. Rec.,* **42,** 212–227.

CARROLL, H. A., and L. S. HOLLINGWORTH. 1940. The systematic error of Herring-Binet in rating gifted children. *J. Educ. Psychol.,* **21,** 1–11.

CATTELL, J. McK. 1915, 1917. Families of American men of science. *Pop. Sci. Mo.,* **86,** 504–515 ; *Sci. Mo.,* **4,** 248–262 ; **5,** 368–378.

———. 1927. The origin and distribution of scientific men. *Science,* **66,** 513–516.

CATTELL, P. 1933. Do the Stanford-Binet IQ's of superior boys and girls tend to decrease or increase with age? *J. Educ. Res.,* **26,** 668–673.

CLEVELAND, E. 1920. Detroit's experiment with gifted children. *Sch. and Soc.*, **12**, 179–183.

——. 1921. Some further studies of gifted children. *J. Educ. Res.*, **4**, 195–199.

COBB, M. V., and L. S. HOLLINGWORTH. 1925. The regression of siblings of children who test at or above 135 IQ (Stanford-Binet). *J. Educ. Psychol.*, **16**, 1–7.

COBB, M. V., and G. A. TAYLOR. 1924. Standard achievement tests with a group of gifted children. *Yearb. Nat. Soc. Stud. Educ.*, 23 (I), 275–289.

COHEN, H. L., and N. G. CORYELL. 1935. *Educating superior students*. New York: American Book.

COHLER, M. J. 1941. Scholastic status of achievers and nonachievers of superior intelligence. *J. Educ. Psychol.*, **32**, 603–610.

COLLMANN, R. D. 1931. The psychogalvanic reactions of exceptional and normal school children. *Teach. Coll. Contr. Educ.*, No. 469.

CONKLIN, A. M. 1940. Failures of highly intelligent pupils; a study of their behavior by means of a control group. *Teach. Coll. Contr. Educ.*, No. 792.

COX, C. M. 1926. *Genetic studies of genius:* Vol. II, *The early mental traits of three hundred geniuses*. Stanford University, Calif.: Stanford University Press.

COX, C. M. *See also* MILES, C. C.

COY, G. L. 1918. The mentality of a gifted child. *J. Appl. Psychol.*, **2**, 299–307.

——. 1923. The interests, abilities and achievements of a special class for gifted children. *Teach. Coll. Contr. Educ.*, No. 131.

——. 1930. The daily programs of thirty gifted children. *J. Genet. Psychol.*, **37**, 123–138.

DANIELSON, C. L. 1929. A study of the effect of a definite course of reading in general literature upon achievement in content subjects with children of superior mental ability. *J. Educ. Psychol.*, **20**, 610–621.

——. 1931. Special classes for highly endowed children. *4th Yearb. Psychol. Educ. Res. Div., Los Angeles City Schools*, 67–87.

DAVIDSON, H. A. 1904. The gift of genius. *J. Ped.*, **16**, 281–297.

DAVIDSON, H. H. 1943. *Personality and economic background; a study of highly intelligent children*. New York: King's Crown Press.

DAVIS, H. 1924. Personal and social characteristics of gifted children. *Yearb. Nat. Soc. Stud. Educ.*, 23(I), 123–144.

DEARBORN, W. F., and P. CATTELL. 1930. The intelligence and achievement of private-school pupils. *J. Educ. Psychol.*, **21**, 197–211.

DECANDOLLE, A. 1885. *Histoire des sciences et des savants depuis deux siècles*. Genève: Georg.

DEPARTMENT OF SUPERINTENDENCE. 1931. How elementary and secondary schools are meeting the needs of individual pupils. *Yearb. Nat. Educ. Ass.*, **9**, 107–146.

DEVOSS, J. C. 1925. Specialization of the abilities of gifted children. In L. M. TERMAN et al., *Genetic studies of genius:* Vol. I, *Mental and physical traits of a thousand gifted children*. Stanford University, Calif.: Stanford University Press.

DOLBEAR, K. E. 1912. Precocious children. *Ped. Sem.*, **19**, 461–491.

DOOLEY, L. 1916. Psychoanalytic studies of genius. *Amer. J. Psychol.*, **27**, 363–417.

DOWNES, F. E. 1912. Seven years with unusually gifted pupils. *Psychol. Clin.*, **6**, 13–18.

DRAG, F. L. 1941. The gifted child: A report of practices in California cities. *Calif. J. Elem. Educ.*, **10**, 8–28.

DRANSFIELD, J. E. 1933. Administration of enrichment to superior children in the typical classroom. *Teach. Coll. Contr. Educ.*, No. 558.

DUFF, J. F. 1929. Children of high intelligence: A follow-up inquiry. *Brit. J. Psychol.*, **19**, 413–439.

DUFF, J. F., and G. H. THOMSON. 1923. The social and geographical distribution of intelligence in Northumberland. *Brit. J. Psychol.*, **14**, 192–198.

DUROST, W. N. 1932. Children's collecting activity related to social factors. *Teach. Coll. Contr. Educ.*, No. 535.

DVORAK, A., and J. J. RAE. 1929. A comparison of the achievement of superior children in segregated and unsegregated first-grade classes. *Elem. Sch. J.*, **29**, 380–387.

DVORAK, H. D. 1923. The mental tests of a superior child. *Ment. Hyg., N. Y.*, **7**, 250–257.

EDUCATIONAL RECORDS BUREAU. 1940. 1939 fall testing program in independent schools. *Educ. Rec. Bull.*, No. 29.

——. 1943. 1942 fall testing program in independent schools. *Educ. Rec. Bull.*, No. 37.

ELLIS, H. 1904. *A study of British genius*. London: Hurst and Blackett.

ELLWOOD, M. 1938. A descriptive study of a gifted child. *Pittsb. Schs. Bull.*, No. 12, 169–173.

ENGLE, T. L. 1935. Achievements of pupils who have had double promotions in elementary school. *Elem. Sch. J.*, **36**, 185–189.

FENTON, N., and L. S. HOWARD. 1924. The challenge of the private school. *J. Educ. Res.*, **9**, 22–28.

FINCH, F. H., and H. A. CARROLL. 1932. Gifted children as high-school leaders. *J. Genet. Psychol.*, **41**, 476–481.

FOSTER, E. M., and E. H. MARTENS. 1938. Statistics of special schools and classes for exceptional children. (Biennial Survey of Education in the United States: 1934–1936, Vol. II, Chap. VI.) [*Bull. U. S. Dept. Interior*, 1937, No. 2 (advance pages).] Washington, D. C.: Government Printing Office.

FREEMAN, F. N. 1924. The treatment of the gifted child in the light of scientific evidence. *Elem. Sch. J.*, **24**, 652–661.

FRENCH, W. C. 1923. A plan of organization for taking care of bright pupils. *Elem. Sch. J.*, **24**, 103–108.

GALTON, F. 1869. *Hereditary genius.* London. (New ed., 1914.) New York: Macmillan.

GARRISON, C. G., A. BURKE, and L. S. HOLLINGWORTH. 1917. The psychology of a prodigious child. *J. Appl. Psychol.*, **1**, 101–110.

GARRISON, K. C. 1940. *The psychology of exceptional children.* New York: Ronald.

GARRISON, S. C., and G. M. PULLIAS. 1923. Bright children. *Psychol. Clin.*, **14**, 259–263.

GESELL, A. 1921. *Exceptional children and public school policy.* New Haven: Yale University Press.

GILLINGHAM, A. 1920. Superior children—their school progress. *J. Educ. Psychol.*, **11**, 327–347.

———. 1923. Educating the gifted child. *Amer. Rev.*, **1**, 401–412.

GODDARD, H. H. 1928. *School training of gifted children.* Yonkers-on-Hudson: World Book.

GOLDBERG, S. 1934. A clinical study of K, IQ 196. *J. Appl. Psychol.*, **18**, 550–560.

GOODENOUGH, F. L. 1926. Racial differences in the intelligence of school children. *J. Exp. Psychol.*, **9**, 388–397.

GRAHAM, B. G., *et al.* 1938. A descriptive study of a gifted child. *Pittsb. Schs. Bull.*, No. 12.

GRAY, H., and W. J. JACOMB. 1921. Size and weight in one hundred and thirty-six boarding school boys. *Amer. J. Dis. Child.*, **22**, 259–271.

GRAY, H. A. 1930. Some factors in the undergraduate careers of young college students. *Teach. Coll. Contr. Educ.*, No. 437.

GRAY, H. A., and L. S. HOLLINGWORTH. 1931. The achievement of gifted children enrolled and not enrolled in special opportunity classes. *J. Educ. Res.*, **24**, 255–261.

GRAY, W. S. 1942. Education of the gifted child: With special reference to reading. *Elem. Sch. J.*, **42**, 736–744.

GREENBERG, B. B. 1939. The education of the intellectually gifted. *J. Except. Child*, **5**, 101–109.

GROSZMANN, M. P. E. 1917. *The exceptional child.* New York: Scribner's.

GUTHRIE, L. G. 1907. Contributions from history and literature to the study of precocious children. *Lancet*, **173**, 1592–1596.

HAGGERTY, M. E. 1925. The incidence of undesirable behavior in public school children. *J. Educ. Res.*, **12**, 102–122.

HAHN, O. 1911. Eigenärtige Begabung eines Dreijährigen. *Z. pädag. Psychol.*, **12**, 291–292.

HARLEY, H. L. 1913. Physical status of the special class for bright children at the University of Pennsylvania summer session, 1912. *Psychol. Clin.*, **7**, 20–23.

HARTLAUB, G. F. 1930. *Der Genius im Kinde: Zeichunungen und Malversuche begabter Kinder.* Breslau: Hirt.

HARTSHORNE, H., and M. MAY. 1928. *Studies in deceit.* (2 vols.) New York: Macmillan.

HECK, A. O. 1930. Special schools and classes in cities of 10,000 and more in the United States. *U. S. Off. Educ. Bull.*, No. 7.

———. 1940. *The education of exceptionl children.* New York: McGraw-Hill.

HENMON, V. A. C., and F. O. HOLT. 1931. A report on the administration of scholastic aptitude tests. *Bull. Univ. Wis.*, No. 1786.

HENRY, T. S. 1920. Classroom problems in the education of gifted children. *Yearb. Nat. Soc. Stud. Educ.*, 19(II).

———. 1924. Annotated bibliography on gifted children and their education. *Yearb. Nat. Soc. Stud. Educ.*, 23(I), 389–443.

HERR, W. A. 1937. Junior high school accelerants and their peers in senior high school. *Sch. Rev.*, **45**, 186–195; 289–299.

HERSCHBERGER, M. 1931. *Follow-up of segregated and non-segregated gifted pupils in Pasadena.* Unpublished report.

High school methods with superior students, 1941. *Nat. Educ. Ass. Research Div. Bull.* 19, 155–197.

HILDRETH, G. 1938a. Characteristics of young gifted children. *J. Genet. Psychol.*, **53**, 287–311.

———. 1938b. The educational achievement of gifted children. *Child. Develpm.*, **9**, 365–371.

———. 1939. Comparison of early Binet records with college aptitude test scores. *J. Educ. Psychol.*, **30**, 365–371.

HILDRETH, G., and C. P. INGRAM. 1942. Selected references from the literature on exceptional children. *Elem. Sch. J.*, **42**, 688–705.

HINKLE, B. M. 1923. *The re-creating of the individual.* New York: Harcourt, Brace.

HINRICHSEN, O. 1939. Hochbegabung, Erfolg und psychische Krankheit. *Psychiat. neurol. Wschr.*, **41**, 239–242.

HIRSCH, N. D. M. 1931. *Genius and creative intelligence.* Cambridge: Sci-Art Publishers.

HIRSCH, W. 1896. *Genius and degeneration.* (Trans., 2d ed.) New York: Appleton.

HIRT, Z. I. 1922. A gifted child. *Train. Sch. Bull.*, **19**, 49–54.

HOLLINGWORTH, L. S. 1922. The subsequent history of E. *J. Appl. Psychol.*, **6**, 205–210.

———. 1926a. Musical sensitivity of children who test above 135 IQ (Stanford-Binet). *J. Educ. Psychol.*, **17**, 95–109.

———. 1926b. *Gifted children: Their nature and nurture.* New York: Macmillan.

———. 1927. Subsequent history of E; ten years after the initial report. *J. Appl. Psychol.*, **11**, 385–390.

———. 1930a. Do intellectually gifted children grow toward mediocrity in stature? *J. Genet. Psychol.*, **37**, 345–360.

HOLLINGWORTH, L. S. 1930b. Playmates for the gifted child. *Child Study,* **8,** 103–104.

——. 1931. The child of very superior intelligence as a special problem in social adjustment. *Ment. Hyg., N. Y.,* **15,** 3–16.

——. 1935. The comparative beauty of the faces of highly intelligent adolescents. *J. Genet. Psychol.,* **47,** 268–281.

——. 1936a. Some suggestions on scholarships. *Ind. J. Columbia Univ.,* **4,** 4.

——. 1936b. The Terman classes at Public School 500. *J. Educ. Sociol.,* **10,** 86–90.

——. 1936c. Development of personality in highly intelligent children. *Yearb. Nat. Elem. Sch. Prin.,* **15,** 272–281.

——. 1936–1937. The founding of Public School 500. Speyer School: *Teach. Coll. Rec.,* **38,** 119–128.

——. 1938. An enrichment curriculum for rapid learners at Public School 500: Speyer School. *Teach. Coll. Rec.,* **39,** 296–306.

——. 1939a. Problems of relationship between elementary and secondary schools in the case of highly intelligent pupils. *J. Educ. Sociol.,* **13,** 90–102.

——. 1939b. What we know about the early selection and training of leaders. *Teach. Coll. Rec.,* **40,** 575–592.

——. 1940. Review of research. *Yearb. Nat. Soc. Stud. Educ.,* 39(I), 43–66.

——. 1942. *Children above 180 IQ, Stanford-Binet.* New York: World Book.

HOLLINGWORTH, L. S., and M. V. COBB. 1928. Children clustering at 165 IQ and children clustering at 145 IQ compared for three years in achievement. *Yearb. Nat. Soc. Stud. Educ.,* 27(II), 3–33.

HOLLINGWORTH, L. S., and H. A. GRAY. 1930. Juvenile achievement as related to size. *Teach. Coll. Rec.,* **32,** 236–244.

HOLLINGWORTH, L. S., and R. M. KAUNITZ. 1934. The centile status of gifted children at maturity. *J. Genet. Psychol.,* **45,** 106–120.

HOLLINGWORTH, L. S., and J. E. MONAHAN. 1926. Tapping rate of children who test above 135 IQ (Stanford-Binet). *J. Educ. Psychol.,* **17,** 505–518.

HOLLINGWORTH, L. S., and M. M. RUST. 1937. Application of the Bernreuter inventory of personality to highly intelligent adolescents. *J. Psychol.,* **4,** 287–293.

HOLLINGWORTH, L. S., and G. A. TAYLOR. 1924. Size and strength of children who test above 135 IQ. *Yearb. Nat. Soc. Stud. Educ.,* 23(I), 221–237.

HOLLINGWORTH, L. S., L. M. TERMAN, and M. ODEN. 1940. The significance of deviates. *Yearb. Nat. Soc. Stud. Educ.,* 39(I), 43–92.

HORN, E. 1924. The curriculum for the gifted: Some principles and an illustration. *Yearb. Nat. Soc. Stud. Educ.,* 23(I), 73–89.

HORN, J. L. 1924. *The education of exceptional children.* New York: Century.

JENKINS, M. D. 1936. A socio-psychological study of Negro children of superior intelligence. *J. Negro Educ.,* **5,** 175–190.

——. 1943. Case studies of Negro children of Binet IQ 160 and above. *J. Negro Educ.,* **12,** 159–166.

JENSEN, D. W. 1927. The gifted child. *J. Educ. Res.,* **15,** 34–35; 126–133; 198–206.

JOHNSON, H. G. 1942. Does the gifted child have a low AQ? *J. Educ. Res.,* **36,** 91–99.

JOHNSON, O. J. 1923. Teacher's judgments of qualities of gifted pupils as related to classroom activities. *Sch. and Soc.,* **17,** 466–469.

JOHNSON, W. B., and L. M. TERMAN. 1940. Some highlights in the literature of psychological sex differences published since 1920. *J. Psychol.,* **9,** 327–336.

JONES, A. M. 1925. An analytical study of one hundred and twenty superior children. *Psychol. Clin.,* **16,** 19–76.

JONES, V. A., and W. A. McCALL. 1926. Application of two techniques in evaluating some policies of dealing with bright children. *Teach. Coll. Rec.,* **27,** 825–835.

KELIHER, A. V. 1931. A critical study of homogeneous grouping. *Teach. Coll. Contr. Educ.,* No. 452.

KENWORTHY, M. E. 1928. Some emotional problems seen in the superior child. *Amer. J. Psychol.,* **4,** 3.

KERSCHENSTEINER, G. 1905. *Die Entwicklung der zeichnerischen Begabung.* Munich: Gruber.

KEYS, N. 1935. Adjustment of under-age students in high school. *Psychol. Bull.,* **32,** 539.

——. 1940. The value of group test IQ's for prediction of progress beyond high school. *J. Educ. Psychol.,* **31,** 81–93.

KIK, C. 1909. Die übernormale Zeichenbegabung bei Kindern. *Z. angew. Psychol.,* **2,** 92–149.

KRAMER, F., and W. STERN. 1908. Psychologische Prüfung eines elfjährigen Mädchens mit besonderer mnemotechnischer Fähigkeit. *Z. angew. Psychol.,* **1,** 291–312.

KRETSCHMER, E. 1931. *The psychology of men of genius.* (Trans. by R. B. CATTELL.) New York: Harcourt, Brace.

KYTE, G. C. 1924. Two types of experimental programs in the education of gifted children. *Yearb. Nat. Educ. Ass., Dept. Elem. Sch. Prin.,* **3,** 395–430.

LÄMMERMANN, H. 1931. Ueber das Verhältnis von Allgemein- und Sonderbegabung und seine Bedeutung für eine organisatorische Differenzierung der Schule. *Z. pädag. Psychol.,* **32,** 377–391.

LAMSON, E. E. 1930. A study of young gifted children in senior high school. *Teach. Coll. Contr. Educ.,* No. 424.

——. 1935. High school achievement of fifty-six gifted children. *J. Genet. Psychol.,* **47,** 233–238.

LANG, A. 1897. Genius in children. *No. Amer. Rev.*, **164**, 32–37.

LANGE-EICHBAUM, W. 1928. *Genie, Irrsinn und Ruhm.* Munich: Reinhardt.

——. 1931. *The problem of genius.* London: Kegan Paul.

LANGENBECK, M. 1915. A study of a five-year-old child. *Ped. Sem.*, **22**, 65–88.

LAYCOCK, S. R. 1933. Adjustments of superior and inferior school children. *J. Soc. Psychol.*, **4**, 353–366.

——. 1940a. Special classes for gifted children. *Understanding the Child*, **9**, 3–6.

——. 1940b. The mental hygiene of exceptional children. *J. Except. Children*, **6**, 244–250.

——. 1942. Helping the bright pupil. *School*, **30**, 561–565.

LAZAR, M. 1935. Reading interests, activities and opportunities of bright, average and dull children. *Teach. Coll. Contr. Educ.*, No. 707.

LEHMAN, B. H. 1928. *Carlyle's theory of the hero: Its sources, development, history, and influence on Carlyle's work.* Durham, N. C.: Duke University Press.

LEHMAN, H. C., and P. A. WITTY. 1927. The play behavior of fifty gifted children. *J. Educ. Psychol.*, **18**, 259–265.

LEWIS, W. D. 1940. A study of superior children in the elementary school. *Peabody Coll. Contr. Educ.*, No. 266.

——. 1941. A comparative study of the personalities, interests, and home backgrounds of gifted children of superior and inferior educational achievement. *J. Genet. Psychol.*, **59**, 207–218.

——. 1943. Some characteristics of very superior children. *J. Genet. Psychol.*, **62**, 301–310.

LINCOLN, E. A. 1933. Preliminary report on the Stanford-Binet IQ changes of superior children. *J. Exp. Educ.*, **1**, 287–292.

——. 1935a. A study of changes in the intelligence quotients of superior children. *J. Educ. Res.*, **29**, 272–275.

——. 1935b. The Stanford-Binet IQ changes of superior children. *Sch. and Soc.*, **41**, 519–520.

LINDLEY, E. H., and W. L. BRYAN. 1900. An arithmetical prodigy. *Psychol. Rev.*, **7**, 135.

LOMBROSO, C. 1891. *The man of genius.* London: Scott.

——. 1901. Determining of genius. *Monist*, **12**, 49–64.

LORGE, I., and L. S. HOLLINGWORTH. 1936. Adult status of highly intelligent children. *J. Genet. Psychol.*, **49**, 215–226.

MACMEEKEN, A. M. 1939. The intelligence of a representative group of Scottish children. *Publ. Scot. Coun. Res. Educ.*, No. 15.

MACMURRAY, D. 1937. A comparison of the intelligence of gifted children and of dull-normal children measured by the Pintner-Paterson Scale, as against the Stanford-Binet scale. *J. Psychol.*, **4**, 273–280.

MALHERBE, E. H. 1921. New measurements in private schools. *Survey*, **46**, 272–273.

MARTENS, E. H. 1933. Gifted children. Teachers' problems with exceptional children. *Pamphlet* 41 (II). Washington, D. C.: U. S. Office of Education.

MATEER, F. 1936. Clinical problems of bright children. *J. Educ. Soc.*, **10**, 91–99.

McCANDLESS, B. R. 1939. The effect of enriched educational experiences upon the growth of intelligence of very intelligent children. *Psychol. Bull.*, **36**, 628.

McELWEE, E. W. 1932. A comparison of the personality traits of 300 accelerated, normal, and retarded children. *J. Educ. Res.*, **26**, 31–34.

——. 1934. Seymour, a boy with 192 IQ. *J. Juv. Res.*, **18**, 28–35.

McGEHEE, W., and W. D. LEWIS. 1940. Parental attitudes of mentally superior, average and retarded children. *Sch. and Soc.*, **51**, 556–559.

MERRILL, M. A. 1938. The significance of IQ's on the revised Stanford-Binet scales. *J. Educ. Psychol.*, **29**, 641–651.

MERSAND, J. 1936. How should the teacher carry on work for the gifted child? *High Points*, **18**, No. 7, 42–50.

MILES, C. C. 1935. Sex in social psychology. In C. MURCHISON (Ed.), *A handbook of social psychology.* Worcester: Clark University Press.

MILES, C. C., and L. S. WOLFE. 1936. Childhood physical and mental health records of historical geniuses. *Psychol. Monogr.* (Dodge Commemorative Number), **47**, 390–400.

MILES, C. C. *See also* COX, C. M.

MITCHELL, F. D. 1907. Mathematical prodigies. *Amer. J. Psychol.*, **18**, 61–143.

MONAHAN, J. E., and L. S. HOLLINGWORTH. 1927. Neuromuscular capacity of children who test above 135 IQ (Stanford-Binet). *J. Educ. Psychol.*, **18**, 88–96.

MOREAU, P. 1891. Les enfants prodiges. *Ann. psychiat. et d'hypnol.*, 97–107.

MORT, P. R. 1939. Leadership in democratic living. *Teach. Coll. Rec.*, **40**, 561–564.

MORT, P. R., and F. G. CORNELL. 1938. Adaptability of public school systems. New York: *Teach. Coll. Bur. of Publ.*, Columbia University.

MUSSELMAN, J. W. 1942. Factors associated with the achievements of high school pupils of superior intelligence. *J. Exp. Educ.*, **11**, 53–68.

MYERS, G. C. 1935. The social problem of the gifted child. *J. Except. Child*, **2**, 39–43.

NATIONAL COMMITTEE ON COORDINATION IN SECONDARY EDUCATION. 1939. Education of gifted children in secondary schools. (Report adopted at Cleveland, Feb. 27, 1939.) *J. Educ. Sociol.*, **13**, 120–126.

NEMZEK, C. L. 1932. Constancy of the IQ's of gifted children. *J. Educ. Psychol.*, **23**, 607–610.

NEVILL, E. M. 1937. Brilliant children: With special reference to their particular difficulties. *Brit. J. Educ. Psychol.*, **7**, 247–258.

NEWLAND, T. E. 1941. The education of exceptional children: The mentally gifted. *Rev. Educ. Res.*, **11**, 277–287.

NISBET, J. F. 1891. *The insanity of genius.* London: Paul.

NOONAN, N., and D. E. NORRIS. 1938. Studies of gifted children. *J. Except. Child,* Jan. (extra issue), 46–56.

OLSON, W. C. 1930. *Problem tendencies in children: A method for their measurement and description.* Minneapolis: University of Minnesota Press.

ORLEANS, J. B. 1940. The gifted pupil at George Washington High School: A survey and a forecast. *High Points,* **22**, 17–42.

OSBURN, W. J., and B. J. ROHAN. 1931. *Enriching the curriculum for gifted children: A book of guidance for educational administrators and classroom teachers.* New York: Macmillan.

O'SHEA, M. V. 1911. Popular misconceptions concerning precocity in children. *Science,* **34**, 666–674.

OSTWALD, W. 1909. *Grosse Männer.* Leipzig: Akademische Verlagsgesellschaft.

PATRICK, M. L. 1924. Some attainments of gifted children in segregated classes at Louisville. *Yearb. Nat. Soc. Stud. Educ.,* 23(I), 262–274.

PEACHMAN, M. C. 1942. Attitudes: Their significance in education for the gifted. *J. Educ. Psychol.,* **33**, 83–98.

PETER, R., W. STERN, et al. 1919. Die Auslese befähigter Volksschüler in Hamburg. *Beih. Z. angew. Psychol.,* **18**.

PETZOLDT, J. 1911. Die Einwände gegen Sonderschulen für hervorragend Befähigte. *Neue Jahrb. Päd.,* **28**, 1–24.

PINTNER, R. 1931. *Intelligence testing: Methods and results.* (2d Ed.) New York: Holt.

POINCARÉ, H. 1914. *Science and method.* (Trans. by F. MAITLAND.) London: Nelson and Sons.

RACE, H. V. 1918. A study of a class of children of superior intelligence. *J. Educ. Psychol.,* **9**, 91–97.

REAVIS, W. C. 1924. The administration of the superior students in the University of Chicago High School. *Yearb. Nat. Soc. Stud. Educ.,* 23(I), 355–365.

REGENSBURG, J. 1926. Emotional handicaps to intellectual achievement in supernormal children. *Ment. Hyg., N. Y.,* **10**, 480–494.

———. 1931. Studies of educational success and failure in supernormal children. *Arch. Psychol., N. Y.,* **20**, No. 129.

REIBMAYR, A. 1908. *Die Entwicklungsgeschichte des Talents und Genies.* Munich: Lehmann.

REID, E. C. 1911–1912. Manifestations of manic-depressive insanity in literary genius. *Amer. J. Insan.,* **68**, 595–632.

REMMERS, H. H. 1930. Distinguished students: What they are and why. Studies in higher education, 15. *Bull. Purdue Univ.,* **31**, 2.

RÉVÉSZ, G. 1916a. *Erwin Nyiregyhazi: Psychologische Analyse eines musikalisch hervorragenden Kindes.* Leipzig: Veit.

———. 1916b. Das musikalische Wunderkind. *Z. pädag. Psychol.,* **19**, 29–34.

———. 1921. *Das frühzeitige Auftreten der Begabung und ihre Erkennung.* Leipzig: Barth.

RICHARDS-NASH, A. A. 1924. The psychology of superior children. *Ped. Sem.,* **31**, 209–246.

RIGG, M. 1938. A follow-up study of sixteen superior students. *Sch. and Soc.,* **48**, 411–412.

ROGERS, A. L. 1928. Educational guidance of pupils in private schools. *Private Sch. Teach. Ass., Phila.,* Pamphlet No. 3.

ROOT, W. T. 1921. A socio-psychological study of fifty-three supernormal children. *Psychol. Monogr.,* **29**, No. 133. Pp. 134.

RUSK, R. R. 1917. A case of precocity. *Child Study,* **10**, 21–27.

RUST, M. M. 1931. The effect of resistance on the intelligence scores of young children. *Child Develpm. Monogr.,* No. 6. Pp. xi + 80.

RYANS, D. G. 1939. An observation on the changes in variability of high, medium and low "intelligence" groups, etc. *J. Genet. Psychol.,* **54**, 467–470.

SANGUINET, E. H. 1929. What modifications in the technique of instruction should be made for superior children? *Educ. Admin. Supervis.,* **15**, 58–66.

SCHOENBECK, E. 1922. Die Begabten in deutschen Unterricht. *Prak. Psychol.,* **3**, 223–230.

SCHORN, M. 1928. Zur psychologie des frühbegabten Kindes. *Z. Psychol.,* **105**, 302–316.

SCHOTT, E. L. 1931. Superior intelligence in patients with nervous and mental illnesses. *J. Abnorm. Soc. Psychol.,* **26**, 94–101.

———. 1932. School maladjustment of some mentally superior patients in a psychiatric clinic. *Psychol. Clin.,* **21**, 202–207.

SCHUESSLER, H., and W. SCHWARZHAUPT. 1921. Die pädagogische und experimentell-psychologische Auslese der Begabten für die Übergangsklasse. *Z. pädag. Psychol.,* **22**, 188–195.

SCHUSTER, E. 1907. The promise of youth and the performance of manhood. *Eugen. Lab. Mem., London,* **3**.

SCOTTISH COUNCIL FOR RESEARCH IN EDUCATION. 1933. *The intelligence of Scottish children.* London: University London Press.

SCRIPTURE, E. W. 1891. Arithmetical prodigies. *Amer. J. Psychol.,* **4**, 1–59.

Sérouya, H. 1927. Eine frühreife philosophische Hochbegabung. *Z. angew. Psychol.,* 29, 236–238.

Shaer, I. 1913. Special classes for bright children in an English elementary school. *J. Educ. Psychol.,* 4, 209–222.

Shields, T. E. 1909. *The making and unmaking of a dullard.* Washington, D. C.: Catholic Education Press.

Shuttleworth, F. K. 1939. The physical and mental growth of girls and boys age six to nineteen in relation to age at maximum growth. *Monogr. Soc. Res. Child Develpm.,* 4, No. 3. Pp. vi + 291.

Simmons, R. McK. 1939. A study of a group of children of exceptionally high intelligence quotient in situations partaking of the nature of suggestion. *Teach. Coll. Contr. Educ.,* No. 788.

Slavin, J. S., and F. Griffith. 1942. Scholastic ratings of honor school pupils. *High Points,* 24, 35–43.

Specht, L. F. 1919. A Terman class in Public School No. 64, Manhattan. *Sch. and Soc.,* 9, 393–398.

Stedman, L. M. 1924. *Education of gifted children.* Yonkers-on-Hudson: World Book.

Stern, W. 1911. The supernormal child. *J. Educ. Psychol.,* 2, 143–149; 181–190.

——. 1918. Die Methode der Auslese befähigter Volksschüler in Hamburg. *Z. pädag. Psychol.,* 19, 132–142.

Street, R. F. 1937. The mentally superior child. *J. Except. Child,* 3, 83–86.

Stumpf, C. 1909. Akustische Versuche mit Pepito Arriola. *Z. angew. Psychol.,* 2, 1–11.

Sully, J. 1886. Genius and precocity. *Pop. Sci. Mo.,* 29, 469–482, 594–604.

Sumption, M. R. 1941. *Three hundred gifted children. A follow-up study of the results of special education of superior children.* Yonkers-on-Hudson: World Book.

Terman, L. M. 1904. A preliminary study in the psychology and pedagogy of leadership. *Ped. Sem.,* 11, 413–451.

——. 1905. A study of precocity and prematuration. *Amer. J. Psychol.,* 16, 145–183.

——. 1906. Genius and stupidity. *Ped. Sem.,* 13, 307–373.

——. 1915. The mental hygiene of exceptional children. *Ped. Sem.,* 22, 529–537.

——. 1916. *The measurement of intelligence.* Boston: Houghton Mifflin.

——. 1917. The IQ of Francis Galton in childhood. *Amer. J. Psychol.,* 28, 209–215.

——. 1918. An experiment in infant education. *J. Appl. Psychol.,* 2, 218–229.

——. 1919. *The intelligence of school children.* Boston: Houghton Mifflin.

——. 1922. A new approach to the study of genius. *Psychol. Rev.,* 29, 310–318.

——. 1924a. The conservation of talent. *Sch. and Soc.,* 19, 359–364.

Terman, L. M. 1924b. The physical and mental traits of gifted children. *Yearb. Nat. Soc. Stud. Educ.,* 23(I), 155–167.

——. 1931. The gifted child. In C. Murchison (Ed.), *A handbook of child psychology.* Worcester: Clark University Press.

——. 1939a. Educational suggestions for follow-up studies of intellectually gifted children. *J. Educ. Sociol.,* 13, 82–89.

——. 1939b. The gifted student and his academic environment. *Sch. and Soc.,* 49, 65–73.

——. 1940. Intelligence in a changing universe. *Sch. and Soc.,* 51, 465–470.

Terman, L. M., *et al.* 1925. *Genetic studies of genius:* Vol. I. *Mental and physical traits of a thousand gifted children.* Stanford University, Calif.: Stanford University Press.

Terman, L. M., and B. S. Burks. 1933. The gifted child. In C. Murchison (Ed.), *A handbook of child psychology.* (2d Ed.) Worcester: Clark University Press.

Terman, L. M., and J. M. Chase. 1920. The psychology, biology and pedagogy of genius. *Psychol. Bull.,* 17, 397–409.

Terman, L. M., and J. C. DeVoss. 1924. The educational achievements of gifted children. *Yearb. Nat. Soc. Stud. Educ.,* 23(I), 169–184.

Terman, L. M., and J. C. Fenton. 1921. Preliminary report on a gifted juvenile author. *J. Appl. Psychol.,* 5, 163–178.

Terman, L. M., and C. C. Miles. 1936. *Sex and personality.* New York: McGraw-Hill.

Terman, L. M., and M. Oden. 1940a. The significance of deviates: II. Status of the California gifted group at the end of sixteen years. *Yearb. Nat. Soc. Stud. Educ.,* 39(I), 67–74.

——. 1940b. The significance of deviates: III. Correlates of adult achievement in the California gifted group. *Yearb. Nat. Soc. Stud. Educ.,* 39(I), 74–89.

Theman, V., and P. A. Witty. 1943. Case studies and genetic records of two gifted Negroes. *J. Psychol.,* 15, 165–181.

Thomson, G. H. 1936. *Intelligence and civilisation.* Edinburgh: University Press.

Thorndike, E. L. 1939. How may we improve the selection, training, and life-work of leaders? *Teach. Coll. Rec.,* 40, 593–605.

——. 1941. Gifted children in small cities. *Teach. Coll. Rec.,* 24, 420–427.

Thorndike, R. L. 1939. Responses of a group of gifted children to the Pressey interest-attitude test. *J. Educ. Psychol.,* 30, 588–594.

——. 1940a. Constancy of the IQ. *Psychol. Bull.,* 37, 167–186.

——. 1940b. Performance of gifted children on tests of developmental age. *J. Psychol.,* 9, 337–343.

——. 1941. Problems in identification, description, and development of the gifted. *Teach. Coll. Rec.,* 24, 402–406.

Thorner, M. W., and G. H. J. Pearson. 1940.

Behavior disorders of intellectual origin occurring in childhood. *Amer. J. Dis. Child.*, **60**, 1245–1251.

THURSTONE, L. L., and T. G. THURSTONE. 1937. The 1936 psychological examination for college freshmen. *Educ. Rec.*, **18**, 252–273.

——. 1938. The 1937 psychological examination for college freshmen. *Educ. Rec.*, **19**, 209–234.

THURSTONE, L. L., T. G. THURSTONE, and D. C. ADKINS. 1939. The 1938 psychological examination. *Educ. Rec.*, **20**, 263–300.

TIEBOUT, H. M. 1943. The misnamed lazy student. *Educ. Rec.*, **24**, 113–129.

TONSOR, C. A. 1941. Failure in the bright school. *High Points*, **23**, 67–70.

TOOPS, H. A. 1928. The selection of graduate assistants. *Person. J.*, **6**, 457–472.

TRAXLER, A. E. 1940. What is a satisfactory IQ for admission to college? *Sch. and Soc.*, **51**, 462–463.

——. 1941. Comparison between IQ's on the new edition of the Kuhlmann-Anderson intelligence tests and Binet IQ's. *Educ. Rec. Bull.*, No. 31.

TROW, W. C. 1941. Who are the gifted? *Educ. Digest*, **7**, 17–20.

VALENTINER, T. 1911. Ein elfjähriger Humorist. *Säemann*, **4**, 218–227.

VAN ALSTYNE, D. 1923. A study of ten gifted children whose school progress was unsatisfactory. *J. Educ. Res.*, **8**, 122–135.

VAN WAGENEN, M. J. 1925. A comparison of the mental ability and school achievement of the bright and dull pupils in the sixth grade of a large school system. *J. Educ. Psychol.*, **16**, 186–192.

VARNER, G. F. 1922. Can teachers select bright and dull children? *J. Educ. Res.*, **6**, 126–132.

WADDLE, C. W. 1924. Case studies of gifted children. *Yearb. Nat. Soc. Stud. Educ.*, 23(I), 185–207.

WARD, L. F. 1906. *Applied sociology.* Boston: Ginn.

WARNER, M. L. 1930. Eugene, a brilliant boy who failed in school. *Psychol. Clin.*, **19**, 143–155.

WASHBURNE, C. W. 1924. The attainments of gifted children under individual instruction. *Yearb. Nat. Soc. Stud. Educ.*, 23(I), 247–261.

WEBB, E. 1915. Character and intelligence. *Brit. J. Psychol. Monogr. Suppl.*, **1**, No. 3. Pp. 99.

WHIPPLE, G. M. 1913. Supernormal children. In P. MONROE (Ed.), *Cyclopedia of Education*, Vol. V. New York: Macmillan. Pp. 464–467.

——. 1919. *Classes for gifted children: An experimental study of method of selection and introduction.* Bloomington, Ill.: Public School Publishing Co.

——. 1920. Some features of the education of gifted children. *Sch. and Soc.*, **12**, 175–179.

WHIPPLE, G. M. 1923. School provision for gifted children in the United States. *Nat. Conf. Soc. Work*, 399–404.

——. 1924. Education of gifted children: historical and introductory. *Yearb. Nat. Soc. Stud. Educ.*, 23(I), 124.

WHITE, R. K. 1930. Note on the psychopathology of genius. *J. Soc. Psychol.*, **1**, 311–315.

——. 1931. The versatility of genius. *J. Soc. Psychol.*, **2**, 460–489.

WHITE HOUSE CONFERENCE ON SPECIAL EDUCATION. 1931. *The handicapped and the gifted.* New York: Century.

WILKINS, W. L. 1936. High school achievement of accelerated pupils. *Sch. Rev.*, **44**, 268–273.

WILLIAMS, T. A. 1911. Intellectual precocity. *Ped. Sem.*, **18**, 85–103.

WITTE, K. 1914. *The education of Karl Witte.* (Trans. by L. WIENER.) New York: Crowell.

WITTY, P. A. 1930. A study of one hundred gifted children. *Univ. Kan. Bull. Educ., State T.C. Stud. Educ.*, **1**, No. 13.

——. 1934. The relative frequency of gifted boys and girls in the secondary school. *Educ. Adm. Supervis.*, **20**, 606–612.

——. 1936. Exploitation of the child of high intelligence quotient. *Educ. Meth.*, **15**, 298–304.

——. 1940a. A genetic study of fifty gifted children. *Yearb. Nat. Soc. Stud. Educ.*, 39 (II), 401–408.

——. 1940b. Contributions to the IQ controversy from the study of superior deviates. *Sch. and Soc.*, **51**, 503–508.

——. 1940c. Evidence regarding the nature of intelligence from the study of superior deviates. In *Addresses and Discussions Presenting the 39th Yearbook of the National Society for the Study of Education.* Salem, Mass.: Newcomb and Gauss.

WITTY, P. A., and M. D. JENKINS. 1936. Intra-race testing and Negro intelligence. *J. Psychol.*, **1**, 179–192.

WITTY, P. A., and H. C. LEHMAN. 1930. Nervous instability and genius: Some conflicting opinions. *J. Abnorm. Soc. Psychol.*, **24**, 486–497.

——. 1932. A study of the reading and reading interests of gifted children. *J. Genet. Psychol.*, **40**, 473–485.

WITTY, P. A., and V. THEMAN. 1943. A follow-up study of the educational attainment of gifted Negroes. *J. Educ. Psychol.*, **34**, 35–47.

WITTY, P. A., and L. WILKINS. 1933. The status of acceleration or grade skipping as an administrative practice. *Educ. Adm. Supervis.*, **19**, 321–346.

WOOD, E. P. 1929. The educational achievement and intelligence of independent school children. *Educ. Rec. Bull.*, No. 2.

WOODROW, H. 1919. *Brightness and dullness in children.* Philadelphia : Lippincott.

WOODS, E. L. 1917. Provision for the gifted child. *Educ. Adm. Supervis.,* **3,** 139–149.

——. 1929. Personality traits of children of superior intelligence in special classes and in regular classes. *3d Yearb. Psychol. Educ. Res. Div., Los Angeles City Schools,* No. 185, 102–109.

——. 1944. The mentally gifted. *Rev. Educ. Res.,* **14,** 224–230.

WOOLLEY, H. T. 1925. Agnes: A dominant personality in the making. *Ped. Sem.,* **32,** 569–598.

WRENN, C. G. 1935a. Aiding the fit. *J. Higher Educ.,* **6,** 357–363.

——. 1935b. Intelligence and the vocational choices of college students. *Educ. Rec.,* **16,** 217–219.

YATES, D. H. 1922. A study of some high school seniors of superior intelligence. *J. Educ. Res. Monogr.,* No. 2. Pp. 75.

YODER, A. H. 1894. The study of the boyhood of great men. *Ped. Sem.,* **3,** 134–156.

ZEIGEL, H., JR. 1927. Achievement of high school honor students in the University of Missouri. *Sch. and Soc.,* **25,** 82–84.

ZILLIG, M. 1929. Zur Psychologie des dichterischschaffenden Kindes. *Z. Psychol.,* **112,** 302–324.

ZORBAUGH, H. W. (Ed.). 1936. Gifted and talented children. *J. Educ. Soc.,* **10,** 65–128.

ZORBAUGH, H. W. 1940. How may the community utilize its gifted children? *Ment. Hyg., N. Y.,* **24,** 1–16.

ZORBAUGH, H. W., and R. K. BOARDMAN. 1936. Salvaging our gifted children. *J. Educ. Sociol.,* **10,** 100–108.

Chapter 19

PSYCHOLOGICAL SEX DIFFERENCES [1]

Lewis M. Terman

in association with

Winifred B. Johnson, George Kuznets, and Olga W. McNemar [2]

This chapter will deal almost exclusively with the literature that has appeared since 1920. Earlier contributions were excluded for several reasons, not the least of which is the fact that many of them have been repeatedly summarized in textbooks and special treatises. Apart from this, we were influenced by the fact that with few exceptions the early studies are unsatisfactory because of the use of questionable techniques, faulty samplings, or inadequate statistical presentation.

We have further limited our survey to quantitative data on subjects below the college age, although in special cases material is included from subjects above this age. As a rule we have excluded studies based on populations of less than fifty in each sex group or on even larger groups that were obviously biased samplings. However, we have sometimes used smaller num-

bers when larger were not available or when the investigation in question provided many observations or measures of each individual subject.

Even within the limits stated above, our survey can make no claim to completeness. We have not included cultures other than the Occidental or extended our search for material beyond available publications in English, German, and French. A vast majority of studies reviewed were published in America or Great Britain, where the Galtonian tradition has favored the objective and statistical approach to the study of human behavior.

The Physical Background of Sex Differences

Sex differences have been found for almost every physical variable, including body build, gross and fine anatomy, physiological functioning, and biochemical composition. Indeed, every cell in a human body bears the stamp of its sex. As this chapter is concerned primarily with psychological sex differences, it is necessary to confine our discussion of physical differences to those which would seem most likely to have correlates in the realm of psychological behavior. The reader who wishes to pursue the matter further may well begin with the excellent graphic and

[1] This chapter is part of a more extensive treatment of sex differences that was made possible by grants-in-aid from the Committee for Research on Problems of Sex, of the National Research Council.

[2] The associate authors carried out the search for data and prepared abstracts and summaries of the pertinent material as follows: Johnson for the sections on the physical background, conative behavior, social behavior, neurotic and emotional response, character traits, and cultural influences; Kuznets for the section on intellectual abilities; and McNemar for the section on interests. The final draft was written by the senior author. References were checked by McNemar.

954

pictorial atlas compiled by Shuttleworth 1938).

Among the physical traits in which sex differences might be expected to reflect themselves in psychological behavior are height, weight, body build, muscular strength, motor skills, vital capacity, and rate of maturation. One wonders what would happen to the sex temperaments as we now know them if these differences were reversed. Conceivably the reversal might have far-reaching effects upon the masculine and feminine rôles and upon social customs and social institutions generally. The probability of these effects' occurring is not negated by the sex overlap on physical traits or by the lack of clear-cut behavioral differences between the large and small or the strong and weak persons within a single sex. The significant fact is that the obvious central tendency toward male superiority in such traits as size, strength, and motor ability tends to set standard patterns of dominance, aggression, and energetic activity for all males and contrasting patterns for all females.

The considerations just mentioned, together with limitations of space, have led us to emphasize sex differences in central tendencies rather than the extent and frequency of sex overlap. There is no intention, however, to minimize the significance of overlap. Present-day concepts of sexuality no longer regard maleness and femaleness as mutually exclusive categories. Sex is not an all-or-none affair; masculinity and femininity are relative terms. The sex of an individual is determined in part by secondary endocrine factors as well as by primary genetic factors. These secondary factors are of such weight as to permit reversal of the genetic sex of domestic fowls (Crew, 1927) and of pigeons (Riddle, 1929) and to permit in human beings a variety of intermediate sexual conditions (Broster *et al.*, 1938). The biochemical forces which activate masculine and feminine behavior are in some degree present in both sexes. All males secrete estrogens and females, androgens; it is the difference in relative amount of these substances that gives to each sex its character (Evans, 1939). As someone has stated it, there are no men, there are no women; there are only sexual majorities.

The varying degrees of physical maleness or femaleness within a given sex may contribute materially to the sex overlap in psychological behavior. It has sometimes been taken for granted that such overlap is *prima facie* evidence of the influence of cultural patterns. Without minimizing cultural influences, we would point out the desirability of further research on the physical correlates of deviations from the sex norms of masculine or feminine behavior. Endocrine experimentation, as well as the characteristic behavior associated with hypogonadal conditions, suggests the influence of physical factors in deviations from the norm of masculine and feminine behavior. Among normal subjects a few low but fairly reliable correlations have been found between physical measures and masculinity-femininity scores on the Terman-Miles M-F test (Terman and Miles, 1936; Gilkinson, 1937). Sheldon (1940) claims to have found significant personality characteristics associated with masculinity and femininity of body build in male college students. Changes in personality in boys with hypogenitalism or adiposity have been reported when injections of testosterone were carried out over a period of months. There was an impression of increased aggressiveness shown by a detachment from the family group and a greater tendency to assertiveness (Marquis, 1940). Sollenberger (1940) found a close relationship between the amount of male sex hormone in the urine of adolescent boys and their maturity of interests and attitudes; in fact the correlations reported in this research are so high as to be suspect.

We turn next to a brief review of sex differences in specific physical variables.

Body Size. Mean weight of boys at birth exceeds that of girls by approximately 5 per cent. This superiority continues to about 11 years, then rapidly decreases. By age 14 the direction of difference is reversed and the mean for boys is around 5 per cent below that for girls. Not until 15 or 16 do boys regain their former position. By age 20 the mean superiority of males is in the neighborhood of 20 per cent.[1]

Mean body length is greater for boys than for girls from birth to about 11 years, the superiority in most of this range being only 1 or 2 per cent. From ages 11 to 14 boys are below girls in mean height, but the greatest difference in this direction is only about 2 per cent. Growth in height rapidly slows down for girls after 15 and almost ceases by 17. Height increase continues fairly rapid for boys to 17 or 18 years and usually does not cease until the early 20's, by which time male superiority amounts to something like 10 per cent.

Vital Capacity. Sex differences in vital capacity are greater than those for height or weight and may be more significant for behavior. Because vital capacity is one of the determiners of the sustained energy output which is possible for an individual, it may be one of the factors underlying sex differences in play interests, drive for achievement, and liking for activity and adventure. The superiority of boys in vital capacity is about 7 per cent by age 6, increases to 10 or 12 per cent at age 10, and to about 35 per cent at age 20. It is

[1] Physical sex differences vary more or less with race and nationality. Unless otherwise noted, the differences referred to in this chapter are for white subjects of predominately western European descent.

particularly significant that the *vital index* or the ratio between vital capacity and weight, is higher for boys at all ages for which measures have been made.

Strength. Muscular strength is another trait in which boys are superior to girls at all ages for which tests have been reported. In strength of grip of right hand the superiority of boys is about 10 per cent at age 7 and increases slowly to age 14. The curve for girls flattens at 16, that for boys about three years later. At age 18 the mean superiority of boys is about 50 to 60 per cent. Sex differences in strength of back and legs are correspondingly great and follow a similar course.

Rate of Maturation. Some of the most marked age shifts in the amount or direction of sex differences are largely functions of the more rapid physical maturation of girls. Maturational differences are especially conspicuous in gonadal functioning. Girls of all races precede boys on the average by twelve to twenty months in pubertal development, and their adolescent growth changes are correspondingly accelerated. In skeletal development girls are superior to boys at birth and increase this superiority at a fairly steady rate until growth is complete. At age 6 girls are a year more advanced in this respect than boys, at age 9 one and a half years, and at 13 about two years. Flory (1935) finds in girls a correlation of .637 ± .048 between age of first menstruation and skeletal-months ratings taken at age 11. Dentition also proceeds more rapidly with girls, but the sex difference here is less than for skeletal development (P. Cattell, 1928).

Sex Ratio and Viability. It is well known that human beings show an excess of male over female births (Parkes, 1926; Crew, 1927; Bakwin, 1929; Dublin and Lotka, 1936). The ratio differs with race, but is usually between 103 and 107 males to 100 females. For stillbirths the ratio is around 130 or 135, and for miscarriages it is almost 200. Data reported by Bakwin (1929) indicate that the sex ratio for mortality increases with improvement in general health conditions; that is, the more recent the figures and the more favorable the climatic and cultural conditions the greater the excess of female survivors. Females are more resistant to most infectious diseases. In the period of infancy (under one year) seventeen of the eighteen foremost causes of death given by the mortality statistics of the United States showed a mortality sex ratio markedly favoring girls. In childhood and adolescence the girl maintains her superior resistance. The exception at this period is tuberculosis, which shows twice as many female as male deaths in the age period 12 to 27 (Frank, 1933).

Stability of Bodily Function. There are a number of facts that suggest greater stability of bodily function in the male. For example, glandular imbalance is much more common in females, with the possible exception of pituitary disturbance (Rowe, 1928; Dublin and Lotka, 1936; Shuttleworth, 1938). Glandular obesity is usually reported as showing a sex ratio of near 10 to 1. The mental diseases to which females are most prone are those associated with fluctuations of bodily function: mania and depression and involutional mental upset. The male shows less fluctuation than the female in body temperature (Burton, 1939; Murlin, 1939), basal metabolism (Burton, 1939), acid-base balance of the blood (Shock and Hastings, 1934), and level of blood sugar (Rowe, 1928). Females are more prone to flushing and fainting. From such differences it would appear that homeostatic mechanisms operate within narrower limits in the male than in the female.

Neuromuscular Tension. There is evidence that the male is geared to muscular reactivity in greater degree than the female. Gatewood and Weiss (1930), measuring the reactions of the newborn in a stabilimeter, find males more reactive to stimulation as shown by greatly increased respiration rate. At the nursery school level boys exceed girls in motility. Goodenough (1930) found a critical ratio of 3.00 for such a difference in a comprehensive time-sampling study of the behavior of 33 nursery school children. Other studies of nursery school behavior have found evidence of greater motor tensions in males; for example, Hattwick (1937) reports that boys more often jump and squeal excessively, are tense at rest, and stay awake at nap time. Infantile tetany occurs twice as often in boys as in girls (Bakwin, 1929). Tics of the muscular-spasm variety seem to be more prevalent in boys than in girls (Terman *et al.*, 1925).

Miscellaneous Physical Differences. In the sensory field the higher incidence of defective color vision among males is well known. With older children and adults auditory defect in the perception of high-frequency tones is more common in males (Beasley, 1938; Ciocco, 1938). Left-handedness, stuttering, and alexia (nonreading) all show a higher incidence for males than for females. (Some believe these three variables to be functionally interrelated.) Epilepsy and mental deficiency are also more common among males (Danby, 1934), though the true difference is probably less than the sex ratio of admissions to state and private institutions would indicate.

Sex Differences in Interests

Plays, Games, and Other Activities. Sex differences are prominent in the play and other spontaneous activities of children in cultures ranging from the very primitive to the most advanced. In part these differences reflect the division of activity that prevails between males and females in the adult population, though not all the plays of children, even among primitives, are imitative of adult behavior. There are certain general types of plays and games which are common to cultures widely separated with respect to the adult occupational activities (Miller, 1928). Endogenous factors that might be expected to contribute to sex differences in children's play activities include physical strength and energy, motor speed and skills, and the temperamental predisposition to given types of emotional and social response.

In a study of the play interests of 554 gifted and 474 unselected children of Grades 3 to 8 Terman *et al.* (1925) reported a "masculinity index" for each of 90 plays, games, and activities. The indices were based on knowledge of, interest in, and time devoted to the various activities by unselected boys and girls. The masculinity ratings of these 90 activities are here given in terms of standard scores in the order from most to least masculine, with the score 13 representing the line of neutrality.

24. Tools.
21. Shooting.
20. Kites, bicycle, marbles, wrestling, boxing, football.
19. Tops, machinery, baseball.
18. Fishing.
17. Bow and arrow, skiing, tug of war, soccer.
16. Stilts, garden work, basketball, pool.
15. Hoops, swimming, rowing, hunting, snap the whip, shinny, racing and jumping.
14. Coasting, hiking, riding, duck on rock, leap-frog, bowling, handball, backgammon, checkers, chess, billiards.
13. (Line of neutrality) Red Rover, pompom pull-away, follow the leader, anty over, roly-poly, fox and geese, croquet, volleyball, dominoes, crokinole, parchesi, tiddledy-winks, snap,

cards, history cards, geography cards word building.
12. Jackstraws, postoffice, blackman, fox and hounds, tennis, authors.
11. Tag, hide and seek, puss in corner, dare base, Simon says, playing church, solving puzzles.
10. Jackstones, skating, drop the handkerchief, blindfold.
9. Ring around the rosy, London Bridge, farmer in the dell, in and out the window, cat and mouse, jumping rope, guessing games, charades.
8. Dancing, sewing, playing store.
7. Knitting or crocheting.
6. Playing school.
5. Cooking, playing house.
4. Hopscotch.
3. Dressing up.
2. Dolls.

An outstanding fact brought out by these masculinity ratings is that nearly all the games that involve strenuous activity are definitely on the masculine end of the scale. Considering indices 12 to 14 as neutral or near neutral, we have above 14 bicycling, wrestling, boxing, football, baseball, skiing, tug of war, soccer, basketball, swimming, rowing, shinny, racing, and jumping, whereas below 12 the only activities at all strenuous are dare base, skating, and jumping rope.

The most extensive data on children's play activities were collected by Lehman and Witty (1927) in a series of surveys involving some 17,000 city children and over 2000 rural children. On a list of 200 play activities the children were told to check anything they had done during the past week just because they wanted to, and to indicate the three things they liked best. The results are difficult to evaluate, as sex differences are shown only in the form of graphs and rank-order lists. However, a number of sex differences are evident. In the first place, boys are more variable than girls in their play life. Boys more often engage in the following types of activity: active, vigorous plays and games; those involving muscular dexterity and skill; games involving competition; and the more highly organized plays and games. Girls, on the other hand, are more conservative in their play life; they participate more often in sedentary activities and in activities involving a restricted range of action. On the whole, the largest sex differences occur for ages 8½ to 10½, inclusive. After 10½ the similarities in activities become more and more evident as chronological age increases, at least more activities are common to the sexes and the range of interest of each sex becomes narrower. The authors' data on best-liked games show much the same trends of sex differences as are revealed by Terman's masculinity indices.

J. C. Foster (1930) asked 738 boys and 385 girls in the first six elementary grades of Minneapolis schools to list the games (10 or less) played within the last year, indicating whether the game was played outdoors or indoors. All games were then classified under the following 11 types: (1) catching, throwing, kicking; (2) chasing and fleeing; (3) hiding and seeking; (4) jumping and hopping; (5) folk dancing and singing; (6) informal dramatization; (7) following directions; (8) table games; (9) very active play; (10) rather inactive play; and (11) group games of the guessing type. There were no very marked sex differences in preference for these 11 classes of games, though the catching, throwing, and kicking games played out of doors constitute at every age a larger percentage for the boys than for the girls of the total number of games. The same is true for this type of game played indoors except at ages 6 and 7. Girls show a greater interest in the outdoor jumping and hopping games, and, except for age 6, a greater interest in informal dramatiza-

tions (indoors). When we consider the individual games, we find that baseball attains a popularity with boys that is equaled only by the popularity of jacks with girls. Playing house and school appear frequently on the girls' lists but not at all on the boys', whereas volleyball and basketball are on the boys' preferred lists but not on the girls'.

Hildreth (1933) reported data on the recreational and play interests of 89 boys and 84 girls in the ninth grade and of 52 boys and 51 girls in the twelfth grade enrolled in one public and one private school. Check lists were given out and subjects were asked to designate the three games they liked best. Rank orders of games and activities differed as between public and private school, showing the need of wide sampling as a basis for generalizations in this field. Football was chosen almost exclusively by boys. Baseball was most popular with boys, but it also ranked among the five games most popular with girls. There was little difference in basketball, handball, or soccer. Bridge, golf, tennis, and croquet rated higher with girls; boxing, chess, and wrestling with boys. Similar data secured for other activities showed swimming and ice skating about equally popular with the sexes. Rating higher with boys were bicycle riding, driving automobiles, fishing, and camping; higher with girls were social dancing, horseback riding, reading, and attending movies. This study illustrates the growing tendency of girls to participate in games formerly monopolized by boys.

Farwell (1930) tested experimentally the reactions of young children to constructive play materials. The subjects were 125 boys and 146 girls enrolled in kindergarten, first grade, and second grade. The children were taken in small groups to a room equipped with several sets of materials for modeling, building, drawing, painting, sewing, cardboard construction, and paper construction. They were introduced to the materials and then allowed 30 minutes to play with them as they chose. The subjects were given 14 such play periods on different days, and observers recorded the percentage of total time each child spent with each of the kinds of play material.

The building material gave the largest sex differences, boys at all age levels devoting about 50 per cent of their time to it as compared with 5 per cent for girls. Girls devoted about 30 per cent of their time to painting and the same amount to modeling. Painting and modeling were also popular with boys, but less so than with girls. The percentages were low with both sexes for all the other activities. Both in clay modeling and in alabastine painting, boys showed more interest in vehicles, the girls more interest in articles of furniture.

As part of an interest blank used by Terman in his study of gifted children (1925) the following question was asked: "Name all the collections you have made; tell how old you were when you made the collection and tell how large it was." Data were secured for approximately 500 gifted children and 500 unselected children of ages 6 to 14. The average for ages 7 to 13 combined was about 1.7 collections per gifted boy and 1.3 per gifted girl. The control group had only about half as many collectors and showed only small sex differences.

The parents of the gifted children were questioned as to specific collections made, and data were thus obtained for 330 boys and 273 girls. Boys were found to collect stamps much oftener than anything else (32 per cent). Pictures, insects, stones or minerals, and shells are next in order (all between 7 and 9 per cent). The girls have no outstanding preference; dolls, which rank first, are collected by only 11 per cent. Following in order for the girls are flowers, pictures, stamps, and stones or minerals.

An item in the Lehman-Witty play quiz (1927) was "collecting stamps, birds' eggs etc." The authors took the responses to this item as an index of children's interest in collecting and concluded that very few children were engaged in any kind of collecting. In fact, the figures they present are seldom as high as 15 per cent for either sex at any age. As a check on this study Whitley (1929) gave to over 2000 of each sex a questionnaire of 60 items dealing with the kinds of things children collect. The median number of items collected at each age is given here for each sex.

Age	7 or less 8	9	10	11	12	13	14	15	16	17	18 or over
Boys	3	6	7	9	9	9	8	7	6	5	5	5
Girls	2	6	8	8	8	9	8	7	7	6	5	7

The sex differences are negligible and inconsistent from age to age. However, the particular types of collections made show large sex differences. The percentages of each sex collecting certain items are as follows for the combined age groups:

	Boys	Girls
Pictures, post cards, photographs	54	71
Marbles	41	10
Stamps	38	22
Stones and rocks	20	14
Pieces of cloth	8	30

Witty and Lehman (1930), in a second investigation, used a check list of 150 items with a total of more than 1300 children of each sex. By this method it was found that about 80 per cent of the boys and nearly 85 per cent of the girls reported collections. The checking technique is obviously better than free recall.

Reading and Movie Interests. Sex differences in reading preferences are among the most interesting to be found in any field. At home, at school, and in public libraries the books to which children are exposed are largely the same for boys and girls, yet marked sex differences in reading preferences are evident as early as the primary school grades and persist to adult years if not through life. These differences can hardly be due entirely to adult pressures, for children are notoriously perverse in reading the kinds of books they find interesting rather than the books urged upon them by teachers and parents. As the child grows up there are doubtless external influences that tend to draw the girl toward a pattern of femininity in her reading and the boy toward a pattern of masculinity, but these pressures are relatively mild compared to those that create sex stereotypes in other fields of behavior. There are girls' games that are practically taboo for boys, but there is no comparable pressure to keep boys from reading fiction or girls from reading adventure stories. The kind of book a child reads is less noticeable than the kind of play he engages in, with the result that reading largely escapes censorship so far as separate standards for the sexes are concerned.

Jordan (1921) studied the reading interests of some 3500 children in Grades 6 through 12 in three towns and one city. Ages were chiefly between 12 and 18. Each child was asked to name in order of preference the five books and the three magazines he liked best of any he had ever read. These were classified under the following categories: novels, stories, adventure, biography, history, poetry, science, travel, information, humor, and miscellaneous. More than 90 per cent of the book choices of each sex are accounted for by three categories: adventure, novels, and stories. The percentages of total choices were:

	Boys	Girls
Adventure	58	18
Novels	18	42
Stories	15	35

Adventure shows the largest sex difference, but the difference is also large in the opposite direction for novels and stories. The interest in novels increased with age for both sexes, the greatest increase being most marked in the range 12 to 16 with boys and 9 to 13 with girls. The sex differences are even greater than the above figures indicate, since, within a particular category, boys and girls read almost entirely different books. The books most preferred by boys in Jordan's 1921 survey were *The Call of the Wild, Boy Scout Series,* and *Treasure Island;* by girls, *Little Women, Girl of the Limberlost,* and *Pollyanna.*

Turning to the data for magazines, we find the interests of both sexes more widely distributed, with six categories accounting for 90 per cent of choices. The percentages were:

	Boys	Girls
Adventure	29	6
Fiction	24	27
Science	16	2
Current events	9	12
Woman's arts	6	40
Juvenile fiction	6	4

Adventure and science are highly masculine and woman's arts even more highly feminine. The most popular magazines in order of preference were: with boys, *American Boy* and *Popular Mechanics;* with girls, *Ladies' Home Journal, Woman's Home Companion, Woman's World,* and *The Delineator.*

Terman and Lima (1926) report the results of an experiment in which 511 gifted and 808 control children of ages 9 to 15 kept a record of their reading over a two-month period. It was found that the girls in both gifted and control groups read 20 to 30 per cent more books than did boys. The girls read enormously more stories of home and school life and decidedly more emotional fiction, whereas the boys read many more stories of adventure or mystery. Percentages of total books read falling in certain categories were:

	Boys	Girls
Stories of adventure or mystery	56	18
Stories of home or school life	2.5	32
Emotional fiction	3.5	16
Informational fiction, including the classics	15	11
Fairy tales, folk tales, and legends	7	10

The authors also obtained information from 602 gifted and 1225 unselected children as to the books they "had most enjoyed reading in the last year." Lists of the 20 books most liked by each sex were:

Boys

*1. Treasure Island
*2. Call of the Wild
3. Tom Sawyer
4. Robinson Crusoe
*5. Three Musketeers
*6. Ivanhoe
7. Huckleberry Finn
8. Penrod
9. Sherlock Holmes
10. Kidnapped
11. Black Beauty
12. Swiss Family Robinson
13. Connecticut Yankee
*14. Tale of Two Cities
15. Count of Monte Cristo
16. Penrod and Sam
17. White Fang
18. Last of the Mohicans
19. Jungle Books
20. Oliver Twist

Girls

1. Little Women
2. Anne of Green Gables
*3. Ivanhoe
4. Little Men
*5. Treasure Island
6. Laddie
*7. Three Musketeers
8. Alice in Wonderland
9. Heidi
10. Pollyanna
11. Secret Garden
12. Rebecca of Sunnybrook Farm
13. David Copperfield
14. Little Lord Fauntleroy
*15. Call of the Wild
16. Eight Cousins
17. Freckles
18. Little Minister
*19. Tale of Two Cities
20. Uncle Tom's Cabin

* Common to both lists.

Without a single exception, all the books in both lists are fiction. Only five titles appear in both lists, the overlap being wholly due to the fact that girls sometimes read boys' books. Boys almost never read girls' books, yet they have a wider range of interests in reading and do less rereading than girls.

Johnson (1932) obtained data on the reading of 888 boys and 968 girls in 19 different Minnesota schools, Grades 6 through 11. The children were asked to keep a detailed record of their reading over a period of one month. *Liberty* and the *Saturday Evening Post* were the most popular magazines with both sexes. The next three in order of preference were for the boys, *American Boy, Boy's Life,* and *Popular Mechanics;* for the girls, *Ladies' Home Journal, Pictorial Review,* and *Literary Digest.* The only large sex difference that appeared when the data were tabulated according to the particular sections of magazines read was for scientific articles (read by 46 per cent of boys and only 17 per cent of girls). Somewhat more girls than boys read the short stories (94 vs 86 per cent) and the humorous sections (94 vs. 80 per cent). In the newspaper both sexes read the comic more than any other section. Of boys, 74 per cent read the sports section; of girls, 34 per cent

Only 30 per cent of boys, compared to 57 per cent of girls, read the children's page. More boys than girls read the crime news (45 vs. 24 per cent) and the national news (30 vs. 19 per cent). More girls than boys read the society news (28 vs. 3 per cent), the home page (8 vs. 1 per cent), and the advertisements (20 vs. 11 per cent). Among the books reported there was not one common to the boys' and girls' lists of ten most frequently read. Eight of the boys' first ten were adventure stories; the books the girls preferred were about home, school, and children.

Adams (1936) has reported a detailed analysis of the use made of the school library by the 17,616 pupils enrolled in 24 high schools. His data show that girls exceed boys in number of books read and in frequency of library attendance. From the author's report on frequency of attendance for various types of nonreference reading we have calculated the following percentages of total attendance spent in each type of reading:

Type Reading	Junior High School		Senior High School	
	Boys	Girls	Boys	Girls
Newspaper	68	44	77	44
Magazines	21	35	17	34
Books	10	18	6	18
Poetry	1	3	0.5	4

Coleman (1931) analyzed the subjects chosen for written compositions by 5000 children in Grades 7 to 12. The children were given three lists of titles, of 36 each (representing 36 categories), and were allowed to choose one title from each list for a composition. Titles that are reliably more popular with boys fall in such categories as current events, famous people, machines, handwork, modern industries, and outdoor activities. Categories appear-

ing reliably more often in girls' choices include children, home life, personal experience, proverbs, religion, sentiment, sympathy, travel, school, literature, art, and human anecdotes. The sex differences here are strikingly like those found for reading interests.

In movie interests we find patterns of sex difference similar to those for reading. Written quizzes given by Mitchell (1929) to about 10,000 children in Grades 5 to 12 showed significant sex differences in five of the ten categories into which choices were classified. The percentages for these were:

	Boys	Girls
Adventure	15.3	6.5
Romance	3.9	19.4
Tragedy	3.3	9.2
War	5.1	1.9
Western	20.4	12.0

Abbott (1927) reported movie preferences of 286 boys and 273 girls in high school. The children were shown 54 films from the "Selected List" of the National Board of Review and were asked to indicate their degree of liking for each. From an analysis of the information the author concludes that both sexes want plot, action, and suspense; that the boys like comedy, dislike romance and too much emotion, whereas the girls like romance and appeal to sympathy, dislike comedy, and show greater sensitiveness to ethical questions.

Seagoe (1931) obtained information from 800 children in the first eight grades relating to preference for movies and actors. Results are not presented for the sexes separately, but the author reports that boys tend to prefer the exciting movie and to like pictures dealing with things, particularly things of mechanical interest; and girls are more interested in human beings and the appearance of their favorite stars.

Data presented by Hicks and Hayes

(1938) show much the same patterns of sex difference in movie preferences as do the studies just reviewed. The same is true of the data by Longstaff (1936) and by Eisenberg (1936) on preferences for radio programs. Eisenberg's data were obtained from 1747 boys and 1598 girls, chiefly in the sixth grade, by means of a questionnaire, compositions, and interviews. Radio programs best liked by boys included stories of strenuous adventure, conquest over great odds, sports, mysteries, and detection of criminals. Girls preferred programs of sentiment and emotion, home scenes, and everyday realities. Boys exceeded girls in liking for dramatizations; girls exceeded boys in liking for musical programs. However, the sexes are more alike than different in their program preferences. Of 28 programs most popular with boys, all but 8 are found in the 28 most popular with girls. There is a correlation of .88 between preferences of boys and of girls.

Preference for School Subjects. Two extensive studies have been reported on the school subject preferences of high school seniors (Book, 1922; Colvin and MacPhail, 1924). Book's populations included 2300 boys and 3400 girls in Indiana. The populations studied by Colvin and MacPhail included a fifth of all high school seniors in Massachusetts, so chosen as to make a representative sampling. In both studies children were asked to name their favorite subject, and the Massachusetts children were also asked to name their least-liked subject. We have brought together in Table 1 the most important data from the two surveys. It will be noted that the order of preferred subjects is the same for boys in the two studies: science, mathematics, history, English, commercial studies, and languages. The order for girls differs in the two studies, but English rates high in both, science low, and languages and history in between. The direction of every sex difference is the same in the two studies. Boys exceed girls in liking for science, mathematics, and history; girls exceed boys in liking for English, languages, and the commercial studies (largely typing and stenography).

Hicks and Hayes (1938) secured data on subjects best liked and least liked by 102 boys and 148 girls in a junior high school, Grades 7 to 9. The sex differences followed about the same pattern as those found for high school seniors. Boys more often than girls prefer mathematics, science, and the social studies (history, civics, and geography); English is far more popular with girls.

Blair (1938) has reported subject preferences expressed by mentally superior and mentally inferior children in junior and senior high school in the state of Washington. His population included approximately 200 of each sex in both superior and inferior groups, or more than 800 subjects in all. The superior and inferior groups had IQ's respectively one sigma above or one sigma below the mean of their class populations. For each subject except history and social science the direction of sex difference is the same in both groups, but in mathematics, science, foreign languages, and especially English the difference is greater for the superior than for the inferior group. The patterns of sex difference resemble those for unselected high school populations.

Terman *et al.* (1925) had 245 gifted children and 226 children of a control group, all of ages 11 to 13, rate on a five-point scale their liking for 29 different school subjects. The following subjects were rated reliably higher by girls than by boys in both gifted and control groups: drawing, modeling, music (especially singing), dramatics, grammar, folk dancing, and penmanship. Subjects rated higher by boys

TABLE 1

School Subject Preferences of High School Senior.

(Data from Book, 1922, and Colvin and MacPhail, 1924

| | Percentage Preferring | | | | Percentage Liking Least | |
| | Indiana | | Massachusetts | | Massachusetts | |
	Boys	Girls	Boys	Girls	Boys	Girls
Science (general science, physics, or chemistry)	30	6	20	6	12	13
Mathematics	28	17	19	5	16	14
History	15	11	17	10	13	22
English	7	29	14	20	15	8
Commercial studies	6	13	10	36	8	21
Languages	3	11	9	16	28	16

in both groups were general science and United States history. However, science, mathematics, and English did not show at this age level the markedly differential appeal for boys and girls that characterizes these subjects in the high school.

School subject preferences of younger children have been reported by Sister Columba (1926) for a population of 792 boys and 872 girls in Grades 3 to 8 in schools (presumably Catholic) of Washington, D. C. The children were asked to name their best-liked and least-liked subject. On reworking the author's data to take account of varying N's, we find for the total group of six grades only two critical ratios above 2.00 for sex differences on best-liked subjects: more girls than boys named religion (CR = 3.98) and more boys than girls named history (CR = 3.28). On subjects least liked, five differences yielded critical ratios above 2.00: more boys than girls named English (CR = 7.48) and spell-

ing (CR = 2.84), whereas more girls than boys named geography (CR = 3.30), history (CR = 2.89), and arithmetic (CR = 2.36). There was no appreciable sex difference on reading or penmanship.

We have also computed critical ratios of the sex differences for each grade separately to see if any consistent trends could be found in the amount and direction of difference from grade to grade. Does the sex difference usually emerge gradually and increase with age, or does it follow some other pattern? Moderately consistent trends were found, especially on subjects least liked, but every subject showed some irregularities and at least one shift in the direction of differences. Religion was better liked by boys in the eighth grade and much better liked by girls in the seventh; history was more favored by girls in the eighth grade and by boys in the seventh. These larger irregularities were not due to chance factors, since the N's ranged from

100 to 200 for each sex in each grade. They suggest rather that a subject's appeal to a given sex may be greatly influenced by instructional methods and subject matter content, both of which vary from grade to grade and from teacher to teacher.

Occupational Interests. The numerous studies that have been made of children's occupational preferences show large differences between the sexes at all age levels. Information of this kind has important bearing on the problems of educational and vocational guidance but it tells us very little about sex differences in real interests. Occupational preferences expressed by boys and girls reflect largely the vocational opportunities open to men and women. This is especially true of the preferences expressed by older children who are beginning to face the future realistically and to shape their ambitions along practical lines. For this reason we shall merely refer the reader to a few typical studies.

Douglass (1922), using the questionnaire method, ascertained the prospective occupation and reasons for choice of approximately half the high school seniors in the state of Washington—1186 males, 1658 females. Alberty (1925) reported the occupational preferences of 1468 boys and 1507 girls enrolled in high school. For more than 300 of each sex the preferences were obtained in three successive years. Girls showed less change of preference than boys, probably because girls have fewer occupations to choose from. Book (1922) reported sex differences in the occupational preferences of 6000 high school seniors in Indiana. Beeson (1928) analyzed the vocational choices of about 2000 high school students in Colorado. Boynton (1936) obtained information from more than 1500 children of Grades 1 to 6 in several Southern communities. Personal interview methods were used for the first three grades and the usual questionnaire technique for the others. The children were asked to indicate "the ONE thing you would rather do than anything else when you get old enough to make your own living." Lehman and Witty (1931) administered the Lehman-Witty vocational attitude quiz to some 13,000 of each sex, ages 8½ to 18½, in two large cities in Kansas, but their material has not been adequately evaluated for sex differences. Williamson and Darley (1935) analyzed the occupational preferences of all Minnesota high school seniors who entered the University of Minnesota during the five-year period 1929–1933. Preferences were classified according to the Brussell occupational scale.

The results of such studies are greatly influenced by geographical location and by the limited knowledge children have about the nature of specific occupations and about their own mental equipment. What we really want to know is how a given child's interests, attitudes, likes, and dislikes resemble or differ from those of persons successfully engaged in particular vocations. This is something neither a child nor an adult can tell us directly, but the information can be secured indirectly by use of a vocational interest test such as that devised by Strong. Carter and Strong (1933) administered this test to 34 pairs of unlike-sexed twins and to a group of 100 non-twins of each sex from the same high school. The age range was 12 to 20 years, with a mean of 16 for both twin and non-twin groups. The scores for the boys were significantly higher on the scales for engineer, chemist, farmer, physicist, and purchasing agent, whereas small differences in the same direction were found for doctor, psychologist, and mathematician. The scales showing significant differences in favor of the girls were those for journalist, advertiser, life insurance salesman, city school superintendent, and certified public accountant. The scales for artist, teacher, minister, and Y.M.C.A. secretary gave significant sex differences in favor of girls for the non-twin cases, but for the twin group these differences were not so great. All but one of the occupational interest scales which show higher scores for boys were in the "science" group. In general it would seem that the girls have more interest in those occupations involving use of language and contact with people.

In an effort to help Pittsburgh high school students analyze their own special vocational aptitudes and work interests, Miner (1922) devised a blank eliciting information on specific types of work classified on the basis of the skill required rather than on vocations as they exist in the industrial framework. The largest sex differences in favor of the girls were for teaching, welfare work, entertaining, and work-

ing with records. Favoring boys were the differences on operating engines, construction work, and scientific work. When students were asked their preferences regarding types of work involving stated characteristics, sex differences were found as shown in Table 2. The differences are all significant: boys prefer responsibility, giving directions, and greater pay in spite of risk or discomfort; girls prefer working indoors and dealing with people rather than with things. These differences are psychologically meaningful and agree closely with the patterns of sex difference found in other areas of children's interests.

Conative Behavior

Among the conative aspects of personality to be considered are aggressive behavior, dominance as measured by tests, negativism, suggestibility, and persistence.

TABLE 2

PREFERENCES FOR WORK REQUIRING STATED CHARACTERISTICS

Work Requiring	Boys		Girls		CR*
	N	Percentage Yes	N	Percentage Yes	
1. Little responsibility vs. much	706	14	796	20	−4.00
2. Calmness rather than enthusiasm	710	37	827	26	4.40
3. Risk or discomfort, but affording greater pay	694	30	832	16	6.42
4. Being indoors rather than out of doors	699	23	816	38	−6.61
5. Planning vs. carrying out other's plans	657	48	775	33	6.02
6. Directing vs. following	664	77	782	58	7.90
7. Dealing with people vs. dealing with things	666	50	799	79	−12.13

* The critical ratios are our computations.

Aggressive and Dominant Behavior. There is considerable evidence that from early childhood boys show more aggression and anger than girls. Goodenough (1931) had mothers keep daily records of the anger outbursts of 26 boys and 19 girls, aged 7 to 82 months. During the period covered the mean number of such outbursts was 45 for boys and 37 for girls. Hattwick's (1937) ratings of 579 nursery school children indicate that in their relations with other children boys more often grab toys (CR = 2.60), attack others (CR = 2.76), or refuse to share (CR = 1.37), whereas girls more often avoid play (CR = 1.97) and give in too easily (CR = 1.30). In their reactions to adults, boys more often refuse to comply (CR = 1.25) or ignore requests (CR = 1.70), whereas girls more often seek praise (CR = 1.04), stay near someone (CR = 4.50), or criticize others (CR = 1.04). The boys exceed girls in all forms of aggressive behavior with the exception of verbal bossing. The author suggests that these sex differences could hardly be due to social pressures, since they were almost equally in evidence at all ages from 2 to 4½ years.

Caille (1933) also reports more aggressive behavior among boys in a group of 36 nursery school children, aged 19 to 49 months (CR = 2.36). Among 104 children aged 2 to 4 years Berne (1930) found boys more given to teasing (CR = 3.7) and social conformance more characteristic of girls (CR = 3.2). In a study of self-ratings by 110 boys and 109 girls in the seventh and eighth grades, Hurlock (1927) reports that more boys than girls describe themselves as daring (18.1 vs. 4.6 per cent), fond of a fight (16.3 vs. 8.2 per cent), or proud (38.2 vs. 19.2 per cent).

Several studies have been made of children's quarrels. One of the most marked sex differences found by Macfarlane, Honzik, and Davis (1937) in their reputation study of young children of the first three grades was the greater frequency among boys of quarrelsome behavior. Children condemn this trait in girls more than in boys: the r between "popular" and "not quarrelsome" is .77 for girls but only .48 for boys.

Using 1600 time samplings of the behavior of 40 nursery school children, Green (1933a) reported an average of 13.4 quarrels for boys as against 10.2 for girls. Boys also quarreled with more children. Another analysis by Green (1933b) showed that boys' quarrels were more often physical, girls' were more often verbal. Dawe's (1934) detailed analysis of 200 quarrels among nursery school subjects gives 13.5 as the mean number of quarrels for boys as against 9.6 for the girls. Dawe notes that boys are more likely than girls to quarrel over possessions, whereas girls more often than boys quarrel because of interference with an activity. Boys do more striking, girls more pulling and pinching. Boys more often precipitate their quarrels, girls more often take retaliative or objecting rôles. Data by Fuxloch (1930) on 500 children of kindergarten and school age indicated that in their free play boys are more pugnacious and more outstanding in leadership than girls. Jersild and Markey (1935) and Roff and Roff (1940) found less sex difference in conflict tendencies at the nursery school level than other investigators have reported.

Measures of dominance and ascendance of the type devised by Allport and by Bernreuter almost invariably yield higher scores for males than for females at the high school and college level. Sex differences in this direction reported by Bernreuter (1933) have critical ratios of 3.38 for high school subjects, 2.74 for college subjects, and 3.97 for older adults. Carter (1935) found a similar sex difference on the Bernreuter dominance scores of 118 pairs of twins enrolled in high schools. Perry (1934) reported a somewhat smaller sex difference on this test in the case of 178 men and 144 women at the junior college level. Another interesting sex difference reported by Perry is that the dominance and self-sufficiency scores of girls were positively correlated with scholarship, whereas no such relationship was found for boys. Bell (1939) reported for large populations sex differences in social adjustment scores yielded by his adjustment inventory. The inventory was so constituted that high scores in social adjustment indicated the presence of considerable social aggressiveness. These scores were higher for males in four separate groups, the critical ratios of the sex differences being as follows: for 251 high school subjects, 2.03; for 414 college subjects, 2.62; for 148 delinquents, 2.07; for 468 adults, 4.35.

Other data indicating the aggressiveness of boys as contrasted with the docility and conformity of girls are found in the section on character (p. 977 ff.).

That sex differences in aggressive and dominant behavior derive in part from gonadal factors is indicated by the changes which accompany sexual maturation and by the behavioral picture that characterizes hypogonadal conditions. The most outstanding trait of boys so afflicted is docility and lack of aggression. The effects of castration on the behavior of male animals are so familiar that their spectacular nature is often overlooked. That reversal of sex differences in the pugnacity and aggressiveness of domestic fowls can be effected by gonadal transplants has been amply demonstrated. Little has been done with human subjects in determining the behavioral effects of particular gonadal conditions. We need more accurate information, for example, on the relationship between dominant behavior and pubertal changes in boys and girls; also on the possible relationship between dominant behavior and the masculinity or femininity of body build in men and women.

Stone and Barker (1939) on the basis of personality tests given to a large population of adolescent girls reported reliable differences in some of the responses of pre- and postmenarcheal groups of a given age. Their data indicated that the menarche brings with it behavior tendencies toward quieter living and toward feminine interests and introverted attitudes. Tryon (1939) reported a change in the opposite direction between the ages of 12 and 15. Among her 12-year-old girls the quiet, sedate, and nonaggressive qualities are regarded as most attractive, whereas among 15-year-olds admiration for ladylike and prim behavior is largely replaced by an ideal that tends toward mental masculinity, with increased approval of daring and leadership qualities. The disagreement between the two studies is more apparent than real: the data of Stone and Barker are more concerned with changes in behavior, those of Tryon with qualities admired.

Negativism and Resistant Behavior. There are many forms of resistant behavior, but we shall limit the present discussion to the negativism displayed by young children in mental test situations. Data on disobedience and rebelliousness toward authority are presented in the section on character traits.

One of the first statistical studies of negativism in test situations was made by Levy and Tulchin (1923) and was based on tests of 983 subjects aged 6 to 63 months. The authors reported girls slightly more resistant than boys at all ages except 30 months. The fact that the direction of sex difference in this study is contrary to what most others have found may be explained by the types of behavior classed by Levy and Tulchin as resistant. They counted in this category every kind of interference with the progress of the test, including crying and inattentiveness. Goodenough (1928) reported ratings of 380 nursery school children on degree of shyness, negativism, and distractibility during the administration of Kuhlmann-Binet tests. There was no sex difference on shyness. Negativism was reliably more common among boys, but this difference was present only at the upper occupational levels. The peak of negativism was at 18 months for girls, at 30 months for boys. Boys were rated throughout as more distractible than girls. The second study by Goodenough (1929), based on tests of 990 subjects, confirmed the earlier findings. Mayer (1935) found negativistic behavior among 245 children of ages 2 to 5½ years, during the administration of the revised Stanford-Binet scales, to be slightly more frequent with boys, but the difference approached statistical significance only at age 4 (CR = 2.1). Nelson's (1931) mental test data for 91 three-year-olds showed boys to be slightly, though not reliably, more resistant.

A somewhat different type of situation was utilized in the studies by Reynolds (1928) and Caille (1933). Reynolds' procedure was to try to get the child to play with blocks while sitting on the experimenter's lap and to engage in imitative plays with the experimenter. The mean score for negativism was slightly, but not reliably, higher for 105 boys than for 124 girls. The age range was from 2 to 5 years. The mean for girls began to drop at 3 years, that for boys at 4 years. Caille's study of 17 boys and 19 girls summarizes evidence of resistance based not only upon mental tests but also upon stenographic records of the speech of each subject during two days of nursery school attendance. Again, resistant behavior was found to be more common with boys.

Suggestibility. Suggestibility may be thought of as the opposite of negativism. The subject was a favorite one for investigation in the earlier decades of experimental psychology but has received little attention during the last twenty years. For a brief summary of the older literature the reader is referred to Whipple (1915). More recent studies of suggestibility among children have been reported by Aveling and Hargreaves (1921), Lodge (1926), White (1930), Hurlock (1930), Messerschmidt (1933), and Wegrocki (1934). In general, the sex differences disclosed by these studies are small, but the direction consistently indicates that girls are more suggestible than boys.

Persistence. Willingness to persist in the performance of tasks or in the overcoming of obstacles would seem to be an important aspect of conative behavior. Unfortunately, attempts to isolate a general factor of persistence have met with little success. Like tests of suggestibility, the different measures of persistence yield low intercorrelations. A subject's score in such a test depends on the specific nature of the activity involved, on its appeal to the subject, and on the manner in which the task is set. We have found little in the experimental literature on persistence that throws much light on sex differences in conative tendencies. The data of Hartshorne and May, summarized in the section on character (p. 981), showed girls more persistent than boys, but Ryans (1939) found a small but consistent difference in the opposite direction. Other references are Chapman (1924), Cushing (1929), Pinard (1932), Shacter (1933), R. B. Cattell (1935), and Wolf (1938).

Social Behavior

A very large part of the child's behavior is social in the broad sense of that term

In this section, however, our discussion will be limited to sociality and spontaneous groupings.

Sociality. It is a common belief that one of the characteristically feminine traits is an absorbing interest in persons and personal relationships. That in fact a sex difference exists in this respect is indicated by data from subjects over a wide range of ages. It should be noted, however, that social interest and social participation are by no means the same variable. A number of researches suggest that the female shows more sociality, in the sense of social desire, but that introvertive tendencies and inferiority feelings often inhibit her social participation.

We have already seen that the greater social interests of girls appear in their play activities, in the books they read, and in their occupational preferences. Terman's (1925) "sociability" ratings of both gifted and unselected children, based on preference for social versus nonsocial plays and games, averaged higher for girls than for boys at every age. "Activity" ratings, on the other hand, averaged higher for boys. Wyman's (1925) word association test used with these same subjects as a measure of interests also showed girls consistently above boys in social interest and as consistently below them in activity interest.

Symonds (1936) had 784 boys and 857 girls in junior and senior high schools rank 15 "major areas of life concern" according to their interest in reading about or discussing them. The largest sex difference was on personal attractiveness, which had a mean rank order of 5.4 for girls as compared with 8.1 for boys. Manners and getting along with others were also ranked somewhat higher by girls. All these differences indicate greater social interests among girls.

Davis (1932) had mothers of children aged 3 to 12 record 50 consecutive questions asked in the parental presence by 39 boys and 34 girls. Girls asked more questions on social relations (CR = 3.04), boys on causal explanation (CR = 3.07).

Orgel and Tuckman (1935) found that among 235 boys and 75 girls in a Hebrew orphanage 39.1 per cent of boys' nicknames and only 6.7 per cent of girls' are based upon some physical peculiarity or defect, whereas affectionate forms of nicknames account for 32 per cent of those given to girls as against only 3.8 per cent of those given to boys. That is, in bestowing nicknames girls manifest more social sensitivity and more personal affection.

Interviews with 666 children, aged 5 to 12, by Jersild, Markey, and Jersild (1933) showed 12 per cent of "first" wishes by girls to concern siblings, companions, or friends, as against 3 per cent of wishes by the boys. Questioned regarding the best thing that ever happened to them, 14.9 per cent of girls as against 8.3 per cent of boys mentioned such things as parental relationships and other human contacts. Regarding the worst thing that ever happened to them, 15.6 per cent of girls and 8.0 per cent of boys mentioned people or undesirable traits of people. Asked what they liked best, 31 per cent of girls and 23 per cent of boys replied in terms of people or associations with people.

Terman and Miles (1936) found much evidence of the greater social orientation of girls among 550 subjects at the seventh-grade, high school, and college levels. From their analysis of sex differences on M-F test items it appears that situations which involve attack on social self-feeling are almost the only field in which girls report more anger than boys. They are more angry at "being socially slighted," "hearing friends unjustly abused," "seeing boys make fun of old people," "seeing someone laugh when a blind man runs into an obstacle," or "seeing a person treated unfairly because of his race." The items expressing care for personal appearance and liking for social gatherings all carried feminine weights in the scoring of this test.

The fact that gifted subjects (Burks, Jensen, and Terman, 1930) showed no appreciable sex difference on the Moss test of social intelligence is probably attributable to the inadequacy of the test, for Butler's study (1934) of 1600 subjects in Grades 8 to 12 showed that girls greatly exceed boys in knowledge of matters having to do with family relationships and social adjustments.

Jealousy is one indication of the value an individual attaches to given social relationships, and studies of jealousy all show that it is more prevalent among girls than among boys. S. Foster (1927) and Sewall (1930) found this to be the case with pre-school children. Ross (1931) reported that in an older group, aged 6 to 11 years, sibling jealousy was much more common among girls (17 per cent as compared to 11 per cent for boys).

The greater sociality of girls is evidenced even in their dreams, which suggests that the sex difference in question is deep-seated. For example, Cason's study (1935) of some 200 subjects ranging in age from 8 years to adulthood showed that girls more often than boys dream of home, family, and other persons. Schubert and Wagner (1936) found that among 355 high school seniors 62.6 per cent of girls as against 30 per cent of boys reported dreams about members of the family or about dead people. For 517 younger children, chiefly 4 to 12 years, Foster and Anderson (1936) reported 24.5 per cent of girls but only 9.8 per cent of boys having dreams of strange or bad people.

Sex differences in sociality have been noted at a very early age. Thus Berne (1930), using a rating scale technique with 82 nursery school children, found that girls show more responsibility for others, more social conformance, and more motherly behavior than do boys. Hübsch and Reininger (1931) reported that, among kindergarten children in Vienna, boys were more concerned with things, girls with personal relationships.

Spontaneous Social Groupings. Most of the investigations of social groupings have dealt with small samples, chiefly at the nursery school level. One of the earlier studies was by Chevaleva-Janovskaja (1927), who analyzed 888 playground groupings of 276 children, aged 3 to 8 years, in Odessa. She reported greater participation in social groups by boys than by girls and a preponderance of unisexual as compared with bisexual groupings among the preschool children. At a later age range girls were found in bisexual groupings more often than in unisexual (56.84 vs. 43.16 per cent).

Challman (1932) recorded 7248 social groupings among 17 boys and 16 girls attending nursery school. These were predominantly unisexual. Girls showed a trend toward more social participation and higher friendship scores than the boys. Green's (1933a) time-sampling study of friendships and quarrels among 21 boys and 19 girls in a nursery school indicated that girls make more social contacts than boys in terms of number of children played with, and that unisex groupings predominate. Another time-sampling study of social behavior at the preschool level was made by Parten (1933). Her subjects were 19 boys and 15 girls who afforded 781 groupings for an analysis. Two thirds of the two-child groups were unisexual. When the data were treated so as to show the five favorite playmates of each child, it was found that 81 per cent of girls' favorites were girls, whereas only 62 per cent of boys' favorites were boys. The most favored playmate of each girl was in every case of the same sex, whereas this was true for only 12 of the 19 boys.

Data on the social groupings of older children have been reported by Wellman (1926) and Campbell (1939). Wellman made observations of the free groupings of 27 boys and 27 girls in a high school population of 113. She found that boys at this age seek a much wider range of companions than do girls. The mean number of companions per child was 22.2 for the boys as compared with 16.5 for the girls. Campbell's study of the clique formations of 75 girls and 77 boys in the ninth grade by means of a modified "guess who" technique showed that boys' social relations are less rigidly structured than those of girls. Boys at this age associate with more persons than girls. Girls are more given to clique association and are more prone than boys to mention unfavorably an acquaintance outside the inner circle. Burks, Jensen, and Terman (1930) reported that at high school age gifted boys oftener than gifted girls have no close chums.

Adolescent crushes have been studied by Hurlock and Klein (1934). Their subjects included 148 boys and 202 girls in the high school, and 54 men and 155 women who were teachers or counselors. The data secured were memory reports elicited by a questionnaire. More females than males reported having experienced one or more crushes (86.6 vs. 71.6 per cent). Nearly all the homosexual crushes were reported by girls.

The studies of social groupings do not impress us as particularly fruitful; their chief contribution is in the quantification of information familiar to almost everyone who has observed children. Perhaps the most important generalization suggested by the data reviewed is that in the preschool years girls appear to exceed boys in the number of social contacts but lose this position to boys in the later years.

Neurotic and Emotional Response

Under this somewhat ill-defined heading we shall summarize data on nervous habits, fear response, and emotionality as measured by personality tests and inventories.

Nervous Habits. Olson (1929) has made one of the most valuable studies of nervous habits in normal children. His subjects were 225 boys and 242 girls in Grades 1 to 6 and 169 children in Grades 7 and 8, each of whom was observed during 20 five-minute periods. The main categories of nervous habits observed gave the following frequencies, in percentages (for 221 boys and 238 girls in the first six grades):

	Boys	Girls	Diff. $\frac{}{PE_{diff.}}$
Oral	47	60	4.1
Nasal	28	27	...
Hirsutal	17	28	4.2
Ocular	11	19	3.5
Aural	13	8	−2.5
Genital	5	3	−1.7

The categories oral, hirsutal, and ocular are reliably more frequent with girls, aural and genital with boys.

Koch (1935) made time-sample observations of the nervous habits of 21 boys and 25 girls attending nursery school. Her data were secured by 400 half-minute periods distributed over eight months. The only reliable sex difference was for the hirsutal-caputal category, for which the average number observed per child was 1.8 for boys and 8.6 for girls.

Blatz and Ringland (1935) have reported a time-sampling study of "tics," a term used by them to include such a wide variety of habits and mannerisms as to involve practically all the children in a normal group. The subjects were 30 boys and 31 girls enrolled in nursery school, kindergarten, and first grade. The mean number of positive notations per child was somewhat higher for girls.

Brackett (1934) recorded time-sampling observations of crying for 17 boys and 12 girls aged 18 to 48 months. The samples are too small to yield reliable sex differences, but there is a trend toward more crying by girls (CR = 1.1).

Wechsler (1931) observed the incidence of nail-biting among 3000 New York children ranging in age from less than 3 years to 18 years. Before 11 years the sex differences were small and inconsistent, from 11 to 13 the incidence was reliably higher among girls, but for ages after 13 it was reliably higher for boys. Wechsler's method of determining presence of nail-biting by a quick glance at the child's hand has been criticized by Olson (1936) as inaccurate.

Macfarlane (1938) reported the incidence of various forms of special behaviors for 60 boys and 60 girls observed at each of the following ages (months): 21, 24, 30, 36, 42, 48, 54, 60. Nail-biting, thumb-sucking, and jealous behavior showed "a small but consistently higher incidence in girls." However, the N's are quite small for the separate categories. On total of extreme behaviors studied there was no appreciable sex difference.

Michaels and Goodman (1934) reported data on enuresis and "other neuropathic traits" for 255 boys and 220 girls, ages 6 to 16, who attended a summer camp. The information was obtained partly from parents and partly from the subjects themselves by observation and questioning. The following percentages were found for various conditions:

	Boys	Girls
Enuresis after age 3	26.1	23.4
Thumb-sucking	17.6	34.1
Nail-biting	45.7	57.1
Speech impediment	23.3	17.0
Tantrums	12.8	16.1
Sleep disturbances	16.1	22.0
Fears	31.1	58.7

The only reliable differences here are the excess of girls with a history of thumb-sucking, nail-biting, and fears.

Michaels and Goodman (1939) summarized case history data on enuresis beyond age 3 for 500 male and 500 female patients in a state psychopathic hospital. In the 193 case histories that were positive 56.5 per cent were of males and 43.5 per cent were of females, a reliable difference. In 122 cases with whom enuresis persisted after 10 years, 61.5 per cent were males and 38.5 per cent females.

Among the 600 nursery subjects studied by Hattwick (1937) the following nervous tendencies were unrelated to sex: enuresis, nail-biting, chewing objects, playing with fingers, picking nose, twitching, holding body tense.

Terman et al. (1925) obtained data from parents, teachers, and medical examinations regarding various nervous conditions in a gifted population of nearly 600, ages 5 to 13. Parents reported 10 per cent of boys and 13 per cent of girls as having "marked fears." Teachers reported "excessive timidity" for 4.9 per cent of boys and 10.5 per cent of girls, and "tendency to worry" for 9 per cent of boys and 12 per cent of girls. The medical records of these subjects showed enuresis still present with 20 boys but with only 5 girls.

If we lump together the numerous kinds of behavior known as nervous habits, it appears that the total incidence of such behavior is higher with girls. For enuresis and perhaps one or two other categories it is higher with boys. Unfortunately, little is known about the interrelationships of the variables in question or about their significance for personality development. The fact that they are so commonly classed together under a single label is no guaranty that they have any functional relationship. What we need is a factor analysis of time-sampling records of such behaviors.

Fear Responses. Jersild and Holmes (1935) presented fear situations in the laboratory to 57 boys and 48 girls aged 2 to 5 years. Mean fear scores for girls are higher than for boys (CR = 2.58). When 29 sex pairs were matched for age the difference was greater (CR = 3.29). In the same monograph these authors reported parental records of children's fear responses over a period of 21 days. The subjects were 85 boys and 68 girls chiefly between 1 and 5 years. This method of estimating fear showed little difference in number of fears for girls and boys: average for boys was 4.9; for girls, 5.2. There were marked sex differences in what constitutes a fear situation. Boys were more afraid of kinesthetic catastrophe; girls were more afraid of strangers and of social mishaps. These differences may be related to the greater muscular activity of boys and the greater social concern of girls.

Hattwick (1937) had three independent judges record behavior tendencies of 300 nursery school children of each sex, aged 2 to 4½ years. Girls were reported oftener in the following categories:

	CR
Stays near adult	4.50
Fears strange people and places	1.04
Fears high places	1.85
Cries easily	1.54
Avoids risk	1.73
Avoids play	1.97

Pintner and Brunschwig (1937) questioned 159 deaf and 345 hearing children of ages 12 to 15 regarding 39 fear situations. Girls of both groups reported more fears than did the boys (CR = 6.15 for the deaf, 4.53 for the hearing group).

Jersild, Markey, and Jersild (1933) and Jersild and Holmes (1935) reported interviews with 400 children, 25 of each sex at each age from 5 to 12 inclusive. Twice as many boys as girls reported no fears, and the girls reported a larger number of different fears. In teachers' ratings secured by Wickman (1928) for more than 1600 school children the girls were more often reported as showing oversensitive behavior and fear behavior.

Kimmins (1920, 1931, 1937) had 6000 London children, ages 5 to 18, report the last dream they could remember. In the range from 8 to 14 years more fear dreams were reported for boys (19 per cent) than for girls (16 per cent). After 14, fears decreased with boys and increased with girls. Little statistical treatment was presented.

In general the evidence is fairly consistent in indicating that girls are more prone to fear response than are boys. In the reports made by the subjects it is possible that the sex difference is in part spurious because of the boy's unwillingness to confess fear experiences. Boys are expected to be brave.

Emotionality as Measured by Tests and Inventories. We refer here to paper-and-pencil tests of the kind devised by Woodworth, Thurstone, Bernreuter, Pressey, Maller, Brown, and others. Although scores on the various tests do not measure exactly the same thing, a core common to all of them may properly be called emotionality.

Mathews (1923) gave a modified Woodworth Personal Data Sheet to 575 boys and 558 girls, aged 9 to 19 years. For all ages combined the median number of "emotionally unstable" replies was about 25 per cent greater for girls than for boys, a difference which is statistically reliable. However, between ages 10 and 17, the median of unstable responses for boys decreased from 35 to 14, whereas for girls it increased from 24 to 37. Only after age 14 were the scores significantly better for the boys. Schubert and Wagner's (1936) Woodworth scores for 229 boys and 248 girls, all high school seniors, showed a much smaller sex difference in the same direction. The same test given by Hartshorne, May, and Maller (1929) to 393 boys and 382 girls in Grades 5 to 8 gave no reliable sex differences. Cady's modification of the Woodworth test was given by Terman et al. (1925) to 532 gifted subjects aged 7 to 14 and to 533 unselected subjects aged 10 to 14. In neither group was there a reliable sex difference at any age.

Bernreuter's (1933) test for neurotic tendency (B1-N), which has much in common with the Woodworth test, yielded scores which were reliably more "neurotic" for females in all the author's standardization groups. The critical ratio in the high school group was 3.94, in the college group 2.21, and in the adult group 3.37. Carter's (1935) application of the Bernreuter test to 128 male and 108 female twins aged 12 to 19 years also showed girls reliably more "neurotic" than boys.

Emotionality, or neurotic tendency, is one of several aspects of maladjustment measured by the Bell Adjustment Inventory. In high school, college, and delinquent populations this inventory yields higher emotionality scores for female than for male groups. For high school groups the CR was 8.51; for college groups, 2.44 (Bell, 1939).

Maller's Character Sketches for testing emotional stability showed about the same sex differences for 103 Parisian children as others have found for children in this country (Kinter-Remmlein, 1933). A comparison of blind and sighted high school students by means of the Clark-Thurstone neurotic inventory (P. A. Brown, 1939) yielded even larger sex differences for the blind than for the normal subjects. The CR between 178 boys and 174 girls in the normal group was 3.44; for 95 boys and 115 girls in the blind group, 7.16. For his

own psychoneurotic inventory F. Brown (1934) found no significant sex differences in a population of 1663 unselected children in Grades 4 to 9. Springer (1938) confirmed this finding. In Springer's study Brown's inventory was given to 800 children of Grades 4 to 9, including 190 boys and 137 girls in a slum district and 237 boys and 236 girls in a good district. Girls of both groups tested slightly more "neurotic" than boys, but the critical ratios were only 1.5 and 1.8.

Sex comparisons are available from a number of studies based on the Pressey test of affectivity. Only one of the subtests in Pressey's battery relates to emotionality, namely, the inventory of worries. Sunne (1925) gave this test to 130 boys and 102 girls in Grades 7 and 8 and found that girls checked reliably more worries than did boys. Collins's (1927) data from Pressey tests of 1500 Scotch and English children aged 11 to 15 showed slightly higher affectivity scores for girls with a marked sex difference in the worries test. Kohn (1937), using the X-O test as revised in 1933, found no sex differences for Pressey scores in an orphanage high school population of 149 boys and 118 girls.

The study of Pintner and Lev (1940) is one of the very few to report boys more prone than girls to worry about social and personal inadequacy. These authors administered an inventory of 53 worry items to 270 boys and 270 girls in Grades 5 and 6. Some of the differences reported are so unexpected as to suggest that errors may have occurred in data tabulation or else that the boys' responses were inspired by a sense of humor. For example, these boys of 11 and 12 years are reported as worrying more than girls about "being late for supper" (CR = 4.31), "not having a pretty home" (CR = 2.67), and "getting married" (CR = 2.44)! In their analysis of sex differences in responses to individual items of the M-F test Terman and Miles (1936) summarized data from 550 subjects on anger, fear, disgust, and pity. The subjects included 250 in the seventh grade, 200 in the eleventh grade, and 100 college students. The inventory called for a rating of degree of emotion aroused in the subject by each of 34 situations for anger, 40 for fear, 36 for disgust, and 28 for pity. In all three populations, and for all four types of emotion, the responses of girls indicated greater affectivity than those of boys. However, for a given emotion the direction of sex difference varied according to the specific situation presented. Whether the emotion in question be anger, fear, disgust, or pity, the items that have low affectivity thresholds for boys are largely different from those that have low thresholds for girls. These qualitative differences, too numerous to review here, are psychologically more interesting than the quantitative differences.

The preponderance of evidence from personality inventories indicates somewhat greater emotionality for females. The amount of sex difference varies from test to test but even when small is almost invariably in one direction. At the same time caution is necessary in the interpretation of pencil-and-paper tests of emotionality. We cannot be sure that boys and girls are equally willing to confess their emotional reactions or that the individual questions in a personality inventory carry always the same meaning for the sexes. However, a study by Darley (1937) indicated that the greater emotionality shown by females may not be spurious. When college students who had been given tests of maladjustment were clinically interviewed by two experienced counselors, it was found that excess of maladjustment among women, as compared with men, was more marked in the clinical diagnoses than in the test scores.

Finally, a word of caution regarding the common use of the term "emotionality" as synonymous with neuroticism. It may well be that the subject who scores high on the usual psychoneurotic inventory is properly described as psychoneurotic or as emotionally unstable. However, as Landis, Zubin, and Katz (1935) have pointed out, it does not follow that the extremely low-scoring subject is emotionally stable. He may be stable, but there is a chance that his hypoemotionality is indicative of a schizophrenic tendency.

Character Traits

We shall discuss sex differences in three variables related to character: (1) the incidence of delinquency, (2) the incidence of character faults as judged by teachers and others, and (3) the results of character tests.

Incidence of Delinquency. Sex differences in the incidence of delinquency are difficult to interpret. The sexes are exposed to different temptations and in different degrees, the criteria of delinquency are not the same for boys and girls, and there is differential treatment of the sexes with respect to arrests and disposal of cases. The available statistics probably minimize the actual amount of delinquency among girls as compared with boys. There is one exception, however, to this tendency: the statistics undoubtedly exaggerate the relative sex delinquency of girls because the social tolerance of sexual misconduct by girls is much lower than it is for boys.

Healy and Bronner (1926) gave the sex ratio in two large series of juvenile court cases as 2.3 boys to 1 girl. There was close agreement between the Chicago and Boston series. Fortes (1933) reported 808 boys and 59 girls in the records of probation officers of East London, Connecticut. This is a ratio of 7.3 to 1. Alper and Lodgen (1936) reported probation data for all but two counties in Pennsylvania. The totals were 2533 boys and 748 girls, a ratio of almost 3 to 1.

Maller (1933) noted a marked change in the sex ratio among juvenile court cases in New York City during the three decades beginning in 1902. The ratio was about 8 to 1 in the first decade, 4 to 1 in the second, and 2.7 to 1 in the third. In thirty years the number of boys brought before the juvenile court decreased by 20 per cent, whereas the number of girls more than doubled. Maller believes that this rapid change is not primarily a function of altered court procedure and attributes the increase in delinquency among girls to the increasing incidence of parental divorce, which is supposed to have a worse effect upon girls than upon boys. We doubt the correctness of this interpretation and suspect that the observed trend is largely due to changes in selective factors.

Statistics from all sources report a higher percentage of boy than of girl delinquents charged with offenses against property, and a higher percentage of girl delinquents charged with sex offenses.

Incidence of Character Faults. The statistical studies of character faults are even more difficult to evaluate than those of delinquency. They are usually based on information supplied by teachers and are subject to many kinds of bias known to affect teacher attitudes.

Haggerty (1925) secured teachers' ratings on the incidence of faults and problem behavior among 800 children in Grades 1 to 8. By weighting the faults according to estimated seriousness the author derived a behavior score for each child. The mean scores were higher (more unfavorable) for boys in every school grade. Wickman (1928), who had assisted in the Haggerty study, reported similar scores for 462 boys

and 412 girls in Cleveland. The mean number of "problems" per child was approximately 10 for boys and 6 for girls. Undesirable kinds of behavior that were reported by teachers at least twice as frequently for boys as for girls included truancy, destruction of property, stealing, profanity, disobedience, defiance, cruelty, bullying, and rudeness. The only kind more frequently reported for girls was the writing of obscene notes. Children regarded by teachers as presenting minor behavior problems included 49 per cent of boys and 35 per cent of girls; those judged to have serious behavior problems were 10 per cent of boys and 3 per cent of girls. Olson (1930) reported similar figures for 1473 boys and 1394 girls.

Williams (1933) secured data in ten cities on 1343 children regarded by their teachers as problem cases. These constituted 2.4 per cent of the school population covered by the survey. In the problem group the ratio of boys to girls was 4 to 1. Types of behavior more common among problem boys than problem girls were "misconduct in school" (46 vs. 22 per cent), disobedience (45 vs. 23 per cent), annoying other children (48 vs. 31 per cent). The incidence of 37 types of undesirable behavior, as judged by teachers, was reported by Hurlock and McDonald (1934) for 438 boys and 352 girls in a junior high school attended largely by Jewish children. More frequent among problem boys than problem girls were lying, cheating, truancy, disobedience, rudeness, and bullying.

The studies just reviewed are so typical of their kind that it would be a waste of time to cite others. It is perhaps not unfair to say that in general they throw more light on teacher attitudes than on sex differences. Ratings secured by Terman (1925) for gifted and control groups, each numbering more than 500, showed that under the most careful procedures the rat-ngs for children contain a "generosity factor" which is differential for sex. Among the twenty-five traits for which these subjects were rated by parents and teachers were four which may be classified as "moral" traits: sympathy, generosity, conscientiousness, and truthfulness. The mean rating on each of these four traits was significantly higher for girls than for boys in both gifted and control groups. That this apparent moral superiority of girls must be largely spurious is suggested by the fact that in the same groups the mean ratings were consistently higher for girls than for boys on such traits as health, physical energy, persistence, common sense, and freedom from vanity. Only on mechanical ingenuity were boys rated significantly higher than girls. The only reasonable inference is that ratings of children by women teachers and mothers are biased in favor of girls.[1]

[1] There are several studies which reveal a "sex halo" in teachers' ratings of children. Hayes (1934) had about 400 of each sex, aged 10 to 15 years, rated on a large number of behaviors. The median rating for girls was higher than for boys at every age, the maximum difference being at 14. Langlie (1937) had 170 high school seniors (85 of each sex) rated by several men teachers, and 135 boys and 300 girls rated by several women teachers, on ability to learn, intellectual initiative, industry, scholastic zeal, dependability, and capacity for college work. Median ratings by both men and women were higher for girls on every trait, although college aptitude tests of these subjects averaged slightly higher for boys. Women favored the girls a little more than did men. Indicative of the greater halo factor in girls' ratings is the higher intercorrelation found for girls than for boys on the various trait ratings.

S. Smith (1939) had 1600 children, including 100 of each sex at each age from 8 to 15, express by vote whether given traits were more characteristic of boys or girls. A majority of both sexes voted that boys more than girls are mean to strange dogs, hard workers, given to teasing, likely to stick to a hard job, better leaders, better puzzle-solvers, good sports. Both sexes voted that girls are more friendly, more honest, more truthful, more likely to do right when not observed, nicer to small children, more generous, and brighter in school. On the fol-

Clinics of child guidance and of juvenile research are another source of information on character faults of children, but again the information is of doubtful value, so far as sex differences are concerned, because of the selective factors that may affect clinic populations. In the main, however, the sex difference trends from such data are similar to those found in the surveys of school populations. For details the reader should consult the report by Schumacher (1933) on 120 consecutive cases of each sex examined in a child guidance clinic, and Ackerson's (1931) analysis of 5000 consecutive cases examined at the Institute for Juvenile Research at Chicago. Percentage frequencies of certain personality problems among 2853 white boys and 1739 white girls in Ackerson's population were:

	Boys	Girls
Restless, overactive	19	16
Irritable temperament	19	14
Touchy	13	10
Distractible	12	9
Personal violence	8	4
Request for sanity diagnosis	7	4
Potential sex delinquency	0.1	3

The percentages for "potential sex delinquency" illustrate the need for caution in drawing conclusions from such data. Taken at their face value, the figures would suggest that the incidence of potential sex delinquency is thirty times as high for girls as for boys!

lowing the sexes disagreed, a majority of boys favoring boys and a majority of girls favoring girls: doing things for others, good memory for stories, selfishness, keeping secrets, being good losers. It is interesting that children showed the same bias as teachers in judging girls to be more honest, more truthful, more likely to do right when not observed, more generous, and brighter in school. However, there were marked age trends: boys' opinions of themselves became relatively more favorable with age, girls' opinions of themselves became relatively less favorable. Conversely, with increasing age boys had a relatively poorer opinion of girls, whereas girls had a relatively better opinion of boys.

Character Tests. One of the first applications of character tests to large groups of children was reported by Terman *et al.* (1925). His subjects included a gifted group of 284 boys and 248 girls, aged 7 to 14 years, and a control group of 258 boys and 275 girls, aged 10 to 14. All were given a battery of seven character tests including two tests of overstatement, two tests of questionable interests, a test of questionable social attitudes, a test of honesty, and a test of emotional stability. The first five were taken from a battery devised by Raubenheimer (1925), the last two from Cady's battery (1923). Only three of the seven tests were of the performance type: the two overstatement tests and the test of honesty. The other four were indirect measures, although they were shown to differentiate between delinquent and non-delinquent groups. Results for the separate tests in Table 3 show that boys in both groups made worse scores than girls on five of the seven tests, that girls made worse scores in the performance test of cheating, and that the sexes did not differ

TABLE 3

SEX DIFFERENCES IN CHARACTER TESTS

(Data from Terman, 1925)

		Gifted Group			Control Group		
		Boys	Girls	CR	Boys	Girls	CR
1. Overstatement A	M	2.03	1.63	1.25	3.38	2.70	1.79
	SD	3.90	3.46		4.47	3.65	
2. Overstatement B	M	5.2	−2.8	3.33	18.1	16.0	.88
	SD	29.4	26.0		28.6	26.5	
3. Questionable interests: book preferences	M	383	325	2.52	516	473	2.08
	SD	276	254		219	260	
4. Questionable interests: character preferences	M	241	193	3.06	340	311	1.36
	SD	213	148		267	222	
5. Social attitudes	M	2.74	1.51	4.73	7.24	5.30	3.88
	SD	3.64	1.99		5.96	5.40	
6. Honesty	M	31.2	35.6	1.52	43.6	43.9	
	SD	31.9	33.2		34.1	35.9	
7. Emotional stability	M	11.8	11.0	1.33	16.2	16.1	
	SD	6.80	7.09		9.36	8.19	
Weighted total	M	139.8	118.8	3.33	219.3	194.1	3.07
	SD	78.45	68.00		93.34	96.77	

in emotional stability as measured by the Woodworth-Cady inventory.

The most extensive data on sex differences in character tests are those reported by Hartshorne and May (1928). Their tests were for the most part direct measures (performance tests) of "good" and "bad" behavior. They include numerous tests of deception, of service and cooperation, of persistence and self-control, and of moral knowledge.

We have brought together in Table 4 the sex differences found by Hartshorne and May on eight types of deception tests. It will be noted that in all but one of these tests a larger proportion of girls than of boys were guilty of deception. The largest differences were for home cheating, party cheating, and lying. A difference not shown in the table was that boys behaved more consistently from test to test than did the girls, which is interpreted by the authors as indicating that boys are better integrated than girls in this area of conduct.

Hartshorne, May, and Maller (1929) also reported sex differences in cooperative behavior and in persistence at tasks. Five tests of cooperation were given to approximately 400 subjects of each sex in Grades 5 to 8. In three of the tests subjects were allowed to choose between keeping and sharing proceeds earned or things given them. Another allowed a choice between doing or not doing tasks for the benefit of hospital children. The fifth tested "endurance in cooperation" by having the subject work at a speed task twelve minutes for himself and a second twelve minutes for his class. The results showed the girls sig-

TABLE 4

Sex Differences in Deceptive Behavior

(Data from Hartshorne and May, 1928)

Character of Test	No. Tested		Percentage Cheating		CR
	Boys	Girls	Boys	Girls	
1. "School cheating" (subjects graded their own papers at school)	934	957	30.9	33.8	1.35
2. "Home cheating" (in grading their own papers at home)	3041	2909	30.3	37.8	6.10
3. "Speed tests" (answering items after time was called)	1020	1209	38.7	34.8	1.90
4. "Motor coordination" (peeping when eyes are supposed to be shut)	788	1128	79.3	85.4	3.41
5. "Puzzle tests" (faked solutions)	93	63	67.8	73.0	.70
6. "Athletic contests" (taken in privacy and scores exaggerated)	200	137	49.5	56.2	1.21
7. "Party tests" (peeping in a social game)	149	87	38.0	68.0	4.69
8. "Lying tests" (denying types of deception previously guilty of in tests)	375	264	13.0	24.0	3.49

nificantly more cooperative in three tests. On the other two tests the boys were slightly more cooperative but the difference was not reliable. On total score of the five tests there was a critical ratio of 1.9 in favor of the girls. However, when the *reputation* of the subjects for cooperativeness was measured by a "guess who" technique and by a check list given to teachers, the sex difference was enormously magnified, the critical ratio being raised from 1.9 to 7.9. The opinions of teachers and of the children themselves (boys as well as girls) were about equally biased in favor of girls.

Persistence was measured in the same population by three types of tests. In one test stories were read to the subject as far as the climax, at which point the climax, in a form very difficult to decipher, was given the child to read. The subject could either persist in reading the climax or go on to a new story. In a second test the subject was given two puzzles at the same time and was told which to begin with. Score was time spent on the first before giving up and turning to the other. In one experiment both puzzles were of the mechanical variety, in another they were magic squares. As a third test of persistence the authors used the scores earned in the "endurance of cooperation" already described.

On total score of the persistence tests the mean for girls was a little higher than for boys (CR = 1.7). On *reputation* for persistence, measured as was reputation for cooperation, the difference was greatly magnified (CR now = 7.6).

Inhibition (or self-control) was measured in the same populations by four tests: "picture inhibition," "puzzle manipulation," "safe manipulation," and "story inhibition." All these involved work tasks for the subject to do in the presence of interesting distractions. On every test the girls showed greater self-control (CR's ranging from 2.6 to 5.5). Almost exactly the same sex difference was found on reputation for inhibition (CR = 5.0). This was the only instance in which reputation scores were not biased in favor of girls.

Finally, the same groups were put through an elaborate set of tests of moral knowledge and moral opinions. On all tests in this battery the mean for girls exceeded that for boys (CR's ranging from 1.98 to 4.31).

The character test data in general indicate that, although sex differences vary according to the specific situation a test involves, there is a tendency for boys to cheat less than girls and for girls to exceed boys in tests of self-control, persistence, cooperativeness, moral knowledge, and moral opinions.

Cultural Influences on Personality

The social influences to which boys and girls are subjected differ in countless and subtle ways. The differential pressures begin early and operate continuously. They are omnipresent in such things as clothing, play activities, restrictions of mobility, experience with money, home and school discipline, parental associations, occupational experience, educational exposures, and innumerable ideals of conduct and of life satisfactions. Unfortunately, there has been little scientific effort to measure the extent to which particular social pressures differ for the sexes or to assess the effects of such differences in molding sex temperaments. The work of Mead is interesting but unconvincing in view of the known difficulties inherent in the subjective estimation of sex differences from brief observation of primitive groups. Investigations of our own culture are needed that would deal not only with cross-section influences but also with changing patterns of influence. For example, although the incidence of suicide for all ages combined is more than three times as high for males as for females, in the period 1911 to 1920 it was higher for females than for males at ages 15 to 19, then dropped so rapidly for girls that by 1925 the adolescent rate had become equal for the sexes. Between 1911 and 1931 the rate for adolescent girls dropped about 65 per cent, that for boys only about 45 per cent (Dublin and Bunzel, 1933).[1] This relatively greater decrease for girls raises interesting questions for which no answer is available. This is but one problem of many that could be mentioned to illustrate the need for research on differential cultural pressures.

It is possible to consider here only a few studies concerned chiefly with sex differences in familial relationships.

Parent-Child Relationships. Parent-child relationships have been given great prominence by Freudians. Although the psychoanalytic contributions on this problem are extremely interesting, they are beyond the scope of a discussion that is concerned primarily with objective evidences amenable to statistical treatment.

One indication of parental attachments is provided by the child's choice of preferred parent. Simpson (1935) interviewed 500 children, 50 of each sex at each age from 5 to 9 years, all of whom were living at home with both parents. The children were questioned about the favorite parent and were shown pictures of home life which elicited responses throwing additional light on attitudes toward parents. Preferring the mother were 69.6 per cent of boys and 61.2 per cent of girls. The difference is fairly reliable, but a large part of it is accounted for by the marked preference of five-year-old girls for the father. Greatest mother preference was shown by children

whose mothers worked away from home and so had acquired a scarcity value. A number of differences in parental treatment of the children were brought out in the interviews. For example, boys were more often spanked by fathers, girls by mothers. Both sexes were given more pennies by the mother.

Mott (1937) asked 67 boys and 57 girls, all six-year-olds, whom in the family they liked best. Both boys and girls named the mother about twice as often as the father. On the other hand, in a study by Hayward (1935) of 180 unselected children (90 of each sex, Grades 4 to 9) and of 140 delinquent children (82 boys and 58 girls) there was little sex difference in preference for parents.

Terman (1938) found a number of sex differences in the reports given by 792 husbands and 792 wives regarding their childhood experiences. The women reported stronger attachment to the father than did the men, more conflict with the mother, less childhood punishment, more unhappiness in childhood, and more adequate sex education. Similar differences were found in other marital studies (Terman and Buttenwieser, 1935; Burgess and Cottrell, 1939). Personal history data and several personality test scores reported by Wang (1932) for 358 college students (203 men and 155 women) gave some evidence of sex difference in the correlates of family background. Introversion in women was associated with lax discipline by the mother and with lack of religious training, but neither of these relationships was found for men. Introversion in men was associated with a history of irregular money allowance, extroversion with regular allowance or regular earnings.

Even in areas of experience provided by parents for both boys and girls, the exact nature of the experience is likely to differ for the sexes. Hanson (1933) found from

[1] The figures are for United States white populations.

interviews with 39 boys and 59 girls, all of whom had an allowance and managed their own money, that a larger proportion of boys than of girls had had experience in borrowing (44 vs. 30 per cent), lending (39 vs. 18 per cent), investing (75 vs. 48 per cent), and buying clothes (53 vs. 29 per cent). On the other hand, more girls than boys kept accounts.

Newell (1936) studied the effects of maternal hostility upon 35 boys and 40 girls of ages 4 to 18. Results are compared with those from a control group of 36 boys and 46 girls. The author concluded that boys are more aggressive if there is consistent hostility on the part of one or both parents, and that girls are submissive if the father is protective or ambivalent. These conclusions rest on judgments of a rather subjective nature and need to be checked against more objective evidence.

Stagner (1938) investigated the rôle of parents in the development of emotional stability and instability. His subjects were college freshmen (28 men, 22 women) who were given two tests of emotional instability and the Stagner-Drought scales for measuring attitudes toward parents. Responses that tended to be associated with emotional stability were:

	Responses by	
	Men	Women
Punished by mother	No	No
Punished by father	Yes	No
Spoiled by mother	Yes	...
Mother demonstrative	No	...
Home life as child happy	Yes	Yes
Father emotional	No	...
Parents happily married	Yes	Yes
Father played much with you	Yes	...
Close-knit family	Yes	...
Mother happy	Yes	Yes
Mother demanded obedience	No	...
Father demanded obedience	...	No
Conflict with mother	No	Yes
Mother at home much	...	Yes
Father at home much	...	No

	Responses by	
	Men	Women
Idealize father	Yes	...
Idealize mother	No	Yes
"Give up" for mother	...	Yes
Ever ashamed of father	No	...

Cavan (1932) gave 900 junior high school children the Woodworth test of neurotic tendency. One question which the subject is asked in this test is whether he sometimes wishes he had never been born. The question was answered affirmatively by 22.8 per cent of boys and 30.3 per cent of girls. Subjects who answered affirmatively scored more neurotic on the Woodworth test than did those who answered negatively; they were also reliably lower in teachers' ratings on moral traits, emotional stability, and social aggressiveness. When the subjects were questioned further about family relationships it was found that the wish never to have been born was significantly related to attitudes toward parents, to home punishments, to mother's nervousness (as reported by subject), and to broken home. Again the relationships were more marked with girls than with boys. Of girls from broken homes, 37.5 per cent expressed the wish as compared with 26.9 per cent from unbroken homes. The corresponding figures for boys were 23.7 per cent and 22.4 per cent. With girls the wish in question was significantly related to number of friends and to number of club memberships; for boys no such relationships were found.

Sibling Relationships. That sibling relationships are capable of influencing sex differences is indicated by several investigators. In a study of 400 school children in Germany, Busemann (1928) reported that children with siblings of the same sex have better school grades than children in mixed sibships; that boys from arge families are more tractable than those from small families, whereas the reverse is true for girls; and that both sexes increase in industry and success with size of sibship. However, a critical examination of the author's methods and data throws doubt on the validity of these conclusions.

Thurstone and Jenkins (1931) studied the sibships of nearly a thousand children brought to a behavior clinic. Their data suggest that if a problem boy comes from a family having two or more problem children, his next older sib is more likely to be a boy, as is also his next younger sib. If a girl comes from such a family her next younger sib is more likely to be a boy, but there is little difference on the sex of her next older sib. If a problem boy comes from a family having one behavior case, his next older sib is more likely to be a boy; if a girl comes from such a family, her next younger sib is also more likely to be a boy. In other words, there is a preponderance of boys among the adjacent sibs of behavior clinic cases. Because of the unknown selective factors that may affect a behavior clinic population a control group is needed to check the validity of this finding. The comparable study by Phillips (1931) of a clinic group of 125 boys and 101 girls agrees closely with the figures of Thurstone and Jenkins for boy patients but not for girl patients. For boys the two sets of figures are:

	Thurstone and Jenkins		Phillips	
	N	Percentage	*N*	Percentage
Next older a boy	552	58.2	39	59.0
Next older a girl	396	41.8	27	40.9
Next younger a boy	589	57.9	36	59.0
Next younger a girl	428	42.1	25	40.9

It is particularly significant that the study by Sletto (1934), who used a control group, also points to sibling influences as a factor in delinquency. His subjects were 939 delinquents (786 boys, 153 girls) and 939 nondelinquents matched for age, sex, and size of sibship. His data show that for boys whose birth order position was between two brothers in three-child families the incidence of delinquency was twice as high as it was for boys who were between two sisters. Similarly, delinquency ratios were higher for girls who had brothers but no sisters than for girls with sisters but no brothers.

Sex Differences in Sensitivity to Environment. The belief seems to be fairly general that girls are more susceptible to environmental influences than are boys. Spencer (1938) investigated mental conflict among 192 high school students—88 boys and 104 girls. Although his method of measuring conflict (too complicated to describe here) yielded higher conflict scores for boys, the scores of girls were more closely related to a number of environmental variables, including broken home, irregular church attendance, and being youngest in the family. Terman's (1938) study of 792 marriages reported separately for husbands and wives the relationships between marital happiness and a number of variables having to do with family background. Relationships which approached statistical significance are listed on p. 986. There was no husband-wife difference in relation of marital happiness to marital happiness of parents, to birth order, to number of opposite sex siblings, or to childhood happiness.

In Germany, Busemann and Harders (1932) compared the school grades of 473 children of unemployed parents with the grades of 1154 whose fathers were fully employed. All subjects in both groups were from families of two children and

	More Closely Related to Happiness of	Direction of Relationship
Much conflict with mother	Wives	Negative
No attachment to father	Husbands	Negative
Greater attachment to father than to mother	Wives	Negative
Childhood happiness below average	Wives	Negative
Parents rebuffed child's sex curiosity	Husbands	Negative
Premarital attitude toward sex that of passionate longing	Husbands	Negative
Much association with opposite sex during adolescence	Husbands	Positive
Very strict religious training	Wives	Negative
Sex instruction very inadequate	Husbands	Negative

ranged in age from 8 to 14 years. The authors concluded that girls suffer more effect than boys from parental unemployment. Actually their data showed that this sex difference is unreliably small and that it disappears altogether when the comparison is made separately for three occupational classes.

Springer (1938) gave the Brown personality inventory to 327 slum children and to 473 children of a good district. Ages were 9 to 15 years. Mean adjustment scores were better for the latter group, and to almost exactly the same extent with boys and girls. There was no evidence that life in a slum district affects one sex more than the other. The adjustment scores reported by Pintner (1940) for 1400 children who were hard of hearing and for a comparable group of normal children indicated that hearing more seriously affects the adjustment of boys than of girls. The difference was not large, but because of the large N's it was statistically significant. For girls the hearing defect was a handicap to adjustment only when hearing was extremely poor.

The evidence now available hardly justifies the broad generalization that girls are more sensitive than boys to environmental influences. We need more information on the differential effects of specific environments.

Mental Abilities

An adequate summary of available data on sex differences in mental abilities would require a fair-sized volume. Notwithstanding the wealth of data, the large populations tested, and the objectivity of scores on which sex comparisons are based, brevity is here permissible for three reasons: (1) much of the material has been previously summarized in textbooks and elsewhere; (2) the results are sufficiently consistent to leave little doubt as to what are the essential facts; and (3) present limitations of space allow only a brief sketch of the results of typical studies in selected areas. The areas chosen for treatment include language development in the preschool child, later vocabulary growth, memory, intelligence as measured by specific tests, and measured achievement in reading, science, and arithmetic. Important areas omitted entirely include musical ability, artistic ability, mechanical ability, and the various kinds of psychomotor skills. Only scant reference can be made to sex differences in the subtests of test batteries.

Early Language Development. The mean age of learning to talk appears to be slightly lower with girls than with boys. According to mothers' reports on 502 gifted children (Terman *et al.*, 1925) the difference was approximately three weeks, or 5.52 times its standard error. In the ame study girls were reported as using hort sentences earlier than boys, but this lifference was not very reliable (*C.R.* = .71). It is not known whether mothers' eports of this kind are subject to a memory bias favoring girls.

Several studies indicate a slight superiority of girls in articulation, intelligibility, and correctness of speech sounds. In a study of speech sounds of 204 preschool children Wellman *et al.* (1931) found differences in correctness of consonant sounds that were fairly reliable at ages 3 and 4 (CR's = 2.6 and 2.5). Differences in the correctness of vowel sounds were not significant. Little and Williams (1937) in a study of speech sounds, intelligibility, and organization based on 177 preschool subjects and 155 orphanage children of preschool age concluded that "there is a general tendency for girls to score higher than the boys in all areas and at most age levels." This conclusion, however, is not supported by the data which he authors presented. In 18 sex comparisons of the preschool group 9 favored girls, 8 favored boys, and one showed no sex difference. Of 15 comparisons for the orphanage group, 9 favored girls, 6 favored boys. The age-sex groups were small, and tests of significance were not given.

The mean length of spoken sentences among preschool children was reported by M. E. Smith (1926) and by McCarthy (1930) to be slightly greater for girls. However, the age-sex groups in both these studies were too small to afford reliable differences. In extent of vocabulary Smith's count of words used by 68 boys and 69 girls under age 2 did not reveal consistent differences in favor of either sex. A vocabulary test devised by this author and used with over 100 children of each sex aged 2 to 6 years showed no reliable sex difference.

Later Vocabulary Growth. Among the recent studies affording sex comparisons on later vocabulary growth the following gave typical results. Gansl (1939) used a 100-item multiple-choice test in all regular classes of Grades 3 to 8 in two New York City public schools. In one school all the means for ages 8 to 14 favored boys, but only at age 12 was the difference statistically significant. In the other school the differences were neither reliable nor consistent. Schiller (1934) did not find a reliable sex difference on the vocabulary subtest of Thorndike's CAVD given to 189 boys and 206 girls in the third and fourth grades of a Brooklyn public school. Similarly small and inconsistent differences were reported by Bryan (1934) for 100 boys and 100 girls at ages 5 and 6; by Garrett, Bryan, and Perl (1935) for ages 9, 12, and 15; by Broom (1930) for 600 junior high school subjects of each sex; by Hales (1932) for a large group of 12- to 16-year-old Australian subjects; and by McIntyre and Wood (1935) for Australian children aged 9 to 12.

Although the studies to date indicate no marked quantitative difference in the total vocabulary of boys and girls at any age up to the late teens, it is probable that significant qualitative differences would be disclosed by a vocabulary test composed of separate lists of words representing different fields of knowledge, such as science, mechanics, sports, literature, the arts, business, and social manners. Greene (1937) devised a test of this type which would yield interesting results if applied to unselected sex groups.

Memory. One form of memory may be tested by the delayed response technique. Allen (1931) reported a study of delayed reactions based upon 52 boys and 48 girls aged almost exactly 12 months. A subject was induced to play with a toy while on his mother's lap. The toy was then taken from the child and dropped in one of three symmetrically arranged boxes on a near-by table, which was then pushed beyond the child's reach. After a specified time the table was pushed back and the child was given 60 seconds to make a response. The author presented data for a number of delay periods, beginning with 10 seconds, but the only sex difference verging on significance (CR = 2.7) was that for the 45-second period of delay in favor of girls. It is to be noted that in this experiment the use of language aids was ruled out by the age of the subjects. In the standardization of the 1937 Stanford-Binet scales a delayed reaction test, with verbal instructions, was given to 204 boys and 200 girls, including approximately 50 of each sex at each of the following ages: 18, 24, 30, and 36 months. For these ages combined the proportion of passes was 83 per cent for girls and 71 per cent for boys. The difference between the percentages is statistically significant (CR = 2.65).[1]

Sex comparisons on digit span are available from many sources and for large populations. The studies are almost unanimous in showing that sex differences are trifling and inconsistent. This holds for the subjects tested at ages 10 to 13 by Dewey, Child, and Ruml (1920); for Goodenough's (1928) sample of 300 subjects aged 2, 3, and 4 years; for 450 subjects aged 7 to 14 years tested by Fischler and Ullert (1929); for Bryan's (1934) 100 subjects of each sex between the ages of 5 and 6; for Easby-Grave's (1924) 500 first-grade children; for Altmaier's (1931) 500 sixth-grade children; and for Leaming's (1922) 600 subjects aged 15 years. The tests by Garrett, Bryan, and Perl (1935) of about 100 subjects of each sex at each of the ages 9, 12,

and 15 gave small but unreliable differences in favor of the boys at all ages. The only study giving consistent differences favoring girls is Woolley's (1926), which was based upon tests of working and school children aged 14 to 18 years. Selective factors may have affected her samples. The standardization data for the 1937 revision of the Stanford-Binet showed only small sex differences in percentages passing the digit-span tests at the various age levels, though it may be significant that 15 out of 18 summed comparisons were slightly favorable to the girls.

In memory span for sentences the data of Fischler and Ullert (1929) showed no sex differences. Those of Bryan (1934) showed an unreliable difference in favor of girls. The standardization data of the 1937 Stanford-Binet scales gave only one reliable sex difference in 28 available comparisons. Below age 5½ the small differences rather consistently favored girls; from 5½ on there was no consistent trend in either direction.

Data on memory for designs and forms were reported by Woolley (1926) for 358 boys and 277 girls aged 18 years; by Garrett, Bryan, and Perl (1935) in their study of age groups 9, 12, and 15; by Fischler and Ullert (1929) for groups aged 7 to 14; by Bryan (1934) for 200 subjects aged 5; and by Holzinger and Swineford (1939) for 146 boys and 155 girls in Grades 7 and 8. None of these investigations yielded reliable or consistent sex differences. The studies just mentioned tested recognition of geometrical forms. Tests of reproducing designs from memory were given the standardization groups on which the 1937 Stanford-Binet revision was based. Although there was not a reliable sex difference in the summed percentages, in 28 of 46 comparisons the results favored boys.

On memory for narratives the direction of sex difference depends upon content of

[1] A detailed analysis of the data on which the 1937 Stanford-Binet revision is based can be found in Q. McNemar, 1942, *The Revision of the Stanford-Binet Scale; an Analysis of the Standardization Data*, Boston: Houghton Mifflin.

he material used and its differential appeal to the sexes. Data supporting this conclusion were reported by Pyle (1925), Dietze and Jones (1931), and Garrett, Bryan, and Perl (1935). The 1937 Stanford-Binet standardization data led to the same conclusion.

General Intelligence. Total scores on various tests of general intelligence have been reported separately for the sexes by many investigators. Although the groups tested are often large they can never be viewed as strictly random samples of the general population, since a number of factors affecting school enrollments are known to operate differentially for the sexes. In general, however, the sex differences found were so small and so inconsistent in direction that no positive claim could be made for the superiority of either sex at any age. An interesting table compiled by Kuznets and McNemar (1940) brought together the pertinent data of 12 studies reporting sex comparisons for large groups and for a wide range of ages on such tests as the 1916 Stanford-Binet, the NIT, Thorndike's IER, the Pressey intelligence test, the McCall multi-mental test, and the Spearman test. Of the 56 sex-age comparisons in this table, 28 favored boys, 25 favored girls, and 3 gave zero difference. The Pressey and the NIT consistently favored girls, whereas the IER no less consistently favored boys.

Sex comparisons not included in the table referred to were reported by Broom (1930) for 1200 subjects in Grades 7, 8, and 9 given the Terman group test; by Armstrong (1932) on 400 subjects given the Otis, the Army performance (individual), and Army Beta; by Madsen (1924) on 880 subjects given the 1916 Stanford-Binet; and by Kaulfers (1928) on 1002 subjects given the 1916 Stanford-Binet. All these studies yielded negative results. On the other hand, Rigg's (1940) data on 10,079 children in Grades 3 to 8 who were given the NIT showed a small but highly reliable difference favoring girls in the combined grade groups. Terman and Merrill (1937) found only small sex differences in IQ's on the L and M scales of the revised Stanford-Binet, but it should be noted that the authors eliminated a number of test items from the trial battery because they seemed to favor unduly one or the other of the sexes.

A large majority of the sex comparisons reported are based upon groups that did not include extreme variants. The Scottish Mental Surveys are exceptions to this rule. The first of these (1933) involved a verbal group test of practically all the children (except the blind or deaf) who were born in Scotland in a given year, totaling over 87,000. The test was administered when the subjects were between 10½ and 11 years of age. The means for the sexes were almost identical. The 1916 Stanford-Binet was given to a subsample of 500 of each sex. After a correction was applied to free the sample from bias due to over-representation of superior children there was no reliable difference between the sexes in mean IQ. In the second Scottish survey (Macmeeken, 1939) the 1916 Stanford-Binet was given to all living children who had been born in Scotland on one of four specified days of 1926 (444 boys and 430 girls). This is the most nearly perfect sampling in the history of psychometrics, for only a single child who should have been tested was missed. Here again the mean IQ's were almost identical for the sexes. Another good sampling was made by Roberts *et al.* (1935), who gave the Otis advanced test to all children of Bath, England, born between specified dates in 1921 and 1924. The sample included 1336 boys and 1217 girls, aged 9½ to 13½ when the tests were administered. The sex difference was minute and unreliable.

The amount and direction of difference on nonverbal and performance tests depend upon the specific nature of the tests used. Data were reported by Pintner (1924) for 924 subjects aged 10 and for 1346 subjects aged 12 given his non-language group test. No reliable sex difference was found. Lincoln's (1927) data on 200 to 400 subjects at each age from 7 to 16 given the Dearborn general examination showed only small and inconsistent differences between the sexes. Goodenough (1926) gave sex comparisons for nearly 1600 subjects, ages 6 to 11 years, on her test of drawing a man. The girls were superior at each age, the critical ratios ranging from 0.5 to 2.7. The previously mentioned Scottish group consisting of 444 boys and 430 girls born on specified days in 1926 was given between the ages of 9 and 11 a battery of eight performance tests including a form board, a manikin, two picture completion tests, cube construction, and Kohs block designs. The difference favored boys (CR = 3.74).

The numerous studies reporting the results of intelligence tests in high schools and colleges are inconclusive for sex differences because of the selective factors that are known to affect enrollments at the upper educational levels. About all one can say is that the more verbal the test the more likely it is to yield higher scores for girls, and that boys are favored by tests which are heavily loaded with scientific and mathematical content.

Achievement in Reading. A survey of representative studies does not suggest that any marked sex differences exist in reading ability or reading achievement. Heilman's (1933) data for all 10-year-old children in the public schools of Denver showed no sex difference for either of the reading subtests of the Stanford Achievement Tests. Schiller (1934) found no reliable sex difference from her application of the Gates silent reading test to third and fourth-grade subjects. Results on the Thorndike-McCall reading test have been reported by Thorndike et al. (1934) for 266 boys and 200 girls aged 13 to 15 years and for 785 boys and 905 girls in the eighth grade of New York City public schools. In the first of these groups there was a reliable difference favoring girls; in the second a reliable difference favoring boys. McIntyre and Wood (1935) administered tests of reading achievement to approximately 33,000 subjects in Australia. The tests provided separate measures of vocabulary, speed of reading, reading for general meaning, reading for detail, and reading for inference. Only on speed of reading were there consistent and reliable sex differences, in this case favoring girls.

Several studies are available in which sex comparisons on reading tests are presented for school groups not classified by age. Jordan (1937) gave such comparisons for two reading tests used in a survey of high school seniors in North Carolina. Girls were superior to boys in both tests; the differences were small, but because of the large population tested one difference was statistically significant. Score distributions reported by Woody (1937, 1938) on the Traxler silent reading test applied to first- and second-year high school students in a Michigan survey yielded mean differences (computed by Kuznets) that favored boys.

We have already noted one study in which sex comparisons by age on speed of reading favored girls. Moore (1940) reported speed scores on the Iowa silent reading test for all white pupils in Grades 6, 8, 10, and 12 in two southern towns. The *N* was approximately 100 of each sex in each of these grades. The only reliable difference (CR = 2.9) favored the girls in Grade 8, and this was accompanied by a reliable difference favoring girls on the Otis test of mental ability (CR = 3.5).

Achievement in Science. Significant differences favoring males are found in practically all studies in which achievement in science has been measured by objective tests. Heilman (1933), in the well-known study of intelligence and achievement of unselected 10-year-olds in Denver, reported a higher mean for 464 boys than for 482 girls on the nature study and science section of the Stanford Achievement Tests (CR = 2.6). Terman *et al.* (1925) reported achievement test scores for sex groups of about 560 gifted children and an equal number of unselected children all in Grades 3 to 8. The gifted sex groups were closely equated for IQ. On 110 items of science information the difference in means consistently favored boys in both the gifted and unselected groups, though in a majority of the 13 comparisons the differences lacked statistical significance because of the small *N*'s at a single age.

Sex differences in science achievement apparently increase as we go up the educational ladder. Jordan (1937) in his survey of North Carolina high school seniors, which included some 8000 boys and 11,000 girls, reported an astronomically large critical ratio in favor of boys on the science section of the achievement test used (CR = 31.7). Learned and Wood (1938) in their valuable study of the achievement of college students reported achievement scores in natural science for 2992 men and 1410 women. The mean was markedly higher for men, the difference being twenty-four times its standard error. It hardly needs to be pointed out that this great superiority of males in achievement scores is no proof that males are better endowed than females with scientific ability; it may be due entirely to difference in interests.

Arithmetical Achievement. Buckingham and MacLatchy (1930) studied the number abilities of approximately 1000 first-grade entrants aged 6 to 6½ years. The subjects were tested in rote counting by ones and by tens, counting 20 objects, number selection, and number identification. In all but 2 of 11 comparisons the difference favored girls, the critical ratios ranging from 1.03 to 2.90. Woody (1931) gave an individual inventory test in arithmetic involving 205 items to approximately 100 children in kindergartens, 600 in Grade 1B, 1800 in Grade 1A, and 300 in Grades 2B and 2A. Boys were superior in all comparisons, but in no case was the difference statistically significant.

On the results of pencil-and-paper tests of arithmetical achievement there is a vast quantity of data available. Reference can here be made to only a few representative studies. Heilman's (1933) study of 10-year-olds in Denver showed girls superior to boys in the arithmetic computation test of the SAT battery (CR = 2.10) and boys superior to girls in the arithmetic reasoning test (CR = 2.68). In his monumental study of the mental and scholastic achievement of London children Burt (1921) reported sex comparisons in seven phases of arithmetical achievement for about 250 of each sex at each age from 8 to 12 years. In oral arithmetic boys were reliably superior at every age. In "mechanical" arithmetic the differences were unreliable except at age 12, where boys were reliably superior. In arithmetic problems the differences were reliably in favor of boys at all ages and were particularly large at ages 11 and 12. In addition, subtraction, multiplication, and division (five age-sex comparisons for each) there were only two reliable differences, both favoring girls in addition. Schiller's (1934) data for 189 boys and 206 girls in Grades 3 and 4 showed no appreciable sex difference in computation, but in arithmetical reasoning boys were reliably superior (CR = 4.17). Cunningham and Price (1935) reported the results of arithmetic tests given to approximately 40,000 children in Australia. In addition, subtraction, multiplication, and division the differences were small and inconsistent. In "mechanical" arithmetic the differences all favored boys but were not statistically significant. In "problem" arithmetic the differences all favored boys and were highly reliable. Grossnickle (1937) gave a test of "concepts in social arithmetic" to 667 boys and 670 girls at the end of the eighth grade. The concepts tested were classified in such categories as banking, taxation, insurance, etc. The sex difference favored boys, and though small in magnitude was statistically significant (CR = 5.4).

The standardization data on which the 1937 Stanford-Binet revision is based afford sex comparisons on concept of one, concept of two, concept of three, concept of four, counting to three, counting 13 pennies, counting taps, knowledge of numbers, making change, and arithmetical reasoning. On concepts of one, two, three, and four there are 16 sex comparisons by age on percentages passing, of which 11 favor girls and 4 favor boys. In the three counting tests the sex difference favors girls in 11 comparisons, the boys in two. In knowledge of numbers the differences are small and inconsistent. In making change all the six comparisons favor boys. The most reliable differences are for the test of arithmetical reasoning, the boys being superior in all the age groups.

From the above studies it appears that in arithmetical achievement the sex differences are small at the lower levels represented by routine computation and that they progressively favor boys as we go toward the more complex levels of arithmetical reasoning.

Sex Differences in Dispersion. The relative variability of the sexes has long been a very hotly debated issue. Among those who have participated in the controversy are Ellis (1894, 1903), Pearson (1897) and Hollingworth (1914). An impartial list of the eminent persons of any country or any period is sure to contain a vast preponderance of men. At the opposite extreme of the ability range more males than females are usually reported in the statistical surveys of mental deficiency. Here, however, the excess of males is not great and might conceivably be accounted for by biased samplings. McNemar and Terman (1936) made an extensive survey of the most reliable and objective data available on variability of the sexes in physical traits, scholastic achievement, and intelligence. The results for achievement are far from consistent but on the whole afford a slight preponderance of evidence favoring greater male variability. In the less well-standardized psychological tests the evidence breaks about evenly for the sexes. However, of 33 comparisons based on such standardized tests as CAVD, NIT, the Pressey group test, and the 1916 Stanford-Binet, 29 showed greater variability for males, the mean of the critical ratios being 1.47. This mean is 8.4 times its standard error. On the other hand, the carefully selected group tested in the standardization of the 1937 Stanford-Binet scales, including about 1500 of each sex, showed no consistent sex differences in dispersion. Perhaps the best data of all come from the two Scottish surveys, both of which show the SD of IQ distribution about one point higher for boys. If the distribution of intelligence can be assumed to follow the Gaussian curve, a difference of one IQ point in variability would show about 9 girls to 6 boys scoring above 140 IQ or below 60 IQ. A school population of 16,800 in Grades 3 to 8 which was sifted by Terman *et al.* (1925) for children of 140 IQ, or higher, yielded 352 boys and 291 girls who reached this standard, a ratio of about 6 to 5. Of these, 65 boys and 48 girls reached or exceeded 160 IQ, a ratio of approximately 5.4 to 4. A large high school population sifted by the Terman group test yielded 257 boys and 121 girls whose scores were judged to be the equivalent of 140 IQ or higher on the Stanford-Binet.

If the greater male variability suggested by the Scottish surveys represents the true facts, the apparent excess of mentally defective males would seem to be accounted for. So small a difference, however, would not account for the enormous excess of males among historical geniuses. Sex differences in motivation and opportunities were no doubt important factors.

Bibliography

REFERENCES CITED

ABBOTT, M. A. 1927. A study of the motion picture preferences of the Horace Mann high schools. *Teach. Coll. Rec.*, 28, 819–835.

ACKERSON, L. 1931. *Children's behavior problems.* Chicago: University of Chicago Press.

ADAMS, E. A. 1936. The use of libraries in junior and senior high schools. *Univ. S. Calif. Educ. Monogr.*, No. 8. Pp. x + 105.

ALBERTY, H. B. 1925. The permanence of the vocational choices of high school pupils. *Industr. Arts Mag.*, 14, 203–207.

ALLEN, C. N. 1931. Individual differences in delayed reactions of infants. *Arch. Psychol., N. Y.*, 19, No. 127.

ALPER, B. S., and G. E. LODGEN. 1936. The delinquent child in Pennsylvania courts. *Ment. Hyg., N. Y.*, 20, 598–604.

ALTMAIER, C. L. 1931. The performance level of children in the sixth grade in two Philadelphia public schools. *Psychol. Clin.*, 19, 233–257.

ARMSTRONG, C. P. 1932. Sex differences in the mental functioning of school children. *J. Appl. Psychol.*, 16, 559–571.

AVELING, F., and H. L. HARGREAVES. 1921. Suggestibility with and without prestige in children. *Brit. J. Psychol.*, 12, 53–75.

BAKWIN, H. 1929. Sex factor in infant mortality. *Human Biol.*, 1, 90–116.

BEASLEY, W. C. 1938. Sex differences and age variations in hearing loss in relation to stage of deafness. *Nat. Health Surv. Bull.*, No. 6.

BEESON, M. F. 1928. A study of vocational preferences of high school students. *Voc. Guid. Mag.*, 7, 115–119.

BELL, H. M. 1939. *The theory and practice of personal counseling.* Stanford University, Calif.: Stanford University Press.

BERNE, E. V. C. 1930. An experimental investigation of social behavior patterns in young children. *Univ. Iowa Stud. Child Welfare*, 4, No. 3.

BERNREUTER, R. G. 1933. The theory and construction of the personality inventory. *J. Soc. Psychol.*, 4, 387–405.

BLAIR, G. M. 1938. Mentally superior and inferior children in the junior and senior high school; a comparative study of their backgrounds, interests, and ambitions. *Teach. Coll. Contr. Educ.*, No. 766.

BLATZ, W. E., and M. C. RINGLAND. 1935. *A study of tics in pre-school children.* Toronto: University of Toronto Press.

BOOK, W. F. 1922. *The intelligence of high school seniors.* New York: Macmillan.

BOYNTON, P. L. 1936. The vocational preferences of school children. *J. Genet. Psychol.*, 49, 411–425.

BRACKETT, C. W. 1934. Laughing and crying of preschool children. *Child Develpm. Monogr.*, No. 14. Pp. xv + 91.

BROOM, M. E. 1930. Sex differences in mental ability among junior high school pupils. *J. Appl. Psychol.*, 14, 83–90.

BROSTER, L. R., *et al.* 1938. *The adrenal cortex and intersexuality.* London: Chapman and Hall.

BROWN, F. 1934. A psychoneurotic inventory for children between nine and fourteen years of age. *J. Appl. Psychol.*, 18, 566–577.

BROWN, P. A. 1939. Responses of blind and seeing adolescents to a neurotic inventory. *J. Psychol.*, 7, 211–221.

BRYAN, A. I. 1934. Organization of memory in young children. *Arch. Psychol., N. Y.*, No. 162.

BUCKINGHAM, B. R., and J. MACLATCHY. 1930. The number abilities of children when they enter grade one. *Yearb. Nat. Soc. Stud. Educ.*, 29(II), 473–549.

BURGESS, E. W., and L. S. COTTRELL. 1939. *Predicting success or failure in marriage.* New York: Prentice-Hall.

BURKS, B., D. W. JENSEN, and L. M. TERMAN. 1930. *Genetic studies of genius:* Vol. III. *The promise of youth; follow-up studies of a thousand gifted children.* Stanford University, Calif.: Stanford University Press.

BURT, C. L. 1921. *Mental and scholastic tests.* London: King.

BURTON, A. C. 1939. Temperature regulation. *Ann. Rev. Physiol.*, 1, 109–130.

BUSEMANN, A. 1928. Geschwisterschaft, Schultuchtigkeit und Charakter. *Z. Kinderforsch.*, 34, 1–52.

BUSEMANN, A., and G. HARDERS. 1932. Die Wirkung väterlicher Erwerbslosigkeit auf die Schulleistungen der Kinder. *Z. Kinderforsch.*, 40, 89–100.

BUTLER, E. I. 1934. A study of the needs of high school students and the effectiveness of a program of learning in selected phases of child development and family relationships. *Univ. Iowa Stud. Child Welfare*, **10**, 169–248.

CADY, V. M. 1923. The estimation of juvenile incorrigibility. *J. Delinq. Monogr.*, No. 2. Pp. 140.

CAILLE, R. K. 1933. Resistant behavior of preschool children. *Child Develpm. Monogr.*, No. 11. Pp. xvi + 142.

CAMPBELL, H. M. 1939. Differences in clique formation among adolescent boys and girls revealed by a "guess who" technique. (Abstract.) *Psychol. Bull.*, **36**, 537.

CARTER, H. D. 1935. Twin-similarities in emotional traits. *Character and Pers.*, **4**, 61–78.

CARTER, H. D., and E. K. STRONG. 1933. Sex differences in occupational interests of high school students. *Person. J.*, **12**, 166–175.

CASON, H. 1935. The nightmare dream. *Psychol. Monogr.*, **46**, No. 209. Pp. 51.

CATTELL, P. 1928. *Dentition as a measure of maturity.* Cambridge: Harvard University Press.

CATTELL, R. B. 1935. On the measure of "perseveration." *Brit. J. Educ. Psychol.*, **5**, 76–92.

CAVAN, R. S. 1932. The wish never to have been born. *Amer. J. Sociol.*, **37**, 547–559.

CHALLMAN, R. C. 1932. Factors influencing friendships among preschool children. *Child Develpm.*, **3**, 146–158.

CHAPMAN, J. C. 1924. Persistence, success and speed in a mental task. *Ped. Sem.*, **31**, 276–284.

CHEVALEVA-JANOVSKAJA, E. 1927. Les groupements spontanés d'enfants à l'âge pré-sholaires. *Arch. Psychol., Genève*, **20**, 219–233.

CIOCCO, A. 1938. Audiometric studies of school children: V. Changes in air conduction acuity after an interval of five years, with particular reference to the effect of age and sex. *Ann. Otol., etc., St. Louis*, **47**, 926–937.

COLEMAN, J. H. 1931. Written composition interests of junior and senior high school pupils. *Teach. Coll. Contr. Educ.*, No. 494.

COLLINS, M. 1927. British norms for the Pressey Cross-out Test. *Brit. J. Psychol.*, **18**, 121–133.

COLUMBA, SR. M. 1926. A study of interests and their relations to other factors of achievement in the elementary school subjects. *Cath. Univ. Amer. Educ. Res. Bull.*, **1**, No. 7.

COLVIN, S. S., and A. H. MACPHAIL. 1924. Intelligence of seniors in the high schools of Massachusetts. *U. S. Bur. Educ. Bull.*, No. 9.

CREW, F. A. E. 1927. *The genetics of sexuality in animals.* New York: Macmillan.

CUNNINGHAM, K. S., and W. T. PRICE. 1935. The standardization of an Australian arithmetic test. *Aust. Coun. Educ. Res. Ser.*, No. 21.

CUSHING, H. M. 1929. A perseverative tendency in pre-school children. A study in personality differences. *Arch. Psychol., N. Y.*, **17**, No. 108.

DANBY, T. A. 1934. The sex incidence of mental deficiency (amentia) with a consideration of mental variation in the sexes. *Ment. Welfare*, **15**, 8–16.

DARLEY, J. G. 1937. Tested maladjustment related to clinically diagnosed maladjustment. *J. Appl. Psychol.*, **21**, 632–642.

DAVIS, E. A. 1932. The form and function of children's questions. *Child Develpm.*, **3**, 57–74.

DAWE, H. C. 1934. An analysis of two hundred quarrels of preschool children. *Child Develpm.*, **5**, 139–157.

DEWEY, E., E. CHILD, and B. RUML. 1920. *Methods and results of testing school children.* New York: Dutton.

DIETZE, A. G., and G. E. JONES. 1931. Factual memory of secondary school pupils for a short article which they read a single time. *J. Educ. Psychol.*, **22**, 586–598; 667–676.

DOUGLASS, A. A. 1922. Vocational interests of high-school seniors. *Sch. and Soc.*, **16**, 79–84.

DUBLIN, L. I., and B. BUNZEL. 1933. *To be or not to be: A study in suicide.* New York: Smith and Haas.

DUBLIN, L. I., and A. J. LOTKA. 1936. *Length of life.* New York: Ronald.

EASBY-GRAVE, C. 1924. Tests and norms at the six year old performance level. *Psychol. Clin.*, **15**, 261–300.

EISENBERG, A. L. 1936. *Children and radio programs.* New York: Columbia University Press.

ELLIS, H. 1894. *Man and woman.* (1st ed.) London: Scott.

———. 1903. Variation in man and woman. *Pop. Sci. Mon.*, **62**, 237–253. Also in Appendix to *Man and woman.* (6th ed.) London: Black, 1926.

EVANS, H. M. 1939. Endocrine glands: Gonads, pituitary, and adrenals. *Ann. Rev. Physiol.*, **1**, 577–652.

FARWELL, L. 1930. Reactions of kindergarten, first- and second-grade children to constructive play materials. *Genet. Psychol. Monogr.*, **8**, 431–562.

FISCHLER, D., and I. ULLERT. 1929. Contribution à l'étude des tests de mémoire immédiate. *Arch. Psychol., Genève*, **21**, 293–306.

FLORY, C. D. 1935. Sex differences in skeletal development. *Child Develpm.*, **6**, 205–212.

FORTES, M. 1933. Notes on juvenile delinquency: I. The age of young delinquents in East London. *Sociol. Rev.*, **25**, 14–24.

FOSTER, J. C. 1930. Play activities of children in the first six grades. *Child Develpm.*, **1**, 248–254.

FOSTER, J. C., and J. E. ANDERSON. 1936. Un

pleasant dreams in childhood. *Child Develpm.*, **7**, 77–84.

FOSTER, S. 1927. A study of the personality make-up and social setting of fifty jealous children. *Ment. Hyg., N. Y.*, **11**, 53–57.

FRANK, L. K. 1933. Childhood and youth. In President's Research Committee on Social Trends, *Recent social trends in the United States.* New York: McGraw-Hill. Vol. II, pp. 751–800.

FUXLOCH, K. 1930. Das Sociologische im Spiel des Kindes. *Beih. Z. angew. Psychol.*, No. 53.

GANSL, I. 1939. Vocabulary: Its measurement and growth. *Arch. Psychol., N. Y.*, No. 236.

GARRETT, H. E., A. I. BRYAN, and R. E. PERL. 1935. The age factor in mental organization. *Arch. Psychol., N. Y.*, No. 176.

GATEWOOD, M. C., and A. P. WEISS. 1930. Race and sex differences in newborn infants. *J. Genet. Psychol.*, **38**, 31–49.

GILKINSON, H. 1937. Masculine temperament and secondary sex characteristics: A study of the relationship between psychological and physical measures of masculinity. *Genet. Psychol. Monogr.*, **19**, 105–154.

GOODENOUGH, F. L. 1926. *Measurement of intelligence by drawings.* Yonkers-on-Hudson: World Book.

——. 1928. *The Kuhlmann-Binet tests for children of preschool age.* (*Inst. Child Welfare Monogr. Ser.*, No. 2.) Minneapolis: University of Minnesota Press. Pp. viii + 146.

——. 1929. The emotional behavior of young children during mental tests. *J. Juv. Res.*, **13**, 204–219.

——. 1930. Inter-relationships in the behavior of young children. *Child Develpm.*, **1**, 29–47.

——. 1931. *Anger in young children.* (*Inst. Child Welfare Monogr. Ser.*, No. 9.) Minneapolis: University of Minnesota Press. Pp. xiii + 278.

GREEN, E. H. 1933*a.* Friendships and quarrels among preschool children. *Child Develpm.*, **4**, 237–252.

——. 1933*b.* Group play and quarreling among preschool children. *Child Develpm.*, **4**, 302–307.

GREENE, E. B. 1937. *Michigan vocabulary profile: Forms I, II.* Ann Arbor: Author.

GROSSNICKLE, F. E. 1937. Concepts in social arithmetic for the eighth grade level. *J. Educ. Res.*, **30**, 475–488.

HAGGERTY, M. E. 1925. The incidence of undesirable behavior in public-school children. *J. Educ. Res.*, **12**, 102–122.

HALES, N. M. 1932. An advanced test of general intelligence. *Aust. Coun. Educ. Res. Ser.*, No. 11.

HANSON, R. L. 1933. An investigation of children's use of money. *Child Develpm.*, **4**, 50–54.

HARTSHORNE, H., and M. A. MAY. 1928. *Studies in deceit:* Book I. *General methods and results;* Book II. *Statistical methods and results.* New York: Macmillan.

HARTSHORNE, H., M. A. MAY, and J. B. MALLER. 1929. *Studies in service and self-control.* New York: Macmillan.

HARTSHORNE, H., M. A. MAY, and F. K. SHUTTLEWORTH. 1930. *Studies in the organization of character.* New York: Macmillan.

HATTWICK, L. A. 1937. Sex differences in behavior of nursery school children. *Child Develpm.*, **8**, 343–355.

HAYES, M. 1934. A scale for evaluating adolescent personality. *J. Genet. Psychol.*, **44**, 206–222.

HAYWARD, R. S. 1935. The child's report of psychological factors in the family. *Arch. Psychol., N. Y.*, **28**, No. 189.

HEALY, W., and A. F. BRONNER. 1926. *Delinquents and criminals, their making and unmaking.* New York: Macmillan.

HEILMAN, J. D. 1933. Sex differences in intellectual abilities. *J. Educ. Psychol.*, **24**, 47–62.

HICKS, J. A., and M. HAYES. 1938. Study of the characteristics of 250 junior high school children. *Child Develpm.*, **9**, 219–242.

HILDRETH, G. 1933. Adolescent interests and abilities. *J. Genet. Psychol.*, **43**, 65–93.

HOLLINGWORTH, L. S. 1914. Variability as related to sex differences in achievement. *Amer. J. Sociol.*, **19**, 510–530.

HOLMES, F. B. 1936. An experimental investigation of a method of overcoming children's fears. *Child Develpm.*, **7**, 6–30.

HOLZINGER, K. J., and F. SWINEFORD. 1939. A study in factor analysis: The stability of a bi-factor solution. *Suppl. Educ. Monogr.*, No. 48. Pp. ix + 91.

HÜBSCH, L., and K. REININGER. 1931. Zur Psychologie des Kinderspiels und der Geschlechtsunterschiede im Kindergartenalter. *Z. angew. Psychol.*, **40**, 97–176.

HURLOCK, E. B. 1927. A study of self-ratings by children. *J. Appl. Psychol.*, **11**, 490–502.

——. 1930. The suggestibility of children. *J. Genet. Psychol.*, **37**, 59–74.

HURLOCK, E. B., and E. R. KLEIN. 1934. Adolescent "crushes." *Child Develpm.*, **5**, 63–80.

HURLOCK, E. B., and L. C. MCDONALD. 1934. Undesirable behavior traits in junior high school students. *Child Develpm.*, **5**, 278–290.

JERSILD, A. T., and F. B. HOLMES. 1935. Children's fears. *Child Develpm. Monogr.*, No. 20. Pp. ix + 356.

JERSILD, A. T., and F. V. MARKEY. 1935. Conflicts between preschool children. *Child Develpm. Monogr.*, No. 21. Pp. xi + 181.

JERSILD, A. T., F. V. MARKEY, and C. L. JERSILD. 1933. Children's fears, dreams, wishes, daydreams, likes, dislikes, pleasant and unpleasant memories. *Child Develpm. Monogr.*, No. 12. Pp. xi + 172.

JOHNSON, B. L. 1932. Children's reading interests as related to sex and grade in school. *Sch. Rev.*, **40**, 257–272.

JORDAN, A. M. 1921. Children's interests in reading. *Teach. Coll. Contr. Educ.*, No. 107.

——. 1937. Sex differences in mental traits. *High Sch. J.*, **20**, 254–261.

KAULFERS, W. 1928. Intelligence of one thousand students of foreign languages. *Sch. and Soc.*, **28**, 597–599.

KIMMINS, C. W. 1920. *Children's dreams.* New York: Longmans, Green.

——. 1931. Children's dreams. In C. MURCHISON (Ed.), *A handbook of child psychology* (1st ed.), pp. 527–554. Worcester: Clark University Press.

——. 1937. *Children's dreams; an unexplored land.* London: Allen and Unwin.

KINTER-REMMLEIN, M. 1933. *Enquête sur un groupe des petits Parisiens; leur idées sur le bien et le mal; leur réactions de coopération et d'altruisme.* Paris: Rodstein.

KOCH, H. L. 1935. An analysis of certain forms of so-called "nervous habits" in young children. *J. Genet. Psychol.*, **46**, 139–170.

KOHN, H. A. 1937. Some experiences with the Pressey X-O test using a group of normal orphan children in a superior institutional environment. *J. Genet. Psychol.*, **51**, 219–222.

KUZNETS, G. M., and O. McNEMAR. 1940. Sex differences in intelligence-test scores. *Yearb. Nat. Soc. Stud. Educ.*, 39(I), 211–220.

LANDIS, C., J. ZUBIN, and S. E. KATZ. 1935. Empirical evaluation of three personality adjustment inventories. *J. Educ. Psychol.*, **26**, 321–330.

LANGLIE, T. A. 1937. Personality ratings: I. Reliability of teachers' ratings. *J. Genet. Psychol.*, **50**, 339–359.

LEAMING, R. E. 1922. Tests and norms for vocational guidance at the fifteen-year-old performance level. *Psychol. Clin.*, **14**, 193–220.

LEARNED, W. S., and B. D. WOOD. 1938. The student and his knowledge. *Carnegie Found. Adv. Teaching Bull.*, No. 29.

LEHMAN, H. C., and P. A. WITTY. 1927. *The psychology of play activities.* New York: Barnes.

——. 1931. Further study of the social status of occupations. *J. Educ. Sociol.*, **5**, 101–112.

LEVY, D. M., and S. H. TULCHIN. 1923. The resistance of infants and children during mental tests. *J. Exp. Psychol.*, **6**, 304–322.

LINCOLN, E. A. 1927. *Sex differences in the growth of American school children.* Baltimore: Warwick and York.

LITTLE, M. F., and H. M. WILLIAMS. 1937. An analytical scale of language achievement. In Development of language and vocabulary in young children. *Univ. Iowa Stud. Child Welfare*, **13**, No. 2, pp. 47–94.

LODGE, J. H. 1926. The illusion of warmth test for suggestibility. *Forum Educ.*, **4**, 180–186.

LONGSTAFF, H. P. 1936. Effectiveness of children's radio programs. *J. Appl. Psychol.*, **20**, 208–220.

MACFARLANE, J. W. 1938. Studies in child guidance: I. Methodology of data collection and organization. *Monogr. Soc. Res. Child Develpm.*, **3**, No. 6. Pp. vii + 254.

MACFARLANE, J. W., M. P. HONZIK, and M. H. DAVIS. 1937. Reputation differences among young school children. *J. Educ. Psychol.*, **28**, 161–175.

MACMEEKEN, A. M. 1939. *The intelligence of a representative group of Scottish children.* London: University of London Press.

MADSEN, I. N. 1924. Some results with the Stanford revision of the Binet-Simon tests. *Sch. and Soc.*, **19**, 559–562.

MALLER, J. B. 1933. The trend of juvenile delinquency in New York City. *J. Juv. Res.*, **17**, 10–18.

MARQUIS, D. G. 1940. Physiological psychology. *Ann. Rev. Physiol.*, **2**, 433–461.

MATHEWS, E. 1923. A study of emotional stability in children. *J. Deling.*, **8**, 1–40.

MAYER, B. A. 1935. Negativistic reactions of preschool children on the new revision of the Stanford-Binet. *J. Genet. Psychol.*, **46**, 311–334.

McCARTHY, D. A. 1930. *The language development of the preschool child.* (*Inst. Child Welfare Monogr. Ser.*, No. 4.) Minneapolis: University of Minnesota Press. Pp. xiii + 174.

McINTYRE, G. A., and W. WOOD. 1935. The standardization of an Australian reading test. *Aust. Coun. Educ. Res. Ser.*, No. 39.

McNEMAR, Q., and L. M. TERMAN. 1936. Sex differences in variational tendency. *Genet. Psychol. Monogr.*, **18**, 1–65.

MESSERSCHMIDT, R. 1933. The suggestibility of boys and girls between the ages of six and sixteen years. *J. Genet. Psychol.*, **43**, 422–437.

MICHAELS, J. J., and S. E. GOODMAN. 1934. Incidence and intercorrelations of enuresis and other neuropathic traits in so-called normal children. *Amer. J. Orthopsychiat.*, **4**, 79–106.

——. 1939. The incidence of enuresis and age of cessation in one thousand neuropsychiatric patients: with a discussion of the relationship between enuresis and delinquency. *Amer. J. Orthopsychiat.*, **9**, 59–71.

MILLER, N. 1928. *The child in primitive society.* New York: Brentano's.

MINER, J. B. 1922. An aid to the analysis of vocational interests. *J. Educ. Res.*, **5**, 311–323.

MITCHELL, A. M. 1929. *Children and movies.* Chicago: University of Chicago Press.

MOORE, J. E. 1940. A further study of sex differences in speed of reading. *Peabody J. Educ.*, **17**, 359–362.

MOTT, S. M. 1937. Mother-father preference. *Character and Pers.*, 5, 302–304.

MURLIN, J. R. 1939. Energy metabolism. *Ann. Rev. Physiol.*, 1, 131–162.

NELSON, J. F. 1931. Personality and intelligence. *Child Develpm. Monogr.*, No. 4. Pp. 62.

NEWELL, H. W. 1936. A further study of maternal rejection. *Amer. J. Orthopsychiat.*, 6, 576–589.

OLSON, W. C. 1929. *The measurement of nervous habits in normal children.* (*Inst. Child Welfare Monogr. Ser.*, No. 3.) Minneapolis: University of Minnesota Press. Pp. xii + 97.

———. 1930. *Problem tendencies in children: A method for their measurement and description.* Minneapolis: University of Minnesota Press.

———. 1936. The diagnosis of oral habits in children from the condition of the hands. *J. Abnorm. (Soc.) Psychol.*, 31, 182–189.

ORGEL, S. Z., and J. TUCKMAN. 1935. Nicknames of institutional children. *Amer. J. Orthopsychiat.*, 5, 276–285.

PARKES, A. S. 1926. The mammalian sex-ratio. *Biol. Rev.*, 2, 1–52.

PARTEN, M. B. 1933. Social play among preschool children. *J. Abnorm. (Soc.) Psychol.*, 28, 136–147.

PEARSON, K. 1897. *Chances of death.* London: Arnold. Vol. I.

PERRY, R. C. 1934. A group factor analysis of the adjustment questionnaire. *Univ. S. Calif. Educ. Monogr.*, No. 5. Pp. xi + 93.

PHILLIPS, A. 1931. Sibship: Intelligence and behavior. *Psychol. Clin.*, 20, 97–115.

PINARD, J. W. 1932. Tests of perseveration: I. Their relation to character. *Brit. J. Psychol.*, 23, 5–19.

PINTNER, R. 1924. Results obtained with the non-language group test. *J. Educ. Psychol.*, 15, 473–483.

———. 1940. An adjustment test with normal and hard of hearing children. *J. Genet. Psychol.*, 56, 367–381.

PINTNER, R., and L. BRUNSCHWIG. 1937. A study of certain fears and wishes among deaf and hearing children. *J. Educ. Psychol.*, 28, 259–270.

PINTNER, R., and J. LEV. 1940. Worries of school children. *J. Genet. Psychol.*, 56, 67–76.

PRESSEY, S. L. 1921. A group scale for investigating emotions. *J. Abnorm. Psychol.*, 16, 55–64.

PRESSEY, S. L., and L. C. PRESSEY. 1933. Development of the interest-attitude tests. *J. Appl. Psychol.*, 17, 1–16.

PYLE, W. H. 1925. The relation of sex differences to the kind of material used. *J. Educ. Psychol.*, 16, 261–264.

RAUBENHEIMER, A. S. 1925. An experimental study of some behavior traits of the potentially delinquent boy. *Psychol. Monogr.*, 34, No. 159. Pp. 107.

REYNOLDS, M. M. 1928. Negativism of preschool children. *Teach. Coll. Contr. Educ.*, No. 288.

RIDDLE, O. 1929. Some interrelations of sexuality, reproduction, and internal secretion. *J. Amer. Med. Ass.*, 92, 943–950.

RIGG, M. G. 1940. The relative variability in intelligence of boys and girls. *J. Genet. Psychol.*, 56, 211–214.

ROBERTS, J. A. F., R. M. NORMAN, and R. GRIFFITHS. 1935. Studies on a child population. *Ann. Eugen., Camb.*, 6, 319–338.

ROFF, M., and L. ROFF. 1940. An analysis of the variance of conflict behavior in preschool children. *Child Develpm.*, 11, 43–60.

ROSS, B. M. 1931. Some traits associated with sibling jealousy in problem children. *Smith Coll. Stud. Soc. Work.*, 1, 364–376.

ROWE, A. W. 1928. Studies of the endocrine glands: I. A general method for the diagnosis of abnormal function. *Endocrinology*, 12, 1–54.

RYANS, D. G. 1939. A note on variations in "persistence" test score with sex, age, and academic level. *J. Soc. Psychol.*, 10, 259–264.

SCHILLER, B. 1934. Verbal, numerical, and spatial abilities of young children. *Arch. Psychol., N. Y.*, No. 161.

SCHUBERT, H. J. P., and M. E. WAGNER. 1936. The relation of individual personal data responses and transiency, place among siblings, and academic ability. *J. Abnorm. (Soc.) Psychol.*, 30, 474–483.

SCHUMACHER, H. C. 1933. An inquiry into the etiology of children's maladjustment. *Amer. J. Orthopsychiat.*, 3, 376–398.

SCOTTISH COUNCIL FOR RESEARCH IN EDUCATION. 1933. *The intelligence of Scottish children: A national survey.* London: University of London Press.

SEAGOE, M. V. 1931. The child's reaction to the movies. *J. Juv. Res.*, 15, 169–180.

SEWALL, M. 1930. Two studies in sibling rivalry: I. Some causes of jealousy in young children. *Smith Coll. Stud. Soc. Work.*, 1, 6–22.

SHACTER, H. S. 1933. A method for measuring the sustained attention of preschool children. *J. Genet. Psychol.*, 42, 339–371.

SHELDON, W. H. 1940. *The varieties of human physique.* New York: Harper.

SHOCK, N. W., and A. B. HASTINGS. 1934. Sex difference in average P.H. bicarbonate, and carbon dioxide tension of blood. *J. Biol. Chem.*, 104, 585.

SHUTTLEWORTH, F. K. 1938. The adolescent period; a graphic and pictorial atlas. *Monogr. Soc. Res. Child Develpm.*, 3, No. 3. Pp. v + 246.

SIMPSON, M. 1935. Parent preference of young

children. *Teach. Coll. Contr. Educ.*, No. 652.

SLETTO, R. F. 1934. Sibling position and juvenile delinquency. *Amer. J. Sociol.*, **39**, 657–669.

SMITH, M. E. 1926. An investigation of the development of the sentence and the extent of vocabulary in young children. *Univ. Iowa Stud. Child Welfare*, **3**, No. 5.

SMITH, S. 1939. Age and sex differences in children's opinion concerning sex differences. *J. Genet. Psychol.*, **54**, 17–25.

SOLLENBERGER, R. T. 1940. Some relationships between the urinary excretion of male hormone by maturing boys and their expressed interests and attitudes. *J. Psychol.*, **9**, 179–189.

SPENCER, D. 1938. *Fulcra of conflict. A new approach to personality measurement.* Yonkers-on-Hudson : World Book.

SPRINGER, N. N. 1938. The influence of general social status on the emotional stability of children. *J. Genet. Psychol.*, **53**, 321–328.

STAGNER, R. 1938. The rôle of parents in the development of emotional instability. *Amer. J. Orthopsychiat.*, **8**, 122–129.

STONE, C. P., and R. G. BARKER. 1939. The attitudes and interests of premenarcheal and postmenarcheal girls. *J. Genet. Psychol.*, **54**, 27–71.

SUNNE, D. 1925. Personality tests : White and Negro adolescents. *J. Appl. Psychol.*, **9**, 256–280.

SYMONDS, P. M. 1936. Sex differences in the life problems and interests of adolescents. *Sch. and Soc.*, **43**, 751–752.

TERMAN, L. M. 1938. *Psychological factors in marital happiness.* New York : McGraw-Hill.

TERMAN, L. M., *et al.* 1925. *Genetic studies of genius:* Vol. I. *Mental and physical traits of a thousand gifted children.* Stanford University, Calif. : Stanford University Press.

TERMAN, L. M., and P. BUTTENWIESER. 1935. Personality factors in marital compatibility. *J. Soc. Psychol.*, **6**, 143–171 ; 267–289.

TERMAN, L. M., and M. LIMA. 1926. *Children's readings.* (1st ed.) New York : Appleton.

TERMAN, L. M., and M. A. MERRILL. 1937. *Measuring intelligence.* Boston : Houghton Mifflin.

TERMAN, L. M., and C. C. MILES. 1936. *Sex and personality: Studies in masculinity and femininity.* New York : McGraw-Hill.

THORNDIKE, E. L., *et al.* 1934. *Prediction of vocational success.* New York : Commonwealth Fund.

THURSTONE, L. L., and R. L. JENKINS. 1931. *Order of birth, parent-age, and intelligence.* Chicago : University of Chicago Press.

THURSTONE, L. L., and T. G. THURSTONE. 1930. A neurotic inventory. *J. Soc. Psychol.*, **1**, 3–30.

TRYON, C. M. 1939. Evaluations of adolescent personality by adolescents. *Monogr. Soc. Res. Child Develpm.*, **4**, No. 4. Pp. x + 83.

WANG, C. K. A. 1932. The significance of early personal history for certain personality traits. *Amer. J. Psychol.*, **44**, 768–774.

WECHSLER, D. 1931. The incidence and significance of fingernail biting in children. *Psychoanal. Rev.*, **18**, 201–209.

WEGROCKI, H. J. 1934. The effect of prestige suggestibility on emotional attitudes. *J. Soc. Psychol.*, **5**, 384–394.

WELLMAN, B. 1926. The school child's choice of companions. *J. Educ. Res.*, **14**, 126–132.

WELLMAN, B. L., I. M. CASE, I. G. MENGERT, and D. E. BRADBURY. 1931. Speech sounds of young children. *Univ. Iowa Stud. Child Welfare*, **5**, No. 2.

WHIPPLE, G. M. 1915. *Manual of mental and physical tests:* Part II. *Complex processes.* Baltimore : Warwick and York.

WHITE, R. S. 1930. Motor suggestion in children. *Child Develpm.*, **1**, 161–185.

WHITLEY, M. T. 1929. Children's interest in collecting. *J. Educ. Psychol.*, **20**, 249–261.

WICKMAN, E. K. 1928. *Children's behavior and teachers' attitudes.* New York : Commonwealth Fund.

WILLIAMS, H. D. 1933. A survey of predelinquent children in ten middle western cities. *J. Juv. Res.*, **17**, 163–174.

WILLIAMSON, E. G., and J. G. DARLEY. 1935. Trends in the occupational choices of high school seniors. *J. Appl. Psychol.*, **19**, 361–370.

WITTY, P. A., and H. C. LEHMAN. 1930. Further studies of children's interest in collecting. *J. Educ. Psychol.*, **21**, 112–127.

WOLF, T. H. 1938. *The effect of praise and competition on the persisting behavior of kindergarten children.* (Inst. Child Welfare Monogr. Ser., No. 15.) Minneapolis : University of Minnesota Press. Pp. vi + 138.

WOODY, C. 1931. The arithmetical backgrounds of young children. *J. Educ. Res.*, **24**, 188–201.

———. 1937, 1938. The sophomore and freshman testing program in the accredited high schools of Michigan. *Bur. Educ. Ref. and Res.*, Bull. 149, Bull. 150.

WOOLLEY, H. T. 1926. *An experimental study of children.* New York : Macmillan.

WYMAN, J. B. 1925. Tests of intellectual, social, and activity interests. In L. M. TERMAN, *et al. Genetic studies of genius.* Stanford University, Calif. : Stanford University Press. Vol. I, pp. 455–483.

ADDITIONAL SELECTED REFERENCES

ACKERSON, L. 1936. On evaluating the relative importance or "seriousness" of various behavior problems in children. *J. Juv. Res.*, **20**, 114–123.

ALLEN, C. N. 1927. Studies in sex differences. *Psychol. Bull.*, **24**, 294–304.

ALLEN, C. N. 1930. Recent studies in sex differences. *Psychol. Bull.*, **27**, 394–407.

——. 1935. Recent research on sex differences. *Psychol. Bull.*, **32**, 343–354.

ARMSTRONG, C. P. 1937. A psychoneurotic reaction of delinquent boys and girls. *J. Abnorm. (Soc.) Psychol.*, **32**, 329–342.

BELL, M. A. 1927. *On sex differences in non-intellectual mental traits.* Unpublished Master's Thesis, Stanford University.

BENNETT, E. E. 1932. What high-school pupils read in school papers. *Sch. Rev.*, **40**, 772–780.

BLATZ, W. E., and E. A. BOTT. 1927. Studies in the mental hygiene of children : I. Behavior of public school children—A description of method. *Ped. Sem.*, **34**, 552–582.

BLOCK, V. L. 1937. Conflicts of adolescents with their mothers. *J. Abnorm. (Soc.) Psychol.*, **32**, 193–206.

BROWN, F. 1937. Neuroticism of institution versus non-institution children. *J. Appl. Psychol.*, **21**, 379–383.

BROWN, P. A. 1938. Responses of blind and seeing adolescents to an introversion-extroversion questionnaire. *J. Psychol.*, **6**, 137–147.

BÜHLER, C. 1927a. Das Problem der Differenz der Geschlechter. (*Dtsch. Mädchenbildung*, Vol. 3.) Leipzig : Teubner.

——. 1927b. Die ersten sozialen Verhaltungsweisen des Kindes. *Quel. Stud. Jugendk.*, No. 5.

CALDWELL, O. W., and G. E. LUNDEEN. 1934. Further study of unfounded beliefs among junior high school pupils. *Teach. Coll. Rec.*, **36**, 35–52.

CAMPBELL, E. H. 1934. The social-sex development of children. *Genet. Psychol. Monogr.*, **21**, 461–552.

CARTER, H. D. 1938. A preliminary study of free association : I. Twin similarities and the technique of measurement. *J. Psychol.*, **6**, 201–215.

CELESTINE, SR. M. 1930. A survey of the literature on the reading interests of children of the elementary grades. *Cath. Univ. Amer. Educ. Res. Bull.*, **5**, Nos. 2 and 3.

COMMINS, W. D. 1928. More about sex differences. *Sch. and Soc.*, **28**, 599–600.

CONRAD, H. S., H. E. JONES, and H. H. HSIAO. 1933. Sex differences in mental growth and decline. *J. Educ. Psychol.*, **24**, 161–169.

DALE, A. B. 1926. Group tests in reasoning ability. *Brit. J. Psychol.*, **16**, 314–338.

DARLEY, J. G. 1937. Scholastic achievement and measured maladjustment. *J. Appl. Psychol.*, **21**, 485–493.

DODGE, A. F. 1937. Social dominance of clerical workers and sales-persons as measured by the Bernreuter Personality Inventory. *J. Educ. Psychol.*, **28**, 71–73.

DRIGGS, H. W. 1934. The vocabulary of letters of boys and girls 12 to 15 years of age inclusive. *J. Exp. Educ.*, **2**, 339–354.

DUDYCHA, G. J., and M. M. DUDYCHA. 1933. Some factors and characteristics of childhood memories. *Child Develpm.*, **4**, 265–278.

DUNN, F. W. 1921. Interest factors in primary reading material. *Teach. Coll. Contr. Educ.*, No. 113.

DUREA, M. A. 1939. A survey of the adjustment of school children. *Child Develpm.*, **10**, 107–114.

FRANKLIN, E. E. 1926. The permanence of vocational interests after three years. *Sch. and Soc.*, **23**, 438–440.

GARRETT, H. E., and T. R. FISHER. 1926. The prevalence of certain popular misconceptions. *J. Appl. Psychol.*, **10**, 411–420.

GERBERICH, J. R. 1930. The gifted pupils of the Iowa High School survey. *J. Appl. Psychol.*, **14**, 566–576.

GOODENOUGH, F. L. 1927. The consistency of sex differences in mental traits at various ages. *Psychol. Rev.*, **34**, 440–462.

GUILFORD, J. P., and R. B. GUILFORD. 1936. Personality factors S, E, and M, and their measurement. *J. Psychol.*, **2**, 109–127.

HANSKE, C. F. 1931. Sex differences in high-school chemistry. *J. Educ. Res.*, **23**, 412–416.

HENMON, V. A. C. 1929. *Achievement tests in the modern foreign languages.* New York : Macmillan.

HORTON, B. J. 1937. The truthfulness of boys and girls in public and private schools. *J. Abnorm. (Soc.) Psychol.*, **31**, 398–405.

HURD, A. W. 1934. Sex differences in achievement in physical science. *J. Educ. Psychol.*, **25**, 70.

KANGLEY, L. 1938. Poetry preferences in the junior high school. *Teach. Coll. Contr. Educ.*, No. 758.

KLOPFER, B. 1939. Personality differences between boys and girls in early childhood. (Abstract.) *Psychol. Bull.*, **36**, 538.

LEVY, D. M., and S. H. TULCHIN. 1925. The resistant behavior of infants and children : II. *J. Exp. Psychol.*, **8**, 209–224.

LILLIE, F. R. 1939. General biological introduction. In E. ALLEN (Ed.), *Sex and internal secretions*, pp. 3–14. (2d ed.) Baltimore : Williams and Wilkins.

LOCKHART, E. G. 1930. The attitudes of children toward law. *Univ. Iowa Stud. Charact.*, **3**, No. 1.

MALLER, J. B. 1929. Cooperation and competition ; an experimental study in motivation. *Teach. Coll. Contr. Educ.*, No. 384.

MCBEE, M. 1935. A mental-hygiene clinic in a high school. *Ment. Hyg., N. Y.*, **19**, 238–280.

MCCRACKEN, T. C., and H. E. LAMB. 1923. *Occupational information in the elementary school.* Boston : Houghton Mifflin.

MILES, C. C. 1935. Sex in social psychology.

In C. MURCHISON (Ed.), *A handbook of social psychology*, pp. 683–797. Worcester: Clark University Press.

MORTON, D. M. 1936. Number forms and arithmetical ability in children. *Brit. J. Educ. Psychol.*, **6**, 58–73.

NIFENECKER, E. A., and H. G. CAMPBELL. 1937. *Review of departmental experience in dealing with problems of school maladjustment:* Part II. *Statistical reference data relating to problems of over-ageness, educational retardation, non-promotion, 1900–1934*. New York: Board of Education, Bureau of Reference, Research and Statistics. (Publ. No. 28.)

PECK, L. 1935. Teachers' reports of the problems of unadjusted school children. *J. Educ. Psychol.*, **26**, 123–138.

PINTNER, R. 1933. A comparison of interests, abilities, and attitudes. *J. Abnorm. (Soc.) Psychol.*, **27**, 351–357.

PINTNER, R., J. B. MALLER, G. FORLANO, and K. AXELROD. 1935. The measurement of pupil adjustment. *J. Educ. Res.*, **28**, 334–346.

REMER, L. L. 1932. Handicaps of school entrants: A study of traits which handicap children entering kindergarten and first grade. *Univ. Iowa Stud. Child Welfare*, **6**, 197–207.

RYANS, D. G. 1939. The measurement of persistence: An historical review. *Psychol. Bull.*, **36**, 715–739.

SCHMIDBERGER, G. 1932. Über Geschlechtsunterschiede in der Rechnenbegabung. *Z. pädag. Psychol.*, **33**, 70–85; 104–165.

SMITH, M. E. 1933. The influence of age, sex, and situation on the frequency, form, and function of questions asked by preschool children. *Child Develpm.*, **4**, 201–213.

SPEER, G. S. 1939. Oral and written wishes of rural and city school children. *Child Develpm.*, **10**, 151–155.

STAGNER, R., and N. DROUGHT. 1935. Measuring children's attitudes toward their parents. *J. Educ. Psychol.*, **26**, 169–176.

STRAKER, A., and R. H. THOULESS. 1940. Preliminary results of Cambridge survey of evacuated children. *Brit. J. Educ. Psychol.*, **10**, 97–113.

SYMONDS, P. M. 1937. Changes in sex differences in problems and interests of adolescents with increasing age. *J. Genet. Psychol.*, **50**, 83–89.

THORNDIKE, E. L. 1926. Sex differences in status and gain in intelligence scores from thirteen to eighteen. *Ped. Sem.*, **33**, 167–181.

TOUTON, F. C. 1924. Sex differences in geometric abilities. *J. Educ. Psychol.*, **15**, 234–247.

TRAXLER, A. E. 1935. Sex differences in rate of reading in the high school. *J. Appl. Psychol.*, **19**, 351–352.

WASHBURNE, C. W., and M. VOGEL. 1926. *What children like to read*. New York: Rand McNally.

WASHBURNE, J. N. 1932. The impulsions of adolescents as revealed by written wishes. *J. Juv. Res.*, **16**, 193–212.

WEINBERG, D. 1932. Contribution à l'étude expérimentale de quelques différences de caractères chez les garçons et les filles. *Bull. Soc. de Sexol.*, **1**, 57–66.

WELLMAN, B. L. 1933. Sex differences. In C. MURCHISON (Ed.), *A handbook of child psychology*, pp. 626–649. (2d ed., rev.) Worcester: Clark University Press.

WILDS, E. H. 1932. Interschool contests in American high schools. *Sch. Rev.*, **40**, 429–441.

A GRAPHIC AGE CONVERSION SCALE

BY

Dorothea McCarthy

Reproduced with the permission of the publisher from
Child Development, March, 1936.

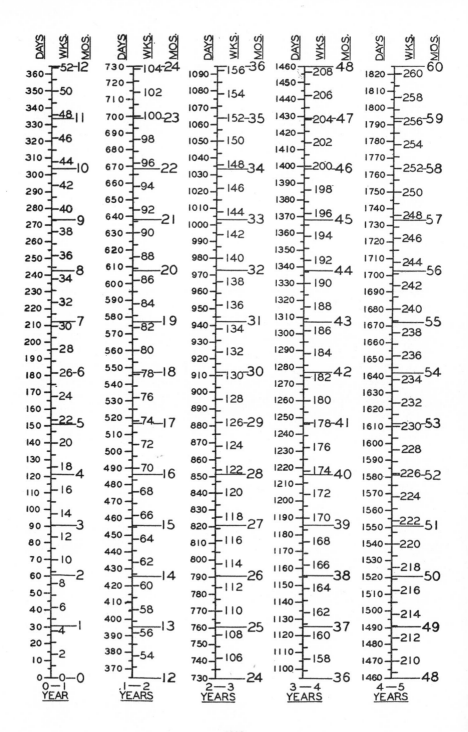

A GRAPHIC AGE CONVERSION SCALE

As there is no uniformity in the method of stating age in the preschool literature, it is difficult to make comparisons in tracing developmental trends when one study reports age in days, another in weeks, another in months, and another in years and months. The line graph on the opposite page is designed, therefore, to aid the reader in dealing with the wide variety of age designations employed in the voluminous literature reviewed by the authors of this manual.

This graphic age conversion scale covers the age range from birth through five years, with one vertical line representing each year. Days are indicated on the scales to the left and weeks and months to the right of the vertical scales. In the construction of the graph each 365-day year was divided into twelve equal months of 30.42 days, and into 52.14 weeks of seven days each. Although the finest units marked on the scale are five-day units, the scale can be read quite easily to the nearest day. It can be seen, for example, that if a given phenomenon is reported at 450 days by one writer, 65 weeks by another, and 15 months by another the three studies are in close agreement on the time of appearance of the phenomenon.

INDEX